INTERMEDIATE FUTURES AND OPTIONS

AN ACTIVE LEARNING APPROACH

INTERMEDIATE FUTURES AND OPTIONS

AN ACTIVE LEARNING APPROACH

Cheng Few Lee
Rutgers University, USA

John Lee
Center for PBBEF Research, USA

Alice Lee
Center for PBBEF Research, USA

World Scientific

NEW JERSEY • LONDON • SINGAPORE • BEIJING • SHANGHAI • HONG KONG • TAIPEI • CHENNAI • TOKYO

Published by

World Scientific Publishing Co. Pte. Ltd.
5 Toh Tuck Link, Singapore 596224
USA office: 27 Warren Street, Suite 401-402, Hackensack, NJ 07601
UK office: 57 Shelton Street, Covent Garden, London WC2H 9HE

Library of Congress Cataloging-in-Publication Data
Names: Lee, Cheng F., author. | Lee, John C., author. | Lee, Alice C., author.
Title: Intermediate futures and options : an active learning approach /
Cheng Few Lee, Rutgers University, USA, John Lee, Center for PBBEF Research, USA,
Alice Lee, Center for PBBEF Research, USA.
Description: New Jersey : World scientific, [2024] | Includes bibliographical references and index.
Identifiers: LCCN 2023028666 | ISBN 9789811280269 (hardcover) |
ISBN 9789811281488 (paperback) | ISBN 9789811280276 (ebook) |
ISBN 9789811280283 (ebook other)
Subjects: LCSH: Futures. | Options (Finance) | Investments.
Classification: LCC HG6024.A3 L44 2024 | DDC 332.64/52--dc23/eng/20230623
LC record available at https://lccn.loc.gov/2023028666

British Library Cataloguing-in-Publication Data
A catalogue record for this book is available from the British Library.

For any available supplementary material, please visit
https://www.worldscientific.com/worldscibooks/10.1142/13515#t=suppl

Desk Editors: Aanand Jayaraman/Lai Ann

Typeset by Stallion Press
Email: enquiries@stallionpress.com

Preface

Based on our teaching and industry experiences, and our research papers and books, we write this book entitled *Intermediate Futures and Options: An Active Learning Approach.* In this book, we use active and interdisciplinary approaches. In terms of the interdisciplinary aspect, we use accounting, corporate finance, investment analysis, statistics, calculus, Ito's Calculus, financial econometrics, fuzzy mathematics, and Microsoft Excel tools. In terms of the active aspect, we use real-world data of accounting, stock rates of return, futures, and options to enable students to create three projects.

This book is an updated and expanded version of our previous book, entitled, *Security Analysis, Portfolio Management, and Financial Derivatives.* In this book, we incorporate some materials of futures and options from *Encyclopedia of Finance* 3rd edition (2022) and from the following books: *Essentials of Excel VBA, Python, and R: Financial Statistics, and Portfolio Analysis* (2023); *Essentials of Excel VBA, Python, and R: Financial Derivatives, Risk Management and Machine Learning* (2023); *Handbook of Investment Analysis, Portfolio Management, and Financial Derivatives* (2023); *Handbook of Financial Econometrics, Mathematics, Statistics, and Machine Learning* (2021); *Financial Econometrics, Mathematics and Statistics* (2019); *Financial Analysis, Planning and Forecasting* (2017); *Handbook of Financial Econometrics and Statistics* (2015); *Statistics for Business and Financial Economics* 3rd ed. (2013); and *Handbook of Quantitative Finance and Risk Management* (2010).

The title, *Intermediate Futures and Options: An Active Learning Approach*, describes both the objective of this textbook and the method we have chosen to achieve the objective. Our goal is to introduce finance, economics, statistics, and mathematics students to the subject of quantitative finance that deals with forwards, futures, options, and other derivatives. Our method is to blend current academic thinking with respect to financial theory, statistics, and mathematics with real-world and case-like examples. Whenever practical, we use real-world information about the financial derivative evaluations and applications.

We initially concentrate on presenting theories and methods along with supporting examples; we then provide numerous questions and problems that allow students to apply their newly gained knowledge. In the first chapter, we discuss basic concepts and definitions which will be used throughout the book; then, we explicitly describe the content of the book as well as the methods of teaching.

This book is designed to be used in either a one-semester or a two-semester derivative course at the master's level or intermediate-level undergraduate program in quantitative finance. We have attempted to make the book more approachable by the extensive use of numerical examples, exhibits, tables, and diagrams.

Ancillary Material

A complete set of ancillary materials is available to adopters of this book:

1. An instructor's manual, written by Cheng Few Lee, Wen-Chi Yeh, and Louis E. Williams, features detailed chapter outlines as well as solutions to end-of-chapter discussion questions and problems.
2. PowerPoints feature chapter outlines, graphs, tables, and important material from each chapter. Excel programs are important tools to conduct the active teaching approach of Intermediate Futures and Options.

Acknowledgments

We gratefully received help from Natalie Krawczyk, Wen-Chi Yeh, Matthew Gregory, Louis Williams, and Sophia Chen in the preparation of this book. We also appreciate the help of Aanand Jayaraman, the Production Manager from World Scientific.

Cheng Few Lee
Alice Lee
John Lee
2023

References

Lee, Cheng F., Alice C. Lee, and John C. Lee. *Handbook of Investment Analysis, Portfolio Management, and Financial Derivatives.* World Scientific, 2023.

Lee, John, and Cheng-Few Lee. *Essentials of Excel VBA, Python, and R: Volume I: Financial Statistics and Portfolio Analysis.* Springer, 2023.

Lee, John, *et al.* Financial analysis, planning, and forecasting. *Essentials of Excel VBA, Python, and R: Volume II: Financial Derivatives, Risk Management and Machine Learning.* Cham: Springer, 2023, pp. 433–455.

Lee, Cheng Few, John C. Lee, and Michael Lee. *Corporate Finance and Strategy: An Active Learning Approach.* World Scientific, 2022.

Lee, Cheng Few and Alice C. Lee. *Encyclopedia of Finance,* 3rd edition. Springer, 2022.

Lee, Cheng Few, and John C. Lee, eds. *Handbook of Financial Econometrics, Mathematics, Statistics, and Machine Learning.* World Scientific, 2021.

Lee, Cheng-Few, Hong-Yi Chen, and John Lee. *Financial Econometrics, Mathematics and Statistics.* Springer, New York, 2019.

Lee, Cheng-Few and John C. Lee. *Financial Analysis, Planning and Forecasting*, 3rd edition. World Scientific, 2017.

Lee, Cheng-Few, and John C. Lee. *Handbook of Financial Econometrics and Statistics.* Springer, 2015.

Lee, Cheng-Few, Lee, John C., and Alice C. Lee. *Statistics for Business and Financial Economics*, 3rd edition, Springer, 2013.

Lee, Cheng-Few, Joseph E. Finnerty, Donald H. Wort, John Lee and Alice C. Lee. *Security Analysis, Portfolio Management, and Financial Derivatives.* World Scientific, 2013.

Lee, Cheng-Few, Alice C. Lee, and John C. Lee. *Handbook of Quantitative Finance and Risk Management.* Ed. Cheng F. Lee. Vol. 1. New York: Springer, 2010.

About the Authors

Professor Cheng Few Lee is a Distinguished Professor of Finance and Economics at Rutgers Business School, Rutgers University, and was chairperson of the Department of Finance from 1988–1995. He has also served on the faculty of the University of Illinois (IBE Professor of Finance) and the University of Georgia. He has maintained academic and consulting ties in Taiwan, Hong Kong, China and the United States for the past five decades. He has been a consultant to many prominent groups, including the American Insurance Group, the World Bank, the United Nations, the Marmon Group Inc., Wintek Corporation, Polaris Financial Group and others.

Professor Lee founded the *Review of Quantitative Finance and Accounting* (RQFA) in 1990 and the *Review of Pacific Basin Financial Markets and Policies* (RPBFMP) in 1998, and he serves as managing editor for both journals. He was also a co-editor of the *Financial Review* (1985–1991) and *The Quarterly Review of Economics and Finance* (1987–1989). In the past 50 years, Professor Lee has written numerous textbooks ranging in subject matters from financial management to corporate finance, security analysis and portfolio management to financial analysis, planning and forecasting, and business statistics. In addition, he has edited several popular books, *Encyclopedia of Finance* (with Alice C. Lee), *Handbook of Quantitative Finance and Risk Management* (with Alice C. Lee and John Lee), *Handbook of Financial Econometrics and Statistics* (with John Lee), *Handbook of Financial Econometrics, Mathematics, Statistics, and Machine Learning* (with John Lee), and *Handbook of Investment Analysis, Portfolio Management and Financial Derivatives* (with Alice C. Lee and John Lee). Professor Lee has also published more than 260 articles in more than 20 different journals on finance, accounting, economics, statistics, and management. Professor Lee has been ranked the most published finance professor worldwide during the period 1953–2008.

Professor Lee was the intellectual force behind the creation of the new Master of Quantitative Finance program at Rutgers University. This program began in 2001 and has been ranked as one of the top 15 quantitative finance programs in the United States. Professor Lee started the Conference on Financial Economics and Accounting in 1989. This conference is a consortium of Rutgers University, New York University, Temple University, University of Maryland, Georgia State University, Tulane University, Indiana University, and University of Toronto. This conference is the most well-known conference in finance and accounting. In addition, Professor Lee also started the conference on Pacific Basin Finance, Economics, Accounting, and Management (PBFEAM) in 1993.

Professor Lee had earned following honors and awards: (a) Special Recognition Award for his dedication and diligence as a founding father of The Financial Economics and Accounting Conference (Founded in 1990), (b) In Recognition of Outstanding Service as Editor of The Financial Review 1986–1991, (c) RBS Dean's Meritorious Award for Lifetime Achievement in Research 2013–2014 in Recognition of Outstanding Research Contributions, (d) Siwei Cheng Award in Quantitative Management by International Academy of Information Technology and Quantitative Management (IAITQM) in April 2013, (e) Member of the Board of Policy Advisors to Research Center On Fictitious Economy and Data Science, Chinese Academy of Science in 2009, (f) Lifetime Achievement Award in Recognition of exceptional contributions and long-term commitment by William Peterson University at 17th Annual International Conference on Applied Business and Economics in November 2021, (g) Fellow of ITQM (International Academy of Information Technology and Quantitative Management) 2022, and (h) Rutgers University 2023 Chancellor-Provost Faculty Excellence Awards.

John C. Lee is a Microsoft Certified Professional in Microsoft Visual Basic and Microsoft Excel VBA. He has a bachelor's and a master's degree in accounting from the University of Illinois at Urbana-Champaign.

John has worked for over 37 years in both the business and technical fields as an accountant, auditor, systems analyst, and business software developer. He is the author of the book *Essentials of Excel, Excel VBA, SAS and Minitab for Statistical and Financial Analyses*, which is a companion text to *Statistics of Business and Financial Economics*, 2nd and 3rd editions, of which he is one of the co-authors. In addition, he has also co-authored the textbooks *Financial Analysis, Planning and Forecasting*, 3rd edition (with Cheng F. Lee), and *Security Analysis, Portfolio Management, and Financial Derivatives* (with Cheng F. Lee, Joseph Finnerty, Alice C. Lee, and Donald Wort). He has also co-authored two books entitled (i) *Essentials of Excel VBA, Python, and R: Financial Statistics and Portfolio Analysis* and (ii) *Essentials of Excel VBA, Python, and R: Financial Derivatives, Financial Management, Risk Management and Machine Learning*. John has been a Senior Technology Officer at the Chase Manhattan Bank and Assistant Vice President at Merrill Lynch. Currently, he is the Director of the Center for PBBEF Research.

Alice C. Lee is an expert in risk management and risk validation. She has a bachelor's degree in computer science from the University of Illinois at Urbana-Champaign and Ph.D. in insurance and finance from the Wharton School, University of Pennsylvania.

She has worked for over 32 years in business and academics. In business, she worked for State Street Corporation, Boston, KPMG Advisory, Financial Risk Management, New Jersey, and other companies. In academics, she taught at San Francisco State University. She is a co-author of the well-known book entitled *Encyclopedia of Finance,* 3rd edition, 2022, by Springer (with Cheng Few Lee). In addition, she has also co-authored the textbooks *Security Analysis, Portfolio Management, and Financial Derivatives* (with Cheng F. Lee, Joseph Finnerty, and Donald Wort) and *Statistics of Business and Financial Economics,* 2nd and 3rd editions. She also co-authored several handbooks in the area of finance with Cheng Few Lee and John C. Lee.

Contents

Part I

Overview

Chapter 1

Introduction

Contents

1.1 Introduction

The main purposes of this chapter are (i) to briefly review forward contracts, future contracts, and option contracts; (ii) to briefly discuss alternative traders, which include hedgers, speculators, and arbitrageurs; (iii) to go over the contents of the book; and (iv) to discuss the methods of teaching this book.

In Section 1.2, we discuss forward contracts and future contracts, and in Section 1.3, we discuss option contracts. Section 1.4 discusses the types of traders. Section 1.5 reviews the contents of the book. Finally, in Section 1.6, we summarize and provide concluding remarks for the chapter.

1.2 Forward and Future Contracts

In this section, we will briefly discuss forward contracts and future contracts. In addition, we also discuss the relationships between these two contracts.

1.2.1 *Forward contracts*

A forward contract is a customizable derivative contract between two parties to buy or sell an asset at a specified price on a future date. Forward contracts can be tailored to a specific commodity, amount, and delivery date. Forward contracts do not trade on a centralized exchange and are considered over-the-counter (OTC) instruments. For example, forward contracts can help producers and users of agricultural products hedge against a change in the price of an underlying asset or commodity. Financial institutions that initiate forward contracts are exposed to a greater degree of settlement and default risk compared to contracts that are marked to market regularly. A forward contract can be used for hedging or speculation, although its non-standardized nature makes it particularly apt for hedging.

Unlike standard futures contracts, a forward contract can be customized to a commodity, amount, and delivery date. Commodities traded can be grains, precious metals, natural gas, oil, or even poultry. A forward contract settlement can occur on a cash or delivery basis. Both forward and futures contracts involve the agreement to buy or sell a commodity at a set price in the future. But there are slight differences between the two. While a forward contract does not trade on an exchange, a futures contract does. Settlement for the forward contract takes place at the end of the contract, while the futures contract settles on a daily basis. Most importantly, futures contracts exist as standardized contracts that are not customized between counterparties.

1.2.2 *Future contracts*

Unlike a forward contract, a futures contract is a standardized financial instrument with a stated amount and specific maturity that is traded on an organized exchange and is resalable up to the close of trading or settlement date. The futures contract defines what asset is to be bought or sold, and how, when, where, and in what quantity it is to be delivered. The terms also specify the currency in which the contract will trade, minimum tick value, the last trading day, and expiry or delivery month. Futures contracts tend to be smaller than forward contracts and are not as flexible in meeting hedging needs.

1.2.3 *Forward contracts vs. futures contracts*

While futures and forward contracts are similar in many respects, their differences are more important to fully understanding the nature and uses of these financial instruments. Both futures and forward contracts specify a transaction to take place at a future date and include precise requirements for the commodity to be delivered, its price, its quantity, the delivery date, and the delivery point. Nevertheless, these two types of contracts for future delivery of a commodity and the markets in which they are traded differ in several significant ways. The differences between forward and future contracts will be discussed in the next chapter in detail.

Although most people are unlikely ever to become involved in the forward market, it is important to understand some of its attributes, particularly as a good deal of the literature on pricing futures contracts typically refers to these two contracts interchangeably. These differences resulting from liquidity, credit risk, search, margin, taxes, and commissions could cause futures and forward contracts not to be priced identically. Some of the major users of forward contracts include the following:

1. *Public utilities*: Public utilities sometimes engage in long-term perpetual forward contracts for the delivery of coal or natural gas.
2. *Savings-and-loan associations*: A typical thrift institution might contract to deliver a pool of mortgages to another thrift in ninety days.
3. *Apparel or toy manufacturers*: Stores often contract for the delivery of the "new fall line" in early spring.
4. *Import–export businesses*: A U.S. exporter may contract for the delivery of a foreign currency in sixty days, after it receives payment in the foreign currency for goods sold overseas.

1.3 Option Contracts

In general, there are three types of options based on equity securities: (1) warrants, (2) publicly traded options, and (3) executive stock options. A warrant is a financial instrument issued by a corporation that gives the purchaser the right to buy a fixed number of shares at a set price for a specified period. There usually is a secondary market where existing warrants may be traded. It must be noted that a warrant is more difficult to price than a traded option. This is because when warrants are exercised, the underlying company changes; it receives a cash inflow and its capital structure is less levered. When a publicly traded option is exercised, on the other hand, the only thing that happens is that the ownership of some shares changes hands.

There are two major differences between a warrant and a publicly traded option. First, the warrant normally matures in three to five years, whereas the maturity of a publicly traded option is normally less than nine months. The second difference is that the warrant is an agreement between the corporation and the warrant's buyer. If the warrant's owner decides to exercise the right to purchase stock, the corporation issues new shares and receives the cash from the sales of those shares. A publicly traded option is an agreement between two individuals who have no relationship with the corporation whose shares underlie the option. When a publicly traded option is exercised, money and shares are exchanged between the individuals and the corporation receives no funds.

Executive stock options provide stock purchase rights as compensation for corporate employees. For services rendered, the manager or the employee has the right to buy a specific number of shares for a set price during a given period. Unlike warrants and publicly traded options, executive stock options cannot be traded. The option's owner has only two choices: exercise the option or let it expire. Like a warrant, should the owner decide to exercise the option, the corporation receives money and issues new shares.

The use of executive stock options for management compensation raises an interesting agency question. The firm's managers may make investment and financing decisions that increase the firm's risk in order to increase the value of their stock options. Such an action could have a detrimental effect on the bondholders and other creditors of the firm.

Publicly traded options are probably the most widely known of the three types of equity option instruments. In 1973, the Chicago Board of Options Exchange (CBOE) was founded to provide a market in these securities. Although it was possible to trade options over the counter before that time, trading volume was relatively low. The opening of the CBOE marked the beginning of a phenomenal growth in the popularity of options as financial instruments. Indeed, in terms of the value of the securities traded, the Chicago Board Options Exchange is challenging the New York and Tokyo Stock Exchanges as the world's largest securities market. There are now five options trading centers in the United States — the CBOE, the American Stock Exchange, the Philadelphia Stock Exchange, the Pacific Stock Exchange, and the New York Stock Exchange — and these exchanges receive steady streams of proposals for new listings.

1.4 Types of Traders

Derivatives have been very successful. The volume of derivative trading has substantially exceeded the volume of trading in spot market. The main reason for this situation is because they have attracted many different types of traders and have a great deal of liquidity. When an investor wants to take one side of a contract, there is usually no problem in finding someone that is prepared to take the other side.

In general, derivatives traders can be classified into (i) hedgers, (ii) speculators, and (iii) arbitrageurs. Hedgers use derivatives such as stock options, currency options, or other options to reduce the risk that they face from potential future movements in a market variable. In addition, futures contracts such as currency futures, index futures, and other futures can also perform such a function. Speculators use them to bet on the future direction of a market variable to make a profit. Arbitrageurs take offsetting positions in two or more instruments to lock in a profit. For example, arbitrageurs of portfolio insurance use the arbitrage process to lock in the profit. In Chapter 13, we will discuss portfolio insurance and synthetic options in detail.

1.4.1 *Hedge and hedgers*

To hedge, in finance, is to take an offsetting position in an asset or investment that reduces the price risk of an existing position. A hedge is therefore a trade that is made with the purpose of reducing the risk of adverse price movements in another asset. Normally, a hedge consists of taking the opposite position in a related security or in a derivative security based on the asset to be hedged.

Derivatives can be effective hedges against their underlying assets because the relationship between the two is more or less clearly defined. Derivatives are securities that move in correspondence to one or more underlying assets. They include options, swaps, futures, and forward contracts. The underlying assets can be stocks, bonds, commodities, currencies, indexes, or interest rates. It is possible to use derivatives to set up a trading strategy in which a loss for one investment is mitigated or offset by a gain in a comparable derivative.

Popular hedging techniques involve taking offsetting positions in derivatives that correspond to an existing position.

Other types of hedges can be constructed via other means like diversification. An example could be investing in both cyclical and countercyclical stocks.

Besides protecting an investor from various types of risk, it is believed that hedging makes the market run more efficiently.

Using a hedge is somewhat analogous to taking out an insurance policy. If you own a home in a flood-prone area, you will want to protect that asset from the risk of flooding — to hedge it, in other words — by taking out flood insurance. In this example, you cannot prevent a flood, but you can plan ahead of time to mitigate the dangers in the event that a flood occurs.

There is a risk–reward trade-off inherent in hedging; while it reduces potential risk, it also chips away at potential gains. Put simply, hedging is not free. In the case of the flood insurance policy example, the monthly payments add up, and if the flood never comes, the policyholder receives no payout. Still, most people would choose to take that predictable, circumscribed loss rather than suddenly lose the roof over their heads.

In the investment world, hedging works in the same way. Investors and money managers use hedging practices to reduce and control their exposure to risks. To appropriately hedge in the investment world, one must use various instruments in a strategic fashion to offset the risk of adverse price movements in the market. The best way to do this is to make another investment in a targeted and controlled way. Of course, the parallels with the insurance example above are limited: in the case of flood insurance, the policyholder would be completely compensated for her loss, perhaps less a deductible. In the investment space, hedging is both more complex and an imperfect science. The portfolio insurance methods which will be discussed in Chapter 13 will show this phenomenon in detail.

1.4.2 *Speculation and speculators*

Speculation can be defined as investment in stocks, derivatives, property, or other ventures in the hope of gain but with the risk of loss.

A speculator can be defined as a person who invests in stocks, property, or other ventures in the hope of making a profit. Speculators generally use futures market or option market to perform their speculative investment. In the derivative market, speculators take the risk which hedgers would rather hedge. Therefore, speculators play an important role in the derivative market for hedgers to hedge their risk.

1.4.3 *Arbitrage and arbitrageurs*

Now, we discuss how the arbitrage process can be used in the financial market. Suppose there are two riskless assets offering rates of return r and r'. Assuming no transaction costs, one of the strongest statements that can be made in positive economics is that

$$r = r'. \tag{1.1}$$

This is based on the law of one price, which says that the same good cannot sell at different prices. In terms of securities, the law of one price says that securities with identical risks must have the same expected return. Essentially, Equation (1.1) is an **arbitrage condition** that must be expected to hold in all but the most extreme circumstances. This is because if $r > r'$, the first riskless asset could be purchased with funds obtained from selling the second riskless asset. This arbitrage transaction would yield a return of $r - r'$ with no risk and no net wealth invested. If investors were to come across such a disequilibrium relationship, they would surely seize the opportunity to make a return of $r - r'$ without having to make any new investment of funds or take on any additional risk. In the process of buying the first asset and selling the second, investors would bid up the former's price and bid down the latter's price. This repricing mechanism would continue up to the point where these two assets' respective prices equaled each other, and thus $r = r'$. This arbitrage process is practically used in foreign exchange markets to make a profit. In addition, this arbitrage process can be theoretically used to determine the asset pricing which will be discussed in Chapter 3 in detail.

Arbitrageurs are a third important group of participants in futures, forward, and options markets. Arbitrage involves locking in a riskless profit by simultaneously entering transactions in two or more markets as we previously discussed.

1.5 Content of the Book and Teaching Method

1.5.1 *Content of the book*

This book contains 22 chapters and is divided into five parts: Part I — Overview; Part II — Forwards and Futures; Part III — Option: Theories and Applications; Part IV — Advanced Analyses of Options; and Part V — Special Topics of Options and Futures.

There are three chapters in Part I. Chapter 1 is the Introduction, and Chapter 2 is Futures, Options, and Swap: An Overview. In this chapter, we discuss the basic concepts and valuation methods of futures, options, and swap. In addition, option-like securities are also discussed in some detail. Finally, we briefly discuss how options, futures, and swap can be used in risk management. Chapter 3 is Introduction to Valuation Theories. In this chapter, we discuss bond and stock valuation. We also discuss M&M Valuation Theory, CAPM, and APT. Finally, we expand upon the basic concept of options, which was discussed in Chapter 2. Overall, Chapters 2 and 3 present an overall view of futures, forward, M&M Valuation Theory, CAPM, and APT.

There are two chapters in Part II. Chapter 4 discusses futures valuation, future market, and how they can be used for hedging. In this chapter, we also compare the similarities and differences between futures and forwards. In addition, we have discussed five hedging strategies, which include (i) the Classic Hedge Strategy; (ii) the Working Hedge Strategy; (iii) the Johnson Minimum-Variance Hedge

Strategy; (iv) the Howard–D'Antonio Optimal Risk–Return Hedge Strategy; and (v) the Optimum Mean-Variance Hedge Strategy. The relationships among these five strategies have also been discussed in some detail. Chapter 5 discusses commodity futures, financial futures, stock index futures, currency, and other futures. The valuations of these futures and their applications in hedging are also discussed in some detail.

There are five chapters in Part III. Chapter 6 discusses the basic valuation of options and option strategies. Chapter 7 discusses option pricing theory and firm valuation, and Chapter 8 discusses the decision tree and Microsoft Excel approach for option pricing model. Chapter 9 discusses normal, log-normal distribution, and option pricing model. And finally, Chapter 10 discusses index option, option on index futures, and currency options.

There are six chapters in Part IV. Chapter 11 presents comparative analysis of the option pricing models. Chapter 12 discusses implied variance, implied distribution, and volatility smiles. Chapter 13 discusses portfolio insurance and synthetic options. Chapter 14 presents bond duration, bond option, and bond portfolio strategies. Chapter 15 presents the integration and detailed derivation of constant elasticity of the variance option pricing model. Chapter 16 discusses warrants and convertible securities.

There are six chapters in Part V. Chapter 17 discusses the application of discriminant analysis, factor analysis, logistics regression, and the KMV-Merton model in credit risk analysis. Chapter 18 presents exotic options. Chapter 19 discusses real option, fuzzy set, and fuzzy real option. Chapter 20 discusses the derivation of the Black–Scholes option pricing model. Chapter 21 presents alternative methods for estimating hedge ratios, and finally, Chapter 22 presents alternative methods for determining option bounds.

1.5.2 *Teaching method*

When we teach derivatives for either undergraduate or graduate courses, we use the first sixteen chapters and Chapter 21. We use active and interdisciplinary approaches to teach this book as we have done in the corporate finance course which has been described in the paper by Lee (2022). In other words, we assign the following three projects: Project 1: Alternative Hedge Ratio Estimation Theory and Empirical Results; Project 2: Financial Statement Analysis and Option Strategies for XYZ Company; and Project 3: Historical Variance, Beta Coefficient, Greek Letters, and Option Valuation. These three projects count for 30% of students' grades. In this course, we use interdisciplinary approaches to teach the course. In other words, we not only teach future and options but also cover financial statement information and risk management, which are described in Chapters 2 and 17. In addition, we also use some basic financial theories related to corporate finance and investment analysis which are discussed in Chapter 3. In addition, we show how calculus and mathematical statistics can be used to understand the derivation of hedge ratio, option pricing model, implied volatility, and volatility smile. For the projects, we extensively ask students to use Excel tools.

1.6 Summary

In this chapter, we first discuss some basic concepts and information to be used in this book. This information includes forward, future, and option contracts, and type of traders. Second, we briefly discuss the contents of the book. Third, we suggest how to use an active and interdisciplinary approach to teach this course.

Questions

1. Define the following terms:

forward contracts	traders
future contracts	arbitrage
option contracts	arbitrageurs
hedge	speculation
hedgers	speculators

2. Discuss the differences among hedgers, speculators, and arbitrageurs.
3. Please briefly discuss the arbitrage process.
4. Please briefly discuss the structure of this book.
5. Please briefly discuss the active and interdisciplinary approach to teach futures and options.

Bibliography

Chen, S. S., C. F. Lee and K. Shrestha (2003). Futures hedge ratios: A review. *The Quarterly Review of Economics and Finance*, 43(3), 433–465.

Hull, J. C. (2017). *Fundamentals of Futures and Options Markets*, 9th ed. New York: Pearson.

Hull, J. C. (2021). *Options, Futures, and Other Derivatives*, 11th ed. New York: Pearson.

John, L. C. and C. F. Lee (2023). *Essentials of Excel VBA, Python, and R: Financial Statistics, and Portfolio Analysis*. New York: Springer Academic Publishers, forthcoming.

John, L. C., C. F. Lee, J. R. Chang and L.-J. Kao (2023). *Essentials of Excel VBA, Python, and R: Financial Derivatives, Risk Management and Machine Learning*. New York: Springer Academic Publishers.

Lee, C. F. (2022). Active and interdisciplinary approach to teach corporate finance. *Review of Pacific Basin Financial Markets and Policies*, 25(3), 1–31.

Lee, C. F. and J. Lee (2015). *Handbook of Financial Econometrics and Statistics*. New York: Springer Academic Publishers.

Lee, C. F. and J. Lee (2020). *Handbook of Financial Econometrics, Mathematics, Statistics, and Machine Learning*. Singapore: World Scientific.

Lee, C. F. and A. C. Lee (2022). *Encyclopedia of Finance*, 3rd ed. New York: Springer Academic Publishers.

Lee, C. F., A. C. Lee, and J. Lee (2010). *Handbook of Quantitative Finance and Risk Management*. New York: Springer Academic Publishers.

Lee, C. F., J. Lee and A. C. Lee (2013). *Statistics for Business and Financial Economics*, 3rd ed. New York: Springer Academic Publishers.

Lee, C. F., Y. Chen and J. Lee (2016). Alternative methods to derive option pricing models: Review and comparison. *Review of Quantitative Finance and Accounting*, 47(2), 417–451.

Lee, C. F., H.-Y. Chen and J. Lee (2019). *Financial Econometrics, Mathematics and Statistics*. New York: Springer Academic Publishers.

Lee, C. F., J. Lee and M. Lee (2022). *Corporate Finance and Strategy: An Active Learning Approach*. Singapore: World Scientific.

Lee, C. F., A. C. Lee and J. Lee (2023). *Handbook of Investment Analysis, Portfolio Management, and Financial Derivatives*. Singapore: World Scientific.

Lee, C. F., J. Finnerty, J. Lee, A. C. Lee and D. Wort (2013). *Security Analysis, Portfolio Management, and Financial Derivatives*, 3rd ed. Singapore: World Scientific.

Lin, F. L. (2023). A comparative analysis of hedging determination for three alternative international equity index futures. *Review of Pacific Basin Financial Markets and Policies*, 26, forthcoming.

Chapter 2

Futures, Options, Swaps, and Risk Management

Contents

2.1 Introduction

For those not familiar with their characteristics and uses, derivative securities such as futures, options, and swaps can appear to be highly speculative — that is, risky — investments. News stories in recent years informed the public of the escapades of highly speculative investments made by personnel at organizations such as Barings Bank PLC; Procter & Gamble; Orange County, California; Gibson Greetings; and Metallgesellschaft.

On the contrary, proper use of derivatives helps companies, as well as investors, to *reduce* risk. Firms that use oil, metals, or grain as production inputs can use derivatives to "lock in" prices today to reduce the risk of future price fluctuations. Financial derivatives can reduce firms' financing costs and can help corporate treasurers reduce the risk of future changes in interest rates or exchange rates.

The seventies and eighties can be regarded as truly revolutionary for financial markets and financial theory. During those decades, derivative securities, such as futures, options, warrants, and swaps, literally caused the markets to explode. It is said that the value of derivatives now traded generally exceeds the value of the New York Stock Exchange by a factor of 10. Much of the growth of these derivatives can be attributed to increased volatility in the financial markets. In addition, with the theoretical development of the Black–Scholes Option pricing model, the way that financial analysts consider risk and return has changed. The main purpose of this chapter is to introduce these relatively new ideas by briefly discussing futures, options, and swaps and applying them to the valuation of option-like securities and the management of corporate risk.

In the next five sections, we will go into more detail concerning the topics of Futures, Options, Option-Like Securities, Swap Contracts, and Risk Management. In Section 2.2, we take a deeper look at futures contracts and how entering futures contracts can hedge exchange rate risks. In Section 2.3, we define what an option contract is and how to value option contracts. In Section 2.4, we will learn about other securities that act like options, for example, warrants, convertible securities, callable bonds, and risky corporate debt. We will then learn the benefits of using interest rate swaps and currency rate swaps to hedge risk in Section 2.5. In Section 2.6, we will describe the importance of managing risk for investors through the various strategies of futures contracts, option contracts, swaps, warrants, convertible bonds, and other hedging procedures. In Section 2.7, we will provide a summary of the chapter. Finally, in Appendix 2A, we briefly discuss financial static ratio analysis.

2.2 Futures Contracts and Hedging

This section defines futures contracts. In Section 2.2.1, we define what a futures contract is and explain the terminology associated it.

Section 2.2.2 provides a brief background on the history of Futures Exchanges both domestically and internationally. In Section 2.2.3, the importance of margin requirements in respect to futures contracts is described. After we discuss maintenance requirements, we will look at Section 2.2.4 and learn about the regulation surrounding the futures markets. In Section 2.2.5, we learn about the advantages of using futures to hedge out risk, especially exchange rate risk. This section will provide a large overview of futures contracts and how futures can be used to hedge risk for investors.

2.2.1 *Nature of contracts*

Many types of securities share similar characteristics with options, which we will discuss in the next section. Perhaps the most significant is a *futures contract*. The International Money Market (IMM) of the Chicago Mercantile Exchange (CME) began trading futures contracts on foreign exchange currency in 1972. In 1982, a market similar to the IMM opened in London. This market, called the London International Financial Futures Exchange (LIFFE), trades futures contracts that are similar to the IMM contracts. In this section, we focus on currency futures. However, several other futures also exist, such as futures on grains and oilseeds, futures on metals and petroleum, and futures on interest rates. Table 2.1 presents futures price quotations of corn futures as examples for these markets.

A **forward contract** is a tailor-made agreement between a corporate customer and a bank that specifies an amount, a place, a date, and an exchange rate for the exchange of one currency for another. These forward contracts are very useful because they can be tailored to fit any situation, but they are very expensive. Unlike a forward contract, a **futures contract** is a standardized financial instrument with a stated amount and specific maturity that is traded on an organized exchange and is resalable up to the close of trading or settlement date. The futures contract defines what asset is to be bought or sold, and how, when, where, and in what quantity it is to be delivered. The terms also specify the currency in which the contract will trade, minimum tick value, and the last trading day and expiry or delivery month. Futures contracts tend to be smaller than forward contracts and are not as flexible in meeting hedging needs.

Table 2.1 is composed of futures quotes provided by the Wall Street Journal for the commodities corn, gold, and crude oil on the

Table 2.1 Futures Quotes for Select Commodities from the *Wall Street Journal* on May 24, 2021

	Open	High	Low	Last Trade	Prior Settlement	Change	Volume	Open Interest
Corn Continuous Contract, C00 (U.S.: CBOT)								
July, 2021	652.25	658.50	645.50	658.00	657.25	−1.50	94,900	629,918
Sept, 2021	566.00	570.50	555.50	569.00	568.50	−4.25	25,996	294,457
Dec, 2021	540.00	542.50	529.00	540.50	540.25	−6.00	60,326	531,115
Mar, 2022	547.25	548.75	535.50	546.50	546.50	−6.75	4,985	110,664
May, 2022	546.00	551.50	538.50	549.25	549.50	−6.50	1,917	33,436
July, 2022	549.00	550.25	537.75	548.25	548.25	−6.00	1,802	54,198
Gold Continuous Contract, GC00 (U.S.: Nymex)								
July, 2021	1,884.30	1,888.70	1,876.80	1,885.20	1,885.50	7.60	844	1,553
Aug, 2021	1,885.60	1,890.00	1,877.90	1,883.50	1,886.70	4.60	51,824	281,810
Dec, 2021	1,887.90	1,893.20	1,881.40	1,888.50	1,890.50	6.00	3,504	47,191
Feb, 2022	1,889.00	1,893.10	1,888.80	1,889.70	1,892.40	5.20	984	7,807
Apr, 2022	1,891.70	1,894.60	1,891.70	1,894.60	1,894.00	8.60	18	837
Aug, 2022	1,891.00	1,893.90	1,886.40	1,897.50	1,897.50	−6.30	1	10
Crude Oil WTI (NYM $/bbl) Front Month, CL.1 (U.S.: Nymex)								
July, 2021	63.87	66.14	63.63	66.03	66.05	2.45	435,983	485,249
Sept, 2021	63.26	65.42	63.07	65.29	65.32	2.30	88,000	197,881
Dec, 2021	61.89	63.85	61.73	63.70	63.73	2.05	75,900	329,438
Mar, 2022	60.70	62.38	60.70	62.28	62.30	1.87	8,255	53,732
May, 2022	60.23	61.55	60.15	61.43	61.51	1.73	2,618	33,961
July, 2022	60.95	60.36	59.05	60.36	60.78	1.31	949	21,625

Source: *Wall Street Journal*, Commodity Market Data, May 24, 2021. https://www.wsj.com/market-data/commodities?mod=nav_top_subsection.

date May 24, 2021. The underlying asset of the futures contract, the contract size, and the way the price is quoted are shown at the top of each section. For the commodity corn, the size of the contract is 5,000 bushels, quoted at cents per bushel. The expiration month of each contract is also listed in the first column. Futures terms related to Table 2.1 are defined in Table 2.2.

The table indicates the opening price, the highest price in trading thus far during the trading day, and the lowest price thus far during the trading day. The opening price represents the prices at which the contracts were trading immediately at the start of trading on May 24, 2021. For the May 2022 Crude Oil contract, the opening price was $60.23 per barrel, with a high of $61.55 per barrel and low of $60.15 per barrel.

The Last Trade column represents the most recent trading price for the contract on the current trading day. The Change column represents the change of the current price of the contract from the previous day's settlement price. The settlement price is the price used to calculate the daily gains and losses and margin requirements. We calculate it as the price at which the contract traded immediately before the day's trading session ended. For the April 2022 Gold contract, the last trade was at $1,894.60 per ounce. This price is $0.60 greater than the settlement price from the previous day. Therefore, we see that the prior settlement for the April 2022 Gold contract was $1,894.00 ($1,894.60 – 0.60 = 1,894.00). Since the change is positive, we subtract the change from the last trade value. If the change was negative, we would add that to the last trade number to find the prior settlement price. We add when the change is negative since the prior settlement price had a higher price than the current's day last trade, meaning the prior settlement price needs to be larger than the current day's last trading price.

The second to last column in Table 2.1 represents the Volume. This column gives the trading volume, or the number of contracts traded in a day, for the given futures contract. It can be contrasted with the open interest, which is the number of contracts outstanding, or in other words, the number of long positions or the number of short positions. If there is a large amount of trading by day traders, then the volume of trading may be greater than the beginning open interest or the closing open interest.

Table 2.2 Futures Terms

Open	The price for the day's first trade, registered during the period designated as the opening of the market.
High	The highest price at which the futures contract sold during the day.
Low	The lowest price at which the futures contract sold during the day.
Settle	Since each contract is marked to market each day, the settlement price or the marking to market price is very important to investors. The settlement price is a figure determined by formula from within the range of closing prices or it may be the closing price.
Change	The amount the settlement price changed from the previous day.
Lifetime high or low	The highest and lowest prices recorded for each contract maturity from the first day it was traded to the present.
Open interest	The quantity of open long positions at the exchange's clearinghouse for each contract.
Volume	The number of contracts actually traded on the exchange for a given trading session.

The price fluctuations of a futures contract are limited by the rules of the exchange on which it trades. The parties (buyer and seller) to the futures contract typically do not know each other. However, neither faces any chance of default on the futures contract because an exchange clearinghouse stands ready to ensure performance of the contract. The major limitations of the futures contract from the viewpoint of corporations or hedgers are the relatively small sizes and the standardized maturities of available contracts.

After expiry, each futures contract will be settled, either by physical delivery (typically for assets underlying commodities) or by a cash settlement (typically for financial underlying stock). The contracts ultimately are not between the original buyer and the original seller, but between the holders at expiry and the exchange. Since contracts potentially pass through many different hands between the point of creation and sale, settling parties often do not know with whom they have ultimately traded.

Table 2.2 presents the definitions of futures contract terms.

2.2.2 *Futures exchanges*

Futures Exchanges are able to provide risk insurance to producers with a risky output and provide insurance to commodity stockholders at low cost. Speculators in the market absorb some of the risk but hedging appears to drive most commodity markets. The equilibrium futures price can be either below or above the (rationally) expected future price.

One of the earliest written records of futures trading is found in Aristotle's *Politics*. Aristotle tells the story of Thalesa, a poor philosopher from Miletus, who developed a "financial device, which involves a principle of universal application." Thales used his skill in forecasting and predicted that the olive harvest would be exceptionally good the next autumn. Confident in his prediction, he made agreements with local olive press owners to deposit his money with them to guarantee him exclusive use of their olive presses when the harvest was ready. Thales successfully negotiated low prices because the harvest was in the future and no one knew whether the harvest would be plentiful or pathetic and because the olive press owners were willing to "hedge" against the possibility of a poor yield. When the harvest time came, and a sharp increase in demand for the use of the olive presses outstripped availability of the presses, he sold his future use contracts of the olive presses at a rate of his choosing and made a large quantity of money. It should be noted, however, that this is a very loose example of futures trading and, in fact, more closely resembles an option contract because Thales was not obligated to use the presses if the yield turned out to be pathetic.

The first modern organized futures exchange began in 1710 at the Dojima Rice Exchange in Osaka, Japan.

The London Metal Market and Exchange Company (London Metal Exchange) was founded in 1877, but the market traces its origins back to 1571 and the opening of the Royal Exchange, London. Before the exchange was created, business was conducted by traders in London coffee houses, using a makeshift ring drawn in chalk on the floor. At first, only copper was traded later followed by lead and zinc (although they were only made official in 1920). The exchange was closed during WWII and did not reopen until 1952. The range of metals traded was extended to include aluminum, nickel, tin, aluminum alloy, steel, cobalt, and molybdenum. The exchange ceased trading plastics in 2011. The total value of the trade is around US$11.6 trillion annually.

Chicago has the largest future exchange in the world, the Chicago Mercantile Exchange. Chicago is located at the base of the Great Lakes, close to the farmlands and cattle country of the Midwest, making it a natural center for transportation, distribution, and trading of agricultural produce. Gluts and shortages of these products caused chaotic fluctuations in price, and this led to the development of a market enabling grain merchants, processors, and agriculture companies to trade in "to arrive" or "cash forward" contracts to insulate them from the risk of adverse price change and enable them to hedge. In March 2008, the Chicago Mercantile Exchange announced its acquisition of NYMEX Holdings, Inc., the parent company of the New York Mercantile Exchange and Commodity Exchange. CME's acquisition of NYMEX was completed in August 2008.

For most exchanges, forward contracts were standard at the time. However, most forward contracts were not honored by both the buyer and the seller. For instance, if the buyer of a corn forward contract made an agreement to buy corn, and at the time of delivery the price of corn differed dramatically from the original contract price, either the buyer or the seller would back out. Additionally, the forward contracts market was very illiquid and an exchange was needed that would bring together a market to find potential buyers and sellers of a commodity instead of making people bear the burden of finding a buyer or seller.

In 1848, the Chicago Board of Trade (CBOT) was formed. Trading was originally in forward contracts; the first contract (on corn) was written on March 13, 1851. In 1865, standardized futures contracts were introduced.

Following the end of the postwar international gold standard in 1972, the CME formed a division called the International Monetary Market (IMM) to offer futures contracts in foreign currencies: British pound, Canadian dollar, German mark, Japanese yen, Mexican peso, and Swiss franc.

In 1881, a regional market was founded in Minneapolis, Minnesota, and in 1883, futures were introduced for the first time. Trading continuously since then, today, the Minneapolis Grain EXchange (MGEX) is the only exchange for hard red spring wheat futures and options.

The 1970s saw the development of the financial futures contracts, which allowed trading in the future value of interest rates. These (in particular the 90-day Eurodollar contracts introduced in 1981) had an enormous impact on the development of the interest rate swap market.

In June 2001, InterContinental Exchange (ICE) acquired the International Petroleum Exchange (IPE), now ICE Futures, which operated Europe's leading open-outcry energy futures exchange. Since 2003, ICE has partnered with the Chicago Climate Exchange (CCX) to host its electronic marketplace. In April 2005, the entire ICE portfolio of energy futures became fully electronic.

In 2005, the Africa Mercantile Exchange (AfMX®) became the first African commodities market to implement an automated system for the dissemination of market data and information online in real time through a wide network of computer terminals. As of the end of 2007, AfMX® had developed a system of secure data storage providing online services for brokerage firms. The year 2010 saw the exchange unveil a novel system of electronic trading, known as After®. After® extends the potential volume of processing of information and allows the Exchange to increase its overall volume of trading activities.

In 2006, the NYSE teamed up with the Amsterdam–Brussels–Lisbon–Paris Exchanges' "Euronext" electronic exchange to form the first transcontinental futures and options exchange. These two developments as well as the sharp growth of internet futures trading platforms developed by a number of trading companies clearly point to a race to total internet trading of futures and options in the coming years.

In terms of trading volume, the National Stock Exchange of India in Mumbai is the largest stock futures trading exchange in the world, followed by JSE Limited in Sandton, Gauteng, South Africa.

2.2.3 *Margin*

Whenever someone enters into a contract position in the futures market, a security deposit, commonly called a **margin requirement**, must be paid. While the futures margin may seem to be a partial payment for the security on which the futures contract is based, it only represents security to cover any losses that may result from adverse price movements. The meaning of the word margin is often quite confusing. We have profit margin, NYSE margin requirement, and so on. Each of these usages of the word margin has a specialized meaning. It is helpful to go over the various definitions of the word margin to ensure that any confusion is avoided.

The minimum margin requirements set by the exchange must be collected by the clearing member firms (members of the exchange involved in the clearinghouse operations) when their customers take positions in the market. In turn, the clearing member firms must deposit a fixed portion of these margins with the clearinghouse. At the end of each trading day, every futures trading account is incremented or reduced by the corresponding increase or decrease in the value of all open interest positions. This daily adjustment procedure is applied to the margin deposit and is called **marking to market**. For example, if an investor is long on a yen futures contract and by the end of the day its market value has fallen \$1,000, he or she would be asked to add an additional \$1,000 to the margin account. Why? Because the investor is responsible for its initial value. For example, if a futures contract is executed at \$10,000 with an initial margin of \$1,000 and the value of the position goes down \$1,000 to \$9,000, the buyer would be required to put in an additional margin of \$1,000 because the investor is responsible for paying \$10,000 for the contract. If the investor is unable to comply or refuses to do so, the clearing member firm that he or she trades through would automatically close out the position. On the other hand, if the contract's value was up \$1,000 for the day, the investor might immediately withdraw the profit if he or she so desired. The procedure of marking to market implies that all potential profits and losses are realized immediately.

Due to the difficulty of calling all customers whose margin accounts have fallen in value for the day, a clearing member firm usually will require that a sum of money be deposited at the initiation of any futures position. This additional sum is called **maintenance margin**. In most situations, the original margin requirement may be established with a risk-free, interest-bearing security such as a T-bill. However, the maintenance margin, which must be in cash, is adjusted for daily changes in the contract value.

As the clearing house is the counterparty to all their trades, they only have to have one margin account. This is in contrast with OTC derivatives, where issues such as margin accounts have to be negotiated with all counterparties.

2.2.4 *Regulation*

Each exchange is normally regulated by a national governmental (or semi-governmental) regulatory agency:

- In Australia, this role is performed by the Australian Securities and Investments Commission.
- On the Chinese mainland by the China Securities Regulatory Commission.
- In Hong Kong by the *Securities and Futures Commission.*
- In India by the Securities and Exchange Board of India and Forward Markets Commission (FMC).
- In Japan by the Financial Services Agency.
- In Pakistan by the Securities and Exchange Commission of Pakistan.
- In Singapore by the *Monetary Authority of Singapore.*
- In the UK, futures exchanges are regulated by the Financial Services Authority.
- In the U.S. by the Commodity Futures Trading Commission.
- In Malaysia by the Securities Commission Malaysia.
- In Spain by the Comisión Nacional del Mercado de Valores (CNMV).
- In Brazil by the Comissão de Valores Mobiliários (CVM).
- In South Africa by the Financial Services Board (South Africa).
- In Mauritius by the Financial Services Commission (FSC).

2.2.5 *Hedging with futures*

Markets that permit individuals, corporations, and banks to protect themselves from foreign exchange risk are necessary during periods of fluctuating exchange rates. A comparison of forward and futures markets is summarized in Table 2.3.

Foreign exchange futures also can be used to hedge exchange rate risk. For example, a German firm that exports its products to the United States will receive U.S. dollar payments in the near future. The financial manager of the German firm can sell the Deutsche Mark currency futures to hedge potential devaluation of the U.S. dollar relative to the Deutsche Mark. The Deutsche Mark currency futures will result in a gain if the value of the dollar falls against the Deutsche Mark.

Table 2.3 Comparison of Forward and Futures Markets

	Forward	Futures
Size of contract	Tailored to individual needs	Standardized
Delivery date	Tailored to individual needs	Standardized
Method of transaction	Established by the bank via telephone contact with limited number of market participants	Determined by open auction among many buyers and sellers on the exchange floor
Participants	Banks, brokers, corporations, and central banks; public speculation not encouraged	Banks, brokers, and corporations; public speculation encouraged
Commissions	Set by spread between bank's buy and sell prices; not easily determined by consumer	Small brokerage fee and negotiated rates on block trades
Security deposit	None, but compensating bank balances required	Small security deposit required
Clearing operation	Handling contingent upon individual banks and brokers	Handled by exchange clearinghouse, daily settlements marked to market
Marketplace	Communications network	Central exchange floor
Economic justification	Facilitate world trade by providing a hedge mechanism	Risk sharing with public participation
Accessibility	Limited to very large customers	Open to anyone
Regulation	Self-regulating	Commodity Futures Trading Commission
Price fluctuations	No daily limit	Daily limit imposed by exchange
Contract liquidity	None	Daily trading

2.3 Options

In this section, we will learn what option contracts are and how they can also be used to manage risk. In Section 2.3.1, the basic definitions concerning options are provided and a brief explanation on the history of option contracts is provided. In Section 2.3.2, we describe what is meant by a call and put option, as well as American versus European options. In Section 2.3.3, we discuss the different exchanges that exist for the trading of options. In Section 2.3.4, we look at a partial listing of option contracts and learn how to pull out important information from exchange quotes. Section 2.3.5 expands on how to value both call and put options, using Equations (2.1) and (2.2). In addition, we learn how option contracts are influenced by the market price of the stock, exercise price of the option, volatility of the stock price, and time until option expiration.

2.3.1 *Basic concepts of options*

In general, there are three types of options based on equity securities: (1) warrants, (2) publicly traded options, and (3) executive stock options. A **warrant** is a financial instrument issued by a corporation that gives the purchaser the right to buy a fixed number of shares at a set price for a specified period. There usually is a secondary market where existing warrants may be traded. It must be noted that a warrant is more difficult to price than a traded option. This is because when warrants are exercised, the underlying company changes; it receives a cash inflow and its capital structure is less levered. When a publicly traded option is exercised, on the other hand, the only thing that happens is that ownership of some shares changes hands.

There are two major differences between a warrant and a publicly traded option. First, the warrant normally matures in three to five years, whereas the maturity of a publicly traded option is normally less than nine months. The second difference is that the warrant is an agreement between the corporation and the warrant's buyer. If the warrant's owner decides to exercise the right to purchase stock, the corporation issues new shares and receives the cash from the sales of those shares. A **publicly traded option** is an agreement between two individuals who have no relationship with the corporation whose shares underlie the option. When a publicly traded option is exercised, money and shares are exchanged between the individuals and the corporation receives no funds.

Executive stock options provide stock purchase rights as compensation for corporate employees. For services rendered, the manager or the employee has the right to buy a specific number of shares for a set price during a given period. Unlike warrants and publicly traded options, executive stock options cannot be traded. The option's owner has only two choices: exercise the option or let it expire. Like a warrant, should the owner decide to exercise the option, the corporation receives money and issues new shares.

The use of executive stock options for management compensation raises an interesting agency question. The firm's managers may make investment and financing decisions that increase the firm's risk in order to increase the value of their stock options. (As we will see, the value of an option is directly related to the variability or riskiness of the underlying asset, which in this case is the firm.) Such an action could have a detrimental effect on the bondholders and other creditors of the firm.

Publicly traded options are probably the most widely known of the three types of equity option instruments. In 1973, the Chicago Board of Options Exchange (CBOE) was founded to provide a market in these securities. Although it was possible to trade options over the counter before that time, trading volume was relatively low. The opening of the CBOE marked the beginning of a phenomenal growth in the popularity of options as financial instruments. Indeed, in terms of the value of the securities traded, the Chicago Board Options Exchange is challenging the New York and Tokyo Stock Exchanges as the world's largest securities market. There are now five options trading centers in the United States — the CBOE, the American Stock Exchange, the Philadelphia Stock Exchange, the Pacific Stock Exchange, and the New York Stock Exchange — and these exchanges receive steady streams of proposals for new listings.

2.3.2 *Option terminology*

There are two basic types of publicly traded options: calls and puts. A **call option** gives the holder the right to buy a particular number of shares of a designated common stock at a specified price, called the **exercise price** (or striking price), on or before a given date, known as the **expiration date**. On the Chicago Board Options Exchange, options typically are created for three-, six-, or nine-month periods. All have the same expiration date: the Saturday following the third Friday of the month of expiration. The owner of the shares of common stock can write or create an option and sell it in the options market, in an attempt to increase the return or income on a stock investment. A more venturesome investor may create an option in this fashion without owing any of the underlying stock. This **naked option writing** exposes the speculator to unlimited risk because he or she may have to buy shares at some point to satisfy the contract at whatever price is reached. This is serious if the value of the underlying asset has a high degree of variability.

A **put option** gives the holder the right to sell a certain number of shares of common stock at a set price on or before the expiration date of the option. In purchasing a put, the owner of the shares has bought the right to sell those shares by the expiration date at the exercise price. As with calls, one can create, or write, a put, accepting the obligation to buy shares.

The owner of a put or call is not obligated to carry out the specified transaction, but has the *option* of doing so. If the transaction is carried out, it is said to have been *exercised*. For example, if you hold a call option on a stock that is currently trading at a price higher than the exercise price, you may want to exercise the option to purchase stock at the exercise price and then immediately resell the stock at a profit. This call option is said to be *in the money*. On the other hand, if the call option is *out of the money* — that is, the stock is trading at a price below the exercise price — you certainly would not want to exercise the option, as it would be cheaper to purchase stock directly. *At the money* means that the stock price is trading at the exercise price of the option.

An **American option** can be exercised at any time up to the expiration date. A **European option** can be exercised only on the expiration date; this makes it simpler to analyze because its term to maturity is known. Because of this simplifying factor, we will concentrate on the valuation of European options. The factors that determine the values of American and European options are the same; all other things being equal, however, an American option is worth more than a European option because of the extra flexibility it grants the option holder.

Although our discussion in this section is limited to options on equities, many other kinds of securities underlie publicly traded options. For example, people also trade options to buy or sell stock indexes, Treasury bonds, futures contracts, foreign currencies, and

Table 2.4 Definitions of Option Terminology

Call	An option to purchase a fixed number of shares of common stock.
Put	An option to sell a fixed number of shares of common stock.
Exercise price	The price at which the underlying security specified in an option contract may be traded.
Expiration date	The time by which the option transaction must be carried out.
Exercise an option	Carry out a transaction specified in an option contract.
American option	An option that can be exercised any time up to the expiration date.
European option	An option that can be exercised only on the expiration date.
At the money	A call or put option with an exercise price equal to the current stock price.
In the money	A call option with an exercise price below the stock price, or a put option with an exercise price above the stock price.
Out of the money	A call option with an exercise price above the stock price, or a put option with an exercise price below the stock price.
Naked options	The writing of a call or put option without owning the underlying asset.

agricultural commodities. Table 2.4 summarizes the terms introduced in this section.

2.3.3 *Option exchanges*

In 1973, the Chicago Board Options Exchange (CBOE) was founded to provide a market for options. The opening of the CBOE created exponential growth in the popularity of options as financial instruments. Most of the trading for options is done on electronic exchanges. Most derivatives exchanges are now fully electronic, so there is no need for traders to physically meet. The International Securities Exchange launched the first all-electronic options market for equities in May 2000. In addition, over 95% of the option orders handled at the Chicago Board Options Exchange are handled electronically. The remaining 5% are complex or large institutional orders that require the skill and knowledge of floor traders.

Today, the amount of option exchanges in the United States and around the world has increased. In addition to CBOE and the International Securities Exchange, there is the BATS Option Market, Boston (BOX) Options Exchange, C2 Options Exchange, ISE Gemini, MIAC Options Exchange, NASDAQ OMX BX, NASDAQ OMX PHLX, Philadelphia Stock Exchange, NASDAQ Options Market, NYSE, AMEX Options (American Stock Exchange), and NYSE Arca Options.

2.3.4 *Option price information*

Table 2.5 presents options quotations for Johnson & Johnson. The price of Johnson & Johnson shares on this date was around $170. The first column gives the **expiration month** for each option. We have included listings for call and put options with exercise prices ranging from $165 to $175 per share, and with expiration dates in May 2021, August 2021, and January 2022.

The next columns provide the closing price, its change from the previous trading day, bid price, asked price, trading volume, and open interest (outstanding contracts) of each option. Column 4 shows the Bid, or the latest price offered by a market maker to buy a particular option. The **Ask** price in Column 5 is the latest price offered by a market maker to sell a particular option. For example, the first contract traded on the May 2021 expiration call with the exercise price of $165. The last trade was at $5.25, meaning that an option to purchase one share of Johnson & Johnson at an exercise price of $165 sold for $5.25. Each option contract (on 100 shares) therefore costs $525.

Note that the prices of call options decrease as the exercise price increases. For example, the May 2021 expiration call with exercise price $175 costs only $0.03. This makes sense, because the right to purchase a share at a higher exercise price is less valuable. Conversely, put prices increase with the exercise price. The right to sell a share of Johnson & Johnson at a price of $165 in May 2021 costs $0.10 while the right to sell at $175 costs $5.05.

Option prices also increase with time until expiration. Clearly, one would rather have the right to buy Johnson & Johnson for $175 at any time until January 2022 rather than at any time until May 2021. Not surprisingly, this shows up in a higher price for the January 2022

Table 2.5 Option Quotes for Johnson & Johnson, May 25, 2021

25-May-21													
Johnson & Johnson (JNJ)								Underlying Stock Price: $170					
	Call							Put					
Expiration	**Last**	**Chg**	**Bid**	**Ask**	**Volume**	**Open Int.**	**Strike**	**Last**	**Chg**	**Bid**	**Ask**	**Volume**	**Open Int.**
May-21	5.25	(0.35)	4.90	5.10	10.00	238.00	165.00	0.10	–	0.09	0.11	497.00	848.00
May-21	0.80	(0.52)	0.76	0.83	377.00	1,740.00	170.00	0.93	0.19	0.87	0.93	441.00	547.00
May-21	0.03	(0.03)	0.03	0.05	363.00	1,487.00	175.00	5.05	0.55	5.05	5.25	3.00	144.00
Aug-21	8.70	–	8.45	8.70	20.00	122.00	165.00	3.34	0.05	3.35	3.50	5.00	79.00
Aug-21	5.52	(0.40)	5.40	5.60	190.00	1,551.00	170.00	5.36	0.16	5.30	5.45	15.00	30.00
Aug-21	3.25	(0.35)	3.25	3.30	160.00	316.00	175.00	8.15	0.35	8.00	8.25	2.00	15.00
Jan-22	12.50	(0.40)	12.20	12.45	110.00	2,029.00	165.00	8.48	0.18	8.35	8.50	14.00	2,382.00
Jan-22	9.55	(0.42)	9.50	9.70	6.00	2,759.00	170.00	10.70	0.15	10.65	10.85	13.00	2,105.00
Jan-22	7.25	(0.45)	7.20	7.40	79.00	3,019.00	175.00	15.60	–	13.35	13.60	–	793.00

expiration options. For example, the call with exercise price $175 expiring in January 2022 sells for $7.25, compared to only $0.03 for the May 2021 call.

2.3.5 *Option valuation*

Let's begin with a simple question. How much is a call option worth on its expiration date? The question is simple because the imminent expiration makes the uncertain future movements of the price of the stock irrelevant. The call must be exercised immediately or not at all. If a call option is out of the money on its expiration date, it will not be exercised; it will become a worthless piece of paper.

On the other hand, if the call option is in the money on its expiration date, it will be exercised. The owner can purchase stock at the exercise price and immediately resell it at the market price, if desired. The option value is the difference between these two prices. On the call option's expiration date, its value is either zero or some positive amount equal to the difference between the market price of the stock and the exercise price of the option.

2.3.5.1 *Basic model*

Symbolically, let P equal the price of the stock and X equal the exercise price of the option. The value of the call, V_c, equals the maximum of zero or P minus X. This relationship can be written as follows:

$$V_c = \text{Max}(0, P - X), \tag{2.1}$$

where Max denotes the larger of the two bracketed terms. For a put option (V_p), $V_p = X - P$ if $X > P$, and $V_p = 0$ if $X < P$. This can be written as follows:

$$V_p = \text{Max}(0, X - P). \tag{2.2}$$

The call position is illustrated in Figure 2.1(a), which considers a call option with an exercise price of $50, which is equal to stock price. Therefore, the call option value is $V_c = 50 - 50 = 0$. The option's value increases as the stock price rises above $50. If, on the expiration date, the stock is trading at $60, then the call option is worth $10.

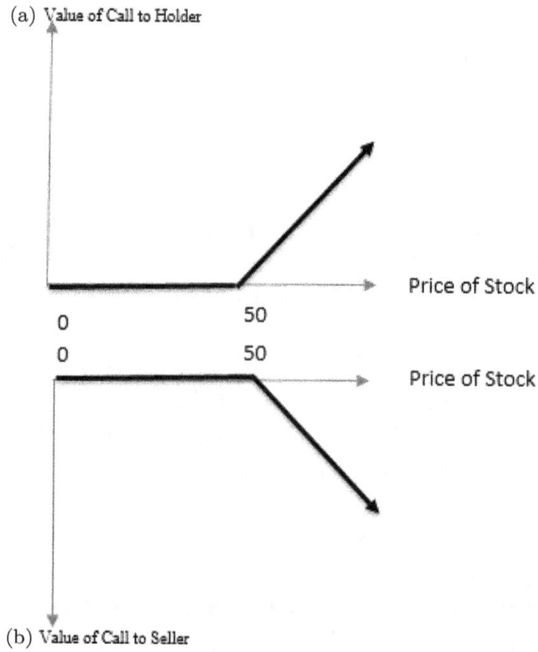

Figure 2.1 Value of $50 Exercise Price Call Option to (a) Holder and (b) Seller

Figure 2.1(b) is the mirror image of Figure 2.1(a); it shows the position of the write of the call option. If the stock is trading below the exercise price on the expiration date, the call option will not be exercised and its seller will incur no loss. However, if stock is trading at $60, the seller of the call option will be required to sell this stock for $50, that is, $10 below the price that could be obtained on the market.

We have seen that once a call option has been purchased, the holder of the option may obtain gains but cannot incur losses beyond the initial premium payment. Correspondingly, the writer of an option may incur losses but cannot achieve any more gains after receiving the premium. In both cases, the **premium** represents the current value of the option. Further, there is no net gain; the profit gained by one balances the loss of the other. Thus, options are zero-sum securities; they transfer wealth rather than create it. To acquire this instrument, the buyer must pay the premium to the writer. This value is the price paid to acquire the chance of future profit, and therefore, it will reflect uncertainty about future market prices of the common stock. Several factors that influence call option values are discussed in the next section. The real value or attractiveness of options has to do with how options can transform risks. So, it is not wealth creation that gives options value but rather the risk transformation factor.

2.3.6 *Variables that influence call option value*

Five factors influence the value of a call option: the market price of the stock, the exercise price of the option, the risk-free interest rate, the volatility of the stock price, and the time that remains before the option's expiration date. We will examine the impact of these factors on call value next.

Market price of the stock. AE in Figure 2.2 shows the curvilinear relationship between a call option's value and the market price of the underlying stock. As already noted, the slope of this relationship increases as market price becomes higher; eventually, each dollar increase in the price of the stock translates into an increase in the value of the call option. In Figure 2.2, AB and CD represent the maximum and the minimum value for the call option, respectively.

Exercise price of the option. Offered two otherwise identical call options on the same stock, you would prefer the one with the lower exercise price. It would generate larger gains from any favorable movement in the price of the stock than the option with the higher exercise price. Therefore, a lower exercise price implies a higher call option value, all other things being equal. In Figure 2.2, C represents the exercise price. In addition, the locations of at-the-money, in-the-money, and out-of-the-money prices are also presented.

Risk-free interest rate. If a call option is eventually exercised, the holder of the option will reap some of the benefits of an increase in the market value of the stock. The option holder will enjoy this gain without having to pay the exercise price immediately. This payment will be made only at some future time, when the call option is actually exercised. In the meantime, this money can be invested in government securities to earn a no-risk return.

This opportunity confers an increment of value on the call option. All else being equal, a higher risk-free interest rate should cause a greater call option value. Moreover, postponing the exercise of the

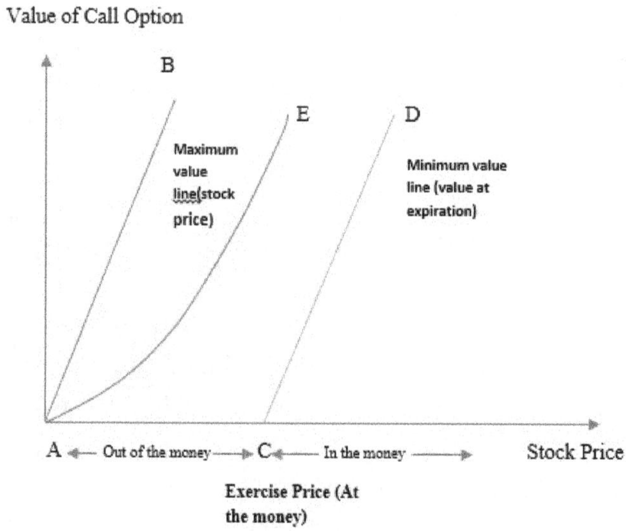

Figure 2.2 Relation of Call Option Value to Market Price of Stock

option for a longer time should increase the risk-free interest earnings. Accordingly, the risk-free interest rate should help to determine a call option's value in conjunction with the time remaining before the expiration date.

Volatility of the stock price. Suppose that you can purchase call options on either Stock A or Stock B each with an exercise price of \$50. Table 2.6 lists probabilities (PR_i) for different market prices (P_i) on the expiration date for each stock. Both mean expected future prices are \$52.[1] However, the price of Stock B is far more likely to differ substantially from the mean than the price of Stock A. The price of such a stock is said to be more volatile.

Following Equation (2.1), the expected payoff (EP) on the expiration date for a call option can be defined as follows:

$$\mathrm{EP} = \sum_{i=1}^{n} (\mathrm{PR}_i) \times \mathrm{Max}(0, P_i - X), \tag{2.3}$$

[1]Mean expected future price (MEFP) is calculated by the following formula:

$$\mathrm{MEFP} = \sum_{i=1}^{n} (P_i)(\mathrm{PR}_i).$$

Table 2.6 Probabilities for Future Prices of Two Stocks

Less Volatile for Stock A			More Volatile for Stock B		
Future Price (P)	**Prob. (PR)**	**(P)(PR)**	**Future Price (P)**	**Prob. (PR)**	**(P)(PR)**
42	0.10	4.2	32	0.10	3.2
47	0.20	9.4	42	0.20	8.4
52	0.40	20.8	52	0.40	20.8
57	0.20	11.4	62	0.20	12.4
62	0.10	6.2	72	0.10	7.2
	1.00	**52.0**		**1.00**	**52.0**

where P_i is the stock price per share at the ith state of nature, X is the exercise price, and PR_i is the probability at the ith state of nature.

The expected payoff on the expiration date for a call option on the more volatile stock is higher than the expected payoff for a call option on the less volatile stock. The option on the less volatile stock will not be exercised at a price below \$50; for the three prices above \$50, its exercise will result in payoff of \$2, \$7, and \$12. Therefore, following Equation (2.3), the expected payoff for the call option on the less volatile stock (EP_A) is as follows:

$$\begin{aligned}\mathrm{EP_A} &= (0.10)(0) + (0.20)(0) + (0.40)(2)\\ &\quad + (0.20)(7) + (0.10)(12)\\ &= \$3.40.\end{aligned}$$

Similarly, for a call option on the more volatile stock, $\mathrm{EP_B}$,

$$\mathrm{EP_B} = (0.10)(0)+(0.20)(0)+(0.40)(2)+(0.20)(12)+(0.10)(2) = \$5.40,$$

where $\mathrm{EP_B} = \$5.40$ is the expected payoff from the call option on the more volatile stock.

Although the mean expected future price is the same for the two stocks, the expected payoff from a call option on the more volatile stock is higher. This conclusion is quite general. For example, it does not require that the exercise price must fall below the expected future stock price.

Time remaining to option's expiration. The above discussions of the risk-free interest rate and stock price volatility both suggest that a longer time remaining before an option's expiration date should accompany a higher call option value, all else being equal. Extra time allows larger gains from postponing payment of the exercise price, and it permits greater volatility in price movements of the stock. These two considerations operate together to increase the value of a call option.

Following the five variables just mentioned, Black and Scholes derived the well-known option pricing model that will be discussed in Chapter 7. In the following section, we will use these option concepts to discuss option-like securities in some detail.

2.4 Option-Like Securities

Some corporate bond and stock issues take on the characteristics of options. Bonds constitute a fixed claim on the corporation, while common stock confers a residual claim and a share in corporate ownership. However, corporations also raise capital by issuing securities that are neither straight debt nor straight equity. In this section, we will discuss the following option-like securities: warrants, callable bonds, convertible securities, and risky corporate debt.

2.4.1 *Warrants*

As mentioned earlier, a **warrant** constitutes an option to purchase a specific number of shares of common stock at a stipulated price for a set period of time directly from the issuing corporation. Typically, a warrant accompanies a bond issue, but it is detachable; it can be traded separately from the bond. A warrant is essentially a call option written by the company that issues the stock. Its value is influenced by the same factors that influence the value of a call option.

In this context, the value of a warrant at expiration (V_w) is defined by the following equation:

$$V_w = \text{Max}[0, NP - -NX], \tag{2.4}$$

where P and X are as defined in Equation (2.1) and N is the number of shares obtainable with each warrant. The valuation of warrant will be discussed in Chapters 7 and 16.

Example 2.1 (Calculating the Value of a Warrant). On the expiration date of a warrant, the common stock of a firm is selling at \$10 per share. The warrant gives the holder the right to buy two shares of stock for \$18. What is the value of the warrant at expiration?

A: Using Equation (2.4), we obtain the following:

$$\begin{aligned} V_w &= \text{Max}(0, NP - NX) \\ &= \text{Max}(0, 2(\$10) - \$18) \\ &= \$2.00/\text{warrant}. \end{aligned}$$

The stock is valued at \$10 per share, or \$20 for two shares. The exercise of the warrant to get two shares costs \$18; therefore, the warrant is worth \$2.

2.4.2 *Convertible securities*

A **convertible security** is a bond or preferred stock issue that typically gives its holder the right to exchange it for a stipulated number of shares of common stock of the issuing corporation during a specified period of time. Therefore, convertible bonds and convertible preferred stock represent options to the security holder. If the price of common stock rises sufficiently, holders of these securities will find it profitable to exercise their conversion rights. As for a warrant, such a right will have some positive value in the market, so the market will accept a lower coupon rate on the corporation's convertible bonds than it would demand for a bond with no conversion privilege.

Convertible bonds are especially attractive when management prefers to raise capital by issuing equity rather than debt, but believes that transient influences have led the market to temporarily undervalue its common stock. If this perception is correct, the stock price will rise and, as a result, debt will be converted to equity. A convertible bond issue may offer an advantage over a bond issue with warrants since managers can predict how much capital the issue will raise.

The exercise of a warrant raises further capital for the firm; conversion simply substitutes equity for debt. The conversion of a bond issue for shares of common stock does not raise new capital, but it does implicitly increase cash flow if the conversion occurs prior to the bond's maturity date, by reducing future coupon payments.

A further distinction between warrants and convertible bonds is that warrants are not callable, while the issuer generally can call a convertible bond. The bondholder can be offered the option of converting it within a short time period or surrendering it at a specific cash price. As with all callable bonds, investors demand higher returns for callable, convertible securities. Firms are willing to pay this higher price in exchange for management flexibility.

We have seen why a corporation might want to issue a hybrid security rather than straight debt and/or equity. What about the investor? These securities may be particularly attractive when investors have trouble assessing the riskiness of a corporation's future business activities. If the corporation embarks on a high-risk enterprise, holders of straight bonds will be in the unappealing position of gaining nothing if the enterprise succeeds and facing greatly increased default risk if it fails.

Warrants or conversion privileges can restore some balance. By exercising a warrant or converting a bond to stock, the bondholder can share in any success resulting from a risky venture. This reduces the importance of assessing the future business risk of a corporation's activities. Now, we will discuss how the conversion privilege can be determined.

Consider an issue of 20-year bonds with face values of $1,000. Each bond is convertible to 50 shares of common stock and the current market price of the stock is $15 per share. The coupon rate on these convertible bonds is 9.5%, while straight debt of the issuing corporation with similar terms currently carries a rate of 12%. This issue can be called by the corporation, at a price of $1,050, at any time after five years. How much do investors pay for the conversion privilege?

The number of shares that can be received in exchange for each bond is set by the **conversion ratio**; the conversion ratio of the issue described above is 50 shares to one bond. Immediate conversion would exchange a bond valued at $1,000 for 50 shares of common stock, so that the effective price of the stock would be $20 per share.

This **conversion price**, in general, equals the following:

$$\text{Conversion price} = \frac{\text{Par value of bond}}{\text{Conversion ratio}}.$$

Many convertible bond contracts specifically state conversion prices. The conversion price of the example bond exceeds the current market price of the shares by one-third. Obviously, it makes no sense to exercise this conversion privilege immediately. However, that privilege may have some value due to the profit that holders of the convertible bond can expect to earn if the price of the stock increases sufficiently.

The value of the conversion privilege is determined by computing the present value of the bond's debt element. Holding the bond to maturity, the bondholder would receive a stream of 20 annual payments of \$95, plus \$1,000 at the end of Year 20. Discounting these payments at a rate of 12% gives a present value of debt, PV_D, of

$$\begin{aligned}\text{PV}_D &= \sum_{t=1}^{20} \frac{\$95}{(1.12)^t} + \frac{\$1{,}000}{(1.12)^{20}} \\ &= \$95 \times \text{PVIFA}(12\%, 20\,\text{years}) + \$1{,}000\ \text{PVIF}(12\%, 20\,\text{years}) \\ &= \$709.60 + \$103.67 = \$813.27.\end{aligned}$$

This often is called the **straight bond value** of the convertible bond. The market value of a convertible bond is somewhat above the higher of the conversion or straight bond values, as shown in Figure 2.3.

Remember, however, that the instrument may be worth more if the conversion privilege is exercised. Since, at issue, the bond can be exchanged for 50 shares of common stock valued by the market at \$15 per share, its conversion value is 50 times \$15 or \$750. The bond value exceeds the conversion value, but it is lower than the price of the bond. If the bond is issued at par, then the difference between the market value of \$1,000 and the larger of the straight bond values (line A in Figure 2.3) or conversion value is \$186.73. This represents the **conversion premium**, or the price (line B in Figure 2.5) that investors pay for the conversion privilege.

As mentioned earlier, the conversion privilege is essentially a call option on shares of common stock, so its value is influenced by all those factors that determine the value of call options. However, one

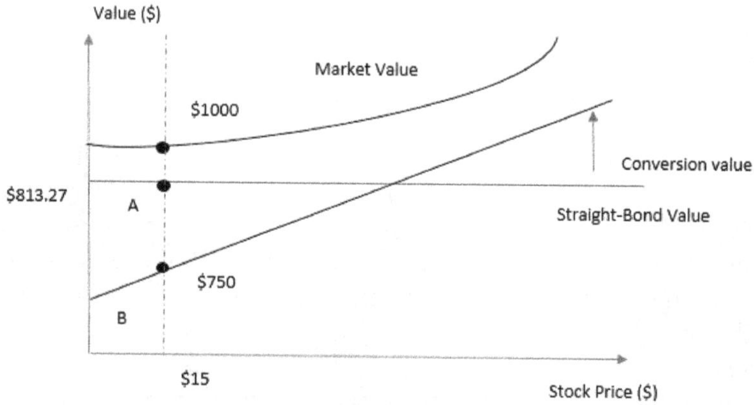

Figure 2.3 Market Value of a Convertible Bond

additional factor also has an effect. If the conversion privilege is exercised, the bond must be surrendered in exchange for stock. Therefore, the exercise price per share of the call option is the market price of the convertible bond divided by the conversion ratio. Over time, market forces will cause the price of the convertible bond to vary, so the exercise price of the implicit call option also will vary. The valuation of convertible bond will be discussed in Chapters 7 and 16.

Example 2.2. (Analyzing the Value of Convertible Bond). JoLee Corp. has a \$1 million, \$1,000 par value, 9% semiannual convertible bond that is maturing in 5 years. The conversion price for the equity is \$20 per share. Today, the common stock is selling for \$18 per share. Similar convertibles have a stated nominal rate (APR) of 10%.

Calculate the conversion ratio, the conversion value, and the minimum price of the bond. As an investor, what would you do with this bond? What is the value of the conversion privilege if the bond is selling at \$1,000?

$$\begin{aligned}\text{A: Conversion ratio} &= \frac{\text{Par value}}{\text{Conversion price}}\\ &= \frac{\$1{,}000}{\$20/\text{share}}\\ &= 50\,\text{shares.}\end{aligned}$$

$$\begin{aligned}\text{Conversion value} &= \text{Conversion ratio} \times \text{Price per share}\\ &= 50 \text{ shares} \times \$18/\text{share}\\ &= \$900.\end{aligned}$$

APR of 10% corresponds to a semiannual periodic rate of 5%

$$\begin{aligned}\text{Bond value} &= \sum_{t=1}^{n} \frac{\text{Interest}}{(1+r)^t} + \frac{\text{Par}}{(1+r)^n}\\ &= \$45 \times \text{PVIFA}(5\%,\ 10\,\text{periods})\\ &\quad + \$1{,}000 \times \text{PVIF}(5\%,\ 10\,\text{periods})\\ &= \$347.48 + \$613.91\\ &= \$961.39.\end{aligned}$$

If the market price is below $900 per bond, you would buy the bond and convert it into common shares. The value of the conversion privilege is the difference between $1,000 and the larger of bond value or conversion value: $1,000 – $961.39 = $38.61.

2.4.3 *Callable bonds*

Corporate bonds often are issued with call provisions that entitle the issuer to buy back the bond from bondholders at some later date, at a specified price. These securities are called callable bonds. We can view the call provision as a call option held by the issuer of the bond. In this case, the excise price is equal to the price at which the bond can be repurchased. In order for bondholders to allow the firm to hold a call option on the security they own, they must be compensated with a higher coupon rate.

2.4.4 *Risky corporate debt*

Sometimes, options are used to value risky corporate debt. Because of the limited liability of stockholders, money borrowed by the firm is backed, at most, by the total value of the firm's assets. One way to view this agreement is to consider that stockholders have sold the entire firm to debt holders but hold a call option with an exercise price equal to the face value of the debt. In this case, if the value of the firm exceeds the value of the debt, stockholders exercise the call option by paying off the bondholders. If the value of the firm is less than the value of the debt, shareholders do not exercise the call option, and all assets are distributed to the bondholders.

Black and Scholes (1973) have used the option pricing model to discuss the relationship between stock, bonds, and firm values.

2.4.5 *Earnings per share with warrants and convertibles*

Warrants and convertible securities can change a firm's earnings per share (EPS) and number of shares outstanding. Investors, managers, accountants, and federal and state government agencies all watch the earnings per share of a corporation. Earnings per share generally means net income after taxes, less preferred stock dividends, divided by the weighted average number of shares of common stock outstanding. In 1969, the Accounting Principles Board, a forerunner of the FASB, issued APB Opinion No. 15, "Earnings per Share." This ruling laid down the rules for calculating the earnings per share for financial reporting purposes. In 1982, the FASB issued Statement No. 55, "Determining Whether a Convertible Security Is a Common Stock Equivalent." The accounting requirements set out in these rulings provide alternative ways of calculating earnings per share if a company has outstanding convertible securities, warrants, stock options, or other contracts that permit it to increase the number of shares of common stock.

The EPS for a firm with a simple capital structure is called basic EPS. A simple capital structure has only one form of voting capital and includes no potential equity, such as warrants or convertibles. The existence of non-convertible preferred stock does not create a complex capital structure.

A corporation that has warrants, convertibles, or options outstanding is said to have a **complex capital structure**. The complexity comes from the difficulty of measuring the number of shares outstanding. This is a function of a known amount of common shares currently outstanding plus an estimate of the number of shares that may be issued to satisfy the holders of warrants, convertibles, and options should they decide to exercise their rights and receive new common shares.

Because of the possible dilution in EPS represented by securities that have the potential to become new shares of common stock, the EPS calculation must account for **Common Stock Equivalents** (CSEs). CSEs are securities that are not common stock, but are equivalent to common stock because they are likely to be converted into common stock in the future. Convertible debt, convertible preferred stock, stock rights, stock options, and stock warrants are all securities that can create new common shares and thus dilute (or reduce) the firm's earnings per share. APB No. 15 mandates the calculation of two types of EPS for a firm with a complex capital structure: primary EPS and fully diluted EPS. It is useful to review the basic accounting concepts dealing with income recognition and ownership at this point:

1. *Basic EPS*. The earnings available to stockholders are divided by the average number of shares actually outstanding during the period.
2. *Primary EPS*. The earnings available to stockholders are divided by the average number of common shares plus the CSEs.
3. *Fully diluted EPS*. Earnings are handled in a manner similar to primary EPS, but all warrants and convertibles are assumed to be exercised or converted. In other words, EPS is assumed to be at maximum dilution.

The relationship between these three types of EPS can be presented as follows:

Primary EPS

EPS = Basic EPS − Impact of CSE − CSE impact of all other dilutive securities

Fully diluted EPS

It is interesting to speculate on whether the market will use primary EPS or fully diluted EPS in valuing shares of stock. If the market expects holders of common stock equivalents to convert them into new equity, then fully diluted EPS is likely to be more meaningful. If the market does not expect conversion, then it is likely to treat convertible bonds like straight debt and focus on primary EPS with no adjustment for new shares. In other words, the market is likely to use basic EPS in such cases.

Convertible bonds that have no chance of being converted are called **hung convertibles**. The idea here is that if investors do not wish to convert their bonds into the firm's equity, the conversion price is hung. The bond is worth more as a bond than it is worth converted into equity. APB No. 15 and FASB No. 55 require a firm to provide EPS information under either circumstance and let the market participant choose which measure is more meaningful.

The financial analyst needs to identify the difference between two firms with a similar primary EPS value and markedly different fully diluted EPS values. In general, hybrid securities in the capital structure cause the difference. Now, based upon the JNJ 2020 annual report, we will present the basic EPS and diluted EPS as follows:

The following is a reconciliation of basic net earnings per share to diluted net earnings per share for the fiscal years ended January 3, 2021, December 29, 2019, and December 30, 2018:

(In Millions Except Per Share Amounts)	2020	2019	2018
Basic net earnings per share	$5.59	5.72	5.70
Average shares outstanding — basic	2,632.8	2,645.1	2,681.5
Potential shares exercisable under stock option plans	118.3	136.3	139.0
Less: shares repurchased under treasury stock method	(80.4)	(97.8)	(92.5)
Convertible debt shares	—	0.7	0.7
Adjusted average shares outstanding — diluted	2,670.7	2,684.3	2,728.7
Diluted net earnings per share	$5.51	5.63	5.61

The diluted net earnings per share calculation for fiscal year 2020 excluded 18 million shares related to stock options, as the exercise price of these options was greater than their average market value. As of January 3, 2021, the Company did not have convertible debt. The diluted net earnings per share calculation for fiscal year 2019 excluded an insignificant number of shares related to stock options, as the exercise price of these options was greater than the average market value of the Company's stock.

The diluted net earnings per share calculation for fiscal year 2019 included the dilutive effect of convertible debt that was offset by the related reduction in interest expense of $1 million after tax. The diluted net earnings per share calculation for fiscal year 2018 included all shares related to stock options, as the exercise price of all options was less than the average market value of the Company's stock.

The diluted net earnings per share calculation for fiscal year 2018 included the dilutive effect of convertible debt that was offset by the related reduction in interest expense of $1 million after tax.

In Appendix 2A, we have used JNJ's financial report data to discuss Liquidity Ratios, Financial Leverage Ratios, Turnover Ratios, Profitability Ratios, Market Value Ratios, and Policy Ratios in some detail. In addition, we also discuss degree of operating leverage, degree of financial leverage, and combined effect. All this information is useful to perform financial analysis for JNJ.

2.5 Swap Contracts and Hedging

In addition to using forward, futures, and option contracts to hedge transactions or transaction exposure, many corporations are engaging in what are called *swap transactions* to accomplish this. A **swap contract** is a private agreement between two companies to exchange a specific cash flow amount at a specific date in the future. If the specific cash flow amount is interest payments, then the contract is an *interest rate swap*; if the specific amount of cash flows is currency payments, then the contract is a *currency swap*. The first currency swap contract was negotiated between IBM and the World Bank in the early eighties. Since that time, the swap market has grown to over $10 trillion.

2.5.1 *Interest rate swaps*

An **interest rate swap** is a financial transaction in which two borrowers exchange interest payments on a particular amount of principal with a specified maturity. The swap enables each party to alter the characteristics of the periodic interest payments that it makes or receives.

The exchange might involve swapping a fixed-rate payment for a variable-rate payment or one type of floating rate for another. All swaps trade only interest payments made on underlying note values; no principal payments need to change hands with a simple interest rate swap.

Figure 2.4 shows the cash flows of a simple interest rate swap for each of the parties involved. The two primary parties to the swap

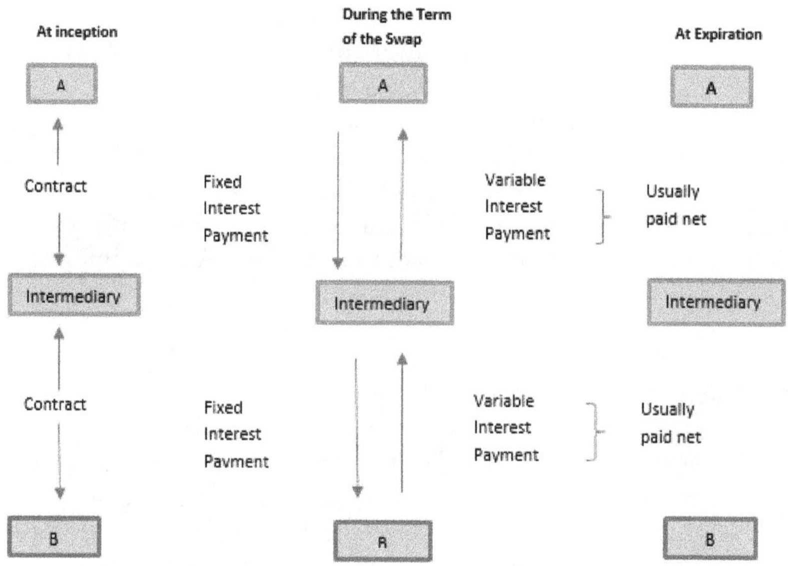

Figure 2.4 Cash Flows from a Simple Interest Swap

are called **counterparties**. Usually, although not always, a financial institution serves as an intermediary between the counterparties.

In this example, Company A exchanges a variable-rate debt for a fixed-rate debt. Company B trades its fixed-rate debt for a variable-rate debt. The intermediary has no exposure to interest rate movements and earns a fee of 0.1%, which is spread between the payments and the receipts of A and B.

In the typical interest rate swap, the counterparty with the fixed-rate debt pays a premium over the rate the other counterparty initially paid on its variable-rate debt. This premium is based upon factors such as terms of the swap, the creditworthiness of the counterparties, and the conditions in the market for fixed-rate and variable-rate debt.

It is unusual for two companies to arrange an interest rate swap themselves. In most cases, intermediaries act as brokers, dealers, or principals to the transaction. As a broker or dealer, the intermediary serves to bring A and B together and collects an arrangement fee. However, in most swaps, the intermediary acts as a principal to both counterparties, assuming the credit risk in the event that one counterparty defaults. When the intermediary acts as the principal to a swap, its compensation is in the form of an arrangement fee and/or the spread between the terms of these two counterparties.

Firm A has a variable-rate debt with an interest rate of LIBOR (London Interbank Offer Rate) +1%, which is borrowed from the money market; Firm B has a fixed-rate debt with a fixed rate of 9.3%, which is borrowed from the capital market. Through the intermediary, Firm A swaps its variable-rate debt for Firm B's fixed-rate debt at interest payment dates. This interest rate swap flowchart is presented in Figure 2.5.

The analysis of this swap is now presented in more detail.

From the information given in Figure 2.5, the interest rate cost of Firm A and Firm B and the fee of the intermediary can be calculated as follows:

		Firm A	Intermediary	Firm B
Pays		Fixed 9.5%	Fixed 9.4%	Fixed 9.3%
		LIBOR + 1%	LIBOR + 1.1%	LIBOR + 1.1%
Receives		LIBOR + 1.1%	Fixed 9.5%	Fixed 9.4%
	L			
	I	Fixed 9.4%		LIBOR + 1%
	B			
			OR + 1.1%	

Net Payment (income) (.1%)

After the swap, Firm A owns a fixed-rate debt with an interest rate of 9.4% and Firm B owns a variable-rate debt with an interest rate of LIBOR +1%. The intermediary earns a fee of 0.1%. Due to this swap, Firm A has eliminated its interest rate exposure risk.

Firm A has entered into the swap; it has three sets of cash flows:

1. It pays FIXED 9.5% to Intermediary.
2. It pays LIBOR +1% to Money Market.
3. It receives LIBOR +1.1% from Intermediary.

For Firm B, the swap could have the effects of transforming a fixed-rate loan into a floating-rate loan. After it has entered into the swap, it has three sets of cash flows:

1. It pays FIXED 9.3% to Capital Market.
2. It pays LIBOR +1.1% to Intermediary.
3. It receives FIXED 9.4% from Intermediary.

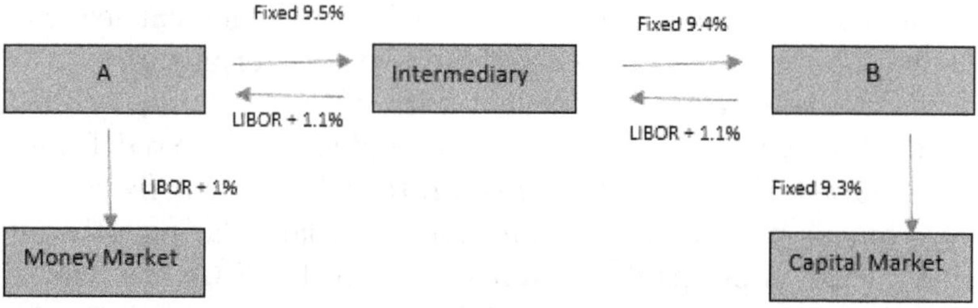

Figure 2.5 Costs of an Interest Rate Swap

For intermediary, there are four cash flows:

1. It pays LIBOR +1.1% to Firm A.
2. It pays FIXED 9.4% to Firm B.
3. It receives FIXED 9.5% from Firm A.
4. It receives LIBOR +1.1% from Firm B.

By using the interest rate swap theory and method discussed in this section, we will discuss different swapping strategies that are available to bond portfolio managers in Chapter 14. Swapping strategies in portfolio management can be classified into the following: (1) pure yield-pickup swap, (2) interest rate anticipations, (3) intermarket swap, and (4) substitution swap. Substitution swap attempts to profit from a change in yield spread between two nearly identical bonds. The trade is based upon a forecasted change in the yield spread between the two bonds, holding the coupon and maturity equal for both bonds. Intermarket Swap works on trading between sector quality coupon categories, based upon a forecasted change in yield spread between two different categories. In this method, the most common forecasting method is to observe historical yield spreads at various points in the interest rate cycle, and then adjust them for current supply–demand effects.

Interest rate anticipation swaps are geared toward the investor who believes the level of interest rate is going to change and wants to benefit from this change. This type of swap is highly speculative, and time as a factor works heavily against the swapper. In a pure yield-pickup swap there is no expectation of market changes, but a simple attempt to increase yield. Essentially, two bonds are examined to establish their difference in Yield To Maturity (YTM), with a further adjustment to consider the impact of interim reinvestment of coupons at an assumed rate or return between now and the maturity date.

2.5.2 *Currency swaps*

In a **currency swap**, two firms agree to exchange an equivalent amount of two different currencies for a specified period of time.

As an example of a typical currency swap, suppose a company from the UK would like to borrow U.S. dollars to finance a foreign investment, but the firm is not known outside the UK. Similarly, a U.S. firm needs British Pounds for its UK subsidiary, but the cost of borrowing in the United States is cheaper than the cost of borrowing in UK for this firm. Both firms face a similar problem. They can borrow at favorable rates, but not in the desired currency. In this case, a currency swap presents one solution. A bank acting as an intermediary can bring these two firms together and arrange a swap of British Pounds for dollars. The UK firm agrees to pay the U.S. Company principal and interest on its dollar borrowings in the U.S., while the U.S. firm agrees to pay the costs of the pound borrowings for its UK subsidiaries. Each firm thus obtains the best possible rate and eliminates exposure to exchange rate changes by agreeing to exchange currencies. Figure 2.6 illustrates the workings of a currency swap.

Figure 2.6 can be used to explain this action: (a) principal exchange, (b) interest payment, and (c) repayment. In this case, the U.S. firm and UK firm agree to exchange an amount of U.S. dollars for an equivalent amount of British Sterling. In a principal exchange, the UK firm pays the U.S. firm an amount of British Sterling and U.S. firm an equivalent amount of U.S. dollars.

Consider a hypothetical five-year currency swap agreement between a U.S. firm and a UK firm entered into on March 1, 2021. We supposed the U.S. firm pays a fixed rate of interest of 4% in sterling and receives a fixed rate of interest of 5% in dollars from the UK. Interest rate payments are made once a year and the principal amounts are \$20 million and £15 million. This is termed a fixed-for-fixed currency swap because the interest rate in each currency is at a fixed rate. The swap is shown in Figure 2.6. Initially, the principle amounts flow in the opposite direction to the arrows in Figure 2.6. At the outset of the swap, the U.S. firm pays \$20 million and receives

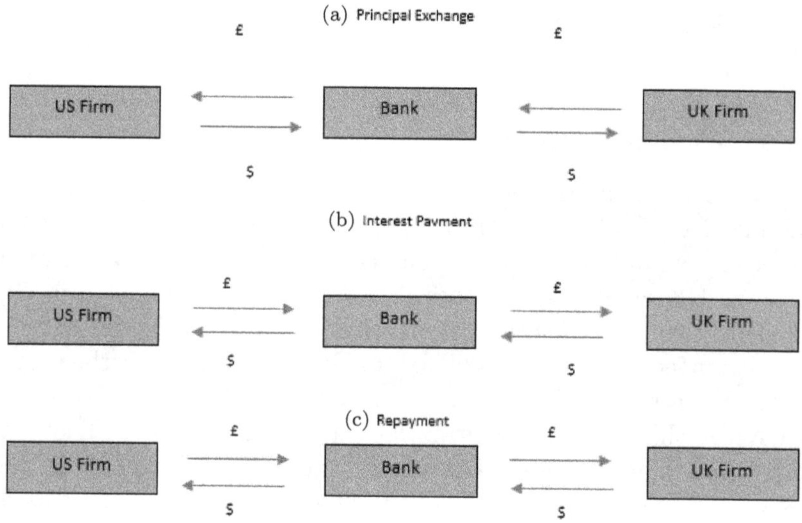

Figure 2.6 Currency Swap

Table 2.7 Cash Flows to U.S. Firm in Currency Swap

Date	Dollar Cash Flows (Millions)	Sterling Cash Flows (Millions)
March 1, 2021	−20.00	+15.00
March 1, 2022	+1.00	−0.60
March 1, 2023	+1.00	−0.60
March 1, 2024	+1.00	−0.60
March 1, 2025	+1.00	−0.60
March 1, 2026	+21.00	−15.60

£15 million. Each year, during the life of the swap contract, the U.S. firm receives $1 million (= 5% * $20 million) and pays £60 million (= 4% * £15 million). At the end of the life of the swap, it pays a principal of £15 million and receives a principal of $20 million. We show these cash flows in Table 2.7.

2.5.3 *Swapping for bond portfolio management*

When a market is in turmoil, great distortions take place. Some bonds drop further than they should, others less. A bond swapper can improve yield and pick up a substantial capital gain. In swapping, timing is very important.

Swapping strategies generally concentrate on highly specialized trading relationships. A commonly accepted method for classifying such swaps is Homer and Leibowitz's four types: (1) pure yield-pickup swap, (2) interest rate anticipations, (3) intermarket swap, and (4) substitution swap. The expected return from any swap is usually based upon several motives, not just one — thus, these "types" of swaps are really just sources of return. Chapter 14 will discuss these four different swaps in detail.

2.6 Risk Management

In Sections 2.2 and 2.4, we discussed how futures and swaps can be used to hedge interest rate risk and exchange rate risk. In this section, we briefly summarize how options, futures, and swaps can be used in corporate risk management.

2.6.1 *Corporate risk management*

Unexpected changes in interest rates, exchange rates, and prices can lead to serious economic consequences for a corporation. For example, changing exchange rates can impact the price that a U.S. importer pays for goods. Because of the great volatility in the financial markets in the last decade, corporations have been devoting a great deal of effort to managing or hedging these types of financial risks. Many of these risk management strategies incorporate the use of options, futures, and swaps.

The basic idea of hedging is to take a position in a derivative security (options, futures, or swaps) so that losses in the spot market will be offset by gains in the derivatives security. For example, a corporation that will be using commercial paper to raise short-term funds in four months may be concerned that interest rates will rise and thus increase the cost of these funds. Because a rise in interest rates will reduce the amount the corporation receives from the issue, it may try to hedge a reduction in the price of its issue. This corporation can hedge the risk of a price decrease caused by an increase in interest rates by buying a futures contract on money market instruments such as Treasury bills or Eurodollars. If interest rates do rise, at least a portion of the losses will be offset by gains from the futures contract.

As another example, a corporation that has borrowed a significant amount of funds at variable interest rate may be concerned about rising short-term interest rates. Rising interest rates will increase the firm's interest costs significantly, and may adversely affect its financial well-being. To reduce its interest rate exposure, the corporation may engage in an interest rate swap in which some of the interest payments on the floating-rate debt are exchanged for interest payments at a fixed rate. This allows the corporation to reduce its short-term interest rate exposure.

2.6.2 *Risk management in the real world*

To give a real-world example, companies such as Johnson & Johnson and Caterpillar are good firms to use in understanding the concepts of risk management. According to Johnson & Johnson's 2020 annual report, the company utilizes financial instruments in managing the impacts of foreign exchange rate changes on cash flows. Johnson & Johnson enters into forward foreign exchange contracts to protect the value of foreign currency assets and liabilities and to hedge future foreign currency transactions primarily related to product costs. The contract gains or losses are offset by the transaction gains or losses. Either way, the gain or loss on the forward contract would be offset by the gain or loss on the underlying transaction, providing no impact on future anticipated earnings and cash flows. In addition, Johnson & Johnson hedges the exposure to fluctuations in currency exchange rates by entering into currency swap contracts. By entering the currency swap contracts, the effect on certain assets and liabilities in foreign currency is also hedged.

It is important to note that Johnson & Johnson does not use financial instruments for trading or speculative purposes. Further, they have a policy of only entering into contracts with parties that have at least an investment-grade credit rating. Johnson & Johnson invests in both fixed-rate and floating-rate interest-earning securities which carry a degree of interest rate risk.

On the topic of option-like securities and risk management, we will look at Caterpillar's 2020 annual report to assess the firm's financial instrument structure. Option-like securities are convertible securities that commonly include bonds and preferred stock that are convertible into common shares. Caterpillar does not have any preferred stock, nor do they have convertible bonds. The company does offer stock-based compensation plans that primarily provide for the granting of stock options, stock-settled Stock Appreciation Rights (SARs), Restricted Stock Units (RSUs), and Performance-based Restricted Stock Units (PRSUs) to officers and other key employees, as well as non-employee directors. Stock options permit a holder to buy Caterpillar stock at the stock's price when the option was granted. SARs permit a holder the right to receive the value in shares of the appreciation in Caterpillar stock that occurred from the date the right was granted up to the date of exercise. RSUs are agreements to issue shares of Caterpillar stock at the time of vesting. PRSUs are similar to RSUs and include performance conditions in the vesting terms of the award.

Not all convertible securities dilute EPS. Retired, converted, or corporate-activity-affected securities that increase the EPS figure are considered anti-dilutive. It is important to distinguish between dilutive and anti-dilutive securities and describe the implications of each for the earnings per share calculation. It is therefore very important to ascertain whether the inclusion of a financial instrument in the EPS calculation has dilutive or anti-dilutive characteristics. In other words, accounting for dilution, or lack thereof, is crucial to evaluate the implications of potentially dilutive securities on EPS. According to U.S. Generally Accepted Accounting Principles (GAAP), anti-dilutive securities are not used in the diluted EPS calculation because it, intuitively, defeats the purpose of the calculation. The relationship between basic EPS and diluted EPS is consistent with the GAAP requirement that anti-dilutive securities are to be excluded from the EPS calculation, as it would cause diluted EPS to become potentially larger than basic EPS. Of course, an anti-dilutive EPS is not allowed for official financial reporting, but it is useful to understand the dilutive EPS calculation for a company.

Risk management is paired with derivative financial instruments on Caterpillar's 2020 annual report. The relevant risk factor categories for the firm include foreign currency exchange rate risk, interest rate risk, and commodity price risk. Foreign currency exchange rate movements create a degree of risk by affecting the U.S. dollar value of sales made and costs incurred in foreign currencies. Interest rate movements create a degree of risk by affecting the amount of Caterpillar's interest payments and the value of its fixed-rate debt. Commodity price movements create risk in impacting the price for certain raw materials that Caterpillar uses in its operations. Caterpillar's earnings and cash flows are subject to fluctuations due to the existence of their risk factors. To manage and mitigate risk exposure, Caterpillar utilizes derivative financial instruments that include foreign currency forward, option and cross-currency contracts, interest rate contracts, and commodity forward and option contracts. Foreign currency forward and option contracts are used to manage unmatched foreign currency cash inflow and outflow, ideally minimizing the risk of exchange rate movements that would reduce the U.S. dollar value of Caterpillar's foreign currency cash flow. Interest rate contracts are used to manage Caterpillar's exposure to interest rate changes, in efforts to minimize the cost of borrowed funds. Commodity forward and option contracts are used to manage commodity risk and reduce the cost of purchased materials, minimizing commodity price volatility. The consolidated statement of financial position location presents the location and fair value of both designated and undesignated derivative instruments.

2.6.3 *Financing and market risk*

Based upon JNJ 2020 annual report on page 32, we now discuss how JNJ manages its financing and risk management.

The Company uses financial instruments to manage the impact of foreign exchange rate changes on cash flows. Accordingly, the Company enters into forward foreign exchange contracts to protect the value of certain foreign currency assets and liabilities and to hedge future foreign currency transactions primarily related to product costs. Gains or losses on these contracts are offset by the gains or losses on the underlying transactions. A 10% appreciation of the U.S. dollar from the January 3, 2021 market rates would increase the unrealized value of the Company's forward contracts by $121 million. Conversely, a 10% depreciation of the U.S. dollar from the January 3, 2021 market rates would decrease the unrealized value of the Company's forward contracts by $148 million. In either scenario, the gain or loss on the forward contract would be offset by the gain or loss on the underlying transaction, and therefore, would have no impact on future anticipated earnings and cash flows.

The Company hedges the exposure to fluctuations in currency exchange rates, and the effect on certain assets and liabilities in foreign currency, by entering into currency swap contracts. A 1% change in the spread between U.S. and foreign interest rates on the Company's interest-rate-sensitive financial instruments would either increase or decrease the unrealized value of the Company's swap contracts by approximately $1,667 million. In either scenario, at maturity, the gain or loss on the swap contract would be offset by the gain or loss on the underlying transaction, and therefore, would have no impact on future anticipated cash flows.

The Company does not enter into financial instruments for trading or speculative purposes. Further, the Company has a policy of only entering into contracts with parties that have at least an investment-grade credit rating. The counterparties to these contracts are major financial institutions and there is no significant concentration of exposure with any one counterparty. Management believes the risk of loss is remote. The Company entered into Credit Support Agreements (CSA) with certain derivative counterparties establishing collateral thresholds based on respective credit ratings and netting agreements. See Note 6 to the Consolidated Financial Statements for additional details on CSA.

The Company invests in both fixed-rate and floating-rate interest-earning securities which carry a degree of interest rate risk. The fair market value of fixed-rate securities may be adversely impacted due to a rise in interest rates, while floating-rate securities may produce less income than predicted if interest rates fall. A 1% (100 basis points) change in spread on the Company's interest-rate-sensitive investments would either increase or decrease the unrealized value of cash equivalents and current marketable securities by approximately $36 million. Total borrowings at the end of 2020 and 2019 were $35.3 billion and $27.7 billion, respectively. The increase in borrowings was the issuance of notes in 2020 when market conditions were favorable. In 2020, net debt (cash and current marketable securities, net of debt) was $10.1 billion compared to net debt of $8.4 billion in 2019. Total debt represented 35.8% of total capital (shareholders' equity and total debt) in 2020 and 31.8% of total capital in 2019. Shareholders' equity per share at the end of 2020 was $24.04 compared to $22.59 at year-end 2019. A summary of borrowings can be found in Note 7 to the Consolidated Financial Statements.

2.6.4 *JNJ's borrowings*

Based upon JNJ 2020 annual report on page 60, the components of long-term debt are presented as follows:

(Dollars in Millions)	2020	Effective Rate %	2019	Effective Rate %
3% Zero Coupon Convertible Subordinated Debentures due 2020	$ —	—	51	3.00
2.95% Debentures due 2020	—	—	549	3.15
1.950% Notes due 2020	—	—	500	1.99
3.55% Notes due 2021	450	3.67	449	3.67
2.45% Notes due 2021	350	2.48	349	2.48
1.65% Notes due 2021	999	1.65	999	1.65
0.250% Notes due 2022 (1B Euro 1.2281)[2]/(1B Euro 1.1096)[3]	1,227[2]	0.26	1,108[3]	0.26
2.25% Notes due 2022	999	2.31	998	2.31
6.73% Debentures due 2023	250	6.73	250	6.73
3.375% Notes due 2023	803	3.17	804	3.17
2.05% Notes due 2023	499	2.09	498	2.09
0.650% Notes due 2024 (750MM Euro 1.2281)[2]/(750MM Euro 1.1096)[3]	919[2]	0.68	829[3]	0.68
5.50% Notes due 2024 (500MM 1.3654 GBP)[2]/(500MM GBP 1.2987)[3]	679[2]	6.75	645[3]	6.75
2.625% Notes due 2025	748	2.63	748	2.63
0.55% Notes due 2025[5]	996	0.57	—	—
2.45% Notes due 2026	1,994	2.47	1,993	2.47
2.95% Notes due 2027	997	2.96	996	2.96
0.95% Notes due 2027[5]	1,494	0.96	—	—
1.150% Notes due 2028 (750MM Euro 1.2281)[2]/(750MM Euro 1.1096)[3]	915[2]	1.21	825[3]	1.21
2.90% Notes due 2028	1,495	2.91	1,494	2.91
6.95% Notes due 2029	297	7.14	297	7.14
1.30% Notes due 2030[5]	1,743	1.30	—	—
4.95% Debentures due 2033	498	4.95	498	4.95
4.375% Notes due 2033	855	4.24	855	4.24
1.650% Notes due 2035 (1.5B Euro 1.2281)[2]/(1.5B Euro 1.1096)[3]	1,827[2]	1.68	1,649[3]	1.68
3.55% Notes due 2036	989	3.59	989	3.59
5.95% Notes due 2037	992	5.99	992	5.99
3.625% Notes due 2037	1,488	3.64	1,487	3.64
5.85% Debentures due 2038	696	5.85	696	5.85
3.400% Notes due 2038	991	3.42	991	3.42
4.50% Debentures due 2040	539	4.63	539	4.63
2.10% Notes due 2040[5]	986	2.14	—	—
4.85% Notes due 2041	297	4.89	297	4.89
4.50% Notes due 2043	496	4.52	495	4.52
3.70% Notes due 2046	1,974	3.74	1,973	3.74
3.75% Notes due 2047	991	3.76	991	3.76
3.500% Notes due 2048	742	3.52	742	3.52
2.250% Notes due 2050[5]	984	2.29	—	—
2.450% Notes due 2060[5]	1,228	2.49	—	—
Other	7	—	18	—
Subtotal	**34,434**[4]	**2.85%**[1]	**27,594**[4]	**3.19**[1]
Less current portion	1,799		1,100	
Total long-term debt	**$32,635**		**26,494**	

(1) Weighted average effective rate.

(2) Translation rate at January 3, 2021.

(3) Translation rate at December 29, 2019.

(4) The excess of the fair value over the carrying value of debt was \$5.4 billion at the end of fiscal year 2020 and \$3.0 billion at the end of fiscal year 2019.

(5) In the fiscal third quarter of 2020, the Company issued senior unsecured notes for a total of \$7.5 billion.

Fair value of the long-term debt was estimated using market prices, which were corroborated by quoted broker prices and significant other observable inputs.

The Company has access to substantial sources of funds at numerous banks worldwide. In September 2020, the Company secured a new 364-day Credit Facility. Total credit available to the Company approximates $10 billion, which expires on September 9, 2021. Interest charged on borrowings under the credit line agreement is based on either bids provided by banks, London Interbank Offered Rates (LIBOR), Secured Overnight Financing Rate (SOFR) Swap Curve, or other applicable market rates as allowed plus applicable margins. Commitment fees under the agreements are not material.

Throughout fiscal year 2020, the Company continued to have access to liquidity through the commercial paper market. Short-term borrowings and the current portion of long-term debt amounted to approximately $2.6 billion at the end of fiscal year 2020, of which $1.8 billion is the current portion of the long-term debt, and the remainder is commercial paper and local borrowings by international subsidiaries.

Throughout fiscal year 2019, the Company continued to have access to liquidity through the commercial paper market. Short-term borrowings and the current portion of long-term debt amounted to approximately $1.2 billion at the end of fiscal year 2019, of which $1.1 billion is the current portion of the long-term debt, and the remainder principally represents local borrowing by international subsidiaries.

Aggregate maturities of long-term debt obligations commencing in 2021 are as follows:

(Dollars in Millions) 2021	2022	2023	2024	2025	After 2025
$1,799	2,226	1,552	1,598	1,744	25,515

It is well known that JNJ's borrowing activities will affect either Liquidity Ratios or Financial Leverage Ratios which will be discussed in Appendix 2A in some detail.

2.7 Summary

In this chapter, we discussed the basic concepts of futures, options, and swaps and how these instruments can be used to hedge risk. In addition, the concept of options was used to illustrate the mechanics of a number of securities that have option-like properties. Corporate securities, such as warrants, convertible bonds, convertible preferred stock, callable bonds, and risky corporate debt can all be analyzed using the basic principles of options. We also discussed the calculation of earnings per share for a company issuing warrants and convertibles. Also, we discussed another important hedging instrument, the swap, including both interest rate swaps and currency swaps.

The main ideas discussed in this chapter are summarized as follows:

1. Futures contracts such as currency futures have similar characteristics as forward contracts. Both forward and futures contracts can be used to hedge risk.
2. Two basic types of options are call option and put option. The value of a call option depends on (a) current stock price per share, (b) exercise price of the option, (c) risk-free interest rate, (d) volatility of the stock price, and (e) time remaining to option's expiration date.
3. Firms frequently issue option-like securities. For example, warrants are long-term call options issued by the firm; convertible bonds give the investor the right to buy the firm's stocks in exchange for the value of the underlying bonds. Callable bonds give the option right to the issuing firms instead of investors.
4. Risky corporate debt issued by a firm can be regarded as an option contract. We can consider that stockholders have sold the entire firm to debt holders but hold a call option with an exercise price equal to the face value of the debt.
5. Swap contracts allow firms to exchange one series of future payments for another. Both interest rate and currency swaps can be used to do risk management for a firm.

Questions and Problems

1. Define the following terms: executive stock option; call option; put option; exercise price; option premium; expiration date; naked option writing; in the money; out of the money; and at the money.
2. Distinguish between an American option and a European option.

3. What happens to the number of shares of stock outstanding when a call option is exercised?
4. What is the major difference between an option and a futures contract?
5. What is a convertible bond? Why would a corporation issue a convertible bond?
6. What is an interest rate swap?
7. Briefly explain how options are valued.
8. What is the relationship between the conversion ratio and the conversion price for a convertible bond?
9. Why will a convertible bond usually sell at a price above its value as equity or debt?
10. What is the difference between a warrant and a convertible bond?
11. What factors determine the value of a warrant?
12. Describe a situation in which a firm should consider issuing a convertible bond.
13. Describe a situation in which a firm should consider issuing warrants.
14. What is the conflict of interest when a manager with executive stock options is making capital budgeting decisions concerning risky projects?
15. What is the problem with a corporate treasurer speculating with options and/or futures in order to increase shareholder wealth?
16. Bankers do not need to explain the risks of using derivative instruments to sophisticated corporate treasurers. Comment on the arguments for and against this statement.
17. Please discuss the financial and market risk analyses for Johnson & Johnson.
18. Based upon Appendix 2A, please discuss important financial ratios.
19. Calculating Expected Value of Call Options
    Find the expected value of a call option with an exercise price of \$100 at the end of the period, given the following information (current stock price is \$100):

Probability	**Stock Price**
0.4	\$150
0.6	80

18. Calculating Value of Call Options
If a call option has an exercise price of $50, how much will it be worth on its exercise date (assuming no transaction costs) if the price of the underlying stock is:
a. $30?
b. $50?
c. $80?

19. Call Option Value for Buyer and Seller
If a call option has an exercise price of $60 and the price of the stock is $40, what is the value of the call:
a. to the holder of the option?
b. to the seller of the option?

20. Expected Value of Call Options
Allison Merrick is considering two call options, each with an exercise price of $20 and identical in all other respects except for the distribution of underlying stock values. The distribution of the values of the underlying stocks of Companies J and K are given below:

Company J		**Company K**	
Future Stock Price	**Probability**	**Future Stock Price**	**Probability**
$10	0.2	$5	0.1
18	0.3	17	0.3
22	0.3	25	0.4
25	0.2	35	0.2

Find the expected payoff for each call option and explain which one you would prefer.

21. Conversion Price of a Bond
LMW Company has issued convertible bonds that have a conversion ratio of 20 shares to one bond. Compute the conversion price for a bond with a par value of $1,000. If the current market price for the stick is $75 per share, does it make sense to convert? Why?

22. Price Conversion Privilege
Jones and Smith Company has just issued convertible bonds that have a coupon rate of 10% and a conversion ratio of 25 shares to one bond. They mature in 20 years and pay semiannual coupons. If similar straight debt has a nominal return of 14%, what price will investors pay for the conversion privilege if the bonds currently are selling in par?

23. Price Conversion Privilege
IKC Corporation has convertible bonds outstanding. The bonds have a coupon rate of 8% and a conversion ratio of 50 shares to one bond. They mature in 10 years and pay semiannual coupons. If similar straight debt has a nominal return of 10%, what price will investors pay for the conversion privilege if the bonds currently are selling at par?
24. Calculating the Value of a Warrant
On the expiration date of a warrant, the common stock of a firm is selling at \$25 per share. The warrant gives the holder the right to buy five shares of stock for \$90. What is the value of the warrant at expiration?

Bibliography

Caterpillar Inc. (2019). Annual Report & Sustainability Report: caterpillar.com/en/investors/reports.html.

Caterpillar Inc. (2020, January). About Caterpillar: https://www.caterpillar.com/en/company.html.

Homer, S. and M. L. Leibowitz (1972). *Inside the Yield Book.* New York, NY: Prentice-Hall and New York Institute of Finance.

Hull, J. C. (2017). *Fundamentals of Futures and Options Markets*, 9th ed. New York: Pearson.

Hull, J. C. (2018). *Options, Futures, and Other Derivatives*, 10th ed. New York: Pearson.

Johnson & Johnson (2019). Annual Report: https://www.jnj.com/about-jnj/annual-reports.

Lee, C. F. and A. C. Lee (2022). *Encyclopedia of Finance*, 3rd ed. New York: Springer.

Lee, C. F. and J. Lee (2017). *Financial Analysis and Planning: Theory and Application.* Singapore: World Scientific.

Lee, C. F., J. C. Lee, J. R. Chang and T. Tai (2016). *Essentials of Microsoft Excel, VBA, SAS, and MINITAB for Statistical and Financial Analyses.* Singapore: World Scientific.

Lee, C. F., J. Finnerty, J. C. Lee, A. C. Lee and D. Wort (2013). *Security Analysis, Portfolio Management, and Financial Derivatives*, 3rd ed. Singapore: World Scientific.

Lee, C. F., J. C. Lee and A. C. Lee (2013). *Statistics for Business and Financial Economics*, 3rd ed. New York: Springer.

Lee, C. F., J. Lee and M. Lee (2022). *Corporate Finance and Strategy: An Active Learning Approach*, 2nd ed. Singapore: World Scientific Publishing Co.

Appendix 2A: Financial Ratio Analysis

In order to make use of financial statements, an analyst needs some form of measurement for analysis. Frequently, ratios are used to relate one piece of financial data to another. The ratio puts the two pieces of data on an equivalent base, which increases the usefulness of the data. For example, net income as an absolute number is meaningless to compare across firms of different sizes. However, if one creates a net profitability ratio (NI/Sales), comparisons are easier to make. Analysis of a series of ratios will give us a clear picture of a firm's financial condition and performance.

Analysis of ratios can take one of two forms. First, the analyst can compare the ratios of one firm with those of similar firms or with industry averages at a specific point in time. This is a type of cross-sectional analysis technique that may indicate the relative financial condition and performance of a firm. One must be careful, however, to analyze the ratios while keeping in mind the inherent differences between a firm's production functions and its operations. Also, the analyst should avoid using "rules of thumb" across industries because the composition of industries and individual firms varies considerably. Furthermore, inconsistency in a firm's accounting procedures can cause accounting data to show substantial differences between firms, which can hinder ratio comparability. This variation in accounting procedures can also lead to problems in determining the "target ratio," which can be found in Lee *et al.* (2022).

The second method of ratio comparison involves the comparison of a firm's present ratio with its past and expected ratios. This form of time series analysis will indicate whether the firm's financial condition has improved or deteriorated. Both types of ratio analysis can take one of the two forms, for example, static determination and its analysis or dynamic adjustment and its analysis.

2A.1 *Static determination of financial ratios*

The static determination of financial ratios involves the calculation and analysis of ratios over a number of periods for one company, or the analysis of differences in ratios among individual firms in one industry. An analyst must be careful of extreme values in either direction, because of the interrelationships between ratios. For instance, a very high liquidity ratio is costly to maintain, causing profitability ratios to be lower than they need to be. Furthermore, ratios must be interpreted in relation to the raw data from which they are calculated, particularly for ratios that sum accounts in order to arrive at the necessary data for the calculation. Even though this analysis must be performed with extreme caution, it can yield important conclusions in the analysis for a particular company. Table 2A.1 presents six alternative types of ratios for Johnson & Johnson. These six ratios are short-term solvency, long-term solvency, asset management, profitability ratios, market value ratios, and policy ratios. We now discuss these six ratios in detail.

2A.1.1 *Short-term solvency or liquidity ratios*

Liquidity ratios are calculated from information on the balance sheet; they measure the relative strength of a firm's financial position. Crudely interpreted, these are coverage ratios that indicate the firm's ability to meet short-term obligations. The current ratio (ratio 1 in Table 2A.1) is the most popular of the liquidity ratios because it is easy to calculate, and it has intuitive appeal. It is also the most broadly defined liquidity ratio, as it does not take into account the differences in relative liquidity among the individual components of current assets. A more specifically defined liquidity ratio is the quick or acid-test ratio (ratio 2), which excludes the least liquid portion of current assets and inventories. In other words, the numerator of this ratio includes cash, marketable securities (MS), and receivables. Cash ratio (ratio 3) is the ratio of the company's total cash and cash equivalents (MS) to its current liabilities. It is most often used as a measure of company liquidity. A strong cash ratio is useful to creditors when deciding how much debt they are willing to extend to the asking party (Investopedia.com).

The net working capital to total asset ratio (ratio 4) is the NWC divided by the total assets of the company. A relatively low value might indicate relatively low levels of liquidity.

2A.1.2 *Long-term solvency or financial leverage ratios*

If an analyst wishes to measure the extent of a firm's debt financing, a leverage ratio is the appropriate tool to use. This group of ratios

Table 2A.1 Alternative Financial Ratios for Johnson & Johnson (2016 to 2019)

Ratio Classification	Formula	JNJ 2019	2018	2017	2016
I. Short-Term Solvency or Liquidity Ratios (Times)					
(1) Current Ratio	(Current asset)/(Current liabilities)	1.26	1.47	1.41	2.47
(2) Quick Ratio	(Cash + MS + Receivables)/(Current liabilities)	0.94	1.08	1.04	2.04
(3) Cash Ratio	(Cash + MS)/(Current liabilities)	0.54	0.63	0.60	1.59
(4) Net Working Capital to Total Asset	(Net working capital)/(Total asset)	0.06	0.10	0.08	0.27
II. Long-Term Solvency or Financial Leverage Ratios (Times)					
(5) Debt-to-Asset	(Total debt)/(Total asset)	0.62	0.61	0.62	0.50
(6) Debt-to-Equity	(Total debt)/(Total equity)	1.65	1.56	1.61	1.01
(7) Equity Multiplier	(Total asset)/(Total equity)	2.65	2.56	2.61	2.01
(8) Times Interest Paid	(EBIT)/(Interest expenses)	54.49	17.91	18.92	28.28
(9) Long-Term Debt Ratio	(Long-term debt)/(Long-term debt + Total equity)	0.31	0.32	0.34	0.24
(10) Cash Coverage Ratio	(EBIT + Depreciation)/(Interest expenses)	76.53	24.80	24.96	33.45
III. Asset Management or Turnover (Activity) Ratios (Times)					
(11) Day's Sales in Receivables (Average Collection Period)	(Account receivable)/(Sales/365)	64.41	63.08	64.41	59.40

(Continued)

Table 2A.1 (*Continued*)

Ratio Classification	Formula	JNJ 2019	2018	2017	2016
(12) Receivable Turnover	(Sales)/(Account receivable)	5.67	5.79	5.67	6.14
(13) Day's Sales in Inventory	(Inventory)/(Cost of goods sold/365)	119.48	115.86	126.18	137.08
(14) Inventory Turnover	(Cost of goods sold)/(Inventory)	3.05	3.15	2.89	2.66
(15) Fixed Asset Turnover	(Sales)/(Fixed assets)	4.65	4.78	4.50	4.52
(16) Total Asset Turnover	(Sales)/(Total assets)	0.52	0.53	0.49	0.51
(17) Net Working Capital Turnover	(Sales)/(Net working capital)	8.81	5.51	6.09	1.86
IV. Profitability Ratios (Percentage)					
(18) Profit Margin	(Net income)/(Sales)	18.42	18.75	1.70	23.01
(19) Return on Assets (ROA)	(Net income)/(Total assets)	9.59	10.00	0.83	11.71
(20) Return on Equity (ROE)	(Net income)/(Total equity)	25.42	25.60	2.16	23.49
V. Market Value Ratios (Times)					
(21) Price-Earnings Ratio	(Market price per share)/(Earnings per share)	30.08	25.96	289.33	18.70
(22) Market-to-Book Ratio	(Market price per share)/(Book value per share)	2.88	2.60	2.39	2.19
(23) Earnings Yield	(Earnings per share)/(Market price per share)	0.03	0.04	0.00	0.05
(24) Dividend Yield	(Dividend per share)/(Market price per share)	0.02	0.02	0.02	0.03

(*Continued*)

Table 2A.1 (*Continued*)

Ratio Classification	Formula	JNJ 2019	2018	2017	2016
(25) PEG Ratio	(Price-earnings ratio)/(Earnings growth rate)	343.85	267.28	−2,277.37	166.27
(26) Enterprise Value-EBITDA Ratio	(Enterprise value)/(EBITDA)	18.97	17.68	18.81	14.46
(27) Dividend Payout Ratio	(Dividend payout)/(Net income)	0.66	0.62	6.88	0.52
VI. Policy Ratios (Percentage)					
(5) Debt-to-Asset	(Total debt)/(Total asset)	62.30	60.93	61.76	50.13
(27) Dividend Payout Ratio	(Dividend payout)/(Net income)	65.59	62.06	687.92	52.12
(28) Sustainable Growth Rate	[(1 - Payout ratio) * ROE]/[1 - (1 - Payout ratio) * ROE]	9.59	10.76	−11.27	12.67

reflects the financial risk posture of the firm. The two sources of data from which these ratios can be calculated are the balance sheet and the statement of earnings.

The balance sheet leverage ratio measures the proportion of debt incorporated into the capital structure. The debt–equity ratio measures the proportion of debt that is matched by equity; thus, this ratio reflects the composition of the capital structure. The debt–asset ratio (ratio 5), on the other hand, measures the proportion of debt-financed assets currently being used by the firm. Other commonly used leverage ratios include the equity multiplier ratio (7) and the time interest paid ratio (8).

Debt to equity (6) is a variation on the total debt ratio. It is total debt divided by total equity.

Long-term debt ratio (9) is long-term debt divided by the sum of long-term debt and total equity.

Cash coverage ratio (10) is defined as the sum of EBIT and depreciation divided by interest. The numerator is often abbreviated as EBITDA.

The income statement leverage ratio measures the firm's ability to meet fixed obligations of one form or another. The time interest paid, which is earnings before interest and taxes over interest expense, measures the firm's ability to service the interest expense on its outstanding debt. A more broadly defined ratio of this type is the fixed-charge coverage ratio, which includes not only the interest expense but also all other expenses that the firm is obligated by contract to pay. (This ratio is not included in Table 2.5 because there is not enough information on fixed charges for these firms to calculate this ratio.)

2A.1.3 *Asset management or turnover (activity) ratios*

This group of ratios measures how efficiently the firm is utilizing its assets. With activity ratios, one must be particularly careful about the interpretation of extreme results in either direction; very high values may indicate possible problems in the long term and very low values may indicate a current problem of low sales or not taking a loss for obsolete assets. The reason that high activity may not be good in the long term is that the firm may not be able to adjust to an even higher level of activity and therefore may miss out on a market opportunity. Better analysis and planning can help a firm get around this problem.

The days in accounts receivable or average collection period ratio (11) indicates the firm's effectiveness in collecting its credit sales. The other activity ratios measure the firm's efficiency in generating sales with its current level of assets, appropriately termed turnover ratios. While there are many turnover ratios that can be calculated, there are three basic ones: inventory turnover (14), fixed assets turnover (15), and total assets turnover (16). Each of these ratios measures a different aspect of the firm's efficiency in managing its assets.

Receivables turnover (12) is computed as credit sales divided by accounts receivable. In general, a higher accounts receivable turnover suggests more frequent payment of receivables by customers.

In general, analysts look for higher receivables turnover and shorter collection periods, *but this combination may imply that the firm's credit policy is too strict*, allowing only the lowest-risk customers to buy on credit. Although this strategy could minimize credit losses, it may hurt overall sales, profits, and shareholder wealth.

Day's sales in inventory ratio (13) estimates how many days, on average, a product sits in the inventory before it is sold.

Net working capital turnover (17) measures how much per dollar of net working capital can generate dollar of sales. For example, if this ratio is 3, this means the per dollar of net working capital can generate $3 of sales.

2A.1.4 *Profitability ratios*

This group of ratios indicates the profitability of the firm's operations. It is important to note here that these measures are based on past performance. Profitability ratios are generally the most volatile, because many of the variables affecting them are beyond the firm's control. There are three groups of profitability ratios: those measuring margins, those measuring returns, and those measuring the relationship of market values to book or accounting values.

Profit margin ratios show the percentage of sales dollars that the firm was able to convert into profit. There are many such ratios that can be calculated to yield insightful results, namely, profit margin (18), return on asset (19), and return on equity (20).

Return ratios are generally calculated as a return on assets or equity. The return on assets ratio (19) measures the profitability of the firm's asset utilization. The return on equity ratio (20) indicates the rate of return earned on the book value of owner's equity. Market value analyses include (i) market value/book value ratio, (ii) price per share/earnings per share (P/E) ratio, and other ratios as indicated in Table 2.5.

Overall, all four different types of ratios (as indicated in Table 2.5) have different characteristics stemming from the firm itself and the industry as a whole. For example, the collection period ratio (which is accounts receivable times 365 over net sales) is clearly the function of the billings, payment, and collection policies of the pharmaceutical industry. In addition, the fixed asset turnover ratios for those firms are different, which might imply that different firms have different capacity utilizations.

2A.1.5 *Market value ratios*

A firm's profitability, risk, quality of management, and many other factors are reflected in its stock and security prices. Hence, market value ratios indicate the market's assessment of the value of the firm's securities.

The price earnings (PE) ratio (21) is simply the market price of the firm's common stock divided by its annual earnings per share. Sometimes called the *earnings multiple*, the PE ratio shows how much the investors are willing to pay for each dollar of the firm's earnings per share. Earnings per share comes from the income statement. Therefore, earnings per share is sensitive to the many factors that affect the construction of an income statement, such as the choice of GAAP to management decisions regarding the use of debt to finance assets. Although earnings per share cannot reflect the value of patents or assets, the quality of the firm's management, or its risk, and stock prices can reflect all of these factors. Comparing a firm's PE ratio to that of the stock market as a whole, or with the firm's competitors, indicates the market's perception of the true value of the company.

Market-to-book ratio (22) measures the market's valuation relative to balance sheet equity. The book value of equity is simply the difference between the book values of assets and liabilities appearing on the balance sheet. The price-to-book-value ratio is the market price per share divided by the book value of equity per share. A higher ratio suggests that investors are more optimistic about the market value of a firm's assets, its intangible assets, and the ability of its managers.

Earnings yield (23) is defined as earnings per share divided by market price per share and is used to measure return on investment. Dividend yield (24) is defined as dividend per share divided by market price per share, which is used to determine whether this company's stock is an income stock or a gross stock. A gross stock dividend yield is very small or even zero. For example, the stock from a utility industry dividend yield is very high.

PEG ratio (25) is defined as price earnings ratio divided by earnings growth rate. The price/earnings-to-growth (PEG) ratio is used to determine a stock's value while taking the company's earnings growth into account and is considered to provide a more complete picture than the PE ratio. While a high PE ratio may make a stock look like a good buy, factoring in the company's growth rate to get the stock's PEG ratio can tell a different story. The lower the PEG ratio, the more the stock may be undervalued given its earnings performance. The PEG ratio that indicates an over or underpriced stock varies by industry and by company type, though a broad rule of thumb is that a PEG ratio below one is desirable. Also, the accuracy of the PEG ratio depends on the inputs used. Sustainable growth rate is usually used to estimate earnings growth rate.

Enterprise value is an estimate of the market value of the company's operating assets, which means all the assets of the firm except cash. Since market values are usually unavailable, we use the right-hand side of the balance sheet and calculate the enterprise value as follows:

$$\begin{aligned}\text{Enterprise value} &= \text{Total market value of equity}\\ &\quad + \text{Book value of total liabilities} - \text{Cash.}\end{aligned}$$

Note that the sum of the value of the market values of the stock and all liabilities equals the value of the firm's assets from the balance sheet identity. Total market value of equity = Market price per share × Basic number of shares outstanding.

Enterprise value is often used to calculate the Enterprise value-EBITDA ratio (26):

$$\text{EBITDA ratio} = \text{Enterprise value/EBITDA},$$

where EBITDA is defined as earnings before interest, taxes, depreciation, and amortization.

This ratio is similar to the PE ratio, but it relates the value of all the operating assets to a measure of the operating cash flow generated by those assets.

2A.1.6 *Policy ratios*

Policy ratios include debt-to-asset ratio, dividend payout ratio, and sustainable growth rate. Dividend payout ratio is defined as (dividend payout)/(net income). The dividend payout ratio is the ratio of the total amount of dividends paid out to shareholders relative to the net income of the company. It is the percentage of earnings paid to shareholders in dividends. The amount that is not paid to shareholders is retained by the company to pay off debt or to reinvest in core operations. It is sometimes simply referred to as the "payout ratio."

2A.1.7 *Estimation of the target of a ratio*

An issue that must be addressed at this point is the determination of an appropriate proxy for the target of a ratio. For an analyst, this can be an insurmountable problem if the firm is extremely diversified, and if it does not have one or two major product lines in industries where industry averages are available. One possible solution is to determine the relative industry share of each division or major product line, then apply these percentages to the related industry averages. Lastly, derive one target ratio for the firm as a whole with which its ratio can be compared. One must be very careful in any such analysis, because the proxy may be extremely over- or underestimated. The analyst can also use Standard Industrial Classification (SIC) codes to properly define the industry of diversified firms. The analyst can then use 3- or 4-digit codes and compute their own weighted industry average.

Often, an industry average is used as a proxy for the target ratio. This can lead to another problem, the inappropriate calculation of an industry average, even though the industry and companies are fairly well defined. The issue here is the appropriate weighting scheme for combining the individual company ratios in order to arrive at one industry average. Individual ratios can be weighted according to equal weights, asset weights, or sales weights. The analyst must determine the extent to which firm size, as measured by asset base or market share, affects the relative level of a firm's ratios and the tendency for other firms in the industry to adjust toward the target level of this ratio. One way this can be done is to calculate the coefficients of variation for a number of ratios under each of the weighting schemes and to compare them to see which scheme consistently has the lowest coefficient variation. This would appear to be the most appropriate weighting scheme. Of course, one could also use a different weighting scheme for each ratio, but this would be very tedious if many ratios were to be analyzed. Note that the median rather than the average or mean can be used to avoid needless complications with respect to extreme values that might distort the computation of averages. Dynamic financial ratio analysis is to compare individual company ratios with industry averages over time. In general, this kind of analysis needs to rely upon regression analysis. Lee and Lee (2017, Chapter 2) have discussed this kind of analysis in detail.

2A.2 *DOL, DFL, and CL*

Besides the static ratio discussed in the previous section, analysts frequently use degree of operating leverage (DOL), degree of financial leverage (DFL), and combined leverage (CL) to analyze how the increase of sales can affect earnings before interest and tax (EBIT) and earning per share (EPS).

In this section, we first define the definitions of DOL, DFL, and DCL in terms of elasticity definition, then we show how the Excel program can be used to calculate these three variables in terms of financial statement data. Chapter 11 of Lee *et al.* (2022) has theoretically and empirically discussed these three variables in further detail.

The Excel program can be used to calculate these three variables in terms of financial statement data in the following manner:

1. The definition of degree of operating leverage is as follows:

$$\text{DOL} = \frac{\%\text{Change in EBIT}}{\%\text{Change in sale}}. \tag{2A.1}$$

To calculate the degree of operating leverage, we first compute the percentage change in EBIT by inputting "(B4–C4)/C4." Then, compute the percentage change in sale by inputting "(B3–C3)/C3." Put them together, we input "=((B4–C4)/C4)/((B3–C3)/C3)" to get DOL = −6.3626.

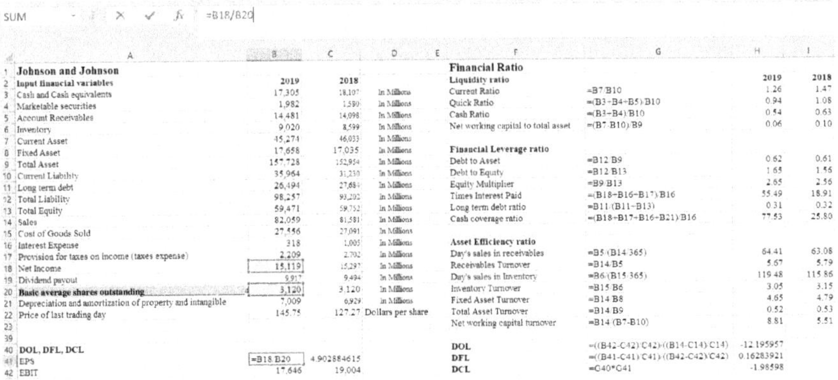

SUM fx =B18/B20

	A	B	C	D	F	G	H	I
1	**Johnson and Johnson**				**Financial Ratio**			
2	**Input financial variables**	**2019**	**2018**		**Liquidity ratio**		**2019**	**2018**
3	Cash and Cash equivalents	17,305	18,107	In Millions	Current Ratio	=B7/B10	1.26	1.47
4	Marketable securities	1,982	1,580	In Millions	Quick Ratio	=(B3+B4+B5)/B10	0.94	1.08
5	Account Receivables	14,481	14,098	In Millions	Cash Ratio	=(B3+B4)/B10	0.54	0.63
6	Inventory	9,020	8,599	In Millions	Net working capital to total asset	=(B7-B10)/B9	0.06	0.10
7	Current Asset	45,274	46,033	In Millions				
8	Fixed Asset	17,658	17,035	In Millions	**Financial Leverage ratio**			
9	Total Asset	157,728	152,954	In Millions	Debt to Asset	=B12/B9	0.62	0.61
10	Current Liability	35,964	31,230	In Millions	Debt to Equity	=B12/B13	1.65	1.56
11	Long term debt	26,494	27,684	In Millions	Equity Multiplier	=B9/B13	2.65	2.56
12	Total Liability	98,257	93,202	In Millions	Times Interest Paid	=(B18+B16+B17)/B16	55.49	18.91
13	Total Equity	59,471	59,752	In Millions	Long term debt ratio	=B11/(B11+B13)	0.31	0.32
14	Sales	82,059	81,581	In Millions	Cash coverage ratio	=(B18+B17+B16+B21)/B16	77.53	25.80
15	Cost of Goods Sold	27,556	27,091	In Millions				
16	Interest Expense	318	1,005	In Millions	**Asset Efficiency ratio**			
17	Provision for taxes on income (taxes expense)	2,209	2,702	In Millions	Day's sales in receivables	=B5/(B14/365)	64.41	63.08
18	Net Income	15,119	15,297	In Millions	Receivables Turnover	=B14/B5	5.67	5.79
19	Dividend payout	9,917	9,494	In Millions	Day's sales in Inventory	=B6/(B15/365)	119.48	115.86
20	**Basic average shares outstanding**	3,120	3,120	In Millions	Inventory Turnover	=B15/B6	3.05	3.15
21	Depreciation and amortization of property and intangible	7,009	6,929	In Millions	Fixed Asset Turnover	=B14/B8	4.65	4.79
22	Price of last trading day	145.75	127.27	Dollars per share	Total Asset Turnover	=B14/B9	0.52	0.53
23					Net working capital turnover	=B14/(B7-B10)	8.81	5.51
39								
40	**DOL, DFL, DCL**				**DOL**	=((B42-C42)/C42)/((B14-C14)/C14)	-12.195957	
41	EPS	=B18/B20	4.902884615		**DFL**	=((B41-C41)/C41)/((B42-C42)/C42)	0.16283921	
42	EBIT	17,646	19,004		**DCL**	=G40*G41	-1.98598	

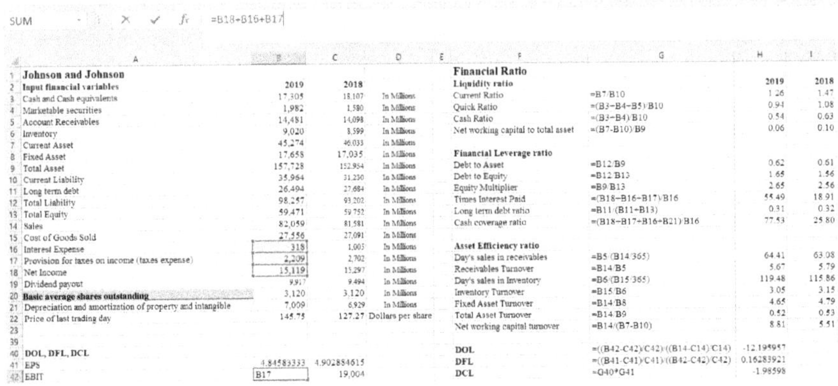

SUM fx =B18+B16+B17

	A	B	C	D	F	G	H	I
1	**Johnson and Johnson**				**Financial Ratio**			
2	**Input financial variables**	**2019**	**2018**		**Liquidity ratio**		**2019**	**2018**
3	Cash and Cash equivalents	17,305	18,107	In Millions	Current Ratio	=B7/B10	1.26	1.47
4	Marketable securities	1,982	1,580	In Millions	Quick Ratio	=(B3+B4+B5)/B10	0.94	1.08
5	Account Receivables	14,481	14,098	In Millions	Cash Ratio	=(B3+B4)/B10	0.54	0.63
6	Inventory	9,020	8,599	In Millions	Net working capital to total asset	=(B7-B10)/B9	0.06	0.10
7	Current Asset	45,274	46,033	In Millions				
8	Fixed Asset	17,658	17,035	In Millions	**Financial Leverage ratio**			
9	Total Asset	157,728	152,954	In Millions	Debt to Asset	=B12/B9	0.62	0.61
10	Current Liability	35,964	31,230	In Millions	Debt to Equity	=B12/B13	1.65	1.56
11	Long term debt	26,494	27,684	In Millions	Equity Multiplier	=B9/B13	2.65	2.56
12	Total Liability	98,257	93,202	In Millions	Times Interest Paid	=(B18+B16+B17)/B16	55.49	18.91
13	Total Equity	59,471	59,752	In Millions	Long term debt ratio	=B11/(B11+B13)	0.31	0.32
14	Sales	82,059	81,581	In Millions	Cash coverage ratio	=(B18+B17+B16+B21)/B16	77.53	25.80
15	Cost of Goods Sold	27,556	27,091	In Millions				
16	Interest Expense	318	1,005	In Millions	**Asset Efficiency ratio**			
17	Provision for taxes on income (taxes expense)	2,209	2,702	In Millions	Day's sales in receivables	=B5/(B14/365)	64.41	63.08
18	Net Income	15,119	15,297	In Millions	Receivables Turnover	=B14/B5	5.67	5.79
19	Dividend payout	9,917	9,494	In Millions	Day's sales in Inventory	=B6/(B15/365)	119.48	115.86
20	**Basic average shares outstanding**	3,120	3,120	In Millions	Inventory Turnover	=B15/B6	3.05	3.15
21	Depreciation and amortization of property and intangible	7,009	6,929	In Millions	Fixed Asset Turnover	=B14/B8	4.65	4.79
22	Price of last trading day	145.75	127.27	Dollars per share	Total Asset Turnover	=B14/B9	0.52	0.53
23					Net working capital turnover	=B14/(B7-B10)	8.81	5.51
39								
40	**DOL, DFL, DCL**				**DOL**	=((B42-C42)/C42)/((B14-C14)/C14)	-12.195957	
41	EPS	4.84583333	4.902884615		**DFL**	=((B41-C41)/C41)/((B42-C42)/C42)	0.16283921	
42	EBIT	B17	19,004		**DCL**	=G40*G41	-1.98598	

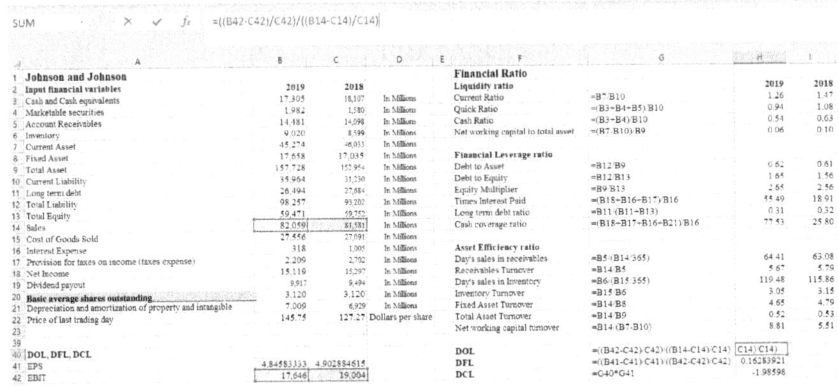

SUM fx =((B42-C42)/C42)/((B14-C14)/C14)

	A	B	C	D	F	G	H	I
1	**Johnson and Johnson**				**Financial Ratio**			
2	**Input financial variables**	**2019**	**2018**		**Liquidity ratio**		**2019**	**2018**
3	Cash and Cash equivalents	17,305	18,107	In Millions	Current Ratio	=B7/B10	1.26	1.47
4	Marketable securities	1,982	1,580	In Millions	Quick Ratio	=(B3+B4+B5)/B10	0.94	1.08
5	Account Receivables	14,481	14,098	In Millions	Cash Ratio	=(B3+B4)/B10	0.54	0.63
6	Inventory	9,020	8,599	In Millions	Net working capital to total asset	=(B7-B10)/B9	0.06	0.10
7	Current Asset	45,274	46,033	In Millions				
8	Fixed Asset	17,658	17,035	In Millions	**Financial Leverage ratio**			
9	Total Asset	157,728	152,954	In Millions	Debt to Asset	=B12/B9	0.62	0.61
10	Current Liability	35,964	31,230	In Millions	Debt to Equity	=B12/B13	1.65	1.56
11	Long term debt	26,494	27,684	In Millions	Equity Multiplier	=B9/B13	2.65	2.56
12	Total Liability	98,257	93,202	In Millions	Times Interest Paid	=(B18+B16+B17)/B16	55.49	18.91
13	Total Equity	59,471	59,752	In Millions	Long term debt ratio	=B11/(B11+B13)	0.31	0.32
14	Sales	82,059	81,581	In Millions	Cash coverage ratio	=(B18+B17+B16+B21)/B16	77.53	25.80
15	Cost of Goods Sold	27,556	27,091	In Millions				
16	Interest Expense	318	1,005	In Millions	**Asset Efficiency ratio**			
17	Provision for taxes on income (taxes expense)	2,209	2,702	In Millions	Day's sales in receivables	=B5/(B14/365)	64.41	63.08
18	Net Income	15,119	15,297	In Millions	Receivables Turnover	=B14/B5	5.67	5.79
19	Dividend payout	9,917	9,494	In Millions	Day's sales in Inventory	=B6/(B15/365)	119.48	115.86
20	**Basic average shares outstanding**	3,120	3,120	In Millions	Inventory Turnover	=B15/B6	3.05	3.15
21	Depreciation and amortization of property and intangible	7,009	6,929	In Millions	Fixed Asset Turnover	=B14/B8	4.65	4.79
22	Price of last trading day	145.75	127.27	Dollars per share	Total Asset Turnover	=B14/B9	0.52	0.53
23					Net working capital turnover	=B14/(B7-B10)	8.81	5.51
39								
40	**DOL, DFL, DCL**				**DOL**	=((B42-C42)/C42)/((B14-C14)/C14)	C14)/C14)	
41	EPS	4.84583333	4.902884615		**DFL**	=((B41-C41)/C41)/((B42-C42)/C42)	0.16283921	
42	EBIT	17,646	19,004		**DCL**	=G40*G41	-1.98598	

2. The definition of degree of financial leverage is as follows:

$$\text{DFL} = \frac{\%\text{Change in EPS}}{\%\text{Change in EBIT}}. \tag{2A.2}$$

To calculate the degree of operating leverage, we firstly compute EPS (Net income/Total shares) by inputting "=B5/B6." And then, we compute the percentage change in EPS by inputting "(B7–C7)/C7," which is the percentage change in EPS. Then, compute the percentage change in EBIT by inputting "(B4–C4)/C4." Put them together, we input "=((B7–C7)/C7)/((B4–C4)/C4)" to get DFL = 0.312132932.

SUM =((B41-C41)/C41)/((B42-C42)/C42)

	A	B	C	D	E	F	G	H	I
1	**Johnson and Johnson**					**Financial Ratio**			
2	**Input financial variables**	**2019**	**2018**			**Liquidity ratio**		**2019**	**2018**
3	Cash and Cash equivalents	17,305	18,107	In Millions		Current Ratio	=B7/B10	1.26	1.47
4	Marketable securities	1,982	1,580	In Millions		Quick Ratio	=(B3+B4+B5)/B10	0.94	1.08
5	Account Receivables	14,481	14,098	In Millions		Cash Ratio	=(B3+B4)/B10	0.54	0.63
6	Inventory	9,020	8,599	In Millions		Net working capital to total asset	=(B7-B10)/B9	0.06	0.10
7	Current Asset	45,274	46,033	In Millions					
8	Fixed Asset	17,658	17,035	In Millions		**Financial Leverage ratio**			
9	Total Asset	157,728	152,954	In Millions		Debt to Asset	=B12/B9	0.62	0.61
10	Current Liability	35,964	31,230	In Millions		Debt to Equity	=B12/B13	1.65	1.56
11	Long term debt	26,494	27,684	In Millions		Equity Multiplier	=B9/B13	2.65	2.56
12	Total Liability	98,257	93,202	In Millions		Times Interest Paid	=(B18+B16+B17)/B16	55.49	18.91
13	Total Equity	59,471	59,752	In Millions		Long term debt ratio	=B11/(B11+B13)	0.31	0.32
14	Sales	82,059	81,581	In Millions		Cash coverage ratio	=(B18+B17+B16+B21)/B16	77.53	25.80
15	Cost of Goods Sold	27,556	27,091	In Millions					
16	Interest Expense	318	1,005	In Millions		**Asset Efficiency ratio**			
17	Provision for taxes on income (taxes expense)	2,209	2,702	In Millions		Day's sales in receivables	=B5/(B14/365)	64.41	63.08
18	Net Income	15,119	15,297	In Millions		Receivables Turnover	=B14/B5	5.67	5.79
19	Dividend payout	9,917	9,494	In Millions		Day's sales in Inventory	=B6/(B15/365)	119.48	115.86
20	**Basic average shares outstanding**	3,120	3,120	In Millions		Inventory Turnover	=B15/B6	3.05	3.15
21	Depreciation and amortization of property and intangible	7,009	6,929	In Millions		Fixed Asset Turnover	=B14/B8	4.65	4.79
22	Price of last trading day	145.75	127.27	Dollars per share		Total Asset Turnover	=B14/B9	0.52	0.53
23						Net working capital turnover	=B14/(B7-B10)	8.81	5.51
39									
40	**DOL, DFL, DCL**					**DOL**	=((B42-C42)/C42)/((B14-C14)/C14)	-12.195957	
41	EPS	4.84583333	4.902884615			**DFL**	=((B41-C41)/C41)/((B42-C42)/C42)	C42)/C42)	
42	EBIT	17,646	19,004			**DCL**	=G40*G41	-1.98598	

3. The definition of degree of combined leverage is as follows:

$$\begin{aligned} \text{DCL} &= \frac{\%\text{Change in EPS}}{\%\text{Change in EBIT}} * \frac{\%\text{Change in EBIT}}{\%\text{Change in sale}} \\ &= \frac{\%\text{Change in EPS}}{\%\text{Change in sale}}. \end{aligned} \tag{2A.3}$$

To calculate the degree of combined leverage, we first compute the percentage change in EPS by inputting "(B7–C7)/C7," which is the percentage change in EPS. Then, compute the percentage change in sale by inputting "(B3–C3)/C3." Put them together, we input "=((B7–C7)/C7)/((B3–C3)/C3)" to get DFL = −1.986. Alternatively, we can also input "= B10 * B11" to get the same result since DCL = DFL * DOL = −1.986.

SUM fx =H40*H41

	A	B	C	D	E	F	G	H	I
1	**Johuson and Johnson**					**Financial Ratio**			
2	**Input financial variables**	**2019**	**2018**			**Liquidity ratio**		**2019**	**2018**
3	Cash and Cash equivalents	17,305	18,107	In Millions		Current Ratio	=B7/B10	1.26	1.47
4	Marketable securities	1,982	1,580	In Millions		Quick Ratio	=(B3+B4+B5)/B10	0.94	1.08
5	Account Receivables	14,481	14,098	In Millions		Cash Ratio	=(B3+B4)/B10	0.54	0.63
6	Inventory	9,020	8,599	In Millions		Net working capital to total asset	=(B7-B10)/B9	0.06	0.10
7	Current Asset	45,274	46,033	In Millions					
8	Fixed Asset	17,658	17,035	In Millions		**Financial Leverage ratio**			
9	Total Asset	157,728	152,954	In Millions		Debt to Asset	=B12/B9	0.62	0.61
10	Current Liability	35,964	31,230	In Millions		Debt to Equity	=B12/B13	1.65	1.56
11	Long term debt	26,494	27,684	In Millions		Equity Multiplier	=B9/B13	2.65	2.56
12	Total Liability	98,257	93,202	In Millions		Times Interest Paid	=(B18+B16+B17)/B16	55.49	18.91
13	Total Equity	59,471	59,752	In Millions		Long term debt ratio	=B11/(B11+B13)	0.31	0.32
14	Sales	82,059	81,581	In Millions		Cash coverage ratio	=(B18+B17+B16+B21)/B16	77.53	25.80
15	Cost of Goods Sold	27,556	27,091	In Millions					
16	Interest Expense	318	1,005	In Millions		**Asset Efficiency ratio**			
17	Provision for taxes on income (taxes expense)	2,209	2,702	In Millions		Day's sales in receivables	=B5/(B14/365)	64.41	63.08
18	Net Income	15,119	15,297	In Millions		Receivables Turnover	=B14/B5	5.67	5.79
19	Dividend payout	9,917	9,494	In Millions		Day's sales in Inventory	=B6/(B15/365)	119.48	115.86
20	**Basic average shares outstanding**	3,120	3,120	In Millions		Inventory Turnover	=B15/B6	3.05	3.15
21	Depreciation and amortization of property and intangible	7,009	6,929	In Millions		Fixed Asset Turnover	=B14/B8	4.65	4.79
22	Price of last trading day	145.75	127.27	Dollars per share		Total Asset Turnover	=B14/B9	0.52	0.53
23						Net working capital turnover	=B14/(B7-B10)	8.81	5.51
39									
40	**DOL, DFL, DCL**					**DOL**	=((B42-C42)/C42)/((B14-C14)/C14)	-12.195957	
41	EPS	4.84583333	4.902884615			**DFL**	=((B41-C41)/C41)/((B42-C42)/C42)	0.16283921	
42	EBIT	17,646	19,004			**DCL**	=G40*G41	=H40*H41	

Chapter 3

Introduction to Important Finance Theories

Contents

3.1 Introduction

Financial theories are important in corporate finance, investment analysis, portfolio management, and derivatives. Finance theories are the basic tools for determining the intrinsic value of alternative financial instruments. This chapter provides a general review of the financial theory to be used in this book.

There are four alternative but interrelated valuation models of financial theory that are useful for the analysis of securities, the management of portfolios, financial management, and derivative. These four theories are as follows:

(1) Bond and stock valuation theory (classical financial theory),
(2) M&M valuation theory and Portfolio theory (neoclassical financial theory),
(3) Capital Asset Pricing Model (CAPM) and Arbitrage Pricing Theory (APT), and
(4) Valuation theories of derivatives (forward, future, and option).

The relationship among these four different theories can be described by Figure 3.1.

Bond valuation is discussed in Section 3.2. Section 3.3 explores common-stock valuation. Section 3.4 discusses M&M valuation theory. Portfolio analysis and its application are discussed in Section 3.5. CAPM and APT are discussed in Section 3.6. Section 3.7 defines the basic concept and valuation methods for forward contracts, future contracts, and option contracts. Finally, Section 3.8 summarizes the

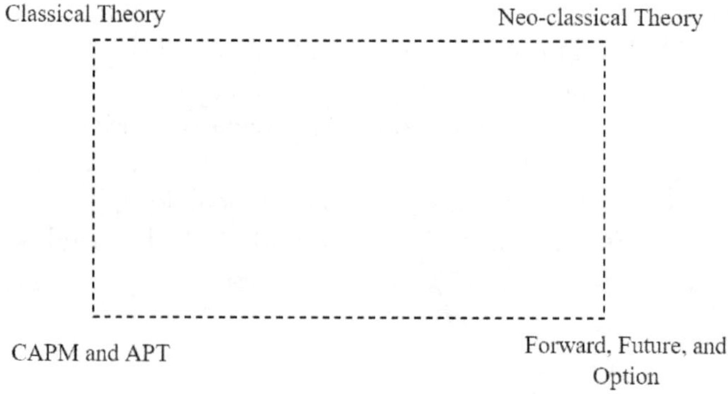

Figure 3.1 Alternative Valuation Theories

chapter. Appendix 3A discusses the minimum-variance approach to derive optimal weight. Appendix 3B discusses the Sharpe performance approach to derive optimal weight. Appendix 3C discusses statistical analysis, beta coefficient, and portfolio analysis. We will apply the concepts, methods, and theories of these three appendixes extensively in this chapter.

3.2 Bond Valuation

Bond valuation is a relatively easy process, as the income stream the bondholder will receive is known with a high degree of certainty. Barring a firm's default, the income stream consists of the periodic coupon payments and the repayments of the principal at maturity. These cash flows must be discounted to the present using the required rate of return for the bond.

The basic principles of bond valuation are represented in the following equation:

$$\mathrm{PV} = \sum_{t=1}^{n} \frac{\mathrm{CF}_t}{(1+k_b)^t}, \tag{3.1}$$

where PV = present value of the bond, n = the number of periods to maturity, CF_t = the cash flow (interest and principal) received in period t, and k_b = the required rate of return of the bondholders (equal to risk-free rate i plus a risk premium).

3.2.1 *Perpetuity*

The first (and most extreme) case of bond valuation involves a **perpetuity**, a bond with no maturity date and perpetual interest payments. Such bonds do exist. In 1814, the English government floated a large bond issue to consolidate the various small issues they had used to pay for the Napoleonic Wars. Such bonds are called *consols*, and the owners are entitled to a fixed amount of interest income annually in perpetuity. In this case, Equation (3.1) collapses into

$$\mathrm{PV} = \frac{\mathrm{CF}}{k_b}. \tag{3.2}$$

Thus, the valuation depends directly on the periodic interest payment and the required rate of return for the bond. Required rates of return, necessitated by a higher rate of inflation or an increase in the perceived risk of the bond, lower the present value, decreasing the bond's market value. For example, if the stated annual interest payment on the perpetuity bond is \$50 and the required rate of return in the market is 10%, the price of the security is stated as follows:

$$\text{PV} = \$50/0.10 = \$500.$$

If its issuing price had been \$1,000, it can be seen that the required rate of return would have been only 5% ($k_b = \text{CF}/\text{PV} = \$50/\$1{,}000 = 0.05$, or 5%).

3.2.2 *Term bonds*

Most bonds are **term bonds**, which mature at some definite point in time. Thus, Equation (3.1) should be respecified to take this fact into account:

$$\text{PV} = \sum_{t=1}^{n} \frac{I_t}{(1+k_b)^t} + \frac{P_n}{(1+k_b)^n}, \tag{3.3}$$

where I_t = the annual coupon interest payment, P_n = the principal amount (face value) of the bond, and n = the number of periods to maturity.

Sample Problem 3.1

If a corporate bond issued by XYZ Company has the following characteristics,

Annual coupon payment	= \$90
Face value	= \$1,000
Number of years till bond matures	= 5
Return required by bondholders	= 12%,

then Equation (3.8) can be used to calculate the theoretical value of this bond.

$$\begin{aligned} \text{PV} &= \frac{\$90}{(1+0.12)} + \frac{\$90}{(1+.012)^2} + \frac{\$90}{(1+0.12)^3} \\ &\quad + \frac{\$90}{(1+0.12)^4} + \frac{\$90}{(1+0.12)^5} + \frac{\$1,000}{(1+0.12)^5} \\ &= \$891.83. \end{aligned}$$

Again, it should be noted that the market price, PV, of a bond is affected by changes in the rate of inflation. If inflation increases, the discount rate must also increase to compensate the investor for the resultant decrease in the value of the debt repayment. The present value of each period's interest payment thus decreases, and the price of the bond falls. The bondholder is always exposed to interest rate risk and the variance of bond prices resulting from fluctuations in the level of interest rates. Interest rate risk, or price volatility of a bond caused by changes in interest rate levels, is directly related to the term to maturity. There are two types of risk premiums associated with interest rate risk as it applies to corporate bonds. The **bond maturity premium** refers to the net return from investing in long-term government bonds rather than the short-term bills. Since corporate bonds generally possess default risk, another of the components of corporate bond rates of return is **default premium**. The bond default premium is the net increase in return from investing in long-term corporate bonds rather than in long-term government bonds.

Additional features of a bond can affect its valuation. **Convertible bonds**, those with a provision for conversion into shares of common stock, are generally more valuable than firm's straight bonds for several reasons. First, the investor receives the potential of positive gains from conversion when the market price of a firm's common stock rises above the conversion price. If the stock price is greater than conversion price, the convertible bond generally sells at or above its conversion value. Second, the bondholder also receives the protection of fixed-income payment, regardless of the current price of the stock — assuring the investor that the price of the bond will be at least equal to that of a straight bond, should stock prices fail to increase sufficiently. Third, for any given firm, the coupon rate of return from its bonds is generally greater than the dividend rate of return (dividend yield) from their common stock — thus causing a measure of superiority for a convertible bond over its conversion into common stock until stock dividends rise above the bond's coupon rate. Even then, the convertible bond may be preferred by investors because of the higher degree of certainty of interest payments as compared to dividends that would decline when earnings fall.

A sinking fund provision may also increase the value of a bond, at least at its time of issue. A sinking fund agreement specifies a schedule by which the sinking fund will retire the bond issue gradually over its life. By providing cash to the sinking fund for use in redeeming the bonds, this provision ensures the investor some potential demand for the bond, thus slightly increasing the liquidity of the investment.

Finally, the possibility that the bond may be called will generally lower the value relative to a non-callable bond. A call provision stipulates that the bond may be retired by the issuer at a certain price, usually above par or face value. Therefore, in periods of large downward interest movements, a company may be able to retire a high coupon bond and issue new bonds with a lower interest payment requirement. A call feature increases the risk to an investor in that his expected high-interest payments may be called away from him, if overall interest rate levels decline.

3.3 Common-Stock Valuation

Common-stock valuation is complicated by an uncertainty of cash flows to the investor, necessarily greater than that for bond valuation.[1]

Not only might the dividends voted to shareholders' each period change in response to management's assessment concerning the current level of earnings stability and future earnings prospects, or other factors, but the price of the stock may also either rise or fall, resulting in either capital gains or losses if the shares are sold. Thus, the

[1]This is true because foregoing interest puts the firm into default, while missing dividend payments does not.

valuation process requires the forecasting of both capital gains and the stream of expected dividends. Both must also be discounted at the required rate of return of the common stockholders:

$$P_0 = \frac{d_1}{1+k} + \frac{d_2}{(1+k)^2} + \cdots + \frac{P_n}{(1+k)^n}, \tag{3.4}$$

where P_0 = the present value, or price, of the common stock per share, d = the dividend payment per share, k = the required rate of return of the common stockholders, and P_n = the price of the stock in period n when sold.

However, P_n can also be expressed as the sum of all discounted dividends to be received from period n forward into the future. Thus, the value at the present time can be expressed as an infinite series of discounted dividend payments:

$$P_0 = \sum_{t=1}^{\infty} \frac{d_t}{(1+k)^t}, \tag{3.5}$$

in which d_t is the dividend payment in period t. Several possibilities exist regarding the growth of dividend payments over time. First, dividends may be assumed to be a constant amount, and the formula for the stock's valuation is simple as shown in Equation (3.2), where CF is the constant dividend and k is the required rate of return of the common stockholder.

Second, dividends may be expected to grow at some constant rate, g. In such a case, a dividend at time t is simply the compound value of the present dividend (i.e., $P_t = (1+g)^t d_0$). Under this assumption, as in the previous section, if $g < k$, the valuation equation can be simplified to

$$P_0 = \frac{d_1}{(k-g)}. \tag{3.6}$$

This equation represents the **Gordon growth model**. Note that a critical condition for this model is that the constant growth of dividends must be less than the constant required rate of return. The zero-growth situation is a special case of this model, in which

$$P_0 = \frac{d_1}{k}. \tag{3.7}$$

Finally, dividends can exhibit a period of supernormal growth (i.e., $g > k$) before declining to the normal growth situation assumed in the Gordon model ($g < k$). Supernormal growth often occurs during the "takeoff" phase in a firm's life cycle. That is, a firm may experience a life cycle analogous to that of a product: first, a low-profit introductory phase, then a takeoff phase of high growth and high profits, leveling off at a plateau during its mature stage, perhaps followed by a period of declining earnings. Computer and electronics manufacturers experienced a period of supernormal growth during the 1960s, as did semiconductor firms during the 1970s. Bioengineering firms appeared to be the super growth firms of the 1980s. Internet firms experienced a high growth during the 1990s. In recent times, solar energy firms appear to be the super growth firms.

Sample Problem 3.2

LBO, Inc., has just paid a dividend of $6 per share. In addition, dividends are expected to grow at a constant rate of 3% per year. If shareholders require a 7% annual rate of return, what should be the current theoretical price of LBO's stock?

Equation (3.6) can be used to calculate the current theoretical price. However, Equation (3.6) uses the dividend expected to be received next year, while the current information relates to the dividend received this year. Because dividends are expected to grow at a constant rate, next year's dividend should just be the future value of this year's dividend compounded at the growth rate of dividends:

$$\begin{aligned} d_1 &= d_0(1+g) \\ &= \$6(1+0.03) \\ &= \$6.18. \end{aligned}$$

Substituting into Equation (3.6) gives the current theoretical price of LBO's stock:

$$\begin{aligned} P_0 &= \frac{\$6.18}{0.07-0.03} \\ &= \$154.50. \end{aligned}$$

The valuation of a supernormal growth stock requires some estimate of the length of the supernormal growth period. The current price of the stock will then consist of two components: (1) the present value of the stock during the supernormal growth period and (2) the present value of the stock price at the end of the supernormal growth period:

$$P_0 = \sum_{t=1}^{n} \frac{d_0(1+g_s)^t}{(1+k)^t} + \frac{\frac{d_{n+1}}{k-g_n}}{(1+k)^n}, \tag{3.8}$$

where g_s = supernormal growth rate, n = the number of periods before the growth drops from supernormal to normal, k = the required rate of return of the stockholders, and g_n = the normal growth rate of dividends (assumed to be constant thereafter).

As we can see from our development of the discounted cash flow financial theory, the primary determinant of value for securities is the cash flow received by the investors. Anything that affects the cash flow, such as the dividend policy, investment policy, financing policy, and production policy of the firm, needs to be evaluated in order to determine a market price.

Some shortcomings of this approach include the overemphasis on the evaluation of the individual firm to the exclusion of portfolio concepts and the interrelationship with the overall market indexes. Most of the classical models are also static in nature, overlooking the concept of dynamic growth. Nevertheless, a fundamental approach to security valuation — the stream of dividends approach — has evolved from this theory.

3.4 M&M Valuation Theory

3.4.1 *Four alternative valuation methods*

Miller and Modigliani (M&M, 1961) have proposed four alternative valuation methods to determine the theoretical value of common stocks. This section discusses these valuation approaches in some detail. M&M's four more or less distinct approaches to the valuation of common stock are as follows: (1) the discounted cash flow approach, (2) the current earnings plus future investment opportunities approach, (3) the stream of dividends approach, and (4) the stream of earnings approach.

Working from a valuation expression referred to by M&M as the "fundamental principle of valuation"

$$P_0 = \frac{1}{1+k}(d_1 + P_1), \tag{3.9}$$

M&M further developed a valuation formula to serve as a point of reference and comparison among the four valuation approaches:

$$V_0 = \sum_{t=0}^{\infty} \frac{1}{(1+k)^{t+1}}(X_t - I_t), \tag{3.10}$$

where V_0 = the current market value of the firm, X_t = net operating earnings in period t, and I_t = new investment during period t.

In this context, the discounted cash flow approach can be expressed as

$$V_0 = \sum_{t=0}^{\infty} \frac{1}{(1+k)^{t+1}}(R_t - O_t), \tag{3.11}$$

in which R_t is the stream of cash receipts by the firm and O_t is the stream of cash outlays of the firm. This fundamental principle is based on the assumption of "perfect markets," "rational behavior," and "perfect certainty" as defined by M&M. Since X_t differs from R_t and I_t differs from O_t only by the cost of goods sold and depreciation expense, if $(R_t - O_t)$ equals $(X_t - I_t)$, then Equation (3.11) is equivalent to Equation (3.10) and the discounted cash flow approach is an extension of Equation (3.9), the fundamental valuation principle. Hence, the security analyst must be well versed in generally accepted accounting principles in order to evaluate the worth of accounting earnings of $(X_t - I_t)$.

The **investment opportunities approach** seems in some ways the most natural approach from the standpoint of an investor. This approach takes into account the ability of the firm's management to issue securities at "normal" market rates of return and invest in the opportunities, providing a rate higher than the normal rate of return. M&M develop from this framework the following expression, which they show can also be derived from Equation (3.10):

$$V_0 = \frac{X_0}{k} + \sum_{t=0}^{\infty} \frac{I_t(k_t^* - k)}{(1+k)^{t+1}}, \tag{3.12}$$

in which X_0 is the perpetual net operation earning and k_t^* is the "higher-than-normal" rate of return on new investment I_t.

From the expression, it can be seen that if a firm cannot generate a rate of return of its new investments higher than the normal rate, k, the price/earnings ratio applied to the firm's earnings will be equal to $1/k$, thus implying simple expansion rather than growth over time. An important variable for security analysis is a firm's price/earning (P/E) ratio (or earnings multiple), defined as

$$\text{P/E ratio} = \frac{\text{Market price}}{\text{Earnings per share}}.$$

Conceptually, the P/E ratio is determined by three factors: (1) the investor's required rate of return (K); (2) the retention ratio of the firm's earning, b, where b is equal to 1 minus the dividend payout ratio; and (3) the firm's expected return on investment (r). Using the constant growth model (Equation (3.6)),

$$\begin{aligned} P_0 &= \frac{d_1}{k-g}, \\ P_0 &= \frac{E_1(1-b)}{k-(br)}, \\ \frac{P_0}{E_1} &= \frac{1-b}{k-(br)}, \end{aligned} \tag{3.13}$$

in which b is the retention rate and E_1 is the next period's expected profit.

The P_0/E ratio is theoretically equal to the payout ratio of a firm, divided by the difference between the investor's required return and the firm's growth rates. In the above relationship, a direct relationship has been identified between P/E ratio and discount cash flow valuation model.

The **stream-of-dividends approach** has been by far the most popular in the literature of valuation; it was developed in the pre-M&M period. Assuming an infinite time horizon, this approach defines the current market price of a share of common stock as equal to the discounted present value of all future dividends:

$$P_0 = \sum_{t=0}^{\infty} \frac{1}{(1+k)^{t+1}}(d_t). \tag{3.14}$$

Restating in terms of total market value

$$V_0 = \sum_{t=0}^{\infty} \frac{1}{(1+k)^{t+1}}(D_t). \tag{3.15}$$

With no outside financing, it can be seen that $D_t = X_t - I_t$ and

$$V_0 = \sum_{t=0}^{\infty} \frac{1}{(1+k)^{t+1}}(X_t - I_t).$$

With outside financing through the issuance of shares of new common stock, it can be shown that

$$V_0 = \sum_{t=0}^{\infty} \frac{1}{(1+k)^{t+1}}(D_t + V_{t+1} - m_{t+1} * P_{t+1}), \tag{3.16}$$

in which m_{t+1} is the number of new shares issued at price P_{t+1}. For the infinite horizon, the value of the firm is equal to the investments it makes and the new capital it raises, or

$$V_{t+1} - (m_{t+1})(P_{t+1}) = I_t - (X_t - D_t).$$

Thus, Equation (3.16) can also be written as

$$V_0 = \sum_{t=0}^{\infty} \frac{1}{(1+k)^{t+1}}(X_t - I_t),$$

which is the same as Equation (3.10).

Given the M&M ideal assumptions, the above result implies irrelevance of dividends because the market value of the dividends provided to the new stockholders must always be precisely the same as the increase in current dividends. This is in direct disagreement with the findings of the discounted cash flow model, where dividends are a major determinant of value. In this case, dividends have no impact on value, and the firm's investment policy is the most important determinant of value. Security analysis should concern itself with the future investment opportunities of the firm and forget about dividends.

M&M also developed the **stream earnings approach**, which takes account of the fact that additional capital must be acquired at some cost in order to maintain the stream of future earnings at its current level. The capital to be raised is I_t and its cost is $K\%$ per period thereafter; thus, the current value of the firm under this approach can be stated as $V_0 = \sum_{t=0}^{\infty} \frac{1}{(1+k)^{t+1}}(X_t - I_t)$ which, again, is Equation (3.10).

Because under none of these four theoretical approaches does the term D_t remain in the final valuation expression and because X_t, I_t, and k are assumed to be independent of D_t, M&M conclude that the current value of a firm is independent of its current and future dividend decisions. The amount gained by stockholders is offset exactly by the decline in the market value of their stock. In the short run, this effect is observed when a stock goes ex-dividend — that is, if the market price of the stock falls by the amount of the dividend on the last day, the old shareholders are entitled to receive a dividend payment. The stock's value is then dependent only upon the expected future earnings stream of the firm. Security analysts spend much time and effort forecasting a firm's expected earnings.

While the above analysis ignores the case in which external financing is obtained through the issuance of debt, in such a situation, M&M's *position* then rests upon their indifference proposition with respect to leverage (M&M, 1958), discussed elsewhere in this chapter. Since that analysis shows that under a set of assumptions consistent with their "fundamental principal of valuation," the real cost of debt in a world of no taxation is equal to the real cost of equity financing, M&M conclude that the means of external financing used to offset the payment of dividends does not affect their hypothesis that dividends are irrelevant.

Prior to M&M's 1961 article, the classical view held that dividend policy was a major determinant of the value of the corporation and that firms should seek their "optimal payout ratios" to maximize their value. M&M's conclusions about the irrelevance of dividend policy collided head-on with the existing classical view. The view that the value of the firm is independent of dividend policy also extends into a world with corporate taxes but without personal taxes.

3.4.2 *Review and extension of M&M Proposition I*

The existence of optimal capital structure has become one of the important issues for academicians and practitioners in finance. While classical finance theorists argue that there is an optimal capital structure for a firm, the new classical financial theory developed by M&M (1958, 1963) has cast doubt upon the existence of such an optimal structure. The specific assumptions that they made, consistent with the dividend irrelevance analysis previously outlined, include the following: (1) capital markets are perfect (frictionless), (2) both individuals and firms can borrow and lend at the risk-free rate, (3) firms use risk-free debt and risky equity, (4) there are only corporate taxes (i.e., there are no wealth taxes or personal income taxes), and (5) all cash flow streams are perpetuities (i.e., no growth).

Developing the additional concepts of risk class and homemade leverage, M&M derived their well-known **Proposition I**, both with and without corporate taxes.[2]

If all firms are in the same risk class, then their expected risky future net operating cash flow ($\dot{X}$) varies only by a scale factor. Under this circumstance, the correlation between two firms' net operating income (NOI) within a risk class should be equal to 1.0. This implies that the rates of return will be equal for all firms in the same risk class, that is,

$$R_{it} = \frac{\dot{X}_{it} - \dot{X}_{it-1}}{X_{it-1}}, \tag{3.17}$$

and because $\dot{X}_{it} = C\dot{X}_{jt}$, where C is the scale factor,

$$R_{jt} = \frac{C\dot{X}_{jt} - C\dot{X}_{jt}}{C\dot{X}_{jt-1}} = R_{it}, \tag{3.18}$$

[2]In 1985, Franco Modigliani won the Nobel Prize for his work on the life cycle of savings and his contribution to what has become known as the M&M theory, discussed in this section.

in which R_{it} and R_{jt} are rates of return for the ith and jth firms, respectively. Therefore, if two streams of cash flow differ by only a scale factor, they will have the same distributions of returns and the same risk, and they will require the same expected return.

The concept of **homemade leverage** is used to refer to the leverage created by individual investors who sell their own debt while **corporate leverage** is used to refer to the debt floated by the corporation. Using the assumption that the cost of homemade leverage is equal to the cost of corporate leverage, M&M (1958) derived their Proposition I both with and without taxes. However, the Proposition I with taxes was not correct, and they subsequently corrected this result in their 1963 paper. Mathematically, M&M's Proposition I can be defined as

$$V_j = (S_j + B_j) = X_j/\rho_k, \tag{3.19}$$

and Proposition I with taxes can be defined as

$$V_j^L = \frac{(1-\tau_j)X_j}{\rho_k^\tau} + \frac{\tau I_j}{r} = V_j^U + \tau B_j. \tag{3.20}$$

In Equation (3.19), B_j, S_j, and V_j are the market value of debt, common shares, and the firm, respectively; X_j is the expected profit before deduction of interest; and ρ_k the required rate of return or the cost of capital in risk class k. In Equation (3.20), ρ_k^τ is the required rate of return used to capitalize the expected returns net of tax for the unlevered firm with long-run average earnings before tax and interest of (X_j) in risk class k; τ_j is the corporate tax rate for the jth firm; I_j is the total interest expense for the jth firm; r is the market interest rate used to capitalize certain cash inflows generated by risk-free debt; B_j is total risk-free debt floated by the jth firm; and V^L and V^U are the market values of the leveraged and unleveraged firms, respectively.

By comparing these two equations, we find that the advantages of a firm with leverage will increase that firm's value by $\tau_j B_j$ — that is, the corporate tax rate times the total debt floated by that firm. One of the important implications of this proposition is that there is no optimal capital structure for the firm unless there are bankruptcy costs associated with its debt flotation. If there are bankruptcy costs, then a firm will issue debt until its tax benefit is equal to the bankruptcy cost, thus providing, in such a case, an optimal capital structure for the firm. In addition to the bankruptcy costs, information signaling (see Leland and Pyle, 1977; Ross, 1977) and differential expectations between shareholders and bondholders can be used to justify the possible existence of an optimal structure of a firm. The existence of optimal capital structure is an important issue for security analysts to investigate because it affects the value of the firm and the value of the firm's securities. Is a firm with a high level of debt more valuable than a similar firm with very little debt? M&M say either it does not matter or that the highly leveraged firm is more valuable.

The important assumptions used to prove the M&M Proposition I with taxes are that (1) there are no transaction costs, (2) homemade leverage is equal to corporate leverage, (3) corporate debt is riskless, and (4) there is no bankruptcy cost. Overall, M&M's Proposition I implies that there is no optimal capital structure. If there is a tax structure that systematically provides a lower after-tax real cost of debt relative to the after-tax real cost of equity, the corporation will maximize the proportion of debt in their capital structure and will issue as much debt as possible to maximize the tax shield associated with the deductibility of interest.

Stiglitz (1969) extends M&M's proposition using a general equilibrium state preference framework. He is able to show that M&M's results do not depend on risk classes, competitive capital markets, or agreement by investors. The only two fundamental assumptions are that there is no bankruptcy and individuals can borrow at the same rate as firms. Stiglitz (1974) develops the argument that there may exist a determinate debt–equity ratio for the economy as a whole, but not for the individual firm.

3.4.3 *Miller's proposition on debt and taxes*

Miller (1977) argues that although there is no optimal capital structure for an individual firm, in the aggregate case, there may be an optimal structure. In balancing bankruptcy cost against tax shelter, an optimal capital structure is derived, just as the classical view has always maintained.

The Tax Reform Act of 1986 taxed dividends and long-term capital gains at the same top rate of 28%. This is a major change from the old 50% rate on dividends and 20% rate on long-term capital gains. The new tax bill has also shifted the major tax burden to corporations and away from individuals. Even though the maximum corporate tax rate will decrease to 34% from the current top rate of 46%, corporations will be paying more taxes because of the loss of the Investment Tax Credits and the Accelerated Cost Recovery System depreciation allowances.

These changes in the tax code will shift the emphasis of corporate management from retaining earnings in order to generate price appreciation and capital gains to the payout of corporate funds in the form of dividends.

In his presidential address at the Annual Meeting of the American Finance Association, Merton Miller (1977) incorporated personal taxes into the M&M (1958, 1963) argument for the relationship between the firm's leverage and cost of capital.

M&M's Proposition I shows that the value of the leveraged firm equals the value of the unleveraged firm plus the tax shield associated with interest payments, as shown by Equation (3.21):

$$V^L = V^U + t_C B, \tag{3.21}$$

where V^L = the value of the leveraged firm, V^U = the value of the unleveraged firm, t_C = the corporate tax rate, and B = the value of the firm's debt.

Miller generalizes the M&M relationship shown in Equation (3.21) to include personal taxes on dividends and capital gains as well as taxes on interest income, to yield

$$V^L = V^U + \left[1 - \frac{(1 - t_C)(1 - t_{ps})}{(1 - t_{pB})}\right] B, \tag{3.22}$$

in which t_{ps} is the personal tax rate on income from stock and t_{pB} is the personal tax rate on income from bonds.

Using Equation (3.22) and the assumption of market equilibrium, and the fact that individual investors can defer income on stocks indefinitely (or that there exists a group of investors who are tax exempt, namely, $t_{ps} = 0$), Miller argues that for the economy as a whole there is an optimal amount of debt, but for individual firms there is no optimal capital structure. Using Equation (3.22), the impact on firm value caused by the tax code changes embodied in the Tax Reform Act of 1986 was examined.

In general, by using the 1963 M&M relationship and the 1977 Miller relationship for tax shields, we can identify an upper and lower bound for the change in value associated with interest tax shields. The upper bound is defined by the M&M arguments as $t_c B$. The lower bound is zero, which can occur under four circumstances. These circumstances have been analyzed in Miller's (1977) original paper and Lee and Lee (2017).

3.5 Portfolio Analysis and Application

A portfolio is any combination of assets or investments. Portfolio analysis is used to determine the return and risk characteristics for any combination of assets. As first described by Harry Markowitz (1959), portfolio analysis involves the identification of specific statistical characteristics that enable managers or investors to systematically reduce risk through diversification, that is, holding more than a single asset in a portfolio.

3.5.1 *Expected rate of return on a portfolio*

The rate of return on a portfolio is simply the weighted average of the returns of individual securities in the portfolio. This is a linear relationship. For example, suppose 40% of the portfolio is invested in security a and 30% is invested in security b and c. If the expected rate of return of securities a, b, and c is 10%, 5%, and 12%, respectively, then the expected rate of return for this portfolio is as follows:

$$\begin{aligned}\overline{R}_p &= W_a\overline{R}_a + W_b\overline{R}_b + W_c\overline{R}_c \\ &= (.4)(.1) + (.3)(.05) + (.3)(.12) \\ &= .091,\end{aligned}$$

where W_a, W_b, and W_c are the propositions of the portfolio invested in securities a, b, and c. The summation of these weights equals 1. $\overline{R}_a$, $\overline{R}_b$, and $\overline{R}_c$ represent expected rates of return on securities a, b, and c, respectively. $\overline{R}_p$ represents the expected rate of return of return for the portfolio, which is the weighted average of the securities' expected rates of return. In general, the expected return on an

N-asset portfolio is defined by Equation (3.23):

$$\overline{R}_p = \sum_{i=1}^{n} W_i \overline{R}_i \quad \left(\text{where } \sum_{i=1}^{n} W_i = 1\right), \tag{3.23}$$

where W_i is the proportion of the individual's investment allocated to security i, and $\overline{R}_i$ is the expected rate of return for security i.

If an investor chooses not to invest the entire portfolio in financial assets, then one of the investor's assets will be cash. Hence, the individual investor must hold 100% of his or her financial wealth in some form of profitable assets and cash.

3.5.2 *Variance and standard deviation of a portfolio*

A portfolio's risk is measured by its standard deviation, or variance. The standard deviation is the square root of the variance. To calculate a portfolio's standard deviation, we should first identify the covariance among the securities in the portfolio. The covariance between two such securities is defined as follows:

$$\begin{aligned} Cov(W_1R_1, W_2R_2) &= \frac{1}{N}\sum_{t=1}^{N}(W_1R_{1t} - W_1\overline{R}_1)(W_2R_{2t} - W_2\overline{R}_2) \\ &= \frac{W_1W_2}{N}\sum_{t=1}^{N}(R_{1t} - \overline{R}_1)(R_{2t} - \overline{R}_2) \\ &= W_1W_2Cov(R_1, R_2), \end{aligned} \tag{3.24}$$

where R_{1t} is the rate of return for the first security in period t and R_{2t} is the rate of return for the second security in period t. $\overline{R}_1$ and $\overline{R}_2$ are average rates of return for the securities, while $Cov(R_1, R_2)$ represents the covariance between R_1 and R_2.

$$\begin{aligned} \sigma_p^2 &= VAR(W_1R_{1t} + W_2R_{2t}) \\ &= \frac{1}{N}\sum_{t=1}^{N}[(W_1R_{1t} + W_2R_{2t}) - (W_1\overline{R}_1 + W_2\overline{R}_2)]^2 \\ &= W_1^2\sigma_1^2 + W_2^2\sigma_2^2 + 2W_1W_2Cov(R_1, R_2). \end{aligned} \tag{3.25}$$

Now that we have shown how to find covariance and variance of a portfolio, we proceed to the standard deviation of returns for a portfolio, which is determined as follows:

$$\sigma_p = \sqrt{\frac{1}{N}\sum_{t=1}^{N}(R_{pt} - \overline{R}_p)^2}, \tag{3.26}$$

where σ_p is the standard deviation of the portfolio's return, R_{pt} is the portfolio's rate of return in period t, and $\overline{R}_p$ is the average portfolio rate of return. Figure 3.2 illustrates two possible distributions for two portfolios with the same expected return but with different degrees of risk. Portfolio B's variability is larger than portfolio A's.

Consequently, investors regard portfolio B as riskier than portfolio A. Therefore, portfolio A is more attractive than portfolio B because it offers less risk with the same expected return.

3.5.3 *The two-asset case*

To explain the fundamental aspect of portfolio risk diversification, we consider the two-asset case. Following Equations (3.25) and (3.26),

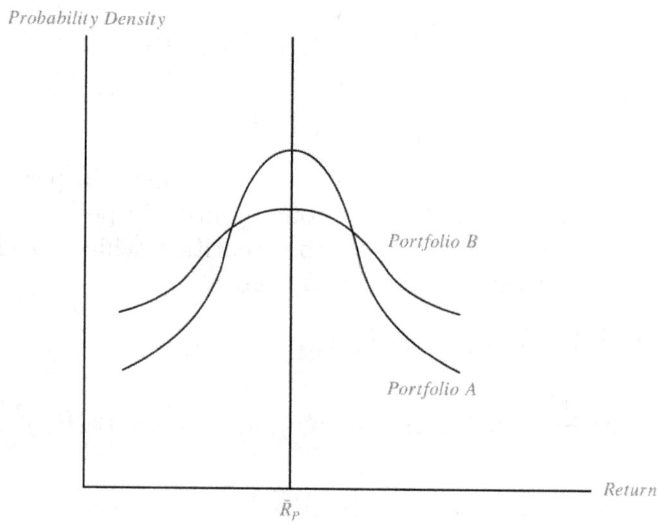

Figure 3.2 Probability Distribution of Returns for Two Portfolios

we define σ_p as follows:

$$\sigma_p = [W_1^2 VAR(R_1) + W_2^2 VAR(R_2) + 2W_1W_2Cov(R_1, R_2)]^{\frac{1}{2}}, \tag{3.27}$$

where $W_1 + W_2 = 1$. The covariance term can be expressed in terms of the correlation coefficient between R_1 and R_2 and the respective standard deviations of R_1 and R_2:

$$Cov(R_1, R_2) = \rho_{12}\sigma_1\sigma_2. \tag{3.28}$$

The correlation coefficient measures the degree of similarity of movement for a time series. The ρ_{ij} is defined over the range of +1 to −1. Figure 3.3 depicts various values of ρ_{ij}. At $\rho_{ij} = 1$, the fluctuation of returns for both series over time is identical; at $\rho_{ij} = 0$, the returns are unrelated; and at $\rho_{ij} = -1$, the fluctuations are moving in opposite directions.

Equation (3.26) is a quadratic equation, and some value of W_1 minimizes σ_p. To obtain this value, we differentiate Equation (3.27)

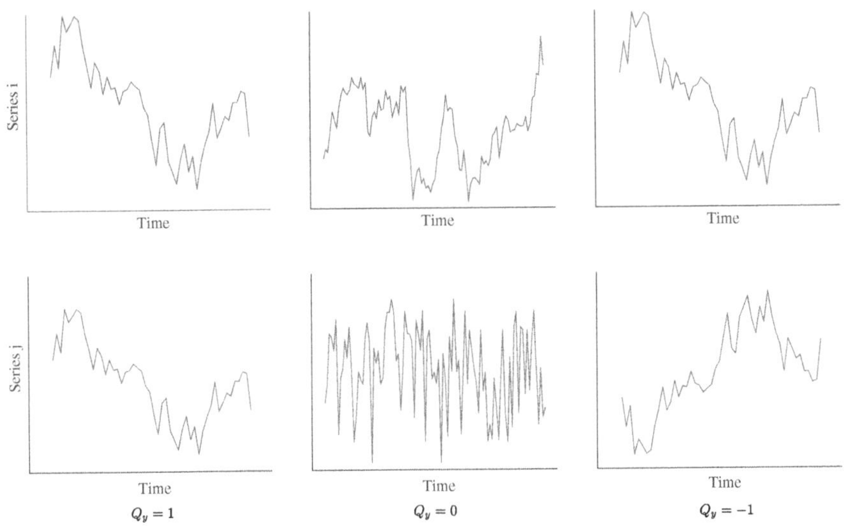

Figure 3.3 Different Patterns of Correlation Coefficient Over Time

with respect to W_1 and set this derivative equal to 0 to solve for W_1[3]:

$$W_1 = \frac{\sigma_2(\sigma_2 - \rho_{12}\sigma_1)}{\sigma_1^2 + \sigma_2^2 - 2\rho_{12}\sigma_1\sigma_2}. \tag{3.29}$$

Equation (3.27) can be used to estimate the optimal weight of security 1. From the constraint $W_1 + W_2 = 1$, the optimal weight of security 2 can also be estimated. From estimated W_1 and W_2, we can estimate $\overline{R}_p$ and σ_p for a two-security minimum-variance portfolio.

3.5.4 *The N-asset case*

An expanded form of Equation (3.27) for a portfolio of N securities is ρ_{ij}, the correlation coefficient between i and j, and n is the number of securities included in the portfolio.

$$\sigma_p = \sqrt{\sum_{i=1}^{n} W_i^2\sigma_i^2 + \sum_{j=1}^{n}\sum_{i=1}^{n} W_i W_j \rho_{ij}\sigma_i\sigma_j \quad i \neq j}, \tag{3.30}$$

where W_i and W_j are the investor's investment allocated to securities i and j, ρ_{ij} is the correlation coefficient between i and j, and n is the number of securities included in the portfolio.

Since Equation (3.30) has n securities, there are n variance terms (i.e., $W_i^2\sigma_i^2$) and $(n^2 - n)$ covariance terms (i.e., $W_i W_j \rho_{ij}\sigma_i\sigma_j$). If $n = 20$, Equation (3.30) will have 20 variance terms and 380 covariance terms.

Using a matrix notation, we can express these terms as follows:

$$\begin{bmatrix} W_1^2\sigma_1^2 & \cdots & \cdots & W_1 W_{20}\sigma_{1,20} \\ \vdots & W_2^2\sigma_2^2 & \vdots & \vdots \\ \vdots & \vdots & \ddots & \vdots \\ W_{20}W_1\sigma_{20,1} & \cdots & \cdots & W_{20}^2\sigma_{20}^2 \end{bmatrix}.$$

[3]In Appendix 3A, we have shown how to obtain optimal weights for a two-security portfolio. In addition, Appendix 3B discusses how the Sharpe performance measure approach can be used to derive the optimal portfolio weights.

This is a variance–covariance matrix for portfolio analysis. Lee *et al.* (2013), Elton *et al.* (2013), and Francis and Kim (2013) have used this kind of matrix to perform portfolio analysis. In addition, they also showed how to obtain the optimal ways for an N-asset portfolio.

3.5.5 *The efficient portfolios*

Under the mean-variance framework, by definition, a security or a portfolio will be efficient if

1. No other portfolio has the same expected return at a lower risk.
2. No other portfolio has a higher expected return at the same risk.

These two rules are called the *dominance principle*, which we discuss in detail later in this chapter.

This suggests that given two investments, A and B, A is preferred to B if $E(A) > E(B)$ and $\text{Var}(A) = \text{Var}(B)$ or $E(A) = E(B)$ and $\text{Var}(A) < \text{Var}(B)$, where $E(A)$ and $E(B)$ are the expected returns of investments A and B, and $\text{Var}(A)$ and $\text{Var}(B)$ are their respective variances, or risk. The mean return and standard deviation of an investment can be calculated and plotted as a single point on a mean standard deviation diagram, as shown in Figure 3.4.

All points below curve EF represent possible portfolio combinations. All points above EF are combinations of risk and returns that do not exist. Point D represents a portfolio of investments with return R_D and risk σ_D. Therefore, point B represents a risk-and-return combination that cannot be obtained with any combination of existing investment opportunities.

The EF curve is also called the efficient frontier, because all points below the curve are dominated by a point found on the curve. The efficient frontier is defined as the set of portfolios that has the maximum return for every given level of risk or the minimum risk for every level of return. Suppose a firm is willing to assume a maximum risk σ_D. It can obtain a return of R_D with portfolio D or move to point C on the frontier and receive a higher return of R_C with that portfolio at the same level of risk. Therefore, portfolio C dominates portfolio D because it is preferred to portfolio D.

A similar argument could be made in terms of risk. If the firm wants to achieve a return of R_A, it would select portfolio A over D, because A represents the same return at a lower level of risk

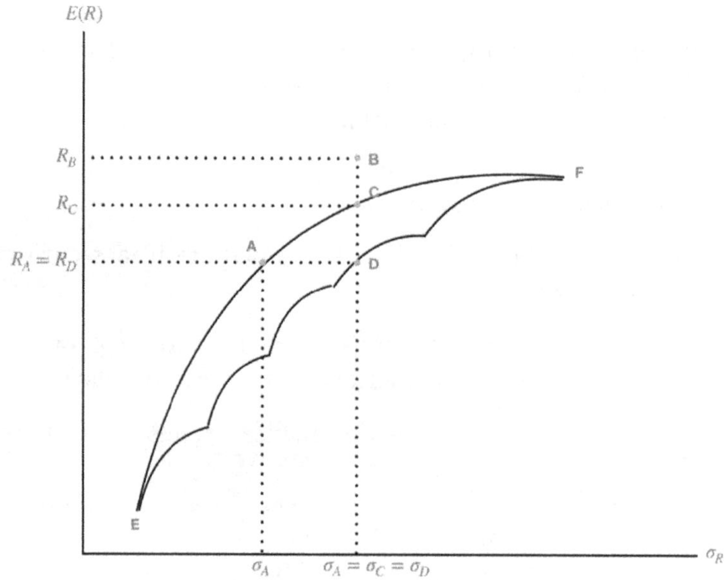

Figure 3.4 Efficient Frontier in Portfolio Analysis

or standard deviation: $\sigma_A < \sigma_D$. Therefore, point D is not efficient but points A and C are. A decision-maker following these arguments would, therefore, select any point on the frontier as being preferable to any interior point.

The amount of curvature of the efficient frontier depends on the correlation between the two assets. If the correlation between assets equals +1, the combinations lie on the straight line. The lower the correlation coefficient, the more curved the efficient frontier.

Sample Problem 3.3

To show how the portfolio concepts and methods discussed in this section can be used in practical analysis, we evaluate the monthly rates of return during January 2010–December 2018 for Johnson & Johnson (JNJ) and International Business Machines Corporation (IBM).

The basic statistical estimates for these two firms are average monthly rates of return and the variance–covariance matrix. The average monthly rates of return are –.0011439 for IBM and –0.008967 for JNJ.

The variance and covariance are listed in Table 3.1.

Table 3.1 Variance–Covariance Matrix

	IBM	**JNJ**
IBM	0.00298732	
JNJ	0.00060082	0.00160289

From Equation (3.29), we have

$$\begin{aligned}W_{IBM} &= \frac{\sigma_{JNJ}^2 - Cov(R_{IMB}, R_{JNJ})}{\sigma_{IBM}^2 + \sigma_{JNJ}^2 - Cov(R_{IMB}, R_{JNJ})}\\ &= \frac{0.0016 - 0.0006}{0.0030 + 0.0016 - 0.0006} = 0.2512\\ W_{JNJ} &= 1 - 0.2512 = 0.7488.\end{aligned}$$

Using the weight estimates and Equations (3.23) and (3.27),

$$E(R_p) = -0.007002, \sigma_p^2 = 0.000226 \quad \text{and} \quad \rho_{12} = 0.2746.$$

When ρ_{12} is less than 1, the combination of the two securities results in a total risk less than the sum of their weighted risk. This is the diversification effect. When ρ_{12} equals 1, the combination of the two securities has no diversification effect at all.

For the correlation coefficient of $\rho_{12} = 0.2746$, we see that a portfolio that combines JNJ and IBM shows a greater diversification effect, and a substantial reduction in risk then would hold each of the securities separately.

Depending on the correlation coefficient between securities, as long as the securities are not positively correlated, the risk of a portfolio as measured by the standard deviation of return will be less than the weighted average of the risks (standard deviations) of the individual securities. In notational form,

$$\sigma_P < W_1\sigma_1 + W_2\sigma_2 \quad \text{if } \rho_{12} \neq 1.$$

This will always be true and represents a significant fact that investors and managers must keep in mind when making financial decisions.

3.5.6 *Corporate application of diversification*

The effects of diversification are not necessarily isolated to security analysis and portfolio management but may have wider applications at the corporate decision-making level. Managers often justify undertaking multiproduct lines because of the effects of diversification. Instead of putting "all eggs in one basket," the investment risks are spread out among many lines of services of products in hopes of reducing overall risk and maximizing returns. To what degree this diversification takes place in other types of corporate decisions depends on the decision-maker's preference for risk and return. The overall goal is to reduce business risk fluctuations of net income.

This type of corporate diversification can also be taken to the multinational level. For example, General Motors has overseas divisions throughout the world that all produce the same product — autos and auto parts. Because GM is a multinational corporation, it can take advantage of diversifying effects of different exchange rates and political and economic climates, because each overseas division is less than perfectly positively correlated with each other.

The strategy of diversifying at the corporate level has been criticized because shareholders can attain diversification in their own portfolios, which makes corporate diversification redundant. There is the agency theory argument that corporate diversification is in fact a form of risk-sharing between stockholders and bondholders, where the bondholders have less risky fixed-income securities due to corporate diversification and the shareholders suffer a loss in the value of their equity position. Finally, there is a reduction in the risk/return deals with options, which deal with mergers and divestitures.

3.6 Capital Asset Pricing Model and Arbitrage Pricing Theory

In this section, we will discuss the theories and applications of the CAPM and APT.

3.6.1 *Capital asset pricing model*

At about the same time when M&M were developing their work, developments in portfolio theory were leading to a model describing the formation of capital asset prices in a world of uncertainty: the **CAPM**.

The CAPM is a generalized version of M&M theory in which M&M theory is provided with a link to the market:

$$E(R_j) = R_f + \beta_j[E(R_m) - R_f], \tag{3.31}$$

where R_j = the rate of return for security j, β_j = a volatility measure relating the rate of return on security j with that of the market over time, R_m = the rate of return for the overall market (typically measured by the rate of return reflected by a market index, such as the S&P 500), and R_f = the risk-free rate available in the market (usually the rate of return on U.S. Treasury bills is used as a proxy).

In the CAPM framework, the valuation of a company's securities is dependent not only upon their cash flows but also upon those of other securities available for investment. It is assumed that much of the total risk, as measured by standard deviation of return, can be diversified away by combining the stock of a firm being analyzed with those of other companies. Unless the cash flows from these securities are perfectly positively correlated, smoothing or diversification will take place. Thus, the security return can be divided into two components: a systematic component that is perfectly correlated with the overall market return and an unsystematic component that is independent of the market return:

$$\text{Security return} = \text{Systematic return} + \text{Unsystematic return}. \tag{3.32}$$

Since the security return is perfectly correlated with the market return, it can be expressed as a constant, **beta**, multiplied by the market return (R_m). The beta is a volatility index, measuring the sensitivity of the security return to changes in the market return. The unsystematic return is residual of the relationship of R_j with R_m.

As has been previously noted, the standard deviation of the probability distribution of a security's rate of return is considered to be an appropriate measure of the total risk of that security. This total risk can be broken down into systematic and unsystematic components, just as noted above for security return:

$$\text{Total security risk} = \text{Systematic risk} + \text{Unsystematic risk}. \quad (3.33)$$

Diversification is achieved only when securities that are not perfectly correlated with one other are combined. The unsystematic risk components tend to cancel each other since they are all residuals from the relationship of security returns with the overall market return. In the process, the portfolio risk measure declines without any corresponding lowering of portfolio return (see Figure 3.5). It is assumed in this illustration that the selection of additional securities as the portfolio size is increased is performed in some random manner, although any selection process other than intentionally choosing perfectly correlated securities will suffice. Unsystematic risk is shown to be gradually eliminated until the portfolio risk is completely market related. While for an actual portfolio the systematic risk will not remain constant as securities are added, the intent is to show that the unsystematic risk portion can be diversified away, leaving the market-related systematic portion as the only relevant measure of risk. Empirical studies have shown that a portfolio of about 20 securities not highly correlated with one another will provide a high degree of diversification. Although capital market theory assumes that all

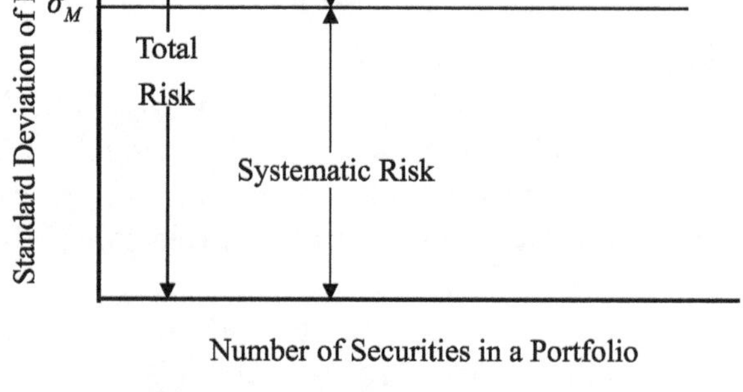

Figure 3.5 Diversification Process

investors will hold the market portfolio, it is neither necessary nor realistic to assume that all investors will be satisfied with the market level of risk. There are basically two ways that investors can adjust their risk level within the CAPM theoretical framework. First, funds for investment can be divided between the market portfolio and risk-free securities. The Capital Market Line (CML) is derived assuming such a trade-off function.

This is illustrated in Figure 3.6, in which point M is the market portfolio and points on the CML below and above M imply lending and borrowing at the risk-free rate, respectively. The second way of adjusting the portfolio risk level is by investing in a fully diversified portfolio of securities (i.e., the correlation coefficient of the portfolio with the market, r_{pm}, is equal to 1.0) that has a weighted average beta equal to the systematic risk level desired:

$$\beta_p = \sum_{j=1}^{n} W_j B_j, \tag{3.34}$$

in which W_j is the proportion of total funds invested in security j. Since in the CAPM systematic risk as measured by beta is the only risk that need be undertaken, it follows that no risk premium should be expected for the bearing of unsystematic risk. With that in mind, the relationship between expected return and risk can be better defined through the illustration of the Security Market Line (SML) in Figure 3.7 in which R_m and β_m are the expected return and risk level of the market portfolio, respectively. In equilibrium, all securities and combinations of securities are expected to lie along this

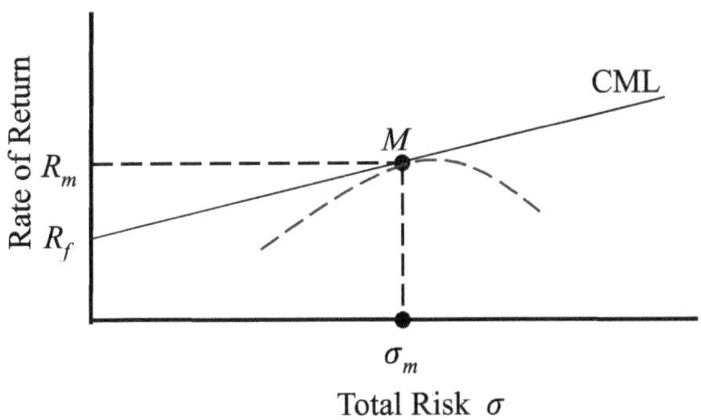

Figure 3.6 Capital Market Line

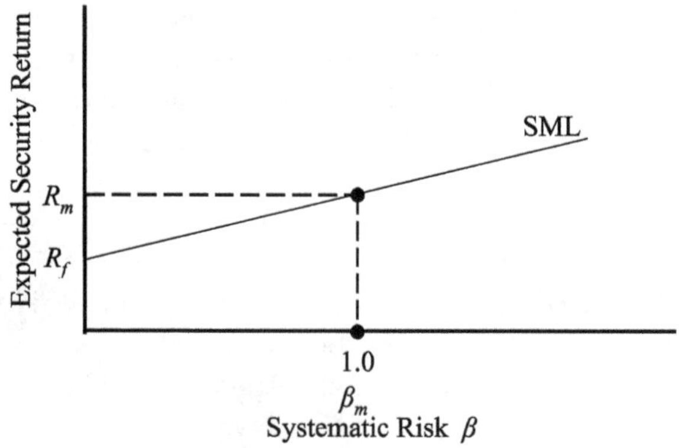

Figure 3.7 Security Market Line

line. In contrast, only fully diversified portfolios would be expected to fall along the CML, because only with full diversification is total risk equal to systematic risk alone. Sample Problem 3.4 provides further illustration, and a much more detailed description of the use of CAPM in making investment decisions is included in later chapters of this book.

Sample Problem 3.4

The following is known about the market and LBO, Inc.:

Three-month T-bill rate = 8%,
Expected return on the S&P 500 = 11%,
Estimated beat for LBO's stock = 1.5.

Substituting into Equation (4.26) solves for the expected return on LBO's stock.

Solution

$$\begin{aligned} E(R_{\text{LBO}}) &= 8\% + 1.5(11\% - 8\%) \\ &= 12.5\%. \end{aligned}$$

3.6.2 *Arbitrage pricing theory*

3.6.2.1 *Arbitrage theory*

Suppose there are two riskless assets offering rates of return r and r'. Assuming no transaction costs, one of the strongest statements that can be made in positive economics is that

$$r = r'. \tag{3.35}$$

This is based on the law of one price, which says that the same good cannot sell at different prices. In terms of securities, the law of one price says that securities with identical risks must have the same expected return. Essentially, Equation (3.35) is an **arbitrage condition** that must be expected to hold in all but the most extreme circumstances. This is because if $r > r'$, the first riskless asset could be purchased with funds obtained from selling the second riskless asset. This arbitrage transaction would yield a return of $r - r'$ with no risk and no net wealth invested. If investors were to come across such a disequilibrium relationship, they would surely seize the opportunity to make a return of $r - r'$ without having to make any new investment of funds or taking on any additional risk. In the process of buying the first asset and selling the second, investors would bid up the former's price and bid down the latter's price. This repricing mechanism would continue up to the point where these two assets' respective prices equaled each other, and thus $r = r'$.

Put in the context of securities that are traded in markets and held in portfolios, consider the following simple example. There exist three assets A, B, and C, all of which are related to the same basic underlying factor. The characteristics of these three assets are shown in Figure 3.8. Securities A and C are both correctly priced given the sensitivity they have to the factor.[4] However, security B appears to be mispriced; it offers a return of 8%, which exceeds the expected return of 7.5% for securities with a sensitivity of 0.5. To take advantage of this mispricing, an investor can perform an arbitrage among the three securities. By buying \$1 worth of security B and short selling \$0.75 of security A and \$0.25 of security C, the investor can generate a risk-free return of 0.5%. This arbitrage is shown in Figure 3.8. The arbitrage allows the investor to earn a return of 0.5% with no risk and no investment. There is only one factor in this example, but the arbitrage argument can be extended to include many factors. As long as there exists a mispricing of one of the securities on one of the

[4]Strictly speaking, A, B, or C or some combination may be mispriced. However, the validity of the argument still holds.

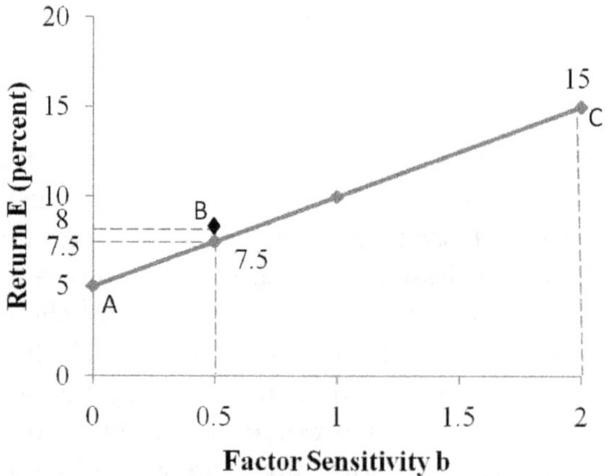

Security	Expected Return (%)	Factor Sensitivity
A	5	0.0
B	8	0.5
C	15	2.0

Figure 3.8 Expected Returns and Factor Sensitivity

factors, an arbitrage opportunity will exist until investors drive the market into equilibrium.

APT utilizes this robust type of argument and extends its application to the pricing of risky assets. The net result of APT's development is a more generalized and less restrictive framework than the CAPM for the pricing of risky assets. More explicitly, to make its equilibrium statement for asset returns, APT does not require quadratic utility functions for investors or joint normality or returns between individual assets and the market portfolio. (APT does not require that market portfolio be mean-variance efficient or even that it exists at all.) Finally, APT is not limited to a single period, as is the original form of the CAPM.

3.6.2.2 *Ross's arbitrage model specification*

This section focuses on two related forms of the arbitrage pricing model. The first of these is the model as originally proposed by Ross (1977).

The initial and probably the most prominent assumption made by APT concerns the return-generating process for assets. Specifically, individuals are assumed to believe (homogeneously) that the random returns on the set of assets being considered are governed by a k-factor generating model of the following form:

$$\tilde{r}_i = E_i + b_{i1}\tilde{\delta}_1 + \cdots + b_{ik}\tilde{\delta}_k + \tilde{\in}_i \quad (i = 1, \ldots, n), \tag{3.36}$$

where $\tilde{r}_i$ = random return on the ith asset, E_i = expected return on the ith asset, $\tilde{\delta}_j$ = jth factor common to the returns of all assets under consideration with a mean of zero, common factors that in essence capture the systematic component of risk in the model, b_{ij} = a coefficient called a *factor loading* that quantifies the sensitivity of asset i's returns to the movements in the common factor $\tilde{\delta}_j$ (and is analogous to the beta in the CAPM), and $\tilde{\in}_i$ = an error term, or unsystematic risk component, idiosyncratic to the ith asset, with mean zero and variance equal to $\tilde{\sigma}^2_{\in}$.

Moreover, it is assumed that the $\tilde{\in}_i$ reflects the random influence of information that is unrelated to other assets. Thus, the following condition is assumed to hold:

$$E\{\tilde{\in}_i \mid \tilde{\in}_j\} = 0, \tag{3.37}$$

as well as $\tilde{\in}_i$ and $\tilde{\in}_j$ independence for all $i \neq j$. Also, for any two securities i and j,

$$E\{\tilde{\in}_i, \tilde{\in}_j\} = 0, \tag{3.38}$$

for all i and j, where $i \neq j$. If this last condition did not hold — that is, if there was too strong a dependence between $\tilde{\in}_i$ and $\tilde{\in}_j$ — it would be equivalent to saying that more than simply the k-hypothesized common factors existed. Finally, it is assumed that the set of n is much greater than the number of factors k.

Before developing Ross's riskless arbitrage argument, it is essential to examine Equation (3.31) more closely and draw some implications from its structure. First, consider the effect of omitting the unsystematic risk terms $\tilde{e}_i$. Equation (3.36) would then imply that each asset i has returns $\tilde{r}$ that are an exact linear combination of the returns on a riskless asset (with constant return) and the returns on k other factors or assets (or column vectors) $\tilde{\delta}_i, \ldots, \tilde{\delta}_k$. Moreover, the riskless return and each of the k factors can be expressed as a linear combination of $k + 1$ other returns — for example, r, through r_{k+1} — in this type of setting. Taking this logic one step further, since any other asset return is a linear combination of the factors, it must also be that a linear combination of the returns of the first $k + 1$ assets must be perfect substitutes for all other assets in the market. Consequently, there must be restrictions on the individual returns generated by the model, since perfect substitutes must be priced equivalently. This sequence of mathematical logic is the core of APT. That is, only a few systematic components of risk exist in the economy, and consequently many portfolios will be close substitutes, thereby demanding the same value.

To initiate Ross's arbitrage argument about APT, it is best to start with the assumption of Equation (3.31). Next, presume an investor who is contemplating an alteration of the currently held portfolio, The difference between any new portfolio and the old portfolio will be quantified by changes in the investment proportions x_i $(i = 1, \ldots, n)$. The x_i, represents the dollar amount purchased or sold of asset i as a fraction of total invested wealth. The investor's portfolio investment is constrained to hold to the following condition:

$$\sum_{i=1}^{n} x_i = 0. \tag{3.39}$$

In words, Equation (3.34) says that additional purchases of assets must be financed by sales of others. Portfolios that require no net investment such as $x \equiv (x_j, \ldots, x_n)$ are called *arbitrage portfolios.* Table 3.2 shows exactly this situation: The proceeds from the short sale of A and C were used to purchase B.

Now, consider an arbitrage portfolio chosen in the following manner. First the portfolio must be chosen to be well diversified by keeping each element, x, of order $1/n$ in size. Second, the x of the portfolio must be selected in such a way as to eliminate all systematic risk (for each h):

$$xb_h \sum_{i=1} x_i b_{ih} = 0 \quad (h = 1, \ldots, k). \tag{3.40}$$

Table 3.2 Arbitrage Results

	Expected Return	Factor Sensitivity
Buy \$1 of B	$(1 \times 8\%) = 8\%$	$(1 \times 0.5) = 0.5$
Sell \$0.75 of A short	$-(0.75 \times 5\%) = -3.75\%$	$-(0.75 \times 0 = 0$
Sell \$0.25 of C short	$-(0.25 \times 15\%) = -3.75\%$	$-(0.25 \times 2) = -0.5$
Total investment = 0	Total return = 0.5%	Total sensitivity = 0

The returns on any such arbitrage portfolios can be described:

$$\begin{aligned} x\tilde{r} &= (xE) + (xb)\tilde{\delta}_1 + \cdots + (xb_k)\tilde{\delta}_k + (x\tilde{\in}) \\ &\approx xE + (xb_1)\tilde{\delta}_1 + \cdots + (xb_k)\tilde{\delta}_k \\ &= xE, \end{aligned}$$

where $x\tilde{r} = \sum_{i=1}^{n} x_i\tilde{r}_i$ and $xE = \sum_{i=1}^{n} x_iE_i$. Note that the term $(x\tilde{\in})$ is (approximately) eliminated by the effect of holding a well-diversified portfolio of n assets, where n is large. Using the law of large numbers, if σ^2 denotes the average variance of the $\tilde{e}_i$ terms, and assuming for simplicity that each x approximately equals $1/n$ and that the $\in_i$ are mutually independent:

$$\begin{aligned} \mathrm{Var}(x\tilde{\in}) &= \mathrm{Var}\left(\frac{1}{n}\sum_i \in_i\right) \\ &= \frac{\mathrm{Var}(\tilde{\in}_i)}{n^2} \\ &= \frac{\sigma^2}{n^2}. \end{aligned}$$

Thus, if n is large, the variance of $x\tilde{\in}$ will be negligible.

Reconsidering the steps up to this point, note that a portfolio has been created that has no systematic or unsystematic risk and using no wealth. Under **conditions of equilibrium** it can be stated unequivocally that *all portfolios of these n assets that satisfy the conditions of using no wealth and having no risk must also earn no return on average.* In other words, there are no free lunches in an efficient market, at least not for any extended period of time. Therefore the expected return on the arbitrage portfolio can be expressed as

$$x\tilde{r} = xE = \sum_{i=1}^{n} x_i E_i = 0. \tag{3.41}$$

Another way to state the preceding statements and results is through linear algebra. In general, any vector x with elements on the order of $1/n$ that is orthogonal to the constant vector and to each of the coefficient vectors b_h $(h = 1, \ldots, k)$ must also be orthogonal to the vector of expected returns. A further algebraic consequence of this statement is that the expected return vector E must be a linear combination of the constant vector and the b vectors. Using algebraic terminology, there exist $k+1$ weights $(\lambda_0, \lambda_1, \ldots, \lambda_k)$ such that

$$E_i = \lambda_0 + \lambda_1 b_{il} + \cdots + \lambda_k b_{ik} \quad \text{for all } I. \tag{3.42}$$

In addition, if there exists a riskless asset with return E_0 which can be said to be the common return on all zero-beta assets — that is, $b_{ih} = 0$ (for all h) — then, $E_0 = \lambda_0$.

Utilizing this definition and rearranging,

$$E_i - E_0 = \lambda_1 b_{il} + \cdots + \lambda_k b_{ik}. \tag{3.43}$$

The pricing relationship depicted in Equation (13.15) is the central conclusion of the APT. Before exploring the consequences of this pricing model through a simple numerical example, it is best to first give some interpretation to the λ_h, the factor risk premium. If portfolios are formed with a systematic risk of 1 relative to factor h and no risk on other factors, then each λ_h can be interpreted as

$$\lambda_h = E^h - E_0. \tag{3.44}$$

In other words, each λ_h can be thought of as the excess return or market risk premium on portfolios with only systematic factor h risk. Hence, Equation (3.39) can be rewritten as

$$E_i - E_0 = (E^1 - E_0)b_{i1} + \cdots + (E^k - E_0)b_{ik}. \tag{3.45}$$

The implications that arise from the arguments concerning APT that have been constructed thus far can be summarized in the following statement: *APT yields a statement of relative pricing on subsets of the universe of assets*. Moreover, note that the arbitrage pricing model of Equation (3.43) or (3.45) can be tested by examining only subsets of the set of all return. Consequently, the market portfolio plays no special role in APT, since any well-diversified portfolio could serve the same purpose. Hence, it can be empirically tested on any set of data, and the results should be generalizable to the entire market. The following three sample problems give further illustration.

Sample Problem 3.5

To reinforce the concepts and workings of the arbitrage mechanism, consider a simple example. Suppose that the returns on two well-diversified portfolios can be described by a linear function in the following arbitrage pricing model (APM) form:

$$(E_i - E_0) = (\lambda_1 b_{i1} + \lambda_2 b_{i2}),$$

or

$$= (E^1 - E_0)b_{i1} + (E^2 - E_0)b_{i2} + (E^3 - E_0)b_{i3},$$

in which E_0 is the constant return on the riskless asset.

Next, assume these portfolios have the following sensitivity coefficients (factor loadings) with the three identified factors as presented in Table 3.3.

Assuming the riskless rate is 7% (E_0), the expected returns and their relative returns per unit of risk as defined by the Treynor performance measure can be expressed in Table 3.4. In addition, a graph can be drawn of each portfolio's expected return versus the averaged value of its sensitivity coefficients, as indicated in the Figure 3.8. This is somewhat analogous to the analysis in CAPM. Please note that

Table 3.3 Sensitivity Coefficients

Portfolio	b_{i1}	b_{i2}	b_{i3}
1	0.6	1.0	0.8
2	0.3	0.7	0.5

Table 3.4 Expected Return per Unit of Risk

Portfolio	E_i (%)	$\frac{(E_i - E_0)}{(\sum_{i=1}^{3} b_{ih}/3)}$
1	12	6.25
2	8	2.00

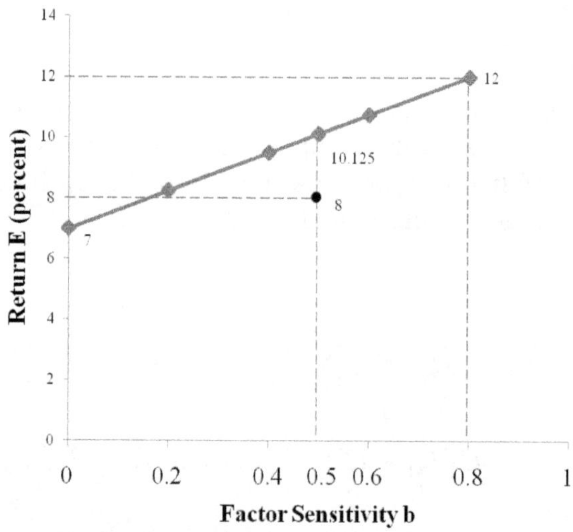

Figure 3.9 Expected Return and Factor Sensitivity

10.125% in Figure 3.9 is calculated as follows:

$$\frac{x-7}{0.5} = \frac{12-7}{0.8},$$

$$x = 10.125,$$

where x is the theoretical expected return related to the factor sensitivity of the second portfolio.

As was demonstrated through the determination of each portfolio's expected return-per-risk measure, the graph again points out that the second portfolio is overpriced.[5] That is, its expected return

[5]Suppose the second portfolio will pay \$10 per year. The price of this portfolio with the expected return 8% is \$10/0.08 = \$125, while the price with the theoretical return 10.125% is \$10/10.125% = \$98.77. The market price (\$125) is higher than its theoretical price (\$98.77), so the second portfolio is overpriced.

Table 3.5 Excess Return of the Investment

	Investment	Systematic Risk (b_{ih})	Expected Return (%)
For portfolio 2, sell short	\$1,000,000	−0.5	−8.0
For portfolio 1, buy	(\$625,000)	$(0.625 \times 0.8) = 0.5$	$(0.625 \times 12.0) = 7.5$
Invest remainder in bills	(\$375,000)	$(0.375 \times 0) = 0$	$(0.375 \times 7.0) = 2.625$
Net investment:	\$0		
Net risk:		0.0	
Total excess return earned:			2.125%

per unit of risk is lower than that of the first portfolio relative to the riskless rate of 7%.

The proper "arbitrage strategy" to follow in order to profit from this apparent mispricing is shown in Table 3.5. However appealing the logic of the previous arbitrage argument, some specific assumptions are required for the APT:

(1) Investors are return maximizers.
(2) Borrowing and lending are done at the riskless rate.
(3) There are no market restrictions such as transaction costs, taxes, or restrictions on short selling.
(4) Investors agree on the number and identity of the factors that are priced.
(5) Riskless profitable opportunities above the risk-free rate are immediately arbitraged away.

Hence, since any market equilibrium must be consistent with no arbitrage profits, every equilibrium will be characterized by a linear relationship between each asset's expected return and its sensitivity to the common priced factors.

Sample Problem 3.6

Given the three portfolios in Table 3.6 with expected return R_i and sensitivity factors b_{i1} and b_{i2}, what is the equation of the plane in terms of R_i, b_{i1}, and b_{i2} space defined by these portfolios?

Table 3.6 Expected Return R_i and Sensitivity Factors b_{i1} and b_{i2}

Portfolio	R_i	b_{i1}	b_{i2}
A	14.0	0.8	0.8
B	10.8	0.6	0.4
C	11.2	0.4	0.6

Solution

The information can be used to derive the equation for the risk–return plan of Equation (3.42) as follows. Substituting returns and sensitivity factor information into Equation (3.42),

$$\begin{aligned}
14 &= \lambda_0 + 0.8\lambda_1 + 0.8\lambda_2 && \text{(i)}\\
10.8 &= \lambda_0 + 0.6\lambda_1 + 0.4\lambda_2 && \text{(ii)}\\
11.2 &= \lambda_0 + 0.4\lambda_1 + 0.6\lambda_2. && \text{(iii)}\\
\text{Subtract (ii) from (i)}: \quad 3.2 &= 0.2\lambda_1 + 0.4\lambda_2. && \text{(iv)}\\
\text{Subtract (ii) from (iii)}: \quad 0.4 &= -0.2\lambda_1 + 0.2\lambda_2. && \text{(v)}
\end{aligned}$$

From Equations (iv) and (v), $\lambda_2 = 6$. From Equation (v), $\lambda_1 = 4$. Finally, from Equation (i), solving for λ_0,

$$\lambda_0 = 14 + 0.8\lambda_1 - 0.8\lambda_2 = 14 + 3.2 - 4.8 = 6.$$

Hence, the equation of the plane describing equilibrium risk–return space can be expressed as follows:

$$E_i = 6 + 4b_{i1} + 6b_{i2}.$$

Sample Problem 3.7

Using the portfolios in Sample Problem 3.6, determine how much arbitrage profit, if any, can be made by buying or selling (short) the following portfolios (individually) as presented in Table 3.7.

Solution

From portfolios A, B, and C, the risk/return relationship is $E_i = 6 + 4b_{i1} + 6b_{i2}$.

For portfolio D, an equivalent portfolio can be composed from a linear combination of portfolios A, B, and C. Given sensitivity factors

Table 3.7 Expected Return R_i and Sensitivity Factors b_{i1} and b_{i2}

Portfolio	R_i (%)	b_{i1}	b_{i2}
D	14.0	0.5	0.7
E	15.2	0.8	1.0
F	9.0	0.6	0.5

$b_{i1} = 0.5$ and $b_{i2} = 0.7$, the expected return would be

$$\begin{aligned} r_0 &= 6 + 4(0.5) + 6(0.7) \\ &= 12.2\%. \end{aligned}$$

Since 12.2% < 14%, portfolio D is underpriced. A riskless, costless arbitrage profit can be made by buying portfolio D and selling an equivalent amount of a portfolio composed of portfolios A, B, and C.

For portfolio E, an equivalent portfolio can be constructed with yield

$$r_{\text{equiv}} = 6 + 4(0.8) + 6(1.0) = 15.2\%.$$

This is exactly the yield of portfolio E; therefore, no arbitrage opportunities remain:

For portfolio F,

$$r_{\text{equiv}} = 6 + 4(0.8) + 6(0.5) = 11.4\%.$$

Since 11.4% > 9%, portfolio F is overpriced. Therefore, portfolio F should be sold, and the equivalent portfolio should be bought.

A riskless, costless arbitrage profit of \$18,000 as indicated in Table 3.8 can be made by buying \$10 million worth of portfolio D and by selling \$10 million of an equivalent portfolio made up of portfolios A, B, and C.

A riskless, costless arbitrage profit of \$24,000 as indicated in Table 3.9 can be made by selling \$10 million worth of portfolio F and by buying \$10 million of an equivalent portfolio made up of portfolios A, B, and C.

Even though the APT is very general and based on few assumptions, it provides little guidance concerning the identification of the

Table 3.8 Arbitrage Profits of Portfolio D and the Equivalent Portfolio

	Initial *CF*	Ending *CF*	Risk Factors b_{i1}	b_{i2}
Portfolio D	−$10,000,000	+$1,140,000	0.5	0.7
Equivalent portfolio	+$10,000,000	−$1,122,000	−0.5	−0.7
	0	+18,000	0	0

Table 3.9 Arbitrage Profits of Portfolio E and the Equivalent Portfolio

	Initial *CF*	Ending *CF*	Sens. Factors b_{i1}	b_{i2}
Portfolio F	+$10,000,000	−$1,090,000	−0.8	−1.0
Equivalent portfolio	−$10,000,000	+$1,114,000	+0.8	+1.0
	0	+24,000	0	0

priced factors. Hence, empirical research must achieve two goals:

(1) Identify the number of factors, and
(2) Identify the various economics underlying each factor.

3.6.3 *Empirical test methodology*

Empirical tests of the APT are evolving at an increasing rate as academicians attempt to verify its conclusions. In particular, recent empirical work in this area has sought to determine whether there exist multiple underlying factors for asset returns — and, if they exist, whether they are associated with risk premiums. It is hypothesized that there exist non-zero $\lambda_1, \ldots, \lambda_k$ such that

$$E_i - E_0 = \lambda_1 b_{i1} + \cdots + \lambda_k b_{ik}, \tag{3.46}$$

for all i. To empirically test this hypothesis, a two-step procedure is typically utilized. In the first step, the statistical technique of factor analysis is used to estimate the expected returns and the factor loading $(b_{i1}, \ldots, b_{ik})$ from time series data of asset returns. In the second step, these estimates are used in the basic cross-sectional pricing equation of the APT to estimate the risk premium (λ_h), thereby performing the hypothesis test.

While this two-step procedure is analogous to familiar CAPM empirical work, it is free of some major conceptual difficulties in CAPM tests. The most important of these is that the APT can be applied to subsets of the universe of assets, eliminating any need to specify as well as justify any particular choice of a proxy for the market portfolio.

It would be ideal to perform the factor analysis in the first step on all asset returns as a whole; nevertheless, the resulting huge covariance matrix would be beyond the normal processing capacity of computers. To compromise with this technical constraint, several approaches have been taken in the empirical studies of APT. However, to date, no one approach has yet been proposed that is free of shortcomings. To better clarify the testing procedures required for APT along with the inherent problems, some of the major empirical studies are now offered, followed by an example of an empirical test of the APT.

The most comprehensive and widely recognized study of the APT is that of Roll and Ross (RR, 1980). These authors use daily returns for a sample of 1,269 selected securities from both the NYSE and AMEX over the period July 3, 1962 to December 31, 1972. RR arranged the sample into 42 groups with 30 securities in each, on the basis of alphabetical order. Next, RR perform maximum-likelihood factor analysis on each of the 42 group to estimate the respective factor loadings. The estimated factor loadings are then used as the explanatory variables in the **second-stage cross-sectional regression test**.

The dominant problem associated with this approach is that the return-generating process cannot be compared across groups. This results from the complexity that factors in different groups might not lie in the same dimensionality. More explicitly, the first factor in one group may not correspond to the first factor in the other group. Quite conceivably then, the first factor in one group might be equivalent to the third factor in the other group. Hence, after the cross-sectional distributions of the loading coefficients are tabulated, there could be a mixing of estimates which apply to different "true" factors. Moreover, there is no way to ascertain that the same three (or four) factors (the number RR found) generate the returns in every group.

A second approach in testing the APT, called the **small-sample approach**, is employed by Chen (1983), and Oldfield and Rogalski (1981). Using the small-sample approach, assets are divided into several groups as before. However, now, factor analysis is applied for only a single group (as opposed to every group) and corresponding factor loadings estimated. The estimates of factor loadings in the remaining groups are inferred from the covariance of their returns with the loading coefficients of the factor analyzed group.

The small-sample approach assures the comparability of factors across groups, a definite strength over the RR approach. However, because only a relatively small number of asset returns are used in the factor estimation procedure, the statistical problem of inefficient estimation is encountered. Moreover, as other researchers have demonstrated, the estimation bias in the original estimation of factor loadings can be magnified further when the remaining loadings are derived. The central consequence of this estimation bias is that "spurious" explanatory factors may be extracted.

To surpass the hindrance of inefficient estimation, Reinganum (1981) applies a third approach, the **portfolio approach**. Here, assets are grouped into portfolios, and factor analysis is performed on the covariance matrix among these portfolio returns instead of the individual asset returns (as in the previous two approaches). The problem with this methodology is that as the number of assets in a portfolio increases, the portfolio returns tend to reflect a single-factor model even when a multifactor model is true. Thus, it is not surprising that the studies using the portfolio approach find but one significant factor.

Thus, it has been shown that any efficient estimation procedure for testing the APT requires the utilization of all assets in the sample. Moreover, the portfolio approach stresses the importance of using the covariance matrix among individual assets in order to avoid the tendency toward a single-factor model. Yet, the constraint of computer capacity makes the comparative analysis of the covariance matrix of the entire population of assets virtually impossible. Consequently, as Roll and Ross's study (1980) points out, dividing the population into a manageable number of smaller groups creates a problem in identifying what the explanatory factors are and determining whether their relative significance across groups is consistent.

3.7 Valuations of Derivatives

The innovation of derivatives products in finance is important in both theory and practice in the subject of finance and accounting. Derivative contracts include forward contracts, future contracts, and option contracts. Following Chapter 2, we will discuss these three contracts in further detail.

3.7.1 *Forward contracts*

A forward contract is a customized contract between two parties to buy or sell an asset at a specified price on a future date. A forward contract can be used for hedging or speculation, although its non-standardized nature makes it particularly apt for hedging.

A currency forward contract is an agreement between a commercial bank and a corporate customer to exchange a specific amount of one currency for another on a specific future date at a specific price or exchange rate. At the initiation of the agreement, no money changes hands; the actual exchange of funds takes place on the future date specified in the forward contract. Forward contracts are very useful because they can be tailored to fit any situation, but they are very expensive.

In financial markets, there are also forward contracts for stock and bond.

We now consider a forward contract on an investment asset, such as stock or bond, with price S_0 that provides no income. Let T be the time to maturity, r be the risk-free rate, and F_0 be the forward price. The relationship between F_0 and S_0 in terms of continuous compounding is as follows:

$$F_0 = S_0 e^{rT}. \tag{3.47}$$

Following the arbitrage process, which has been discussed in the previous section, if $F_0 > S_0 e^{rT}$, arbitrageurs can buy the asset and short forward contracts on the asset. If $F_0 < S_0 e^{rT}$, they can short the asset and enter into long forward contracts on it. For example, $S_0 = \$40$, $r = 0.05$, and $T = 0.25$, so that Equation (3.47) gives

$$F_0 = 40\mathrm{e}^{0.05(0.25)} = \$40.50.$$

A long forward contract and a spot purchase both lead to the asset being owned at time T. The forward price is higher than the spot price because of the cost of financing the spot purchase of the asset during the life of the forward contract.

Sample Problem 3.8

Consider a 4-month forward contract to buy a zero-coupon bond that will mature 1 year from today. (This means that the bond will have 8 months to go when the forward contract matures.) The current price of the bond is \$930. We assume that the 4-month risk-free rate of interest (continuously compounded) is 6% per annum. Because zero-coupon bonds provide no income, we can use Equation (5.1) with $T = 4/12$, $r = 0.06$, and $S_0 = 930$. The forward price, F_0, is given by

$$F_0 = 930e^{0.06(4/12)} = \$948.79.$$

This would be the delivery price in a contract negotiated today.

Now, we consider a forward contract on an investment asset that will provide a perfectly predictable cash income to the holder. Examples are stocks paying known dividends and coupon-bearing bonds. We adopt the same approach as in the previous example. We first look at a numerical example and then review the formal argument.

Consider a long forward contract to purchase a coupon-bearing bond whose current price is \$900. We will suppose that the forward contract matures in 9 months. We will also suppose that a coupon payment of \$40 is expected after 4 months. We assume that the 4-month and 9-month risk-free interest rates (continuously compounded) are, respectively, 3% and 4% per annum. In Appendix 3A, we have presented a continuously compounding and discounting process and formula.

Suppose first that the forward price is relatively high at \$910. An arbitrageur can borrow \$900 to buy the bond and short a forward contract. The coupon payment has a present value of $40e^{-0.03(4/12)} =$ \$39.60. Of the \$900, \$39.60 is therefore borrowed at 3% per annum for 4 months so that it can be repaid with the coupon payment. The remaining \$860.40 is borrowed at 4% per annum for 9 months. The amount owing at the end of the 9-month period is $860.40e^{0.04(0.75)} =$ \$886.60. A sum of \$910 is received for the bond under the terms of the forward contract. The arbitrageur therefore makes a net profit of

$$910.00 - 886.60 = \$23.40.$$

Suppose next that the forward price is relatively low at \$870. An investor can short the bond and enter into a long forward contract. Of the \$900 realized from shorting the bond, \$39.60 is invested for 4 months at 3% per annum so that it grows into an amount sufficient to pay the coupon on the bond. The remaining \$860.40 is invested for 9 months at 4% per annum and grows to \$886.60. Under the terms of the forward contract, \$870 is paid to buy the bond and the short position is closed out. The investor therefore gains

$$886.60 - 870 = \$16.60.$$

The first strategy produces a profit when the forward price is greater than \$886.60, whereas the second strategy produces a profit when the forward price is less than \$886.60. It follows that if there are no arbitrage opportunities then the forward price must be \$886.60.

Now, we can generalize from this example to argue that, when an investment asset will provide income with a present value of I during the life of a forward contract, we have

$$F_0 = (S_0 - I)e^{rT}. \tag{3.48}$$

Equation (3.43) is evaluated in terms of continuous compounding.

For example, $S_0 = 900.00$, $I = 40\mathrm{e}^{-0.03(4/12)} = 39.60$, $r = 0.04$, and $T = 0.75$, so that

$$F_0 = (900.00 - 39.60)\mathrm{e}^{0.04(0.75)} = \$886.60.$$

This is in agreement with our earlier calculation. Equation (3.48) applies to any investment asset that provides a known cash income.

If $F_0 > (S_0 - I)\mathrm{e}^{rT}$, an arbitrageur can lock in a profit by buying the asset and shorting a forward contract on the asset; if $F_0 < (S_0 - I)\mathrm{e}^{rT}$, an arbitrageur can lock in a profit by shorting the asset and taking a long position in a forward contract. If short sales are not possible, investors who own the asset will find it profitable to sell the asset and enter into long forward contracts.

3.7.2 *Future contracts*

In Chapter 2, we have discussed forward contracts and future contracts. In the previous section, we have discussed forward contracts in some detail. Future contacts are similar to forward contracts. Now, we will define the future contracts as follows. A futures contract is a legal agreement to buy or sell a particular commodity asset, or security at a predetermined price at a specified time in the future. Futures contracts are standardized for quality and quantity to facilitate trading on a futures exchange. In Chapter 2, we have used a real-world commodity future contract example to define the terminology use. In addition, we also compare the similarity and difference between future contracts and forward contracts. In Chapters 4 and 5, we will discuss the valuation formula of commodity future, financial future, and other futures in detail. In addition, in Chapters 4 and 5, we also explore different methods to estimate hedge ratio and the applications of the hedge ratio.

3.7.3 *Option contracts*

Option contracts give their holders the right to buy and sell a specific asset at some specified price on or before a specified date. Since these contracts can be valued in relation to common stock, the basic concepts involved have a number of applications to financial theory and to the valuation of other financial instruments. (A more theoretical discussion of option pricing theory is included in Chapters 7, 8, and 9.)

While there are a variety of option contracts — for example, call options, put options, combinations of calls and puts, convertible securities, and warrants — this chapter's discussion is limited to **call options**. A call option gives the holder the right to buy a share of stock at a specified price, known as the exercise price, and the basic American option can be exercised at any time through the expiration date. The value of the option at expiration is the difference between the market price of the underlying stock and its exercise price (with a minimum value of zero, of course).

While several factors affect the value of an option, the most important factor is the price volatility of the stock — the greater the volatility, the greater the value of the option, other things remaining the same. We will also note that the longer the time left before expiration

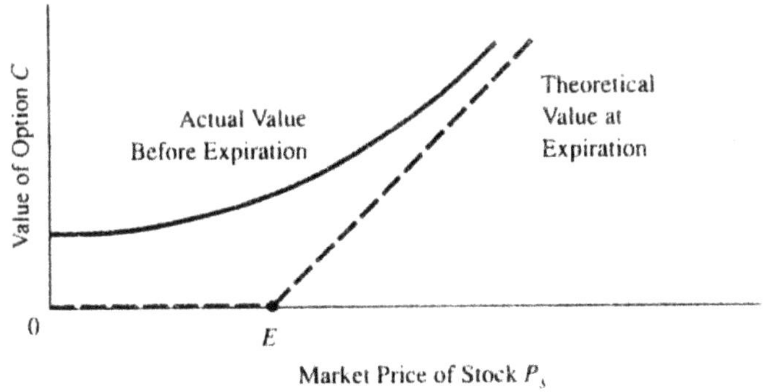

Figure 3.10 Theoretical and Actual Values of a Call Option

and the higher the level of interest rates in the market, the greater the option value, all other things held the same.

The theoretical value of a call option at expiration is the difference between the market price of the underlying common stock, p_s, and the exercise price of the option, E, or zero, whichever is greater:

$$C = \text{Max}(P_s - E,\ 0). \tag{3.49}$$

When the price of the stock is greater than the exercise price, the option has a positive theoretical value which will increase dollar for dollar with the price of the stock. When the market price of the stock is equal to or less than the exercise price, the option has a theoretical value of zero, as shown in Figure 3.10. Nevertheless, as long as some time remains before expiration, the actual market price of the option (referred to as the option premium at the time of issue) is likely to be greater than its theoretical value. This increment above the theoretical value is called the *time value* or *speculative value* of the option, and its size will depend primarily on the perceived likelihood of a profitable move on the price of the stock before expiration of the option. Sample Problem 3.9 provides further illustration.

Sample Problem 3.9

A call option written on LBO, Inc.'s stock has an exercise price of \$95. Calculate the value of the call option when the option expires if the price of the stock at expiration is (a) \$106 and (b) \$92.

Solution

According to Equation (3.30), the call option can take on only two values. If the call option expires "in the money," its value will be the difference between the stock price and the exercise price. If the call option expires "out of the money," its value will be equal to zero because the option holder does not have to exercise this option.

(a) Call expires "in the money":

$$\begin{aligned} C &= \$106 - \$95 \\ &= \$11. \end{aligned}$$

(b) Call expires "out of the money," so option will not be exercised:

$$C = \$0.$$

The full range of possible values for the market price of the option is from the theoretical value on the low side to the market price of the stock itself on the high side. For the option price to be equal to the stock price, an infinite time to expiration would be implied. For the option price to be equal to the theoretical value only, imminent expiration would be implied. For virtually all options for which the value would be determined, however, the option price would fall somewhere between these two extremes. Because an option costs less than its underlying stock, the percentage change in option price is greater than the percentage change in stock price, given some increase in the market price of the stock. Thus, a leveraged rate of return can be earned by investment in the option rather than the stock. As stock price continues to increase, the difference between the percentage change in option price and the percentage change in stock price will tend to converge.

Thus far, it has been shown that the value of an option will be a function of the underlying stock price, the exercise price of the option, and the time to maturity. Yet, there is still another factor that is probably the single most important variable affecting the speculative value of the option. That is the **price volatility** of the underlying stock. The greater the probability of significant change in the price of the stock, the more likely it is that the option can be exercised at a profit before expiration. Sample Problem 3.10 provides further illustration.

Sample Problem 3.10

At the beginning of some time period, investment may be considered in options on stock A and stock B, both of which have an exercise price of $48. If the probabilities of stock price at the end of the period are as indicated in Table 3.10, the theoretical values of option A and option B can also be determined using Equation (3.44). While the expected value of the stock prices for A and B is the same, $50, the expected theoretical values are $3.40 for option A and $7.40 for option B.

$$\begin{aligned}\textbf{Option A} &= (0)(0.1) + (0)(0.2) + (2)(0.4) + (7)(0.2) + (12)(0.1)\\ &= \$3.40.\\ \textbf{Option B} &= (0)(0.1) + (0)(0.2) + (2)(0.4) + (12)(0.2) + (22)(0.1)\\ &= \$7.40.\end{aligned}$$

The greater expected value of the option with greater stock price volatility that is shown, therefore, results from the fact that the value of an option cannot be less than zero. Consequently, the value of an option is not a function of the expected value of the stock price at a point in time but a function of the volatility of stock price.

There is another factor affecting the speculative premium for options. This is the level of interest rates in the market — specifically for option analysis, the *call money* rate charged by brokers for the use of margin in common-stock accounts. As this concept is discussed later, it is sufficient here to point out that the leverage achieved through option investment is similar to that achieved through direct margin purchase of the underlying common stock, but without the explicit interest cost involved in the latter. Thus,

Table 3.10 Stock Price and Option Price

Probability	**0.1**	**0.2**	**0.4**	**0.2**	**0.1**
Price of stock A ($)	40	45	50	55	60
Theoretical value of option A ($)	0	0	2	7	12
Price of stock B ($)	30	40	50	60	70
Theoretical value of option B ($)	0	0	2	2	22

Exercise price of option A = Exercise price of option B = $48 the higher the call money rate, the greater the savings from the use of options and the greater the speculative value of the option.

To summarize, there are five variables necessary to determine the value of an American call option (ignoring dividends on the common stock, the effect of which is discussed in Chapter 14):

1. *Stock price*
2. *Exercise price*: The relationship between these two prices determines whether the option has a positive theoretical value.
3. *Time to maturity*: The longer the time to maturity, the greater the speculative value of the option because the chances for a profitable movement in the price of the stock are increased.
4. *Volatility of stock price*: There is a positive relationship between the volatility of the underlying stock price and the speculative value of the option because with greater volatility, there is greater potential for gain on the upside and greater benefit from the downside protection involved with the option.
5. *Interest rate*: The higher the call money rate for direct margin purchase of common stock, the greater the relative value of being able to achieve equal amounts of leverage through the alternative of option purchase.

The factors that affect the value of an option can be written in a functional form:

$$C = f(S,\ X, \sigma^2, T, r_f), \tag{3.50}$$

where C = value of the option, S = stock price, X = exercise price, σ^2 = variance of the stock, T = time to expiration, and r_f = risk-free rate.

The value of the option increases as a function of the value of the stock for a given exercise price and maturity date — the lower the exercise price, the greater the value of the option; and the longer the time to maturity, the higher the value of the option. The holder of an option will prefer more variance in the price of the stock. The greater the variance (price volatility), the greater the probability that the stock price will exceed the exercise price and thus benefit the holder.

Considering two related financial securities — common stock and the option on the common stock — it is possible to illustrate how a risk-free hedged position can be developed. In this way, unprofitable price movements in one of the securities will be offset by profitable price movements in the other. The hedge ratio determines the portion of stock held long in relation to the options in the short position (or vice-versa). With a complete hedge, the value of the hedged position can be shown to be the same regardless of the stock price outcome. In efficient financial markets, the rate of return earned on perfectly hedged positions will be the risk-free rate. Consequently, it is then possible to determine the appropriate option price at the beginning of the period. If the actual market price is above or below this value, arbitrage would then drive the option price toward its correct level. In Chapter 14, this process and the development of the Black and Scholes (1973) continuous type of option pricing model and Cox, Ross, and Rubinstein's (1979) discrete type of binomial option pricing model will be analyzed in some detail. Option pricing models and their applications are discussed (in great detail) in Chapters 14, 15, and 21.

3.8 Summary

We have first reviewed and summarized alternative valuation theories, which include classical theory, M&M theory, CAPM, APT, forward contracts, future contracts, and option contracts. These theories can directly and indirectly become guidelines for further study of financial management, investment analysis, portfolio management, and financial derivatives. Based upon the theory discussed in this chapter, we will explore and expand the forward contracts, future contracts, option contracts, valuations, and their applications in later chapters of this book.

Questions and Problems

1. What is arbitrage? Why is it such an important concept in security analysis and portfolio management?
2. Calculate the value of a security that will pay $10/year in perpetuity, if investors require an 8% return.
3. Calculate the value of a bond that has an annual coupon rate of 9% and a maturity value of $1,000. Assume the bond matures in five years and that bondholders require an 11% return.

4. What is a callable bond? Other things being equal, which bond will have greater value, a callable bond or a non-callable bond?
5. Evaluate the following statement: "Because investors purchase a security for its expected cash flow, the dividend policy of a firm will affect the value of the firm's stock."
6. You are given the following information:

$$\text{Return on three-month T-bills} = 6\%.$$

$$\text{Expected return on S\&P 500} = 9\%.$$

   (a) Draw the security market line.
   (b) Calculate the expected rate of return on a stock with a beta equal to 1.5.

7. Define the following terms:

   (a) forward contract
   (b) future contract
   (c) call option
   (d) put option
   (e) exercise price

8. What are the advantages of purchasing a call option on IBM stock rather than purchasing the stock itself? Are there any disadvantages?
9. Evaluate the following statement: "Because most individuals dislike risk, the higher the variance of IBM's stock price, the lower the value of put and call options written on IBM's stock."
10. What is the call money rate? Carefully explain the relationship between the call money rate and the value of an option.
11. What is a perpetuity? What would a bond that pays $110 per year in perpetuity be worth if bondholders required a 12% return?
12. Briefly explain M&M's Proposition I and its importance to modern financial theory.
13. What is portfolio insurance? Identify and explain the various strategies that can be used to insure a portfolio.
14. What is the difference between hedging and portfolio insurance?

15. A manager is running a $10-million portfolio. She has decided to allocate $5 million to risky assets and $5 million to risk-free assets. She has set the floor of the portfolio at $7 million.
    (a) What is the cushion for this portfolio?
    (b) What is the exposure for this portfolio?
    (c) What is the multiple for this portfolio?
16. Given the information in Question 3, if the market for risky assets increases by 30%:
    (a) What is the value of the total portfolio?
    (b) What is the new multiple?
    (c) What should the portfolio manager do to restore the portfolio to its target multiple?
17. Given the information in Question 3, if the market for risky assets decreases by 10%:
    (a) What is the value of the total portfolio?
    (b) What is the new multiple?
    (c) What should the portfolio manager do to restore the portfolio to its target level?
18. What does the term *path dependence* mean? Why is it important for portfolio insurance strategies to be path independent?
19. Define a synthetic option. Explain how the option position is adjusted in a rising or falling market.
20. What is a delta value? Why is it important?

Bibliography

Barnea, A., R. A. Haugen and L. W. Senbet (1981). Market imperfections, agency problems, and capital structure: A review. *Financial Management*, 10(Summer), 7–22.

Black, F. and M. Scholes (1973). The pricing of options and corporate liabilities. *Journal of Political Economy*, 81(May–June), 637–654.

Bodie, Z., A. Kane and A. Marcus (2013). *Investments*, 10th ed. New York, NY: McGraw-Hill/Irwin.

Brealey, R., S. Myers and F. Allen (2020). *Principles of Corporate Finance.* New York, NY: McGraw-Hill Book Company.

Chen, N. F. (1983). Some empirical tests of the theory of arbitrage pricing. *Journal of Finance*, 38(December), 1393–1414.

Copeland, T. E. and J. F. Weston (2004). *Financial Theory and Corporate Policy*, 4th ed. Reading, MA: Addison-Wesley Publishing Company.

Cox, J. C., S. A. Ross and M. Rubinstein (1979). Option pricing: A simplified approach. *Journal of Financial Economics*, 7(September), 229–263.

DeAngelo, H. and L. DeAngelo (2006). The irrelevance of the MM dividend irrelevance theorem. *Journal of Financial Economics*, 79, 293–315.

DeAngelo, H. and R. W. Masulis (1980). Optimal capital structure under corporate and personal taxation. *Journal of Financial Economics*, 8(March), 3–29.

Fama, E. F. and M. H. Miller (1972). *Theory of Finance*. New York, NY: Holt, Rinehart and Winston.

Galai, D. and R. W. Masulis (1976). The option pricing model and the risk factor of stock. *Journal of Financial Economics*, 3(March), 53–81.

Hsia, C. C. (1981). Coherence of the modern theories of finance. *The Financial Review*, 16(Winter), 27–42.

Hull, J. (2022). *Options, Futures, and Other Derivatives*, 10th ed. Reading, MA: Pearson.

Jensen, M. C. and W. H. Meckling (1978). Can the corporation survive? *Financial Analysts Journal*, 34(January/February), 31–37.

Lee, C. F. (1983). *Financial Analysis and Planning: Theory and Application. A Book of Readings*. Reading, MA: Addison-Wesley Publishing Company.

Lee, C. F. (1985). *Financial Analysis and Planning: Theory and Applications*. Reading, MA: Addison-Wesley Publishing Company.

Lee, C. F. and J. E. Finnerty (1990). *Corporate Finance: Theory, Method, and Applications*. New York: Harcourt Brace Jovanovich.

Lee, C. F. and J. C. Junkus (1983). Financial analysis and planning: An overview. *Journal of Economics and Business*, 34(August), 257–283.

Lee, C. F. and J. C. Lee (2016). *Financial Analysis, Planning and Forecasting: Theory and Application*, 3rd ed. Hackensack, NJ and Singapore: World Scientific.

Lee, C. F. and J. Lee (2021). *Handbook of Financial Econometrics, Mathematics, Statistics, and Machine Learning*. Singapore: World Scientific.

Lee, C. F. and A. C. Lee (2023). *Encyclopedia of Finance*. Berlin: Springer.

Lee, C. F., A. C. Lee and J. Lee (2010). *Handbook of Quantitative Finance and Risk Management*. Berlin: Springer.

Lee, C. F., J. C. Lee and M. Lee (2022). *Corporate Finance and Strategy: An Active Learning Approach*. Singapore: World Scientific.

Lee, C. F., A. C. Lee and J. Lee (2023). *Handbook of Investment Analysis, Portfolio Management, and Financial Derivatives*. Singapore: World Scientific.

Lee, C. F. and Y. C. Yeh (2023). Three project analyses of Johnson & Johnson (JNJ) in terms of Excel programs, Working paper.

Leland, H. and D. H. Pyle (1977). Informational asymmetries, financial structure and financial intermediation. *Journal of Finance*, 32(September), 371–387.

Miller, M. H. (1977). Debt and taxes. *Journal of Finance*, 32(May), 101–175.

Miller, M. H. (1988). The Modigliani–Miller proposition after 30 years. *Journal of Economic Perspectives*, 2(Fall), 99–120.

Miller, M. H. and F. Modigliani (1961). Dividend policy growth and the valuation of share. *Journal of Business*, 34, 411–433.

Modigliani, F. and M. Miller (1958). The cost of capital, corporation finance and the theory of investment. *American Economic Review*, 48(June), 261–297.

Modigliani, F. and M. Miller (1963). Corporate income taxes and the cost of capital: A correction. *American Economic Review*, 53(June), 433–443.

Oldfield Jr, G. S. and R. J. Rogalski (1981). Treasury bill factors and common stock returns. *The Journal of Finance*, 36(2), 337–350.

Reilly, F. K. and K. C. Brown (2011). *Investment Analysis and Portfolio Management*, 10th ed. Orlando, FL: Dryden Press.

Reinganum, M. R. (1981). Misspecification of capital asset pricing: Empirical anomalies based on earnings' yields and market values. *Journal of Financial Economics*, 9(1), 19–46.

Roll, R. and S. A. Ross (1980). An empirical investigation of the arbitrage pricing theory. *The Journal of Finance*, 35(5), 1073–1103.

Ross, S. A. (1977). The determination of financial structure: The incentive signalling approach. *Bell Journal of Economics*, (Spring), 23–40.

Ross, S., A. R. W. Westerfield and J. Jaffe (2019). *Corporate Finance*, 12th ed. New York, NY: McGraw-Hill/Irwin.

Shelton, J. (1981). Equal access and Miller's equilibrium. *Journal of Financial and Quantitative Analysis*, 16(November), 603–623.

Stiglitz, J. E. (1969). A re-examination of the Modigliani-Miller theorem. *The American Economic Review*, 54(December), 784–793.

Stiglitz, J. E. (1974). On the irrelevance of corporate financial policy. *The American Economic Review*, 54(December), 851–866.

Weston, J. F. (1981). Developments in finance theory. *Financial Management*, 10(Tenth Anniversary Issue), 5–22.

Yeh, W.-C. (2022). Three Excel programs for financial analysis planning and forecasting. These program can be found in: http://centerforpbbefr.rutgers.edu/.

Appendix 3A: Minimum-Variance Approach to Derive Optimal Weight

If there is a two-security portfolio, its variance can be defined as

$$\sigma_p^2 = w_1^2\sigma_1^2 + w_2^2\sigma_2^2 + 2w_1w_2Cov(r_1, r_2), \tag{3A.1}$$

where w_1 and w_2 are weight associated with securities 1 and 2, respectively.

σ_1^2 and σ_2^2 are variance of securities 1 and 2, respectively.

The problem is choosing optimal w_1 to minimize the portfolio variance, σ_p^2

$$\underset{w_1}{Min}\,.\sigma_p^2. \tag{3A.2}$$

We can solve the minimization problem by differentiating the σ_p^2 with respect to w_1, and setting the derivative equal to zero and we can obtain the answer as follows:

$$w_1 = \frac{\sigma_2^2 - Cov(r_1, r_2)}{\sigma_1^2 + \sigma_2^2 - 2Cov(r_1, r_2)}. \tag{3A.3}$$

The detailed procedure to obtain this answer can be found in Chapter 7 of Lee *et al.* (2022).

Appendix 3B: Sharpe Performance Approach to Derive Optimal Weight

In Appendix 3A, we derived the optimal portfolio weight in terms of the minimum-variance approach. In this case, we assume that the investor is only concerned with the risk without considering the return. If the investor is concerned with both return and risk, then the Sharpe performance measure approach can be used to derive the optimal weights, which will be discussed in this appendix.

The solution for the weights of the optimal risky portfolio includes two securities which can be found by solving the following maximization problem:

$$\underset{w_1}{Max}\ S_p = \frac{E(r_p) - r_f}{\sigma_p},$$

where $E(r_p)$ = expected rates of return for portfolio P, r_f = risk free rates of return, S_p = Sharpe performance measure, and σ_p is as defined in Equation (3C.1) of Appendix 3C.

We can solve the maximization problem by differentiating the S_p with respect to w_1, and setting the derivative equal to zero, that is, we can solve Equation (3B.1) and obtain the answer as presented in Equation (3B.2).

$$\frac{\partial S_p}{\partial w_1} = 0. \tag{3B.1}$$

$$w_1 = \frac{[E(r_1) - r_f]\sigma_2^2 - [E(r_2) - r_f]Cov(r_1, r_2)}{\begin{aligned}[E(r_1) - r_f]\sigma_2^2 + [E(r_2) - r_f]\sigma_1^2 - [E(r_1) - r_f \\ + E(r_2) - r_f]Cov(r_1, r_2).\end{aligned}} \tag{3B.2}$$

In this appendix, we discussed the Sharpe Performance Measure approach in terms of two security case. This kind of method can be extended to n securities case. Chiou, Lee, and Chang (2008) have used this approach to investigate whether international diversification is beneficial to investors. In addition, Chapter 7 of Lee *et al.* (2022) has shown this approach in detail.

Appendix 3C: Statistical Analyses, Beta Coefficient, Performance Measures, and Portfolio Analyses

3C.1 *Summary statistics of monthly returns for JNJ, IBM, and S&P 500*

In this appendix, we will use the 5-year monthly stock returns of JNJ, IBM, and S&P 500 index. By using this monthly return data, we can calculate the monthly average returns, monthly standard deviations, monthly skewness, monthly kurtosis, and variance–covariance matrix.

For JNJ's monthly average return, we enter "=AVERAGE (B2:B51)" into the Excel program to get the average return from June 01, 2017 to July 01, 2022. The monthly average return for JNJ is 0.0094. With the same idea, we can calculate monthly average returns for IBM and S&P 500, and the excel program shows 0.0051 and 0.0132, respectively. Based upon the information presented in the following table, we know that JNJ did not perform as well as market, but JNJ performed better than IBM.

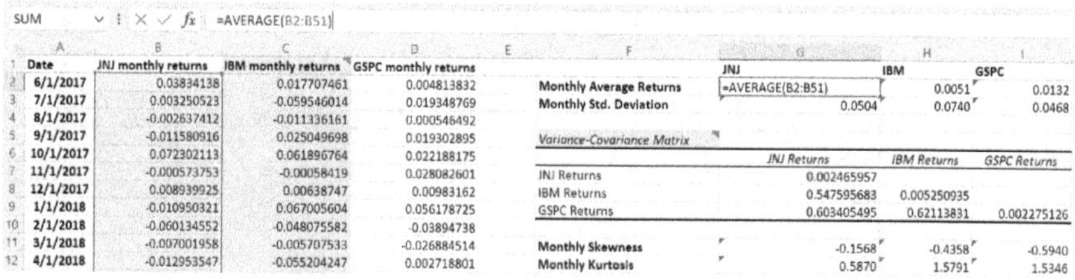

SUM =AVERAGE(B2:B51)

	Date	JNJ monthly returns	IBM monthly returns	GSPC monthly returns
2	6/1/2017	0.03834138	0.017707461	0.004813832
3	7/1/2017	0.003250523	-0.059546014	0.019348769
4	8/1/2017	-0.002637412	-0.011336161	0.000546492
5	9/1/2017	-0.011580916	0.025049698	0.019302895
6	10/1/2017	0.072302113	0.061896764	0.022188175
7	11/1/2017	-0.000573753	-0.00058419	0.028082601
8	12/1/2017	0.008939925	0.00638747	0.00983162
9	1/1/2018	-0.010950321	0.067005604	0.056178725
10	2/1/2018	-0.060134552	-0.048075582	-0.03894738
11	3/1/2018	-0.007001958	-0.005707533	-0.026884514
12	4/1/2018	-0.012953547	-0.055204247	0.002718801

	JNJ	IBM	GSPC
Monthly Average Returns	=AVERAGE(B2:B51)	0.0051	0.0132
Monthly Std. Deviation	0.0504	0.0740	0.0468

Variance-Covariance Matrix

	JNJ Returns	IBM Returns	GSPC Returns
JNJ Returns	0.002465957		
IBM Returns	0.547595683	0.005250935	
GSPC Returns	0.603405495	0.62113831	0.002275126

	JNJ	IBM	GSPC
Monthly Skewness	-0.1568	-0.4358	-0.5940
Monthly Kurtosis	0.5870	1.5791	1.5346

For JNJ's monthly standard deviation, we enter "=STDEV. S(B2:B51)" into the Excel program, and the program shows the standard deviation is 0.0504 from June 01, 2017 to July 01, 2022. Similarly, we can calculate monthly standard deviations for IBM and S&P 500, and the program shows 0.074 and 0.0468, respectively. Based upon the information presented in the following table, we found both JNJ and IBM are risker than the S&P 500 index.

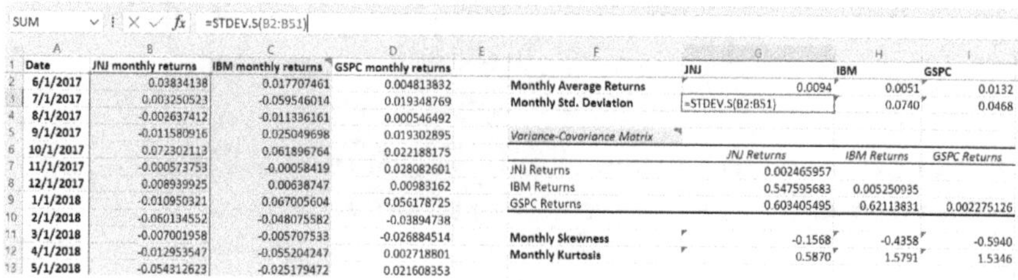

SUM =STDEV.S(B2:B51)

	Date	JNJ monthly returns	IBM monthly returns	GSPC monthly returns
2	6/1/2017	0.03834138	0.017707461	0.004813832
3	7/1/2017	0.003250523	-0.059546014	0.019348769
4	8/1/2017	-0.002637412	-0.011336161	0.000546492
5	9/1/2017	-0.011580916	0.025049698	0.019302895
6	10/1/2017	0.072302113	0.061896764	0.022188175
7	11/1/2017	-0.000573753	-0.00058419	0.028082601
8	12/1/2017	0.008939925	0.00638747	0.00983162
9	1/1/2018	-0.010950321	0.067005604	0.056178725
10	2/1/2018	-0.060134552	-0.048075582	-0.03894738
11	3/1/2018	-0.007001958	-0.005707533	-0.026884514
12	4/1/2018	-0.012953547	-0.055204247	0.002718801
13	5/1/2018	-0.054312623	-0.025179472	0.021608353

	JNJ	IBM	GSPC
Monthly Average Returns	0.0094	0.0051	0.0132
Monthly Std. Deviation	=STDEV.S(B2:B51)	0.0740	0.0468

Variance-Covariance Matrix

	JNJ Returns	IBM Returns	GSPC Returns
JNJ Returns	0.002465957		
IBM Returns	0.547595683	0.005250935	
GSPC Returns	0.603405495	0.62113831	0.002275126

	JNJ	IBM	GSPC
Monthly Skewness	-0.1568	-0.4358	-0.5940
Monthly Kurtosis	0.5870	1.5791	1.5346

For JNJ's monthly skewness, we enter "=SKEW.P(B2:B51)" into the Excel program, and we get JNJ's skewness as −0.1568 as presented in the following table:

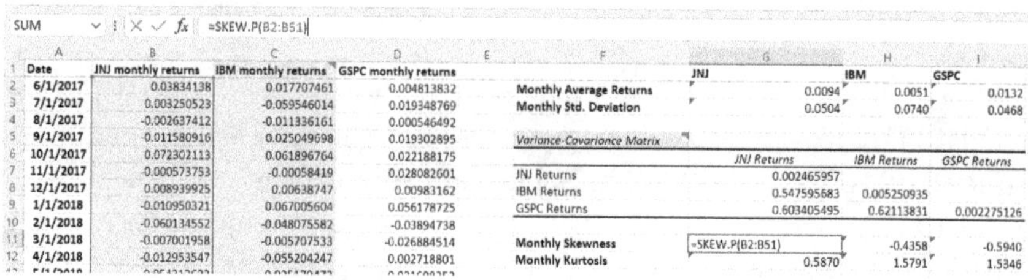

SUM =SKEW.P(B2:B51)

	Date	JNJ monthly returns	IBM monthly returns	GSPC monthly returns
2	6/1/2017	0.03834138	0.017707461	0.004813832
3	7/1/2017	0.003250523	-0.059546014	0.019348769
4	8/1/2017	-0.002637412	-0.011336161	0.000546492
5	9/1/2017	-0.011580916	0.025049698	0.019302895
6	10/1/2017	0.072302113	0.061896764	0.022188175
7	11/1/2017	-0.000573753	-0.00058419	0.028082601
8	12/1/2017	0.008939925	0.00638747	0.00983162
9	1/1/2018	-0.010950321	0.067005604	0.056178725
10	2/1/2018	-0.060134552	-0.048075582	-0.03894738
11	3/1/2018	-0.007001958	-0.005707533	-0.026884514
12	4/1/2018	-0.012953547	-0.055204247	0.002718801

	JNJ	IBM	GSPC
Monthly Average Returns	0.0094	0.0051	0.0132
Monthly Std. Deviation	0.0504	0.0740	0.0468

Variance-Covariance Matrix

	JNJ Returns	IBM Returns	GSPC Returns
JNJ Returns	0.002465957		
IBM Returns	0.547595683	0.005250935	
GSPC Returns	0.603405495	0.62113831	0.002275126

	JNJ	IBM	GSPC
Monthly Skewness	=SKEW.P(B2:B51)	-0.4358	-0.5940
Monthly Kurtosis	0.5870	1.5791	1.5346

Table 3C.1 Summary Statistics of Monthly Returns for JNJ, IBM, and S&P 500

	JNJ	IBM	S&P 500
Monthly Average Returns	0.0094	0.0051	0.0132
Monthly Std. Deviation	0.0504	0.0740	0.0468
Monthly Skewness	−0.1568	−0.4358	−0.5940
Monthly Kurtosis	0.5870	1.5791	1.5346

For JNJ's monthly kurtosis, we enter "=KURT(B2:B51)" into the Excel program, and we get JNJ's kurtosis as 0.5870 as presented in the following table:

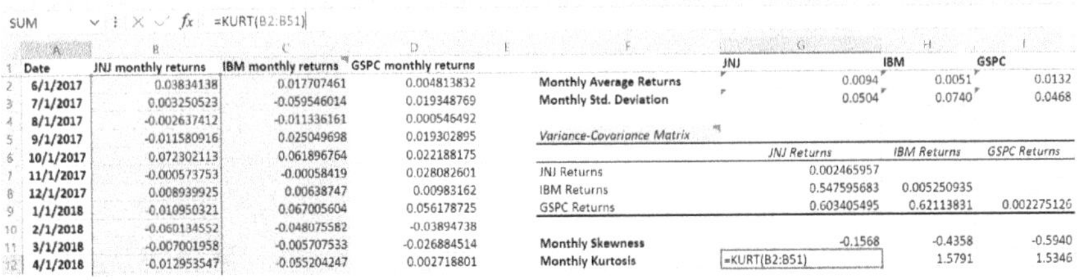

SUM =KURT(B2:B51)

Date	JNJ monthly returns	IBM monthly returns	GSPC monthly returns
6/1/2017	0.03834138	0.017707461	0.004813832
7/1/2017	0.003250523	-0.059546014	0.019348769
8/1/2017	-0.002637412	-0.011336161	0.000546492
9/1/2017	-0.011580916	0.025049698	0.019302895
10/1/2017	0.072302113	0.061896764	0.022188175
11/1/2017	-0.000573753	-0.00058419	0.028082601
12/1/2017	0.008939925	0.00638747	0.00983162
1/1/2018	-0.010950321	0.067005604	0.056178725
2/1/2018	-0.060134552	-0.048075582	-0.03894738
3/1/2018	-0.007001958	-0.005707533	-0.026884514
4/1/2018	-0.012953547	-0.055204247	0.002718801

	JNJ	IBM	GSPC
Monthly Average Returns	0.0094	0.0051	0.0132
Monthly Std. Deviation	0.0504	0.0740	0.0468

Variance-Covariance Matrix

	JNJ Returns	*IBM Returns*	*GSPC Returns*
JNJ Returns	0.002465957		
IBM Returns	0.547595683	0.005250935	
GSPC Returns	0.603405495	0.62113831	0.002275126

	JNJ	IBM	GSPC
Monthly Skewness	-0.1568	-0.4358	-0.5940
Monthly Kurtosis	=KURT(B2:B51)	1.5791	1.5346

Combining all the information presented in the previous four tables, we can obtain the summary statistics for JNJ, IBM, and S&P 500 as shown in Table 3C.1.

3C.2 *Variance–covariance matrix for JNJ, IBM, and S&P 500*

To obtain the variance–covariance matrix, we calculate variance for JNJ, IBM, and S&P 500, and the covariance for JNJ vs. IBM, JNJ vs. S&P 500, and IBM vs. S&P 500. For the variance of JNJ, we enter "=VARP('Stock Returns'!$B$2:$B$63)" into the Excel program, and get JNJ's monthly return variance as 0.002465957 as presented in the following table:

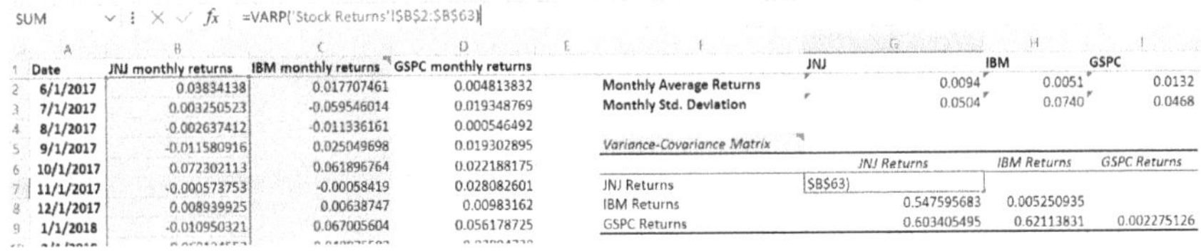

SUM =VARP('Stock Returns'!$B$2:$B$63)

Date	JNJ monthly returns	IBM monthly returns	GSPC monthly returns
6/1/2017	0.03834138	0.017707461	0.004813832
7/1/2017	0.003250523	-0.059546014	0.019348769
8/1/2017	-0.002637412	-0.011336161	0.000546492
9/1/2017	-0.011580916	0.025049698	0.019302895
10/1/2017	0.072302113	0.061896764	0.022188175
11/1/2017	-0.000573753	-0.00058419	0.028082601
12/1/2017	0.008939925	0.00638747	0.00983162
1/1/2018	-0.010950321	0.067005604	0.056178725

	JNJ	IBM	GSPC
Monthly Average Returns	0.0094	0.0051	0.0132
Monthly Std. Deviation	0.0504	0.0740	0.0468

Variance-Covariance Matrix

	JNJ Returns	*IBM Returns*	*GSPC Returns*
JNJ Returns	$B$63)		
IBM Returns	0.547595683	0.005250935	
GSPC Returns	0.603405495	0.62113831	0.002275126

Table 3C.2 Variance–Covariance Matrix

	JNJ Returns	IBM Returns	GSPC Returns
JNJ Returns	0.002465957		
IBM Returns	0.001970476	0.005250935	
GSPC Returns	0.001429239	0.002146888	0.002275126

For the covariance between JNJ and IBM, we enter "=COVARIANCE.P(B2:B63, C2:C63)" into the Excel program, and get the covariance 0.001970476 as indicated in the following table:

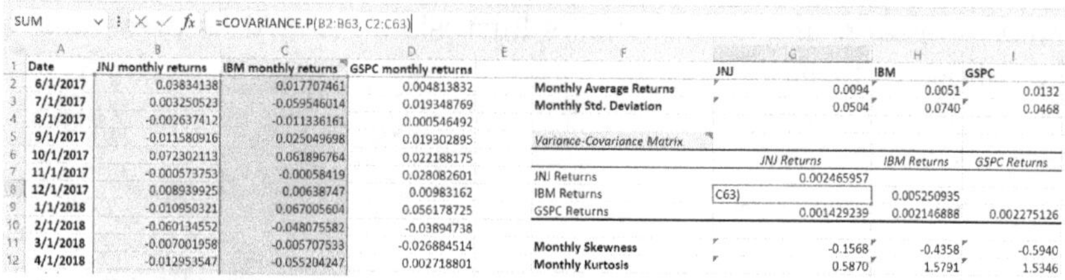

By combing the previous two tables, we obtain the variance–covariance matrix for all JNJ, IBM, and S&P 500 as presented in Table 3C.2. From Table 3C.2, we note that the variances for JNJ, IBM, and S&P 500 are 0.002465957, 0.005250935, and 0.002275126, respectively. In addition, 0.001429239 and 0.002146888 are covariances for JNJ and S&P 500 and IBM and S&P 500, respectively.

3C.3 *Beta coefficient calculations for JNJ and IBM*

Based upon the monthly rates of return that we described previously, we can regress monthly return of JNJ on market rate of return and regress monthly return of IBM on market rate of return. In the Excel program, we select "Data" and then click on "Data Analysis." Under data analysis, we choose "Regression" and click "OK"; we obtained the following table:

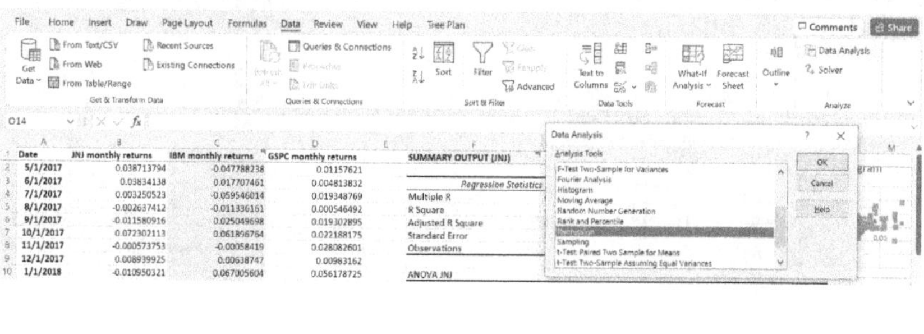

In "Regression," we select JNJ monthly returns in the "Input Y Range," and then S&P 500 monthly returns in the "Input X Range." Similarly, we put market index in the X variable, and company data in the Y variable. We obtain another output from the Excel program.

Date	JNJ monthly returns	IBM monthly returns	GSPC monthly returns
5/1/2017	0.038713794	-0.047788238	0.01157621
6/1/2017	0.03834138	0.017707461	0.004813832
7/1/2017	0.003250523	-0.059546014	0.019348769
8/1/2017	-0.002637412	-0.011336161	0.000546492
9/1/2017	-0.011580916	0.025049698	0.019302895
10/1/2017	0.072302113	0.061896764	0.022188175
11/1/2017	-0.000573753	-0.00058419	0.028082601
12/1/2017	0.008939925	0.00638747	0.00983162
1/1/2018	-0.010950321	0.067005604	0.056178725
2/1/2018	-0.060134552	-0.048075582	-0.03894738
3/1/2018	-0.007001958	-0.005707533	-0.026884514
4/1/2018	-0.012953547	-0.055204247	0.002718801
5/1/2018	-0.054312623	-0.025179472	0.021608353
6/1/2018	0.021902033	-0.000418878	0.0048424
7/1/2018	0.092137914	0.037437137	0.036021586
8/1/2018	0.016374824	0.010695079	0.030263219
9/1/2018	0.032673447	0.043443698	0.004294301
10/1/2018	0.013172191	-0.236624528	-0.069403359
11/1/2018	0.049360605	0.076583187	0.017859382
12/1/2018	-0.115916885	-0.073648248	-0.091776956
1/1/2019	0.031228377	0.182546091	0.078684405

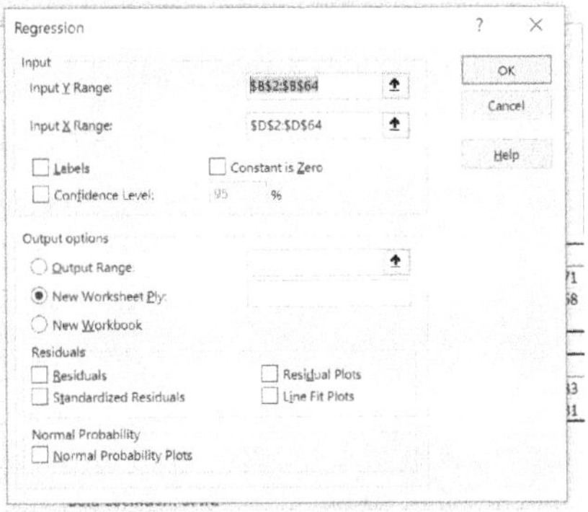

After clicking "OK," the Excel program will provide a new sheet and show the regression results for running the regression on JNJ and S&P 500. We can find that the alpha value in this regression is 0.003465096 and the beta is 0.628772176.

SUMMARY OUTPUT

Regression Statistics	
Multiple R	0.602202
R Square	0.362647
Adjusted F	0.352199
Standard I	0.040085
Observatic	63

ANOVA

	df	*SS*	*MS*	*F*	*gnificance F*
Regressior	1	0.055771	0.055771	34.70839	1.78E-07
Residual	61	0.098018	0.001607		
Total	62	0.153789			

	Coefficients	*andard Err*	*t Stat*	*P-value*	*Lower 95%*	*Upper 95%*	*ower 95.0%*	*pper 95.0%*
Intercept	0.003465	0.005136	0.674688	0.502423	-0.0068	0.013735	-0.0068	0.013735
X Variable	0.628772	0.106727	5.891383	1.78E-07	0.415357	0.842187	0.415357	0.842187

Table 3C.3 presents both regression intercepts and slopes of JNJ and IBM.

Table 3C.3 Alphas and Betas for JNJ and IBM

	JNJ	IBM
Regression Intercept (Alpha)	0.003465096	−0.004653991
Regression Slope (Beta)	0.628772176	0.942533144

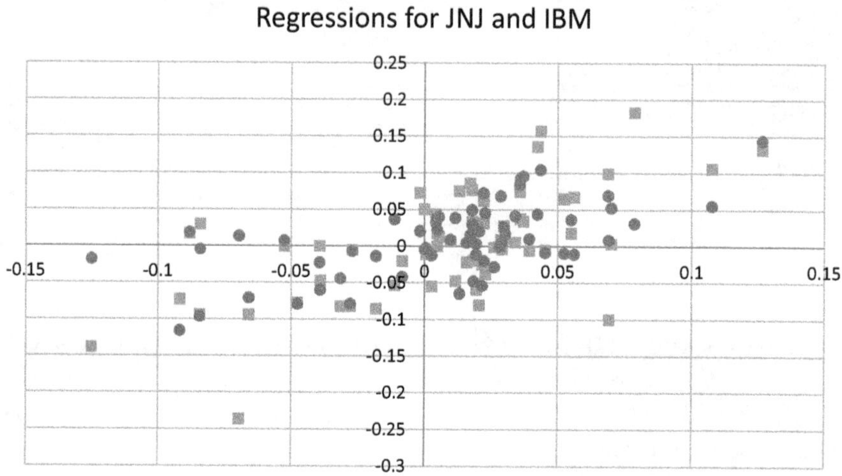

Figure 3C.1 Regressions for JNJ and IBM

Figure 3C.1 shows the regression scatter diagram for both JNJ and IBM. The filled square box presents IBM's regression and the filled circle presents JNJ's regression. Because the regression slope for IBM is 0.943, which is larger than JNJ's slope 0.629, the scatter diagram line for IBM is steeper than JNJ.

3C.4 *Sharpe, Treynor, and Jensen performance measures*

By using the monthly rates of return of Johnson & Johnson, IBM, and S&P 500, we estimate Sharpe performance, Treynor performance, and Jensen performance measures. To estimate these performance measures, we assume that the monthly risk-free rate is 0.0025.

For the Sharpe performance measure, we enter "=(G2-$G$15)/G3" into the Excel program. Then, we get the Sharpe performance measure as 0.1375 for JNJ. Similarly, we get the Sharpe performance measures for IBM and S&P 500.

SUM f_x =(G2-$G$15)/G3

	A	B	C	D
1	**Date**	**JNJ monthly returns**	**IBM monthly returns**	**GSPC monthly returns**
2	**6/1/2017**	0.03834138	0.017707461	0.004813832
3	**7/1/2017**	0.003250523	-0.059546014	0.019348769
4	**8/1/2017**	-0.002637412	-0.011336161	0.000546492
5	**9/1/2017**	-0.011580916	0.025049698	0.019302895
6	**10/1/2017**	0.072302113	0.061896764	0.022188175
7	**11/1/2017**	-0.000573753	-0.00058419	0.028082601
8	**12/1/2017**	0.008939925	0.00638747	0.00983162
9	**1/1/2018**	-0.010950321	0.067005604	0.056178725
10	**2/1/2018**	-0.060134552	-0.048075582	-0.03894738
11	**3/1/2018**	-0.007001958	-0.005707533	-0.026884514
12	**4/1/2018**	-0.012953547	-0.055204247	0.002718801
13	**5/1/2018**	-0.054312623	-0.025179472	0.021608353
14	**6/1/2018**	0.021902033	-0.000418878	0.0048424
15	**7/1/2018**	0.092137914	0.037437137	0.036021586
16	**8/1/2018**	0.016374824	0.010695079	0.030263219
17	**9/1/2018**	0.032673447	0.043443698	0.004294301
18	**10/1/2018**	0.013172191	-0.236624528	-0.069403359
19	**11/1/2018**	0.049360605	0.076583187	0.017859382
20	**12/1/2018**	-0.115916885	-0.073648248	-0.091776956
21	**1/1/2019**	0.031228377	0.182546091	0.078684405
22	**2/1/2019**	0.02675068	0.027600121	0.02972893
23	**3/1/2019**	0.029838359	0.033403017	0.017924288

F	G	H	I
	JNJ	**IBM**	**GSPC**
Monthly Average Returns	0.0094	0.0051	0.0132
Monthly Std. Deviation	0.0504	0.0740	0.0468
Variance-Covariance Matrix			
	JNJ Returns	*IBM Returns*	*GSPC Returns*
JNJ Returns	0.002465957		
IBM Returns	0.001970476	0.005250935	
GSPC Returns	0.001429239	0.002146888	0.002275126
Monthly Skewness	-0.1568	-0.4358	-0.5940
Monthly Kurtosis	0.5870	1.5791	1.5346
Coefficient Variantion	5.3428	14.5001	3.5548
Monthly Risk Free Rate	0.00250		
Performance Measure			
Sharpe Performance Measure	=(G2-$G$15)/G3	0.0352	0.2279
Treynor Performance Measure	0.011	0.003	0.011
Beta	0.629	0.943	1
Jensen Performance Measure	0.000	-0.007	0.000

For the Treynor performance measure, we need to obtain the regression coefficient, which is the beta value for JNJ. In the previous session, we got the regression betas for JNJ as 0.629 and IBM as 0.943. Thus, we enter the values in the G21 and G22 cells in the Excel sheet. Next, we enter "=(G2-$G$15)/G21" to calculate the Treynor performance measure for JNJ. Then, we obtain the Treynor performance measure as 0.011 for JNJ. We can apply the same idea to get the Treynor performance measures for IBM and S&P 500. The beta value for S&P 500 is assumed to be 1.

SUM f_x =(G2-$G$15)/G21

	A	B	C	D
1	**Date**	**JNJ monthly returns**	**IBM monthly returns**	**GSPC monthly returns**
2	**6/1/2017**	0.03834138	0.017707461	0.004813832
3	**7/1/2017**	0.003250523	-0.059546014	0.019348769
4	**8/1/2017**	-0.002637412	-0.011336161	0.000546492
5	**9/1/2017**	-0.011580916	0.025049698	0.019302895
6	**10/1/2017**	0.072302113	0.061896764	0.022188175
7	**11/1/2017**	-0.000573753	-0.00058419	0.028082601
8	**12/1/2017**	0.008939925	0.00638747	0.00983162
9	**1/1/2018**	-0.010950321	0.067005604	0.056178725
10	**2/1/2018**	-0.060134552	-0.048075582	-0.03894738
11	**3/1/2018**	-0.007001958	-0.005707533	-0.026884514
12	**4/1/2018**	-0.012953547	-0.055204247	0.002718801
13	**5/1/2018**	-0.054312623	-0.025179472	0.021608353
14	**6/1/2018**	0.021902033	-0.000418878	0.0048424
15	**7/1/2018**	0.092137914	0.037437137	0.036021586
16	**8/1/2018**	0.016374824	0.010695079	0.030263219
17	**9/1/2018**	0.032673447	0.043443698	0.004294301
18	**10/1/2018**	0.013172191	-0.236624528	-0.069403359
19	**11/1/2018**	0.049360605	0.076583187	0.017859382
20	**12/1/2018**	-0.115916885	-0.073648248	-0.091776956
21	**1/1/2019**	0.031228377	0.182546091	0.078684405
22	**2/1/2019**	0.02675068	0.027600121	0.02972893
23	**3/1/2019**	0.029838359	0.033403017	0.017924288

F	G	H	I
	JNJ	**IBM**	**GSPC**
Monthly Average Returns	0.0094	0.0051	0.0132
Monthly Std. Deviation	0.0504	0.0740	0.0468
Variance-Covariance Matrix			
	JNJ Returns	*IBM Returns*	*GSPC Returns*
JNJ Returns	0.002465957		
IBM Returns	0.001970476	0.005250935	
GSPC Returns	0.001429239	0.002146888	0.002275126
Monthly Skewness	-0.1568	-0.4358	-0.5940
Monthly Kurtosis	0.5870	1.5791	1.5346
Coefficient Variantion	5.3428	14.5001	3.5548
Monthly Risk Free Rate	0.00250		
Performance Measure			
Sharpe Performance Measure	0.1375	0.0352	0.2279
Treynor Performance Measure	=(G2-$G$15)/G21	0.003	0.011
Beta	0.629	0.943	1
Jensen Performance Measure	0.000	-0.007	0.000

Table 3C.4 Performance Measures*

	JNJ	IBM	S&P 500
Sharpe Performance Measure	0.1375	0.0352	0.2279
Treynor Performance Measure	0.011	0.003	0.011
Jensen Performance Measure	0.000	−0.007	0.000

Note: *We assume that the monthly risk-free rate is 0.0025 to calculate this performance measure.

For the Jensen performance measure, we enter "=(G2-$G$15)-G21*($I$2-$G$15)" in the Excel program. Then, we obtain the Jensen performance measure as 0.000 for JNJ. We can apply the same idea to get the Jensen performance measures for IBM and S&P 500.

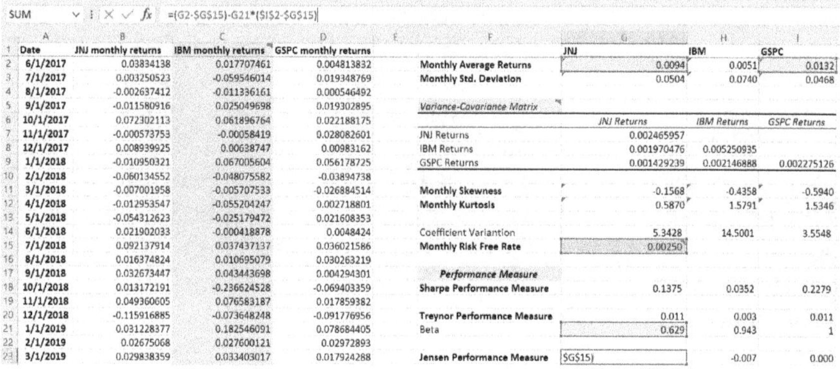
SUM =(G2-$G$15)-G21*($I$2-$G$15)

	A	B	C	D	F	G	H	I
1	Date	JNJ monthly returns	IBM monthly returns	GSPC monthly returns		JNJ	IBM	GSPC
2	6/1/2017	0.03834138	0.017707461	0.004813832	Monthly Average Returns	0.0094	0.0051	0.0132
3	7/1/2017	0.003250523	-0.059546014	0.019348769	Monthly Std. Deviation	0.0504	0.0740	0.0468
4	8/1/2017	-0.002637412	-0.011336161	0.000546492				
5	9/1/2017	-0.011580916	0.025049698	0.019302895	Variance-Covariance Matrix			
6	10/1/2017	0.072302113	0.061896764	0.022188175		JNJ Returns	IBM Returns	GSPC Returns
7	11/1/2017	-0.000573753	-0.00058419	0.028082601	JNJ Returns	0.002465957		
8	12/1/2017	0.008939925	0.00638747	0.00983162	IBM Returns	0.001970476	0.005250935	
9	1/1/2018	-0.010950321	0.067005604	0.056178725	GSPC Returns	0.001429239	0.002146888	0.002275126
10	2/1/2018	-0.060134552	-0.048075582	-0.03894738				
11	3/1/2018	-0.007001958	-0.005707533	-0.026884514	Monthly Skewness	-0.1568	-0.4358	-0.5940
12	4/1/2018	-0.012953547	-0.055204247	0.002718801	Monthly Kurtosis	0.5870	1.5791	1.5346
13	5/1/2018	-0.054312623	-0.025179472	0.021608353				
14	6/1/2018	0.021902033	-0.000418878	0.0048424	Coefficient Variantion	5.3428	14.5001	3.5548
15	7/1/2018	0.092137914	0.037437137	0.036021586	Monthly Risk Free Rate	0.00250		
16	8/1/2018	0.016374824	0.010695079	0.030263219				
17	9/1/2018	0.032673447	0.043443698	0.004294301	Performance Measure			
18	10/1/2018	0.013172191	-0.236624528	-0.069403359	Sharpe Performance Measure	0.1375	0.0352	0.2279
19	11/1/2018	0.049360605	0.076583187	0.017859382				
20	12/1/2018	-0.115916885	-0.073648248	-0.091776956	Treynor Performance Measure	0.011	0.003	0.011
21	1/1/2019	0.031228377	0.182546091	0.078684405	Beta	0.629	0.943	1
22	2/1/2019	0.02675068	0.027600121	0.02972893				
23	3/1/2019	0.029838359	0.033403017	0.017924288	Jensen Performance Measure	$G$15)	-0.007	0.000

The empirical results for all performance measures are presented in Table 3C.4.

3C.5 *Calculation of the optimal portfolio weights*

3C.5.1 *Optimal weights in terms of variance minimization*

For the approach of variance minimization, we use the following formulas. All the input variables are already obtained from previous sessions.

$$W_A = \frac{\sigma_B^2 - Cov(R_A, R_B)}{\sigma_A^2 + \sigma_B^2 - Cov(R_A, R_B)},$$

$$W_B = 1 - W_A,$$

where W_A = represents JNJ and W_B = represents IBM in our example, σ_A^2 = JNJ's monthly returns' variance, σ_B^2 = IBM's monthly returns' variance, and $Cov(R_A, R_B)$ = covariance between JNJ and IBM's monthly returns.

By applying the formula in the Excel program, we enter "=(B9-B10)/(B8+B9-B10)" to calculate the variance minimization for JNJ. Excel shows the number is 0.571.

SUM fx =(B5-B6)/(B4+B5-B6)

	A	B	C	D	E	F
1	**Variance Minimization**				**Sharpe Performance Maximization**	
2						
3	**Input**				**Input**	
4	Variance_A (JNJ)	0.0025			ExcessReturns_1 (JNJ)	0.0069
5	Variance_B (IBM)	0.0053			ExcessReturns_2 (IBM)	0.0026
6	Covariance	0.0020			Variance_1	0.0025
7					Variance_2	0.0053
8	**Output**				Covariance	0.0020
9	W_A (JNJ)	B4+B5-B6)				
10	W_B (IBM)	0.42913			**Output**	
11					W_1 (JNJ)	1.301331
12					W_2 (IBM)	-0.30133

3C.5.2 *Optimal weights in terms of Sharpe performance measure maximization*

For the approach of Sharpe performance measure maximization, we follow the following formulas. And the excess returns are defined as the difference between the average monthly return and the monthly risk-free return.

$$W_1 = \frac{[E(R_1) - R_f]\sigma_2^2 - [E(R_2) - R_f]\, Cov(R_1, R_2)}{[E(R_1) - R_f]\sigma_2^2 + [E(R_2) - R_f]\sigma_1^2 - [E(R_1) - R_f + E(R_2) - R_f]\, Cov(1)},$$

$$W_2 = 1 - W_1,$$

where W_1 represents JNJ and W_2 represents IBM in our example, σ_1^2 = JNJ's monthly returns' variance, σ_2^2 = IBM's monthly returns' variance, $E(R_1)$ = monthly average return of JNJ, $E(R_2)$ = monthly average return of IBM, R_f = monthly average returns of S&P 500, and $Cov(R_1, R_2)$ = covariance between JNJ and IBM's monthly returns.

By applying the formula in the Excel program, we first calculate the excess returns for JNJ and IBM, which are the companies' monthly average returns minus market average return (S&P 500 in this case).

SUM fx ='Stock Returns'!G2-'Stock Returns'!G15

	A	B	C	D	E	F	G	H	I
1	**Variance Minimization**				**Sharpe Performance Maximization**				
2									
3	**Input**				**Input**				
4	Variance_A (JNJ)	0.0025			ExcessReturns_1 (JNJ)	='Stock Returns'!G2-'Stock Returns'!G15			
5	Variance_B (IBM)	0.0053			ExcessReturns_2 (IBM)	0.0026			
6	Covariance	0.0020			Variance_1	0.0025			
7					Variance_2	0.0053			
8	**Output**				Covariance	0.0020			
9	W_A (JNJ)	0.57087							
10	W_B (IBM)	0.42913			**Output**				
11					W_1 (JNJ)	1.301331			
12					W_2 (IBM)	-0.30133			

Next, we enter "=(F8*F11-F9*F12)/(F8*F11+F9*F10-(F8+F9)*F12)" to calculate the Sharpe Performance Maximization for JNJ. Excel shows the number is 1.301.

SUM fx =(F4*F7-F5*F8)/(F4*F7+F5*F6-(F4+F5)*F8)

	A	B	C	D	E	F
1	**Variance Minimization**				**Sharpe Performance Maximization**	
2						
3	**Input**				**Input**	
4	Variance_A (JNJ)	0.0025			ExcessReturns_1 (JNJ)	0.0069
5	Variance_B (IBM)	0.0053			ExcessReturns_2 (IBM)	0.0026
6	Covariance	0.0020			Variance_1	0.0025
7					Variance_2	0.0053
8	**Output**				Covariance	0.0020
9	W_A (JNJ)	0.57087				
10	W_B (IBM)	0.42913			**Output**	
11					W_1 (JNJ)	F5)*F8)
12					W_2 (IBM)	-0.30133

Table 3C.5 Variance Minimization and Sharpe Performance Maximization

	Variance Minimization		Sharpe Performance Maximization	
Inputs	Variance_A (JNJ)	0.0025	ExcessReturns_1 (JNJ)	0.0069
	Variance_B (IBM)	0.0053	ExcessReturns_2 (IBM)	0.0026
	Covariance	0.0020	Variance_1	0.0025
			Variance_2	0.0053
			Covariance	0.0020
Output	**W_A (JNJ)**	**0.5701**	**W_1 (JNJ)**	**1.301**
	W_B (IBM)	**0.429**	**W_2 (IBM)**	**−0.301**

Table 3C.5 shows the overall results for both JNJ and IBM.

Part II

Forwards and Futures

Chapter 4

Futures Valuation and Hedging

Contents

4.1 Introduction

A basic assumption of finance theory is that investors are risk averse. If we equate risk with uncertainty, can we question the validity of this assumption? What evidence is there?

As living, functional proof of the appropriateness of the risk aversion assumption, there exist entire markets whose sole underlying purpose is to allow investors to display their uncertainties about the future. These particular markets, which primarily focus on the future, are called just that, **futures markets**. These markets allow for the transfer of risk from hedgers (risk-averse individuals) to speculators (risk-seeking individuals), a key element necessary for the existence of futures markets is the balance between the number of hedgers and speculators who are willing to transfer and accept risk.

A **future contract** is a standardized legal agreement between a buyer and a seller, who promise now to exchange a specified amount of money for goods or services at a future time. Of course, there is nothing really unusual about a contract made in advance of delivery. For instance, whenever something is ordered rather than purchased on the spot, a futures (or forward) contract is involved. Although the price is determined at the time of the order, the actual exchange of cash for the merchandise takes place later. For some items, the lag is a few days, while for others (such as a car) it may be months. Moreover, a futures contract imparts a legal obligation to both parties of the contract to fulfill the specifications. To guarantee fulfillment of this obligation, a "good-faith" deposit, also called **margin**, may be required from the buyer (and the seller, if he or she does not already own the product).

To ensure consistency in the contracts and to help develop liquidity, futures exchanges have been established. These exchanges provide a central location and a standardized set of rules in order to enhance the credibility of these markets and thus generate an orderly, liquid arena for the price determination of individual commodities at distinct points in the future.

A substantial increase in the number of types of futures contracts offered by the exchanges has been occurring over the last decade. At the same time, the growth in futures trading volume has been phenomenal. Two explanations can be offered for this increase in futures activity. These increases can be intuitively correlated with the growing levels of uncertainty in many facets of the economic environment — for example, inflation and interest rates. A second view is based on the argument that even though the world has not become any more uncertain, the increased integration of financial and real markets has increased the risk exposure of any given individual. The tremendous growth in the home mortgage and consumer debt financial markets has allowed the purchase of more and more expensive and real assets. This increase in the rise of individual financial leverage has increased individual exposure to interest rate fluctuations, thereby increasing the requirements for risk-sharing across markets or between individuals with varied portfolios. Futures markets have the potential to help people manage or transfer the uncertainties that plague the world today.

This chapter examines the basic types of futures contracts offered and the functioning of futures markets. In addition, the uses of financial and index futures are illustrated, and the theoretical pricing concepts related to these financial instruments are discussed. The important terms associated with futures contracts and futures markets are defined and the futures market is compared to the forward market. An analysis of futures market follows. A theory of valuation is introduced, and the chapter closes with a discussion of various hedging strategies and concepts.

Section 4.2 discusses the differences between futures and forward markets, and Section 4.3 gives an overview of futures markets. Section 4.4 provides the components and mechanics of futures markets, where Section 4.5 covers the valuation of futures contracts. In Section 4.6, hedging concepts and strategies are introduced. A summary is given in Section 4.7, discussing the key information from this chapter. Appendix 4A discusses basic futures terminology, and Appendix 4B covers the derivation of the minimum-variance hedge ratio. Finally, Appendix 4C discusses single-stock futures (SSF) and their specific valuation.

4.2 Futures versus Forward Markets

While futures and forward contracts are similar in many respects, their differences are more important to fully understanding the nature and uses of these financial instruments. Both futures and forward contracts specify a transaction to take place at a future date and include precise requirements for the commodity to be delivered, its price, its quantity, the delivery date, and the delivery point. Nevertheless, these two types of contracts for future delivery of a commodity and the markets in which they are traded differ in a number of significant ways, some of which are included in Table 4.1.

Although most people are unlikely ever to become involved in the forward market, it is important to understand some of its attributes, particularly as a good deal of the literature on pricing futures contracts typically refers to these two contracts interchangeably.

Table 4.1 A Comparison of Futures and Forward Markets

Futures Market	Forward Market
1. Trading is conducted in a competitive arena by "open outcry" of bids, offers, and amounts.	1. Trading is done by telex or telephone, with participants generally dealing directly with broker-dealers.
2. Contract terms are standardized with all buyers and sellers negotiating only with respect to price.	2. All contract terms are negotiated privately by the parties.
3. Nonmember participants deal through brokers (exchange members) who represent them on the exchange floor.	3. Participants deal typically on a principal-to-principal basis.
4. Participants include banks, corporations, financial institutions, individual investors, and speculators.	4. Participants are primarily institutions dealing with one other and other interested parties dealing through one or more dealers.
5. The clearinghouse of the exchange becomes the opposite side to each cleared transaction; therefore, the credit risk for a futures-market participant is always the same and there is no need to analyze the credit of other market participants.	5. A participant must examine the credit risk and establish credit limits for each opposite party.
6. Margin deposits are to be required of all participants.	6. Typically, no money changes hands until delivery, although a small margin deposit might be required of nondealer customers on certain occasions.
7. Settlements are made daily through the exchange clearinghouse. Gains on open positions may be withdrawn, and losses are collected daily.	7. Settlement occurs on date agreed upon between the parties to each transaction.
8. Long and short positions are usually liquidated easily.	8. Forward positions are not as easily offset or transferred to other participants.
9. Settlements are normally made in cash, with only a small percentage of all contracts resulting in actual delivery.	9. Most transactions result in delivery.
10. A single, round-trip (in and out of the market) commission is charged. It is negotiated between broker and customer and is relatively small in relation to the value of the contract. Commissions range from \$18 to over \$100 per round-turn.	10. No commission is typically charged if the transaction is made directly with another dealer. A commission is charged to both buyer and seller, however, if transacted through a broker.
11. Trading is regulated by the exchange and by a federal agency, the Commodity Futures Trading Commission (CFTC).	11. Trading is mostly unregulated.
12. The delivery price is the spot price.	12. The delivery price is the forward price.

Specifically, it might be inferred from Table 4.1 that differences resulting from liquidity, credit risk, search, margin, taxes, and commissions could cause futures and forward contracts not to be priced identically. Some of the major users of forward contracts include the following:

1. *Public utilities*: Public utilities sometimes engage in fairly long-term perpetual forward contracts for the delivery of coal or natural gas.
2. *Savings-and-loan associations*: A typical thrift institution might contract to deliver a pool of mortgages to another thrift in ninety days.
3. *Apparel or toy manufacturers*: Stores often contract for the delivery of the "new fall line" in early spring.
4. *Import–export businesses*: A U.S. exporter may contract for the delivery of a foreign currency in sixty days, after it receives payment in the foreign currency for goods sold overseas.

4.3 Futures Markets: Overview

In the most general sense, the term **commodity futures** is taken to embrace all existing futures contracts. Nevertheless, for purposes of clarity and classification, its meaning here is restricted to a limited segment of the total futures markets. Accordingly, futures contracts can be classified into three main types:

1. Commodity futures,
2. Financial futures, and
3. Index futures.

Within this classification, commodity futures include all agriculturally related futures contracts with underlying assets, such as corn, wheat, rye, barley, rice, oats, sugar, coffee, soybeans, frozen orange juice, pork bellies, live cattle, hogs, and lumber. Also within the commodity futures framework are futures contracts written on precious metals, such as gold, silver, copper, platinum, and palladium, and contracts written on petroleum products, including gasoline, crude oil, and heating oil. Many of the futures contracts on metals and petroleum products have been introduced as recently as the early 1980s.

Producers, refineries, and distributors, to name only a few potential users, employ futures contracts to assure a particular price or supply — or both — for the underlying commodity at a future date.

Futures market participants are divided into two broad classes: hedgers and speculators. **Hedging** refers to a futures market transaction made as a temporary substitute for a cash market transaction to be made at a later date. The purpose of hedging is to take advantage of current prices by using futures transactions. For example, banks and corporations can be hedgers when they use futures to fix future borrowing and lending rates.

Futures market **speculation** involves taking a short or long futures position solely to profit from price changes. If you think that interest rates will rise because of an increase in inflation, you can sell T-bill futures and make a profit if interest rates do rise and the value of T-bills falls. Sample Problem 4.1 provides further illustration.

Sample Problem 4.1

An investor has a portfolio of T-bills with a face value of $1 million, currently worth $950,000 in the cash market. A futures contract with a face value of $1,000,000 worth of T-bills is currently selling for $95\frac{16}{32}$ per hundred dollars. Interest rates rise and the value of the T-bills falls to $946.875, while the value of the T-bill futures contract falls to $95\frac{6}{32}$ per hundred dollars. If the investor were to hedge the T-bill position with T-bill futures, what would be the net result of this interest rate change on the value of the hedged position? If the investor were to speculate that interest rates would fall, what is the next effect of the portfolio value?

Solution

Tables 4.2 and 4.3 show the results of hedging and speculative positions, respectively. Table 4.2 presents how $950,000 T-bills in cash markets can be hedged by selling ten futures contracts worth $955,000 in period t. In period $t + 1$, the T-bill value loses $3,125. However, the futures contract value goes up by $3,125. Therefore, the net value change of the hedged portfolio is equal to zero.

Table 4.3 shows the speculative position for an investor of a $950,000 T-bill in cash markets. Instead of selling futures contracts

Table 4.2 Hedged Position for Sample Problem 4.1

Time	T-Bill Value in Cash Market	Time	Futures Value	
t	\$950,000	t	Sell ten T-bill contracts at $95\frac{16}{32}$ (1,000,000 × 0.955).	\$955.000
$t+1$	\$946,875	$t+1$	Buy ten T-bill contracts at $95\frac{6}{32}$ (1,000,000 × 0.951875).	\$951,875
Loss in cash market	−\$3,125		Gain on short position in futures	+\$3,125
Net change in value of hedged portfolio = \$0				

Table 4.3 Speculative Position for Sample Problem 4.1

Time	T-Bill Value in Cash Market	Time	Futures Value	
t	\$950,000	t	Buy ten T-bill contracts at $95\frac{16}{32}$ (1,000,000 × 0.955).	\$955.000
$t+1$	\$946,875	$t+1$	Sell ten T-bill contracts at $95\frac{6}{32}$ (1,000,000 × 0.951875).	\$951,875
Loss in cash market	−\$3,125		Loss on sale	−\$3,125
Net change in value of unhedged portfolio plus speculation loss = \$6,250				

to hedge the T-bill, the investor buys \$955,000 T-bill futures contracts in period t. In period $t + 1$, this investor loses \$3,125 in cash markets, and also loses \$3,125 in futures markets. In this situation, the net value change in the unhedged portfolio is a loss of \$6,250.

Financial futures are a trading medium initiated with the introduction of contracts on foreign currencies at the International Monetary Market (IMM) in 1972. In addition to future on foreign currencies, financial futures include contracts based on Treasury bonds (T-bonds), Treasury bills (T-bills), Treasury notes (T-notes), bank certificates of deposit, Eurodollars, and GNMA mortgage securities. These latter types of financial futures contracts are also referred to as *interest rate futures* since their underlying asset is an interest-bearing security. While foreign currency futures arose with the abolition of the Bretton Woods fixed exchange rate system during the early 1970s, interest rate futures surged in popularity and number following the change in U.S. monetary policy in October 1979. The effect of the Federal Open Market Committee's decision to deemphasize the traditional practice of "pegging" interest rates was to greatly increase the volatility of market interest rates. Thus, interest rate changes have become a highly prominent risk to corporations, investors, and financial institutions. (Figures 4.1(a) and 4.1(b) exhibit the changing volatility of T-bill prices and rates of return from 1990 to 2021.)

Index futures represent the newest and boldest innovation in the futures market to date. An index futures contract is one for which the underlying asset is actually a portfolio of assets — for example, the Major Market Index (MMI) includes twenty stocks traded on the NYSE and the S&P index includes the five hundred stocks of the S&P index. Contracts on more diverse types of indexes include a high-quality bond index, an interest rate index composed of interest-bearing market securities, and the consumer price index.

The S&P 500 index, requiring delivery of the five hundred stocks constituting the S&P 500 stock index, would certainly have dampened enthusiasm for this and similar index contracts. Because of this, an index futures contract is settled on the basis of its cash value when the contract matures. The cash value of the contract is equal to the closing index value on its last trading day times a dollar amount of \$500.

Many portfolio managers are taking advantage of index futures to alter their portfolios risk–return distributions. Some applications that have arisen are discussed later in this chapter.

4.4 Components and Mechanics of Futures Markets

This section discusses components and mechanics of futures markets: the exchanges, the clearinghouse, margin, order execution, and T-bill futures transactions.

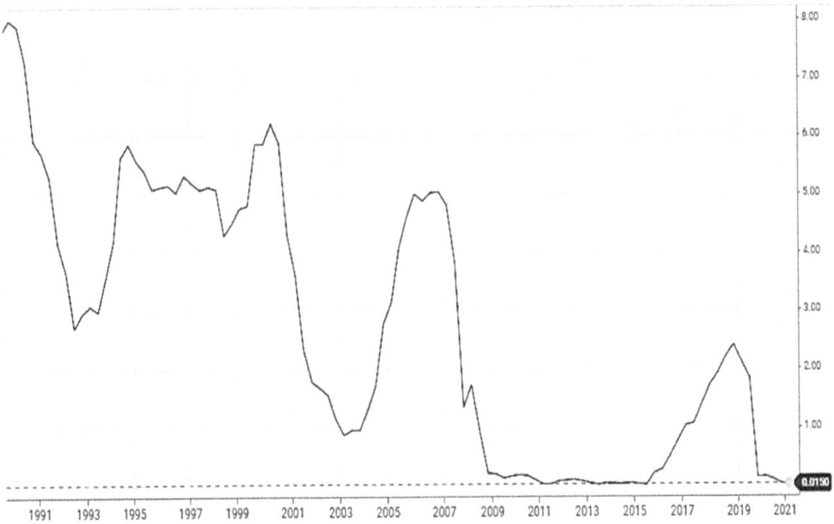

(a)

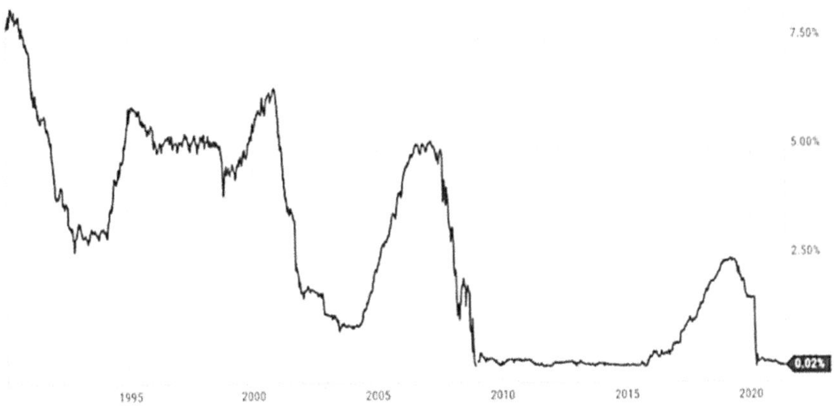

(b)

Figure 4.1 (a) Monthly Prices of Three-Month T-Bill (1990–2021). (b) Monthly Three-Month T-Bill Returns (1990–2021)

Source: (a) CNBC Market Quotes. https://www.cnbc.com/quotes/US3M. (b) YCharts Economic Indicators. https://ycharts.com/indicators/3_month_treasury_rate/.

4.4.1 *The exchanges*

A **futures exchange**, just like a stock exchange, is the arena for the actual daily trading of futures contracts. The exchange is a non-profit organization whose members include those allowed to trade on its floor. Members include individual traders, brokerage firms, and other types of institutions. The exchange's governing rules and procedures are determined by its members, who serve on various policy committees and elect the officers of the exchange.

The fees paid by an exchange's members support not only the daily operation of its trading venue but also other functions and services performed by staff members for the exchange, such as research, public relations, presentations and seminars for users, lobbying of government, and planning for the exchange's future.

Another term for an exchange membership is a seat. A prospective member may buy a full seat, allowing him or her to trade any of the offered futures contracts. To encourage volume on newer or less liquid contracts, most exchanges usually also offer a partial seat, permitting its owner to trade only a designated number of contracts. Usually, to get onto an exchange to trade, an investor needs to buy or lease a seat from a current owner. The value of an exchange seat can vary substantially; for example, the high and low prices for a full seat on the IMM exchange range from \$300,000 to \$100,000, respectively. Such exchanges are entrusted with clearinghouse responsibilities that are vital to the efficient operation of the futures market.

4.4.2 *The clearinghouse*

Central to the operation of organized futures markets is the **clearinghouse** or clearing corporation for the exchange. Whenever someone enters a position in a futures contract on the long or short side, the clearinghouse always takes the opposite side of the contract. That is, it becomes a buyer to every seller and a seller to every buyer. The advantages of having a central organization providing this role are threefold:

1. The clearinghouse eliminates concern over the creditworthiness of the party on the other side of the transaction.
2. It frees the original trading partners from the obligation of delivery or offset with each other.
3. It provides greater flexibility in opening or closing a position.

For example, if an investor originally bought a T-bill futures contract in January that matures in March, but in February desired to liquidate his position by selling the same contract at the current market price, he would not have to find the original seller of the contract. Instead, he need only call up his broker with instructions to place an order to sell at the market price in the trading pit, allowing any other trader to buy the contract. On the other hand, if the investor decided to hold his T-bill futures contract to its March expiration and take delivery of the $1,000,000 of thirteen-week T-bills that the contract calls for, he would not need to locate the original seller of the contract. Rather, he need only notify the exchange's clearinghouse of his intentions; upon the contract's expiration, the clearinghouse would randomly select someone with an open short position in the same contract to make delivery.

The clearinghouse guarantees the integrity of such transactions by its guaranty fund, increased from $33 million to $36 million in July 1989 for the Chicago Mercantile Exchange. The fund is made up of contributions from clearing member firms and is available to be drawn upon in the event of a clearing member's failure to discharge financial obligations to the exchange's clearinghouse. The clearinghouse also oversees the daily marking to market of required margin deposits for all open accounts.

4.4.3 *Margin*

Whenever someone enters into a contract position in the futures market, a security deposit, commonly called a **margin requirement**, must be paid. While the futures margin seems to be a partial payment for the security on which the futures contract is based, it only represents security to cover any losses that could result from adverse price movements.

The minimum margin requirements set by the exchange must be collected by the clearing member firms (members of the exchange involved in the clearinghouse operations) when their customers take positions in the market. In turn, the clearing member firms must deposit a fixed portion of these margins with the clearinghouse. At the end of each trading day, every futures trading account is incremented or reduced by the corresponding increase or decrease in the value of all open futures positions. This daily adjustment procedure is applied to the margin deposit and is called **marking to market**.

For example, if an investor is long on a T-bill futures contract, and by the end of a day its market value has fallen \$1,000, he or she would be asked to add an additional \$1,000 to the margin account. Why? Because the investor is responsible for its initial value. For example, if a futures contract is executed at \$10,000 with initial margin of \$1,000 and the value of the position goes down \$1,000 to \$9,000, the buyer would be required to put in an additional margin of \$1,000. If the buyer refuses to do so, the clearing member firm that the clearing member firm that he or she trades through would automatically close out the position. On the other hand, if the contract's value was up \$1,000 for the day, the investor might immediately withdraw the profit if he or she so desired. The procedure of marking to market implies that all potential profits and losses are immediately realized.

Due to the difficulty of calling all customers whose margin accounts have fallen in value for the day, a clearing member firm will usually require that a sum of money be deposited at the initiation of any futures position. This additional sum is called **maintenance margin**. In most situations, the original margin requirement may be established with a risk-free, interest-bearing security such as a T-bill. However, the maintenance margin, which must be in cash, is adjusted for daily changes in the contract value.

Margin requirements may vary among brokerage houses and may certainly differ for the type of futures trading engaged in. The largest margin deposit is required of a speculator — that is, someone who has an outright long or short position in the futures, with no corresponding position in a related security or the actual underlying asset. This results from the fact that the speculator takes on the most risk and stands to lose the most. However, for someone who owns the asset underlying the futures contract and enters the market in order to hedge the spot position, margin requirements are significantly lower. That is, the hedger's spot position stands as collateral, and the overall position is subject to a much smaller degree of price risk. Lower margins are also required from *spreaders* — traders taking an opposite futures position in a distant contract month or a related contract, or who are taking a position in an option on the futures contract. For instance, if a spreader is long the September 1988 T-bill futures, and short the same but more distant March 1989 contract, the margin requirement would be lower than that required for an outright speculative position.

Although *margin calls* can be an inconvenience, are disruptive to cash flow, and involve an interest opportunity cost, the actual size of the required margin deposit is very small compared to the value of the contract it controls. For a T-bill futures contract worth $1,000,000, the required margin might be as little as $2,700. This is a leverage factor of 37×. For the much more volatile stock index futures, such as the contract on the S&P 500 index, a speculative position requiring $8,500 in total margin would typically control a position worth $75,000 to $85,000. This is still a leverage factor of roughly 10×, one reason that futures contracts are growing in popularity.

4.4.4 *Order execution*

Each order to buy and sell futures contracts comes to the exchange floor either by telephone or by a computerized order entry system. It is received by a member firm at its communications desk and is time-stamped. The person receiving the order is called a *phone clerk*.

The phone clerk then hands the order to a *runner*, who relays it to the appropriate trading area or *pit*. Futures contracts are traded in separate pits, which are divided into a number of sections designated for trading in specific contract months.

The runner gives the order to the firm's *floor broker*, who handles the firm's trades in a specific contract or delivery month and takes responsibility for executing the order. If the order is to buy, the floor broker sounds out a bid for the appropriate type and number of futures contracts at the requested price to the other brokers and traders in the pit. If the order is to sell, the floor broker sounds out an offer. Once someone calls back an acknowledgment to the broker's bid or offer, the order is executed.

When the order is executed, the floor broker endorses its time, price, and size while a specially trained employee of the exchange, the *pit observer*, records the price for immediate entry into the exchange's computerized price-reporting system. The system then instantaneously transmits information to market participants around the world.

Finally, the executed order is returned from the trading pit to the phone clerk again via the runner. Once more, at the firm's communications desk, the phone clerk time-stamps the executed order and immediately confirms its execution to the customer who entered it.

In all, the entire order-handling process on the exchange floor takes as little as two to three minutes.

As an aside, the time-stamping serves to indicate how long the firm took to execute or *fill* the order. Some orders — such as a market order, where the firm is instructed to buy or sell at the going market price — are typically allowed only three minutes for complete execution, and the firm can be penalized by the customer through the exchange if the order is not completed in the time allowed.

4.4.5 *A sample T-bill futures transaction*

Suppose that on October 2, 1990, a trader buys one December 1990 T-bill futures contract at the opening index price of 94.83. Once the transaction is complete, the trader is contractually obligated to buy a $1 million face-value thirteen-week T-bill yielding 100 − 94.83 = 5.17% on a discount basis on the contract delivery date, which is December 18, 1990. At the time of the initial transaction, however, the trader pays only a commission and deposits the required margin with the broker.

Suppose the futures price falls two basis points during the next day's trading session; this means that the discount rate on T-bills for future delivery has been increased. Each basis-point change in the T-bill index is worth $25. The trader in this case will lose $50 if he or she sells the contract at the closing price. The procedure of handling this loss is now the focus for discussion.

The practice of marking futures contracts to market at the end of each trading session means that the trader is forced to realize this loss even if the trader does not sell the contract, because $50 is subtracted from the trader's margin account. This money is then transferred to the seller's margin account. After the contract is marked to market, the trader is still obligated to buy a T-bill on December 18, 1990, but now at a discount yield of 5.19%. In effect, the trader pays $50 less for the T-bill at delivery because he has paid $50 to the potential seller by marking to market. Every day, the old futures contract is essentially canceled and replaced by a new contract with a delivery price equal to the new futures price — that is, the settlement price at the end of the day.

If the trader chooses to hold the contract to maturity, the contract is marked to market one last time at the close of trading on December

18. All longs with open positions at that time must be prepared to buy the deliverable T-bill at a price determined by the closing futures price.

The final settlement price or purchase price for an International Money Market T-bill contract is determined as follows. First, the total discount is calculated from the face value of the T-bill:

$$\text{Discount} = \frac{\text{Days to maturity} \times [(100 - \text{Index}) \times 0.01] \times \$1{,}000{,}000}{360}$$

where $(100-\text{Index}) \times 0.01$ is the futures discount yield expressed as a fraction. Second, the purchase price is computed by subtracting the old discount from the face value of the deliverable bill. For example, if the final index price is \$94.81, the settlement price for the delivery is

$$\$986{,}880.83 = \$1{,}000{,}000 - \frac{91 \text{ days } \times 0.0519 \times \$1{,}000{,}000}{360}$$

where $0.0519 = [100 - \text{Index}] \times 0.01$.

Because buying a futures contract during the last trading session is essentially equivalent to buying a T-bill in the spot market, futures prices tend to converge to the spot price of the deliverable security on the final day of futures trading for a given contract. Otherwise, risk-free arbitrage results. Thus, the settlement futures discount yield should equal the spot market discount yield at the end of the trading day. Sample Problem 4.2 provides further illustration.

Sample Problem 4.2

What is the settlement value for delivery for an IMM T-bill contract when the final index is 93?

Solution

$$\begin{aligned}
\text{Discount} &= \frac{\text{Days to maturity} \times [(100 - \text{Index}) \times 0.01] \times \$1{,}000{,}000}{360} \\
&= \frac{91 \times [(100 - 93) \times 0.01] \times \$1{,}000{,}000}{360} \\
&= \$17{,}194.44. \\
\text{Settlement value} &= \$1{,}000{,}000 - \text{Discount} \\
&= \$1{,}000{,}000 - \$17{,}194.44 \\
&= \$982{,}305.56.
\end{aligned}$$

The minimum yield change for T-bill futures contracts is one basis point (0.001), or a hundredth of 1%. To calculate the change in dollar value for a change of one basis point, the discount relationship can be modified. For example, for a 90-day IMM T-bill contract, each change of one basis point is equivalent to a change of $25.

$$\begin{aligned}\Delta(\$) &= \frac{\text{Days to maturity} \times \Delta(\text{basis points}) \times \$1{,}000{,}000}{360} \\ &= \frac{90 \times 0.001 \times \$1{,}000{,}000}{360} \\ &= \$25.\end{aligned}$$

The two important variables in the above relationship are the days to maturity and the face value of the contract.

4.5 The Valuation of Futures Contracts

The discussions of each of the three classifications of futures contracts have pointed out pricing idiosyncrasies and have examined specific pricing models for particular types of contracts. Nevertheless, the underlying tenets of any particular pricing model have their roots in a more general theoretical framework of valuation. Consequently, the focus is now on the traditional concepts of futures contracts valuation as a prelude to more specific discussions in supplementary chapters.

4.5.1 *The arbitrage argument*

An instant before the futures contract matures, its price must be equal to the spot (cash) price of the underlying commodity, or

$$F_{t,T} = S_t, \tag{4.1}$$

where $F_{t,T}$ = the price of the futures contract at time t, which matures at time T, where $T > t$ and $T - t$ is a very small interval of time, and S_t = the spot price of the underlying commodity at time t.

If Equation (4.1) did not hold, and the arbitrage condition would prevail, more specifically, when $t = T$ at the maturity of the contract, all trading on the contract ceases and the futures price equals the spot price. If an instant before maturity $F_{t,T} < S_t$, one could realize a sure profit (an arbitrage profit) by simultaneously buying the futures contract (which is undervalued) and selling the spot commodity (which is overvalued). The arbitrage profit would equal

$$S_t - F_{t,T}. \tag{4.2}$$

However, if $F_{t,T} > S_t$ is the market condition an instant before maturity, smart traders would recognize this arbitrage condition and sell futures contracts and buy the spot commodity until $t = T$ and $F_{t,T} = S_t$. In fact, the effect of selling the futures and buying the spot would bid their prices down and up, respectively. Thus, the arbitrage process would alleviate any such pricing disequilibrium between the futures contract and its underlying spot commodity.

4.5.2 *Interest costs*

The previous simplified argument demonstrated that the futures and spot prices must be equal an instant before the contract's maturity. This development assumes no costs in holding the spot commodity or carrying it (storing it) across time. If such a market condition held, Equation (4.1) could be extended to apply to any point of time where $t < T$. However, by having to buy or sell the spot commodity to carry out the arbitrage process, the trader would incur certain costs. For instance, if the spot commodity were purchased because it is undervalued relative to the futures, the trader or *arbitrageur* would incur an opportunity or interest cost. Any funds he or she tied up in the purchase of the commodity could alternatively be earning some risk-free interest rate R_f through investment in an interest-bearing risk-free security. Therefore, the futures price should account for the interest cost of holding the spot commodity over time, and consequently Equation (4.1) can be modified to

$$F_{t,T} = S_t(1 + R_{f,T-t}), \tag{4.3}$$

where $R_{f,T-t}$ is the risk-free opportunity cost or interest income that is lost by tying up funds in the spot commodity over the interval $T-t$. Sample Problem 4.3 provides further illustration.

Sample Problem 4.3

On September 1, the spot price of a commodity is \$100. The current risk-free rate is 12%. What is the value on September 1 of a futures contract that matures on October 1 with a price of \$100?

Solution

$$F_{t,T} = S_t(1 + R_{f,T-t}),$$

$$F_{t,T} = \$100\left(1 + \frac{0.12}{12}\right),$$

$$F_{\text{Sept. 1. Oct. 1}} = \$101.$$

Since the investment is for one month only, the annualized rate of 12% must be converted to a monthly rate of 1%; this is done for $R_{f,T-t}$ by dividing the annual rate by twelve.

4.5.3 *Carrying costs*

Since theories on the pricing of futures contracts were developed long before the introduction of financial or index futures, the costs of storing and insuring the spot commodity were considered relevant factors in the price of a futures contract. That is, someone who purchased the spot commodity to hold from time t to a later period T incurs the costs of actually housing the commodity and insuring it in case of fire or theft. In the case of livestock such as cattle or hogs, the majority of this cost would be in feeding. The holder of a futures contract avoids these costs borne by the spot holder, making the value of the contract relative to the spot commodity increase by the amount of these carrying costs. Therefore, Equation (4.3) can be extended:

$$F_{t,T} = S_t(1 + R_{f,T-t}) + C_{T-t}, \tag{4.4}$$

where C_{T-t} is the carrying cost associated with the spot commodity for the interval $T - t$. Sample Problem 4.4 provides further illustration.

Sample Problem 4.4

Extending the problem in Sample Problem 4.3, if the carrying cost is \$0.04 per dollar of value per month, what is the value of the futures contract on September 1?

Solution

$$F_{t,T} = S_t(1 + R_{f,T-t}) + C_{T-t},$$

$$F_{t,T} = \$100\left(1 + \frac{0.12}{12}\right) + \$100(\$0.04/\text{month})(1\,\text{month}),$$

$$F_{\text{Sept. 1. Oct. 1}} = \$105.$$

4.5.4 *Supply and demand effects*

As for other financial instruments or commodities, the price of a futures contract is affected by expectations of future supply and demand conditions. The effects of supply and demand for the current spot commodity (as well as for the future spot commodity) have not yet been considered in this analysis.

If the probability exists that future supplies of the spot commodity might significantly differ from current supplies, then this will affect the futures price. The discussion up to this point has assumed that the aggregate supply of the commodity was fixed over time and that demand remained constant; however, for agricultural, financial, and index futures, this is a very unrealistic assumption. For instance, if it is expected that the future available supply of wheat for time T will decline because of poor weather, and demand is expected to remain unchanged, one would then expect the future spot price of wheat to be higher than the current spot price. Furthermore, a futures contract on wheat that matures at time T can also be considered to represent the expected spot price at time T and consequently should reflect the expected change in supply conditions. In a more extreme fashion, if it is assumed there is no current supply of wheat, then the futures price would reflect only future supply conditions and the expected future spot price at time T. This can be expressed as follows:

$$F_{t,T} = E_t(\tilde{S}_T), \tag{4.5}$$

where $E_t(\tilde{S}_T)$ is the spot price at a future point T expected at time t, where $t < T$. The tilde above S_T indicates that the future spot price is a random variable because future factors such as supply cannot presently be known with certainty.

Equation (4.5) is called the **unbiased expectations hypothesis** because it postulates that the current price of a futures contract maturing at time T represents the market's expectation of the future spot price at time T. Which of these expression for the price of a futures contract at time t will hold in the market — the arbitrage pricing relationship in Equation (4.4) or the unbiased expectations hypothesis in Equation (4.5)? The answer is that, because the markets are assumed to be efficient, the market price of the futures contract will take on the minimum value of either of these two pricing relationship, or

$$F_{t,T} = \text{Min}[E_t(\tilde{S}_T), S_t(1 + R_{f,T-t}) + C_{T-t}]. \tag{4.6}$$

Sample Problem 4.5 provides further illustration.

Sample Problem 4.5

Continuing Sample Problems 4.3 and 4.4, suppose that the consensus expectation is that the price of the commodity at time T will be \$103. What is the price that anyone would pay for a futures contract on September 1?

Solution

$$\begin{aligned} F_{t,T} &= \text{Min}[E_t(\tilde{S}_T), S_t(1 + R_{f,T-t}) + C_{T-t}], \\ F_{t,T} &= \text{Min}(\$103, \$105), \\ F_{\text{Sept. 1. Oct. 1}} &= \$103. \end{aligned}$$

For any storable commodity on a given day t, the futures price $F_{t,T}$ will be higher than the spot price S_t on day t; $F_{t,T} > S_t$. The amount by which the futures price exceeds the spot price $(F_{t,T} - S_t)$ is called the **premium**. In most cases, this premium is equal to the sum of financial costs $S_t R_{f,T-t}$ and carrying costs C_{T-t}. The condition of $F_{t,T} > S_t$ is associated with a commodity market called a **normal carrying-change market**.

In general, the difference between the futures price $F_{t,T}$ and spot price S_t is called the **basis**:

$$\textbf{Basis} = F_{t,T} - S_t. \tag{4.7}$$

4.5.5 *The effect of hedging demand*

John Maynard Keynes (1930), who studied the futures markets as a hobby, proposed that for some commodities there was a strong tendency for hedgers to be concentrated on the short side of the futures market. That is, to protect themselves against the risk of a price decline in the spot commodity, the spot holder or producer (such as a farmer) would hedge the risk by selling futures contracts on his or her particular commodity. This demand for hedging, producing an abundant supply of futures contracts, would force the market price below that of the expected spot price at maturity (time T). Moreover, the hedgers would be transferring their price risk to speculators. This difference between $E_t(\tilde{S}_T)$ and $F_{t,T}$ when $F_{t,T} < E_t(\tilde{S}_T)$ can be thought of as a risk premium paid to the speculators for holding the long futures position and bearing the price risk of the hedger. This risk premium can be formulated as follows:

$$E_t(R_P) = E_t(\tilde{S}_T) - F_{t,T}, \tag{4.8}$$

where $E_t(R_P)$ is the expected risk premium paid to the speculator for bearing the hedger's price risk.

Keynes described this pricing phenomenon as **normal backwardation**. When the opposite conditions exist — hedgers are concentrated on the long side of the market and bid up the futures spot pricing $F_{t,T}$ over the expected future spot $E_t(\tilde{S}_T)$ — the pricing relationship is called **contango** (i.e., $E_t(R_P) = F_{t,T} - E_t(\tilde{S}_T)$). To reflect the effect of normal backwardation or contango on the current futures price, the $E_t(\tilde{S}_T)$ term in Equation (4.8) must be adjusted for the effects of hedging demand:

$$F_{t,T} = \text{Min}[E_t(\tilde{S}_T) + E(R_P), S_t(1 + R_{f,T-t}) + C_{T-t}]. \tag{4.9}$$

Equation (4.9) expresses a broad pricing framework for the value of a futures contract. Over the life of the futures contract, the futures price must move toward the cash price, because at the maturity of the futures contract the futures price will be equal to the current cash price. If hedgers are in a net short position, then futures prices must lie below the expected future spot price, and futures prices would be expected to rise over the life of the contract. However, if hedgers are net long, then the futures price must lie above the expected futures spot price and the price of the futures would be

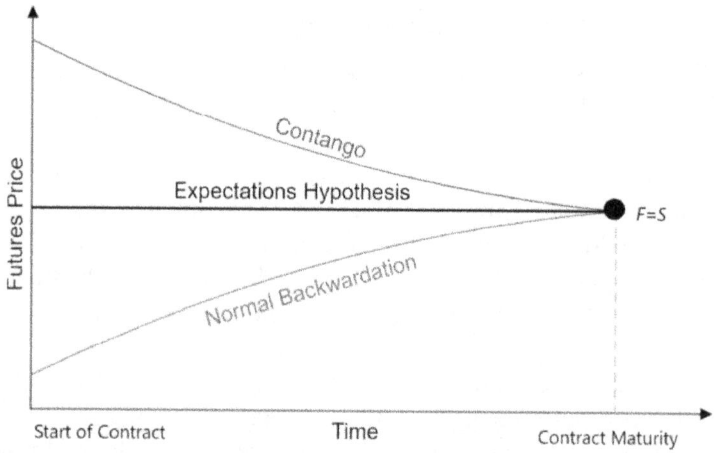

Figure 4.2 Bounds for Futures Prices

expected to fall. Either a falling futures price (normal backwardation) or a rising futures price (contango) determines the boundaries within which the actual futures price will be located. This region is shown in Figure 4.2.

However, numerous other factors can alter and distort the relationship shown by Equation (4.9). For instance, the analysis implicitly assumes that interest rates remain constant from time t to the contract's maturity date at time T. However, since market interest rates fluctuate, an increasing or decreasing term structure of interest rates would bias the price of the futures contract higher or lower. In fact, the more accurate one's forecast of future interest rates, the more accurate the current valuation of the futures contract.

Empirical research casts rather strong doubt on the size of the expected risk premium component of futures prices, particularly for financial and index futures.

In fact, the expectation of speculators along with actual futures contract supply and demand conditions in the pit can combine to reverse the effect expected by Keynes. This results in part from the makeup of futures' users, a clear majority of whom are not hedgers as suggested by Keynes. Additionally, a futures contract for which an illiquid level of trading volume exists would put the bid and offer prices for the contract further apart. A seller of such a futures contract would require more than the theoretical fair price as compensation for the risk undertaken. The risk is of prices starting to rise in an illiquid market in which the position cannot be immediately closed out. It costs money to maintain the position; therefore, a premium is required to cover this cost.

4.6 Hedging Concepts and Strategies

The underlying motivation for the development of futures markets is to aid the holders of the spot commodity in hedging their price risk and costs; consequently, the discussion now focuses on such an application of futures market. Four methodologies based on various risk–return criteria are examined; moreover, to fully clarify the hedger's situation, some of the common problems and risks that arise in the hedging process are analyzed.

4.6.1 *Hedging risks and costs*

As mentioned previously, hedging refers to a process designed to alleviate the uncertainty of future price changes for the spot commodity. Typically, this is accomplished by taking an opposite position in a futures contract on the same commodity that is held. If an investor owns the spot commodity, as is usually the case (a long position), the appropriate action in the futures market would be to sell a contract (a short position). However, disregarding for the moment the correct number of futures contracts to enter into, a problem arises if the prices of the spot commodity and the futures contract on this commodity do not move in a perfectly correlated manner. This nonsynchronicity of spot and futures prices is related to the basis and is called the **basis risk**.

The basis has been defined as the difference between the futures and spot prices. Basis risk is the chance that this difference will not remain constant over time. Four types of risk contribute to basis risk; these are defined in Table 4.4. These four types of risks prevent the hedger from forming a perfect hedge (which would have zero risk). Even though the hedger is reducing the amount of risk, it has not been reduced to zero. It is often said that hedging replaces price risk with basis risk.

Table 4.4 The Components of Basis Risk

Type of Risk	Components
Expiration-date risk	Futures contracts are not usually available for every month. If a hedger needed a futures contract for July and the only contracts that were available were for March, June, September, and December, the hedger would have to select either the June or September contract. Either of these contracts would have a different price series than a July contract (if one existed). Hence, the hedger cannot form a perfect hedge and is faced with the chance that the basis may change.
Location risk	The hedger requires delivery of the futures contract in location Y, but the only futures contracts available are for delivery in location X. Hence, the hedger cannot form a perfect hedge because of the transportation costs from X to Y; this may cause the basis to change.
Quality risk	The exact standard or grade of the commodity required by the hedger is not covered by the futures contract. Therefore, the price movement of commodity grade A may be different from the price movement of commodity grade B, which will cause the basis to change and prevent the hedger from forming a perfect hedge.
Quantity risk	The exact amount of the commodity needed by the hedger is not available by a single futures contract or any integer multiple thereof. Hence, the amount of the commodity is not hedged exactly; this prevents the hedger from forming a perfect hedge, and the underhedged or overhedged amount is subject to risk.

The potential causes of basis risk are not necessarily limited to those identified in Table 4.4. Hence, basis risk is the prominent source of uncertainty in the hedging process. Among other probable causes are (1) supply–demand conditions and (2) cross-hedging consequences.

Even if the futures contract is written on the exact commodity that the hedger holds, differing supply and demand conditions in the spot market and futures market could cause the basis to vary over time. Occasionally, speculators in the futures market will bid the futures price above or below its equilibrium position, due perhaps to the excitement induced by an unexpected news release. Of course, the market forces of arbitrage will eventually bring the spot and futures prices back in line. The limiting case is at the expiration of the futures contract, when its price must converge to the spot price.

Consequently, the disequilibrating influence on the basis stemming from supply–demand forces can be alleviated by entering a futures contract that matures on the exact day that the hedger intends to sell the spot commodity. But although most futures contracts are quite flexible, it is unlikely that any contract would correlate so precisely with the hedger's needs. In some cases (such as for agricultural commodities, where futures contracts are offered that mature each month), the basis risk due to non-simultaneous maturities is not so great. However, for other commodities, particularly financial instruments, futures contracts maturing three months apart are more typically offered. Thus, at the time the hedger needs to sell the spot commodity in the market, any protection in price risk over the hedging period could conceivably be wiped out by a temporary adverse change in the basis.

Cross-hedging refers to hedging with a futures contract written on a non-identical commodity (relative to the spot commodity). While not often necessary with agricultural futures, cross-hedging is frequently the best that can be done with financial and index futures. Changes in the basis risk induced by the cross-hedge are caused by less than perfect correlation of price movements between the spot and futures prices — even at maturity. That is, because the spot commodity and futures contract commodity are different, their respective prices will tend to be affected (even though minutely at times) by differing market forces. While the futures price must equal the price of its underlying spot commodity at the contract's maturity date, this condition does not necessarily hold when the hedger's commodity is not the "true" underlying asset. Therefore, even when the liquidation of the spot commodity coincides with the maturity of the futures contract, there is no guarantee of obtaining the original price of the commodity that held at the initiation of the hedge.

Sample Problem 4.6

Basis risk is illustrated in Table 4.5. The spot price is \$100 and the futures price is \$105 on day t. The top half of the exhibit shows what can happen if the spot price falls at day $t + 1$, and the bottom half shows what happens if the spot price rises at day $t+1$. It is assumed that the hedger is trying to create a fully hedged position in each of the cases presented.

If the basis is unchanged, the hedged position will neither gain nor lose. This situation is shown in Table 4.5, and we can see that this situation can happen for either a price drop or price increase. As can be seen in Table 4.5, the gain or loss on the hedged position is related to the change in the basis. Now, we will discuss the gain or loss from a cash price drop or a cash price increase. When the cash price drops, spot markets lose \$5. For the future market, it will be a gain of \$4 if we buy the future at \$101. It will be a gain of \$6 if we buy the future market price at \$99. Hence, if the futures market makes \$4, then the hedged position can lose \$1. When we buy the \$99 futures price, then the hedged portfolio will make \$1.

We will now discuss the case of a cash price increase. From Table 4.5, we can see when the base can be equal to zero, +\$1, or −\$1. When the base is +\$1, the hedge portfolio loses \$1. When the base is −\$1, the hedged portfolio makes \$1. Hence, the asset position has exposure to price risk equal to zero and the only risk the hedger faces is a change in the basis.

4.6.2 *The classic hedge strategy*

The implicit assumption of the classic hedge ratio equal to one is that the prices of the spot commodity (in this case, the stock portfolio) and the futures contract will remain perfectly correlated over the entire hedge period. Then, if the stock market does turn down as expected, any losses in the portfolio due to price declines in its composite stocks will be exactly offset by the gain on the futures position. Conversely, if stock prices rise, the portfolio's gains will be offset by

Table 4.5 Examples of Basis Risk

Spot Market			**Futures Market**		**Basis ($F - S$)**
Drop in cash price					
t	buy	100	sell	105	5
$t+1$	sell	95	buy	100	5
		−5		5	Basis change = 0
Value of hedged portfolio = 0			No change in basis		
t	buy	100	sell	105	5
$t+1$	sell	95	buy	101	6
		−5		4	Basis change = +1
Value of hedged portfolio = −1			Basis increases		
t	buy	100	sell	105	5
$t+1$	sell	95	buy	99	4
		−5		6	Basis change = −1
Value of hedged portfolio = +1			Basis decreases		
Increase in cash price					
	buy	100	sell	105	5
	sell	105	buy	110	5
		5		−5	Basis change = 0
Value of hedged portfolio = 0			No change in basis		
	buy	100	sell	105	5
	sell	105	buy	111	6
		5		−6	Basis change = +1
Value of hedged portfolio = −1			Basis increases		
	buy	100	sell	105	5
	sell	105	buy	109	4
		5		−4	Basis change = −1
Value of hedged portfolio = +1			Basis decreases		

equal losses on the futures position. Therefore, the portfolio manager attempts to lock in current profits by taking on a hedge position. Such a strategy implies that the objective of the classic hedge is risk minimization or elimination.

Table 4.6 The Classic Hedge Strategy

	Cash-Market Position	**Future-Market Position (index = 150)**
July 1, 1989	$7,500,000 in well-diversified stock portfolio	Short (sell) 100 contracts, equal to 100 × ($500 × 150) = $7,500,000.
August 1, 1989	Scenario I: Stock prices fall (index = 145)	
	$7,250,000 value of portfolio	Buy 100 contracts, equal to 100 × ($500 × 145) = $7,250,000
	Net Results from Hedging	
	Gain or (loss) ($250,000)	Gain or (loss) $250,000
	Net Gain = $0	
	Scenario II: Stock prices rise (index = 155)	
	$7,750,000 value of portfolio	Buy 100 contracts, equal to 100 × ($500 × 55) = $7,750,000
	Net Results from Hedging	
	Gain or (loss) $250,000	Gain or (loss) ($250,000)
	Net Gain = $0	

Sample Problem 4.7

The S&P 500 Index futures contract is used as the hedging instrument.

Table 4.6 describes both the cash market positions and future market positions. It is clear that the hedged portfolio's net gain will be zero, whether the stock index price falls from $150 to $145 or rises from $150 to $155. In other words, when the index price goes down from $150 to $145, the cash market loss is $250,000; however, the future market gains $250,000. Similarly, when futures prices go up to $155, cash markets earn $250,000, but the futures market loses $250,000.

To apply the **classic hedge strategy** to the hedging problem, an opposite and equal position is taken in the futures market for the underlying commodity. More specifically, if a cautious portfolio manager believed that the stock market was going to turn downward for the next month and she wanted to lock in previously unrealized capital gains on her $7.5 million stock portfolio, she would sell $7.5 million worth of stock index futures contracts. Furthermore, that portfolio manager would keep her initial futures position constant over the entire hedge period.

It is difficult to imagine the consequences of this strategy if the spot and futures prices are not perfectly correlated. In fact, if the spot and futures contract commodities are not identical, or if the hedging horizon does not coincide with the maturity of the futures contract, perfectly correlated spot and futures prices will always be the exception and not the rule.

Hence, there are identifiable risks associated with hedging. Two such types are (1) the risk of margin calls and (2) liquidity. Hedgers, like all participants in futures markets, must mark to market each day. In the simplified example, the decline (increase) in the value of the futures position is offset by gains (decreases) from the cash position. Nevertheless, gains from the cash position are typically not realized immediately, while futures contracts are marked to market at the end of each trading session. Thus, the practice of marking to market causes an imbalance in the cash flow of the hedger, who must balance paper gains in the cash market against realized (cash) outflows in the futures market. And although futures contracts are usually more liquid than the underlying cash instrument, liquidity may be a problem for some contracts. Hence, hedgers who find it impossible to execute orders for the purchase or sale of a futures contract may need to be able to satisfy the delivery requirements of their hedge.

Liquidity is most likely a problem for futures contracts with delivery dates more than a year away. Trading activity in futures contracts is heaviest in contracts for the nearby delivery months. Trading in the most distant contract is typically very thin, hence less liquid.

Because of these problems with hedging, researchers have tried to incorporate the risk of hedging into the way the relative futures position is determined.

4.6.3 *The working hedge strategy*

The **working hedge strategy**, formulated by Holbrook Working (1953), makes explicit the speculative aspect of hedging. That is, in any hedged position, the basis will not be constant over time. Therefore, the hedger in a certain sense is speculating on the future

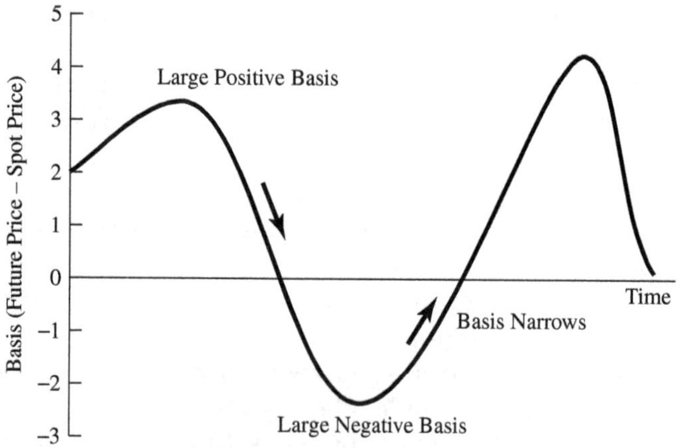

Figure 4.3 A Hypothetical Basis Relationship Over Time

course of the basis. Yet, it is expected that the changes in the basis will involve a smaller degree of risk than the corresponding price risk of the unhedged position.

This speculative aspect to hedging is exploited in Working's model by simultaneously determining positions in the spot and futures markets in order to capture increased return arising from relative movements in spot and futures prices. By studying the year-to-year constancy of the relation between spot and futures prices in various markets, Working discerned that a large *positive basis* (spot price less than futures price) was likely to be followed by a large negative change in the basis (basis narrows), and, conversely, a large negative basis by a large positive change in the basis. Figure 4.3 graphs a hypothetical basis relationship over time and designates the points considered indicative of large positive or negative basis.

The implications of Working's 1953 model for the hedger are as follows. A short position in futures (of equal magnitude to the commodity held) is entered into only if the basis is sufficiently wide and positive. Thus, on the expectation that this large positive basis will narrow over time, the hedger will (it is hoped) profit from the combined spot and futures position.

Sample Problem 4.8

As an example of the implementation of this hedging rule, assume that the manager of a well-diversified portfolio of stocks — worth \$7.5 million — sees a difference between the stock index futures price for the S&P 500 near-term contract and the spot price of \$2.85 on July 1 (\$152.85 - \$150.00). Her portfolio is highly correlated with the S&P 500 index, and she sells ninety-eight contracts to achieve an approximately equally valued position in the futures — with a value of \$7,489,650. Table 4.7 summarizes the results of this hedge strategy one month later. As Table 4.7 shows for this simplified example, the hedger, by entering a short futures position when the basis was sufficiently positive, nearly triples (\$2.85) the return on her portfolio. However, if the basis had widened over the hedging horizon, the net gain on the hedged position would have been reduced correspondingly.

On August 1, 1989, the spot price is equal to \$150.50 and the future price is \$152. Therefore, the spot value increased from \$7.5 million to \$7.525 million, and the future position changed from \$7,489,650 to \$7,448,000. From the bottom of Table 4.7, we know that the spot market makes \$25,000 and the futures market makes \$41,650. The gross profit from this hedged position is \$66,650.

Table 4.7 The Working Hedge Strategy

	Spot-Market Position (Spot Price = \$150)	**Futures-Market Position (Futures Price = \$152.88)**
July 1, 1989	\$7,500,000 in well-diversified stock portfolio	Sell 98 contracts, equal to 98 × (\$500 × 152.85) = \$7,489,650. Basis = 2.85
August 1, 1989	\$7,525,000 value of portfolio	Buy 98 contracts, equal to 98 × (\$500 × 152.00) = \$7,448,000. Basis = 1.50
Results from Hedging	Gain or (less) \$25,000	Gain or (loss) \$41,650
	Gross Profit = \$66,650	

For the most part, the Working strategy provides a relatively simple decision rule to facilitate speculation on the basis. Moreover, the hedger should create a hedged position with the futures only if the basis is sufficiently wide and positive at the beginning of the hedge period. Both the decision to hedge and the size of the hedging commitment are essentially predetermined and therefore relatively easy to implement. Finally, in order to evaluate the Working strategy versus the classic one-to-one hedge, the following *ex post* measure of hedging effectiveness has been suggested:

$$\text{GP} = (S_2 - S_1) - H(F_2 - F_1), \tag{4.10}$$

where GP = gross profit, H = hedge ratio, S_1, S_2 = beginning and end-of-period spot prices, and F_1, F_2 = beginning and end-of-period futures prices.

In the example, gross profit is $66,650. This sum could then be compared to either the gross profit (or loss) from an unhedged position or to the gross profit generated from an alternative hedging strategy.

4.6.4 *The Johnson minimum-variance hedge strategy*

Developed within the framework of modern portfolio theory, the **Johnson hedge model** (1960) retains the traditional objective of risk minimization but defines risk as the variance of return on a two-asset hedge portfolio. As in the two-parameter world of Markowitz (1959), the hedger is assumed to be infinitely risk averse (i.e., the investor desires zero variance). Moreover, with the risk minimization objective defined as the variance of return of the combined spot and futures position, the Johnson hedge ratio is expressed in terms of expectations of variances and covariances for price changes in the spot and futures markets.

The Johnson hedge model can be expressed in regression form as follows:

$$\Delta S_t = a + H\Delta F_t + e_t, \tag{4.11}$$

where ΔS_t= change in the spot price at time t, ΔF_t = change in the futures price at time t, a = constant, H = hedged ratio, and e_t = residual term at time t.

Furthermore, the hedge ratio measure can be better understood by defining it in terms of its components:

$$\frac{X_f^*}{X_s} = \frac{\sigma_{\Delta S,\Delta F}}{\sigma_{\Delta F}^2} = H, \tag{4.12}$$

where X_f^* and X_s = the dollar amount invested in futures and spot, respectively, $\sigma_{\Delta S,\Delta F}$ = the covariance of spot and futures price changes, and $\sigma_{\Delta F}^2$ = the variance of futures price changes.

Thus, H, the minimum-variance hedge ratio computed in variability, is also a measure of the relative dollar amount to be invested in futures per dollar of spot holdings. In a sense, it is a localized beta coefficient similar in concept to the beta of a stock *a la* capital asset pricing theory.

Equation (4.12), H can be rewritten as follows:

$$H = \sigma_{\Delta S,\Delta F}/\sigma_{\Delta F}^2 = \rho(\sigma_{\Delta S}/\sigma_{\Delta F}). \tag{4.12a}$$

As a measure of hedging effectiveness, Johnson utilizes the squared simple correlation coefficient between spot and futures price changes, ρ^2. More formally, Johnson's hedging effectiveness measure can be ascertained by first establishing the following expression:

$$\text{HE} = 1 - \frac{V_H}{V_u}, \tag{4.13}$$

where V_u = variance of the unhedged spot position = $X_s^2\sigma_{\Delta S}^2$, $\sigma_{\Delta S}^2$ = variance of spot price changes, and V_H = the variance of return for the hedged portfolio = $X_s^2\sigma_{\Delta S}^2(1-\rho^2)$.

By substituting the minimum-variance hedge position in the futures, X_f^*,

$$\text{HE} = \left[1 - \frac{X_S^2\sigma_{\Delta S}^2(1-\rho^2)}{X_S^2\sigma_{\Delta S}^2}\right] = \rho^2. \tag{4.14}$$

It is well known that ρ^2 is the R^2 for the simple regression of Equation (4.11).

In simpler terms then, the Johnson measure of hedging effectiveness is the R^2 of a regression of spot price changes on futures price changes. To utilize this hedging method, it is necessary to regress historical data of spot price changes on futures price changes. The resulting beta coefficient from the regression would be the localized Johnson hedge ratio, and the regression R^2 would represent the expected degree of variance minimization using this hedge ratio over the hedging horizon. "Localized" and "expected" must be emphasized because, first of all, although the Johnson hedge ratio can be reestimated, it nonetheless is a static measure based on historical data. What held for the past may not hold precisely for the future. Moreover, large price moves may distort this hedge ratio considerably. Hence, R^2 is what can be expected based on the past in terms of variance reduction for the total hedge position. It should not be expected to hold exactly. (A sample computation of a hedge ratio using the Johnson model is presented in a later section.)

4.6.5 *The Howard–D'Antonio optimal risk–return hedge strategy*

The classic one-to-one hedge is a naïve strategy based upon a broadly defined objective of risk minimization. The strategy is naïve in the sense that a hedging coefficient of one is used regardless of past or expected correlations of spot and futures price changes. Working's strategy brings out the speculative aspects of hedging by analyzing changes in the basis and accordingly exercising discrete judgment about when to hedge and when not to hedge. The underlying objective of Working's decision rule for hedgers is one of profit maximization. Finally, Johnson (1960), in applying the mean-variance criteria of modern portfolio theory, emphasizes the risk minimization objective but defines risk in terms of the variance of the hedged position. Although Johnson's method improves on the naïve strategy of a one-to-one hedge, it essentially disregards the return component associated with a particular level of risk. Rutledge (1972) uses both mean and variance information to derive the hedge ratio.

In a recent paper by Howard and D'Antonio (1984), a hedge ratio and measure of hedging effectiveness are derived in which the hedger's risk and return are both explicitly taken into account. Moreover, some of the variable relationships derived from their analysis help explain some of the idiosyncrasies of hedging that occur in practice.

Using a mean-variance framework, the **Howard–D'Antonio strategy** begins by assuming that the "agent" is out to maximize the expected return for a given level of portfolio risk. With a choice of putting money into three assets — a spot position, a futures contract, and a risk-free asset — the agent's optimal portfolio will depend on the relative risk–return characteristics of each asset. For a hedger, the optimal portfolio may contain a short futures position, a long futures position, or no futures position at all. In general, the precise futures position to be entered into will be determined by (1) the risk-free rate, (2) the expected returns and the standard deviations for the spot and futures positions, and (3) the correlation between the return on the spot position and the return on the futures.

Howard and D'Antonio arrive at the following expressions for the hedge ratio and the measure of hedging effectiveness:

$$\text{Hedge ratio } H = \frac{(\lambda - \rho)}{\gamma\pi(1 - \lambda\rho)} \tag{4.15}$$

and

$$\text{Hedging effectiveness HE} = \sqrt{\frac{1 - 2\lambda\rho + \lambda^2}{1 - \rho^2}}, \tag{4.16}$$

where $\pi = \sigma_f/\sigma_s$ = relative variability of futures and spot returns, $\alpha = \bar{r}_f/(\bar{r}_s - i)$ = relative excess return on futures to that of spot, $\gamma = P_f/P_s$ = current price ratio of futures to spot, $\lambda = \alpha/\pi = (\bar{r}_f/\sigma_f)/[(\bar{r}_s - i)/\sigma_s]$ = risk-to-excess-return relative of futures versus the spot position, P_s, P_f = the current price per unit for the spot and futures, respectively, ρ = simple correlation coefficient between the

Table 4.8 The Hedging Implications of Different Relative Magnitudes of λ and ρ

Relative Magnitude	Hedge Ratio	Implied Futures Position
$\lambda < \rho$	$H < 0$	Short
$\lambda = \rho$	$H = 0$	None
$\lambda > \rho$	$H > 0$	Long

spot and futures returns, σ_s = standard deviation of spot returns, σ_f = standard deviation of futures returns, $\bar{r}_s$ = mean return on the spot over some recent past interval, $\bar{r}_f$ = mean return on the futures over some recent past interval, and i = risk-free rate.

By analyzing the properties of λ, these authors discern some important insights for the coordinated use of futures in a hedge portfolio. Numerically, λ expresses the relative attractiveness of investing in futures versus the spot position. When $\lambda < 1$, $\lambda = 1$, and $\lambda > 1$, the futures contract offers less, the same, and more excess return per unit of risk than the spot position, respectively. Since this analysis is being undertaken from a hedger's point of view, it is assumed that $\lambda < 1$. An assumption that $\lambda > 1$ would inappropriately imply that theoretically it is possible to hedge the futures position with the spot asset.

First, consider the effect of the relationship of λ to ρ on the optional hedge ratio, H. Table 4.8 summarizes the hedging implications for different magnitudes of the ratio of the risk–return relative λ to the simple correlation coefficient of spot and futures returns ρ. Of particular note is the case when $\lambda = \rho$. Such a condition implies that no benefit exists for going short or long in futures. Furthermore, this result rather clearly demonstrates that the holding of futures as a hedge against price risk is not simply related to ρ but is also dependent on the relative return–risk relationship between the futures and the spot asset.

Next, a careful examination of Howard and D'Antonio's hedging effectiveness measure in Equation (4.6) is warranted. It is important to note that this hedging effectiveness measure HE is different from the measures studied so far because it takes into account the risk–return relationship between futures and spot as well as the correlation of returns. The Howard–D'Antonio HE measure indicates the degree (in terms of return) to which the hedger (investor) could enhance the portfolio by entering into the appropriate futures position, as indicated by Equation (4.14). For instance, if $\lambda = 0.60$ and $\rho = 0.80$, then HE $= 1.054$, meaning that a hedger could expect to enhance the excess return of the portfolio of the risk-free and spot assets by 5.4% by going short ($\lambda < \rho$) the number of futures contracts indicated by Equation (4.15).

The relationship among ρ, λ, and HE is seen more clearly in Figure 4.4 and is summarized in Table 4.9. As can be seen from Figure 4.4, HE is symmetrical about $\lambda = \rho$. Moreover, it is shown that as ρ approaches 1, HE increases. That is, the hedging properties of futures improve as ρ approaches 1. However, this effect is entirely contingent on $\lambda \neq \rho$. Even if $\rho \neq 1$, there will be no benefit to holding a futures contract if $\lambda = \rho$.

The last result is at odds with past studies on hedging, especially Johnson's (1960) work. Yet, the implications from this result can help provide insight into the cross-hedging process. While past studies have indicated that the correlation of futures and spot price movements is the determinant of a hedge's effectiveness and would almost necessarily attribute superior hedging qualities to a futures contract on the true underlying asset (a straight hedge), these results indicate that the effectiveness of one's hedge — be it a cross-hedge or a straight hedge — depends on the relationship between λ and ρ.

From a practitioner's perspective, it is also important to note that even when $\lambda \neq \rho$, a hedged position using the futures may not provide a real net improvement in the risk–return performance of a portfolio. Unless HE is significantly greater than 1, other factors such as transaction costs, taxes, the potential for margin calls, and liquidity may negate the overall benefit of hedging with futures. This point, along with the previous results about hedging, helps explain why certain futures contracts highly correlated with their underlying assets are not used extensively as hedging vehicles as might be expected.

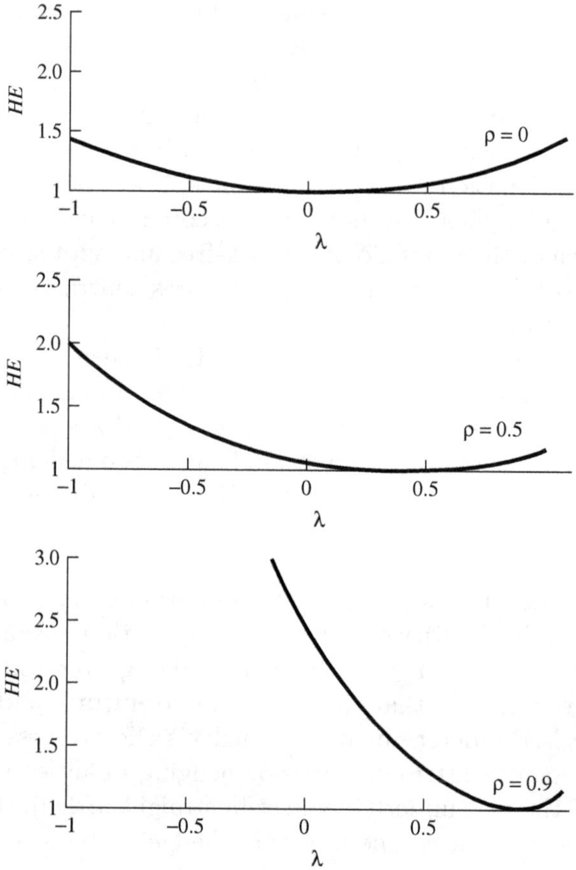

Figure 4.4 Hedging Effectiveness (HE) versus the Risk–Return Relative for Various Correlations
Source: Howard, C. T. and L. J. D'Antonio (1984). A risk-return measure of hedging effectiveness. *Journal of Financial and Quantitative Analysis*, 19(March), 109. Reprinted with permission.

Chen *et al.* (2003) have shown that the optimal number of futures positions, C_f^*, is given by the following:

$$C_f^* = -C_s \frac{\left(\frac{S}{F}\right)\left(\frac{\sigma_s}{\sigma_f}\right)\left[\frac{\sigma_s}{\sigma_f}\left(\frac{E(R_f)}{E(R_s) - R_F}\right) - \rho\right]}{\left[1 - \frac{\sigma_s}{\sigma_f}\left(\frac{E(R_f)\,\rho}{E(R_s) - R_F}\right)\right]}. \tag{4.17}$$

Table 4.9 The Relationship of λ, ρ, and HE

Effect on the HE Measure		Benefit of Hedging with Futures
$\lambda < \rho$	$HE > 1.0$	Positive
$\lambda = \rho$	$HE = 1.0$	None
$\lambda > \rho$	$HE > 1.0$	Positive

From the optimal futures position, Chen *et al.* (2003) have derived the optimal hedge ratio as follows:

$$h_3 = -\frac{\left(\frac{\sigma_s}{\sigma_f}\right)\left[\frac{\sigma_s}{\sigma_f}\left(\frac{E(R_f)}{E(R_s)-R_F}\right)-\rho\right]}{\left[1-\frac{\sigma_s}{\sigma_f}\left(\frac{E(R_f)\rho}{E(R_s)-R_F}\right)\right]}. \tag{4.18}$$

Again, if $E(R_f) = 0$, then h_3 reduces to the following:

$$h_3 = \left(\frac{\sigma_s}{\sigma_f}\right)\rho, \tag{4.19}$$

which is similar to the minimum-variance hedge ratio as presented in Equation (4.12a). Please note that the hedge ratio of Equation (4.19) is calculated in terms of S and F instead of ΔS and ΔF.

4.6.6 *Optimum mean-variance hedge strategy*

Various studies have incorporated both risk and return in the derivation of the hedge ratio. For example, Hsin *et al.* (1994) derive the optimal hedge ratio that maximizes the following utility function:

$$\underset{C_f}{Max}\, V(E(R_h),\sigma;A) = E(R_h) - 0.5A\sigma_h^2, \tag{4.20}$$

where A represents the risk aversion parameter. It is clear that this utility function incorporates both risk and return. Therefore, the hedge ratio based on this utility function would be consistent with the mean-variance framework. The optimal number of futures contract and the optimal hedge ratio are given by the following:

$$h_2 = -\frac{C_f^* F}{C_s S} = -\left[\frac{E(R_f)}{A\sigma_f^2} - \rho\frac{\sigma_s}{\sigma_f}\right]. \tag{4.21}$$

One problem associated with this type of hedge ratio is that in order to derive the optimum hedge ratio, we need to know the individual's risk aversion parameter. Furthermore, different individuals will choose different optimal hedge ratios, depending on the values of their risk aversion parameter.

Since the MV hedge ratio is easy to understand and simple to compute, it will be interesting and useful to know under what condition the above hedge ratio would be the same as the MV hedge ratio. It can be seen from Equations (4.12) and (4.21) that if $A \to \infty$ or $E(R_f) = 0$, then h_2 would be equal to the MV hedge ratio h_J^*. The first condition is simply a restatement of the infinitely risk-averse individuals. However, the second condition does not impose any condition on the risk averseness, and this is important. It implies that even if the individuals are not infinitely risk averse, then the MV hedge ratio would be the same as the optimal mean-variance hedge ratio if the expected return on the futures contract is zero (i.e., futures prices follow a simple martingale process). Therefore, if futures prices follow a simple martingale process, then we do not need to know the risk aversion parameter of the investor to find the optimal hedge ratio.

4.6.7 *Numeric examples*

In this section, we will use a numerical example to show the relationship between the Johnson MV hedge ratio, the optimum MV hedge ratio, and the Sharpe hedge ratio.

If $\sigma_s = 0.01$, $\sigma_f = 0.02$, $E(R_f) = 0.02$, $E(R_s) = 0.015$, $A = 200$, $R_F = 0.02$, and $\rho = 0.6$, then we can use Equations (4.12), (4.21), and (4.18) to calculate the Johnson minimum-variance hedge ratio, optimal mean-variance hedge ratio, and Sharp hedge ratio.

Johnson MV hedge ratio

$$= h_J^* = \frac{Cov(R_s, R_f)}{\text{Var}(R_f)} = \rho\frac{\sigma_s}{\sigma_f} = 0.6 \times \frac{0.01}{0.02} = 0.3.$$

Optimal MV hedge ratio

$$= h_2 = -\frac{C_f^* F}{C_s S} = -\left[\frac{E(R_f)}{A\sigma_f^2} - \rho\frac{\sigma_s}{\sigma_f}\right]$$

$$= -\left[\frac{0.02}{200 \times 0.02^2} - 0.6 \times \frac{0.01}{0.02}\right] = 0.05.$$

Sharp hedge ratio

$$= h_3 = -\frac{\left(\frac{\sigma_s}{\sigma_f}\right)\left[\frac{\sigma_s}{\sigma_f}\left(\frac{E(R_f)}{E(R_s)-R_F}\right) - \rho\right]}{\left[1 - \frac{\sigma_s}{\sigma_f}\left(\frac{E(R_f)\rho}{E(R_s)-R_F}\right)\right]}$$

$$= -\frac{\left(\frac{0.01}{0.02}\right)\left[\frac{0.01}{0.02}\left(\frac{0.02}{0.015-0.02}\right) - 0.6\right]}{\left[1 - \frac{0.01}{0.02}\left(\frac{0.02\times 0.3}{0.015-0.02}\right)\right]}$$

$$= -\frac{0.5\,(0.5 \times (-4) - 0.6)}{1 - 0.5 \times (-2.4)} = \frac{1.3}{2.2} = 0.59.$$

From this example, we find that if A approaches ∞, then the optimal minimum-variance hedge ratio equals 0.3. Similarly, if $E(R_f)$ equals zero, then the Sharpe hedge ratio equals 0.3. Therefore, we can conclude that both optimal MV hedge ratio and Sharpe hedge ratio are generalized cases of Johnson MV hedge ratio.

4.7 Summary and Concluding Remarks

This chapter has focused on the basic concepts of futures markets. Important terms were defined and basic models to evaluate futures contracts were discussed. The differences between futures and forward markets also received treatment. Finally hedging concepts and strategies were analyzed and alternative hedging ratios were investigated in detail. These concepts and valuation models can be used in security analysis and portfolio management related to futures and forward contracts. Chapter 21 will expand on the hedge theory hedge method and hedge ratios in further detail. The next chapter investigates in depth commodity futures, financial futures, and index futures.

Questions and Problems

1. Define the following terms:

   (a) basis (b) backwardation
   (c) contango (d) hedger
   (e) speculator (f) arbitrager

2. Carefully explain the difference between a futures contract and a forward contract.
3. Explain the importance of futures markets.
4. Carefully discuss the importance of the clearinghouse in futures markets.
5. What is marking to market? How does marking to market affect the cash flows of a futures contract?
6. What is the relationship between the price of the futures contract and the spot price of the underlying commodity as the expiration of the futures contract is approached?
7. Carefully explain how the interest rate determines the relationship between future and spot prices.
8. Carefully explain how carrying costs determine the relationship between future and spot prices.
9. On February 1, the spot price of a commodity is $250 and the current risk-free rate is 9%. What is the value on February 1 of a futures contract that matures on March 1 and on April 1?
10. Carefully explain the difference between hedging and speculation.
11. Suppose an investor has a portfolio of T-bills with a face value of $1 million, currently worth $960,000. Assume the T-bills in this portfolio mature in three months. A three-month T-bill futures contract is currently selling for $96\frac{24}{32}$. Assume that interest rates rise and the value of the T-bills falls to $950,125, while the value of the T-bills futures contract falls to $96\frac{8}{32}$.

    (a) Use the T-bill futures to hedge your T-bill position.
    (b) Is it possible to create a riskless hedge for this example?
    (c) If it is not possible to create a riskless hedge, what does this say about the market for T-bills and T-bill futures?
    (d) Calculate the net change in the value of the hedged portfolio.

12. Calculate the change in settlement for a T-bill contract for a 6-basis-point change in the yield. Assume the contract matures in 180 days.
13. What is the settlement value for an IMM T-bill contract when the final index is 94?
14. Suppose the spot price for hog bellies is 44 cents per pound on July 1. What is the value on July 1 of a futures contract that matures on September 1 with a price of 44 cents per pound? Assume that the risk-free rate is 8%.
15. Recalculate the value of the futures contract presented in Sample Problem 4.4 if the carrying cost changes to \$0.02 per pound per month.
16. Explain the logic behind the following formula:

$$F_{t,T} = \text{Min}[E_t(\tilde{S}_T), S_t(1 + R_{f,T-t}) + C_{T-t}].$$

17. Explain the role of each of the following in the futures market:
    (a) hedger
    (b) speculator
    (c) arbitrager

    If any one of these groups is not participating in the futures market, what happens to the market? Answer this question for each group.
18. What are the various risk components of basis risk? What can be done about reducing or eliminating them?
19. What is the economic rationale for the existence of futures markets?
20. What is the difference between a forward market and a futures market?
21. An investor with \$10 million in T-bills wishes to hedge his position. Given the following information, what is the gain or loss on the cash and futures position?

at $t = 0$	T-bills sell at 98% of par.
	Futures contract (\$1 million face) is $98\frac{1}{4}$.
at $t \leq t + 1$	Interest rates have fallen.
	T-bills sell at $98\frac{1}{2}$% of par.
	Futures contract (\$1 million face) is $98\frac{3}{4}$.

22. Compare and contrast the uses of the word *margin* in the stock market and in the futures market.

23. What is the current futures price of commodity X if the spot prices of X is \$10 and the futures contract has two months to delivery? The current interest rate is 12%.
24. Given the information in Question 23 and a carrying cost of \$0.10 per dollar value per month, what is the current futures price?
25. Given the information in Questions 23 and 24, if the spot price for X is expected to be \$10, what is the futures price at $t = 0$? If the spot price of X is expected never to change, perhaps it is guaranteed by some sort of government program. Would you trade in futures contracts for X?
26. Given the following information, what is the basis at $t = 0$? What is the basis at $t \leq 1$? Why has the basis changed?

$t = 0$	Spot price = \$10	$t \leq 1$	Spot price = 9.75
	Futures price = \$11.50		Futures price = \$10.75

$$\text{Basis} = \text{Future} - \text{Spot}$$

$$f = \text{S}(1 + r) + \text{Carrying costs}$$

27. Using the Howard–D'Antonio model, what is the hedge ratio if

$$\lambda = 0.5$$

$$\rho = 0.9$$

$$\gamma = 1.01$$

$$\pi = 1.2$$

What is the hedging effectiveness?

Bibliography

Black, F. (1976). The pricing of commodity contracts. *Journal of Financial Economics*, 3(September), 167–179.

Castelino, M. (1989). Basis volatility: Implications for hedging. *Journal of Financial Research*, 12(2), 157–172.

Castelino, M. and J. Francis (1982). Basis speculation in commodity futures: The maturity effect. *Journal of Futures Markets*, 2(2), 195–207.

Chen, S. S., C. F. Lee and K. Shrestha (2003). Futures hedge ratios: A review. *The Quarterly Review of Economics and Finance*, 43(3), 433–465.

Chen, S. S., C. F. Lee and K. Shrestha (2004). An empirical analysis of the relationship between the hedge ratio and hedging horizon: A simultaneous estimation of the short- and long-run hedge ratios. *Journal of Futures Markets*, 24(4), 359–386.

Cheng, E. (1985). Returns of speculators and the theory of normal backwardation. *Journal of Finance*, 40(March), 193–208.

Chicago Board of Trade (1987). *GNMA Futures*. Chicago Board of Trade.

Chicago Board of Trade (1987). *Ten-Year Treasury Futures*. Chicago Board of Trade.

Chicago Board of Trade (1987). *U.S. Treasury Bond Futures*. Chicago Board of Trade.

Chou, W. L., K. F. Denis and C. F. Lee (1996). Hedging with the Nikkei index futures: The conventional model versus the error correction model. *The Quarterly Review of Economics and Finance*, 36(4), 495–505.

Cornell, B. and K. French (1983). Taxes and the pricing of stock index futures. *Journal of Finance*, 38(June), 675–694.

Cox, J., J. Ingersoll and S. Ross (1981). The relation between forward and futures prices. *Journal of Financial Economics*, 9(December), 321–346.

Daigler, T. (1988). Futures bibliography. *Journal of Futures Markets*, 8(Spring), 131–143.

Dusak, K. (1973). Futures trading and investor returns: An investigation of commodity market risk premiums. *Journal of Political Economy*, 81(November/December), 1306–1313.

Ederington, L. H. (1979). The hedging performance of the new futures markets. *Journal of Finance*, 34(March), 157–170.

Elton, E., M. Gruber and J. Rentzler (1984). Intraday tests of the efficiency of the T-bill futures market. *Review of Economics and Statistics*, 66(February), 129–137.

Fama, E. (1976). Forward rates as predictors of future spot rates. *Journal of Financial Economics*, 3(October), 361–377.

Figlewski, S. (1986). *Hedging with Financial Futures for Institutional Investors*. New York: Ballinger Publishing Co.

Howard, C. T. and L. J. D'Antonio (1984). A risk-return measure of hedging effectiveness. *Journal of Financial and Quantitative Analysis*, 19(March), 101–112.

Hsin, C. W., J. Kuo and C. F. Lee (1994). A new measure to compare the hedging effectiveness of foreign currency futures versus options. *Journal of Futures Markets*, 14(6), 685–707.

Hsin, C. W., J. Kuo and C. F. Lee (1995). An empirical test of minimum-risk foreign currency hedges with futures and options. *Advances in Investment Analysis and Portfolio Management*, III, 100–125.

International Monetary Market (1988). *Opportunities in Interest Rates: T-Bill Futures.* IMM.

International Monetary Market (1988). *Inside CD Futures.* IMM.

International Monetary Market (1988). *Inside Eurodollar Futures.* IMM.

International Monetary Market (1988). *Inside SP500 Stock Index Futures.* IMM.

International Monetary Market (1988). *International Monetary Market.* IMM.

International Monetary Market (1988). *Understanding Futures in Foreign Exchange.* IMM.

International Monetary Market (1988). *The S & P 100 Stock Index Futures Contract: Flexibility for Today's Investor.* IMM.

Jacob, N. L. and R. R. Pettit (1984). *Investments.* New York: Richard D. Irwin, Inc.

Jarrow, R. and G. Oldfield (1981). Forward contracts and futures contracts. *Journal of Financial Economics*, 8(December), 373–382.

Johnson, L. L. (1960). The theory of hedging and speculation in commodity futures. *Review of Economic Studies*, 27(March), 139–151.

Junkus, J. C. and C. F. Lee (1985). Use of three stock index futures in hedging decisions. *Journal of Futures Markets*, 5(2), 201–222.

Kamara, A. (1982). Issues in futures markets: A survey. *Journal of Futures Markets*, 2(Fall), 261–294.

Keynes, J. M. (1930). *A Treatise on Money, 2.* New York: Macmillan & Co.

Khoury, S. J. (1983). *Investing Management: Theory and Application.* New York: Macmillan Publishing Co., Inc.

Kolb, R. (1984). *Understanding Futures Markets.* New York: Scott, Foresman and Co.

Koppenhaver, G. D. and C. F. Lee (1987). Alternative instruments for hedging inflation risk in the banking industry. *Journal of Futures Markets*, 7(6), 619–636.

Lee, C. F., E. L. Bubnys and Y. Lin (1987). Stock index futures hedge ratios: Test on horizon effects and functional form. *Advances in Futures and Options Research*, 2(1), 291–311.

Lee, C. F., K. Wang and Y. L. Chen (2009). Hedging and optimal hedge ratios for international index futures markets. *Review of Pacific Basin Financial Markets and Policies*, 12(4), 593–610.

Lin, F. L. (2023). A comparative analysis of hedging determination for three alternative international equity index futures. *Review of Pacific Basin Financial Markets and Policies*, Forthcoming.

Loosigian, A. M. (1980). *Interest Rate Futures.* New York: Dow Jones-Irwin Inc.

Markowitz, H. (1959). *Portfolio Selection.* New York: John Wiley and Sons, Inc.

Modest, D. M. and M. Sundaresan (1983). The relationship between spot and futures prices in stock index futures markets: Some preliminary evidence. *The Journal of Futures Markets*, 3(Spring), 15–42.

Powers, M. and D. Vogel (1981). *Inside the Financial Futures Markets.* New York: John Wiley and Sons, Inc.

Rutledge, D. J. S. (1972). Hedgers' demand for futures contracts: A theoretical framework with applications to the United States Soybean Complex. *Food Research Institute Studies*, 11(March), 237–256.

Schwarz, E., J. Hill and T. Schneeweis (1986). *Financial Futures: Fundamentals Strategies, and Applications.* New York: Richard D. Irwin.

Sharpe, W. F. (1987). *Investments*, 3rd ed. New York.: Prentice-Hall, Inc.

Telser, L. (1981). Why there are organized futures markets. *Journal of Law and Economics*, 24(April), 1–22.

Telser, L. (1986). Futures and actual markets: How they are related. *Journal of Business*, 59(April), 5–20.

Toevs, A. and D. Jacob (1986). Futures and alternative hedge ratio methodologies. *Journal of Portfolio Management*, 12(Spring), 60–70.

Weiner, N. S. (1981). The hedging rationale for a stock index futures contract. *Journal of Futures Market*, 1(Spring), 59–76.

Weiner, N. S. (1984). *Stock Index Futures.* New York: John Wiley and Sons, Inc.

Working, H. (1953). Hedging reconsidered. *Journal of Farm Economics*, 35(June), 544–561.

Appendix 4A: Basic Futures Terminology

Although related to other securities markets, such as those for stocks or bonds, the futures market is unique not only in nature but also with regard to some of its terminology. In this appendix, we define some commonly used terms for these markets as follows in Table 4A.1.

Table 4A.1 Basic Futures Terminology

Term	Definition
Arbitrage	The simultaneous purchase and sale of similar financial instruments or commodity futures in order to benefit from an anticipated change (correction) in their price relationship.
Basis	The difference between futures price and the spot price. Basis is one kind of risk in investment: it is explored in this chapter.
Bid	An offer to purchase at a specified price.
Car	A loose term sometimes used to describe the quantity of a contract — for example, "I am long a car of bellies."
Cash commodity	The actual physical commodity, as distinguished from a futures commodity. A commodity delivered at the time of sale is a cash commodity, while a commodity to be delivered at a specific future date is a future commodity.
Clearinghouse	The third party of every futures contract, which guarantees that every futures contract will be carried out even if one of the parties defaults. The clearinghouse also facilitates trading of futures contracts before they are due for delivery.
Contract amount	The number of units of the good or service to be delivered.
Contract month	The month in which a futures contract is scheduled to mature by making or accepting a delivery.
Contract specification	The precise definition of the good or service to be delivered in the futures contract.
Delivery	The tender and receipt of an actual commodity or financial instrument, or cash in settlement of a futures contract.
Delivery point	A point designated by a futures exchange at which the financial instrument or commodity covered by futures contract may be delivered in fulfillment of such a contract.
Equity	The residual dollar value of a futures trading account (over and above margin requirements), assuming its liquidation at the going market price.

Table 4A.1 (*Continued*)

Term	Definition
Floor broker	A licensed member of the exchange who is paid a fee for executing orders for clearing members or their customers.
Floor trader	An exchange member who generally trades only for his or her own account, or for an account controlled by him or her. (Also called "local.")
Forward contract	A prespecified contract similar to a futures contract except that it is tailored to suit the particular needs of the individual parties. Forward contracts are not generally traded on exchanges because they lack standardization, they do not have the daily mark-to-market requirement, and they typically require no transfers of money until delivery.
Futures contract	A legally binding, standardized agreement made within the confines of an exchange trading area, specifying the good or service involved, the quantity, and the future date and price at which the contract is to be fulfilled.
Hedger	A market participant who has or will have a position in the cash commodity and who attempts to eliminate or reduce risk exposure by taking an offsetting position in the futures or forward market.
Liquidation	Any transaction that offsets or closes out a long or short position. (Also called "evening up" or "offset.")
Long position	The purchase of a futures contract in anticipation of taking eventual delivery of the commodity (or financial instrument) or an expected increase in the underlying asset's price.
Margin	A cash amount of funds that must be deposited with the broker for each futures contract as a guarantee of its fulfillment.
Margin call	A demand for additional cash funds for each futures position held because of an adverse price movement.
Mark to market	The daily adjustment of a futures trading account to reflect profits or losses due to daily changes in the value of the futures contract.

(*Continued*)

Table 4A.1 (*Continued*)

Term	Definition
Open contracts	Contracts that have been bought or sold without the transactions having been completed by subsequent sale or purchase, or by making or taking actual delivery of the financial instrument or physical commodity. Measured by "open interest," as reported in the press.
Settlement price	A figure determined by the closing price range that is used to calculate daily gains and losses in futures market accounts (and thus margin calls) and invoice prices for deliveries.
Short position	The sale of a futures contract in anticipation of a fall in the price of the underlying asset. Also obligates delivery of the commodity or financial instrument (and payment) if the position is left open to maturity.
Speculator	A market participant who is willing (for a price) to take on the risk the hedger wishes to eliminate. This trader goes long or short on a contract without having, or intending to take, an opposite position in the cash market.
Spot price	The current price of the commodity if purchased in the cash or "spot" market.
Spread	Refers to the simultaneous purchase and sale of futures contracts for (1) the name commodity or instrument with different maturity months or (2) commodities in different but related markets.
Tick	Refers to a change in price, either up or down. The amount varies with each contract.
Volume	The number of transactions in a futures contract made during a specified period of time.

Appendix 4B: Derivation of Minimum-Variance Hedge Ratio

By combining investments in the spot market and futures market to form a portfolio, we can eliminate (or reduce) fluctuations in its value by hedging. Consider a portfolio consisting of C_s units of a long spot position and C_f units of a short futures position.[1] Following Lee *et al.* (2013) and Chen *et al.* (2003), let S_t and F_t denote the spot and futures prices at time t, respectively. Since the futures contracts are

[1]Without loss of generality, we assume that the size of the future contract is 1.

used to reduce the fluctuations in spot positions, the resulting portfolio is known as the hedged portfolio. If the hedge ratio is discussed in terms of price changes (profits), then the profit on the hedged portfolio, ΔV_H, and the hedge ratio, H, are respectively given by the following:

$$\Delta V_H = C_s \Delta S_t - H C_f \Delta F_t \quad \text{and} \quad H = \frac{C_f}{C_s}, \tag{4B.1}$$

where $\Delta S_t = S_{t+1} - S_t$ and $\Delta F_t = F_{t+1} - F_t$.

The most widely used static hedge ratio is the minimum-variance (MV) hedge ratio. Johnson (1960) derives this hedge ratio by minimizing the portfolio risk, where the risk is given by the variance of changes in the value of the hedged portfolio as follows:

$$\text{Var}(\Delta V_H) = C_s^2 \text{Var}(\Delta S) + C_f^2\, \text{Var}(\Delta F) - 2C_s C_f H\, Cov(\Delta S, \Delta F).$$

The MV hedge ratio, in this case, is given by the following:

$$H_J^* = \frac{C_f}{C_s} = \frac{Cov(\Delta S, \Delta F)}{\text{Var}(\Delta F)}. \tag{4B.2}$$

Alternatively, if we use $\text{Var}(R_h)$ to represent the risk of hedged portfolio return (R_h), then the MV hedge ratio is obtained by minimizing $Var(R_h)$ which is given by the following:

$$\text{Var}(R_h) = \text{Var}(R_s) + h^2 \text{Var}(R_f) - 2h Cov(R_s, R_f),$$

where h is the so-called hedge ratio, and R_s and R_f are so-called one-period returns on the spot and futures positions, respectively. In this case, the MV hedge ratio is given by the following:

$$h_J^* = \frac{Cov(R_s, R_f)}{\text{Var}(R_f)} = \rho \frac{\sigma_s}{\sigma_f}, \tag{4B.3}$$

where ρ is the correlation coefficient between R_s and R_f, and σ_s and σ_f are standard deviations of R_s and R_f, respectively.

The attractive features of the MV hedge ratio are that it is easy to understand and simple to compute. However, in general, the MV hedge ratio is not consistent with the mean-variance framework since it ignores the expected return on the hedged portfolio. For the

MV hedge ratio to be consistent with the mean-variance framework, either the investors need to be infinitely risk averse or the expected return on the futures contract needs to be zero.

Appendix 4C: Single-Stock Futures and Their Valuation

In this appendix, we will learn about Single-Stock Futures (SSF) and how these alternate securities can be used by investors to increase their profitability while managing their exposure. Single-Stock futures possess many of the same qualities of traditional futures contracts, yet also have their differences. We will look more into the nature of Single-Stock Futures, as well as their advantages in this appendix.

Single-stock futures are futures contracts on individual stocks. There are currently over 80 well-known stock futures such as IBM, eBay, and Philip Morris. These futures products provide investors with a cost-effective vehicle for participating in U.S. equities markets.

A stock futures contract is an agreement to deliver shares of a specific stock at a designated date in the future, called the expiration date. Most stock futures contracts are not held until expiration because traders typically offset their position — selling if the trader is long or buying if the trader is short.

The price of an equity futures typically tracks the price of the underlying instrument nearly tick for tick, so trading strategies followed in the stock market are generally transferable to the stock futures market. Single-stock futures may therefore be used with a broad range of trading strategies and for a variety of portfolio management needs.

When a stock future is traded, both the buyer and seller put up a good-faith deposit called margin. The margin requirement for security futures is generally 20% of the underlying value of the securities, although this requirement may be lower if the investor also holds certain offsetting positions in cash equities, stock options, or other security futures in the same securities account.

4C.1 *Nature of SSF contracts*

Each single-stock futures contract represents 100 shares of underlying stock. That is the contract size used at the London International Financial Futures Exchange (LIFFE) and by the Chicago Board Options Exchange (CBOE) for equity options. There are no daily price limits for SSF contracts. Like other securities that are exchange traded, physical delivery of underlying security takes place on the third business day following the Expiration Day.

In Table 4C.1, we see the market quotes for Single-Stock Futures from Yahoo! for May 25, 2021. Both tables show the trading of SSF on the Yahoo! Finance website, the bottom table just representing what stocks experience more frequent trading. The first column represents the **symbol** for each of the SSF. In the bottom table, we see that there are quotes on Allstate (ALL1C), Cisco Systems (CSCO1C), American Express (AXP), and many others. The second column, **expiration month**, states the month of expiration for each of the stock futures depicted, in this case either March or December. The third column, **days to expiration**, expands on Column 2 and provides a quantitative measure of the days left in the futures contract. The fourth and seventh columns, **Future Bid Size** and **Future Ask Size** describe the size of the futures contract in question. As we can see for the EA1D futures contract in the second table, there is a bid/ask size of 10. The **Future Bid** illustrates the price that people are willing to buy the SSF contracts at, and the **Future Ask** is the price at which people are willing to sell. Looking at the **Dividend** column, we see that most of the stocks do not offer a dividend, except for ALL1C. In the following section, we will see that when pricing single-stock futures, we need to account for dividends by subtracting them out of the equation due to the fact that SSF contract holders are not entitled to a dividend. The last column represents the **time** at which each trade occurred.

4C.2 *Pricing single-stock futures*

Single-stock futures values are priced by the market in accordance with a theoretical pricing model based on the following formula:

$$\begin{aligned}\text{Futures price} &= \text{Underlying stock price}\\ &\quad \times (1 + \text{Annualized interest rate}) - \text{Dividend}.\end{aligned}$$

Table 4C.1 SSF Quotes from Yahoo!

Symbol	Expiration Month	Days to Expiration	Future BID Size	Future BID	Future ASK	Future ASK Size	Dividend (%)	Time
Yahoo! ETF Futures on 5-25-2021								
XLF1D	Dec	220	29,200	37.47	37.48	47,300	1.63	4:00:00
XLE1D	Dec	220	3,200	51.63	51.64	1,800	4.23	4:00:00
SPY1D	Dec	220	1,300	418.23	418.16	1,400	1.33	4:00:00
QQQ1D	Dec	220	1,200	332.68	332.73	1,400	0.52	4:00:00
IWM1D	Dec	220	1,800	219.21	219.22	1,000	0.90	4:00:00
DIA1D	Dec	220	900	343.11	343.19	800	1.64	4:00:00
10 Active Futures at Yahoo! on 5-25-2021								
EA1D	Mar	310	800	143.24	143.29	1,200	0.49	4:00:00
AA1C	Dec	220	1,000	35.06	35.11	1,400	N/A	4:00:00
ALL1C	Dec	220	800	135.36	135.39	800	2.36	4:00:00
AUY1D	Mar	310	38,800	5.16	5.17	36,900	2.02	4:00:00
AXP1C	Dec	220	1,300	158.09	157.86	900	1.08	4:00:00
CCL1C	Dec	220	1,400	28.62	28.63	1,000	N/A	4:00:00
COHU1D	Dec	220	800	36.37	36.41	800	N/A	4:00:00
COST1C	Dec	220	1,000	385.43	385.44	800	0.82	4:00:00
CS1D	Dec	220	28,000	10.78	10.80	43,500	1.01	4:00:00
CSCO1C	Dec	220	2,900	53.29	53.30	36,200	2.77	4:00:00

Source: Yahoo! Finance; May 25, 2021; Real-Time Stock Quotes — https://finance.yahoo.com/portfolio/p_2/view/view_1.

For stocks that contain a dividend, we get the following equation:

$$F = S \cdot (1 + r) - \text{Div}, \tag{4C.1}$$

where F is the single-stock futures contract price, S is the underlying stock price, r is the annualized interest rate, and Div is the expected dividend.

Another valuation of single-stock futures can be found through the following:

$$F = [S - \text{PV}(\text{Div})] \cdot \mathrm{e}^{r \cdot (T-t)}, \tag{4C.2}$$

where F is single-stock futures contract price, S is the underlying stock price, PV(Div) is the present value of any dividends entitled to the holder of the underlying between T and t, r is the interest rate, and e is the base of the natural log.

For stocks that do not contain a dividend, we can price SSF using the following equation:

$$F = S \cdot (1 + r), \tag{4C.3}$$

where F is the single-stock futures contract price, S is the underlying stock price, and r is the annualized interest rate.

Another valuation of single-stock futures can be found through the following:

$$F = S \cdot e^{r \cdot (T-t)}, \tag{4C.4}$$

where F is single-stock futures contract price, S is the price of the underlying (the stock price), $T - t$ is the days to expiration, r is the interest rate, and e is the base of the natural log.

Most of the time, single-stock futures will trade at a premium to the stock price adjusted for the broker loan rate. The premium reflects the interest earned on the capital saved by not posting the full value of the underlying stock. Since futures holders are not entitled to collect dividends, the futures price must be adjusted downward by the expected amount of dividend payments prior to expiration. In the case where a large dividend payment is expected, the futures contract may theoretically trade at a discount to the actual cash price.

4C.3 *Advantages of single-stock futures*

There are many advantages to an investor who chooses to use Single-Stock Futures. Some of these advantages are as follows:

4C.3.1 *Selling a stock short*

One advantage to selling a stock short is the ease and diminished expense of taking a short position in a single stock. Selling a stock short in the stock market is relatively complicated and expensive. A short sale in a stock necessitates locating the shares to borrow and paying the broker loan rate of interest. You must then wait for an uptick to sell the stock short. Waiting for an uptick to sell a stock short in a declining market can be frustrating and costly. By the time a particular stock upticks, it could be substantially below the price at which you wanted it sold. However, in the futures market with the SSF contract, you can sell a stock short just as easily as you can buy one. When you sell a stock short using an SSF contract, you do not have to wait for an uptick. You can sell when you want, without going to the trouble of finding the stock and without the expense of paying the broker loan rate of interest on the shares borrowed.

4C.3.2 *Risk management*

Selling SSF contracts can also greatly contribute to risk management in an investor's portfolio with possible tax benefits. Instead of selling specific stocks in one's portfolio during market downturns, an investor could sell an equal amount of shares in SSF as a hedge against his or her stock position. The ability to hedge a particular stock facilitates holding onto the underlying position in the stock market for longer periods of time, thereby potentially providing investors substantial tax savings in long-term versus short-term gains.

4C.3.3 *Speculation*

An investor without owning any stock could use SSF to speculate outright on an anticipated increase or decrease in the price of a stock.

4C.3.4 *Margins*

One major difference between stocks and futures centers on the role of margins. For stocks, margins, which are set by the Federal Reserve's Regulation T, have been at 50% for retail investors and 15% for dealers since 1974. A stock investor buying on margin borrows the difference, and can either pay the loan down or offset it when the security is sold. Futures margins, which are set by the exchange, do not represent a down payment on an asset, but are rather a performance bond from the investor to the exchange clearinghouse. Margins vary quite widely as a percentage of the underlying asset, but generally are quite low. For example, the underlying value of the S&P 500 future is hovering around $335,000, but the initial margin for a speculator is only $23,438, or less than 7%. The futures investor does not have to pay interest on the remaining 93%; indeed, futures investors can deposit T-bills and earn interest on 90% of the deposit with a 10% haircut in their margin accounts.

4C.3.5 *Cost advantage*

SSF are traded in 100-share blocks, virtually mirroring the price movement in the single stock on which the futures contract is based. A $1 move in an individual stock equals $100 in an SSF contract. There is a big cost advantage here. In order to control shares in a stock, you need to post at least 50% margin and pay interest on the balance. In SSF, all that is required is approximately 20%, or less than half the margin required in the stock market. Additionally, there is no interest charge on buying or selling a stock on margin in SSF. Essentially, you will earn or lose the same in an SSF contract as you would when buying 100 shares of stock.

4C.3.6 *Commission savings*

In all probability, the transaction costs in buying or selling an SSF contract amount to less than buying or selling the same 100 shares of stock in the stock market.

4C.3.7 *Spread differentials*

SSF offers investors additional investment strategies. For example, if an investor feels the price of one stock will decline or rise in relation to another stock, he or she can buy an SSF contract on one stock and sell an SSF contract on another, hoping to profit from the spread differential between the two stocks any time up to the contract's expiration.

4C.3.8 *No clearing fees on foreign markets*

The investor can also gain cross-border exposure without the expense of going through foreign clearing systems. This will circumvent many of the difficulties faced by investors attempting to trade across jurisdictional boundaries by providing access to UK, European, and US shares on a single trading platform.

Universal Stock futures transactions will be clear of costs of accessing settlement systems across international borders.

4C.3.9 *Greater versatility*

SSF allows a trader to potentially profit no matter what direction the market moves. If a trader is of the opinion that the stock market is going to fall, a trader can sell a contract. A profit will be made if the trader then buys that contract back later when the price decreases. This avoids the hassle of stock borrowing.

Chapter 5

Commodity Futures, Financial Futures, and Stock Index Futures

Contents

5.1 Introduction

From the viewpoint of a security analyst and portfolio manager, knowledge of alternative future instruments is important because these instruments allow the analyst and manager to invest for profit and/or to hedge for risk. How to use futures as portfolio insurance is discussed in Chapter 13.

Following the basic concepts, valuation, and hedging strategies of futures instruments and markets discussed in Chapter 4, Chapter 5 investigates commodity futures, financial futures, and index futures.

Section 5.2 introduces commodity futures, and Section 5.3 discusses futures quotations. Financial futures are covered in Section 5.4, and Section 5.5 presents stock index futures. The summary in Section 5.6 covers the key concepts learned in this chapter.

5.2 Commodity Futures

Futures trading in the United States originated in the early 1800s for agricultural commodities. With no organized trading exchanges at that time, these original **commodity futures** contracts were, originally, forward agreements. The use of forward contracts evolved from necessity as spot markets increasingly proved their inability to handle excess supply or demand for commodities. However, these forward contracts also proved to have their limitations in that they were not sufficiently liquid for hedgers.

Today, there are over fourteen commodity exchanges offering futures contracts on more than thirty different commodities. In the United States, the two major futures exchanges are the Chicago Mercantile Exchange (CME) and the InterContinental Exchange (ICE). Why are futures contracts traded on some commodities? And why are some commodities excluded from futures trading? Remember that price risk is the underlying reason for the existence of futures markets. Any good (or service) that has a volatile price, either due to macroeconomic or environmental factors that can affect future supply and demand conditions, is a prime candidate to be traded in a futures market.

For example, think of agricultural crops for a moment. The annual supply of a particular crop can be devastatingly affected by adverse weather conditions. So, if heavy rains and unexpectedly cold weather damaged a large portion of the wheat crop, supply would be reduced and prices that processors have to pay would rise. Conversely, if weather conditions turned out better than expected and the wheat harvest was very large, an overabundant supply of the crop would push prices down, hurting the farmer. Thus, for good reason, the agricultural industry was the first to utilize forward-pricing arrangements to aid in transferring the inherent price risks to those more willing to bear it.

There are alternatives to consider for the farmer in dealing with price uncertainty. Assume it is spring and crop planting is taking place. The farmer observes that although market prices are comfortably high, the wheat harvest may be large enough to force prices to become significantly lower. If prices drop, the farmer will lose money on the invested efforts and expenses. If the farmer does nothing and waits to see what happens to prices, the risk is substantial, especially if the odds increase that weather conditions will be better than expected. The farmer's other alternative would be to hedge the price risk in the futures market. To do this, the farmer would go into the futures market (through a commodities broker) and sell (go short) wheat futures contracts that expire at the same time that the crop would be brought to market. By taking such an action, the farmer is indicating satisfaction with the current contracted price, as taking a position in the futures market essentially "locks in" the contracted futures price. Sample Problem 5.1 provides an illustration of hedging price risk, where a wheat farmer is exploring their alternatives within the futures market.

Sample Problem 5.1

Suppose that Farmer Smith is planting enough wheat to yield 50,000 bushels to bring to market in July. Furthermore, Farmer Smith observes that while current market prices are quite attractive at $5.00 per bushel, a record wheat crop is expected.

So, Farmer Smith decides to hedge his price risk by going into the futures market and effectively selling his crop ahead of time through the sale of ten wheat futures contracts (a contract represents 5,000 bushels) at $5.00 per bushel, expiring in July. Assuming there is no basis risk, the outcomes of this transaction for falling and rising prices over the interim period are shown in Table 5.1.

While Sample Problem 5.1 is simplified, its purpose is to demonstrate how the futures market is used and how the locking in of a price is achieved through hedging. That is, the farmer received $5.00 per bushel at market time whether prices went lower or higher over the interim. Of course, it would be logical to wonder who would buy the futures contracts from the farmer if prices were expected to fall. As a matter of fact, it is the market participants known as the **speculators** who would do so. Contrary to the farmer, who as a hedger took a position in the futures market opposite to the actual commodity, instead, the speculator would buy the futures contracts from the farmer on the chance that prices would actually rise and not fall as expected. If prices rose, the speculator, who is long the contract,

Table 5.1 Hedging the Price Risk by Futures Market

	Cash Market	Futures Market
Prices fall	March 1: Plants 50,000 bu (spot price = \$5.00/bu)	Sells ten contracts at \$5.00
	July 15: Sells 50,000 but at \$4.50/bu	Buys ten contracts at \$4.50
	Profit (loss) = (\$0.50/bu) × 50,000 bu = (\$25,000)	Profit (loss) = (\$0.50/bu) × 10 × 5,000 bu = (\$25,000)
		Net gain = 0
Prices rise	March 1: Plants 50,000 bu (spot price = \$5.00/bu)	Sells ten contracts at \$5.00
	July 15: Sells 50,000 bu at \$5.50/bu	Buys ten contracts at \$5.50
	Profit (loss) = (\$0,50/bu) × 50,000 bu = \$25,000	Profit (loss) = (\$0,50/bu) × 10 × 5,000 bu = (\$25,000)
		Net gain = 0

would profit handsomely because of the leverage involved. However, the large potential return is balanced by a large potential loss should prices fall.

It should be known that hedging works both ways. In this example, Table 5.1 shows that when the price falls, hedging is beneficial to the hedger. When the price rises, the spot market makes \$2,500. However, the future market loses \$2,500, reducing the profit that could be made in the spot market to zero.

The speculator's role in the futures market has been questioned throughout the history of futures markets. Essentially, what the speculator appears to be doing is gambling. Yet, without the speculator, the futures markets would cease to function efficiently, if at all. That is, the farmer (hedger) who goes into the market to hedge the price risk is, essentially, transferring it to someone else, the speculator. When the hedger needs to liquidate a futures position by buying ten contracts (as in the example), the speculator is there to sell them. So, the speculator contributes to the functioning of futures markets in two invaluable ways: (1) risk transference and (2) liquidity.

Finally, remember that the speculator does not intend to provide such invaluable economic services for no return; the speculator takes on price risk and provides liquidity in return for potential profits.

For any futures contract, there are numerous specifications and trading characteristics concerning the goods to be delivered. Table 5.2 lists these specifications and characteristics by contract

Table 5.2 Agriculture, Energy, Index, Interest Rate, Metals, Currency, and Other Futures

Complete Commodities & Futures Data		
Intraday Futures Prices		
All Contracts in These Categories; Plus, Options and More Charting		
Agriculture	**Interest Rate**	**Other**
Food, Fiber	Americas	Currency
Livestock, Meat	Europe	Lumber
Corn, Oats, Rice	Euro	Weather
Oilseeds	Eurodollar, Yen	
Wheat	Asian, Pacific	
Ethanol	**Metals**	
Energy	Copper	
Electricity	Gold	
Petroleum	Platinum	
Index	Silver	
U.S.		
International		
Spot Prices		
Cash Commodity Prices		Spot Lumber & Panel Prices
Settlement Prices, Indexes & Other Statistics		
API Energy Data: Weekly Snapshot	London Metals Exchange Prices	Electricity Price Indexes
Commodities Indexes	Performance by Asset Class	Electricity Production
Futures Settlements		
Futures Options — Closing Snapshot		
Agricultural	Interest Rate	Energy
Currency	Livestock	Metals
Index		

Source: *The Wall Street Journal.*

and exchange, displaying the commodity futures prices as they are printed daily in the press.

5.3 Futures Quotations

As indicated in Table 5.2, *The Wall Street Journal* reports daily information on various types of futures contracts. For example, the corn futures price data, on May 27, 2021, is presented in Table 5.3. There are a number of important terms and quotations related to futures contracts (and used in *The Wall Street Journal*) that are useful to know; these terms will be defined in Table 5.4.

Also of concern are *commodity*, *exchanges*, *contract size*, and *prices*. For example, the commodity trade is corn. The exchange refers to the place where the futures contracts are traded: CBT signifies the Chicago Board of Trade. The contract size refers to the amount of spot commodity that the contract represents — for example, 5,000 bushels of corn. The price is the manner in which

Table 5.3 Corn Future Prices: Globex (CBOT) — 5/27/2021

Click for Chart	Current Session								Prior Day		Opt's
	Open	High	Low	Last	Time	Set	Chg	Vol	Set	Op Int	
Cash	-	669 4/8	669 4/8	669 4/8	21:09 May 26	669 4/8s*	4 2/8	-	665 2/8	-	n/a
Jul'21	626 0/8	664 4/8	621 2/8	664 4/8	13:19 May 27	664 4/8s	40 0/8	147969	624 4/8	612617	Call Put
Sep'21	548 6/8	586 6/8	546 0/8	585 4/8	13:19 May 27	585 4/8s	38 2/8	55854	547 2/8	314717	Call Put
Dec'21	523 0/8	557 0/8	521 0/8	555 0/8	13:19 May 27	555 0/8s	34 2/8	111990	520 6/8	535356	Call Put
Mar'22	529 0/8	563 2/8	527 6/8	561 4/8	13:19 May 27	561 4/8s	34 2/8	10535	527 2/8	115724	Call Put
May'22	531 4/8	565 4/8	531 0/8	564 0/8	13:19 May 27	564 0/8s	34 0/8	7513	530 0/8	33166	Call Put
Jul'22	531 0/8	564 4/8	530 0/8	563 0/8	13:19 May 27	563 0/8s	33 2/8	6341	529 6/8	54833	Call Put
Sep'22	486 4/8	512 6/8	486 4/8	511 0/8	13:14 May 27	511 0/8s	24 6/8	1218	486 2/8	9737	Call Put
Dec'22	473 0/8	497 0/8	472 6/8	493 2/8	13:19 May 27	493 2/8s	20 0/8	3837	473 2/8	46372	Call Put
Mar'23	480 0/8	500 0/8	480 0/8	499 4/8	13:05 May 27	499 4/8s	19 4/8	48	480 0/8	1914	Call Put
May'23	495 0/8	501 2/8	495 0/8	501 2/8	11:41 May 27	501 2/8s	20 0/8	12	481 2/8	96	Call Put
Jul'23	487 0/8	505 4/8	487 0/8	503 0/8	12:56 May 27	503 0/8s	18 6/8	19	484 2/8	781	Call Put
Sep'23	-	458 0/8	458 0/8	458 0/8	14:00 May 27	458 0/8s	18 6/8	-	439 2/8	96	Call Put
Dec'23	434 0/8	448 0/8	434 0/8	446 2/8	12:49 May 27	446 2/8s	13 0/8	66	433 2/8	2454	Call Put
Jul'24	-	457 2/8	457 2/8	457 2/8	14:00 May 27	457 2/8s	13 0/8	-	444 2/8	24	Call Put
Dec'24	413 0/8	419 2/8	413 0/8	418 6/8	12:51 May 27	418 6/8s	6 2/8	42	412 4/8	405	Call Put

Source: FuturesTradingCharts.com.

Table 5.4 Futures Terms

Term	**Definition**
Open	The price for the day's first trade, registered during the period designated as the opening of the market.
High	Highest price at which the commodity sold during the day.
Low	Lowest price at which the commodity sold during the day.
Settle	Since each contract is marked to market each day, the settlement price or the marking-to-market price is very important to investors. The settlement price is a figure determined by formula from within the closing range or it may be the closing price.
Change	The amount the settlement price changed from the previous day.
Lifetime high or low	The highest and lowest prices recorded for each contract maturity from the first day it was traded to the present.
Open interest	The number represents the quantity of open long positions at the exchange's clearinghouse for each contract.
Volume	The number of contracts actually traded on the exchange for a given trading session.

the prices are quoted; for instance, corn at 162 means corn sells for \$1.62 per bushel. Specifications for commodity futures are listed in Table 5.2.

5.4 Financial Futures

Financial futures take many forms. The following discussion focuses on foreign currency futures and interest rate futures, which include T-bill futures, T-bond futures, and other interest rate futures.

Financial futures are standardized futures contracts whose market prices are established through open outcry and hand signals in regulated commodity exchange. They represent a legally enforceable commitment to buy and sell a prespecified quantity and quality of a specific financial instrument during a predetermined future delivery month.

5.4.1 *Foreign currency futures*

Foreign currency futures and their valuation theory are discussed in this section. A foreign currency futures contract is similar to other commodity futures contracts. It promises future delivery of a standard amount of a foreign currency at a specified time, place, and price. This instrument can be used to hedge foreign exchange risk for investors and firms involved in the import and export business.

Evolution. The concept of financial futures on currencies emerged as an anticipatory reaction to the end of the Bretton Woods Agreement, which called for the elimination of fixed parities between major currencies. In effect, on May 16, 1972, the International Monetary Market (IMM) division of the CME opened and offered the first organized trading of standardized futures contracts on foreign currencies. The application of the futures market and its trading mechanics to financial products was supported by a number of economists at the time, including Milton Friedman.

The need for these exchange rate hedging tools has intensified in the last decade. The change in U.S. monetary policy in October 1979, which went from essentially "pegging" interest rates to letting them float in accordance with market forces, resulted in a significant increase in the volatility of market interest rates. The effects of highly volatile U.S. interest rates were felt heavily in other countries as well. Consequently, the already volatile foreign exchange rate market became even more turbulent, as investors and governments moved their funds from one currency to another in search of higher returns.

As interest rates change in one country, so does the value of its currency relative to those of other countries. Therefore, a U.S. corporation that contracts to purchase materials from some foreign firm with payment to be made three months from now is exposing itself to foreign exchange risk. If at the end of the three-month period the U.S. dollar's value falls against the home currency of the foreign firm, the U.S. company will actually end up paying more for the materials than originally intended.

Advantages. Although forward markets have existed for some time to help alleviate exchange rate or currency risk, they generally do not offer the liquidity or flexibility of the futures market. The establishment of foreign currency futures has provided a means by which Interbank dealers can hedge their positions in spot or forward markets. Moreover, because each trade is guaranteed by the exchange's clearinghouse, participants need not analyze the credit risk of a large number of market counterparts, as might be necessary in establishing a forward contract. The funds of participants are protected by daily settlement of the change in position values; they are also safeguarded by the exchange's clearinghouse, whose members together guarantee all trades. Finally, futures markets allow dealers to trade anonymously and provide price insurance and arbitrage opportunities in the spot and forward markets.

IMM is one of the exchanges that offer futures contracts on foreign currencies. Presently, the foreign currencies for which futures contracts are traded include British pounds (ticker code BP); Canadian dollars (CD); Eurodollars (EUR); Chinese yuan (CY); Japanese yen (JY); and Swiss francs (SF). Trading volume is concentrated in the futures on pounds, marks, Swiss francs, yen, and the Canadian dollar. Currency futures data are presented in Table 5.5. The currency exchange rates are shown in Table 5.6.

When dealing with foreign exchange rates, it is important to realize that the price of a currency is in terms of a second currency. Both the numerator and denominator of the price ratio are in terms of money. For example, in Table 5.6, the Canadian dollar is worth \$0.8288 (\$1.2066 Canadian dollars per U.S. dollar). All foreign exchange rates are related as reciprocals.

Futures market quotes for foreign exchange are also shown in Table 5.5. The futures market is different from the forward market. In the futures market, the maturity date of a given contract is fixed by the rules of the exchange. As each day passes, the futures contract gets closer to maturity. In the forward market, thirty-, sixty-, and ninety-day contracts (or any other number of days) are available. However, contracts in the futures market mature four times a year (June, September, December, and March). In the forward market, they mature every day. In the forward market, the contract size is determined between the buyer and seller. In the futures market, only contracts of standardized amounts are traded.

Table 5.5 Currency Futures Data

Contract Name	Last	Change	Open	High	Low	Volume	Time (CT)
U.S. Dollar Index (Jun '21)	89.97	-0.06	90.075	90.18	89.895	17,955	14:34
U.S. Dollar Index (Sept '21)	89.959	-0.071	90.1	90.175	89.9	508	5/27/2021
Bitcoin Futures (Jun '21)	38,755	145	39,220	40,565	37,410	4,658	14:34
Bitcoin Futures (Jul '21)	38,845	105	39,200	40,680	37,730	261	14:34
Euro FX (Jun '21)	1.22025	0.00055	1.2197	1.2218	1.21785	148,437	14:34
Euro FX (Sept '21)	1.22235	0.0005	1.2219	1.2237	1.22	6,034	14:05
Australian Dollar (Jun '21)	0.77445	-0.0002	0.7745	0.77585	0.77235	65,860	14:34
Australian Dollar (Sept '21)	0.7748	-0.00015	0.7748	0.7761	0.7729	635	14:01
British Pound (Jun '21)	1.4208	0.0083	1.4121	1.4221	1.4091	96,264	14:34
British Pound (Sept '21)	1.4208	0.0082	1.411	1.422	1.4093	2,137	14:34
Canadian Dollar (Jun '21)	0.82865	0.0032	0.82495	0.8294	0.8235	59,586	14:34
Canadian Dollar (Sept '21)	0.8287	0.00325	0.825	0.8293	0.82355	1,556	14:24
Japanese Yen (Jun '21)	0.91095	-0.00555	0.9165	0.91715	0.90975	122,918	14:34
Japanese Yen (Sept '21)	0.9115	-0.00565	0.9169	0.91745	0.9104	853	13:59
Swiss Franc (Jun '21)	1.1153	0.0007	1.1145	1.1164	1.1104	22,499	14:34
Swiss Franc (Sept '21)	1.1182	0.001	1.1162	1.1182	1.1138	124	12:59
Mexican Peso (Jun '21)	0.04996	-0.0002	0.05016	0.05035	0.0498	40,415	14:34
Mexican Peso (Sept '21)	0.04948	-0.00017	0.04975	0.04976	0.04943	1,714	13:00
New Zealand Dollar (Jun '21)	0.7297	0.0006	0.7286	0.7311	0.7266	26,834	14:34
New Zealand Dollar (Sept '21)	0.7296	0.0008	0.728	0.7306	0.7265	68	12:52
South African Rand (Jun '21)	0.0725	2.50E–05	0.072475	0.072925	0.0723	2,165	13:59
Brazilian Real (Jun '21)	0.19045	0.00245	0.1872	0.1908	0.1872	13,483	14:34
Russian Ruble (Jun '21)	0.01358	0	0.01357	0.013605	0.01356	2,777	14:00

Source: Downloaded from Barchart.com as of 05-27-2021 02:44 pm CDT.

Table 5.6 Exchange Rates — 5/27/2021

Currency	Value	Change	Net Change	Time (EDT)
Americas				
USD-CAD	1.2066	−0.0057	−0.47%	3:59 PM
USD-MXN	19.9759	0.0949	+0.48%	3:59 PM
USD-BRL	5.2544	−0.0576	−1.08%	3:58 PM
USD-CLP	728.8500	−0.8900	−0.12%	1:29 PM
USD-COP	3, 732.1600	−11.4100	−0.30%	1:59 PM
USD-PEN	3.8478	−0.0062	−0.16%	2:29 PM
USD-VEF	—	—	–	—
USD-CRC	617.5000	0.0100	+0.00%	3:02 PM
USD-ARS	94.5354	0.0504	+0.05%	1:59 PM
EMEA				
EUR-USD	1.2198	0.0006	+0.05%	4:02 PM
GBP-USD	1.4202	0.0083	+0.59%	4:02 PM
USD-CHF	0.8967	−0.0015	−0.17%	4:02 PM
USD-SEK	8.2674	−0.0468	−0.56%	4:02 PM
USD-DKK	6.0965	−0.0025	−0.04%	4:02 PM
USD-NOK	8.3419	−0.0264	−0.32%	4:02 PM
USD-CZK	20.8615	0.0046	+0.02%	4:02 PM
USD-SKK	24.6997	−0.0083	−0.03%	4:02 PM
USD-PLN	3.6806	−0.0094	−0.25%	4:02 PM
USD-HUF	285.3800	−1.4100	−0.49%	4:02 PM
USD-RUB	73.5240	−0.0724	−0.10%	4:02 PM
USD-TRY	8.4940	0.0360	+0.43%	4:03 PM
USD-ILS	3.2422	−0.0056	−0.17%	3:58 PM
USD-KES	107.5100	−0.0600	−0.06%	10:59 AM
USD-ZAR	13.7672	0.0066	+0.05%	4:02 PM
USD-MAD	8.8405	0.0084	+0.10%	4:02 PM
APAC				
USD-JPY	109.7900	0.6400	+0.59%	4:04 PM
EUR-JPY	133.9300	0.8500	+0.64%	4:04 PM
HKD-JPY	14.1473	0.0865	+0.62%	4:04 PM
USD-HKD	7.7608	−0.0015	−0.02%	4:04 PM

(*Continued*)

Table 5.6 (*Continued*)

Currency	Value	Change	Net Change	Time (EDT)
USD-SGD	1.3241	−0.0001	−0.01%	4:04 PM
AUD-JPY	85.0230	0.5090	+0.60%	4:03 PM
AUD-USD	0.7744	0.0001	+0.01%	4:04 PM
NZD-USD	0.7297	0.0015	+0.21%	4:04 PM
USD-TWD	27.7810	−0.0240	−0.09%	3:59 AM
USD-KRW	1,117.9000	1.0500	+0.09%	2:29 AM
USD-PHP	48.0060	−0.1450	−0.30%	3:59 AM
USD-IDR	14,287.5000	−40.0000	−0.28%	3:58 AM
USD-INR	72.5875	−0.1887	−0.26%	5:59 AM
USD-CNY	6.3833	−0.0075	−0.12%	11:29 AM
USD-MYR	4.1403	−0.0032	−0.08%	5:48 AM
USD-THB	31.2960	0.0530	+0.17%	4:04 PM
JPY-MYR	3.7709	−0.0252	−0.66%	4:03 PM

Source: Bloomberg Markets.

Pricing foreign currency futures. The arbitrage argument used to establish the price of a currency futures contract relative to the spot price is called **interest rate parity** (which will be addressed in Appendix 5A). In the case of the U.S. dollar/British pound,

$$F_{t,T} = S_t \frac{(1 + R^{\$}_{t,T})}{(1 + R^{£}_{t,T})}, \tag{5.1}$$

where $F_{t,T}$ = equilibrium price at time t for a currency futures contract maturing at time T, S_t = spot price at time t for the foreign currency (to which the futures contract applies), $R^{\$}_{t,T}$ = U.S. interest rate on risk-free securities maturing at time T, and $R^{£}_{t,T}$ = British interest rate on risk-free securities maturing at time T.

Sample Problem 5.2 provides further illustration.

Sample Problem 5.2

As an example, suppose the U.S. dollar is currently quoted in the spot currency market for the British pound at \$1.80/£. Interest rates in the United States and Britain for three months are 3% and 4%, respectively. What is the price of a three-month deposit futures contract for pounds?

Solution

Substituting all information into Equation (5.1),

$$F_{t,3\,\mathrm{mo}} = (\$1.80/£)\left(\frac{1+0.03}{1+0.04}\right)$$
$$= \$1.70/£.$$

Empirical tests have shown that the pricing relationship described by interest rate parity holds very closely in the foreign currency markets. The following is offered for clarification.

In the previous section on pricing theory for futures prices, spot prices of foreign currency were described as following a random walk. Thus, money as a liquid financial instrument incorporates anticipations of its future value into its current value. This is analogous to the manner in which future stock prices and dividend estimates are reflected in today's stock price. Using this rational expectations hypothesis and momentarily assuming no inventory costs,

$$S_t = E_t(S_T), \tag{5.2}$$

or, today's price reflects the expected price for the foreign currency at time T.

Equation (5.2) can be reversed as follows:

$$E_t(S_T) = S_t. \tag{5.3}$$

Hence, the best estimate for the spot price at some future point in time T is the current spot price of the currency. Since the currency futures price at time t for a contract maturing at time T reflects the expected spot price for the foreign currency at time T (assuming no carrying costs),

$$F_{t,T} = E_t(S_T). \tag{5.4}$$

Consequently,

$$F_{t,T} = S_t. \tag{5.5}$$

So, without carrying costs, the current futures price equals the current spot price for any foreign currency. Sample Problem 5.3 provides further illustration.

Sample Problem 5.3

To see how the carrying cost (or relative opportunity cost) associated with interest has an effect on the valuation of foreign currency futures, assume that the spot and one-year futures prices for the British pound are \$1.30 and \$1.33, respectively. Suppose an American investor who bought \$1,300,000 worth or pounds (£1,000,000) then invests £1,000,000 at the 10% riskless rate yielded by one-year British government securities. Furthermore, in order to hedge himself against fluctuations in the dollar–pound exchange rate, the investor sells £1,000,000 worth of one-year futures contracts on pounds at 1.33 (equal to the value of forty contracts). Assuming the investor holds his futures position to its maturity and then delivers the initial £1,000,000 investment to close the position, the following is a summary of the transactions and closing position value:

January 1, 1989	
Buy \$1.3 million worth of pounds.	
Invest proceeds at 10% British rate.	
Sell £1,000,000 worth of futures at \$1.33.	
January 1, 1990	
Proceeds from earned interest	\$130,000
Deliver £1,000,000 against short futures Position at \$1.33/£1.00.	\$1,330,000
Gross revenue	\$1,460,000
Less initial investment	\$1,300,000
Net profit	\$160,000
Annual return	12.3%.

From all these transactions, the investor earns an annualized return of 12.3% on the original investment of \$1,300,000. This return is composed of the interest earned on the riskless British government security and the 0.03 difference in spot and one-year futures prices for the pound (i.e., the investor sold the pound at \$1.33 but only paid \$1.30).

If the investor can borrow U.S. dollars at a rate less than 12.3%, then a riskless arbitrage opportunity is available. For instance, if the U.S. lending rate is 11%, the investor could borrow the initial capital of \$1,300,000 and after one year repay the interest of 11% and clear a 1.3% risk-free return. However, this opportunity will not pass unnoticed. Arbitragers will buy pounds (bidding their price up), invest the pounds in one-year British government securities yielding

10% (bidding their price up and yield down), and sell an equivalent number of futures contracts (forcing their price down). Finally, these arbitrage portfolios will be financed by borrowing U.S. dollars at the going 11% rate (forcing the rate to increase). All pressures discussed in this problem will continue until the arbitrage opportunity has dissipated. That point will be attained when

$$S_t(1 + R^{\$}_{t,T}) = F_{t,T}(1 + R^{£}_{t,T}), \tag{5.6}$$

where $R^{\$}_{t,T}$ and $R^{£}_{t,T}$ are interest rates on securities with the same maturity as the futures contract (one year, in this case).

Rearranging Equation (5.6) to solve for $F_{t,T}$, the futures price for a one-year contract on British pounds, we have

$$F_{t,T} = S_t \frac{(1 + R^{\$}_{t,T})}{(1 + R^{£}_{t,T})}. \tag{5.7}$$

This is the interest rate parity relationship from Equation (5.1). Thus, the equilibrium one-year futures price for British pounds that would eliminate the arbitrage opportunity in the example can be computed as follows:

$$\begin{aligned} F_{t,T} &= (\$1.30/£)\left(\frac{1 + 0.11}{1 + 0.10}\right) \\ &= \$1.3118/£. \end{aligned}$$

5.4.2 *Interest rate futures*

Financial futures-related, interest-rate-sensitive instruments such as the U.S. Treasury debt futures, Eurodollar futures, 30-day Federal Funds futures, the Secured Overnight Financing Rate (SOFR) futures, and others are the focus of this section. Sample daily price quotations for interest rate futures are shown in Table 5.7. In the following sub-sections, we will discuss U.S. Treasury debt futures, bank certificate of deposit futures, and Eurodollar futures.

5.4.2.1 *U.S. Treasury debt futures*

The U.S. Treasury issues debt securities to finance government operations and the federal deficit. These securities are backed by the government and are considered to be free of default risk. All Treasury

Table 5.7 Interest Rate Futures Data — 5/27/2021

Category	Product	Contract	Last	Change	Open	High	Low	Globex Volume
Stirs	Eurodollar Futures	Mar-22	99.845	0	99.84	99.845	99.83	138,284
	30-Day Federal Funds Futures	Oct-21	99.92	0.005	99.92	99.92	99.915	3,139
	q-Month SOFR Futures	Oct-21	99.965	0	99.965	99.97	99.965	1,775
	3-Month SOFR Futures	Dec-21	99.96	−0.005	99.96	99.965	99.955	20,252
	MPC SONIA Futures	Aug-21	0	0	0	0	0	0
	Quarterly IMM SONIA Futures	Sept-21	0	0	0	0	0	31
U.S. Treasuries	2-Year T-Note Futures	Jun-21	110.137	(0.001)	110.135	110.138	110.132	342,257
	3-Year T-Note Futures	Jun-21	116.102	0.002	116.097	116.102	116.085	8,591
	5-Year T-Note Futures	Jun-21	124.115	(0.025)	124.120	124.142	124.087	525,095
	10-Year T-Note Futures	Jun-21	132.235	(0.055)	132.270	132.300	132.180	961,117
	Ultra 10-Year U.S. Treasury Note Futures	Jun-21	146.135	(0.100)	146.220	146.260	146.040	221,557
	U.S. Treasury Bond Futures	Jun-21	157.30	(0.20)	158.14	158.18	157.16	221,669
	Ultra U.S. Treasury Bond Futures	Jun-21	186.16	(0.26)	187.09	187.14	185.20	110,243
Swap Futures	2-Year USD MAC Swap Futures	Jun-21	0	0	0	0	0	0
	5-Year USD MAC Swap Futures	Jun-21	97.317	(0.030)	98.005	98.005	97.295	1,144

7-Year USD MAC Swap Futures	Jun-21	0	0	0	0	0	0
10-Year USD MAC Swap Futures	Jun-21	91.290	(0.100)	92.000	92.000	91.260	1,641
20-Year USD MAC Swap Futures	Jun-21	0	0	0	0	0	0
30-Year USD MAC Swap Futures	Jun-21	0	0	0	0	0	0
2-Year Eris Swap Futures	Jun-21	0	0	0	0	0	0
3-Year Eris Swap Futures	Jun-21	0	0	0	0	0	0
4-Year Eris Swap Futures	Jun-21	0	0	0	0	0	0
5-Year Eris Swap Futures	Jun-21	97.985	−0.12	97.985	97.985	97.985	5
7-Year Eris Swap Futures	Jun-21	0	0	0	0	0	0
10-Year Eris Swap Futures	Jun-21	91.83	−0.41	92.02	92.02	91.83	21
12-Year Eris Swap Futures	Jun-21	0	0	0	0	0	0
15-Year Eris Swap Futures	Jun-21	0	0	0	0	0	0
20-Year Eris Swap Futures	Jun-21	0	0	0	0	0	0
30-Year Eris Swap Futures	Jun-21	0	0	0	0	0	0

Source: CME Group Market Data. https://www.cmegroup.com/market-data/delayed-quotes/interest-rates.html.

debt is virtually identical except for differing maturities and yields. Corporations, financial institutions, investment funds, and state and local governments all utilize short-term U.S. Treasury securities as a repository for temporary surpluses of cash. Individual, institutional, and foreign investors use longer-term U.S. Treasury securities to secure their capital and insure its return for more extended periods of time. U.S. Treasury debt can be classified into three types, depending on the time to maturity: (1) U.S. Treasury bills, with a time to maturity of one year, (2) U.S. Treasury notes, with a time to maturity of more than one year up to and including ten years, and (3) U.S. Treasury bonds, with a time to maturity of more than ten years.

One of the attractive features of U.S. Treasury securities is that they can easily be resold, because a strong secondary market exists for them. More than thirty primary dealers in government securities around the country (approved by the Federal Reserve Board) maintain a large and very liquid market for the purchase and sale of outstanding government securities (mostly those of the Treasury).

Considering the existence of such a well-developed secondary market, it might be surprising that futures markets do exist for those cash securities. The reason is interest rate risk. Moreover, the homogeneity, relative risk, and correlation with the rates on other risky market debt securities make U.S. Treasury securities an ideal instrument on which to trade futures for hedging purposes.

Treasury bill (T-bill) futures are traded at the IMM, while T-note futures and T-bond futures are offered by the CBT. Potential users of these contracts include the following:

1. Banks,
2. Government securities dealers,
3. Investment bankers,
4. Bond-fund managers,
5. Pension fund managers,
6. Trust fund managers,
7. Corporate treasurers,
8. Insurance company portfolio managers,
9. Speculators, and
10. Arbitragers.

The potential applications of T-bill, T-note, and T-bond futures include the following:

1. Locking in yields on futures purchases of T-bills, T-notes, or T-bonds,
2. Protecting the value of a portfolio comprising government securities,
3. Hedging participation in auctions for T-bills, T-notes, and T-bonds,
4. Hedging corporate debt issuance,
5. Cross-hedging other domestic and Eurodollar financial instruments,
6. Pursuing speculative opportunity with risk capital,
7. Profiting from price differentials (arbitrage), and
8. Discovering current and forward price information.

Characteristics of T-bill futures. A futures contract on ninety-day T-bills was initiated by the IMM on January 6, 1976. This futures contract calls for the delivery of a ninety-day T-bill with a face value of $1,000,000. Prices are quoted in terms of the IMM index (see Table 5.7). T-bills (as well as T-notes and T-bonds) are traditionally quoted in terms of their yield to maturity. Since interest rates (or yields) and prices of debt securities move inversely, the common perception that a long position makes money as the quoted values increase does not apply to such instruments. That is, if someone bought a ninety-day T-bill with a 10.00% yield and yields then rose, the investor would lose money on a long position.

The IMM quote system for its interest rate securities is essentially an index based on the difference between the actual T-bill price and 100.00. Hence, a T-bill yield of 10% would be quoted on the IMM at 90.00. This method fits the traditional quotation procedures in futures trading where the bid price is lower than the offer (to sell) price. Furthermore, each 0.01 move in the price of a T-bill futures contract is equal to one basis point, which is equal to $25.

Figure 5.1 illustrates the delivery process within a clearinghouse system. In the figure, 1S and 2S show the process of the selling clearing member producing the order to expect instructions and the notice of delivery, respectively. This similar process is done for the buying clearing member, as 1B and 2B illustrate the order to expect instructions and the notice of delivery receipt, respectively. Processes 3S and 3B are done for both the selling and the buying clearing member, respectively, giving the order to expect instructions to the clearing member's specific bank. Continuing processes 2S and 2B, the notice of delivery and the notice of delivery receipt, respectively, are both sent to the IMM clearinghouse. Then, the IMM clearinghouse sends the instructions for delivery to the seller's bank and the instructions for accepting delivery are sent to the buyer's bank. These processes are done prior to the maturity date of the futures contract.

When the IMM T-bill futures contract reaches the maturity date, the seller of the contract may have to make delivery of the underlying T-bill. The major function of the clearinghouse is to see that the transfer and payment take place in a timely fashion. Figure 5.1

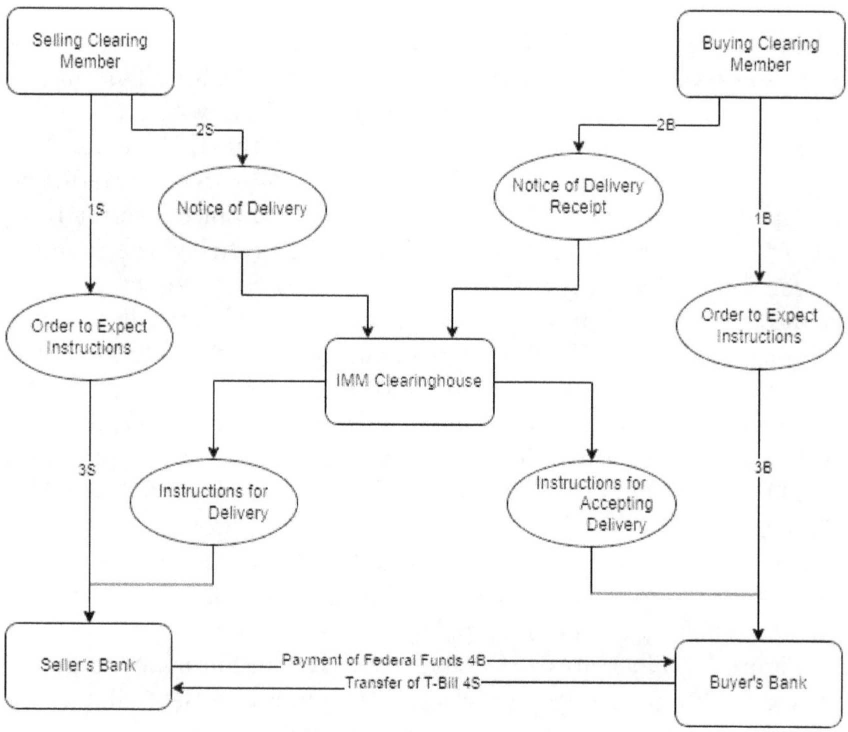

Figure 5.1 Delivery of an IMM T-Bill Futures Contract

illustrates these final processes in 4S and 5B, where the transfer of T-bill and the payment of federal funds are done, respectively. Should either party default in any way, the clearinghouse will complete the transaction and then seek to recover from the defaulting party.

Pricing T-bill futures contracts. Studies by Poole (1978) and Rendleman and Carabini (1979) determined upper and lower bounds for the theoretical price of a T-bill futures contract. In following their derivation, which is based upon an arbitrage relationship between the spot and futures markets, first consider the situation an investor faced with the following choice: (1) Invest in a 182-day T-bill or (2) Invest in a 91-day T-bill and buy a futures contract maturing 91 days hence. In a perfectly efficient market, the investor should be indifferent between these equivalent investments, since both offer the same return.

Following Appendix 5B, the relationship between P_{Fu}, P_n, and P_m can be written as follows:

$$P_{Fu} = \frac{P_n}{P_m}, \tag{5.8}$$

where P_{Fu} = price of a T-bill futures contract, quoted as the difference between \$100 and the annualized discount from par assuming 360 days in a year, P_n = spot price of an n-day T-bill, and P_m = spot price of an m-day T-bill ($n > m$).

Equation (5.8) can be altered to account for transaction costs such as commissions and a greater than zero bid–ask dealer spread (or bid–offer). In doing so, the boundary conditions for the price of a T-bill futures contract are obtained:

$$100\frac{P_n^A}{P_m^B} - CC \leq P_{Fu} \leq 100\frac{P_n^A}{P_m^B} + CC,$$

where CC = round-trip commission costs per \$100 of face value, P_n^A = the price at which a dealer will sell an n-day T-bill, and P_m^B = the price at which a dealer will buy an m-day T-bill.

Sample Problem 5.4 provides further illustration.

Sample Problem 5.4

Using Equation (5.8), compute the theoretical futures price for the IMM December 1989 contract as of June 7, 1988. Assume that the deliverable bill (in period) against the futures contract is the T-bill maturing on March 21, 1989, with a bid price of 10.67 and ask price of 10.59. Also assume \$0.004 per \$100 of face value as the round-trip commission cost.

Solution

1. Determine the T-bill rate corresponding to the m period — the interval between June 7, 1989 and the third Thursday of December 1989, the delivery date of the contract (that is, $m = 188$ days).
2. Find the price of this T-bill maturing in (approximately) 188 days (December 27) from the U.S. T-bill data listed earlier. Its bid price is 10.47 and its ask price is 10.41.
3. Now, calculate P_{Fu} without commission costs using Equation (5.13) and an average of the bid and ask prices for the m period and n period and n-period T-bills:

$$P_{Fu} = \frac{100 - [10.63 \times (279/360)]}{100 - [10.44 \times (188/360)]}$$

$$= \frac{100 - 8.238}{100 - 5.452} = \frac{91.762}{84.548} = 0.97053.$$

Now, to get the quarterly yield (price) for the futures,

$$100 - 97.053 = 2.947.$$

And the annualized yield,

$$2.947 \times \frac{360}{91} = 11.658.$$

Finally, compute the theoretical futures price P_{Fu}:

$$P_{Fu} = 100 - 11.658 = 88.342.$$

In comparing this price with the market price of 88.32 for the December 1989 T-bill futures contract, it becomes clear that the calculated price is upwardly biased. This disparity could be due to neglect of transaction costs such as commissions. So, the commission costs will be calculated on an annualized basis (like the futures price) and subtracted from the computed price:

$$0.004 \times \frac{360}{91} = 0.016$$

and

$$P_{Fu} = 88.342 - 0.016 = 88.326.$$

Characteristics of T-note and T-bond futures. T-bond futures as on the CBT require the delivery of a U.S. Treasury bond with a face value of $100,000 and mature in at least fifteen years. Prices are quoted as a percentage of par. With daily trading volume in excess of around 400,000 contracts on average, the T-bond futures contract is currently the most successful futures contract ever. The depth of trading in this contract is revealed by the existence of outstanding T-bond contracts with maturities of over fifteen years into the future.

Growing in popularity is the **T-note futures** contract, also offered by the CBT. One of the underlying stimuli for its success is the growing proportion of total Treasury debt, which is represented by T-note securities. The T-note futures contract specifies the delivery of a U.S. Treasury note with a face value of $100,000 and a maturity of no less than 6.5 years and no more than ten years from the date of delivery. Additional contract specifications for T-note and T-bond futures are listed in Table 5.8. The impacts of federal reserve activity on the market price of Treasury securities are discussed in Table 5.9.

5.4.2.2 *Bank certificate of deposit futures*

Certificates of deposit, more commonly referred to as **large negotiable CDs**, were created in the early 1960s by the larger U.S. banks. At the time, banks were hungry for cash to fund an unexpected surge in loan demand. CDs were meant to tap the short-term surplus funds of corporations — money that up to this point had largely been invested in low-yielding Treasury securities — by offering higher yields and more flexible terms.

Since its introduction, the CD instrument has been tremendously successful. Moreover, CDs have become a means of permanently

Table 5.8 Contract Specifications of T-Bonds and T-Note Futures

	Bond Futures	10-yrs Note Futures	5-yrs Note Futures	2-yrs Note Futures
Face Amount	\$100.000	\$100.000	\$100.000	\$200.000
Maturity	15 years +	6 1/2 to 10 years	4 1/2 to 5 years	1 1/2 to 2 years
Notional Coupon	6% coupon	6% coupon	6% coupon	6% coupon
Minimum Tick	1/32	1/64	1/64	1/128
Minimum Tick Value	\$31.25	\$15.625	\$15.625	\$15.625

Source: *Chicago Board of Trade (CBOT) Reference Guide.* CBOT U.S. Treasury Futures and Options. https://insigniafutures.com/Docs/CBOT_Treasuries.pdf.

increasing the size of the major money center banks. The concept of managing the size of the bank with CDs has come to be known as **liability management**.

The success of CDs can be associated with their two primary attributes: (1) CDs allow major U.S. banks greater control over the size of their banks and over net earnings and (2) CDs provide a higher return for the bank's corporate customers as well as allowing them specific maturities for investing their excess cash. However, using CDs to fund loans with different maturities subjects the bank to interest rate risk. For instance, when short-term rates are lower than long-term rates (an upward-sloping yield curve), the bank will want to lend long and borrow short to maximize the spread between the rates at which they lend and borrow funds. This interest rate spread is the bank's primary source of income. Yet, to keep the long-term loan funded, the bank will have to roll over its short-term borrowings (liabilities) until the long-term loan (asset) matures. Should short-term rates rise over this interim period, the bank will be forced to fund its long-term loan at a higher and higher cost, thereby reducing its profitability.

Unlike the secondary markets for Treasury securities (which are liquid on both sides, making it easy to buy or sell), the secondary market for cash CDs is not particularly efficient. One reason is the lack of homogeneity of CDs, making them difficult to price. Moreover, because banks do not issue CDs at predictable times and with

Table 5.9 Impacts of Federal Reserve Activity

Fed Activities	Market Price of Treasury Securities	Explanation
Fed raises discount rate	Lower	An increase in the borrowing rate for banks from the Fed usually results in increased rates for the bank's customers. This action is used to slow credit expansion.
Fed lowers discount rate	Higher	Usually results in decreased rates to bank borrowers.
Fed does repurchase agreement	Higher	Fed puts money into the banking system by purchasing collateral and agreeing to resell later, essentially a lending transaction. With more money available for lending, the expectation is for downward pressure on customer rates.
Fed does match sales	Lower	This is the opposite transaction to the above. The Fed is essentially borrowing available liquidity, putting upward pressure on customer rates.
Fed buys bills	Higher	Fed lends money to the banking system, essentially increasing the supply of loanable funds that should put download pressure on customer rates
Fed sells bills	Lower	Essentially decreases supply of loanable funds in the economy creating competition for funds and upward pressure on rates.

Source: *Chicago Board of Trade (CBOT) Reference Guide.* CBOT U.S. Treasury Futures and Options. https://insigniafutures.com/Docs/CBOT_Treasuries.pdf.

specific maturities, it is nearly impossible to short a CD. Hence, dealing or trading in cash CDs is a risky activity. This has spurred the introduction of CD futures to help accommodate the hedging needs of banks.

CD futures have increasingly grown in use by banks to hedge interest rate risk created by the asset–liability gap described earlier. As of early 1988, the IMM was the only exchange to offer CD futures contracts. The size of each contract was $1,000,000 and the delivery instrument is a CD with restrictions on its defining parameters.

Contract prices are quoted in terms of the IMM index with a minimum price fluctuation of one basis point (which is 0.01 or \$25). The rest of the details of CD futures contract specifications are summarized in the table in Sample Problem 5.5, which concerns a short hedge with CD futures to minimize a bank's interest rate risk.

Sample Problem 5.5

A short hedge with CD futures. With current short-term rates lower than current long rates, the ABC bank finds it more profitable to fund the six-month commercial loan made on June 12 with a three-month CD. To keep the loan funded, however, the bank will have to roll over or issue another three-month CD for roughly the same or original amount. The bank's forecast of interest rates over the next three months indicates a flattering of the yield curve caused by an increase in short-term rates.

In order to reduce the interest rate risk that their asset–liability gap has created, the bank decides to hedge with CD futures. Using futures, the bank is attempting to lock in the current (and lower) CD rate and maximize the return on its asset (the loan). The transactions are summarized in the following table. Note that we assumed a one-to-one (dollar-per-dollar) hedge ratio for the calculations. As the results from this hypothetical example indicate, CD futures offer a viable mechanism for hedging interest rate risk. In this case, ABC bank nearly eliminated the higher funding cost for its loan by the profit on its futures position.

CD rates are quoted in various terms to maturity — including one-, three-, and five-year terms to maturity. In 2021, the interest rates on CD products were at their lowest point in history. This was a result and continuation of the 2020 pandemic response by the Federal Reserve, when Chairman Jerome Powell initiated an interest rate cut to nearly 0%. The average one and five-year CD rates for 2021 are presented in Figure 5.2, where it can be seen that rates continued their downward trend into 2021. Moving forward into 2022, rates are expected to begin their upward trend. The rate hikes will cause the CD rates to increase back to normal levels. As can be seen in Figure 5.2, the interest rates on CDs of different terms to maturity will vary but the rates generally move together. In other words, the percentage change will be similar for both one- and five-year term CDs.

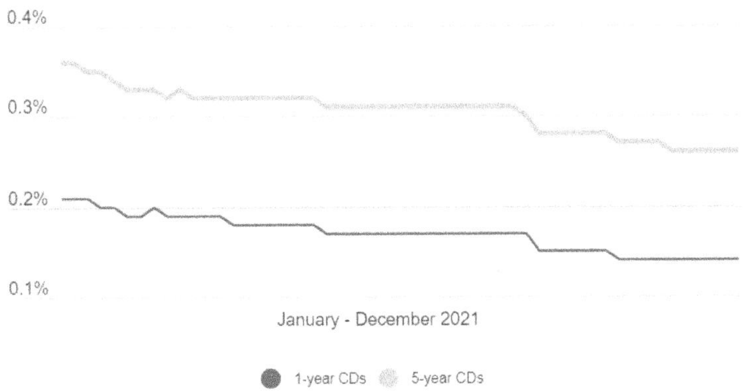

Figure 5.2 National Average Bank CD Interest Rates (2021)

Source: Bankrate national survey.

5.4.2.3 *The Eurodollar futures market*

A **Eurodollar** is any dollar on deposit outside the United States. Typically, this refers to dollar balances on the books of the London branches of the U.S. and other major world-class banks. On occasion, Eurodollars are also deposited in other locations, such as Nassau or the Grand Cayman Islands. An important aspect of these deposits is that, because of their location outside of the U.S., they do not fall under U.S. jurisdiction. Therefore, Eurodollars are not governed by the same regulations that apply to domestic deposits, set by the Federal Reserve.

Evolution. The Eurodollar market evolved in the 1950s in response to Federal Reserve restrictions on the maximum allowable interest rate to be paid on a deposit. Foreign merchant banks were able to pay a larger rate on dollar deposits than was allowed by Regulation Q and still make an arbitrage profit by selling dollars in their own country on a forward basis for a return even higher than that offered to the dollar depositors. To defend themselves against a loss of deposits, U.S. banks eventually reacted to this unconventional banking practice by allowing their London branches to enter this market and also take in dollar deposits.

By the mid-1960s, the Eurodollar market had grown significantly and funds became available for dollar-denominated loans to be made by European banks to commercial lenders. Moreover, in 1966, Eurodollar CDs were issued by banks in the United Kingdom to increase the attractiveness of the Euro market to depositors and to meet the increased demand for funds from the United States. These securities were negotiable instruments among the investor and the (foreign) banking institution. As the Eurodollar markets developed and matured, formal lines of credit and sovereign risk limitations were formalized by participants.

A bank lending funds in the Eurodollar market is exposed to essentially three risks:

(1) Interest rate risk,
(2) Credit risk, and
(3) Sovereign risk.

The interest rate risk involved with a Eurodollar loan is virtually identical to that in previous explanations and examples. Credit risk, while present to some extent in the U.S. cash CD market, is a larger concern in the Eurodollar market because of the difficulties that can arise when trying to analyze a foreign borrower's financial position. Finally, sovereign risk is unique to the arena of international lending. **Sovereign risk** refers to the unfavorable consequences that can have impact on a bank's investment if a foreign government is overthrown, becomes economically unstable, or passes detrimental regulations affecting the movement of funds. Most banks will have sovereign risk limitations restricting the total amount placed on deposit with (or loaned to) institutions in any one country.

The relationship between three-month rates offered on Eurodollar deposits (as measured by the LIBOR rate), U.S. CDs, and U.S. T-bills can be visualized for a ten-year period in Figure 5.3. A number of aspects of the relationship between these three securities can be noted from this chart. Most prominent among the rate relationships is that Eurodollar rates are higher than CD rates, which are higher than T-bill rates — a ranking consistent with the level of risk inherent in these securities. Not so obvious is the variation in the spread (difference) between Eurodollar rates and CD rates, which do not simply rise together when rates rise and fall together when rates fall. Rather, changes in the interest rate spread are affected by a variety of unpredictable market forces and decisions of U.S. and foreign governments. For example, increasing U.S. interest rates tend

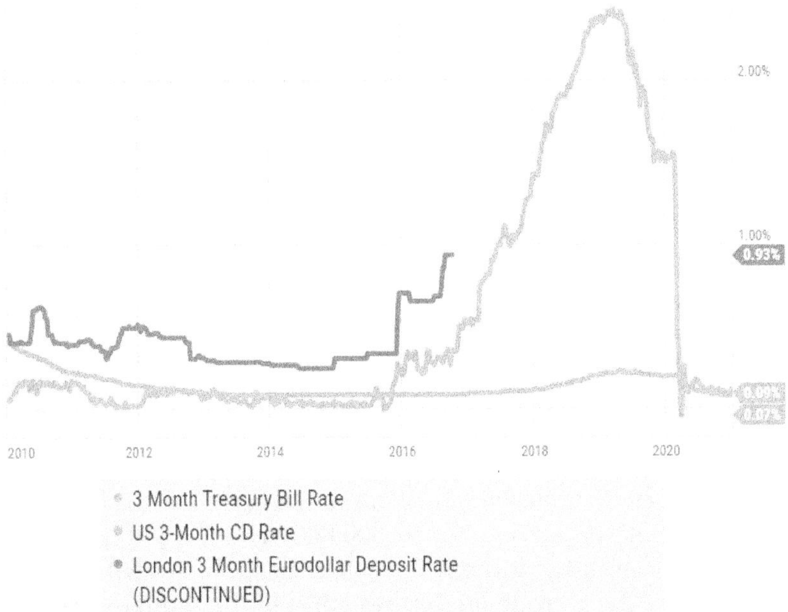

Figure 5.3 Three-Month Rates on U.S. CDs, U.S. T-Bills, and Eurodollar Deposits, January 2010–2021 (Monthly Data)

Source: YCharts. https://ycharts.com/charts/fundamental_chart/.

to strengthen the dollar, narrowing the spread between Eurodollars and domestic CD rates. Unlike the behavior of the spread between Eurodollar and CD rates, the Eurodollar rates and Treasury rates have a less predictable tendency to rise together as rates rise.

The rationale for briefly discussing the Eurodollar market and the relationship of its rates to domestic rates is to provide a basis for understanding exactly what Eurodollar futures are, as well as to make it easier to understand why Eurodollar futures exist and how they can be used. Hence, the focus now turns to the Eurodollar futures contract and market.

Eurodollar futures. Eurodollar futures are traded on the IMM and the London International Financial Exchange (LIFFE). Due to similarities and a desire to keep the analysis as simple as possible, the sole focus here is on the IMM contract. The Eurodollar futures

Table 5.10 Eurodollar Futures Quotes — 5/27/2021

Month	Last	Change	Prior Settle	Open	High	Low	Vol.
Jun-21	99.8825	0.01	99.8725	99.8725	99.8825	99.87	193,892
Jul-21	99.885	0.015	99.87	99.87	99.89	99.87	42,465
Aug-21	99.885	0.015	99.87	99.87	99.885	99.865	9,240
Sept-21	99.875	0.005	99.87	99.865	99.885	99.865	199,895
Oct-21	99.87	0.01	99.86	99.855	99.87	99.855	1,003
Nov-21	99.85	0.005	99.845	99.84	99.85	99.84	74
Dec-21	99.83	0.005	99.825	99.82	99.835	99.815	197,807
Mar-22	99.845	0.005	99.84	99.84	99.845	99.83	141,423
Jun-22	99.8	0	99.8	99.8	99.805	99.79	116,267
Sept-22	99.73	−0.01	99.74	99.74	99.74	99.72	143,927
Dec-22	99.615	−0.02	99.635	99.635	99.635	99.605	215,897
Mar-23	99.555	−0.015	99.57	99.57	99.575	99.54	155,273

Source: CME Group Eurodollar Futures and Options. https://www.cmegroup.com/trading/interest-rates/stir/eurodollar_quotes_globex.html.

contract has, as its underlying instrument, a three-month Eurodollar time deposit in the amount of \$1,000,000. However, this contract, like those of the index futures, is settled in cash. As with CD and T-bill futures, the Eurodollar futures contract is quoted in terms of the IMM index. For example, using Table 5.10, a quote of 99.73 for the September 2022 contract is equivalent to a current contract value of \$997,300. Further information about Eurodollar futures contracts can be found in Figure 5.4.

The primary use of Eurodollar futures as a hedging vehicle is similar to that of other hedging vehicles; they are capable of protecting against detrimental changes in interest rates. Sample Problem 5.6 is offered to help clarify their application.

Sample Problem 5.6

A long hedge with Eurodollar futures. Suppose that the London branch of a U.S. bank anticipates a decline in rates from September 16 to December 16. Furthermore, on June 12th the bank makes a three-month loan in the Eurodollar market and finances the loan with the funds from a six-month Eurodollar CD. When the three-month loan matures, the bank will relend the principal and interest received for another three months. Such a reverse liability–asset gap is partially the result of a downward-sloping yield curve where short-term rates are higher than longer-term rates.

CONTRACT UNIT	$2,500 x Contract IMM Index
PRICE QUOTATION	Contract IMM Index = 100 minus R R = three-month London interbank offered rate for spot settlement on 3rd Wednesday of contract month. E.g., a price quote of 97.45 signifies a deposit rate of 2.55 percent per annum. One interest rate basis point = 0.01 price points = $25 per contract.
TRADING HOURS	Sunday - Friday 6:00 p.m. - 5:00 p.m.ET (5:00 p.m. - 4:00 p.m. CT). Monday - Thursday 5:00 p.m. - 6:00 p.m. ET (4:00 p.m. - 5:00 p.m. CT) daily maintenance period.
MINIMUM PRICE FLUCTUATION	Nearby expiry: 1/4 of one interest rate basis point / 0.0025 price points = $6.25 All other expiries: 1/2 of one interest rate basis point / 0.005 price points = $12.50 The new nearby expiry begins trading at 0.0025 price points on the last trading day of the current nearby expiry.
PRODUCT CODE	CME Globex: GE CME ClearPort: ED Clearing: ED
LISTED CONTRACTS	Quarterly contracts (Mar, Jun, Sep, Dec) listed for 40 consecutive quarters and the nearest 4 serial contract months. List a new quarterly contract for trading on the last trading day of the nearby expiry.
SETTLEMENT METHOD	Financially Settled
TERMINATION OF TRADING	Trading terminates at 11:00 a.m. London time on the 2nd London business day prior to the 3rd Wednesday of the contract month.
SETTLEMENT PROCEDURES	Eurodollar Future Settlement Procedures
POSITION LIMITS	CME Position Limits
EXCHANGE RULEBOOK	CME 452
BLOCK MINIMUM	Block Minimum Thresholds
PRICE LIMIT OR CIRCUIT	Price Limits
ALL OR NONE MINIMUM	All or None Minimums
VENDOR CODES	Quote Vendor Symbols Listing

Figure 5.4 Eurodollar Futures Contract

Source: CME Group. https://www.cmegroup.com/trading/interest-rates/stir/eurodollar.html.

Since the bank's profit is the spread between the higher rate at which they loan money and the lower rate at which they borrow money, a decline in the former without a corresponding decline in the latter will adversely affect profitability. In this scenario where declining rates are expected by the end of the first three-month loan, the bank is prone to reinvestment rate risk.

To alleviate the problem, the bank chooses to fix the reinvestment rate for the latter three-month investment horizon through a long position in Eurodollar Futures. On June 12th, the Eurodollar contract for September delivery was priced at an index of 86.53 (100% – 13.47%), the six-month Eurodollar CD rate was 13%, and the initial three-month loan was made at the LIBOR rate of 14%. Table 5.11 summarizes the transactions results. Note that a dollar-per-dollar hedge ratio for this example is assumed.

Table 5.11 Hedging Interest Rate Risk by Future Market

	Spot-Market Transaction	**Futures-Market Transaction**
June 12	Issue a $1,000,000 six-month Euro CD at 13.00 percent	Buy one Eurodollar futures contract for September delivery at 86.53 (13.47 percent)
	Loan the $1,000,000 in the Euro market for three months at 14.00 percent	
September 14: interest rates fall as expected	Return the $1,000,000 principal plus interest of $33,299 at the current LIBOR rate of 12.00 percent (a net reinvestment rate decline of 2.00 percent)	Sell one Eurodollar futures contract at 88.00(12.00 percent)
Results	Bought futures contract at	86.53 (13.47 percent)
	Sold futures contract at	
	Profit on the contract (+147 basis points)	88.00 1.47 (1.47 percent)
	Dollar value of profit from futures transaction (each basis point is worth $25): 147 × $25 × 1 contract	$3,675
	Loss caused by decline in LIBOR lending rate: $[(1.02)^{0.25} - 1] \times \$1{,}033{,}299$	($5,128)
	Total net loss	($1,453)

As Table 5.11 indicates, the use of the futures position to hedge the interest rate risk allows the bank to reduce its reinvestment rate loss by 71%. Use of a more sophisticated hedge ratio such as Howard and D'Antonio's might have resulted in an even stronger position in futures, further cutting the bank's losses.

5.5 Stock Index Futures

Stock index futures offer the investor a medium for expressing an opinion on the general course of the market. In addition, these contracts can be used by portfolio managers in a variety of ways to alter the risk–return distribution of their stock portfolios. For instance, much of a sudden upward surge in the market could be missed by the institutional investor due to the time it takes to get money into the stock market. By purchasing stock–index futures contracts, the institutional investor can enter the market immediately and then gradually unwind the long futures position as he or she is able to get more funds invested in stocks. Conversely, after a run up in the value of the stock portfolio (assuming it is well diversified and correlates well with one of the major indexes), a portfolio manager might desire to lock in the profits until after being required to report the quarterly return on the portfolio. By selling an appropriate number of stock index futures contracts, the institutional investor could offset any losses on the stock portfolio with corresponding gains on the futures position. Before presenting examples using stock index futures, the origination of these contracts, the different types offered, and their theoretical pricing models are reviewed.

The first stock index futures contract was offered by the Kansas City Board of Trade (KCBT) on the Value Line Composite Stock Index (VLCI) on February 24, 1982. Contracts on the S&P 500 stock index and NYSE composite stock index were soon offered by the IMM (a division of the Chicago Mercantile Exchange) and the NYSE, respectively. A futures contract on the S&P 100 stock index began trading on the IMM in January of 1983, and most recently the CBT initiated trading in a futures contract based on the AMEX Major Market Index (MMI). The MMI is a portfolio of twenty stocks from the Dow Jones Industrial Average and, not surprisingly, correlates very well with the highly visible DJIA index.

The calculation of the market value for a stock index futures contract on any given day is simply a matter of multiplying the current index price for the contract by the appropriate dollar amount. Each of the U.S. stock index futures is listed in order of market popularity. Each contract bought and sold on a particular day is included in the calculation of daily trading volume. Table 5.12 shows prices, volume, and open interest for the S&P 500 index. Further, Table 5.12 includes the June 2021 to June 2022 futures quote information for the index. Figure 5.5 illustrates the S&P 500 price quote information listed in Table 5.12, as it is a futures quote chart for the years 2011 to 2021. This information was gathered from *The Wall Street Journal* on May 27, 2021.

As Table 5.12 and Figure 5.5 show and illustrate the S&P 500 futures price quotes, respectively, Figure 5.6 shows the contract specifications of S&P 500 Futures. Open interest represents the number of open contract positions on a given day with only one side counted. That is, when the buyer and seller make their transaction, only one position is counted as being open, not two. S&P 500 futures are by far the most highly traded of the contracts, with daily volume typically in excess of 50,000 and open interest between one-thousand and 2.6 million for the period. At the other extreme, the S&P 100 futures have far less daily contract trading volume, on average, and open interest is generally much lower than that of the S&P 500.

The importance of trading volume data is that is represents the relative liquidity of the various index futures contracts. This is important information for users (particularly hedgers) trying to decide which would best suit their purposes. The higher a contract's liquidity, the easier to enter and exit positions and to trade in larger lots of contracts without overly impacting price. Of course, the extent to which an institutional investor's stock portfolio correlates with each of the underlying stock indexes will also influence the decision of which futures contract to hedge with.

All index futures contracts call for cash settlement or delivery. This means that on the expiration date of the contract, no security or portfolio of securities is delivered. Rather, the difference in the value of the contract between buying and selling is delivered in cash. For example, if the S&P 500 contract was purchased

Table 5.12 S&P 500 Future Quotes (CME) — 5/27/2021

Month	Last	Chg.	Open	High	Low	Settlement	Vol.	Open Int.
Jun-21	4,211.25	18.15	4,193	4,211.5	4,177.75	4,199	1,163,991	2,599,672
Sept-21	4,200.5	17.4	4,183	4,200.5	4,168	4,189	6,962	64,574
Dec-21	4,191	18.1	4,171.25	4,191.25	4,158.5	4,179.3	43	45,422
Mar-22	4,174.3	−17.8	4,123.5	4,125	4,123.5	4,174.3	0	1,029
Jun-22	4,162	−26.3	4,110	4,110	4,110	4,162	0	40,722

Source: *The Wall Street Journal.*

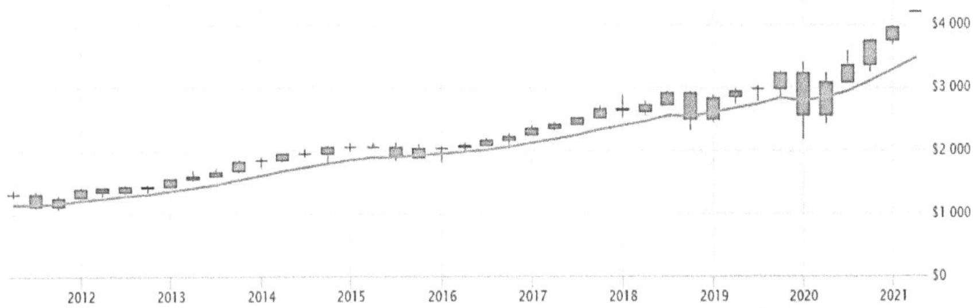

Figure 5.5 S&P 500 Future Chart (CME): 2011–2021*

Note: *Quarterly frequency, candlestick display, 10-period exponential moving average trend line.
Source: *The Wall Street Journal.*

when the index was 300 and delivered when the index was 310, the purchaser would receive \$5,000 from the seller (310 × \$500 = \$155,000 settlement value minus 300 × \$500 = \$150,000 purchase value).

5.5.1 *Pricing stock index futures contracts*

Although the theoretical pricing of these contracts has not yet reached a conclusive level, an examination of the components of the models offered to date will further an understanding of the general pricing factors involved.

A paper by Modest and Sundaresan (1983) proposes theoretical pricing boundaries for a stock index futures contract based on arbitrage conditions. First, for the case where no dividends are paid by the stocks in the underlying index, interest rates are non-stochastic, and there are no transaction costs, the price of a futures contract can

CONTRACT UNIT	$50 x S&P 500 Index
PRICE QUOTATION	U.S. dollars and cents per index point
TRADING HOURS	**CME Globex:** Sunday - Friday 6:00 p.m. - 5:00 p.m. ET with trading halt 4:15 p.m. - 4:30 p.m. BTIC: Sunday - Friday 6:00 p.m. - 4:00 p.m. ET TACO: Sunday - Friday 6:00 p.m. - 9:30 a.m. ET. Monday - Thursday 11:00 a.m. - 5:00 p.m. ET; no 11:00 a.m.- 5:00 p.m. ET session on Friday. Monday - Thursday 5:00 p.m. - 6:00 p.m. ET daily maintenance period. **CME ClearPort:** Sunday - Friday 6:00 p.m. - 5:00 p.m. ET TACO: Sunday 6:00 p.m. - Monday 9:30 a.m. ET. Monday - Thursday 11:00 a.m. - 5:00 p.m. ET and 6:00 p.m. - 9:30 a.m. ET. Friday 11:00 a.m. - 5:00 p.m. ET.
MINIMUM PRICE FLUCTUATION	0.25 index points = $12.50 Calendar spreads: 0.05 index points = $2.50 BTIC: 0.05 index points = $2.50 TACO: 0.05 index points = $2.50
PRODUCT CODE	CME Globex: ES CME ClearPort: ES Clearing: ES BTIC: "EST","ESQ"
LISTED CONTRACTS	Quarterly contracts (Mar, Jun, Sep, Dec) listed for 5 consecutive quarters
SETTLEMENT METHOD	Financially Settled
TERMINATION OF TRADING	Trading terminates at 9:30 a.m. ET on the 3rd Friday of the contract month. BTIC trading terminates at 4:00 p.m. ET on the Thursday before the 3rd Friday of contract month. TACO trading terminates at 9:30 a.m. ET on the Thursday before the 3rd Friday of the contract month.
SETTLEMENT PROCEDURES	Settlement Procedures
POSITION LIMITS	Position Limits
EXCHANGE RULEBOOK	CME 358
BLOCK MINIMUM	Block Table
PRICE LIMIT OR CIRCUIT	Price Limits
VENDOR CODES	Quote Vendor Symbols

Figure 5.6 S&P 500 Future Contract

Source: CME Group, http://www.cmegroup.com/.

be stated as follows:

$$F_{t,T} = S_t(1 + R_{f,T-t}). \tag{5.9}$$

The argument for this relationship was presented earlier. Next, Modest and Sundaresan extend Equation (5.9) to a set of boundary conditions by taking into account transaction costs. To simplify, let the price of a discount bound $[1/(1 + R_{f,T-t})]$ be stated as $[1/(1 + R_{f,T-t})]$. So, now,

$$\frac{S_t + C_{LS} + C_{SF}}{B_{t,T}} \geq F_{t,T} \geq \frac{S_t - C_{SS} - C_{LF}}{B_{t,T}}, \tag{5.10}$$

where S_t = market value of the underlying stock index at time t, $F_{t,T}$ = theoretically bounded price for a stock index futures contract at time t, that matures at time T, where $T > t$, $B_{t,T}$ = price of a discount bound = $1/(1 + R_{f,T-t})$, C_{LS} = cost of being long in the spot index, C_{SF} = cost of being short in the futures contract, C_{SS} = cost of being short in the spot index (which may include foregone interest on the short-sale proceeds), and C_{LF} = cost of being long in the futures contract.

There are two steps to be taken to establish the validity of the arbitrage argument behind Equation (5.10). The first step is to show that $B_{t,T}F_{t,T} < (S_t + C_{LS} + C_{SF})$ [equivalent to $F_{t,T} \leq (S_t + C_{LS} + C_{SF})/B_{t,T}$]. To do so, suppose that the reverse is true. Then, at time t, the following transactions can be undertaken to guarantee riskless profits:

1. Buy the spot index by investing $\$(S_t + C_{LS})$.
2. Sell futures short by incurring $\$C_{SF}$.

At time T, cover the short position in the futures by delivering the stock index (assuming this was allowed) and receive $F_{t,T}$ for certain. The present value at time t for the futures price received at time T is $B_{t,T}F_{t,T}$. Thus, if $B_{t,T}F_{t,T} > S_t + C_{L,S} + C_{SF}$, then arbitrage profits would be available. Hence,

$$B_{t,T}F_{t,T} < S_t + C_{L,S} + C_{SF}.$$

The second step is to show that $B_{t,T}F_{t,T} \geq (S_t - C_{SS} - C_{LF})$, or equivalently that $F_{t,T} \geq (S_t - C_{SS} - C_{LF})/B_{t,T}$. Once again, assume that the reverse pricing condition is true and pursue the following transactions at time t to obtain riskless profits:

1. Sell the spot index short. This produces an inflow of $\$(S_t - C_{SS})$.
2. Buy futures (long position) incurring–$\$C_{LF}$.

At time T, collect the stock in the futures market by paying $F_{t,T}$ and covering the short position. The inflow at time t is $(S_t - C_{SS} - C_{LF})$, and its value at time T is simply the same amount compounded from t to T by $B_{t,T}$ (i.e., divide the dollar sum by $B_{t,T}$, the price of a discount bound, which in the case of non-stochastic rates is the future value interest factor). The outflow at time T is $F_{t,T}$; so, if $(S_t - C_{SS} - C_{LF})/B_{t,T} > F_{t,T}$, then arbitrage profits can be made. Therefore, efficient markets infer that the opposite condition is true.

To adjust the bounds for dividends paid out by the stocks in the spot index, simply subtract their discounted value from each side of the boundaries. Why? Since the holder of a stock index futures contract does not receive the dividends paid out by the underlying stock index, its value must be diminished by their present value. Assuming that dividends d are non-stochastic and paid out at known futures periods, such that $t < \tau < T$, their value can be discounted back to the present by a discount factor of $B_{t,t+T}$. Summing the present value of all future dividends paid by the spot index between t and T, the pricing boundary conditions can be adjusted downward in Equation (5.10):

$$\frac{S_t + C_{LS} - \left(\sum_{\tau=1}^{T-t} B_{t,T} + \tau d\tau\right)}{B_{t,T}} \geq F_{t,T}$$
$$\geq \frac{S_t - C_{SS} - C_{LF} - \left(\sum_{\tau=1}^{T-t} B_{t,T} + \tau d\tau\right)}{B_{t,T}}. \qquad (5.11)$$

In Equation (5.11), d equals cash dividend paid. Other notations have been defined as earlier. Figures 5.7 and 5.8 show how well the price for S&P 500 futures contract matures in June 1982 followed the boundary conditions in Equation (5.11). Figure 5.7 assumes that 0% of any proceeds from a short sale of the spot index was available for use. Figure 5.8 assumes that 50% of such proceeds should be used by the investor for reinvestment. As can be seen, allowance for the use of 50% of short-sale proceeds increases the bounds and indicates

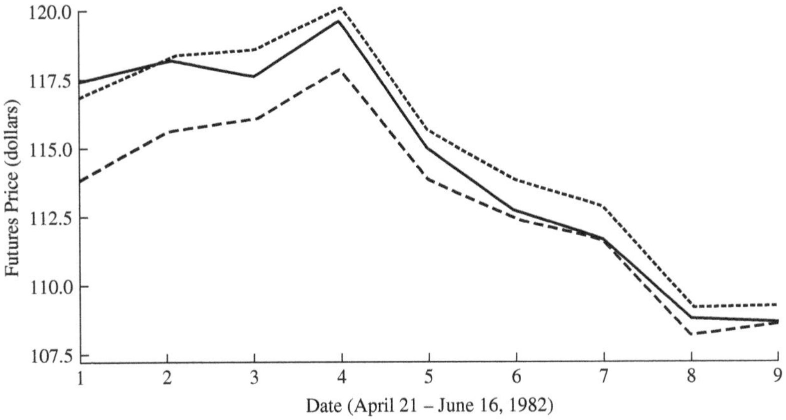

Figure 5.7 Futures Prices and Bounds for S&P 500 Contracts Maturing June 1982: Zero Use of Proceeds, Adjustments for Dividends

Source: Lee *et al.* (2013, p. 592).

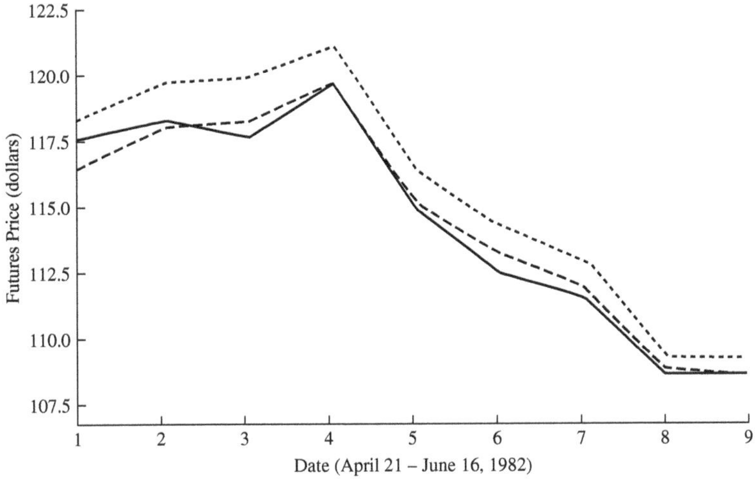

Figure 5.8 Futures Prices and Bounds for S&P 500 Contracts Maturing June 1982: Half Use of Proceeds, No Adjustments for Dividends

Source: Lee *et al.* (2013, p. 592).

that either they are upwardly biased or that the June 1982 futures contract was slightly undervalued during this period.

An analysis of the components in Equation (5.11) can help discern how the futures price should be affected by a change in any one of the variables.

$\frac{\partial F_{t,T}}{\partial B_{t,T}} > 0$ As the price of a discount bond increases or equivalently, interest rate falls, the futures price will increase. (5.12a)

$\frac{\partial F_{t,T}}{\partial S_t} > 0$ As the underlying spot price increases, the futures price will increase. (5.12b)

$\frac{\partial F_{t,T}}{\partial d} < 0$ As future dividend payments are expected to increase, the futures price declines. (5.12c)

$\frac{\partial F_{t,T}}{\partial C} < 0$ As relevant transaction costs rise, the futures price will fall. (5.12d)

If more than one of the denominator variables changes at the same time, the expression cannot be generalized for the resulting effect on the futures price. The precise change in the futures price will depend on the relative size of the two or more changing parameters. Nevertheless, it can be concluded that a correct valuation for a stock index futures contract requires accurate forecasts of future interest rates and dividends. Sample Problem 5.7 provides further illustration.

Sample Problem 5.7

Hedging with stock index futures. In this example, an institutional investor is going to use S&P 500 stock index futures contracts to hedge an expected market decline over the coming month. Assume the following: (1) the S&P 500 stock index is an exact proxy of the composition of the investor's stock portfolio, (2) no transaction costs are involved in entering or exiting either market, and (3) that the investor uses the Howard–D'Antonio hedge ratio equation (Equation (4.15)) to determine how many futures contracts to sell. The figures used to compute the hedge ratio are from daily data over a two-month period.

The first step is to calculate the hedge ratio and corresponding hedging effectiveness measure. So, use the following figures:

i = 0.10 (the risk-free rate on 13-week T-bills),
$\bar{r}_f$ = 0.2241 (average daily return, annualized, for the nearby futures),
$\bar{r}_s$ = 0.2025 (average daily return, annualized, for the S&P 500 index),
σ_f = 0.1851 (standard deviation of daily returns on the nearby futures),
σ_s = 0.0792 (standard deviation of daily returns on the S&P 500 index),
ρ = 0.9815 (correlation coefficient among the returns on the S&P 500 index and nearby S&P 500 futures contract),
$\pi = \sigma_f/\sigma_s = 2.3371$,
$\alpha = r_f/(r_s - i) = 2.1863$,
$\lambda = \alpha/\pi = 0.9355$ (risk–return relative),
P_f = 167.60 (current futures price for September contract),
P_s = 165.54 (current value of S&P 500 index), and
$\gamma = P_f/P_s = 1.0124$.

The hedge ratio is as follows:

$$\text{HHD} = \frac{(\lambda - \rho)}{\gamma\pi(1 - \lambda\rho)} = \frac{0.9355 - 0.9815}{1.0124(2.3371)[1 - (0.9355)(0.9815)]}$$
$$= -0.238.$$

The hedging effectiveness measure [Chapter 4, Equation (4.16)] is as follows:

$$\text{HE} = \sqrt{\frac{1 - 2\lambda\rho + \lambda^2}{1 - \rho^2}} = \sqrt{\frac{1 - 2(0.9355)(0.9815) + (0.92355)}{1 - (0.9815)^2}}$$
$$= 1.0284.$$

Assuming the investor's stock portfolio is 100 × the value of the S&P 500 index, the investor should sell twenty-four futures contracts to hedge the portfolio. Based on the past risk–return relationship between the futures and the spot markets, the institutional investor can expect to enhance the excess return to risk on his or her portfolio by 2.8% over the hedging period [(1.0284 – 1) × 100%]. Table 5.13 summarizes the transactions and results from the hedge.

Table 5.13 Transactions and Results

	Spot-Market Transaction	Futures-Market Transaction
August 1	Holding a stock portfolio duplicating the S&P 500 index but 100 × its spot value or 100 × \$500 × 165.54 = \$8,277,000	Sell 24 September-delivery S&P 500 futures contracts at a price of 167.60 (market value of 24 × \$500 × 167.60 = \$2,011,200)
September 1: stock-market prices fall as expected	S&P 500 index falls to 163.04; value of portfolio is now 100 × \$500 × 163.04 = \$8,152,000	Buy 24 September S&P 500 futures contracts at a price of 163.60 (market value = 24 × \$500 × 163.60 = \$1,963,200)
Results	Sell 24 contracts at	167.60
	Buy 24 contracts at	163.60
	Net profit on futures (+400 basis points)	4.00
	Dollar value of profit (each basis point worth \$5): 400 × \$5 × 24 contracts or \$2,011,200 – \$1,963,200	\$48,000
	Net loss on stock portfolio (\$8,152,000 – \$8,277,000)	(\$125,000)
	Net loss on hedge	(\$77,000)
	Portfolio loss reduced by hedge (percent)	38

Utilizing the Howard and D'Antonio hedging strategy, the loss on the spot position was reduced by 38%.

5.5.2 *Stock index futures: Does the tail wag the dog?*

The rise in program trading based on a comparatively narrow blue-chip stock market barometer, the **MMI**, is said to be fueling the volatile price swings in the stock market, a case of the tail wagging the dog. The MMI is a price-weighted index of twenty very actively traded stocks, sixteen of which are included in the Dow Jones 30 Industrials. Because of its relatively small size, the MMI is expected to be more easily arbitrable than other stock index futures contracts. Basically, program trading is taking a position (long or short) in a portfolio of stocks comprising the index and simultaneously taking an opposite position in the index futures contracts. The objective of the program trade is to create a risk-free position that earns a return in excess of the currently available risk-free return.

These so-called program trades may move both the futures and the spot market. The chain of causality may work as follows:

1. Investors believe the stock market will rise and they purchase futures contracts in expectation of higher equity values. The purchase of futures contracts is preferable because they entail no initial investment and lower transaction costs than a position in the stock market.
2. The rise in futures prices causes an imbalance between the prices of the futures and the underlying index; as this premium between the futures and the index increases, it may become more profitable to execute a program trade.
3. The simultaneous sale of the futures and purchase of the underlying index will cause the premium between the futures and the index to shrink.

Changes in other factors, such as interest rates, can also have an effect on the equilibrium relationship between the index price and the futures price, thereby changing the premium or discount between the two markets. Program traders can take advantage of any change in the spread between the markets. It does not matter what causes the change in spread, either internal factors like changes in investor expectations or external factors such as interest rate changes. All program trading does is to bring cash and futures prices together. The program trade may be an essential mechanism insuring that futures prices and the underlying equity prices are efficiently determined. Chapter 21 discusses the relationship between portfolio insurance and program trading.

To date, most of the literature on the impact of futures trading on the cash market has focused on the changes in the spot price volatility because of the initiation or cessation of futures trading. A common conclusion of these studies is that the futures market has a smoothing effect on the cash market by stabilizing the spot price. The recent uproar about the "triple witching hour" and the so-called crises at expiration caused by the expiration of stock index futures and options at the close on the third Friday of March, June,

September, and December brings to question the smoothing influence that futures contracts have on the underlying index.

If the market is efficient, prices adjust instantaneously to reflect all relevant information, and knowledge of such information cannot lead to excess risk-adjusted returns. The central concept in the efficient market hypothesis is the fair-game model. A sequence of past returns over time is fair game if today's price reflects the then-available information, making it impossible to earn excess risk-adjusted returns by trading on that information. If the information set today contains all of the information known and used by the market participants in the spot market in determining the spot price, one of the components of the information set is the previous change in the price of futures contracts.

Using intraday spot and futures prices of the CBT's MMI over the period August 1984 to August 1986, Finnerty and Park (1871) provide the following and subsequent spot price changes. A majority of the contracts studied showed a significant relationship between the change in the futures price and the subsequent spot price change (Table 5.14). This supports the notion that the tail is wagging the dog. This result was present for both the Maxi and the regular MMI contracts. Of interest is the fact that when each of the contracts was first traded, there existed a period of time when there was no relationship between the change in the futures price and subsequent change in the index. For the Maxi contract, this was the first four months of trading, from September to December 1985. And for the MMI during the first nine months of trading, six out nine contracts showed no relationship between futures and subsequent spot price changes. This could indicate either that arbitrage opportunities were not available during the initial trading of the contracts, or that program traders were unable immediately to take advantage of the opportunities if they were available.

However, after the initial start-up periods, the results indicate that there exists a strong relationship between futures and subsequent index price changes in seven out of the last seven months for the Maxi and thirteen out of the last fifteen months for the MMI contracts. These results indicate that it is reasonable to answer in the affirmative: the tail is wagging the dog, at least in the case of the MMI and Maxi MMI.

Table 5.14 Linkage between Futures Price Changes and Subsequent Spot Price Changes

Maxi Major Market Index		**Major Market Index**	
Number of contracts studied	11		24
Number showing significance at the 10 percent level	7		16
Number showing significance if results were random	1		2
Number significant before December 1985/number of contracts	0/4	Number significant before April 1985/number of contracts	3/9
Number significant after December 1985/number of contracts	7/7	Number significant after April 1985/number of contracts	13/15

5.6 Summary

In one sense, uncertainty and risk are equivalent; thus, the more uncertain something is the more risky it is. The futures markets evolved to alleviate one particular kind of risk — that associated with unexpected price changes. The purpose of this chapter has been to help explain what futures contracts are, how markets for them operate, and most importantly, how they can be applied to the hedging of price risk for securities.

Although futures contracts originated on agricultural commodities, the 1970s saw the introduction of futures for financial instruments. Deregulation of the domestic financial sector, the 1979 change in monetary policy, elimination of fixed foreign exchange rates, the growing interrelatedness of the world economy, and bouts with high levels of inflation are some of the major reasons for the growing need for and popularity of financial futures.

The general methodology for using futures to reduce price risk (or equivalently, interest rate risk) should seem quite straightforward. If long the spot commodity or instrument, then sell or short the related futures contract in order to lock in a price (or rate). Nevertheless, exactly how to determine the appropriate hedge ratio and evaluate the effectiveness of the hedge has no all-conclusive answer.

Questions and Problems

1. Carefully explain why a market for foreign currency futures emerged.
2. What is interest rate parity? What is the relationship between the concept of interest rate parity and the futures and spot prices for foreign currency?
3. Assume that the six-month interest rate in the United States is 5% while the rate is 7% in Japan. If the spot price of dollars in terms of yen is 124 yen/dollar, what is the price of a six-month futures contract for dollars?
4. Suppose IBM is planning to issue thirty-year bonds to finance a new plant. Assume that it plans to issue these bonds in three months. Is there any way IBM can protect itself from unexpected increases in interest rates?
5. Carefully explain the function speculators serve in the futures markets.
6. Assume that sixty-day spot Treasury bills sell for $97.75, while ninety-day spot Treasury bills sell for $96.50. If the price of a thirty-day Treasury bill future that matures in thirty days is $98.50, are there any arbitrage opportunities? If so, create a strategy to exploit this opportunity.
7. I. M. Ritch has a stock portfolio worth $50,000. He plans to use it for a down payment on a house he will be purchasing in six months. Is there any way Mr. Ritch can protect himself from an adverse change in stock prices? Are there any conditions that must be met for this strategy to work?
8. Calculate the implied forward rate of a T-bill with a life of 182 days if the 91-day T-bill rate is 9% and the nine-month T-bill rate is 10.5%.
9. What are Eurodollars? Why do they exist?
10. Carefully explain why a bank might choose to have a long position in Eurodollar futures.
11. Carefully explain the difference between a long hedge and a short hedge. When would an investor wish to use a long hedge? A short hedge?
12. Juan Valdez is a coffee grower who is planning to harvest 112,500 pounds of coffee on June 1. The current price for coffee is $1.34

per pound. A futures contract on coffee that matures on June 1 also costs \$1.34.

(a) To hedge his position in coffee, should Mr. Valdez buy or sell futures contracts?
(b) If a contract consists of 37,500 pounds of coffee, how many contracts does Mr. Valdez need to buy or sell to hedge his position perfectly?
(c) Show the net gain or loss if the price of coffee rises to \$1.50 per pound on July 1.
(d) Show the net gain or loss if the price of coffee falls to \$1.20 per pound.

13. The spot price for a T-bill that matures in 91 days is 98.875, while the spot price for a T-bill that matures in 273 days is 95.125.

 (a) Calculate the theoretical price of a futures contract for a 182-day T-bill with delivery in 91 days.
 (b) Recompute your answer in (a) assuming that there is a round-trip commission cost of \$0.006 per \$100 of face value.

14. Because the yield curve was upward sloping, Friendly Bank decided it would be more profitable to finance three-year car loans with a six-month CD. Since a car loan matures in three years and a CD in only six months, it will be necessary for the bank to roll over or issue additional CDs to keep the load funded.

 (a) If Friendly Bank forecasts an increase in future short-term interest rates, should it use a long or short hedge to maximize the return on its loan?
 (b) Assume that the bank has two hundred \$10,000 car loans to finance. How many CD futures does it need to buy or sell?

15. Assume that Friendly Bank has financed a six-month commercial loan using the funds from a five-year CD. When the loan matures in six months, the bank will relend the money to another company for another six months.

 (a) If the yield curve is inverted (downward sloping), should Friendly Bank use a long or a short hedge?
 (b) Carefully explain how this will work.

Bibliography

Anderson, R. W. and J. P. Danthine (1981). Cross-hedging. *Journal of Political Economy*, 89(November/December), 1182–1196.

Bacon, P. W. and R. Williams (1976). Interest rate futures: New tools for the financial manager. *Financial Management*, 5(Spring), 32–38.

Benninga, S. and M. Smirlock (1985). An empirical analysis of the delivery option, marking to market and the pricing of T-bond futures. *Journal of Futures Markets*, 5(Fall), 361–374.

Black, F. L. (1976). The pricing of commodity contracts. *Journal of Financial Economics*, 3(June), 167–179.

Capozza, D. and B. Cornell (1979). Treasury bill pricing in the spot and futures markets. *Review of Economics and Statistics*, 61(November), 513–520.

Cassel, G. (1916a). The present situation of foreign exchange I. *Economic Journal*, 26(March), 62–65.

Cassel, G. (1916b). The present situation of foreign exchange II. *Economic Journal*, 26(September), 319–323.

Cornell, B. and K. French (1983a). The pricing of stock index futures. *Journal of Futures Markets*, 3(March), 1–14.

Cornell, B. and K. French (1983b). Taxes and the pricing of stock index futures. *Journal of Finance*, 38(June), 675–694.

Cornell, B. and M. Reinganum (1981). Forward and futures prices: Evidence from the foreign exchange markets. *Journal of Finance*, 36(September), 1035–1045.

Cox, J., J. Ingersoll Jr, and S. Ross (1981). The relation between forward and futures prices. *Journal of Financial Economics*, 9(September), 321–346.

Chen, S. S., C. F. Lee and K. Shrestha (2003). Futures hedge ratios: A review. *The Quarterly Review of Economics and Finance*, 43(3), 433–465.

Chen, S. S., C. F. Lee and K. Shrestha (2004). An empirical analysis of the relationship between the hedge ratio and hedging horizon: A simultaneous estimation of the short- and long-run hedge ratios. *Journal of Futures Markets*, 24(4), 359–386.

Chou, W. L., K. F. Denis and C. F. Lee (1996). Hedging with the Nikkei index futures: The conventional model versus the error correction model. *The Quarterly Review of Economics and Finance*, 36(4), 495–505.

Duncan, W. H. (1977). Treasury bill futures: Opportunities and pitfalls. *Review*, Federal Reserve Bank of Dallas (July), 1–5.

Ederington, L. (1979). The hedging performance of the new futures markets. *Journal of Finance*, 34(March), 157–170.

Fabozzi, F. and G. Kipnis (1984). *Stock Index Futures.* New York: Dow Jones-Irwin.

Figlewski, S. (1985). Hedging with stock index futures: Theory and application in a new market. *Journal of Futures Markets*, 5(Summer), 183–200.

Figlewski, S. and S. J. Kon (1982). Portfolio management with stock index futures. *Financial Analysts Journal*, 20(January/February), 52–60.

Finnerty, J. and H. Park (1987). Does the tail wag the dog? *Financial Analysts Journal*, 43(March/April), 57–60.

Fisher, I. (1907). *The Rate of Interest.* New York: Macmillan.

Francis, J. and M. Castelino (1982). Basis speculation in commodity futures: The maturity effect. *Journal of Futures Markets*, 2(Summer), 195–206.

Gay, R., R. Kolb and R. Chiang (1983). Interest rate hedging: An empirical test of alternate strategies. *Journal of Financial Research*, 6(March), 187–197.

Gay, R. and D. J. S. Rutledge (1971). The economics of commodity futures markets: A survey. *Review of Marketing and Agricultural Economics*, 34(March), 57–108.

Hansen, L. P. and R. J. Hordrick (1980). Forward exchange rate as optimal predictors of future spot rates: An econometric analysis. *Journal of Political Economy*, 88(October), 829–853.

Hill, J. and T. Schneeweis (1984). Reducing volatility with financial futures. *Financial Analysts Journal*, 40(November/December), 34–40.

Hilliard, J. (1984). Hedging interest rate risk with futures portfolios under term structure effects. *Journal of Finance*, 39(December), 1547–1570.

Hsin, C. W., J. Kuo and C. F. Lee (1994). A new measure to compare the hedging effectiveness of foreign currency futures versus options. *Journal of Futures Markets*, 14(6), 685–707.

Hsin, C. W., J. Kuo and C. F. Lee (1995). An empirical test of minimum-risk foreign currency hedges with futures and options. *Advances in Investment Analysis and Portfolio Management*, III, 495–505.

Junkus, J. C. and C. F. Lee (1985). Use of three stock index futures in hedging decisions. *Journal of Futures Markets*, 5(2), 201–222.

Kamara, A. (1982). Issues in futures markets: A survey. *Journal of Futures Markets*, 2(Fall), 261–294.

Koppenhaver, G. D. and C. F. Lee (1987). Alternative instruments for hedging inflation risk in the banking industry. *Journal of Futures Markets*, 7(6), 619–636.

Keynes, J. M. (1930). *A Treatise on Money.* New York: Macmillan.

Khoury, S. (1984). *Speculative Markets.* New York: Macmillan.

Kolb, R. (1985). *Understanding Futures Markets.* New York: Scott, Foresman and Co.

Kolb, R. and R. Chiang (1981). Improving performance using interest rate futures. *Financial Management*, 10(Autumn), 77–85.

Kolb, R. W. and R. Chiang (1982). Duration, immunization, and hedging with interest rate futures. *Journal of Financial Research*, 5(2), 161–170.

Laufman, P. (1986). *Handbook of Futures Markets: Commodity, Financial Stock Indices and Options.* New York: John Wiley and Sons.

Lee, C. F., E. L. Bubnys and Y. Lin (1987). Stock index futures hedge ratios: Test on horizon effects and functional form. *Advances in Futures and Options Research*, 2(1), 291–311.

Lee, C. F., J. E. Finnerty, D. H. Wort, J. Lee and A. C. Lee (2013). *Security Analysis, Portfolio Management, and Financial Derivatives.* Singapore: World Scientific Publishers, Inc.

Lee, C. F., K. Wang and Y. L. Chen (2009). Hedging and optimal hedge ratios for international index futures markets. *Review of Pacific Basin Financial Markets and Policies*, 12(4), 593–610.

Lin, F. L. (2023). A comparative analysis of hedging determination for three alternative international equity index futures. *Review of Pacific Basin Financial Markets and Policies*, 26(1), 1–22.

Loosigian, A. M. (1980). *Interest Rate Futures.* New York: Dow Jones-Irwin.

Modest, D. M. and M. Sundaresan (1983). The relationship between spot and futures prices in stock-index futures markets: Some preliminary evidence. *Journal of Futures Markets*, 3(Spring), 13–42.

Nelson, R. and R. Collins (1985). A measure of hedging performance. *Journal of Futures Markets*, 5(Spring), 45–55.

Poole, W. (1978). Using T-bill futures to gauge interest rate expectations. *Economic Review*, Federal Reserve Bank of San Francisco (Spring), 7–19.

Powers, M. (1984). *Inside the Financial Futures Markets.* New York: John Wiley and Sons.

Rendleman, R. and C. Carabini (1979). The efficiency of the T-bill futures. *Journal of Finance*, 34(September), 895–914.

Rishard, S. and M. Sundaresan (1981). A continuous time equilibrium model of forward prices and futures prices in a multigood economy. *Journal of Financial Economics*, 9(September), 347–372.

Rothstein, N. (ed.) (1986). *Handbook of Financial Futures.* New York: McGraw-Hill.

Rutledge, D. J. S. (1972). Hedgers' demand for futures contracts: A theoretical framework with applications to the United States Soybean Complex. *Food Research Institute Studies*, 11(March), 237–256.

Schwarz, E., J. Hill and T. Schneeweis (1986). *Financial Futures: Fundamental Strategies and Applications.* New York: Irwin.
Senchack, A. J., Jr and J. C. Easeterwood (1983). Cross hedging CDs with treasury bill futures. *Journal of Futures Markets*, 3(Winter), 429–438.
Weiner, N. S. (1981). The hedging rationale for a stock index futures contract. *Journal of Futures Market*, 1(Spring), 59–76.

Appendix 5A: The Traditional Theory of International Parity

The writings of Keynes, Cassel, and Irving Fisher implicitly require four conditions for international currency parity:

1. Financial markets are perfect. There are no controls, transaction costs, taxes, and so on.
2. Goods markets are perfect. Shipment of goods anywhere in the world is costless.
3. There is a single consumption good common to everyone.
4. The future is known with certainty.

Interest rate parity. For any two countries, the difference in their domestic interest rates must be equal to the forward exchange rate differential:

$$\frac{1+R_i^t}{1+R_j^t} = \frac{F_{ij}^t}{S_{ij}^t}, \tag{5A.1}$$

where R_i^t and R_j^t = the interest rate for countries i and j, respectively, in time t, F_{ij}^t = the forward exchange rate of currency i in units of currency j quoted at time t for delivery at $t+1$, and S_{ij}^t = the spot exchange rate of currency i in units of currency j at time t.

Keynes (1930) developed this relationship by using only the first assumption.

Purchasing power parity. Cassel (1961) derived a **purchasing power parity** theorem based on the first and third assumptions. According to the laws of one price in perfect markets, identical goods must have the same real price everywhere. Since it is assumed that every country consumes the same good (or basket of goods), a given currency has the same purchasing power in every country:

$$\frac{P_i^t}{P_j^t} = S_{ij}^t, \tag{5A.2}$$

where S_{ij}^t = the spot rate between countries i and j at time t, and P_i^t and P_j^t = price level in countries i and j at time t, respectively.

Fisherian relation. Using the first, third, and fourth assumptions, Irving Fisher (1930) showed that the nominal interest rate in every country will be equal to the real rate of interest plus the expected future inflation rate (this is called the **Fisherian relation**):

$$(1 + R_j^t) = (1 + r_j^t)(1 + I_j^t), \tag{5A.3}$$

where r_j^t = the real rate of interest in country j at time t, R_j^t = the nominal rate of interest at time t, and I_j^t = the inflation rate at time t.

The implication of this relationship is that if the real rate of interest is equal everywhere, then the inflation differential between countries is fully reflected in their nominal interest rates.

Forward parity. The forward exchange rate (F_{ij}^t) must be equal to the spot exchange rate at some future point in time (S_{ij}^{t+1}):

$$S_{ij}^{t+1} = F_{ij}^t. \tag{5A.4}$$

This relationship (**forward parity**) must be true given the first three relationships derived above; otherwise, arbitrage opportunities would exist. Sample Problem 5.4 provides further illustration.

Note that $I + I_j^t = P_i^{t+1}/P_j^t$. Then, assuming that $1 + r_j^t = 1 + r_i^t$, it follows that

$$\frac{(1 + R_j^t)}{(1 + R_i^t)} = \frac{P_i^t}{P_j^t}\frac{P_j^{t+1}}{P_i^{t+1}} = \frac{S_{ij}^t}{S_{ij}^{t+1}}, \tag{5A.5}$$

which is equal to 1 plus the rate of currency appreciation (or depreciation).

In order to understand the pricing of futures contracts, the four relationships above must be used as building blocks. The linkages among interest rates, price levels, expected inflation, and exchange rates are all relevant in pricing a foreign currency contract.

Appendix 5B: Derivation of Equation (5.8)

To derive Equation (5.8), we assume the market is in equilibrium. Now, let

Y_m = yield on a 91-day T-bill, $m = 1$,
Y_n = yield on a 182-day T-bill, $n = 2$,
$Y_{Fu,m}$ = yield on a futures contract maturing m days from now, and
$Y_{Fw,n-m}$ = implied forward rate on a T-bill with a life equal to $n-m$.

If the market is to be in equilibrium, then

$$\begin{aligned}[(1+Y_m)(1+Y_{Fu,m})]^{1/n} &= [(1+Y_m)(1+Y_{Fw,n-m})]^{1/n} \\ &= (1+Y_n). \end{aligned} \tag{5B.1}$$

In other words, investing in a 91-day T-bill and then buying a futures contract maturing in 91 more days is equivalent to initially investing in a 182-day T-bill.

Arbitrage conditions will arise if

$$\begin{aligned} Y_{Fu,m} &< Y_{Fw,n-m}, \\ Y_{Fu,m} &> Y_{Fw,n-m}. \end{aligned} \tag{5B.2}$$

To compute $Y_{Fw,n-m}$, the implied forward rate of a T-bill with a life of $n-m$, the following example is utilized. Assume that the 182-day T-bill rate is 11% and the three-month T-bill rate is 10%. The implied three-month forward rate is then

$$Y_{Fw,3} = \frac{(1+Y_n)^{n/m}}{(1+Y_m)} - 1 = \frac{(1+0.11)^2}{(1+0.10)} - 1. \tag{5B.3}$$

If an arbitrager observed that the futures rate was above 12% (or had a price less than 88.00), he or she could profit from the following strategy:

1. Borrow money at 11% (assuming lending and borrowing rates are equal) by selling short a six-month T-bill.
2. Buy a three-month T-bill.
3. Simultaneously, buy one T-bill futures contract with a time to maturity of three months.

Combining the spot and futures T-bill positions results in a synthetic six-month T-bill with a yield exceeding that realized on the actual six-month T-bill. For instance, if the futures contract has a rate of 13%, the six-month annualized return on the synthetic position is

$$\sqrt{(1+0.10)(1+0.13)-1} = 11.48\%.$$

The **arbitrage profit** is equal to the realized yield on the synthetic position less the cost of establishing that position or 11.48% − 11.00% = 0.48%. On a $1,000,000 position, the arbitrager would have made $4,800 essentially risk-free.

Of course, this scenario could be reversed for a situation where the observed futures rate was less than 12% (or had a price greater than 88.00). Based on these examples, the theoretical price for a T-bill future can be derived from Equation (5B.1). First, by taking its inverse,

$$\frac{1}{(1+Y_m)} \times \frac{1}{(1+Y_{Fu,m})} = \frac{1}{(1+Y_n)^n}, \tag{5B.4}$$

or, equivalently

$$P_m \times P_{Fu} = P_n, \tag{5B.5}$$

where P_n is the price of an n-day T-bill paying $1 at maturity.

Part III

Option: Theories and Applications

Chapter 6

Options, Put–Call Parities, and Option Strategies

Contents

6.1 Introduction

The use of stock options for risk reduction and return enhancement has expanded at an astounding pace over the last two decades. Among the causes of this growth, two are most significant. First, the establishment of the Chicago Board Option Exchange (CBOE) in 1973 brought about the liquidity necessary for successful option trading, through public listing and standardization of option contracts. The second stimulus emanated from academia. In the same year that the CBOE was established, Professors Fischer Black and

Myron Scholes published a paper in which they derived a revolutionary option pricing model. The power of their model to predict an option's fair price has since made it the industry standard.

The development of option valuation theory shed new light on the valuation process. Previous pricing models such as CAPM were based on very stringent assumptions, such as there being an identifiable and measurable market portfolio, as well as various imputed investor attributes, such as quadratic utility functions. Furthermore, previous theories priced only market risk since investors were assumed to hold well-diversified portfolios. The strength of the Black–Scholes and subsequent option pricing models is that they rely on far fewer assumptions. In addition, the option valuation models price total risk and do not require any assumptions concerning the direction of the underlying securities price. The growing popularity of the option concept is evidenced by its application to the valuation of a wide array of other financial instruments (such as common stock and bonds) as well as more abstract assets including leases and real estate agreements.

This chapter aims to establish basic knowledge of options and the markets in which they are traded. It begins with the most common types of options, calls, and puts, explaining their general characteristics and discussing the institutions where they are traded. In addition, the concepts relevant to the new types of options on indexes and futures are introduced. The next focus is the basic pricing relationship between puts and calls, known as put–call parity. The final study concerns how options can be used as investment tools. The chapter on option valuation that follows utilizes all these essential concepts to afford a deeper conceptual understanding of valuation theory.

In Section 6.2, we will define the option market and related terms. The put–call parity is introduced in Section 6.3. The risk–return characteristics of options are discussed in Section 6.4, and Section 6.5 covers the Excel approach to analyze the option strategies. Finally, a chapter summary is given in Section 6.6.

6.2 The Option Market and Related Definitions

This section discusses option market and related definitions of options, which are needed to understand option valuations and option strategies.

6.2.1 *What is an option?*

An **option** is a contract conveying the right to buy or sell a designated security at a stipulated price. The contract normally expires at a predetermined time. The most important element of an option contract is that there is no obligation placed upon the purchaser: It is an "option." This attribute of an option contract distinguishes it from other financial contracts. For instance, while the holder of an option has the opportunity to let his or her claim expire unused if so desired, futures and forward contracts obligate their parties to fulfill certain conditions.

6.2.2 *Types of options and their characteristics*

A **call option** gives its owner the right to buy the underlying asset, while a **put option** conveys to its holder the right to sell the underlying asset.

An option is specified by five essential parts:

(1) the type (call or put),
(2) the underlying asset,
(3) the exercise price,
(4) the expiration date, and
(5) the option price.

While the most common type of underlying asset for an option is an individual stock, other underlying assets for options exist as well. These include futures contracts, foreign currencies, stock indexes, and US debt instruments. In the case of common stock options (on which this discussion is exclusively centered), the specified quantity to which the option buyer is entitled to buy or sell is 100 shares of the stock per option.

The **exercise price** (also called the **striking price**) is the price stated in the option contract at which the call (put) owner can buy (sell) the underlying asset up to the expiration date, the final calendar date on which the option can be traded. Options on common stocks have expiration dates three months apart in one of three fixed cycles:

(1) January/April/July/October,
(2) February/May/August/November, and
(3) March/June/September/December.

The normal expiration date is the third Saturday of the month. (The third Friday is the last trading date for the option.)

As an example, an option referred to as an "ABC June 25 call" is an option to buy 100 shares of the underlying ABC stock at $25 per share, up to its expiration date in June. Option prices are quoted on a per-share basis. Thus, a stock option that is quoted at $5 would cost $500 ($5 × 100 shares), plus commission and a nominal SEC fee.

A common distinction among options pertains to when they can be exercised. Exercising an option is the process of carrying out the right to buy or sell the underlying asset at the stated price. American options allow the exercise of this right at any time from when the option is purchased up to the expiration date. On the other hand, European options allow their holder the right of exercise only on the expiration date itself. The distinction between an American and European option has nothing to do with the location at which they are traded. Both types are currently bought and sold in the United States. There are distinctions in their pricing and in the possibility of exercising them prior to expiration.

Finally, when discussing options, the two parties to the contract are characterized by whether they have bought or sold the contract. The party buying the option contract (call or put) is the option buyer (or holder), while the party selling the option is the option seller (or writer). If the writer of an option does not own the underlying asset, he or she is said to write a naked option.

Tables 6.1–6.4 show a listing of publicly traded options for Johnson & Johnson (JNJ) on February 18, 2022.

6.2.3 *Relationships between the option price and the underlying asset price*

A call (put) option is said to be **in the money** if the underlying asset is selling above (below) the exercise price of the option. An **at-the-money** call (put) is one whose exercise price is equal to the current price of the underlying asset. A call (put) option is **out of the money** if the underlying asset is selling below (above) the exercise price of the option.

Table 6.1 Call and Put Options Expired on May 20, 2022

Stock Price on February 18, 2022 = \$163.36						
Strike	**Symbol**	**Last**	**Bid**	**Ask**	**Vol.**	**Open Int**
Call Options Expired on May 20, 2022						
140	JNJ220520C00140000	25.6	25.25	28.95	3	3
155	JNJ220520C00155000	8.07	7.1	11.25	—	—
160	JNJ220520C00160000	10.17	9.7	10.65	222	127
165	JNJ220520C00165000	7	6.7	7.15	229	241
170	JNJ220520C00170000	4.53	4.1	4.6	126	313
175	JNJ220520C00175000	2.5	2.27	2.94	935	407
180	JNJ220520C00180000	1.43	1.28	1.7	439	152
185	JNJ220520C00185000	0.75	0.52	0.85	4	5
190	JNJ220520C00190000	0.46	0.32	0.55	1	1
Put Options Expired on May 20, 2022						
130	JNJ220520P00130000	1.07	0.47	2.12	—	—
135	JNJ220520P00135000	0.98	0.53	0.99	1	22
140	JNJ220520P00140000	2.15	0.51	1.37	6	10
145	JNJ220520P00145000	1.41	0.84	1.69	21	80
150	JNJ220520P00150000	1.92	1.55	2.01	27	384
155	JNJ220520P00155000	2.68	2.5	2.84	74	150
160	JNJ220520P00160000	4.01	3.65	4.15	145	264
165	JNJ220520P00165000	5.75	5.65	6.1	205	431
170	JNJ220520P00170000	13.75	7.8	8.45	1	251

Suppose ABC stock is selling at \$30 per share. An ABC June 25 call option is in the money ($\$30-25>0$), while an ABC June 35 call option is out of the money ($\$30-35<0$). Of course, the expiration dates could be any month without changing the option's standing as in, at, or out of the money.

An option premium exists in buying and selling options contracts, represented by the ask and bid price, respectively. Typically found on the options chain, the option premium is either the price paid to buy the option, or the price received for writing or selling the option. Essentially, an investor pays a premium to own a contract and they receive a premium when writing a contract. Option premiums consist of two price components: intrinsic and extrinsic value. The intrinsic value of an option premium represents the inherent profit that is

Table 6.2 Call and Put Options Expired on June 17, 2022

Stock Price on February 18, 2022 = $163.36						
Strike	**Symbol**	**Last**	**Bid**	**Ask**	**Vol.**	**Open Int**
Call Options Expired on June 17, 2022						
150	JNJ210917C00150000	17.41	16.15	16.95	5	1,740
155	JNJ210917C00155000	14.33	12.25	13.1	4	1,195
160	JNJ210917C00160000	9.6	9.05	9.45	1	1,177
165	JNJ210917C00165000	6.3	6.3	6.7	32	1,762
170	JNJ210917C00170000	4.35	4.05	4.45	7	2,779
175	JNJ210917C00175000	2.65	2.45	2.85	15	5,022
180	JNJ210917C00180000	1.51	1.38	1.89	23	6,524
185	JNJ210917C00185000	1.02	0.69	1.12	11	4,531
190	JNJ210917C00190000	0.55	0.45	1.23	52	3,110
195	JNJ210917C00195000	0.33	0.22	0.4	1	815
Put Options Expired on June 17, 2022						
125	JNJ210917P00125000	1.7	1.71	1.85	40	1,106
130	JNJ210917P00130000	2.17	2.18	2.45	2	758
135	JNJ210917P00135000	3.05	2.76	3.25	3	270
140	JNJ210917P00140000	4.05	3.85	4.35	2	626
145	JNJ210917P00145000	5.3	4.9	5.6	2	645
150	JNJ210917P00150000	7.15	6.9	7.35	401	987
155	JNJ210917P00155000	9	8.8	9.3	2	358
160	JNJ210917P00160000	11.3	10.7	11.6	7	1,032
165	JNJ210917P00165000	13.03	13.5	14.5	7	590
170	JNJ210917P00170000	15.45	15.7	17.8	12	157

expressed in the contract, determined in calculating the difference between the current stock price and the strike price. The extrinsic value of an option premium represents the actual costs associated with owning options, and symbolizes compensation for the risks of writing the option contract.

The relationship between the price of an option and the price of the underlying asset indicates both the amount of intrinsic value and time value inherent in the option's price, as shown in Equation (6.1):

$$\text{Intrinsic value} = \text{Underlying asset price} - \text{Option exercise price}. \tag{6.1}$$

Table 6.3 Call and Put Options Expired on July 15, 2022

Strike	Symbol	Last	Bid	Ask	Vol.	Open Int
Stock Price on February 18, 2022 = $163.36						
Call Options Expired on July 15, 2022						
150	JNJ220715C00150000	12.1	17.45	20.2	54	87
155	JNJ220715C00155000	15.42	14.2	15.45	6	177
160	JNJ220715C00160000	11.7	11.1	11.9	29	1,033
165	JNJ220715C00165000	8.7	7.65	8.85	9	625
170	JNJ220715C00170000	6	5.4	6.3	88	290
175	JNJ220715C00175000	4.1	3.55	4.05	47	1,029
180	JNJ220715C00180000	2.63	2.15	2.91	12	701
185	JNJ220715C00185000	0.92	1.16	1.6	71	1,155
190	JNJ220715C00190000	0.66	0.68	1.38	3	256
195	JNJ220715C00195000	0.55	0.37	0.75	6	115
Put Options Expired on July 15, 2022						
125	JNJ220715P00125000	1.47	0.47	1.17	1	35
130	JNJ220715P00130000	1.6	0.79	1.41	1	382
135	JNJ220715P00135000	1.37	1	2.61	9	251
140	JNJ220715P00140000	1.9	1.44	1.93	1	158
145	JNJ220715P00145000	2.45	2.14	2.76	36	690
150	JNJ220715P00150000	3.25	2.67	3.6	41	585
155	JNJ220715P00155000	4.2	4.3	4.75	11	657
160	JNJ220715P00160000	6.05	5.15	6.3	1	385
165	JNJ220715P00165000	8	7.55	8.3	15	164
170	JNJ220715P00170000	10.95	10.25	10.9	18	195

For a call (put) option that is in the money (underlying asset price > exercise price), its intrinsic value is positive. And for at-the-money and out-of-the-money options, the intrinsic value is zero. An option's time value is the amount by which the option's premium (or market price) exceeds its intrinsic value. For a call or put option,

$$\text{Time value} = \text{Option premium} - \text{Intrinsic value}, \tag{6.2}$$

where intrinsic value is the maximum of zero or stock price minus exercise price. Thus, an option premium or market price is composed of two components: intrinsic value and time value. In-the-money options are usually most expensive because of their large

Table 6.4 Call and Put Options Expired on October 17, 2022

Stock Price on February 18, 2022 = $163.36						
Strike	**Symbol**	**Last**	**Bid**	**Ask**	**Vol.**	**Open Int**
Call Options Expired on October 17, 2022						
135	JNJ221021C00135000	32.3	31.7	34.8	—	1
150	JNJ221021C00150000	20.25	20.3	21.75	22	22
165	JNJ221021C00165000	11.1	10.6	11.75	3	60
175	JNJ221021C00175000	6.7	5.65	6.9	43	22
180	JNJ221021C00180000	4.85	3.75	6.1	2	27
Put Options Expired on October 17, 2022						
110	JNJ221021P00110000	1.07	0.62	1.05	1	2
115	JNJ221021P00115000	1.56	0.83	1.96	1	21
125	JNJ221021P00125000	2.8	1.34	2.25	3	5
130	JNJ221021P00130000	3.4	0.89	5	—	—
135	JNJ221021P00135000	3.5	1.5	6.05	—	—
145	JNJ221021P00145000	4.5	3.7	4.75	3	5
155	JNJ221021P00155000	11.1	6.4	7.55	19	63

intrinsic-value component. An option with an at-the-money exercise price will have only time value inherent in its market price. Deep out-of-the-money options have zero intrinsic value and little time value, and consequently are the least expensive. Deep in-the-money cases also have little time value, and time value is the greatest for at-the-money options. In addition, time value (as its name implies) is positively related to the amount of time the option has to expiration. The theoretical valuation of options focuses on determining the relevant variables that affect the time value portion of an option premium and the derivation of their relationship in option pricing.

In general, the call price should be equal to or exceed the intrinsic value:

$$C \geq \text{Max}(S - E, 0),$$

where C = the value of the call option, S = the current stock price, and E = the exercise price.

Figure 6.1 illustrates the relationship between an option's time value and its exercise price. When the exercise price is zero, the time value of an option is zero. Although this relationship is described quite well in general by Figure 6.1, the exact relationship is somewhat ambiguous. Moreover, the identification of options with a mispriced time value portion in their total premium motivates interest in a theoretical pricing model.

One more aspect of time value that is very important to discuss is the change in the amount of time value an option has as its duration shortens. As previously mentioned, options with a longer time to maturity and those near to the money have the largest time value components. Assuming that a particular option remains near to the money as its time to maturity diminishes, the rate of decrease in its time value, or what is termed the effect of time decay, is of interest. How time decay affects an option's premium is an important question for the valuation of options and the application of option strategies. To best see an answer to this question, refer to Figure 6.2.

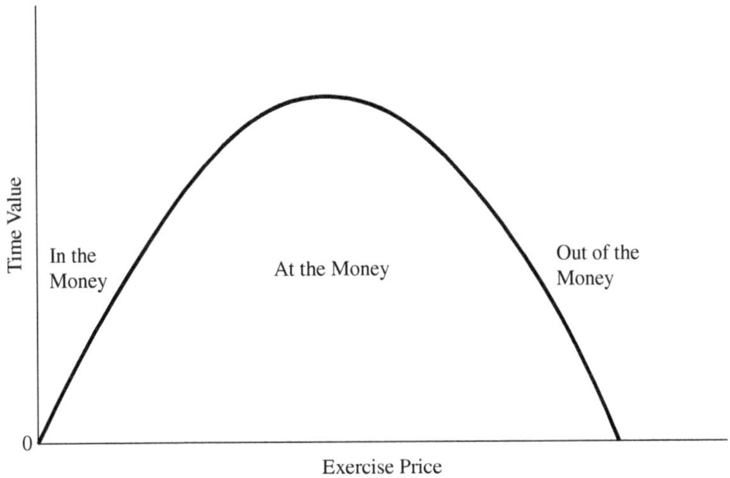

Figure 6.1 The Relationship between an Option's Exercise Price and Its Time Value

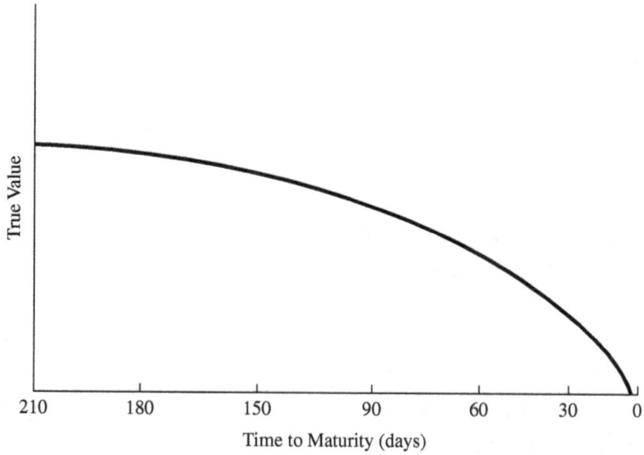

Figure 6.2 The Relationship between Time Value and Time to Maturity for a Near-to-the-Money Option (Assuming a Constant Price for the Underlying Asset)

In general, the value of call options with the same exercise price increases as time to expiration increases: $C(S_1, E_1, T_1) \leq C(S_1, E_1, T_2)$, where $T_1 \leq T_2$ and T_1 and T_2 are the time to expiration.

Note that for the simple case in Figure 6.2 the effect of time decay is smooth up until the last month before expiration, when the time value of an option begins to decay very rapidly. Why this effect occurs is made clearer in the next chapter, when the components of the option pricing model are examined. Sample Problem 6.1 shows the effect of time decay.

Sample Problem 6.1

It is January 1, the price of the underlying ABC stock is \$20 per share, and the time premiums are shown in Table 6.5. What is the value for the various call options?

Solution

$$\begin{aligned}\text{Call premium} &= \text{Intrinsic value} + \text{Time premium}\\ C_{15,\text{Jan}} &= \text{Max}(20 - 15, 0) + 0.50\\ &= \$5.50 \text{ per share or } \$550 \text{ for 1 contract.}\end{aligned}$$

Table 6.5 Time Premiums: Sample Problem 6.1

Exercise Price X	January	April	July
15	\$0.50	\$1.25	\$3.50
20	\$1.00	\$2.00	\$5.00
25	\$0.50	\$1.25	\$3.50

Table 6.6 Call Premiums: Sample Problem 6.1

Exercise Price X	January	April	July
15	\$5.50	Max(20−15, 0) + 1.25 = \$6.25	Max(20−15, 0) + 3.50 = \$8.50
20	Max(20−20, 0) + 1.00 = \$1.00	Max(20−20, 0) + 2.00 = \$2.00	Max(20−20, 0) + 5.00 = \$5.00
25	Max(20−25, 0) + 5.00 = \$0.50	Max(20−25, 0) + 1.25 = \$1.25	Max(20−25, 0) + 3.50 = \$3.50

The calculation of the call premiums, at exercise price X, for the other values is shown in Table 6.6.

6.2.4 *Additional definitions and distinguishing features*

Options may be specified in terms of their classes and series. A **class of options** refers to all call and put options on the same underlying asset. For example, all AT&T call and put options at various exercise prices and expiration months form one class. A **series** is a subset of a class and consists of all contracts of the same class (such as AT&T) having the same expiration date and exercise price.

When an investor either buys or sells an option (i.e., is long or short) as the initial transaction, the option exchange adds this opening transaction to what is termed the **open interest** for an option series. Essentially, open interest represents the number of contracts outstanding at a particular point in time. If the investor reverses the initial position with a closing transaction (i.e., sells the option if he or she originally bought it or vice versa), then the open interest for the particular option series is reduced by one.

While open interest is more of a static variable, indicating the number of outstanding contracts at one point in time, **volume** represents a dynamic characteristic. More specifically, volume indicates the number of times a particular option is bought and sold during a particular trading day. Volume and open interest are measures of an option's liquidity, the ease with which the option can be bought and sold in large quantities. The larger the volume and/or open interest, the more liquid the option.

Again, an option holder who invokes the right to buy or sell is exercising the option. Whenever a holder exercises an option, a writer is assigned the obligation to fulfill the terms of the option contract by the exchange on which the option is traded. If a call holder exercises the right to buy, a **call writer** is assigned the obligation to sell. Similarly, when a put holder exercises the right to sell, a **put writer** is assigned the obligation to buy.

The seller or writer of a call option must deliver 100 shares of the underlying stock at the specified exercise price when the option is exercised. The writer of a put option must purchase 100 shares of the underlying stock when the put option is exercised. The writer of either option receives the premium or price of the option for this legal obligation. The maximum loss an option buyer can experience is limited to the price of the option. However, the maximum loss from writing a naked call is unlimited; the maximum loss possible from writing a naked put is the exercise price less the original price of that put. To guarantee that the option writer can meet these obligations, the exchange clearinghouse requires margin deposits.

The payment of cash dividends affects both the price of the underlying stock and the value of an option on the stock. Normally, no adjustment is made in the terms of the option when a cash dividend is paid. However, strike price or number of shares may be adjusted if the underlying stock realizes a stock dividend or stock split. For example, an option on XYZ Corporation with an exercise price of \$100 would be adjusted if XYZ Corporation stock split two for one. The adjustment in this case would be a change in the exercise price from \$100 to \$50, and the number of contracts would be doubled. In the case of a non-integer split (such as three for two), the adjustment is made to the exercise price and the number of shares covered by the option contracts. For example, if XYZ Corporation had an exercise price of \$100 per share and had a three-for-two split, the option would have the exercise price adjusted to \$66.66, and the number of shares would be increased to 150. Note that the old exercise value of the option, \$10,000 (\$100 × 100 shares), is maintained by the adjustment (\$$66\frac{2}{3}$ × 150 shares).

6.2.5 *Types of underlying asset*

Although most people would identify common stocks as the underlying asset for an option, a variety of other assets and financial instruments can assume the same function. In fact, options on agricultural commodities were introduced by traders in the United States as early as the mid-1800s. After a number of scandals, agricultural commodity options were banned by the government. They were later reintroduced under tighter regulations and in a more standardized tradable form. Today, futures options on such agricultural commodities as corn, soybeans, wheat, cotton, sugar, live cattle, and live hogs are actively traded on a number of exchanges.

The biggest success for options has been realized for options on financial futures. Options on the S&P 500 index futures contracts, NYSE index futures, foreign currency futures, 30-year US Treasury bond futures, and gold futures have all realized extraordinary growth since their initial offerings back in 1982. Options on futures are very similar to options on the actual asset, except that the futures options give their holders the right (not the obligation) to buy or sell predetermined quantities of specified futures contracts at a fixed price within a predetermined period.

Options on the actual asset have arisen in another form as well. While a number of options have existed for various stock index futures contracts, options now also exist on the stock index itself. Because of the complexity of having to provide all the stocks in an index at the spot price, should a call holder exercise his or her buy right, options on stock indexes are always settled in cash. That is, should a call holder exercise his or her right to buy because of a large increase in the underlying index, that holder would be accommodated by a cash amount equal to the profit on his contract, or the current value of the option's premium. Although the options on the S&P 100 stock index at the CBOE are the most popular among traders, numerous index options are now traded as well. These include options on the S&P 500 index, the S&P OTC 250 index, the

NYSE composite and AMEX indexes (computer technology, oil and gas, and airline), the Philadelphia Exchange indexes (gold/silver), the Value Line index, and the NASDAQ 100 index.

6.2.6 *Institutional characteristics*

Probably two of the most important underlying factors leading to the success of options have been the standardization of contracts through the establishment of option exchanges and the trading anonymity brought about by the Option Clearing Corporations and clearinghouses of the major futures exchanges.

An important element for option trading is the interchangeability of contracts. Exchange contracts are not matched between individuals. Instead, when an investor or trader enters into an option contract, the Option Clearing Corporation (or clearinghouse for the particular futures exchange) takes the opposite side of the transaction. So, rather than having to contact a particular option writer to terminate an option position, a buyer can simply sell it back to the exchange at the current market clearing price. This type of anonymity among option market participants is what permits an active secondary market to operate.

The sources of futures options traded on the various futures exchanges mentioned earlier are determined by the **open-auction bidding**, probably the purest form of laissez-faire price determination that can be seen today. With the open-auction bidding-price mechanism there are no market makers, only a large octagonal pit filled with traders bidding among themselves to buy and sell contracts. While some traders buy and sell only for themselves, many of the participants are brokers representing large investment firms. Different sides of the pit usually represent traders who are dealing in particular expiration months. As brokers and other pit participants conduct trade, they mark down what they bought or sold, how much, at what price, and from whom. These cards are then collected by members of the exchange who record the trades and post the new prices. The prices are displayed on "scoreboards" surrounding the pit.

While stock options and options on commodities and indexes are traded in a similar fashion, one major difference prevails — the presence of **market makers**. Market makers are individuals who typically trade one type of option for their own account and are responsible for ensuring that a market always exists for their particular contract. In addition, some option exchanges utilize **board brokers** as well. These individuals are charged with the maintenance of the book of limit orders (orders from outside investors that are to be executed at particular prices or when the market goes up or down by a prespecified amount). Essentially, market makers and board brokers on the options exchanges share the duties performed by the specialists on the major stock exchanges.

Although stocks can be bought with as little as 50% margin, no margin is allowed for buying options — the cost of the contract must be fully paid. Because options offer a high degree of leverage on the underlying asset, additional leveraging through margins is considered by regulators to be excessive. However, if more than one option contract is entered into at the same time — for instance, selling and buying two different calls — then, of course, a lower cost is incurred, since the cost of one is partially (or wholly) offset by the sale of the other.

6.3 Put–Call Parities

This section addresses a very important concept, called **put–call parity** (for option valuation). The discussion includes European options, American options, and future options.

6.3.1 *European options*

As an initial step to examining the pricing formulas for options, it is essential to discuss the relationships between the prices of put and call options on the same underlying asset. Such relationships among put and call prices are referred to as the *put–call parity theorems.* Stoll (1969) was the first to introduce the concept of put–call parity. Dealing strictly with European options, he showed that the value of a call option would equal the value of a portfolio composed of a long put option, its underlying stock, and a short discounted exercise price. Before stating the basic put–call parity theorem as originally devised by Stoll, it must be assumed that the markets for options, bonds, and stocks (or any other underlying asset we choose) are frictionless.

Theorem 6.1. *Put–call parity for European options with no dividends*

$$C_{t,T} = P_{t,T} + S_t - EB_{t,T}, \tag{6.3}$$

where $C_{t,T}$ = value of a European call option at time t that matures at time $T(T > f)$, $P_{t,T}$ = value of a European put option at time t that matures at time T, S_t = value of the underlying stock (asset) to both the call and put options at time t, E = exercise price for both the call and put options, and $B_{t,T}$ = price at time t of a default-free bond that pays \$1 with certainty at time T (if it is assumed that this risk-free rate of interest is the same for all maturities and equal to r — in essence a flat-term structure — then $B_{t,T} = e^{-r(T-t)}$, under continuous compounding), or $B_{t,T} = 1/(1+r)^{T-t}$ for discrete compounding.

Equation (6.3) uses the following principle. If the options are neither dominant or dominated securities, and if the borrowing and lending rates are equal, then the return patterns of a European call and a portfolio composed of a European put, a pure discount bond with a face value equal to the options exercise price E, and the underlying stock (or asset) are the same.[1]

In understanding why the put–call parity theorem holds, and to support the theorem, two additional properties of option pricing must be provided:

Property 1: At maturity (time T), the call option is worth the greater of $S_T - E$ dollars or zero dollars:

$$C_T = \text{Max}(0, S_T - E). \tag{6.4}$$

As an example, suppose that the call option has an exercise price of \$30. At maturity, if the stock's (asset's) price is \$25, then the value of the call is the maximum of (0, 25 − 30) or (0, −5), which

[1]Any security x is dominant over any security y if the rate of return on x is equal to or greater than that of y for all states of nature and is strictly greater for at least one state. For an expanded discussion of this subject, see Merton (1973) and Smith (1976).

of course is zero. If an option sells for less than $(S, -E)$, its intrinsic value, an arbitrage opportunity will exist. Investors would buy the option and short sell the stock, forcing the mispricing to correct itself. Consequently, this first property implies that a call option's value is always greater than zero. An equivalent property and argument exist for the value of a put option as well.

Property 2: At maturity, the value of a put option is the greater of $E - S_T$ dollars or zero dollars:

$$P_T = \text{Max}(0, E - S_T). \tag{6.5}$$

Using the same line of reasoning and argument as for the call option, the second property also implies that the value of a put option is never less than zero. Table 6.7 provides proof of this first put–call parity theorem. Suppose at time t, two portfolios are formed: Portfolio B is just a long call option on a stock with price S_t an exercise price of E, and a maturity date at T. Portfolio A consists of purchasing 100 shares of the underlying stock (since stock options represent one hundred shares), purchasing (going long) one put option on the same stock with exercise price E and maturity date T, and borrowing at the risk-free rate an amount equal to the present value of the exercise price or $EB_{t,T}$ with face value of E. (This portion of the portfolio finances the put, call, and stock positions.)

Table 6.7 Call Parity for a European Option with No Dividends

	Time T (Maturity)		
Time t Strategy	$S_T > E$	$S_T = E$	$S_T < E$
Portfolio A:			
1. Buy 100 shares of the stock (S_t).	S_T	S_T	S_T
2. Buy a put (P_t, maturity at T with exercise price E).	0	0	$E - S_T$
3. Borrow $EB_{t,T}$ dollars.	$-E$	$-E$	$-E$
Portfolio A value at time T	$(S_T - E)$	0	0
Portfolio B:			
1. Buy a call (C_t maturing at T with exercise price E).	$(S_T - E)$	0	0

At maturity date T, the call option (Portfolio B) has value only if $S_T > E$, which is in accordance with Property 1. For Portfolio A, under all these conditions, the stock price and maturing loan values are the same, whereas the put option has value only if $E > S_T$. Under all three possible outcomes for the stock price S_T, it can be seen that the values of Portfolios A and B are equal. Proof has been established for the first put–call parity theorem. Sample Problem 6.2 provides further illustration.

Sample Problem 6.2

A call option with one year to maturity and an exercise price of \$110 is selling for \$5. Assuming discrete compounding, a risk-free rate of 10%, and a current stock price of \$100, what is the value of a European put option with a strike price of \$110 and one-year maturity?

Solution

$$P_{t,T} = C_{t,T} + EB_{t,T} - S_t,$$

$$P_{0,1yr} = \$5 + \$110\left(\frac{1}{(1.1)^1}\right) - \$100,$$

$$P_{0,1yr} = \$5.$$

6.3.2 *American options*

Indeed, this first put–call parity theorem holds only under the most basic conditions (i.e., no early exercise and no dividends). Jarrow and Rudd (1983) give an extensive coverage of the effects of more complicated conditions on put–call parity. These authors demonstrate that the effect of known dividends is simply to reduce, by the discounted value (to time t) of the dividends, the amount of the underlying stock purchased. In considering stochastic dividends, the exactness of this pricing relationship breaks down and depends on the degree of certainty that can be maintained about the range of future dividends. Put–call parity for American options is also derived under various dividend conditions. Jarrow and Rudd demonstrate that as a result of the American option's early exercise feature, strict pricing relationships give way to boundary conditions dependent on the size and certainty of future dividends, as well as the level of interest rates and the size of the exercise price. To summarize, they state that for sufficiently high interest rates and/or exercise prices, it may be optimal to exercise the put prior to maturity (with or without dividends). So, the basic put–call parity for an American option with no dividends and constant interest rates is described by the following theorem.

Theorem 6.2. *Put–call parity for an American option with no dividends*

$$P_{t,T} + S - EB_{t,T} > C_{t,T} > P_{t,T} + S_t - E. \tag{6.6}$$

Increasing the generality of conditions results in increasing boundaries for the equilibrium relationship between put and call options. The beauty of these arguments stems from the fact that they require only that investors prefer more wealth to less. If more stringent assumptions are made, then the bounds can be made tighter. For an extensive derivation and explanation of these theorems, see Jarrow and Rudd (1983). Sample Problem 6.3 provides further illustration.

Sample Problem 6.3

A put option with one year to maturity and an exercise price of \$90 is selling for \$15; the stock price is \$100. Assuming discrete compounding and a risk-free rate of 10%, what are the boundaries for the price of an American call option?

Solution

$$P_{t,T} + S - EB_{t,T} > C_{t,T} > P_{t,T} + S_t - E,$$

$$\$15 + \$100 - \$90\left(\frac{1}{(1.1)^1}\right) > C_{t,T} > \$15 + \$100 - \$90,$$

$$\$33.18 > C_{t,1yr} > \$25.$$

6.3.3 *Futures options*

As a final demonstration of put–call parity, the analysis is extended to the case where the underlying asset is a futures contract. The topic of futures contracts and their valuation will be more fully examined in the next chapter. Nevertheless, this chapter takes time to apply put–call parity when the options are on a futures contract because of the growing popularity and importance of such futures options. A futures contract as described in Chapter 12 is a contract in which the party entering into the contract is obligated to buy or sell the underlying asset at the maturity date for some stipulated price. While the difference between European and American options still remains, the complexity of dividends can be ignored since futures contracts do not pay dividends. Put–call parity for a European futures option (when interest rates are constant) is as follows:

Theorem 6.3. *Put–call parity for a European futures option*

$$C_{t,T} = P_{t,T} + B_{t,T}(F_{t,T} - E), \tag{6.7}$$

where $F_{t,T}$ is the price at time t for a futures contract maturing at time T (which is the underlying asset to both the call and put options).

Option pricing properties 1 and 2 for call and put options apply in an equivalent sense to futures options as well. However, to understand this relationship as stated in Equation (6.7), it must be assumed that the cost of a futures contract is zero. While a certain margin requirement is required, the majority of this assurance deposit can be in the form of interest-bearing securities. Hence, as an approximation, a zero cost for the futures contract is not unrealistic.

Again, the easiest way to prove this relationship is to follow the same path of analysis used in proving Theorem 1. Table 6.8 indicates that the argument for this theorem's proof is similar, with only a few notable exceptions. The value of the futures contract at time T (maturity) is equal to the difference between the price of the contract at time T and the price at which it was bought, or $F_{TT} - F_{t,T}$. This is an outcome of the fixed duration of a futures contract as opposed to the perpetual duration of common stock. Second, because no money is required to enter into the futures contract, the exercise price is reduced by the current futures price and the total is lent at the risk-free rate. (Actually this amount is either lent or borrowed depending on the relationship between $F_{t,T}$ and E at time t. If $F_{t,T} - E < 0$, then this amount will actually be borrowed at the risk-free rate.)

Why are there options on spot assets as well as options on futures contracts for the spot assets? After all, at expiration, the basis of a futures contract goes to zero and futures prices equal spot prices;

Table 6.8 Put–Call Parity for a European Futures Option

	Time *T* (Maturity)		
Time *t* Strategy	$F_{TT} > E$	$F_{TT} = E$	$F_{TT} < E$
Portfolio A:			
1. Buy a futures contract ($F_{t,T}$).	$F_{TT} - F_{t,T}$	$F_{TT} - F_{t,T}$	$F_{TT} - F_{t,T}$
2. Buy a put ($P_{t,T}$ on $F_{t,T}$ with exercise price E and maturity T).	0	0	$E - F_{TT}$
3. Lend $B_{t,T}$ $(F_{t,T} - E)$ dollars.	$(F_{t,T} - E)$	$(F_{t,T} - E)$	$(F_{t,T} - E)$
Portfolio A's value at time T	$(F_{TT} - E)$	0	0
Portfolio B:			
1. Buy a call ($C_{t,T}$ on $F_{t,T}$ with exercise price E and maturity T).	$(F_{TT} - E)$	0	0

thus, options in the spot and options on the future are related to the same futures value, and their current values must be identical. Yet, a look at the markets shows that options on spot assets and options on futures for the same assets sell at different prices. One explanation for this is that investors who purchase options on spot must pay a large sum of money when they exercise their options, whereas investors who exercise an option on a future need only pay enough to meet the initial margin for the futures contract. Therefore, if the exercise of the option is important to an investor, that investor would prefer options on futures rather than options on spot and would be willing to pay a premium for the option on the future, whereas the investor who has no desire to exercise the option (remember, the investor can always sell it to somebody else to realize a profit) is not willing to pay for this advantage and so finds the option on spot more attractive.

6.3.4 *Market application*

Put options were not listed on the CBOE until June 1977. Before that time, brokers satisfied their clients' demands for put option risk–return characteristics by a direct application of put–call parity. By combining call options and the underlying security, brokers could construct a **synthetic put**.

To illustrate, the put–call parity theorem is used when a futures contract is the underlying asset. Furthermore, to simulate the option broker's circumstances on July 1, 1984, the equation is merely rearranged to yield the put's "synthetic" value:

$$P_{t,T} = C_{t,T} - B_{t,T}F_{t,T} + B_{t,T}E. \tag{6.8}$$

So, instead of a futures contract being purchased, it is sold. Assume the following values and use the S&P 500 index futures as the underlying asset:

$C_{t,T}$ = \$3.35,
$F_{t,T}$ = 154.85 (September contract),
E = 155.00, and
$B_{t,T}$ = 0.9770 (current price of a risk-free bond that pays \$1 when the option and the futures contract expire, average of bid and ask prices for T-bills from *The Wall Street Journal*).

According to Equation (6.8), the put's price should equal the theorem price: $P_{t,T}$ = \$3.497. The actual put price on this day (July 1, 1984) with the same exercise price and expiration month was $P_{t,T}$ = \$3.50. With repeated comparisons of the theorem using actual prices, it becomes clear that put–call parity is a powerful equilibrium mechanism in the market.

6.4 Risk–Return Characteristics of Options and Option Strategies

One of the most attractive features of options is the myriad of ways in which they can be employed to achieve a particular combination of risk and return. Whether through a straight option position in combination with the underlying asset or some portfolio of securities, options offer an innovative and relatively low-cost mechanism for altering and enhancing the risk–return trade-off. In order to better grasp these potential applications, this section analyzes call and put options individually and in combination, relative to their potential profit and loss and the effects of time and market sentiment.

6.4.1 *Risk–return characteristics of options*

6.4.1.1 *Long call*

The purchase of a call option is the simplest and most familiar type of option position. The allure of calls is that they provide the investor a great deal of leverage. Potentially, large percentage profits can be realized from only a modest price rise in the underlying asset. In fact, the potential profit from buying a call is unlimited. Moreover, the option purchaser has the right but no obligation to exercise the contract. Therefore, should the price of the underlying asset decline over the life of the call, the purchaser need only let the contract expire worthless. Consequently, the risk of a long call position is limited. Figure 6.3 illustrates the profit profile of a **long call** position. The following summarizes the basic risk–return features for a long call position:

Profit potential: unlimited.
Loss potential: limited (to cost of option).
Effect of time decay: negative (decrease option's value).
Market expectation: bullish.

As the profit profile indicates, the time value of a long call declines over time. Consequently, an option is a wasting asset. If the underlying asset's price does not move above the exercise price

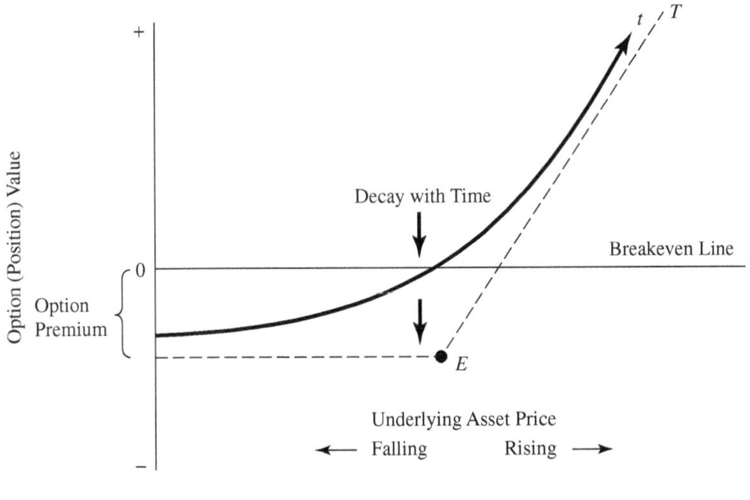

Figure 6.3 Profit Profile for a Long Call

of the option E by its expiration date T, the buyer of the call will lose the value of his initial investment (the option premium). Consequently, the longer an investor holds a call, the more time value the option loses, thereby reducing the price of the option. This leads to another important point — taking on an option position. As with any other investment vehicle, the purchaser of a call expresses an opinion about the market for the underlying asset. Whereas an investor can essentially express one of three different sentiments (bullish, neutral, or bearish) about future market conditions, the long call is strictly a bullish position. That is, the call buyer only wins if the underlying asset rises in price. However, depending on the exercise price of the call, the buyer can express differing degrees of bullishness. For instance, since out-of-the-money calls are the cheapest, a large price increase in the underlying asset will make these calls the biggest percentage gainers in value. So an investor who is extremely bullish would probably go with an out-of-the-money call, since its intrinsic value is small and its value will increase along with a large increase in the market.

6.4.1.2 *Short call*

Selling a call (writing it) has risk–reward characteristics, which are the inverse of the long call. However, one major distinction arises when writing calls (or puts) rather than buying them. That is, the writer can either own the underlying asset upon which he or she is selling the option (a **covered write**), or simply sell the option without owning the asset (a **naked write**). The difference between the two is of considerable consequence to the amount of risk and return taken on by the seller. Let us first examine the profit profile and related attributes of the naked **short call**, displayed in Figure 6.4.

When the writer of a call does not own the underlying asset, his or her potential loss is unlimited. Why? Because if the price of the underlying asset increases, the value of the call also increases for the buyer. The seller of a call is *obliged* to provide a designated quantity of the underlying asset at some prespecified price (the exercise price) at any time up to the maturity date of the option. So, if the asset starts rising dramatically in price and the call buyer exercises his or her *right*, the naked call writer must go into the market to buy the underlying asset at whatever the market price. The naked call

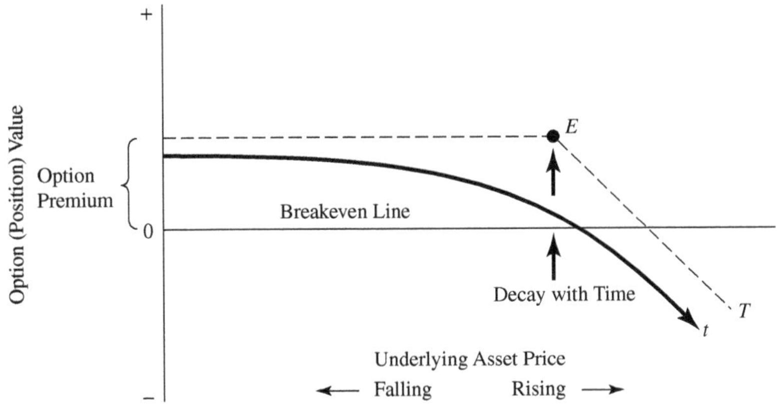

Figure 6.4 Profit Profile for a Short Call

writer suffers the loss of buying the asset at a price S and selling it at a price E when $S > E$ (less the original premium collected). When common stock is the underlying asset, there is no limit to how high its price could go. Thus, the naked call writer's risk is unlimited as well. Indeed, the naked call writer could have reversed the position by buying back the original option he sold — that is, zeroing out the position; however, this is also done at a loss. The following summarizes the basic risk–return features for a naked short call position:

Profit potential: Limited (to option premium).
Loss potential: Unlimited.
Effect of time decay: Positive (makes buyer's position less valuable).
Market expectation: Bearish to neutral.

The naked short call position is obviously a bearish position. If the underlying asset's price moves down, the call writer keeps the entire premium received for selling this call, since the call buyer's position becomes worthless. Once again, the naked call writer can express the degree of bearishness by the exercise price at which he or she sells the call. By selling an in-the-money call, the writer stands to collect a higher option premium. Conversely, selling an out-of-the-money call conveys only a mildly-bearish-to-neutral expectation. If the underlying asset's price stays where it is, the value of the buyer's position, which is solely time value, will decay to zero; and the call writer will collect the entire premium (though a substantially smaller premium than for an in-the-money call).

While the passing of time has a negative effect on the value of a call option for the buyer, it has a positive effect for the seller. One aspect of an option's time value is that in the last month before the option expires, its time value decays most rapidly — the reason being that time value is related to the probability that the underlying asset's price will move up or down enough to make an option position increase in value. This probability declines at an accelerating (exponential) rate as the option approaches its maturity date. The consideration of time value, then, is a major element when investing in or hedging with options. Unless an investor is extremely bullish, it would probably be unwise to take a long position in a call in its last month before maturity. Conversely, the last month of an option's life is a preferred time to sell since its time value can more easily and quickly be collected.

Now, consider the other type of short call position, covered call writing. Because the seller of the call owns the underlying asset in this case, the risk is truncated. The purpose of writing a call on the underlying asset when it is owned is twofold. First, by writing a call option, one always decreases the risk of owning the asset. Second, writing a call can increase the overall realized return on the asset. The profit profile for a covered short call (or a covered write) in Figure 6.5 provides further illustration. The following summarizes the basic risk–return features for the covered short call position:

Profit potential: Limited (Exercise price − Asset price + Call premium).
Loss potential: Limited (Asset price − Call premium).
Effect of time decay: Positive.
Market expectation: Neutral to mildly bullish.

By owning the underlying asset, the covered call writer's loss on the asset for a price decline is decreased by the original amount of the premium collected for selling the option. The total loss on the position is limited to the extent that the asset is one of limited liability, such as a stock, and cannot fall below zero. The maximum profit on the combined asset and option position is higher if the option was written alone, but lower simply owning the asset with

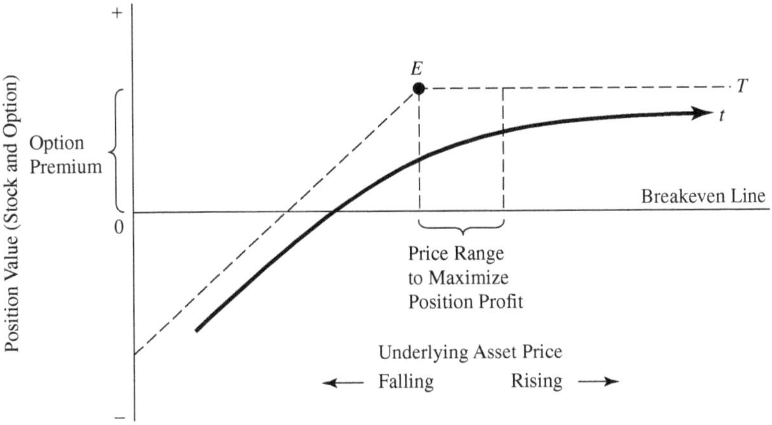

Figure 6.5 Profit Profile for a Covered Short Call

no short call written on it. Once the asset increases in price by a significant amount, the call buyer will very likely exercise the right to purchase the asset at the prespecified exercise price. Thus, covered call writing is a tool or strategy for enhancing an asset's realized return while lowering its risk in a sideways market.

6.4.1.3 *Long put*

Again, the put option conveys to its purchasers the right to sell a given quantity of some asset at a prespecified price on or before its expiration date. Similar to a long call, a **long put** is also a highly leveraged position, but the purchaser of the put makes money on the investment only when the price of the underlying asset declines. While a call buyer has unlimited profit potential, a put buyer has limited profit potential since the price of the underlying asset can never drop below zero. Yet, like the long call position, the put buyer can never lose more than the initial investment (the option's premium). The profit profile for a long put is seen in Figure 6.6. The following summarizes the basic risk–return features for the profit profile of a long put position:

Profit potential: Limited (asset price must be greater than zero).
Loss potential: Limited (to cost of put).
Effect of time decay: Negative or positive.
Market expectation: Bearish.

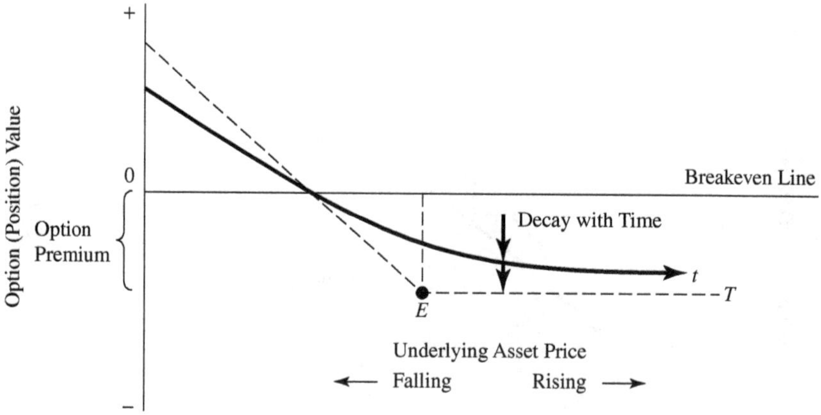

Figure 6.6 Profit Profile for a Long Put

An interesting pricing ambiguity for this bearish investment is how the put's price is affected by the time decay. With the long call, there is a clear-cut relation — that is, the effect of the time decay is to diminish the value of the call. The relationship is not so clear with the long put. Although at certain prices for the underlying asset the value of the long put position decreases with time, there exist lower asset prices for which its value will increase with time. It is the put's ambiguous relationship with time that makes its correct price difficult to ascertain. (This topic will be further explored in Chapter 17.)

One uniquely attractive attribute of the long put is its negative relationship with the underlying asset. In terms of the capital asset pricing model, it has a negative beta (though usually numerically larger than that of the underlying asset, due to the leverage affect). Therefore, the long put is an ideal hedging instrument for the holder of the underlying asset who wants to protect against a price decline. If the investor is wrong and the price of the asset moves up instead, the profit from the asset's price increase is only moderately diminished by the cost of the put. More on hedging and related concepts is discussed in Chapter 17.

6.4.1.4 *Short put*

As was true for the short call position, put writing can be covered or uncovered (naked). The risk–return features of the uncovered (naked) **short put** are discussed first.

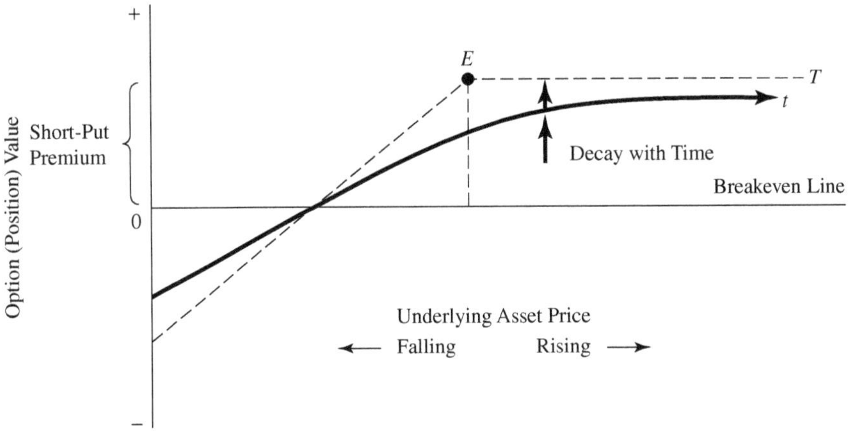

Figure 6.7 Profit Profile for an Uncovered Short Call

For taking on the obligation to buy the underlying asset at the exercise price, the put writer receives a premium. The maximum profit for the uncovered put writer is this premium, which is initially received. Figure 6.7 provides further illustration.

While the loss potential is limited for the uncovered put writer, it is nonetheless still very large. Thus, someone neutral on the direction of the market would sell out-of-the-money (lower exercise price) puts. A more bullish sentiment would suggest that at-the-money options be sold. The investor who is convinced that the market will go up should maximize return by selling a put with a larger premium. As with the long put, the time decay effect is ambiguous and depends on the price of the underlying asset. The following summarizes the basic risk–return features for the profit profile of an uncovered short put position:

Profit potential: Limited (to put premium).
Loss potential: Limited (asset price must be greater than zero).
Effect of time decay: Positive or negative.
Market expectation: Neutral to bullish.

Referring again to Figure 6.5 for the combined short call and long asset position, notice the striking resemblance of its profit profile at expiration to that of the uncovered short put. This relationship can be seen mathematically by using put–call parity. That is, the synthetic put price $P_T = E_c + C_T - S_T$, or at expiration the value of the put should equal the exercise price of the call option plus the call option's value minus the value at time T of the underlying asset. Buying (writing) a call and selling (buying) the underlying asset (or vice versa) allow an investor to achieve essentially the same risk–return combination as would be received from a long put (short put). This combination of two assets to equal the risk and return of a third is referred to as a synthetic asset (or synthetic option in this case). Synthesizing two financial instruments to resemble a third is an arbitrage process and is a central concept of finance theory.

Now, a look at covered short puts is in order to round out the basics of option strategies. For margin purposes and in a theoretical sense, selling a put against a short asset position would be the sale of a covered put. However, this sort of position has a limited profit potential that is obtained if the underlying asset is anywhere below the exercise price of the put at expiration. This position also has unlimited upside risk, since the short position in the asset will accrue losses while the profit from the put sale is limited. Essentially, this position is equivalent to the uncovered or naked short call, except that the latter has less expensive transaction costs. Moreover, because the time value for put options is generally less than that of calls, it will be advantageous to short the call.

Strictly speaking, a short put is covered only if the investor also owns a corresponding put with exercise price equal to or greater than that of the written put. Such a position, called a spread, is discussed later in this chapter.

6.4.2 *Risk–return characteristics of option strategies*

6.4.2.1 *Long straddle*

A straddle is a simultaneous position in both a call and a put on the same underlying asset. A **long straddle** involves purchasing both the call and the put. By combining these two seemingly opposing options, an investor can get the best risk–return combination that each offers. The profit profile for a long straddle in Figure 6.8 illustrates the nature of this synthetic asset. The following summarizes the basic risk–return features for the profit profile of a long straddle position:

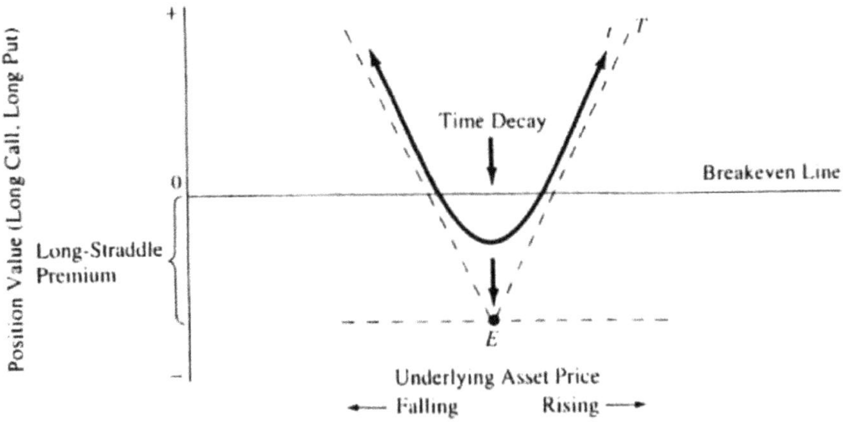

Figure 6.8 Profit Profile for a Long Straddle

Profit potential: Unlimited on upside, limited on downside.
Loss potential: Limited (to cost of call and put premiums).
Effect of time decay: Negative.
Market sentiment: Bullish or bearish.

The long straddle's profit profile makes clear that its risk–reward picture is simply that of the long call overlapped by the long put, with each horizontal segment truncated (represented by the horizontal dashed lines on the bottom). An investor will profit on this type of position as long as the price of the underlying asset moves sufficiently up or down to more than cover the original cost of the option premiums. Thus, a long straddle is an effective strategy for someone expecting the volatility of the underlying asset to increase in the future. In the same light, the investor who buys a straddle expects the underlying asset's volatility of price to be greater than that imputed in the option price.

Since time decay is working against the value of this position, it might be unwise to purchase a straddle composed of a call and put in their last month to maturity when their time decay is greatest. It would be possible to reduce the cost of the straddle by purchasing a high-exercise-price call and a low-exercise put (out-of-the-money options); however, the necessary up or down movement in the asset's price in order to profit is larger. Sample Problem 6.4 provides further illustration.

Sample Problem 6.4

Situation: An investor feels the stock market is going to break sharply up or down but is not sure which way. However, the investor is confident that market volatility will increase in the near future. To express his position, the investor puts on a long straddle using options on the S&P 500 index, buying both at-the-money call and put options on the September contract. The current September S&P 500 futures contract price is 155.00. Assume the position is held to expiration.

Transaction:

1. Buy 1 September 155 call at \$2.00	(\$1,000)
2. Buy 1 September 155 put at \$2.00	(\$1,000)
Net initial investment (position value)	(\$2,000)

Results:

1. If futures price = 150.00:	
(a) 1 September call expires at \$0	(\$1,000)
(b) 1 September put expires at \$5.00	\$2,500
(c) Less initial cost of put	(\$1,000)
Ending position value (net profit)	\$500
2. If futures price = 155.00:	
(a) 1 September call expires at \$0	(\$1,000)
(b) 1 September put expires at \$0	(\$1,000)
Ending position value (net loss)	\$2,000
3. If futures price = 160.00:	
(a) 1 September call expires at \$5.00	\$2,500
(b) 1 September call expires at \$0	(\$1,000)
(c) Less initial cost of put	(\$1,000)
Ending position value (net profit)	\$500

Summary:

Maximum profit potential: Unlimited. If the market had contributed to move below 150.00 or above 160.00, the position would have continued to increase in value.

Maximum loss potential: \$2,000, the initial investment.

Breakeven points: 151.00 and 159.00, for the September S&P 500 futures contract.[2]

Effect of time decay: Negative, as evidenced by the loss incurred, with no change in futures price (result 2).

6.4.2.2 *Short straddle*

For the most part, the short straddle implies the opposite risk–return characteristics of the long straddle. A short straddle is a simultaneous position in both a short call and a short put on the same underlying asset. Contrary to the long straddle position, selling a straddle can be an effective strategy when an investor expects little or no movement in the price of the underlying asset. A similar interpretation of its use would be that the investor expects the future volatility of the underlying asset's price that is currently impounded in the option premiums to decline. Moreover, since the time decay is a positive effect for the value of this position, one appropriate time to set a short straddle might be in the last month to expiration for the combined call and put. Figure 6.9 shows the short straddle's profit profile, and Sample Problem 6.5 provides further illustration. The following summarizes the basic risk–return features for the profit profile of a short straddle position:

Profit potential: Limited (to call and put premiums).
Loss potential: Unlimited on upside, limited on downside.
Effect of time decay: Positive.
Market expectation: Neutral.

---

[2]Breakeven points for the straddle are calculated as follows:
Upside BEP = Exercise price + Initial net investment (in points)

$$159.00 = 155.00 + 4.00$$

Downside BEP = Exercise price − Initial net investment (in points)

$$159.00 = 155.00 + 4.00$$
$$151.00 = 155.00 - 4.00$$

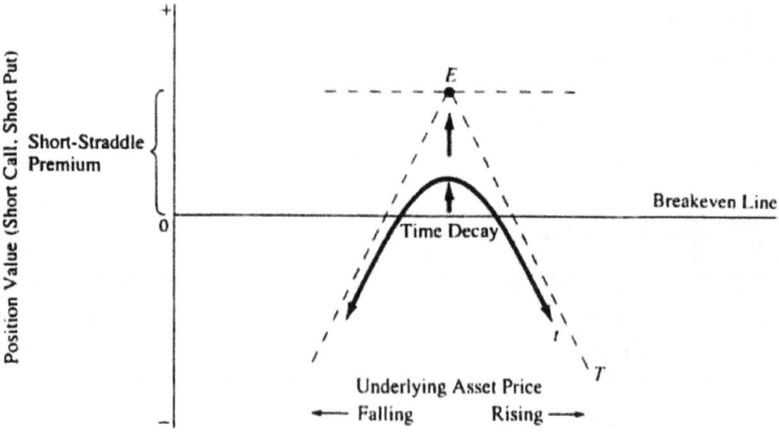

Figure 6.9 Profit Profile for a Short Straddle

Sample Problem 6.5

Situation: An investor feels the market is overestimating price volatility at the moment and that prices are going to remain stable for some time. To express his opinion, the investor sells a straddle consisting of at-the-money call and put options on the September S&P 500 futures contract, for which the current price is 155.00. Assume the position is held to expiration.

Transaction:

1.	Sell 1 September 155 call at $2.00 (× $500 per point)	$1,000
2.	Sell 1 September 155 put at $2.00	$1,000
	Net initial inflow (position value)	$2,000

Results:

1.	If futures price = 150.00:	
	(a) 1 September 155 call expires at 0	$1,000
	(b) 1 September 155 put expires at $5.00	($2,500)
	(c) Plus initial inflow from sale of put	$1,000
	Ending position value (net loss)	($500)

2. If futures price = 155.00:

(a) 1 September 155 call expires at 0	\$1,000
(b) 1 September 155 put expires at 0	\$1,000
Ending position value (net profit)	\$2,000

3. If futures price = 160.00:

(a) 1 September 155 call expires at \$5.00	(\$2,500)
(b) 1 September put expires at 0	\$1,000
(c) Plus initial inflow from sale of call	\$1,000
Ending position value (net loss)	(\$500)

Summary:

Maximum profit potential: \$2,000, result 2, where futures price does not move.

Maximum loss potential: Unlimited. If futures price had continued up over 160.00 or down below 145.00, this position would have kept losing money.

Breakeven points: 151.00 and 159.00, an eight-point range for profitability of the position.[3]

Effect of time decay: Positive, as evidenced by result 2.

6.4.2.3 *Long vertical (bull) spread (LVBS)*

When dealing strictly in options, a spread is a combination of any two or more of the same type of options (two calls or two puts, for instance) on the same underlying asset. A vertical spread specifies that the options have the same maturity month. Finally, a long vertical spread designates a position for which one has bought a low-exercise-price call (or a low-exercise-price put) and sold a high-exercise-price call (or a high-exercise-price put) that both mature in the same month. A long vertical spread is also known as a **bull** spread because of the bullish market expectation of the investor who enters into it. Actually, the long vertical spread (or bull spread) is not a strongly bullish position, because the investor limits the profit potential in selling the high-exercise-price call (or high-exercise-price put). Rather, this is a popular position when it is expected that the market will more likely go up than down. Therefore, the bull

[3]Breakeven points for the short straddle are calculated in the same manner as for the long straddle: exercise price plus initial prices of options.

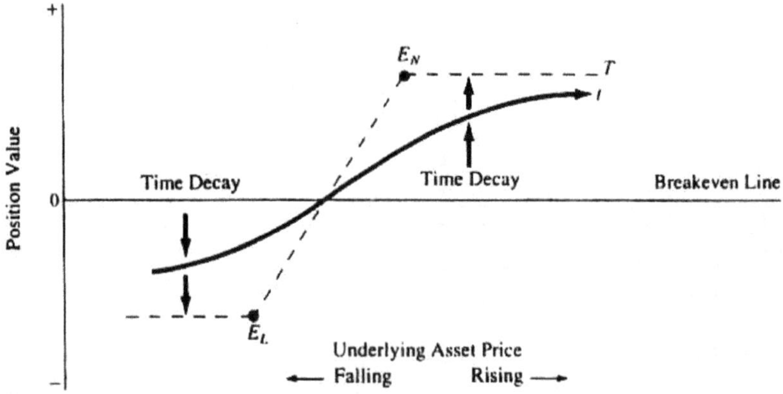

Figure 6.10 Profit Profile for a Long Vertical Spread

spread conveys a bit of uncertainty about future market conditions. Of course, the higher the exercise price at which the call is sold, the more bullish the position. An examination of the profit profile for the long vertical spread (see Figure 6.10) can tell more about its risk–return attributes. The following summarizes the basic risk–return features for the profit profile of a long vertical spread position:

Profit potential: Limited (up to the higher exercise price).
Loss potential: Limited (down to the lower exercise price).
Effect of time decay: Mixed.
Market expectation: Cautiously bullish.

Although profit is limited by the shorted call on the upside, the loss potential is also truncated at the lower exercise price by the same short call. There are other reasons for this being a mildly bullish strategy. The effect of time decay is ambiguous up to the expiration or liquidation of the position. That is, if the asset price, S_t, is near the exercise price of the higher-price option E_H, then the position acts more like a long call and time decay effect is negative. Conversely, if S_t is near the exercise price of the lower-price option E_L, then the bull spread acts more like a short call and the time decay effect is neutral.

Consequently, unless an investor is more than mildly bullish, it would probably be unwise to put on a bull spread with the low-exercise-price call near the current price of the asset while both options are in their last month to expiration. Sample Problem 6.6 provides further illustration.

Sample Problem 6.6

Situation: An investor is moderately bullish on the West German mark. He would like to be long but wants to reduce the cost and risk of this position in case he is wrong. To express his opinion, the investor puts on a long vertical spread by buying a lower-exercise-price call and selling a higher-exercise-price call with the same month to expiration. Assume the position is held to expiration.

Transaction:

1.	Buy 1 September 0.37 call at 0.0047 (× 125.000 per point)	($587.50)
2.	Sell 1 September 0.38 call at 0.0013	$162.50
	Net initial investment (position value)	($425.00)

Results:

1.	If futures price = 0.3700:	
	(a) 1 September 0.37 call expires at 0	($587.50)
	(b) 1 September 0.38 call expires at 0	$162.50
	Ending position value (net loss)	($425.00)
2.	If futures price = 0.3800:	
	(a) 1 September 0.37 call expires at 0.0100	$1,250.00
	(b) 1 September 0.38 call expires at 0	$162.50
	Less initial cost of 0.37 call	($587.50)
	Ending position value (net profit)	$825.00
3.	If futures price = 0.3900:	
	(a) 1 September 0.38 call expires at 0.0200	$2,500.00
	(b) 1 September put expires at 0	($1,250.00)
	Less initial premium of 0.37 call	($587.50)
	Plus initial premium of 0.38 call	$162.50
	Ending position value (net profit)	$825.00

Summary:

Maximum profit potential: \$825.00, result 2.
Maximum loss potential: \$425.00, result 1.
Breakeven point: 0.3734.[4]
Effect of time decay: Mixed; positive if price is at high end of range and negative if at low end.

Generally, a spread combines any two, or more, of the same type of options on same asset. As previously mentioned, a vertical spread specifies that the options have the same maturity month. Specifically, a long vertical spread designates positions that both mature in the same month, for which one has bought a low-exercise-price call, or a low-exercise put. Also known as a bull spread, a long vertical spread holds that a bullish market expectation exists in the investor who enters into the position. The profit potential is limited in selling the high-exercise-price call or put, limited up to the higher exercise price. The loss potential is limited down to the lower exercise price and the effect of time decay is mixed. In summary, market expectations are cautiously bullish under this spread and this is a popular position when bullish market expectations are stronger than bearish perceptions.

6.4.2.4 *Short vertical (bear) spread*

The **short vertical spread** is simply the reverse of the corresponding long position. That is, an investor buys a high-exercise-price call (or put) and sells a low-exercise-price call (or put), both having the same time to expiration left. As the more common name for this type of option position is bear spread, it is easy to infer the type of market sentiment consistent with this position. The profit profile for the short vertical spread is seen in Figure 6.11.

As the profit profile indicates, this strategy is profitable as long as the underlying asset moves down in price. Profit is limited to a price decline in the asset down to the lower exercise price, while risk is limited on the upside by the long call position. From the time

---

[4]Breakeven point for the long vertical spread is computed as lower exercise price plus price of long call minus price of short call ($0.3734 = 0.3700 + 0.0047 - 0.0013$).

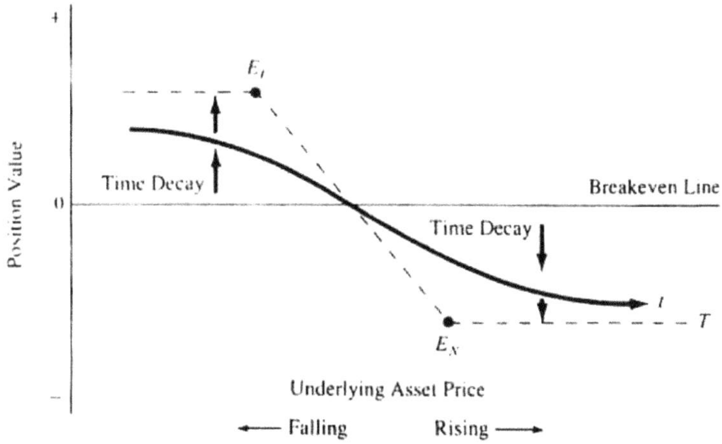

Figure 6.11 Profit Profile for a Short Vertical Spread

decay effects shown, a mildly bearish investor might consider using options in the last month to expiration with the E_L option near the money. The following summarizes the basic risk–return features for the profit profile of a short vertical spread position:

Profit potential: Limited (down to E_L).
Loss potential: Limited (up to E_H).
Effect of time decay: Mixed (opposite to that of long vertical spread).
Market sentiment: Mildly bearish.

6.4.2.5 *Calendar (time) spreads*

A **calendar spread** (also called a **time** or **horizontal spread**) consists of the sale of one option and the simultaneous purchase of another option with the same exercise price but a longer term to maturity. The objective of the calendar spread is to capture the faster erosion in the time premium portion of the shorted nearer-term-to-maturity option. By taking a position in two of the same type options (two calls or two puts), both with the same exercise price, the investor utilizing this strategy expresses a neutral opinion on the market. In other words, the investor is interested in selling time rather than predicting the price direction of the underlying asset. Thus, a calendar spread might be considered appropriate for a

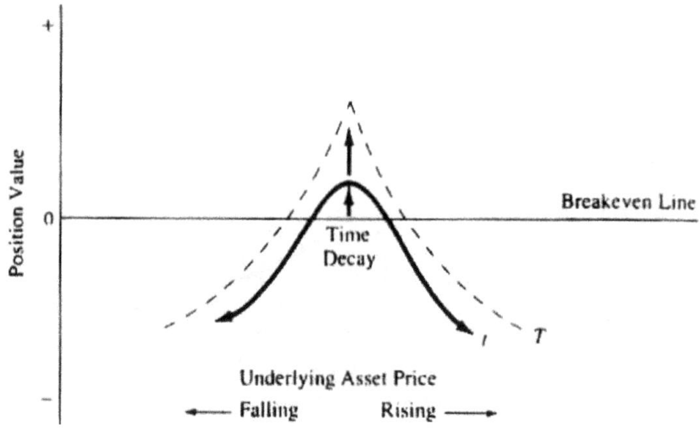

Figure 6.12 Profit Profile for a Neutral Calendar Spread

sideways-moving or quiet market. However, if the underlying asset's price moves significantly up or down, the calendar spread will lose part of its original value. Figure 6.12 displays the calendar spread's profit profile and related risk–return attributes.

The profit profile shows that this strategy will make money for a rather narrow range of price movement in the underlying asset. While similar in nature to the short straddle (both are neutral strategies), the calendar spread is more conservative. The reason being it has both a lower profit potential and lower (limited) risk than the short straddle. The lower potential profit is the result of only benefiting from the time decay in one option premium instead of two (the call and the put) for the short straddle. Moreover, taking opposite positions in the same type of option at the same exercise price adds a loss limit on each side against adverse price moves. The following summarizes the basic risk–return features for the profit profile of a neutral calendar spread position:

Profit potential: Limited.
Loss potential: Limited (to original cost of position).
Effect of time decay: Positive. (Option sold loses value faster than option bought.)
Market sentiment: Neutral.

The calendar spread does not have to be neutral in sentiment. By diagonalizing this spread, it is possible to express an opinion on the market. For instance, by selling a near-term higher-exercise-price option and purchasing a longer-term lower-exercise-price option, the investor is being bullish in position. Such a position is thus referred to as a bullish calendar spread. Why is it bullish? Remember that with the neutral calendar spread, we are concerned solely with benefiting from the faster time decay in the premium of the shorted near-term option. Any significant movement in price upward, for instance, would have not been profitable because it would have slowed the time decay and increased the intrinsic value of the shorted near-term option. In fact, we would eventually lose money because the difference in premiums between the near-term and the longer-term options (the spread) would narrow as the underlying asset's price increased. However, the bullish calendar spread is much like a long vertical (or bull) spread in that a modest increase in price for the asset up to the higher exercise price will be profitable. At the same time, though, the bullish calendar spread also reaps some of the benefits from the greater time decay in the nearer-term option's premium. While this strategy might sound superior to the straight bull spread, it really depends on market conditions. With a bullish calendar spread, its gain from time decay will probably not be as great as that from a neutral calendar spread, nor will its bullish nature be as profitable as a straight bull spread in the event of a modest price increase for the underlying asset. The real-world application will be discussed in the next section.

6.5 Excel Approach to Analyze the Option Strategies[2]

In this section, we will show how the excel program can be used to analyze the option strategies. To show how option strategies can be executed in terms of the excel program, we choose the option that expired on June 17, 2022, which is presented in Table 6.1. Tables 6.9 and 6.10 present call and put option data that expired on June 17, 2022. The data will be used to show how seven strategies can be performed in this session. JNJ stock closed at $163.36 on February 18, 2022.

[2]The Excel program used in this section is presented in Appendix 6A.

Table 6.9 Call Option Expired on June 17, 2022

Symbol	Strike	Bid	Ask
JNJ220617C00150000	150	16.15	16.95
JNJ220617C00155000	155	12.25	13.1
JNJ220617C00160000	160	9.05	9.45
JNJ220617C00165000	165	6.3	6.7
JNJ220617C00170000	170	4.05	4.45
JNJ220617C00175000	175	2.45	2.85
JNJ220617C00180000	180	1.38	1.89
JNJ220617C00185000	185	0.69	1.12
JNJ220617C00190000	190	0.45	1.23
JNJ220617C00195000	195	0.22	0.4

Table 6.10 Put Option Expired on June 17, 2022

Symbol	Strike	Bid	Ask
JNJ210416P00135000	125	0.69	1.03
JNJ210416P00140000	130	0.85	1.42
JNJ210416P00145000	135	1.3	2.35
JNJ210416P00150000	140	1.56	2.08
JNJ210416P00155000	145	2.46	2.77
JNJ210416P00160000	150	3.4	3.6
JNJ210416P00165000	155	4.5	4.85
JNJ210416P00170000	160	6.1	6.5
JNJ210416P00175000	165	8.35	8.65
JNJ210416P00180000	170	11	11.65

6.5.1 *Long straddle*

In general, a straddle is a simultaneous position in both a call and a put on the same underlying asset. As previously mentioned, a long straddle involves purchasing both the call and the put. In combining the opposite options positions, investors may get the best risk–return combination offered by each position. For a long straddle position, profit potential is unlimited on upside and limited on downside. The loss potential is limited to the cost of call and put premiums, and the effect of time decay is negative. The market sentiment is bullish or bearish, as the position is relatively neutral at its core. Therefore, the goal of a long straddle is to profit from a very strong price move in any direction. Thus, a long straddle strategy is best used when the volatility of an asset is expected to increase in the future.

Assume that an investor expects the volatility of JNJ stock to increase in the future, and then can use a long straddle to profit. The investor can purchase a call option and a put option with the same exercise price at \$160. The investor will profit on this type of position as long as the price of the underlying asset moves sufficiently up or down to more than cover the original cost of the option premiums. Let S_0, S_T, and X denote the stock purchase price, future stock price at the expiration time T, and the strike price, respectively. Given $X = \$160$, and the premiums for the call option \$9.45 and put option \$6.50, Table 6.11 shows the values for long straddle at different stock prices at time T. The payoff of the long call is the stock price per share minus exercise price per share, which is \$160. If the future stock price is lower than the exercise price for a call option, then the payoff is zero because the investor will not exercise the call option. The payoff of the long put is exercise price per share minus stock price per share. If the future stock price is higher than the exercise price for a put option, then the payoff is zero because the investor will not exercise the put option. The payoff of a long straddle is the sum of the payoff of call and put options. Profit for both the long call and long put is the payoff minus premiums, and profit of a long straddle is the sum of the profits from long call and long put. The profit profile of the long straddle position is constructed in Figure 6.13.

6.5.2 *Short straddle*

As previously mentioned, a straddle is a simultaneous position in both a call and a put on the same underlying asset. A short straddle position has the same risk–return characteristics as that of a long straddle strategy. A short straddle strategy holds a simultaneous position in both a short call and a short put on the same asset, selling both options where a long straddle would buy. Unlike a long straddle, selling a straddle can be effective when volatility expectations are low, forecasting little or no price movement in the asset. Similarly, future expectations of asset price volatility, currently impounded in the option premiums, are estimated to decline. The effect of time decay is positive for the value of this position. Therefore, a time

Table 6.11 Value of Long Straddle Position at Option Expiration

Long a Call at Strike Price	**$160.00**	**Premium (Ask)**	**$9.45**
Long a Put at Strike Price	**$160.00**	**Premium (Ask)**	**$6.50**

Stock	Long Call (X = $160)		Long Put (X = $160)		Long Straddle	
Price	Payoff	Profit	Payoff	Profit	Payoff	Profit
125	0	−9.45	35	28.5	35	19.05
130	0	−9.45	30	23.5	30	14.05
135	0	−9.45	25	18.5	25	9.05
140	0	−9.45	20	13.5	20	4.05
145	0	−9.45	15	8.5	15	−0.95
150	0	−9.45	10	3.5	10	−5.95
155	0	−9.45	5	−1.5	5	−10.95
160	0	−9.45	0	−6.5	0	−15.95
165	5	−4.45	0	−6.5	5	−10.95
170	10	0.55	0	−6.5	10	−5.95
175	15	5.55	0	−6.5	15	−0.95
180	20	10.55	0	−6.5	20	4.05
185	25	15.55	0	−6.5	25	9.05
190	30	20.55	0	−6.5	30	14.05
195	35	25.55	0	−6.5	35	19.05
200	40	30.55	0	−6.5	40	24.05

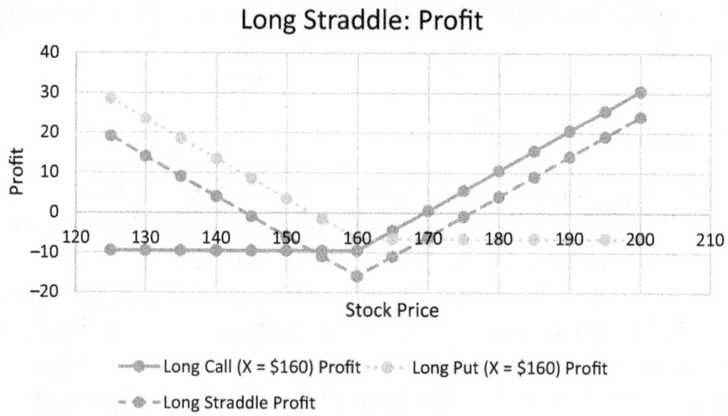

Figure 6.13 Profit Profile for Long Straddle

to set a short straddle can be the last month to expiration for the combined call and put.

Contrary to the long straddle strategy, an investor will use a short straddle via a short call and a short put on JNJ stock with the same exercise price \$160 when he or she expects little or no movement in the price of the JNJ stock. Given $X = \$160$, and the premiums for the call option \$9.05 and put option \$6.1, Table 6.12 shows the values for a short straddle at different stock prices at time T. The payoff of a short call is the exercise price per share, which is \$160, minus stock price per share. If the future stock price is lower than the exercise price for a call option, then the payoff is zero because the investor will not exercise the call option. The payoff of a short put is stock price per share minus exercise price per share. If the future stock price is higher than the exercise price for a put option, then the payoff is zero because the investor will not exercise the put option. The payoff of a short straddle is the sum of the payoffs of short call and short put options. Profit for both call and put is payoff minus premiums, and the profit of a short straddle is the sum of the profits from a short call and short put. The profit profile of the short straddle position is constructed in Figure 6.14.

In summary, a short straddle options strategy consists of selling both a call option and a put option with the same strike price and expiration date, utilized when an investor believes the asset price will not materially fluctuate over the life of the identical-term options contracts.

6.5.3 *Long vertical (bull) spread*

In general, a spread combines any two, or more, of the same type of options on the same asset. A vertical spread specifies that the options have the same maturity month. Specifically, a long vertical spread designates positions that both mature in the same month, for which one has bought a low-exercise-price call or a low-exercise put. Also known as a bull spread, a long vertical spread holds that a bullish market expectation exists in the investor who enters into the position. The profit potential is limited in selling the high-exercise-price call or put, limited up to the higher exercise price. The loss potential is limited down to the lower exercise price and the effect of time decay is mixed. In summary, market expectations are cautiously

Table 6.12 Value of Short Straddle Position at Option Expiration

Short a Call at Strike Price			**$160.00 Premium (Bid)**		**$9.05**	
Short a Put at Strike Price			**$160.00 Premium (Bid)**		**$6.10**	
Stock	**Short Call (X = $160)**		**Short Put (X = $160)**		**Short Straddle**	
Price	**Payoff**	**Profit**	**Payoff**	**Profit**	**Payoff**	**Profit**
125	0	9.05	−35	−28.9	−35	−19.85
130	0	9.05	−30	−23.9	−30	−14.85
135	0	9.05	−25	−18.9	−25	−9.85
140	0	9.05	−20	−13.9	−20	−4.85
145	0	9.05	−15	−8.9	−15	0.15
150	0	9.05	−10	−3.9	−10	5.15
155	0	9.05	−5	1.1	−5	10.15
160	0	9.05	0	6.1	0	15.15
165	−5	4.05	0	6.1	−5	10.15
170	−10	−0.95	0	6.1	−10	5.15
175	−15	−5.95	0	6.1	−15	0.15
180	−20	−10.95	0	6.1	−20	−4.85
185	−25	−15.95	0	6.1	−25	−9.85
190	−30	−20.95	0	6.1	−30	−14.85
195	−35	−25.95	0	6.1	−35	−19.85
200	−40	−30.95	0	6.1	−40	−24.85

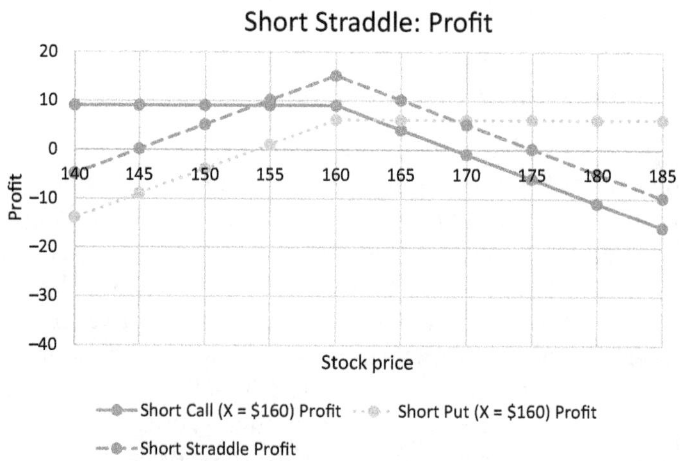

Figure 6.14 Profit Profile for Short Straddle

bullish under this spread and this is a popular position when bullish market expectations are stronger than bearish perceptions.

This strategy combines a long call (or put) with a low strike price and a short call (or put) with a high strike price. For example, an investor purchases a call with the exercise price \$155 and sells a call with the exercise price \$165. Given $X_1 = \$155$, $X_2 = \$165$, and the premium for the long call option is \$13.1 and the short call option is \$6.3, Table 6.13 shows the values for Long Vertical Spread at different stock prices at time T. The payoff of long a call is the stock price per share minus exercise price per share, which is \$155. If the future stock price is lower than the exercise price for a call option, then the payoff is zero because the investor will not exercise the call option. The payoff of short a call is exercise price per share, which is \$165, minus stock price per share. The payoff of a long vertical spread is the sum of the payoff of long call and short call options. Profit for both a long call and a short call is the payoff minus premiums, and profit of a long vertical spread is the sum of the profits from a long call and short call. The profit profile of the Long Vertical Spread is constructed in Figure 6.15.

6.5.4 *Short vertical (bear) spread (SVBS)*

As previously mentioned, a spread combines any two, or more, of the same type of options on the same asset. A short vertical (bear) spread is an options strategy implemented by mildly bearish investors, with the goal of maximizing profits while minimizing losses to net the investor a profit when the price of the security declines. This strategy involves simultaneously purchasing and selling either puts or calls for the same contract, with the same expiration date, but at different strike prices. Also called a bear call spread, the strategy is constructed by selling one call option at a lower strike price and purchasing one call option at a higher strike price. Selected when the outlook on the underlying stock is bearish and the outlook regarding its volatility is indifferent, the maximum expiration profit and loss for this strategy is limited.

Contrary to a long vertical spread, this strategy combines a long call (or put) with a high strike price and a short call (or put) with a low strike price. For example, an investor purchases a call with the exercise price \$160 and sells a call with the exercise price \$155. Given

Table 6.13 Value of Long Vertical Spread Position at Option Expiration

Long a Call at Strike Price	**$155**	**Premium (Ask)**	**$13.10**
Short a Call at Strike Price	**$165**	**Premium (Bid)**	**$6.30**

Stock	**Long Call (X = $155)**		**Short Call (X = $165)**		**Long Vertical Spread**	
Price	**Payoff**	**Profit**	**Payoff**	**Profit**	**Payoff**	**Profit**
125	0	−13.1	0	6.3	0	−6.8
130	0	−13.1	0	6.3	0	−6.8
135	0	−13.1	0	6.3	0	−6.8
140	0	−13.1	0	6.3	0	−6.8
145	0	−13.1	0	6.3	0	−6.8
150	0	−13.1	0	6.3	0	−6.8
155	0	−13.1	0	6.3	0	−6.8
160	5	−8.1	0	6.3	5	−1.8
165	10	−3.1	0	6.3	10	3.2
170	15	1.9	−5	1.3	10	3.2
175	20	6.9	−10	−3.7	10	3.2
180	25	11.9	−15	−8.7	10	3.2
185	30	16.9	−20	−13.7	10	3.2
190	35	21.9	−25	−18.7	10	3.2
195	40	26.9	−30	−23.7	10	3.2
200	45	31.9	−35	−28.7	10	3.2

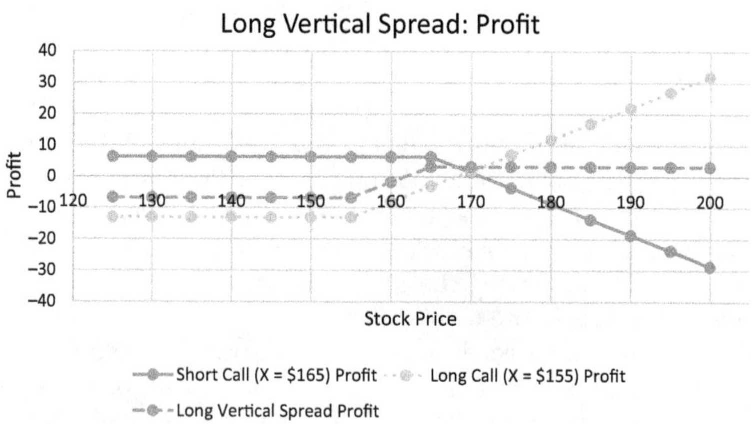

Figure 6.15 Profit Profile for Long Vertical Spread

Table 6.14 Value of Short Vertical Spread Position at Option Expiration

Long a Call at Strike Price	**\$160**	**Premium (Ask)**	**\$9.45**
Short a Call at Strike Price	**\$155**	**Premium (Bid)**	**\$12.25**

Stock	**Long Call (X = \$160)**		**Short Call (X = \$155)**		**Short Vertical Spread**	
Price	**Payoff**	**Profit**	**Payoff**	**Profit**	**Payoff**	**Profit**
125	0	−9.45	0	12.25	0	2.8
130	0	−9.45	0	12.25	0	2.8
135	0	−9.45	0	12.25	0	2.8
140	0	−9.45	0	12.25	0	2.8
145	0	−9.45	0	12.25	0	2.8
150	0	−9.45	0	12.25	0	2.8
155	0	−9.45	0	12.25	0	2.8
160	0	−9.45	−5	7.25	−5	−2.2
165	5	−4.45	−10	2.25	−5	−2.2
170	10	0.55	−15	−2.75	−5	−2.2
175	15	5.55	−20	−7.75	−5	−2.2
180	20	10.55	−25	−12.75	−5	−2.2
185	25	15.55	−30	−17.75	−5	−2.2
190	30	20.55	−35	−22.75	−5	−2.2
195	35	25.55	−40	−27.75	−5	−2.2
200	40	30.55	−45	−32.75	−5	−2.2

$X_1 = \$160$, $X_2 = \$155$, and the premium for the long call option is \$9.45 and the short call option is \$12.25, Table 6.14 shows the values for short vertical spread at different stock prices at time T. The payoff of long a call is the stock price per share minus exercise price per share, which is \$160. The payoff of short a call is exercise price per share, which is \$155, minus stock price per share. The payoff of a short vertical spread is the sum of the payoff of long call and short call options. Profit for both a long call and a short call is the payoff minus premiums, and profit of a short vertical spread is the sum of the profits from the call and put. The profit profile of the short vertical spread is constructed in Figure 6.16.

6.5.5 *Protective put*

A protective put involves the purchase of stock, combined with a put option that guarantees minimum proceeds that are equal to the

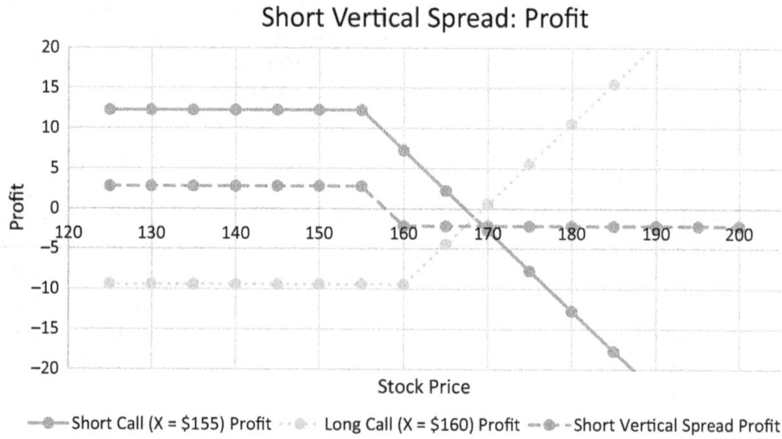

Figure 6.16 Profit Profile for Short Vertical Spread

put's exercise price. The protective put involves buying a put to hedge a stock already in the portfolio. If the put is bought at the same time as the stock, the strategy is called a married put. The married put and protective put strategies are identical, except for the time when the stock is acquired. A synthetic call is simply a generic term for this combination, constructed by purchasing 100 shares of the underlying stock and purchasing one put option. Increases in volatility can positively affect the value of the put option, and the maximum profit for this strategy is unlimited with a limit on losses.

Assume that an investor wants to invest in the JNJ stock on February 18, 2022, but does not desire to bear any potential loss for prices below \$155. The investor can purchase JNJ stock and at the same time buy the put option with a strike price of \$155. Given $S_0 = \$163.36$, $X = \$155$, and the premium for the put option \$4.85 (the ask price), Table 6.15 shows the values for Protective Put at different stock prices at time T. The payoff of long a put is the exercise price per share, which is \$155, minus stock price per share. The payoff of buying one share of stock is the stock price. The payoff of the protective put value is the sum of the payoffs of a long put and one share of stock. The profit for a put is payoff minus premiums, and the profit for one share of stock is the stock price per share minus the stock price at the moment the investor purchased, which is \$163.36

Table 6.15 Value of Protective Put Position at Option Expiration

Long a Put at Strike Price	**$155**	**Premium (Ask) $4.85**
Buy One Share of Stock	**Market Value Per Share**	**Price (Feb. 18) $163.36**

Stock Price	**Long Put (X = $155)**		**One Share of Stock**		**Protective Put Value**	
	Payoff	**Profit**	**Payoff**	**Profit**	**Payoff**	**Profit**
125	30	25.15	125	−38.36	155	−13.21
130	25	20.15	130	−33.36	155	−13.21
135	20	15.15	135	−28.36	155	−13.21
140	15	10.15	140	−23.36	155	−13.21
145	10	5.15	145	−18.36	155	−13.21
150	5	0.15	150	−13.36	155	−13.21
155	0	−4.85	155	−8.36	155	−13.21
160	0	−4.85	160	−3.36	160	−8.21
165	0	−4.85	165	1.64	165	−3.21
170	0	−4.85	170	6.64	170	1.79
175	0	−4.85	175	11.64	175	6.79
180	0	−4.85	180	16.64	180	11.79
185	0	−4.85	185	21.64	185	16.79
190	0	−4.85	190	26.64	190	21.79
195	0	−4.85	195	31.64	195	26.79
200	0	−4.85	200	36.64	200	31.79

in this example. The profit of the protective put value is the sum of the profits from a long put and one share of stock. The profit profile of the Protective Put position is constructed in Figure 6.17.

6.5.6 *Covered call*

This strategy involves investing in a stock and selling a call option on the stock at the same time. The value at the expiration of the call will be the stock value minus the value of the call. The call is "covered" because the potential obligation of delivering the stock is covered by the stock held in the portfolio. Suppose a manager of a stock fund holds a share of JNJ stock on February 18, 2022 and she plans to sell the JNJ stock if its price hits $165. Then, she can write a share of a call option with a strike price of $165 to establish the position. She shorts the call and collects premiums. Given that S_0 = $163.36, X = $165, and the premium for the call option is $6.3 (the bid price), Table 6.16 shows the values for a covered call

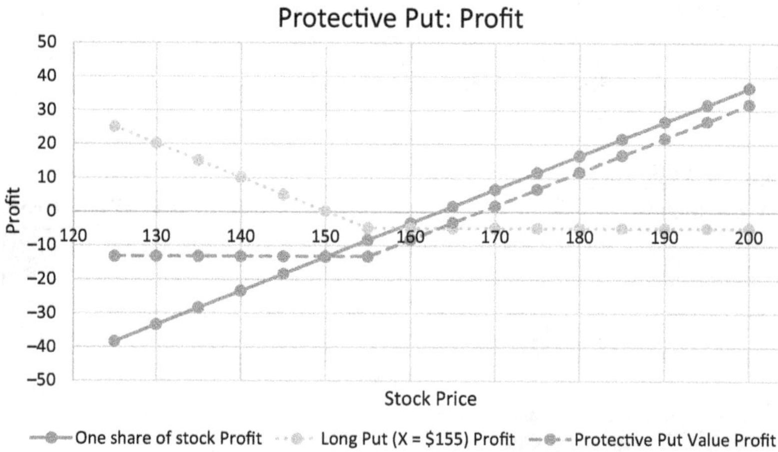

Figure 6.17 Profit Profile for Protective Put

Table 6.16 Value of Covered Call Position at Option Expiration

Write a Call at Strike Price	**$165**	**Premium (Bid)**	**$6.30**
Buy One Share of Stock		**Price (Feb. 18)**	**$163.36**

Stock Price	**Written Call (X = $165) Payoff**	**Written Call (X = $165) Profit**	**One Share of Stock Payoff**	**One Share of Stock Profit**	**Covered Call Payoff**	**Covered Call Profit**
125	0	6.3	125	−38.36	125	−32.06
130	0	6.3	130	−33.36	130	−27.06
135	0	6.3	135	−28.36	135	−22.06
140	0	6.3	140	−23.36	140	−17.06
145	0	6.3	145	−18.36	145	−12.06
150	0	6.3	150	−13.36	150	−7.06
155	0	6.3	155	−8.36	155	−2.06
160	0	6.3	160	−3.36	160	2.94
165	0	6.3	165	1.64	165	7.94
170	−5	1.3	170	6.64	165	7.94
175	−10	−3.7	175	11.64	165	7.94
180	−15	−8.7	180	16.64	165	7.94
185	−20	−13.7	185	21.64	165	7.94
190	−25	−18.7	190	26.64	165	7.94
195	−30	−23.7	195	31.64	165	7.94
200	−35	−28.7	200	36.64	165	7.94

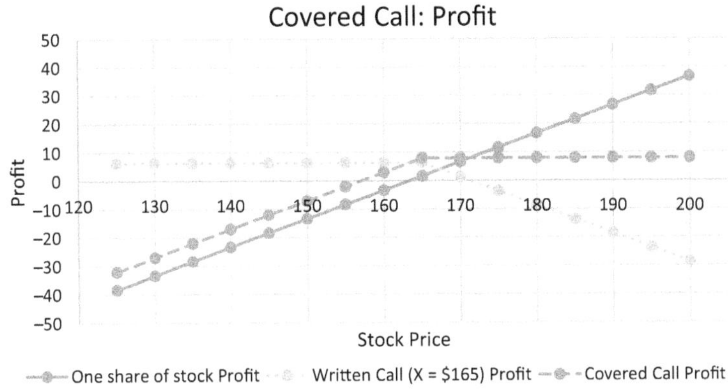

Figure 6.18 Profit Profile for Covered Call

at different stock prices at time T. The payoff of short a call is the exercise price per share, which is \$165, minus stock price per share. The payoff of buying one share of stock is the stock price. The payoff of the covered call is the sum of the payoffs of a short call and one share of stock. The profit for the call is payoff minus premiums, and the profit for one share of stock is the stock price per share minus the stock price at the moment the investor purchased, which is \$163.36 in this example. The profit of the covered call is the sum of the profits from a short call and one share of stock. The profit profile of the covered call position is constructed in Figure 6.18. It can be shown that the payoff pattern of the covered call is exactly equal to shorting a put. Therefore, the covered call has frequently been used to replace shorting a put in dynamic hedging practice.

As previously mentioned, a covered call is a strategy involves investing in a stock and selling a call option on the stock at the same time. Covered calls are far less risky than naked calls. The worst scenario is having to sell shares that are already owned at a below their current market value. Generally, a covered call is created by purchasing 100 shares of stock and selling one call option, selected when the outlook on the stock is neutral and lower volatility is expected. The maximum profit for this strategy is limited, and the maximum loss is limited to the amount of the stock purchase minus the amount received from the sale of the call option. When a call option seller owns the security, the option is “covered” because the financial instrument can be delivered without purchasing it on the open market.

In summary, the covered call strategy is slightly bullish but is near neutral. It is best for stocks with low volatility and low expected increases in stock price. Larger companies with an established market presence are ideal for this strategy, as there is not much protection against significant drops in stock price.

6.5.7 *Collar value*

A collar option strategy is also called a hedge wrapper, utilized to reduce both positive and negative returns of an asset. In limiting the returns to a specified range, a collar strategy holds a position that protects against potential volatility. Created through the usage of a protective put and covered call option, the strategy involves holding an underlying stock, buying an out-of-the-money put option, and selling an out-of-the-money call option. In other words, a collar strategy consists of purchasing a stock, writing a call, and buying a put. The written call is done at a higher strike price than the long put, providing a short call premium that is equal to the bid price and a long put premium that is equal to the ask price.

Our analysis in this subsection will focus on the long collar strategy, but it should be known that a short collar strategy does exist. Generally, a long collar is constructed by purchasing 100 shares of the underlying stock, purchasing one put option, and selling one call option at a strike price that is higher than the put. Selected when the outlook on the underlying stock is bullish, the maximum profit and loss for this strategy is limited.

As previously mentioned, a collar combines a protective put and a short call option to bracket the value of a portfolio between two bounds. For example, an investor holds the JNJ stock selling at \$163.36. Buying a protective put using the put option with an exercise price of \$155 places a lower bound of \$155 on the value of the portfolio. At the same time, the investor can write a call option with an exercise price of \$165. The call and the put sell at \$6.3 (the bid price) and \$4.85 (the ask price), respectively, making the net outlay for the two options only \$1.45. Table 6.17 shows the values of the collar position at different stock prices at time T. The payoff of short a call is the exercise price per share, which is \$165, minus stock price

Table 6.17 Value of Collar Position at Option Expiration

Write a Call at Strike Price	**\$165**	**Premium (Bid)**	**\$6.30**
Long a Put at Strike Price	**\$155**	**Premium (Ask)**	**\$4.85**
Buy One Share of Stock		**Price (Feb. 18)**	**\$163.36**

Stock	Write Call (X = \$165)		Long Put (X = \$155)		One Share of Stock		Collar Value	
Price	Payoff	Profit	Payoff	Profit	Payoff	Profit	Payoff	Profit
125	0	6.3	30	25.15	125	−38.36	155	−6.91
130	0	6.3	25	20.15	130	−33.36	155	−6.91
135	0	6.3	20	15.15	135	−28.36	155	−6.91
140	0	6.3	15	10.15	140	−23.36	155	−6.91
145	0	6.3	10	5.15	145	−18.36	155	−6.91
150	0	6.3	5	0.15	150	−13.36	155	−6.91
155	0	6.3	0	−4.85	155	−8.36	155	−6.91
160	0	6.3	0	−4.85	160	−3.36	160	−1.91
165	0	6.3	0	−4.85	165	1.64	165	3.09
170	−5	1.3	0	−4.85	170	6.64	165	3.09
175	−10	−3.7	0	−4.85	175	11.64	165	3.09
180	−15	−8.7	0	−4.85	180	16.64	165	3.09
185	−20	−13.7	0	−4.85	185	21.64	165	3.09
190	−25	−18.7	0	−4.85	190	26.64	165	3.09
195	−30	−23.7	0	−4.85	195	31.64	165	3.09
200	−35	−28.7	0	−4.85	200	36.64	165	3.09

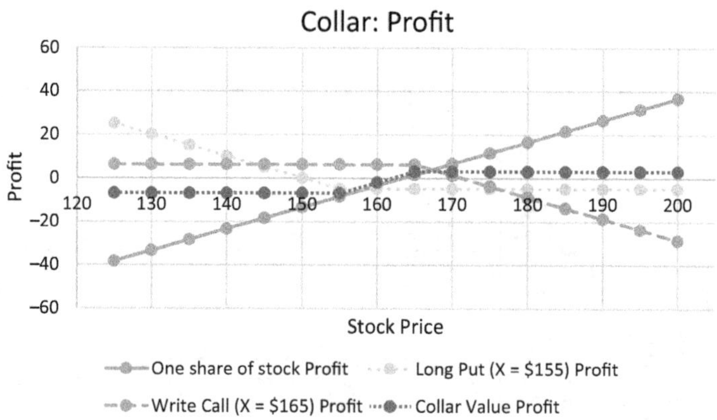

Figure 6.19 Profit Profile for Collar

per share. The payoff of long a put is the exercise price per share, which is $155, minus stock price per share. The payoff of buying one share of stock is the stock price. The payoff of the collar value is the sum of the payoffs of a short call, a long put, and one share of stock. The profit profile of the collar position is shown in Figure 6.19.

In general, we are concerned with the long collar strategy for bullish expectations. With that said, Caterpillar does not reach profitability under this strategy at the selected strike prices and stock price range. As we can see, the characteristics of the written call are what produce a potentially profitable position. Therefore, we can say that this strategy primarily gets its downside protection from the long put position, with target value protection coming largely from the short call position and upside protection in the owned stock. Thus, this strategy is consistent with its bullish reputation and is most useful when the short call strike price is larger than the share price of owned stock.

6.6 Summary

This chapter has introduced some of the essential differences between the two most basic kinds of option, calls and puts. A delineation was made of the relationship between the option's price or premium and that of the underlying asset. The option's value was shown to be composed of intrinsic value, or the underlying asset price less the exercise price, and time value. Moreover, it was demonstrated that the time value decays over time, particularly in the last month to maturity for an option.

In this chapter, we use Johnson & Johnson's call and put option data and show how seven option strategies can be executed. In Chapter 3, we used JNJ's financial data to perform financial statement analysis. By integrating the materials covered in Chapter 3 and this chapter, we conduct an evaluation of Johnson & Johnson including both internal and external aspects, assessing relevant internal benchmarks and useful external comparisons. Considering past accomplishments and current advantages in Johnson & Johnson's market proved to be useful in determining the business's outlook for the future. The basic financial analysis of Johnson & Johnson's financial statements provided the necessary insight to perform a fundamental analysis of the company, its competitors, and the industry. Fundamental analysis enabled us to formulate a future perspective for the company, providing more meaning to various alternative options and strategies.

Index and futures options were studied to introduce these important financial instruments. Put–call parity theorems were developed for European, American, and futures options in order to show the basic valuation relationship between the underlying asset and its call and put options. Finally, investment applications of options and related combinations were discussed, along with relevant risk–return characteristics. A thorough understanding of this chapter is essential as a basic tool to successfully study option valuation models in the next chapter.

Questions and Problems

1. Define the following terms:

(a) call option	(g) exercise price
(b) put option	(h) put–call parity
(c) striking price	(i) intrinsic value
(d) straddle	(j) European option
(e) option	(k) American option
(f) spread	(l) time value

2. Compare the following pairs of investment strategies:
   (a) Which is riskier, buying or selling a call option?

(b) Which is riskier, writing a naked call option or writing a covered call option?
(c) Other things being equal, which option has greater value, an American call option or a European call option?
(d) Other things being equal, which option should have greater value, the option written on a low-beta stock or the option written on a high-beta stock?

3. Plot profit versus the stock price for a call option with an exercise price of $100 and a premium of $3.
4. HHH, Inc. is a company doing medical research. It has decided to place all of its resources into finding a cure for AIDS. If HHH is successful, the value of its stock will increase tenfold. If the company is unsuccessful, it will be bankrupt in 10 years. (a) If you believe that there is an SO-percent chance of success, is there an investment strategy you can devise using put and call options to exploit this situation? (b) How might your answer in (a) change if you believe that there is only a 33% chance of success?
5. Carefully explain the difference between a vertical bull spread and a vertical bear spread. When would you use the vertical bull spread? When would you use the vertical bear spread?
6. You would like to purchase a put option on XYZ Company's stock. If only call options exist on XYZ Company's stock, explain how you could create your own put option.
7. What is the benefit of purchasing a call option over purchasing the underlying stock? What are the disadvantages?
8. Carefully explain why the value of an option can never be negative.
9. Compare an option to a futures contract. How are they similar? How are they different?
10. What is a butterfly spread? When would an investor purchase a calendar spread?
11. Plot the profit opportunities for an investor who purchases a long straddle. Assume that the exercise price on the put and call options is $100.
12. Use the information given in the previous question to plot the profit opportunities for a short straddle. Compare these two positions.

13. Explain what is meant by an option that is

    (a) in the money.
    (b) at the money.
    (c) out of the money.

14. Explain how the time value of an option behaves as the option moves closer to expiration.
15. Given a stock valued at $25 on February 1, 1989 and the following information about call option premiums, what is the time value for each of the options?

Exercise Price	March	June	September
20	$5.75	$6.75	$7.50
25	$1.00	$2.00	$3.00
30	$0.25	$0.50	$0.75

16. What impact does the payment of cash dividends by XYZ Company have on the put options of XYZ Company? How does it affect the call options of XYZ Company?
17. Discuss the uses of an option on foreign currencies.
18. Why would you never exercise an index option before the exercise date?
19. Explain the logic behind the put–call parity relationship shown in Table 6.7.
20. A call option with six months to maturity and an exercise price of 20 is selling for $3. Assuming discrete compounding, a risk-free rate of interest of 8%, and a current stock price of $19, what is the value of a European put option with a strike price of 20 and one year to maturity?
21. For a stock with a price of $10, a put option with three months to maturity and an exercise price of $12 is selling for $3. Assuming discrete compounding and a risk-free rate of 8%, what are the boundaries of the price for an American call option?
22. What are the major advantages of an option on futures over an option on an underlying asset?

23. What is a synthetic put? Why would a synthetic put be useful if you have listed put options?
24. Compare the risk–return features of a long call with a short naked call. If these two types of call positions were to be continued indefinitely, what would be the result?
25. Compare the risk–return features for a short covered call with an uncovered short put. Be sure to discuss the time decay.
26. An investor wants to use a long straddle, the current market index being 150. He buys the three-month 150 call for \$5.00 and the three-month 150 put at \$4.50. If the market rises to 180 at the end of three months, what is the investor's profit or loss? If the market falls to 125 at the end of three months, what is the investor's profit or loss? If the market stays at 150 at the end of three months, what is the profit or loss?
27. Calculate the breakeven points (upside and downside) for the straddle described in the previous problem.
28. An investor wants to use a short straddle; the current market index is 100. He sells a one-month 100 call for \$1.50 and a one-month 100 put for \$1.75. At the end of one month, the market index is: (a) 100, (b) 90, or (c) 80. What is the profit or loss for (a), (b), and (c)?
29. If an investor sells a high-exercise-price call and buys a low-exercise-price call of the same month to expiration, what does he or she hope for the price of the underlying asset?
30. How do you profit from a neutral calendar spread?
31. Firm A's common stock has been trading in a narrow price range for the past month. An investor is convinced that the price is going to break far out of that range in the next three months. However, this investor does not know whether the price will go up or down. The current price of the stock is \$90 per share and the price of a three-month call option at an exercise price of \$90 is \$8.

    (a) Assuming the risk-free rate is 6% per year, what is the price of a three-month put option on firm A's stock at an exercise price of \$90? (Assume the stock pays no dividend.)

(b) What would be a simple option strategy to exploit your conviction about the stock price movement in the next three months? How far would it have to move in either direction for you to make a profit on your initial investment?

32. Firm B's common stock has been trading in a narrow price range around \$60 per share for a while. You believe the price is going to stay in the range for the next three months. The price of a three-month put option with an exercise price of \$60 is \$5.

    (a) Assuming the risk-free rate is 6% per year, what is the price of a three-month call option on firm B's stock at an exercise price of \$60 if it is in the money? (Assume the stock pays no dividend.)
    (b) What would be a simple option strategy to exploit your conviction about the stock price movement in the next three months? What is the most money you can make on this position? How far would it have to move in either direction before you lose money?

33. A manager in firm C receives 10,000 shares of company stock as part of his compensation package. The current market price of the stock is \$50 per share. At this current price, this manager would receive \$500,000 for the stock. This manager is considering buying a second house in April but is worried about the value of his stock holding. If the value of the stock holding falls below \$450,000, he will not be able to come up with the down payment for the house. However, if the value of the stock rises above \$550,000, he would be able to have a small cash reserve even after he makes his down payment. Please evaluate the following two strategies with respect to this manager's investment goal. What are the advantage and disadvantage of each strategy?

    (a) **Strategy A:** Write April call options on firm C's share with strike price \$55. These calls are currently selling at \$4 each.
    (b) **Strategy B:** Long April put options on firm C's share with strike price \$45. These calls are currently selling at \$4 each.

34. Please discuss why owning a corporate bond is similar to shorting a put option. And the same for a call option.

35. An investor is holding the following option portfolio. She is writing an April expiration call option on Dell with exercise price 80. She is also writing an April Dell put option with exercise price 75. The costs of the above options are \$1 and \$0.5, respectively.
    (a) Graph the payoff of this portfolio at option expiration as a function of Dell's stock price at that time.
    (b) What is the profit/loss on this position if Dell is selling at \$78 on the option maturity data? What if Dell is selling at 88?
    (c) At what two stock prices will you just break even on your investment?
36. Consider the following portfolio. An investor writes a put option with exercise price 70 and buys a put option on the same stock with the same maturity date with exercise price 86.
    (a) Graph the *value* of the portfolio at the option maturity date.
    (b) Graph the *profit* of the portfolio. Determine which option costs more.
37. A GM put option with strike price \$50 trading on the Acme options exchange sells for \$3. However, a GM put with the same maturity selling on the Apex options exchange but with strike price \$52 also sells for \$3. If an investor plans to hold the option position to maturity, devise a zero-net-investment arbitrage strategy to exploit the pricing anomaly. Please graph the diagram at maturity for your position.
38. John purchased a stock index fund currently selling at \$500 per share. He also purchases an at-the-money European put option on the fund for \$15 with exercise price \$500 and three-month time to expiration because he is worried about the losses. Investor A's financial adviser, Alice, points out that he is spending too much money on the put option. The adviser notes that three-month puts with the strike prices of \$480 cost only \$10 and suggests that investor A use the cheaper put.
    (a) For both John and Alice, draw the profit diagram for the stock-plus-put position for various stock prices in three months.

(b) When does Alice's strategy do better? When does it do worse?
(c) Which strategy has larger systematic risk?

39. An investment manager writes a call option with strike price \$30 and buys a call option with strike price \$40. The options are on the same stock and have the same maturity date. One of the calls sells for \$2 and the other one sells for \$6.
(a) Draw both payoff and profit graphs for this strategy at the option maturity date.
(b) What is the breakeven point for this strategy? Is this manager bullish or bearish on the stock?

Bibliography

Amram, M. and N. Kulatilaka (2001). *Real Options.* New York, NY: Oxford University Press.

Ball, C. and W. Torous (1983). Bond prices dynamics and options. *Journal of Financial and Quantitative Analysis*, 18(December), 517–532.

Bhattacharya, M. (1980). Empirical properties of the Black–Scholes formula under ideal conditions. *Journal of Financial and Quantitative Analysis*, 15(December), 1081–1106.

Black, F. (1972). Capital market equilibrium with restricted borrowing. *Journal of Business*, 45(July), 444–445.

Black, F. (1985). Fact and fantasy in the use of options. *Financial Analysts Journal*, 31(July/August), 36–72.

Black, F. and M. Scholes (1973). The pricing of options and corporate liabilities. *Journal of Political Economy*, 31(May/June), 637–654.

Bodhurta, J. and G. Courtadon (1986). Efficiency tests of the foreign currency options market. *Journal of Finance*, 41(March), 151–162.

Bookstaber, R. M. (1981). *Option Pricing and Strategies in Investing.* Reading, MA: Addison-Wesley Publishing Company.

Bookstaber, R. M. and R. Clarke (1983). *Option Strategies for Institutional Investment Management.* Reading, MA: Addison-Wesley Publishing Company.

Brennan, M. and E. Schwartz (1977). The valuation of American put options. *Journal of Finance*, 32(May), 449–462.

Cox, J. C. (1979). Option pricing: A simplified approach. *Journal of Financial Economics*, 8(September), 229–263.

Cox, J. C. and M. Rubinstein (1985). *Option Markets.* Englewood Cliffs, NJ: Prentice-Hall.

Eckardt, W. and S. Williams (1984). The complete options indexes. *Financial Analysts Journal*, 40(July/August), 48–57.

Ervine, J. and A. Rudd (1985). Index options: The early evidence. *Journal of Finance*, 40(June), 743–756.

Finnerty, J. (1978). The Chicago Board Options Exchange and market efficiency. *Journal of Financial and Quantitative Analysis*, 13(March), 28–38.

Galai, D. and R. W. Masulis (1976). The option pricing model and the risk factor of stock. *Journal of Financial Economics*, 3(March), 53–81.

Galai, D., R. Geske and S. Givots (1988). *Option Markets.* Reading, MA: Addison-Wesley Publishing Company.

Gastineau, G. (1979). *The Stock Options Manual.* New York, NY: McGraw-Hill.

Geske, R. and K. Shastri (1985). Valuation by approximation: A comparison of alternative option valuation techniques. *Journal of Financial and Quantitative Analysis*, 20(March), 45–72.

Hull, J. (2005). *Options, Futures, and Other Derivatives*, 6th ed. Upper Saddle River, NJ: Prentice Hall.

Jarrow, R. A. and A. Rudd (1983). *Option Pricing.* Homewood, IL: Richard D. Irwin.

Jarrow R. and S. Turnbull (1999). *Derivatives Securities*, 2nd ed. Cincinnati, OH: South-Western College Pub.

Lee, C. F. (2009). *Handbook of Quantitative Finance and Risk Management.* New York, NY: Springer.

Lee, C. F. and A. C. Lee (2006). *Encyclopedia of Finance.* New York, NY: Springer.

Li, J., Y. Yao, Y. Chen and C. F. Lee (2018). Option prices and stock market momentum: Evidence from China. *Quantitative Finance*, 18(9), 1517–1529.

Liaw, K. T. and R. L. Moy (2000). *The Irwin Guide to Stocks, Bonds, Futures, and Options.* New York, NY: McGraw-Hill Co.

Macbeth, J. and L. Merville (1979). An empirical examination of the Black–Scholes call option pricing model. *Journal of Finance*, 34(December), J173–J186.

McDonald, R. L. (2005). *Derivatives Markets*, 2nd ed. Boston, MA: Addison Wesley.

Merton, R. (1973). Theory of rational option pricing. *Bell Journal of Economics and Management Science*, 4(Spring), 141–183.

Rendleman, R. J., Jr and B. J. Barter (1979). Two-state option pricing. *Journal of Finance*, 34(September), 1093–1110.
Ritchken, P. (1987). *Options: Theory, Strategy and Applications*. Glenview, IL: Scott, Foresman.
Rubinstein, M. and H. Leland (1981). Replicating options with positions in stock and cash. *Financial Analysts Journal*, 37(July/August), 63–72.
Rubinstein, M. and J. Cox (1985). *Option Markets*. Englewood Cliffs, NJ: Prentice-Hall.
Sears, S. and G. Trennepohl (1982). Measuring portfolio risk in options. *Journal of Financial and Quantitative Analysis*, 17(September), 391–410.
Smith, C. (1976). Option pricing: A review. *Journal of Financial Economics*, 3(January), 3–51.
Stoll, H. (1969). The relationships between put and call option prices. *Journal of Finance*, 24(December), 801–824.
Summa, J. F. and J. W. Lubow (2001). *Options on Futures*. New York, NY: John Wiley & Sons.
Trennepohl, G. (1981). A comparison of listed option premium and Black–Scholes model prices: 1973–1979. *Journal of Financial Research*, 4(Spring), 11–20.
Weinstein, M. (1983). Bond systematic risk and the options pricing model. *Journal of Finance*, 38(December), 1415–1430.
Welch, W. (1982). *Strategies for Put and Call Option Trading*. Cambridge, MA: Winthrop.
Whaley, R. (1982). Valuation of American call options on dividend paying stocks: Empirical tests. *Journal of Financial Economics*, 10(March), 29–58.
Zhang, P. G. (1998). *Exotic Options: A Guide to Second Generation Options*, 2nd ed. Singapore: World Scientific.

Appendix 6A: Seven Option Strategies with Excel Approach

In this appendix, we use the call and put option price data that were published on February 18, 2022, with the expiration date of June 17, 2022, as examples to show seven option strategies. The seven option strategies are long straddle, short straddle, long vertical (bull) spread, short vertical (bear) spread, protective put, covered call, and collar value. The following figure lists 10 contracts that we picked for call options and 10 contracts for put options from Yahoo! Finance.

Call

Symbol	Strike	Bid	Ask
JNJ220617C00150000	150	16.15	16.95
JNJ220617C00155000	155	12.25	13.1
JNJ220617C00160000	160	9.05	9.45
JNJ220617C00165000	165	6.3	6.7
JNJ220617C00170000	170	4.05	4.45
JNJ220617C00175000	175	2.45	2.85
JNJ220617C00180000	180	1.38	1.89
JNJ220617C00185000	185	0.69	1.12
JNJ220617C00190000	190	0.45	1.23
JNJ220617C00195000	195	0.22	0.4

Put

Symbol	Strike	Bid	Ask
JNJ210416P00135000	125	0.69	1.03
JNJ210416P00140000	130	0.85	1.42
JNJ210416P00145000	135	1.3	2.35
JNJ210416P00150000	140	1.56	2.08
JNJ210416P00155000	145	2.46	2.77
JNJ210416P00160000	150	3.4	3.6
JNJ210416P00165000	155	4.5	4.85
JNJ210416P00170000	160	6.1	6.5
JNJ210416P00175000	165	8.35	8.65
JNJ210416P00180000	170	11	11.65

6A.1 *First strategy: Long straddle*

In this strategy, the investor purchases a call option at a strike price of \$160 and purchases a put option at the same strike price. From the previous figure, we can find that the premium for buying a call option at \$160 is \$9.45 (see ask column), and the premium for buying a put at \$160 is \$6.5 (see ask column). Collecting all the information and putting it into an excel spread sheet, we can assume the future stock price range, which you expect the stock price might look like in the future. For JNJ as our example, the stock price was \$163.36 on February 18, 2022. Therefore, we can assume that the future stock price might go down to \$125 and go up to \$200, and this is the future stock price range for us to analyze the future payoff and profit for call and put option strategies.

The payoff of a long call is the stock price per share minus exercise price per share, which is $160. If the future stock price is lower than the exercise price for a call option, then the payoff is zero because the investor will not exercise the call option. The payoff of a long put is exercise price per share minus stock price per share. If the future stock price is higher than the exercise price for a put option, then the payoff is zero because the investor will not exercise the put option. The payoff of a long straddle is the sum of the payoff of call and put options (sum of Columns B and D). Profit for both a long call and a long put is the payoff minus premiums, and profit of a long straddle is the sum of the profits from a long call and long put (sum of Columns C and E).

	A	B	C	D	E	F	G	H
1	Long a call at strike price $160				9.45	Premium (see ask column)		
2	Long a put at strike price $160				6.5	Premium (see ask column)		
3								
4	Stock	Long Call (X = $160)		Long Put (X = $160)		Long Straddle		
5	Price	Payoff	Profit	Payoff	Profit	Payoff	Profit	
6	125	0	-9.45	35	28.5	35	19.05	
7	130	0	-9.45	30	23.5	30	14.05	
8	135	0	-9.45	25	18.5	25	9.05	
9	140	0	-9.45	20	13.5	20	4.05	
10	145	0	-9.45	15	8.5	15	-0.95	
11	150	0	-9.45	10	3.5	10	-5.95	
12	155	0	-9.45	5	-1.5	5	-10.95	
13	160	0	-9.45	0	-6.5	0	-15.95	
14	165	5	-4.45	0	-6.5	5	-10.95	
15	170	10	0.55	0	-6.5	10	-5.95	
16	175	15	5.55	0	-6.5	15	-0.95	
17	180	20	10.55	0	-6.5	20	4.05	
18	185	25	15.55	0	-6.5	25	9.05	
19	190	30	20.55	0	-6.5	30	14.05	
20	195	35	25.55	0	-6.5	35	19.05	
21	200	40	30.55	0	-6.5	40	24.05	

By calculating all the numbers in the Excel sheet, the chart for a long straddle will show up automatically. Otherwise, we can also draw a similar chart from "insert" in the Excel and choose the "2-D line" feature with all the long call, long put, and long straddle data. The profit profile of the long straddle is constructed in the following:

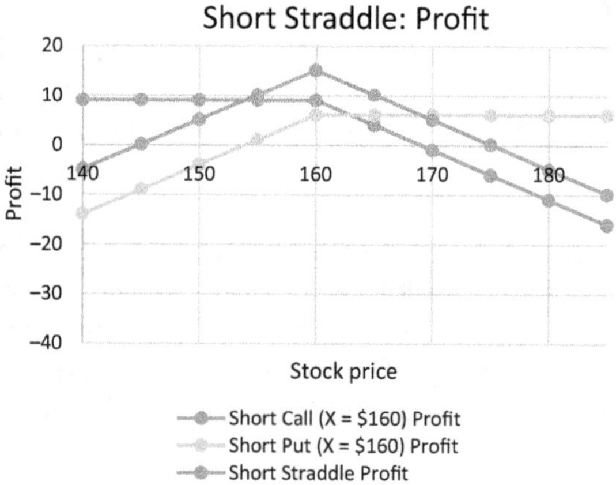

6A.2 *Second strategy: Short straddle*

In this strategy, the investor sells a call option at a strike price of \$160 and sells a put option at the same strike price. From the 10 strategies that we picked, we can find the premium for selling a call option at \$160 is \$9.05 (see bid column), and the premium for selling a put at \$160 is \$6.1 (see bid column). Collecting all the information and putting it into an excel spread sheet, we can assume the future stock price range, which is the same concept that we show in the first strategy. For JNJ as our example, the stock price was \$163.36 on February 18, 2022. Therefore, we can assume that the future stock price might go down to \$125 and go up to \$200, and this is the future stock price range for us to analyze the future payoff and profit for call and put option strategies.

The payoff of a short call is the exercise price per share, which is \$160, minus stock price per share. If the future stock price is lower than the exercise price for a call option, then the payoff is zero because the investor will not exercise the call option. The payoff of a short put is stock price per share minus exercise price per share. If the future stock price is higher than the exercise price for a put option, then the payoff is zero because the investor will not exercise the put option. The payoff of a short straddle is the sum of the payoffs of short call and short put options (sum of Columns B and D). Profit for both a call and a put is payoff minus premiums, and the profit of a short straddle is the sum of the profits from call and put.

	A	B	C	D	E	F	G	H
1	Short a call at strike price $160				9.05	Premium (see bid column)		
2	Short a put at strike price $160				6.1	Premium (see bid column)		
3								
4	Stock	Short Call (X = $160)		Short Put (X = $160)		Short Straddle		
5	Price	Payoff	Profit	Payoff	Profit	Payoff	Profit	
6	125	0	9.05	-35	-28.9	-35	-19.85	
7	130	0	9.05	-30	-23.9	-30	-14.85	
8	135	0	9.05	-25	-18.9	-25	-9.85	
9	140	0	9.05	-20	-13.9	-20	-4.85	
10	145	0	9.05	-15	-8.9	-15	0.15	
11	150	0	9.05	-10	-3.9	-10	5.15	
12	155	0	9.05	-5	1.1	-5	10.15	
13	160	0	9.05	0	6.1	0	15.15	
14	165	-5	4.05	0	6.1	-5	10.15	
15	170	-10	-0.95	0	6.1	-10	5.15	
16	175	-15	-5.95	0	6.1	-15	0.15	
17	180	-20	-10.95	0	6.1	-20	-4.85	
18	185	-25	-15.95	0	6.1	-25	-9.85	
19	190	-30	-20.95	0	6.1	-30	-14.85	
20	195	-35	-25.95	0	6.1	-35	-19.85	
21	200	-40	-30.95	0	6.1	-40	-24.85	

Just as we mentioned for the first strategy, the chart for a short straddle will show up automatically after entering all the data. Otherwise, we can also draw a similar chart from "insert" in the Excel and choose the "2-D line" feature with all the short call, short put, and short straddle data. The profit profile of the short straddle is constructed in the following:

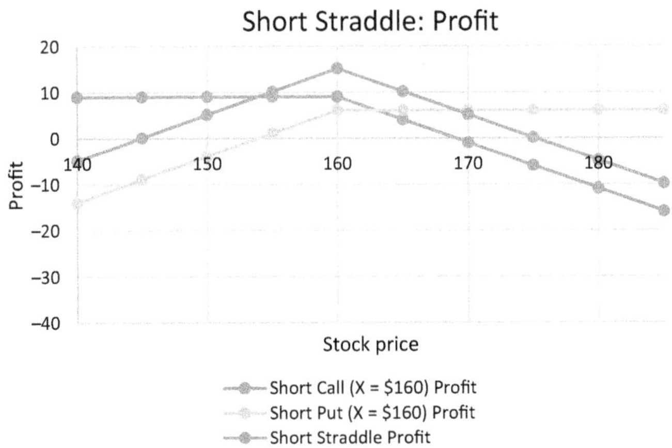

6A.3 *Third strategy: Long vertical (bull) spread*

In this strategy, the investor purchases a call option at a strike price of \$155 and sells a call option at a strike price of \$165, which is slightly higher than the long call price. From the 10 strategies that we picked, we can find that the premium for buying a call option at \$155 is \$13.1 (see ask column), and the premium for selling a call at \$165 is \$6.3 (see bid column). Collecting all the information and putting it into an excel spread sheet, we can assume the future stock price range, which is the same concept that we show in the first strategy.

The payoff of long a call is the stock price per share minus exercise price per share, which is \$155. If the future stock price is lower than the exercise price for a call option, then the payoff is zero because the investor will not exercise the call option. The payoff of short a call is exercise price per share, which is \$165, minus stock price per share. The payoff of a long vertical spread is the sum of the payoff of long call and short call options (sum of Columns B and D). Profit for both a long call and a short call is the payoff minus premiums, and profit of a long vertical spread is the sum of the profits from a long call and short call.

	A	B	C	D	E	F	G	H
1	Long a call at strike price \$155				13.1	Premium (see ask column)		
2	Short a call at strike price \$165				6.3	Premium (see bid colum)		
3								
4	Stock	Long Call (X = \$155)		Short Call (X = \$165)		Long Vertical Spread		
5	Price	Payoff	Profit	Payoff	Profit	Payoff	Profit	
6	125	0	-13.1	0	6.3	0	-6.8	
7	130	0	-13.1	0	6.3	0	-6.8	
8	135	0	-13.1	0	6.3	0	-6.8	
9	140	0	-13.1	0	6.3	0	-6.8	
10	145	0	-13.1	0	6.3	0	-6.8	
11	150	0	-13.1	0	6.3	0	-6.8	
12	155	0	-13.1	0	6.3	0	-6.8	
13	160	5	-8.1	0	6.3	5	-1.8	
14	165	10	-3.1	0	6.3	10	3.2	
15	170	15	1.9	-5	1.3	10	3.2	
16	175	20	6.9	-10	-3.7	10	3.2	
17	180	25	11.9	-15	-8.7	10	3.2	
18	185	30	16.9	-20	-13.7	10	3.2	
19	190	35	21.9	-25	-18.7	10	3.2	
20	195	40	26.9	-30	-23.7	10	3.2	
21	200	45	31.9	-35	-28.7	10	3.2	

Similar to the previous examples, the profit profile of the long vertical spread is constructed in the following:

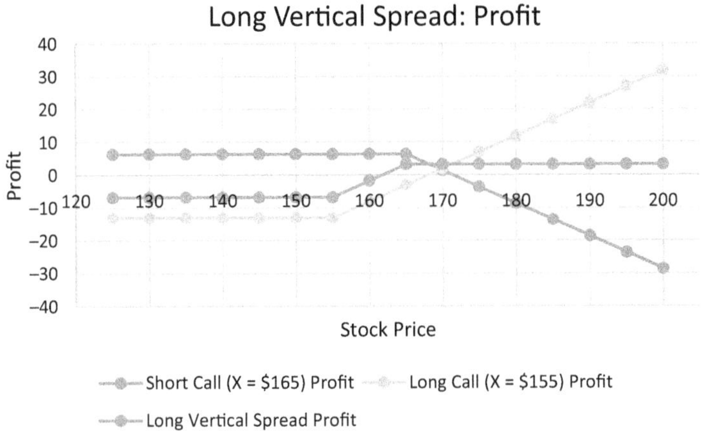

6A.4 *Fourth strategy: Short vertical (bear) spread (SVBS)*

In this strategy, the investor purchases a call option at a strike price of \$160 and sells a call option at a strike price of \$155, which is slightly lower than the long call price. From the 10 strategies that we picked, we can find that the premium for buying a call option at \$160 is \$9.45 (see ask column), and the premium for selling a call at \$155 is \$12.25 (see bid column). Collecting all the information and putting it into an excel spread sheet, we can assume the future stock price range, which is the same concept that we show in the first strategy.

The payoff of long a call is the stock price per share minus exercise price per share, which is \$160. The payoff of short a call is exercise price per share, which is \$155, minus stock price per share. The payoff of a short vertical spread is the sum of the payoff of long call and short call options (sum of Columns B and D). Profit for both a long call and a short call is the payoff minus premiums, and profit of a short vertical spread is the sum of the profits from a long call and short call.

	A	B	C	D	E	F	G	H
1	Long a call at strike price $160				9.45	Premium (see ask column)		
2	Short a call at strike price $155				12.25	Premium (see bid colum)		
3								
4	Stock	Long Call (X = $160)		Short Call (X = $155)		Short Vertical Spread		
5	Price	Payoff	Profit	Payoff	Profit	Payoff	Profit	
6	125	0	-9.45	0	12.25	0	2.8	
7	130	0	-9.45	0	12.25	0	2.8	
8	135	0	-9.45	0	12.25	0	2.8	
9	140	0	-9.45	0	12.25	0	2.8	
10	145	0	-9.45	0	12.25	0	2.8	
11	150	0	-9.45	0	12.25	0	2.8	
12	155	0	-9.45	0	12.25	0	2.8	
13	160	0	-9.45	-5	7.25	-5	-2.2	
14	165	5	-4.45	-10	2.25	-5	-2.2	
15	170	10	0.55	-15	-2.75	-5	-2.2	
16	175	15	5.55	-20	-7.75	-5	-2.2	
17	180	20	10.55	-25	-12.75	-5	-2.2	
18	185	25	15.55	-30	-17.75	-5	-2.2	
19	190	30	20.55	-35	-22.75	-5	-2.2	
20	195	35	25.55	-40	-27.75	-5	-2.2	
21	200	40	30.55	-45	-32.75	-5	-2.2	

The profit profile of the short spread is constructed in the following:

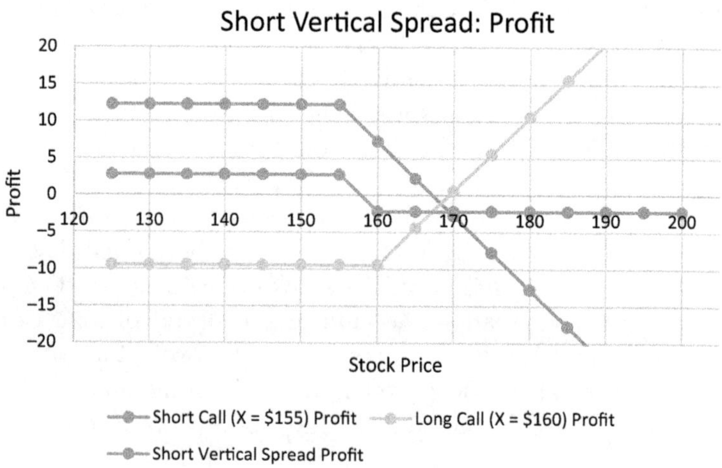

6A.5 *Fifth strategy: Protective put*

In this strategy, the investor purchases a put option at a strike price of \$155 and purchases one share of stock. The stock price is based on the moment that the investor buys a stock, which is \$163.36 for one JNJ share of stock price on February 18, 2022. From the 10 strategies that we picked, we can find that the premium for buying a put option at \$155 is \$4.85 (see ask column). Collecting all the information and putting it into an excel spread sheet, we can assume the future stock price range, which is the same concept that we show in the first strategy.

The payoff of long a put is the exercise price per share, which is \$155, minus stock price per share. The payoff of buying one share of stock is the stock price. The payoff of the protective put value is the sum of the payoffs of a long put and one share of stock (sum of Columns B and D). The profit for a put is payoff minus premiums, and the profit for one share of stock is the stock price per share minus the stock price at the moment the investor purchased, which is \$163.36 in this example. The profit of the protective put value is the sum of the profits from a long put and one share of stock.

	A	B	C	D	E	F	G	H
1	Long a Put at strike price $155				4.85	Premium (see ask column)		
2	Buy one share of stock				163.36	Stock price on Feb. 18		
3								
4	Stock	Long Put (X = $155)		One share of stock		Protective Put Value		
5	Price	Payoff	Profit	Payoff	Profit	Payoff	Profit	
6	125	30	25.15	125	-38.36	155	-13.21	
7	130	25	20.15	130	-33.36	155	-13.21	
8	135	20	15.15	135	-28.36	155	-13.21	
9	140	15	10.15	140	-23.36	155	-13.21	
10	145	10	5.15	145	-18.36	155	-13.21	
11	150	5	0.15	150	-13.36	155	-13.21	
12	155	0	-4.85	155	-8.36	155	-13.21	
13	160	0	-4.85	160	-3.36	160	-8.21	
14	165	0	-4.85	165	1.64	165	-3.21	
15	170	0	-4.85	170	6.64	170	1.79	
16	175	0	-4.85	175	11.64	175	6.79	
17	180	0	-4.85	180	16.64	180	11.79	
18	185	0	-4.85	185	21.64	185	16.79	
19	190	0	-4.85	190	26.64	190	21.79	
20	195	0	-4.85	195	31.64	195	26.79	
21	200	0	-4.85	200	36.64	200	31.79	

The profit profile of the protective put position is constructed in the following:

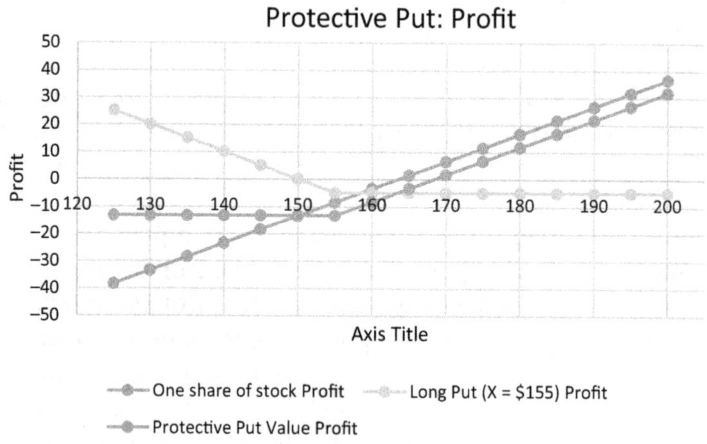

6A.6 *Sixth strategy: Covered call*

In this strategy, the investor writes a call option at a strike price of \$165 and purchases one share of stock. Similar to the fifth strategy, the stock price is based on the moment that the investor buys a stock, which is \$163.36 for one JNJ share of stock price on February 18, 2022. From the 10 strategies that we picked, we can find that the premium for selling a call option at \$165 is \$6.3 (see bid column). Collecting all the information and putting it into an excel spread sheet, we can assume the future stock price range, which is the same concept that we show in the first strategy.

The payoff of short a call is the exercise price per share, which is \$165, minus stock price per share. The payoff of buying one share of stock is the stock price. The payoff of the covered call is the sum of the payoffs of a short call and one share of stock (sum of Columns B and D). The profit for a call is payoff minus premiums, and the profit for one share of stock is the stock price per share minus the stock price at the moment the investor purchased, which is \$163.36 in this example. The profit of the covered call is the sum of the profits from a short call and one share of stock.

	A	B	C	D	E	F	G
1	Write (=Sell) a call at strike price $165				6.3	Premium (see bid column)	
2	Buy one share of stock				163.36	Stock price on Feb. 18	
3							
4	Stock	Written Call (X = $165)		One share of stock		Covered Call	
5	Price	Payoff	Profit	Payoff	Profit	Payoff	Profit
6	125	0	6.3	125	-38.36	125	-32.06
7	130	0	6.3	130	-33.36	130	-27.06
8	135	0	6.3	135	-28.36	135	-22.06
9	140	0	6.3	140	-23.36	140	-17.06
10	145	0	6.3	145	-18.36	145	-12.06
11	150	0	6.3	150	-13.36	150	-7.06
12	155	0	6.3	155	-8.36	155	-2.06
13	160	0	6.3	160	-3.36	160	2.94
14	165	0	6.3	165	1.64	165	7.94
15	170	-5	1.3	170	6.64	165	7.94
16	175	-10	-3.7	175	11.64	165	7.94
17	180	-15	-8.7	180	16.64	165	7.94
18	185	-20	-13.7	185	21.64	165	7.94
19	190	-25	-18.7	190	26.64	165	7.94
20	195	-30	-23.7	195	31.64	165	7.94
21	200	-35	-28.7	200	36.64	165	7.94

The profit profile of the covered call position is constructed in the following:

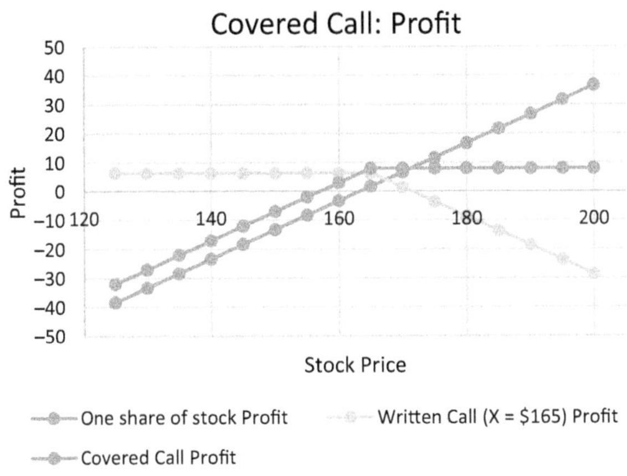

6A.7 *Seventh strategy: Collar value*

In this strategy, the investor writes a call option at a strike price of $165, purchases a put option at a strike price of $155, and purchases one share of stock. From the 10 strategies that we picked, we can find that the premium for selling a call option at $165 is $6.3 (see bid column), and buying a put option at $155 is $4.85 (see ask column). Collecting all the information and putting it into an excel spread sheet, we can assume the future stock price range, which is the same concept that we show in the first strategy.

The payoff of short a call is the exercise price per share, which is $165, minus stock price per share. The payoff of long a put is the exercise price per share, which is $155, minus stock price per share. The payoff of buying one share of stock is the stock price (sum of Columns B and D). The payoff of the collar value is the sum of the payoffs of a short call, long put, and one share of stock.

	A	B	C	D	E	F	G	H	I
1	Write a call at strike price $165				6.3	Premium (see bid column)			
2	Long a Put at strike pirce $ 155				4.85	Premium (see ask column)			
3	Buy one share of stock				163.36	Stock price on Feb. 18			
4									
5	Stock	Write Call (X =		Long Put (X = $155)		One share of stock		Collar Value	
6	Price	Payoff	Profit	Payoff	Profit	Payoff	Profit	Payoff	Profit
7	125	0	6.3	30	25.15	125	-38.36	155	-6.91
8	130	0	6.3	25	20.15	130	-33.36	155	-6.91
9	135	0	6.3	20	15.15	135	-28.36	155	-6.91
10	140	0	6.3	15	10.15	140	-23.36	155	-6.91
11	145	0	6.3	10	5.15	145	-18.36	155	-6.91
12	150	0	6.3	5	0.15	150	-13.36	155	-6.91
13	155	0	6.3	0	-4.85	155	-8.36	155	-6.91
14	160	0	6.3	0	-4.85	160	-3.36	160	-1.91
15	165	0	6.3	0	-4.85	165	1.64	165	3.09
16	170	-5	1.3	0	-4.85	170	6.64	165	3.09
17	175	-10	-3.7	0	-4.85	175	11.64	165	3.09
18	180	-15	-8.7	0	-4.85	180	16.64	165	3.09
19	185	-20	-13.7	0	-4.85	185	21.64	165	3.09
20	190	-25	-18.7	0	-4.85	190	26.64	165	3.09
21	195	-30	-23.7	0	-4.85	195	31.64	165	3.09
22	200	-35	-28.7	0	-4.85	200	36.64	165	3.09

The profit profile of the collar value position is shown in the following:

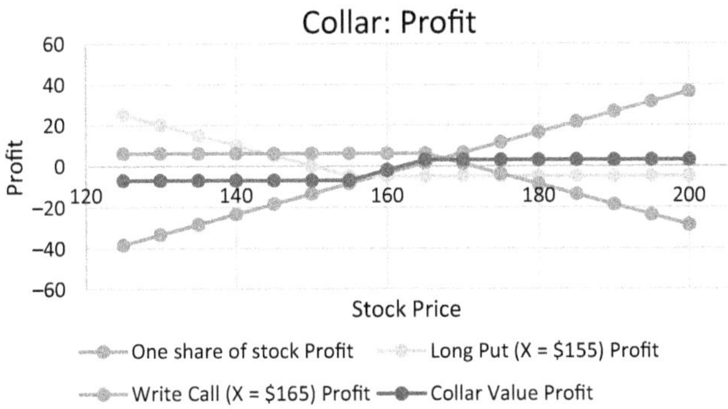
Collar: Profit
60
40
20
0
−20
−40
−60
Profit
120
140
160
180
200
Stock Price
One share of stock Profit
Long Put (X = $155) Profit
Write Call (X = $165) Profit
Collar Value Profit

Chapter 7

Option Pricing Theory and Firm Valuation

Contents

7.1 Introduction

We begin by looking at the basic concepts of options in Section 7.1, then go on to discuss factors that affect the value of options in Section 7.2. Hedging, hedge ratio, and option valuation are discussed in Section 7.3. Section 7.4 discusses how option pricing theory is used to investigate the capital structure question. We close the chapter with a look as the type of option called the warrant in Section 7.5. A summary of this chapter is discussed in Section 7.6. Appendix 7A shows **the derivation and applications of the binomial option pricing model (OPM)**. Appendix 7B shows how **the derivation and applications of delta for both call and put options** can be done. Appendix 7C shows how Black's model (1976) can be used to evaluate options on futures.

7.2 Basic Concepts of Options

In general, there are three types of equity options: (1) warrants, (2) executive stock options, and (3) publicly traded options. A *warrant* is a financial instrument issued by a corporation that gives the purchaser the right to buy a fixed number of shares at a set price for a specific period. There are two major differences between a warrant and a publicly traded option. The first is that the maturity of the warrant is normally less than nine months. The second difference is that the warrant is an agreement between the corporation and the warrant's buyer. This means that if the warrant's owner decides to exercise his right and purchase stock, the corporation issues new shares and receives the cash from the sale of those shares. The *publicly traded option* is an agreement between two individuals who have no relationship with the corporation whose shares are being optioned. When the publicly traded option is exercised, money is exchanged for shares between individuals and the corporation receives no funds, only a new owner.

Executive stock options are a means of compensation for corporate employees. For services rendered, the manager or the employee has the right to buy a specific number of shares for a set price during a given period. Unlike warrants and publicly traded options, executive stock options cannot be traded. The option's owner has only two choices: exercise the option or let it expire. Like a warrant, should the owner decide to exercise the option, the corporation receives money and issues new shares.

The use of executive stock options for management compensation raises an interesting agency question. The firm's managers may make investment and financing decisions that increase the firm's risk in order to increase the value of their stock options. Such actions could have a detrimental effect on the bondholders and other creditors of the firm. Thus, we will see that the value of an option is directly related to the variability or riskiness of the underlying asset, which in this case in the firm.

Publicly traded options are probably the most widely known of the three types of equity option instruments. An important date in the history of these options is 1973, when the Chicago Board Options Exchange was founded. Although it was possible to trade options over the counter before that time, trading volume was relatively low. This date marks the beginning of a phenomenal growth in the popularity of options as a financial instrument. Indeed, in terms of the value of securities traded, the Chicago Board Options Exchange is running neck and neck with the New York and Tokyo stock exchanges as the world's largest securities market. There are now five options trading centers in the United States — the Chicago Board Option Exchange, the American Stock Exchange, the Philadelphia Stock Exchange, the Pacific Stock Exchange, and the New York Stock Exchange — and there is a steady stream of proposals for new listings on these exchanges.

The share volume of trading and the general acceptance of these financial instruments render options valuation an important subject for study. However, even more significant for our purposes, the theory of options valuation has important applications in financial management and in the valuation of other financial instruments. Black and Scholes (1973) point out that those corporate securities can be viewed as options or contingent claims on firm value. In viewing a firm's securities as options, we need to evaluate the interdependencies of bonds and stocks. As we have seen, a bond's price is the present value of future interest and principal payments, and a stock's price is determined by future dividends. The contingent-claims approach to security valuation differs in that it considers the valuation of all of the firm's classes of securities simultaneously. Bonds and stocks are valued in terms on the value placed on the firm's assets; that is, their value is contingent on the firm's assets or investments.

Banz and Miller (1978) developed an approach to making capital budgeting decisions based on a contingent claims framework. They created a method for calculating the net present value (NPV) of an investment based on estimates derived from using an option valuation model. In this chapter, we consider the question of option valuation and how options are used to make financial management decisions. However, before doing so, we must become acquainted with some of the terminology of options trading.

There are two basic types of options: puts and calls. A *call* gives the holder the right to buy a particular number of shares of a designated common stock at a specified price, called the *exercise price* (or strike price), on or before a given date, known as the *expiration date.* Hence, the owner of shares of common stock can create an option and sell it in the options market, thereby increasing the return or income on his or her stock investment. Such an option specifies both an exercise price and an expiration date. On the Chicago Board of Options Exchange, options are typically created for three, six, or nine months. The actual expiration date is the third Saturday of the month of expiration. A more venturesome investor may create an option in this fashion without owning any of underlying stock. This is called *naked option writing* and can be very risky, especially if the value of the underlying asset has a high degree of variability.

A *put* gives the holder the right to sell a certain number of shares of common stock at a set price on or before the expiration date of the option. In purchasing a put, the owner of shares has bought the right to sell these shares by the expiration date at the exercise price. As with calls, the creator can own the underlying shares (covered writing) or not (naked writing).

The owner of a put or call is not obligated to carry out the specified transaction, but has the *option* of doing so. If the transaction is carried out, it is said to have been *exercised.* For example, if you hold a call option on a stock that is currently trading at a price higher than the exercise price, the stock could be immediately resold at a profit. (Or you could sell the option or hold it in the hope of further gains.) This call option is said to be "in the money." On the other hand, if the call option is "out of the money" — that is, the stock is trading at a price — you certainly would not want to exercise the option, as it would be cheaper to purchase the stock directly.

An American option can be exercised at any time up to the expiration date. A simpler instrument to analyze is the European option, which can only be exercised on the expiration date. In this case, the term to maturity of the option is known. Because of this simplifying factor, we will concentrate on the valuation of the European option. The factors determining the values of the two types of options are the same, although all other things equal, an American option is worth more than a European option because of the extra flexibility permitted to the option holder.

Although our discussion is limited to equity options, many kinds of publicly traded options are available. Those include options in stick indexes, options on treasury bonds, options on future contracts, options on foreign currencies, and options on agricultural commodities.

The proceeding discussion presented quite a lot of new terminology. For convenience, we list and define those terms in the following:

Call	An option to purchase a fixed number of shares of common stock.
Put	An option to sell a fixed number of shares of common stock.
Exercise price contract	Trading price set for the transaction as specified in an option.
Expiration date	Time by which the option transaction must be carried out.
Exercise option	Carrying out the transaction specified in an option.
American option	An option in which the transaction can only be carried out at any time up to the expiration date.
European option	An option in which the transaction can only be carried out in the expiration date.
Call option "in the money"	If the stock price is above the exercise price.
Put option "in the money"	If the stock price is below the exercise price.
Call option "out of the money"	If the stock price is below the exercise price.
Put option "out of the money"	If the stock price is above the exercise price.

7.2.1 *Option price information*

Exhibit 23.1 presents options quotations for Johnson & Johnson. The price of Johnson & Johnson shares on this date was around $170. The first column gives the expiration month for each option. We have included listings for call and put options with exercise prices ranging from $165 to $175 per share, and with expiration dates in August 2021. The next columns provide the closing prices, the change from the previous trading day, bid price, asked price, trading volume, and open interest (outstanding contracts) of each option. Column 4 shows the Bid, or the latest price offered by a market maker to buy a particular option. The Ask price in Column 5 is the latest price offered by a market maker to sell a particular option. For example, the first contract traded on the August 2021 expiration call was with an exercise price of $165. The last trade was at $8.70, meaning that an option to purchase one share of Johnson & Johnson at an exercise price of $165 sold for $8.70. Each option contract (on 100 shares) therefore costs $870. The specific factors that determine option value are discussed next (Table 7.1).

How much should you pay for a put or call option? The answer is not easy to determine. However, it is possible to list the various factors that determine option value.

We begin with a simple question. How much is a call option worth on its expiration date? The question is simple because we are in a deterministic world. The uncertain future movement of the price of the stock in question is irrelevant. The call must be exercised immediately or not at all. If a call option is out of the money on its expiration date, it will not be exercised and the call becomes a worthless piece of paper. On the other hand, if the call option is in

Table 7.1 Option Quotes for Johnson & Johnson (Underlying Stock Price: $170), May 25, 2021

	Call					Put			
Expiration	**Last**	**Chg**	**Bid**	**Ask**	**Strike**	**Last**	**Chg**	**Bid**	**Ask**
Aug-21	8.70	—	8.45	8.70	165.00	3.34	0.05	3.35	3.50
Aug-21	5.52	(0.40)	5.40	5.60	170.00	5.36	0.16	5.30	5.45
Aug-21	3.25	(0.35)	3.25	3.30	175.00	8.15	0.35	8.00	8.25

the money on its expiration date, it will be exercised. Stock can be purchased at the exercise price, and immediately resold at the market price, if so desired. The option value is the difference between these two prices. On the call option's expiration date, its value will be either 0 or some positive amount equal to the difference between the market price of the stock and the exercise price of the option. Symbolically, let P = price of stock, V_c = value of call option, and E = exercise price. Then, $V_c = P - E$ if $E \geq P$, and $V_c = 0$ if $P < E$. This relationship can be written as

$$V_c = \text{Max}(0, P - E),$$

where Max denoted the larger of the two bracketed terms. For a put option (V_p), $V_p = E - P$ if $E > P$, and $V_p = 0$ if $E \leq P$. This can be written as

$$V_p = \text{Max}(0, E - P).$$

The call position is illustrated in Figure 7.1(a), where we consider a call option with an exercise price of \$50. The figure shows the option value as a function of stock price to the option holder. For any price of the stock up to \$50, the call option is worthless. The option's value increases as the stock price rises above \$50. Hence, if on the expiration date the stock is trading at \$60, the call option is worth \$10.

Figure 7.1(b), which is the mirror image of Figure 7.1(a), shows the option position from the view point of the writer of the call option. If the stock is trading below the exercise price on the expiration date, the call option will not be exercised and its seller incurs no loss. However, if the stock is trading at \$60, the seller of the call option will be required to sell this stock for \$50, which is \$10 below the price that could be obtained on the market.

We have seen that once a call option has been purchased, the holder of the option has the possibility of obtaining gains but cannot incur losses. Correspondingly, the writer of the option may incur losses but cannot achieve any gains after receiving the premium. Further, there is no net gain in the sense that the profit incurred by one will balance the loss of the other. Thus, options are zero-sum securities — they merely transfer wealth rather than create it. To acquire this instrument, a price must be paid to the writer, and it is

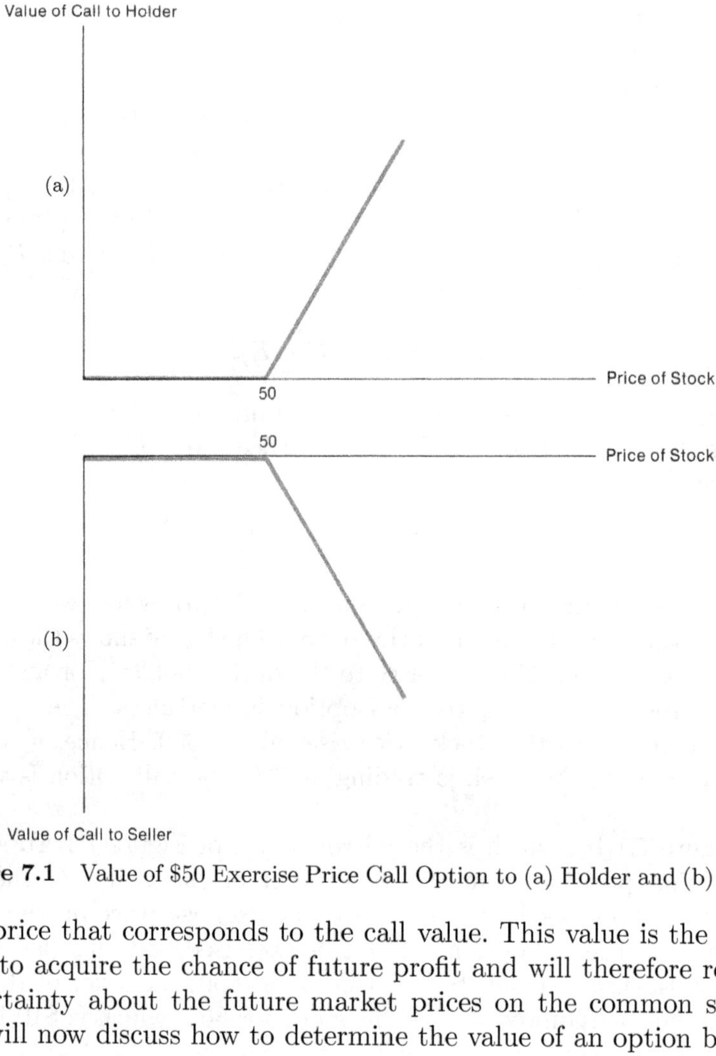

Figure 7.1 Value of $50 Exercise Price Call Option to (a) Holder and (b) Seller

this price that corresponds to the call value. This value is the price paid to acquire the chance of future profit and will therefore reflect uncertainty about the future market prices on the common stock. We will now discuss how to determine the value of an option before its expiration date.

7.3 Factors Affecting Option Value

7.3.1 *Determining the value of a call option before the expiration date*

Suppose that you are considering the purchase of a call option, with an exercise price of $50, on a share of common stock. Let us try to determine what factors should be taken into account in trying to assess the value of such an option prior to the expiration date. As we have seen, the problem is trivial at the expiration date. However, determining the value of an option prior to expiration is more complex.

An important factor in this determination is the current price per share of the stock. Indeed, it is most straightforward to think of option value as a function of the market price. Given this framework, we can see fairly quickly how to set bounds on the value of a call option.

Lower bound: The value of a call cannot be less than the payoff that would accrue if it were exercised immediately. We can think of Figure 7.1 as showing the payoff from immediate exercise of a call as a function on the current price of the stock. In our example, this payoff is zero for any market price below \$50, and the payoff is larger than 0 if the market price is above \$50. Suppose that the current stock price is \$60 per share, and you are offered a call option for \$8. This is certain to be profitable because you could immediately exercise the call and then resell the stock at a \$10 gain. Subtracting the cost of the call option would yield a profit of \$2. Of course, market participants are well aware of this, so the excess of demand over supply for such immediate profits is unattainable.

Upper bound: The value of a call cannot be more than the market price of the stock.

Suppose that, at the same cost, you are offered two alternatives:

(a) purchase a share of stock, or
(b) purchase an option on the same share of stock.

Looking into the future, option (b) will either be exercised or discarded as worthless. If the option is exercised, its value will be the difference between the future stock prices less the exercise price. This will be less than the future stock price, which is the value derived from option (a). Similarly, if the option turns out to have no value, this cannot be preferable to holding the stock, which, while it may have fallen in price, will have retained some value. Therefore, option (b) cannot be preferable to option (a), so the option value cannot exceed the market price of the stock.

These conclusions are illustrated in Figure 7.2, which relates the call option value to the market price of the stock. The *ACD* line

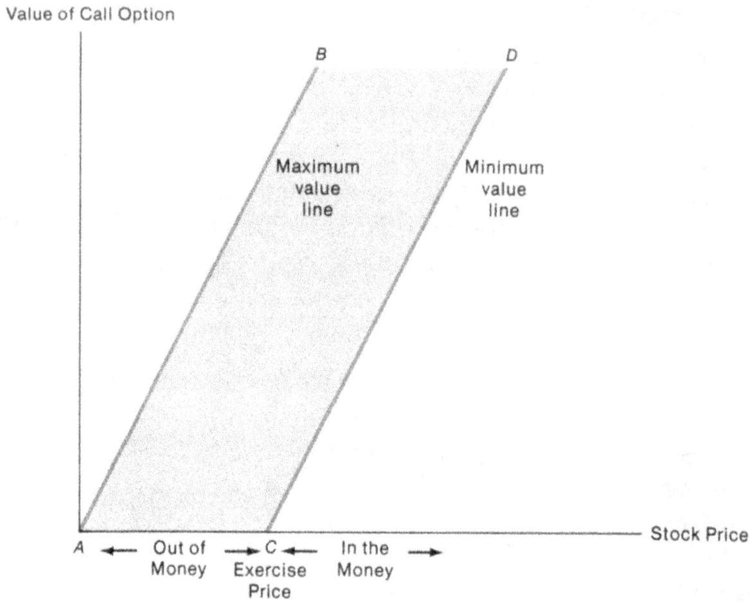

Figure 7.2 Value of Call Option

shows the payoff that would be obtained if the option were exercised immediately. The AB line is the set of points at which the call value equals the market price of the stock. The call value must lie between these boundaries, that is, in the shaded area depicted in Figure 7.2.

So far, we have been able to determine a fairly wide range in which the option value must lie for any given value of the market price of the stock. Let us now see if we can be more precise in formulating the shape of the relationship between call option value and market price stock. The following considerations should help in forming the appropriate picture of Figure 7.3:

(1) *If the market price of the stock is 0, the call value will also be* 0, *as indicated by point A.* This extreme case arises only when there is no hope that the stock will ever have any value, for otherwise investors would be prepared to pay some price, however small, for the stock. It follows, in such a dire circumstance, that the call option will never be exercised, and so it too has no value.

(2) *All other things equal, as the stock price increases, so does the call value (see lines AB and CD).* A call with an exercise price of $50

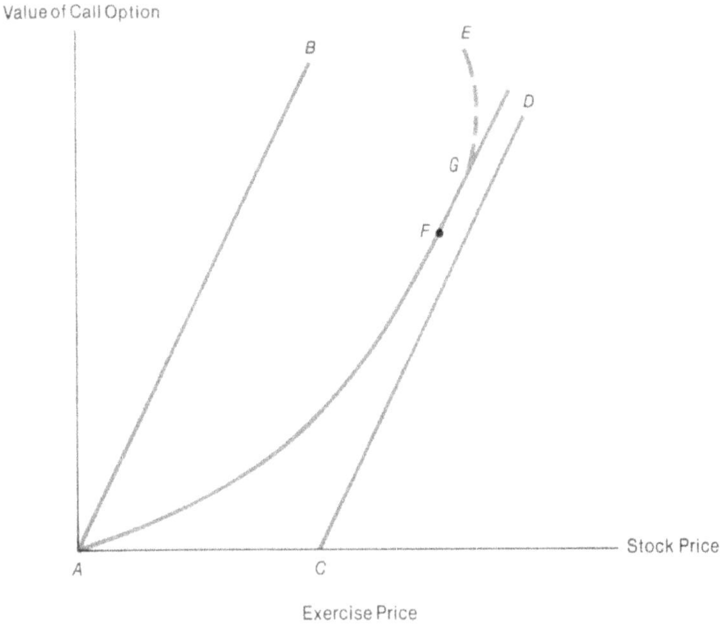

Figure 7.3 Call Option Value as a Function of Stock Price

would be worth more if the current market price was $40 than if it was $35, all else equal. The probability that the market price will eventually exceed the exercise price by any given amount is higher in the former case than in the latter, and so, consequently, is the payoff expected from the holding call.

(3) *If the price of the stock is high in relation to the exercise price, each dollar increase in price induces an increase of very nearly the same amount in the call value (shown by the slope of the line at point F)*. Suppose that the market price of the stock exceeds the exercise price of a call by such a large amount that it is virtually impossible for the stock price to fall below the exercise price before the expiration date. Then, any change in stock price will induce a change of the same amount in the payoff expected from the call, since it is certain that the option will be exercised. The point is that if it is known that an option will eventually be exchanged for stock, this is tantamount to already owning stock. The call holder has effectively purchased the stock without paying the full amount for it right away. The balance

owned is the exercise price to be paid at the expiration date. It follows that the value of the call option is the market value of the stock less the present value of the exercise price. Note that in our previous notation, this will exceed $P - E$ if the exercise price does not have to be paid until some time in the future, because of the time value of money.

(4) *The call value rises at an increasing rate as the value of the stock price rises, as shown by curvature AFG (NOTE TAKE OUT).* The segment AF shows that as the stock price increases, the call value increases by a lesser amount. The segment FE shows the call price increasing by a larger amount than the increase in the stock price. Theoretically, this is impossible, because if it occurs, eventually the call price would exceed the price of the underlying stock.

Putting these four considerations together, we show in Figure 7.3 a typical curve relating call option value to the market price of a stock. Beginning at the origin, when both quantities are 0, the curve shows the call value increasing as market price increases. Eventually, the curve becomes virtually parallel to the two 45-degree lines, forming the boundaries of the possible values region. This is a result of the fourth consideration listed above.

The curve graphed in Figure 7.3 shows the relationship between the call option value and the market price of the stock, when all other relevant factors influencing call option value are constant. Next, we must try to see what these other factors might be and assess their impact on call value.

We consider, in turn, five factors that influence the value of a call option:

(1) **Market price of the stock:** In Figure 7.3, we have seen the curvilinear relationship between call option value and market price of the stock. All other things equal, the higher the market price, the higher the call option value on the stock. As already noted, the slope of this relationship increases as market price becomes higher, to the point where, eventually, each dollar increase in the stock price translates into an increase of about the same amount in the call option value on that stock.

(2) **The exercise price:** If offered two otherwise identical call options on the same stock, you would prefer the call with the lower exercise price. This would involve larger gains from any favorable movement in the price of the stock than would an option with a higher exercise price. Therefore, we conclude that the lower the exercise price, the higher the call option value, all other things equal.

(3) **The risk-free interest rate:** If a call option is eventually exercised, the holder of the option will reap some of the benefits of an increase in the market value of the stock. However, the holder will do so without having to immediately pay the exercise price. This payment will only be made at some future time when the call option is actually exercised. In the meantime, this money can be invested in government securities to earn a no-risk return. This opportunity confers an increment of value on the call option; the higher the risk-free rate of interest, the greater this incremental value or lower the present value of the exercise price. Therefore, we would expect to find, all else equal, that the higher the risk-free rate of interest, the greater the call option value. Moreover, the longer the exercise of the option is postponed, the greater the risk-free interest earnings. Accordingly, we would expect the risk-free interest rate to determine call option value in conjunction with the time remaining before the expiration date.

(4) **The volatility of the stock price:** Suppose that you are offered the opportunity to purchase one of two call options, each with an exercise price of \$50. Table 7.2 lists probabilities for different market prices on the expiration date for each of the two stocks.

In each case, the mean (expected) future price is the same. However, for the second stock, prices that differ substantially from the mean are far more likely than for the first stock. The price of such a stock is said to be relatively volatile. We now show that the expected price of such a stock is said to be relatively volatile. We now show that the expected payoff on the expiration date is higher for a call option on the more volatile stock than for a call option on the less volatile stock. For less volatile stock, the option will not be exercised for prices below \$50, but for the three higher prices, its exercise will result in payoffs of \$2, \$7, and \$12. Therefore, we find

Table 7.2 Probabilities for Future Prices of Two Stocks

Less Volatile Stock		More Volatile Stock	
Future Price ($)	**Probability**	**Future Price ($)**	**Probability**
42	.10	32	.15
47	.20	42	.20
52	.40	52	.30
57	.20	62	.20
62	.10	72	.15

Expected payoff from call option on less volatile stock = $(0)(0.10) + (0)(0.20) + (2)(0.40) + (7)(0.20) + (12)(0.10) = \$3.40$.

Similarly, for a call option on more volatile stock,

Expected payoff from call option on more volatile stock = $(0)(0.15) + (0)(0.20) + (2)(0.30) + (12)(0.20) + (22)(0.15) = \$6.30$.

We find, then, that although the expected future price is the same for the two stocks, the expected payoff is higher from a call option on the more volatile stock. This conclusion is quite general. For example, it does not depend on our having set the exercise price below the expected future stock price. The reader is invited to verify that the same qualitative finding would emerge if the exercise price were $55. We can conclude that, all other things remaining the same, the greater the volatility in the price of the stock, the higher the call option value on that stock.

One useful way to measure volatility is through the *variance* in day-to-day changes in the stock price. Figure 7.4 illustrates our assertion about the influence of stock price volatility on call option value. The figure shows the relationship between call value and current market price for three stocks. The three curves have the same general form depicted in Figure 7.3. However, note that for any given current market price of the stock, the higher the variance of day-to-day price changes, the greater the call option value.

The notion of volatility in future stock market prices is related to the length of the time horizon being considered. Specifically, if the variance of day-to-day changes is σ^2, the variance in the change from the present to t days is $\sigma^2 t$ if the price changes are serially independent. Therefore, the further ahead the expiration date, the

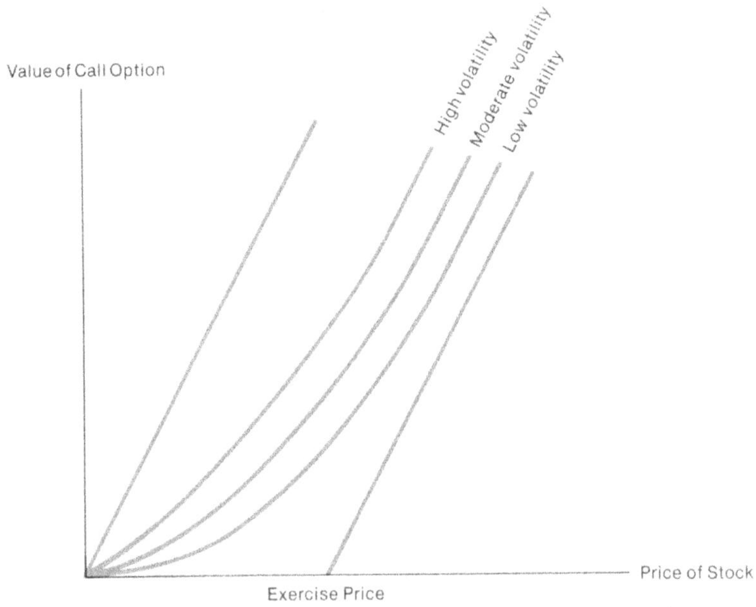

Figure 7.4 Call Option Value as Function of Stock Price for High-, Moderate-, and Low-Volatility Stocks

greater the volatility in price movements. This suggests that for a European option, which can only be exercised on the expiration date, the relevant measure of volatility is $\sigma^2 t$ where t is the number of days remaining to the expiration date. The larger this quantity, the greater the call option value.

(5) **Time remaining to expiration date:** We have seen in factors 3 and 4 two reasons to expect that the longer the time remaining before the expiration date, the higher the call option value, all else equal. The reason is that the extra time allows larger gains to be derived from postponing payment of the exercise price and permits greater volatility in price movements of the stock. These two considerations both operate in the same direction — toward increasing the call option value.

We have seen that five factors influence the value of a call option. The interaction of these various factors in determining option value is rather complex. We present a formula that, under certain assumptions, can be shown to determine a call option value as a function of these five parameters. However, before proceeding to this somewhat complicated relationship, we discuss a simple situation in which option valuation is more straightforward. This is useful in explaining further the dependence of option value on the risk-free rate of interest.

Our aim here is to show, for a special set of assumptions, that an investor can guarantee a particular return from a combined strategy of holding shares in a stock and writing call options on that stock, even though there is some uncertainty about the future price of the stock. The essential simplifying assumption required to generate this result is that there are only two possible values for the future price per share of the stock. In addition, for convenience, we will use European options, with an expiration date in one year. Further, we assume that the stock pays no dividend and that there are no transactions costs.

Within this framework, consider the factors in Table 7.3. An investor can purchase shares for \$100 each and write European call options with an exercise price of \$100. There are two possible prices of the stock on the expiration date, with uncertainty as to which will materialize.

In Table 7.4, we list the consequences to the investor for the two expiration date stock prices. If the higher price prevails, each share of stock will be worth \$125. However, the call options will be exercised at a cost per share to the writer of the difference between the stock price and the exercise price. In Table 7.4, this is a negative value

Table 7.3 Data for a Hedging Example

Current price per share:	\$100
Future price per share:	\$125 with probability 0.6
	\$85 with probability 0.4
Exercise price of call option:	\$100

Table 7.4 Possible Expiration Date Outcomes for Hedging Example

Expiration-Date Stock Price	Value per Share of Stock Holdings	Value per Share of Options Written
\$125	\$125	−\$25
\$85	\$85	\$0

of \$25 from having written the call option. If the lower of the two possible stock prices materializes on the expiration date, each share owned will be worth \$85, and it will have cost nothing to write the option because it will not be exercised.

Suppose that the investor wants to form a *hedged portfolio* by both purchasing stock and writing call options, so as to guarantee as large a total value of holdings per dollar invested as possible, whatever the stock price on the expiration date. The hedge is constructed to be riskless, since any profit (or loss) from the stock is exactly offset with a loss (or profit) from the call option. This is called a *perfect* or *riskless hedge* and can be accomplished by purchasing H number of shares for each option written. We now determine H. If H shares are purchased and one option written, the total value on the expiration date will be \$125H – \$25 at the higher market price and \$85H – \$0 at the lower price. Suppose we choose H so that these two amounts are equal; that is,

$$125H - 25 = 85H,$$

or

$$H = \frac{25}{40} = \frac{5}{8}.$$

Then, the same total value results whatever the stock's expiration date market price. This ratio is known as the *hedge ratio* of stocks to options, the implication being that a hedged portfolio is achieved by writing eight options for each five shares purchased. More generally, it follows from the above argument that the hedge ratio is given by

$$H = \frac{P_U - E}{P_U - P_L},$$

where P_U = upper share price; P_L = lower share price; E = exercise price of option; and E is assumed to be between P_U and P_L.

Returning to our example, suppose that five shares are purchased and an option on eight shares is written. If the expiration date price is \$125, then the total value of the investor's portfolio is

$$(5)(125) - (8)(25) = \$425.$$

If the expiration date stock price is \$85, the total value is

$$(5)(85) + (8)(0) = \$425.$$

As predicted, the two are identical, so that this value is assured.

Next, we must consider the investor's income from the writing of call options. Let V_c denote the price per share of a call option. Then, the purchase of five shares costs \$500, but \$8 V_c is received from writing call options on eight shares, so that the net outlay will be \$500 − \$8 V_c. For this outlay, a value one year hence of \$425 is assured. However, there is another simple mechanism for guaranteeing such a return. An investment could be made in government securities at the risk-free interest rate. Suppose that this rate is 8% per annum. On the expiration date, an initial investment of \$500 − \$8 V_c will be worth \$1.08(500 − 8 V_c). If this is to be equal to the value of the hedged portfolio, then

$$1.08(500 - 8V_c) = 425,$$

so that

$$H = \frac{Max(0, P_U - E) - Max(0, P_L - E)}{P_U - P_L} = \frac{25 - 0}{125 - 85}.$$

Therefore, we conclude that if the price per share for the call option is \$13.31, the hedging strategy will yield an assured rate of return equal to the risk-free interest rate.

In a competitive market, this is the price that will prevail, and therefore is the value of the call option. Suppose that the price of the call option was above \$13.31. By forming a hedged portfolio in the manner just described, investors could ensure a return in excess of the risk-free rate. Such an opportunity would attract many to sell options, thus driving down the price. Conversely, if the price of the option was below \$13.31, it would be possible to achieve a return guaranteed to be in excess of the risk-free rate by both purchasing call options and selling short the stock. The volume of demand thus created for the call option would drive up its price. Hence, in a competitive market, \$13.31 is the only sustainable price for this option.

Our example shows that a hedged portfolio can achieve an assured rate of return of 8%. Note that our analysis depends on the level of the risk-free rate. If that rate is 10% per annum, the call option value is \$14.20. This illustrates the dependence of call option value on the risk-free interest rate.

7.4 Determining the Value of Options

7.4.1 *Expected value estimation*

A higher *expected rate of return*, as compared with the hedged portfolio, can be achieved by the exclusive purchase either of shares or of call options. Suppose that a single share is purchased for \$100. One year hence, the expected value of that share is

$$\text{Expected value of share} = (0.6)(125) + (0.4)(85) = \$109.$$

Hence, the expected rate of return from a portfolio consisting entirely of holdings of this stock is 9%. Similarly, suppose that a call option is purchased for \$13.31. The expected value of this option on the expiration date is

$$\text{Expected value of call} = (0.6)(25) + (0.4)(0) = \$15.$$

Hence, the expected rate of return is

$$\text{Expected rate of return on call} = \frac{15 - 13.31}{13.31} \times 100 = 12.7\%.$$

The increased expected rates of return from holding exclusively these two types of securities should not be surprising. They simply represent increases required by investors for assuming additional risk.

We have shown how call option valuation can be determined within a simple framework in which only two values for the future market price of a stock are possible. We must move on to more realistic situations that involve a range of future market prices.

The value of a put option is determined by the same factors that determine the value of a call option, except that the factors have different relationships to the value of a put than they have to the value of a call. Figure 7.5 shows the relationship between put option value and stock price.

The value of a put option is

$$V_P = MAX(E - P, 0),$$

where V_P = value of the put, E = exercise price, and P = value of the underlying stock. The maximum value of a put is equal to the exercise price of the option when the stock price is 0. This is shown by the line "Maximum value of the put" in Figure 7.5. The minimum

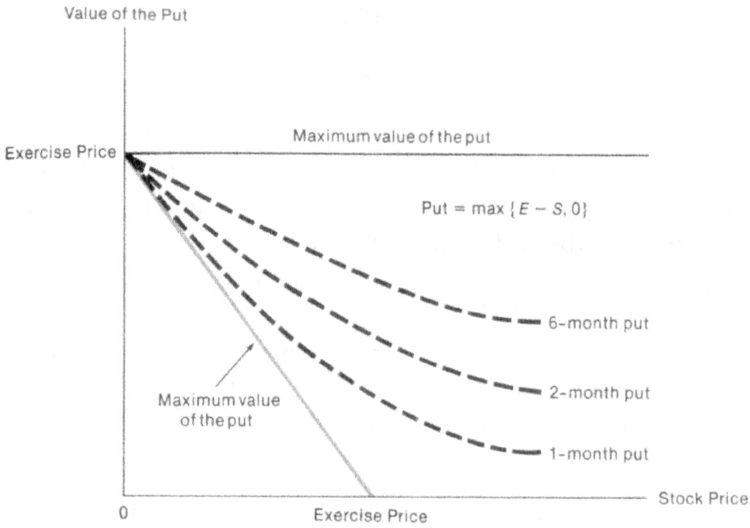

Figure 7.5 Put Option Value

value of the put is 0, which occurs when the stock price exceeds the exercise price.

7.4.2 *The Black–Scholes option pricing model*

The notion that the price of a call option should be such that the rate of return on a fully hedged portfolio is equal to the risk-free rate of interest has been used by Black and Scholes (1973) to derive a more generally applicable procedure for valuing an option. The assumption that only two future prices are possible is dropped for a more realistic view of future price movements. The complete set of assumptions on which the Black–Scholes formula is based is given in the following:

- Only European options are considered.
- Options and stocks can be traded in any quantities in a perfectly competitive market; there are no transaction costs and all relevant information is freely available to market participants.
- Short-selling of stocks and options in a perfectly competitive market is possible.

- The risk-free interest rate is known and is constant up to the expiration date. Market participants are able to borrow or lend at this rate.
- No dividends are paid on the stock.
- The stock price follows a random path in continuous time such that the variance of the rate of return is constant over time and known to market participants. The logarithm of future stock prices follows a normal distribution.

Under these assumptions, Black and Scholes show that the call option value on a share of stock is given by

$$V_c = P[N(d_1)] - e^{-rt}E[N(d_2)], \tag{7.1}$$

where V = value of option, P = current price of stock, r = continuously compounded annual risk-free interest rate, t = time in years to expiration date, E = exercise price, e = 2.71828 is a constant, and $N(d_1)$ = probability that a standard normal random variable is less than or equal to d_i $(i = 1, 2)$, with

$$d_1 = \frac{ln\left(\frac{P}{E}\right) + \left(r + \frac{\sigma^2}{2}\right)t}{\sigma\sqrt{t}}, \tag{7.2a}$$

and

$$d_2 = \frac{ln\left(\frac{P}{E}\right) + \left(r - \frac{\sigma^2}{2}\right)t}{\sigma\sqrt{t}} = d_1 - \sigma\sqrt{t}, \tag{7.2b}$$

where σ^2 = variance of annual rate of return on the stock, continuously compounded, and logarithms are to base e. A binomial distribution approach to derive the OPM can be found in Appendix 7A. In Appendix 7B, we will show how to derive delta for both call and put options. In this appendix, we will also give three examples to show how the delta of both call and put options can be found in real-world, practical situations. In addition, this appendix will also present a Black and Scholes put option formula.

The variance calculated from the monthly rate of return of a stock is the historical variance. Besides the historical variance, we can use implied variance. The implied variance can be calculated by substituting a call premium on the left-hand side of Equation (7.1) and assuming σ^2 is unknown and to be estimated from Equation (7.1). Then, we estimate this unknown variance in terms of Equation (7.1). The procedure of estimating implied variance will be discussed in Chapter 12 of this book.

Although the specific form of the Black–Scholes option pricing formula is complicated, its interpretation is straightforward. The first term of Equation (7.1) is the value of an investor's right to that portion of the probability distribution of the stock's price that lies above the exercise price. This term equals the expected value of this portion of the stock's price distribution. $N(d_1)$ can be graphically described by Figure 7.6.

The second term in Equation (7.1) is the present value of the exercise price times the probability that the exercise price will be paid (the option will be exercised at maturity). Overall, the Black–Scholes model involves the present value of a future cash flow, a common concern in finance. The Black–Scholes model equates option value to the present expected value of the stock price minus the present value of the cost of exercising the option. More important for our purposes than the particular formula is the manner in which the model relates option value to the five factors discussed in the previous section. These relationships are as follows:

(1) All other things equal, the higher the current market price of the stock, the higher the call option value.
(2) All other things equal, the higher the exercise price, the lower the option value.
(3) All other things equal, the higher the risk-free interest rate, the higher the option value.
(4) All other things equal, the greater the time to the expiration date, the higher the option value.
(5) All other things equal, the greater the volatility of the stock price (as measured by σ^2), the higher the option value.

According to the Black–Scholes model, although the call option value depends on the variance of rate of return, it does not depend on the stock's expected rate of return. This is because a change in expected rate of return affects stock price but not the relative value of the option and the stock. Recall from our earlier discussion that formation of the hedged portfolio was independent of expected

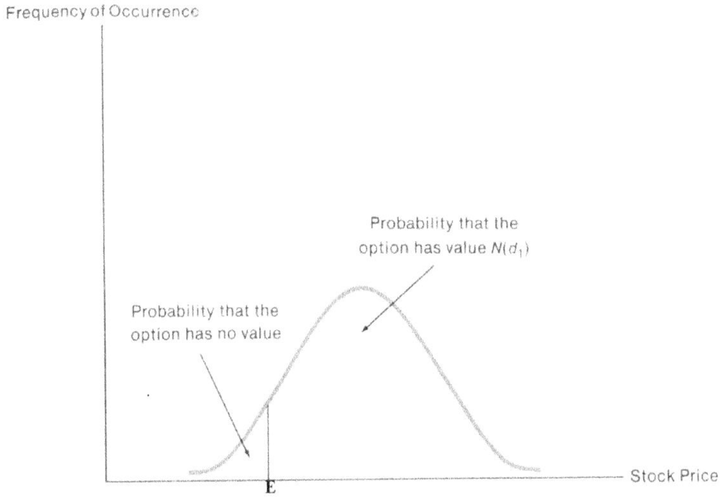

Figure 7.6 Probability Distribution of Stock Prices

return. For example, changing the two probabilities in Table 7.3 has no effect on call option value.

The following example illustrates the computation of option value using the Black–Scholes formula.

Example 7.1. Suppose that the current market price of a share of stock is \$90 and an option is written to purchase the stock for \$100 in six months. The current risk-free rate of interest is 8% per annum. Since the time to the expiration date is half a year, we have, in the notation of the Black–Scholes model, $P = 90$; $E = 100$; $r = .08$; and $t = .50$.

All of this information is readily available to market participants. More problematic is an assessment of the likely volatility of returns on the stock over the next six months. One possible approach is to estimate this volatility using data on past price changes. For instance, we could compute the variance of daily changes in the logarithm of price (daily rate of return) over the last 100 trading days. Multiplying the result by the number of trading days in the year would then yield an estimate of the required variance on an annual basis. For this stock, suppose that such a procedure yields the standard deviation

$$\sigma = .6.$$

This value or some alternative (perhaps developed subjectively) can then be substituted, together with the values of the other four factors, in Equation (7.1) to obtain an estimate of the market value of the call option. We now illustrate these calculations. First, we need the natural logarithm of P/E. This is

$$ln\left(\frac{P}{E}\right) = ln(.9) = -.1054.$$

It follows that

$$\begin{aligned} d_1 &= \frac{ln\left(\frac{P}{E}\right) + rt + \sigma^2 \frac{t}{2}}{\sigma\sqrt{t}} \\ &= \frac{-.1054 + (.08)(.50) + \frac{1}{2}(.36)(.50)}{.6\sqrt{.50}} \\ &= .06. \\ d_2 &= \frac{ln\left(\frac{P}{E}\right) + rt - \sigma^2 \frac{t}{2}}{\sigma\sqrt{t}} \\ &= \frac{-.1054 + (.08)(.50) - \frac{1}{2}(.36)(.50)}{.6\sqrt{.50}}. \\ &= -.37 \end{aligned}$$

Using the table of the cumulative distribution function of the standard normal distribution in the Appendix B at the back of this book, we find the probability that a standard normal random variable less than 0.06 is

$$N(d_1) = N(.06) = .5239.$$

and the probability that a standard normal random variable is less than -0.37 is

$$N(d_2) = N(-.37) = 1 - N(.37) = .3557.$$

The detailed discussion of how to obtain $N(d_1)$ and $N(d_2)$ can be found in Chapter 19.

These numbers represent the probability that the stock price will be at least equal to the exercise price — 52% of the time over the life of the option — and the probability of exercise −35%. We also require

$$e^{-rt} = e^{-(.08)(.5)} = .9608.$$

Finally, on substitution into Equation (7.1), we find

$$\begin{aligned} V_c &= PN(d_1) - e^{rt}EN(d_2) \\ &= (90)(.5239) - (.9608)(100)(.3557) = \$12.98. \end{aligned}$$

Therefore, according to the Black–Scholes model, the call option should be priced at $12.98 per share.

A further implication of the Black–Scholes model is that the quantity $N(d_1)$ provides the hedge ratio for a hedged portfolio of stocks and written options. We see, then, that to achieve such a portfolio, 0.5239 shares of stock should be purchased for each option written.

7.4.3 *Taxation of options*

The taxation of option gains, losses, and income is a fairly complex and constantly changing part of the tax law. However, tax treatment can have a large impact on the usefulness of options for the individual investor. Income (premiums) received by the option writer is taxed as normal income, just as if the option writer were providing a service.

Options can be used to defer gains into the future, which reduces the investor's current tax liability. For example, an investor with a short-term gain on a stock can purchase a put to protect against a drop in the stock price. This allows the investor to hold the stock and not realize the gain until sometime in the future, perhaps the next year, thereby deferring the payment of tax from the present until some future period. Hence, the tax position of the investor is also a factor in determining the value or usefulness of options. However, because we do not have a homogeneous tax structure, it is difficult to incorporate the tax effect into a formulation such as the Black–Scholes model.

7.4.4 *American options*

In our analysis of options, we have assumed the options are European and thus may only be exercised on the expiration date, and that no dividends are paid on the stock before the expiration date. Merton (1973) has shown that if the stock does not pay dividends, it is suboptimal to exercise an American call option before the expiration date. Therefore, if American and European call options on a non-dividend-paying stock are otherwise identical, they should have the same value.

The effect of dividends on a call option depends on whether the firm is expected to pay dividends before the option's expiration date. Such action should reduce the option's value — the greater the expected dividend, the larger the reduction in option value. The reason is that a dividend payment amounts to the transfer to stockholders of part of the firm's value. However, the option holders do not share the dividend payment amount. The larger this reduction in firm value, all other things equal, the lower the expected future price of the stock, because that price reflects firm value at any point in time. Therefore, the higher the dividend, the smaller the probability of any gains from exercising a call option on common stock and, hence, the lower the value of the option. The extreme case occurs if the firm is liquidated and the entire amount of funds realized from the liquidation is distributed as dividends to common stockholders. Once such a distribution is made, the stock and the call option have zero value.

If the firm pays dividends, the value of an American call option on its stock will exceed that of an otherwise identical European option. The reason is that the holder of the American call can exercise the option just before the ex-dividend date and thus receive the dividend payment. If the benefits from such an exercise outweigh the interest income that would have been earned on the exercise price had the option been held to the expiration date, it benefits the holder of an American call to exercise the option. Since this opportunity is not available to the holder of a European option, the American option should have a higher value.

The solution to valuing an option on a stock that pays dividends can be approximated by replacing P, the stock price in the Black–Scholes formula, with the stock price minus the present value of the known future dividend. This is justified because if the option is not exercised before maturity, the option holder will not receive the dividends, in which case the holder should subtract the present value of the dividend from the stock price.

7.5 Option Pricing Theory and Capital Structure

In this section, we show how option pricing theory can be used to analyze the value of the components of a firm's capital structure. Suppose that management of an unlevered corporation decides to issue bonds. For simplicity, we assume these to be zero coupon bonds with face value B to be paid at the maturity date. When the bonds mature, bondholders must be paid an amount B, if possible. If this money cannot be raised, bondholders have a first claim on the firm's assets and will be paid the firm's entire value, V_f which in this case will be less than B. Let us look at this arrangement from the point of view of the firm's stockholders. By using debt, stockholders can be regarded as having sold the firm to bondholders, with an option to purchase it back by paying an amount B at the maturity date of the bonds. Thus, the stockholders hold a call option on the firm, with expiration date at the date of maturity of the bonds. If the firm's value exceeds the value of the debt on the expiration date, the debt will be retired, so that stockholders will have exercised their call option. On the other hand, if the firm's value is less than the face value of the debt, stockholders' limited liability allows them to leave the firm in the hands of the bondholders. The call option will not be exercised, so that the stock will be worth nothing. However, stockholders will have no further obligations to bondholders. Therefore, on the date of expiration, the value of this call option, or, equivalently, the value of stockholders' equity, will be $V = V_f - B$ if $V_f > B$ and 0 if $V_f < B$. Thus, we can write

$$V = \text{MAX}(0, V_f - B), \tag{7.3}$$

where V = value of stockholders' call option on the firm; V_f = value of the firm; and B = face value of debt. This relationship is shown in Figure 7.7. As we can see, this is exactly the relationship shown in Figure 7.1(a) for the value of a call option.

We see, then, that the theory of options can provide us with insights into the valuation of debt and stockholders' equity. This analysis indicates that the stockholders own a call option on the firm's assets. At any time, they could exercise this option by delivering the face value of the bonds to pay off the bondholders and realize

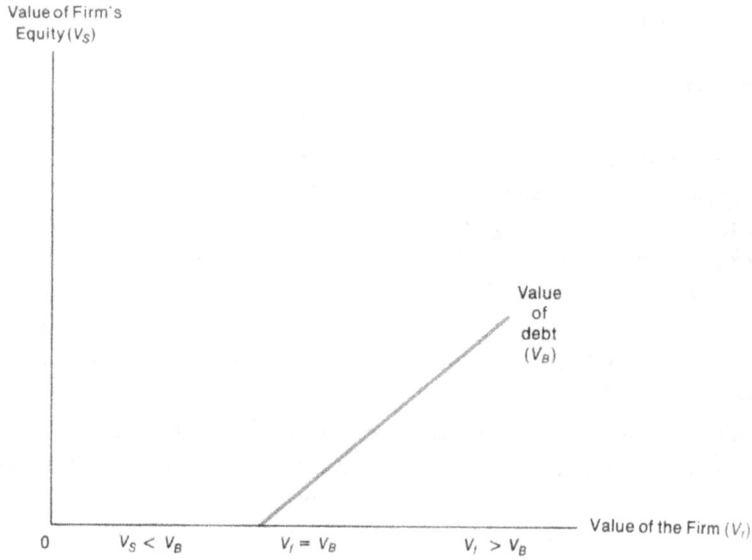

Figure 7.7 Option Approach to Capital Structure

the value of their option. This point is illustrated in the following example, where we employ the Black–Scholes model.

Example 7.2. An unlevered corporation is valued at \$14 million. The corporation issues debt, payable in six years, with a face value of \$10 million. The standard deviation of the continuously compounded rate of return on the total value of this corporation is 0.2. Assume that the risk-free rate of interest is 8% per annum.

In our previous notation, the current market price of the asset (in this case, the firm) is \$14 million, and the exercise price of the option is the face value of the debt. Therefore, we have $P = 14$, $E = 10$, $r = 0.08$, $t = 6$, and $\sigma = 0.2$, where we are measuring value in units of a million dollars.

We will use the Black–Scholes formula, Equation (7.1), to compute the value of stockholders' equity, that is, the value of the stockholders' call option on the firm. First, we require the natural logarithm of P/E, so that

$$ln\left(\frac{P}{E}\right) = ln(1.4) = .3365.$$

Next, we find

$$d_1 = \frac{ln\left(\frac{P}{E}\right) + rt + \sigma^2 \frac{t}{2}}{\sigma\sqrt{t}}$$

$$= \frac{.3365 + (.08)(6) + \frac{1}{2}(.2)(6)}{.2\sqrt{6}} = 1.91,$$

and

$$d_2 = \frac{ln\left(\frac{P}{E}\right) + rt - \sigma^2 \frac{t}{2}}{\sigma\sqrt{t}}$$

$$= \frac{.3365 + (.08)(6) - \frac{1}{2}(.2)(6)}{.2\sqrt{6}} = 1.42$$

From tabulated values of the cumulative distribution function of the standard normal random variable, we find

$$N(d_1) = N(1.91) = .9719.$$

and

$$N(d_2) = N(1.42) = .9222.$$

We also require

$$e^{-rt} = e^{-(.08)(6)} = .6188.$$

On substitution in Equation (7.1), we find the value of stockholders' equity

$$V = PN(d_1) - e^{-rt}EN(d_2)$$
$$= (14)(.9719) - (.6188)(10)(.9222) = \$7.90\,\text{million}.$$

Since the total value of the firm is \$14 million, the value of the debt is

$$\text{Value of debt} = \$14 - \$7.9 = \$6.10\,\text{million}.$$

Assuming the market is efficient, this firm could sell debt with a face value of \$10 million for \$6.1 million. These receipts could be distributed to stockholders, leaving them with equity worth \$7.9 million.

We now turn to examine the effects of two factors on our calculations.

7.5.1 *Proportion of debt in capital structure*

Let us compare our results of Example 7.2 with an otherwise identical situation, but where now only \$5 million face value of debt is to be issued. With $E = 5$ so that $P/E = 2.8$, we find $\ln(P/E)$ to be 1.0296. Using the same procedure as in Example 7.2, $d_1 = 3.33$ and $d_2 = 2.84$, so that $N(d_1) = .9996$ and $N(d_2) = .9977$. Using Equation (7.1), the value of stockholders' equity is

$$\begin{aligned} V &= PN(d_1) - e^{-rt}EN(d_2) \\ &= (14)(.9996) - (.6188)(5)(.9977). \\ &= \$10.91\,\text{million.} \end{aligned}$$

Therefore, the value of the debt is

$$\text{Value of debt} = 14 - 10.91 = \$3.09\,\text{million.}$$

In Table 7.5, we compare, from the point of view of bondholders, the cases where the face values of issued debt are \$5 million and \$10 million. We see from the table that increasing the proportion of debt in the capital structure decreases the value of each dollar of face value of debt. If all the debt is issued at one time, this phenomenon, which simply reflects the increase in bondholders' risk as debt increases, will result in the demand for correspondingly higher interest rates. As our example illustrates, if the corporation sells only \$5 million of face-value bonds, a price of \$618,000 per million dollars in face value will be paid for these bonds. However, if bonds with face value of \$10 million are to be issued, this price will fall to \$610,000. In such a case, the market for bonds operates such that the risk to bondholders of future default is considered in establishing the price of the zero coupon bonds, or more generally the interest rate attached to any bonds.

Table 7.5 Effect of Different Levels of Debt on Debt Value

Face Value of Debt (\$ Millions)	Actual Value of Debt (\$ Millions)	Actual Value per Dollar Debt Face Value of Debt
5	3.09	\$0.618
10	6.10	\$0.610

Suppose, however, that our company issues bonds with face value of \$5 million, at a cost to bond purchasers of \$3.09 million. One year later, this corporation decides to issue more debt. In valuing this new debt, potential purchasers of bonds will assess the risk of default. One factor taken into consideration will be the *total* level of debt of the corporation, that is, the amount of existing debt as well as the size of the new issue. Hence, the market price for the new bonds will reflect riskiness. Consider, however, the position of existing bondholders. The interest rates to be paid to these holders of old debt have already been established. The issue of new debt is going to increase the chance of default on all loans. Consequently, the value of existing bonds must fall when new bonds are issued. Therefore, the issue of new bonds entails a decrease in the wealth of existing bondholders. The beneficiaries are the stockholders of the company whose wealth increases by a corresponding amount. We see, then, that there is a conflict of interest between existing bondholders and holders of common stock. All other things equal, existing bondholders will prefer that no further debt be issued, while stockholders will prefer to see more debt issued. This provides an illustration of the agency problem. Purchasers of bonds will require covenants restricting the freedom of action of corporate management in order to protect the value of their investment.

7.5.2 *Riskiness of business operations*

Let us return to the corporation of Example 7.2, which is about to issue debt with a face value of \$10 million. Leaving the other variables unchanged, suppose that the standard deviation of the continuously compounded rate of return on the corporation's total value is 0.4, rather than 0.2. This implies that the corporation is operating in an environment of greater business risk. Setting $\sigma^2 = .4$, with all other relevant variables as specified in Example 7.2, we find $d_1 = 1.32$ and $d_2 = .34$, so that $N(d_1) = .9066$ and $N(d_2) = .6331$. From Equation (7.1), we find the value of stockholders' equity to be

$$\begin{aligned} V &= PN(d_1) - e^{-rt}EN(d_2) \\ &= (14)(.9066) - (.6188)(10)(.6331) \\ &= \$8.77\,\text{million}. \end{aligned}$$

Table 7.6 Effect of Different Levels of Business Risk on the Value of $10 Million Face Value of Debt

Variance of Rate of Return	Value of Equity ($ Millions)	Value of Debt ($ Millions)
0.2	7.90	6.10
0.4	8.77	5.23

Thus, the value of the debt is

$$\text{Value of debt} = 14 - 8.77 = \$5.23\,\text{million}.$$

Table 7.6 summarizes the comparison between these results and those of Example 7.2. We see that this increase in business risk, with its associated increase in the probability of default on the bonds, leads to a reduction from $6.10 million to $5.23 million in the market value of the $10 million face value of debt. To the extent that potential purchasers of bonds are able to anticipate the degree of business risk, the higher interest rate on the bonds reflects the risk involved. The greater the degree of risk, the higher the interest rate that must be offered to sell a particular amount of debt.

However, suppose that having issued debt, corporate management embarks on new projects with a higher level of risk than could have been foreseen by the purchasers of the bonds. As we have just seen, this will lower the value of existing bonds. This decrease in bondholders' wealth accrues as a gain in wealth to holders of common stock. Once again, we find a conflict of interest between stockholders and bondholders. Once debt has been sold, it will be in the interests of stockholders for the firm to operate with a high degree of business risk, while bondholders will prefer lower levels of risk. Thus, the degree of business risk represents another example of an agency problem. Bondholders will want protection against the possibility that management will take on riskier than anticipated projects, and will demand protective covenants against such actions.

Because of this factor, the issue of a large volume of debt is likely to be accompanied by constraints on the freedom of management action in the firm's operation.

7.5.3 *Option pricing approach to determine the optimal capital structure*

Chapter 6 of Lee *et al.* (2009) discussed the traditional approach to determine the optimal capital structure. Leland (1994) proposed an option approach to determine the optimal capital structure. Chen *et al.* (2010) discussed traditional and option approaches to determine optimal capital structure. The option approach extended the M&M Proposition 1 with tax from the certainty to uncertainty case which includes the possibility of bankruptcy.

7.6 Warrants

A *warrant* is an option issued by a corporation to individual investors to purchase, at a stated price, a specified number of the shares of common stock of that corporation. Warrants are issued in two principal sets of circumstances:

(1) In raising venture capital, either to start a new company or to substantially increase the scope of operations of an existing company, warrants are often issued to lenders as an additional inducement to the promised interest payments or to purchasers of new stock issues.
(2) Often, when issuing bonds, a company will increase the bonds' attractiveness by attaching warrants. Thus, as well as receiving interest payments on the bonds, their purchasers obtain an option to buy stock in the corporation at a specified price. As we have seen, such options will have some value, and so their attachment to bonds should lead to a lowering of the interest rate paid on a fixed quantity of bonds or an increase in the number of bonds that can be sold at a given interest rate.

Since a warrant is essentially a call option on a specified number of shares of common stock, the principles underlying the valuation of call options are also applicable to the valuation of warrants. Suppose that a warrant entitles its holder to purchase N shares of common stock at a total cost E. If, at the expiration date, the price per share of common stock is P, then shares of total value NP can be purchased at cost E. If NP exceeds E, the option to purchase will be exercised, and the difference between these quantities is the value of the warrant. On the other hand, if NP is less than E, it will not pay to exercise the option, so that the warrant will be worthless. The warrant's value on the expiration date can then be expressed as

$$V_w = \text{MAX}(0, NP - E),$$

where V = value of warrant, N = number of shares that can be purchased, P = market price per share of stock, and E = exercise price for the purchase of N shares of stock

Prior to the expiration date, for reasons discussed earlier in this chapter, the warrant's value will exceed this theoretical value. The same factors affecting the value of an ordinary call option are also relevant here. Thus, all other things equal, warrant value will increase with increases in the volatility of the stock price, in the risk-free interest rate, and in the time to the expiration date. However, the basic version of the Black–Scholes model generally will not be directly applicable, as it pertains to the valuation of warrants. The reason is that, generally, warrants differ in important respects from ordinary call options. These factors are as follows:

(1) The life of a call option typically is just a few months. However, the life of a warrant is several years. While it may not be unreasonable to expect volatility of rate of return to remain constant for a few months, it is less likely that it will do so for several years.
(2) Over a period of several years, it is likely that dividends will be paid. As we have seen, dividend payments, which do not accrue to warrant holders, reduce the value of options to purchase stock.
(3) For many warrants, the exercise price is not fixed to the expiration date, but changes at designated points in time. It may well pay to exercise the option to purchase shares immediately before such a change.
(4) It may be that the number of shares that all warrant holders are entitled to purchase represents a considerable fraction of the total number of shares of the corporation. Thus, if these options are all exercised, and total earnings are unaffected, then earnings per share will be diluted.

Let us look at this last point in more detail. Since by using warrants, a corporation can extract more favorable terms from bondholders, it follows that, in return, the company must have transferred something of value to these bondholders. This transfer can be visualized as giving the bondholders a stake in the corporation's equity. Thus, we should regard equity as comprising both stockholdings and warrant value. We will refer to this total equity, prior to the exercise of the options, as *old equity* so that

$$\text{Old equity} = \text{Stockholders' equity} + \text{Warrants}.$$

Suppose that the warrants are exercised. The corporation then receives additional money from the purchase of new shares, so that total equity is

$$\text{New equity} = \text{Old equity} + \text{Exercise money}.$$

We denote by N the number of shares outstanding and by N_w the number of shares that warrant holders can purchase. If the options are exercised, there will be a total of $N + N_w$ shares, a fraction $N_w/(N_w + N)$ of which is owned by former warrant holders. These holders then own this fraction of the new equity; that is,

$$H(\text{New equity}) = H(\text{Old equity}) + H(\text{Exercise money}),$$

where

$$H = \frac{N_w}{N_w + N}.$$

Thus, a fraction, $N_w/(N_w+N)$, of the exercise money is effectively returned to the former warrant holders. In fact, they have really spent $[1 - N_w/(N_w + N)] = N/(N_w + N)$ of the exercise money to acquire a fraction, $N_w/(N_w + N)$, of the old equity. Therefore, in valuing the warrants, the Black–Scholes formula must be modified. We need to make the appropriate substitutions in Equation (7.1) for the current stock price, P, and the exercise price of the option, E:

$$P = \left(\frac{N_w}{N_w + N}\right) \text{(value of old equity)}.$$

$$E = \left(\frac{N}{N_w + N}\right) \text{(exercise money)}.$$

It also follows that the appropriate measure of volatility, σ^2, is the variance of rate of return on the total old equity (including the value of warrants), not simply on stockholders' equity.

Suppose that a firm has one million shares outstanding, currently selling at \$100 per share. There are also 500,000 warrants with an exercise price of \$80 per share. The warrants are worth \$20, or the current stock price, \$100, less the exercise price of \$80. The value of the old equity is

$$\text{Old equity} = 100\,\text{m} + 20(0.5\,\text{m}) = \$110\,\text{million}.$$

If the warrants are exercised, the firm will receive \$40 million (\$80 × 0.5 m) of new equity, so that the new equity is

$$\text{New equity} = \$110\,\text{m} + \$40\,\text{m} = \$150\,\text{million}.$$

When they exercise their warrants, the warrant holders will own one-third of the shares outstanding, that is,

$$H = \frac{N_w}{N_w + N} \quad \text{or} \quad \frac{500{,}000}{500{,}000 + 1{,}000{,}000},$$

and the old shareholders will own the remaining two-third of the shares outstanding.

The warrant holders now have an investment worth \$50 million, or

$$\frac{1}{3}(150\,\text{m}) = \frac{1}{3}(110\,\text{m}) + \frac{1}{3}(40\,\text{m}) = 50\,\text{million}.$$

It makes sense for the warrant holders to exercise their warrant; they spend \$40 million for shares that are worth \$50 million. In terms of the warrant value, the market should be willing to pay \$20 per warrant for 500,000 warrants, or \$10 million.

In Chapter 16, we will discuss warrants and convertible bonds. A *convertible bond* is a security that gives its owner the right to exchange it for a given number of shares of common stock any time before the maturity date of the bond. Hence, a convertible bond is actually a portfolio of two securities: a bond and a warrant. The value of a convertible bond is the value of the bond portion of the portfolio plus the value of the warrant. This issue of warrants and convertible bonds will be discussed in Chapter 16 in further detail.

7.7 Summary

In Chapter 7, we have discussed the basic concepts of call and put options and have examined the factors that determine the value of an option. One procedure used in option valuation is the Black–Scholes model, which allows us to estimate option value as a function of stock price, option exercise price, time-to-expiration date, and risk-free interest rate. The option pricing approach to investigating capital structure is also discussed, as is the value of warrants.

In Appendix 7A, we present the derivation and application of the binomial OPM. In Appendix 7B, we show how the delta for both call and put options can be derived.

Questions and Problems

1. Find the expected value of an option with an exercise price of \$100 at the end of the period, given the following information: Current stock price is \$100.
2. A riskless hedge position can be constructed by buying a stock and writing options on the stock. Using the information in Problem 1 (assume the risk-free interest rate is 10%):

   (a) Find the optimal hedge ratio.
   (b) Find the equilibrium option price.

3. The price of Goodsell Company stock on January 1 is \$100 per share. A call option maturing on April 1 has a \$100 exercise price. The standard deviation of Goodsell stock is 20% per year. What is the call option value if the risk-free rate is 10%?
4. Suppose an unleveraged firm is valued at \$10 million. The firm issues debt, payable in nine years, with a face value of \$7 million. The standard deviation of the rate of return on the total value of this firm is 0.4, and the risk-free interest rate is 8% per annum. Using the option valuation model, calculate the value of stockholders' equity.
5. How does the price of a call option respond to the following changes, other things equal?

   (a) Stock price increase.
   (b) Exercise price increase.

(c) Risk-free interest rate increase.
(d) Extension of the expiration date.
(e) Volatility of the stock price increase.

6. If a call option has an exercise price of $50, then over what stock price range would it be:
   (a) Out of the money?
   (b) In the money?
7. If a put option has an exercise price of $50, then over what stock price range would it be:
   (a) Out of the money?
   (b) In the money?
8. Would an American option generally sell at a price higher or lower than a European option? Explain.
9. If a call option has an exercise price of $50, how much will it be worth on its exercise date (assuming no transaction costs) if the price of the underlying stock is
   (a) $30?
   (b) $50?
   (c) $80?
10. If a call option has an exercise price of $60 and the price of the stock is $40, what is the value of the call option to the
    (a) Holder of the option?
    (b) The seller of the option?
11. Allison Merrick is considering two call options, each having exercise prices of $20 and being identical in all other respects except for the distribution of underlying stock values. The distributions of the values of the underlying stocks of Companies J and K are given in Table 7.7.

Table 7.7 Distributions of the Values of Companies J and K

Probability	Stock J	Probability	Stock K
0.2	$15	0.1	$12
0.3	$18	0.3	$17
0.3	$22	0.4	$25
0.2	$25	0.2	$35

Find the expected payoff for each and explain which one you would prefer.

12. The current price per share is \$80 which can either go up to \$100 or down to \$60. The probabilities of upward and downward movement of the stock price are 0.6 and 0.4, respectively. Given an exercise price of \$80 on a call option and an optimal hedge ratio of 0.4:

    (a) Find the lower bound of the stock price.
    (b) Find the expected value of the call option.
    (c) Demonstrate that the hedged portfolio is riskless.

13. The standard deviation of the return on the stock of Company A is .5 per year. A call option written on this stock is maturing six months from now and has an exercise price of \$80. If the current stock price is \$80 and the risk-free rate of interest is \$8, find the optimal hedge ratio for a portfolio of stocks and options using the Black–Scholes model. (*Note*: This is equivalent to finding $N(d_1)$ in the Black–Scholes model.)
14. A firm has outstanding debt of \$12 million which matures 5 years from now. The standard deviation of the rate of return of the firm's value is .3. The value of another otherwise identical firm with zero debt is \$20 million. Find the value of the firm's outstanding debt, given that the risk-free interest rate is 8%.
15. $S_0 = 100$, $X = 120$, and $R_f = 10\%$. There are two possibilities for S_T, \$140 and \$70. Derive a two-state put option value in this problem.

    (a) Show that the range of S is 70, whereas that of P is 40 across state.
    (b) Form a portfolio of four shares of stocks and seven puts. What is the (non-random) payoff to this portfolio? What is the present value of the portfolio?
    (c) Given that the stock is currently selling at 100, solve for the value of the put.

16. Use the Black–Scholes formula to find the value of a call option on the following stock and then use the put–call parity to calculate the put option value on the stock in the previous problem with the same exercise price and maturity as the call option.

Time to maturity	6 months
Standard deviation	20% per year
Exercise price	\$50
Stock price	\$50
Interest rate	5%

17. A call option with strike price \$50 on a stock currently priced at $S = \$65$ is selling for \$10. Using a volatility estimate of $\sigma = 0.30$, you find that $N(d1) = 0.6$ and $N(d2) = 0.4$. The risk-free interest rate is 0. Is the implied volatility based on the option price more or less than 0.3? Explain.
18. The hedge ratio of an at-the-money call option on Dell is 0.3. The hedge ratio of an at-the-money put option is −0.6. What is the hedge ratio of an at-the-money straddle position on Dell?
19. A collar is established by buying a share of stock for \$50, buying a six-month put option with exercise price \$45, and writing a six-month call option with exercise price \$55. Based on the volatility of the stock, you calculate that for a strike price of \$45 and maturity of six months, $N(d1) = 0.7$, whereas for the exercise price of \$55, $N(d1) = 0.3$.

    (a) What will be the gain or loss on the collar if the stock price increases by \$1?
    (b) What happens to the delta of the portfolio if the stock price becomes very large or very small?

20. John is very bullish on Microsoft, much more so than the rest of the market. In each question, choose the portfolio strategy that will give you the largest dollar profit if John's bullish forecast turns out to be correct. Please briefly discuss your answer.

    (a) **Choice A:** \$20,000 invested in calls with $X = 50$.

        Choice B: \$20,000 invested in Microsoft.

    (b) **Choice A:** 20 call options contracts (for 100 shares each) with $X = 50$.

        Choice B: 2,000 shares of Microsoft stock.

21. Suppose you are a provider of portfolio insurance and are establishing a three-year program. The portfolio you manage is currently worth \$100 million and you hope to provide a minimum

return of 0%. The equity portfolio has a standard deviation of 35% per year and T-bills pay 7% per year. Assume the portfolio pays no dividend. How much of the portfolio should be placed in equity? How much of the portfolio should be placed in bills?

22. Dennis wants to hold a protective put position on stock A to lock in a guaranteed minimum value of \$100 at year-end. Stock A currently sells for \$100. Over the next year, the stock price will increase by 30% or decrease by 10%. The T-bill rate is 7%. Unfortunately, no put options are traded on stock A.

    (a) If the desired put option were traded, how much would it cost to purchase?
    (b) What would have been the cost of the protective put portfolio?
    (c) What portfolio position in stock and T-bills will ensure a payoff that would be provided by a protective put with $X = 100$? Please show that the payoff to this portfolio and the cost of establishing the portfolio match that of the desired protective put.

23. Richard is attempting to value a call option with an exercise price of \$100 and one year to expiration. The underlying stock pays no dividends, its current price is \$100, and Richard believes it has a 50% chance of increasing to \$110 and a 50% chance of decreasing to \$90. The risk-free rate of interest is 6%. Calculate the call option's value using the two-state stock price model.
24. Consider an increase in the volatility of the stock in the previous problem. Suppose that if the stock increases in price, it will increase to \$120, and that if it falls, it will fall to \$80. Show that the value of the call option is now higher than the value derived previously.
25. Tim believes that market volatility will be 20% annually for the next three years. Three-year at-the-money call and put options on the market index sell at an implied volatility of 22%. What options portfolio can Tim establish to speculate on its volatility belief without taking a bullish or bearish position on the market? Using Tim's estimate of volatility, three years' at-the-money options have $N(d1) = 0.2$.

26. Suppose that call options on IBM stock with time to maturity six months and strike price \$60 are selling at an implied volatility of 30%. IBM stock currently is \$60 per share, and the risk-free rate is 6%. If you believe the true volatility of the stock is 38%, how can you trade on your belief without taking on exposure to the performance of IBM? How many shares of stock will you hold for each option contract purchased or sold?
27. Suppose a firm sells call options on \$1.6 million worth of a stock portfolio with beta = 1.8. The option delta is 0.6. It wishes to hedge out its resultant exposure to a market advance by buying a market index portfolio.

    (a) How many dollars' worth of the market index portfolio should the firm purchase to hedge its position?
    (b) What if the firm instead uses market index puts to hedge its exposure? Should it buy or sell puts? Each put option is on 100 units of the index, and the index at current prices represents \$1,000 worth of stock.

28. John is holding call options on a stock. The stock's beta is 0.6, and John is concerned that the stock market is about to fall. The stock is currently selling for \$5 and John holds 1 million options on the stock (i.e., John holds 10,000 contracts for 100 shares each). The option delta is 0.9. How much of the market index portfolio must you buy or sell to hedge your market exposure?

Bibliography

Amram, M. and N. Kulatilaka (2001). *Real Options.* New York, NY: Oxford University Press.

Banz, R. and M. Miller (1978). Prices for state contingent claims: Some estimates and applications. *Journal of Business*, 51, 653–672.

Bhattachayra, M. (1980). Empirical properties of the Black–Scholes formula under ideal conditions. *Journal of Financial and Quantitative Analysis*, 15(December), 1081–1105.

Black, F. (1972). Capital market equilibrium with restricted borrowing. *Journal of Business*, 45(July), 444–445.

Black, F. (1976). The pricing of commodity contracts. *Journal of Financial Economics*, 3(January–March), 167–178.

Black, F. and M. Scholes (1973). The pricing of options and corporate liabilities. *Journal of Political Economy*, 31(May–June), 637–659.

Bookstaber, R. M. (1981). *Option Pricing and Strategies in Investing*. Reading, MA: Addison-Wesley.

Chen, S. S., C. F. Lee and H. H. Lee (2010). Alternative methods to determine optimal capital structure: Theory and application, in C. F. Lee, A. C. Lee and J. Lee (eds.), *Handbook of Quantitative Finance and Risk Management*, pp. 933–951. New York, NY: Springer.

Cox, J. C. and M. Rubinstein (1985). *Option Markets*. Englewood Cliffs, NJ: Prentice-Hall.

Finnerty, J. (1978). The Chicago Board Options Exchange and market efficiency. *Journal of Financial and Quantitative Analysis*, 13(March), 29–38.

Galai, D. and R. W. Masulis (1976). The option pricing model and the risk factor of stock. *Journal of Financial Economics*, 3, 53–81.

Hull, J. (2015). *Options, Futures, and Other Derivatives*, 9th ed. Upper Saddle River, NJ: Prentice Hall.

Jarrow, R. and S. Turnbull (1999). *Derivatives Securities*, 2nd ed. Cincinnati, OH: South-Western College Pub.

Lee, C. F. (2020). Financial econometrics, mathematics, statistics, and financial technology: An overall view. *Review of Quantitative Finance and Accounting*, 54(4), 1529–1578.

Lee, C. F. and J. C. Lee (2017). *Financial Analysis, Planning and Forecasting: Theory and Application*, 2nd ed. Singapore: World Scientific Publishing Company.

Lee, C. F. and A. C. Lee (2022). *Encyclopedia of Finance*, 3rd ed. New York, NY: Springer.

Lee, C. F. and C. S.-M. Lin (2010). Two alternative binomial option pricing model approaches to derive Black–Scholes option pricing model, in C. F. Lee, A. C. Lee and J. Lee (eds.), *Handbook of Quantitative Finance and Risk Management*, pp. 409–420. New York, NY: Springer.

Lee, C. F., A. C. Lee and J. Lee (2010). *Handbook of Quantitative Finance and Risk Management*. New York, NY: Springer.

Lee, C. F., C. Yibin and J. C. Lee (2016). Alternative methods to derive option pricing models: Review and comparison. *Review of Quantitative Finance and Accounting*, 47(2), 417–451.

Lee, C. F., Y. Chen and J. Lee (2016). Alternative methods to derive option pricing models: Review and comparison. *Review of Quantitative Finance and Accounting*, 47(2), 417–451.

Lee, C. F., H.-Y. Chen and J. Lee (2019). *Financial Econometrics, Mathematics and Statistics.* New York: Springer Academic Publishers.

Leland, H. E. (1994). Corporate debt value, bond covenants and optimal capital structure. *Journal of Finance*, 49, 1213–1252.

Li, J., Y. Yao, Y. Chen and C. F. Lee (2018). Option prices and stock market momentum: Evidence from China. *Quantitative Finance*, 18(9), 1517–1529.

Liaw, K. T. and R. L. Moy (2000). *The Irwin Guide to Stocks, Bonds, Futures, and Options.* New York, NY: McGraw-Hill Companies.

MacBeth, J. and L. Merville (1979). An empirical examination of the Black–Scholes call option pricing model. *The Journal of Finance*, 34(December), 1173–1186.

McDonald, R. L. (2013). *Derivatives Markets*, 3rd ed. Boston, MA: Addison Wesley.

Merton, R. (1973). An inter-temporal capital asset pricing model. *Econometrica*, 41(September), 867–887.

Rendleman, R. J., Jr and B. J. Barter (1979). Two-state option pricing. *Journal of Finance*, 24, 1093–1110.

Ritchken, P. (1987). *Option: Theory, Strategy, and Applications.* Glenview, IL: Scott, Foresman.

Summa, J. F. and J. W. Lubow (2001). *Options on Futures.* New York, NY: John Wiley & Sons.

Trennepohl, G. (1981). A comparison of listed option Premia and Black–Scholes model prices: 1973–1979. *Journal of Financial Research*, 4(Spring), 11–20.

Zhang, P. G. (1998). *Exotic Options: A Guide to Second Generation Options*, 2nd ed. Singapore: World Scientific.

Appendix 7A: Derivation and Applications of the Binomial Option Pricing Model

In this appendix, we show how the binomial distribution is combined with some basic finance concepts to generate a model for determining the price of stock options.

7A.1 *The simple binomial OPM*

Before discussing the binomial option model, we must recognize its two major underlying assumptions. First, the binomial approach assumes that trading takes place in discrete time — that is, on a period-by-period basis. Second, it is assumed that the stock price (the price of the underlying asset) can take on only two possible values each period; it can go up or go down.

Say we have a stock whose current price per share S can advance or decline during the next period by a factor of either u (up) or d (down). This price either will increase by the proportion $u-1 \geq 0$ or will decrease by the proportion $1-d$, $0 < d < 1$. Therefore, the value S in the next period will be either uS or dS. Next, suppose that a call option exists on this stock with a current price per share of C and an exercise price per share of X and that the option has one period left to maturity. This option's value at expiration is determined by the price of its underlying stock and the exercise price X. The value is either

$$C_u = \text{Max}(0, uS - X) \tag{7A.1}$$

or

$$C_d = \text{Max}(0, dS - X). \tag{7A.2}$$

Why is the call worth $\text{Max}(0, uS-X)$ if the stock price is uS? The option holder is not obliged to purchase the stock at the exercise price of X, so he or she will exercise the option only when it is beneficial to do so. This means the option can never have a negative value. When is it beneficial for the option holder to exercise the option? When the price per share of the stock is greater than the price per share X, which he or she can purchase the stock by using the option to purchase the stock. Thus, if the stock price uS exceeds the exercise price X, the investor can exercise the option and buy the stock. Then, he or she can immediately sell it for uS, making a profit of $uS - X$ (ignoring commission). Likewise, if the stock price declines to dS, the call is worth $\text{Max}(0, dS - X)$.

Also for the moment, we will assume that the risk-free interest rate for both borrowing and lending is equal to $r\%$ over the one time period and that the exercise price of the option is equal to X.

To intuitively grasp the underlying concept of option pricing, we must set up a *risk-free portfolio* — a combination of assets that produces the same return in every state of the world over our chosen investment horizon. The investment horizon is assumed to be one period (the duration of this period can be any length of time, such as an hour, a day, or a week). To do this, we buy h share of the stock and sell the call option at its current price of C. Moreover, we choose the value of h such that our portfolio will yield the same payoff whether the stock goes up or down.

$$h(uS) - C_u = h(dS) - C_d. \tag{7A.3}$$

By solving for h, we can obtain the number of shares of stock we should buy for each call option we sell:

$$h = \frac{C_u - C_d}{(u-d)S}. \tag{7A.4}$$

Here, h is called the *hedge ratio*. Because our portfolio yields the same return under either of the two possible states for the stock, it is without risk and therefore should yield the risk-free rate of return, $r\%$, which is equal to the risk-free borrowing and lending rate; the condition must be true, otherwise it would be possible to earn a risk-free profit without using any money. Therefore, the ending portfolio value must be equal to $(1+r)$ times the beginning portfolio value, $hS - C$:

$$(1+r)(hS - C) = h(uS) - C_u = h(dS) - C_d. \tag{7A.5}$$

Note that S and C represent the beginning values of the stock price and the option price, respectively.

Setting $R = 1 + r$, rearranging to solve for C, and using the value of h from Equation (7A.4), we get

$$C = \left[\left(\frac{R-d}{u-d}\right)C_u + \left(\frac{u-R}{u-d}\right)C_d\right] \Big/ R, \tag{7A.6}$$

where $d < r < u$. To simplify this equation, we set

$$p = \frac{R-d}{u-d} \quad \text{so} \quad 1 - p = \left\{\frac{u-R}{u-d}\right\}. \tag{7A.7}$$

Thus, we get the option's value with one period to expiration:

$$C = [pC_u + (1-p)C_d]/R. \tag{7A.8}$$

This is the binomial call option valuation formula in its most basic form. In other words, this is the binomial valuation formula with one period to expiration of the option.

Table 7A.1 Possible Option Value at Maturity

Today			
Stock (S)	**Option (C)**		**Next Period (Maturity)**
		$uS = \$110$	$C_u = \text{Max}(0, uS - X) = \text{Max}(0, 110 - 100) = \text{Max}(0, 10) = \$10$
\$100	C		
		$dS = \$90$	$C_d = \text{Max}(0, dS - X) = \text{Max}(0, 90 - 100) = \text{Max}(0, -10) = \$0$

To illustrate the model's qualities, let us plug in the following values, while assuming the option has one period to expiration. Let

$$\begin{aligned} X &= \$100, \\ S &= \$100, \\ u &= (1.10), \text{ so } uS = \$110, \\ d &= (.90), \text{ so } dS = \$90, \\ R &= 1 + r = 1 + 0.07 = 1.07. \end{aligned}$$

First, we need to determine the two possible option values at maturity, as indicated in Table 7A.1.

Next, we calculate the value of p as indicated in Equation (7A.7).

$$p = \frac{1.07 - .90}{1.10 - .90} = .85 \quad \text{so} \quad 1 - p = \frac{1.10 - 1.07}{1.10 - .90} = .15.$$

Solving the binomial valuation equation as indicated in Equation (7A.8), we get

$$\begin{aligned} C &= [.85(10) + .15(0)]/1.07 \\ &= \$7.94. \end{aligned}$$

The correct value for this particular call option today, under the specified conditions, is \$7.94. If the call option does not sell for \$7.94, it will be possible to earn arbitrage profits. That is, it will be possible for the investor to earn a risk-free profit while using none of his or her own money. Clearly, this type of opportunity cannot continue to exist indefinitely.

7A.2 *The generalized binomial OPM*

Suppose we are interested in the case where there is more than one period until the option expires. We can extend the one-period binomial model to the consideration of two or more periods. Because we are assuming that the stock follows a binomial process, from one period to the next it can only go up by a factor of u or go down by a factor of d. After one period, the stock's price is either uS or dS. Between the first and second periods, the stock's price can once again go up by u or down by d, so the possible prices for the stock two periods from now are uuS, udS, and ddS. This process is demonstrated in the tree diagram from (Figure 7A.1) in Example 7A.1 in this appendix.

Note that the option's price at expiration, two periods from now, is a function of the same relationship that determined its expiration price in the one-period model; more specifically, the call option's maturity value is always

$$C_T = \text{Max}[0, S_T - X], \tag{7A.9}$$

where T designated the maturity date of the option.

To derive the option's price with two periods to go ($T = 2$), it is helpful as an intermediate step to derive the value of C_u and C_d with one period to expiration when the stock price is either uS or dS, respectively:

$$C_u = [pC_{uu} + (1 - p)C_{ud}]/R \tag{7A.10}$$

$$C_d = [pC_{du} + (1 - p)C_{dd}]/R. \tag{7A.11}$$

Equation (7A.10) tells us that if the value of the option after one period is C_u, the option will be worth either C_{uu} (if the stock price goes up) or C_{ud} (if stock price goes down) after one more period (at its expiration date). Similarly, Equation (7A.11) shows that if the value of the option is C_d after one period, the option will be worth either C_{du} or C_{dd} at the end of the second period. Replacing C_u and

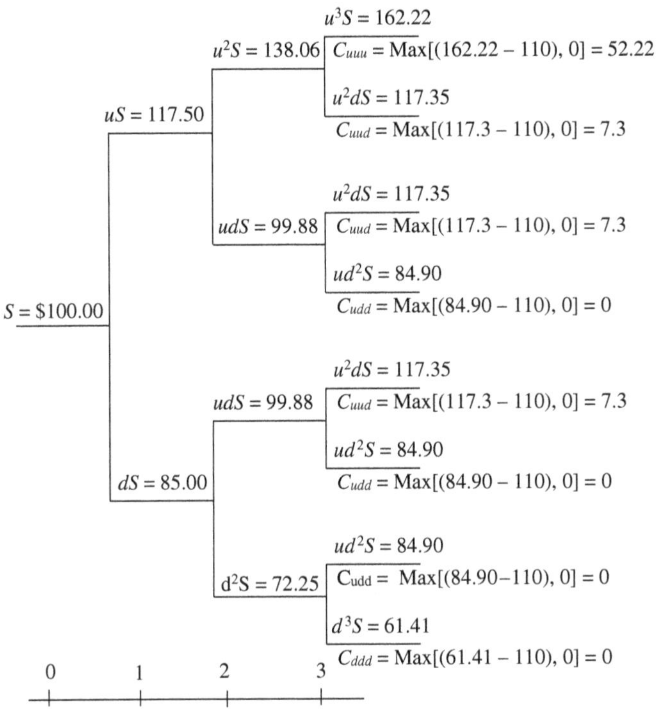

Figure 7A.1 Price Path of Underlying Stock and Value of Call Option

C_d in Equation (7A.8) with their expressions in Equations (7A.10) and (7A.11), respectively, we can simplify the resulting equation to yield the two-period equivalent of the one-period binomial pricing formula, which is

$$C = [p^2 C_{uu} + 2p(1-p)C_{ud} + (1-p)^2 C_{dd}]/R^2. \tag{7A.12}$$

In Equation (7A.12), we used the fact that $C_{ud} = C_{du}$ because the price will be the same in either case.

We know the values of the parameters S and X. If we assume that R, u, and d will remain constant over time, the possible maturity values for the option can be determined exactly. Thus, deriving the option's fair value with two periods to maturity is a relatively simple process of working backward from the possible maturity values.

To derive the three-period model, we now define C_{uu}, C_{ud}, and C_{dd} which appear in Equation (7A.12).

$$\begin{aligned} C_{uu} &= [pC_{uuu} + (1-p)C_{uud}]/R, && \text{(a)} \\ C_{ud} &= [pC_{uud} + (1-p)C_{udd}]/R, && \text{(b)} \\ C_{dd} &= [pC_{udd} + (1-p)C_{ddd}]/R. && \text{(c)} \end{aligned}$$

Then, we substitute Equations (a), (b), and (c) into Equation (7A.12). Then, we obtain the three-period call option formula as follows:

$$\begin{aligned} C &= [p^2[pC_{uuu} + (1-p)C_{uud}] + 2p(1-p)[pC_{uud} + (1-p)C_{udd}] \\ &\quad + (1-p)^2[pC_{udd} + (1-p)C_{ddd}]]/R^3 \\ &= [p^3C_{uuu} + p^2(1-p)C_{uud} + 2p^2(1-p)C_{uud} + 2p(1-p)^2C_{udd} \\ &\quad + p(1-p)^2C_{udd} + (1-p)^3C_{ddd}]/R^3 \\ &= [p^3C_{uuu} + 3p^2(1-p)C_{uud} + 3p(1-p)^2C_{udd} + (1-p)^3C_{ddd}]/R^3. \end{aligned} \tag{7A.13}$$

Now, we provide an example of applying Equation (7A.13) to estimate a three-period call option value.

Example 7A.1. *A decision tree approach to analyzing future stock price and determining value of call option*

By making some simplifying assumptions about how a stock's price can change from one period to the next, it is possible to forecast the future price of the stock by means of a decision tree. To illustrate this point, let us consider the following example.

Suppose the price of Company A's stock is currently \$100. Now, let us assume that from one period to the next, the stock can go up by 17.5% or go down by 15%. In addition, let us assume that there is a 50% chance that the stock will go up and a 50% chance that the stock will go down. It is also assumed that the price movement of a stock (or of the stock market) today is completely independent of its movement in the past; in other words, the price will rise or fall today by a random amount. A sequence of these random increases and decreases is known as a **random walk**.

In addition, suppose a call option has three periods to expiration. The underlying asset is stock A, the exercise price is \$110, and the risk-free rate is 16%.

Given this information, we can lay out the paths that the stock's price may take. Figure 7A.1 shows the possible stock prices for Company A for three periods.

Note that in Period 1, there are two possible outcomes: The stock can go up in value by 17.5% to \$117.50 or down by 15% to \$85.00. In Period 2, there are four possible outcomes. If the stock went up in the first period, it can go up again to \$138.06 or down in the second period to \$99.88. Likewise, if the stock went down in the first period, it can go down again to \$72.25 or up in the second period to \$99.88. Using the same argument, we can trace the path of the stock's price for all three periods.

In addition, we can use Equation (7A.13) to determine the value of the call option.

$$
\begin{aligned}
p &= \frac{R-d}{u-d} = \frac{(1.16)-1.15}{1.175-1.15} = 0.4, \quad \text{and} \\
1-p &= \frac{u-R}{u-d} = \frac{1.175-1.16}{1.175-1.15} = 0.6 \\
C &= [p^3 C_{uuu} + 3p^2(1-p)C_{uud} + 3p(1-p)^2 C_{udd} \\
&\quad + (1-p)^3 C_{ddd}]/R^3 \\
&= [(0.4)^3 52.22 + 3(0.4)^2(0.6)(7.3) + 3(0.4)(0.6)^2(0) \\
&\quad + (0.6)^3(0)]/(1.16)^3 \\
&= [(0.4)^3 52.22 + 3(0.4)^2(0.6)(7.3)]/(1.16)^3 \\
&= 3.4880.
\end{aligned}
$$

The cumulative binomial density function can be defined as

$$
B(k;n,p) = \sum_{k=0}^{n} \frac{n!}{k!(n-k)!} p^{n-k}(1-p)^k, \tag{7A.14}
$$

where n is the number of periods,

k is the number of successful trials,

$$n! = n(n-1)(n-2)\cdots(1),$$
$$k! = k(k-1)(k-2)\cdots(1), \text{ and}$$
$$(n-k)! = (n-k)(n-k-1)(n-k-2)\cdots(1).$$

We can use the cumulative binomial distribution as defined in Equation (7A.14) to generalize Equation (7A.13) into an N period binomial OPM.

Then, we can extend the binomial approach to its more generalized form, with n periods' maturity:

$$C = \frac{1}{R^n}\sum_{k=0}^{n}\frac{n!}{k!(n-k)!}p^k(1-p)^{n-k}\,\text{Max}[0, u^k d^{n-k}S - X]. \quad (7A.15)$$

When $n = 2$ and $n = 3$, it can be shown that Equation (7A.15) can be reduced to Equation (7A.12) and Equation (7A.13), respectively.

To actually get this form of the binomial model, we could extend the two-period model to three periods, then from three periods to four periods, and so on. Equation (7A.15) would be the result of these efforts. To show how Equation (7A.14) can be used to assess a call option's value, we modify the example as follows: $S = \$100$, $X = \$100$, $R = 1.07$, $n = 3$, $u = 1.1$, and $d = .90$.

First, we calculate the value of p from Equation (7A.7) as 0.85, so $1 - p$ is 0.15. Next, we calculate the four possible ending values for the call option after three periods in terms of $\text{Max}[0, u^k, d^{n-k}S - X]$:

$$C_{uuu} = \text{Max}[0, (1.1)^3(.90)^0(100) - 100] = 33.10 = u^3d^0(100) - 100.$$
$$C_{uud} = \text{Max}[0, (1.1)^2(.90)(100) - 100] = 8.90 = u^2d^1(100) - 100.$$
$$C_{udd} = \text{Max}[0, (1.1)(.90)^2(100) - 100] = 0 = u^1d^2(100) - 100.$$
$$C_{ddd} = \text{Max}[0, (1.1)^0(.90)^3(100) - 100] = 0 = u^0d^3(100) - 100.$$

Now, we insert these numbers (C_{uuu}, C_{uud}, C_{udd}, and C_{ddd}) into the model and sum the terms:

$$\begin{aligned}C &= \frac{1}{(1.07)^3}\left[\frac{3!}{0!3!}(.85)^0(.15)^3X0 + \frac{3!}{1!2!}(.85)^1(.15)^2X0\right.\\&\quad\left.+\frac{3!}{2!1!}(.85)^2(.15)^1X8.90 + \frac{3!}{3!0!}(.85)^3(.15)^0X33.10\right]\\&= \frac{1}{1.225}\left[0+0+\frac{3X2X1}{2X1X1}(.7225)(.15)(8.90)\right.\\&\quad\left.+\frac{3X2X1}{3X2X1X1}X(.61413)(1)(33.10)\right]\\&= \frac{1}{1.225}[(.32513X8.90) + (.61413X33.10)]\\&= \$18.96.\end{aligned}$$

This example can be directly solved by using Equation (7A.13) as follows:

By substituting $C_{uuu} = 33.10$, $C_{uud} = 8.90$, $C_{udd} = 0$, and $C_{ddd} = 0$ into Equation (7A.13),

$$\begin{aligned}C &= [(0.85)^3(33.10) + 3(0.85)^2(1-0.85)(8.90)\\&\quad + 3(0.85)(1-0.85)^2(0) + (0.85)^0(1-0.85)^3(0)]/(1.07)^3\\&= 18.95.\end{aligned}$$

Even using two methods, we get the same number. However, Method 1 is more general than Method 2. Method 1 can be used to calculate $n = 4, 5, 6$, and so on. Therefore, Method 1 is more general than Method 2.

As this example suggests, working out a multiple-period problem by hand with this formula can become laborious as the number of periods increases. Fortunately, programming this model into a computer is not too difficult.

Now, let us derive a binomial OPM, which is similar to the Black and Scholes model defined in Equation (7.1), in terms of the cumulative binomial density function. If $[u^k,\ d^{n-k}S - X] > 0$, then Equation

(7A.15) can be rewritten as follows:

$$C = \frac{1}{R^n}\sum_{k=0}^{n}\frac{n!}{k!(n-k)!}p^k(1-p)^{n-k}[u^k d^{n-k}S - X]. \qquad (7A.15')$$

By expanding Equation (7A.15′) into two terms, we get Equation (7A.16) as follows:

$$C = S\left[\sum_{k=m}^{n}\frac{n!}{k!(n-K)!}p^K(1-p)^{n-k}\frac{u^k d^{n-k}}{R^n}\right] - \frac{X}{R^n}\left[\sum_{k=m}^{n}\frac{n!}{k!(n-k)!}p^k(1-p)^{n-k}\right]. \qquad (7A.16)$$

As mentioned before, in order to remove the Max operator, we assume that $u^k d^{n-k}S - X$ is positive, which we can do by changing the counter in the summation from $k = 0$ to $k = m$. What is m? It is the minimum number of upward stock movements necessary for the option to terminate "in the money" (i.e., $u^k d^{n-k}S - X > 0$). How can we interpret Equation (7A.15)? Consider the second term in brackets; it is just a cumulative binomial distribution with parameters of n and p. Likewise, via a small algebraic manipulation, we can show that the first term in the brackets is also a cumulative binomial distribution. This can be done by defining $P' \equiv (u/R)p$ and $1 - P' \equiv (d/R)(1-p)$. Thus,

$$P^k(1-p)^{n-k}\frac{u^k d^{n-k}}{R^n} = p'^k(1-p')^{n-k} = \left[\left(\frac{u}{R}\right)p\right]^k \times \left[\left(\frac{d}{R}\right)(1-p)\right]^{n-k}.$$

Therefore, the first term in brackets is also a cumulative binomial distribution with parameters of n and p'. We can write the binomial call option model as

$$C = SB_1(n, p', m) - \frac{X}{R^n}B_2(n, p, m), \qquad (7A.17)$$

where

$$B_1(n,p',m) = \sum_{k=m}^{n} C_k^n p'^k (1-p')^{n-k},$$

$$B_2(n,p,m) = \sum_{k=m}^{n} C_k^n p^k (1-p)^{n-k},$$

and m is the minimum amount of time the stock has to go up for the investor to finish *in the money* (i.e., for the stock price to become larger than the exercise price).

In this appendix, we showed that by employing the definition of a call option and by making some simplifying assumptions, we could use the binomial distribution to find the value of a call option. Lee *et al.* (2016) and Lee and Lin (2010) have shown how to use the binomial OPM approach to derive the Black–Scholes OPM. In the next chapter, we will show how the binomial distribution is related to the normal distribution and how this relationship can be used to derive one of the most famous valuation equations in finance, the Black–Scholes OPM. In Chapter 20, we have shown how we can use Itô's calculus and normal–lognormal approach to derive the OPM.

Appendix 7B: Derivation and Applications of Delta for Both Call and Put Options

In this appendix, we will first show how the delta of both call and put options can be derived. Then, we will show how the calculation of delta can be applied to real-world decision-making. In Chapter 11, we will show the derivation and applications of delta for stock with cash dividend payments.

From the Black–Scholes OPM, we know the price of call option on a non-dividend stock can be written as follows:

$$C_t = S_t N(d_1) - Xe^{-r\tau} N(d_2). \tag{7B.1}$$

By using put–call parity and Equation (7B.1), we can derive the price of put options on non-dividend stocks as follows:

$$P_t = Xe^{-r\tau} N(-d_2) - S_t N(-d_1), \tag{7B.2}$$

where

$$d_1 = \frac{\ln\left(\frac{S_t}{X}\right) + \left(r + \frac{\sigma_s^2}{2}\right)\tau}{\sigma_s\sqrt{\tau}},$$

$$d_2 = \frac{\ln\left(\frac{S_t}{X}\right) + \left(r - \frac{\sigma_s^2}{2}\right)\tau}{\sigma_s\sqrt{\tau}} = d_1 - \sigma_s\sqrt{\tau},$$

$$\tau = T - t,$$

$N(\cdot)$ is the cumulative density function of normal distribution.

$$N(d_1) = \int_{-\infty}^{d_1} f(u)du = \int_{-\infty}^{d_1} \frac{1}{\sqrt{2\pi}} e^{-\frac{u^2}{2}} du.$$

First, we calculate

$$N'(d_1) = \frac{\partial N(d_1)}{\partial d_1} = \frac{1}{\sqrt{2\pi}} e^{-\frac{d_1^2}{2}} \tag{7B.3}$$

$$\begin{aligned} N'(d_2) &= \frac{\partial N(d_2)}{\partial d_2} \\ &= \frac{1}{\sqrt{2\pi}} e^{-\frac{d_2^2}{2}} \\ &= \frac{1}{\sqrt{2\pi}} e^{-\frac{(d_1-\sigma_s\sqrt{\tau})^2}{2}} \\ &= \frac{1}{\sqrt{2\pi}} e^{-\frac{d_1^2}{2}} \cdot e^{d_1\sigma_s\sqrt{\tau}} \cdot e^{-\frac{\sigma_s^2\tau}{2}} \\ &= \frac{1}{\sqrt{2\pi}} e^{-\frac{d_1^2}{2}} \cdot e^{\ln\left(\frac{S_t}{X}\right) + \left(r + \frac{\sigma_s^2}{2}\right)\tau} \cdot e^{-\frac{\sigma_s^2\tau}{2}} \\ &= \frac{1}{\sqrt{2\pi}} e^{-\frac{d_1^2}{2}} \cdot \frac{S_t}{X} \cdot e^{r\tau}. \end{aligned} \tag{7B.4}$$

Equations (7B.3) and (7B.4) will be used to derive delta for both call and put options. For a European call option on a non-dividend stock, delta can be defined as follows:

$$\Delta = N(d_1). \tag{7B.5}$$

The derivation of Equation (7B.5) is in the following:

$$\begin{aligned}
\Delta = \frac{\partial C_t}{\partial S_t} &= N(d_1) + S_t \frac{\partial N(d_1)}{\partial S_t} - Xe^{-r\tau} \frac{\partial N(d_2)}{\partial S_t} \\
&= N(d_1) + S_t \frac{\partial N(d_1)}{\partial d_1} \frac{\partial d_1}{\partial S_t} - Xe^{-r\tau} \frac{\partial N(d_2)}{\partial d_2} \frac{\partial d_2}{\partial S_t} \\
&= N(d_1) + S_t \frac{1}{\sqrt{2\pi}} e^{-\frac{d_1^2}{2}} \cdot \frac{1}{S_t \sigma_s \sqrt{\tau}} \\
&\quad - Xe^{-r\tau} \frac{1}{\sqrt{2\pi}} e^{-\frac{d_1^2}{2}} \cdot \frac{S_t}{X} \cdot e^{r\tau} \cdot \frac{1}{S_t \sigma_s \sqrt{\tau}} \\
&= N(d_1) + S_t \frac{1}{S_t \sigma_s \sqrt{2\pi\tau}} e^{-\frac{d_1^2}{2}} - S_t \frac{1}{S_t \sigma_s \sqrt{2\pi\tau}} e^{-\frac{d_1^2}{2}} \\
&= N(d_1).
\end{aligned}$$

For a European put option on a non-dividend stock, delta can be shown as

$$\Delta = N(d_1) - 1. \tag{7B.6}$$

The derivation of Equation (7B.6) is

$$\begin{aligned}
\Delta = \frac{\partial P_t}{\partial S_t} &= \mathrm{X}\mathrm{e}^{-r\tau} \frac{\partial N(-d_2)}{\partial S_t} - N(-d_1) - S_t \frac{\partial N(-d_1)}{\partial S_t} \\
&= \mathrm{X}\mathrm{e}^{-r\tau} \frac{\partial (1 - N(d_2))}{\partial d_2} \frac{\partial d_2}{\partial S_t} - (1 - N(d_1)) \\
&\quad - S_t \frac{\partial (1 - N(d_1))}{\partial d_1} \frac{\partial d_1}{\partial S_t} \\
&= -\mathrm{X}\mathrm{e}^{-r\tau} \frac{1}{\sqrt{2\pi}} e^{-\frac{d_1^2}{2}} \cdot \frac{S_t}{X} \cdot e^{r\tau} \cdot \frac{1}{S_t \sigma_s \sqrt{\tau}} \\
&\quad - (1 - N(d_1)) + S_t \frac{1}{\sqrt{2\pi}} e^{-\frac{d_1^2}{2}} \cdot \frac{1}{S_t \sigma_s \sqrt{\tau}} \\
&= -S_t \frac{1}{S_t \sigma_s \sqrt{2\pi\tau}} e^{-\frac{d_1^2}{2}} - N(d_1) - 1 + S_t \frac{1}{S_t \sigma_s \sqrt{2\pi\tau}} e^{-\frac{d_1^2}{2}} \\
&= N(d_1) - 1.
\end{aligned}$$

It is well known that delta for call and put options are hedge ratios for both call and put options. Now, we will present three examples to show how delta of call and put options can be applied in real-world situations.

Example 7B.1. Tim believes that market volatility will be 20% annually for the next three years. Three-year at-the-money call and put options on the market index sell at an implied volatility of 22%. What options portfolio can Tim establish to speculate on its volatility belief without taking a bullish or bearish position on the market? Using Tim's estimate of volatility, three years' at-the-money options have hedge ratio, $N(d_1) = 0.2$.

The answer of this question is now discussed. Since Tim believes that the market assessment of volatility is too high, Tim should sell options because the analysis suggests the options are overpriced with respect to true volatility. The delta of the call is 0.2, while that of the put is $0.2 - 1 = -0.8$. Therefore, Tim should sell puts and calls in the ratio of 0.2 to 0.8. For example, if Tim sells 4 calls and 1 puts, the position will be delta neutral: Delta $= (4 \times 0.2) + [1 \times (-0.8)] = 0$.

Example 7B.2. Suppose that call options on IBM stock with time to maturity of six months and strike price of \$60 are selling at an implied volatility of 30%. IBM stock currently is \$60 per share and the risk-free rate is 6%. If you believe the true volatility of the stock is 38%, how can you trade on your belief without taking on exposure to the performance of IBM? How many shares of stock will you hold for each option contract purchased or sold?

The solution of this question is now discussed. First, we can use the true volatility (38%) to calculate the hedge ratio for IBM as follows:

$$
\begin{aligned}
N(d_1) &= N\left(\frac{\ln(S_0/X) + (r + \sigma^2/2)T}{\sigma\sqrt{T}}\right) \\
&= N\left(\frac{\ln(60/60) + (.06 + .38^2/2).5}{.38\sqrt{.5}}\right) = .5972.
\end{aligned}
$$

The hedge ratio calculated from true volatility is 0.5972. In addition, you believe the calls are underpriced (selling at an implied volatility that is too low). Therefore, you will short 0.5972 shares for each call you buy.

Example 7B.3. Suppose a firm sells call options on \$1.6 million worth of a stock portfolio with beta = 1.8. The option delta is 0.6. It wishes to hedge out its resultant exposure to a market advance by buying a market index portfolio.

(a) How many dollars' worth of the market index portfolio should the firm purchase to hedge its position?
(b) What if the firm instead uses market index puts to hedge its exposure? Should it buy or sell puts? Each put option is on 100 units of the index, and the index at current prices represents \$1,000 worth of stock.

We now discuss the answer for both question (a) and (b) as follows:

(a) To calculate the hedge ratio, suppose that the market index increases by 1%. Then, the stock portfolio would be expected to increase by the following:

$$1\% \times 1.8 = 1.8\% \text{ or } 0.018 \times \$1{,}600{,}000 = \$28{,}800.$$

Given the option delta of 0.8, the option portfolio would increase by

$$\$28{,}800 \times 0.6 = \$17{,}280.$$

The firm's liability from writing these options would increase by the same amount. The market index portfolio would increase in value by 1%. Therefore, the firm should purchase \$1,728,000 of the market index portfolio in order to hedge its position so that a 1% change in the index would result in a \$17,280 change in the value of the portfolio.
(b) The delta of a put option is as follows:

$$0.6 - 1 = -0.4.$$

Therefore, for every 1% the market increases, the index will rise by 10 points and the value of the put option contract will change by

$$\text{Delta} \times 10 \times \text{Contract multiplier} = -0.4 \times 10 \times 100 = -\$400$$

Therefore, the firm should write: \$12,000/\$400 = 30 put contracts.

In this appendix, we have shown how the delta for both call and put options can be mathematically derived. In addition, we present three examples to show how the delta of both call and put options can be applied. In Chapters 11 and 12, we will explore the topics discussed in this appendix in further detail.

Appendix 7C: Application of Black Model to Options on Futures

Fourth, Black (1976) showed that the original call option formula for stocks can be easily modified to be used in pricing call options on futures. The formula is as follows:

$$C(T, F, \sigma^2, X, r) = \mathrm{e}^{-rT}[FN(d_1) - XN(d_2)], \tag{7C.1}$$

$$d_1 = \frac{\ln(F/X) + \frac{1}{2}\sigma^2 T}{\sigma\sqrt{T}}, \tag{7C.2}$$

$$d_2 = \frac{\ln(F/X) - \frac{1}{2}\sigma^2 T}{\sigma\sqrt{T}}. \tag{7C.3}$$

In Equation (7C.1), F now denotes the current futures price. The other four variables are as before — time to maturity, volatility of the underlying futures price, exercise price, and risk-free rate. Note that Equation (7C.1) differs from Equation (7B.1), which can be found in Appendix 7B, only in one respect: By substituting $\mathrm{e}^{-rT}F$ for S in the original Equation (7B.1), Equation (7C.1) is obtained. This holds because the investment in a futures contract is zero, which causes the interest rate in Equations (7C.2) and (7C.3) to drop out.

Chapter 8

Decision Tree and Microsoft Excel Approach for the Option Pricing Model

Contents

8.1 Introduction

The Binomial Option Pricing Model (OPM) derived by Rendleman and Barter (RB, 1979), and Cox *et al.* (CRR, 1979) is one the most famous models used to price options. Only the Black–Scholes model (1973) is more famous. One problem with learning the binomial OPM is that it is computationally intensive. This results in a very complicated formula to price an option.

The complexity of the binomial OPM makes it a challenge to learn the model. Most books teach the binomial option model by describing the formula. This is not very effective because it usually requires the learner to mentally keep track of many details, many times to the point of information overload. There is a well-known principle in psychology that the average number of things that a person can remember at one time is seven.

In Appendix 7A, we graphically and mathematically calculated call option values by the n-period decision tree. This chapter will first demonstrate that it is possible to create large Decision Trees for the binomial pricing model using Microsoft Excel. A 10-period Decision Tree would require 2,047 call calculations and 2,047 put calculations. This chapter will also show the Decision Tree for the price of a stock and the price of a bond, each requiring 2,047 calculation. Therefore, there would be 8,188 $(2,047 \times 4)$ calculations for a complete set of 10-period Decision Trees.

Second, this chapter will present the binomial option model in a less mathematical manner. By using Decision Trees, we can price call and put options without keeping track of many things at one time. Finally, this chapter will show the relationship between the binomial OPM and the Black–Scholes OPM.

Section 8.1 discusses the basic concepts of call and put options. Section 8.2 demonstrates the one-period call and put OPMs. Section 8.3 presents the two-period OPM. Section 8.4 demonstrates how to use the Microsoft Excel workbook *binomialBS_OPM.xls* to create the Decision Trees for an n-period Binomical OPM. Section 8.5 demonstrates the use of the Black–Scholes model. Section 8.6 shows the relationship between the binomial option pricing model and the Black–Scholes OPM. Section 8.7 demonstrates how to use the Microsoft Excel workbook *binomialBS_OPM.xls* to demonstrate the relationship between the binomial OPM and the Black–Scholes OPM.

This chapter uses a Microsoft Excel workbook called *binomialBS_OPM.xls* that contains the Visual Basic for Applications (VBA) code to create the Decision Trees for the binomial OPM. The VBA code is provided in Appendix 8A. The password for the workbook is *bigsky* for those who want to study the VBA code.[1]

8.2 Call and Put Options

A *call option* gives the owner the right but not the obligation to buy the underlying security at a specified price. The price at which the owner can buy the underlying price is called the *exercise price*. A call option becomes valuable when the exercise price is less than the current price of the underlying stock price.

For example, a call option on an XYZ Company stock with an exercise price of $20 when the stock price of an XYZ Company stock is $25 is worth $5. The reason it is worth $5 is because a holder of the call option can buy the XYZ Company stock at $20 and then sell the XYZ Company stock at the prevailing price of $25 for a profit of $5. Also, a call option on an XYZ Company stock with an exercise price of $30 when the stock price of an XYZ Company stock is $15 is worth $0.

A *put option* gives the owner the right but not the obligation to sell the underlying security at a specified price. A put option becomes valuable when the exercise price is more than the current price of the underlying stock price.

For example, a put option on an XYZ Company stock with an exercise price of $20 when the stock price of an XYZ Company stock is $15 is worth $5. The reason it is worth $5 is because a holder of the put option can buy the XYZ Company stock at the prevailing price of $15 and then sell the XYZ Company stock at the put price of $20 for a profit of $5. Also, a put option on an XYZ Company stock with an exercise price of $20 when the stock price of an XYZ Company stock is $25 is worth $0.

Figures 8.1 and 8.2 are charts showing the value of call and put options of the above XYZ Company stock at varying prices.

---

[1]The Microsoft Excel workbook will be available upon request (JohnLeeExcelVBA@gmail.com).

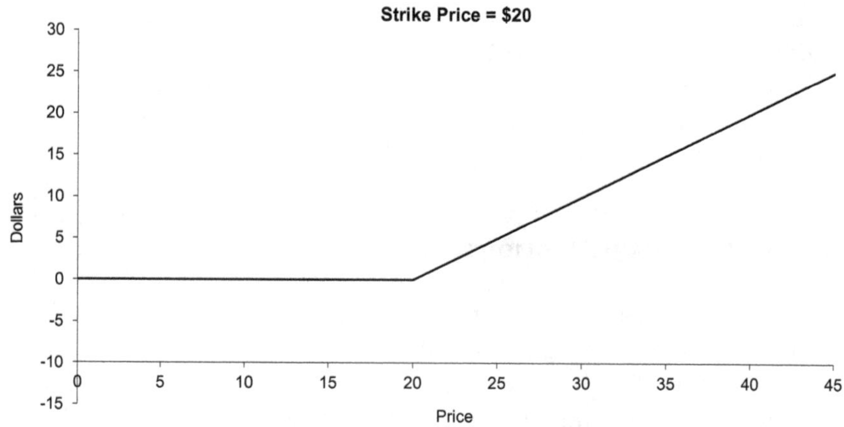

Figure 8.1 Value of XYZ Company Call Option

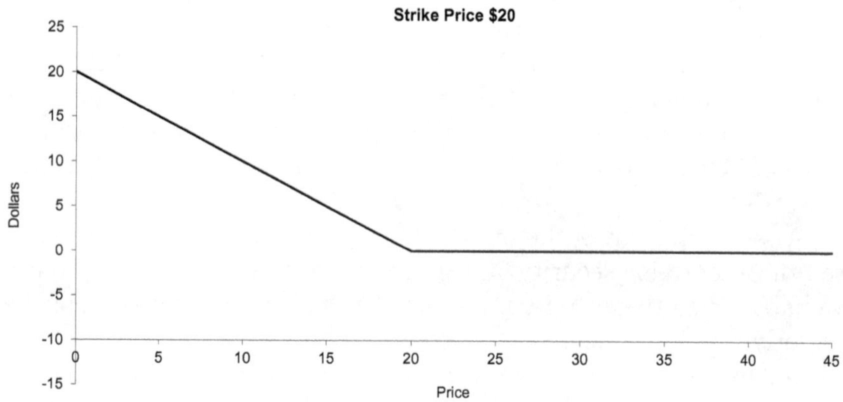

Figure 8.2 Value of XYZ Company Put Option

8.3 Synthetic Option Approach for the One-Period Option Pricing Model

What should be the value of these options? Let us look at a case where we are only concerned with the value of options for one period. In the next period, a stock price can either go up or go down. Let us look at a case where we know for certain that an XYZ Company stock with a price of $20 will either go up 5% or go down 5% in the next period and the exercise after one period is $20. Figures 8.3–8.5

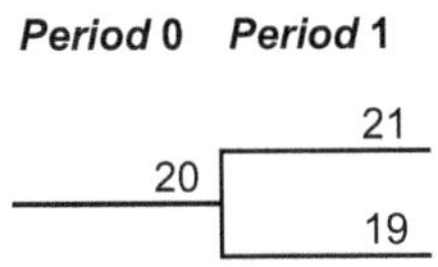

Figure 8.3 Stock Price

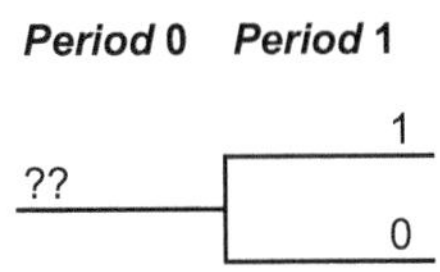

Figure 8.4 Call Option Price

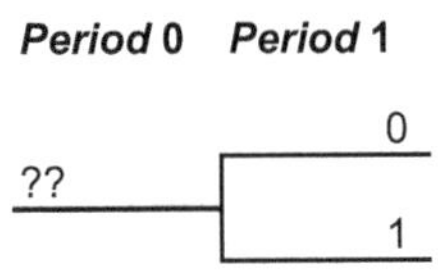

Figure 8.5 Put Option Price

show the Decision Tree for the XYZ Company stock price, the XYZ Company call option price, and the XYZ Company put option price, respectively.

Let us first consider the issue of pricing an XYZ Company call option. Using a one-period Decision Tree, we can illustrate the price of an XYZ Company stock if it goes up 5% and the price of an XYZ Company stock if it goes down 5%. Since we know the possible ending values of the XYZ Company stock, we can derive the possible ending values of a call option. If the stock price increases to \$21, the price of the XYZ Company call option will then be \$1 (\$21 – \$20). If the XYZ Company stock price decreases to \$19, the value of the call option will be worth \$0 because it would be below the exercise price of \$20. We have just discussed the possible ending value of an XYZ Company call option in Period 1. But, what we are really interested in is what the value is now of the XYZ Company call option knowing the two resulting values of the XYZ Company call option.

8.3.1 *Synthetic call option*

To help determine the value of a one-period XYZ Company call option, it is useful to know that it is possible to replicate the resulting two states of the value of the XYZ Company call option by buying a combination of stocks and bonds. The following is the formula to replicate the situation where the price increases to \$21. We will assume that the interest rate for the bond is 3%:

$$21\text{S} + 1.03\text{B} = 1,$$

$$19\text{S} + 1.03\text{B} = 0.$$

We can use simple algebra to solve for both S and B. The first thing that we need to do is to rearrange the second equation as follows:

$$1.03\text{B} = -19\text{S}.$$

With the above equation, we can rewrite the first equation as

$$21\text{S} + (-19\text{S}) = 1,$$

$$2\text{S} = 1,$$

$$\text{S} = 0.5.$$

We can solve for B by substituting the value 0.5 for S in the first equation.

$$21(0.5) + 1.03\text{B} = 1,$$

$$10.5 + 1.03\text{B} = 1,$$

$$1.03\text{B} = -9.5,$$

$$\text{B} = -9.223.$$

Therefore, from the above simple algebraic exercise, we should at period 0 buy 0.5 shares of XYZ Company stock and borrow 9.223 at 3% to replicate the payoff of the XYZ Company call option. This means the value of an XYZ Company call option should be $0.5 \times 20 - 9.223 = 0.777$. This example shows how we can use a synthetic option approach to evaluate a call option value.

If this was not the case, there would then be arbitrage profits. For example, if the call option were sold for \$3, there would be a profit of 2.223. This would result in an increase in the selling of the XYZ Company call option. The increase in the supply of XYZ Company call options would push the price down for the call options. If the call option were sold for \$0.50, there would be a saving of 0.277. This saving would result in the increased demand for the XYZ Company call option. This increased demand would result in the price of the call option increasing. The equilibrium point would be \$0.777.

Using the abovementioned concept and procedure, Benninga (2000) has derived a one-period call option model as

$$C = q_u \operatorname{Max}[uSX, 0] + q_d \operatorname{Max}[dS - X, 0], \tag{8.1}$$

where

$$\begin{aligned} q_u &= \frac{(1+i)-d}{(1+i)(u-d)}, \\ q_d &= \frac{u-(1+i)}{(1+i)(u-d)}, \\ u &= \text{increase factor}, \\ d &= \text{down factor, and} \\ i &= \text{interest rate}. \end{aligned}$$

If we let $i = r$, $R = (1+r)$, $p = (R-d)/(u-d)$, $1-p = (u-R)(u-d)$, $C_u = \operatorname{Max}[uS - X, 0]$, and $C_d = \operatorname{Max}[dS - X, 0]$, then we have

$$C = [pC_u + (1-p)C_d]/R, \tag{8.2}$$

where C_u = call option price after increase, and C_d = call option price after decrease.

Equation (8.2) is identical to Equation (7A.8) in Chapter 7.

The following is the calculation of the value of the above one-period call option where the strike price, X, is \$20 and the risk-free interest rate is 3%. We will assume that the price of a stock for any given period will either increase or decrease by 5%:

$$\begin{aligned}
X &= \$20,\\
S &= \$20,\\
u &= 1.05,\\
d &= 0.95,\\
R &= 1 + r = 1 + 0.03,\\
p &= (1.03 - 0.95)/(1.05 - 0.95),\\
C &= [0.8(1) + 0.2(0)]/1.03 = \$0.777.
\end{aligned}$$

Therefore, from the above calculations, the value of the call option is \$7.94. Figure 8.6 shows the resulting Decision Tree for the above call option.

8.3.2 *Synthetic put options*

Like the call option, it is possible to replicate the resulting two states of the value of the put option by buying a combination of stocks and bonds. The following is the formula to replicate the situation where the price decreases to \$19:

$$\begin{aligned}
21\text{S} + 1.03\text{B} &= 0,\\
19\text{S} + 1.03\text{B} &= 1.
\end{aligned}$$

We will use simple algebra to solve for both S and B. The first thing we will do is to rewrite the second equation as follows:

$$1.03\text{B} = 1.5 - 19\text{S}.$$

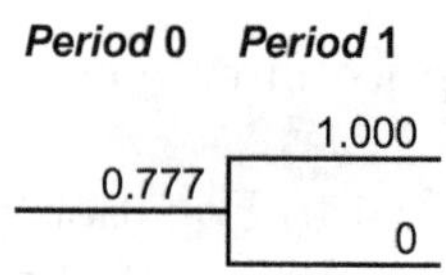

Figure 8.6 Call Option Price

The next thing to do is to substitute the above equation to the first put option equation. Doing this would result in the following:

$$21\text{S} + 1.5 - 19\text{S} = 0.$$

The following solves for S:

$$\begin{aligned} 2\text{S} &= -1.5, \\ \text{S} &= -0.5. \end{aligned}$$

Now, let us solve for B by putting the value of S into the first equation. This is shown as follows:

$$\begin{aligned} 21(-0.5) + 1.03\text{B} &= 0, \\ 1.03\text{B} &= 10.5, \\ \text{B} &= 10.194. \end{aligned}$$

From the above simple algebra exercise, we have S $= -0.5$ and B $=$ 10.194. This tells us that we should in period 0 lend \$10.194 at 3% and sell 0.5 shares of stock to replicate the put option payoff for period 1. And, the value of the XYZ Company put option should be $20(-0.5) + 10.194 = 0.194$.

Using the same arbitrage argument that we used in the discussion of the call option, 0.194 has to be the equilibrium price of the put option.

As with the call option, Benninga (2000) has derived a one-period put option model as

$$P = q_u \,\text{Max}[X - uS, 0] + q_d \,\text{Max}[X - dS, 0], \tag{8.3}$$

where

$$\begin{aligned} q_u &= \frac{(1+i) - d}{(1+i)(u-d)}, \\ q_d &= \frac{u - (1+i)}{(1+i)(u-d)}, \\ u &= \text{increase factor}, \\ d &= \text{down factor, and} \\ i &= \text{interest rate}. \end{aligned}$$

If we let $i = r$, $R = (1+r)$, $p = (R-d)/(u-d)$, $1-p = (u-R)/(u-d)$, $P_u = \text{Max}[X - uS, 0]$, and $P_d = \text{Max}[X - dS, 0]$, then we have

$$P = [pP_u + (1-p)P_d]/R, \tag{8.4}$$

where P_u = put option price after increase, and P_d = put option price after decrease.

The following is the calculation of the value of the above one-period put option where the strike price, X, is \$30 and the risk-free interest rate is 3%:

$$P = [0.8(0) + 0.2(1)]/1.03 = \$0.194.$$

From the above calculation, the put option pricing Decision Tree would look like the following.

Figure 8.7 shows the resulting Decision Tree for the above put option.

There is a relationship between the price of a put option and the price of a call option. This relationship is called the put–call parity. Equation (8.5) shows the relationship between the price of a put option and the price of a call option:

$$P = C + X/R - S, \tag{8.5}$$

where C = call price, X = strike price, $R = 1 +$ interest rate, and S = stock price.

The following uses the put–call parity to calculate the price of the XYZ Company put option:

$$\begin{aligned} P &= \$0.777 + \$20/(1.03) - -\$20 \\ &= 0.777 + 19.417 - 20 \\ &= 0.194. \end{aligned}$$

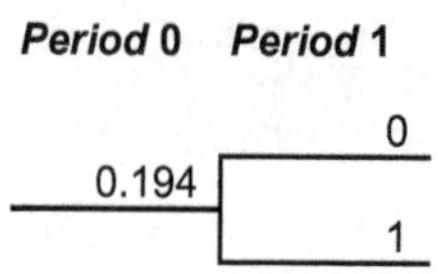

Figure 8.7 XYZ Company Put Option Price

8.4 Two-Period Option Pricing Model

We now will look at pricing options for two periods. Figure 8.8 shows the stock price Decision Tree based on the parameters indicated in the last section. This Decision Tree was created based on the assumption that a stock price will either increase by 5% or decrease by 5%.

How do we price the value of a call and put option for two periods?

The highest possible value for our stock based on our assumption is \$22.05. We get this value first by multiplying the stock price at period 0 by 105% to get the resulting value of \$21 of Period 1. We then again multiply the stock price in period 1 by 105% to get the resulting value of \$22.05. In Period 2, the value of a call option when a stock price is \$22.05 is the stock price minus the exercise price, \$22.05 – \$20, or \$2.05. In Period 2, the value of a put option when a stock price is \$22.05 is the exercise price minus the stock price, \$20 – \$22.05, or −\$2.05. A negative value has no value to an investor so the value of the put option would be \$0.

The lowest possible value for our stock based on our assumptions is \$18.05. We get this value first by multiplying the stock price at period 0 by 95% (decreasing the value of the stock by 5%) to get the resulting value of \$19.0 of Period 1. We then again multiply the stock price in Period 1 by 95% to get the resulting value of \$18.05. In Period 2, the value of a call option when a stock price is \$18.05 is the stock price minus the exercise price, \$18.05 – \$20, or −\$1.95. A negative value has no value to an investor so the value of a call option would be \$0. In Period 2, the value of a put option when a stock price is \$18.05 is the exercise price minus the stock price, \$20 – \$18.05, or \$1.95. We can derive the call and put option value for the other possible value of the stock in Period 2 in the same fashion.

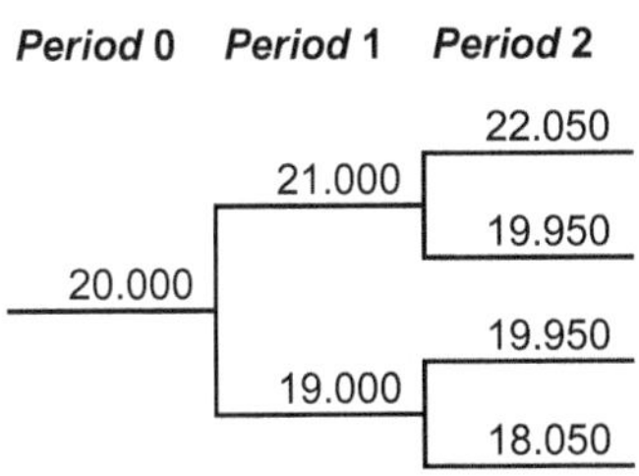

Figure 8.8 XYZ Company Stock Price

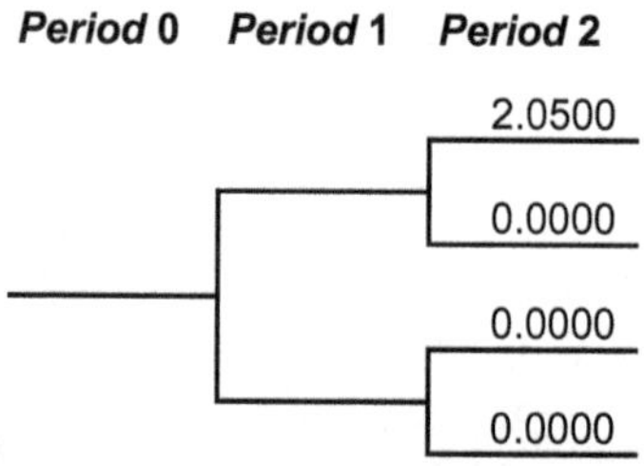

Figure 8.9 XYZ Company Call Option

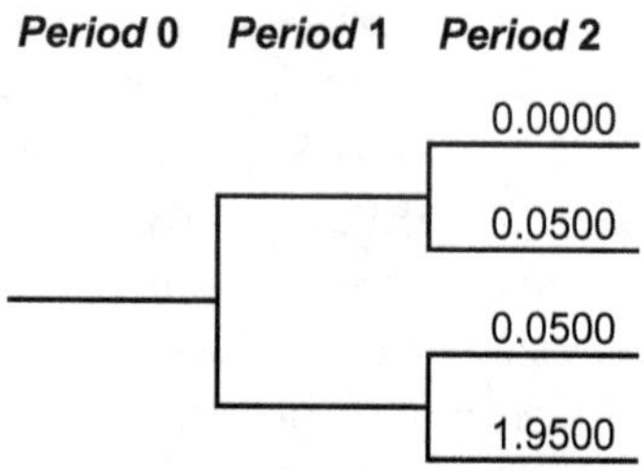

Figure 8.10 XYZ Company Put Option

Figures 8.9 and 8.10 show the possible call and put option values, respectively, for Period 2.

We cannot calculate the value of the call and put option in Period 1 the same way we did in Period 2 because it is not the ending value of the stock. In Period 1, there are two possible call values. One value is when the stock price increased and one value is when the stock price decreased. The call option Decision Tree shown in Figure 8.9 shows two possible values for a call option in Period 1. If we just focus on the value of a call option when the stock price increases from Period 1, we will note that it is like the Decision Tree for a call option for one period. This is shown in Figure 8.11.

Using the same method for pricing a call option for one period, the price of a call option when stock price increases from Period 0 will be \$1.5922. The resulting Decision Tree is shown in Figure 8.12.

In the same fashion, we can price the value of a call option when a stock price decreases. The price of a call option when a stock price decreases from period 0 is \$0. The resulting Decision Tree is shown in Figure 8.13.

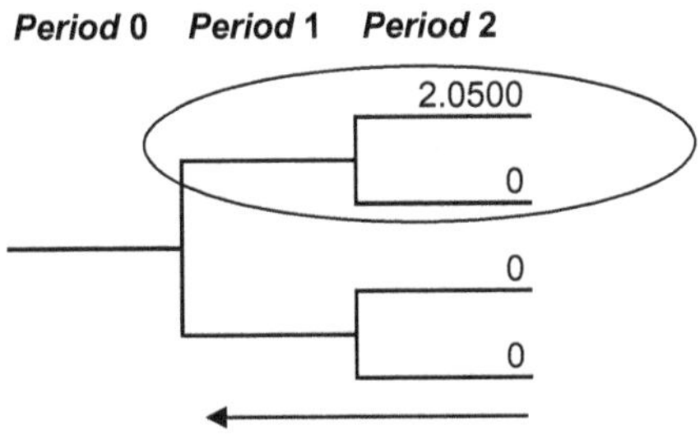

Figure 8.11 XYZ Company Call Option

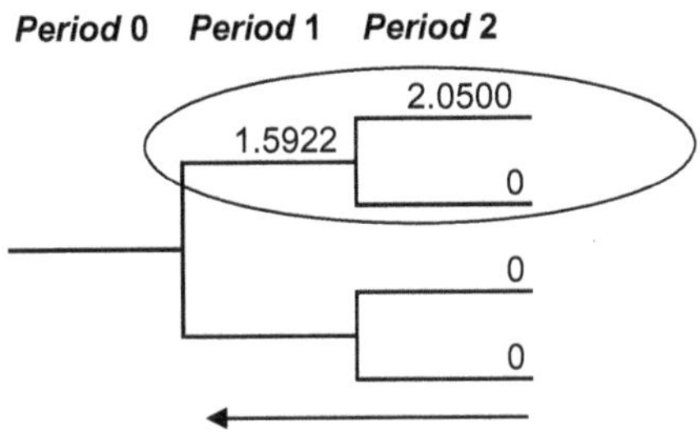

Figure 8.12 XYZ Company Call Option

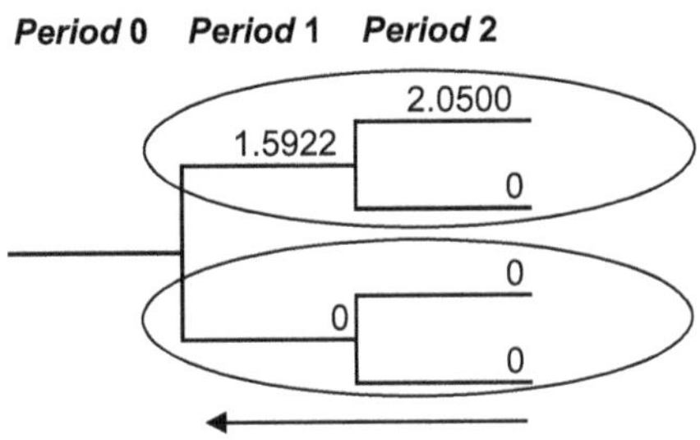

Figure 8.13 XYZ Company Call Option

In the same fashion, we can price the value of a call option in Period 0. The resulting Decision Tree is shown in Figure 8.14.

We can calculate the value of a put option in the same manner as we did while calculating the value of a call option. The Decision Tree for a put option is shown in Figure 8.15.

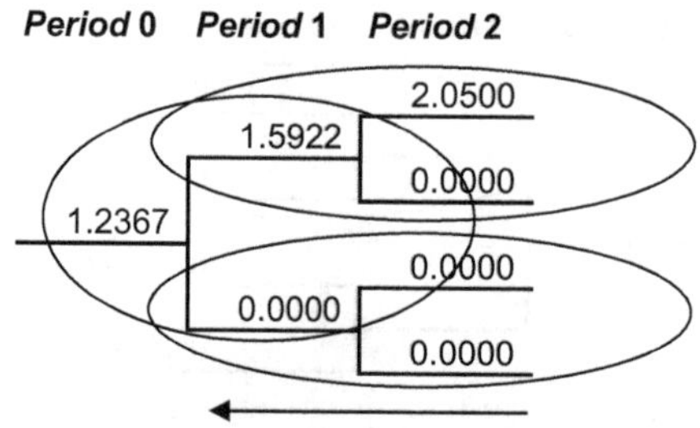

Figure 8.14 XYZ Company Call Option

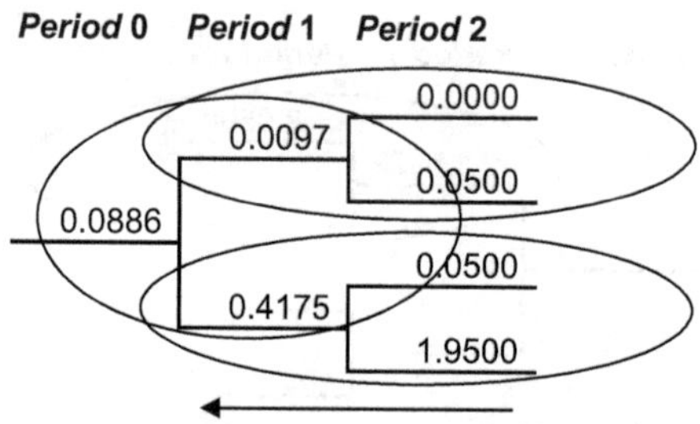

Figure 8.15 XYZ Company Put Option

8.5 Using Microsoft Excel to Create the Binomial Option Trees

In the previous section, we priced the value of a call and put option by pricing backward, from the last period to the first period. This method of pricing call and put options will work for any n-period. To price the value of a call option for two periods required seven sets of calculations. The number of calculations increases dramatically as n increases. Table 8.1 lists the number of calculations for a specific number of periods.

After two periods, it becomes very cumbersome to calculate and create the Decision Trees for a call and put option. In the previous section, we saw that calculations were very repetitive and mechanical. To solve this problem, this chapter will use Microsoft Excel to do the calculations and create the Decision Trees for the call and put options. We will also use Microsoft Excel to calculate and draw the related Decision Trees for the underlying stock and bond.

Table 8.1 Number of Calculations for a Specific Number of Periods

Periods	Calculations
1	3
2	7
3	17
4	31
5	63
6	127
7	255
8	511
9	1,023
10	2,047
11	4,065
12	8,191

To solve this repetitive and mechanical calculation of the Binomial OPM, we will look at a Microsoft Excel file called *binomialBS_OPM.xls*. We will use this Microsoft Excel workbook to produce four Decision Trees for the XYZ Company stock that was discussed in the previous sections. The four Decision Trees are as follows:

(1) Stock Price,
(2) Call Option Price,
(3) Put Option Price, and
(4) Bond Price.

This section will demonstrate how to use the *binomialBS_OPM.xls* Excel file to create the four Decision Trees. Figure 8.16 shows the Excel file *binomialBS_OPM.xls* after the file is opened. Pushing the button shown in Figure 8.16 will get the dialog box shown in Figure 8.17.

The dialog box shown in Figure 8.17 shows the parameters for the *Binomial OPM.* These parameters are changeable. The dialog box in Figure 8.17 shows the default values.

Pushing the *calculate* button shown in Figure 8.17 will produce the four Decision Trees shown in Figures 8.18–8.21.

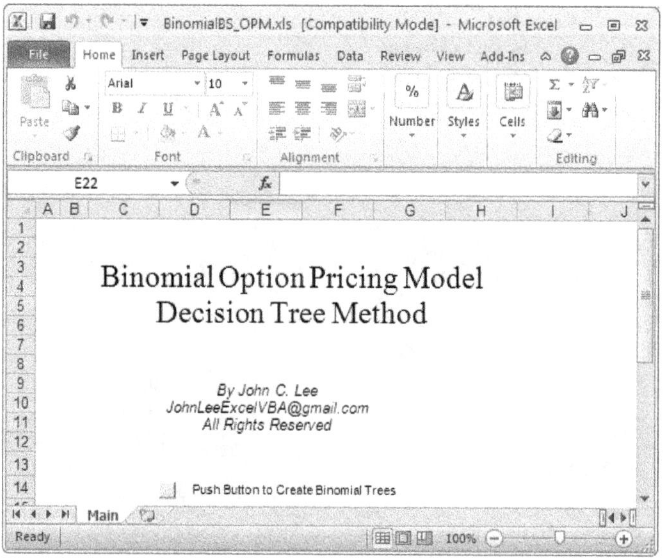

Figure 8.16 Excel File BinomialBS_OPM.xls

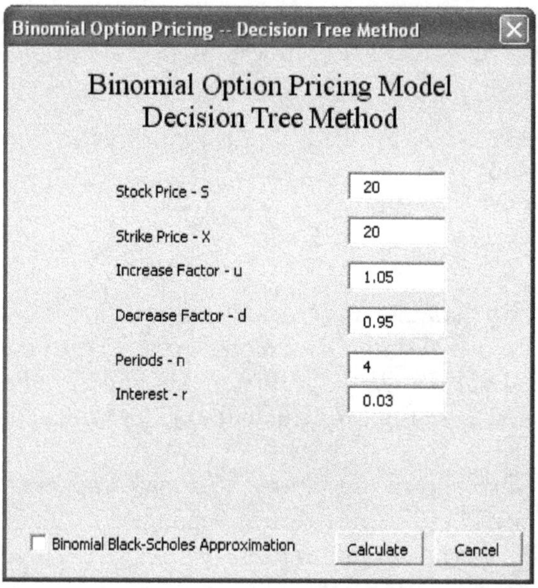

Figure 8.17 Dialog Box Showing Parameters for the Binomial OPM

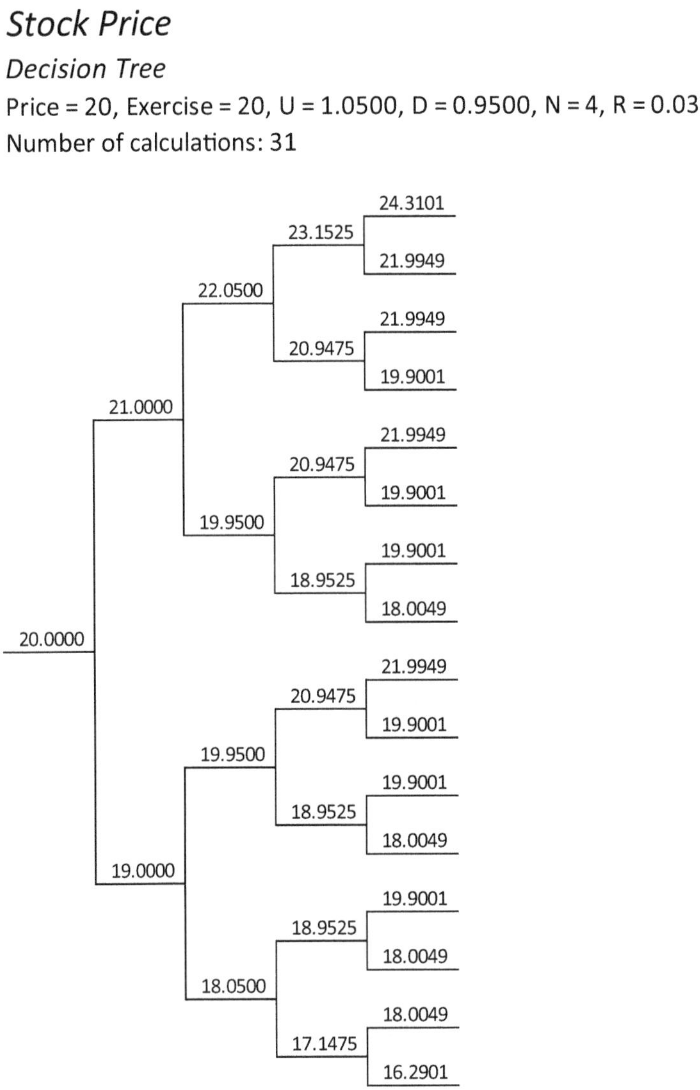

Figure 8.18 Stock Price Decision Tree

Table 8.1 indicated that 31 calculations were required to create a Decision Tree that has four periods. This section showed four Decision Trees. Therefore, the Excel file did $31 \times 4 = 121$ calculations to create the four Decision Trees.

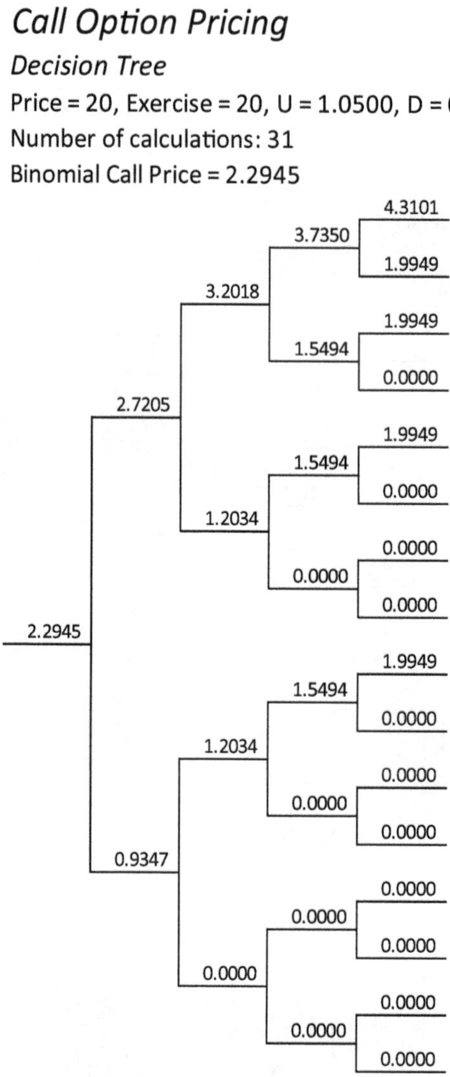

Figure 8.19 Call Option Pricing Decision Tree

Benninga (2000, p. 260) has defined the price of a call option in a Binomial OPM with n periods as

$$C = \sum_{i=0}^{n} \binom{n}{i} q_u^i q_d^{n-i} \max[S(u)^i(d)^{n-i}, 0], \tag{8.6}$$

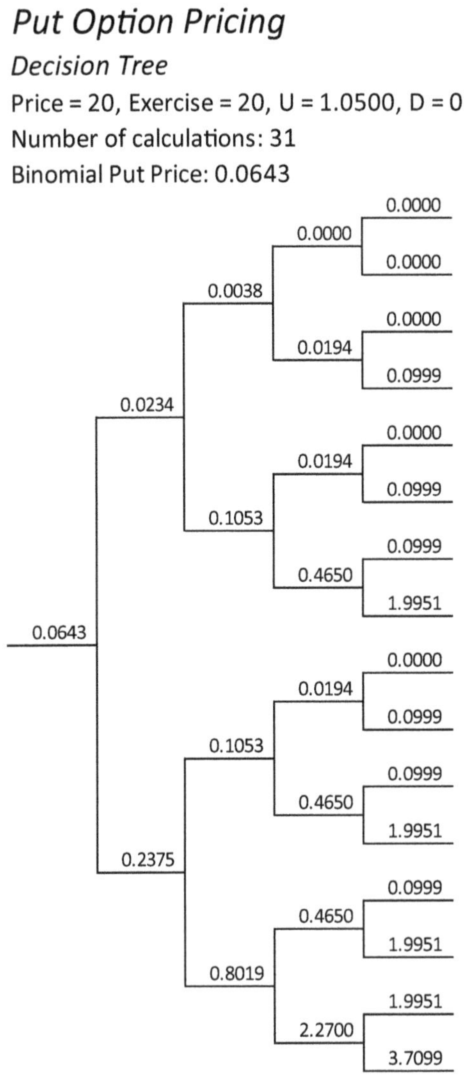

Figure 8.20 Put Option Pricing Decision Tree

and the price of a put option in a Binomial OPM with n-periods as

$$P = \sum_{i=0}^{n} \binom{n}{i} q_u^i q_d^{n-i} \max[X - S(u)^i (d)^{n-i}, 0]. \tag{8.7}$$

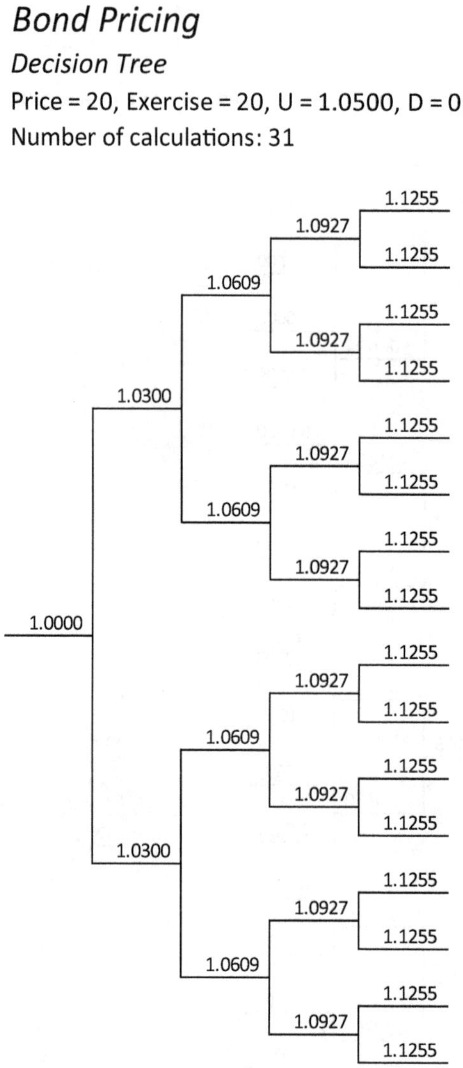

Figure 8.21 Bond Pricing Decision Tree

Lee *et al.* (2000, p. 237) have defined the pricing of a call option in a Binomial OPM with n-period as

$$C = \frac{1}{R^n}\sum_{k=0}^{n}\frac{n!}{k!(n-k!)}p^k(1-p)^{n-k}\max[0,(u)^k(d)^{n-k},S-X]. \quad (8.8)$$

The definition of the pricing of a put option in a Binomial OPM with n-period would then be defined as

$$P = \frac{1}{R^n} \sum_{k=0}^{n} \frac{n!}{k!(n-k)!} p^k (1-p)^{n-k} \max[0, X - (u)^k (d)^{n-k}, S]. \quad (8.9)$$

8.6 Black–Scholes Option Pricing Model

The most famous OPM is the Black–Scholes OPM. In this section, we will demonstrate the usage of the Black–Scholes OPM. In latter sections, we will demonstrate the relationship between the Binomial OPM and the Black–Scholes pricing model. The Black–Scholes model prices European call and put options. The Black–Scholes model for a European call option is

$$C = \mathrm{SN}(d_1) - X\mathrm{e}^{-rT} N(d_2), \quad (8.10)$$

where

C = Call price,
S = Stock price,
r = Risk-free interest rate,
T = Time to maturity of option in years,
$N(\cdot)$ = Standard normal distribution,
σ = Stock volatility.
$d1 = \frac{\ln(S/X) + \left(r + \frac{\sigma^2}{2}\right)T}{\sigma\sqrt{T}}$, and
$d2 = d1 - \sigma\sqrt{T}$.

Let us manually calculate the price of a European call option in terms of Equation (8.10) with the following parameter values: $S = 20$, $X = 20$, $r = 3\%$, $T = 4$, $\sigma = 20\%$.

Solution

$$d1 = \frac{\ln(S/X) + \left(r + \frac{\sigma^2}{2}\right)T}{\sigma\sqrt{T}} = \frac{\ln(30/30) + \left(.03 + .\frac{2^2}{2}\right)(4)}{.2\sqrt{4}}$$

$$= \frac{(.03 + .02) * 4}{.4} = \frac{.2}{.4} = .5,$$

$$d2 = .5 - .2\sqrt{4} = .1.$$

$$N(d_1) = 0.69146, \quad N(d_2) = 0.5398, \quad \mathrm{e}^{-rT} = 0.8869$$

$$C = (20) * (0.69146) - (20) * (0.8869) * 0.5398$$
$$= 13.8292 - 9.5749724 = 4.2542276.$$

The Black–Scholes put–call parity equation is

$$P = C - S + Xe^{-rT}.$$

The put option value for the stock would be

$$P = 4.25 - 20 + 20(0.8869)$$
$$= 4.25 - 20 + 17.738$$
$$= 1.988.$$

8.7 Relationship between the Binomial Option Pricing Model and the Black–Scholes Option Pricing Model

We can use either the Binomial model or Black–Scholes to price an option. They both should result in similar numbers. If we look at the parameters in both models, we will note that the Binomial model has an *Increase Factor* (u), a *Decrease Factor* (d), and n-period parameters that the Black–Scholes model does not have. We also note that the Black–Scholes model has the σ and T parameters that the Binomial model does not have. Benninga (2008) suggests the following translation between the Binomial and Black–Scholes parameters:

$$\Delta t = T/n \quad R = e^{r\Delta t} \quad U = e^{\sigma\sqrt{\Delta t}} \quad D = e^{-\sigma\sqrt{\Delta t}}.$$

In the Excel program, shown in Appendix 8A, we use Benniga's (2008) *Increase Factor* and *Decrease Factor* definitions. They are defined as follows:

$$q_u = \frac{R - d}{R(u - d)}, \quad q_d = \frac{u - R}{R(u - d)},$$

where $u =$ 1+ Percentage of price increase, $d =$ 1− Percentage of price increase, and $R =$ 1+ Interest rate.

8.8 Decision Tree Black–Scholes Calculation

We will now use the *BinomialBS_OPM.xls* Excel file to calculate the Binomial and Black–Scholes call and put values illustrated in Section 8.5. Note that in Figure 8.22 the *Binomial Black–Scholes Approximation* checkbox is checked. Checking this box will cause T and σ parameters to appear and will adjust the *Increase Factor — u and Decrease Factor — d* parameters. The adjustment was done as indicated in Section 8.7.

Notice in Figures 8.23 and 8.24 that the Binomial OPM value does not agree with the Black–Scholes OPM. The Binomial OPM value will get very close to the Black–Scholes OPM value once the Binomial parameter n gets very large. Benninga (2008) demonstrated that the Binomial value will be close to the Black–Scholes when the Binomial n parameter gets larger than 500.

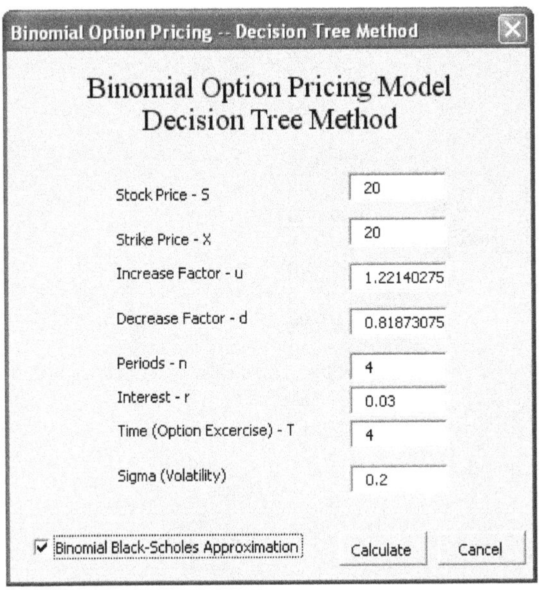

Figure 8.22 Dialog Box Showing Parameters for the Binomial OPM

Call Option Pricing

Decision Tree

Price = 20, Exercise = 20, U = 1.2214, D = 0.8187, N = 4, R = 0.03

Number of calculations: 31

Binomial Call Price = 4.0670

Black-Scholes Call Price = 4.2536, d1 = 0.5000, d2 = 0.1000, N(d1) = 0.6915, N(d2) = 0.5398

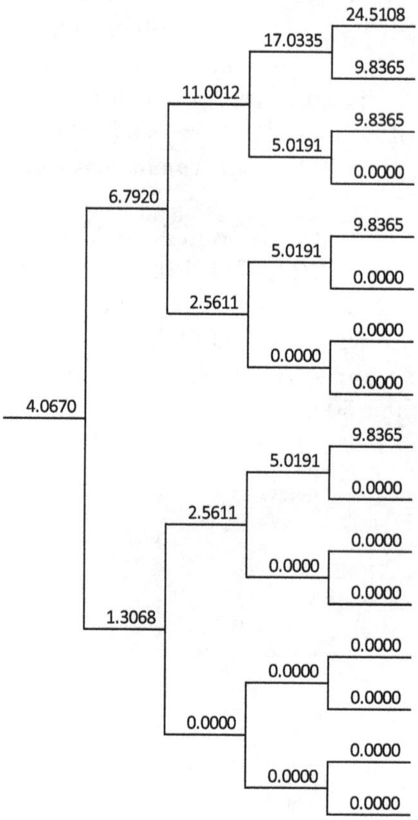

Figure 8.23 Decision Tree Approximation of Black–Scholes Call Pricing

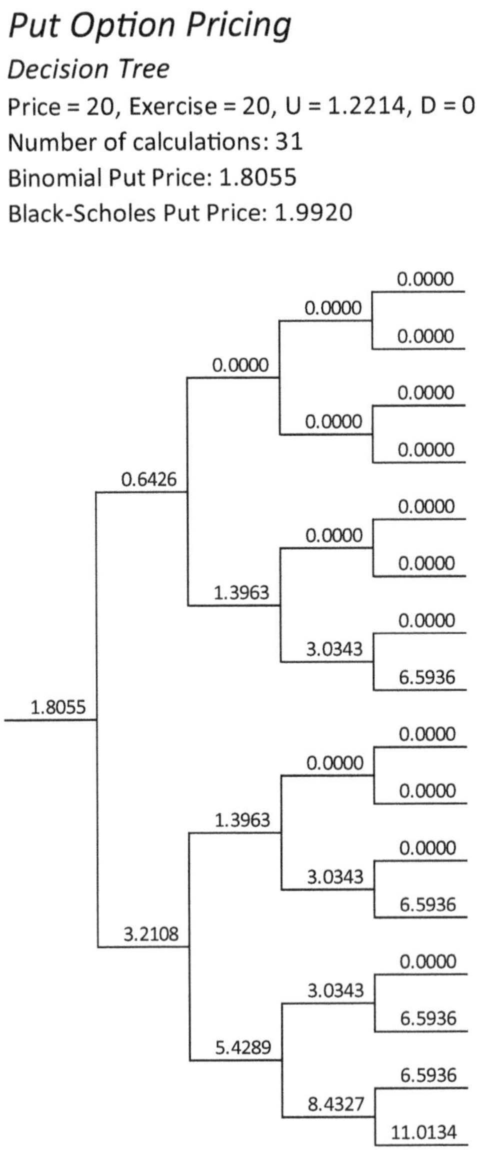

Figure 8.24 Decision Tree Approximation of Black–Scholes Put Pricing

8.9 Summary

This chapter demonstrated, with the aid of Microsoft Excel and Decision Trees, the Binomial Option model in a less mathematical fashion. This chapter allowed the reader to focus more on the concepts by studying the associated Decision Trees, which were created by Microsoft Excel. This chapter also demonstrated that using Microsoft Excel releases the reader from the computation burden of the Binomial Option Model.

This chapter also published the Microsoft Excel VBA code that created the Binomial Option Decision Trees. This is a good option for those who are interested in studying the many advanced Microsoft Excel VBA programming concepts that were used to create the Decision Trees. One major computer science programming concept used by the Excel VBA program in this chapter is recursive programming. Recursive programming is the ideal of a procedure calling itself many times. Inside the procedure, there are statements to decide when not to call itself.

This chapter also used Decision trees to demonstrate the relationship between the Binomial OPM and the Black–Scholes OPM.

Questions and Problems

1. What is the binomial distribution? What is cumulative density function of binomial distribution?
2. Please graphically and mathematically derive a binomial call option model when the time period (n) is 3.
3. What are the parameters used in the Binomial model? What are the parameters used in the Black–Scholes model? How are the parameters of the two models related?
4. Explain how to form a risk-free portfolio by purchasing H shares of the stock for each call option written. How to get the hedge ratio from this risk-free portfolio?
5. In Table 8.1, please graphically explain why there are seven calculations when the number of periods equals three.

6. You are given the following information about a stock:

   Stock Price $S = \$100$
   Strike Price $X = \$102$
   Increase Factor $u = 1.15$
   Decrease Factor $d = 0.90$
   Period (the number of months) $n = 5$
   Interest Rate (per month) $r = 0.005$
   Calculate the value of the call option if the stock goes up in three out of the five months.

7. If the parameters of Question 6 change as follows, please calculate the call option value again:

   (a) when $u = 1.20$
   (b) when $d = 0.85$
   (c) when $X = \$95$
   (d) when $S = \$110$

8. Answer Question 6 again, finding the value of the option if the stock goes up in two out of the five months.
9. Given the parameters in Question 6, calculate the value of the put option if the stock goes down in four out of the five months.

Bibliography

Benninga, S. (2008). *Financial Modeling.* Cambridge, MA: MIT Press.

Black, F. and M. Scholes (1973). The pricing of options and corporate liabilities. *Journal of Political Economy*, 31(May–June), 637–659.

Cox, J., S. A. Ross and M. Rubinstein (1979). Option pricing: A simplified approach. *Journal of Financial Economics*, 7, 229–263.

Daigler, R. T. (1994). *Financial Futures and Options Markets Concepts and Strategies.* New York, NY: Harper Collins.

Jarrow, R. and S. TurnBull (1996). *Derivative Securities.* Cincinnati, OH: South-Western College Publishing.

Lee, C. F. (2009). *Handbook of Quantitative Finance.* New York, NY: Springer.

Lee, C. F. (2020). Financial econometrics, mathematics, statistics, and financial technology: An overall view. *Review of Quantitative Finance and Accounting*, 54(4), 1529–1578.

Lee, J. C. (2001). Using Microsoft Excel and decision trees to demonstrate the binomial option pricing model. *Advances in Investment Analysis and Portfolio Management*, 8, 303–329.

Lee, C. F. and A. C. Lee (2006). *Encyclopedia of Finance.* New York, NY: Springer.

Lee, J. and C. F. Lee (2023). *Essentials of Excel VBA, Python, and R: Financial Statistics, Portfolio Analysis, and Financial Management.* New York: Springer Academic Publishers.

Lee, C. F., Y. Chen and J. Lee (2016). Alternative methods to derive option pricing models: Review and comparison. *Review of Quantitative Finance and Accounting*, 47(2), 417–451.

Lee, Cheng-Few, Chiung-Min Tsai, and Alice C. Lee (2013). Asset pricing with disequilibrium price adjustment: theory and empirical evidence. *Quantitative Finance*, 13(2), 227–239.

Lee, C. F., H.-Y. Chen and J. Lee (2019). *Financial Econometrics, Mathematics and Statistics.* New York: Springer Academic Publishers.

Lee, C. F., J. C. Lee and A. C. Lee (2000). *Statistics for Business and Financial Economics.* Singapore: World Scientific.

Lee, C. F., J. Lee and A. C. Lee (2013). *Statistics for Business and Financial Economics*, 3rd ed. New York: Springer Academic Publishers.

Lee, J. C., C. F. Lee, R. S. Wang and T. I. Lin (2004). On the limit properties of binomial and multinomial option pricing models: Review and integration, in *Advances in Quantitative Analysis of Finance and Accounting New Series*, Vol. 1. Singapore: World Scientific.

Lee, J., C. F. Lee, J. R. Chang and L.-J. Kao (2023). *Essentials of Excel VBA, Python, and R: Financial Derivatives, Risk Management and Machine Learning.* New York: Springer Academic Publishers.

Lo, A. W. and J. Wang (2000). Trading volume: Definition, data analysis, and implications of portfolio theory. *Review of Financial Studies*, 13, 257–300.

Rendleman Jr, R. J. and B. J. Barter (1979). Two-state option pricing. *Journal of Finance*, 34(5), 1093–1110.

Walkenbach, J. (2003). *Excel 2003 Power Programming with VBA.* Indianapolis, IN: Wiley Publishing, Inc.

Wells, E. and S. Harshbarger (1997). *Microsoft Excel 97 Developer's Handbook.* Redmond, WA: Microsoft Press.

Appendix 8A: Excel VBA Code — Binomial Option Pricing Model

It is important to note that the thing that makes Microsoft Excel powerful is that it offers a powerful professional programming language called VBA. This section shows the VBA code that generated the Decision Trees for the Binomial Option pricing model. This code is in the form *frmBinomiaOption.* The procedure *cmdCalculate_Click* is the first procedure to run.

```
'/*************************************************************************
'/          Relationship Between the Binomial OPM
'/          and Black-Scholes OPM:
'/          Decision Tree and Microsoft Excel Approach
'/
'/                 by John Lee
'/                 JohnLeeExcelVBA@gmail.com
'/                 All Rights Reserved
'/*************************************************************************
Option Explicit
Dim mwbTreeWorkbook As Workbook
Dim mwsTreeWorksheet As Worksheet
Dim mwsCallTree As Worksheet
Dim mwsPutTree As Worksheet
Dim mwsBondTree As Worksheet
Dim mdblPFactor As Double
Dim mBinomialCalc As Long
Dim mCallPrice As Double   'jcl 12/8/2008
Dim mPutPrice As Double   'jcl 12/8/2008

'/*************************************************
'/Purpose:  Keep track the numbers of binomial calc
'/*************************************************
Property Let BinomialCalc(l As Long)
   mBinomialCalc = l
End Property
Property Get BinomialCalc() As Long
   BinomialCalc = mBinomialCalc
End Property
Property Set TreeWorkbook(wb As Workbook)
   Set mwbTreeWorkbook = wb
End Property
Property Get TreeWorkbook() As Workbook
   Set TreeWorkbook = mwbTreeWorkbook
End Property
```

```
Property Set TreeWorksheet(ws As Worksheet)
    Set mwsTreeWorksheet = ws
End Property
Property Get TreeWorksheet() As Worksheet
    Set TreeWorksheet = mwsTreeWorksheet
End Property
Property Set CallTree(ws As Worksheet)
    Set mwsCallTree = ws
End Property
Property Get CallTree() As Worksheet
    Set CallTree = mwsCallTree
End Property
Property Set PutTree(ws As Worksheet)
    Set mwsPutTree = ws
End Property
Property Get PutTree() As Worksheet
    Set PutTree = mwsPutTree
End Property
Property Set BondTree(ws As Worksheet)
    Set mwsBondTree = ws
End Property
Property Get BondTree() As Worksheet
    Set BondTree = mwsBondTree
End Property
Property Let CallPrice(dCallPrice As Double)
    '12/8/2008
    mCallPrice = dCallPrice
End Property
Property Get CallPrice() As Double
    Let CallPrice = mCallPrice
End Property
Property Let PutPrice(dPutPrice As Double)
    '12/10/2008
    mPutPrice = dPutPrice
End Property
Property Get PutPrice() As Double
    '12/10/2008
    Let PutPrice = mPutPrice
End Property

Property Let PFactor(r As Double)
    Dim dRate As Double

    dRate = ((1 + r) - Me.txtBinomialD) / (Me.txtBinomialU - Me.txtBinomialD)

    Let mdblPFactor = dRate
End Property
Property Get PFactor() As Double
    Let PFactor = mdblPFactor
End Property

Property Get qU() As Double
    Dim dblDeltaT As Double
    Dim dblDown As Double
    Dim dblUp As Double
    Dim dblR As Double

    dblDeltaT = Me.txtTimeT / Me.txtBinomialN
    dblR = Exp(Me.txtBinomialr * dblDeltaT)
    dblUp = Exp(Me.txtSigma * VBA.Sqr(dblDeltaT))
    dblDown = Exp(-Me.txtSigma * VBA.Sqr(dblDeltaT))


    qU = (dblR - dblDown) / (dblR * (dblUp - dblDown))
End Property

Property Get qD() As Double

    Dim dblDeltaT As Double
    Dim dblDown As Double
    Dim dblUp As Double
```

```
    Dim dblR As Double

    dblDeltaT = Me.txtTimeT / Me.txtBinomialN
    dblR = Exp(Me.txtBinomialr * dblDeltaT)
    dblUp = Exp(Me.txtSigma * VBA.Sqr(dblDeltaT))
    dblDown = Exp(-Me.txtSigma * VBA.Sqr(dblDeltaT))

    qD = (dblUp - dblR) / (dblR * (dblUp - dblDown))
End Property


Private Sub chkBinomialBSApproximation_Click()
    On Error Resume Next
        'Time and Sigma only BlackScholes parameter
        Me.txtTimeT.Visible = Me.chkBinomialBSApproximation
        Me.lblTimeT.Visible = Me.chkBinomialBSApproximation
        Me.txtSigma.Visible = Me.chkBinomialBSApproximation
        Me.lblSigma.Visible = Me.chkBinomialBSApproximation
        txtTimeT_Change

End Sub

Private Sub cmdCalculate_Click()
    Me.Hide
    BinomialOption
    Unload Me
End Sub

Private Sub cmdCancel_Click()
    Unload Me
End Sub


Private Sub txtBinomialN_Change()
    'jcl 12/8/2008
    On Error Resume Next
    If Me.chkBinomialBSApproximation Then
        Me.txtBinomialU = Exp(Me.txtSigma * Sqr(Me.txtTimeT / Me.txtBinomialN))
        Me.txtBinomialD = Exp(-Me.txtSigma * Sqr(Me.txtTimeT / Me.txtBinomialN))
    End If
End Sub



Private Sub txtTimeT_Change()

    'jcl 12/8/2008
    On Error Resume Next
    If Me.chkBinomialBSApproximation Then
        Me.txtBinomialU = Exp(Me.txtSigma * Sqr(Me.txtTimeT / Me.txtBinomialN))
        Me.txtBinomialD = Exp(-Me.txtSigma * Sqr(Me.txtTimeT / Me.txtBinomialN))
    End If
End Sub

Private Sub UserForm_Initialize()


    With Me

        .txtBinomialS = 20
        .txtBinomialX = 20
        .txtBinomialD = 0.95
        .txtBinomialU = 1.05
        .txtBinomialN = 4
        .txtBinomialr = 0.03
        .txtSigma = 0.2
        .txtTimeT = 4


        Me.chkBinomialBSApproximation = False
    End With
```

```
    chkBinomialBSApproximation_Click
    Me.Hide
End Sub

Sub BinomialOption()
    Dim wbTree As Workbook
    Dim wsTree As Worksheet
    Dim rColumn As Range
    Dim ws As Worksheet

    Set Me.TreeWorkbook = Workbooks.Add
    Set Me.BondTree = Me.TreeWorkbook.Worksheets.Add
    Set Me.PutTree = Me.TreeWorkbook.Worksheets.Add
    Set Me.CallTree = Me.TreeWorkbook.Worksheets.Add
    Set Me.TreeWorksheet = Me.TreeWorkbook.Worksheets.Add

    Set rColumn = Me.TreeWorksheet.Range("a1")

    With Me
        .BinomialCalc = 0
        .PFactor = Me.txtBinomialr
        .CallTree.Name = "Call Option Price"
        .PutTree.Name = "Put Option Price"
        .TreeWorksheet.Name = "Stock Price"
        .BondTree.Name = "Bond"
    End With

    DecisionTree rCell:=rColumn, nPeriod:=Me.txtBinomialN + 1, _
             dblPrice:=Me.txtBinomialS, sngU:=Me.txtBinomialU, _
             sngD:=Me.txtBinomialD

    DecitionTreeFormat
    TreeTitle wsTree:=Me.TreeWorksheet, sTitle:="Stock Price "
    TreeTitle wsTree:=Me.CallTree, sTitle:="Call Option Pricing"
    TreeTitle wsTree:=Me.PutTree, sTitle:="Put Option Pricing"
    TreeTitle wsTree:=Me.BondTree, sTitle:="Bond Pricing"

    Application.DisplayAlerts = False
    For Each ws In Me.TreeWorkbook.Worksheets
        If Left(ws.Name, 5) = "Sheet" Then
            ws.Delete
        Else
            ws.Activate
            ActiveWindow.DisplayGridlines = False
            ws.UsedRange.NumberFormat = "#,##0.0000_);(#,##0.0000)"
        End If
    Next
    Application.DisplayAlerts = True
    Me.TreeWorksheet.Activate
End Sub
Sub TreeTitle(wsTree As Worksheet, sTitle As String)
    wsTree.Range("A1:A5").EntireRow.Insert (xlShiftDown)
    With wsTree
        With .Cells(1)
             .Value = sTitle
             .Font.Size = 20
             .Font.Italic = True
        End With
        With .Cells(2, 1)
            .Value = "Decision Tree"
            .Font.Size = 16
            .Font.Italic = True
        End With
        With .Cells(3, 1)
            .Value = "Price = " & Me.txtBinomialS & _
                  ",Exercise = " & Me.txtBinomialX & _
                  ",U = " & Format(Me.txtBinomialU, "#,##0.0000") & _
                  ",D = " & Format(Me.txtBinomialD, "#,##0.0000") & _
                  ",N = " & Me.txtBinomialN & _
                  ",R = " & Me.txtBinomialr
```

```
            .Font.Size = 14
        End With
        With .Cells(4, 1)
            .Value = "Number of calculations: " & Me.BinomialCalc
            .Font.Size = 14
        End With


        If wsTree Is Me.CallTree Then
            With .Cells(5, 1)
                .Value = "Binomial Call Price= " & Format(Me.CallPrice, "#,##0.0000")
                .Font.Size = 14
            End With

          If Me.chkBinomialBSApproximation Then
            wsTree.Range("A6:A7").EntireRow.Insert (xlShiftDown)

            With .Cells(6, 1)
                .Value = "Black-Scholes Call Price= " & Format(Me.BS_Call, "#,##0.0000") _
                        & ",d1=" & Format(Me.BS_D1, "#,##0.0000") _
                        & ",d2=" & Format(Me.BS_D2, "#,##0.0000") _
                        & ",N(d1)=" & Format(WorksheetFunction.NormSDist(BS_D1), "#,##0.0000")
_
                        & ",N(d2)=" & Format(WorksheetFunction.NormSDist(BS_D2), "#,##0.0000")
                .Font.Size = 14
            End With
           End If
        ElseIf wsTree Is Me.PutTree Then
            With .Cells(5, 1)
                .Value = "Binomial Put Price: " & Format(Me.PutPrice, "#,##0.0000")
                .Font.Size = 14
            End With
           If Me.chkBinomialBSApproximation Then
            wsTree.Range("A6:A7").EntireRow.Insert (xlShiftDown)

            With .Cells(6, 1)
                .Value = "Black-Scholes Put Price: " & Format(Me.BS_PUT, "#,##0.0000")
                .Font.Size = 14
            End With
           End If
        End If

    End With
End Sub
Sub BondDecisionTree(rPrice As Range, arCell As Variant, iCount As Long)
    Dim rBond As Range
    Dim rPup As Range
    Dim rPDown As Range

    Set rBond = Me.BondTree.Cells(rPrice.Row, rPrice.Column)
    Set rPup = Me.BondTree.Cells(arCell(iCount - 1).Row, arCell(iCount - 1).Column)
    Set rPDown = Me.BondTree.Cells(arCell(iCount).Row, arCell(iCount).Column)

    If rPup.Column = Me.TreeWorksheet.UsedRange.Columns.Count Then
        rPup.Value = (1 + Me.txtBinomialr) ^ (rPup.Column - 1)
        rPDown.Value = rPup.Value
    End If

    With rBond
        .Value = (1 + Me.txtBinomialr) ^ (rBond.Column - 1)
        .Borders(xlBottom).LineStyle = xlContinuous
    End With
        rPDown.Borders(xlBottom).LineStyle = xlContinuous
        With rPup
            .Borders(xlBottom).LineStyle = xlContinuous
            .Offset(1, 0).Resize((rPDown.Row - rPup.Row), 1). _
                Borders(xlEdgeLeft).LineStyle = xlContinuous
        End With

End Sub
```

```
Sub PutDecisionTree(rPrice As Range, arCell As Variant, iCount As Long)
    Dim rCall As Range
    Dim rPup As Range
    Dim rPDown As Range

    Set rCall = Me.PutTree.Cells(rPrice.Row, rPrice.Column)
    Set rPup = Me.PutTree.Cells(arCell(iCount - 1).Row, arCell(iCount - 1).Column)
    Set rPDown = Me.PutTree.Cells(arCell(iCount).Row, arCell(iCount).Column)

    If rPup.Column = Me.TreeWorksheet.UsedRange.Columns.Count Then
        rPup.Value = WorksheetFunction.Max(Me.txtBinomialX - arCell(iCount - 1), 0)
        rPDown.Value = WorksheetFunction.Max(Me.txtBinomialX - arCell(iCount), 0)
    End If

    With rCall

            '12/10/2008
            If Not Me.chkBinomialBSApproximation Then
                .Value = (Me.PFactor * rPup + (1 - Me.PFactor) * rPDown) / (1 + Me.txtBinomialr)
            Else
                .Value = (Me.qU * rPup) + (Me.qD * rPDown)
            End If

             Me.PutPrice = .Value  '12/8/2008

            .Borders(xlBottom).LineStyle = xlContinuous
    End With

    rPDown.Borders(xlBottom).LineStyle = xlContinuous
    With rPup
        .Borders(xlBottom).LineStyle = xlContinuous
        .Offset(1, 0).Resize((rPDown.Row - rPup.Row), 1). _
        Borders(xlEdgeLeft).LineStyle = xlContinuous
    End With

End Sub
Sub CallDecisionTree(rPrice As Range, arCell As Variant, iCount As Long)
    Dim rCall As Range
    Dim rCup As Range
    Dim rCDown As Range

    Set rCall = Me.CallTree.Cells(rPrice.Row, rPrice.Column)
    Set rCup = Me.CallTree.Cells(arCell(iCount - 1).Row, arCell(iCount - 1).Column)
    Set rCDown = Me.CallTree.Cells(arCell(iCount).Row, arCell(iCount).Column)

    If rCup.Column = Me.TreeWorksheet.UsedRange.Columns.Count Then
        With rCup
            .Value = WorksheetFunction.Max(arCell(iCount - 1) - Me.txtBinomialX, 0)
            .Borders(xlBottom).LineStyle = xlContinuous
        End With
        With rCDown
                .Value = WorksheetFunction.Max(arCell(iCount) - Me.txtBinomialX, 0)
                .Borders(xlBottom).LineStyle = xlContinuous
        End With
    End If

    With rCall

        If Not Me.chkBinomialBSApproximation Then
            .Value = (Me.PFactor * rCup + (1 - Me.PFactor) * rCDown) / (1 + Me.txtBinomialr)
        Else
            .Value = (Me.qU * rCup) + (Me.qD * rCDown)
        End If

        Me.CallPrice = .Value  '12/8/2008

        .Borders(xlBottom).LineStyle = xlContinuous
    End With

    rCup.Offset(1, 0).Resize((rCDown.Row - rCup.Row), 1). _
```

```
                Borders(xlEdgeLeft).LineStyle = xlContinuous

End Sub

Sub DecitionTreeFormat()
   Dim rTree As Range
   Dim nColumns As Integer
   Dim rLast As Range
   Dim rCell As Range
   Dim lCount As Long
   Dim lCellSize As Long
   Dim vntColumn As Variant
   Dim iCount As Long
   Dim lTimes As Long
   Dim arCell() As Range
   Dim sFormatColumn As String
   Dim rPrice As Range


   Application.StatusBar = "Formatting Tree.. "
   Set rTree = Me.TreeWorksheet.UsedRange
   nColumns = rTree.Columns.Count


   Set rLast = rTree.Columns(nColumns).EntireColumn.SpecialCells(xlCellTypeConstants, 23)
   lCellSize = rLast.Cells.Count
   For lCount = nColumns To 2 Step -1
      sFormatColumn = rLast.Parent.Columns(lCount).EntireColumn.Address
      Application.StatusBar = "Formatting column " & sFormatColumn
      ReDim vntColumn(1 To (rLast.Cells.Count / 2), 1)

      Application.StatusBar = "Assigning values to array for column " & _
         rLast.Parent.Columns(lCount).EntireColumn.Address
      vntColumn = rLast.Offset(0, -1).EntireColumn.Cells(1).Resize(rLast.Cells.Count / 2,1)
      rLast.Offset(0, -1).EntireColumn.ClearContents

      ReDim arCell(1 To rLast.Cells.Count)
      lTimes = 1
      Application.StatusBar = "Assigning cells to arrays. Total number of cells: "&lCellSize
      For Each rCell In rLast.Cells
         Application.StatusBar = "Array to column " & sFormatColumn & " Cells " & rCell.Row
         Set arCell(lTimes) = rCell
         lTimes = lTimes + 1
      Next

      lTimes = 1

      Application.StatusBar = "Formatting leaves for column " & sFormatColumn
      For iCount = 2 To lCellSize Step 2

         Application.StatusBar = "Formatting leaves for cell " & arCell(iCount).Address
         If rLast.Cells.Count <> 2 Then
            Set rPrice = arCell(iCount).Offset(-1 * ((arCell(iCount).Row - arCell(iCount-
              1).Row) / 2), -1)
            rPrice.Value = vntColumn(lTimes, 1)
         Else
            Set rPrice = arCell(iCount).Offset(-1 * ((arCell(iCount).Row - arCell(iCount-
              1).Row) / 2), -1)
            rPrice.Value = vntColumn
         End If


         arCell(iCount).Borders(xlBottom).LineStyle = xlContinuous
         With arCell(iCount - 1)
            .Borders(xlBottom).LineStyle = xlContinuous
            .Offset(1, 0).Resize((arCell(iCount).Row - arCell(iCount - 1).Row), 1). _
               Borders(xlEdgeLeft).LineStyle = xlContinuous
         End With
         lTimes = 1 + lTimes
```

```
            CallDecisionTree rPrice:=rPrice, arCell:=arCell, iCount:=iCount
            PutDecisionTree rPrice:=rPrice, arCell:=arCell, iCount:=iCount
            BondDecisionTree rPrice:=rPrice, arCell:=arCell, iCount:=iCount
        Next

        Set rLast = rTree.Columns(lCount - 1).EntireColumn.SpecialCells(xlCellTypeConstants,
23)
        lCellSize = rLast.Cells.Count
    Next ' / outer next

    rLast.Borders(xlBottom).LineStyle = xlContinuous
    Application.StatusBar = False
End Sub

'/*****************************************************************
'/Purpse: To calculate the price value of every state of the binomial
'/       decision tree
'/*****************************************************************
Sub DecisionTree(rCell As Range, nPeriod As Integer, _
            dblPrice As Double, sngU As Single, sngD As Single)
    Dim lIteminColumn As Long

    If Not nPeriod = 1 Then
        'Do Up
        DecisionTree rCell:=rCell.Offset(0, 1), nPeriod:=nPeriod - 1, _
                dblPrice:=dblPrice * sngU, sngU:=sngU, _
                sngD:=sngD
        'Do Down
        DecisionTree rCell:=rCell.Offset(0, 1), nPeriod:=nPeriod - 1, _
                dblPrice:=dblPrice * sngD, sngU:=sngU, _
                sngD:=sngD
    End If


    lIteminColumn = WorksheetFunction.CountA(rCell.EntireColumn)


    If lIteminColumn = 0 Then
        rCell = dblPrice

    Else
        If nPeriod <> 1 Then
            rCell.EntireColumn.Cells(lIteminColumn + 1) = dblPrice
        Else
            rCell.EntireColumn.Cells(((lIteminColumn + 1) * 2) - 1) = dblPrice
            Application.StatusBar = "The number of binomial calcs are : " & Me.BinomialCalc-

            & " at cell " & rCell.EntireColumn.Cells(((lIteminColumn + 1) * 2) - 1).Address
        End If

    End If
    Me.BinomialCalc = Me.BinomialCalc + 1

End Sub
Function BS_D1() As Double
    Dim dblNumerator As Double
    Dim dblDenominator As Double

    On Error Resume Next
    dblNumerator = VBA.Log(Me.txtBinomialS / Me.txtBinomialX) + _
            ((Me.txtBinomialr + Me.txtSigma ^ 2 / 2) * Me.txtTimeT)
    dblDenominator = Me.txtSigma * Sqr(Me.txtTimeT)


    BS_D1 = dblNumerator / dblDenominator

End Function
Function BS_D2() As Double

    On Error Resume Next
```

```
   BS_D2 = BS_D1 - (Me.txtSigma * VBA.Sqr(Me.txtTimeT))

End Function
Function BS_Call() As Double

   BS_Call = (Me.txtBinomialS * WorksheetFunction.NormSDist(BS_D1)) _
          - Me.txtBinomialX * Exp(-Me.txtBinomialr * Me.txtTimeT) * _
          WorksheetFunction.NormSDist(BS_D2)

End Function
'Used put-call parity theorem to price put option
Function BS_PUT() As Double

   BS_PUT = BS_Call - Me.txtBinomialS + _
          (Me.txtBinomialX * Exp(-Me.txtBinomialr * Me.txtTimeT))
End Function
```

Chapter 9

Normal, Log-Normal Distribution, and Option Pricing Model

Contents

9.1 Introduction

The normal (or Gaussian) distribution is the most important distribution in probability and statistics. One of the justifications for using the normal distribution is the central limit theorem. Also, most of the statistical theory is based on the normality assumption. However, in finance research, the log-normal distribution plays an important role. Part of the reason is the fact that in finance, we are dealing with random quantities which are positive in nature. Hence, taking the natural logarithm is quite reasonable. Also, empirical data often support the assumption of log-normality for a random quantity such as the stock price movements.

In Sections 9.1 and 9.2, we discuss the normal distribution and the log-normal distribution, respectively. Section 9.3 explains the relationship between the log-normal distribution and the normal distribution. In Section 9.4, the multivariate normal and log-normal distributions are introduced. Section 9.5 applies the normal distribution to the binomial distribution. Section 9.6 covers the applications of the log-normal distribution in option pricing. Section 9.7 introduces the bivariate normal distribution. In Section 9.8, we price the American call options by the bivariate normal distribution and illustrate the calculation process by giving an example. In Section 9.9, we derive the price bounds of options written on the stocks with or without dividends. In Section 9.10, we summarize and conclude our findings from the previous sections.

9.2 The Normal Distribution

A random variable X is said to be normally distributed with mean μ and variance σ^2 if it has the probability density function (PDF)

$$f(x) = \frac{1}{\sqrt{2\pi}\sigma} e^{-\frac{1}{2}\left(\frac{x-\mu}{\sigma}\right)^2}, \ \sigma > 0. \tag{9.1}$$

The normal distribution is symmetric around μ, which is the mean and the mode of the distribution. It is easy to see that the PDF of $Z = \frac{X-\mu}{\sigma}$ is

$$g(z) = \frac{1}{\sqrt{2\pi}} e^{-\frac{z^2}{2}}, \tag{9.2}$$

which is the PDF of the standard normal and is independent of the parameters μ and σ^2.

The cumulative distribution function (CDF) of Z is

$$P(Z \leq z) = N(z), \tag{9.3}$$

which has been well tabulated. Also, a software package or system such S-plus will provide the value $N(z)$ instantly. For a discussion of some approximations for $N(z)$, the reader is referred to Johnson and Kotz (1972).

$$P(X \leq x) = P\left(\frac{X-\mu}{\sigma} \leq \frac{x-\mu}{\sigma}\right) = N\left(\frac{x-\mu}{\sigma}\right). \tag{9.4}$$

The normal distribution as given in Equation (9.1) is very important in practice. It is very useful in describing phenomena such as the scores of tests and heights of students in a certain school. It is useful in serving as an approximation for binomial distribution. It is also quite useful in studying option pricing.

Next, we discuss some properties of the normal distribution. If X is normally distributed with mean μ and variance σ^2, then the Moment Generating Function (MGF) of X is

$$M_x(t) = e^{\mu t + t^2\sigma^2/2}, \tag{9.5}$$

which is useful in deriving the moment of X. Equation (9.5) is also useful in deriving the moments of the log-normal distribution. From Equation (9.5), it is easy to verify that

$$E(X) = \mu \quad \text{and} \quad Var(X) = \sigma^2.$$

If $X_1, \ldots, X_n$ are independent, normally distributed random variables, then any linear function of these variables is also normally distributed. In fact, if X_i is normally distributed with mean μ_i and variance σ_i^2, then $\sum_{i=1}^n a_i X_i$ is normally distributed with mean $\sum_{i=1}^n a_i \mu_i$ and variance $\sum_{i=1}^n a_i^2 \sigma_i^2$, when $a_i's$ are constants. If X_1 and X_2 are independent, and each is normally distributed with mean 0 and variance σ^2, then $(X_1^2 - X_2^2)/(X_1^2 + X_2^2)$ is also normally distributed.

9.3 The Log-Normal Distribution

A random variable X is said to be log-normally distributed with parameters μ and σ^2 if

$$Y = \log X, \tag{9.6}$$

is normally distributed with mean μ and variance σ^2. It is clear that X has to be a positive random variable. This distribution is quite useful in studying the behavior of stock prices.

For the log-normal distribution as described above, the PDF is

$$g(x) = \frac{1}{\sqrt{2\pi}\sigma x} e^{-\frac{1}{2\sigma^2}(\log x - \mu)^2}, \quad x > 0. \tag{9.7}$$

The log-normal distribution is sometimes called the antilog-normal distribution, because it is the distribution of the random variable X which is the antilog of the normal random variable Y. However, "log-normal" is most used in literature. When applied to economic data, especially production function, it is often called the Cobb–Douglas distribution.

Next, we discuss some properties of the log-normal distribution, as defined in Equation (9.6). The rth moment of X is

$$\mu'_r = E(X^r) = E(e^{rY}) = e^{\mu r + \frac{r^2\sigma^2}{2}}. \tag{9.8}$$

It is noted that we have utilized the fact the MGF of the normal random variable Y with mean μ and variance σ^2 is $M_Y(t) = e^{\mu t + \frac{t^2\sigma^2}{2}}$. Thus, $E(e^{rY})$ is simply $M_Y(r)$, which is the right-hand side of Equation (9.8). From Equation (9.8), we have

$$E(X) = e^{\mu + \frac{\sigma^2}{2}}, \tag{9.9}$$

$$Var(X) = e^{2\mu} e^{\sigma^2} [e^{\sigma^2} - 1]. \tag{9.10}$$

It is noted that the moment sequence $\{\mu'_r\}$ does not belong only to log-normal distribution. Thus, the log-normal distribution cannot be defined by its moments.

The CDF of X is

$$P(X \leq x) = P(\log X \leq \log x) = N\left(\frac{\log x - \mu}{\sigma}\right), \tag{9.11}$$

because $\log X$ is normally distributed with mean μ and variance σ^2.

The distribution of X is unimodal with the mode at

$$\text{mode}(X) = e^{(\mu-\sigma^2)}. \tag{9.12}$$

Let x_α be the (100)α percentile for the log-normal distribution and z_α be the corresponding percentile for the standard normal, then

$$P(X \le x_\alpha) = P\left(\frac{\log X - \mu}{\sigma} \le \frac{\log x_\alpha - \mu}{\sigma}\right) = N\left(\frac{\log x_\alpha - \mu}{\sigma}\right). \tag{9.13}$$

Thus, $z_\alpha = \frac{\log x_\alpha - \mu}{\sigma}$, implying that

$$x_\alpha = e^{\mu+\sigma z_\alpha}. \tag{9.14}$$

Thus, the percentile of the log-normal distribution can be obtained from the percentile of the standard normal.

From Equation (9.13), we also see that

$$median(X) = e^{\mu}, \tag{9.15}$$

as $z_{0.5} = 0$. Thus, $median(X) > \text{mod}\, e(X)$. Hence, the log-normal distribution is not symmetric.

9.4 The Log-Normal Distribution and Its Relationship to the Normal Distribution

By comparing the PDF of normal distribution given in Equation (9.1) and the PDF of log-normal distribution given in Equation (9.7), we know that

$$f(x) = \frac{f(y)}{x}. \tag{9.16}$$

In addition, from Equation (9.6), it is easy to see that

$$dx = xdy. \tag{9.17}$$

The CDF for the log-normal distribution can be expressed as

$$\begin{aligned} F(a) &= \Pr(X \le a) = \Pr(\log X \le \log a) \\ &= \Pr\left(\frac{\log X - \mu}{\sigma} \le \frac{\log a - \mu}{\sigma}\right) \\ &= N(d) \end{aligned} \tag{9.18}$$

where

$$d = \frac{\log a - \mu}{\sigma}, \tag{9.19}$$

and $N(d)$ is the CDF of the standard normal distribution which can be obtained from the Normal Table; $N(d)$ can also be obtained from S-plus or other software packages. Alternatively, the value of $N(d)$ can be approximated by the following formula:

$$N(d) = a_0 e^{-\frac{d^2}{2}}(a_1 t + a_2 t^2 + a_3 t^3), \tag{9.20}$$

where

$$t = \frac{1}{1 + 0.33267d}$$
$$a_0 = 0.3989423, \ a_1 = 0.4361936, \ a_2 = -0.1201676, \ a_3 = 0.9372980.$$

In case we need $\Pr(X > a)$, then we have

$$\Pr(X > a) = 1 - \Pr(X \leq a) = 1 - N(d) = N(-d). \tag{9.21}$$

for any h, $E(X^h) = E(e^{hY})$, the hth moment of X, the following MGF of Y, which is normally distributed with mean μ and variance σ^2,

$$M_Y(t) = e^{\mu t + \frac{1}{2}t^2\sigma^2}. \tag{9.22}$$

For example,

$$\mu_X = E(X) = E(e^Y) = M_Y(1) = e^{\mu + \frac{1}{2}t^2\sigma^2},$$
$$E(X^h) = E(e^{hY}) = M_Y(h) = e^{\mu h + \frac{1}{2}t^2\sigma^2}. \tag{9.23}$$

Hence,

$$\begin{aligned} \sigma_X^2 &= E(X^2) - (EX)^2 = e^{2\mu + 2\sigma^2} - e^{2\mu + \sigma^2} \\ &= e^{2\mu + \sigma^2}(e^{\sigma^2} - 1). \end{aligned} \tag{9.24}$$

Thus, the fractional and negative moment of a log-normal distribution can be obtained from Equation (9.23).

The mean of a log-normal random variable can be defined as

$$\int_0^{\infty} xf(x)dx = e^{\mu+\frac{\sigma^2}{2}}. \tag{9.25}$$

If the lower bound a is larger than 0, then the partial mean of x can be shown as

$$\int_0^{\infty} xf(x)dx = \int_{\log(a)}^{\infty} f(y)e^y dy = e^{\mu+\frac{\sigma^2}{2}} N(d), \tag{9.26}$$

where

$$d = \frac{\mu - \log(a)}{\sigma} + \sigma.$$

This implies that the partial mean of a log-normal variable is the mean of x times an adjustment term, $N(d)$.

9.5 Multivariate Normal and Log-Normal Distributions

The normal distribution with the PDF given in Equation (9.1) can be extended to the p-dimensional case. Let $\boldsymbol{X} = (X_1, \ldots, X_p)'$ be a $p \times 1$ random vector. Then, we say that $\boldsymbol{X} \sim N_p(\boldsymbol{\mu}, \Sigma)$, if it has the PDF

$$f(\boldsymbol{x}) = (2\pi)^{-p/2} |\,\Sigma\,|^{-1/2} \exp\left[-\frac{1}{2}(\boldsymbol{x} - \boldsymbol{\mu})'\,\Sigma^{-1}(\boldsymbol{x} - \boldsymbol{\mu})\right]. \tag{9.27}$$

In Equation (9.27), $\boldsymbol{\mu}$ is the mean vector and Σ is the covariance matrix which is symmetric and positive definite. The moment-generating function of $\boldsymbol{X}$ is

$$M_x(t) = E(e^{t'x}) = e^{t'\mu+\frac{1}{2}t'\Sigma t}, \tag{9.28}$$

where $t = (t_1, \ldots, t_p)'$ is a $p \times 1$ vector of real values.

From Equation (9.28), it can be shown that

$$E(\boldsymbol{X}) = \boldsymbol{\mu} \quad \text{and} \quad Cov(\boldsymbol{X}) = \Sigma.$$

If $\mathbf{C}$ is a $q \times p$ matrix of rank $q \leq p$, then $\mathbf{CX} \sim N_q(\mathbf{C}\mu, \mathbf{C}\Sigma\mathbf{C}')$. Thus, linear transformation of a normal random vector is also a multivariate normal random vector.

Let $\mathbf{X} = \begin{pmatrix} \mathbf{X}^{(1)} \\ \mathbf{X}^{(2)} \end{pmatrix}$, $\mu = \begin{pmatrix} \mu^{(1)} \\ \mu^{(2)} \end{pmatrix}$, and $\Sigma = \begin{pmatrix} \Sigma_{11} & \Sigma_{12} \\ \Sigma_{21} & \Sigma_{22} \end{pmatrix}$, where $\mathbf{X}^{(i)}$ and $\mu^{(i)}$ are $p_i \times 1$, $p_1 + p_2 = p$, and Σ_{ij} is $p_i \times p_j$.

Then, the marginal distribution of $X^{(i)}$ is also a multivariate normal with mean vector $\mu^{(i)}$ and covariance matrix Σ_{ii}, that is, $\mathbf{X}^{(i)} \sim N_{p_i}(\mu^{(i)}, \Sigma_{ii})$. Furthermore, the conditional distribution of $\mathbf{X}^{(1)}$ given $\mathbf{X}^{(2)} = x^{(2)}$, where $x^{(2)}$ is a known vector, is normal with mean vector $\mu_{1\cdot 2}$ and covariance matrix $\Sigma_{11\cdot 2}$
where

$$\mu_{1\cdot 2} = \mu^{(1)} + \Sigma_{12}\Sigma_{22}^{-1}\left(x^{(2)} - \mu^{(2)}\right), \tag{9.29}$$

and

$$\Sigma_{11\cdot 2} = \Sigma_{11} - \Sigma_{12}\Sigma_{22}^{-1}\Sigma_{21}, \tag{9.30}$$

that is, $\mathbf{X}^{(1)} \Big| \mathbf{X}^{(2)} = x^{(2)} \sim N_{p_1}(\mu_{1\cdot 2}, \Sigma_{11\cdot 2})$.

We next consider a bivariate version of correlated log-normal distribution.

Let $\begin{pmatrix} Y_1 \\ Y_2 \end{pmatrix} = \begin{pmatrix} \log(X_1) \\ \log(X_2) \end{pmatrix} \sim N\left(\begin{pmatrix} \mu_1 \\ \mu_2 \end{pmatrix}, \begin{pmatrix} \sigma_{11} & \sigma_{12} \\ \sigma_{21} & \sigma_{22} \end{pmatrix}\right)$.

The joint PDF of X_1 and X_2 can be obtained from the joint PDF of Y_1 and Y_2 by observing that

$$dx_1 dx_2 = x_1 x_2 dy_1 dy_2, \tag{9.31}$$

which is an extension of Equation (9.17) to the bivariate case.

Hence, the joint PDF of X_1 and X_2 is

$$\begin{aligned} g(x_1, x_2) = \frac{1}{2\pi |\Sigma| x_1 x_2} \exp\Bigg\{ &-\frac{1}{2}\left[(\log x_1, \log x_2) - \mu\right]' \\ &\times \Sigma^{-1}\left[(\log x_1, \log x_2) - \mu\right] \Bigg\}. \end{aligned} \tag{9.32}$$

From the property of the multivariate normal distribution, we have $Y_i \sim N(\mu_i, \sigma_{ii})$. Hence, X_i is log-normal with

$$E(X_i) = e^{\mu_i + \frac{\sigma_{ii}}{2}}, \tag{9.33}$$

$$Var(X_i) = e^{2\mu_i} e^{\sigma_{ii}}[e^{\sigma_{ii}} - 1]. \tag{9.34}$$

Furthermore, by the property of the moment generating for the bivariate normal distribution, we have

$$\begin{aligned}E(X_1X_2) &= E(e^{Y_1+Y_2})\\ &= e^{\mu_1+\mu_2+\frac{1}{2}(\sigma_{11}+\sigma_{22}+2\sigma_{12})}\\ &= E(X_1)E(X_2)\cdot\exp(\rho\sqrt{\sigma_{11}\sigma_{22}}).\end{aligned} \tag{9.35}$$

Thus, the covariance between X_1 and X_2 is

$$\begin{aligned}Cov(X_1,X_2) &= E(X_1X_2) - E(X_1)E(X_2)\\ &= E(X_1)E(X_2)\cdot(\exp(\rho\sqrt{\sigma_{11}\sigma_{22}})-1)\\ &= \exp\left(\mu_1+\mu_2+\frac{1}{2}(\sigma_{11}+\sigma_{22})\right)\cdot(\exp(\rho\sqrt{\sigma_{11}\sigma_{22}})-1).\end{aligned} \tag{9.36}$$

From the property of conditional normality of Y_1 given $Y_2 = y_2$, we also see that the conditional distribution of Y_1 given $Y_2 = y_2$ is log-normal.

The extension to the p-variate log-normal distribution is trivial. Let $\boldsymbol{Y} = (Y_1,\ldots,Y_p)'$, where $Y_i = \log X_i$. If $\boldsymbol{Y} \sim N_p(\boldsymbol{\mu},\Sigma)$, where $\boldsymbol{\mu} = (\mu_1\cdots\mu_p)'$, $\Sigma = (\sigma_{ij})$.

The joint PDF of $X_1,\ldots,X_p$, can be obtained from the following theorem.

Theorem 9.1. (Anderson, 2003)

Let the PDF of $Y_1,\ldots,Y_p$ be $f(y_1,\ldots,y_p)$, and consider the p-valued functions

$$x_i = x_i(y_1,\ldots,y_p),\ i = 1,\ldots,p. \tag{9.37}$$

We assume that the transformation from the y-space to the x-space is one to one with the inverse transformation

$$y_i = y_i(x_1,\ldots,x_p),\ i = 1,\ldots,p. \tag{9.38}$$

Let the random variables $X_1,\ldots,X_p$ be defined by

$$X_i = x_i(Y_1,\ldots,Y_p),\ i = 1,\ldots,p. \tag{9.39}$$

Then, the PDF of $X_1, \ldots, X_p$ is

$$g(x_1, \ldots, x_p) = f(y_1(x_1, \ldots, x_p), \ldots, y_p(x_1, \ldots, x_p))J(x_1, \ldots, x_p), \tag{9.40}$$

where $J(x_1, \ldots, x_p)$ is the Jacobian of transformations

$$J(x_1, \ldots, x_p) = \text{mod} \begin{vmatrix} \frac{\partial y_1}{\partial x_1} & \cdots & \frac{\partial y_1}{\partial x_p} \\ \vdots & \ddots & \vdots \\ \frac{\partial y_p}{\partial x_1} & \cdots & \frac{\partial y_p}{\partial x_p} \end{vmatrix}, \tag{9.41}$$

where "mod" means a modulus or absolute value.

Applying the above theorem with $f(y_1, \ldots, y_p)$ being a p-variate normal, and

$$J(x_1, \ldots, x_p) = \text{mod} \begin{vmatrix} \frac{1}{x_1} & 0 & \cdots & 0 \\ 0 & \frac{1}{x_2} & \cdots & 0 \\ \vdots & & \ddots & \vdots \\ 0 & \cdots & & \frac{1}{x_p} \end{vmatrix} = \prod_{i=1}^{p} \frac{1}{x_i}, \tag{9.42}$$

we have the following joint PDF of $X_1, \ldots, X_p$

$$g(x_1, \ldots, x_p) = (2\pi)^{-p/2} |\Sigma|^{-\frac{p}{2}} \left(\prod_{i=1}^{p} \frac{1}{x_i} \right)$$

$$\exp\left\{ -\frac{1}{2} \left[(\log x_1, \ldots, \log x_p) - \mu \right]' \Sigma^{-1} \left[(\log x_1, \ldots, \log x_p) - \mu \right] \right\}. \tag{9.43}$$

It is noted that when $p = 2$, Equation (9.43) reduces to the bivariate case given in Equation (9.32).

Then, the first two moments are

$$E(X_i) = e^{\mu_i + \frac{\sigma_{ii}}{2}}, \tag{9.44}$$

$$Var(X_i) = e^{2\mu_i} e^{\sigma_{ii}} [e^{\sigma_{ii}} - 1]. \tag{9.45}$$

$$Cor(X_i, X_j) = \exp\left(\mu_i + \mu_j + \frac{1}{2}(\sigma_{ii} + \sigma_{jj}) \right) \cdot (\exp(\rho_{ij}\sqrt{\sigma_{ii}\sigma_{jj}}) - 1), \tag{9.46}$$

where ρ_{ij} is the correlation between Y_i and Y_j.

For more details concerning properties of the multivariate log-normal distribution, the reader is referred to Johnson and Kotz (1972).

9.6 The Normal Distribution as an Application to the Binomial and Poisson Distribution

The cumulative normal density function tells us the probability that a random variable Z will be less than some value x. Note in Figure 9.1 that $P(Z < x)$ is simply the area under the normal curve from $-\infty$ up to point x.

One of the many applications of the cumulative normal distribution function is in valuing stock options. A call option gives the option holder the right to purchase, at a specified price known as the exercise price, a specified number of shares of stock during a given time period. A call option is a function of the following five variables:

(1) Current price of the firm's common stock (S),
(2) Exercise price (or strike price) of the option (X),
(3) Term to maturity in years (T),
(4) Variance of the stock's price (σ^2), and
(5) Risk-free rate of interest (r).

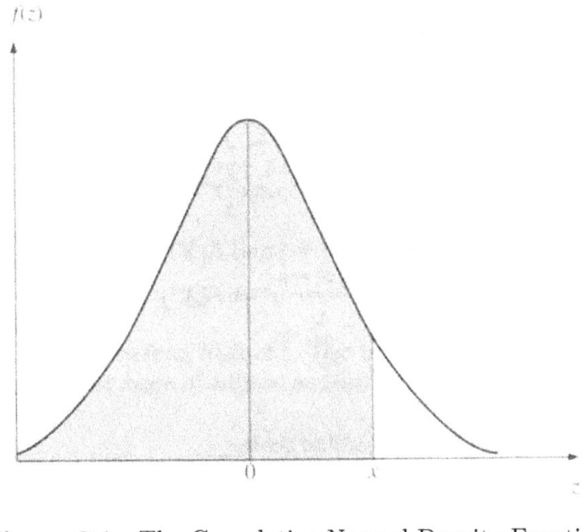

Figure 9.1 The Cumulative Normal Density Function

The binomial option pricing model defined in Equation (9.22) can be written as

$$\begin{aligned} C &= S\left[\sum_{k=m}^{T} \frac{T!}{k!(T-k)!} p'^{k}(1-p')^{T-k}\right] \\ &\quad - \frac{X}{(1+r)^T}\left[\sum_{k=m}^{T} \frac{T!}{k!(T-k)!} p^{k}(1-p)^{T-k}\right] \\ &= SB(T, p', m) - \frac{X}{(1+r)^T} B(T, p, m), \end{aligned} \tag{9.47}$$

and $C = 0$ if $m > T$, where S = current price of the stock, T = term to maturity in years, and m = minimum number of upward movements in stock price that is necessary for the option to terminate "in the money."

$$p = \frac{R-d}{u-d} \quad \text{and} \quad 1-p = \frac{u-R}{u-d},$$

X = option exercise price (or strike price), $R = 1 + r = 1+$ risk-free rate of return, $u = 1+$ percentage of price increase, $d = 1+$ percentage of price decrease, and $p' = \left(\frac{u}{R}\right) p$.

$$B(n, p, m) = \sum_{k=m}^{n} {}_{n}C_{k} p^{k}(1-p)^{n-k}.$$

By a form of the central limit theorem, we showed in Section 9.7 as $T \to \infty$, the option price C converges to C below[1]

$$C = SN(d_1) - XR^{-T}N(d_2), \tag{9.48}$$

[1]See Cox, J., S. Ross and M. Rubinstein (1979). Option pricing: A simplified approach. *Journal of Financial Economics*, 7, 229–263.

where C = price of the call option, $d_1 = \frac{\log(\frac{S}{X_{r-t}})}{\sigma\sqrt{t}} + \frac{1}{2}\sqrt{t}$, $d_2 = d_1 - \sigma\sqrt{t}$, and $N(d)$ is the value of the cumulative standard normal distribution, t is the fixed length of calendar time to expiration, h is the elapsed time between successive stock price changes, and $T = ht$.

If future stock prices are constant over time, then $\sigma^2 = 0$. It can be shown that both $N(d_1)$ and $N(d_2)$ are equal to 1 and that Equation (9.48) becomes

$$C = S - Xe^{-rT}. \tag{9.49}$$

Alternatively, Equations (9.48) and (9.49) can be understood in terms of the following steps:

Step 1: The future price of the stock is constant over time.

Because a call option gives the option holder the right to purchase the stock at the exercise price X, the value of the option, C, is just the current price of the stock less the present value of the stock's purchase price. Mathematically, the value of the call option is

$$C = S - \frac{X}{(1+r)^T}. \tag{9.50}$$

Note that Equation (9.50) assumes discrete compounding of interest, whereas Equation (9.49) assumes continuous compounding of interest. To adjust Equation (9.50) for continuous compounding, we substitute e^{-rT} for $\frac{1}{(1+r)^T}$ to get

$$C = S - Xe^{-rT}. \tag{9.51}$$

Step 2: Assume the price of the stock fluctuates over time (S_t).

In this case, we need to adjust Equation (9.49) for the uncertainty associated with that fluctuation. We do this by using the cumulative normal distribution function. In deriving Equation (9.48), we assume that S_t follows a log-normal distribution, as discussed in Section 9.3.

The adjustment factors $N(d_1)$ and $N(d_2)$ in the Black–Scholes option valuation model are simply adjustments made to

Equation (9.49) to account for the uncertainty associated with the fluctuation of the price of the stock.

Equation (9.48) is a continuous option pricing model. Compare this with the binomial option price model given in Equation (9.47), which is a discrete option pricing model. The adjustment factors $N(d_1)$ and $N(d_2)$ are cumulative normal density functions. The adjustment factors $B(T, p', m)$ and $B(T, p, m)$ are complementary binomial distribution functions.

We can use Equation (9.48) to determine the theoretical value, as of November 29, 1991, of one of IBM's options with maturity on April 1992. In this case, we have $X = \$90$, $S = \$92.50$, $\sigma = 0.2194$, $r = 0.0435$, and $T = \frac{5}{12} = 0.42$ (in years).[2] Armed with this information, we can calculate the estimated d_1 and d_2:

$$x = \frac{\left\{\ln\left(\frac{92.5}{90}\right) + \left[(.0435) + \frac{1}{2}(0.2194)^2\right](0.42)\right\}}{(0.2194)(0.42)^{\frac{1}{2}}} = 0.392,$$

$$x - \sigma\sqrt{t} = x - (0.2194)(0.42)^{\frac{1}{2}} = 0.25.$$

In Equation (9.45), $N(d_1)$ and $N(d_2)$ are the probabilities that a random variable with a standard normal distribution takes on a values less than d_1 and d_2, respectively. The values for $N(d_1)$ and $N(d_2)$ can be found by using the tables in the back of this book for the standard normal distribution, which provide the probability that a variable Z is between 0 and x (see Figure 9.2).

To find the cumulative normal density function, we need to add the probability that Z is less than zero to the value given in the standard normal distribution table. Because the standard normal distribution is symmetric around zero, we know that the probability that Z is less than zero is 0.5, so

$$P(Z < x) = P(Z < 0) + P(0 < Z < x) = 0.5 + \text{value from table.}$$

[2]Values of $X = \$90$, $S = \$92.50$, $r = 0.0435$ were obtained from Section C of the *Wall Street Journal* on December 2, 1991. $\sigma = 0.2194$ is estimated in terms of monthly rate of return during the period January 1989 to November 1991.

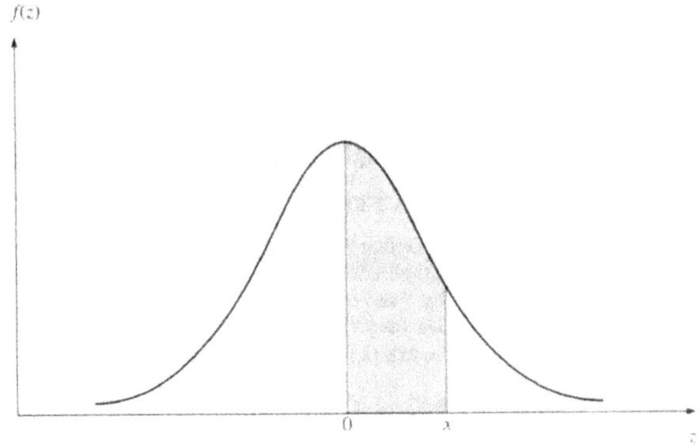

Figure 9.2 Probability of a Variable Z Between 0 and x

We can now compute the values of $N(d_1)$ and $N(d_2)$.

$$\begin{aligned} N(d_1) &= P(Z < d_1) = P(Z < 0) + P(0 < Z < d_1) \\ &= P(Z < .392) = 0.5 + 0.1517 = 0.6517. \\ N(d_2) &= P(Z < d_2) = P(Z < 0) + P(0 < Z < d_2) \\ &= P(Z < 0.25) = 0.5 + 0.0987 = 0.5987. \end{aligned}$$

Then, the theoretical value of the option is

$$\begin{aligned} C &= (92.5)(0.6517) - [(90)(0.5987)]/e^{(0.0435)(0.42)} \\ &= 60.282 - 53.883/1.0184 = \$7.373. \end{aligned}$$

and the actual price of the option on November 29, 1991 was \$7.75.

9.7 Applications of the Log-Normal Distribution in Option Pricing

To derive the Black–Scholes formula, it is assumed that there are no transaction costs, no margin requirements, and no taxes; that all shares are infinitely divisible; and that continuous trading can be accomplished. It is also assumed that the economy is risk neutral and the stock price follows a log-normal distribution. Denote the current stock price by S and the stock price at the end of jth period by S_j.

Then, $\frac{S_j}{S_{j-1}} = \exp[K_j]$ is a random variable with a log-normal distribution, where K_j is the rate of return in jth period and is a random variable with normal distribution. Let K_t have the expected value μ_k and variance σ_k^2 for each j. Then, $K_1 + K_2 + \cdots + K_t$ is a normal random variable with expected value $t\mu_k$ and variance $t\sigma_k^2$. Thus, we can define the expected value (mean) of $\frac{S_t}{S} = \exp[K_1 + K_2 + \cdots + K_t]$ as

$$E\left(\frac{S_t}{S}\right) = \exp\left[t\mu_k + \frac{t\sigma_k^2}{2}\right]. \tag{9.52}$$

Under the assumption of a risk-neutral investor, the expected return $E\left(\frac{S_t}{S}\right)$ is assumed to be $\exp(rt)$ (where r is the riskless rate of interest). In other words,

$$\mu_k = r - \frac{\sigma_k^2}{2}. \tag{9.53}$$

In the risk-neutral assumptions of Cox and Ross (1976) and Rubinstein (1976), the call option price C can be determined by discounting the expected value of the terminal option price by the riskless rate of interest:

$$C = \exp[-rt]E[Max(S_T - X, 0)], \tag{9.54}$$

where T is the time of expiration and X is the striking price.

Note that

$$\begin{aligned} Max(S_T - X, 0) &= \left(S\left(\frac{S_T}{S} - \frac{X}{S}\right)\right), \quad \text{for} \quad \frac{S_T}{S} > \frac{X}{S} \\ &= 0 \qquad\qquad\qquad\qquad\quad \text{for} \quad \frac{S_T}{S} < \frac{X}{S}. \end{aligned} \tag{9.55}$$

Equations (9.54) and (9.55) say that the value of the call option today will be either $S_t - X$ or 0, whichever is greater. If the price of stock at time t is greater than the exercise price, the call option will expire in the money. This simply means that an investor who owns the call option will exercise it. The option will be exercised regardless of whether the option holder would like to take physical possession of the stock. If the investor would like to own the stock, the cheapest way to obtain the stock is by exercising the option. If the investor would not like to own the stock, he or she will still exercise the option and immediately sell the stock in the market. Since the price the investor paid (X) is lower than the price he or she can sell the stock for (S_t), the investor realizes an immediate profit of $S_t - X$. If the price of the stock (S_t) is less than the exercise price (X), the option expires out of the money. This occurs because in purchasing shares of the stock the investor will find it cheaper to purchase the stock in the market than to exercise the option.

Let $X = \frac{S_T}{S}$ be log-normally distributed with parameters $\mu = tr - \frac{t\sigma_k^2}{2}$ and $\sigma^2 = t\sigma_k^2$. Then,

$$\begin{aligned}C &= \exp[-rt]E[Max(S_t - X)] \\ &= \exp[-rt]\int_{\frac{X}{S}}^{\infty} S\left[x - \frac{X}{S}\right]g(x)dx \\ &= \exp[-rt]S\int_{\frac{X}{S}}^{\infty} xg(x)dx - \exp[-rt]S\frac{X}{S}\int_{\frac{X}{S}}^{\infty} g(x)dx, \quad (9.56)\end{aligned}$$

where $g(x)$ is the probability density function of $X_t = \frac{S_t}{S}$.

Substituting $\mu = tr - t\sigma_k^2/2$, $\sigma^2 = t\sigma_k^2$, and $a = \frac{X}{S}$ into Equations (9.18) and (9.26) in Section 9.4, we obtain

$$\int_{\frac{X}{S}}^{\infty} xg(x)dx = e^{rt}N(d_1), \quad (9.57)$$

$$\int_{\frac{X}{S}}^{\infty} g(x)dx = N(d_2), \quad (9.58)$$

where

$$d_1 = \frac{tr - \frac{t}{2}\sigma_k^2 - \log(\frac{X}{S})}{\sqrt{t}\sigma_k} + \sqrt{t}\sigma_k = \frac{\log\left(\frac{S}{X}\right) + \left(r + \frac{1}{2}\sigma_k^2\right)t}{\sqrt{t}\sigma_k} \quad (9.59)$$

and

$$d_2 = \frac{\log\left(\frac{S}{X}\right) + \left(r - \frac{1}{2}\sigma_k^2\right)t}{\sqrt{t}\sigma_k} = d_1 - \sqrt{t}\sigma_k. \quad (9.60)$$

Substituting Equation (9.58) into Equation (9.56), we obtain

$$C = SN(d_1) - X\exp[-rt]N(d_2). \quad (9.61)$$

This is Equation (9.48) defined in Section 9.6.

We have defined a put option as a contract conveying the right to sell a designated security at a stipulated price. It can be shown that the relationship between a call option (C) and a put option (P) can be defined as

$$C + Xe^{-rt} = P + S. \tag{9.62}$$

Substituting Equation (9.33) into Equation (9.34), we obtain the put option formula as

$$P = Xe^{-rt}N(-d_2) - SN(-d_1), \tag{9.63}$$

where S, C, r, t, d_1, and d_2 are identical to those defined in the call option model.

9.8 The Bivariate Normal Density Function

In correlation analysis, we assume a population where both X and Y vary jointly. It is called a joint distribution of two variables. If both X and Y are normally distributed, then we call this known distribution a bivariate normal distribution.

We can define the PDF of the normally distributed random variables X and Y as

$$f(X) = \frac{1}{\sigma_X\sqrt{2\pi}} \exp\left[\frac{-(X - \mu_X)}{2\sigma_X^2}\right], \quad -\infty < X < \infty, \tag{9.64}$$

$$f(Y) = \frac{1}{\sigma_Y\sqrt{2\pi}} \exp\left[\frac{-(Y - \mu_Y)}{2\sigma_Y^2}\right], \quad -\infty < Y < \infty, \tag{9.65}$$

where μ_X and μ_Y are population means for X and Y, respectively; σ_X and σ_Y are population standard deviations of X and Y, respectively; $\pi = 3.1416$; and exp represents the exponential function.

If ρ represents the population correlation between X and Y, then the PDF of the bivariate normal distribution can be defined as

$$f(X, Y) = \frac{1}{2\pi\sigma_X\sigma_Y\sqrt{1-\rho^2}} \exp(-q/2),$$
$$-\infty < X < \infty, -\infty < Y < \infty, \tag{9.66}$$

where $\sigma_X > 0, \sigma_Y > 0$, and $-1 < \rho < 1$,

$$q = \frac{1}{1-\rho^2}\left[\left(\left(\frac{X-\mu_X}{\sigma_X}\right)^2 - 2\rho\left(\frac{X-\mu_X}{\sigma_X}\right)\left(\frac{Y-\mu_Y}{\sigma_Y}\right)\right.\right.$$
$$\left.\left. + \left(\frac{X-\mu_Y}{\sigma_Y}\right)^2\right)\right].$$

It can be shown that the conditional mean of Y, given X, is linear in X and given by

$$E(Y \mid X) = \mu_Y + \rho\left\{\frac{\sigma_Y}{\sigma_X}\right\}(X - \mu_X). \tag{9.67}$$

It is also clear that given X, we can define the conditional variance of Y as

$$\sigma(Y \mid X) = \sigma_Y^2(1 - \rho^2). \tag{9.68}$$

Equation (9.67) can be regarded as describing the population linear regression line. For example, if we have a bivariate normal distribution of heights of brothers and sisters, we can see that they vary together and there is no cause-and-effect relationship. Accordingly, a linear regression in terms of the bivariate normal distribution variable is treated as though there was a two-way relationship instead of an existing causal relationship. It should be noted that regression implies a causal relationship only under a "prediction" case.

Equation (9.66) represents a joint PDF for X and Y. If $\rho = 0$, then Equation (9.66) becomes

$$f(X, Y) = f(X)f(Y). \tag{9.69}$$

This implies that the joint PDF of X and Y is equal to the PDF of X times the PDF of Y. We also know that both X and Y are normally distributed. Therefore, X is independent of Y.

Example 9.1

Using a mathematics aptitude test to predict grade in statistics

Let X and Y represent scores in a mathematics aptitude test and numerical grade in elementary statistics, respectively. In addition, we assume that the parameters in Equation (9.66) are

$$\mu_X = 550 \ \sigma_X = 40 \ \mu_Y = 80 \ \sigma_Y = 4 \ \rho = 0.7.$$

Substituting this information into Equations (9.67) and (9.68), respectively, we obtain

$$E(Y \mid X) = 80 + 0.7(4/40)(X - 550) = 41.5 + 0.07X, \quad (9.70)$$

$$\sigma^2(Y \mid X) = (16)(1 - 0.49) = 8.16. \quad (9.71)$$

If we know nothing about the aptitude test score of a particular student (say, John), we have to use the distribution of Y to predict his elementary statistics grade.

$$95\% \text{ interval} = 80 \pm (1.96)(4) = 80 \pm 7.84.$$

That is, we predict with 95% probability that John's grade will fall between 87.84 and 72.16.

Alternatively, suppose we know that John's mathematics aptitude score is 650. In this case, we can use Equations (9.70) and (9.71) to predict John's grade in elementary statistics:

$$E(Y \mid X = 650) = 41.5 + (0.07)(650) = 87$$

and

$$\sigma^2(Y \mid X) = (16)(1 - 0.49) = 8.16.$$

We can now base our interval on a normal probability distribution with a mean of 87 and a standard deviation of 2.86:

$$95\% \text{ interval} = 87 \pm (1.96)(2.86) = 87 \pm 5.61.$$

That is, we predict with 95% probability that John's grade will fall between 92.61 and 81.39.

Two things have happened to this interval. First, the center has shifted upward to consider the fact that John's mathematics aptitude score is above average. Second, the width of the interval has been narrowed from $87.84 - 72.16 = 15.68$ grade points to $92.61 - 81.39 = 11.22$ grade points. In this sense, the information about John's mathematics aptitude score has made us less uncertain about his grade in statistics.

9.9 American Call Options

In this section, we will discuss two alternative methods to pricing American call options. These two methods are (i) bivariate normal distribution method and (ii) Black's approximation method.

9.9.1 *Bivariate normal distribution method*

An option contract which can be exercised only on the expiration date is called European call. If the contract of a call option can be exercised at any time of the option's contract period, then this kind of call option is called American call.

When a stock pays a dividend, the American call is more complex. Following Whaley (1981), the valuation equation for American call option with one known dividend payment can be defined as

$$\begin{aligned} C(S,T,X) &= S^x[N_1(b_1) + N_2(a_1, -b_1; -\sqrt{t/T})] \\ &\quad - Xe^{-rt}[N_1(b_2)e^{r(T-t)} + N_2(a_2, -b_2; -\sqrt{t/T})] \\ &\quad + De^{-rt}N_1(b_2), \end{aligned} \tag{9.72a}$$

where

$$a1 = \frac{\ln\left(\frac{S^x}{X}\right) + \left(r + \frac{1}{2}\sigma^2\right)T}{\sigma\sqrt{T}}, \quad a2 = a1 - \sigma\sqrt{T}, \tag{9.72b}$$

$$b1 = \frac{\ln\left(\frac{S^x}{S_t^*}\right) + \left(r + \frac{1}{2}\sigma^2\right)t}{\sigma\sqrt{t}}, \quad b2 = b1 - \sigma\sqrt{t}, \tag{9.72c}$$

$$S^x = S - De^{-rt}, \tag{9.73}$$

S^x represents the correct stock net price of the present value of the promised dividend per share (D); t represents the time dividend to be paid.

S_t^* is the ex-dividend stock price for which

$$C(S_t^*, T-t) = S_t^* + D - X, \text{ and} \tag{9.74}$$

S, X, r, σ^2, and T have been defined previously in this chapter.

Both $N_1(b_1)$ and $N_2(b_2)$ are cumulative univariate normal density function; $N_2(a, b; \rho)$ is the cumulative bivariate normal density function with upper integral limits, a and b, and correlation coefficient, $\rho = -\sqrt{t/T}$.

American call option on a non-dividend-paying stock will never optimally be exercised prior to expiration. Therefore, if no dividend payments exist, Equation (9.72) will reduce to the European Option pricing model with no dividend payment.

We have shown how the cumulative univariate normal density function can be used to evaluate the European call option in previous sections of this chapter. If a common stock pays a discrete dividend during the option's life, the American call option valuation equation requires the evaluation of a cumulative bivariate normal density function. While there are many available approximations for the cumulative bivariate normal distribution, the approximation provided here relies on Gaussian quadratures. The approach is straightforward and efficient, and its maximum absolute error is 0.00000055.

Following Equation (9.66), the probability that x' is less than a and that y' is less than b for the standardized cumulative bivariate normal distribution is

$$
\begin{aligned}
&P(X' < a, Y' < b) \\
&= \frac{1}{2\pi\sqrt{1-\rho^2}} \int_{-\infty}^{a} \int_{-\infty}^{b} \exp\left[\frac{2x'^2 - 2\rho x'y' + y'^2}{2(1-\rho^2)}\right] dx'dy',
\end{aligned}
$$

where $x' = \frac{x-\mu_x}{\sigma_x}$, $y' = \frac{y-\mu_y}{\sigma_y}$, and p is the correlation between the random variables x' and y'.

The first step in the approximation of the bivariate normal probability $N_2(a, b; \rho)$ is as follows:

$$
\phi(a, b; \rho) \approx 0.31830989\sqrt{1-\rho^2} \sum_{i=1}^{5} \sum_{j=1}^{5} w_i w_j f(x_i', x_j'), \tag{9.75}
$$

where

$$
f(x_i', x_j') = \exp[a_1(2x_i' - a_1) + b_1(2x_j' - b_1) + 2\rho(x_i' - a_1)(x_j' - b_1)].
$$

The pairs of weights (w) and corresponding abscissa values (x') are

i, j	w	x'
1	0.24840615	0.10024215
2	0.39233107	0.48281397
3	0.21141819	1.0609498
4	0.033246660	1.7797294
5	0.00082485334	2.6697604

This portion is based upon Appendix 13.1 of Stoll, H. R. and R. E. Whaley (1993). *Futures and Options*. Cincinnati, OH: Southwestern Publishing.

and the coefficients a_1 and b_1 are computed using

$$a_1 = \frac{a}{\sqrt{2(1-\rho^2)}} \quad \text{and} \quad b_1 = \frac{b}{\sqrt{2(1-\rho^2)}}.$$

The second step in the approximation involves computing the product $ab\rho$; if $ab\rho \leq 0$, compute the bivariate normal probability, $N_2(a, b; \rho)$, using the following rules:

$$\begin{aligned}
&(1) \text{ If } a \leq 0,\ b \leq 0, \quad \text{and} \quad \rho \leq 0, \\
&\qquad \text{then} \quad N_2(a, b; \rho) = \phi(a, b; \rho); \\
&(2) \text{ If } a \leq 0,\ b \geq 0, \quad \text{and} \quad \rho > 0, \\
&\qquad \text{then} \quad N_2(a, b; \rho) = N_1(a) - \phi(a, -b; -\rho); \\
&(3) \text{ If } a \geq 0,\ b \leq 0, \quad \text{and} \quad \rho > 0, \\
&\qquad \text{then} \quad N_2(a, b; \rho) = N_1(b) - \phi(-a, b; -\rho); \\
&(4) \text{ If } a \geq 0,\ b \geq 0, \quad \text{and} \quad \rho \leq 0, \\
&\qquad \text{then} \quad N_2(a, b; \rho) = N_1(a) + N_1(b) - 1 + \phi(-a, -b; \rho).
\end{aligned} \tag{9.76}$$

If $ab\rho > 0$, compute the bivariate normal probability, $N_2(a, b; \rho)$, as

$$N_2(a, b; \rho) = N_2(a, 0; \rho_{ab}) + N_2(b, 0; \rho_{ab}) - \delta, \tag{9.77}$$

where the values of $N_2(\bullet)$ on the right-hand side are computed from the rules, for $ab\rho \leq 0$

$$\rho_{ab} = \frac{(\rho a - b)Sgn(a)}{\sqrt{a^2 - 2\rho ab + b^2}}, \quad \rho_{ba} = \frac{(\rho b - a)Sgn(b)}{\sqrt{a^2 - 2\rho ab + b^2}},$$

$$\delta = \frac{1 - Sgn(a) \times Sgn(b)}{4}$$

and

$$Sgn(x) = \begin{cases} 1 & x \geq 0 \\ -1 & x < 0 \end{cases},$$

$N_1(d)$ is the cumulative univariate normal probability.

Example 9.2

An American call option whose exercise price is \$48 has an expiration time of 90 days. Assume the risk-free rate of interest is 8% annually, the underlying price is \$50, the standard deviation of the rate of return of the stock is 20%, and the stock pays a dividend of \$2 exactly for 50 days. (a) What is the European call value? (b) Can the early exercise price predicted? (c) What is the value of the American call?

(a) The current stock net price of the present value of the promised dividend is

$$S^x = 50 - 2e^{-0.08(50/365)} = 48.0218.$$

The European call value can be calculated as

$$C = (48.0218)N(d_1) - 48e^{-0.08(90/365)}N(d_2),$$

where

$$d_1 = \frac{[\ln(48.208/48) + (0.08 + 0.5(0.20)^2)(90/365)]}{0.20\sqrt{90/365}} = 0.25285$$

$$d_2 = 0.292 - 0.0993 = 0.15354.$$

From standard normal table, we obtain

$$N(0.25285) = 0.5 + 0.3438 = 0.599809.$$

$$N(0.15354) = 0.5 + 0.3186 = 0.561014.$$

So, the European call value is

$$C = (48.516)(0.599809) - 48(0.980)(0.561014) = 2.40123.$$

(b) The present value of the interest income that would be earned by deferring exercise until expiration is

$$X(1 - e^{-r(T-t)}) = 48(1 - e^{-0.08(90-50)/365}) = 48(1 - 0.991) = 0.432.$$

Since $d = 2 > 0.432$, the early exercise is not precluded.

(c) The value of the American call is now calculated as

$$\begin{aligned} C &= 48.208[N_1(b_1) + N_2(a_1, -b_1; \sqrt{50/90})] \\ &\quad - 48e^{-0.08(90/365)}[N_1(b_2)e^{-0.08(40/365)} + N_2(a_2, -b_2; -\sqrt{50/90})] \\ &\quad + 2e^{-0.08(50/365)}N_1(b_2). \end{aligned} \tag{9.78}$$

since both b_1 and b_2 depend on the critical ex-dividend stock price S_t^*, which can be determined by

$$C(S_t^*, 40/365; 48) = S_t^* + 2 - 48.$$

By using trial and error, we find that $S_t^* = 46.9641$. An Excel program used to calculate this value is presented in Table 9.1.

Table 9.1 Calculation of S_t^* (Critical Ex-dividend Stock Price)

S^* (critical ex-dividend stock price)	46	46.962	46.963	46.9641	46.9	47
X (exercise price of option)	48	48	48	48	48	48
r (risk-free interest rate)	0.08	0.08	0.08	0.08	0.08	0.08
σ (volatility of stock)	0.2	0.2	0.2	0.2	0.2	0.2
$T - t$ (expiration date − exercise date)	0.10959	0.10959	0.10959	0.10959	0.10959	0.10959
d_1	−0.4773	−0.1647	−0.1644	−0.164	−0.1846	−0.1525
d_2	−0.5435	−0.2309	−0.2306	−0.2302	−0.2508	−0.2187
D (dividend)	2	2	2	2	2	2
c (value of European call option to buy one share)	0.60263	0.96319	0.96362	0.9641	0.93649	0.9798
p (value of European put option to sell one share)	2.18365	1.58221	1.58164	1.58102	1.61751	1.56081
$C(S_t^*, T-t; X) - St^* - D + X$	0.60263	0.00119	0.00062	2.3E−06	0.03649	−0.0202

Calculation of S_t^* (Critical Ex-dividend Stock Price)			
*Number**	A	B	C*
1	Option Pricing Model		
2		—	
3	S^*(critical ex-dividend stock price)	46	
4	X(exercise price of option)	48	
5	r(risk-free interest rate)	0.08	
6	volatility of stock	0.2	
7	$T{-}t$(expiration date-exercise date)	*0.10959*	= (90 − 50)/365
8	d_1	*−0.4773*	= (LN(C3/C4)+(C5+C6^2/2)* (C7))/(C6*SQRT(C7))
9	d_2	*−0.5435*	= (LN(C3/C4)+(C5–C6^2/2)* (C7))/(C6*SQRT(C7))
10	D(divent)	*2*	
11		—	
12	c(value of European call option to buy one share)	*0.60263*	= C3*NORMSDIST(C8)−C4* EXP(−C5*C7)* NORMSDIST(C9)
13	p(value of European put option to sell one share)	*2.18365*	= C4*EXP(−C5*C7)* NORMSDIST(−C9)– C3*NORMSDIST(−C8)
14		—	
15	$C(S_t^*, T-t; X) - S_t^* - D + X$	*0.60263*	$= C12 - C3 - C10 + C4$

Note: *The number of the row and the column in the Excel sheet.

Substituting $S^x = 48.208$, $X = \$48$, and S_t^* into Equations (9.72b) and (9.72c), we can calculate a_1, a_2, b_1, and b_2 as follows:

$$a_1 = d_1 = 0.25285.$$

$$a_2 = d_2 = 0.15354.$$

$$b_1 = \frac{\ln(\frac{48.208}{46.9641}) + (0.08 + \frac{0.2^2}{2})(\frac{50}{365})}{(0.20)\sqrt{50/365}} = 0.4859.$$

$$b_2 = 0.485931 - 0.074023 = 0.4119.$$

In addition, we also know $\rho = -\sqrt{50/90} = -0.7454$.

From the above information, we now calculate related normal probability as follows:

$$N_1(b_1) = N_1(0.4859) = 0.6865.$$

$$N_1(b_2) = N_1(0.7454) = 0.6598.$$

Following Equation (9.77), we now calculate the value of N_2 (0.25285, −0.4859; −0.7454) and N_2 (0.15354, −0.4119; −0.7454) as follows:

Since $ab\rho > 0$ for both cumulative bivariate normal density function, we can use equation $N_2(a, b; \rho) = N_2(a, 0; \rho_{ab}) + N_2(b, 0; \rho_{ba}) - \delta$ to calculate the value of both $N_2(a, b; \rho)$ as follows:

$$\rho_{ab} = \frac{[(-0.7454)(0.25285) + 0.4859](1)}{\sqrt{(0.25285)^2 - 2(0.7454)(0.25285)(-0.4859) + (0.4859)^2}}$$
$$= 0.87002.$$
$$\rho_{ba} = \frac{[(-0.7454)(-0.4859) - 0.25285](1)}{\sqrt{(0.25285)^2 - 2(0.7454)(0.25285)(-0.4859) + (0.4859)^2}}$$
$$= -0.31979.$$
$$\delta = (1 - (1)(-1))/4 = 1/2.$$

$$\begin{aligned} &N_2(0.292, -0.4859; -0.7454) \\ &\quad = N_2(0.292, 0.0844) + N_2(-0.5377, 0.0656) - 0.5 \\ &\quad = N_1(0) + N_1(-0.5377) - \Phi(-0.292, 0; -0.0844) \\ &\qquad - \Phi(-0.5377, 0; -0.0656) - 0.5 = 0.07525. \end{aligned}$$

Using the Microsoft Excel program presented in Appendix 9A, we obtain

$$N_2(0.1927, -0.4119; -0.7454) = 0.06862.$$

Then, substituting the related information into the Equation (9.78), we obtain $C = \$3.08238$ and all related results are presented in Appendix 9B.

9.9.2 *Black's approximation method with one dividend payment*

To evaluate whether there exist early exercise opportunities for the American option with one dividend payment or not, we should check whether the present value of interest income is larger or smaller than the cash dividend payment. If the cash dividend is larger than the present value of interest income, then there will be a chance to exercise this American option early. There are two alternative methods to evaluate an American option with one dividend payment with early exercise.

Method 1: Precise Method, which has been discussed in Section 9.9.2.

Method 2: Black's Approximation Method

There are three steps to perform Black's approximation method.

Step 1: Evaluate the European call option with one dividend payment as indicated in the following:

$C = (48.0218)(0.599809) - 48(0.980)(0.561014) = 2.40123$

Please note that the contract period for this situation is $T = 90$. The detailed procedure of this calculation can be found in Section 9.9.2.

Step 2: We assume there will be early exercise at $t = 50$, then the calculation can be performed as follows:

$$S_0 = 50,\ E = K = 48,\ r = 0.08,\ \sigma = 0.20,\ T = 50/365 = 0.137.$$

$$d_1 = \frac{\ln\left(\frac{50}{48}\right) + \left(0.08 + \frac{0.2^2}{2}\right)(0.137)}{0.2\sqrt{0.137}} = 0.74.$$

$$d_2 = \frac{\ln\left(\frac{50}{48}\right) + \left(0.08 - \frac{0.2^2}{2}\right)(0.137)}{0.2\sqrt{0.137}} = 0.66.$$

From the normal table

$$B(d_1) = 0.7693,\ N(d_2) = 0.7462$$

And the call price is

$$50(0.7693) - 48e^{-0.08(0.137)}(07462) = 3.04.$$

Step 3: Compare the call option value obtained from Step 1 (2.40123) with the call option value obtained from Step 2 (3.04). Because $2.40123 < 3.04$, then the approximation value of American option with one dividend payment is \$3.04.

However, the value obtain from the precise method is 3.08238. The procedure of calculating the precise value can be found in the previous section of the chapter. The precise value 3.08238 is larger than the value obtained from the approximation method (3.04).

1. The first point concerns the timing of the early exercise decision and tends to make the precise method greater than Black's approximation method. In Black's approximation method, the assumption is that the holder has to decide today whether the option will be exercised after 50 days or after 90 days; the precise method allows the decision on early exercise at the 50-day point to depend upon the stock price.
2. The second point concerns the way in which volatility is applied and tends to make Black's approximation method greater than the precise method. In Black's approximation method, we assume exercise takes place after 50 days, and the volatility is applied to the stock price less than the present value of the stock dividend; when we assume exercise takes place after 90 days, the volatility applied to stock price is less than the present value of dividend. In the precise method, it is always applied to the stock price less the present value of dividend.

9.10 Price Bounds for Options

9.10.1 *Options written on non-dividend-paying stocks*

To derive the lower price bounds and the put–call parity relations for options on non-dividend-paying stocks, simply set the cost-of-carry rate, b, equal to the risk-less rate of interest, r. Note that the only cost of carrying the stock is interest.

The lower price bounds for the European call and put options are

$$c(S,T;X) \geq \max[0, S - Xe^{-rT}] \tag{9.79a}$$

and

$$p(S,T;X) \geq \max[0, Xe^{-rT} - S], \tag{9.79b}$$

respectively, and the lower price bounds for the American call and put options are

$$C(S,T;X) \geq \max[0, S - Xe^{-rT}] \tag{9.80a}$$

and

$$P(S,T;X) \geq \max[0, Xe^{-rT} - S], \tag{9.80b}$$

respectively. The put–call parity relation for the non-dividend-paying European stock options is

$$c(S,T;X) - p(S,T;X) = S - Xe^{-rT}, \tag{9.81a}$$

and the put–call parity relation for American options on non-dividend-paying stocks is

$$S - X \leq C(S,T;X) - P(S,T;X) \leq S - Xe^{-rT}. \tag{9.81b}$$

For non-dividend-paying stock options, the American call option will not rationally be exercised early, while the American put option may be done so.

9.10.2 *Options written on dividend-paying stocks*

If dividends are paid during the option's life, the above relations must reflect the stock's drop in value when the dividends are paid. To manage this modification, we assume that the underlying stock pays a single dividend during the option's life at a time that is known with certainty. The dividend amount is D and the time to ex-dividend is t.

If the amount and the timing of the dividend payment are known, the lower price bound for the European call option on a stock is

$$c(S,T;X) \geq \max[0, S - De^{-rt} - Xe^{-rT}]. \tag{9.82a}$$

In this relation, the current stock price is reduced by the present value of the promised dividend. Because a European-style option cannot be exercised before maturity, the call option holder has no opportunity to exercise the option while the stock is selling cum dividend. In other words, to the call option holder, the current value of the underlying stock is its observed market price less the amount that the promised dividend contributes to the current stock value, that is, $S - De^{-rt}$. To prove this pricing relation, we use the same arbitrage transactions, except we use the reduced stock price $S - De^{-rt}$ in place of S. The lower price bound for the European put option on a stock is

$$p(S,T;X) \geq \max[0, Xe^{-rT} - S - De^{-rt}]. \tag{9.82b}$$

Again, the stock price is reduced by the present value of the promised dividend. Unlike the call option case, however, this serves to increase the lower price bound of the European put option. Because the put option is the right to sell the underlying stock at a fixed price, a discrete drop in the stock price, such as that induced by the payment of a dividend, serves to increase the value of the option. An arbitrage proof of this relation is straightforward when the stock price, net of the present value of the dividend, is used in place of the commodity price.

The lower price bounds for American stock options are slightly more complex. In the case of the American call option, for example, it may be optimal to exercise just prior to the dividend payment because the stock price falls by an amount D when the dividend is paid. The lower price bound of an American call option expiring at the ex-dividend instant would be 0 or $S - Xe^{-rt}$, whichever is greater. On the other hand, it may be optimal to wait until the call option's expiration to exercise. The lower price bound for a call option expiring normally is Equation (9.82a). Combining the two results, we get

$$C(S, T; X) \geq \max[0, S - Xe^{-rt},\ S - De^{-rt} - Xe^{-rT}]. \tag{9.83}$$

The last two terms on the right-hand side of Equation (9.83) provide important guidance in deciding whether to exercise the American call option early, just prior to the ex-dividend instant. The second term in the squared brackets is the present value of the early exercise proceeds of the call. If the amount is less than the lower price bound of the call that expires normally, that is, if

$$S - Xe^{-rt} \leq S - De^{-rT} - Xe^{-rt}, \tag{9.84}$$

the American call option will not be exercised just prior to the ex-dividend instant.

To see why, simply rewrite Equation (9.84) so it reads

$$D < X[1 - e^{-r(T-t)}]. \tag{9.85}$$

In other words, the American call will not be exercised early if the dividend captured by exercising prior to the ex-dividend date is less than the interest implicitly earned by deferring exercise until expiration.

Figure 9.3 depicts a case in which early exercise could occur at the ex-dividend instant, t. Just prior to ex-dividend, the call option may

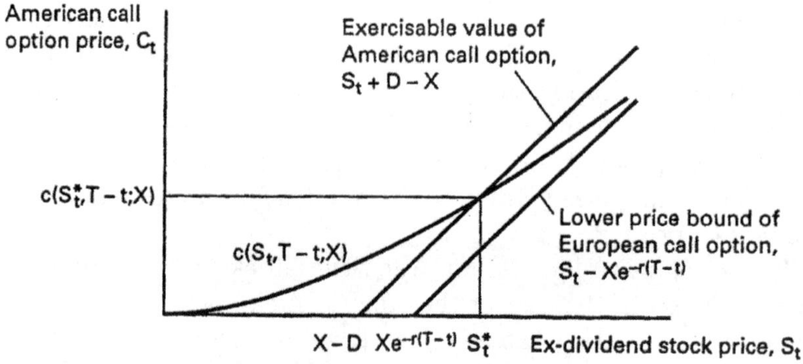

Figure 9.3 American Call Option Price as a Function of the Ex-dividend Stock Price Immediately Prior to the Ex-dividend Instant. Early Exercise May Be Optimal

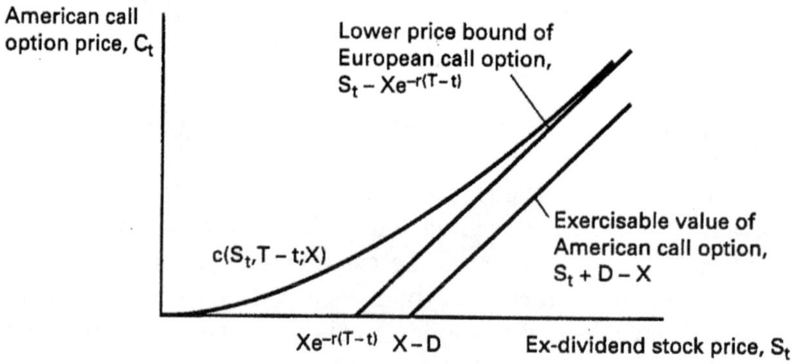

Figure 9.4 American Call Option Price as a Function of the Ex-dividend Stock Price Immediately Prior to the Ex-dividend Instant. Early Exercise Will Not Be Optimal

be exercised yielding proceeds S_t+D-X, where S_t is the ex-dividend stock price. An instant later, the option is left unexercised with value $c(S_t, T-t; X)$, where $c(\cdot)$ is the European call option formula. Thus, if the ex-dividend stock price, S_t, is above the critical ex-dividend stock price where the two functions intersect, S_t^*, the option holder will choose to exercise his or her option early just prior to the ex-dividend instant. On the other hand, if $S_t \leq S_t^*$, the option holder will choose to leave her position open until the option's expiration.

Figure 9.4 depicts a case in which early exercise will not occur at the ex-dividend instant, t. Early exercise will not occur if the functions $S_t + D - X$ and $c(S_t, T - t; X)$ do not intersect, as is depicted in Figure 9.4. In this case, the lower boundary condition of the European call, $S_t - Xe^{-r(T-t)}$, lies above the early exercise proceeds, $S_t + D - X$, and hence the call option will not be exercised early. Stated explicitly, early exercise is not rational if

$$S_t + D - X < S_t - Xe^{-r(T-t)}.$$

This condition for no early exercise is the same as Equation (9.84), where S_t is the ex-dividend stock price and where the investor is standing at the ex-dividend instant, t. The condition can also be written as

$$D < X[1 - e^{-r(T-t)}]. \tag{9.85}$$

In other words, if the ex-dividend stock price decline — the dividend — is less than the present value of the interest income that would be earned by deferring exercise until expiration, early exercise will not occur. When condition (9.85) is met, the value of the American call is simply the value of the corresponding European call.

The lower price bound of an American put option is somewhat different. In the absence of a dividend, an American put may be exercised early. In the presence of a dividend payment, however, there is a period just prior to the ex-dividend date when early exercise is suboptimal. In that period, the interest earned on the exercise proceeds of the option is less than the drop in the stock price from the payment of the dividend. If t_n represents a time prior to the dividend payment at time t, early exercise is suboptimal, where $(X - S)e^{-r(t-t_n)}$ is less than $(X - S + D)$. Rearranging will not occur between t_n and t if the condition defined in Equation (9.86) holds[3]:

$$t_n > t - \frac{\ln(1 + \frac{D}{X-S})}{r}. \tag{9.86}$$

[3]It is possible that the dividend payment is so large that early exercise prior to the dividend payment is completely precluded. For example, consider the case where $X = 50$, $S = 40$, $D = 1$, $t = 0.25$, and $r = 0.10$. Early exercise is precluded if $r = 0.25 - \ln[1 - l/(50 - 40)]/0.10 = -0.7031$. Because the value is negative, the implication is that there is no time during the current dividend period (i.e., from 0 to t) where it will not pay the American put option holder to wait until the dividend is paid to exercise his option.

Early exercise will become a possibility again immediately after the dividend is paid. Overall, the lower price bound of the American put option is

$$P(S,T;X) \geq \max[o, X - (S - De^{-rt})]. \tag{9.83b}$$

Put–call parity for European options on dividend-paying stocks also reflects the fact that the current stock price is deflated by the present value of the promised dividend, that is,

$$c(S,T;X) - p(S,T;X) = S - De^{-rt} - Xe^{-rT}. \tag{9.87}$$

That the presence of the dividend reduces the value of the call and increases the value of the put is again reflected here by the fact that the term on the right-hand side of Equation (9.87) is smaller than it would be if the stock paid no dividend.

Put–call parity for American options on dividend-paying stocks is represented by a pair of inequalities, that is,

$$S - De^{-rt} - X \leq C(S,T;X) - P(S,T;X) \leq S - De^{-rt} - Xe^{-rT}. \tag{9.88}$$

To prove the put–call parity relation (9.88), we consider each inequality in turn. The left-hand side condition of Equation (9.88) can be derived by considering the values of a portfolio that consists of buying a call, selling a put, selling the stock, and lending $X + De^{-rt}$ risklessly. Table 9.2 contains these portfolio values.

In Table 9.2, it can be seen that, if all of the security positions stay open until expiration, the terminal value of the portfolio will be positive, independent of whether the terminal stock price is above or below the exercise price of the options. If the terminal stock price is above the exercise price, the call option is exercised, and the stock acquired at exercise price X is used to deliver, in part, against the short stock position. If the terminal stock price is below the exercise price, the put is exercised. The stock received in the exercise of the put is used to cover the short stock position established at the outset. In the event the put is exercised early at time T, the investment in the riskless bonds is more than sufficient to cover the payment of the exercise price to the put option holder, and the stock received from the exercise of the put is used to cover the stock sold when the

Table 9.2 Arbitrage Transactions for Establishing Put–Call Parity for American Stock Options

$$S - De^{-rt} - X \leq C(S, T; X) - P(S, T; X)$$

Position	Initial Value	Ex-dividend Day (t)	Put Exercised Early (γ) Intermediate Value	Put Exercised Normally (T) Terminal Value $\tilde{S}_T \leq X$	 $\tilde{S}_T > X$
Buy American Call	$-C$		$\tilde{C}_\gamma$	0	$\tilde{S}_T - X$
Sell American Put	P		$-(X - \tilde{S}_\gamma)$	$-(\tilde{X} - S_T)$	0
Sell Stock	S	$-D$	$-\tilde{S}_\gamma$	$-\tilde{S}_T$	$-\tilde{S}_T$
Lend De^{-rt}	De^{-rt}	D		Xe^{rT}	Xe^{rT}
Lend X	$-X$		$Xe^{r\gamma}$		
Net Portfolio Value	$-C + P + S$ $-De^{-rt} - X$	0	$\tilde{C}_\gamma + X(e^{r\gamma} - 1)$	$X(e^{rT} - 1)$	$X(e^{rT} - 1)$

portfolio was formed. In addition, an open call option position that may still have value remains.

In other words, by forming the portfolio of securities in the proportions noted above, we have formed a portfolio that will never have a negative future value. If the future value is certain to be non-negative, the initial value must be non-positive or the left-hand inequality of Equation (9.88) holds.

The right-hand side of Equation (9.88) may be derived by considering the portfolio used to prove European put–call parity. Table 9.2 contains the arbitrage portfolio transactions. In this case, the terminal value of the portfolio is certain to equal zero, should the option positions stay open until that time. In the event the American call option holder decides to exercise the call option early, the portfolio holder uses his long stock position to cover his stock obligation on the exercised call and uses the exercise proceeds to retire his outstanding debt. After these actions are taken, the portfolio holder still has an open long put position and cash in the amount of $X[1 - e^{-r(T-t)}]$. Since the portfolio is certain to have non-negative outcomes, the initial value must be non-positive or the right-hand inequality of Equation (9.88) must hold. In Chapter 22, we will discuss option bounds for both European and American options in further detail.

9.11 Summary

In this chapter, we first introduced univariate and multivariate normal distribution and log-normal distribution. Then, we showed how normal distribution can be used to approximate binomial distribution. Finally, we used the concepts normal and log-normal distributions to derive Black–Scholes formula under the assumption that investors are risk neutral.

In this chapter, we first reviewed the basic concept of the Bivariate normal density function and present the Bivariate normal CDF. The theory of American call stock option pricing model for one dividend payment is also presented. The evaluations of stock option models without dividend payment and with dividend payment are discussed. Finally, we provided an excel program for evaluating the American option pricing model with one dividend payment.

Questions and Problems

1. Briefly explain the relationship between normal distribution and binomial distribution in valuing stock call options.
2. Briefly describe the relationship between the expected stock return and risk-free rate under the risk-neutral assumption.
3. What does the Black–Scholes stock option model assume about the probability distribution of the stock price?
4. Let X follow the normal distribution with mean $\mu = 0$ and variance $\sigma^2 = 1$. Find the following probabilities:

   (a) $P(X > 1.65)$.
   (b) $P(X < -2.38)$.
   (c) $P(X > -1.37)$.
   (d) $P(-2.43 < X < 1.72)$.

5. As the assumption in Question 1, find the following values of z :

   (a) $P(X < z) = 0.99$.
   (b) $P(X > z) = 0.05$.
   (c) $P(z < X < 0) = 0.0130$.
   (d) $P(-z < X < z) = 0.5408$.

6. Let Y follow the normal distribution with a mean of 5 and a standard deviation of 2. Find the probabilities as follows:

   (a) Y is between 5 and 9.
   (b) Y is between -1 and 3.
   (c) Y is greater than 6.
   (d) Y is less than 10.

7. The manager in the local bank discovers that people come in to cash their pay checks on Friday. The amount of money withdrawn on Friday follows a normal distribution with 6 million as the mean and 1 million as the standard deviation. The bank manager wants to make sure that the amount of money in the bank can cover 99.9% of the Friday withdrawals. What is the minimum amount of money he or she should plan to have on hand?
8. A consumer rights organization wants to find out whether a local dairy farm actually puts 20 ounces of milk into a container that is labeled 20 ounces. Assume the milk put into the container by local dairy farm follows a normal distribution with a mean of 20.05 and a standard deviation of 0.05.

   (a) What is the probability that a certain container contains more than 20 ounces of milk?
   (b) The consumer rights organization bought 400 bottles of milk. What is the probability that among them, it found fewer than 12 bottles that do not contain enough milk?

9. Use the Black–Scholes option formula to price the value of a call option under the following information:

   $S = \$105,$
   $X = \$110,$
   $r = 0.05,$
   $t = 0.8,$
   $\sigma = 0.45.$

10. In Question 9, what is the value of a call option when $X = \$90$? Briefly describe the relationship between the strike price and call option in terms of the probability following the log-normal distribution.

Bibliography

Anderson, T. W. (2003). *An Introduction to Multivariate Statistical Analysis*, 3rd ed. New York, NY: Wiley-Interscience.

Cox, J. C. and S. A. Ross (1976). The valuation of options for alternative stochastic processes. *Journal of Financial Economics*, 3(January–March), 145–166.

Cox, J., S. Ross and M. Rubinstein (1979). Option pricing: A simplified approach. *Journal of Financial Economics*, 7, 229–263.

Johnson, N. L. and S. Kotz (1970). *Distributions in Statistics: Continuous Univariate Distributions 2*. New York, NY: Wiley.

Johnson, N. L. and S. Kotz (1972). *Distributions in Statistics: Continuous Multivariate Distributions*. New York, NY: Wiley.

Lee, C. F. (2020). Financial econometrics, mathematics, statistics, and financial technology: An overall view. *Review of Quantitative Finance and Accounting*, 54(4), 1529–1578.

Lee, C. F., Y. Chen and J. Lee (2016). Alternative methods to derive option pricing models: Review and comparison. *Review of Quantitative Finance and Accounting*, 47(2), 417–451.

Lee, C. F., H.-Y. Chen and J. Lee (2019). *Financial Econometrics, Mathematics and Statistics*. New York: Springer Academic Publishers.

Lee, C. F., J. Lee and A. C. Lee (2013). *Statistics for Business and Financial Economics*, 3rd ed. New York: Springer Academic Publishers.

Lee, J., C. F. Lee, J. R. Chang and L.-J. Kao (2023). *Essentials of Excel VBA, Python, and R: Financial Derivatives, Risk Management and Machine Learning*. New York: Springer Academic Publishers.

Rubinstein, M. (1976). The valuation of uncertain income streams and the pricing of options. *Bell Journal of Economics and Management Science*, 7, 407–425.

Stoll, H. R. (1969). The relationship between put and call option prices. *Journal of Finance*, 24(December), 801–824.

Whaley, R. E. (1981). On the valuation of American call options on stocks with known dividends. *Journal of Financial Economics*, 9, 207–211.

Appendix 9A: Microsoft Excel Program for Calculating Cumulative Bivariate Normal Density Function

```
Option Explicit

Public Function Bivarncdf(a As Double, b As Double, rho As Double) As Double

    Dim rho_ab As Double, rho_ba As Double
    Dim delta As Double

    If (a * b * rho) <= 0 Then

        If (a <= 0 And b <= 0 And rho <= 0) Then
            Bivarncdf = Phi(a, b, rho)
        End If

        If (a <= 0 And b >= 0 And rho > 0) Then
            Bivarncdf = Application.WorksheetFunction.NormSDist(a) - Phi(a, -b, -rho)
        End If

        If (a >= 0 And b <= 0 And rho > 0) Then
            Bivarncdf = Application.WorksheetFunction.NormSDist(b) - Phi(-a, b, -rho)
        End If

        If (a >= 0 And b >= 0 And rho <= 0) Then
            Bivarncdf = Application.WorksheetFunction.NormSDist(a) +
Application.WorksheetFunction.NormSDist(b) - 1 + Phi(-a, -b, rho)
        End If
    Else

        rho_ab = ((rho * a - b) * IIf(a >= 0, 1, -1)) / Sqr(a ^ 2 - 2 * rho * a * b + b ^ 2)
        rho_ba = ((rho * b - a) * IIf(b >= 0, 1, -1)) / Sqr(a ^ 2 - 2 * rho * a * b + b ^ 2)
        delta = (1 - IIf(a >= 0, 1, -1) * IIf(b >= 0, 1, -1)) / 4
        Bivarncdf = Bivarncdf(a, 0, rho_ab) + Bivarncdf(b, 0, rho_ba) - delta

    End If
End Function

Public Function Phi(a As Double, b As Double, rho As Double) As Double

    Dim a1 As Double, b1 As Double
    Dim w(5) As Double, x(5) As Double
    Dim i As Integer, j As Integer
    Dim doublesum As Double

    a1 = a / Sqr(2 * (1 - rho ^ 2))
    b1 = b / Sqr(2 * (1 - rho ^ 2))

    w(1) = 0.24840615
    w(2) = 0.39233107
    w(3) = 0.21141819
    w(4) = 0.03324666
    w(5) = 0.00082485334
```

```
    x(1) = 0.10024215
    x(2) = 0.48281397
    x(3) = 1.0609498
    x(4) = 1.7797294
    x(5) = 2.6697604

    doublesum = 0

    For i = 1 To 5

        For j = 1 To 5
        doublesum = doublesum + w(i) * w(j) * Exp(a1 * (2 * x(i) - a1) + b1 * (2 * x(j) - b1) +
2 * rho * (x(i) - a1) * (x(j) - b1))
        Next j
    Next i

    Phi = 0.31830989 * Sqr(1 - rho ^ 2) * doublesum

End Function
```

Appendix 9B: Microsoft Excel Program for Calculating American Call Options

Number*	A	B	C*
1	Option Pricing Calculation		
2			
3	S (current stock price) =	50	
4	S_t^* (critical ex-dividend stock price) =	46.9641	
5	S(current stock price NPV of promised dividend) =	48.0218	= B3–B11*EXP(−B7*B10)
6	X (exercise price of option) =	48	
7	R(risk-free interest rate) =	0.08	
8	σ(volatility of stock) =	0.2	
9	T(expiration date) =	0.24658	
10	T(exercise date) =	0.13699	
11	D(dividend) =	2	
12	d_1 (non-dividend-paying) =	0.65933	= (LN(B3/B6) + (B7 + 0.5*B8^2)*B9)/ (B8*SQRT (B9))
13	d_2 (non-dividend-paying) =	0.56001	= B12–B8*SQRT(B9)

(*Continued*)

(*Continued*)

Number*	A	B	C*
14	d_1^* (critical ex-dividend stock price) =	−0.16401	= (LN(B4/B6) + (B7 + 0.5*B8^2)* (B9–B10))/(B8*SQRT (B9–B10))
15	d_2^* (critical ex-dividend stock price) =	−0.23022	= B14–B8*SQRT(B9–B10)
16	d_1 (dividend-paying) =	0.25285	= (LN(B5/B6) + (B7 + 0.5*B8^2)* (B9))/(B8*SQRT(B9))
17	d_2 (dividend-paying) =	0.15354	= B16–B8*SQRT(B9)
18	$a_1 =$	0.25285	= (LN((B3–B11*EXP(−B7*B10))/ B6) + (B7 + 0.5*B8^2)* (B9))/ (B8*SQRT(B9))
19	$a_2 =$	0.15354	= B18–B8*SQRT(B9)
20	$b_1 =$	0.48593	= (LN((B3–B11*EXP(−B7*B10))/ B4) + (B7 + 0.5*B8^2)* (B10))/(B8*SQRT(B10))
21	$b_2 =$	0.41191	= B20–B8*SQRT(B10)
22			
23	$C(S_t^*, T-t; X) =$	0.9641	= B4*NORMSDIST (B14)–B6* EXP (−B7*(B9–B10))* NORMSDIST(B15)
24	$C(S_t^*, T-t; X)$ $-S_t^* - D + X =$	2.3E−06	= B23–B4–B11+B6
25			
26	$N_1(a_1) =$	0.59981	= NORMSDIST(B18)
27	$N_1(a_2) =$	0.56101	= NORMSDIST(B19)
28	$N_1(b_1) =$	0.68649	= NORMSDIST(B20)
29	$N_1(b_2) =$	0.6598	= NORMSDIST(B21)
30	$N_1(-b_1) =$	0.31351	= NORMSDIST(-B20)
31	$N_1(-b_2) =$	0.3402	= NORMSDIST(-B21)
32	$\rho =$	−0.74536	= − SQRT(B10/B9)
33	$a = a_1;\ b = -b_1$		
34	$\Phi(a, -b; -\rho) =$	0.20259	= phi(−B20,0,−B37)
35	$\Phi(-a, b; -\rho) =$	0.04084	= phi(−B18,0,−B36)
36	$\rho ab =$	0.87002	= ((B32*B18–(−B20))*IF(B18 >= 0, 1, −1))/SQRT(B18^2 − 2* B32*B18*–B20+(−B20)^2)
37	$\rho ba =$	−0.31979	= ((B32*–B20–(B18))*IF(−B20 >=0,1,−1))/SQRT (B18^2– 2*B32*B18*−B20+(−B20)^2)
38	$N_2(a, 0; \rho ab) =$	0.45916	= bivarncdf(B18,0, B36)
39	$N_2(b, 0; \rho ba) =$	0.11092	= bivarncdf(−B20,0,B37)
40	$\delta =$	0.5	= (1 − IF(*B*18 >= 0,1,−1)*IF(−B20 >= 0,1,−1))/4

(*Continued*)

(*Continued*)

Number*	A	B	C*
41	$a = a_2$; $b = b_2$		
42	Φ(a, −b; −ρ) =	0.24401	= phi(−B21,0,−B45)
43	Φ(−a, b; −ρ) =	0.02757	= phi(−B19,0,−B44)
44	$\rho ab =$	0.94558	= ((B32*B19–(−B21))*IF(B19 >=0,1,−1))/SQRT (B19^2–2*B32*B19*–B21+(−B21)^2)
45	$\rho ba =$	−0.48787	= ((B32*–B21–(B19))*IF(−B21 >=0,1,−1))/SQRT (B19^2–2*B32*B19*−B21+(−B21)^2)
46	$N_2(a, 0; \rho ab) =$	0.47243	= bivarncdf(B19,0, B44)
47	$N_2(b, 0; \rho ba) =$	0.09619	= bivarncdf(−B21,0,B45)
48	$\delta =$	0.5	= (1–IF(B19 >=0,1,−1)* IF(−B21>=0,1,−1))/4
49			
50	$N_2(a_1, -b_1; \rho) =$	0.07007	= bivarncdf(B18,−B20,B32)
51	$N_2(a_2, -b_2; \rho) =$	0.06862	= bivarncdf(B19,−B21,B32)
52			
53	c (value of European call option to buy one share)	2.40123	= B5*NORMSDIST (B16)–B6*EXP(−B7*B9)*NO RMSDIST(B17)
54	p(value of European put option to sell one share)	1.44186	= −B5*NORMS DIST(−B16)+B6*EXP(−B7* B9)*NO RMSDIST(−B17)
55	c(value of American call option to buy one share)	3.08238	= (B3–B11*EXP(−B7*B10)) * (NORMSDIST(B20) +bivarncdf (B18,−B20,−SQRT(B10/B9)))–B6*EXP (−B7*B9)*(NORMSDIST (B21)* EXP(B7*(B9–B10)) + bivarncdf(B19,−B21,−SQRT (B10/B9)))+B11*EX P(−B7*B10)* NORMSDIST(B21)

Note: *The number of the row and the column in the Excel sheet.

Chapter 10

Index Option, Option on Index Futures, and Currency Option

Contents

10.1 Introduction

In previous chapters, we have discussed the valuations of forwards, futures, and options. In this chapter, we will discuss the valuation of index options, option on index futures, and currency option. In Section 10.2, we will discuss five major market indexes. These market indexes are the Dow Jones Industrial Average, Standard & Poor's Composite 500 Index, the New York Stock Exchange Composite Index, the Wilshire 5000 Equity Index, and Standard & Poor's Composite 100 Index. Index options will be discussed in Section 10.3.

Further, Section 10.4 covers the option on index futures, and the alternative international parity theory is introduced in Section 10.5. The currency option is presented in Section 10.6. Lastly, we will summarize this chapter in Section 10.7.

10.2 Market Indexes

In this section, we will discuss five important market indexes: Dow Jones Industrial Average, Standard & Poor's Composite 500 Index, the New York Stock Exchange Composite Index, the Wilshire 5000 Equity Index, and Standard & Poor's Composite 100 Index.

10.2.1 *Dow Jones Industrial Average*

The DJIA is probably the best known and most widely quoted of all the market indexes. Its latest value is broadcast many times a day, even on the least news-oriented top-40 radio stations. The Financial News Cable Network reports it every 90 seconds during a trading day. It is also probably the most criticized representation of the overall market among the available major stock indexes. The DJIA is a price-weighted arithmetic average of 30 large, well-known industrial stocks, all of which are listed on the New York Stock Exchange (NYSE). The computation involves summing the current prices of the 30 stocks and then dividing by a divisor that is adjusted to allow for any stock splits or large stock dividends:

$$DJIA = \sum_{i=t}^{3()} \frac{P_{it}}{DV_t}, \tag{10.1}$$

where P_{it} = the closing price of stock i on day t, and DV_t = the adjusted divisor on day t.

As can be seen in Table 10.1, the adjustment process is designed to keep the index value the same as it would have been if the split had not occurred. Similar adjustments have been made when it has been found necessary to replace one of the component stocks with the stock of another company. The consistency and comparability of index values at different points in time are thus protected. Nevertheless, the

Table 10.1 Adjustment of DJIA Divisor to Allow for a Stock Split

Stock	Price before Split	Price after 2-for-1 Stock Split by Stock A
A	60	30
B	30	30
C	20	20
D	10	10
	120	90
	Average $= \frac{120}{4} = 30$	Adjustment of Divisor $= \frac{90}{30} = 3$
		Average $= \frac{90}{3} = 30$
	Divisor before Split $= 4$	Divisor before Split $= 3$

adjustment process used for the DJIA has not been accepted without criticism. Since price weighting itself causes high-priced stocks to dominate the series, this same effect can cause a shift in this balance when fast-growing firms split their stock. For example, a 20% increase in the price of Stock A from Table 6.1 would have caused a 10% increase in the value of the sample index before the split, while a 20% increase in Stock B would have caused only a 5% increase in the index value. After the two-for-one split of Stock A, a 20% increase in either Stock A or Stock B would produce the same effect on the index value (a 6.7% increase), illustrating a downward shift in the importance of Stock A relative to the other stocks in the sample. This type of an effect could lead to the fastest-growing stocks having the least importance in determining the index values.

Other criticisms of the DJIA center on its emphasis on using only large, mature, "blue-chip" firms (and a small number of them at that) that do not seem to be like most companies in the market. The attitude of the multitudes that watch its daily movement seems to be "as the DJIA goes, so goes the economy." Since studies measuring the correlation of daily price changes of the DJIA with other broader indexes of NYSE stocks have found correlation coefficients ranging from 0.89 to 0.92, this attitude may be justified in the short run.[1]

[1]See Reilly, F. K. and C. K. Brown (2012). *Investments Analysis and Portfolio Management.* Cincinnati: South-Western Cengage Learning.

10.2.2 *Standard & Poor's Composite 500 Index*

The second most popular market index, **Standard & Poor's Composite 500 Index (S&P 500)**, is a value-weighted index of 400 industrial stocks, 40 utility stocks, 20 transportation stocks, and 40 financial stocks. It is computed as follows:

$$\text{S\&P}_t = \frac{\sum P_{it}Q_{it}}{\sum P_{i()}Q_{i()}} \times 10, \tag{10.2}$$

where P_{it} = price of stock i in period t, Q_{it} = number of shares outstanding for stock i in period t, $P_{\text{i}()}$ = price of stock i in the base period (), and $Q_{\text{i}()}$ = number of shares outstanding for stock i in base period (), and the base period is 1941–1943.

Since 1976, when the makeup of the S&P 500 was changed to include financial stocks, the index had for the first time included stocks from the over-the-counter (OTC) market. ("Over the counter" recalls the trading practices of the 1800s, when buyers and sellers of unlisted stocks traded their stocks over the bank counter.) This was necessary because many of the stocks of major financial institutions are traded on the OTC market.

While the S&P 500 is much more comprehensive in makeup — thus more representative of the overall market — than the DJIA, its total number of components is still small compared to the theoretically available market portfolio of all investment opportunities. The value-weighting computational approach is also subject to the criticism that firms with the largest market values have the most influence on the computed level. While this is certainly true, it is also true of the market portfolio itself, and should not be a problem except to the extent that the S&P 500 sample does not sufficiently reflect the makeup of the market portfolio. This cannot be properly evaluated empirically because of the impossibility of specifying the market portfolio accurately. In any case, the S&P 500 has gained added significance recently because of the development of options, futures contracts, and options on futures contracts for this index.[2] This has created a new opportunity for

[2]Other indexes for which options and futures contracts have been developed include the NYSE Composite Index, the Value Line Stock Index, and a subset of the S&P 500, the S&P 100.

portfolio managers by providing a new means to adjust the risk and return of a portfolio to desired levels. By adjusting the proportion of the futures position to the valuation of the portfolio, the portfolio manager can theoretically attain any risk–return combination desired. These opportunities are discussed in further detail in later chapters.

10.2.3 *New York Stock Exchange Composite Index*

Another commonly used value-weighted index is the **New York Stock Exchange Composite Index**, inaugurated in 1966 and consisting of the market values of all of the common stocks listed on the NYSE. While it includes many more stocks than the S&P 500 (over 2,000), this index can still be criticized as a proxy for the market portfolio because it contains none of the companies that cannot be listed, or choose not to be listed, on the NYSE. In addition, this index does not strictly consist of U.S. companies. Around 400 companies that are included in the NYSE Composite Index are foreign businesses. Although the index only includes companies that are listed on the NYSE, and includes both U.S. and foreign companies, this index is considered useful for investors seeking diversified and quality investments in large-cap companies.

10.2.4 *Wilshire 5000 Equity Index*

The **Wilshire 5000 Equity Index**, prepared by Wilshire Associates of Santa Monica, California, is a value-weighted and equal-weighted index that is increasing in usage because it contains most equity securities available for investment, including all NYSE and AMEX issues plus the most active stocks on the OTC market.

The following formula is used to compute the index:

$$I_t = I_{t-1}\left(\frac{\sum_{j=1}^{n}(S_{jt})P_{jt}}{\sum_{j=1}^{n}(S_{jt-1})P_{jt-1}}\right), \tag{10.3}$$

where I_t = index value for the tth period, n = number of stocks in index, P_{jt} = price of the jth security for the tth period, and S_{jt} = shares outstanding of the jth security for the tth period.

In the event that P_{jt} is not available for a given security, that security is dropped from the summations. If P_{jt-1} is not available but P_{jt} is — that is, a security has just resumed trading — the last available price is substituted for P_{jt-1}.

10.2.5 *Standard & Poor's Composite 100 Index*

Very recently, a subset of the S&P 500 called the **S&P 100** was developed for use in the futures and options markets. Although it may seem strange in the context of the increasing development of broader indexes that this more narrowly based index would be formed, it will become clear that the basis for its popularity is related to margin requirement in the options market. Sample Problem 6.2 provides further illustration.

Example 10.1. To illustrate the five indexes just discussed, daily quotations from *Yahoo Finance* for January 10 to January 25, 2022, are presented in Table 10.2. These quotations are the prices of the index at market close — adjusted for splits, dividends, and capital gains distributions.

Table 10.2 Major Stock Indexes for January 11, 2022–January 25, 2022

Indexes	DJIA	Nasdaq	S&P 500	Wilshire 5000	S&P 100
11-Jan	36,252.02	15,153.45	4,713.07	47,750.80	2,175.44
12-Jan	36,290.32	15,188.39	4,726.35	47,807.05	2,182.25
13-Jan	36,113.62	14,806.81	4,659.03	47,079.63	2,146.00
14-Jan	35,911.81	14,893.75	4,662.85	47,103.44	2,149.93
18-Jan	35,368.47	14,506.90	4,577.11	46,141.10	2,110.13
19-Jan	35,028.65	14,340.26	4,532.76	45,673.16	2,090.13
20-Jan	34,715.39	14,154.02	4,482.73	45,142.14	2,068.11
21-Jan	34,265.37	13,768.92	4,397.94	44,219.81	2,024.95
24-Jan	34,364.50	13,855.13	4,410.13	44,455.17	2,026.16
25-Jan	34,297.73	13,539.29	4,356.45	43,843.05	2,003.70

10.3 Index Option

Index option is the option on stock index instead of individual stocks. Many different index options currently trade in the United States. The most popular contracts are those on the S&P 500 Index and the S&P 100 Index (CBOE). Index options may be European or American. The contract on the S&P 500 is European, whereas that on the S&P 100 is American. For example, one CBOE contract is to buy or sell 100 times the index at the specified strike price of 280. If it is exercised when the value of the index is 292, the writer of the contract pays the holder $(292 - 280) \times 100 = \$1,200$. This cash payment is based on the index value at the end of the day in which the exercise instructions are issued. Not surprisingly, investors usually wait until the end of a day before issuing these instructions.

In valuing index, assume that it could be treated as a security paying a known dividend yield. Therefore, the European style of index call options can be evaluated in terms of the European style of stock call option formula defined as

$$C = S'N(d_1) - Xe^{-rt}N(d_2), \tag{10.4}$$

where $S' = Se^{-qt}$, S = spot exchange rate, q = dividend yield, r = risk-free rate, X = exercise price, σ = standard deviation of spot exchange rate, t = time to expiration, $d_1 = [\ln(S/X) + (r - q + \frac{1}{2}\sigma^2)t]/\sigma\sqrt{t}$, and $d_2 = d_1 - \sigma\sqrt{t}$.

Example 10.2 (Index option valuation). Consider a European call option on the S&P 500 that is two months from maturity. The current value of the index is 950, the exercise price is 900, the risk-free interest rate is 6% per annum, and the volatility of the index is 15 per annum. Dividend yields of 0.2% and 0.3% are expected in the first and the second month, respectively. In this case, $S = 950$, $X = 900$, $r = 0.06$, $\sigma = 0$, and $T = 2/12$. The total dividend yield during the option's life is $0.2 + 0.3 = 0.5\%$. This is 3% per annum. Hence, $q = 0.03$ and

$$d_1 = \frac{\left[\ln(950/900) + (0.06 - 0.03 + (0.15)^2(.5))\left(\frac{2}{12}\right)\right]}{(0.15)\sqrt{2/12}}$$

$$= \frac{.054 + .007}{.061} = 1.$$

$$d_2 = 1 - (.15)\sqrt{2/12} = .93.$$

From the Normal Distribution table, we obtained that

$$N(d_1) = 0.8413 \quad N(d_2) = 0.8238,$$

so that the call price, C, is given by Equation (10.4):

$$C = 950(0.8413)e^{-0.03\times 2/12} - 900(.8238)e^{-0.006\times 2/12}$$

$$= 795.24 - 734.01 = 61.23.$$

One contract would cost $\$61.23 \times 100 = \$6,123$.

If the absolute amount of the dividend that will be paid on the stocks underlying the index (rather than the dividend yield) is assumed to be known, the basic Black–Scholes formula can be used with the initial stock price reduced by the present value of the dividends.

Example 10.3. Consider a European call option on the S&P 500 that is three months from maturity. The current value of index is 1,000, the exercise price is 950, the risk-free rate is 6% per annum, and the volatility of the index is 15% per annum. Total dividend yields during the option's life will be 1%. What is the value of the index call option?

The European style of index call options can be evaluated as

$$C = S'N(d_1) - Xe^{-rt}N(d_2),$$

where $S' = Se^{-qt}$, S = spot exchange rate, q = dividend yield per year, r = risk-free rate, X = exercise price, σ = standard deviation of spot exchange rate, and t = time to expiration, $d_1 = [\ln(S/X) + (r - q + \frac{1}{2}\sigma^2)t]/\sigma\sqrt{t}$, and $d_2 = d_1 - \sigma\sqrt{t}$.

$S = 1,000$, $X = 950$, $r = 6\%$, $\sigma = 15\%$, $t = 3/12 = 0.25$, total dividend yield during 3 months is 1%, so dividend yield per annum is 4% (i.e., $q = 4\%$).

$$d_1 = \left[\ln(1000/950) + \left(0.06 - 0.04 + \frac{1}{2}(0.15)^2\right)\right.$$
$$\left.\times (0.25)\right] \Big/ (0.15)\sqrt{0.25} = 0.7881.$$

$$d_2 = d_1 - \sigma\sqrt{t} = 0.7881 - (0.15)\sqrt{0.25} = 0.7131.$$

$$N(d_1) = N(0.7881) = 0.7847, N(d_2) = N(0.7131) = 0.7621$$

$$C = 1000e^{-0.04(0.25)}(0.7847) - 950e^{-0.06(0.25)}(0.7621) = 63.6495.$$

10.4 Option on Index Futures

For a review of the literature on option pricing, see the two papers by Smith (1976, 1979). It is appropriate here to make a few remarks on the Black–Scholes option pricing model to clarify its significance and its limitation.

First, the Black–Scholes model for a European call as originally derived, and as reported here, is based on several simplifying assumptions:

(1) The stock price follows an Itô equation.
(2) The market operates continuously.
(3) There are no transaction costs in buying or selling the option or the underlying stock.
(4) There are no taxes.
(5) The riskless rate is known and constant.
(6) There are no restrictions on short sales.

Several researchers have extended the original Black–Scholes model by modifying these assumptions. Merton (1973) generalized the model to include dividend payments, exercise price changes, and the case of a stochastic interest rate. Roll (1977) had solved the problem of valuing a call option that can be exercised prior to its expiration date when the underlying stock is assumed to make known dividend payments before the option matures. Ingersoll (1976) studied the effect of differential taxes on capital gains and income, while Scholes (1976) determined the effects of the tax treatment of options on the pricing model. Furthermore, Merton (1976) and Cox and Ross (1976) showed that if the stock price movements are discontinuous, under certain assumptions, the valuation model still holds. These and other modifications of the original Black–Scholes analysis indicate that the model is quite robust about the relaxation of its fundamental assumptions.

Second, it is worth repeating that the use of Itô's calculus and the important insight concerning the appropriate concept of equilibrium by creating a riskless hedge portfolio have let Black and Scholes obtain a closed-form solution for option pricing. In this closed-form solution, several variables do not appear, such as (1) the expected rate of return of the stock, (2) the expected rate of return of the option, (3) a measure of investor's risk preference, (4) investor expectations, and (5) equilibrium conditions for the entire capital market.

Third, the Black–Scholes pricing model has found numerous applications. Among these are the following: (1) pricing the debt and equity of a firm; (2) the effects of corporate policy and, specially, the effects of mergers, acquisitions, and scale expansions on the relative values of the debt and equity of the firm; (3) the pricing of convertible bonds; (4) the pricing of underwriting contracts; (5) the pricing of leases; and (6) the pricing of insurance. Smith (1976, 1979) summarized most applications and indicates the original reference. See also Brealey and Myers (1988).

Fourth, Black (1976) showed that the original call option formula for stocks can be easily modified to be used in pricing call options on futures. The formula is

$$C(T, F, \sigma^2, X, r) = \mathrm{e}^{-rT}[FN(d_1) - XN(d_2)], \tag{10.5}$$

$$d_1 = \frac{\ln(F/X) + \frac{1}{2}\sigma^2 T}{\sigma\sqrt{T}}, \tag{10.6}$$

$$d_2 = \frac{\ln(F/X) - \frac{1}{2}\sigma^2 T}{\sigma\sqrt{T}}. \tag{10.7}$$

In Equation (10.5), F now denotes the current futures price. The other four variables are as before — time to maturity, volatility of the underlying futures price, exercise price, and risk-free rate. Note that Equation (10.5) differs from Equation (10.4) only in one respect: by substituting $e^{-rT}F$ for S in the original Equation (10.4), Equation (10.5) is obtained. This holds because the investment in a futures contract is zero, which causes the interest rate in Equations (10.6) and (10.7) to drop out.

Fifth, three important papers by Harrison and Kreps (1979) and Kreps (1981, 1982) consider some foundational issues that arise in conjunction with the arbitrage theory of option pricing. The important point to consider is this: The ability to trade securities frequently can enable a few multiperiod securities to span many states of nature. In the Black–Scholes theory, there are two securities and uncountable many states of nature, but because there are infinitely many trading opportunities and because uncertainty resolves nicely, markets are effectively complete. Thus, even though there are far fewer securities than states of nature, markets are complete and risk is allocated efficiently. An interesting result of Harrison and Kreps (1979) is that certain self-trading strategies can create something out of nothing when there are infinitely many trading opportunities. The doubling strategies are the well-known illustrations of this phenomenon. Harrison and Kreps introduce the concept of a simple strategy to eliminate free lunches and conjecture that a non-negative wealth constraint could rule out the doubling strategies. Duffie and Huang (1985) gave an interpretation of admissible strategy as a limit of a sequence of simple strategies and used an integrability condition on the trading strategies. Dybvig and Huang (1986) showed that under certain conditions, the non-negative wealth constraints are functionally equivalent.

Finally, for an intensive survey of numerous empirical tests, see Galai (1983).

Example 10.4. Assume that the current price of futures on Japanese yen is 100 and the exercise price on the futures is 85. Volatility of the futures price is 13%. The risk-free rate in the U.S. is 3.2% per annum. And the future option is going to mature one year from now. What is the value of the future call option?

Solution

$$C(T, F, \sigma^2, X, r) = \mathrm{e}^{-rT}[FN(d_1) - XN(d_2)],$$

where

$$d_1 = \frac{\ln\left(\frac{F}{N}\right) + \frac{1}{2}\sigma^2 T}{\sigma\sqrt{T}},$$

$$d_2 = \frac{\ln(F/N) - \frac{1}{2}\sigma^2 T}{\sigma\sqrt{T}}.$$

Given that $F = \$100$, $X = \$85$, $\sigma = 13\%$, $r = 3.2\%$, and $T = 1$, then $d_1 = 1.3151$, $d_2 = 1.1851$ and $N(d_1) = 0.9058$, $N(d_2) = 0.8820$ Therefore, $C = 15.11$.

10.5 Alternative International Parity Theory

10.5.1 *The traditional theory of international parity*

The writings of Keynes, Cassel, and Irving Fisher implicitly require four conditions for international currency parity:

(1) Financial markets are perfect. There are no controls, transaction costs, taxes, and so on.
(2) Goods markets are perfect. Shipment of goods anywhere in the world is costless.
(3) There is a single consumption good common to everyone.
(4) The future is known with certainty.

10.5.1.1 *Interest rate parity*

The arbitrage argument used to establish the price of a currency futures contract relative to the spot price is called **interest rate parity** (which will be addressed again shortly). In the case of the U.S. dollar/British pound,

$$F_{t,T} = S_t \frac{(1 + R_{t,T}^{\$})}{(1 + R_{t,T}^{£})}, \tag{10.8}$$

where $F_{t,T}$ = equilibrium price at time t for a currency futures contract maturing at time T, S_t = spot price at time t for the foreign currency (to which the futures contract applies), $R^{\$}_{t,T}$ =U.S. interest rate on risk-free securities maturing at time T, and $R^{£}_{t,T}$ = British interest rate on risk-free securities maturing at time T.

Sample example 10.6 provides further illustration.

10.5.1.2 *Purchasing power parity*

According to the laws of one price in perfect markets, identical goods must have the same real price everywhere. Since it is assumed that every country consumes the same good (or basket of goods), a given currency has the same purchasing power in every country:

$$\frac{P_i^t}{P_j^t} = S_{ij}^t,$$

where S_{ij}^t = the spot rate between countries i and j at time t, and P_i^t and P_j^t = price level in countries i and j at time t, respectively.

Example 10.5. As an example, suppose the U.S. dollar is currently quoted in the spot currency market for the British pound at \$1.80/£. Interest rates in the United States and Britain for three months are 3% and 4%, respectively. What is the price of a three-month deposit futures contract for pounds?

Solution

Substituting all information into Equation (10.8),

$$\begin{aligned} F_{t,3\,\text{mo}} &= (\$1.80/£)\left(\frac{1+0.03}{1+0.04}\right) \\ &= \$1.70/£. \end{aligned}$$

Empirical tests have shown that the pricing relationship described by interest rate parity holds very closely in the currency markets. The following is offered for clarification.

In the previous section on pricing theory for futures prices, spot prices of foreign currency were described as following a random walk.

Thus, money as a liquid financial instrument incorporates anticipations of its future value into its current value. This is analogous to the manner in which future stock prices and dividend estimates are reflected in today's stock price. Using this rational expectations hypothesis and momentarily assuming no inventory costs,

$$S_t = E_t(S_T), \tag{10.9}$$

or today's price reflects the expected price for the foreign currency at time T.

Equation (10.9) can be reversed:

$$E_t(S_T) = S_t. \tag{10.10}$$

Hence, the best estimate for the spot price at some future point in time T is the current spot price of the currency. Since the currency futures price at time t for a contract maturing at time T reflects the expected spot price for the foreign currency at time T (assuming no carrying costs),

$$F_{t,T} = E_t(S_T). \tag{10.11}$$

Consequently,

$$F_{t,T} = S_t.$$

So, without carrying costs, the current futures price equals the current spot price for any foreign currency. Sample example 10.6 provides further illustration.

Example 10.6. To see how the carrying cost (or relative opportunity cost) associated with interest has an effect on the valuation of foreign currency futures, assume that the spot and one-year futures prices for the British pound are \$1.30 and \$1.33, respectively. Suppose an American investor who bought \$1.3 million worth of pounds (£ 1 million) then invests £ 1 million at the 10% riskless rate yielded by one-year British government securities. Furthermore, in order to hedge himself or herself against fluctuations in the dollar–pound exchange rate, the investor sells £ 1 million worth of one-year futures contracts on pounds at 1.33 (equal to the value of 40 contracts). Assuming the investor holds his futures position to its maturity and then delivers the initial £ 1 million investment to close the position, the following is a summary of the transactions and closing position value:

February 1, 2021	
Buy $1.3 million worth of pounds.	
Invest proceeds at 10% British rate.	
Sell £ 1 million worth of futures at $1.33.	
February 1, 2022	
Proceeds from earned interest	$150,000
Deliver £ 1 million against short futures Position at $1.33/£ 1.00	$1,330,000
Gross revenue	$1,460,000
Less initial investment	$1,300,000
Net profit	$160,000
Annual return	12.3%

From all these transactions, the investor earns an annualized return of 12.3% on the original investment of $1.3 million. This return is composed of the interest earned on the riskless British government security and the 0.03 difference in spot and one-year futures prices for the pound (i.e., the investor sold the pound at $1.33 but only paid $1.30).

If the investor can borrow U.S. dollars at a rate less than 12.3%, then a riskless arbitrage opportunity is available. For instance, if the U.S. lending rate is 11.0%, the investor could borrow the initial capital of $1.3 million and after one year repay the interest of 11% and clear a 1.3% risk-free return. However, this opportunity will not pass unnoticed. Arbitragers will buy pounds (bidding their price up), invest the pounds in one-year British government securities yielding 10% (bidding their price up and yield down), and sell an equivalent number of futures contracts (forcing their price down). Finally, these arbitrage portfolios will be financed by borrowing U.S. dollars at the going 11.0% rate (forcing the rate to increase). All pressures discussed in this problem will continue until the arbitrage opportunity has dissipated. That point will be attained when

$$S_t(1 + R^{\$}_{t,T}) = F_{t,T}(1 + R^{£}_{t,T}), \tag{10.12}$$

where $R^{\$}_{t,T}$ and $R^{£}_{t,T}$ are interest rates on securities with the same maturity as the futures contract (one year, in this case).

Rearranging Equation (10.6) to solve for $F_{t,T}$, the futures price for a one-year contract on British pounds, we have

$$F_{t,T} = S_t \frac{(1 + R^{\$}_{t,T})}{(1 + R^{£}_{t,T})}. \tag{10.13}$$

This is the interest rate parity relationship from Equation (15.1). Thus, the equilibrium one-year futures price for British pounds that would eliminate the arbitrage opportunity in the example can be computed as

$$\begin{aligned} F_{t,T} &= (\$1.30/£)\left(\frac{1 + 0.11}{1 + 0.10}\right) \\ &= \$1.3118/£. \end{aligned}$$

10.6 Currency Option

A currency option is an option on the spot exchange rate instead of either individual stock or the stock index. An exchange rate is the price of one currency in terms of another currency. For example, the exchange rate between the Japanese yen and U.S. dollar was 115.262 on January 31, 2022.

The valuation model for the European type of currency call option can be defined as

$$C = Se^{-r_f t}N(d_1) - Xe^{-rt}N(d_2), \tag{10.14}$$

where S = spot exchange rate, r = domestic risk-free rate, r_f = foreign risk-free rate, X = exercise price, σ = standard deviation of spot exchange rate, and t = time to expiration,

$$d_1 = \frac{ln\left(\frac{P}{E}\right) + (r - r_f)\,t + \sigma^2 \frac{t}{2}}{\sigma\sqrt{t}} \quad \text{and}$$

$$d_2 = \frac{ln\left(\frac{P}{E}\right) + (r - r_f)\,t - \sigma^2 \frac{t}{2}}{\sigma\sqrt{t}} = d_1 - \sigma\sqrt{t}.$$

By comparing the standard Black and Scholes option pricing model, it is found that Equation (22.13) can be obtained by replacing q with r_f.

Example 10.7 (Valuation of currency option).
Consider a four-month European call option on the Japanese yen. Suppose that the current exchange rate is 130, the exercise price is 125, the risk-free rate in the United States is 6% per annum, and the risk-free rate in Japan is 2% per annum. The volatility of foreign exchange rate is 15%.

Substituting $S = 130$, $X = 125$, $r = 0.06$, r_f =0.02, $\sigma = .15$, $T = 4/12$ into Equation (10.14), we obtain

$$d_1 = \frac{\ln\left(\frac{130}{125}\right) + (0.06 - 0.02 + \left(\frac{(.15)^2}{2}\right)\left(\frac{4}{12}\right)}{(.15)\sqrt{\frac{4}{12}}}$$

$$= \frac{.0392 + .0171}{.0866} = .6501.$$

$$d_2 = .6501 - (.15)\sqrt{\frac{4}{12}} = .5635.$$

From the standard normal distribution table, we obtain

$$N(.65) = .7422\, N(.56) = 0.7123.$$

Substituting all related information into Equation (22.13), we obtain

$$\begin{aligned} C &= 130e^{-\frac{.02}{3}}(.7422) - (125)e^{-\frac{.06}{3}}(.7123) \\ &= 95.8395 - 87.2746 \\ &= 8.5649. \end{aligned}$$

10.7 Summary

In this chapter, we first discussed five major market indexes. These market indexes are the Dow Jones Industrial Average, Standard & Poor's Composite 500 Index, the New York Stock Exchange Composite Index, the Wilshire 5000 Equity Index, and Standard & Poor's Composite 100 Index. Based upon the indexes covered in the previous sections, we first discussed the valuation of index options. Then, the valuation of options on index futures was discussed in some detail.

The three alternative international parity theories are covered in this chapter in detail. Based upon these concepts, we discuss the concept of currency option and their valuations.

Questions and Problems

1. Define the following terms:

(a) exchange rate risk	(b) interest rate parity
(c) purchasing power parity	(d) the Fisher effect
(e) spot rate	(f) forward rate
(g) direct foreign investment	(h) international portfolio investment
(i) ADR	

2. What are the returns to a U.S. investor for the investments shown in the table?

	Foreign Return (%)	Currency Change (%)
A	12	2
B	10	−5
C	7	0
D	10	−20

3. Can currency risk be diversified away for the U.S. investor?
4. The spot rate for the French franc is $\$1 = 6\text{FF}$. The inflation rate is 5% in the United States and 10% in France. What is the expected future spot rate for the franc in dollars?
5. What are the advantages of an ADR for the U.S. investor?

6. Consider that a European call option on the Japanese yen is maturing one year from now. Suppose that the current exchange rate is 80, the exercise price is 85, the risk-free rate in the United States is 3% per annum, and the risk-free rate in Japan is 2% per annum. The volatility of foreign exchange rate is 15%. What is the value of the currency call option?
7. Consider a European call option on the S&P 500 that is three months from maturity. The current value of the index is 1,000, the exercise price is 950, the risk-free interest rate is 6% per annum, and the volatility of the index is 15 per annum. Total dividend yields during the option's life will be 1%. What is the value of the index call option?
8. Suppose you have $1,200 and invest in a Japanese company, ABC. The stock price of ABC is ¥200 per share. The exchange rate at that time is ¥100. That is, ¥100 can exchange to $1. One year later, the ABC stock price is ¥250 per share and pays ¥20 dividends per share, and the exchange rate is ¥90. What is the rate of return on your investment in terms of the Japanese yen? What is the rate of return on your investment in terms of the U.S. dollar?

Bibliography

Abeysekera, S. P. and A. Mahajan (1985). The international arbitrage pricing theory: An empirical investigation. Working paper, presented June 1985, Western Finance Association Annual Meeting.

Adler, M. and B. Dumas (1983). International portfolio choice and corporate finance: A synthesis. *Journal of Finance*, 38(June), 925–984.

Adler, M. and D. Simon (1986). Exchange risk surprises in international portfolios. *Journal of Portfolio Management*, 12(Winter), 44–53.

Ang, J. and R. Pohlman (1978). A note on the price behavior of far eastern stocks. *Journal of International Business Studies*, 9(Spring), 103–107.

Bae, K., W. Bailey and C. X. Mao (2006). Stock market liberalization and the information environment. *Journal of International Money and Finance*, 25, 404–428.

Beck, T., A. Demirgüç-Kunt and R. Levine (2003). Law, endowments, and finance. *Journal of Financial Economics*, 70, 137–181.

Bekaert, G. and C. R. Harvey (1995). Time-varying world market integration. *Journal of Finance*, 50, 403–444.

Bekaert, G. and C. R. Harvey (1997). Emerging equity market volatility. *Journal of Financial Economics*, 43, 29–77.

Bekaert, G. and C. R. Harvey (2000). Foreign speculators and emerging equity markets. *Journal of Finance*, 55, 565–614.

Bekaert, G. and C. R. Harvey (2003). Emerging markets finance. *Journal of Empirical Finance*, 10, 3–56.

Bekaert, G. and G. Wu (2000). Asymmetric volatility and risk in equity markets. *Review of Financial Studies*, 13, 1–42.

Bekaert, G., C. R. Harvey and A. Ng (2005). Market integration and contagion. *Journal of Business*, 78, 39–70.

Bekaert, G., R. Hodrick and X. Zhang (2009). International stock return comovements. *Journal of Finance*, 64(December), 2591–2626.

Bekaert, G., C. R. Harvey, C. T. Lundblad and S. Siegel (2008). What segments equity markets? Working paper, Columbia University.

Black, F. (1974). International capital market equilibrium with investment barriers. *Journal of Financial Economics*, 1(December), 337–352.

Black, F. (1978). The ins and outs of foreign investment. *Financial Analysts Journal*, 34(May/June), 25–32.

Bodie, Z., A. Kane and A. J. Marcus (2011). *Investments*, 9th ed. New York: McGraw-Hill.

Bollerslev, T. (1986). Generalized autoregressive conditional heteroscedasticity. *Journal of Econometrics*, 31, 307–327.

Bomberger, W. A. and W. J. Frazer (1981). Interest rates, uncertainty, and the Livingston data. *Journal of Finance*, 36(June), 661–679.

Box, G. E. P., G. M. Jenkins and G. C. Reinsel (1994). *Time Series Analysis: Forecasting and Control*, 3rd ed. Upper Saddle River, NJ: Prentice Hall.

Breeden, D. T. (1979). An intertemporal asset pricing model with stochastic consumption and investment opportunities. *Journal of Financial Economics*, 7(September), 265–296.

Carrieri, F., V. Errunza and S. Sarkissian (2004). Industry risk and market integration. *Management Science*, 50, 207–221.

Chen, S. and C. F. Lee (1981). The sampling relationship between Sharpe's performance measure and its risk proxy: Sample size, investment horizon and market conditions. *Management Science*, 27, 607–618.

Chen, S. and C. F. Lee (1986). The effects of the sample size, the investment horizon and market conditions on the validity of composite performance measures: A generalization. *Management Science*, 32, 1410–1421.

Chiou, W. P., A. C. Lee and C. A. Chang (2009). Do investors still benefit from international diversification with investment constraints? *Quarterly Review of Economics and Finance*, 49, 448–483.

Chiou, W. P., A. C. Lee and C. F. Lee (2009). Variation in stock return risks: An international comparison. *Review of Pacific Basin Financial Markets and Policies*, 12, 245–266.

Chiou, W. P., A. C. Lee and C. F. Lee (2010). Stock return, risk and legal environment around the world. *International Review of Economics and Finance*, 19, 95–105.

Cho, D. C., C. S. Eun and L. W. Senbet (1986). International arbitrage pricing theory: An empirical investigation. *Journal of Finance*, 41(June), 313–329.

Cohn, R. A. and J. J. Pringle (1973). Imperfection in international financial markets: Implications for risk premium and the cost of capital to firms. *Journal of Finance*, 28(March), 59–66.

Cornell, B. (1977). Spot rates, forward rates, and exchange market efficiency. *Journal of Financial Economics*, 5(August), 55–65.

Cornell, B. (1980). Inflation, relative price changes, and exchange risk. *Financial Management*, 9(Autumn), 30–34.

De Santis, G. and S. İmrohoroğlu (1997). Stock returns and volatility in emerging financial markets. *Journal of International Money and Finance*, 16, 561–579.

Demirgüç-Kunt, A. and V. Maksimovic (1998). Law, finance, and firm growth. *Journal of Finance*, 53, 2107–2137.

Demirgüç-Kunt, A. and V. Maksimovic (2002). Bank-based and market-based financial systems: Evidence from firm-level data. *Journal of Financial Economics*, 65, 337–363.

Dumas, B., J. Fleming and R. E. Whaley (1998). Implied volatility functions: Empirical tests. *Journal of Finance*, 53, 2059–2106.

Errunza, V. R. and L. Senbet (1981). The effects of international operations on the market value of the firm: Theory and evidence. *Journal of Finance*, 36(May), 401–417.

Eun, C. S. (1989). International portfolio diversification, in D. K. Eiteman and A. I. Stonehill (eds.), *Multinational Business Finance*. New York, NY: Addison-Wesley.

Eun, C. S. and B. Resnick (1984). Estimating the correlation structure of international share prices. *Journal of Finance*, 39(December), 1311–1324.

Eun, C. S. and B. Resnick (1987). International diversification under estimation risk: Actual vs. potential gains, in S. Khoury and A. Gosh (eds.), *Recent Developments in International Banking and Finance*, pp. 135–147. Lexington, MA: Lexington Books.

Eun, C. S. and B. Resnick (1988). Estimating the dependence structure of share prices: A comparative study of the U.S. and Japan. *The Financial Review*, 23(November), 387–401.

Fama, E. F. and A. Farber (1979). Money bonds and foreign exchange. *American Economic Review*, 69(September), 639–650.

Frankel, J. and R. Levich (1975). Covered interest arbitrage: Unexploited profits? *Journal of Political Economy*, 83(April), 325–338.

Grauer, F., R. Litzenberger and R. Stehle (1976). Sharing rules and equilibrium in an international capital market under uncertainty. *Journal of Financial Economics*, 3(June), 233–256.

Grubel, H. G. (1968). International diversified portfolios: Welfare gains and capital flows. *American Economic Review*, 58(December), 1299–1314.

Grubel, H. G. and K. Fadner (1971). The interdependence of international equity markets. *Journal of Finance*, 26(March), 89–94.

Guerard, J. B. (2010). *Handbook of Portfolio and Construction: Contemporary Applications of Markowitz Techniques*. New York, NY: Springer.

Hamilton, J. D. and G. Lin (1996). Stock market volatility and the business cycle. *Journal of Applied Econometrics*, 11, 573–593.

Harvey, C. (1991). The world price of covariance risk. *Journal of Finance*, 46, 111–157.

Haugen, R. A., E. Talmor and W. N. Torous (1991). The effect of volatility changes on the level of stock prices and subsequent expected returns. *Journal of Finance*, 46, 985–1007.

Hawawini, G. (1984). *European Equity Markets: Price Behavior and Efficiency*. Salomon Brothers Center, New York University.

Ibbotson, R., L. Siegel and K. Love (1985). World wealth: Market values and returns. *Journal of Portfolio Management*, 11(Fall), 4–23.

Jacob, N. L. and R. R. Pettit (1984). *Investments*. Homewood, IL: Richard D. Irwin, Inc.

Jacquillat, B. and B. Solnik (1978). Multinationals are poor tools for diversification. *Journal of Portfolio Management*, 4(Winter), 8–12.

Jaffe, J. and R. Westerfield (1985). Patterns in Japanese common stock returns: Day of the week and turn of the year effects. *Journal of Finance and Quantitative Analysis*, 20(June), 259–278.

John, L. M., L. M. Donald, E. P. Jerald and W. M. Dennis (2007). *Managing Investment Portfolios: A Dynamic Process*, 3rd ed. New York: CFA Institute.

Jorion, R. (1985). International portfolio diversification with estimation risk. *Journal of Business*, 58(July), 259–278.

Karolyi, G. A. and R. M. Stulz (2003). Are financial assets priced locally or globally? *Handbook of the Economics of Finance*, 1B, 975–1020.

Kato, K. and J. S. Schallheim (1985). Seasonal and size anomalies in the Japanese stock market. *Journal of Financial and Quantitative Analysis*, 20(June), 243–260.

Kim, E. H. and V. Singal (2000). Stock markets openings: Experience of emerging Economies. *Journal of Business*, 73, 25–66.

La Porta, R., F. Lopez-de-Silanes, A. Shleifer and R. Vishny (1998). Law and finance. *Journal of Political Economy*, 106, 1113–1155.

La Porta, R., F. Lopez-de-Silanes, A. Shleifer and R. Vishny (1999). The quality government. *Journal of Law, Economics, and Organization*, 15, 222–279.

La Porta, R., F. Lopez-de-Silanes, A. Shleifer and R. Vishny (2000). Investor protection and corporate governance. *Journal of Financial Economics*, 58, 141–186.

Lee, C. F. (2020). Financial econometrics, mathematics, statistics, and financial technology: An overall view. *Review of Quantitative Finance and Accounting*, 54(4), 1529–1578.

Lee, W. Y. and K. Sachdeva (1977). The role of multinational firm in the integration of segmented capital markets. *Journal of Finance*, 32(May), 479–492.

Lee C. F., Chen, H.-Y. and Lee, J. (2019). *Financial Econometrics, Mathematics and Statistics*. New York: Springer Academic Publishers.

Lessard, D. R. (1973). International portfolio diversification: A multivariate analysis for a group of Latin American countries. *Journal of Finance*, 28(June), 619–633.

Lessard, D. R. (1976). World, country, and industry relationships in equity returns: Implications for risk reduction through international diversification. *Financial Analysis Journal*, 32(January/February), 32–38.

Levy, H. and M. Sarnat (1970). International diversification of investment portfolios. *American Economic Review*, 60(September), 668–675.

Madhavan, A., M. Richardson and M. Roomans (1997). Why do security prices change? A transaction-level analysis of NYSE stocks. *Review of Financial Studies*, 10, 1035–1064.

Maldonado, R. and A. Saunders (1981). International portfolio diversification and international stability of international stock market relationships. *Financial Management*, 10(Autumn), 54–63.

Pindyck, R. S. (1984). Risk, inflation, and the stock market. *American Economic Review*, 74, 335–351.

Proffitt, D. and N. Seitz (1983). The performance of internationally diversified mutual funds. *Journal of the Midwest Finance Association*, 12(March), 39–53.

Reilly, F. K. and C. K. Brown (2012). *Investments Analysis and Portfolio Management*. Cincinnati: South-Western Cengage Learning.

Robichek, A. A. and M. R. Eaker (1978). Foreign exchange hedging and capital asset pricing model. *Journal of Financial*, 33(June), 1011–1018.

Roll, R. (1977). A critique of asset pricing theories tests. Part I: On past and potential testability of the theory. *Journal of Economics*, 4(March), 129–176.

Roll, R. (1979). Violations of purchasing power parity and their implications for efficient international commodity markets, in M. Sarnat and G. Szego (eds.), *International Finance and Trade*. Cambridge, MA: Bollinger.

Roll, R. and B. Solnik (1977). A pure foreign exchange asset pricing model. *Journal of International Economics*, 13(May), 161–179.

Senchack, A. and W. Beedles (1980). Is indirect international diversification desirable? *Journal of Portfolio Management*, 6(Winter), 49–57.

Solnik, B. (1974a). An equilibrium model of the international capital market. *Journal of Economic Theory*, 8(August), 500–525.

Solnik, B. (1974b). An international model of security price behavior. *Journal of Financial and Quantitative Analysis*, 9(September), 537–554.

Solnik, B. (1974c). The international pricing of risk: An empirical investigation of the world capital market structure. *Journal of Finance*, 29(May), 365–378.

Solnik, B. (1974d). Why not diversity internationally rather than domestically? *Financial Analysis Journal*, 29(July/August), 48–54.

Solnik, B. (1977). Testing international asset pricing: Some pessimistic views. *Journal of Finance*, 32(May), 503–512.

Solnik, B. (1988). *International Investments*. Reading, MA: Addison-Wesley.

Stehle, R. (1977). An empirical test of the alternate hypothesis of national and international pricing of risky assets. *Journal of Finance*, 32(May), 493–507.

Stockman, A. (1980). A theory of exchange rate determination. *Journal of Political Economy*, 88(August), 673–699.

Stulz, R. (1981a). A model of international asset pricing. *Journal of Financial Economics*, 9(December), 383–406.

Stulz, R. (1981b). On the effects of barriers to international investment. *Journal of Finance*, 36(September), 923–934.

Stulz, R. M. and R. Williamson (2003). Culture, openness, and finance. *Journal Financial Economics*, 70, 313–349.

Subrashmanyam, M. (1975). On the optimality of international capital market integration. *Journal of Financial Economics*, 2(August), 3–28.

Veronesi, P. (1999). Stock market overreaction to bad news in good times: A rational expectations equilibrium model. *Review of Financial Studies*, 12, 975–1007.

Witter, D. (1984). Dean Witter World Wide Investment Trust. Prospectus, June 1984.

Part IV

Advanced Analyses of Options

Chapter 11

Comparative Static Analysis of the Option Pricing Models

Contents

11.1 Introduction

In Chapter 7, we have discussed how the call option value can be affected by stock price per share, exercise price per share, the contract period of the option, the risk-free rate, and the volatility of the stock return. In this chapter, we will mathematically analyze these kinds of relationships. Parts of these mathematical relationships are called "Greek letters" by finance professionals. Here, we specifically derive Greek letters for call (put) options on non-dividend stock and dividends-paying stock. Some examples will be provided to explain applications of these Greek letters. Sections 11.2 to 11.5 discuss the derivations and applications of Delta, Theta, Gamma, Vega, and Rho, respectively. Section 11.6 derives the partial derivative of stock options with respect to their exercise prices. Section 11.7 describes the relationship between Delta, Theta, and Gamma, and their implications in delta-neutral portfolio. Finally, in Section 11.8, we summarize and conclude this chapter.

11.2 Delta (Δ)

The delta of an option, Δ, is defined as the rate of change of the option price with respect to the rate of change of the underlying asset price:

$$\Delta = \frac{\partial \Pi}{\partial S},$$

where Π is the option price and S is underlying asset price. We next show the derivation of delta for various kinds of stock options.

11.2.1 *Derivation of delta for different kinds of stock options*

From the Black–Scholes option pricing model, we know the price of a call option on a non-dividend stock can be written as

$$C_t = S_t N(d_1) - Xe^{-r\tau} N(d_2), \tag{11.1}$$

and the price of put option on a non-dividend stock can be written as

$$P_t = Xe^{-r\tau} N(-d_2) - S_t N(-d_1), \tag{11.2}$$

where

$$d_1 = \frac{\ln\left(\frac{S_t}{X}\right) + \left(r + \frac{\sigma_s^2}{2}\right)\tau}{\sigma_s\sqrt{\tau}},$$

$$d_2 = \frac{\ln\left(\frac{S_t}{X}\right) + \left(r - \frac{\sigma_s^2}{2}\right)\tau}{\sigma_s\sqrt{\tau}} = d_1 - \sigma_s\sqrt{\tau},$$

$$\tau = T - t,$$

$N(\cdot)$ is the cumulative density function of normal distribution.

$$N(d_1) = \int_{-\infty}^{d_1} f(u)du = \int_{-\infty}^{d_1} \frac{1}{\sqrt{2\pi}} e^{-\frac{u^2}{2}} du$$

First, we calculate

$$N'(d_1) = \frac{\partial N(d_1)}{\partial d_1} = \frac{1}{\sqrt{2\pi}} e^{-\frac{d_1^2}{2}}. \tag{11.3}$$

$$\begin{aligned}
N'(d_2) &= \frac{\partial N(d_2)}{\partial d_2} \\
&= \frac{1}{\sqrt{2\pi}} e^{-\frac{d_2^2}{2}} \\
&= \frac{1}{\sqrt{2\pi}} e^{-\frac{(d_1 - \sigma_s\sqrt{\tau})^2}{2}} \\
&= \frac{1}{\sqrt{2\pi}} e^{-\frac{d_1^2}{2}} \cdot e^{d_1\sigma_s\sqrt{\tau}} \cdot e^{-\frac{\sigma_s^2\tau}{2}} \\
&= \frac{1}{\sqrt{2\pi}} e^{-\frac{d_1^2}{2}} \cdot e^{\ln\left(\frac{S_t}{X}\right) + \left(r + \frac{\sigma_s^2}{2}\right)\tau} \cdot e^{-\frac{\sigma_s^2\tau}{2}} \\
&= \frac{1}{\sqrt{2\pi}} e^{-\frac{d_1^2}{2}} \cdot \frac{S_t}{X} \cdot e^{r\tau}.
\end{aligned} \tag{11.4}$$

Equations (11.2) and (11.3) will be used repetitively in determining the following Greek letters when the underlying asset is a non-dividend-paying stock.

For a European call option on a non-dividend stock, delta can be shown as

$$\Delta = N(d_1). \tag{11.5}$$

The derivation of Equation (11.5) is in the following:

$$\begin{aligned}
\Delta = \frac{\partial C_t}{\partial S_t} &= N(d_1) + S_t \frac{\partial N(d_1)}{\partial S_t} - Xe^{-r\tau} \frac{\partial N(d_2)}{\partial S_t} \\
&= N(d_1) + S_t \frac{\partial N(d_1)}{\partial d_1} \frac{\partial d_1}{\partial S_t} - Xe^{-r\tau} \frac{\partial N(d_2)}{\partial d_2} \frac{\partial d_2}{\partial S_t} \\
&= N(d_1) + S_t \frac{1}{\sqrt{2\pi}} e^{-\frac{d_1^2}{2}} \cdot \frac{1}{S_t \sigma_s \sqrt{\tau}} \\
&\quad - Xe^{-r\tau} \frac{1}{\sqrt{2\pi}} e^{-\frac{d_1^2}{2}} \cdot \frac{S_t}{X} \cdot e^{r\tau} \cdot \frac{1}{S_t \sigma_s \sqrt{\tau}} \\
&= N(d_1) + S_t \frac{1}{S_t \sigma_s \sqrt{2\pi\tau}} e^{-\frac{d_1^2}{2}} - S_t \frac{1}{S_t \sigma_s \sqrt{2\pi\tau}} e^{-\frac{d_1^2}{2}} \\
&= N(d_1).
\end{aligned}$$

For a European put option on a non-dividend stock, delta can be shown as

$$\Delta = N(d_1) - 1. \tag{11.6}$$

The derivation of Equation (11.6) is

$$\begin{aligned}
\Delta = \frac{\partial P_t}{\partial S_t} &= Xe^{-r\tau} \frac{\partial N(-d_2)}{\partial S_t} - N(-d_1) - S_t \frac{\partial N(-d_1)}{\partial S_t} \\
&= Xe^{-r\tau} \frac{\partial (1 - N(d_2))}{\partial d_2} \frac{\partial d_2}{\partial S_t} - (1 - N(d_1)) \\
&\quad - S_t \frac{\partial (1 - N(d_1))}{\partial d_1} \frac{\partial d_1}{\partial S_t} \\
&= -Xe^{-r\tau} \frac{1}{\sqrt{2\pi}} e^{-\frac{d_1^2}{2}} \cdot \frac{S_t}{X} \cdot e^{r\tau} \cdot \frac{1}{S_t \sigma_s \sqrt{\tau}} \\
&\quad - (1 - N(d_1)) + S_t \frac{1}{\sqrt{2\pi}} e^{-\frac{d_1^2}{2}} \cdot \frac{1}{S_t \sigma_s \sqrt{\tau}} \\
&= -S_t \frac{1}{S_t \sigma_s \sqrt{2\pi\tau}} e^{-\frac{d_1^2}{2}} - N(d_1) - 1 + S_t \frac{1}{S_t \sigma_s \sqrt{2\pi\tau}} e^{-\frac{d_1^2}{2}} \\
&= N(d_1) - 1.
\end{aligned}$$

If the underlying asset is a dividend-paying stock providing a dividend yield at rate q, Black–Scholes formulas for the prices of a European call option on a dividend-paying stock and a European put option on a dividend-paying stock are

$$C_t = S_t e^{-q\tau} N(d_1) - X e^{-r\tau} N(d_2) \tag{11.7}$$

and

$$P_t = X e^{-r\tau} N(-d_2) - S_t e^{-q\tau} N(-d_1), \tag{11.8}$$

where

$$d_1 = \frac{\ln\left(\frac{S_t}{X}\right) + \left(r - q + \frac{\sigma_s^2}{2}\right)\tau}{\sigma_s\sqrt{\tau}},$$

$$d_2 = \frac{\ln\left(\frac{S_t}{X}\right) + \left(r - q - \frac{\sigma_s^2}{2}\right)\tau}{\sigma_s\sqrt{\tau}} = d_1 - \sigma_s\sqrt{\tau}.$$

To make the following derivations more easily, we calculate Equations (11.9) and (11.10) in advance:

$$N'(d_1) = \frac{\partial N(d_1)}{\partial d_1} = \frac{1}{\sqrt{2\pi}} e^{-\frac{d_1^2}{2}}, \tag{11.9}$$

$$\begin{aligned}
N'(d_2) &= \frac{\partial N(d_2)}{\partial d_2} \\
&= \frac{1}{\sqrt{2\pi}} e^{-\frac{d_2^2}{2}} \\
&= \frac{1}{\sqrt{2\pi}} e^{-\frac{(d_1 - \sigma_s\sqrt{\tau})^2}{2}} \\
&= \frac{1}{\sqrt{2\pi}} e^{-\frac{d_1^2}{2}} \cdot e^{d_1\sigma_s\sqrt{\tau}} \cdot e^{-\frac{\sigma_s^2\tau}{2}} \\
&= \frac{1}{\sqrt{2\pi}} e^{-\frac{d_1^2}{2}} \cdot e^{\ln\left(\frac{S_t}{X}\right) + \left(r - q + \frac{\sigma_s^2}{2}\right)\tau} \cdot e^{-\frac{\sigma_s^2\tau}{2}} \\
&= \frac{1}{\sqrt{2\pi}} e^{-\frac{d_1^2}{2}} \cdot \frac{S_t}{X} \cdot e^{(r-q)\tau}.
\end{aligned} \tag{11.10}$$

For a European call option on a dividend-paying stock, delta can be shown as

$$\Delta = e^{-q\tau}N(d_1). \tag{11.11}$$

The derivation of Equation (11.11) is

$$\begin{aligned}
\Delta = \frac{\partial C_t}{\partial S_t} &= e^{-q\tau}N(d_1) + S_t e^{-q\tau}\frac{\partial N(d_1)}{\partial S_t} - Xe^{-r\tau}\frac{\partial N(d_2)}{\partial S_t} \\
&= e^{-q\tau}N(d_1) + S_t e^{-q\tau}\frac{\partial N(d_1)}{\partial d_1}\frac{\partial d_1}{\partial S_t} - Xe^{-r\tau}\frac{\partial N(d_2)}{\partial d_2}\frac{\partial d_2}{\partial S_t} \\
&= e^{-q\tau}N(d_1) + S_t e^{-q\tau}\frac{1}{\sqrt{2\pi}}e^{-\frac{d_1^2}{2}} \cdot \frac{1}{S_t\sigma_s\sqrt{\tau}} \\
&\quad - Xe^{-r\tau}\frac{1}{\sqrt{2\pi}}e^{-\frac{d_1^2}{2}} \cdot \frac{S_t}{X} \cdot e^{(r-q)\tau} \cdot \frac{1}{S_t\sigma_s\sqrt{\tau}} \\
&= e^{-q\tau}N(d_1) + S_t e^{-q\tau}\frac{1}{S_t\sigma_s\sqrt{2\pi\tau}}e^{-\frac{d_1^2}{2}} \\
&\quad - S_t e^{-q\tau}\frac{1}{S_t\sigma_s\sqrt{2\pi\tau}}e^{-\frac{d_1^2}{2}} \\
&= e^{-q\tau}N(d_1).
\end{aligned}$$

For a European call option on a dividend-paying stock, delta can be shown as

$$\Delta = e^{-q\tau}[N(d_1) - 1]. \tag{11.12}$$

The derivation of Equation (11.12) is

$$\begin{aligned}
\Delta = \frac{\partial P_t}{\partial S_t} &= Xe^{-r\tau}\frac{\partial N(-d_2)}{\partial S_t} - e^{-q\tau}N(-d_1) - S_t e^{-q\tau}\frac{\partial N(-d_1)}{\partial S_t} \\
&= Xe^{-r\tau}\frac{\partial(1 - N(d_2))}{\partial d_2}\frac{\partial d_2}{\partial S_t} - e^{-q\tau}(1 - N(d_1)) \\
&\quad - S_t e^{-q\tau}\frac{\partial(1 - N(d_1))}{\partial d_1}\frac{\partial d_1}{\partial S_t} \\
&= -Xe^{-r\tau}\frac{1}{\sqrt{2\pi}}e^{-\frac{d_1^2}{2}} \cdot \frac{S_t}{X} \cdot e^{(r-q)\tau} \cdot \frac{1}{S_t\sigma_s\sqrt{\tau}} \\
&\quad - e^{-q\tau}(1 - N(d_1)) + S_t e^{-q\tau}\frac{1}{\sqrt{2\pi}}e^{-\frac{d_1^2}{2}} \cdot \frac{1}{S_t\sigma_s\sqrt{\tau}}
\end{aligned}$$

$$= -S_t e^{-q\tau} \frac{1}{S_t \sigma_s \sqrt{2\pi\tau}} e^{-\frac{d_1^2}{2}} + e^{-q\tau}(N(d_1) - 1)$$

$$+ S_t e^{-q\tau} \frac{1}{S_t \sigma_s \sqrt{2\pi\tau}} e^{-\frac{d_1^2}{2}}$$

$$= e^{-q\tau}(N(d_1) - 1).$$

11.2.2 *Application of delta* (Δ)

Figure 11.1 shows the relationship between the price of a call option and the price of its underlying asset. The delta of this call option is the slope of the line at the point of A corresponding to the current price of the underlying asset.

By calculating the delta ratio, a financial institution that sells options to a client can make a delta-neutral position to hedge the risk of changes of the underlying asset price. Suppose that the current stock price is \$100, the call option price on stock is \$10, and the current delta of the call option is 0.4. A financial institution sold 10 call options to its client, so that the client has a right to buy 1,000 shares at time to maturity. To construct a delta hedge position, the financial institution should buy $0.4 \times 1{,}000 = 400$ shares of stock. If the stock price goes up to \$1, the option price will go up by \$0.40. In this situation, the financial institution has a \$400 (\$1 $\times$ 400 shares) gain in its stock position and a \$400 (\$0.40 $\times$ 1,000 shares) loss in its option position. The total payoff of the financial institution is

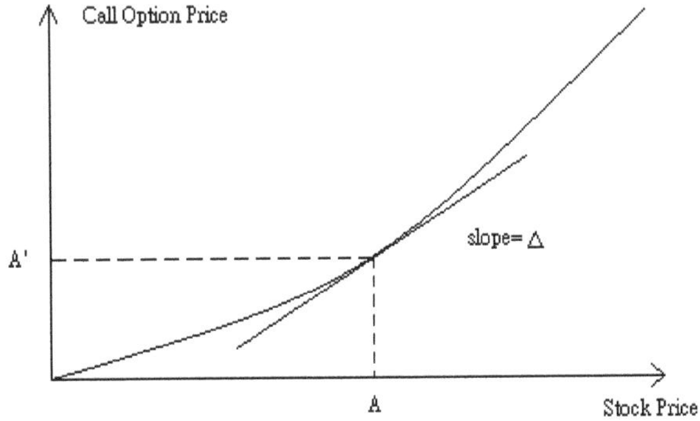

Figure 11.1 The Relationship between the Price of a Call Option and the Price of Its Underlying Asset

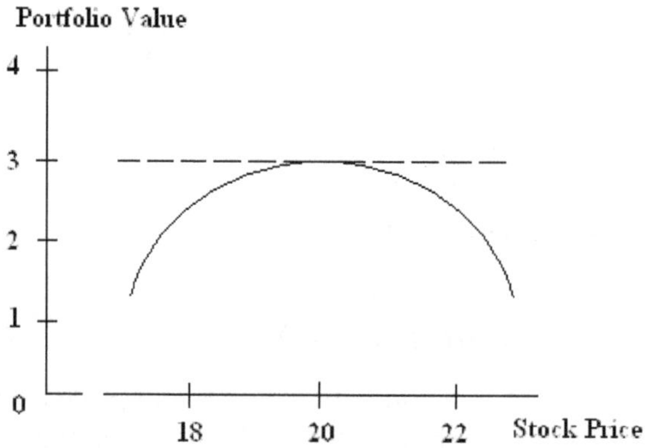

Figure 11.2 Changes of Delta Hedge

zero. On the other hand, if the stock price goes down by \$1, the option price will go down by \$0.40. The total payoff of the financial institution is also zero.

However, the relationship between option price and stock price is not linear, so delta changes over different stock prices. If an investor wants to retain his portfolio in delta neutral, he should adjust his hedged ratio periodically. The more frequent adjustments he does, the better delta hedging he gets.

Figure 11.2 exhibits the change in delta affecting the delta hedges. If the underlying stock has a price equal to \$20, then the investor who uses only delta as a risk measure will consider that his or her portfolio has no risk. However, as the underlying stock prices change, either up or down, the delta changes as well and thus he or she will have to use different delta hedging. The delta measure can be combined with other risk measures to yield better risk measurement. We will discuss it further in the following sections.

11.3 Theta (Θ)

The theta of an option, Θ, is defined as the rate of change of the option price with respect to the passage of time:

$$\Theta = \frac{\partial \Pi}{\partial t},$$

where Π is the option price and t is the passage of time.

If $\tau = T - t$, theta (Θ) can also be defined as minus one timing the rate of change of the option price with respect to time to maturity. The derivation of such a transformation is easy and straightforward:

$$\Theta = \frac{\partial \Pi}{\partial t} = \frac{\partial \Pi}{\partial \tau}\frac{\partial \tau}{\partial t} = (-1)\frac{\partial \Pi}{\partial \tau},$$

where $\tau = T - t$ is time to maturity. For the derivation of theta for various kinds of stock options, we use the definition of negative differential on time to maturity.

11.3.1 *Derivation of theta for different kinds of stock options*

For a European call option on a non-dividend stock, theta can be written as

$$\Theta = -\frac{S_t \sigma_s}{2\sqrt{\tau}} \cdot N'(d_1) - rX \cdot e^{-r\tau} N(d_2). \tag{11.13}$$

The derivation of Equation (11.13) is

$$\begin{aligned}
\Theta = -\frac{\partial C_t}{\partial \tau} &= -S_t \frac{\partial N(d_1)}{\partial \tau} + (-r) \cdot X \cdot e^{-r\tau} N(d_2) + X e^{-r\tau} \frac{\partial N(d_2)}{\partial \tau} \\
&= -S_t \frac{\partial N(d_1)}{\partial d_1}\frac{\partial d_1}{\partial \tau} - rX \cdot e^{-r\tau} N(d_2) + X e^{-r\tau} \frac{\partial N(d_2)}{\partial d_2}\frac{\partial d_2}{\partial \tau} \\
&= -S_t \frac{1}{\sqrt{2\pi}} e^{-\frac{d_1^2}{2}} \cdot \left(\frac{r + \frac{\sigma_s^2}{2}}{\sigma_s \sqrt{\tau}} - \frac{\ln\left(\frac{S_t}{X}\right)}{2\sigma_s \tau^{3/2}} - \frac{r + \frac{\sigma_s^2}{2}}{2\sigma_s \sqrt{\tau}} \right) \\
&\quad - rX \cdot e^{-r\tau} N(d_2) + X e^{-r\tau} \cdot \left(\frac{1}{\sqrt{2\pi}} e^{-\frac{d_1^2}{2}} \cdot \frac{S_t}{X} \cdot e^{r\tau} \right) \\
&\quad \cdot \left(\frac{r}{\sigma_s \sqrt{\tau}} - \frac{\ln(\frac{S_t}{X})}{2\sigma_s \tau^{3/2}} - \frac{r + \frac{\sigma_s^2}{2}}{2\sigma_s \sqrt{\tau}} \right)
\end{aligned}$$

$$= -S_t \frac{1}{\sqrt{2\pi}} e^{-\frac{d_1^2}{2}} \cdot \left(\frac{r + \frac{\sigma_s^2}{2}}{\sigma_s \sqrt{\tau}} - \frac{\ln\left(\frac{S_t}{X}\right)}{2\sigma_s \tau^{3/2}} - \frac{r + \frac{\sigma_s^2}{2}}{2\sigma_s \sqrt{\tau}} \right)$$

$$- rX \cdot e^{-r\tau} N(d_2) + S_t \frac{1}{\sqrt{2\pi}} e^{-\frac{d_1^2}{2}}$$

$$\cdot \left(\frac{r}{\sigma_s \sqrt{\tau}} - \frac{\ln\left(\frac{S_t}{X}\right)}{2\sigma_s \tau^{3/2}} - \frac{r + \frac{\sigma_s^2}{2}}{2\sigma_s \sqrt{\tau}} \right)$$

$$= -S_t \frac{1}{\sqrt{2\pi}} e^{-\frac{d_1^2}{2}} \cdot \left(\frac{\frac{\sigma_s^2}{2}}{\sigma_s \sqrt{\tau}} \right) - rX \cdot e^{-r\tau} N(d_2)$$

$$= -\frac{S_t \sigma_s}{2\sqrt{\tau}} \cdot N'(d_1) - rX \cdot e^{-r\tau} N(d_2).$$

For a European put option on a non-dividend stock, theta can be shown as

$$\Theta = -\frac{S_t \sigma_s}{2\sqrt{\tau}} \cdot N'(d_1) + rX \cdot e^{-r\tau} N(-d_2). \tag{11.14}$$

The derivation of Equation (11.14) is

$$\Theta = -\frac{\partial P_t}{\partial \tau} = -(-r) \cdot X \cdot e^{-r\tau} N(-d_2)$$

$$- Xe^{-r\tau} \frac{\partial N(-d_2)}{\partial \tau} + S_t \frac{\partial N(-d_1)}{\partial \tau}$$

$$= -(-r)X \cdot e^{-r\tau}(1 - N(d_2))$$

$$- Xe^{-r\tau} \frac{\partial (1 - N(d_2))}{\partial d_2} \frac{\partial d_2}{\partial \tau} + S_t \frac{\partial (1 - N(d_1))}{\partial d_1} \frac{\partial d_1}{\partial \tau}$$

$$= -(-r)X \cdot e^{-r\tau}(1 - N(d_2)) + Xe^{-r\tau}$$

$$\cdot \left(\frac{1}{\sqrt{2\pi}} e^{-\frac{d_1^2}{2}} \cdot \frac{S_t}{X} \cdot e^{r\tau} \right) \cdot \left(\frac{r}{\sigma_s \sqrt{\tau}} - \frac{\ln\left(\frac{S_t}{X}\right)}{2\sigma_s \tau^{3/2}} - \frac{r + \frac{\sigma_s^2}{2}}{2\sigma_s \sqrt{\tau}} \right)$$

$$- S_t \frac{1}{\sqrt{2\pi}} e^{-\frac{d_1^2}{2}} \cdot \left(\frac{r + \frac{\sigma_s^2}{2}}{\sigma_s \sqrt{\tau}} - \frac{\ln\left(\frac{S_t}{X}\right)}{2\sigma_s \tau^{3/2}} - \frac{r + \frac{\sigma_s^2}{2}}{2\sigma_s \sqrt{\tau}} \right)$$

$$= rX \cdot e^{-r\tau}(1 - N(d_2)) + S_t \frac{1}{\sqrt{2\pi}} e^{-\frac{d_1^2}{2}}$$

$$\cdot \left(\frac{r}{\sigma_s \sqrt{\tau}} - \frac{\ln\left(\frac{S_t}{X}\right)}{2\sigma_s \tau^{3/2}} - \frac{r + \frac{\sigma_s^2}{2}}{2\sigma_s \sqrt{\tau}} \right)$$

$$- S_t \frac{1}{\sqrt{2\pi}} e^{-\frac{d_1^2}{2}} \cdot \left(\frac{r + \frac{\sigma_s^2}{2}}{\sigma_s \sqrt{\tau}} - \frac{\ln(\frac{S_t}{X})}{2\sigma_s \tau^{3/2}} - \frac{r + \frac{\sigma_s^2}{2}}{2\sigma_s \sqrt{\tau}} \right)$$

$$= rX \cdot e^{-r\tau}(1 - N(d_2)) - S_t \frac{1}{\sqrt{2\pi}} e^{-\frac{d_1^2}{2}} \cdot \left(\frac{\frac{\sigma_s^2}{2}}{\sigma_s \sqrt{\tau}} \right)$$

$$= rX \cdot e^{-r\tau}(1 - N(d_2)) - \frac{S_t \sigma_s}{2\sqrt{\tau}} \cdot N'(d_1)$$

$$= rX \cdot e^{-r\tau} N(-d_2) - \frac{S_t \sigma_s}{2\sqrt{\tau}} \cdot N'(d_1).$$

For a European call option on a dividend-paying stock, theta can be shown as

$$\Theta = q \cdot S_t e^{-q\tau} N(d_1) - \frac{S_t e^{-q\tau} \sigma_s}{2\sqrt{\tau}} \cdot N'(d_1) - rX \cdot e^{-r\tau} N(d_2). \tag{11.15}$$

The derivation of Equation (11.15) is

$$\Theta = -\frac{\partial C_t}{\partial \tau} = q \cdot S_t e^{-q\tau} N(d_1) - S_t e^{-q\tau} \frac{\partial N(d_1)}{\partial \tau}$$

$$+ (-r) \cdot X \cdot e^{-r\tau} N(d_2) + X e^{-r\tau} \frac{\partial N(d_2)}{\partial \tau}$$

$$= q \cdot S_t e^{-q\tau} N(d_1) - S_t e^{-q\tau} \frac{\partial N(d_1)}{\partial d_1} \frac{\partial d_1}{\partial \tau}$$

$$- rX \cdot e^{-r\tau} N(d_2) + X e^{-r\tau} \frac{\partial N(d_2)}{\partial d_2} \frac{\partial d_2}{\partial \tau}$$

$$= q \cdot S_t e^{-q\tau} N(d_1) - S_t e^{-q\tau} \frac{1}{\sqrt{2\pi}} e^{-\frac{d_1^2}{2}}$$

$$\cdot \left(\frac{r - q + \frac{\sigma_s^2}{2}}{\sigma_s \sqrt{\tau}} - \frac{\ln(\frac{S_t}{X})}{2\sigma_s \tau^{3/2}} - \frac{r - q + \frac{\sigma_s^2}{2}}{2\sigma_s \sqrt{\tau}} \right)$$

$$- rX \cdot e^{-r\tau} N(d_2) + Xe^{-r\tau} \cdot \left(\frac{1}{\sqrt{2\pi}} e^{-\frac{d_1^2}{2}} \cdot \frac{S_t}{X} \cdot e^{(r-q)\tau} \right)$$

$$\cdot \left(\frac{r - q}{\sigma_s \sqrt{\tau}} - \frac{\ln(\frac{S_t}{X})}{2\sigma_s \tau^{3/2}} - \frac{r - q + \frac{\sigma_s^2}{2}}{2\sigma_s \sqrt{\tau}} \right)$$

$$= q \cdot S_t e^{-q\tau} N(d_1) - S_t e^{-q\tau} \frac{1}{\sqrt{2\pi}} e^{-\frac{d_1^2}{2}}$$

$$\cdot \left(\frac{r + \frac{\sigma_s^2}{2}}{\sigma_s \sqrt{\tau}} - \frac{\ln\left(\frac{S_t}{X}\right)}{2\sigma_s \tau^{3/2}} - \frac{r + \frac{\sigma_s^2}{2}}{2\sigma_s \sqrt{\tau}} \right) - rX \cdot e^{-r\tau} N(d_2)$$

$$+ S_t e^{-q\tau} \frac{1}{\sqrt{2\pi}} e^{-\frac{d_1^2}{2}} \cdot \left(\frac{r}{\sigma_s \sqrt{\tau}} - \frac{\ln\left(\frac{S_t}{X}\right)}{2\sigma_s \tau^{3/2}} - \frac{r + \frac{\sigma_s^2}{2}}{2\sigma_s \sqrt{\tau}} \right)$$

$$= q \cdot S_t e^{-q\tau} N(d_1) - S_t e^{-q\tau} \frac{1}{\sqrt{2\pi}} e^{-\frac{d_1^2}{2}} \cdot \left(\frac{\frac{\sigma_s^2}{2}}{\sigma_s \sqrt{\tau}} \right)$$

$$- rX \cdot e^{-r\tau} N(d_2)$$

$$= q \cdot S_t e^{-q\tau} N(d_1) - \frac{S_t e^{-q\tau} \sigma_s}{2\sqrt{\tau}} \cdot N'(d_1) - rX \cdot e^{-r\tau} N(d_2).$$

For a European call option on a dividend-paying stock, theta can be shown as

$$\Theta = rX \cdot e^{-r\tau} N(-d_2) - qS_t e^{-q\tau} N(-d_1) - \frac{S_t e^{-q\tau} \sigma_s}{2\sqrt{\tau}} \cdot N'(d_1). \quad (11.16)$$

The derivation of Equation (11.16) is

$$\Theta = -\frac{\partial P_t}{\partial \tau} = -(-r) \cdot X \cdot e^{-r\tau} N(-d_2) - Xe^{-r\tau} \frac{\partial N(-d_2)}{\partial \tau}$$

$$+ (-q) S_t e^{-q\tau} N(-d_1) + S_t e^{-q\tau} \frac{\partial N(-d_1)}{\partial \tau}$$

$$= rX \cdot e^{-r\tau}(1 - N(d_2)) - Xe^{-r\tau}\frac{\partial(1 - N(d_2))}{\partial d_2}\frac{\partial d_2}{\partial \tau}$$

$$- qS_t e^{-q\tau}N(-d_1) + S_t e^{-q\tau}\frac{\partial(1 - N(d_1))}{\partial d_1}\frac{\partial d_1}{\partial \tau}$$

$$= rX \cdot e^{-r\tau}(1 - N(d_2)) + Xe^{-r\tau} \cdot \left(\frac{1}{\sqrt{2\pi}}e^{-\frac{d_1^2}{2}} \cdot \frac{S_t}{X} \cdot e^{(r-q)\tau}\right)$$

$$\cdot \left(\frac{r-q}{\sigma_s\sqrt{\tau}} - \frac{\ln\left(\frac{S_t}{X}\right)}{2\sigma_s\tau^{3/2}} - \frac{r-q+\frac{\sigma_s^2}{2}}{2\sigma_s\sqrt{\tau}}\right)$$

$$- qS_t e^{-q\tau}N(-d_1) - S_t e^{-q\tau}\frac{1}{\sqrt{2\pi}}e^{-\frac{d_1^2}{2}}$$

$$\cdot \left(\frac{r-q+\frac{\sigma_s^2}{2}}{\sigma_s\sqrt{\tau}} - \frac{\ln\left(\frac{S_t}{X}\right)}{2\sigma_s\tau^{3/2}} - \frac{r-q+\frac{\sigma_s^2}{2}}{2\sigma_s\sqrt{\tau}}\right)$$

$$= rX \cdot e^{-r\tau}(1 - N(d_2)) + S_t e^{-q\tau}\frac{1}{\sqrt{2\pi}}e^{-\frac{d_1^2}{2}}$$

$$\cdot \left(\frac{r-q}{\sigma_s\sqrt{\tau}} - \frac{\ln\left(\frac{S_t}{X}\right)}{2\sigma_s\tau^{3/2}} - \frac{r-q+\frac{\sigma_s^2}{2}}{2\sigma_s\sqrt{\tau}}\right)$$

$$- qS_t e^{-q\tau}N(-d_1) - S_t e^{-q\tau}\frac{1}{\sqrt{2\pi}}e^{-\frac{d_1^2}{2}}$$

$$\cdot \left(\frac{r-q+\frac{\sigma_s^2}{2}}{\sigma_s\sqrt{\tau}} - \frac{\ln\left(\frac{S_t}{X}\right)}{2\sigma_s\tau^{3/2}} - \frac{r-q+\frac{\sigma_s^2}{2}}{2\sigma_s\sqrt{\tau}}\right)$$

$$= rX \cdot e^{-r\tau}(1 - N(d_2)) - qS_t e^{-q\tau}N(-d_1)$$

$$- S_t e^{-q\tau}\frac{1}{\sqrt{2\pi}}e^{-\frac{d_1^2}{2}} \cdot \left(\frac{\frac{\sigma_s^2}{2}}{\sigma_s\sqrt{\tau}}\right)$$

$$= rX \cdot e^{-r\tau}(1 - N(d_2)) - qS_t e^{-q\tau}N(-d_1) - \frac{S_t e^{-q\tau}\sigma_s}{2\sqrt{\tau}} \cdot N'(d_1)$$

$$= rX \cdot e^{-r\tau}N(-d_2) - qS_t e^{-q\tau}N(-d_1) - \frac{S_t e^{-q\tau}\sigma_s}{2\sqrt{\tau}} \cdot N'(d_1).$$

11.3.2 *Application of theta* (Θ)

The value of options is the combination of time value and stock value. When time passes, the time value of the option decreases. Thus, the rate of change of the option price with respect to the passage of time, theta, is usually negative.

Because the passage of time on an option is not uncertain, we do not need to make a theta hedge portfolio against the effect of the passage of time. However, we still regard theta as a useful parameter, because it is a proxy of gamma in the delta-neutral portfolio. We will discuss that specific detail in the following sections.

11.4 Gamma (Γ)

The gamma of an option, Γ, is defined as the rate of change of delta with respect to the rate of change of the underlying asset price:

$$\Gamma = \frac{\partial \Delta}{\partial S} = \frac{\partial^2 \Pi}{\partial S^2},$$

where Π is the option price and S is the underlying asset price.

Because the option is not linearly dependent on its underlying asset, a delta-neutral hedge strategy is useful only when the movement of the underlying asset price is small. Once the underlying asset price moves wider, gamma-neutral hedge is necessary. Next, we show the derivation of gamma for various kinds of stock options.

11.4.1 *Derivation of gamma for different kinds of stock options*

For a European call option on a non-dividend stock, gamma can be shown as

$$\Gamma = \frac{1}{S_t \sigma_s \sqrt{\tau}} N'(d_1). \tag{11.17}$$

The derivation of Equation (11.17) is

$$\Gamma = \frac{\partial^2 C_t}{\partial S_t^2} = \frac{\partial \left(\frac{\partial C_t}{\partial S_t}\right)}{\partial S_t}$$

$$= \frac{\partial N(d_1)}{\partial d_1} \cdot \frac{\partial d_1}{\partial S_t}$$

$$= N'(d_1) \cdot \frac{\frac{1}{S_t}}{\sigma_s\sqrt{\tau}}$$

$$= \frac{1}{S_t\sigma_s\sqrt{\tau}}N'(d_1).$$

For a European put option on a non-dividend stock, gamma can be shown as

$$\Gamma = \frac{1}{S_t\sigma_s\sqrt{\tau}}N'(d_1). \tag{11.18}$$

The derivation of Equation (11.18) is

$$\Gamma = \frac{\partial^2 P_t}{\partial S_t^2} = \frac{\partial\left(\frac{\partial P_t}{\partial S_t}\right)}{\partial S_t}$$

$$= \frac{\partial(N(d_1)-1)}{\partial d_1} \cdot \frac{\partial d_1}{\partial S_t}$$

$$= N'(d_1) \cdot \frac{\frac{1}{S_t}}{\sigma_s\sqrt{\tau}}$$

$$= \frac{1}{S_t\sigma_s\sqrt{\tau}}N'(d_1).$$

For a European call option on a dividend-paying stock, gamma can be shown as

$$\Gamma = \frac{e^{-q\tau}}{S_t\sigma_s\sqrt{\tau}}N'(d_1). \tag{11.19}$$

The derivation of Equation (11.19) is

$$\Gamma = \frac{\partial^2 C_t}{\partial S_t^2} = \frac{\partial\left(\frac{\partial C_t}{\partial S_t}\right)}{\partial S_t}$$

$$= \frac{\partial(e^{-q\tau}N(d_1))}{\partial S_t}$$

$$= e^{-q\tau} \cdot \frac{\partial N(d_1)}{\partial d_1} \cdot \frac{\partial d_1}{\partial S_t}$$

$$= e^{-q\tau} \cdot N'(d_1) \cdot \frac{\frac{1}{S_t}}{\sigma_s\sqrt{\tau}}$$

$$= \frac{e^{-q\tau}}{S_t\sigma_s\sqrt{\tau}} N'(d_1).$$

For a European call option on a dividend-paying stock, gamma can be shown as

$$\Gamma = \frac{e^{-q\tau}}{S_t\sigma_s\sqrt{\tau}} N'(d_1). \tag{11.20}$$

The derivation of Equation (11.20) is

$$\Gamma = \frac{\partial^2 P_t}{\partial S_t^2} = \frac{\partial\left(\frac{\partial P_t}{\partial S_t}\right)}{\partial S_t}$$

$$= \frac{\partial(e^{-q\tau}(N(d_1) - 1))}{\partial S_t}$$

$$= e^{-q\tau} \cdot \frac{\partial\left[(N(d_1) - 1)\right]}{\partial d_1} \cdot \frac{\partial d_1}{\partial S_t}$$

$$= e^{-q\tau} \cdot N'(d_1) \cdot \frac{\frac{1}{S_t}}{\sigma_s\sqrt{\tau}}$$

$$= \frac{e^{-q\tau}.}{S_t\sigma_s\sqrt{\tau}} N'(d_1).$$

11.4.2 *Application of gamma* (Γ)

One can use delta and gamma together to calculate the changes of the option due to changes in the underlying stock price. This change can be approximated by the following relations:

$$\text{change in option value} \approx \Delta \times \text{change in stock price} + \frac{1}{2} \times \Gamma \times (\text{change in stock price})^2.$$

From the above relation, one can observe that the gamma makes the correction for the fact that the option value is not a linear function of underlying stock price. This approximation comes from the Taylor series expansion near the initial stock price. If we let V be option value, S be stock price, and S_0 be initial stock price, then the Taylor series expansion around S_0 yields the following:

$$\begin{aligned}
V(S) &\approx V(S_0) + \frac{\partial V(S_0)}{\partial S}(S - S_0) + \frac{1}{2!}\frac{\partial^2 V(S_0)}{\partial S^2}(S - S_0)^2 \\
&\quad + \cdots + \frac{1}{2!}\frac{\partial^n V(S_0)}{\partial S^n}(S - S_0)^n \\
&\approx V(S_0) + \frac{\partial V(S_0)}{\partial S}(S - S_0) + \frac{1}{2!}\frac{\partial^2 V(S_0)}{\partial S^2}(S - S_0)^2 + o(S).
\end{aligned}$$

If we only consider the first three terms, the approximation is then

$$\begin{aligned}
V(S) - V(S_0) &\approx \frac{\partial V(S_0)}{\partial S}(S - S_0) + \frac{1}{2!}\frac{\partial^2 V(S_0)}{\partial S^2}(S - S_0)^2 \\
&\approx \Delta(S - S_0) + \frac{1}{2}\Gamma(S - S_0)^2.
\end{aligned}$$

For example, if a portfolio of options has a delta equal to \$10,000 and a gamma equal to \$5,000, the change in the portfolio value if the stock price drops to \$34 from \$35 is approximately

$$\begin{aligned}
\text{change in portfolio value} &\approx (\$10000) \times (\$34 - \$35) \\
&\quad + \frac{1}{2} \times (\$5000) \times (\$34 - \$35)^2 \\
&\approx -\$7500.
\end{aligned}$$

The above analysis can also be applied to measure the price sensitivity of interest-rate-related assets or a portfolio to interest rate changes. Here, we introduce *Modified Duration* and *Convexity* as risk measures corresponding to the above delta and gamma. Modified duration measures the percentage change in asset or portfolio value resulting from a percentage change in interest rate.

$$\begin{aligned}
\text{Modified Duration} &= \left(\frac{\text{Change in price}}{\text{Change in interest rate}}\right) \Big/ \text{Price} \\
&= -\Delta/P.
\end{aligned}$$

Using the modified duration,

$$\begin{aligned}\text{Change in Portfolio Value} &= \Delta \times \text{Change in interest rate}\\ &= (-\textit{Duration} \times \text{P})\\ &\quad \times \text{Change in interest rate.}\end{aligned}$$

we can calculate the value changes of the portfolio. The above relation corresponds to the previous discussion of delta measure. We want to know how the price of the portfolio changes given a change in interest rate. Similar to delta, modified duration only shows the first-order approximation of the changes in value. In order to account for the nonlinear relation between the interest rate and portfolio value, we need a second-order approximation similar to the gamma measure before; this is then the convexity measure. Convexity is the interest rate gamma divided by price,

$$\textit{Convexity} = \Gamma/\text{P},$$

and this measure captures the nonlinear part of the price changes due to interest rate changes. Using the modified duration and convexity together allows us to develop first- as well as second-order approximations of the price changes similar to the previous discussion.

$$\begin{aligned}\text{Change in Portfolio Value} &\approx -\textit{Duration} \times \text{P} \times (\text{change in rate})\\ &\quad + \frac{1}{2} \times \textit{Convexity} \times \text{P}\\ &\quad \times (\text{change in rate})^2.\end{aligned}$$

As a result, ($-$Duration $\times P$) and (Convexity $\times P$) act like the delta and gamma measure, respectively, in the previous discussion. This shows that these Greeks can also be applied in measuring risk in interest-rate-related assets or portfolios.

Next, we discuss how to make a portfolio gamma neutral. Suppose the gamma of a delta-neutral portfolio is Γ, the gamma of the option in this portfolio is Γ_o, and ω_o is the number of options added to the delta-neutral portfolio. Then, the gamma of this new portfolio is

$$\omega_o \Gamma_o + \Gamma.$$

To make a gamma-neutral portfolio, we should trade $\omega_o^* = -\Gamma/\Gamma_o$ options. Because the position of the option changes, the new portfolio is not delta neutral. We should change the position of the underlying asset to maintain delta neutrality.

For example, the delta and gamma of a particular call option are 0.7 and 1.2, respectively. A delta-neutral portfolio has a gamma of −2,400. To make a delta-neutral and gamma-neutral portfolio, we should add a long position of $2,400/1.2 = 2,000$ shares and a short position of $2,000 \times 0.7 = 1,400$ shares in the original portfolio.

11.5 Vega (ν)

The vega of an option, ν, is defined as the rate of change of the option price with respect to the volatility of the underlying asset:

$$\nu = \frac{\partial \Pi}{\partial \sigma},$$

where Π is the option price and σ is volatility of the stock price. We next show the derivation of vega for various kinds of stock options.

11.5.1 *Derivation of vega for different kinds of stock options*

For a European call option on a non-dividend stock, vega can be shown as

$$\nu = S_t\sqrt{\tau} \cdot N'(d_1). \tag{11.21}$$

The derivation of Equation (11.21) is

$$\begin{aligned}
\nu = \frac{\partial C_t}{\partial \sigma_s} &= S_t\frac{\partial N(d_1)}{\partial \sigma_s} - Xe^{-r\tau}\frac{\partial N(d_2)}{\partial \sigma_s} \\
&= S_t\frac{\partial N(d_1)}{\partial d_1}\frac{\partial d_1}{\partial \sigma_s} - Xe^{-r\tau}\frac{\partial N(d_2)}{\partial d_2}\frac{\partial d_2}{\partial \sigma_s} \\
&= S_t\frac{1}{\sqrt{2\pi}}e^{-\frac{d_1^2}{2}} \cdot \left(\frac{\sigma_s^2\tau^{3/2} - \left[\ln\frac{S_t}{X} + (r + \frac{\sigma_s^2}{2})\tau\right] \cdot \tau^{\frac{1}{2}}}{\sigma_s^2\tau}\right) \\
&\quad - Xe^{-r\tau}\left(\frac{1}{\sqrt{2\pi}}e^{-\frac{d_1^2}{2}} \cdot \frac{S_t}{X} \cdot e^{r\tau}\right) \cdot \left(\frac{-\left[\ln\frac{S_t}{X} + (r + \frac{\sigma_s^2}{2})\tau\right] \cdot \tau^{\frac{1}{2}}}{\sigma_s^2\tau}\right)
\end{aligned}$$

$$
\begin{aligned}
&= S_t \frac{1}{\sqrt{2\pi}} e^{-\frac{d_1^2}{2}} \cdot \left(\frac{\sigma_s^2 \tau^{3/2} - \left[\ln \frac{S_t}{X} + \left(r + \frac{\sigma_s^2}{2}\right)\tau\right] \cdot \tau^{\frac{1}{2}}}{\sigma_s^2 \tau} \right) \\
&\quad - S_t \frac{1}{\sqrt{2\pi}} e^{-\frac{d_1^2}{2}} \cdot \left(\frac{-\left[\ln \frac{S_t}{X} + (r + \frac{\sigma_s^2}{2})\tau\right] \cdot \tau^{\frac{1}{2}}}{\sigma_s^2 \tau} \right) \\
&= S_t \frac{1}{\sqrt{2\pi}} e^{-\frac{d_1^2}{2}} \cdot \left(\frac{\sigma_s^2 \tau^{3/2}}{\sigma_s^2 \tau} \right) \\
&= S_t \sqrt{\tau} \cdot N'(d_1).
\end{aligned}
$$

For a European put option on a non-dividend stock, vega can be shown as

$$
\nu = S_t \sqrt{\tau} \cdot N'(d_1). \tag{11.22}
$$

The derivation of Equation (11.22) is

$$
\begin{aligned}
\nu = \frac{\partial P_t}{\partial \sigma_s} &= X e^{-r\tau} \frac{\partial N(-d_2)}{\partial \sigma_s} - S_t \frac{\partial N(-d_1)}{\partial \sigma_s} \\
&= X e^{-r\tau} \frac{\partial (1 - N(d_2))}{\partial d_2} \frac{\partial d_2}{\partial \sigma_s} - S_t \frac{\partial (1 - N(d_1))}{\partial d_1} \frac{\partial d_1}{\partial \sigma_s} \\
&= -X e^{-r\tau} \left(\frac{1}{\sqrt{2\pi}} e^{-\frac{d_1^2}{2}} \cdot \frac{S_t}{X} \cdot e^{r\tau} \right) \cdot \left(\frac{-\left[\ln \frac{S_t}{X} + (r + \frac{\sigma_s^2}{2})\tau\right] \cdot \tau^{\frac{1}{2}}}{\sigma_s^2 \tau} \right) \\
&\quad + S_t \frac{1}{\sqrt{2\pi}} e^{-\frac{d_1^2}{2}} \cdot \left(\frac{\sigma_s^2 \tau^{3/2} - \left[\ln \frac{S_t}{X} + (r + \frac{\sigma_s^2}{2})\tau\right] \cdot \tau^{\frac{1}{2}}}{\sigma_s^2 \tau} \right) \\
&= -S_t \frac{1}{\sqrt{2\pi}} e^{-\frac{d_1^2}{2}} \cdot \left(\frac{-\left[\ln \frac{S_t}{X} + (r + \frac{\sigma_s^2}{2})\tau\right] \cdot \tau^{\frac{1}{2}}}{\sigma_s^2 \tau} \right) \\
&\quad + S_t \frac{1}{\sqrt{2\pi}} e^{-\frac{d_1^2}{2}} \cdot \left(\frac{\sigma_s^2 \tau^{3/2} - \left[\ln \frac{S_t}{X} + \left(r + \frac{\sigma_s^2}{2}\right)\tau\right] \cdot \tau^{\frac{1}{2}}}{\sigma_s^2 \tau} \right)
\end{aligned}
$$

$$
\begin{aligned}
&= S_t \frac{1}{\sqrt{2\pi}} e^{-\frac{d_1^2}{2}} \cdot \left(\frac{\sigma_s^2 \tau^{3/2}}{\sigma_s^2 \tau} \right) \\
&= S_t \sqrt{\tau} \cdot N'(d_1).
\end{aligned}
$$

For a European call option on a dividend-paying stock, vega can be shown as

$$
\nu = S_t e^{-q\tau} \sqrt{\tau} \cdot N'(d_1). \tag{11.23}
$$

The derivation of Equation (11.23) is

$$
\begin{aligned}
\nu = \frac{\partial C_t}{\partial \sigma_s} &= S_t e^{-q\tau} \frac{\partial N(d_1)}{\partial \sigma_s} - X e^{-r\tau} \frac{\partial N(d_2)}{\partial \sigma_s} \\
&= S_t e^{-q\tau} \frac{\partial N(d_1)}{\partial d_1} \frac{\partial d_1}{\partial \sigma_s} - X e^{-r\tau} \frac{\partial N(d_2)}{\partial d_2} \frac{\partial d_2}{\partial \sigma_s} \\
&= S_t e^{-q\tau} \frac{1}{\sqrt{2\pi}} e^{-\frac{d_1^2}{2}} \cdot \left(\frac{\sigma_s^2 \tau^{3/2} - \left[\ln \frac{S_t}{X} + (r - q + \frac{\sigma_s^2}{2})\tau \right] \cdot \tau^{\frac{1}{2}}}{\sigma_s^2 \tau} \right) \\
&\quad - X e^{-r\tau} \left(\frac{1}{\sqrt{2\pi}} e^{-\frac{d_1^2}{2}} \cdot \frac{S_t}{X} \cdot e^{(r-q)\tau} \right) \\
&\quad \cdot \left(\frac{- \left[\ln \frac{S_t}{X} + (r - q + \frac{\sigma_s^2}{2})\tau \right] \cdot \tau^{\frac{1}{2}}}{\sigma_s^2 \tau} \right) \\
&= S_t e^{-q\tau} \frac{1}{\sqrt{2\pi}} e^{-\frac{d_1^2}{2}} \cdot \left(\frac{\sigma_s^2 \tau^{3/2} - \left[\ln \frac{S_t}{X} + \left(r - q + \frac{\sigma_s^2}{2} \right) \tau \right] \cdot \tau^{\frac{1}{2}}}{\sigma_s^2 \tau} \right) \\
&\quad - S_t e^{-q\tau} \frac{1}{\sqrt{2\pi}} e^{-\frac{d_1^2}{2}} \cdot \left(\frac{- \left[\ln \frac{S_t}{X} + \left(r - q + \frac{\sigma_s^2}{2} \right) \tau \right] \cdot \tau^{\frac{1}{2}}}{\sigma_s^2 \tau} \right) \\
&= S_t \frac{1}{\sqrt{2\pi}} e^{-\frac{d_1^2}{2}} \cdot \left(\frac{\sigma_s^2 \tau^{3/2}}{\sigma_s^2 \tau} \right) \\
&= S_t e^{-q\tau} \sqrt{\tau} \cdot N'(d_1).
\end{aligned}
$$

For a European call option on a dividend-paying stock, vega can be shown as

$$\nu = S_t e^{-q\tau}\sqrt{\tau}\cdot N'(d_1). \tag{11.24}$$

The derivation of Equation (11.24) is

$$\begin{aligned}
\nu = \frac{\partial P_t}{\partial \sigma_s} &= Xe^{-r\tau}\frac{\partial N(-d_2)}{\partial \sigma_s} - S_t e^{-q\tau}\frac{\partial N(-d_1)}{\partial \sigma_s} \\
&= Xe^{-r\tau}\frac{\partial(1-N(d_2))}{\partial d_2}\frac{\partial d_2}{\partial \sigma_s} - S_t e^{-q\tau}\frac{\partial(1-N(d_1))}{\partial d_1}\frac{\partial d_1}{\partial \sigma_s} \\
&= -Xe^{-r\tau}\left(\frac{1}{\sqrt{2\pi}}e^{-\frac{d_1^2}{2}}\cdot\frac{S_t}{X}\cdot e^{(r-q)\tau}\right) \\
&\quad\cdot\left(\frac{-\left[\ln\frac{S_t}{X}+(r-q+\frac{\sigma_s^2}{2})\tau\right]\cdot\tau^{\frac{1}{2}}}{\sigma_s^2\tau}\right) \\
&\quad + S_t e^{-q\tau}\frac{1}{\sqrt{2\pi}}e^{-\frac{d_1^2}{2}}\cdot\left(\frac{\sigma_s^2\tau^{3/2}-\left[\ln\frac{S_t}{X}+\left(r-q+\frac{\sigma_s^2}{2}\right)\tau\right]\cdot\tau^{\frac{1}{2}}}{\sigma_s^2\tau}\right) \\
&= -S_t e^{-q\tau}\frac{1}{\sqrt{2\pi}}e^{-\frac{d_1^2}{2}}\cdot\left(\frac{-\left[\ln\frac{S_t}{X}+\left(r-q+\frac{\sigma_s^2}{2}\right)\tau\right]\cdot\tau^{\frac{1}{2}}}{\sigma_s^2\tau}\right) \\
&\quad + S_t e^{-q\tau}\frac{1}{\sqrt{2\pi}}e^{-\frac{d_1^2}{2}}\cdot\left(\frac{\sigma_s^2\tau^{3/2}-\left[\ln\frac{S_t}{X}+\left(r-q+\frac{\sigma_s^2}{2}\right)\tau\right]\cdot\tau^{\frac{1}{2}}}{\sigma_s^2\tau}\right) \\
&= S_t e^{-q\tau}\frac{1}{\sqrt{2\pi}}e^{-\frac{d_1^2}{2}}\cdot\left(\frac{\sigma_s^2\tau^{3/2}}{\sigma_s^2\tau}\right) \\
&= S_t e^{-q\tau}\sqrt{\tau}\cdot N'(d_1).
\end{aligned}$$

11.5.2 *Application of vega (ν)*

Suppose a delta-neutral and gamma-neutral portfolio has a vega equal to ν and the vega of a particular option is ν_o. Similar to gamma, we can add a position of $-\nu/\nu_o$ in the option to make a vega-neutral portfolio. To maintain delta neutrality, we should change the underlying asset position. However, when we change the option position, the new portfolio is not gamma neutral. Generally, a portfolio with one option cannot maintain its gamma neutrality and vega neutrality at the same time. If we want a portfolio to be both gamma neutral and vega neutral, we should include at least two kinds of options on the same underlying asset in our portfolio.

For example, a delta-neutral and gamma-neutral portfolio contains option A, option B, and an underlying asset. The gamma and vega of this portfolio are −3,200 and −2,500, respectively. Option A has a delta of 0.3, gamma of 1.2, and vega of 1.5. Option B has a delta of 0.4, gamma of 1.6, and vega of 0.8. The new portfolio will be both gamma neutral and vega neutral when adding ω_A of option A and ω_B of option B into the original portfolio.

$$\begin{aligned} \text{Gamma Neutral:} &\ -3200 + 1.2\omega_A + 1.6\omega_B = 0. \\ \text{Vega Neutral:} &\ -2500 + 1.5\omega_A + 0.8\omega_B = 0. \end{aligned}$$

From the two equations shown above, we can get the solution that $\omega_A = 1,000$ and $\omega_B = 1,250$. The delta of new portfolio is $1,000 \times .3 + 1,250 \times 0.4 = 800$. To maintain delta neutrality, we need to short 800 shares of the underlying asset.

11.6 Rho (ρ)

The rho of an option is defined as the rate of change of the option price with respect to the interest rate:

$$\text{rho} = \frac{\partial \Pi}{\partial r},$$

where Π is the option price and r is the interest rate. The rho for an ordinary stock call option should be positive because a higher interest rate reduces the present value of the strike price which in turn increases the value of the call option. Similarly, the rho of an ordinary put option should be negative by the same reasoning. We next show the derivation of rho for various kinds of stock options.

11.6.1 *Derivation of rho for different kinds of stock options*

For a European call option on a non-dividend stock, rho can be shown as

$$\text{rho} = X\tau \cdot e^{-r\tau}N(d_2). \tag{11.25}$$

The derivation of Equation (11.25) is

$$\begin{aligned}
\text{rho} = \frac{\partial C_t}{\partial r} &= S_t\frac{\partial N(d_1)}{\partial r} - (-\tau)\cdot X\cdot e^{-r\tau}N(d_2) - Xe^{-r\tau}\frac{\partial N(d_2)}{\partial r}\\
&= S_t\frac{\partial N(d_1)}{\partial d_1}\frac{\partial d_1}{\partial r} + X\tau\cdot e^{-r\tau}N(d_2) - Xe^{-r\tau}\frac{\partial N(d_2)}{\partial d_2}\frac{\partial d_2}{\partial r}\\
&= S_t\frac{1}{\sqrt{2\pi}}e^{-\frac{d_1^2}{2}}\cdot\left(\frac{\sqrt{\tau}}{\sigma_s}\right) + X\tau\cdot e^{-r\tau}N(d_2) - Xe^{-r\tau}\\
&\quad\cdot\left(\frac{1}{\sqrt{2\pi}}e^{-\frac{d_1^2}{2}}\cdot\frac{S_t}{X}\cdot e^{r\tau}\right)\cdot\left(\frac{\sqrt{\tau}}{\sigma_s}\right)\\
&= S_t\frac{1}{\sqrt{2\pi}}e^{-\frac{d_1^2}{2}}\cdot\left(\frac{\sqrt{\tau}}{\sigma_s}\right) + X\tau\cdot e^{-r\tau}N(d_2) - S_t\frac{1}{\sqrt{2\pi}}e^{-\frac{d_1^2}{2}}\cdot\left(\frac{\sqrt{\tau}}{\sigma_s}\right)\\
&= X\tau\cdot e^{-r\tau}N(d_2).
\end{aligned}$$

For a European put option on a non-dividend stock, rho can be shown as

$$\text{rho} = -X\tau \cdot e^{-r\tau}N(-d_2). \tag{11.26}$$

The derivation of Equation (11.26) is

$$\begin{aligned}
\text{rho} = \frac{\partial P_t}{\partial r} &= (-\tau)\cdot X\cdot e^{-r\tau}N(-d_2)\\
&\quad + Xe^{-r\tau}\frac{\partial N(-d_2)}{\partial r} - S_t\frac{\partial N(-d_1)}{\partial r}\\
&= -X\tau\cdot e^{-r\tau}(1-N(d_2)) + Xe^{-r\tau}\frac{\partial(1-N(d_2))}{\partial d_2}\frac{\partial d_2}{\partial r}\\
&\quad - S_t\frac{\partial(1-N(d_1))}{\partial d_1}\frac{\partial d_1}{\partial r}
\end{aligned}$$

$$= X\tau \cdot e^{-r\tau}(1 - N(d_2)) - Xe^{-r\tau} \cdot \left(\frac{1}{\sqrt{2\pi}}e^{-\frac{d_1^2}{2}} \cdot \frac{S_t}{X} \cdot e^{r\tau}\right)$$

$$\cdot \left(\frac{\sqrt{\tau}}{\sigma_s}\right) + S_t\frac{1}{\sqrt{2\pi}}e^{-\frac{d_1^2}{2}} \cdot \left(\frac{\sqrt{\tau}}{\sigma_s}\right)$$

$$= X\tau \cdot e^{-r\tau}(1 - N(d_2)) - S_t\frac{1}{\sqrt{2\pi}}e^{-\frac{d_1^2}{2}} \cdot \left(\frac{\sqrt{\tau}}{\sigma_s}\right)$$

$$+ S_t\frac{1}{\sqrt{2\pi}}e^{-\frac{d_1^2}{2}} \cdot \left(\frac{\sqrt{\tau}}{\sigma_s}\right)$$

$$= -X\tau \cdot e^{-r\tau}N(-d_2).$$

For a European call option on a dividend-paying stock, rho can be shown as

$$\text{rho} = X\tau \cdot e^{-r\tau}N(d_2). \tag{11.27}$$

The derivation of Equation (11.27) is

$$\text{rho} = \frac{\partial C_t}{\partial r} = S_t e^{-q\tau}\frac{\partial N(d_1)}{\partial r} - (-\tau) \cdot X \cdot e^{-r\tau}N(d_2) - Xe^{-r\tau}\frac{\partial N(d_2)}{\partial r}$$

$$= S_t e^{-q\tau}\frac{\partial N(d_1)}{\partial d_1}\frac{\partial d_1}{\partial r} + X\tau \cdot e^{-r\tau}N(d_2) - Xe^{-r\tau}\frac{\partial N(d_2)}{\partial d_2}\frac{\partial d_2}{\partial r}$$

$$= S_t e^{-q\tau}\frac{1}{\sqrt{2\pi}}e^{-\frac{d_1^2}{2}} \cdot \left(\frac{\sqrt{\tau}}{\sigma_s}\right) + X\tau \cdot e^{-r\tau}N(d_2)$$

$$- Xe^{-r\tau} \cdot \left(\frac{1}{\sqrt{2\pi}}e^{-\frac{d_1^2}{2}} \cdot \frac{S_t}{X} \cdot e^{(r-q)\tau}\right) \cdot \left(\frac{\sqrt{\tau}}{\sigma_s}\right)$$

$$= S_t e^{-q\tau}\frac{1}{\sqrt{2\pi}}e^{-\frac{d_1^2}{2}} \cdot \left(\frac{\sqrt{\tau}}{\sigma_s}\right) + X\tau \cdot e^{-r\tau}N(d_2)$$

$$- S_t e^{-q\tau}\frac{1}{\sqrt{2\pi}}e^{-\frac{d_1^2}{2}} \cdot \left(\frac{\sqrt{\tau}}{\sigma_s}\right)$$

$$= X\tau \cdot e^{-r\tau}N(d_2).$$

For a European put option on a dividend-paying stock, rho can be shown as

$$\text{rho} = -X\tau \cdot e^{-r\tau}N(-d_2). \tag{11.28}$$

The derivation of Equation (11.28) is

$$\begin{aligned}
\text{rho} = \frac{\partial P_t}{\partial r} &= (-\tau) \cdot X \cdot e^{-r\tau} N(-d_2) \\
&\quad + Xe^{-r\tau} \frac{\partial N(-d_2)}{\partial r} - S_t e^{-q\tau} \frac{\partial N(-d_1)}{\partial r} \\
&= -X\tau \cdot e^{-r\tau}(1 - N(d_2)) + Xe^{-r\tau} \frac{\partial(1 - N(d_2))}{\partial d_2} \frac{\partial d_2}{\partial r} \\
&\quad - S_t e^{-q\tau} \frac{\partial(1 - N(d_1))}{\partial d_1} \frac{\partial d_1}{\partial r} \\
&= X\tau \cdot e^{-r\tau}(1 - N(d_2)) - Xe^{-r\tau} \cdot \left(\frac{1}{\sqrt{2\pi}} e^{-\frac{d_1^2}{2}} \cdot \frac{S_t}{X} \cdot e^{(r-q)\tau}\right) \\
&\quad \cdot \left(\frac{\sqrt{\tau}}{\sigma_s}\right) + S_t e^{-q\tau} \frac{1}{\sqrt{2\pi}} e^{-\frac{d_1^2}{2}} \cdot \left(\frac{\sqrt{\tau}}{\sigma_s}\right) \\
&= X\tau \cdot e^{-r\tau}(1 - N(d_2)) - S_t e^{-q\tau} \frac{1}{\sqrt{2\pi}} e^{-\frac{d_1^2}{2}} \cdot \left(\frac{\sqrt{\tau}}{\sigma_s}\right) \\
&\quad + S_t e^{-q\tau} \frac{1}{\sqrt{2\pi}} e^{-\frac{d_1^2}{2}} \cdot \left(\frac{\sqrt{\tau}}{\sigma_s}\right) \\
&= -X\tau \cdot e^{-r\tau} N(-d_2).
\end{aligned}$$

11.6.2 *Application of rho (ρ)*

Assume that an investor would like to see how interest rate changes affect the value of a three-month European put option she holds with the following information. The current stock price is \$65 and the strike price is \$58. The interest rate and the volatility of the stock are 5% and 30% per annum, respectively. The rho of this European put can be calculated as follows:

$$\begin{aligned}
\text{Rho}_{\text{put}} &= X\tau e^{-r\tau} N(d_2) = (\$58)(0.25)e^{-(0.05)(0.25)} N \\
&\quad \times \left(\frac{\ln(65/58) + \left[0.05 - \frac{1}{2}(0.3)^2\right](0.25)}{(0.3)\sqrt{0.25}}\right) \cong -3.168.
\end{aligned}$$

This calculation indicates that given a 1% increase in interest rate, say from 5% to 6%, the value of this European call option will decrease to 0.03168 (0.01 × 3.168). This simple example can be further applied to stocks that pay dividends using the derivation results shown previously.

11.7 Derivation of Sensitivity for Stock Options with respect to Exercise Price

For a European call option on a non-dividend stock, the sensitivity can be shown as

$$\frac{\partial C_t}{\partial X} = -e^{-r\tau}N(d_2). \tag{11.29}$$

The derivation of Equation (11.29) is

$$\begin{aligned}
\frac{\partial C_t}{\partial X} &= S_t\frac{\partial N(d_1)}{\partial X} - e^{-r\tau}N(d_2) - Xe^{-r\tau}\frac{\partial N(d_2)}{\partial X} \\
&= S_t\frac{\partial N(d_1)}{\partial d_1}\frac{\partial d_1}{\partial X} - e^{-r\tau}N(d_2) - Xe^{-r\tau}\frac{\partial N(d_2)}{\partial d_2}\frac{\partial d_2}{\partial X} \\
&= S_t\frac{1}{\sqrt{2\pi}}e^{-\frac{d_1^2}{2}} \cdot \frac{1}{\sigma_s\sqrt{\tau}} \cdot \left(-\frac{1}{X}\right) - e^{-r\tau}N(d_2) \\
&\quad - Xe^{-r\tau}\left(\frac{1}{\sqrt{2\pi}}e^{-\frac{d_1^2}{2}} \cdot \frac{S_t}{X} \cdot e^{r\tau}\right)\frac{1}{\sigma_s\sqrt{\tau}} \cdot \left(-\frac{1}{X}\right) \\
&= \frac{1}{\sigma_s\sqrt{2\pi\tau}}e^{-\frac{d_1^2}{2}}\left(-\frac{S_t}{X}\right) - e^{-r\tau}N(d_2) - \frac{1}{\sigma_s\sqrt{2\pi\tau}}e^{-\frac{d_1^2}{2}}\left(-\frac{S_t}{X}\right) \\
&= -e^{-r\tau}N(d_2).
\end{aligned}$$

For a European put option on a non-dividend stock, the sensitivity can be shown as

$$\frac{\partial P_t}{\partial X} = e^{-r\tau}N(-d_2). \tag{11.30}$$

The derivation of Equation (11.30) is

$$\begin{aligned}
\frac{\partial P_t}{\partial X} &= e^{-r\tau}N(-d_2) + Xe^{-r\tau}\frac{\partial N(-d_2)}{\partial X} - S_t\frac{\partial N(-d_1)}{\partial X} \\
&= e^{-r\tau}(1-N(d_2)) + Xe^{-r\tau}\frac{\partial(1-N(d_2))}{\partial d_2}\frac{\partial d_2}{\partial X} \\
&\quad - S_t\frac{\partial(1-N(d_1))}{\partial d_1}\frac{\partial d_1}{\partial X} \\
&= e^{-r\tau}(1-N(d_2)) - Xe^{-r\tau}\left(\frac{1}{\sqrt{2\pi}}e^{-\frac{d_1^2}{2}}\cdot\frac{S_t}{X}\cdot e^{r\tau}\right)\frac{1}{\sigma_s\sqrt{\tau}} \\
&\quad \cdot\left(-\frac{1}{X}\right) + S_t\frac{1}{\sqrt{2\pi}}e^{-\frac{d_1^2}{2}}\cdot\frac{1}{\sigma_s\sqrt{\tau}}\cdot\left(-\frac{1}{X}\right) \\
&= e^{-r\tau}(1-N(d_2)) + \frac{1}{\sigma_s\sqrt{2\pi\tau}}e^{-\frac{d_1^2}{2}}\left(\frac{S_t}{X}\right) - \frac{1}{\sigma_s\sqrt{2\pi\tau}}e^{-\frac{d_1^2}{2}}\left(\frac{S_t}{X}\right) \\
&= e^{-r\tau}N(-d_2).
\end{aligned}$$

For a European call option on a dividend-paying stock, the sensitivity can be shown as

$$\frac{\partial C_t}{\partial X} = -e^{-r\tau}N(d_2). \tag{11.31}$$

The derivation of Equation (11.31) is

$$\begin{aligned}
\frac{\partial C_t}{\partial X} &= S_te^{-q\tau}\frac{\partial N(d_1)}{\partial X} - e^{-r\tau}N(d_2) - Xe^{-r\tau}\frac{\partial N(d_2)}{\partial X} \\
&= S_te^{-q\tau}\frac{\partial N(d_1)}{\partial d_1}\frac{\partial d_1}{\partial X} - e^{-r\tau}N(d_2) - Xe^{-r\tau}\frac{\partial N(d_2)}{\partial d_2}\frac{\partial d_2}{\partial X} \\
&= S_te^{-q\tau}\frac{1}{\sqrt{2\pi}}e^{-\frac{d_1^2}{2}}\cdot\frac{1}{\sigma_s\sqrt{\tau}}\cdot\left(-\frac{1}{X}\right) - e^{-r\tau}N(d_2) \\
&\quad - Xe^{-r\tau}\left(\frac{1}{\sqrt{2\pi}}e^{-\frac{d_1^2}{2}}\cdot\frac{S_t}{X}\cdot e^{(r-q)\tau}\right)\frac{1}{\sigma_s\sqrt{\tau}}\cdot\left(-\frac{1}{X}\right) \\
&= \frac{1}{\sigma_s\sqrt{2\pi\tau}}e^{-\frac{d_1^2}{2}}\left(-\frac{S_te^{-q\tau}}{X}\right) - e^{-r\tau}N(d_2) \\
&\quad - \frac{1}{\sigma_s\sqrt{2\pi\tau}}e^{-\frac{d_1^2}{2}}\left(-\frac{S_te^{-q\tau}}{X}\right) \\
&= -e^{-r\tau}N(d_2).
\end{aligned}$$

For a European put option on a dividend-paying stock, the sensitivity can be shown as

$$\frac{\partial P_t}{\partial X} = e^{-r\tau}N(-d_2). \tag{11.32}$$

The derivation of Equation (11.32) is

$$\begin{aligned}
\frac{\partial P_t}{\partial X} &= e^{-r\tau}N(-d_2) + Xe^{-r\tau}\frac{\partial N(-d_2)}{\partial X} - S_t e^{-q\tau}\frac{\partial N(-d_1)}{\partial X} \\
&= e^{-r\tau}(1 - N(d_2)) + Xe^{-r\tau}\frac{\partial(1 - N(d_2))}{\partial d_2}\frac{\partial d_2}{\partial X} \\
&\quad - S_t e^{-q\tau}\frac{\partial(1 - N(d_1))}{\partial d_1}\frac{\partial d_1}{\partial X} \\
&= e^{-r\tau}(1 - N(d_2)) - Xe^{-r\tau}\left(\frac{1}{\sqrt{2\pi}}e^{-\frac{d_1^2}{2}} \cdot \frac{S_t}{X} \cdot e^{(r-q)\tau}\right)\frac{1}{\sigma_s\sqrt{\tau}} \\
&\quad \cdot \left(-\frac{1}{X}\right) + S_t e^{-q\tau}\frac{1}{\sqrt{2\pi}}e^{-\frac{d_1^2}{2}} \cdot \frac{1}{\sigma_s\sqrt{\tau}} \cdot \left(-\frac{1}{X}\right) \\
&= e^{-r\tau}(1 - N(d_2)) + \frac{1}{\sigma_s\sqrt{2\pi\tau}}e^{-\frac{d_1^2}{2}}\left(\frac{S_t e^{-q\tau}}{X}\right) \\
&\quad - \frac{1}{\sigma_s\sqrt{2\pi\tau}}e^{-\frac{d_1^2}{2}}\left(\frac{S_t e^{-q\tau}}{X}\right) \\
&= e^{-r\tau}N(-d_2).
\end{aligned}$$

11.8 Relationship between Delta, Theta, and Gamma

So far, the discussion has introduced the derivation and application of each individual Greek and how they can be applied in portfolio management. In practice, the interaction or trade-off between these parameters is of concern as well. For example, recall that the Black–Scholes–Merton differential equation with a non-dividend paying stock can be written as

$$\frac{\partial \Pi}{\partial t} + rS\frac{\partial \Pi}{\partial S} + \frac{1}{2}\sigma^2 S^2\frac{\partial^2 \Pi}{\partial S^2} = r\Pi,$$

where Π is the value of the derivative security contingent on stock price, S is the price of stock, r is the risk-free rate, σ is the volatility of the stock price, and t is the time to expiration of the derivative. Given the earlier derivation, we can rewrite the Black–Scholes partial differential equation (PDE) as

$$\Theta + rS\Delta + \frac{1}{2}\sigma^2 S^2 \Gamma = r\Pi.$$

This relation gives us the trade-off between delta, gamma, and theta. For example, suppose there are two delta-neutral ($\Delta = 0$) portfolios, one with positive gamma ($\Gamma > 0$)and the other one with negative gamma($\Gamma < 0$) and they both have a value of \$1 ($\Pi = 1$). The trade-off can be written as

$$\Theta + \frac{1}{2}\sigma^2 S^2 \Gamma = r.$$

For the first portfolio, if gamma is positive and large, then theta is negative and large. When gamma is positive, changes in stock prices result in a higher value of the option. This means that when there is no change in stock prices, the value of the option declines as we approach the expiration date. As a result, the theta is negative. On the other hand, when gamma is negative and large, changes in stock prices result in a lower value of the option. This means that when there is no stock price change, the value of the option increases as we approach the expiration, and theta is positive. This gives us a trade-off between gamma and theta and they can be used as proxy for each other in a delta-neutral portfolio.

11.9 Summary

In this chapter, we have shown the partial derivatives of stock option with respect to five variables. Delta (Δ), the rate of change of option price with respect to the change in price of underlying asset, is first derived. After delta is obtained, gamma (Γ) can be derived as the rate of change of delta with respect to the underlying asset price. Another two risk measures are theta (Θ) and rho (ρ); they measure the change in option value with respect to passing time and interest rate, respectively. Finally, one can also measure the change in option value with respect to the volatility of the underlying asset and this gives us the vega (v). The applications of these Greek letters in portfolio management have also been discussed. In addition, we use the Black–Scholes PDE to show the relationship between these risk measures. In sum, risk management is one of the important topics in finance for both academics and practitioners. Given the recent credit crisis, one can observe that it is crucial to properly measure the risk related to even the more complicated financial assets. The comparative static analysis of option pricing models gives an introduction to portfolio risk management. Further discussion of the comparative statics analysis can be found in Hull (2011) and McDonald (2005).

Questions and Problems

1. What does the $\Delta = 0.7$ of a call option mean?
2. Briefly describe the meanings of theta and gamma.
3. Describe the relationship between volatility of stock price and option price via vega.
4. How can one calculate the changes of option price by using delta and gamma together?
5. What is the value of the delta of an at-the-money call option when $r = 5\%$ per year, $\sigma_s = 15\%$, and the maturity $\tau = 2$?
6. Calculate delta, gamma, vega, theta, and rho of a call option on a non-dividend-paying stock under the following information: $S = \$110$, $X = \$100$, $r = 0.05$, $\sigma_s = 15\%$, and $\tau = 7$ months.
7. Based on the information provided in Question 6, if the stock pays dividend with 1% dividend yield, please calculate delta, gamma, vega, theta, and rho.
8. Derive the relationship between the deltas of a call option and of a put option by put–call parity.
9. Describe the relationship between the gamma of a call option and the gamma of a put option.
10. Given the following table of an option portfolio,

Type	Position	Delta	Gamma	Vega
Call	−1,500	0.3	0.4	1.6
Call	−100	0.9	1.3	0.2
Put	−1,000	−0.5	0.9	0.3
Call	−300	0.7	2.5	1.5

let a traded option be available with delta = 0.8, gamma = 2.0, vega = 0.8.

(a) What position in the traded option and the options in the table can make the portfolio with delta neutral?
(b) What position in the traded option and the options in the table can make the portfolio with gamma neutral?
(c) What position in the traded option and the options in the table can make the portfolio with both delta and gamma neutral?

Bibliography

Bjork, T. (1998). *Arbitrage Theory in Continuous Time.* New York, NY: Oxford University Press.

Boyle, P. P. and D. Emanuel (1980). Discretely adjusted option hedges. *Journal of Financial Economics*, 8(3), 259–282.

Duffie, D. (2001). *Dynamic Asset Pricing Theory.* Princeton, NJ: Princeton University Press.

Fabozzi, F. J. (2007). *Fixed Income Analysis*, 2nd ed. New York, NY: Wiley.

Figlewski, S. (1989). Options arbitrage in imperfect markets. *Journal of Finance*, 44(5), 1289–1311.

Galai, D. (1983). The components of the return from hedging options against stocks. *Journal of Business*, 56(1), 45–54.

Hull, J. and A. White (1987). Hedging the risks from writing foreign currency options. *Journal of International Money and Finance*, 6(2), 131–152.

Hull, J. (2011). *Options, Futures, and Other Derivatives*, 8th ed. Upper Saddle River, NJ: Pearson.

Karatzas, I. and S. E. Shreve (2000). *Brownian Motion and Stochastic Calculus.* Berlin: Springer.

Klebaner, F. C. (2005). *Introduction to Stochastic Calculus with Applications.* London: Imperial College Press.

Lee, C. F., Y. Chen and J. Lee (2016). Alternative methods to derive option pricing models: Review and comparison. *Review of Quantitative Finance and Accounting*, 47(2), 417–451.

McDonald, R. L. (2005). *Derivatives Markets*, 2nd ed. Boston, MA: Addison-Wesley.

Shreve, S. E. (2004). *Stochastic Calculus for Finance II: Continuous Time Model.* New York, NY: Springer.

Tuckman, B. (2002). *Fixed Income Securities: Tools for Today's Markets*, 2nd ed. New York, NY: Wiley.

Chapter 12

Implied Variance, Volatility Smile, and CEV Option Pricing Model

Contents

12.1 Introduction

Implied variance is very important information in financial derivative. For example, the VIX, which is traded in future exchange, is the implied variance of the S&P 500 index option. There are two approaches to estimate implied variance, the non-closed-form solution method, which needs to rely upon a complicated computer program to solve it, and the linearized approximation method.

In Section 12.2, we will discuss an Exact Closed-Form Solution for the Implied Standard Deviation, which uses the Tailor Expansion Method to Linearize the Option Pricing Model (OPM). In Section 12.3, we will discuss the Implied Standard Deviation formula under a single call option. Excel programs are also presented in this section for calculating the implied standard deviation. In Section 12.4, we will discuss formulas for Implied Standard Deviation under Different Exercise Prices. In Section 12.5, we will discuss the volatility smile. In Section 12.6, we will discuss the relationship between the Black and Scholes OPM and the constant elasticity volatility (CEV) OPM. In Section 12.7, we will briefly discuss how the MATLAB program can be used to calculate implied variance for both the Black–Scholes model and CEV of the OPM. Finally, in Section 12.7, we summarize the results of this chapter. In Appendix 12A, we will discuss Corrado and Miller's linearized method. Appendix 12B discusses the MATLAB approach to estimate implied variance. Appendix 12C discusses non-central χ^2 and the OPM, and Appendix 12D compares the performance of the Black–Scholes model and the CEV model.

12.2 An Exact Closed-Form Solution for the Implied Standard Deviation: A Special Case

12.2.1 *Modification of option pricing model for estimating implied variance*

Black and Scholes call option formula can be defined as

$$C = S[N(d_1)] - e^{-rT}E[N(d_2)], \tag{12.1}$$

where C = value of option, S = current price of stock, r = continuously compounded annual risk-free interest rate, T = time in years to expiration date, E = exercise price, e = 2.71828 is a constant, and $N(d_1)$ = probability that a standard normal random variable is less than or equal to $d_i (i = 1,\ 2)$, with

$$d_1 = \frac{ln\left(\frac{S}{E}\right) + \left(r + \frac{\sigma^2}{2}\right)T}{\sigma\sqrt{T}} \tag{12.2a}$$

and

$$d_2 = \frac{ln\left(\frac{S}{E}\right) + \left(r - \frac{\sigma^2}{2}\right)T}{\sigma\sqrt{T}} = d_1 - \sigma\sqrt{T}, \tag{12.2b}$$

where σ^2 = variance of annual rate of return on the stock, continuously compounded, and logarithms are to base e.

Substituting $rT = \ln(\mathrm{e}^{rT})$ into Equation (12.2a), we obtain the following:

$$\begin{aligned} d_1 &= \frac{\ln\left(\frac{S}{E}\right) + \ln\left(\mathrm{e}^{rT}\right)}{\sigma\sqrt{T}} + \frac{\frac{1}{2}\sigma^2 T}{\sigma\sqrt{T}} = \frac{\ln\left(\left(\frac{S}{E}\right)\left(\mathrm{e}^{rT}\right)\right)}{\sigma\sqrt{T}} + \frac{\sigma\sqrt{T}}{2} \\ &= \frac{\ln\left(\frac{S}{K}\right)}{\sigma\sqrt{T}} + \frac{\sigma\sqrt{T}}{2}. \end{aligned} \tag{12.3a}$$

Similarly,

$$d_2 = d_1 - \sigma\sqrt{T} = \ln(S/K)/(\sigma\sqrt{T}) - \sigma\sqrt{T}/2. \tag{12.3b}$$

Substituting Equations (12.3a) and (12.3b) into Equation (12.1), we can obtain

$$\begin{aligned} \mathrm{C} = \mathrm{S}[\mathrm{N}(\ln(S/K)/(\sigma\sqrt{T}) + \sigma\sqrt{T}/2)] \\ - \mathrm{K}[\mathrm{N}(\ln(S/K)/(\sigma\sqrt{T}) - \sigma\sqrt{T}/2)], \end{aligned} \tag{12.4}$$

where C is the call premium, S is the underlying asset value, the present value of the exercise price K is equal to $E\mathrm{e}^{-rT}$, E is the exercise price, r is the instantaneous risk-free rate, T is the time to the maturity, σ is the standard deviation of the underlying asset rate of return on an annual basis, and $N(x)$ is the standard cumulative normal distribution function up to x. Equation (12.4) is an equation to be used to estimate implied variance, which will be discussed in Section 12.3.

12.2.2 *Implied variance under the condition that the stock price equals the present value of the exercise price*

Under the condition that the stock price equals the present value of the exercise price (i.e., $S = K = E\mathrm{e}^{-rT}$), Brenner and Subrahmanyam (1988) derive the following simple formula to compute the implied standard deviation:

$$\sigma\sqrt{T} = \sqrt{2\pi}C/S. \tag{12.5}$$

This formula is derived by applying Taylor series expansion at zero in the B/S model up to the first-order term, and the higher-order terms are ignored. Since the higher-order terms are omitted, Equation (12.5) is an approximation rather than an exact solution. The accuracy of the ISD calculated by Equation (12.5) depends not only on the deviation of the stock price S from the present value of exercise price K but also on the magnitude of the standard deviation σ.

However, when the underlying asset price equals the present value of the exercise price, the B/S model becomes[1]

$$\begin{aligned} C &= S[N(\sigma\sqrt{T}/2) - N(-\sigma\sqrt{T}/2)] \\ &= S[1 - 2N(-\sigma\sqrt{T}/2)] \\ &= S[2N(\sigma\sqrt{T}/2) - 1]. \end{aligned} \tag{12.6}$$

Thus, an exact closed-form solution for the ISD is[2]

$$\begin{aligned} \sigma\sqrt{T} &= -2N^{-1}[(S - C)/(2S)] \\ &= 2N^{-1}[(S + C)/(2S)]. \end{aligned} \tag{12.7}$$

Since the cumulative normal distribution is a monotonic increasing function, its inverse cumulative normal functions in Equation (12.7) must exist and be unique. Therefore, Equation (12.7) must be an exact and unique closed-form solution for the ISD if the present

---

[1]Note that $N(-\sigma\sqrt{T}/2) = 1 - N(\sigma\sqrt{T}/2)$.

[2]Given $S = K$, the BS model becomes $C = S[N(\sigma\sqrt{T}/2) - N(-\sigma\sqrt{T}/2)] = S[N(\sigma\sqrt{T}/2) - (1 - (N(\sigma\sqrt{T}/2))] = -S + 2SN(\sigma\sqrt{T}/2)$, solving the ISD yields Equation (12.7).

value of the exercise price equals the underlying asset price. It is noteworthy that the Taylor expansion plays no role in deriving Equation (12.7) and there is no truncation of the remainder terms. Hence, when the assumption $S = K = Ee^{-rT}$ holds, using Equation (12.7) to calculate the ISD results in the true ISD and there is no estimation error. Previous formulas are approximate because they are derived[3] by truncating the remainder terms in Taylor's formula. The estimate error always exists. Equation (12.7) is the best formula for ISD and dominates all other formulas if the $S = K$. $-(N(\sigma\sqrt{T}/2))] = -S + 2SN(\sigma\sqrt{T}/2)$, solving the ISD yields Equation (12.23).

Equation (12.7) is useful to calculate the exact ISD in this special case because of the popularity of Excel in which the inverse standard cumulative normal function is imbedded.

Given Equation (12.6), the sensitivity of the call option of the exercise price and the hedge ratio at the $S = K$ are determined by

$$\partial C/\partial K = -N(-\sigma\sqrt{T}/2) = -1/2 + C/(2S), \tag{12.8}$$

$$\partial C/\partial S = N(\sigma\sqrt{T}/2) = 1/2 + C/(2S). \tag{12.9}$$

Equation (12.8) is the sensitivity of the call option value from the striking price at $K = Ee^{-rT} = S$. Equation (12.9) is the hedge ratio (delta) at the underlying asset price S equaling the present value K of the exercise price. Equation (12.8) shows that the $\partial C/\partial K$ must be greater than $-1/2$, while Equation (12.9) demonstrates that the delta must be greater than $1/2$. Equations (12.8) and (12.9) provide closed-form and exact solutions for the $\partial C/\partial K$ and delta. Given the closed-form and exact solution of the ISD in Equation (12.7), it is possible to find all of the closed-form and exact solutions for all of the Greeks of options at $S = K$. The following theorem summarizes the results of Equations (12.7) to (12.9).

Theorem: Under the Black and Scholes call OPM, if underlying asset price S equals the present value K of exercise price, then there is an exact closed-form solution for the ISD and is given by Equation (12.7). *Further, $\partial C/\partial K$ and the hedge ratio at $S = K$ are given by Equations* (12.8) *and* (12.9), *respectively.*

[3]The function used to calculate the inverse cumulative normal function is named as "NORMSINV" in f_x of Excel.

12.3 An Implied Standard Deviation Formula under a Single Call Option

Following Ang *et al.* (2013), this section derives a formula to estimate the ISD by applying the Taylor series expansion on a single call option. We show that the improved formula for ISD derived by Corrado and Miller (1996) (CM) can be improved further without any replacements. Applying Taylor's formula to both cumulative normal distributions in Equation (12.4) at $L = \ln(S/K)/(\sigma\sqrt{T})$ yields

$$\begin{aligned} N(L+\sigma\sqrt{T}/2) &= N(L) + N'(L)\sigma\sqrt{T}/2 + N''(L)(\sigma\sqrt{T}/2)^2/2 + e_1 \\ &= N(L) + N'(L)(\sigma\sqrt{T}/2)[1 - \ln(S/K)/4] + e_1 \end{aligned} \tag{12.10}$$

and

$$\begin{aligned} N(L-\sigma\sqrt{T}/2) &= N(L) - N'(L)\sigma\sqrt{T}/2 + N''(L)(\sigma\sqrt{T}/2)^2/2 + e_2 \\ &= N(L) - N'(L)(\sigma\sqrt{T}/2)(1 + \ln(S/K)/4) + e_2, \end{aligned} \tag{12.11}$$

where e_1 and e_2 are the remainder terms of Taylor's formulas. Equations (12.10) and (12.11) are obtained by the fact that $N''(x) = -N'(x)x$.

Given $N(0) = 1/2$, $N'(0) = 1/\sqrt{2\pi}$, $N'''(0) = -N'(0)$, $N''(0) = 0 = N''''(0)$. We apply Taylor's formula to the $N[\ln(S/K)/(\sigma\sqrt{T})]$ and $N'[\ln(S/K)/(\sigma\sqrt{T})]$ in Equations (12.10) and (12.11) at 0:

$$\begin{aligned} N(L) &= N(0) + N'(0)(L) + N''(0)(L)^2/2 + e_3 \\ &= 1/2 + L/\sqrt{2\pi} + e_3, \end{aligned} \tag{12.12}$$

$$\begin{aligned} N'(L) &= N'(0) + +N''(0)(L) + N'''(0)(L)^2/2 + e_4 \\ &= 1/\sqrt{2\pi} - L^2/(2\sqrt{2\pi}) + e_4, \end{aligned} \tag{12.13}$$

where e_3 and e_4 are the remainder terms of Taylor's formulas. Substituting Equations (12.10)–(12.13) into Equation (12.4), dropping all of the remainder terms, Equation (12.4) becomes

$$\begin{aligned} C = {} & (S-K)/2 + L[(S-K)(1+[\ln(S/K)/4]^2) \\ & - \ln(S/K)(S+K)/4]/\sqrt{2\pi} \\ & + (\sigma\sqrt{T}/2)[S+K-\ln(S/K)(S-K)/4]/\sqrt{2\pi}. \end{aligned} \quad (12.14)$$

Equation (12.14) is a quadratic equation of $\sigma\sqrt{T}$ and can be rewritten as

$$\begin{aligned} & \sigma^2 T[4(S+K) - (S-K)\ln(S/k)] - 4\sigma\sqrt{T}\sqrt{2\pi}(2C - S + K) \\ & + 8\ln(S/K)[(S-K)(1+(\ln(S/K)/4)^2) \\ & - (S+K)\ln(S/K)/4] = 0. \end{aligned} \quad (12.15)$$

Solving $\sigma\sqrt{T}$ from Equation (12.15) yields

$$\sigma\sqrt{T} = [b \pm \sqrt{b^2 - ac}]/a, \quad (12.16)$$

where $a = 4(S+K) - (S-K)\ln(S/K)$, $b = 2\sqrt{2\pi}(2C - S + K)$, and $c = 8\ln(S/K)[(S-K)(1+(\ln(S/K)/4)^2) - (S+K)\ln(S/K)/4]$. A merit of Equation (12.16) is to circumvent the ad hoc substitution present in Corrado and Miller and improve the accuracy of ISD's estimation.

Since Equations (12.12) and (12.13) are the Taylor series at the zero point, and the remainder terms e_1 to e_4 in Equations (12.10) to (12.11) are omitted in deriving Equation (12.14), the ISD calculated by Equation (12.16) is not an exact formula. Therefore, the effectiveness of using Equation (12.16) to estimate the ISD depends on the deviation of the underlying asset price from the present value of the exercise price. The merits of this formula are that Equation (12.4) is derived without arbitrary substitution (see Appendix 12A) as given by Corrado and Miller (1996). Corrado and Miller's formula, to calculate implied variance, can be defined as follows:

$$\begin{aligned} \sigma\sqrt{T} = {} & \sqrt{2\pi}[C - (S-K)/2 \\ & + \sqrt{(C-(S-K)/2)^2 - (S-K)^2/\pi}]/(S+K)]. \end{aligned} \quad (12.17)$$

All notations of Equation (12.17) are the same as Equation (12.16). The detailed explanation of this equation can be found in Appendix 12A.

Table 12.1 presents the excel program to calculate implied standard deviation in terms of Equation (12.16). Table 12.2 presents the excel program to calculate the implied standard deviation in terms of Equation (12.17).

The source of data for Tables 12.1 and 12.2 comes from IBM Company from April 21.

Table 12.1 Excel Program to Calculate Implied Standard Deviation in Terms of Equation (12.16)

Inputs		
Dividend (q)	0	
Stock price (S)	161.53	
Exercise price (X)	160	
Risk-free rate (r)	0.025	
Time (t)	0.0952	
Call option value (c)	4.111850351	
$K = X^{*}\text{e}\hat{}(-rt)$	159.6195008	
$S' = S^{*}\text{e}\hat{}(-qt)$	161.53	
a	2,569.150544	
b	−126.5987946	
c	0.181850353	
Delta	14,158.45106	
Sigma1	0.154875382	$(-b+\text{sqrt(delta)})/2a^{*}\ \text{sqrt}(t)$
Sigma2	0.004798787	$(-b-\text{sqrt(delta)})/2a^{*}\ \text{sqrt}(t)$
Inputs		
Dividend (q)	0	
Stock price (S)	161.53	
Exercise price (X)	160	
Risk-free rate (r)	0.025	
Time (t)	0.095238095	
Put option value (P)	2.191993056	
$K = X^{*}\ \text{e}\hat{}(-rt)$	159.6195008	
$S' = S^{*}\ \text{e}\hat{}(-qt)$	161.53	
a	2,569.150544	
b	−126.2234794	
c	0.181850353	
Delta	14,063.56301	
Sigma1	0.154386826	$(-\ b+\text{sqrt(delta)})/2a^{*}\text{sqrt}(t)$
Sigma2	0.004813973	$(-\ b-\text{sqrt(delta)})/2a^{*}\text{sqrt}(t)$

Table 12.2 Excel Program to Calculate Implied Standard Deviation in Terms of Equation (12.17).

Estimating Implied Volatility (or ISD) in BS Option Values	
Share price (S)	**161.53**
Exercise price (X)	**160.00**
Int rate-cont (r)	**2.00%**
Dividend yield (q)	**0.00%**
Time now (0, years)	0.00
Time maturity (T, years)	**0.10**
Option life (T, years)	0.10
Volatility (s)	**15.49%**
iopt	**1**
BS option value	4.428610134
Observed option price	**3.37**
ISD Estimate (Corrado and Miller)	**11.83%**
S^* exp($-q^*$ T)	161.53
X^* exp($-r^*$ T)	159.70
Calc0	2.45
Calc1	4.95
Calc2	4.68

If we try to estimate implied standard deviation by the nonlinear OPM, we can use the MATLAB program to achieve this goal. Appendix 12B will show how the MATLAB approach can be used to estimate implied standard deviation in terms of the Black–Scholes model. In addition, this approach can be used to estimate implied standard deviation in terms of the CEV model. The detailed discussion of the CEV model can be found in Appendix 12C.

12.4 Formulas for Implied Standard Deviation under Different Exercise Prices

In this section, we derive two formulas to estimate the ISD from call options with different exercise prices. The derived formulas can apply to a wide range of exercise prices that deviate from the underlying asset price. The advantage of using options with different exercise prices in this section is to obtain a no-error first term in the expansion, thus giving more accurate formulas for ISD. The first term in the Taylor expansion usually provides the major component of the true function and the remaining terms provide correction to adjust and approximate the true function. For example, if the call option value C_1 with exercise price E_1 is expanded at the exercise price E_2, the first term of the Taylor series expansion is the given option value C_2 on E_2. Similarly, the first term of the Taylor expansion on option value C_2 on E_2 at exercise price E_1 is C_1. Since both C_1 and C_2 are given, there is no need to expand the first terms again.

Consider two call options C_1 and C_2 on the same time to maturity with prices of E_1 and E_2 (where $E_1 < E_2$); their present value are K_1 and K_2, respectively. Applying Taylor's expansion to Equation (12.4) at K_2 for C_1 and at K_1 for C_2, respectively, yields

$$C_1 = C_2 - N(\ln(S/K_2)/(\sigma\sqrt{T}) - \sigma\sqrt{T}/2)(K_1 - K_2) + \varepsilon_1, \tag{12.18}$$

$$C_2 = C_1 - N(\ln(S/K_1)/(\sigma\sqrt{T}) - \sigma\sqrt{T}/2)(K_2 - K_1) + \varepsilon_2. \tag{12.19}$$

Here, ε_1 and ε_2 are the remainder terms of C_1 at K_2 and C_2 at K_1 from Equation (12.4), respectively. Dividing both sides of Equations (12.18) and (12.19) by (K_2-K_1) and simple manipulations produces the same left-hand side of $(C_1-C_2)/(K_2-K_1)$. Then, applying the inverse function of the cumulative normal function on both sides, and after using Taylor's formula, yields the following equations:

$$N^{-1}[(C_1 - C_2)/(K_2 - K_1)] = \ln(S/K_1)/(\sigma\sqrt{T}) - \sigma\sqrt{T}/2 + \eta_1, \tag{12.20}$$

$$N^{-1}[(C_1 - C_2)/(K_2 - K_1)] = \ln(S/K_2)/(\sigma\sqrt{T}) - \sigma\sqrt{T}/2 + \eta_2, \tag{12.21}$$

where η_1 and η_2 are the remainder terms of Taylor's formulas derived from Equations (12.18) and (12.19), respectively. After dropping the remainder terms, ISD solved individually from either Equation (12.20) or (12.21) could be more volatile than that solved simultaneously with both equations. Combining Equations (12.20) and

(12.21) could cause the effects of the remainder term $(\eta_1+\eta_2)$ to partially offset and thus reduce their variability. Dropping the remainder term $(\eta_1 + \eta_2)$, a simple manipulation produces the following equation:

$$(\sigma\sqrt{T})^2 + 2N^{-1}[(C_1 - C_2)/(K_2 - K_1)](\sigma\sqrt{T}) - \ln[S^2/(K_1K_2)] = 0. \tag{12.22}$$

Equation (12.22) is a quadratic equation of the ISD and thus can be solved as

$$\begin{aligned}\sigma\sqrt{T} &= -N^{-1}[(C_1 - C_2)/(K_2 - K_1)] \\ &\quad \pm \sqrt{[N^{-1}((C_1 - C_2)/(K_2 - K_1))]^2 + \ln(S^2/K_1K_2)}.\end{aligned} \tag{12.23}$$

There are two solutions for the ISD in Equation (12.22), yet the ISD must only take one of them. It is clear that, if $(C_1 - C_2)/(K_2 - K_1) \geq 1/2$, the inverse of cumulative normal function on it must be non-negative. Consequently, ISD must take the value with the positive sign in Equation (12.23), or else ISD will become negative, which violates the positive requirement for ISD. On the other hand, if $(C_1 - C_2)/(K_2 - K_1) < 1/2$ and $K_1 < S < K_2$, the ISD must take the positive sign in Equation (12.23) too. The negative sign only applies when S is less than K_1. It is clear that if stock price is less than the lower exercise K_1 (i.e., then both call options are out of the money) and if we had chosen the value with the plus sign in Equation (12.23), ISD calculated by Equation (12.23) will be overstated.

Furthermore, if K_2 approaches K_1, then $(C_1 - C_2)/(K_2 - K_1)$ in Equation (12.23) tends to $-\partial C/\partial K$ and $\ln(S^2/K_1K_2)$ tends to zero. Given positive ISD, ISD calculated by Equation (12.23) must converge to $-2N^{-1}(-\partial C/\partial K)$ (see Equation (12.8)). Convergence implies that the ISD in Equation (12.23) must take the negative sign for the exercise prices. Note that the ISD in Equation (12.23) is not an exact solution because the remainder terms η_1 and η_2 were dropped out in the derivation of Equation (12.22).

Equation (12.23) provides a formula to calculate the ISD. All of the parameters on the right-hand sides of Equation (12.23) are given. A merit of this formula is that a sufficient condition to calculate ISD by Equation (12.23) only requires that there exist any two consecutive call option values with different exercise prices. Although it may not always hold that the call option value at $S = K$, it is easier to obtain any consecutive two traded call option values and their exercise prices in practice. In particular, Equation (12.23) is applicable to a wide range of exercise prices if their call options are observable. Of course, its accuracy will depend on the magnitude of the deviation between these two exercise prices. The closer these two exercise prices, the lower the remainder of Taylor's formulas in Equations (12.18) and (12.19). Consequently, the ISD estimated by Equation (12.23) is more accurate than in previous models. In particular, formulas by both Corrado and Miller (1996) and Li (2005) are only valid when calculated near at the money. Outside this range, both formulas' performance is poor if not applicable.

Similar to Equation (12.22), if there is a third call option C_3 with the discounted exercise price K_3, then the following equation (12.24) must hold for K_2, K_3 and C_2, C_3:

$$\begin{aligned}(\sigma\sqrt{T})^2 &+ 2N^{-1}[(C_2 - C_3)/(K_3 - K_2)](\sigma\sqrt{T}) \\ &- \ln[S^2/(K_2K_3)] = 0. \end{aligned} \tag{12.24}$$

Given the constant variance assumption in the Black and Scholes option model, the following equation (12.25) is thus derived by subtracting Equation (12.23) from Equation (12.24):

$$\begin{aligned}\sigma\sqrt{T} = \ln(K_3/K_1)/[2(N^{-1}&((C_1 - C_2)/(K_2 - K_1)) - N^{-1} \\ &\times ((C_2 - C_3)/(K_3 - K_2)))]. \end{aligned} \tag{12.25}$$

An advantage of using Equation (12.25) rather than Equation (12.23) to estimate the ISD is to circumvent the sign issue that appears in Equation (12.23). However, a drawback of using Equation (12.24) is that there must exist at least three instead of two call options for Equation (12.23). Equation (12.25) provides a simple formula to calculate ISD because all option values and exercise prices are given, and the inverse function of the standard cumulative normal function is also available in the Excel spreadsheet. Instead of calculating a complex function of cosine and inverse cosine functions in the formula in Li (2005), Equation (12.23) provides a more convenient approach to calculate ISD. Furthermore, Li's formula suffers from a limited applicable range as stated earlier.

12.5 Volatility Smile

The existence of a volatility smile is due to the fact that the Black–Scholes formula cannot precisely evaluate either the call or put option value. The main reason is that the Black–Scholes formula assumes the stock price per share is log-normally distributed. If we introduce extra distribution parameters into the option pricing determination formula, we can obtain the CEV option pricing formula. This formula can be found in Section 12.6 of this chapter. In Appendix 12D, we also cite the empirical work done by Lee *et al.* (2004) and Chen *et al.* (2009) to show that the CEV model performs better than the Black–Scholes model in evaluating either call or put option value.

How close are the market prices of options to those predicted by the Black–Scholes–Merton model? Do traders really use the Black–Scholes–Merton model when determining a price for an option? Are the probability distributions of asset prices really log-normal? In this chapter, we answer these questions. We explain that traders do use the Black–Scholes–Merton model, but not in exactly the way that Black, Scholes, and Merton originally intended. This is because they allow the volatility used to price an option to depend on its strike price and time to maturity.

A plot of the implied volatility of an option as a function of its strike price is known as a volatility smile. In this chapter, we describe the volatility smiles that traders use in equity and foreign currency markets. We explain the relationship between a volatility smile and the probability distribution being assumed for the future asset price. We also discuss how option traders vary volatility with option maturity and how they use volatility surfaces as pricing tools.

Put–call parity can be used to show that the implied volatility of a European call option must be the same as that of a European put option when both have the same strike price and time to maturity. This is convenient. It means that the volatility smile for European call options must be the same as that for European put options. The implied volatility of an American option is in most cases very similar to that of a European option with the same strike price and time to maturity. As a result, we can say that the volatility smiles we will present apply — at least approximately — to all European and American options with a particular time to maturity.

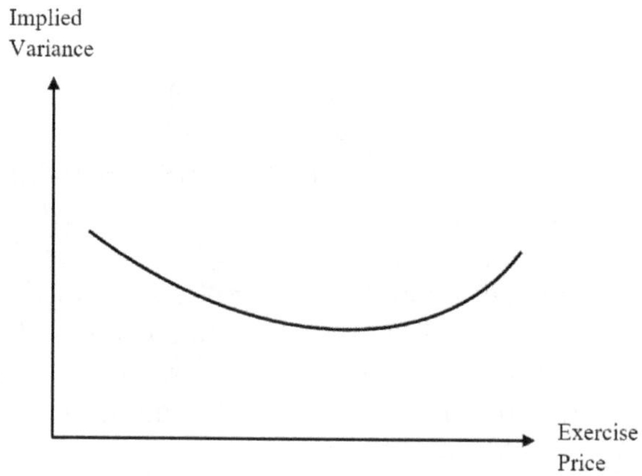

Figure 12.1 Volatility Smile for Foreign Currency Options

12.5.1 *Foreign currency options*

The volatility smile for foreign currency options has the general form shown in Figure 12.1. The implied variance is relatively low for at-the-money options, but becomes progressively higher as the option moves either into the money or out of the money.

12.5.1.1 *Reasons for the smile in foreign currency options*

Why are exchange rates not log-normally distributed? Two of the conditions for an asset price to have a log-normal distribution are as follows:

1. The volatility of the asset is constant.
2. The price of the asset changes smoothly with no jumps.

Neither of these conditions is satisfied for an exchange rate. The volatility of an exchange rate is far from constant, and exchange rates frequently exhibit jumps. The effect of both non-constant volatility and jumps is that extreme outcomes become more likely. As we will discuss in Appendix 12D, the CEV model did not assume variance is constant. In other words, the variance is a function of the stock price per share. In addition, the CEV model can take care of the jump of foreign exchange better than the Black–Scholes model.

The impact of jumps and non-constant volatility depends on the option maturity. As the maturity of the option is increased, the percentage impact of non-constant volatility on prices becomes more pronounced, but its percentage impact on implied volatility usually becomes less pronounced. The percentage impact of jumps on both prices and the implied volatility becomes less pronounced as the maturity of the option is increased. The result of all this is that the volatility smile becomes less pronounced as option maturity increases.

12.5.2 *Equity options*

The volatility smile for equity options has been studied by Rubinstein (1985, 1994) and Jackwerth and Rubinstein (1996). Prior to 1987, there was no marked volatility smile. Since 1987, the volatility smile used by traders to price equity options (both those on individual stocks and those on stock indices) has had the general form shown in Figure 12.2. This is sometimes referred to as *volatility skew*. The volatility decreases as the strike price increases. The volatility used to price an option with a low strike price (i.e., a deep-out-of-the-money put or deep-in-the-money call) is significantly higher than that used to price an option with a high strike price (i.e., a deep-in-the-money put or deep-out-of-the-money call).

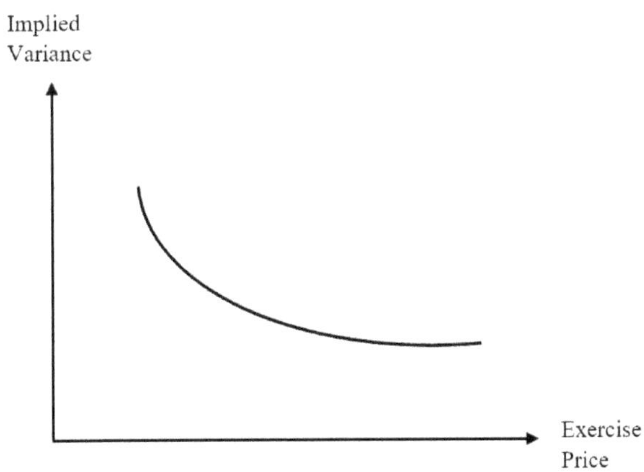

Figure 12.2 Volatility Smile for Equities

12.5.3 *Implied volatility and volatility smile by using Johnson & Johnson (JNJ) stock options as an example*

12.5.3.1 *Implied volatility*

We need to collect several inputs from Johnson & Johnson (JNJ) to calculate implied volatility. We selected an option contract on February 18, 2022, and the expiration date for this option is June 17, 2022. We assume that JNJ does not issue dividend payments during this period, so the dividend (D) is \$0. The stock price (S) was 163.36 on February 18, 2022. We can calculate the time to maturity of this option as the number of days from today until the option expires and divided by 365 days for a year. Therefore, time to maturity (t) is $119/365 = 0.326$. During the contract period, we pick one contract with the exercise price (X) of \$160. Under this contract, the ask call option premium is \$9.45. For the risk-free rate (r), we assume the rate is 3% during this contract period. By following Equation (12.4), we calculate the present value of the exercise price K as 158.96 and the present value of the exercise price as \$162.30.

Input	
Dividend (D)	\$0.00
Stock price (S)	\$163.36
Exercise price (X)	\$160.00
Risk-free rate (r)	3.00%
Time to maturity (t)	0.3260
Call option price (C)	\$9.45
$K = X^*$ (e^($-rt$))	\$158.96
$S' = S^*$ (e^($-rt$))	\$162.30

After combining all the inputs information, we are able to calculate the implied volatility by using Equation (12.16):

$$a = 4(S + K) - (S - K)\ln(S/K) = 1{,}289.16$$
$$b = 2\sqrt{2\pi}(2C - S + K) = -145.3855$$
$$c = 8\ln(S/K)[(S - K)(1 + (\ln(S/K)/4)^2) - (S + K)\ln(S/K)/4] = 0.006$$

From Equation (12.16), sigma is defined as $\sigma = [-b \pm \sqrt{b^2 - 4ac}]/[2a\sqrt{t}]$. Thus, we have two sigmas under this equation, where sigma1 is with $[-b + \sqrt{b^2 - 4ac}]/[2a\sqrt{t}]$ and sigma2 is with $[-b - \sqrt{b^2 - 4ac}]/[2a\sqrt{t}]$. We calculate delta, which is the $\sqrt{b^2 - 4ac}$ before calculating the sigma to simplify the process:

$$\text{Delta} = \sqrt{b^2 - 4ac} = 18{,}658.9852$$
$$\text{Sigma1} = [-b + \text{Delta}]/[2a\sqrt{t}] = 0.1915$$
$$\text{Sigma2} = [-b - \text{Delta}]/[2a\sqrt{t}] = 0.0060$$

In this table, sigma1 and sigma2 represent implied variance for JNJ stock with two different calculation formulas.

Output	**Equation (12.16)**
a	1,289.1603
b	−145.3855
c	0.4805
Delta	18,658.9852
Sigma1	0.1915
Sigma2	0.0060

12.5.3.2 *Volatility smile*

A volatility smile is the combination of several implied volatilities in the same maturity period. Following the process from Section 12.5.3.1, we select an option contract on February 18, 2022, and the expiration date for this option is June 17, 2022. We combine the exercise price from \$150 to \$180 to calculate different implied volatilities.

	Exercise Price (X)	**Call Option Premium (C)**
Input 1	\$150	16.95
Input 2	\$155	13.1
Input 3	\$160	9.45
Input 4	\$165	6.7
Input 5	\$170	4.45
Input 6	\$175	2.85
Input 7	\$180	1.89

Input 1		Input 2		Input 3	
Dividend (D)	$0.00	Dividend (D)	$0.00	Dividend (D)	$0.00
Stock Price (S)	$163.36	Stock Price (S)	$163.36	Stock Price (S)	$163.36
Exercise Price (X)	$160.00	Exercise Price (X)	$150.00	Exercise Price (X)	$155.00
Risk-Free Rate (r)	3.00%	Risk-Free Rate (r)	3.00%	Risk-Free Rate (r)	3.00%
Time to Maturity (t)	0.3260	Time to Maturity (t)	0.3260	Time to Maturity (t)	0.3260
Call Option Premium (C)	$9.45	Call Option Premium (C)	$16.95	Call Option Premium (C)	$13.10
$K = X^*$ (e^($-rt$))	$158.44	$K = X^*$ (e^($-rt$))	$148.54	$K = X^*$ (e^($-rt$))	$153.49
$S' = S^*$ (e^($-rt$))	$163.36	$S' = S^*$ (e^($-rt$))	$163.36	$S' = S^*$ (e^($-rt$))	$163.36

Output 1	Equation (12.16)	Output 2	Equation (12.16)	Output 3	Equation (12.16)
a	1,287.0605	a	1,246.1907	a	1,266.7905
b	−140.1977	b	−191.3062	b	−163.7466
c	0.6012	c	5.6398	c	2.4601
Delta	16,560.3694	Delta	8,485.2079	Delta	14,347.0350
Sigma1	0.1829	Sigma1	0.1992	Sigma1	0.1960
Sigma2	0.0078	Sigma2	0.0697	Sigma2	0.0304

Input 4		Input 5		Input 6	
Dividend (D)	$0.00	Dividend (D)	$0.00	Dividend (D)	$0.00
Stock Price (S)	$163.36	Stock Price (S)	$163.36	Stock Price (S)	$163.36
Exercise Price (X)	$165.00	Exercise Price (X)	$170.00	Exercise Price (X)	$175.00
Risk-Free Rate (r)	3.00%	Risk-Free Rate (r)	3.00%	Risk-Free Rate (r)	3.00%
Time to Maturity (t)	0.3260	Time to Maturity (t)	0.3260	Time to Maturity (t)	0.3260
Call Option Premium (C)	$6.70	Call Option Premium (C)	$4.45	Call Option Premium (C)	$2.85
$K = X^*$ (e^($-rt$))	$163.39	$K = X^*$ (e^($-rt$))	$168.35	$K = X^*$ (e^($-rt$))	$173.30
$S' = S^*$ (e^($-rt$))	$163.36	$S' = S^*$ (e^($-rt$))	$163.36	$S' = S^*$ (e^($-rt$))	$163.36

Output 4	Equation (12.16)	Output 5	Equation (12.16)	Output 6	Equation (12.16)
a	1,307.0161	a	1,326.6716	a	1,346.0400
b	−134.6965	b	−139.2218	b	−156.7816
c	0.0000	c	0.5995	c	2.3473
Delta	18,142.9957	Delta	16,201.4138	Delta	11,941.9981
Sigma1	0.1805	Sigma1	0.1759	Sigma1	0.1731
Sigma2	0.0000	Sigma2	0.0079	Sigma2	0.0309

Input 7	
Dividend (D)	\$0.00
Stock Price (S)	\$163.36
Exercise Price (X)	\$180.00
Risk-Free Rate (r)	3.00%
Time to Maturity (t)	0.3260
Call Option Premium (C)	\$1.89
$K = X^*(\text{e}\hat{}(-rt))$	\$178.25
$S' = S^*(\text{e}\hat{}(-rt))$	\$163.36
Output 7	**Equation (12.16)**
a	1,365.1336
b	−187.1753
c	5.1958
Delta	6,662.9359
Sigma1	0.1724
Sigma2	0.0677

By changing the exercise price and the call option premium, we can get several combinations of implied volatilities.

Volatility Smile

Exercise Price	Option Price	Sigma1	Sigma2
\$150.00	\$16.95	0.2150	0.0602
\$155.00	\$13.10	0.2071	0.0258
\$160.00	\$9.45	0.1915	0.0060
\$165.00	\$6.70	0.1873	0.0001
\$170.00	\$4.45	0.1814	0.0094
\$175.00	\$2.85	0.1775	0.0336
\$180.00	\$1.89	0.1757	0.0715

Figure 12.3 presents the volatility smile based upon sigma1 and sigma2. It is clear that the volatility smile is more severe in terms of sigma2.

One possible explanation for the smile in equity options concerns leverage. As a company's equity declines in value, the company's leverage increases. This means that the equity becomes riskier and its

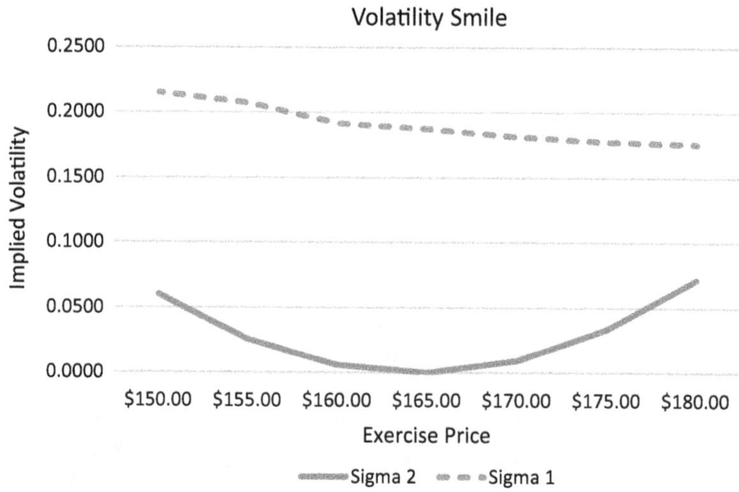

Figure 12.3 Volatility Smile of Equity Option for JNJ

volatility increases. As a company's equity increases in value, leverage decreases. The equity then becomes less risky and its volatility decreases.

12.6 Relationship between the Black and Scholes OPM and CEV OPM

Lee *et al.* (2013) have shown that $Y = \sum_{i=1}^{n}\left(\frac{X_i-\mu}{\sigma_x}\right)^2$ is distributed as χ^2 with n degree of freedom. This is a central χ^2 distribution. In addition, Lee *et al.* (2013) also showed that $Y' = \sum_{i=1}^{n} X_i^2$ is distributed as non-central χ^2 with n degree of freedom and a non-central parameter

$$\lambda = \frac{1}{2}\sum \mu_i^2.$$

If $\mu = 0$, the distribution of Y' reduces to the central χ^2 distribution.

Black–Scholes OPM assumed that the variance of stock rate of return (σ^2) is constant. If the variance of stock rate of return is a function of stock price per share, $\sigma^2 S^{\beta-2}$, then the OPM can be generalized as

$$C = S\left[1 - \chi^2\left(2n; 2 + \frac{2}{2-\beta}, 2m\right)\right] - Xe^{-r(T-t)}\left[\chi^2\left(2m; \frac{2}{\beta-2}, 2n\right)\right], \quad (\beta < 2), \qquad (12.26)$$

where $[\chi^2(2m; \frac{2}{\beta-2}, 2n)]$ is a cumulative non-central chi-square density function.

$$C = S\left[1 - \chi^2\left(2m; \frac{2}{2-\beta}, 2n\right)\right] - Xe^{-r(T-t)}\left[\chi^2\left(2n; 2 + \frac{2}{\beta-2}, 2m\right)\right], \quad (\beta < 2), \qquad (12.27)$$

where T = time of expiration of option, t = current time, r = risk-free rate. $\chi^2(W, V, \lambda)$ is the cumulative non-central chi-square distribution function with W, V, and λ being the upper limit of the integral, degree of freedom, and non-centrality, respectively. In addition m, n, and K can be defined as follows:

$$m = KS^{2-\beta}e^{(2-\beta)\mu(T-t)}$$
$$n = KS^{2-\beta}$$
$$K = \frac{2\mu}{\sigma^2(2-\beta)(e^{(2-\beta)\mu(T-t)} - 1)}. \qquad (12.28)$$

Equations (12.26), (12.27), and (12.28) represent the CEV OPM.

If $\beta = 2$, both m and n approach infinity. Then, it can be shown that both Equations (12.26) and (12.27) reduce to the Black–Scholes option pricing formula. That is, the cumulative density function of non-central chi-square distribution reduces to cumulative density function of normal distribution. Other cases of CEV model can be found in Appendix 12C and Chapter 15.

Forecasting implied that variance is an important topic for risk management. Chapter 4 of Tai's (2014) dissertation has used both the Black–Scholes OPM and the CEV OPM to estimate implied variance and then forecast the implied volatility. She found that the implied volatility estimate from the CEV model has its advantage relative to the implied variance estimate from the Black–Scholes OPM.

12.7 Summary

In this chapter, we first discussed different methods to estimate implied variance, then we discussed the volatility smile related to the Black–Scholes OPM, and we also discussed the existence of a volatility smile for currency option and equity option when Black–Scholes is used. Then, we showed that the CEV OPM generally performs better than the Black–Scholes OPM. In Chapter 15, we will discuss the detailed derivation of the CEV model.

These topics will be further discussed in the appendixes. In Appendix 12A, we will discuss Corrado and Miller's Approach to Estimate Implied Standard Deviation. The MATLAB Approach to Estimate Implied Variance is discussed in Appendix 12B. In Appendix 12C, we will discuss Non-central χ^2 and the OPM. Finally, a Comparison of the Performance of the Black–Scholes Model and the CEV Model is presented in Appendix 12D.

Questions and Problems

1. Define the following terms:
   (a) implied variance
   (b) volatility smile
   (c) CEV option pricing model
   (d) central chi-square
   (e) non-central chi-square
2. Discuss the alternative method of estimating implied variance.
3. Discuss how volatility smile can be estimated.
4. Please discuss the reasons for the volatility smile in foreign currency option in some detail.
5. Following the procedure discussed in Section 12.5.3.2 and using the updated call option of JNJ data, estimate the volatility smile.

6. If $\mu = 90$, $\beta = 1$, $S = \$100$, $X = \$80$, $T = 6$ months, $t = 3$ months, and risk-free rate = 5%, please use Equation (12.26) to calculate the call option value.

Bibliography

Ang, J. S., G. D. Jou and T.-Y. Lai (2012). A comparison of formulas to compute implied standard deviation. *Encyclopedia of Finance*, 2nd ed. New York, NY: Springer.

Black, F. and M. Scholes (1973). The pricing of options and corporate liabilities. *Journal of Political Economy*, 81(May/June), 637–654.

Chen, R. R. and C. F. Lee (1993). A constant elasticity of variance (CEV) family of stock price distributions in option pricing: Review and integration. *Journal of Financial Studies*, 1(1), 29–51.

Chen, R. R., C. F. Lee and H. H. Lee (2009). Empirical performance of the constant elasticity variance option pricing model, in Cheng-Few Lee and John Lee (eds.), *Handbook of Financial Econometrics, Mathematics, Statistics, and Machine Learning*, pp. 1903–1942. Singapore: World Scientific.

Corrado, C. J. and T. W. Miller (1996). A note on a simple, accurate formula to compute implied standard deviations. *Journal of Banking and Finance*, 20, 595–603.

Hsu, Y. L., T. I. Lin and C. F. Lee (2008). Constant elasticity of variance (CEV) option pricing model: Integration and detailed derivation. *Mathematics and Computers in Simulation*, 79(1), 60–71.

Lai, T. Y., C. F. Lee and A. L. Tucker (1992). An alternative method for obtaining the implied standard deviation. *Journal of Financial Engineering*, 1(December), 369–375.

Lee, C. F. and J. Lee (2015). *Handbook of Financial Econometrics and Statistics*. New York: Springer Academic Publishers.

Lee, C. F. and J. Lee (2020). *Handbook of Financial Econometrics, Mathematics, Statistics, and Machine Learning*. Singapore: World Scientific.

Lee, C. F. and O. Sokolinskiy (2015). R-2GAM stochastic volatility model: Flexibility and calibration. *Review of Quantitative Finance and Accounting*, 45(3), 463–483.

Lee, C. F., A. C. Lee and J. Lee (2010). *Handbook of Quantitative Finance and Risk Management*. New York: Springer Academic Publishers.

Lee, C. F., J. C. Lee and A. C. Lee (2013). *Statistics for Business*, 3rd ed. New York: Springer Academic Publishers.

Lee, C. F., T. P. Wu and R. R. Chen (2004). The constant elasticity of variance models: New evidence from S&P 500 index options. *Review of Pacific Basin Financial Markets and Policies*, 07(02), 173–190.

Merton, R. C. (1973). The theory of rational option pricing. *Bell Journal of Economics and Management Science*, 4, 141–183.
Tai, T. (2014). Essays of capital structure, risk management, and options on index futures, Rutgers Unpublished Dissertation.

Appendix 12A: Corrado and Miller's Approach to Estimate Implied Standard Deviation

Based upon Black and Scholes OPM, Brenner and Subrahmanyam (1988) derive the following formulae of ISD under the condition that the stock price S equals the present value K of the exercise price E:

$$\sigma\sqrt{T} = \sqrt{2\pi}C/S. \tag{12A.1}$$

Corrado and Miller (1996) expand the cumulative normal distribution in the Black and Sholes model up to the third order and omit the rest of the reminders. The resulting Taylor expansion of the OPM on the zero point results in a quadratic equation of the ISD. They then solve for the ISD from the quadratic equation and derive the following formulae (12A.2) of ISD (their equation (6) in Corrado and Miller (1996), page 597):

$$\sigma\sqrt{T} = \sqrt{2\pi}[(C - (S-K)/2)/(S+K)] + \sqrt{2\pi[(C-(S-K)/2)/(S+K)]^2 - 2(S-K)\ln(S/K)/(S+K)}. \tag{12A.2}$$

Corrado and Miller stated, "The accuracy of the equation (6) can be significantly improved by minimizing its concavity as follows. First, for simplicity only, we substitute the logarithmic approximation $\ln(S/X) \simeq 2(S-X)/(S+X)$ into equation (6) and then replaced the value "4" with parameter α to obtain this restatement of the quadratic formula":

$$\sigma\sqrt{T} = \sqrt{2\pi}[(C - (S-K)/2)/(S+K)] + \sqrt{2\pi[(C-(S-K)/2)/(S+K)]^2 - \alpha[(S-K)/(S+K)]^2}. \tag{12A.3}$$

This α is called tweaking parameter by Corrado and Miller (2004). To minimize the concavity of their equation (7) (here, Equation (12A.3) at the stock price equal to the present value X of the exercise price), they derive a formula for α in terms normal density function and cumulate normal function with ISD. They solve the α (α is a function of unknown variable of ISD; for further details see their equations (8) and (9) on page 598 of their book) and then substitute $\alpha = 2$ to obtain the following formula of the ISD equation (12A.4) (equation (10) in Corrado and Miller):

$$\sigma\sqrt{T} = \sqrt{2\pi}[C - (S-K)/2 + \sqrt{(C-(S-K)/2)^2 - (S-K)^2/\pi}]/(S+K)]. \tag{12A.4}$$

As shown by Corrado and Miller, their equation (10) (here, Equation (12A.4)) is more accurate than their equation (6) (here, Equation (12A.2)).

Appendix 12B: MATLAB Approach to Estimate Implied Variance

Usually, implied variance can be obtained from a call or put option model by an optimization technique. For each individual option, the implied variance can be obtained by first choosing an initial estimate σ_0, and then Equation (12B.1) is used to iterate toward the correct value:

$$C_{j,t}^M - C_{j,t}^T(\sigma_0) = \left.\frac{\partial C_{j,t}^T}{\partial s}\right|_{s_0} (s - s_0) + e_{j,t}, \tag{12B.1}$$

where $C_{j,t}^M$ = market price of call option j at time t, σ = true or actual implied standard deviation, σ_0 = initial estimate of implied standard deviation, $C_{j,t}^T(\sigma_0)$ = theoretical price of call option j at time t given $\sigma = \sigma_0$, $\left.\frac{\partial C_{j,t}^T}{\partial \sigma}\right|\sigma_0$ = partial derivative of the call option with respect to the standard deviation σ at $\sigma = \sigma_0$, and $e_{j,t}$ = error term.

The partial derivative of the call option with respect to the standard deviation $\frac{\partial C_{j,t}^T}{\partial \sigma}$ from the Black–Scholes model is as follows:

$$\frac{\partial C_{t,j}^F}{\partial \sigma} = Xe^{-r\tau}\sqrt{\tau}N'(d_1) = Xe^{-r\tau}\frac{\sqrt{\tau}}{\sqrt{2\pi}}e^{-d_1^2/2}. \tag{12B.2}$$

It is also called Vega of option.

The iteration proceeds by reinitializing σ_0 to equal σ_1 at each successive stage until an acceptable tolerance level is attained. The tolerance level used is as follows:

$$\left|\frac{\sigma_1 - \sigma_0}{\sigma_0}\right| < .001. \tag{12B.3}$$

The MATLAB finance toolbox provides a function *blsimpv* to search for implied volatility. The algorithm used in the *blsimpv* function is Newton's method, just like the procedure described in Equation (12B.1). This approach minimizes the difference between the observed market option value and the theoretical value of the BS model, and obtains the ISD estimate until a tolerance level is attained.

The complete command of the function *blsimpv* is as follows: Volatility = *blsimpv*(Price, Strike, Rate, Time, Value, Limit, Yield, Tolerance, Class). And the command with default setting is as follows: Volatility = *blsimpv*(Price, Strike, Rate, Time, Value).

There are nine inputs in total, while the last four of them are optional. Detailed explanations of all the inputs are as follows:

Inputs:

Price — Current price of the underlying asset.
Strike — Strike (i.e., exercise) price of the option.
Rate — Annualized continuously compounded risk-free rate of return over the life of the option, expressed as a positive decimal number.
Time — Time to expiration of the option, expressed in years.
Value — Price (i.e., value) of a European option from which the implied volatility of the underlying asset is derived.

Optional Inputs:

Limit — *Positive scalar representing the upper bound of the implied volatility search interval. If empty or missing, the default is 10, or 1,000% per annum.*
Yield — *Annualized continuously compounded yield of the underlying asset over the life of the option, expressed as a decimal number. For example, this could represent the dividend yield and foreign risk-free interest rate for options written on stock indices and currencies, respectively. If empty or missing, the default is zero.*
Tolerance — *Positive scalar implied volatility termination tolerance. If empty or missing, the default is 1e–6.*
Class — *Option class (i.e., whether a call or put) indicating the option type from which the implied volatility is derived. This may be either a logical indicator or a cell array of characters. To specify call options, set Class = true or Class = {'Call'}; to specify put options, set Class = false or Class =* {'Put'}*. If empty or missing, the default is a call option.*

Output:

Volatility — *Implied volatility of the underlying asset derived from European option prices, expressed as a decimal number. If no solution can be found, a NaN (i.e., Not-a-Number) is returned.*

Example

Consider a European call option trading at $5 with an exercise price of $95 and 3 months until expiration. Assume the underlying stock pays 5% annual dividends, which is trading at $90 at this moment, and the risk-free rate is 3% per annum. Under these conditions, the command used in MATLAB will be either of the following two:

Volatility = *blsimpv*(90, 95, 0.03, 0.25, 5, [], 0.05, [], {'Call'})
Volatility = *blsimpv*(90, 95, 0.03, 0.25, 5, [], 0.05, [], true)

Note that this function provided by MATLAB's toolbox can only estimate implied volatility from a single option. For more than one option, the user needs to write their own programs to estimate implied variances.

Appendix 12C: Non-central χ^2 and the Option Pricing Model

Following the CEV model, defined in Section 12.6, we discuss three possible special cases associated with Equations (12.26) and (12.27).

(1) If $\beta = 2$, both m and n approach infinity. Then, it can be shown that both Equations (12.26) and (12.27) reduce to the Black–Scholes option pricing formula. That is, cumulative density function of non-central chi-square distribution reduces to cumulative density function of normal distribution.

(2) If $\beta = 1$, it can be shown that Equations (12.26) and (12.27) reduce to

$$C = (S - Xe^{-r(T-t)})N(y_1) + (S + Xe^{-r(T-t)})N(y_2) + \nu[n(y_1) - n(y_2)], \tag{12C.1}$$

where

$$\nu = \sigma\sqrt{\frac{1 - e^{-2r(T-t)}}{2r}}$$

$$y_1 = \frac{S - Xe^{-r(T-t)}}{\nu}$$

$$y_2 = \frac{-S - Xe^{-r(T-t)}}{\nu}$$

$N(y_1)$ and $N(y_2)$ = cumulative standardized normal distribution function in terms of y_1 and y_2, respectively. $n(y_1)$ and $n(y_2)$ = standardized normal density function in terms of y_1, and y_2, respectively.

(3) If $\beta = 0$, it can be shown that Equations (12.26) and (12.27) reduce to

$$C = SN[q(4)] - Xe^{-r(T-t)}N[q(0)], \tag{12C.2}$$

where

$$q(w) = \frac{1 + h(h-1)\left(\frac{w+2y}{(w+y)^2}\right) - h(h-1)(2 - h(1-3h) \times \left(\frac{(w+2y)^2}{2(w+y)^4}\right) - \left(\frac{z}{(w+y)}\right)^h}{\left\{2h^2\left(\frac{w+2y}{(w+y)^2}\right)(1 - (1-h)(1-3h)\left(\frac{w+2y}{(w+y)^2}\right)\right\}^{1/2}}$$

$$h(w) = 1 - \frac{2}{3}(w+y)(w+3y)(w+2y)^{-2}$$

$$y = \frac{4rS}{\sigma^2(1-e^{-r(T-t)})} \quad \text{and} \quad z = \frac{4rX}{\sigma^2(e^{-r(T-t)}-1)}.$$

The elasticity of variance ($\sigma^2 S^{\beta-2}$) with respect to stock price per share S is

$$\begin{aligned} \eta_s &= \left[\frac{\partial(\sigma^2 S^{\beta-2})}{\partial S}\right]\left[\frac{S}{\sigma^2 S^{\beta-2}}\right] \\ &= \left[\frac{(\beta-2)\sigma^2 S^{\beta-2})}{S}\right]\left[\frac{S}{\sigma^2 S^{\beta-2}}\right] = \beta - 2. \end{aligned} \tag{12C.3}$$

This implies that the OPM defined in Equations (12.26) and (12.27) is a constant elasticity of variance type of OPM.

The CEV type of OPM can be reduced to the following special models:

(a) $\beta = 2$, Equations (12.26) and (12.27) reduce to the Black–Scholes model.
(b) $\beta = 1$, Equations (12.26) and (12.27) reduce to the absolute model as defined in Equation (12C.1).
(c) $\beta = 0$, Equations (12.26) and (12.27) reduce to the square root model as defined in Equation (12C.2).

Appendix 12D: Comparing the Performance of the Black–Scholes Model and the CEV Model

Lee *et al.* (2004) apply an efficient algorithm for computing non-central chi-square distribution function to the CEV OPM. The Black–Scholes model prices are used as a benchmark for comparison. Three traditional measures are used to compare the sample fit and forecasting accuracy of the CEV model and the Black–Scholes model. First is the root mean squared error (RMSE) between the market and the model fitted (in sample) or model predicted (out of sample) option prices:

$$\text{RMSE} = \sqrt{\frac{1}{n}\sum_{i=1}^{n}(C_{\text{market}} - C_{\text{model}})^2}. \tag{12D.1}$$

Second is the Mean Absolute Error (MAE) between the market and the model fitted (in sample) or model predicted (out of sample) option prices:

$$\text{MAE} = \frac{1}{n}\sqrt{\sum_{i=1}^{n} |C_{\text{market}} - C_{\text{model}}|}\,. \tag{12D.2}$$

Third is the mean absolute percentage error (MAPE) between the market and the model fitted (in sample) or model predicted (out of sample) option prices:

$$\text{MAPE} = \frac{1}{n}\sqrt{\sum_{i=1}^{n} \left|\frac{C_{\text{market}} - C_{\text{model}}}{C_{\text{market}}}\right|}. \tag{12D.3}$$

When viewing the results, it should be remembered that when the differences between the market prices and model prices are measured in absolute value using the MAE, they are larger for in-the-money options because the option prices are usually greater for in-the-money options. When the differences are measured as a percentage of market prices using the MAPE, they are larger for out-of-the-money options because the market prices are usually small for out-of-the-money options.

Table 12D.1 In-Sample Moneyness-Based RMSE, MAE, and MAPE Values for the Black–Scholes Model and the CEV Model

Moneyness (S/K)	Model	RMSE	MAE	MAPE
DITM (≥1.06)	BS	1.7556	1.1889	0.0207
	CEV	1.7704	1.2044	0.0209
ITM (1.03–1.06)	BS	1.2872	0.8712	0.0292
	CEV	1.2203	0.8311	0.0279
ATMI (1.00–1.03)	BS	0.9263	0.6364	0.0409
	CEV	0.8028	0.5733	0.0367
ATMO (0.97–1.00)	BS	0.8155	0.5775	0.1153
	CEV	0.5655	0.4216	0.0855
OTM (0.94–0.97)	BS	0.8834	0.6159	0.2260
	CEV	0.5112	0.3692	0.1706
DOTM (< 0.94)	BS	1.3575	0.8971	0.3230
	CEV	0.7098	0.4877	0.1837

Table 12D.2 In-Sample Moneyness- and Maturity-Based RMSE, MAE, and MAPE Values for the Black–Scholes Model and the CEV Model

Moneyness (S/K)	Maturity	Model	RMSE	MAE	MAPE
DITM (≥1.06)	<60	BS	1.8662	1.2999	0.023
		CEV	1.865	1.2877	0.0227
ITM (1.03-0.06)	<60	BS	1.3915	0.9024	0.0336
		CEV	1.3384	0.8693	0.0325
ATMI (1.00-0.03)	<60	BS	0.823	0.5988	0.0475
		CEV	0.7137	0.5089	0.0401
ATMO (0.97-0.00)	<60	BS	0.6906	0.5081	0.1606
		CEV	0.4928	0.3738	0.1224
OTM (0.94-0.97)	<60	BS	0.5747	0.3814	0.3761
		CEV	0.3588	0.2696	0.2705
DOTM (<0.94)	<60	BS	0.5971	0.409	0.6836
		CEV	0.2919	0.2577	0.4064
DITM (≥1.06)	60-180	BS	1.5707	0.9732	0.0164
		CEV	1.5936	0.9944	0.0169
ITM (1.03-1.06)	60-180	BS	1.0793	0.7615	0.023
		CEV	1.0004	0.7307	0.0221
ATMI (1.00-1.03)	60-180	BS	0.9326	0.6313	0.0334
		CEV	0.8329	0.6158	0.0336
ATMO (0.97-1.00)	60-180	BS	0.8513	0.6123	0.0702
		CEV	0.5855	0.438	0.0474
OTM (0.94-0.97)	60-180	BS	0.9086	0.6984	0.226
		CEV	0.5024	0.379	0.1233
DOTM (<0.94)	60-180	BS	0.7537	0.5376	0.3566
		CEV	0.4102	0.3263	0.2203
DITM (≥1.06)	≥180	BS	1.3469	1.0283	0.0166
		CEV	1.5255	1.2862	0.0211
ITM (1.03-1.06)	≥180	BS	1.353	1.1121	0.025
		CEV	1.225	0.988	0.022
ATMI (1.00-1.03)	≥180	BS	1.4405	0.9218	0.0271
		CEV	1.1746	0.842	0.0256
ATMO (0.97-1.00)	≥180	BS	1.2468	0.8473	0.0395
		CEV	0.892	0.6377	0.0465
OTM (0.94-0.97)	≥180	BS	1.4111	1.0176	0.0822
		CEV	0.8392	0.6377	0.0465
DOTM (S/K <0.94)	≥180	BS	1.6868	1.1837	0.278
		CEV	0.8771	0.6171	0.1445

Three benchmark measures are used to compare the performance of the Black–Scholes model and the CEV model. They are RMSE, MAPE, and MAE. The CEV model outperforms the BS model in all three measures. Table 12D.1 lists the in-sample moneyness-based RMSE, MAE, and MAPE values for the Black–Scholes model and the CEV model. The CEV model outperforms the BS model in the out-of-the-money category particularly. Table 12D.2 lists the in-sample moneyness- and maturity-based RMSE, MAE, and MAPE values for the Black–Scholes model and the CEV model. The CEV model outperforms the BS model in most categories, especially the out-of-the-money category.

Chapter 13

Portfolio Insurance and Synthetic Options

Contents

13.1 Introduction

Previous chapters of this book have discussed concepts, valuation models, and theory to evaluate stocks, bonds, futures, options, and futures options. This chapter discusses how futures, options, and futures options can be used in portfolio insurance (dynamic hedging). In addition, the techniques of combining stocks and futures to derive synthetic options are explored.

Portfolio insurance is a strategy that may allow portfolio managers and investors to limit downside risk while maintaining upside potential. In this context, the word *insurance* is somewhat misleading: Portfolio insurance is not a true form of insurance, where the insured pays a premium to someone who accepts the risk of some adverse event. Rather, portfolio insurance is an asset-allocation or hedging strategy that allows the investor to alter the amount of risk he or she is willing to accept by giving up some return.

This chapter first looks at the basic concept of portfolio insurance in Section 13.2. The synthetic-option approach for the one-period option pricing model is discussed in Section 13.3, then Section 13.4 covers the strategies and implementation of portfolio insurance. In Section 13.5, a comparison of alternative portfolio insurance strategies is given. The impact of portfolio insurance on the stock market and pricing of equities is presented in Section 13.6, with empirical studies of portfolio insurance discussed in Section 13.7. Lastly, a chapter summary in Section 13.8 is provided.

13.2 Basic Concepts of Portfolio Insurance

Portfolio insurance refers to any strategy that protects the value of a portfolio of assets. It can be used for stock, bonds, or real assets. If the value of the asset declines, the insurance or hedge will increase in value to help offset the decline in price of hedged assets. If the price of the asset increases, the increase of the insured portfolio will be less than the increase in the asset but will nevertheless still increase.

Table 13.1 illustrates how portfolio insurance works. In this example, the underlying asset is purchased for \$95 and \$5 is spent on portfolio insurance. The minimum amount that the insured investor can realize is \$95, but the uninsured portfolio can fall in value to a low of \$75 if the market falls. If the value of the asset increases, the value of the insured portfolio will increase, but at a smaller rate. Figure 13.1 illustrates the profit and loss of the insured and uninsured portfolio.

Table 13.1 Mechanics of Portfolio Insurance: An Example

Initial Investment	**$100.00**
Cost of Portfolio Insurance	**−$5.00**
Amount of Investment Going toward Securities	**$95.00**
Amount Invested = $100	

Value of Portfolio at Year End ($)	**Return on Uninsured Portfolio (%)**	**Value of Insured Portfolio ($)**	**Net Return on Insured Portfolio (%)**
75.00	−25	95.00	−5
80.00	−20	95.00	−5
85.00	−15	95.00	−5
90.00	−10	95.00	−5
95.00	−5	95.00	−5
100.00	0	95.00	−5
105.00	5	100.00	0
110.00	10	105.00	5
115.00	15	110.00	10
120.00	20	115.00	15
125.00	25	120.00	20
130.00	30	125.00	25

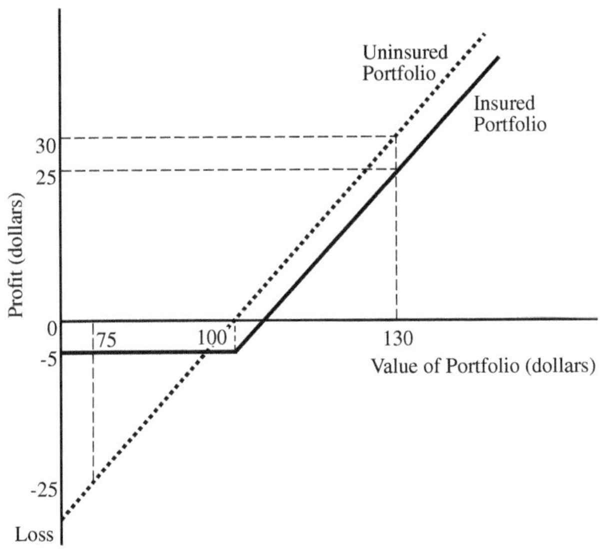

Figure 13.1 Gains and Losses of Insured and Uninsured Portfolios: An Example

Rubinstein (1985) stated that the portfolio shown in Figure 13.1 has the three properties of an insured portfolio:

(1) The loss is limited to a prescribed level.
(2) The rate of return on the insured portfolio will be a predictable percentage of the rate of return on the uninsured portfolio.
(3) The investments of the portfolio are restricted to a market index and cash. The expected return on the market index is above the expected return from holding cash, and the insurance is fairly priced. This guarantees that the insured portfolio has a higher expected return than the uninsured portfolio.

Figure 13.2 provides that portfolio insurance allows market participants to alter the return distribution to fit investors' needs and preferences for risk. Figure 13.2 shows the effect of insurance on the expected returns of a portfolio. Note that the expected return of the uninsured portfolio is greater than the expected return of the uninsured portfolio, according to the third property listed above. It should be noted that in an efficient market at a fair price the insurance will be used until the expected return on insured and uninsured portfolios is the same.

The uninsured portfolio has greater upside potential as well as greater downside risk, whereas the insured portfolio limits the

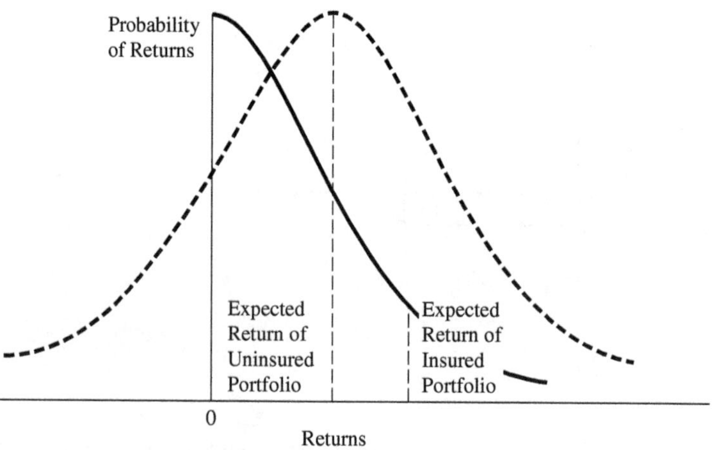

Figure 13.2 Expected Returns on Insured and Uninsured Portfolios

downside loss to the cost of the hedge. The upside potential of the insured portfolio is always below that of the uninsured portfolio. The cost of the insurance is the lower return for the insured portfolio should prices increase. While some investors would prefer the greater upside potential that the uninsured portfolio offers, risk-averse investors would prefer the limited-risk characteristics that the hedged portfolio offers.

In general, portfolio insurance can be thought of as holding two portfolios. The first portfolio can be viewed as the safe or riskless portfolio with value equal to the level of protection desired. This level is called the **floor** and is the lowest value the portfolio can have. For certain strategies, this can be held constant or allowed to change over time as market conditions or needs change. The second portfolio consists of the difference between the total value of the portfolio and the floor, commonly called the **portfolio cushion**. These assets consist of a leveraged position in risky assets. To insure the portfolio, the cushion should be managed so as to never fall below zero in value because of the limited-liability property of common stock. Figure 13.3 shows the relationship between the total value of the portfolio, the cushion, and the floor. The actual investment or allocation of the portfolio funds between risky and risk-free assets is determined by changing market conditions or the changing requirements of the portfolio manager.

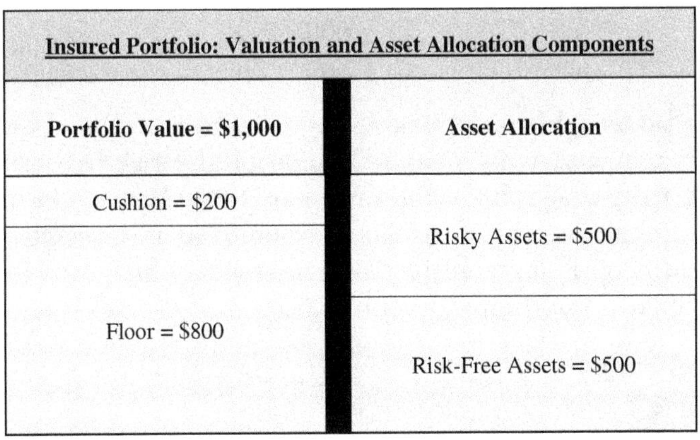

Figure 13.3 Components of an Insured Portfolio Valued at $1,000

A simple example of changing the mix between risky and risk-free assets in response to market changes offers the opportunity to demonstrate the dynamic nature of portfolio insurance. As shown in Figure 13.3, half the current portfolio is invested in risky assets and half in risk-free assets. The exposure at this point is \$500. The cushion is \$200. If this is a reasonable relationship that the portfolio manager wishes to maintain, the relationship between these two, defined as the **multiple**, can be calculated as follows:

$$\text{Multiple} = \frac{\text{Exposure}}{\text{Cushion}}, \tag{13.1}$$

$$m = \frac{e}{c}$$

$$= \frac{500}{200} = 2.5. \tag{13.2}$$

As the market for the risky assets changes, the exposure and the cushion value change, causing a change in the multiple. Given a predetermined trigger or change in multiple, the portfolio manager can trade to restore the balance between the cushion and the exposure. If, for example, the market value of the risky asset rises 20%, the value of the cushion increases to \$300 and the value of the risky assets rises to \$600. The total value of the portfolio is the value of the risky assets plus the value of the risk-free assets (\$500 + \$600, or \$1,100). The value of the floor remains at \$800 so that the cushion goes to \$300 (\$1,100 − \$800). The multiple has fallen to

$$m = \frac{e}{c} = \frac{600}{300} = 2. \tag{13.3}$$

If the target multiple is 2.5, an adjustment must be made by the portfolio manager, who must sell some of the risk-free assets and purchase risky assets until the multiple is 2.5. Hence, the manager needs to rebalance the portfolio so that \$750 is invested in risky assets and \$350 is invested in risk-free assets. This mix will restore the multiple to the desired level of 2.5:

$$m = \frac{e}{c} = \frac{750}{300} = 2.5. \tag{13.4}$$

Figure 13.4 shows the portfolio after rebalancing.

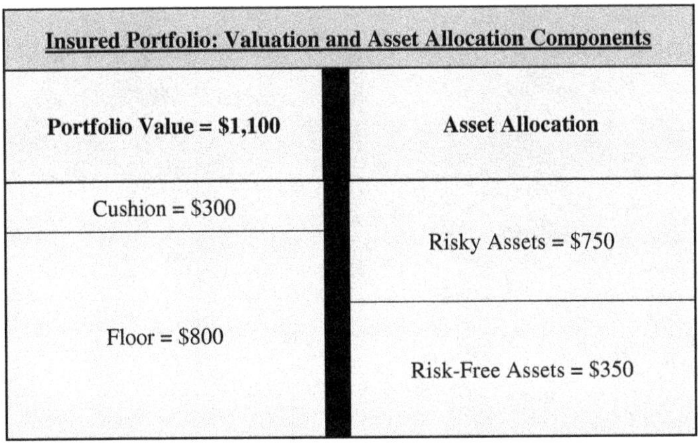

Figure 13.4 Components of an Insured Portfolio Rebalanced after a Market Rise

Increasing the portfolio's risky assets as the market rises allows the manager to participate in the bull market. As long as the market continues its rise, the manager continues to shift assets to the risky-asset portfolio to participate in the market gain. However, when the market turns bearish and begins to go down, the manager needs to sell off risky assets and invest in risk-free assets. For example, if the market declined by $16\frac{2}{3}\%$ back to its original level at the beginning of this example, the value of the risky assets would be \$625 (\$750 × 0.8333). At this new level, the multiple would be

$$m = \frac{e}{c} = \frac{625}{175} = 3.56. \tag{13.5}$$

The target multiple of 2.5 is below the actual multiple of 3.56, so the portfolio manager must sell some of the risky assets and place the proceeds into risk-free assets. The total value of the portfolio has fallen to \$975 (\$625 + \$350). The value of the cushion has fallen to \$175 (\$975 − \$800). In order to have a multiple of 2.5, the risky assets have to be reduced to

$$m = \frac{e}{175} = 2.5,$$
$$e = \$437.50. \tag{13.6}$$

Insured Portfolio: Valuation and Asset Allocation Components	
Portfolio Value = $975	**Asset Allocation**
Cushion = $175	Risky Assets = $437.50
Floor = $800	Risk-Free Assets = $537.50

Figure 13.5 Components of an Insured Portfolio Rebalanced after a Market Fall

Hence, $187.50 of the risky assets must be sold and this amount must be invested in the risk-free assets. The position of the insured portfolio after this rebalancing is shown in Figure 13.5.

As the market falls, the portfolio manager sells off risky assets and invests the proceeds in risk-free assets, thereby reducing exposure to a falling market. In general, this strategy can best be described as "run with your winners and cut your losses." *Underlying this discussion are the assumptions that the rise and fall of the market take place over a time interval long enough for the portfolio manager* to *rebalance the position, and that the market has sufficient liquidity to absorb the value of the risky assets.* This may not always be the case, however. October 19, 1987, commonly called Black Monday, and October 26, 1987, commonly called Blue Monday, as well as October 13, 1989, are examples of a rapid fall in prices in a very illiquid market for risky assets.

This general discussion of portfolio insurance is based on an article by Perold (1986). The simplicity of this approach makes it an ideal way to explain the general way of accomplishing portfolio insurance or portfolio hedging. Perold has called this **constant proportion portfolio insurance (CPPI)**. As can be seen, it involves holding the risk-free asset in an amount equal to the level of protection desired (floor), plus holding the remainder of the portfolio in a risky asset. The multiple of the risky asset to the cushion is then held in a constant proportion.

As will be seen, there are a number of ways of insuring or hedging a portfolio to keep the multiple constant. These are discussed in the next section.

13.3 Synthetic-Option Approach for the One-Period Option Pricing Model

What should be the value of these options? Let us look at a case where we are only concerned with the value of options for one period. In the next period, a stock price can either go up or go down. Let us look at a case where we know for certain that an XYZ Company stock with a price of \$20 will either go up 5% or go down 5% in the next period and the exercise after one period is \$20. Figures 13.6–13.8 show the Decision Tree for the XYZ Company stock price, the XYZ Company call option price, and the XYZ Company put option price, respectively.

Let us first consider the issue of pricing an XYZ Company call option. Using a one-period Decision Tree, we can illustrate the price of an XYZ Company stock if it goes up 5% and the price of an XYZ Company stock if it goes down 5%. Since we know the possible ending values of the XYZ Company stock, we can derive the possible ending values of a call option. If the stock price increases to \$21, the price of the XYZ Company call option will then be \$1 (\$21 – \$20). If the XYZ

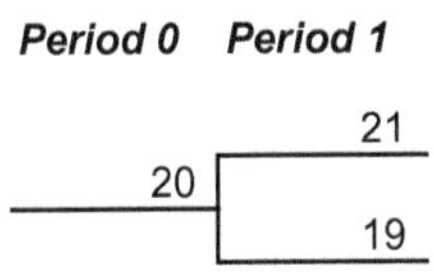

Figure 13.6 Stock Price

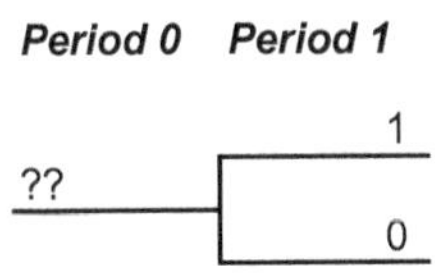

Figure 13.7 Call Option Price

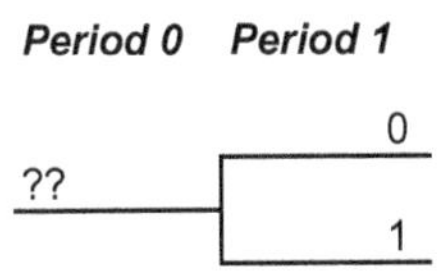

Figure 13.8 Put Option Price

Company stock price decreases to \$19, the value of the call option will be worth \$0 because it would be below the exercise price of \$20. We have just discussed the possible ending value of an XYZ Company call option in Period 1. But, what we are really interested in is what the value is now of the XYZ Company call option knowing the two resulting values of the XYZ Company call option.

13.3.1 *Synthetic-call option*

To help determine the value of a one-period XYZ Company call option, it is useful to know that it is possible to replicate the resulting two states of the value of the XYZ Company call option by buying a combination of stocks and bonds. Provided in the following is the formula to replicate the situation where the price increases to \$21. We will assume that the interest rate for the bond is 3%:

$$21\text{S} + 1.03\text{B} = 1,$$

$$19\text{S} + 1.03\text{B} = 0.$$

We can use simple algebra to solve for both S and B. The first thing that we need to do is to rearrange the second equation as follows:

$$1.03\text{B} = -19\text{S}.$$

With the above equation, we can rewrite the first equation as

$$21\text{S} + (-19\text{S}) = 1.$$

$$2\text{S} = 1.$$

$$\text{S} = 0.5.$$

We can solve for B by substituting the value 0.5 for S in the first equation:

$$21(0.5) + 1.03\text{B} = 1,$$

$$10.5 + 1.03\text{B} = 1,$$

$$1.03\text{B} = -9.5,$$

$$\text{B} = -9.223.$$

Therefore, from the above simple algebraic exercise, we should at period 0 buy 0.5 shares of XYZ Company stock and borrow 9.223

at 3% to replicate the payoff of the XYZ Company call option. This means the value of an XYZ Company call option should be $0.5 \times 20 - 9.223 = 0.777$. This example shows how we can use a synthetic-option approach to evaluate a call options value.

If this were not the case, there would then be arbitrage Company profits. For example, if the call option were sold for \$3, there would be a profit of 2.223. This would result in the increase in the selling of the XYZ Company call option. The increase in the supply of XYZ Company call options would push the price down for the call options. If the call option were sold for \$0.50, there would be a saving of 0.277. This saving would result in the increase in demand for the XYZ Company call option. This increase in demand would result in the price of the call option increasing. The equilibrium point would be \$0.777.

Using the abovementioned concept and procedure, Benninga (2000) has derived a one-period call option model as

$$C = q_u \text{Max}[uSX, 0] + q_d \text{Max}[dS - X, 0], \tag{13.7}$$

where

$$\begin{aligned} q_u &= \frac{(1+i) - d}{(1+i)(u-d)}, \\ q_d &= \frac{u - (1+i)}{(1+i)(u-d)}, \\ u &= \text{increase factor}, \\ d &= \text{down factor, and} \\ i &= \text{interest rate.} \end{aligned}$$

If we let $i = r$, $R = (1+r)$, $p = (R-d)/(u-d)$, $1-p = (u-R)/(u-d)$, $C_u = \text{Max}[uS - X, 0]$, and $C_d = \text{Max}[dS - X, 0]$, then we have

$$C = [pC_u + (1-p)C_d]/R, \tag{13.8}$$

where C_u = call option price after increase, and C_d = call option price after decrease.

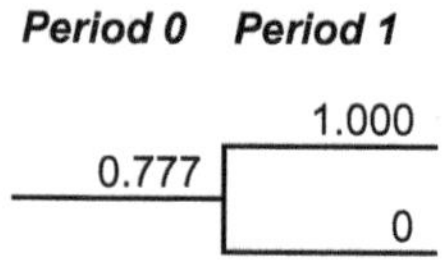

Figure 13.9 Call Option Price

In the following, the value of the above one-period call option is calculated where the strike price, X, is \$20 and the risk-free interest rate is 3%. We will assume that the price of a stock for any given period will either increase or decrease by 5%.

$$X = \$20,$$
$$S = \$20,$$
$$u = 1.05,$$
$$d = 0.95,$$
$$R = 1 + r = 1 + 0.03,$$
$$p = (1.03 - 0.95)/(1.05 - 0.95),$$
$$C = [0.8(1) + 0.2(0)]/1.03 = \$0.777.$$

Therefore, from the above calculations, the value of the call option is \$7.94. Figure 13.9 shows the resulting Decision Tree for the above call option.

13.3.2 *Synthetic-put options*

Like the call option, it is possible to replicate the resulting two states of the value of the put option by buying a combination of stocks and bonds. The following is the formula to replicate the situation where the price decreases to \$19:

$$21\text{S} + 1.03\text{B} = 0,$$
$$19\text{S} + 1.03\text{B} = 1.$$

We will use simple algebra to solve for both S and B. The first thing we will do is to rewrite the second equation as follows:

$$1.03\text{B} = 1.5 - 19\text{S}.$$

The next thing to do is to substitute the above equation to the first put option equation. Doing this would result in the following:

$$21\text{S} + 1.5 - 19\text{S} = 0.$$

The following solves for S:

$$2\text{S} = -1.5,$$

$$\text{S} = -0.5.$$

Now, let us solve for B by putting the value of S into the first equation. This is shown in the following:

$$21(-0.5) + 1.03\text{B} = 0,$$

$$1.03\text{B} = 10.5,$$

$$\text{B} = 10.194.$$

From the above simple algebra exercise, we have $\text{S} = -0.5$ and $\text{B} = 10.194$. This tells us that we should in period 0 lend \$10.194 at 3% and sell 0.5 shares of stock to replicate the put option payoff for Period 1. And the value of the XYZ Company put option should be $20(-0.5) + 10.194 = 0.194$.

Using the same arbitrage argument that we used in the discussion of the call option, 0.194 has to be the equilibrium price of the put option.

As with the call option, Benninga (2000) has derived a one-period put option model as

$$P = q_u \text{Max}[X - uS, 0] + q_d \text{Max}[X - dS, 0], \tag{13.9}$$

where

$$q_u = \frac{(1+i) - d}{(1+i)(u-d)},$$

$$q_d = \frac{u - (1+i)}{(1+i)(u-d)},$$

$u =$ increase factor,

$d =$ down factor, and

$i =$ interest rate.

If we let $i = r$, $R = (1 + r)$, $p = (R - d)/(u - d)$, $1 - p = (u - R)/(u - d)$, $P_u = \text{Max}[X - uS, 0]$, and $P_d = \text{Max}[X - dS, 0]$, then we have

$$P = [pP_u + (1 - p)P_d]/R, \tag{13.10}$$

where P_u = put option price after increase, and P_d = put option price after decrease.

In the following, the value of the above one-period put option is calculated where the strike price, X, is \$30 and the risk-free interest rate is 3%:

$$P = [0.8(0) + 0.2(1)]/1.03 = \$0.194.$$

From the above calculation, the put option pricing Decision Tree would look like the following.

Figure 13.10 shows the resulting Decision Tree for the above put option.

There is a relationship between the price of a put option and the price of all call options. This relationship is called the put–call parity. Equation (13.11) shows the relationship between the price of a put option and the price of a call option:

$$P = C + X/R - S, \tag{13.11}$$

where C = call price, X = strike price, R = 1+ interest rate, and S = stock price.

The following uses the put–call parity to calculate the price of the XYZ Company put option:

$$\begin{aligned} P &= \$0.777 + \$20/(1.03) - \$20 \\ &= 0.777 + 19.417 - 20 \\ &= 0.194. \end{aligned}$$

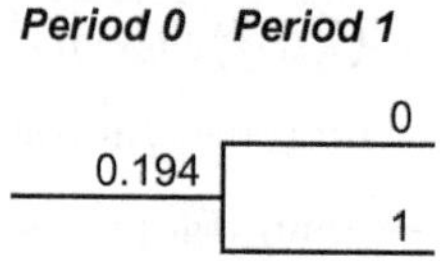

Figure 13.10 XYZ Company Put Option Price

13.4 Strategies and Implementation of Portfolio Insurance

Portfolio insurance allows the investor to participate in the appreciation of value of a risky portfolio while limiting the potential losses of the portfolio. This is very similar to the features available from an investment in options. There are four basic strategies to implementing a portfolio insurance program: (1) the use of stop-loss orders, (2) the purchase of exchange-traded put options, (3) the creation of synthetic-put options, and (4) dynamic hedging using futures contracts. All of these strategies are detailed in the following.

13.4.1 *Stop-loss orders*

A **stop-loss order** is a conditional market order to sell portfolio stock if the value of the stock drops to a given level. For example, if you held an index portfolio when the market index is at $100 and you expected the market to rise, you could limit your downside risk by placing a stop-loss order at $95. If the market fell to $95, your stop-loss order would become a market sell order, and the portfolio would be sold at the prevailing market price. The use of a stop-loss order does not guarantee that you would get exactly $95; you could get more or less. Still, you would begin to liquidate your position at a predetermined level. As you can see, the placement of stop-loss orders is a kind of crude portfolio insurance in that it allows you to make money if the market goes up and cuts your losses (approximately) to a predetermined level should the market fall.

As pointed out by Rubinstein (1985), the major problem of using stop-loss orders to approximate portfolio insurance is the path dependence of this technique — that is, if the market falls, the stop-loss order is executed, and the portfolio is sold, the portfolio manager needs to make a decision about when to get back into the market. The worst thing that could happen would be for the market to rebound immediately after the execution of the stop-loss order and sale of the portfolio. In such a case, the portfolio would consist of 100% cash. Because of this cash position, the portfolio would not benefit from the increase in stock price as the market rises. On the other hand, if the market were to continue to fall after the execution of the stop-loss order, the portfolio manager with 100% cash would be in a position enhanced by the portfolio insurance — that is, 100% cash in a falling market. Hence, the success of the portfolio insurance strategy is dependent on the subsequent market movement. Ideally, portfolio insurance should work regardless of the subsequent movement of the market; thus, it should be **path independent**. Clearly, in the case of stop-loss orders, it is path dependent, and this strategy is not a very useful form of portfolio insurance.

13.4.2 *Portfolio insurance with listed put options*

Put options can be purchased on a stock index on various exchanges and used for creating an insured portfolio. Table 13.2 lists the indexes and exchanges on which options are available. If the market falls, the drop in the value of the portfolio will be offset by the gain in value of the put option. On the other hand, if the market increases in value, the portfolio will increase in value but the premium paid for the put option will be lost. For example, a portfolio manager with a $100-million portfolio purchases 4,000 Major Market Index (MMI) options with an exercise price of $250 with the cost of each option at $500. If the market value of the portfolio declines by $10 million by the expiration date of the option and the MMI index drops to $225, the portfolio manager can exercise the puts to offset the losses on the stock portfolio. The portfolio manager delivers the 4,000 put options and receives $10 million. Since the puts cost $2 million, the net gain on the puts is $8 million. The $8 million gain on the puts offsets some of the $10 million loss on the portfolio, for a net loss of $2 million. If the portfolio increases in value by $20 million and the MMI index closes above $250, the net gain on the portfolio will be $20 million from the increase in equity value minus the $2 million premium paid for the options — a net gain of $18 million. The portfolio returns for this example are depicted in Figure 13.11.

A perfect hedge is usually not possible because the correlation between the market index and the portfolio may not be perfect. This is called the **tracking problem**. The greater the correlation between the portfolio and the index, the more effective the hedge. The lower the correlation, the less effective the hedge as a portfolio insurance strategy.

Table 13.2 Listed Options on Market Indexes

Chicago Mercantile Options Exchange	**Chicago Board Exchange**	**American Stock Exchange**
S&P 500 Index	S&P 100 Index S&P 500 Index	Major Market Index Computer Technology Index Oil Index Institutional Index
Philadelphia Stock Exchange	**New York Stock Exchange**	**Pacific Exchange**
Utilities Index Value Line Index National OTC Index	NYSE Composite Index NYSE Beta Index	Financial News Composite Index

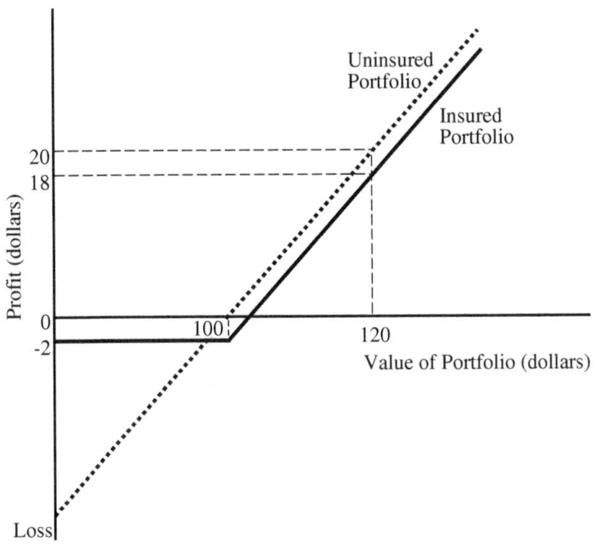

Figure 13.11 Gains and Losses of Insured and Uninsured Portfolios

In the example, it was assumed that the beta coefficient between the portfolio and the MMI was equal to one. If the beta in reality were not equal to one, more or less put contracts would be needed to insure the portfolio. For a beta less than one, fewer puts would be needed, and for a beta greater than one, more puts would be needed. For example, if the portfolio had a beta of 1.20, 20% more put options would be needed to hedge the portfolio.

The price change of the market index and the value of the portfolio, as well as the movement of the price of the option on the index, are all related. The success of a portfolio insurance strategy depends on correct determination of the hedge ratio. The hedge ratio is the ratio of the value of the portfolio to the value of the options contracts used to hedge the portfolio:

$$\text{Hedge ratio} = \frac{\text{Number of contracts} \times \text{Face value of contracts}}{\text{Face value of portfolio}}.$$

In discussing the use of put options for portfolio insurance, two characteristics were assumed about the nature of the options used:

(1) They are available with long maturities or with maturities that match the portfolio manager's investment horizon.
(2) They are exercisable only at maturity — that is, they are European-type options.

Unfortunately, all the index options listed in Table 13.2 are American options. American options can be exercised at any time before expiration, and hence have higher values to certain investors. This is so because American options have all the advantages of European options plus the privilege of early exercise. First, the portfolio manager who uses American options for portfolio insurance finds that he or she is paying for the early exercise privilege when in fact he or she does not really need it. Second, listed options are not protected against normal cash dividend payments. When a firm's stock goes ex-dividend, the price of the stock is expected to fall by the amount of the dividend payment. This expected fall in the price of the stock is not offset by any changes in the option contract; hence, the market price of the option will be affected by the ex-dividend behavior of the stock's price. As a result, options can be used to insure the capital appreciation component of the stock return but not the dividend component. Third, all listed options have a maximum maturity of nine months, with most of the trading taking place in the near contracts with maturities of three months or less. Given these problems, the usefulness of index put options for portfolio insurance is somewhat questionable.

13.4.3 *Portfolio insurance with synthetic options*

Rubinstein and Leland (1981) suggest a strategy that replicates the returns on a call option by continuously adjusting a portfolio consisting of stock and a risk-free asset (T-bill, cash). This is called a synthetic-call-option strategy; it involves increasing the investment in stock by borrowing when the value of stocks is increasing, and selling stock and paying off borrowing or investing in the risk-free asset when market values are falling. The key variable in this strategy is the delta value, which measures the change in the price of a call option with respect to the change in the value of the portfolio of risky stocks (see also Chapter 11). For deep-in-the-money options, the delta value will be close to one because a \$1 change in the stock value will result in approximately a \$1 change in the option value. Thus, to replicate the option with cash and stock, almost one share must be purchased and the amount borrowed will be approximately equal to the exercise price. For deep-out-of-the-money options, the value of the delta will be close to zero, and the replicating portfolio will contain very few shares and little or no borrowing. Hence, in its simplest form, the delta value largely depends on the relationship between the exercise price and the stock price. As the market moves to new levels, the value of the delta will change; hence, the synthetic-option portfolio must be rebalanced periodically to maintain the proper mix between equity and borrowing or cash.

In a similar manner, a portfolio manager can create replicated put options through a combination of selling short the asset and lending. The amount of stock sold short is equal to the delta value minus one. As the market decreases in value, more of the equity is sold (the short position increases), with the proceeds invested at the risk-free rate. If the market increases in value, money is borrowed to buy the stock and reduce the short position.

The logic behind a call-replicating strategy is shown in Figure 13.12, when the exercise price of the option and the current share

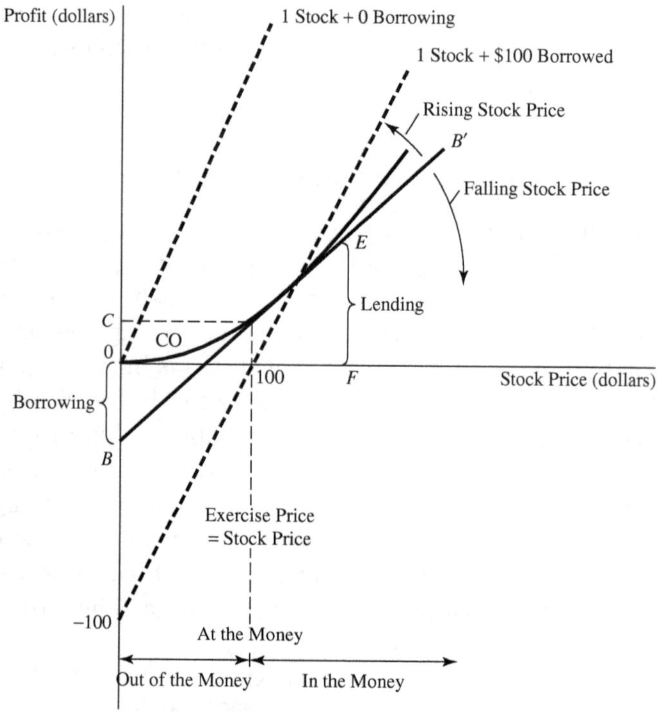

Figure 13.12 Synthetic-Call Option

price are $100. The straight line starting from the origin and labeled "1 Stock + 0 Borrowing" is the value of an unleveraged long position in the stock. When the stock is worth zero, the option is worth zero, and for every $1 increase in the value of the stock, the value of the position increases by $1. The straight line that starts from −100 on the profit axis (labeled "1 Stock + $100 Borrowed") is the leveraged position in which one share of stock is owned and the exercise price of the call ($100) is borrowed. The curved line labeled CO is the value of the call option and is an increasing function of the stock price. When the option is deep out of the money, changes in the stock price do not have much effect on the value of the call option (delta is small); hence, the line is almost horizontal. However, as the stock price increases, the rate of change in the call price (the slope of CO) increases until it approaches one for an in-the-money call. The slope of CO is the number of shares to be held in the replicating portfolio.

At low stock prices, few shares are held; at higher share price, more shares are held.

The amount of borrowing needed to replicate the portfolio is represented by the dotted line BB'. The intercept of BB' and the stock price axis represents the amount of borrowing and the line segment EF represents the amount of paying off borrowing or holding a risk-free asset. As the stock price rises, the dashed line BB' pivots counterclockwise, taking on increasing slope and an intercept farther from zero along the vertical axis. As the stock price falls, the BB' line pivots clockwise, with decreasing slope and an intercept closer to zero. The value C of the call option is shown on the profit axis. Thus, at any stock price, the value of the portfolio invested in stock is the value of the call C plus the amount of borrowing B minus the amount borrowed B or C. The line CO shows how the value of the insured portfolio reacts to changes in the stock price. As the stock price increases (decreases), the slope of the curved line becomes steeper (flatter) and the amount of borrowing increases (decreases).

If the call is in the money at the expiration date, the investor will own one share in the replicating portfolio and owe an amount equal to the exercise price. If the call finishes out of the money, no stock will be owned and the borrowing will be fully repaid. This is equivalent to the position of the call buyer at expiration. Hence, a purchased call position can be replicated by a strategy of buying shares plus borrowing, where shares are bought (sold) and the borrowing is increased (decreased) as the stock price rises (falls). The accuracy of the replicating strategy depends on four considerations. First, since the strategy may involve frequent trading, it is necessary that transaction costs be low. Second, it must be possible to borrow whatever amount is required. Third, trading in the stock may not provide continuous prices; there may be jumps or gaps. In this case, the strategy will not be able to exactly replicate the price movement of a traded call. Fourth, there may be uncertainty surrounding future interest rates, stock volatility, or dividends. This may affect the price of a traded call with an accompanying change in stock price. Hence, the value of the replicated option would not change, while the traded option price would change.

Figure 13.13 shows a synthetic-put position in which the stock and exercise prices are \$100. As the stock value increases (decreases), the slope of a line tangent to the put-value curve becomes flatter

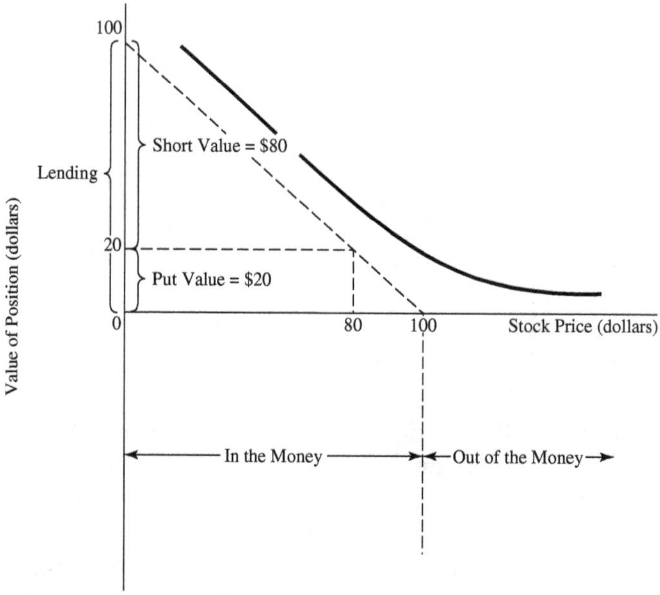

Figure 13.13 Synthetic-Put Option

(steeper) and the number of shares sold short in the synthetic put decreases (increases). The intersection of the value axis gives the lending amount. The lending position increases as the stock declines in value because more proceeds are available from the short sale of the stock. If the put is in the money at expiration, the investor will be short one share of the stock (e.g., $80) and will simultaneously lend the amount equal to the exercise price, $100. The total value of this position will equal the value of the listed put, $20.

13.4.4 *Portfolio insurance with dynamic hedging*

As a practical matter, rather than buying, selling, or short-selling stocks, a portfolio manager may trade (buy or sell) stock index futures to adjust the exposure of a portfolio. If the stock market is declining, futures contracts are sold to effectively reduce the position in the portfolio. The selling of stock index futures has the same effect on the portfolio as the sale of stocks and the investment in a risk-free asset. As the market turns around and begins to go up in value, the portfolio manager purchases futures contracts to cover the short position by liquidating the investment in the risk-free asset. This procedure is called **dynamic hedging**. Whether it works depends upon a high degree of correlation between the value of index futures contracts and the value of the underlying index. For most time periods, there is a very high degree of co-movement between the index and the futures contract. However, this may not always be the case.

Suppose that a portfolio manager wishes to insure a portfolio of well-diversified stocks with a value of \$1 million, and the portfolio beta is 1.1 when measured relative to the S&P 500. (This means that if the S&P 500 goes up or down by 1%, the change in the value of the portfolio will be 1.1%.) If the portfolio manager is worried about a market decline, he or she can insure his or her portfolio by selling S&P 500 index futures contracts. By selling futures contracts, the fall in value of the portfolio would be offset by gains in the futures market. If the strategy for portfolio insurance incorporates the beta, the following relationship is necessary to determine the number of contracts required to insure the portfolio:

$$\text{Number of contracts} = \frac{\text{Value of portfolio}}{\text{Value of futures contracts}} \times \beta. \quad (13.12)$$

Assume the S&P 500 index is selling at \$110, and the portfolio is worth \$1 million on day 1. If the market falls by 10%, the value of the portfolio falls 11% to \$890,000, the value of the S&P 500 futures contract falls to \$99, and the scenario is as follows:

(1) The portfolio has lost \$110,000.
(2) Each S&P 500 futures contract sold can be repurchased for \$99 × 500 or \$49,500, for a gain of \$5,500 (\$55,000 − \$49,500).

In order to have a perfect hedge, the portfolio manager would need \$110,000/5,500 = 20 contracts. Using Equation (13.12), we see that adjusting the number of contracts for the volatility or beta of the portfolio yields the following:

$$\text{Number of contracts} = \frac{\$1{,}000{,}000}{\$110 \times 500} \times 1.1 = 20\,\text{contracts}$$

This result of a perfect hedge is dependent upon two critical assumptions:

(1) The relationship of the volatility of the portfolio to the volatility of the index remains the same or the beta does not change.

(2) The movement of the price of the futures contract is in lock step with the movement of the index; they are perfectly correlated.

In spite of the problems for portfolio insurance associated with the validity of these critical assumptions, the use of futures contracts for portfolio hedging is widespread. The main reason why futures have been accepted as a trading vehicle for portfolio insurance is the low trading costs. This and the reasons provided in the following have led to rapid growth in the use of futures contracts for insuring portfolios during the early part of the 1980s:

(1) Low trading costs allow for rapid and frequent adjustments in implementing the portfolio strategy.
(2) Futures markets are liquid enough for insurance programs for large institutional portfolios.
(3) The use of futures allows for independence between management of the risky assets in the portfolio and the portfolio insurance.

13.5 Comparison of Alternative Portfolio Insurance Strategies

This section compares alternative portfolio insurance strategies — that is, synthetic options, listed put options, and dynamic hedging.

13.5.1 *Synthetic options*

As previously discussed, **synthetic options** are not options but a strategy for allocating assets that replicate the return on a call option. There are four advantages to using a dynamic-hedging strategy instead of synthetic-option approach. First, the futures contracts have lower transaction costs than stocks. Kidder, Peabody reports that index funds pay one-way transaction costs of $125 for $100,000 of stock, or 0.125% (they assume a commission of $0.05 per share at an average price of $40), and institutional clients pay approximately $0.06 per share.[1] In contrast, one-way futures transaction costs for institutional investors are $15 per $100,000, or 0.015%. Thus, the

[1]Hill, J. M. (1987). *Portfolio Insurance: Volatility Risk and Futures Mispricing.* New York, NY: Kidder Peabody Financial Futures Department.

transaction costs for futures are one-eighth to one-tenth of the cost of trading stocks, thereby reducing the cost of dynamic hedging compared with synthetic options. Second, liquidity is much greater in the futures market than in options or stock markets. For example, during the large downside movement in the stock market on September 11–12, 1986, the consulting firm of Leland O'Brien Rubinstein Associates sold more than $500 million of stock index futures.[2] Such large transactions could not be made in options markets.

The third advantage is that futures contracts are highly levered and less cash is necessary to carry out a dynamic-hedging strategy. As little as $2,000 can control each futures contract. The fourth advantage is that because stocks are not sold, the management of the stock portfolio is independent of the portfolio insurance. In contrast, managers must be active when implementing a synthetic option because the underlying stock is bought or sold to replicate the returns on an option.

The main disadvantage of dynamic hedging with respect to synthetic options is the tracking error that might occur because the futures are not perfectly correlated with the stock. This is not a problem with synthetic options because the stock itself is purchased or sold.

Another disadvantage of implementing either a dynamic-hedging or synthetic-option strategy is that they require continuous monitoring to insure that the delta of the replicated put equals the delta of a theoretical option. The replicated put must be rebalanced at certain intervals to maintain a proper mix of stock and futures. Here, a trade-off results: The more frequent the rebalancing, the better the replication of the theoretical put; however, more frequent rebalancing also results in higher transaction costs. Thus, determining when to rebalance the portfolio is a major decision when implementing a synthetic-option or dynamic-hedging strategy in the presence of transaction costs.

There might be a price advantage or disadvantage to a dynamic-hedging strategy due to futures mispricing. When shorting futures for hedging purposes, the manager hopes that the futures sell at

---

[2] Anders, G. (1986). Investors rush for portfolio insurance. *The Wall Street Journal* (October 14), p. 6.

a premium and the basis (the cash price minus the futures price) widens. By selling futures when they are expensive and buying them back at a lower price, a profit results on the hedge. On the other hand, losses on the hedge will probably result if "cheap" futures are sold for hedging purposes. Tables 13.3 and 13.4 illustrate these concepts. Suppose that a manager holds a portfolio worth \$250 and shorts futures on the same portfolio that are worth \$260. The basis is $\$250 - \$260 = -\$10$. Because the basis is equal to zero at expiration, the negative basis will have to increase.

In this example, the investor makes a profit of \$10 on the hedge, regardless of how the portfolio performs. The profit is a result of selling "expensive" futures and waiting for the basis to increase. In contrast, suppose that an investor with a portfolio worth \$250 shorts futures worth \$245. In this example, the investor will lose money if he waits until expiration, because the basis will decrease.

Here, the basis decreases and losses result for the hedger. Cheap futures will increase the costs of implementing a dynamic-hedging strategy and expensive futures will reduce the costs. The dynamic hedger hopes to sell futures selling at a premium and buy the futures at a discount.

Table 13.3 Profit or Loss of Expensive Futures

Value of Stock at Expiration of Futures	Value of Futures at Expiration	Profit or Loss on Stock	Profit or Loss on Futures	Profit or Loss
\$270	\$270	+\$20	−\$10	+\$10
\$230	\$230	−\$20	+\$30	+\$10

Table 13.4 Profit or Loss of Cheap Futures

Value of Stock at Expiration of Futures	Value of Futures at Expiration	Profit or Loss on Stock	Profit or Loss on Futures	Profit or Loss
\$270	\$270	+\$20	−\$25	−\$5
\$230	\$230	−\$20	+\$15	−\$5

The synthetic-call approach is usually used when implementing a portfolio insurance strategy without futures. Thus, more of the risky asset is purchased when performance is favorable and the stock is sold when the asset declines. When implementing a dynamic-hedging strategy, the underlying stocks are not bought or sold, but rather stock index futures are shorted to create a put option on the portfolio. In both cases, insurance is created for the portfolio, but the methods are different. In the synthetic-option case, the underlying portfolio behaves like a call option. For the dynamic-hedging case, the portfolio is not altered, only the futures position is changed to create a put option. A further discussion of the synthetic-call approach can be found in Becker (1988).

13.5.2 *Listed put options*

Portfolio insurance with **listed put options** does not require continuous monitoring because the delta of the listed option is automatically changed when the price of the underlying asset changes. Because of the automatic adjustment of the delta value, a listed put strategy requires less monitoring and lower trading frequency than a synthetic-option or dynamic-hedging strategy.

There are a number of problems with using stock index puts for portfolio insurance. First, because index options have at most a nine-month life, an investor may have to buy these short-term options even though the planning horizon might be much longer. These cumulative purchases of puts would result in a much greater cost than a longer-term option. This is due to the fact that for the long-term one-year put to be in the money, the market price must be below the exercise price after one year. In contrast, the value of the short-term options will have a positive value if the market price finished below the exercise price after nine months.

Second, the purchaser of portfolio insurance is not interested in exercising the option early, because this would leave the portfolio uninsured. The purchaser of insurance would prefer European options over American options because European options are cheaper. (However, the most popular index option, the OEX S&P 100, is American.) This early-exercise feature is of no value to the purchaser of portfolio insurance and adds to the cost of the insurance.

The third problem is that large portfolio managers cannot purchase put options for insurance purposes because options markets do not provide the liquidity necessary to purchase large amounts of put options. Low liquidity might be even more of a problem for deep in- or out-of-the-money options or options that expire in the six- to nine-month range of maturities.

Like futures, there might be a lacking problem between the underlying stock or stocks and the instrument underlying the portfolio.

A replicated-option approach requires more management than a listed put option strategy. The dynamic-hedging approach uses the highly liquid futures market to rebalance the portfolio. On the other hand, portfolio managers of large portfolios cannot purchase listed puts for portfolio insurance because of lack of liquidity in the options market. Futures mispricing will increase or decrease the cost of dynamic hedging; if the short hedger shorts expensive futures, profits will result from the hedges. If expensive futures are shorted, losses will be incurred.

13.5.3 *Dynamic hedging and listed put options*

The first difference between dynamic hedging and listed put options for portfolio insurance is that the delta value of a put option changes automatically while it must be adjusted continuously in a dynamic-hedging framework. Thus, dynamic hedging requires continuous monitoring and more frequent trading than listed puts.

Second, insurance costs (the premium paid for the option) for a listed put strategy are known and paid up front. After the put is purchased, no more adjustment or monitoring is necessary. In contrast, insurance costs are unknown at the beginning of the period and are realized as the dynamic-hedging strategy is implemented. The cost of a dynamic-hedging strategy is the forgone profits that result from shorting futures. For example, suppose that a portfolio consists of \$10,000 of stock and that \$50,000 of futures contracts are shorted to replicate a put option (assume that this is one futures contract) (Table 13.5).

In the second period, the value of the portfolio increased to \$120,000, whereas the value of the futures contract appreciated to \$60,000. If no futures were held, profit on the portfolio would be \$20,000; however, the dynamic hedger lost \$10,000 on the futures.

Table 13.5 Dynamic Hedging

	Portfolio Value	Futures Value	Profit on Portfolio	Loss on Futures	Profit on Insured Portfolio
Period 1	\$100,000	\$50,000			
Period 2	\$120,000	\$60,000	\$20,000	−\$10,000	+\$10,000

Thus, the cost of the dynamic-hedging strategy is the gain on the insured portfolio minus the gain on the uninsured portfolio (\$10,000 − \$20,000 = −\$10,000).

Another difference is that listed option strategy is confined to fixed-interval exercise prices. In contrast, a dynamic-hedging strategy can be implemented around any exercise price.

Changing volatility can affect the cost of a portfolio insurance strategy. For options, the cost of put protection is higher if the volatility declines. This is because the purchaser of the put locks in the volatility at the time of purchase. Thus, if the volatility declines, the put value declines. In contrast, an increase in volatility lowers the cost of put protection because the price of the put increases.

With a dynamic-hedging strategy, costs are lowered if volatility declines because the delta value will be reduced and not as many futures will be sold.

A replicated-option approach can be used for any asset portfolios of stocks, various types of bonds, agricultural commodities, currencies, or metals. Since options markets are limited, replicated options must be created to simulate the returns of these investments.

13.6 Impact of Portfolio Insurance on the Stock Market and Pricing of Equities

Portfolio insurance is not formal insurance in the sense of a guarantee against loss. Rather, it is a method of hedging a portfolio either by selling a certain portion of the risky assets themselves or futures contracts on stock indexes, when the market falls. Both techniques ultimately have the same effect, but index futures tend to be more popular because they entail smaller transaction costs.

When the stock market rises as it did almost uninterruptedly from December 1986 to August 1987, the hedge was hardly used as investors participated in the bull market. But when stocks began to fall in autumn 1987, investors started selling futures, usually contracts tied to the S&P 500 index, thereby making up any losses from falling prices by the gain on the futures contracts. The portfolio insurer sells futures contracts at index levels that, in a falling market, are higher than they will be later. The money from the sale of the futures is then invested in money market instruments until it is needed to buy back the futures contracts at lower prices in the future when the market has bottomed out.

Consider the following sequence of events involving the linkages between the sale of futures contracts for portfolio insurance and the market index:

(1) Your portfolio, valued at \$100, is equally divided between the risk-free asset and risky assets. The market index is 1,000, and there is no futures discount from the index level.
(2) The market declines to an index of 900, and futures give a discount from the index of 10. As the market declines, portfolio insurance requires reducing your investment in the risky asset. This can be done by selling stock directly or by selling futures on the index. You increase your investment in the risk-free asset to \$55, leaving your investment in the risky asset long stocks 45, short index 5.
(3) Market arbitrageurs can now take advantage of mispricing between the index level and the price of futures because the investor has sold futures contracts, thereby increasing the discount between the futures price and the market index level. The discount has gone from 0 to -10. These so-called program traders begin to sell stocks and buy index futures to lock in a risk-free return. This causes the market index to fall; and in a falling market, the investor will want to reduce his exposure to the risky asset by selling futures and investing the funds in the risk-free asset. This action will increase the discount between the index and the futures value and again encourage program traders to execute arbitrage trades. Once the cycle starts, it may be difficult to stop.

Could the scenario described in the last few paragraphs ever really take place? Unfortunately, the answer is yes. On Monday, October 19, 1987 — ever after to be known as Black Monday — this is precisely what happened on the New York Stock Exchange. Figures 13.14–13.16 show the precipitous drop of 508 points on the Dow Jones index that took place on Black Monday. Figure 13.15 shows that for most of the day futures were selling at a discount to the index. What is more revealing is that every time the discount got wider, the index started to fall faster. The bottom panels in Figures 13.15 and 13.16 show the percentages of trading volume for futures and the NYSE. It is apparent that a substantial amount of the record trading was being done by institutions trying to implement their portfolio insurance strategies. What is especially unfortunate about Black Monday is that no one foresaw what would happen if every institution implemented a similar portfolio strategy simultaneously. Even the generally liquid NYSE could not handle the crushing volume of orders to sell as a result of portfolio insurance strategies.

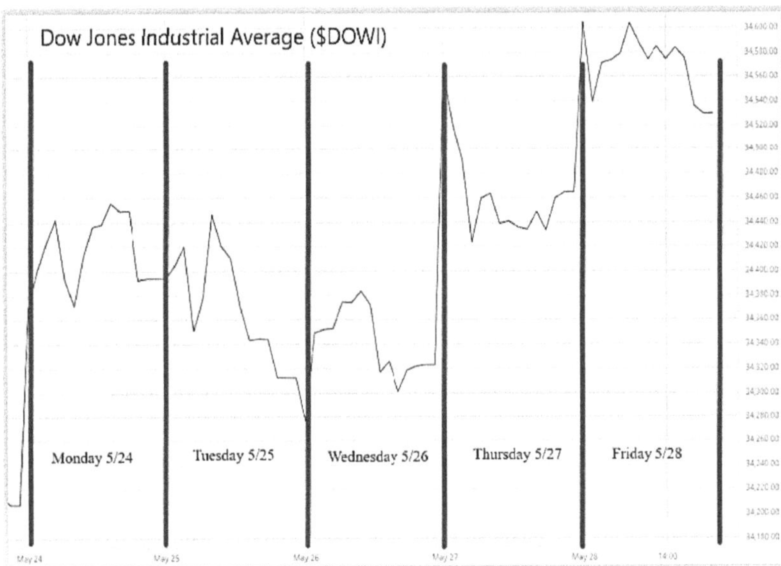

Figure 13.14 Daily Movement of the Dow Jones Industrial Average (May 24–29, 2021)*

Note: *Week prior to Memorial Day weekend 2021.

Source: Barchart Interactive. Chart created.

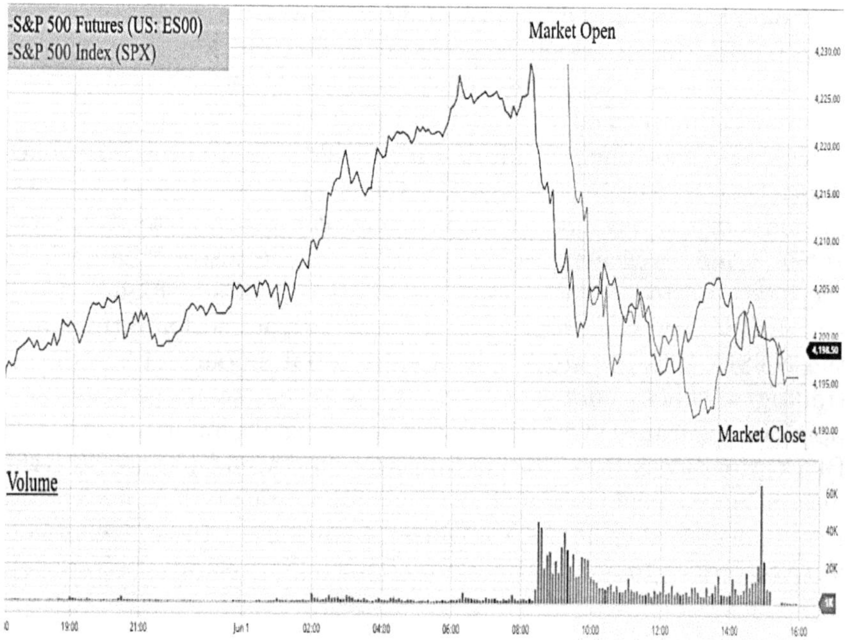

Figure 13.15 S&P 500 Index and Futures Contracts, Tuesday, June 1, 2021*
Note: *Day after Memorial Day Weekend 2021.
Source: Barchart Interactive Chart. Chart created.
https://www.barchart.com/futures/quotes/ES*0/interactive-chart.

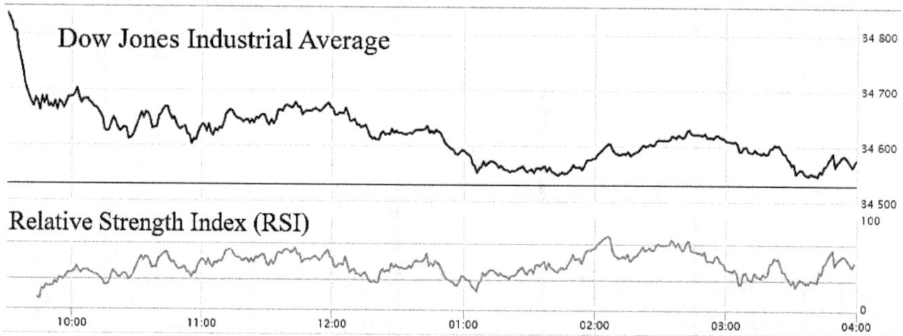

Figure 13.16 Dow Jones Industrial One-Minute Chart, Tuesday, June 1, 2021*
Note: *Day after Memorial Day Weekend 2021.
Source: *The Wall Street Journal*. https://www.wsj.com/market-data/quotes/index/DJIA/advanced-chart.

Most recently, Blume *et al.* (1989) have shown the breakdown in the linkage between futures prices and the spot index on October 19 and October 20, 1987. In addition, they have found breakdowns in the linkage among NYSE stocks.

13.6.1 *Regulation and the Brady Report*

In the aftermath of the October 1987 crash, the role of regulation in both the futures and the stock markets was hotly debated. Table 13.6 shows the relationships of the Congress, Federal agencies, and the Federal Reserve with the two leading futures and stock exchanges. Some have argued that the separate regulation of futures and stocks contributed to the severity of the October 1987 crash. The role of portfolio insurance and index arbitrage in linking the futures and stock markets has brought into question the separation of regulatory authority. At the present time, what form the future regulatory structure will take is a matter of conjecture. One reasoned answer has been presented by the Brady Commission report. This report is likely to provide the framework for the debate of how to regulate US security markets.

The Brady Report makes five primary recommendations:

(1) Information systems should be established to monitor transactions and conditions in related markets.
(2) Clearing methods should be unified across marketplaces to reduce financial risk.
(3) Margins should be made consistent across marketplaces to control speculation and financial leverage.
(4) One agency should coordinate the few but critical regulatory issues that have an impact across the related market segments and throughout the financial system. The Federal Reserve is considered a reasonable candidate for this role.
(5) Circuit-breaker mechanisms such as price limits and coordinated trading halts should be formulated and implemented to protect the market system.

How many of these recommendations are acted upon in restructuring the futures and stock markets remains to be seen. However,

Table 13.6 Regulating the Markets

Regulatory Agency	Institutions Regulated	Other Notable Authority
Depository Regulators		
Federal Reserve	Bank holding companies and certain subsidiaries (e.g., foreign subsidiaries), financial holding companies, securities holding companies, and savings and loan holding companies. Primary regulator of state banks that are members of the Federal Reserve System, foreign banking organizations operating in the United States, Edge Corporations, and any firm or payment system designated as systemically significant by the FSOC	Operates discount window ("lender of last resort") for depositories; operates payment system; conducts monetary policy
Office of the Comptroller of the Currency (OCC)	Primary regulator of national banks, U.S. federal branches of foreign banks, and federally chartered thrift institutions	
Federal Deposit Insurance Corporation (FDIC)	Federally insured depository institutions. Primary regulator of state banks that are not members of the Federal Reserve System and state-chartered thrift institutions	Operates deposit insurance for banks; resolves failing banks
National Credit Union Administration (NCUA)	Federally chartered or federally insured credit unions	Operates deposit insurance for credit unions; resolves failing credit unions
Securities Markets Regulators		
Securities and Exchange Commission (SEC)	Securities exchanges; broker-dealers; clearing and settlement agencies; investment funds, including mutual funds; investment advisers, including hedge funds with assets over \$150 million; and investment companies. Nationally recognized statistical rating organizations. Security-based swap (SBS) dealers, major SBS participants, and SBS execution facilities. Securities sold to the public	Approves rulemakings by self-regulated organizations

Commodity Futures Trading Commission (CFTC)	Futures exchanges, futures commission merchants, commodity pool operators, commodity trading advisors, derivatives clearing organizations, and designated contract markets. Swap dealers, major swap participants, swap execution facilities, and swap data repositories	Approves rulemakings by self-regulated organizations
Government-Sponsored Enterprise Regulators		
Federal Housing Finance Agency (FHFA)	Fannie Mae, Freddie Mac, and Federal Home Loan Banks	Acting as conservator (since September 2008) for Fannie and Freddie
Farm Credit Administration (FCA)	Farm Credit System, Farmer Mac	
Consumer Protection Regulator		
Consumer Financial Protection Bureau (CFPB)	Non-bank mortgage-related firms, private student lenders, payday lenders, and larger "consumer financial entities" determined by the CFPB. Statutory exemptions for certain markets. Rulemaking authority for consumer protection for all banks; supervisory authority for banks with over $10 billion in assets	

Source: Congressional Research Service (2020). Who regulates whom? An overview of the U.S. Financial Regulatory Framework (March 10). https://fas.org/sgp/crs/misc/R44918.pdf.

it is clear that practices such as portfolio insurance that link different markets together have forced a study of the problems of a segmented regulatory system.

13.7 Empirical Studies of Portfolio Insurance

Much of the early research on portfolio insurance focused on simulation models to see whether synthetic-option strategies could successfully limit losses on portfolios of risky assets. In the early to mid-1980s, most of the empirical research on portfolio insurance was conducted by financial institutions such as Drexel, Burnham, Lambert, and Salomon Brothers. However, more articles on the subject have appeared recently in journals such as *The Financial Analyst's Journal* and *Journal of Portfolio Management.*

13.7.1 *Leland* (1985)

Leland (1985) developed a replication strategy in the presence of transaction costs and tested this approach by using a simulation. As Leland pointed out, because transaction costs increase without limit as the revision period becomes shorter, it may be very costly to assure a given level of accuracy in the synthetic option. In addition, "transaction costs associated with replicating strategies are path-dependent: they depend not only on the initial and final stock prices, but also on the entire sequence of stock prices in between." Another problem with trying to create portfolio insurance in the presence of transaction costs is that transaction costs are correlated with the market. Leland posed the question, "In the presence of transaction costs, is there an alternative to the Black–Scholes replicating strategy which will overcome these problems?"

Leland proposed a procedure that adjusts upward the volatility estimate to the replicating procedure. The modification is a positive function of transaction costs and the replication period. This increase in the volatility estimate is due to the fact that each time a transaction occurs, the associated trading costs cause the purchase cost to be higher and the selling proceeds to be lower than without these costs. With transaction costs, the cost of purchasing stock is higher than without these costs; similarly, the price of selling the stock is lower, inclusive of these costs. "This accentuation of up or down movements of the stock price can be modeled as if the volatility of the actual stock price was higher." The adjustment to volatility is

$$\sigma_A^2 = \sigma^2 \left(1 + \frac{\sqrt{2/\pi}k}{\sigma\sqrt{t}}\right), \tag{13.13}$$

where σ_A^2 = the transaction-cost adjusted volatility, σ = he annualized standard deviation of the natural logarithm of the price, k = round-trip transaction costs as a proportion of the volume of transaction, and t = the revision interval as a proportion of a year.

The modification to the volatility estimate has the following characteristics:

(1) Transaction costs remain bounded as the revision period becomes short.
(2) The strategy replicates the option return inclusive of transaction costs, with an error that is uncorrelated with the market and approaches zero as the revision period becomes short.
(3) Expected turnover and associated transaction costs of the modified replicating strategy can easily be calculated, given the revision interval. Since the error inclusive of transaction costs is uncorrelated with the market, these transaction costs put bounds on the option prices.

The delta value of this strategy takes into account transaction costs and will be higher than without transaction costs. As can be seen from Equation (13.13), the volatility estimate increases as the revision period and transaction costs increase. Leland believes that the modified replication strategy is superior to following the Black–Scholes strategy and paying transaction costs that result from the strategy because the expected error is negative, "reflecting the fact that transaction costs are not 'covered' by the initial option price." He assumes that the Black–Scholes strategy will result in higher turnover than the modified strategy because the latter "is based on a higher volatility which tends to 'smooth' the required trading."

Leland uses a simulation to determine the effectiveness of this strategy. The risk-free rate in the simulation is 10%; the expected return for the stock is 16%, with a standard deviation of 20%. Leland uses rebalancing periods of one week, four weeks, and eight weeks to replicate options expiring in three months, six months, and twelve months, respectively. Here, H is the difference between the listed call and the synthetic option after the revision period, Δt:

$$\Delta H = \Delta C - [C_s S + r(C - C_s S)], \tag{13.14}$$

where ΔC is the change in the listed call option over the revision period, C_s is the delta value and is the number of shares in the replicated portfolio, and r is the interest rate over the revision period. If the replicated option perfectly matches the changes in the listed option, ΔH will equal zero. For each of the revision periods, the mean and standard deviation of the errors are calculated.

Using simulated data with no transaction costs, the Black–Scholes strategy replicates the option with mean errors equal to zero for a revision period of one week. The standard deviation increases as the time until expiration decreases. As expected, the mean error increases as the revision period increases, with the greatest error occurring for the eight-week rebalancing period.

Leland uses his modification to the volatility estimate to calculate the accuracy of option replication with transaction costs. He compares the errors from the modified strategy with a Black–Scholes replicating scheme in which delta values and borrowing amounts are derived from the Black–Scholes model and then transaction costs are added on. In every case, the preciseness of the modified strategy exceeds the accuracy of the Black–Scholes design when round-trip transaction costs of 1% are used.

13.7.2 *Asay and Edelsburg* (1986)

Asay and Edelsburg used Monte Carlo simulations to determine how closely a synthetic-option strategy can match the returns on options on Treasury bill futures. They state that there are three objections to a synthetic-option plan. First, changing delta values mean that positions must be continuously adjusted for the returns to be similar. However, rebalancing may not be possible if prices change overnight. If the position changes, too few or too many shares will be held in the underlying asset and the returns will not be the same as in the option position. The second problem with a synthetic strategy is that transaction costs may be significant, particularly if the rebalancing period is short.

The third problem is that the position could be whipsawed. **Whipsawing** occurs when the underlying asset increases enough to trigger rebalancing. After more shares are added, the underlying asset decreases in value, and the additional shares are sold at a lower price than what was paid for them. A common remedy for this problem is to use a larger adjustment gap or filter rule; however, the wrong number of shares could be held if the filter rule were increased, particularly if the stock moved in a linear manner. Whipsawed positions commonly occur when the asset fluctuates around a constant level. Asay and Edelsburg used a Monte Carlo simulation of an option on a Treasury bill future to determine if these and other problems would cause a divergence between the theoretical and synthetic positions. Profits and losses on the synthetic option are compared with those that would be earned through the purchase and sale of the option at the theoretical price if it were held to maturity. The profit on the replicated option is equal to the value of the option at maturity minus the price paid for option. They use adjustment gaps of 5–50 basis points in the simulated one-year interest rate futures to trigger rebalancing.

Fifty simulations on six-month options were run. The option prices generated by the synthetic approach were very close to the options purchased at their theoretical values. Larger adjustment gaps proved more accurate when the futures traded in a narrow range, but the larger gaps were "disastrous" when the futures moved in one direction. Thus, they were unable to recommend a best adjustment gap. Asay and Edelsburg found the transaction cost of the replicating strategy to be insignificant.

To determine the amount of mispricing due to using an incorrect volatility estimate, they used a "correct" volatility measure for the listed option and an "incorrect" measure for the synthetic option. They found that input of a wrong estimate into the option pricing model seems "to have only a minimal effect through the resulting incorrect hedge ratio." The authors concluded that problems such as transaction costs, whipsawing, and frequent rebalancing do not negate the effectiveness of the synthetic option on Treasury bill futures.[3]

13.7.3 *Eizman* (1986)

The purpose of Eizman's paper is to determine which rebalancing strategy is the most effective in a dynamic-hedging portfolio insurance framework. He considered three rebalancing disciplines: (1) to fully rebalance the required stock/cash mix at discrete time intervals, (2) to fully rebalance every time the market changes by a specified percentage, and (3) to rebalance only when the actual mix lags the required mix by more than a specified lag factor in either direction, "and then rebalance only to the extent of bringing the actual mix up to a lag factor away from the required mix ⋯."

Log-normal returns to generate one-year puts are obtained using a multiyear Monte Carlo simulation. Eizman assumes a standard deviation of 13%, an interest rate of 8%, futures transaction costs of 0.15%, and a dividend yield of 4%. Put premiums and delta values for the synthetic put were generated by the Black–Scholes model. Then, average annual transaction costs and average annual replication errors are calculated. In all three strategies, there is a trade-off between transaction costs and accuracy; the liberal adjustment strategies had lower transaction costs and higher replication errors.

For the discrete time adjustment strategy, he rebalanced monthly, weekly, semiweekly, daily, and hourly. The transaction costs increased and replication errors decreased as the rebalance periods shortened. He used a utility function of Min $(X+Y)$, where X is average annual transaction costs and r is average annual replication error, to determine the most effective rebalance period. Using this criterion, the best method is the weekly method, with the semiweekly strategy coming in second.

For the second strategy, market moves from 5% to 0% were used to trigger rebalancing. Again, larger percentage rebalance periods lead to lower transaction costs and larger errors. The third discipline, in

[3]Asay, M. and C. Edelsburg (1986). Can a dynamic strategy replicate the returns of an option? *Journal of Futures Markets*, 6(Spring), 63–70. Copyright © 1986 by John Wiley and Sons, Inc. Reprinted by permission of John Wiley and Sons, Inc.

which the portfolio is rebalanced only if the actual futures/stock mix lags the required mix by more than a prescribed percentage, works the best, according to Eizman. Under this method, the adjustment is made so that the actual mix is brought up to the 3% boundary and not up to the required mix. The lag that provided the best cost/error trade-off was 3%.

13.7.4 *Rendleman and McEnally* (1987)

This study addresses the issue of portfolio insurance cost. It tries to answer the following questions:

(1) What is the probability that the portfolio will earn no more than its insured floor return?
(2) What are the expected returns and utilities of return of the insured portfolio versus those of a reasonable alternative strategy?
(3) What are the probabilities that the insured portfolio or the alternative will have the higher return?
(4) Over the long run, how will the accumulation of value from the insured portfolio stack up against the alternative?

They used a Monte Carlo simulation with a 16% expected return and a 10% interest rate. The Black–Scholes model is used to derive delta values for the put option. In addition, a logarithmic utility function is specified to measure the utility of a portfolio insurance strategy. Rendleman and McEnally simulate one- and three-year put options using minimum returns of 5%, 0%, and −5%, stock volatility of 20% and 18%, and interest rates of 10% and 6%. Various simulations are run and the costs of the put positions are calculated along with expected utility for the insured portfolio and an uninsured portfolio.

Probability distributions are generated to determine the probability that the insured and uninsured portfolios have a return greater than the minimum floor. They concluded that the "insured portfolio is . . . more likely than the optimal portfolio to achieve only the guaranteed minimum return." In addition, they found that portfolio insurance strategies ". . . suffer in comparison with an 'optimal' portfolio designed to maximize the rate of growth of portfolio value over time." Using the various inputs on the simulations, they determined that the insured portfolio can expect to have a lower return than a similar optimal portfolio. They concluded that portfolio insurance strategies are optimal only when investors are highly risk averse.

13.7.5 *Garcia and Gould* (1987)

The main goal of this article is to compute the costs of a synthetic-call portfolio insurance strategy. They do not deal with dynamic hedging because ". . . sufficient historical experience is not yet available to simulate meaningfully the results from long equities/short futures implementations." They use closing prices of the S&P 500 index from January 1, 1963 to December 31, 1983. They generate returns for 240 overlapping years by taking 20 January-to-January returns, then 20 February-to-February returns, and so on. This is the first published portfolio insurance study to use real data as opposed to simulated data.

The returns for hedged and unhedged portfolios were calculated. Over the period of the study, the arithmetic mean of the unhedged S&P 500 returns was 9.63% with a standard deviation of 16.22%; the mean return for a portfolio insurance strategy with a 0% floor and 0.5% transaction costs was 7.08 with a lower standard deviation of 9.33%. The mean return for the strategy with a −5% floor was 8.18% with a standard deviation of 11.80%.

Opportunity costs of the portfolio insurance were calculated. If the return on the unhedged portfolio was 10% and the return on the hedged portfolio was 0.10%, the opportunity cost is 5%. They concluded that with a zero-floor insurance, investors gain 10.27% in a down year. When the market is up, hedged portfolios forgo 7.21%.

They concluded that the cost of portfolio insurance is 170 basis points for zero-floor insurance and 83 basis points for a −5% strategy, and that a dynamically balanced portfolio will not outperform a buy-and-hold (BH) portfolio.

13.7.6 *Zhu and Kavee* (1988)

They evaluated and compared the performances of the two traditional portfolio strategies, the synthetic-put approach of Rubinstein and Leland (1981) and the constant proportion approach of

Black and Jones (1987). They employed a Monte Carlo simulation methodology, assuming log-normally distributed daily returns with an annual mean return of 15% and paired with different values for market volatility, in order to discover whether these strategies can really guarantee the floor return and how much investors have to pay for the protection.

Both strategies are able to reshape the return distribution so as to reduce downside risk and retain a certain part of the upside gains. However, they demonstrated that a certain degree of protection can be achieved at a considerable cost. There are two types of costs in implementing a portfolio insurance strategy. The first is the explicit cost, that is, the transactions costs. The other is the implicit cost, which is the average return forgone in exchange for protection against the downside risk. When the market becomes volatile, the protection error of the synthetic-put approach increases, and the transaction costs may be unbearable. On the contrary, while the constant proportion approach may have lower transaction costs, its implicit cost may still be substantial.

13.7.7 *Perold and Sharpe* (1988)

Using simulated stocks and bills prices, they examined and compared how the four dynamic asset allocation strategies, namely, the BH, constant mix (CM), CPPI, and option-based portfolio insurance (OBPI), perform in bull, bear, and flat markets and in volatile and not-so-volatile markets.

CPPI and OBPI strategies sell stocks as the market falls and buy stocks as the market rises. This dynamic allocation rule represents the purchase of portfolio insurance and has a convex payoff function, which results in a better downside protection and a better upside potential than a BH strategy. However, they do worse in relatively trendless, volatile markets.

On the contrary, a CM strategy — holding a constant fraction of wealth in stocks — buys stocks as the market falls and sells them as it rises. This rebalancing rule effectively represents the sale of portfolio insurance and has a concave payoff function, which leads to less downside protection than, and not as much upside as, a BH strategy. However, it does best in relatively trendless and volatile markets.

They suggested that no one particular type of dynamic strategy is best in all situations. Financial analysts can help investors understand the implications of various strategies, but they cannot, and should not, choose a strategy without a substantial understanding of an investor's circumstances and desires.

13.7.8 *Rendleman and O'Brien* (1990)

They addressed the issue that the misestimation of volatility input can have a significant impact on the final payoffs of a portfolio using a synthetic-put strategy. In an OBPI strategy, the daily portfolio adjustments depend on the delta of the put option on the risky asset. In the original Black and Scholes (1973) valuation equation, the delta at each day is a function of the following variables:

$$D_t = f(S_t, \bar{k}_0, \bar{r}_0, \sigma_0, T), \tag{13.15}$$

where S_t is the price of the risky asset at date t, k_0 the strike price, r_0 the annual continuously compounded riskless rate of interest, σ_0 the *ex ante* volatility parameter at the beginning of the insurance period, and T the maturity of the option.

Assume that at the beginning of the insurance period, one manager predicts a high-volatile market and a 20% annualized volatility, while a second manager predicts a low-volatile market and a 10% volatility. The delta for the first manager is higher which means he would buy more insurance and allocate less to a position in the risky asset. Assume that the *ex post* volatility turns out to be 10%. The second manager will have made the proper allocation between risky and riskless assets. In contrast, the high-estimate manager will have invested too little in the risky asset. This misallocation would lose the opportunity of participating in the price appreciation in a strong market. Thus, a manager who underestimates volatility will typically end up buying less insurance than is necessary to ensure a given return, while a manager who overestimates volatility will buy more insurance than is necessary and forgo gains.

As for the issue of portfolio rebalancing, they examined adjustment frequencies by time intervals, namely, daily, weekly, monthly, and bimonthly. The effect (error) is measured as the difference of the horizon insurance values between non-continuous and continuous trading. They suggested that weekly rebalancing produces an amount of error that appears to be tolerable by most portfolio managers.

More importantly, they addressed the biggest potential risk of implementing portfolio insurance strategies — the gap risk — by simulating the performance of the OBPI strategy over the period of the October 1987 market crash. They indicated that most insured portfolios would have fallen short of their promised values because the managers would not be able to adjust the portfolio in time before a big drop in the market. The gap risk will be discussed further in the financial stability section.

13.7.9 *Loria, Pham, and Sim* (1991)

They simulated the performance of a synthetic-put strategy using futures contracts based on the Australian All Ordinaries Index for the period from April 1984 to March 1989. Their study contains 20 consecutive non-overlapping three-month insurance periods whose expiration dates coincide with the expiration dates of each SPI futures contract traded on the Sydney Futures Exchange. Four implementation scenarios are examined: a zero floor versus 5% floor which corresponds to a portfolio return of 0% and −5% per annual, respectively, and a realized volatility versus Leland's (1985) modified volatility. They reported that there is no perfect guarantee of loss prevention under any scenario. Even in the scenario with a 5% floor and modified volatility, two out of 20 contracts do not meet the desired floor. In addition, the OBPI strategy is most effective under severe market conditions. In other periods characterized by insignificant market declines, the value of the insured portfolio is below that of the market portfolio. They suggested futures mispricing may be one potential culprit for this outcome.

13.7.10 *Do and Faff* (2004)

This empirical paper is an extension of Loria *et al.* (1991). They examined two approaches (the OBPI and CPPI) and conducted simulations across two implementation strategies (via Australia stock index and bills, and via SPI futures and stock index). Furthermore, they considered the use of implied volatility as an input into the model, and the use of a zero floor versus 5% floor. The dataset consists of 59 non-overlapping three-month insurance periods, which span from October 1987 to December 2002. Thus, their key contributions relative to Loria *et al.* (1991) are the examination of a futures-based CPPI, a fine-tuned algorithm that allows for dividend payments, the consideration of *ex ante* volatility information, and more up-to-date data.

In terms of floor protection, the futures-based portfolio insurance implementation generally dominates its index-and-bill rival in both floor specifications, which reflects the low transaction costs in the futures market. Furthermore, the perfect floor protection is possible when implied volatility is used rather than using *ex post* volatilities. From the cost of insurance perspective, the futures-based strategy generally induces a lower cost of insurance than its index-and-bill rival in both floor specifications, which reflects the same reason as above. However, the cost of insurance is higher when implied volatility is used compared to *ex post* volatilities. The possible explanation is that the implied volatility is often higher than the same period *ex post* volatility, which results in over-hedging. As for the performances between the OBPI and CPPI approaches, there is no strong evidence to distinguish between them. Within the futures-based implementation, the synthetic put appears to dominate the CPPI with respect to floor protection, while the latter appears to slightly outperform in terms of upside participation.

They also examined whether portfolio insurance strategies work under stress conditions by assessing the strategies' effectiveness during tranquil and turbulent periods. Tranquil periods are defined as ones that return more than −4% and have a realized volatility of less than 15%; violation of either one or both of these conditions is regarded as indicating a turbulent period. All portfolio insurance strategies achieve 100% floor protection during tranquil periods, whereas the futures-based OBPI approach records the highest portfolio return. During turbulent times, futures-based portfolio insurance continues to perform quite well. The 1987 stock market crash makes the assessment difficult because of trading halts. However, assuming the futures continued to trade during that crisis, from the algorithm's perspective, the futures-based CPPI maintains a positive return, while the OBPI results in a negative return.

13.7.11 *Cesari and Cremonini* (2003)

This study is an extensive comparison of a wide variety of traditional portfolio insurance strategies. There are basically five dynamic asset allocation strategies: (1) BH, (2) CM, (3) constant proportion (without and with the lock-in of profits, CP and CPL), (4) the option-based approach (with three variations: BCDT, NL, and PS), and (5) technical strategy (with two kinds of stop-loss mechanisms: MA and MA2); therefore, nine strategies in total are considered.

For each strategy, eight measures for risk, return, and risk-adjusted performance are calculated, namely, mean return, standard deviation, asymmetry, kurtosis, downside deviation, Sharpe ratio, Sortino ratio, and return at risk. The strategies are then compared in different market situations (bear, no-trend, and bull markets) and with different market volatility periods (low, medium, and high periods), taking into account transaction costs and discrete rebalancing of portfolios. The three market situations are defined accordingly if market average returns fall into the three ranges — (−30%, −5%), (−5%, +5%), and (+5%, +30%) — and the three ranges for the volatile periods are (10%, 15%), (15%, 25%), and (25%, 30%), respectively. Transaction costs are treated in two ways: a proportional cost to the value traded and a correction to the Leland's (1985) option volatility. Two main rebalancing disciplines are used: a time discipline with weekly adjustment and a price discipline with adjustment only when prices are increased/decreased by 2.5% with respect to the previous rebalance time.

Monte Carlo simulations of MSCI World, North America, Europe, and Pacific stock market returns show that no strategy is dominant in all market situations. However, in bear and no-trend markets, CP and CPL strategies appear to be the best choice. In a bull market or in no-trend but with high volatility market, the CM strategy is preferable. If the market phase is unknown, CP, CPL, and BCDT strategies are recommended. In addition, these results are independent of the volatility level and the risk-adjusted performance measure adopted.

13.7.12 *Herold, Maurer, and Purschaker* (2005)

By constructing a fixed-income portfolio, in which the risky asset is the JPMorgan government bond index and the riskless asset is cash (one-month yield), they compared the hedging performances between the traditional CPPI strategy and the risk-based (specifically, VaR-based) strategy with a one-year investment horizon that begins at each year from 1987 to 2003. CPPI avoids losses in the bear years of 1994 and 1999. The mean return is inferior to (about 40 bp below) that of the risk-based strategy. CPPI also produces a higher turnover.

13.7.13 *Hamidi, Jurczenko, and Maillet* (2007)

Although they proposed a conditional CPPI multiplier determined either by VaR or by ES, only a VaR-based measure is studied in this empirical work, and the ES measure is absent for future research.

The dataset contains 29 years of daily returns of the Dow Jones Index, from January 2, 1987 to May 20, 2005, 4,641 observations in total. They used a rolling window of 3,033 returns to estimate the VaR, and there are 1,608 VaRs in the out-of-sample period. They resorted to eight methods of VaR calculation: one non-parametric method using the historical simulation approach; three parametric methods based on distributional assumptions, namely, the normal VaR, the Risk Metrics VaR based on the normal distribution, and the GARCH VaR based on the Student-t distribution; and four semiparametric methods using quantile regression to estimate the conditional autoregressive VaR (CAViaR), namely, the symmetric Absolute Value CAViaR, the Asymmetric Slope CAViaR, the IGARCH(1,1) CAViaR, and the Adaptive CAViaR.

According to the 1,608 back-testing results, the Asymmetric Slope CAViaR is the best model to fit the data. After having calculated the VaR values, the conditional multipliers can be determined. The estimations spread between 1.5 and 6, which are compatible with multiple values used by practitioners in the market (between 3 and 8).

Using the time-varying CPPI multipliers estimated by different methods, and a "multi-start" analysis — the fixed one-year investment horizon beginning at every day of the out-of-sample period — they found that the final returns of these insured portfolios are not significantly different.

13.7.14 *Ho, Cadle, and Theobald* (2008)

This empirical study presents a complete structure of comparing traditional portfolio insurance strategies (OBPI, CPPI) with modern risk-based portfolio insurance strategies (VaR-, ES-based RBPI). By constructing a currency portfolio, in which the risky asset is the Australian dollar and the riskless asset is a US dollar overnight deposit, they compared the dynamic-hedging performances between the traditional and the modern strategies with a one-year investment horizon that begins at each year from 2001 to 2007.

When implementing the OBPI strategy, the delta is calculated based on the modified Black–Scholes formula, $D_t = f(S_t, \bar{k}_0,\ r_t,\ \sigma_t,\ T)$. That is, daily annualized historical volatilities are used as inputs in the put replication process instead of the constant *ex ante* or the implied volatility in the original model to mitigate the volatility misestimation problem. Besides, the latter two parameters would make the portfolio daily returns more volatile. The interest rates are also updated daily for the same reason. When CPPI is implemented, the possible upper bounds of the multiplier are examined via the extreme value theory, which ranges from 4 to 6 corresponding to different confidence levels. When risk-based approaches are employed, both a historical distribution and a normal distribution with exponentially weighted volatility of risky asset returns are assumed. A daily rebalancing principle is adopted in their research without any modification to show the original results of hedging.

The performances are evaluated from six differing perspectives. In terms of the Sharpe ratio and the volatility of portfolio returns, the CPPI is the best performer, while the VaR based upon the normal distribution is the worst. From the perspective that the return distribution of the hedged portfolio is shifted to the right and in terms of both the average and the cumulative portfolio returns across years, the ES-based strategy using the historical distribution ranks first. Moreover, the ES-based strategy results in a lower turnover within the investment horizon, thereby saving transaction costs.

13.8 Summary

This chapter first looked at the basic concept of portfolio insurance, then covered the strategies and implementation of portfolio insurance. Further, a comparison of alternative portfolio insurance strategies was provided. Also, the impact of portfolio insurance on the stock market and the pricing of equities was presented, followed by a discussion of the empirical studies of portfolio insurance.

This chapter has discussed basic concepts and methods of portfolio insurance for stocks. Strategies and implementation of portfolio insurance have also been explored in detail. Other issues related to portfolio insurance and dynamic hedging have also been studied.

Portfolio insurance was described not as an insurance technique but rather as an asset-allocation or hedging technique. The general methods of portfolio insurance — (1) stop-loss orders, (2) market-traded index options, (3) synthetic options, and (4) futures trading — were discussed. One of the major issues facing investors and regulators during the later 1980s was introduced — the effect of portfolio insurance on the stock market.

Overall, this chapter has integrated most of the material discussed in previous chapters. It can be regarded as a synthesis of the whole book although other chapters follow.

Questions and Problems

1. What is portfolio insurance? Identify and explain the various strategies that can be used to insure a portfolio.
2. What is the difference between hedging and portfolio insurance?
3. A manager is running a $10-million portfolio. She has decided to allocate $5 million to risky assets and $5 million to risk-free assets. She has set the floor of the portfolio at $7 million.

   (a) What is the cushion for this portfolio?
   (b) What is the exposure for this portfolio?
   (c) What is the multiple for this portfolio?

4. Given the information in Question 3, if the market for risky assets increases by 30%:

   (a) What is the value of the total portfolio?
   (b) What is the new multiple?
   (c) What should the portfolio manager do to restore the portfolio to its target multiple?

5. Given the information in Question 3, if the market for risky assets decreases by 10%:

   (a) What is the value of the total portfolio?
   (b) What is the new multiple?

(c) What should the portfolio manager do to restore the portfolio to its target level?

6. What does the term *path dependence* mean? Why is it important for portfolio insurance strategies to be path independent?
7. Define a synthetic option. Explain how the option position is adjusted in a rising or falling market.
8. What is a delta value? Why is it important?
9. A portfolio manager has $10 million invested in a well-diversified portfolio of common stock with a portfolio beta of 0.9 measured relative to the S&P 500. How many S&P 500 futures contracts are needed to insure the portfolio if the futures are currently selling for $105?
10. How could the strategy of hedging with futures contracts not provide a perfect hedge?
11. Compare and contrast portfolio insurance with options to portfolio insurance with futures.
12. Identify and discuss the linkage between trading futures contracts for portfolio insurance and market volatility. Does the tail wag the dog?
13. What is the difference between margin on equities and margin on futures?

Bibliography

Anders, G. (1986). Investors risk for portfolio insurance. *The Wall Street Journal* (October 14), p. 6.

Asay, M. and C. Edelsburg (1986). Can a dynamic strategy replicate the returns of an option? *The Journal of Futures Markets*, 6(Spring), 63–70.

Becker, K. (1988). Rebalancing strategies for synthetic call options. Doctoral dissertation, University of Illinois.

Benninga, S. and M. Blume (1985). On the optimality of portfolio insurance. *The Journal of Finance*, 40(December), 1341–1352.

Benninga, S. (2008). *Financial Modeling*. Cambridge, MA: MIT Press.

Bertrand, P. and J. L. Prigent (2005). Portfolio insurance strategies: OBPI versus CPPI. *Finance*, 26(1), 5–32.

Black, F. and M. Scholes (1973). The pricing of options and corporate liabilities. *Journal of Political Economy*, 81, 637–659.

Black, F. and R. Jones (1986). *Simplifying Portfolio Insurance*. New York, NY: Goldman Sachs.

Black, F. and R. Jones (1987). Simplifying portfolio insurance. *Journal of Portfolio Management*, 14, 48–51.

Blume, M. E., A. C. Mackinlay and B. Terker (1989). Order imbalances and stock price movements on October 19 and 20, 1987. *Journal of Finance*, 44(September), 827–848.

Bodie, Z., A. Kane and A. J. Marcus (2021). *Investments*, 12th ed. New York: McGraw-Hill.

Brennan, M. J. and R. Solanki (1981). Optimal portfolio insurance. *Journal of Financial and Quantitative Analysis*, 16(September), 279–300.

Cesari, R. and D. Cremonini (2003). Benchmarking, portfolio insurance and technical analysis: A Monte Carlo comparison of dynamic strategies of asset allocation. *Journal of Economic Dynamics & Control*, 27, 987–1011.

Do, B. H. and R. W. Faff (2004). Do futures-based strategies enhance dynamic portfolio insurance? *Journal of Futures Markets*, 6(June), 591–608.

Dreher, W. (1988). Does portfolio insurance ever make sense? *Journal of Portfolio Management*, 14(Summer), 25–32.

Eizman, E. S. (1986). Rebalance disciplines for portfolio insurance. *Journal of Portfolio Management*, 13(Fall), 59–62.

Finnerty, J. and H. Park (1988). How to profit from program trading. *Journal of Portfolio Management*, 14(Winter), 40–46.

Finnerty, J. and H. Park (1987). Stock index futures: Does the tail wag the dog? *Financial Analysts Journal*, 43(March/April), 57–61.

Garcia, C. B. and F. J. Gould (1987). An empirical study of portfolio insurance. *Financial Analysts Journal*, 43(July/August), 44–54.

Grossman, S. (1988). An analysis of the implications for stock and futures price volatility of program trading and dynamic hedging strategies. *Journal of Business*, 61(July), 275–298.

Grossman, S. (1988). Insurance seen and unseen: The impact on markets. *Journal of Portfolio Management*, 14(Summer), 5–8.

Hamidi, B., E. Jurczenko and B. Maillet (2007). An extended expected CAViaR approach for CPPI. Working paper, Variances, University of Paris-1.

Herold, U., R. Maurer and N. Purschaker (2005). Total return fixed-income portfolio management: A risk-based dynamic strategy. *Journal of Portfolio Management*, 31(Spring), 32–43.

Hill, J. (1987). *Portfolio Insurance: Volatility Risk and Futures Mispricing.* New York, NY: Kidder, Peabody, and Co.

Ho, L. C. (2022). Portfolio insurance strategies, in C. F. Lee and A. C. Lee (eds.), *Encyclopedia of Finance*, 3rd ed. New York, NY: Springer.

Ho, L. C., J. Cadle and M. Theobald (2022). An analysis of risk-based asset allocation and portfolio insurance strategies, in C. F. Lee and A. C. Lee (eds.), *Encyclopedia of Finance*, 3rd ed. New York, NY: Springer.

Ho, L. C., J. Cadle and M. Theobald (2010). Portfolio insurance strategies: Review of Theory and empirical studies, in C. F. Lee, A. C. Lee and J. Lee (eds.), *Handbook of Quantitative Finance and Risk Management*, pp. 319–332. New York, NY: Springer.

John, L. M., L. M. Donald, E. P. Jerald and W. M. Dennis (2007). *Managing Investment Portfolios: A Dynamic Process*, 3rd ed. New York: CFA Institute.

Kritzman, M. (1986). What's wrong with portfolio insurance? *The Journal of Portfolio Management*, 13(Fall), 13–16.

Lee, C.-F. and A. C. Lee (2022). *Encyclopedia of Finance*, 3rd ed. New York: Springer.

Lee, C. F., A. C. Lee and J. Lee (2023). *Handbook of Investment Analysis, Portfolio Management, and Financial Derivatives.* Singapore: World Scientific.

Leland, H. E. (1980). Who should buy portfolio insurance? *Journal of Finance*, 35(May), 581–594.

Leland, H. E. (1985). Option pricing and replication with transaction costs. *Journal of Finance*, 40(December), 1283–1307.

Loria, S., T. M. Pham and A. B. Sim (1991). The performance of a stock index futures-based portfolio insurance scheme: Australian evidence. *Review of Futures Markets*, 10(3), 438–457.

Luskin, D. (1988). *Portfolio Insurance: A Guide to Dynamic Hedging.* New York: Wiley.

Malkiel, B. (1988). The Brady Commission Report: A critique. *Journal of Portfolio Management*, 14(Summer), 9–13.

Nolan E., M. A. Sola and S. Crouch (2010). *The Insured Portfolio: Your Gateway to Stress-Free Global Investments.* New York: Wiley.

O'Brien, T. (1988). The mechanics of portfolio insurance. *Journal of Portfolio Management*, 14(Spring), 40–47.

Perold, A. F. (1986). Constant proportion portfolio insurance. Working paper, New York: Harvard Business School.

Perold, A. R. and W. F. Sharpe (1988). Dynamic strategies for asset allocation. *Financial Analysts Journal*, 44(1), 16–27.

Presidential Task Force on Market Mechanisms (1988). *Tire Brady Report.* Washington, DC: U.S. Government Printing Office, New York.

Rendleman, R. J. and R. W. McEnally (1987). Assessing the cost of portfolio insurance. *Financial Analysts Journal*, 43(May/June), 27–37.

Rendleman Jr, R. J. and T. J. O'Brien (1990). The effects of volatility misestimation on option-replication portfolio insurance. *Financial Analysts Journal*, 46(3), 61–70.

Rubinstein, M. (1985). Alternative paths to portfolio insurance. *Financial Analysts Journal*, 41(July/August), 42–52.

Rubinstein, M. and H. Leland (1981). Replicating options with positions in stock and cash. *Financial Analysts Journal*, 37(July/August), 63–72.

Singleton, C. and R. Grieves (1984). Synthetic puts and portfolio insurance strategies. *Journal of Portfolio Management*, 10(Spring), 63–69.

Tilley, J. A. and G. O. Latainer (1985). A synthetic option framework for asset allocation. *Financial Analysts Journal*, 41(May/June), 32–41.

Zhu, Y. and R. C. Kavee (1988). Performance of portfolio insurance strategies. *Journal of Portfolio Management*, 14(3), 48–54.

Chapter 14

Bond Duration, Bond Option, and Bond Portfolio Strategies

Contents

14.1 Introduction

The duration of a bond has been widely used to measure the volatility of bonds and the relationship of the price of a bond and its duration. In this chapter, we will first analyze the duration, convexity of duration, and application of duration in bond valuation. Second, we will show how Black's (1976) model can be used to analyze the value of bond options. In addition, this chapter also shows how duration can be used to analyze portfolio strategies. Finally, this chapter will also present a technique that is commonly used in bond portfolio management and discusses the impact that portfolio theory has had on bond portfolio management.

In Section 14.2, we will analyze maturity and duration, and the convexity of duration will be discussed in Section 14.3. Bond option valuation will be shown in Section 14.4. Section 14.5 will discuss bond portfolio strategies, and contingent immunization will be demonstrated in Section 14.6. A case study of bond portfolio will be shown in Section 14.7. Finally, Section 14.8 will summarize the results of this chapter.

14.2 Maturity and Duration

The traditional role of bonds as an asset category has changed dramatically due to fluctuation of interest rates and the resultant price volatility. The use of bond maturity to reduce interest rate risk in bond portfolios through maturity matching has become increasingly inadequate. By the 1970s, several researchers had recognized that maturity is an incomplete measure of the life and risk of a coupon bond.

In 1971, Fisher and Weil (1971) recommended a practical measurement tool that could help immunize bond portfolios against interest rate risk, and in 1973, Hopewell and Kaufman demonstrated that it could also be used as a measure of price risk for bonds. This concept is **duration**, which has emerged as an important tool for the measurement and management of interest rate risk. Bierwag, Kaufman, and Toevs (BKT) noted in 1982 that only the introduction of beta in the 1960s has generated as much interest in the investment community as has duration.

The purpose of this section is to review briefly the historical development of duration and to examine its potential use by investors in alternative bond portfolio immunization strategies, as well as to look at certain reservations that should be considered when using duration to immunize bond portfolios.

In 1938, Frederick Macaulay developed the concept of duration as part of an overall analysis of interest rates and bond prices. He was attempting to develop a more meaningful summary measure of the life of a bond that would correlate well with changes in bond price; he arrived at a weighted average of the time to each bond payment, with the weights being the present values of each payment relative to the total present value of all the flows:

$$D = \frac{\sum_{t=0}^{n} t\left[\frac{C_t}{(1+k_d)^t}\right]}{\sum_{t=0}^{n} \frac{C_t}{(1+k_d)^t}}, \tag{14.1}$$

where C_t = the coupon interest payment in periods 1 through $n-1$, C_n = the sum of the coupon interest payment and the face value of the bond in period n, k_d = the YTM or required rate of return of the bondholders in the market, and t = the time period in years.

Thus, for the first semiannual payment in the series between 0 and n, t would equal 0.5. The denominator of this equation is equal to the current price of the bond as estimated by the present value of all future cash flows.

The duration of a bond with a fixed maturity date declines just as maturity does with the passage of time. The duration of a coupon bond, however, is always shorter than its maturity. Only for pure discount (zero-coupon) bonds will duration equal maturity. Duration is also affected by the size of the coupon and its YTM, decreasing as either increases.

It is useful to place the concept of duration in the perspective of other summary measures of the timing of an asset's cash flow. Because the cash flows from bonds are specific, both as to timing and amount, analysts have derived a precise measure of the timing for bonds. The most commonly used timing measure is term to maturity (TM), the number of years prior to the final payment on the bond. The advantage of TM is that it is easily identified and measured. However, the disadvantage is that TM ignores interim cash flows. Moreover, TM ignores the substantial difference in coupon rates and the difference in sinking funds.

14.2.1 *Weighted average term to maturity*

In an attempt to rectify the deficiency of TM, a measure that considered the interest payments and the final principal payment was constructed. The **weighted average term to maturity (WATM)** computes the proportion of each individual payment as a percentage of all payments and makes this proportion the weight for the year the payment is made:

$$\text{WATM} = \frac{\text{CF}_1}{\text{TCF}}(1) + \frac{\text{CF}_2}{\text{TCF}}(2) + \cdots + \frac{\text{CF}_n}{\text{TCF}}(n), \qquad (14.2)$$

where CF_t = the cash flow in year t, t = the year when cash flow is received, n = maturity, and TCF = the total cash flow from the bond.

Sample Problem 14.1 provides further illustration.

Sample Problem 14.1

Suppose a 10-year, 4% bond will have total cash flow payments of \$1,400. Thus, the \$40 payment in CF_1 will have a weight of 0.0287 (\$40/\$1,400), each subsequent interest payment will have the same weight, and the principal in year 10 will have a weight of 0.74286 (\$1,040/1,400). Therefore,

$$\text{WATM} = \frac{\$40}{\$1400}(1) + \frac{\$40}{\$1400}(2) + \frac{\$40}{\$1400}(3) + \cdots + \frac{\$40}{\$1400}(9) + \frac{\$1040}{\$1400}(10) = 8.71\,\text{years}.$$

The WATM is definitely less than the TM, because it takes account of all interim cash flows in addition to the final payment. Moreover, a bond with a larger coupon has a shorter WATM because a larger proportion of its total cash flows is derived from the coupon payments prior to maturity — that is, the coupon-weighted average of the larger coupon is larger than the smaller coupon bond. The weighted average term can be utilized to take into account sinking fund payments, thus lowering the WATM.

14.2.2 *WATM versus duration measure*

A major advantage of WATM is that it considers the timing of all cash flows from the bond, including interim and final payments. One disadvantage is that it does not consider the time value of the flows. The interest payment of the first period is valued the same as the last period.

The **duration measure** is simply a weighted average maturity, where the weights are stated in present value terms. In the same format as the WATM, duration is

$$\mathrm{D} = \frac{\mathrm{PVCF}_1}{\mathrm{PVTCF}}(1) + \frac{\mathrm{PVCF}_2}{\mathrm{PVTCF}}(2) + \cdots + \frac{\mathrm{PVCF}_n}{\mathrm{PVTCF}}(n), \qquad (14.3)$$

where PVCF_t = the present value of the cash flow in year t discounted at current yield to maturity, t = the year when cash flow is received, n = maturity, and PVTCF = the present value of total cash flow from the bond discounted at current YTM.

The time in the future when a cash flow is received is weighted by the proportion that the present value of that cash flow contributes to the total present value or price of the bond. Similar to the WATM, the duration of a bond is shorter than its TM because of the interim interest payment. Duration is inversely related to the coupon of the bond. The one variable that does not influence the average TM but can affect duration is the prevailing market yield. Market yield does not affect WATM because this measure does not consider the present value of flows. Nevertheless, market yield affects both the numerator of WATM and TM. As a result, there is an inverse relation between a change in the market yield and a bond's duration.

Tables 14.1 and 14.2, taken from Reilly and Sidhu's (1980) article, "The many uses of bond duration," illustrate the difference between the timing measures. These two tables show the WATM and the duration, respectively. Due to the consideration of the time value of money in the duration measurement, duration is the superior measuring technique.

WATM is always longer than the duration of a bond, and the difference increases with the market rate used in the duration formula. This is consistent with the duration property of an inverse relation between duration and the market rate.

Table 14.1 WATM (Assuming Annual Interest Payments)

Bond A $1,000, 10 Years, 4%				Bond B $1,000, 10 Years, 8%			
(1) Year	(2) Cash Flow($)	(3) Cash Flow/TCF	(4) (1) × (3)	(5) Year	(6) Cash Flow($)	(7) Cash Flow/TCF	(8) (5) × (7)
1	40	0.02857	0.02857	1	80	0.04444	0.04444
2	40	0.02857	0.05714	2	80	0.04444	0.08888
3	40	0.02857	0.08571	3	80	0.04444	0.13332
4	40	0.02857	0.11428	4	80	0.04444	0.17776
5	40	0.02857	0.14285	5	80	0.04444	0.22220
6	40	0.02857	0.17142	6	80	0.04444	0.26664
7	40	0.02857	0.19999	7	80	0.04444	0.31108
8	40	0.02857	0.22856	8	80	0.04444	0.35552
9	40	0.02857	0.28713	9	80	0.04444	0.39996
10	1,040	0.74286	7.42860	10	1,080	0.60000	6.00000
Sum	$1,400	1.00000	8.71425	Sum	$1,800	1.00000	7.99980
WATM = 8.71 years				WATM = 8.00 years			

Source: Reilly and Sidhu (1980). The many uses of bond duration. *Financial Analysts Journal*, 36(July/August), 60.

14.2.3 *Yield to maturity*[1]

Based upon Chapter 5, **yield to maturity** is an average maturity measurement in its own way because it is calculated using the same rate to discount all payments to the bondholder — thus, it is an average of spot rates over time. For example, if the spot rate for period two, r_2, is greater than that for period one, r_1, the YTM on a two-year coupon bond would be between r_1 and r_2 — an underestimate of the two-year spot rate. Likewise, the opposite condition would overestimate the two-year spot rate. With the high volatility of interest rates that has existed in recent years, the difference can

[1]Malkiel (1962) and Bodie *et al.* (2011) have carefully discussed the sensitivity of bond prices to changes in market interest rate, that is, interest rate sensitivity. They have carefully proposed several propositions to describe this kind of relationship. It is well known that bond characteristics such as coupon rate and yield to maturity affect interest rate sensitivity. Therefore, the yield to maturity discussed in Chapter 5 and this section can be used to analyze the interest rate sensitivity of bond prices.

Table 14.2 Duration (Assuming 8% Market Yield)

(1) Year	(2) Cash Flow	(3) PV at 8%	(4) PV of Flow	(5) PV as % of Price	(6) (1) × (5)
Bond A					
1	40	0.9259	37.04	0.0506	0.0506
2	40	0.8573	34.29	0.0469	0.0938
3	40	0.7938	31.75	0.0434	0.1302
4	40	0.7350	29.40	0.0402	0.1608
5	40	0.6806	27.22	0.0372	0.1860
6	40	0.6302	25.21	0.0345	0.2070
7	40	0.5835	23.34	0.0319	0.2233
8	40	0.5403	21.61	0.0295	0.2360
9	40	0.5002	20.01	0.0274	0.2466
10	1,040	0.4632	481.73	0.6585	6.5850
Sum			$731.58	1.0000	8.1193
Duration = 8.12 years					
Bond B					
1	80	0.9259	74.07	0.0741	0.0741
2	80	0.8573	68.59	0.0686	0.1372
3	80	0.7938	63.50	0.0635	0.1906
4	80	0.7350	58.80	0.0588	0.1906
5	80	0.6806	54.44	0.0544	0.2720
6	80	0.6302	50.42	0.0504	0.3024
7	80	0.5835	46.68	0.0467	0.3269
8	80	0.5403	43.22	0.0432	0.3456
9	80	0.5002	40.02	0.0400	0.3600
10	1,080	0.4632	500.26	0.5003	5.0030
Sum			$1000.00	1.0000	7.2470
Duration = 7.25 years					

be dramatic. For example, in Britain during 1977, the 20-year spot rate of interest was approximately 20%, while the YTM on 20-year coupon bonds was only 13%. The reason for the larger discrepancy was that YTM was calculated as an average of the relatively low short-term spot rates and the relatively high long-term spot rates.

Until the 1970s, when interest rate and bond price volatility increased dramatically, the significance of the superiority of duration over average measurement of bond portfolio risk was required for immunization against interest rate risk. Studies comparing the success of portfolios immunized with a duration strategy and a maturity strategy have shown that duration outperforms maturity 75% of the time for a variety of planning periods. Duration also produces lower variances between realized and promised returns than either the maturity strategy or the naïve strategy of annually rolling over 20-year bonds.

The motivation for bond investment is to secure a fixed cash flow over a particular investment horizon. Asset and liability portfolios of financial institutions often generate future cash flow patterns that must conform to certain solvency and profitability restrictions. For example, insurance companies and pension funds, with definite future commitments of funds, invest now so that their future cash flow stream will match well with their future commitment stream. Bond immunization strategies are designed to guarantee the investor in default-free and option-free bonds a rate of return that approximates the promised rate (or YTM). Nevertheless, the YTM will be equal to the RY only if the interim coupon payments are reinvestable at the YTM. If interest rates change, the RY will be lower or higher than YTM, depending upon the relationship between the bond's measured duration D and the investor's expected holding period H. A simple formula in which RY is computed as a weighted average of the YTM and the average RR available for coupon payments:

$$\text{RY} = \left(\frac{D}{H}\right)(\text{YTM}) + \left(1 - \frac{D}{H}\right)(\text{RR}), \tag{14.4}$$

where RY = realized yield, and RR = reinvestment rate.

Therefore, the RY would equal the YTM only if the duration on the bond were kept equal to the time horizon of the investor. An increase in the RR would increase the return from reinvested coupons but would at the same time decrease the bond value. Only holding the bond to maturity would prevent this value reduction from affecting the RY. Therefore, the overall impact of RR increases depends upon the extent to which the income effect offsets the value reduction. On the other hand, a decrease in the RR will decrease the return from reinvested coupons, but it will increase the bond values in the market. As shown in Equation (14.4), these opposite impacts on RY will exactly offset each other only when D equals H.

If a more complete time spectrum of zero-coupon bonds of all types were readily available, bond portfolio immunization would be a relatively simple process. Simply by choosing bonds with maturities equal to the length of an investor's investment horizon, the rate of return would always be as promised by the YTM, regardless of interest rate changes. Beginning with Treasury bond sales of February 15, 1985, the US Treasury has been cooperating with Wall Street firms in the stripping of coupon payments from new Treasury issues through separate registration of coupon and maturity payments, thus manufacturing a series of zero-coupon issues. However, since this applies only to Treasury issues, it is still necessary for investors to use duration models to immunize portfolios of non-Treasury bonds.

To immunize a bond portfolio, investors must match the duration of the portfolio with the length of their investment horizons. This must be accomplished within their assumed stochastic process of interest rate movements and changes in the yield curve. If the yield curve changes during the holding period, the immunization process will break down and the RY will not equal the YTM as promised.

Since the hoped-for results of the passive duration immunization method can be upset by interest rate shifts, some investors may prefer to try to predict interest rate changes and undertake an active immunization strategy. This would involve the formation of bond portfolios with durations intentionally longer or shorter than the investment planning period. Since it is usually assumed that the market consensus about future interest rates is the most likely possibility, investors should pursue active strategies only if their forecasts of rates differ from those of the market. The investor, who expects the interest rate to be higher than the market forecast, should form a bond portfolio with a duration shorter than the length of the investment horizon. If successful, the income gains from reinvestment of coupons and maturing bonds will exceed the value loss on unmatured bonds: RY will exceed the YTM promised. If unsuccessful, the reinvestment return will not be enough to offset the value loss and RY will be less than YTM.

If the investor expects interest rates to be lower than the market forecast, the procedure would be the reverse of that described above — that is, to purchase a bond portfolio with a duration longer than the investment horizon. If successful, the lower reinvestment returns will be more than offset by the bond value gains. Thus, the active immunization strategy relies solely upon the ability of the investor to predict the direction of future interest rate changes and to take full advantage of market opportunities for realized returns greater than market rates. While this provides the investor with an opportunity for substantial returns, it can also result in substantial losses. Because of this, Leibowitz and Weinberger (LW, 1981) derived a "stop loss" active immunization strategy which they called contingent immunization. In this method, the portfolio manager pursues higher returns through active management unless the value of the portfolio declines to a level that threatens a minimum target return. At this point, the portfolio is switched into a pure immunization mode designed to provide the minimum target specified at the outset. Other researchers have developed similar strategies that rely on two portfolios — one actively and the other passively immunized. Interest changes could take place that would virtually wipe out the active portfolio, but they would not greatly affect the minimum target return of the two-portfolio combination.

14.2.4 *The Macaulay model*

The duration model that is still most widely used because of its simplicity is the **Macaulay model**. However, basic limitations affect the use of this model. First, the current and forward spot rates are assumed to be equal over a specific planning horizon — that is, the yield curve is assumed to be flat. This is also one of the basic weaknesses of the YTM measurement. Second, this model provides an accurate measure of interest rate risk only when there is a single parallel shift in the term of structure of interest rates — that is, there is only one shift within the holding period and it does not involve a change in yield curve shape.

Most studies surveyed seem to indicate that the Macaulay model assumptions are unrealistic and too restrictive. Cox *et al.* (1979) noted that it does not take into account the dynamic nature of the term structure observed in the real world, in which yield curves can and do change in shape as well as location. As a result, a number of more complex duration models have been developed to measure risk when multiple term structure shifts can affect the shape and location of the yield curve. Because the actual underlying stochastic process governing interest rate changes is not known, only empirical analysis can determine whether the extra complexity of these models justifies their usage. Bierwag *et al.* (1982) extensively tested the Macaulay model along with four more complex duration models and found that duration-matching strategies generated realized returns consistently closer to promised yields than a maturity-matching strategy. Even more interesting, the Macaulay measure appeared to perform as well as the more complex models. Their findings suggest that single-factor duration matching is a feasible immunization strategy that works reasonably well, even with the less complex (and thus less costly) Macaulay model.

Duration appears a better measure of a bond's life than maturity because it provides a more meaningful relationship with interest rate changes. This relationship has been expressed by Hopewell and Kaufman (1973) as follows:

$$\frac{\Delta P}{P} = \frac{D}{(1+i)}\Delta i = D * \Delta i_2, \tag{14.5}$$

where Δ = "change in", P = bond price, D = duration, and i = market interest rate or bond yield.

For example, a bond with five years' duration will decline in price by approximately 10% when market yield increases by 2%. Note that $\Delta P/P$ on the left-hand side of Equation (14.5) is the percentage change in price, and Δi is the absolute change in yield level and not percentage change.

Other useful generalizations can be made concerning the relationships of duration to various bond characteristics as follows:

1. The higher the coupon, the shorter the duration, because the face-value payment at maturity will represent a smaller proportional present-value contribution to the makeup of the current bond value. In other words, bonds with small coupon rates will experience larger capital gains or losses as interest rates change.

Table 14.3 Duration, Maturity, and Coupon Rate

Maturity (Years)	Coupon Rate 0.02	0.04	0.06	0.08
1	0.995	0.990	0.985	0.981
5	4.756	4.558	4.393	4.254
10	8.891	8.169	7.662	7.286
20	14.981	12.98	11.904	11.232
50	19.452	17.129	16.273	15.829
100	17.567	17.232	17.120	17.064
∞	17.667	17.667	17.667	17.667

Additionally, for all bonds except zero-coupon-rate bonds, as the maturity of the bond lengthens, the duration at the limit will approach (1 + YTM)/YTM. Table 14.3 shows the relationship between duration, maturity, and coupon rates for a bond with YTM of 6%. At the limit (maturity goes to infinity), the duration will approach 17.667 (i.e., $(1 + 0.06)/0.06$).

As can be seen in Table 14.3, the limit is independent of the coupon rate: It is always 17.667. However, when the coupon rate is the same as or greater than the yield rate (the bond is selling at a premium), duration approaches the limit directly. Conversely, for discount-priced bonds (coupon rate is less than YTM), duration can increase beyond the limit and then recede to the limit. In the case of the bond with the 2% coupon at a maturity of 50 years, the duration is 19.452 — and this approaches the limit as maturity keeps increasing. These relationships are shown in Figure 14.1.

Regardless of coupon size, it is nearly impossible to find bonds with durations in excess of 20 years; most bonds have a limit of about 15 years.

2. The higher the YTM, the shorter the duration, because YTM is used as the discount rate for the bond's cash flows, and higher discount rates diminish the proportional present-value contribution of more distant payments. As has been shown, at the limit, duration is equal to $(1 + \text{YTM})/\text{YTM}$; in Table 14.4, the relationship between duration and YTM is shown.

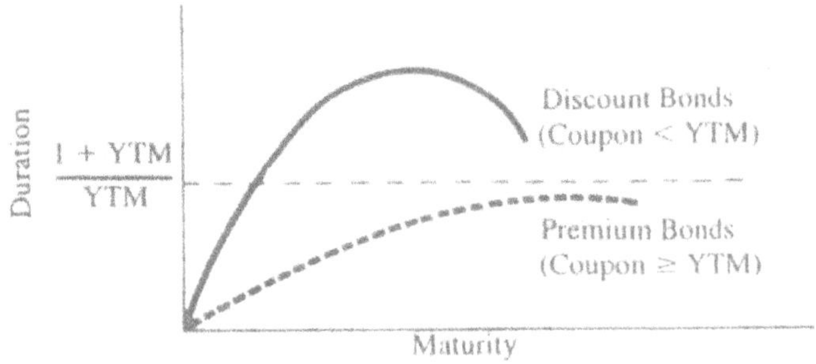

Figure 14.1 Duration and Maturity for Premium and Discount Bonds

Table 14.4 Duration and YTM

YTM	**Duration at Limit (Maturity $\to \infty$)**
0.02	51
0.04	26
0.08	13.5
0.10	11
0.20	6
0.30	4.33
0.50	3

3. A typical sinking fund (one is which the bond principal is gradually retired over time) will reduce in duration. Duration can be reduced by the sinking fund or call provision. A large proportion of current bond issues do have sinking funds, and these can definitely affect a bond's duration. An example will illustrate this fact. A 10-year 4% bond with a sinking fund of 10% of face value per year starting at the end of the fifth year has a duration of 7.10 years as compared to the duration of 8.12 years of a similar bond without a sinking fund. Table 14.5 provides further illustration.

   The effect of a sinking fund on the time structure of cash flows for a bond is certain to the issuer of the bond, since the firm must make the payments: They represent a legal cash flow requirement that will affect the firm's cash flow. However, the sinking fund may not affect the investor since the money put into the sinking fund

Table 14.5 Duration with and without Sinking Funds (Assuming 8% Market Yield)

	Cash Flow	Present-Value Factor	Present Value of Cash Flow	Weight	Duration
Bond A — No Sinking Fund					
1	$40	0.9259	$37.04	0.0506	0.0506
2	40	0.8573	34.29	0.0469	0.0938
3	40	0.7938	31.75	0.0434	0.1302
4	40	0.7350	29.40	0.0402	0.1608
5	40	0.6806	27.22	0.0372	0.1860
6	40	0.6302	25.21	0.0345	0.2070
7	40	0.5835	23.34	0.0319	0.2233
8	40	0.5403	21.61	0.0295	0.2360
9	40	0.5002	20.01	0.0274	0.2466
10	1,040	0.4632	481.73	0.6585	6.5850
Sum			$731.58	1.0000	8.1193
Duration = 8.12 years					
Bond A — Sinking Fund (10% per year from fifth year)					
1	$40	0.9259	$37.04	0.04668	0.04668
2	40	0.8573	34.29	0.04321	0.08642
3	40	0.7938	31.75	0.04001	0.12003
4	40	0.7350	29.40	0.03705	0.14820
5	140	0.6806	95.28	0.12010	0.60050
6	140	0.6302	88.23	0.11119	0.66714
7	140	0.5835	81.69	0.10295	0.72065
8	140	0.5403	75.64	0.09533	0.76264
9	140	0.5002	70.03	0.08826	0.79434
10	540	0.4632	250.13	0.31523	3.15230
Sum			$793.48	1.00000	7.09890
Duration = 7.10 years					

Source: Reilly and Sidhu (1980, pp. 61–62).

may not necessarily be used to retire outstanding bonds. Even if it is, it is not certain that a given investor's bonds will be called for retirement.

4. For bonds of less than five years to maturity, the magnitudes of duration changes are about the same as those for maturity changes. For bonds of 5 to 15 years' maturity, changes in the

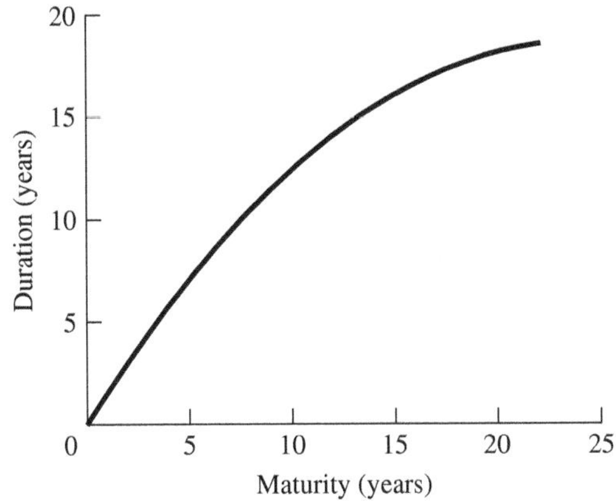

Figure 14.2 Duration versus Maturity

magnitude of duration are considerably less than those of maturity. For bonds with more than 20 years to maturity, changes in the magnitude of duration are very small relative to changes in maturity. As can be seen in Figure 14.2, in the range of zero to five years, the relationship between duration and maturity is shown approximately by a straight line with a slope of 45 degrees. In the range of five to ten years, the slope of the line is less, indicating a smaller change in duration for a given change in maturity. And for more than 20 years, the line is almost horizontal, showing a smaller change in duration for a given change in maturity.

5. In contrast to a sinking fund, all bondholders will be affected if a bond is called. The duration of a callable bond will be shorter than a non-callable bond.

When a bond is callable, the cash flow implicit in the YTM figure is subject to possible early alteration. Most corporate bonds issued today are callable, but with a period of call protection before the call option can be exercised. At the expiration of this period, the bond may be called at a specified call price, which usually involves some premium over par.

To provide some measure of the return in the event that the issuer exercises the call option at some future point, the yield to call is calculated instead of the YTM. This computation is based on the assumption that the bond's cash flow is terminated at the "first call date" with redemption of principal at the specified call price. The crossover yield is defined as that yield where the YTM is equal to the yield to call. When the price of the bond rises to some value above the call price, and the market yield declines to value below the crossover yield, the yield to call becomes the minimum yield. At this price and yield, the firm will probably exercise a call option when it is available. When prices go below the call price, the YTM is the minimum yield. Sample Problem 14.2 provides further illustration.

Sample Problem 14.2

To calculate the crossover yield for an 8%, 30-year bond selling at par with 10-year call protection, the annual return flow divided by the average investment can be used as an approximation for the yield. The implied crossover yield is 8.46%:

$$\text{Crossover yield: } \frac{80 + \frac{1080-1000}{10}}{\frac{1080+1000}{2}} = 8.46\%.$$

In one year's time, the bond's maturity will be 29 years with nine years to call. If the market rate has declined to the point where the YTM of the bond is 7%, which is below the crossover yield of 8.46%, the bond's yield to call will be 6%:

$$\text{Yield to call} = \frac{80 + \frac{1000-1123.43}{9}}{\frac{1080+1123.43}{2}} = 6\%.$$

If a bond portfolio manager ignored the call option and computed the duration of this bond to maturity at a market yield of 7%, the duration would be 12.49 years. If the duration was computed recognizing the call option at a price of $1,080 and using the yield to call of 6%, it would be 6.83 years.

Since a majority of corporate bonds have a call option, the effect of the call option upon a bond's duration could have an effect on the bond manager's investment decision. Therefore, the bond's duration, both disregarding the call option and regarding the call option, must be considered in an investment decision. That is, if interest rates stabilize or continue to rise, the call option duration is of less importance than the bond's duration disregarding the call option. If interest rates fall, the call option duration is of more importance.

14.3 Convexity of Duration

The duration rule in Equation (14.5) is a good approximation for small changes in bond yield, but it is less accurate for large changes. Equation (14.5) implies that the percentage change in bond price is linearly related to change in yield to maturity. If this linear relationship does not hold, then Equation (14.5) can be generalized as

$$\frac{\Delta P}{P} = -D * \Delta i + 0.5 \times Convexity \times (\Delta i)^2, \tag{14.6}$$

In Equation (14.6), the first term on the right-hand side is the same as the duration rule, Equation (14.5). The second term is the modification for convexity. Note that for a bond with positive convexity, the second term is positive, regardless of whether the yield rises or falls.

The more accurate Equation (14.6), which accounts for convexity, always predicts a higher bond price than Equation (14.5). Of course, if the change in yield is small, the convexity term, which is multiplied by $(\Delta i)^2$ in Equation (14.6), will be extremely small and will add little to the approximation. In this case, the linear approximation given by the duration rule will be sufficiently accurate. Thus, convexity is more important as a practical matter when potential interest rate changes are large. Sample Problem 14.3 provides further illustration.

Sample Problem 14.3

Figure 14.3 is drawn by the assumptions that the bond with 20-year maturity and 7.5% coupon sells at an initial yield to maturity of 7.5%. Because the coupon rate equals yield to maturity, the bond sells at par value, or $1,000. The modified duration and convexity of the bond are 10.95908 and 155.059, calculated by Equation (14.1) and the approximation formula in Equation (**??**), respectively.

If the bond's yield increases from 7.5% to 8.0% ($\Delta i = 0.005$), the price of the bond actually falls to $950.9093. Based on the duration rule, the bond price falls from $1,000 to $945.2046 with a decline of 5.47954% by Equation (14.5) as follows:

$$\frac{\Delta P}{P} = -D * \Delta i = -10.95908 * 0.005 = -.0547954, \text{ or } -5.47954\%.$$

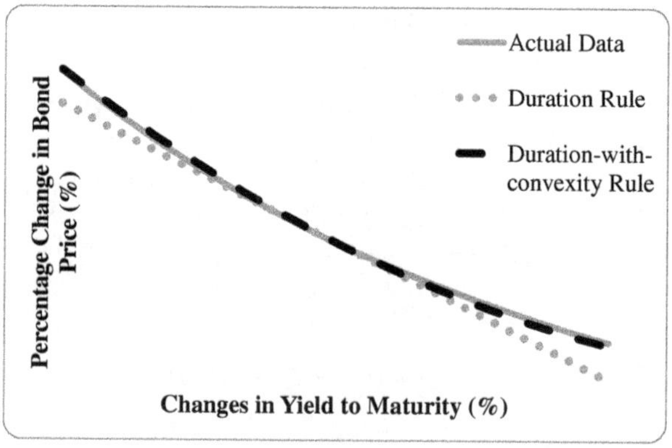

Figure 14.3 The Relationship between Percentage Changes in Bond Price and Changes in YTM

If we use Equation (14.6) instead of Equation (14.5), the bond price falls from \$1,000 to \$947.1482 with a decline of 5.28572%:

$$\begin{aligned}\frac{\Delta P}{P} &= -D * \Delta i + 0.5 \times \mathit{Convexity} \times (\Delta i)^2 \\ &= -10.95908 \times 0.005 + 0.5 \times 155.059 \times (0.005)^2 \\ &= -0.0528572, \text{ or } -5.28572\%\end{aligned}$$

The duration rule used by Equation (14.5) is close to the case with accounting for convexity in terms of Equation (14.6).

However, if the change in yield is larger, 3% ($\Delta i = 0.03$), the price of the bond actually falls to \$753.0727 and convexity becomes an important matter of pricing the percentage change in bond price. Without accounting for convexity, the price of the bond on the dash line actually falls from \$1,000 to \$671.2277 with a decline of 32.8772% based on the duration rule in Equation (14.5) as follows:

$$\frac{\Delta P}{P} = -D * \Delta i = -10.95908 * 0.03 = -.328772, \text{ or } -32.8772\%.$$

According to the duration-with-convexity rule, Equation (14.6), the percentage change in bond price is calculated in the following equation:

$$\begin{aligned}\frac{\Delta P}{P} &= -D * \Delta i + 0.5 \times \mathit{Convexity} \times (\Delta i)^2 \\ &= -10.95908 \times 0.03 + 0.5 \times 155.059 \times (0.03)^2 \\ &= -0.258996, \text{ or } -25.8996\%.\end{aligned}$$

The bond price \$741.0042 estimated by the duration-with-convexity rule is close to the actual bond price \$753.0727 rather than the price \$671.2277 estimated by the duration rule. As the change in interest rate becomes larger, the percentage change in bond price calculated by Equation (14.5) is significantly different from that calculated by Equation (14.6). Saunders and Cornett (2011) have discussed why convexity is important in the risk management of financial institutions.

14.4 Bond Option

A bond option is an option to buy or sell a particular bond by a particular date for a particular price. In addition to trading in the over-the-counter market, bond options are frequently embedded in bonds when they are issued to make them more attractive to either the issuer or potential purchasers. Embedded bonds include callable bonds and convertible bonds.

14.4.1 *Embedded bond options*

One example of a bond with an embedded bond option is a callable bond. This is a bond that contains provisions allowing the issuing firm to buy back the bond at a predetermined price at certain times in the future. The holder of such a bond has sold a call option to the issuer. The strike price or call price in the option is the predetermined price that must be paid by the issuer to the holder. Callable bonds cannot usually be called for the first few years of their life. (This is known as the lock-out period.) After that, the call price is usually a decreasing function of time. For example, in a 12-year callable bond, there might be no call privileges for the first 3 years. After that, the issuer might have the right to buy the bond back at a price of 110 in years 4 and 5 of its life, at a price of 108.5 in years 6 and 7, at a price of 106 in years 8 and 9, at a price of 103 in years 10 and 11, and at a price of 102 in year 12. The value of the call option is reflected in the quoted yields on bonds. Bonds with call features generally offer higher yields than bonds with no call features.

Another type of bond with an embedded option is a puttable bond. This contains provisions that allow the holder to demand early redemption at a predetermined price at certain times in the future. The holder of such a bond has purchased a put option on the bond as well as the bond itself. Because the put option increases the value of the bond to the holder, bonds with put features provide lower yields than bonds with no put features. A simple example of a puttable bond is an 8-year bond where the holder has the right to be repaid at the end of 4 years. (This is sometimes referred to as a retractable bond.)

Loan and deposit instruments also often contain embedded bond options. For example, a 7-year fixed-rate deposit with a financial institution that can be redeemed without penalty at any time contains an American put option on a bond. (The deposit instrument is a bond that the investor has the right to put back to the financial institution at its face value at any time.) Prepayment privileges on loans and mortgages are similarly call options on bonds.

Finally, a loan commitment made by a bank or other financial institution is a put option on a bond. Consider, for example, the situation where a bank quotes a 7-year interest rate of 4% per annum to a potential borrower and states that the rate is good for the next 5 months. The client has, in effect, obtained the right to sell a 7-year bond with a 4% coupon to the financial institution for its face value any time within the next 5 months. The option will be exercised if rates increase.

14.4.2 *European bond options*

Many over-the-counter bond options and some embedded bond options are European. The assumption made in the standard market model for valuing European bond options is that the forward bond price has a constant volatility σ_B. That allows Black's option on future model to be used to evaluate bond option. Following Black's (1976) call option on future model can be defined as follows:

$$C(T, F, \sigma^2, X, r) = e^{-rT}[FN(d_1) - XN(d_2)], \tag{14.7a}$$

$$d_1 = \frac{\ln\left(\frac{F}{x}\right) + \frac{1}{2}\sigma^2 T}{\sigma\sqrt{T}}, \tag{14.7b}$$

$$d_2 = \frac{\ln\left(\frac{F}{x}\right) - \frac{1}{2}\sigma^2 T}{\sigma\sqrt{T}}. \tag{14.7c}$$

In Equation (14.7a), F denotes the current futures price. The other four variables are T = time to maturity, σ = volatility of the underlying futures price, X = exercise price, and r = risk-free rate.

Now, in Equation (14.7a), we redefine σ equal to σ_B, F is redefined as F_B, X is redefined as K, and e^{-rT} is redefined as $P(0,T)$. Then, we can define call option and put option for the bond as follows:

$$c = P(0,T)[F_B N(d_1) - KN(d_2)], \tag{14.8}$$

$$p = P(0,T)[KN(-d_2) - F_B N(-d_1)], \tag{14.9}$$

where $P(0,T) = e^{-rT}$, r = risk-free rate, T = time to maturity, K = strike price, $d_1 = \frac{+\sigma_B^2 T/2}{\sigma_B\sqrt{T}}$, and $d_2 = d_1 - \sigma_B\sqrt{T}$.

In Chapter 3, we have discussed the forward bond contract and the evaluation formula in detail. Following Chapter 3, the forward bond contract price can be calculated using the following formula:

$$F_B = (B_0 - I)/P(0,T), \tag{14.10}$$

where B_0 is the bond price at time zero and I is the present value of the coupons that will be paid during the life of the option. In this formula, both the spot bond price and the forward bond price are cash prices rather than quoted prices. The relationship between cash and quoted bond prices can be explained as follows:

The strike price K in Equations (14.8) and (14.9) should be the cash strike price. In choosing the correct value for K, the precise terms of the option are therefore important. If the strike price is defined as the cash amount that is exchanged for the bond when the option is exercised, K should be set equal to this strike price. If, as is more common, the strike price is the quoted price applicable when the option is exercised, K should be set equal to the strike price plus accrued interest at the expiration date of the option. Traders refer to the quoted price of a bond as the clean price and the cash price as the dirty price. Sample Problem 14.4 provides further illustration.

Sample Problem 14.4

Consider a 10-month European call option on a 9.75-year bond with a face value of $1,000. (When the option matures, the bond will have 8 years and 11 months remaining.) Suppose that the current cash bond price is $960, the strike price is $1,000, the 10-month risk-free interest rate is 10% per annum, and the volatility of the forward bond price for a contract maturing in 10 months is 9% per annum. The bond pays a coupon of 10% per year (with payments made semiannually). Coupon payments of $50 are expected in 3 months and 9 months. (This means that the accrued interest is $25 and the quoted bond price is $935.) We suppose that the 3-month and 9-month risk-free interest rates are 9.0% and 9.5% per annum, respectively. The present value of the coupon payments is, therefore,

$$50e^{-0.25(0.09)} + 50e^{-0.75(0.095)} = \$95.45.$$

The bond forward price from Equation (14.10) is given by

$$F_B = (960 - 95.45)e^{0.1(0.8333)} = 939.68.$$

(a) If the strike price is the cash price that would be paid for the bond on exercise, the parameters for Equation (14.8) are $F_B = 939.68$, $K = 1{,}000$, $P(0,T) = e^{-0.1\times(10/12)} = 0.9200$, $\sigma_B = 0.09$, and $T = 10/12$. The price of the call option is $9.49.

(b) If the strike price is the quoted price that would be paid for the bond on exercise, 1 month's accrued interest must be added to K because the maturity of the option is 1 month after a coupon date. This produces a value for K of

$$1{,}000 + 100 \times 0.08333 = 1{,}008.33.$$

The values for the other parameters in Equation (14.8) are unchanged (i.e., $F_B = 939.68$, $P(0,T) = 0.9200$, $\sigma_B = 0.09$, and $T = 0.8333$). The price of the option is \$7.97.

Figure 14.4 shows how the standard of the logarithm of a bond's price changes as we look further ahead. The standard deviation is zero today because there is no uncertainty about the bond's price today. It is also zero at the bond's maturity because we know that the bond's price will equal its face value at maturity. Between today and the maturity of the bond, the standard deviation first increases and then decreases.

The volatility σ_B that should be used when a European option on the bond is valued is

$$\sigma_B = \frac{\text{Standard deviation of logarithm of bond price at maturity of option}}{\sqrt{\text{Time to maturity of option}}}.$$

For a particular underlying bond, the life of the option is increased. In general, σ_B declines as the life of the option increases. Figure 14.5 describes the relationship between σ_B and life of options.

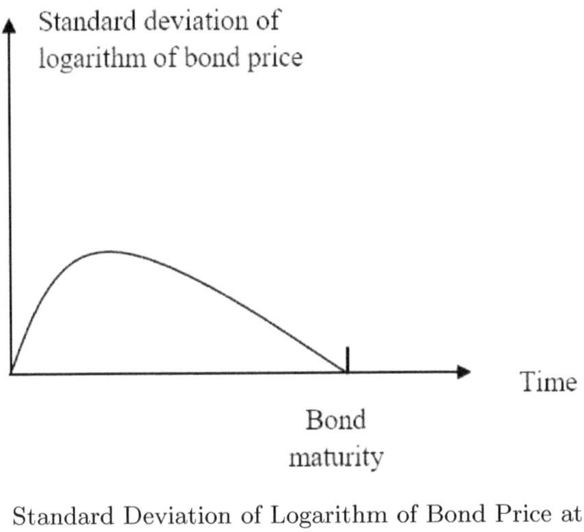

Figure 14.4 Standard Deviation of Logarithm of Bond Price at Future Times

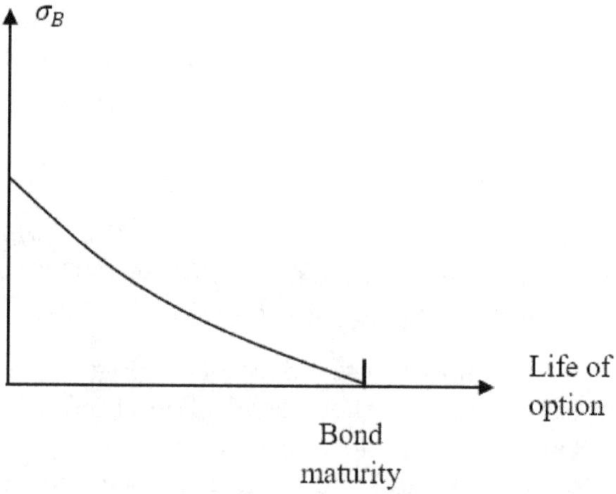

Figure 14.5 Variation of Forward Bond Price Volatility σ_B with Life of Option When Bond Is Kept Fixed

14.4.3 *Yield volatilities*

The volatilities that are quoted for bond options are often yield volatilities rather than price volatilities. The duration concept, introduced in the previous section, is used by the market to convert a quoted yield volatility into a price volatility. Suppose that D is the modified duration of the bond underlying the option at the option maturity, as defined in the previous section. The relationship between the change of forward bond price F_B and the change of forward yield y_F can be defined as

$$\frac{\Delta F_B}{F_B} \approx -D\Delta y_F$$

or

$$\frac{\Delta F_B}{F_B} \approx -Dy_F\frac{\Delta y_F}{y_F},$$

where ΔF_B = change of forward bond price, Δy_F = change of forward bond yield, and D = modify duration.

Volatility is a measure of the standard deviation of percentage changes in the value of a variable. This equation therefore suggests that the volatility of the forward bond price σ_B used in Black's model can be approximately related to the volatility of the forward bond yield σ_y by

$$\sigma_B = Dy_0\sigma_y, \tag{14.11}$$

where y_0 is the initial value of y_F, and σ_y = standard deviation of y_F.

When a yield volatility is quoted for a bond option, the implicit assumption is usually that it will be converted to a price volatility using Equation (14.11), and that this volatility will then be used in conjunction with Equation (14.8) or (14.9) to obtain the option's price. Suppose that the bond underlying a call option will have a modified duration of 5 years at option maturity, the forward yield is 8%, and the forward yield volatility quoted by a broker is 20%. This means that the market price of the option corresponding to the broker quote is the price given by Equation (14.8) when the volatility variable σ_B is $5 \times 0.08 \times 0.2 = 0.08$ or 8% per annum. Figure 14.5 shows that forward bond volatilities depend on the option considered. Forward yield volatilities as we have just defined them are more constant. This is why traders prefer them.

14.5 Bond Portfolio Strategies

How are yield curves useful for investors and analysts? The primary ways in which they are used in the market include the following: (1) to improve the forecasting of interest rates, (2) as a measure to help identify mispriced debt securities, (3) to "ride the yield curve," and (4) to help investors manage their portfolio maturity structures. This section concerns the third and fourth uses of yield curves.

14.5.1 *Riding the yield curve*

Riding the yield curve is an investment strategy designed to take advantage of yield curve shapes that are expected to be maintained for a period of time. Given the yield curve shape, an investor then decides whether to purchase a debt security that matures at the end of his or her time horizon or to purchase a longer-term debt security which can be sold at time T. (The investor may also purchase securities that mature before T and reinvest out to T.) If the yield curve is upward sloping and is expected to remain stable over the investor's horizon period, purchasing a longer-term security and holding on to it as the end of the horizon period approaches would lead to an increasing selling price (bond value) as the yield declines. Even though reinvestment rates (RRs) for coupons would also be declining, the total realized yield (RY) would be higher than the direct investment in a shorter-term security that matures at the end of the holding period. Similar strategies could be illustrated for other yield curve shapes. The problem with successfully using such strategies is that yield curves do not remain unchanged for long periods of time; they can and do change abruptly and seemingly without warning. The best advice to those with a specific horizon period but little forecasting skill would likely be to invest in short-maturity bonds to maintain reinvestment flexibility.

14.5.2 *Maturity structure strategies*

A common practice among bond portfolio managers is to evenly space the maturity of their securities. Under the **staggered maturity plan**, bonds are held to maturity, at which time the principal is reinvested in another long-term maturity instrument. Little managerial expertise is required to maintain the portfolio, and the maturing bonds and regular interest payments provide some liquidity.

An alternative to a staggered portfolio is the dumbbell strategy. Dumbbell portfolios are characterized by the inclusion of some proportion of short- and intermediate-term bonds that provide a liquidity buffer to protect a substantial investment in long-term securities. In Figure 14.6, it is apparent why this is called the dumbbell strategy — the resulting graph looks like a weight lifter's dumbbell.

The dumbbell portfolio divides its funds between two components. The shortest maturity is usually less than three years, and the longest maturities are more than 10 years. The portfolio is weight at both ends of the maturity spectrum (again like a dumbbell). The logic and mechanics of the dumbbell strategy are straightforward: the short-term Treasury notes (T-notes) provide the least risk and highest liquidity, while long-term bonds provide the highest return. The best risk/return portfolio combination may very well be a combination of these extremes. Assuming an upward-sloping

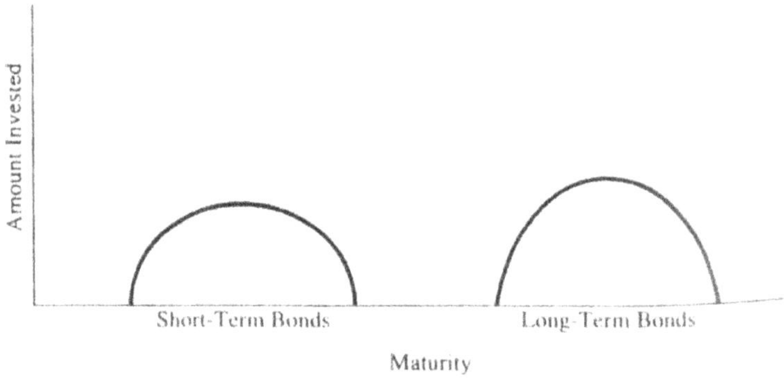

Figure 14.6 Dumbbell Maturity Strategy

yield curve, no intermediate bonds will be held since they have (1) less return than the longest maturity bonds, and (2) less liquidity and safety than the shortest T-note.

The performance of staggered and dumbbell strategies differs with respect to price fluctuations and return. During periods when interest rates are expected to increase, the return will most likely be over for a dumbbell portfolio than for a staggered portfolio. When rates are constant or cyclical and the yield curve is upward sloping, the dumbbell is superior to the staggered portfolio in yield; nevertheless, the price fluctuation will be greater for a dumbbell than for a staggered-maturity structure.

14.5.3 *Swapping*

When a market is in turmoil, great distortions take place. Some bonds drop further than they should, others less. A bond swapper can improve yield and pick up a substantial capital gain. In swapping, timing is very important.

Swapping strategies generally concentrate on highly specialized trading relationships. A commonly accepted method for classifying such swaps is Homer and Leibowitz's four types: (1) pure yield-pickup swap, (2) interest rate anticipations, (3) intermarket swap, and (4) substitution swap. The expected return from any swap is usually based upon several motives, not just one — thus, these "types" of swaps are really just sources of return.

14.5.3.1 *Substitution swap*

The substitution swap is the simplest of all. The swap attempts to profit from a change in yield spread between two nearly identical bonds. The trade is based upon a forecasted change in the yield spread between the two nearly bonds. The forecast is generally based upon the past history of the yield–spread relationship between the two bonds, with the assumption that any aberration from the past relationship is temporary, thereby allowing profit by buying the bond with the lower (higher) yield if the spread will become wider (or narrower). This trade is later reversed, leaving the investor in the original position, but with a trading profit from the relative changes in prices.

The substitution swap is simple in concept. Both the H-bond (the bond now held) and the P-bond (the proposed purchase) have equal coupon and maturity. The swap is executed at a time when the bonds are mispriced relative to each other. This mispricing is expected to be corrected by the end of the workout period. Sample Problem 14.5 provides further illustration.

Sample Problem 14.5

Substitution Swap. Suppose the investor holds a 30-year Aa utility 7% coupon bond (the H-bond), currently priced at par. He is offered to swap another 30-year Aa utility 7% coupon bond (the P-bond) at a yield to maturity (YTM) of 7.10%. Assume the workout period is one year. During this period, the prevailing RR for coupon remains unchanged at 7%. At the end of the workout period, both the H-bond and the P-bond are priced at par to yield 7%. See the evaluation worksheet (Table 14.6).

The worksheet gain of 129 basis points in realized compound yield is achieved only during the single year of the workout period. To obtain such a realized compound yield over the extended 30-year period, the investor must continue to swap an average of once a year, picking up 10 basis points with each swap, or at least averaging such a pickup on balance.

At the very worst, the workout period may take the entire 30 years, at which time the realized compound-yield gain would be 4.3 basis points. This is less than the initial 10-basis-point gain in YTM because the same RR will prevail for reinvesting the coupons of both the H-bond and the P-bond. This RR benefits the bond with the

Table 14.6 Evaluation Worksheet for a Sample Substitution Swap

	***H*-Bond** **30-Year 7s @7.00%**	***P*-Bond** **30-Year 7s @7.10%**
Workout Time: 1 Year RR: 7%		
Original investment per bond	$1,000.00	$987.70
Two coupons during year	70.00	70.00
Interest on one coupon @ 7% for one-half year	1.23	1.23
Principal value at end of year @ 7.00 YTM	1,000.00	1,000.00
Total accrued	1,071.23	1,071.23
Total gain	71.23	83.53
Gain per invested dollar	0.07123	0.08458
Realized compound yield (%)	7.00	8.29
Value of swap	129 basis points in one year	

Source: Homer, S. and M. L. Leibowitz (1972). *Inside the Yield Book*, p. 84. New York: Prentice-Hall and New York Institute of Finance.

Table 14.7 Effect of Workout Time on Substitution Swap: 30-Year 7s Swapped from 7% YTM to 7.10% YTM

Workout Time	**Realized Compound Yield Gain**
30 years	4.3 basis points/year
20	6.4
10	12.9
5	25.7
2	64.4
1	129.0
6 months	258.8
3 months	527.2

Source: Homer and Leibowitz (1972, p. 85).

lower starting yield relative to the bond with the higher starting yield. Thus, it pulls the total returns together. The relative benefit of the RR to the lower-yield issue will be greater at low future RRs and less at high future rates.

As the workout time is reduced, the relative gain in realized compound yield over the workout period rises dramatically, as seen in Table 14.7. The substitution swap may not work out exactly as anticipated due to (1) a slower workout time than anticipated, (2) adverse

Table 14.8 Effect of Major Rate Changes on the Substitution Swap: 30-Year 7s Swapped from 7% to 7.1%, Realized Compound Yields — Principal Plus Interest

RR and YTM (%)	1-Year Workout			30-Year Workout		
	H-Bond	*P*-Bond	Gain (Basis Points)	*H*-Bond	*P*-Bond	Gain (Basis Points)
5	34.551	36.013	146.2	5.922	5.965	4.3
6	19.791	21.161	137.0	6.445	6.448	4.3
7	7.00	8.29	129.0	7.000	7.043	4.3
8	(4.117)	(2.896)	122.1	7.584	7.627	4.3
9	(13.811)	(12.651)	116.0	8.196	8.239	4.3

Source: Homer and Leibowitz (1972, p. 87).

interim spreads, (3) adverse changes in overall rates, and (4) the *P*-bond's not being a true substitute. In the substitution swap, major changes in overall market yields affect the price and reinvestment components of both the *H*-bond and *P*-bond. However, as these effects tend to run parallel for both the *H*-bond and *P*-bond, the relative gain from the swap is insensitive even to major rate changes, as seen in Table 14.8.

14.5.3.2 *Intermarket spread swap*

The intermarket spread swap works on trading between sector–quality–coupon categories, based upon a forecasted change in yield spread between two different categories. The most common forecasting method is to observe historical yield spreads at various points in the interest rate cycle, and then to adjust for current supply-and-demand effects. However, this is most difficult, as shown by the 1977–1978 period of extremely narrow spreads between AA's and US government issues. Many managers bought government issues early in 1977, expecting the spread to widen, only to have to sit on their position through the next 18 months as both inflation and government spending continued unabated.

In the intermarket spread swap, the offered *P*-bond is essentially a different bond from the investor's *H*-bond, and the yield spread between the two bonds is largely determined by the yield spread between two segments of the bond market itself. The investor believes the "intermarket" yield spread is temporarily out of line, and the swap is executed in the hope of profiting when the discrepancy in this spread is resolved.

The intermarket spread swap can be executed in two directions. The swap can be made into a P-bond having a greater YTM than the H-bond. This is done either for the extra yield (in the belief that the spread will not widen) or in the belief that the intermarket spread will narrow, resulting in a lower relative YTM for the P-bond, and thus a higher relative price for the P-bond. The investor is always assured of a gain of the initial-basis-point spread, less any adjustment to the YTM of the swapped bond due to reinvestments at a higher coupon rate by maturity. Sample Problem 14.6 provides further illustration.

Sample Problem 14.6

Intermarket Spread Swap. Suppose an investor holds the 30-year 4s priced at 67.18 to yield 6.50% and views the 30-year 7s at par as appropriate for an intermarket spread swap. This investor feels that the 50-basis-point spread is excessive and anticipates a shrinkage of 10 basis points over the coming year. The price of the H-bond (4s) is kept constant for ease in computation. Table 14.9 illustrates this situation.

Table 14.9 Evaluation Worksheet for a Sample Intermarket Spread Swap in a Yield-Pickup Direction

	H-Bond 30-Year 4s @ 6.50%	**P-Bond 30-Year 7s @ 7.00%**
Initial YTM (%)	6.50	7.00
YTM at workout	6.50	6.90
Spread narrows 10 basis points from 50 basis points to 40 basis points.		
Workout Time: 1 Year RR: 7%		
Original investment per bond	\$671.82	\$1,000.00
Two coupons during year	40.00	70.00
Interest on one coupon @ 7% for 6 months	0.70	1.23
Principal value at end of year	675.55	1,012.46
Total accrued	716.25	1,083.69
Total gained	44.43	83.69
Gain per invested dollar	0.0661	0.0837
Realized compound yield (%)	6.508	8.200
Value of swap	169.2 basis points in one year	

Source: Homer and Leibowitz (1972, p. 90).

The 24.5-basis-point gain over 30 years (see Table 14.10) is less than the initial 50-basis-point gain due to the fact that the same RR benefits the bond with lower starting yield relative to the bond with the higher starting yield. Thus, it pulls the total returns together.

The **yield-give up** version of the intermarket spread swap works against the investor over time. Therefore, when a swap involves a loss in yield, there is a high premium to be placed on achieving a favorable spread change within a relatively short workout period. Here, the investor trades the higher YTM H-bond for a lower YTM bond (P-bond). The investor will profit only if the yield spread widens, leading to relatively lower P-bond prices, which would more than offset the yield loss.

As an example, assume the H-bond is the 30-year 7s priced at par, and the P-bond is the 30-year 4s period at 67.18 to yield 6.50%. The investor believes that the present 50-basis-point spread is too narrow and will widen, as shown in Table 14.11.

General market moves over the short term would have little effect on the swap's value provided the spread changes as originally anticipated. The potential risk of this swap must be viewed in the context of changes in overall rate levels and the realignment of spread relationships among the many market components. As can be seen in Table 14.12, there is a high premium to be placed on achieving a favorable spread change within a relatively short workout period.

Table 14.10 Effect of Various Spread Realignments and Workout Times on the Sample Yield-Pickup Intermarket Swap: Basis-Point Gain (Loss) in Realized Compound Yields (Annual Rate)

	Workout Time				
Spread Shrinkage	**6 Months**	**1 Year**	**2 Years**	**5 Years**	**30 Years**
40	1,083.40	539.9	273.0	114.3	24.5
30	817.0	414.6	215.8	96.4	24.5
20	556.2	291.1	159.1	78.8	24.5
10	300.4	169.2	103.1	61.3	24.5
0	49.8	49.3	47.8	44.0	24.5
(10)	(196.0)	(69.3)	(6.9)	26.8	24.5
(20)	(437.0)	(186.0)	(61.0)	9.9	24.5
(30)	(673.0)	(301.2)	(114.5)	(6.9)	24.5
(40)	(904.6)	(414.8)	(167.4)	(23.4)	24.5

Source: Homer and Leibowitz (1972, p. 91).

Table 14.11 Evaluation Worksheet for a Sample Intermarket Spread Swap with Yield Give up

	H-Bond 30-Year 7s @7%	*P*-Bond 30-Year 4s @6.50%
Initial YTM (%)	7	6.5
YTM at workout	7	6.4
Spread Growth: 10 Basis Points		
Workout Time: 1 Year RR: 7%		
Original investment per bond	\$1,000.00	\$671.82
Two coupons during year	70.00	40.00
Interest on one coupon @ 7% for 6 months	1.23	0.70
Principal value at end of year	1,000.00	685.34
Total accrued	1,071.23	726.04
Total gained	71.23	54.22
Gain per invested dollar	0.0712	0.0807
Realized compound yield (%)	7	7.914
Value of swap	91.4 basis points in one year	

Source: Homer and Leibowitz (1972, p. 88).

Table 14.12 Effect on Various Spread Realignments and Workout Times on the Sample Yield-Give up Intermarket Swap: Basis-Point Gain (Loss) in Realized Compound Yields (Annual Rate)

	Workout Time				
Spread Shrinkage	**6 Months**	**1 Year**	**2 Years**	**5 Years**	**30 Years**
40	1,157.6	525.9	218.8	41.9	(24.5)
30	845.7	378.9	150.9	20.1	(24.5)
20	540.5	234.0	83.9	(1.5)	(24.5)
10	241.9	91.4	17.6	(22.9)	(24.5)
0	(49.8)	(49.3)	(47.8)	(44.0)	(24.5)
(10)	(335.3)	(187.7)	(112.6)	(64.9)	(24.5)
(20)	(614.9)	(324.1)	(176.4)	(85.6)	(24.5)
(30)	(888.2)	(458.4)	(239.1)	(106.0)	(24.5)
(40)	(1,155.5)	(590.8)	(302.1)	(126.3)	(24.5)

Source: Homer and Leibowitz (1972, p. 89).

14.5.3.3 *Interest rate anticipation swap*

The investor who feels that the overall level of interest rates is going to change will want to affect a swap that will net a relative gain if this happens. Most commonly, these swaps consist of shortening maturities if higher long-term yields are expected, and lengthening maturities if lower long-term yields are expected.

The decisive factor is the expected long rate: The change in the long rate will almost always be the chief determinant of the value of the swap. Maturity swaps are highly speculative. If yields do not rise or fall as expected in a short period of time, often a large penalty due to the immediate loss in yield will occur. If the yield curve is positive, as one moves from long to short, a large yield loss occurs. Conversely, if the curve is negative, moving from short to long involves little or no yield pickup and sometimes a yield loss. Time works heavily against the swapper. Nevertheless, these periods of maximum yield loss are usually the best times to make maturity swaps in both directions.

In evaluating maturity swaps, capital gains or losses will be critical over the first year or so. As time goes on, coupon income and compounded interest become more important. The concept of duration easily explains this fact, for as time increases, the present-value factor declines. Therefore, capital gains or losses are valued at the lower present-value factor. Sample Problem 14.7 provides further illustration.

Sample Problem 14.7

Interest-Rate-Anticipation Swap. Suppose an investor holds a 7% 30-year bond selling at par. He expects the rate to rise from 7% to 9% within the year. Therefore, a trade is made into a 5% T-note maturing in one year and selling at par, as in Table 14.13.

The portfolio manager who shortens maturities drastically at a large loss in yield within the long range must expect a substantial increase in yields within the short range — otherwise his long-range yield loss will exceed his short-term gain. The swapper into longs at a big yield increase has time in his favor, but over the near term, he can fare badly if long yields rise further. Finally, the swapper from short to long at a yield loss also has time against him.

Table 14.13 Evaluation Worksheet for a Sample Interest-Rate-Anticipation Swap

	***H*-Bond 30-Year 7s @ 100**	***P*-Bond 30-Year 5s @ 100**
Anticipated Rate Change: 9%		
Workout Time: 1 Year		
Original investment per bond	$1,000.00	$1,000
Two coupons during year	70.00	50
Interest on one coupon @ 7% for 6 months	1.23	
Principal value at end of year	748.37	
Total accrued	819.60	–
Total gained	(180.4)	1,000.00
Gain per invested dollar	(0.1804)	1,050
Realized compound yield (%)	(13.82)	50
		0.05
		5.00
Value of swap	1,885 basis points in one year	

Source: Homer and Leibowitz (1972, p. 94).

14.5.3.4 *Pure yield-pickup swap*

In a pure yield-pickup swap, there is no expectation of market changes, but a simple attempt to increase yield. Basically, two bonds are examined to establish their difference in YTM, with a further adjustment to consider the impact of interim reinvestment of coupons at an assumed rate or return between now and the maturity date. Sample Problem 14.8 provides further illustration.

Sample Problem 14.8

Pure Yield-Pickup Swap. Suppose an investor swaps from the 30-year 4s at 671.82 to yield 6.50% into 30-year 7s at 100 to yield 7% for the sole purpose of picking up the additional 105 basis points in current income or the 50 basis points in the YTM. The investor is not motivated by a judgment that the intermarket spread will shrink or that yields will rise or fall. He has no explicit concept of a workout period — he intends to hold the 7s to maturity.

Table 14.14 Evaluation Worksheet for a Sample Pure Yield-Pickup Swap

	***H*-Bond** 30-Year 4s @ 6.50%	***P*-Bond** 30-Year 7s @ 7.00%
	(one bond)	(0.67182 of one bond)
Coupon income over 30 years	\$1,200.00	\$1,410.82
Interest on interest at 7%	2,730.34	3,210.02
Amortization	328.18	0
Total return	\$4,258.52	\$4,620.84
Realized compound yield (%)	6.76	7.00
Value of swap	24 basis points per annum at 7% RR	

Source: Homer and Leibowitz (1972, p. 99).

To evaluate a swap of this sort, which is based on holding the P-bond to maturity, three factors must be taken into account: (1) the coupon income, (2) the interest on interest, and (3) the amortization to par. Interim market price changes may be ignored. A simple addition of the three money flows just listed, divided by the dollars invested, will give a total return in dollars which, with the aid of a compound-interest table, will give the total realized compound yield as a percentage of each dollar invested, as shown in Table 14.14.

Although the principal invested in both issues is only \$671.82 per bond, over a period of 30 years, the switch results in a gain of \$210.82 per bond in coupon income, a gain of \$479.68 per bond in interest on interest, and a loss of \$328.18 per bond in capital gain. These three factors add up to a net gain of \$362.32 per bond, or a net gain of 24 basis points per year.

14.6 Contingent Immunization

Contingent immunization allows a bond portfolio manager to pursue the highest yields available through active strategies while relying on the techniques of bond immunization to assure that the portfolio will achieve a given minimal return over the investment horizon. Using this strategy, the portfolio manager attempts to earn returns in excess of the immunized return, but at the same time, attempts to constrain or control losses that may result from poor forecasts of interest rate movements.

Risk control is the major objective of contingent immunization. At the inception of the strategy, the manager determines the degree of risk he or she is willing to accept. If a sequence of interest rate movements causes the portfolio to approach the predetermined risk level, the manager alters the portfolio's duration to completely immunize it from any further risk. On the other hand, if the interest rate movements provide additional returns, the portfolio manager does nothing.

The difference between the minimal, or floor, rate of return and the rate of return on the market is called the cushion spread. Equation (14.8) shows the relationship between the market rate of return R_m and the cushion C to be the floor rate of return, R_{FL}:

$$R_{FL} = R_m - C. \tag{14.12}$$

Interest rate movement favorable to the bond portfolio manager's position will enlarge the spread — that is, R_m goes up and the portfolio is long bonds, thereby increasing the realized return. Adverse interest rate movements will reduce the cushion spread $R_m - C$ up to the point that $R_{FL} = R_m$. At this point, the portfolio manager will immunize the portfolio, which will ensure that the realized return will equal R_{FL}.

Figure 14.7 is a graphical presentation of contingent immunization. The realized change in the market rate of return is shown on the horizontal axis, and the potential rate of return for the portfolio is shown on the vertical axis. The potential return is a function of the market return, the floor return, and the cushion. If the interest rate change is +2%, the portfolio manager shifts to an immunization strategy that locks in the R_{FL} at 10% for the planning horizon. Regardless of interest rate movements thereafter, the portfolio will realize a return of 10%. If interest rates were to go down, the portfolio would earn a return in excess of the R_{FL} because of the manager's ability to have a portfolio with a duration larger than the investment horizon.

The contingent immunization approach allows the portfolio manager the ability to follow the active investment strategies discussed earlier in this chapter. At the same time, the manager is able to protect a minimum return by using a duration-based immunization strategy. There is an old saying in the market: "Let your winners

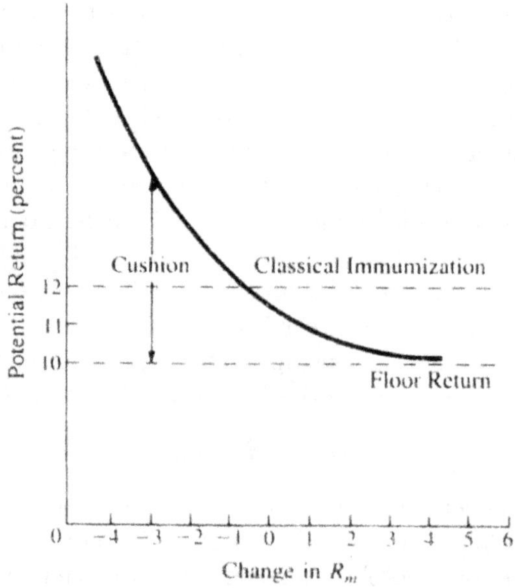

Figure 14.7 Contingent Immunization

run and cut your losses." This is exactly the philosophy behind the contingent immunization strategy.

14.7 A Case Study of Bond Portfolio

Ron Allen is the President of Merchant's Bank and Trust Co.[2] Mr. Allen has been the CEO of the $80-million community bank for less than a year. The bank has always been successful and, in years past, provided its stockholders with a slightly better return than its peers. However, the return on the bank's investment portfolio had suffered somewhat in the early 1980s because of its inability to cope with the dramatic rise and continued fluctuation of interest rates. Now, Allen wants the bank to become more of an investment manager than simply a buyer and seller of bonds. It is Allen's belief

[2]This case study is based on Altmix (1984). Raymond A. Altmix is currently Vice President, First of America Bank-Kankakee.

Table 14.15 Weighted Present Value

(1) Year	(2) Coupons	(3) $\frac{1}{(1+i)^n}$	(4) (2) × (3) Unweighted PV	(5) (1) × (4) Weighted PV
1	100.00	0.9091	90.91	90.91
2	100.00	0.8264	82.64	165.28
3	100.00	0.7513	75.13	225.39
4	100.00	0.6830	68.30	273.20
5	1,100.00	0.6211	683.01	3,415.05
	1,500.00		1,000.00	4,169.83
	4,169.83 ÷ 1,000.00 = 4.17 years duration			

that by using duration theory he can achieve a bond portfolio that is not as sensitive to changes in rates and yet will still produce a better-than-average return.

Duration is the weighted average number of years until an initial cash investment is recovered, with the weight expressed as the relative present value of each payment of interest and principal. For example, suppose a bank bought a five-year, $1,000 bond with a 10% coupon at par. If the going rate of interest remains at 10%, what would be the duration of the bond? The bond would produce a cash income in the amount of $100.00 per year for five years before maturing. To calculate the weighted present value, it is necessary to find the present value of each payment and multiply it by the number of periods until the payment is received. In the first year, the bank will receive $100.00 in coupon income. Discounted at 10%, the present value of the payment is $90.01 (see Table 14.15). Column 3, the present-value interest factor (PVIF), is obtained by using the formula $1/(1+i)^n$, in which n is the number of compounding periods and i is the interest rate.

The present value of the second year's coupon income of $100 will be $82.64. The value is multiplied by two — that is, the number of years until receipt; the weighted present value of $165.28 is obtained. The present value of the third-year cash flow is $75.13; the weighted present value is $225.39. For the fourth year, the present value is $68.30 and the weighted present value is $273.20. For the last year, it is necessary to calculate both the present value of the

$100 coupon and that of the maturing $1,000 bond. This sum is equal to $683.01, which when multiplied by five equals $3,415.05. As presented in Table 14.16, the cumulative weighted present values total $4,169.83. When this total is divided by the unweighted present value of the bond, $1,000, we have the duration of the bond, 4.1698 years. Thus, the initial duration of a five-year, 10% bond selling at par is 4.17 years. (This example assumes that no costs are incurred in buying and selling bonds and in reinvesting the funds received as bond coupons are paid.)

The basic problem that Mr. Allen faces, as with any bond portfolio manager, is obtaining a given rate of return to satisfy the yield requirements of a specific date — that is, the investment horizon. If the market rates never changed between the purchase and the maturity of a bond, it would be possible to acquire a bond that would guarantee overall return of a portfolio manager's investment horizon. However, the term structure of interest rates is dynamic and the market rates are constantly changing. Because of the changes in the term structure, bond portfolio managers are faced with interest rate risk. Interest rate risk is the combination of two risks, price risk and coupon reinvestment risk.

Price risk occurs if interest rates change before the target date and the bond is sold prior to maturity. At that time, the market price will differ from the value at the time of purchase. If rates increase after the purchase date, the price the bond would be sold at would be below what had been anticipated. If the rates decline, the realized price would be above what had been expected.

Increases in interest rates will reduce the market value of a bond below its par value. But it will increase the return from the reinvestment of the coupon interest payments. Conversely, decreases in interest will increase the market value of a bond above its par value but decrease the return on the reinvestment of the coupons. In order for a bond to be protected from the changes in interest rates after purchase, the price risk and coupon reinvestment must offset each other.

Of equal importance is **coupon reinvestment risk**. It is the expected yield calculated by assuming that all coupon cash flows would be reinvested at the same yield that existed at the time of purchase. If rates begin to fall, it would be impossible to reinvest the coupon at a rate high enough to produce the anticipated yield. Obviously, if rates increase, the coupon cash flow will be reinvested at higher rates and produce a return above expectations. Duration is the time period at which the price risk and coupon reinvestment risk of a bond are of equal magnitude but opposite in direction. The result is that the expected yield is realized.

The duration strategy may protect the bank's bond portfolio from these unexpected changes in the yield. Merchant's Bank set its desired holding period at four years in order to protect the portfolio. This means that the duration of the bond portfolio should equal four years. In order to give the portfolio a four-year duration, the weighted average duration is set at the desired length and the bank invests all future cash flows with duration equal to the remaining expected value.

An example of the effect of attempting to protect a portfolio by matching the investment horizon and the duration of a bond portfolio is contained in Table 14.16 using a single bond. Merchant's Bank has an investment horizon of four years. The current YTM for a four-year bond is 10.50%. Therefore, the ending wealth ratio should be 1.4909 $(1/(1.105)^4)$. This assumes a completely protected portfolio. Two investment strategies are computed in Table 14.16. The first is the maturity strategy, where the TM is set at four years. The second is the duration strategy, where the duration is four years. In this case, the bank would acquire a five-year, 10.5% bond that has a duration of 4.13 years, assuming a 10.5% YTM. For this example, it is assumed that there is a single interest rate change at the end of year two and the market yield goes from 10.5% to 8% through the fourth year.

As Table 14.16 shows, the wealth ratio for the maturity strategy fell short of the desired ending wealth ratio on this particular bond. This is due to the interest rate change in year two, which results in a lower RR. In the maturity strategy, the price risk of the bond itself is eliminated because the bond matures in the fourth year. However, the duration strategy actually created a wealth ratio above what was expected. This is because the return that was lost in the reinvestment was offset by the increase in the value of the bond in its

Table 14.16 Comparison of the Maturity Strategy and Duration Strategy for a Five-Year Bond

Year	Cash Flow	RR (%)	Value
Maturity Strategy			
1	105.00	10.5	105.00
2	105.00	10.5	221.03
3	105.00	8.0	343.71
4	105.00	8.0	1,476.01
Duration Strategy			
1	105.00	10.5	105.00
2	105.00	10.5	221.03
3	105.00	8.0	343.71
4	1,125.10*	8.0	1,496.31
			2,166.05
Expected wealth ratio is 1,491.00.			

Note: *The bond could be sold at its market value of $1,125.12, which is the value for a 10.5% bond with one year to maturity priced to yield 8%.

fourth year. In this case, a premium would be paid for a bond with a coupon $2\frac{1}{2}\%$ over the market rate by the purchaser in a secondary market.

The fact that a premium would be paid for this five-year bond at the end of four years is an important factor in the effectiveness of the duration concept. There is a direct relationship between the duration of a bond and the price volatility for the bond assuming given changes in the market rates of interest. This relationship can be expressed in the following formula:

$$\text{BPC} = -D * (r),$$

where BPC = the percent of change in price for the bond, D^* = the adjusted duration of the bond in years, equal to $D/(1+r)$, and r = the change in the market yield in basis points divided by 100 (e.g., a 50-basis-point decline would be -0.5).

Using the values from Table 14.16, the percentage of change in the price of the five-year bond can be calculated. The duration is

4.13 years and interest rate ranges from 8% to 10.5%.

$$
\begin{aligned}
D^* &= 3.738 \\
\text{BPC} &= -3.738(100/100) \\
&= -3.738(1) \\
&= -3.738.
\end{aligned}
$$

In this example, the price of the bond should decline by about 3.7% for every 100-basis-point increase in market rates. The accuracy of the formulas may vary depending on the length of duration. However, the important point is in the relationship between duration and interest rate risk. The longer the duration of a bond, the greater the price volatility of the bond for changes in interest rates.

Developing an interest rate forecast is essential in any bond portfolio manager's program. To aid them in the development of this forecast, Merchant's Bank has secured the services of two well-known investment firms. Both firms publish monthly forecasts that will be used along with forecasts provided by Mr. Allen's staff. Investment Firm A predicts that short-term interest rates, over 0–6 months, will average between $9\frac{1}{2}\%$ and 11%, and long-term rates will fluctuate between 11% and 12%. Firm B has a similar forecast for short-term rates, but Firm B predicts a downward-sloping yield curve with long-term interest rates in the 9–10% range. Mr. Allen's problem here is that the firms' forecasts of long-term interest rates move in opposite directions. If interest rates increase, the bank's bond portfolio will not perform well unless it is protected using duration. However, if interest rates fall, the return provided by using duration strategy will not be as good as using maturity strategy. In this case, Mr. Allen may miss an opportunity to earn above-average returns.

Mr. Allen now must develop an interest rate forecast for his Board of Directors. At the same time, he will attempt to show them that duration can be an effective management tool. Merchant's Bank and Trust Co. has $750,000 in bonds maturing from the existing portfolio. Table 14.17 is a list of bonds Mr. Allen is considering for purchase. His decisions, based on the future of interest rates, will be closely monitored by the Board of Directors. It is important that Mr. Allen consider the advantages and disadvantages of using duration as a bond portfolio management tool.

Table 14.17 Bonds Being Considered for Purchase by Merchant's Bank and Trust Co.

Amount*	Name	Rate (%)	Maturity
$150,000	Agency A	10.90	3
$200,000	Government 1	10.85	3
$100,000	Government 2	11.00	4
$100,000	Agency B	11.10	4
$150,000	Agency C	11.25	4
$100,000	Government 3	11.25	5
$200,000	Agency D	11.35	5
$250,000	Agency E	11.40	5
$100,000	Agency F	11.30	5
$200,000	Government 4	11.25	6
$150,000	Agency G	11.70	6
$200,000	Government 5	12.50	10

Note: *All bonds are purchased at par and are assumed to have an annual coupon.

14.8 Summary

In this chapter, we have first discussed concepts, definitions, and applications of maturity, duration, and convexity of duration. By using the formula of duration and the Black model, which has been discussed in Appendix 7C, we have shown how bond options can be evaluated.

The management of a fixed-income portfolio involves techniques and strategies that are unique to the specific area of bonds. This chapter has discussed riding the yield curve, swaps, and duration as three techniques that are familiar to all managers of fixed-income portfolios. A comparison of these techniques is also carefully discussed in this chapter.

Questions and Problems

1. Define the following terms:

   (a) riding the yield curve (b) swapping
   (c) workout period (d) duration
   (e) immunization (f) crossover yield
   (g) bond option (h) yield volatilities

2. What is the duration of bond A if it has the following characteristics?

$$\begin{array}{ll} \text{PV} = \$1,000 & \text{Principal} = \$1,000 \\ \text{Coupon rate} = 15\% & \text{YTM} = 15\% \\ n = 3 \text{ years} & \end{array}$$

3. What kinds of risks does duration involve?
4. What is the value of a substitution swap for the following two bonds?

***H*-(Hold) Bond**	***P*-(Purchaser) Bond**
20-year 10% purchased at par	20-year 10% priced at \$950
Workout time: 1 year	
RR: 10%	

5. What is the value of an intermarket swap for the following two bonds?

***H*-(Hold) Bond**	***P*-(Purchaser) Bond**
Price of bond: 5% @ beginning \$680	Price of bond: 10% @ beginning \$1,000
YTM: 10%	YTM: 11%
YTM at workout: 10%	YTM: 10%
Workout time: 1 year	
RR: 10%	
Price of bond in one year: \$685	Price of bond in one year: \$1,105

6. What impact does a longer workout period have on the value of swaps?
7. Explain an interest-rate-anticipation swap. What are the trade-offs that the bond investor is relying on?
8. What is the relationship between maturity and duration for a zero-coupon bond? What is the relationship between maturity and duration for a coupon bond selling at par? What is the relationship between maturity and duration for a coupon bond selling at a discount? What is the relationship between maturity and duration for a coupon bond selling at a premium?

9. What is the relationship between WATM and duration?
10. Calculate the duration and WATM for the following bonds. What impact do changing market interest rates have on duration and WATM?

Bond A	Bond B	Bond C
Principal $1,000 Maturity 5 years Coupon 5% PV $957.60	Principal $1,000 Maturity 5 years Coupon 5% PV $1,044.65	Principal $1,000 Maturity 5 years Coupon 5% PV $1,000

11. If you expect interest rates to fall, how should you structure your bond portfolio with respect to duration and holding period?
12. For a given maturity, how does coupon rate affect the duration of a bond?
13. How is the duration of a callable bond related to the duration of a non-callable bond?
14. Explain the convexity of a bond. What is the relationship between convexity and bond price? What is the difference between the duration rule with and without convexity?
15. What is the crossover yield of a bond with a 10% coupon selling at $1,100 with a call protection of 10 years?
16. What is the duration of a 20-year 10% bond selling at par that is callable in 5 years at $1,050?
17. Assume that a bond with 8-year maturity and 6% coupon sells at an initial yield to maturity of 6%, that is, the bond sells at par value, $1,000. What is the duration and modified duration of the bond? What is the approximation value and exact value of convexity?
18. For the given bond in Question 16, what are the bond prices estimated by the duration rule and duration-with-convexity rule when the yield to maturity increases from 6% to 8%? What is the actual bond price when the yield to maturity is 8%?
19. According to the assumption of bond in Question 16, what are the percentage changes in bond price based on the duration rule and duration-with-convexity rule when the yield to maturity declines from 6% to 5.5%?

20. Please use the following information to evaluate bond option. Number to be given.

Bibliography

Altmix, R. A. (1984). Duration, bond portfolio protection: Case study. Unpublished manuscript.

Bierwag, G. O. (1983). Immunization strategies for funding multiple liabilities. *Journal of Financial and Quantitative Analysis*, 18(March), 113–123.

Bierwag, G. O. (1987). *Duration Analysis: Managing Interest Rate Risk.* Cambridge, MA: Ballinger Publishing Co.

Bierwag, G. O., G. G. Kaufman and D. Khang (1978). Duration and bond portfolio analysis: An overview. *Journal of Financial and Quantitative Analysis*, 13(November), 671–681.

Bierwag, G. O., G. G. Kaufman and A. Toevs (1982). Single-factor duration models in a discrete general equilibrium framework. *Journal of Finance*, 37(May), 325–338.

Black, F. (1976). The pricing of commodity contracts. *Journal of Financial Economics*, 3(January–March), 167–178.

Bodie, Z., A. Kane and A. J. Marcus (2011). *Investments*, 9th ed. New York: McGraw-Hill.

Bookstaber, R. (1985). *The Complete Investment Book.* Glenview, IL: Scott, Foresman and Co.

Boquist, J. A., G. Racette and G. G. Schlarbaum (1975). Duration and risk assessment for bonds and common stocks. *Journal of Finance*, 30(December), 1360–1365.

Chua, J. (1984). A closed form formula for calculating bond duration. *Financial analysts Journal*, 40(May/June), 76–78.

Cox, J., J. E. Ingersoll and S. A. Ross (1979). Duration and measurement of basis risk. *Journal of Business*, 52(January), 51–61.

Fisher, L. and R. Weil (1971). Coping with the risk of interest rate fluctuations: Returns to bondholders from naïve and optimal strategies. *Journal of Business*, 44(October), 408–431.

Fong, H. and F. Fabozzi (1985). *Fixed Income Portfolio Management.* Homewood, IL: Dow Jones-Irwin.

Fabozzi, F. (2005). *The Handbook of Fixed Income Securities*, 7th ed. New York: McGraw-Hill.

Fabozzi, F. (2009). *Bond Markets, Analysis, and Strategies*, 7th ed. New York: Prentice Hall.

Hawawini, G. (ed.) (1982). *Bond Duration and Immunization: Early Developments and Recent Contributions.* New York and London: Garland Publishing.

Hessel, C. and L. Huffman (1981). The effect of taxation on immunization rules and duration estimation. *Journal of Finance*, 36(December), 1127–1142.

Homer, S. and M. L. Leibowitz (1972). *Inside the Yield Book.* New York: Prentice-Hall, and New York Institute of Finance.

Hopewell, M. and G. G. Kaufman (1973). Bond price volatility and terms to maturity: A generalized respecification. *American Economic Review*, 63(September), 749–753.

Ingersoll, J., J. Skelton and R. Weil (1978). Duration: Forty years later. *Journal of Financial and Quantitative Analysis*, 13(November), 627–650.

John, L. M., L. M. Donald, E. P. Jerald and W. M. Dennis (2007). *Managing Investment Portfolios: A Dynamic Process*, 3rd ed. New York: CFA Institute.

Lanstein, R. and W. Sharpe (1978). Duration and security risk. *Journal of Financial and Quantitative Analysis*, 13(November), 653–668.

Leibowitz, M. L. (1982). Contingent immunization, Part I: Risk control procedures. *Financial Analysts Journal*, 38(November/December), 17–32.

Leibowitz, M. L. (1983). Contingent immunization, Part II: Problem cases. *Financial Analysts Journal*, 39(January/February), 35–50.

Leibowitz, M. L. and A. Weinberger (1981). The uses of contingent immunization. *Journal of Portfolio Management*, 8(Fall), 51–55.

Malkiel, B. (1962). Expectations, bond prices, and the term structure of interest rates. *Quarterly Journal of Economics*, 76(May), 197–218.

Macaulay, F. (1938). *Some Theoretical Problems Suggested by the Movement of Interest Rates, Bond Yields, and Stock Prices in the U.S. Since 1865.* New York: National Bureau of Economic Research.

McEnally, R. (1977). Duration as a practical tool in bond management. *Journal of Portfolio Management*, 3(Summer), 53–57.

Reilly, F. K. and R. S. Sidhu (1980). Many uses of bond duration. *Financial Analysts Journal*, 36(July/August), 58–72.

Saunders, A. and M. M. Cornett (2010). *Financial Institutions Management*, 7th ed. New York: McGraw-Hill.

Saunders, A. and M. M. Cornett (2011). *Financial Markets and Institutions*, 5th ed. New York: McGraw-Hill.

Weil, R. (1973). Macaulay's duration: An appreciation. *Journal of Business*, 46(October), 589–592.

Yawitz, J. (1977). The relative importance of duration and yield volatility on bond price volatility. *Journal of Money Credit and Banking*, 9(February), 97–102.

Chapter 15

Constant Elasticity of Variance Option Pricing Model: Detailed Derivation and Implied Variance Estimation*

Contents

*This chapter is a modification of the paper by Hsu *et al.* (2008). Constant elasticity of variance (CEV) option pricing model: Integration and detailed derivation. *Mathematics and Computers in Simulation*, 79(1), 60–71.

15.1 Introduction

In Chapter 12, we have discussed the specification and application of the Black–Scholes option pricing model and constant electricity option pricing model. In this chapter, we will discuss the detailed derivation of the CEV model. In Section 15.2, we will discuss the CEV Diffusion and its Transition Probability Density Function. A review of the Non-central Chi-Square Distribution will be presented in Section 15.3. Section 15.4 will present the Non-central Chi-Square Approach to the Option Pricing Model. Section 15.5 will summarize the results of this chapter. Appendix 15A presents Feller's Lemma. Appendix 15B shows how to use Excel program to estimate the implied variance of CEV model.

15.2 The CEV Diffusion and its Transition Probability Density Function

The CEV option pricing model assumes that the stock price is governed by the diffusion process

$$dS = \mu S dt + \sigma S^{\frac{\beta}{2}} dZ, \quad \beta < 2, \tag{15.1}$$

where dZ is a Wiener process and σ is a positive constant. Since the return variance $\upsilon(S,t) = \sigma^2 S^{\beta-2}$, then the elasticity is $\beta - 2$ as follows:

$$\frac{d\upsilon(S,t)/dS}{\upsilon(S,t)/S} = \beta - 2,$$

which implies that $d\upsilon(S,t)/\upsilon(S,t) = \beta - 2dS/S$. Upon integration on both sides, we have $\log \upsilon(S,t) = (\beta - 2)\log S + \log \sigma^2$, or $\upsilon(S,t) = \upsilon(S,t) = \sigma^2 S^{\beta-2}$.

If $\beta = 2$, then the elasticity is zero and the stock prices are lognormally distributed as in the Black and Scholes model. If $\beta = 1$, then Equation (15.1) is the model proposed by Cox and Ross (1976).

In this chapter, we will focus on the case of $\beta < 2$ since many pieces of empirical evidence (see Campbell, 1987; Glosten *et al.*, 1993; Brandt and Kang, 2004) have shown that the relationship between the stock price and its return volatility is negative. The transition density for $\beta > 2$ is given by Emanuel and MacBeth (1982) and the corresponding CEV option pricing formula can be derived through a similar strategy. For more details, see Chen and Lee (1993).

In order to derive the CEV option pricing model, we need the transition probability density function $f(S_T|S_t, T > t)$ of the stock price at time T given the current stock price S_t. For the transition probability density function $f(S_T|S_t)$, we will start with the Kolmogorov forward and backward equations.

Assume X_t follows the diffusion process

$$dX = \mu(X,t)dt + \sigma(X,t)dZ \tag{15.2}$$

and $P = P(X_t, t)$ is the function of X_t and t, then P satisfies the partial differential equations of motion. From Equation (15.2), we have the Kolmogorov backward equation

$$\frac{1}{2}\sigma^2(X_0,t_0)\frac{\partial^2 P}{\partial X_0^2} + \mu(X_0,t_0)\frac{\partial P}{\partial X_0} + \frac{\partial P}{\partial t_0} = 0 \tag{15.3}$$

and the Kolmogorov forward (or Fokker–Planck) equation

$$\frac{1}{2}\frac{\partial^2}{\partial X_t^2}\left[\sigma^2(X,t)P\right] - \frac{\partial P}{\partial X_t}\left[\mu(X_t,t)P\right] - \frac{\partial P}{\partial t} = 0. \tag{15.4}$$

Consider the following parabolic equation:

$$(P)_t = (axP)_{xx} - ((bx+h)P)_x, \quad 0 < x < \infty, \tag{15.5}$$

where $P = P(x,t)$, and are constants with $a > 0, (P)_t$ is the partial derivative of P with respect to t, $()_x$ and $()_{xx}$ are the first and second partial derivatives, respectively, of $()$ with respect to x. This can be interpreted as the Fokker–Planck equation of a diffusion problem in which $bx + h$ represents the drift, and ax represents the diffusion coefficient.

Lemma 15.1. (*Feller, 1951*): *Let $xf(x,t\,|x_0)$ be the probability density function for x and t conditional on x_0. The explicit form of the fundamental solution to the above parabolic equation is given by*

$$f(t,x\,|x_0) = \frac{b}{a(e^{-bt}-1)}\left(\frac{e^{-bt}x}{x_0}\right)^{(h-a)/2a} \exp\times\left\{\frac{-b(x+x_0e^{bt})}{a(e^{bt}-1)}\right\}$$
$$\times I_{1-h/a}\left(\frac{2b}{a(1-e^{-bt})}(e^{-bt}xx_0)^{\frac{1}{2}}\right), \tag{15.6}$$

where $I_x(x)$ is the modified Bessel function of the first kind of order k and is defined as

$$I_k(x) = \sum_{r=0}^{\infty}\frac{(x/2)^{2r+k}}{r!\Gamma(r+1+k)}. \tag{15.7}$$

Proof. See Appendix 15A. □

Before pursuing further, we will first consider the special case in which $\beta = 1$, which is the model considered by Cox and Ross (1976). In this situation, we have

$$dS = \mu(S,t)dt + \sigma(S,t)dZ, \tag{15.8}$$

where $\sigma(S,t) = \sigma\sqrt{S}$.

Now, suppose also that each unit of the stock pays out in dividends in the continuous stream $b(S,t)$ so that the required mean becomes $\mu(S,t) = rS - b(S,t) = rS-(aS+h)$, where $b(S,t) = aS+h$ and r is the risk-free interest rate. Then, $dS = [(r-a)S-h]dt + \sigma\sqrt{S}dz$ and the differential option price equation becomes

$$\frac{1}{2}\sigma^2 S\frac{\partial^2 P}{\partial S^2} + [(r-a)S-h]\frac{\partial P}{\partial S} + \frac{\partial P}{\partial t} = rP, \tag{15.9}$$

and the corresponding Kolmogorov forward equation for the diffusion process (Equation 15.8) is

$$\frac{1}{2}\frac{\partial^2}{\partial S_t^2}(\sigma^2 S_T P) + \frac{\partial}{\partial S_T}[((r-a)S-h)P] - \frac{\partial P}{\partial t} = 0, \tag{15.10}$$

which is obtained by using Equation (15.14) with $\mu(x_t,t) = (r-a)S-h$.

Comparing with Equation (15.6), we set $a = \sigma^2/2$, $x = S_T, x_0 = S_t$, $b = r-\sigma^2/2, h = -h$ and $t = \tau = (T-t)$. Thus, we have the following transition probability density function for the Cox–Ross model:

$$
\begin{aligned}
f(S_T\,|S_t, T > t) = {} & \frac{2(r-\sigma^2/2)}{\sigma^2[e^{(r-\sigma^2/2)\tau}-1]} \times \left(\frac{S_t e^{(r-\sigma^2/2)\tau}}{S_T}\right)^{(1+2h/\sigma^2)/2} \\
& \times \left\{\frac{-2(r-\sigma^2/2)[S_T + S_t e^{(r-\sigma^2/2)\tau}]}{\sigma^2[e^{(r-\sigma^2/2)\tau}-1]}\right\} I_{1+2h/\sigma^2} \\
& \times \left(\frac{4(r-\sigma^2/2)(S_t S_T e^{(r-\sigma^2/2)\tau})^{\frac{1}{2}}}{\sigma^2[e^{(r-\sigma^2/2)\tau}-1]\sigma^2}\right). \qquad (15.11)
\end{aligned}
$$

We next consider the CEV diffusion,

$$
dS = \mu(S,t) + \sigma(S,t)dZ, \qquad (15.12)
$$

where

$$
\mu(S,t) = rS - aS \qquad (15.13)
$$

and

$$
\sigma(S,t) = \sigma S^{\beta/2} dZ, \;\; 0 \le \beta < 2. \qquad (15.14)
$$

Then,

$$
dS = (r-a)Sdt + \sigma S^{\frac{\beta}{2}} dZ. \qquad (15.15)
$$

Let $Y = Y(S,t) = S^{2-\beta}$. By Ito's Lemma with

$$
\frac{\partial Y}{\partial S} = (2-\beta)S^{1-\beta}, \;\; \frac{\partial Y}{\partial t} = 0, \;\; \frac{\partial^2 Y}{\partial S^2} = (2-\beta)(1-\beta)S^{-\beta},
$$

we have

$$
dY = \left[(r-a)(2-\beta)Y - \frac{1}{2}\sigma^2(\beta-1)(\beta-2)\right] dt + \sigma^2(2-\beta)^2 Y dZ. \qquad (15.16)
$$

The Kolmogorov forward equation for Y becomes

$$\begin{aligned}\frac{\partial P}{\partial t} &= \frac{1}{2}\frac{\partial^2}{\partial Y^2}\left[\sigma^2(2-\beta)YP\right] \\ &\quad - \frac{\partial}{\partial Y}\left\{\left[(r-a)(2-\beta)Y + \frac{1}{2}\sigma^2(\beta-1)(\beta-2)\right]P\right\}.\end{aligned} \tag{15.17}$$

Then, $f(S_T|S_t, T>t) = f(Y_T\,|y_t, T>t)|J|$ where $J = (2-\beta)S^{1-\beta}$. By Feller's Lemma with $a = \frac{1}{2}\sigma^2(2-\beta)^2, b = (r-a)(2-\beta)$, $h = \frac{1}{2}\sigma^2(\beta-2)(1-\beta), x = \frac{1}{T}, x_0 = 1$ and $t = \tau = (T-t)$, we have

$$\begin{aligned}f(S_T|S_t, T>t) &= (2-\beta)k^{*1/(2-\beta)}(xz^{1-\beta})^{1/(2(2-\beta))} \\ &\quad \times e^{-x-z}I_{1/(2-\beta)}(2(xz)^{1/2}),\end{aligned} \tag{15.18}$$

where

$$k^* = \frac{2(r-a)}{\sigma^2(2-\beta)[e^{(r-a)(2-\beta)\tau}-1]},\quad x = k^*S_t^{2-\beta}e^{(r-a)(2-\beta)\tau},\quad z = k^*S_T^{2-\beta}.$$

Cox (1975) obtained the following option pricing formula:

$$\begin{aligned}C &= S_te^{-r\tau}\sum_{n=0}^{\infty}\frac{e^{-x}x^nG(n+1+1/(2-\beta), k^*K^{2-\beta})}{\Gamma(n+1)} \\ &\quad - Ke^{-r\tau}\sum_{n=0}^{\infty}\frac{e^{-x}x^{n+1/(2-\beta)}G(n+1, k^*K^{2-\beta})}{\Gamma(n+1+1/(2-\beta))},\end{aligned} \tag{15.19}$$

where $G(m,v) = [\Gamma(m)]^{-1}\int_v^{\infty}e^{-u}u^{m-1}du$ is the standard complementary gamma distribution function.

For a proof of the above formula, see Chen and Lee (1993). We next present the detailed derivations of the option pricing formula as presented by Schroder (1989). Since the option pricing formula is expressed in terms of the non-central Chi-square complementary distribution function, a brief review of the non-central Chi-square distribution is presented in the next section.

15.3 Review of Non-central Chi-Square Distribution

If $Z_1, \ldots, Z_v$ are standard normal random variables, and $\delta_1, \ldots, \delta_v$ are constants, then

$$Y = \sum_{i=1}^{v} (Z_i + \delta_i)^2 \tag{15.20}$$

is the non-central Chi-square distribution with degrees of freedom and non-centrality parameter $\lambda = \sum_{j=1}^{v} \delta_j^2$, and is denoted as $\chi_v'^2(\lambda)$. When $\delta_j = 0$ for all j, then Y is distributed as the central Chi-square distribution with v degrees of freedom, and is denoted as χ_v^2. The cumulative distribution function of $\chi_v'^2(\lambda)$ is

$$\begin{aligned} F(x; v, \lambda) &= P(\chi_v'^2(\lambda) \leq x) \\ &= e^{-\lambda/2} \sum_{j=0}^{\infty} \frac{(\lambda/2)j}{j! 2^{v/2} \Gamma(v/2 + j)} \times \int_0^x y^{v/2+j-1} e^{-\frac{y}{2}} dy, \quad x > 0. \end{aligned} \tag{15.21}$$

An alternative expression for $F(x; v, \lambda)$ is

$$F(x; v, \lambda) = \sum_{j=0}^{\infty} \left(\frac{(\lambda/2)^j e^{-\lambda/2}}{j!} \right) P(\chi_{v+2j}^2 \leq x). \tag{15.22}$$

The complementary distribution function of $\chi_v'^2(\lambda)$ is

$$Q(x; v, \lambda) = 1 - F(x; v, \lambda), \tag{15.23}$$

where $F(x; v, \lambda)$ is given in either Equation (15.21) or Equation (15.22).

The probability density function of $\chi_v'^2(\lambda)$ can be expressed as a mixture of central Chi-square probability density functions:

$$\begin{aligned} P_{\chi_v'^2(\lambda)}(x) &= e^{-\lambda/2} \sum_{j=0}^{\infty} \frac{\left(\frac{1}{2}\lambda\right)^j}{j!} p_{\chi_{v+2j}^2}(x) \\ &= \frac{e^{-(x+\lambda)/2}}{2^{v/2}} \sum_{j=0}^{\infty} \frac{x^{v/2+j-1} \lambda^j}{\Gamma(v/2 + j) 2^{2j} j!}. \end{aligned} \tag{15.24}$$

An alternative expression for the probability density function of $\chi_v'^2(\lambda)$ is

$$P_{\chi_v'^2(\lambda)}(x) = \frac{1}{2}\left(\frac{x}{\lambda}\right)^{(v-2)/4} \exp\left\{-\frac{1}{2}(\lambda + x)\right\} \times I_{(v-2)/2}(\sqrt{\lambda x}),\ x > 0, \tag{15.25}$$

where I_k is the modified Bessel function of the first kind of order k and is defined as

$$I_k(z) = \left(\frac{1}{2}z\right)^k \sum_{j=0}^{\infty} \frac{(z^2/4)^j}{j!\Gamma(k + j + 1)}. \tag{15.26}$$

It is noted that for integer k,

$$I_k(z) = \frac{1}{\pi}\int_0^{\pi} e^{z\cos(k\theta)} \cos(k\theta)d\theta = I_{-k}(z). \tag{15.27}$$

The non-central Chi-square distribution satisfies the reproductive property with respect to n and λ. If $X_1, \ldots, X_k$ are independent random variables with X_t distributed as $\chi_{n_i}'^2(\lambda_i)$, then

$$Y = \sum_{i=1}^{k} X_i \sim \chi'^2_{\sum_{i=1}^{k} n_i}\left(\sum_{i=1}^{k} \lambda_i\right). \tag{15.28}$$

15.4 The Non-central Chi-Square Approach to Option Pricing Model

Cox (1975) derived the renowned CEV option pricing model and Schroder (1989) subsequently extended the model by expressing the CEV option pricing formula in terms of the non-central Chi-square distribution. However, neither of them has given details of their derivations as well as the mathematical and statistical tools in deriving the formulae.

Following Schroder (1989), with the transition probability density function given in Equation (15.18), the option pricing formula under the CEV model is

$$\begin{aligned}C &= E(\max(0, S_T - K)) \quad \tau = T - t\\ &= e^{-r\tau}\int_K^{\infty} f(S_T\,|S_t,\, T > t)(S_T - K)dS_T\\ &= e^{-r\tau}\int_K^{\infty} S_T f(S_T\,|S_t,\, T > t)dS_T\\ &\quad - e^{-r\tau}K\int_K^{\infty} f(S_T\,|S_t,\; T > t)dS_T\\ &= C_1 - C_2. \end{aligned} \tag{15.29}$$

15.4.1 *Detailed derivations of C1 and C2*

Making the change of variable $w = k^* S_T^{2-\beta}$, we have

$$dS_T = (2-\beta)^{-1} k^{*-1/(2-\beta)} w^{(\beta-1)/(2-\beta)} dw.$$

Thus, with $y = k^* K^{2-\beta}$, we have

$$\begin{aligned}C_1 &= e^{-r\tau}\int_y^{\infty} e^{-x-w}(x/w)^{1/(4-2\beta)} \times I_{\frac{1}{2-\beta}}(2\sqrt{xw})(w/k^*)^{1/(2-\beta)}dw\\ &= e^{-r\tau}\int_y^{\infty} e^{-x-w}(x/w)^{1/(4-2\beta)}\\ &\quad \times I_{\frac{1}{2-\beta}}(2\sqrt{xw})(w/x)^{1/(2-\beta)}(x/k^*)^{1/(2-\beta)}dw\\ &= e^{-r\tau}(x/k^*)^{1/(2-\beta)}\int_y^{\infty} e^{-x-w}(x/w)^{-1/(4-2\beta)} \times I_{\frac{1}{2-\beta}}(2\sqrt{xw})dw\\ &= e^{-r\tau}S_t e^{(r-a)\tau}\int_y^{\infty} e^{-x-w}(w/x)^{1/(4-2\beta)} \times I_{\frac{1}{2-\beta}}(2\sqrt{xw})dw,\\ &= e^{-a\tau}S_t\int_y^{\infty} e^{-x-w}(w/x)^{1/(4-2\beta)} \times I_{\frac{1}{2-\beta}}(2\sqrt{xw})dw, \end{aligned} \tag{15.30}$$

and

$$C_2 = Ke^{-r\tau}\int_y^{\infty}(2-\beta)k^{*1/(2-\beta)}(xw^{1-2\beta})^{\frac{1}{4-2\beta}}e^{-x-w}$$

$$\times I_{\frac{1}{2-\beta}}(2\sqrt{xw})\frac{k^{*-1/(2-\beta)}}{2-\beta}w^{\frac{\beta-1}{2-\beta}}dw$$

$$= Ke^{-r\tau}\int_y^{\infty}x^{\frac{1}{4-2\beta}}w^{(1-2\beta+2\beta-2)/(4-2\beta)}e^{-x-w}\times I_{\frac{1}{2-\beta}}(2\sqrt{xw})dw$$

$$= Ke^{-r\tau}\int_y^{\infty}e^{-x-w}(x/w)^{1/(4-\beta)}I_{\frac{1}{2-\beta}}(2\sqrt{xw})dw. \quad (15.31)$$

Recall that the probability density function of the non-central Chi-square distribution with non-centrality λ and degree of freedom υ is

$$P_{\chi_{\upsilon}'^2(\lambda)}(x) = \frac{1}{2}(x/\lambda)^{(\upsilon-2)/4}I_{(\upsilon-2)/2}(\sqrt{\lambda x})e^{-(\lambda+x)/2}$$

$$= P(x;\upsilon,\lambda).$$

Let $Q(x;\upsilon,\lambda) = \int_x^{\infty}P_{\chi_{\upsilon}'^2(\lambda)}(y)dy$. Then, letting $w' = 2w$ and $x' = 2x$, we have

$$C_1 = S_te^{-a\tau}\int_y^{\infty}e^{-(x+w)/2}\left(\frac{w}{x}\right)^{1/(4-2\beta)}I_{\frac{1}{2-\beta}}(2\sqrt{xw})dw$$

$$= S_te^{-a\tau}\int_{2y}^{\infty}e^{-(x'+w')/2}\left(\frac{w'}{x'}\right)^{1/(4-2\beta)}I_{\frac{1}{2-\beta}}(2\sqrt{x'w'})dw'$$

$$= S_te^{-a\tau}Q(2y;\upsilon,x'),$$

$$= S_te^{-a\tau}Q\left(2y;2+\frac{2}{2-\beta},2x\right), \quad (15.32)$$

obtained by noting that $(\upsilon-2)/2, 1/(2-\beta)$, implying $\upsilon = 2+2/(2-\beta)$. Analogously, with $w' = 2w$, $x' = 2x$, and $I_n(z) = I_{-n}(z)$, we have

$$C_2 = Ke^{-r\tau}\int_y^{\infty}e^{-x-w}\left(\frac{x}{w}\right)^{1/(4-2\beta)}I_{\frac{1}{2-\beta}}(2\sqrt{xw})dw$$

$$= Ke^{-r\tau}\int_{2y}^{\infty}e^{-(x'+w')/2}\left(\frac{x'}{w'}\right)^{1/(4-2\beta)}\times I_{\frac{1}{2-\beta}}(2\sqrt{x'w'})dw'$$

$$= Q\left(2y;2-\frac{2}{2-\beta},2x\right), \quad (15.33)$$

obtained by noting that $(\upsilon^* - 2)/2 = -1/(2-\beta)$, implying $\upsilon^* = 2 - 2/(2-\beta)$. Thus,

$$C = S_r e^{-a\tau} Q\left(2y; 2 + \frac{2}{2-\beta}, 2x\right) - K e^{-r\tau} Q\left(2y; 2 + \frac{2}{2-\beta}, 2x\right). \tag{15.34}$$

It is noted that $2-2/(2-\beta)$ can be negative for $\beta < 2$. Thus, further work is needed. Using the monotone convergence theorem and the integration by parts, we have

$$\begin{aligned}\int_y^\infty P(2y, 2\upsilon, 2k)dk &= \int_y^\infty e^{-z-k}(z/k)^{\upsilon-1}\sqrt{kz}^{\upsilon-1} \\ &\quad \times \sum_{n=0}^\infty \frac{(zk)^n}{n!\Gamma(n+\upsilon-1+1)}dk \\ &= \int_y^\infty \frac{e^{-z}z^{n+\upsilon-1}}{\Gamma(n+\upsilon)}\int_y^\infty \frac{e^{-k}k^n}{\Gamma(n+1)}dk \\ &= \sum_{n=0}^\infty g(n+\upsilon, z)G(n+1, y) \\ &= \sum_{n=0}^\infty g(n+\upsilon-1, z)\sum_{i=1}^\infty g(i, y). \qquad (15.35)\end{aligned}$$

Now, we also have the result $G(n, y) = \sum_{i=1}^\infty g(i, y)$, which can be shown by observing that

$$\begin{aligned}G(n, y) &= \int_y^\infty \frac{e^{-k}k^{n-1}}{\Gamma(n)}dk = -\int_y^\infty \frac{k^{n-1}}{\Gamma(n)}de^{-k} \\ &= \frac{y^{n-1}e^{-y}}{\Gamma(n)} + \int_y^\infty \frac{k^{n-2}e^{-k}}{\Gamma(n-1)}dk \\ &= \sum_{i=1}^n \frac{y^{i-1}e^{-y}}{\Gamma(i)} = \sum_{i=1}^n g(i, y).\end{aligned}$$

The above result can also be expressed as

$$G(m+1, t) = G(m+1, t) + G(m, t). \tag{15.36}$$

Next, applying the monotone convergence theorem, we have

$$\begin{aligned}
Q(z;\upsilon,k) &= \int_z^\infty \frac{1}{2}\left(\frac{y}{k}\right)^{(\upsilon-2)/4} I_{\frac{\upsilon-2}{2}}(\sqrt{ky})e^{-(k+y)/2}dy \\
&= \int_z^\infty \frac{1}{2}\left(\frac{y}{k}\right)^{(\upsilon-2)/4}\left(\frac{1}{2}\sqrt{ky}\right)^{(\upsilon-2)/2} \\
&\quad \times \sum_{n=0}^{\infty}\frac{(ky/4)^n}{n!\Gamma\left(\frac{\upsilon+2n}{2}\right)}e^{-(k+y)/2}dy \\
&= \sum_{n=0}^{\infty} e^{-k/2}\frac{k^n\left(\frac{1}{2}\right)^n}{\Gamma(n+1)} \times \int_z^\infty \frac{(1/2)^{(\upsilon+2n)/2}}{\left(\frac{1}{2}\right)^{-(\upsilon+2n)/2}\Gamma\left(\frac{\upsilon+2n}{2}\right)}dy \\
&= \sum_{n=0}^{\infty} e^{-k/2}\frac{(k/2)^n}{\Gamma(n+1)} \times \int_z^\infty \frac{(1/2)^{(\upsilon+2n)/2}}{\Gamma\left(\frac{\upsilon-2n}{2}\right)}e^{-y/2}y^{\frac{\upsilon+2n}{2}-1}dy \\
&= \sum_{n=0}^{\infty} e^{-k/2}\frac{(k/2)^n}{\Gamma(n+1)}Q(z;\upsilon+2n,0), \qquad (15.37)
\end{aligned}$$

where

$$\begin{aligned}
Q(x;\upsilon+2n,0) &= \int_z^\infty \frac{(1/2)^{(\upsilon+2n)/2}}{\Gamma\left(\frac{\upsilon+2n}{2}\right)}e^{-y/2}y^{\frac{\upsilon+2n}{2}-1}dy \\
&= \int_{z/2}^\infty \frac{1}{\Gamma\left(\frac{\upsilon+2n}{2}\right)}e^{-y}y^{\frac{\upsilon+2n}{2}-1}dy \\
&= G(n+\upsilon/2, z/2).
\end{aligned}$$

Furthermore, from the property of $G(\cdot,\cdot)$ as shown in Equation (15.36), we have

$$\begin{aligned}
Q(z;\upsilon,k) &= \sum_{n=0}^{\infty} g(n+1,k/2)G(n+\upsilon/2,z/2) \\
&= \sum_{n=0}^{\infty} g(n,k/2)G\left(n+\frac{\upsilon-2}{2},z/2\right). \qquad (15.38)
\end{aligned}$$

Hence,

$$Q(2z;2\upsilon,2k) = \sum_{n=0}^{\infty} g(n,k)G(n+\upsilon-1,z).$$

Again from the property of $G(\cdot,\cdot)$ as given by Equation (15.36), we have

$$\begin{aligned}
Q(2z;2\upsilon,2k) &= g(1,k)G(\upsilon,z) + g(2,k)G(\upsilon+1,z) \\
&\quad + g(3,k)G(\upsilon+2,z) + \cdots \\
&= g(1,k)[G(\upsilon-1,z) + g(\upsilon,z)] + g(2,k)[G(\upsilon-1,z) \\
&\quad + g(\upsilon+1,z)] + g(3,k)[G(\upsilon-1,z) + g(\upsilon,z) \\
&\quad + g(\upsilon+1,z) + g(\upsilon+2,z)] + \cdots \\
&= [G(\upsilon-1,z) + g(\upsilon,z)]\sum_{n=1}^{\infty} g(n,k) \\
&\quad + g(\upsilon+1,z)\sum_{n=2}^{\infty} g(n,k) + g(\upsilon+2,z)\sum_{n=3}^{\infty} g(n,k) + \cdots \\
&= G(\upsilon-1,z) + g(\upsilon,z) + g(\upsilon+1,z)[1-g(1,k)] \\
&\quad + g(\upsilon+2,z)\,[1-g(1,k)-g(2,k)] + \cdots \\
&= G(\upsilon-1,z) + \sum_{n=0}^{\infty} g(\upsilon+n,z) - g(\upsilon+1,z)[g(1,k)] \\
&\quad - g(\upsilon+2,z)[g(1,k)+g(2,k)] + \cdots \\
&= 1 - g(\upsilon+1,z)[g(1,k)t] - g(\upsilon+2,z) \\
&\quad \times [g(1,k) + g(2,k)] - \cdots .
\end{aligned}$$

We conclude that

$$Q(2z;2\upsilon,2k) = 1 - \sum_{n=1}^{\infty} g(n+\upsilon,z)\sum_{i=1}^{n} g(i,k). \tag{15.39}$$

From Equations (15.35) and (15.39), we observe that

$$\int_{y}^{\infty} P(2z;2\upsilon,2k)dk = 1 - Q(2z;2(\upsilon-1),2y). \tag{15.40}$$

Thus, we can write C_2 as

$$\begin{aligned}C_2 &= Ke^{-r\tau}\int_y^{\infty} P\left(2x; 2+\frac{2}{2-\beta}, 2w\right)dw\\&= Ke^{-r\tau}Q\left(2y; 2-\frac{2}{2-\beta}, 2x\right)\\&= Ke^{-r\tau}\left(1-Q\left(2x; \frac{2}{2-\beta}, 2y\right)\right).\end{aligned} \tag{15.41}$$

From Equation (15.41), we immediately obtain

$$Q\left(2y; 2-\frac{2}{2-\beta}, 2x\right) + Q\left(2x; \frac{2}{2-\beta}, 2y\right) = 1, \tag{15.42}$$

implying

$$Q(z; 2n, k) + Q(k; 2-2n, z) = 1, \tag{15.43}$$

with degrees of freedom $2-2n$ of $Q(k; 2-2n, z)$ can be a non-integer.

From Equation (15.42), we can obtain that the non-central Chi-square $Q(2y; 2-2/(2-\beta), 2x)$ with $2-2/(2-\beta)$ degrees of freedom and the non-centrality parameter $2x$ can be represented by another non-central Chi-square distribution $1-Q(2x; 2-2/(2-\beta), 2y)$ with degrees of freedom $2/(2-\beta)$ and the non-centrality parameter $2y$. The standard definition of non-central Chi-square distribution in Section 15.4 has integer degrees of freedom. If the degree of freedom is not an integer, we can use Equation (15.43) to transfer the original non-central Chi-square distribution into another non-central Chi-square distribution. Thus, we obtain an option pricing formula for the CEV model in terms of the complementary non-central Chi-square distribution function $Q(z; v, k)$ which is valid for any value of β less than 2, as required by the model.

Substituting Equation (15.41) into Equation (15.34), we obtain

$$C = S_t e^{-a\tau}Q\left(2y; 2+\frac{2}{2-\beta}, 2x\right) - Ke^{-r\tau}\left(1-Q\left(2x; \frac{2}{2-\beta}, 2y\right)\right), \tag{15.44}$$

where $y = k^*K^{2-\beta}$, $x = k^*S_t^{2-\beta}\, e^{(r-a)(2-\beta)\tau}$, $k^* = 2(r-a)/(\sigma^2(2-\beta)(e^{(r-a)(2-\beta)\tau}-1))$ and a is the continuous proportional dividend rate. The corresponding CEV option pricing formula for $\beta > 2$ can be derived through a similar manner. When $\beta > 2$ (see Emanuel and MacBeth, 1982; Chen and Lee, 1993), the call option formula is as follows:

$$C = S_t e^{-a\tau} Q\left(2x; \frac{2}{\beta - 2}, 2y\right) - Ke^{-r\tau}\left(1 - Q\left(2y; 2 + \frac{2}{\beta - 2}, 2x\right)\right). \tag{15.45}$$

We note that from the evaluation of the option pricing formula C, especially C_2, as given in Equation (15.34), we have

$$2k^* S_T^{2-\beta} \sim \chi_v'^2(\lambda), \tag{15.46}$$

where

$$v = 2 - \frac{2}{2 - \beta},$$
$$\lambda = 2k^* S_t^{2-\beta} e^{(r-a)(2-\beta)\tau}.$$

Thus, the option pricing formula for the CEV model as given in Equation (15.44) that can be obtained directly from the payoff function

$$\max(S_T - K, 0) = \begin{cases} S_T - K, & \text{if } S_T > K \\ 0, & \text{otherwise} \end{cases} \tag{15.47}$$

by taking the expectation of Equation (15.47), with S_T having the distribution given by Equation (15.46).

Before concluding this subsection, we consider that the non-central Chi-square distribution will approach log-normal as β tends to 2. Since either λ or v approaches to infinity, the standardized variable

$$\frac{\chi_v'^2(\lambda) - (v + \lambda)}{\sqrt{2(v + 2\lambda)}},$$

tends to $N(0,1)$ as either $v \to \infty$ or $\lambda \to \infty$. Using the fact that $(x^a - 1)/a$ will approach to $\ln x$ as $a \to \infty$, it can be verified that

$$\begin{aligned}
\frac{\chi_v'^2(\lambda) - (v+\lambda)}{\sqrt{2(v+2\lambda)}} &= \frac{2k^* S_T^{2-\beta} - (v+\lambda)}{\sqrt{2(v+2\lambda)}} \\
&= \frac{\begin{array}{c} 2r^\bullet S_T^{2-\beta} - (1-\beta)\sigma^2(e^{r^\bullet \tau(2-\beta)} - 1) \\ -2r^\bullet S_t^{2-\beta} e^{r^\bullet \tau(2-\beta)} \end{array}}{\sigma^2(e^{r^\bullet \tau(2-\beta)} - 1)} \\
&\quad \cdot \sqrt{\frac{\sigma^2\left(e^{r^\bullet \tau(2-\beta)} - 1\right)/(2-\beta)}{(1-\beta)\sigma^2(e^{r^\bullet \tau(2-\beta)} - 1) + 4r^\bullet S_t^{2-\beta} e^{r^\bullet \tau(2-\beta)}}} \\
&= \frac{\ln S_T - [\ln S_t + (r^\bullet - \sigma^2/2)\tau]}{\sigma\sqrt{\tau}},
\end{aligned}$$

where $r^\bullet = r - a$. Thus,

$$\ln S_T \,|\ln S_t \sim N(\ln S_t + (r - a - \sigma^2/2)\tau, \sigma^2\tau), \tag{15.48}$$

as $\beta \to 2^-$. Similarly, Equation (15.48) also holds when $\beta \to 2^+$. From Equation (15.45), we have $2k^* S_T^{2-\beta} \sim \chi_v'^2(\lambda)$, where $v = 2 + 2/(\beta - 2)$ if $\beta > 2$. Thus, we clarify the result of Equation (15.48).

15.4.2 *Some computational considerations*

As noted by Schroder (1989), Equation (28.39) allows the following iterative algorithm to be used in computing the infinite sum when z and k are not large. First, initialize the following four variables (with $n = 1$):

$$gA = \frac{e^{-z} z^v}{\Gamma(1+v)} = g(1+v, z),$$

$$gB = e^{-k} = g(1,k),$$

$$Sg = gB,$$

$$R = 1 - (gA)(Sg).$$

Then, repeat the following loop beginning with $n = 2$ and increase increment n by one after each iteration. The loop is terminated when the contribution to the sum, R, is declining and is very small.

$$gA = gA\left(\frac{z}{n+\upsilon-1}\right) = g(n+\upsilon, z),$$

$$gB = gB\left(\frac{k}{n-1}\right) = g(n,k),$$

$$Sg = Sg + gB = g(1,k) + g(n,k),$$

$$R = R - (gA)(Sg) = \text{the}\, n\text{th partial sum}.$$

As each iteration gA equals $g(n+\upsilon, z), gB$ equals $g(n,k)$ and Sg equals $g(1,k) + \cdots + g(n,k)$. The computation is easily done.

As for an approximation, Sankaran (1963) showed that the distribution of $(\chi_{\upsilon}^{\prime 2}/(\upsilon+k))^h$ is approximately normal with the expected value $\mu = 1 + h(h-1)P - h(2-h)mP^2/2$ and variance $\sigma^2 = h^2P(1+mP)$, where $h = 1 - \frac{2}{3}(\upsilon+k)(\upsilon+3k)(\upsilon+2k)^{-2}$, $P = (\upsilon+2k)/(\upsilon+k)^2$ and $m = (h-1)(1-3h)$. Using the approximation, we have approximately

$$\begin{aligned} Q(z,\upsilon,k) &= Pr(\chi^{\prime 2} > z) \\ &= Pr\left(\frac{\chi^{\prime 2}}{\upsilon+k} > \frac{z}{\upsilon+k}\right) \\ &= Pr\left(\left(\frac{\chi^{\prime 2}}{\upsilon+k}\right)^h > \left(\frac{z}{\upsilon+k}\right)^h\right) \\ &= \Phi\left(\frac{1 - hP\left[1-h+0.5(2-h)mP\right] - \left(\frac{z}{\upsilon+k}\right)^h}{h\sqrt{2P(1+mP)}}\right). \end{aligned}$$

In Chapter 12, we have shown how Excel program can be used to estimate implied variance of Black–Scholes option pricing model. In Appendix 15B we show how Excel program can be used to estimate implied variance of CEV option pricing model.

15.5 Summary and Concluding Remark

In Chapter 12, we have discussed implied variance, volatility smile, and CEV option pricing model. In addition, we also show how Excel program can be used to estimate implied variance of Black–Scholes model. In this Chapter, we show how Excel program can be used to estimate implied variance of CEV model.

In Chapter 20, we will show how Ito calculus can be used to derive Black–Scholes option pricing model in detail. Overall, Chapters 12, 15, and 20 can be used to show students how Black–Scholes option pricing model and CEV option pricing model can be theoretically derived and applied to real-world analyses.

Questions and Problems

1. Please define the following terms:
   (a) diffusion process; (b) Ito's lemma; (c) standard complementary gamma distribution function; (d) non-central chi-square distribution; (e) Feller's lemma; (f) implied variance.
2. Please discuss the steps of deriving CEV type of option pricing model in some detail.
3. Please discuss the relationship between Black and Scholes OPM and CEV type of OPM.
4. Please based upon Appendix 15B to describe how the implied variance of CEV pricing model can be calculated in terms of Excel program.

Bibliography

Brandt, M. W. and Q. Kang (2004). On the relationship between the conditional mean and volatility of stock returns: A latent VAR approach. *Journal of Financial Economics*, 72, 217–257.

Campbell, J. (1987). Stock returns and the term structure. *Journal of Financial Economics*, 18, 373–399.

Chen, R. R. and C. F. Lee (1993). A constant elasticity of variance (CEV) family of stock price distributions in option pricing: Review and integration. *Journal of Financial Studies*, 1, 29–51.

Cox, J. (1975). Notes on option pricing I: Constant elasticity of variance diffusion, Unpublished Note, Standford University, Graduate School of Business. Also, *Journal of Portfolio Management* (1996), 23, 5–17.

Cox, J. and S. A. Ross (1976). The valuation of options for alternative stochastic processes. *Journal of Financial Economics*, 3, 145–166.

Emanuel, D. and J. MacBeth (1982). Further results on the constant elasticity of variance call option pricing formula. *Journal of Financial and Quantitative Analysis*, 17, 533–554.
Feller, W. (1951). Two singular diffusion problems. *Annals of Mathematics*, 54, 173–182.
Glosten, L., R. Jagannathan and D. Runkle (1993). On the relation between the expected value and the volatility of the nominal excess returns on stocks. *Journal of Finance*, 48, 1779–1802.
Hsu, Y. L., T. I. Lin and C. F. Lee (2008). Constant elasticity of variance (CEV) option pricing model: Integration and detailed derivation. *Mathematics and Computers in Simulation*, 79(1), 60–71.
Lee, J., J. R. Chang, L. J. Kao and C. F. Lee (2023). *Essentials of Excel VBA, Python, and R*. New York: Springer International Publishing.
Lee, C. F., Y. Chen and J. Lee (2016). Alternative methods to derive option pricing models: Review and comparison. *Review of Quantitative Finance and Accounting*, 47(2), 417–451.
Lee, C. F. and J. Lee (2015). *Handbook of Financial Econometrics and Statistics*. New York: Springer Academic Publishers.
Lee, C. F. and J. Lee (2020). *Handbook of Financial Econometrics, Mathematics, Statistics, and Machine Learning*. Singapore: World Scientific.
Lee, C. F., A. C. Lee and J. Lee (2010). *Handbook of Quantitative Finance and Risk Management*. New York: Springer Academic Publishers.
Lee, C. F., A. C. Lee and J. Lee (2023). *Handbook of Investment Analysis, Portfolio Management, and Financial Derivatives*. Singapore: World Scientific.
Lee, C. F., T. P. Wu and R. R. Chen (2004). The constant elasticity of variance models: New evidence from S&P 500 index options. *Review of Pacific Basin Financial Markets and Policies*, 7(2), 173–190.
Sankaran, M. (1963). Approximations to the non-central Chi-square distribution. *Biometrika*, 50, 199–204.
Schroder, M. (1989). Computing the constant elasticity of variance option pricing formula. *Journal of Finance*, 44, 211–219.

Appendix 15A: Proof of Feller's Lemma

We need some preliminary results in order to prove Equation (15.6).

Proposition 15A.1 *$f(z) = e^{Av/z}z^{-1}$ is the Laplace transformation of $I_0(2(Avx)^{1/2})$, where $I_k(x)$ is the Bessel function*

$$I_k(x) = \sum_{r=0}^{\infty} \frac{(x/2)^{2r+k}}{r!(r+1+k)}.$$

Proof. By the definition of Laplace transformation and the monotone convergence theorem, we have

$$\begin{aligned}
f(z) &= \int_0^\infty e^{-zx} I_0(2(Avx)^{1/2})dx \\
&= \int_0^\infty e^{-zx} \sum_0^\infty \frac{(Avx)^{1/2}}{r!\Gamma(r+1)} \\
&= \int_0^\infty e^{-zx} \left\{1 + \frac{(Avx)}{\Gamma(2)} + \frac{(Avx)^2}{2!\Gamma(3)} \right. \\
&\qquad \left. + \cdots + \frac{(Avx)^n}{n!\Gamma(n+1)} + \cdots \right\} \\
&= \frac{1}{z} + \frac{Av}{z^2} + \frac{(Av)^2}{2!z^3} + \cdots + \frac{(Av)^n}{n!z^{n+1}} + \cdots \\
&= \frac{1}{z}\left\{1 + \frac{Av}{z} + \frac{(Av)^2}{2!z^2} + \cdots + \frac{(Av)^n}{n!z^n}\right\} \\
&= e^{Av/z} z^{-1}.
\end{aligned}$$

□

Proposition 15A.2 *Consider the parabolic differential equation*

$$P_t = (axP)_{xx} - ((bx+h)P)_x, \quad 0 < x < \infty \tag{15.49}$$

where a, b, h are constants, $0 < h < a$, then the Laplace transformation of $f(t, x, x_0)$ with respect to x takes the form

$$\begin{aligned}
w(t, s; x_0) &= \int_0^\infty e^{-sx} f(t, x; x_0)dx \\
&= \left(\frac{b}{sa(e^{bt}-1)+b}\right)^{h/a} \exp\left\{\frac{-sbx_0e^{bt}}{sa(e^{bt}-1)+b}\right\} \\
&\quad \times \Gamma\left(1 - \frac{h}{a}; \frac{b^2x_0e^{bt}}{a(e^{bt}-1)(sa(e^{bt}-1)+b)}\right),
\end{aligned} \tag{15.50}$$

where $\Gamma(n; z) = \Gamma^{-1}(n)\int_0^z e^{-x}x^{n-1}dx$.

Proof. The proof of the lemma is too tedious and hence is omitted. For more details, please see Lemma 7 of Feller (1951).

We now turn to prove Equation (15.56). From Equation (15.50), let $A = \frac{bx_0}{a(1-e^{-bt})}$ and $z = \frac{1}{b}(sa(e^{bt}-1)+b)$. The $w(t,s;x_0)$ in Equation (15.50) can be rewritten as

$$w(t,s;x_0) = \frac{z^{-h/a}e^{-(1-1/z)A}}{\Gamma(1-h/a)}\int_0^{A/z} e^{-x}x^{-h/a}dx$$

$$= \frac{z^{-h/a}e^{-(1-1/z)A}}{\Gamma(1-h/a)} \times \int_0^1 e^{-Ax'/z}(Ax'/z)^{-h/a}(A/z)^{1-h/a}dx'$$

$$= \frac{A^{1-h/a}e^{-A}}{\Gamma(1-h/a)}\int_0^1 e^{A(1-x)'/z}(x')^{-h/a}z^{-1}dx'$$

$$= \frac{A^{1-h/a}e^{-A}}{\Gamma(1-h/a)}\int_0^1 e^{Av/z}(1-v)^{-h/a}z^{-1}dv.$$

By Proposition 28.1, we know that $f(z) = e^{Av/z}z^{-1}$ is the Laplace transformation of $I_0(2(AvX)^{1/2})$ and by the Fubini theorem, we have

$$w(t,s;x_0) = \frac{A^{1-h/a}e^{-A}}{\Gamma(1-h/a)}\int_0^1 (1-v)^{-h/a} \times \left[\int_0^\infty e^{-zx}I_0(2(Avx)^{1/2})dx\right]dv$$

$$= \frac{A^{1-h/a}e^{-A}}{\Gamma(1-h/a)} \times \int_0^\infty\int_0^1 (1-v)^{-h/a}e^{-zx}I_0(2(Avx)^{1/2})dxdv$$

$$= \frac{A^{2-h/a}e^{-A}}{\Gamma(1-h/a)x_0e^{bt}} \times \int_0^\infty \int_0^1 (1-v)^{-h/a}e^{-sx'}e^{-Ax'/(x_0e^{bt})} \times I_0(2A(e^{-bt}vx'/x_0)^{1/2})dvdx'.$$

Hence, upon comparing the two formulae for $w(t,s;x_0)$ and by the monotone convergence theorem, we have

$$f(t,x;x_0) = \frac{b}{\Gamma(1-h/a)a(e^{bt}-1)}\left[\frac{bx_0}{a(e^{bt}-1)}\right]^{1-h/a} \times \exp\left\{\frac{-b(x+x_0e^{bt})}{a(e^{bt}-1)}\right\}\int_0^1 (1-v)^{-h/a}I_0 \times \left(\frac{2b\left(e^{-bt}vxx_0\right)^{1/2}}{a\left(1-e^{-bt}\right)}\right)dv$$

$$
\begin{aligned}
&= \frac{b}{\Gamma(1-h/a)a(e^{bt}-1)}\left[\frac{bx_0}{a(e^{bt}-1)}\right]^{1-h/a} \\
&\quad \times \exp\left\{\frac{-b(x+x_0e^{bt})}{a(e^{bt}-1)}\right\}\int_0^1 (1-\upsilon)^{-h/a} \\
&\quad \times \sum_{r=0}^{\infty}\frac{\left[b(e^{-bt}\upsilon x x_0)^{1/2}/(a(1-e^{-bt}))\right]^{2r}}{r!\Gamma(r+1)} \\
&= \frac{b}{\Gamma(1-h/a)a(e^{bt}-1)}\left[\frac{bx_0}{a(e^{bt}-1)}\right]^{1-h/a} \\
&\quad \times \exp\left\{\frac{-b\left(x+x_0e^{bt}\right)}{a\left(e^{bt}-1\right)}\right\} \\
&\quad \times \sum_{r=0}^{\infty}\frac{\left[b(e^{-bt}x x_0)^{1/2}/(a(1-e^{-bt}))\right]^{2r}}{r!\Gamma(r+1)} \\
&\quad \times \int_0^1 (1-\upsilon)^{-h/a}\upsilon^r d\upsilon \\
&= \frac{b}{\Gamma(1-h/a)a(e^{bt}-1)}\left[\frac{bx_0}{a(e^{bt}-1)}\right]^{1-h/a} \\
&\quad \times \exp\left\{\frac{-b\left(x+x_0e^{bt}\right)}{a\left(e^{bt}-1\right)}\right\} \\
&\quad \times \sum_{r=0}^{\infty}\frac{\left[b(e^{-bt}x x_0)^{1/2}/(a(1-e^{-bt}))\right]^{2r}}{r!\Gamma(r+1)} \\
&\quad \times \frac{\Gamma(r+1)\Gamma(1-h/a)}{\Gamma(r+1+1-h/a)}.
\end{aligned}
$$

This completes the proof. □

Appendix 15B: Excel Program to Estimate European Call Option Price and Implied Variance with CEV Model

Following the CEV formula (Eq. (12.26)) in Chapter 12, we defined a diffusion model proposed by John Hull (2021) where risk-neutral process for a stock price S is

$$dS = (r - q)Sdt + \sigma S^{\alpha} dw,$$

where r is the risk-free rate, q is the dividend yield, σ is a volatility parameter, α is positive, and dw is a Wiener process.

The valuation formula for a European call option under the CEV model is

$$c = S_0 e^{-qT}[1 - \chi^2(a; b + 2, c)] - Ke^{-rT}\chi^2(a; b, c),$$

when $0 < \alpha < 1$, and

$$c = S_0 e^{-qT}[1 - \chi^2(a; -b + 2, c)] - Ke^{-rT}\chi^2(a; 2 - b, c),$$

when $\alpha > 1$, with

$$a = \frac{[Ke^{-(r-q)T}]^{2(1-\alpha)}}{(1-\alpha)^2 v}, \quad b = \frac{1}{1-\alpha}, \quad c = \frac{S^{2(1-\alpha)}}{(1-\alpha)^2 v},$$

where $v = \frac{\sigma^2}{2(r-q)(\alpha-1)}[e^{2(r-q)(\alpha-1)T} - 1]$ and $\chi^2(x; k, \lambda)$ is the cumulative probability with a non-central chi-square distribution with parameter k and λ degree of freedom less than x.

In order to price a European option under a CEV model, we need a non-central chi-square distribution. The following figure shows the charts of the non-central chi-square distribution with 5 degrees of freedom for non-central parameter $\delta = 0, 2, 4, 6$.

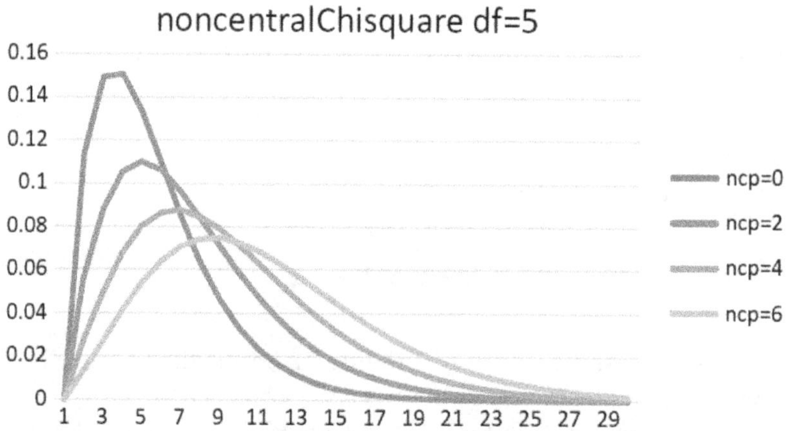

Excel Program to Estimate European Call Option Price with CEV Model

Using the theory in this chapter, we can write a call option price under the CEV model utilizing the following figure:

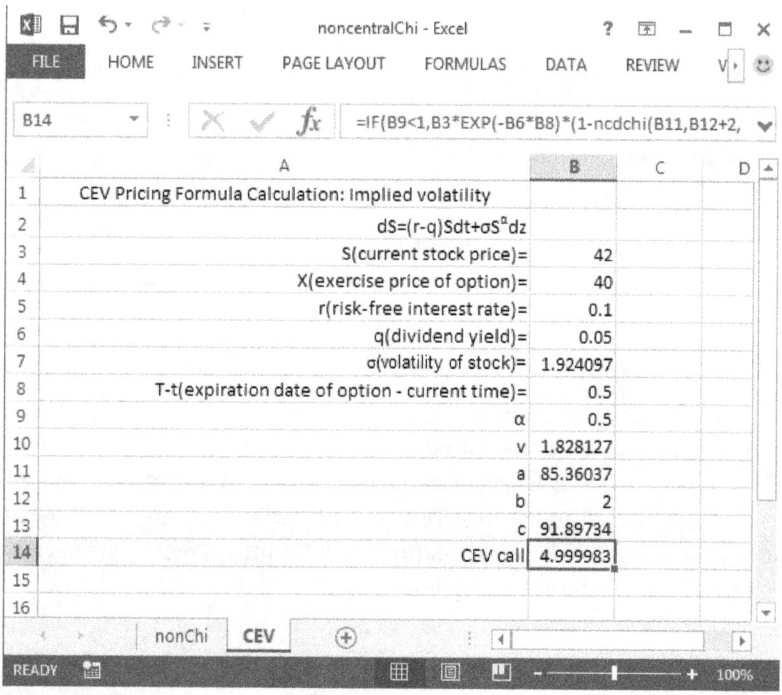

Hence, the formula for the CEV call option in B14 is as follows:

$$
\begin{aligned}
= \mathrm{IF}(&\mathrm{B9} < 1, \mathrm{B3} * \mathrm{EXP}(-\mathrm{B6} * \mathrm{B8}) \\
&*(1 - \mathrm{ncdchi}(\mathrm{B11}, \mathrm{B12} + 2, \mathrm{B13})) \\
&- \mathrm{B4} * \mathrm{EXP}(-\mathrm{B5} * \mathrm{B8}) * \mathrm{ncdchi}(\mathrm{B13}, \mathrm{B12}, \mathrm{B11}), \\
&\mathrm{B3} * \mathrm{EXP}(-\mathrm{B6} * \mathrm{B8}) * (1 - \mathrm{ncdchi}(\mathrm{B13}, -\mathrm{B12}, \mathrm{B11})) \\
&- \mathrm{B4} * \mathrm{EXP}(-\mathrm{B5} * \mathrm{B8}) * \mathrm{ncdchi}(\mathrm{B11}, 2 - \mathrm{B12}, \mathrm{B13})).
\end{aligned}
$$

The ncdchi is the non-central chi-square cumulative distribution function. The function, IF, is used to separate the two conditions for this formula: $0 < \alpha < 1$ and $\alpha > 1$.

We can write a function to price the call option under the CEV model. The following code accomplishes this:

```
Function CEVCall(S, X, r, q, T, sigma, alpha)
'   CEV Call Option Value
    Dim v As Double
    Dim aa As Double
    Dim bb As Double
    Dim cc As Double
    v = (Exp(2 * (r - q) * (alpha - 1) * T) - 1) *
        (sigma ^ 2) / (2 * (r - q) * (alpha - 1))
    aa = ((X * Exp(-(r - q) * T)) ^ (2 * (1 - alpha))) /
         (((1 - alpha) ^ 2) * v)
    bb = 1 / (1 - alpha)
    cc = (S ^ (2 * (1 - alpha))) / (((1 - alpha) ^ 2) * v)
    If alpha < 1 Then
    CEVCall = Exp(-q * T) * S * (1 - ncdchi(aa, bb + 2,
              cc)) - Exp(-r * T) * X * ncdchi(cc, bb, aa)
    Else
    CEVCall = Exp(-q * T) * S * (1 - ncdchi(cc, -bb, aa))
              - Exp(-r * T) * X * ncdchi(aa, 2 - bb, cc)
    End If
End Function
```

Use this function to value the following call option:

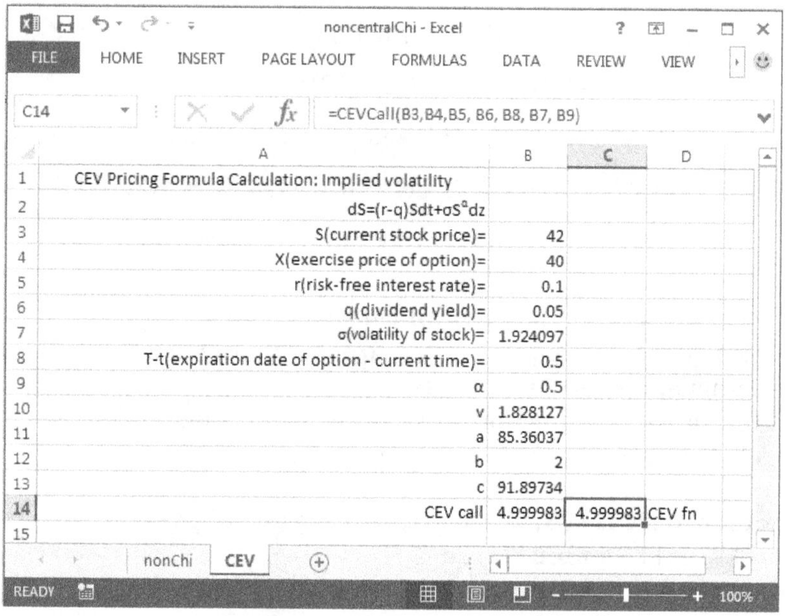

The CEV call option formula in C14 is as follows:

$$= \text{CEVCall}(\text{B3}, \text{B4}, \text{B5}, \text{B6}, \text{B8}, \text{B7}, \text{B9})$$

The value of the CEV call option in C14 is equal to B14.

Next, we want to use the Goal Seek procedure to calculate the implied volatility. To do this, we can see the following figure.

Set cell: B14
To value: 4
By changing cell: $B$7

After pressing the OK button, we can get the sigma value in B7.

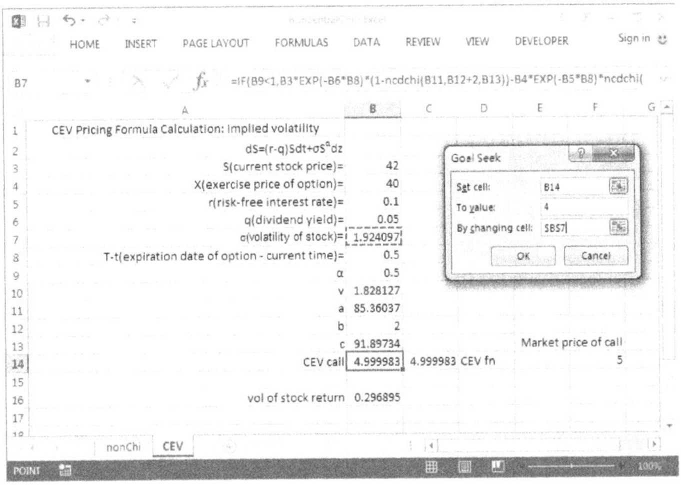

Excel Program to Estimate Implied Variance with CEV Model

If we want to calculate implied volatility of stock return, we show this result in B16 of the following figure. The formula of implied volatility of stock return in B16 is as follows:

$$= \text{B7} * \text{B3} \wedge (\text{B9} - 1)$$

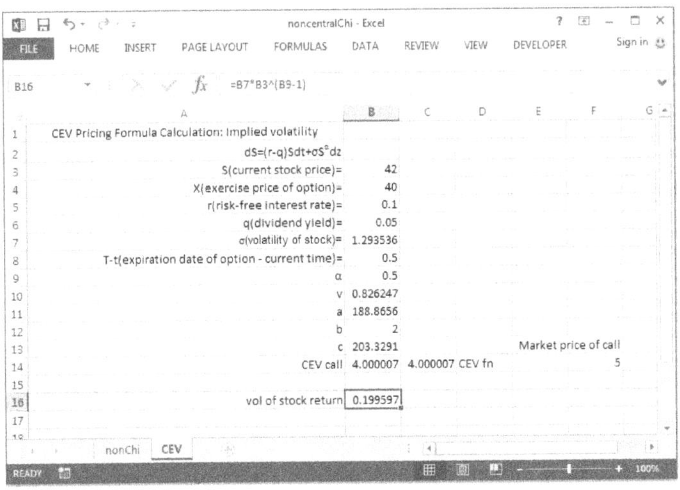

We use the bisection method to write a function to calculate the implied volatility of the CEV model. The following code can accomplish this task:

```
Function CEVIVBisection(S, X, r, q, T, alpha, callprice,
      a, b)
'   Estimate implied volatility by Bisection
'   Uses BSCall fn
      Dim yb, ya, c, yc
      yb = CEVCall(S, X, r, q, T, b, alpha) - callprice
      ya = CEVCall(S, X, r, q, T, a, alpha) - callprice
      If yb * ya > 0 Then
      CEVIVBisection = CVErr(xlErrValue)
    Else
       Do While Abs(a - b) > 0.000000001
          c = (a + b) / 2
          yc = CEVCall(S, X, r, q, T, c, alpha)
               - callprice
          ya = CEVCall(S, X, r, q, T, a, alpha)
               - callprice
          If ya * yc < 0 Then
             b = c
          Else
             a = c
          End If
        Loop
       CEVIVBisection = (a + b) / 2
    End If
End Function
```

After typing the parameters in the above function, we can get the sigma and implied volatility of stock return. The result is shown in the following.

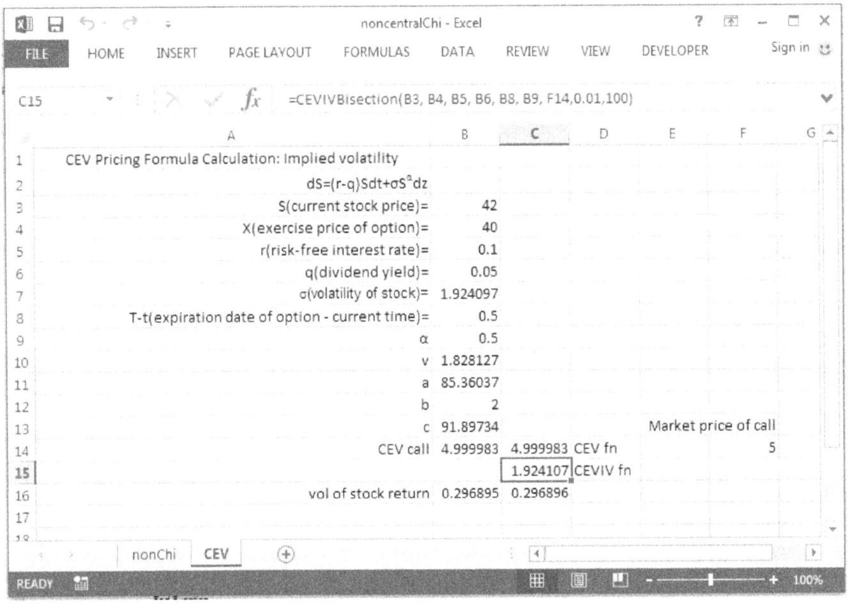

The formula of sigma in the CEV model in C15 is as follows:

$$= \text{CEVIVBisection}(\text{B3, B4, B5, B6, B8, B9, F14}, 0.01, 100),$$

The value of sigma in C15 is similar to B7 calculated by the Goal Seek procedure. In the same way, we can calculate volatility of stock return in C16. The value of volatility of stock return in C16 is also near B16.

Chapter 16

Warrants and Convertible Securities

Contents

16.1 Introduction

A hybrid security has characteristics of both debt and equity, which has been discussed in Chapter 2. In this chapter, we discuss various types of hybrid securities and examine the factors that determine their market value. We have already discussed the valuation of bonds, stocks, and options in earlier chapters. Our approach to valuing hybrid securities is to use those valuation methods to reach an estimate of the value of a warrant or a convertible bond.

A warrant is generally issued in conjunction with a bond as a sweetener to make the debt issue more attractive to investors so that they will require a lower coupon interest rate. A warrant gives the holder the right to purchase a specific number of shares of common stock at a stipulated price for a specific period. Convertible bonds (and convertible preferred stock) are securities that can be exchanged for a stipulated number of shares of common stock during a specific period.

In effect, holders of these hybrid debt securities have made loans to the issuing corporation. However, in contrast to ordinary bondholders, they have the opportunity to profit if the firm flourishes to the extent that the market value of its common stock increases by an appreciable amount. Naturally, there is some cost associated with such an opportunity, so that convertible bonds or bonds with warrants will have lower coupon interest rates than straight (non-convertible) debt. In this chapter, we look at how the market values such securities, which are intermediate between debt and equity. We will also see the risk associated with hybrids in between the risk of straight debt and straight equity. We also discuss the features that render hybrid securities attractive to both the issuing corporation and the investors, and the effect of these securities on the firm's EPS.

In Section 16.2, we discuss hybrid securities. Section 16.3 discusses warrants and their valuations. Section 16.4 discusses convertible bonds and their valuations. Alternative models for evaluating convertible bond are discussed in Section 16.5, and beta coefficients for convertible bonds are discussed in Section 16.6. In Section 16.7, we discuss earnings per share when warrants and convertibles are issued, and finally, Section 16.8 summarizes the chapter. Appendix 16A discusses cost of capital for convertibles and impacts of call and conversion.

16.2 Hybrid Securities

Bonds constitute a fixed claim on the corporation, while common stock confers a residual claim and a share in corporate ownership. However, corporations also raise capital through the issue of securities that are neither straight debt nor straight equity. Our purpose in this chapter is to discuss such hybrid securities. Specifically, we consider warrants and convertible securities.

A warrant is normally issued with debt and constitutes an option to purchase a specific number of shares of common stock at a stipulated price for a set period of time. Typically, a warrant is detachable, which means that it can be traded separately from the bond. Based upon our discussion of call options in Chapters 7 and 8, a warrant is essentially a call option, and its value is influenced by the same factors that influence the value of a call option.

Why would a corporation issue a warrant along with bonds, and what is the attraction to investors of these securities? From the point of view of the issuing corporation, to the extent that the market puts a positive value on the warrant, the bond with a warrant will be valued more highly than an otherwise identical straight bond. Therefore, through the attachment of warrants, the corporation will be able to sell debt at a lower interest rate.

In issuing warrants, a corporation does not know how much capital will eventually be raised through the exercise of the associated options. However, the amount raised will be directly related to the extent of profitable business activity generated by the corporation over the exercise period. If the corporation is relatively unsuccessful, its stock price is likely to stagnate and the options will not be exercised. On the other hand, if the corporation is successful, and in response to this success the stock price rises, the options are more likely to be exercised, generating additional capital presumably at a time when it is most needed.

The foregoing discussion assumes that the market is not changing. Even if the firm doesn't undergo any change, the general level of market movement could affect the probability of the warrant being exercised.

Convertible securities are bonds or preferred stock that can be exchanged for a stipulated number of shares of common stock of a corporation during a specific period of time. If the price of the common stock rises sufficiently, holders of these securities will find it profitable to exercise this conversion right. As in our discussion of warrants, this right will have some positive value in the market, so that a corporation will be required to pay a lower coupon rate on convertible bonds than on bonds with no conversion privilege.

Convertible bonds are also attractive when management prefers to raise capital through the issue of equity rather than debt, but believes that — as a result of transient influences — the common stock is temporarily undervalued by the market if this perception is correct, the stock price will rise, and, as a result, debt will be converted to equity. A possible further advantage of a convertible securities issue over the issue of bonds with warrants is that management knows how much capital will be raised. The exercise of a warrant raises further capital; the conversion of a bond for shares of common stock does not raise new capital. However, there is an implicit increase of cash flow, if the conversion occurs prior to the maturity date, through the saving of future coupon payments; the conversion simply substitutes equity for debt.

A further distinction between warrants and convertible bonds is that warrants are not callable, while a convertible bond can generally be called. The bondholder can be offered conversion within a short time period or surrender of the bond at a specific cash price. As with the pricing of callable and non-callable bonds, the pricing of callable convertibles and non-callable convertibles is different. Investors demand a higher return for a callable security, and firms are willing to pay this higher price because of the increase in management flexibility.

We have seen why a corporation might find it attractive to issue hybrid securities rather than straight debt and/or equity. What of the investor? These securities may be particularly attractive in the bond market when it is difficult for investors to assess the riskiness of a corporation's future business activities. If it is feared that the corporation is about to embark on high-risk enterprises, the holder of a straight bond will be in the unappealing position of gaining nothing if these enterprises are successful and facing greatly increased default risk if they are unsuccessful. However, a more even-handed situation is established if the bonds are issued either with warrants or with a conversion privilege. Through the exercise of the option involved, the bondholder will share in any success resulting from a risky venture. In this case, it is less important to market participants to be able to assess future business risk of a corporation's activities. Hence, the payoff characteristics of convertible bonds and other hybrid securities allow for a resolution of risk determination that is considered an agency problem by Barnea *et al.* (1985), as discussed later in this chapter.

16.3 Warrants and Their Valuation

Consider an issue of 20-year bonds, with a face value of \$1,000. The issuing corporation consults its investment bankers and is advised that in order to raise the desired amount of capital, a coupon interest rate of 14% per annum would be required for a straight bond issue. However, the common stock of this corporation is currently trading at \$35 per share, and the investment bankers advise that if 20 warrants — each allowing the purchase at \$40 of a share of common stock any time in the next 10 years — are attached, the bonds can be marketed with a coupon interest rate of 10%. As is standard practice, the exercise price of the warrant would be adjusted for any future stock splits, but the warrant holder would receive no share in future dividend distributions. As is again usual, the warrants would be detachable, so that they could be traded separately.

We begin by determining the implied market value of these warrants, discussing later the factors that determine this value. The bondholder will receive a stream of 20 annual interest payments of \$100, plus the \$1,000 face value of the bond in 20 years. The investment bankers' advice is that investors discount these payments at a rate of 13% per annum. Therefore, the present value of the debt element of the bond is

$$\begin{aligned}\text{Present value of debt} &= \sum_{t=1}^{20} \frac{100}{(1.13)^t} + \frac{1{,}000}{(1.13)^{20}} \\ &= 702.50 + 87 = \$789.50. \qquad (16.1)\end{aligned}$$

Thus, it is estimated that the market values the straight debt component of this issue at \$789.50. Because it is also estimated that these bonds can be sold for \$1,000, the warrants attached to each bond are valued at \$210.50, or \$10.53 per warrant.

We now ask how this valuation of the warrant might have been derived. In effect, the warrant is an American call option with an expiration date 10 years hence. Galai and Scheneller (1978) study the relationship between the value of a call option and the price of the stock. Specifically, we see the following:

1. The value of a call option must be between two bounds. The upper bound is the market price of the stock, and the lower bound is the greater of 0 and the difference between the price of the stock and the exercise price of the option.

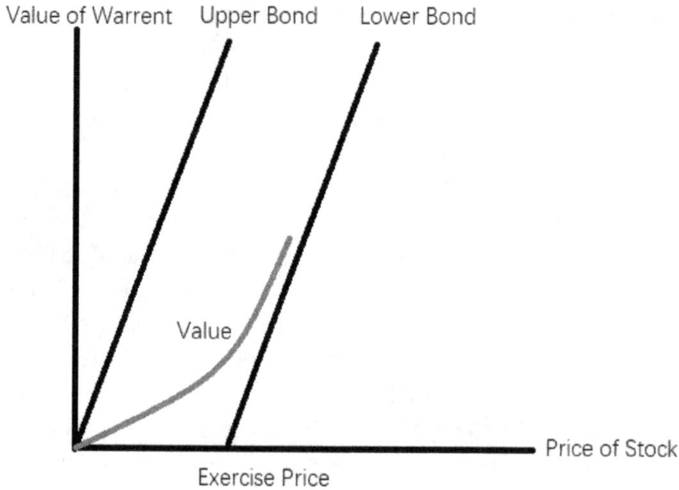

Figure 16.1 Warrant Value as a Function of Stock Price

2. The value of the call option, all other things equal, rises at an increasing rate with increases in the stock price to the point where, when the stock price is high, the value of the option will increase at very nearly the same rate as the stock price.

These considerations suggest the relationship between warrant value and stock price shown in Figure 16.1. All other things equal, the value of a warrant is an increasing function of the price of the stock, in the manner illustrated in Figure 16.1. In addition, Galai and Scheneller (1978) discuss several other factors influencing the value of a call option as follows:

1. The lower the exercise price, the higher the value of the call option.
2. The greater the volatility of the stock price, the higher the value of the call option.
3. The longer the time to the expiration date, the higher the value of the call option.
4. The higher the risk-free rate of interest, the higher the value of the call option.

In Chapters 22 and 23 of Lee *et al.* (2022), we will see how these factors interact in the Black–Scholes valuation model for call options.

These factors are also relevant in the valuation of warrants. However, the purchaser of warrants should also be aware of two other factors that affect the warrant value. First, the holder of a warrant does not receive dividend payments from the issuing corporation, a factor ignored in the Black–Scholes option valuation model. Whenever a dividend is paid, the value of a warrant decreases, since the price of the stock falls on the ex-dividend date. Therefore, it may be better to exercise early if it is anticipated that management will increase the level of dividend payments in the future. Second, if numerous warrant options are exercised, this could lead to an appreciable increase in the number of shares outstanding. Consequently, earnings per share may be less than would otherwise have been the case. This potential dilution in earnings per share tends to lower the value of a warrant. Given a dilution in EPS, price per share may fall, which reduces the value of the warrant.

Let N^b, P^b, and V^b be the before-exercise number of shares outstanding, common stock price per share before exercise, and total equity value before exercise, respectively, let N^w be the number of warrants, and let W^b be the value of one warrant. The value of the firm's old equity is

$$V^b = N^b P^b + N^w W^b. \tag{16.2}$$

If all the warrants are exercised, then the warrant holders will pay the firm $N^w E$ (E = exercise price) and the equity value will rise to

$$V^a = V^b + N^w E, \tag{16.3}$$

where V^a represents the total equity value after the warrants have been exercised.

The total value of the warrants after all warrants have been exercised is

$$N^w W^a = h(V^b + N^w E) - N^w E, \tag{16.4}$$

where $h = \frac{N^w}{N^b+N^w}$ = the proportion of V^a owned by warrant holders.

Equation (16.4) implies that the after-exercise warrant value (W^a) is

$$W^a = \frac{V^b - N^b E}{N^b + N^w}. \quad (16.5)$$

Thus, the warrant holder should exercise if[1]

$$hV^b > (1 - h)N^w E. \quad (16.6)$$

In this case, warrant holders gain if the old equity value exceeds the amount they pay at exercise.

If warrants are exercised, then the market price per share (P^a) can be defined as

$$P^a = \frac{V^b + N^w E}{N^b + N^w}. \quad (16.7)$$

It is worthwhile for warrant holders to exercise the warrants $P^a > E$.

16.4 Convertible Bonds and Their Valuation[2]

Consider an issue of 20-year bonds with a face value of $1,000, each bond convertible to 50 shares of common stock. The current market price of the stock is $15 per share. The coupon rate on these convertible bonds is 9.5%, while similar straight debt of the issuing corporation currently carries a rate of 12%. This issue is protected against stock splits, but can be called by the corporation, at a price of $1,050, at any time after 5 years.

---

[1]Equation (16.5) implies that warrant holders should exercise if

$$V^b > N^b E. \quad \text{(a)}$$

Multiplying both sides of (a) by h, we obtain

$$hV^b > hN^b E, \quad \text{(b)}$$

substituting $h = \frac{N^w}{(N^b + N^w)}$ into the right-hand side of equation (b) and rearranging the terms, we obtain

$$hV^b > (1 - h)N^w E,$$

which is Equation (16.6).

[2]The convertible bonds discussed in this section can be converted only into the firm's own stock. However, convertible bonds can also convert into other

The number of shares that can be received in exchange for each bond is called the *conversion ratio*; in our example, the conversion ratio is 50 shares to one bond. If the exchange was made immediately, a bond valued at $1,000 would be surrendered in exchange for 50 shares of common stock, so that the effective price would be $20 per share. This is known as the *conversion price*, which, in general, is

$$\text{Conversion price} = \frac{\text{Par value of bond}}{\text{Conversion ratio}}. \tag{16.8}$$

Many contracts specifically state the conversion price. In this example, the conversion price exceeds the current market price of the shares by one-third. Obviously, it makes no sense to exercise this conversion privilege immediately. However, that privilege may be of some value, since holders of the convertible bond can profit if the price of the stock increases sufficiently.

Let us see how much investors are being asked to pay for the conversion privilege. As in the previous section, this calculation can be made by computing the present value of the bond's debt element. Holding the debenture of maturity, the bondholder would receive a stream of 20 annual payments of $95, plus $1,000 at the end of 20 years. These payments must be discounted at a rate of 12%, so that

$$\begin{aligned}\text{Present value of debt} &= \sum_{t=1}^{20} \frac{95}{(1.12)^t} + \frac{1{,}000}{(1.12)^{20}} \\ &= 709.6 + 103.7 = \$812.30. \end{aligned} \tag{16.9}$$

This is often called the *bond value* of the convertible bond.

We must also consider a second possibility: The instrument may be worth more if the conversion privilege is exercised. Since, at issue, the bond can be exchanged for 50 shares of common stock valued by the market at $15 per share, we say that its conversion value is (50)(15) = $750. We see that the bond value exceeds the conversion value but is lower than the price of the bond. If the bond is issued

---

firms' stock. For example, the *Asian Wall Street Journal* (November 26, 1987) reported that a Taiwan Company, Yuen Fong Yu, issued a convertible bond that allows investors to convert this bond into Chung Hwa Pulp Corporation's common stock.

at par, then the difference between the market value of $1,000 and the larger of the bond value or conversion value is $186.70. This represents the price that investors pay for the conversion privilege. As mentioned earlier, the conversion privilege is a call option on the shares of corporate common stock, and its value is influenced by all those factors that determine the value of call options. However, one factor should be noted in the present case. If the conversion privilege is exercised, the bond must be surrendered in exchange for stock. Therefore, the exercise price per share of the call option is the value of the convertible bond divided by the conversion ratio. Over time, market forces will cause the price of a convertible bond to vary, and so the exercise price of the implicit call option will also vary.

To see how the market values convertibles bonds, consider again bond value and conversion value. The market value of a convertible bond should be at least as high as bond value and conversion value. The bond value is simply that price at which the bond would sell if it could not be converted to common stock, and the conversion privilege cannot have negative worth. Also, if the convertible bond sold for less than its conversion value, investors could make an immediate profit by purchasing the bond, converting it, and selling the shares of stock. Investors would jump at such an opportunity, and the additional demand would drive up the price of the convertible bond. We have thus established that both the bond value and the conversion value constitute lower bounds to the value of a convertible bond.

To see what constitutes the boundary value of a convertible bond, consider the relationship between bond and conversion values and that of the issuing corporation as illustrated in Figure 16.2. First consider Figure 16.2(a). If the corporation is worth nothing, then so are its stocks and bonds. As corporate value increases, we can expect a proportionate increase in the value of common stock and hence in the conversion value of the convertible bond. Initially, as corporate value increases, bond value will increase more rapidly than conversion value, as investors' fears of default subside. However, at higher corporate values, the rate of increase of bond value slows rapidly, asymptotically approaching risk-free debt. Thus, as seen in Figure 16.2(a), the conversion value and bond value curves will cross at A, so that at a

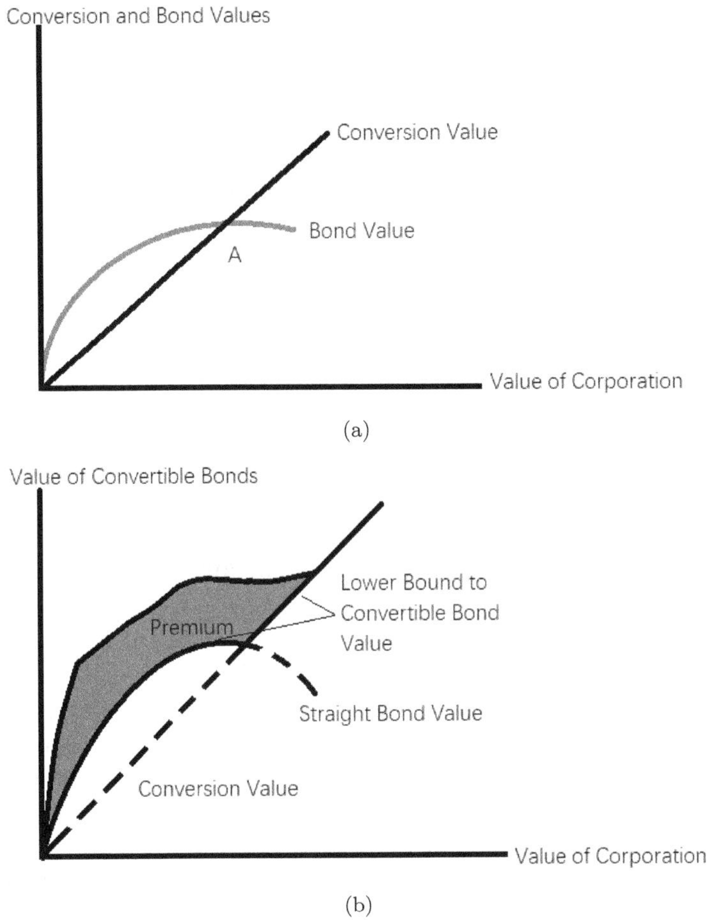

Figure 16.2 Relationship of Convertible Bond Value and Corporation Value under Different Conditions

sufficiently high corporate value, the conversion value of a convertible bond will exceed its bond value.

As we have seen, the value of a convertible bond must be at least as high as both its conversion value and its bond value. This lower bound to convertible bond value, as a function of the value of the corporation, is illustrated in Figure 16.2(b).

In practice, the market value of a convertible bond will usually exceed this lower bound as shown in Figure 16.2(b), the excess being the amount that investors are willing to pay for the conversion privilege (premium). The Black–Scholes option pricing model, which will be discussed in Chapters 22 and 23, can be used to evaluate the market value of the premium. Along with the Black–Scholes determinants of option values, investors must also consider foregone dividends, if the conversion privilege is not exercised, and the possibility of dilution in corporate ownership. Another important consideration is any call provision in the convertible bond issue. Mikkelson (1981) showed that stock prices tend to increase dramatically prior to management's exercise of the call provision.

To illustrate some of the factors involved in convertible bond valuation, consider a newly issued 20-year convertible bond with a $1,000 face value and a coupon rate of 9.5%. This bond may be converted to 50 shares of common stock, which is selling at $15 per share. The bond can be called, at a price of $1,050, any time after 5 years. It is estimated that if capital were to be raised through a straight debt issue, a coupon interest rate of 12% would be required. It is believed that investors expect 10% annual growth in the value of this firm's stock. A dividend yield of 5% is currently being paid, and it is expected that this yield will be 5.5% next year. Thus, using the Gordon dividend model, common stockholders require a rate of return of 15.5%.

Since the bond can be exchanged for 50 shares of common stock, then the conversion value for this convertible bond at the time of issue is

$$\text{Conversion value} = (50)(15) = \$750. \tag{16.10}$$

This is the same bond for which we calculated a debt value of $813.30 at the beginning of this section.

Thus, at the time of issue, the debt value exceeds the conversion value of the bond. However, since the convertible bond is sold for $1,000, investors are, in effect, paying $1,000 − $813.30 = $186.70 for the conversion privilege.

We can examine this valuation by looking at the internal rate of return that is being demanded by purchasers of this bond. Consider an investor who is planning to hold this convertible bond for 5 years, during which time it is callable. Since the price of common stock is expected to grow at 10% per annum, then after 5 years,

$$\text{Expected conversion value} = (750)(1.10)^5 = \$1{,}208. \qquad (16.11)$$

Hence, this investor expects to receive five annual interest payments of \$95, plus common stock valued at \$1,208 at the end of this period. Discounting these receipts at internal rate of return r yields the market value of the convertible bond, so that

$$1{,}000 = \sum_{t=1}^{5} \frac{95}{(1+r)^t} + \frac{1{,}208}{(1+r)^5}. \qquad (16.12)$$

The solution of this equation, in terms of r, is $r = 1.27$. We thus conclude that the required internal rate of return on the convertible bond is 12.7%. Note that this rate is between the 12% rate required by bondholders and the 15% rate required by common stockholders. This finding is to be expected because a convertible bond is less risky than common stock but riskier than a straight bond.

In summary, the basic value concepts and definitions used to value convertible bonds in terms of our example are as follows:

- Face value = market price of issuance = \$1,000,
- Straight debt value = \$813.30,
- Conversion value = \$1,050,
- Call price = \$1,050, and
- Expected conversion value = \$1,208.

However, the theoretical value of this convertible bond can also be calculated by using an understandable formula; this formula and its implications will be discussed in the following section. Cost of capital for convertibles and impacts of call and conversion can be found in Appendix 16A. Lee *et al.* (2013) and Lee and Lee (2017) have discussed convertible securities in further detail.

16.5 Alternative Models for Evaluating Convertible Bond[3]

16.5.1 *Introduction*

A convertible bond which is entitled to a set of fixed claims is a bond that can be converted into common stocks at the owner's option subject to conditions specified in the indenture. Therefore, convertible bonds are two instruments in one: One is the straight debt instrument, which guarantees a fixed payment for the life of the bond. The second instrument is the equity portion, which allows the bondholder to reap the gains due to increase in the equity value by conversion. By issuing convertible bonds, the firms can lower the cost of debt funding compared to straight debt alone. For investors, convertible bonds offer greater stability of income than common stock.

There are two varieties of convertible bonds: callable versus non-callable convertibles. Usually, callable convertibles have the same provisions as their non-callable counterparts, except they are subject to redemption by the issuing company at the prevailing call price prior to maturity. In most cases, the call provision is standard in indentures and is especially important in case of convertibles. As one can think of a non-callable convertible as a special case of callable convertible with a sufficiently large call price, in this study, convertibles with call provision are always assumed.

In general, the price of a convertible is determined by three state variables and four decision variables. The three state variables are as follows: (1) the price behavior of the firm's market value or common stock; (2) the value of the corresponding straight bond; and (3) the credit risk of the issuing firm. The four decision variables are as follows: (1) the call policy of a company with convertibles outstanding as when to announce a call, the call price for redemption payment, the specification of the call notice,... etc.; (2) the conversion policy includes the date of conversion, the conversion price as how much one share of common stock costs at conversion, or equivalently, one share of debenture can be convert into how many shares of common

[3]This section is the modification of Chapter 68 from *Encyclopedia of Finance*, 3rd ed., by Cheng-Few Lee and Alice C. Lee. Published by Springer in 2022.

stock; (3) the put provision that allows the investor to sell the convertible bond to the issuer for specific prices on specific dates prior to maturity; and (4) the capital structure of the firms, for example, whether there are any other senior claims of the firms.

In the literature, various assumptions are employed regarding the aforementioned three state variables. The assumptions span from deterministic to stochastic. By assuming a constant interest rate r and deterministic stock price growing at a constant rate g, the graphical method of Brigham (1966) is a representative of the deterministic approach. The graphical method to evaluate a convertible bond discussed in the previous section is similar to Brigham's deterministic approach. To describe the dynamics of these state variables more rigorously, stochastic models are developed, which can be further divided into calculus and option pricing approach. In the calculus approach, one considers the issuing firm's market value (or stock price) on a specific date in the future as a random variable, while in the option pricing approach, the dynamics of the issuing firm's market value (or stock price) for a time period in the future is modeled as a random process. The representatives of the calculus approach include Baumol *et al.* (1966), Poensgen (1965, 1966), and Frankle and Hawkins (1975). The option pricing approach dominates the pricing of convertible bonds, which is pioneered by Brennan and Schwartz (1977, 1980) and Ingersoll (1977a, 1977b).

Both the deterministic and calculus approach ignore the possibility of bankruptcy by the issuing firm; therefore, the convertible bonds might be mispriced. The option pricing approach, on the other hand, considers the likelihood of default based on either type of default models: the structural model (Merton, 1974; Black and Cox, 1976) or the reduced-form model (Jarrow and Turnbull, 1995). In the one-factor structural model, the issuing firm's market value follows a geometric Brownian motion. Later, Brennan and Schwartz (1980) proposed a two-factor structural model with a stochastic interest rate. Nyborg (1996) extends Brennan and Schwartz's two-factor structural model by including a put provision and floating coupons feature.

In contrast to the structural model, the more recent works of literature use a reduced-form model in which stochastic stock price instead of the firm's market value is modeled. These include the works by Goldman Sachs (1994), Ho and Pfeffer (1996), Tsiveriotis and Fernandes (1998), Davis and Lischka (1999), Takahashi (2001), Ayache *et al.* (2003), and Lau and Kwok (2004).

This work reviews the literature on convertible debt valuation including static stochastic and dynamic stochastic models. The outline of the session is as follows. Section 16.5.2 states the calculus models with static stochastic stock price and/or straight bond price. Section 16.5.3 gives the option pricing approach by modeling the dynamics of a firm's market value as a stochastic process. In Section 16.5.4, a numerical approach, for example, the tree approach, for the valuation of convertible bonds in reduced-form models is given. Section 16.8 concludes.

16.5.2 *Calculus approach: Static stochastic models*

Baumol *et al.* (1966) present a convertible security valuation model that separates the interaction between debt and equity attributes in the valuation of convertible securities by considering the time-t value $c = \max(C_s, C_b)$ of a convertible as

$$C_s = ps + \int_0^{\overline{B}/ps} f(i, t_0)[\overline{B} - i(t)ps]di(t), \tag{16.13}$$

$$c_b = \overline{B} + \int_{\overline{B}/ps}^{\infty} f(i, t_0)[i(t)ps - \overline{B}]di(t), \tag{16.14}$$

where $\overline{B}$ = equivalent straight debt value; s = number of equity securities issued upon conversion; p = price of the equity security at present t_0; $i(t)$ = date-t to date-t_0 equity security's price relative; and $f(i, t_0)$ = subjective probability assessment of $i(t)$ at t_0, when $t > t_0$. Equation (16.13) specifies that C_s is composed of two values: the conversion value ps and the insurance value of the debt character as the stochastic price relative $i(t)$ varies between 0 and $\overline{B}/ps$ at the end of time horizon t. Equation (16.14) states that C_b is a combination of two values: the straight debt value $\overline{B}$ and the value assigned to the conversion feature as the stochastic price relative $i(t)$ varies between $\overline{B}/ps$ and ∞ at the end of time horizon t.

Later, Baumol *et al.* (1966) extended their previous model by introducing the *ex-ante* notion that the convertible security holder is interested in the future conversion value of the convertible security as follows:

$$C = \int_0^{\infty} i(t) ps f(i, t_0) di(t) + \int_0^{\overline{B}/ps} f(i, t_0)[\overline{B} - i(t)ps] di(t). \tag{16.15}$$

In this model, the first term represents the conversion value in all possible states of the price relative $i(t)$ from 0 to ∞, while the second term represents the insurance value of the debt character as the stochastic price relative $i(t)$ varies between 0 and $\overline{B}/ps$.

Both in Brigham (1966) and Baumol *et al.* (1966), the market interest rate is flat, and the bond's straight debt value was treated as an exogenously determined constant. By including the nature of interest rate changes, an explicit characterization of the random nature of a convertible security's bond value would lead to a robust model of the market setting of convertible securities. In Poensgen (1965), both the stochastic stock price and stochastic straight debt value are explicitly considered. To be more specific, on an arbitrary date when conversion is possible, Poensgen (1965) suggests the expected price of the convertible security as

$$E(P) = \int_0^{\infty} \begin{bmatrix} y \displaystyle\int_0^{y} h\left(\frac{x}{y}\right) dx \\ + \displaystyle\int_y^{\infty} xh\left(\frac{x}{y}\right) dx \end{bmatrix} g(y) dy, \tag{16.16}$$

where $x =$ the stock price (or conversion value); $y =$ the straight debt value; $h(x/y) =$ the conditional probability of x for a particular bond value y; and $g(y) =$ the probability of occurrence of the bond value y (unconditional). Note that the probability of joint occurrence of the stock price x and bond value y is $h(x, y) = h(x/y)g(y)$. It can be shown that Equation (16.16) is logically equivalent to the following:

$$E(P) = \int_0^\infty \Bigg[\underbrace{\int_0^\infty xh(x,y)dx}_{\text{Expected stock value}} + \underbrace{\int_0^y (y-x)h(x,y)dx}_{\text{Value of floor guarantee}} \Bigg] dy, \quad (16.17)$$

$$E(P) = \underbrace{\int_0^\infty \int_0^\infty yg(y)dy}_{\text{Expected straight debt value}} + \underbrace{\int_0^\infty \int_y^\infty (x-y)h(x,y)dxdy}_{\text{Expected value of the conversion option}}. \quad (16.18)$$

Equation (16.17) specifies that the value of the convertible security is the expected stock price plus the value attached to the floor guarantee for a stochastic straight debt value, y. This formulation is identical to Equation (16.15) by Baumol *et al.* (1966) model except for the assumption by Poensgen (1965) that y is a random variable. Alternatively, in Equation (16.18), the first term evaluates the value of a straight debt, while the second term evaluates the value of a warrant with exercise price y by integrating over all possible straight debt value, y.

By showing that there was no statistically significant correlation between bond yield variability and stock prices, Poensgen (1965) claims that Equation (16.18) is analytically equal to

$$E(P) = \int_0^\infty yg(y)dy + \int_y^\infty (x-y)f(x)dx, \quad (16.19)$$

where $f(x)$ is the probability density function of x. Based on Equation (16.20), Poensgen (1965) suggests that the distribution of stock prices, x, is truncated on the left by the straight debt value. This assertion facilitates Poensgen's (1965) subsequent empirical work dealing with the truncated distribution of convertible security returns. Nevertheless, the integration in Equation (16.19) does not equal that in Equation (16.18). Therefore, the subsequent work of Poensgen (1965) on the truncated distribution of convertible security returns is not of great help.

Later, Frankle and Hawkins (1975) adopted Poensgen's valuation model for convertible securities to explore the link between the beta of a convertible security and the beta of the underlying common stock by assuming independence of the stock and straight bond prices so as to obtain

$$E(CB) = \int_0^y yh(x)dx + \int_y^\infty xh(x)dx, \tag{16.20}$$

where $E(CB)$ = expected price of the convertible security; y = straight debt value, x = log of the stock price relative; and $h(x)$ = log-normal distribution of stock price relatives. By assuming a constant straight debt value and following the previous direction of Poensgen (1965) by asserting that the probability density function of the log of the stock price relatives is truncated at a constant value a, Frankle and Hawkins (1975) present the expected log return on the convertible bond as

$$E_{en(i(t))CB} = a\int_{-\infty}^{a} \frac{1}{\sqrt{2\pi\sigma_x}} e^{-(1/2)[(x-\mu_x)/\sigma_x]^2}dx + \int_a^\infty x\frac{1}{\sqrt{2\pi\sigma_x}} e^{-(1/2)[(x-\mu_x)/\sigma_x]^2}dx. \tag{16.21}$$

Frankle and Hawkins (1975) proceed to derive an explicit form for the beta of a convertible security based on the beta of the underlying common stock. This relationship is presented as follows:

$$\text{Beta} = \rho\frac{\sigma_x}{\sigma_m}\left[1 - \phi\left(\frac{a}{\sigma_x}\right)\right], \tag{16.22}$$

where ρ = correlation coefficient between x and the market m; σ_x = standard deviation of common stock return; σ_m = standard deviation of market return; and ϕ = the cumulative normal function. It is noted by Frankle and Hawkins that Equation (16.22) implies that the beta of a convertible security is less than or equal to that of its underlying common stock. Thus, Frankle and Hawkins (1975) derive an upper bound for the convertible security's beta. Nevertheless, the result by Frankle and Hawkins (1975) in Equation (16.22) is false as Equation (16.20) is falsely derived. Further efforts need to be done for a valid relationship between the beta of a convertible security and that of its underlying common stock.

The next major advance in convertible security valuation evolved from the option pricing theory originated by Black–Scholes (1973) and the risky zero-coupon bond's pricing by Merton (1974). In the option pricing approach, the firm's market value over time is modeled as a stochastic process, and three possibilities of the termination of a convertible bond are considered: conversions by the bondholders, maturity of the bond, called back or default of the firm. The following section considers the option pricing approach for the valuation of convertible bonds.

16.5.3 *Option pricing approach: Dynamic stochastic model*

When pricing a convertible bond, one needs to consider the conversion and put strategies of bondholders, the call back policy, and the default mechanism of the firm. For simplicity, we'll not consider the put option in this study. Therefore, in the following, we focus on the three decision variables of a convertible bond: the conversion strategy, call back policy, and default mechanism.

Ingersoll (1977a) is the first to derive the optimal conversion strategy for bondholders and optimal call policy for the firm in a perfect, frictionless market with no dividends and constant conversion terms. According to Ingersoll (1977a), for a firm with a capital structure consisting of equities and convertible bonds only, the optimal conversion strategy satisfies the following lemma:

Lemma 16.1. *If the perfect market, no dividends, and constant conversion term assumptions are valid, then a callable convertible will never be converted except at maturity or a call.*

Lemma 16.2. *If the conditions for the above lemma hold, the optimal call strategy is to call when the firm's market value reaches the call price divided by the dilution factor γ, the fraction of the equity that the bond holders possess if they convert.*

One advantage of Ingersoll's result (1977a) is that it captures the dilution effect as convertible bonds are converted into common stocks (Schönbucher, 2003). With this advantage, Ingersoll (1977a) decomposed the price of a non-callable convertible bond G into a straight discount bond F (with the same principal as the convertible bond) and a warrant W as

$$G(V, \tau; B, 0, \gamma) = F(V, \tau; B, 0) + W(\gamma V, \tau; B), \tag{16.23}$$

where B is the balloon payment, τ is the time to maturity, c is coupon payment, γ is the dilution factor, and $W(\gamma V, \tau; B)$ is the warrant price with underlying price γV and exercise price B. The initial condition for W satisfies

$$W(\gamma V, 0; B) = \max(\gamma V_T - B, 0),$$

where V_T is the firm value at maturity. By assuming the firm's market value V follows a geometric Brownian motion and default occurs if V falls below an exogenously determined barrier (Merton, 1974; Black and Cox, 1976; Longstaff and Schwartz, 1995; Briys and Varenne, 1997), or an endogenously determined barrier due to the strategic decision of the firm (Leland, 1994; Leland and Toft, 1996), Ingersoll (1977a) derived analytically the values of the straight discount bond F and the warrant W using the option pricing theory for a risky debt.

In the case of a callable convertible bond, the bond's price H is decomposed into a straight discount bond F, a warrant W, and an additional term representing the cost of the call which reduces the value of the callable convertible bond relative to its non-callable counterpart as

$$\begin{aligned} &H(V, \tau; K(\tau), 0, \gamma) \\ &\quad = F(V, \tau; B, 0) + W(\gamma V, \tau; B) \\ &\qquad + Z^{2(r-\rho)/\sigma^2}[F(\gamma V', \tau; B', 0) - F(\gamma V', \tau; B'/\gamma, 0)], \end{aligned} \tag{16.24}$$

where $K(\tau)$ is the call price of the convertible and $Z = K(\tau)/\gamma V$, $B' = Be^{(r-\rho)\tau}$; $V' = Ve^{(r-\rho)\tau}$. In another paper by Brennan and Schwartz (1977), the partial differential equation for the price of a convertible with call provisions and dividends is derived based on the following conversion and call strategies:

Lemma 16.3. *It will never be optimal to convert a convertible bond except immediately prior either to a dividend date or to an adverse change in the conversion terms, or maturity.*

Lemma 16.4. *The firm's optimal call strategy is to call the bond as soon as its value, if it is not called, is equal to the call price.*

Later, in addition to the simplistic capital structure assumed by Ingersoll (1977a) and Brennan and Schwartz (1977) consisting solely of equity and convertible bonds, Brennan and Schwartz (1980) included senior straight debts in a firm's capital structure and develop a two-factor structure model with a stochastic firm's market value and interest rate for the valuation of a convertible bond. Brennan and Schwartz (1980) found that often the additional factor representing stochastic interest rates had little impact on the prices of convertible bonds. Later, Nyborg (1996) extended the two-factor model of Brennan and Schwartz (1980) with a put provision and floating coupons feature.

Nevertheless, due to the complexity of the convertible's contractual provisions and the number of parameters used for estimate the value of convertible scurety is large, therefore, the aforementioned approach can be impractical and there might be no analytical solutions for the valuation of a convertible bond. Instead, practitioners often use the equity price as the underlying for the valuation of a convertible bond and some numerical approaches are employed. In the following section, the prevalent numerical approach, that is, the tree method, is given.

16.5.4 *Numerical approach: Tree method*

The most widely used numerical approach for the pricing of a convertible is the tree approach. The approach has the capability to handle various convertible bond provisions. The main procedure of the tree approach for convertible bond pricing is stated as follows:

First, consider the firm's stochastic price S as the underlying, which follows a lognormal Ito process of the form

$$dS = \mu(S, t)S\, dt + \sigma S dW, \tag{16.25}$$

where $\mu(S, t)$ is the drift term, σ is the volatility, and W is a standard Brownian motion. A binomial tree is built in a risk-neutral world for the development of the stochastic price S in Equation (16.25) according to the Cox–Ross–Rubinstein model (1979). Each node on the tree represents a possible future stock price. Then, a backward induction procedure starting from the maturity is applied, and a maximum convertible bond value on each node is decided according to the stock price and the action taken according to the provisions, for example, convert, put, call, hold, or redeem the bond. Finally, the current value of convertible bond can be calculated. The credit risk of the convertible bond is considered by setting a risky discount rate with the credit spread of the issuer (Goldman Sachs, 1994) or adding a default node (Hull, 2009) with the default probability which is decided by the default intensity of the issuer.

A more complex model with multi-factors, such as adding a stochastic interest rate, or with time-varying default intensity, volatility, and interest rate, is also applicable with the tree model (Ho and Pfeffer, 1996; Hung and Wang, 2002; Ammann *et al.*, 2003; Carayannopoulos and Kalimipalli, 2003; Chambers and Lu, 2007). Ho and Pfeffer (1996) employed a two-dimensional binomial tree for the stochastic stock price and interest rate in their two-factor model, in which all the cash flows are discounted at the risky rate (i.e., risk-free plus credit spread). Correlated default intensity and stock price are discussed in Andersen and Buffum (2003). However, Brennan and Schwartz (1980) and Goldman Sachs (1994) indicated that the major factor which decides the convertible bond value is the equity price. Adding an additional factor, such as dynamic interest rate, into consideration had little impact on the value of the convertible bond.

16.6 Beta Coefficients for Convertible Bonds

Using the concept that a convertible bond is a portfolio of a bond and a warrant, Beatty *et al.* (1988) show the relationship of the systematic risk of the convertible, bond, and warrant as follows:

$$\beta_{CV} = \frac{B}{B+W}(\beta_B) + \frac{W}{B+W}(\beta_W), \tag{16.26}$$

where β_{CV}, β_B, and β_W are the beta coefficients for the convertible, bond, and warrant, respectively.

We showed that the value of a warrant is proportional to the value of a call option, or

$$W = C(1-g), \tag{16.27}$$

where W and C are the values of a warrant and a call option, and $(1-g)$ is a proportionality factor that takes into account the dilution effects of the new shares issued when the warrant is exercised.

Because the return on the warrant is also proportional to the return on the call option, the systematic risk of the warrant (β_W) must equal the systematic risk of the call option (β_C), or

$$\beta_W = \beta_C. \tag{16.28}$$

Lee and Lee (2017) have shown that the beta on the call option is related to the beta of the underlying asset as follows:

$$\beta_C = \left(\frac{S}{C} \times \frac{\partial C}{\partial S}\right)\beta_s, \tag{16.29}$$

where S and C are the market values of the stock and the options; $\partial C/\partial S$ is the partial derivative of C with respect to S; and β_s is the systematic risk of the equity. In this equation, $(\frac{S}{C} \times \frac{\partial C}{\partial S})$ measures the elasticity between the value of the call option and the value of the underlying stock.

Putting all of this together, we can show that the beta of a convertible is

$$\beta_{CV} = \frac{B}{B+W}\beta_B + \frac{W}{B+W}\left(\frac{S}{C} \times \frac{\partial C}{\partial S}\right)\beta_s. \tag{16.30}$$

Thus, the systematic risk of a convertible bond is a weighted average of the systematic risk of a regular bond and the systematic risk of the firm's equity times an elasticity term. In general, the beta of a convertible bond will be less than the beta of the firm's equity and greater than the beta of its debt.

16.7 Earnings Per Share (EPS) When Warrants and Convertibles are Issued

Warrants and convertibles have the potential to change a firm's EPS and number of shares. We now turn our attention as to how warrants and convertibles affect EPS and the number of shares outstanding.

Investors, managers, accountants, and federal and state governments are concerned with the earnings per share of a corporation. By earnings per share, we generally mean the net income after taxes less preferred stock dividends divided by the weighted average number of shares of common stock outstanding. In 1969, the Accounting

Principles Board, a forerunner of the FASB, issued *APB Opinion No. 15*, "Earnings per Share." This ruling lays down the rules for calculating the earnings per share for financial reporting purposes. In 1982, the FASB issued *Statement No. 55*, "Determining Whether a Convertible Security Is a Common Stock Equivalent." These accounting requirements provide alternative ways of calculating earnings per share if a company has convertible securities, warrants, stock options, or other contracts that permit the number of shares of common stock to be increased.

A simple capital structure has only one form of voting equity capital and no other forms or potential forms of equity, such as warrants or convertibles. The existence of preferred stock does not create a complex capital structure. Figure 16.3 shows an EPS calculation for a firm with a simple capital structure and a constant number of shares outstanding as well as an EPS calculation for a firm with a changing number of shares outstanding.

As you can see in this exhibit, the issuance or repurchase of common shares during a particular period affects the average number of shares outstanding and thereby changes the firm's EPS. In Figure 16.3, months were used as the denominator of the weighting fractions. However, weeks or months can also be used if this is more pertinent to the timing of the changes in the number of shares.

A corporation that has warrants, convertibles, or options outstanding is said to have a *complex capital structure*. The capital structure is complex because the measure of shares outstanding is a function of a known amount of common shares currently outstanding plus an estimate of the potential number of shares that must be issued to satisfy the holders of warrants, convertibles, and options should they decide to exercise their rights and receive new common shares. Because of the possible dilution in EPS represented by securities that have the potential to become new shares of common stock, we must consider *common stock equivalents* (CSEs). CSEs are securities that are not common stock but are equivalent to common stock because they are likely to be converted into common stock in the future. Convertible debt, convertible preferred stock, stock rights, stock options, and stock warrants are all securities that can create new common shares and thus dilute the firm's earnings per share. This dilution effect means that the CSE securities will reduce a firm's EPS.

Constant Number of Shares Outstanding	
Revenue	$10,000,000
Less *expenses*	–7,500,000
Operating income	$ 2,500,000
Less *interest*	–300,000
Taxable income	$ 2,200,000
Less *taxes (50%)*	–1,100,000
Net income	$ 1,100,000
Less *Preferred Dividends*	–100,000
	$ 1,000,000

Earnings available to common shareholders ($1,000,000) dividend by number of shares outstanding (1,000,000) = $1 EPS.

Varying Number of Shares Outstanding

Date	**Share Increase (Decrease)**	**Total Shares**	**Fraction of Year That Balance Was Unchanged**	**Weighted Average Number of Shares Outstanding**
1/1/1988	—	1,000,000	2/12	166,666.67
2/28/1988	200,000 new issue	1,200,000	4/12	400,000.00
6/30/1988	400,000 repurchased	800,000	2/12	133,333.33
9/1/1988	200,000 new issue	1,000,000	4//12	333,333.33
12/31/1988		1,000,000		
			12/12	1,033,333.33

Earnings available to common shareholders ($1,000,000) divided by weighted average of shares outstanding (1,033,333) = $.97 EPS.

Figure 16.3 EPS Calculation for Simple Capital Structure

APB 15 provides two types of EPS for firms with a complex capital structure: primary EPS and fully diluted EPS. Primary EPS is computed by dividing adjusted earnings by the weighted average shares of common stock and common stock equivalents, or

$$\text{Primary EPS} = \frac{\begin{array}{c}\text{Income–Preferred stock dividends}\\ +\text{After-tax effect of bond interest expense if}\\ \text{bonds are CSE}\end{array}}{\text{Weighted average of common shares and CSE}}. \tag{16.31}$$

Fully diluted EPS is computed by dividing the adjusted earnings by the maximum number of potential common shares, given the

Complex Capital Structure Data:

Convertible bonds, 10% interest, $1,000 par value, issued at par $10,000,000 on 1/1/1990 at a AA bond rate of 16%, maturity on 12/32/2009, convertible into ten shares of common stock, 100,000 primary shares.

Preferred stock, 10% interest, $100 par value, 10,000 shares issued at $1,000,000.

Convertible preferred stock, 8% interest, $100 per share, 10,000 shares convertible into one share of common per share of preferred, $1,000,000 issued at a AA bond rate of 10%, 10,000 fully diluted shares.

Common stock $1 per share, outstanding 1,000,000 shares $1,000,000; 10,000 warrants outstanding, each convertible into two shares of common stock at $50 per share; current market price of the warrant is $165, current market price of stock is $105 per share, 1,020,000 primary shares.

Primary EPS		**Fully Diluted EPS**	
Operating income	$2,600,000		$2,600,000
Less interest	−1,000,000		−1,000,000
Taxable income	$1,600,000		$1,600,000
Less taxes (50%)	−800,000		−800,000
Net income	$800,000		$800,000
Less preferred dividends	−180,000	Less preferred stock dividends if preferred stock is not CSE	−100,000
	$620,000		$700,000
After-tax effect if bonds are CSE [1,000,000 (1 − .5)]	$500,000	After-tax effect if bonds are CSE	+500,000
	$1,120,000		$1,200,000
$\frac{\$1{,}120{,}000}{1{,}120{,}000} = \$1$ per share		$\frac{\$1{,}200{,}000}{1{,}130{,}000} = \$1.06$ per share	

Figure 16.4 Primary EPS and Fully Diluted EPS

requirements of *APB 15*:

Fully diluted EPS

$$= \frac{\begin{array}{c}\text{Net income–Preferred stock dividends if}\\ \text{preferred stock is not a CSE + After-tax effort of}\\ \text{bond interest expense if bonds are CSE}\end{array}}{\begin{array}{c}\text{Weighted average of common shares and CSE}\\ \text{assuming maximum dilution}\end{array}}. \quad (16.32)$$

If all hybrid securities are considered to be dilutive CSEs, then primary EPS would be equal to fully diluted EPS. Figure 16.4 gives EPS calculations for both primary and fully diluted EPS.

It is interesting to speculate on whether the market will use primary EPS or fully diluted EPS in valuing shares of stock. If the market expects the common stock equivalent to be converted to new equity, then fully diluted EPS is more meaningful, whereas if the market does not expect the common stock equivalents to be converted, then it would treat convertible bonds like debt and make no adjustment for new shares and use primary EPS. Convertible bonds that have no chance of being converted are called *hung convertibles. APB 15* and *FASB 55* provide EPS information under either circumstance and let the market participant choose which measure is more meaningful.

From the perspective of the financial analyst, it is important to be able to identify the difference between two firms with the same primary EPS and markedly different fully diluted EPS. In general, hybrid securities in the capital structure cause the difference.

16.8 Summary

Hybrid securities give both investors and financial managers greater flexibility in their interactions in the financial markets. Understanding these securities requires an understanding of option pricing.

Our knowledge of how these securities affect firm value, from a financial viewpoint, differs greatly from accounting for their existence. We need a more thorough understanding of these hybrids and how the investor values them before we can adequately define the types of information we need about these kinds of securities.

In this chapter, we have discussed how the issue of warrants and convertible bonds can affect the EPS of a firm. Then, we discuss how to use both traditional and option approaches to evaluate warrant and convertible bonds. Beta coefficient of convertible bond is also discussed in this chapter in some detail. Finally, cost of capital for convertibles and impacts of call and conversion are also discussed in this chapter.

Questions and Problems

1. Define the following terms:
   a. Hybrid securities
   b. Warrants
   c. Conversion ratio

   d. Conversion price
   e. Premium of convertible bond
   f. Conversion value and expected conversion value
   g. Beta coefficient of convertible bonds
2. Describe how the required internal rate of return on the convertible bond can be estimated.
3. XYZ Company has 5 million shares outstanding and an expected market value of 30 million dollars. When its warrants mature and the company wants to issue 500,000 new shares, assuming each warrant can be used to purchase one new share, what exercise price will not affect the existing shareholders' wealth?
4. How is the market value of a convertible bond determined?
5. The earnings per share for XYZ Company is \$3. XYZ's P/E ratio is 15 and its payout ratio is 1/3. Company XYZ wishes to offer \$20 million of 10%, 20-year convertible debentures with an initial conversion premium of 15% and a call price of \$110. XYZ currently has \$2 million common share outstanding and a 34% tax rate:
   a. What is the conversion price?
   b. What is the conversion ratio per \$1,000 debenture?
   c. What is the initial conversion value of each debenture?
   d. How many new shares of common stock must be issued if all debentures are converted?
6. Alice Lee is debating whether to invest \$1,200 in warrants or in common stock of XYZ Company. The current market price of XYZ's stock is \$30. She could purchase warrants that entitle her to buy one share of stock per warrant for \$25. These warrants have a market price of \$3. In 1 year, the market price of the stock may rise to \$35 per share or fall to \$25 per share. What do you advise Lee to do?
7. One of the owners of XYZ Company's warrants wonders whether it is now advantageous to exercise those warrants. The warrant allows the owner to purchase 3.5 shares of common stock at \$40 per share.
   a. Should the owner exercise the warrant if the market price of common stock is \$50?
   b. What is the market value of the owner's warrant when the stock price is \$50?

8. A convertible bond issue of $1 million has the following characteristics:

   Par value of bond = $1,000
   Maturity of debt is 7 years
   Coupon rate (paid annually) is 13%
   Current stock price = $90
   Conversion price = $100
   Assuming that the current coupon rate of a similar straight bond is 16%, calculate the following values:

   a. Conversion ratio
   b. Bond value
   c. Conversion value
   d. Conversion premium
   e. Price of convertible bond if the stock price is:
      i. $80
      ii. $100
      iii. $125

9. VSA Corp. is issuing 12-year convertible bonds with a face value of $.25 million. The par value and annual interest would be $1,000 and $75 per bond, respectively. The coupon rate of a similar bond without conversion provision is 10%. The convertible bond is callable at $1,075 any time after 6 years. The growth rate in VSA's stock prices is expected to be 8% and the current dividend yield is 10%. The current market price of the company's shares is $32. The conversion ratio is 25. Calculate the expected conversion value at $t = 6$ and find the internal rate of return required by the investors.
10. The straight bond issue of a corporation carries a coupon rate of 11.50%. If the firm also gives 15 warrants along with each bond, the coupon rate would be 9.25%. A warrant would entitle the holder to buy one share of common stock at $12.50 during the next 3 years. Calculate the value of warrants if the par value of the convertible bond is $1,000 and the maturity is 10 years.
11. RFC currently has 90,000 shares of common stock and 10,000 warrants outstanding. A warrant holder can purchase one share at $31.50 for each warrant held. The current stock price is $40 per share.

a. Calculate the per-share loss to old shareholders if the option is exercised by the warrant holders.
b. Find the exercise price that would result in no loss or gain to the old shareholders.

12. A warrant entitles its holder to purchase 2 shares of a company's common stock at \$15 per share. Calculate the value of one warrant if the current stock price is:
    a. \$13
    b. \$17
13. Dave is planning to invest \$500. He has two alternatives: common stock and warrants of a blue chip company. The current market prices of stock and warrants are \$20 and \$2, respectively. A warrant holder is entitled to buy one share of this firm at \$17.50.
    a. Calculate the rate of return on the stock and warrant investments held for 1 year if the prices at $t = 1$ are as follows:
        i. Stock = \$30; Warrants = \$10
        ii. Stock = \$16; Warrants = \$1
    b. Explain the results of the two alternatives of investing in stock and warrants.

Bibliography

Ammann, M., A. Kind, and C. Wilde (2003). Are convertible bonds underpriced? An analysis of the French market, *Journal of Banking and Finance*, 27, 635–653.

Andersen, L. and D. Buffum (2003). Calibration and implementation of convertible bond models, *Journal of Computational Finance*, 7(1), 1–34.

Ayache, E., P. A. Forsyth, & K. R. Vetzal (2003). The valuation of convertible bonds with credit risk. *Journal of Derivatives*, 11, 9–29.

Barnea, A., R. A. Haugen and L. Senbet (1985). *Agency Problems and Financial Contracting*. New York: Prentice-Hall.

Baumol, W. J., B. G. Malkiel, and R. E. Quandt (1966). The valuation of convertible securities, *The Quarterly Journal of Economics*, 80, 48–60.

Beatty, R. P., C. F. Lee and K. C. Chen (1988). On the nonstationarity of convertible bond betas: Theory and evidence. *Quarterly Review of Economics and Business*, 26(Fall), 15–27.

Black, F. and M. Scholes (1973). The pricing of options and corporate liabilities. *The Journal of Political Economy*, 81(3), 637–654.

Black, Fischer, and John C. Cox (1976). Valuing corporate securities: Some effects of bond indenture provisions. *The Journal of Finance*, 31(2), 351–367.

Brennan, M. J. and E. S. Schwartz (1980). Analyzing convertible bonds. *Journal of Financial and Quantitative Analysis*, 15, 907–929.

Brennan, M. J. and E. S. Schwartz (1977). Convertible bonds: Valuation and optimal strategies for call and conversions. *Journal of Finance*, 32(5), 1699–1715.

Brigham, E. F. (1966). An analysis of convertible debentures. *Journal of Finance*, 21(1), 35–54.

Carayannopoulos, P. and M. Kalimipalli (2003). Convertible bond prices and inherent biases, *Journal of Fixed Income*, 13, 64–73.

Chambers, D. R. and Q. Lu (2007). A tree model for pricing convertible bonds with equity, interest rate, and default risk, *Journal of Derivatives*, 14, 25–46.

Cox, J. C., S. A. Ross and M. Rubinstein (1979). Option pricing: A simplified approach, *Journal of Financial Economics*, 7, 229–263.

Eric Briys and François de Varenne, (1997). Valuing risky fixed rate debt: An extension, *The Journal of Financial and Quantitative Analysis*, 32(2), pp. 239–248.

Ho T., and D. Pfeffer (1996). Convertible bonds: Model, value attribution and analytics, *Financial Analysts Journal*, 52(5), 35–44.

Hull, J. C. (2009). *Options, Futures, and Other Derivatives.* 7th edition. Upper Saddle River, New Jersey: Pearson Education.

Hung, M. W., and J. Y. Wang (2002). Pricing convertible bonds subject to default risk, *The Journal of Derivatives*, 67–87.

Galai, D. and N. Schneller (1978). The pricing of warrants and the value of the firm. *Journal of Finance*, 33(5), 133–142.

Ingersoll, J. (1977a). A contingent claims valuation of convertible securities. *Journal of Financial Economics*, 4(3), 289–321.

Ingersoll, J. (1977b). An examination of corporate call policies on convertible securities. *Journal of Finance*, 32(2), 463–478.

Jarrow, R. A., and S. Turnbull (1995). Pricing derivatives on financial securities subject to credit risk, *Journal of Finance*, 50, 53–85.

Lau, K. W., and Y. K. Kwok (2004). Anatomy of option features in convertible bonds. *Journal of Futures Markets*, 24, 513–532.

Lee, C. F. and J. Lee (2017). *Financial Analysis, Planning and Forecasting: Theory and Applications*, 3rd ed. Singapore: World Scientific.

Lee, C. F., J. Finnerty, J. Lee, A. C. Lee and D. Wort (2013). *Security Analysis, Portfolio Management, and Financial Derivatives.* Singapore: World Scientific Publishers, Inc.

Lee, C. F., J. C. Lee and M. Lee (2022). *Corporate Finance and Strategy: An Active Learning Approach.* Singapore: World Scientific.

Lee, C.-F. and A. C. Lee (2022). *Encyclopedia of Finance*, 3rd ed. New York: Springer.

Lee, C.-F., K.-W. Lee and G. H.-H. Yeo (2009). Investor protection and convertible debt design. *Journal of Banking & Finance*, 33(6), 985–995.

Leland, H. E. (1994). Corporate debt value, bond covenants, and optimal capital structure. *Journal of Finance*, 49, 1213–1252.

Leland, H. E., and Toft, K. B. (1996). Optimal capital structure, endogenous bankruptcy, and the term structure of credit spreads. *Journal of Finance*, 51, 987–1019.

Longstaff, Francis A., and Eduardo S. Schwartz (1995). A simple approach to valuing risky fixed and floating rate debt. *The Journal of Finance*, 50(3), 789–819.

Merton, R. (1974). On the pricing of corporate debt: The risk structure of interest rates, *Journal of Finance*, 29(2), 449–470.

Mikkelson, A. W. H. (1981). Convertible calls and security returns. *Journal of Financial Economics*, 9(3), 237–264.

Nyborg, K. (1996). The use and pricing of convertible bonds, *Applied Mathematical Finance*, 3, 167–190.

Poensgen, O. H. (1965). The valuation of convertible bonds, Part 1, *Industrial Management Review*, 7, 76–92.

Poensgen, O. H. (1966). The valuation of convertible bonds, Part 2, *Industrial Management Review*, 7, 83–88.

Schönbucher, Philipp J. (2003). Credit derivatives pricing models: models, pricing and implementation. New Jersey: John Wiley & Sons.

Takahashi, A., T. Kobayashi, and N. Nakagawa (2001). Pricing convertible bonds with default risk: a Duffie-Singleton approach, *Journal of Fixed Income*, 11, 9–20.

Tsiveriotis, K., and C. Fernandes (1998). Valuing convertible bonds with credit risk, *Journal of Fixed Income*, 8(2), 95–102.

Appendix 16A: Cost of Capital for Convertibles and Impacts of Call and Conversion

16A.1 *Cost of capital for convertibles*

A convertible bond is equivalent to a portfolio of two securities: a bond and a warrant. The bond portion pays interest and returns the principal of maturity, and the warrant portion serves as a call on the value of the firm's equity. Hence, the value of a convertible bond is

$$CV = B + W, \tag{16A.1}$$

where CV is the market value of a convertible bond; B is the market value of a bond; and W is the market value of a warrant. Therefore, the cost of capital for the convertible bond must be a weighted average of the two component securities, or

$$K_{cv} = \left(\frac{B}{B+W}\right) k_b(1 - \tau_c) + \left(\frac{W}{B+W}\right) k_w, \tag{16A.2}$$

where $k_b(1 - \tau_c)$ is the after-tax cost of the bond and k_w is the total cost of the warrant. This being the case, the traditional argument for using convertibles as a form of cheap debt requires that the lower coupon rate on convertible bonds is sufficient to offset the higher cost associated with the warrant. If we look at the after-tax cost of convertible bonds compared to straight debt, we see that the $k_b(1-\tau_c)$ of the convertible bond is less than the cost of the straight debt. If the difference between $k_b(1-\tau_c)$ for the convertible bond and straight debt is greater than k_w, then the total cost of the convertible bond is less than the total cost of the straight debt. If the difference is less than k_w, then the convertible bond is more costly.

16A.2 *Impacts of call and conversion*

All convertible bonds have a call feature, which gives the firm the right to force the owner of the convertible to either convert the convertible bond into equity or liquidate the investment in the bond for a cash payment. Thus, firm management must have a policy for when to force conversion. The optimal call policy is that a convertible bond (preferred) should be called as soon as its conversion value is equal to or greater than the market value of the equity received on conversion or the current market price times number of shares received. To guarantee conversion, management should wait until the conversion value is sufficiently greater than the call price.[4]

[4]Brigham (1966) surveyed companies and found that many managers set a policy of waiting until the conversion value is at least 20% greater than the call price.

The call provision is equivalent to a call option written by the investor who purchases the callable convertible bond from the firm, that is, the bonds may be repurchased by the firm any time during the life of the security at the prevailing call or exercise price.

If we assume perfect markets, investors should convert the bond in one of four situations: (1) at the maturity of the convertible, (2) when the convertible is called, (3) when the conversion price increases, or (4) when the current dividend yield on the equity is greater than the yield on the convertible bond. The first two situations are *forced conversions*, because it is not in the best interest of the investor to give up the convertible security at these times. In these cases, the investor can receive cash when the bond matures or can receive cash by selling the bond in the marketplace. We are assuming it is better to convert than to receive the call value. For example, if the investor takes cash, he or she must then purchase shares of stock in the market, which increases transaction costs that are usually avoided in the conversion process. The third and fourth situations are voluntary conversions because it is beneficial for the investor to give up the convertible bond for an equity position.

Mikkelson (1981) presents the implications of a call of a convertible security on shareholder wealth. The principal effects of a call and conversion of debt are a reduction in the amount of outstanding conversion privileges, a decrease in the firm's financial leverage, and an increase in the number of common shares outstanding. The investment or asset structure of the firm is unaffected by the conversion in the short run. Figure 16A.1 presents a summary of Mikkelson's arguments concerning how a call and a conversion affect the wealth of the firm's bondholders and shareholders and the value of the firm.

Type of Change due to Conversion	Stockholder Wealth	Bondholder Wealth	Firm Value
Change in tax liabilities	–	–	–
Change in relative priority of outstanding claims	–	+	0
Change in incentive for management to transfer wealth	?	+	+
Decrease in bankruptcy cost	+	+	+
Decrease in amount of conversion privileges outstanding	?	–	–
Increase in shares outstanding	–	0	–
Total effect	?	?	?

Figure 16A.1 The Effects of Conversion of a Convertible Bond on Stockholder and Bondholder Wealth and Firm Value

From Figure 16A.1, it is clear that the total net effect of a conversion is not easily identifiable. What is required is a case-by-case analysis of each situation to determine the relative importance of each type of change and its effect on the shareholder, the bondholder, and firm value. If managers act to maximize shareholder wealth, the net effect should be positive. A negative effect on shareholder wealth with a positive effect on firm value suggests that the bondholders or management are benefiting from the conversion of the convertible debt.

However, as a general rule, we would normally consider that the cost of convertible bond, K_{cv}, is higher than the cost of straight debt, k_b.

Barnea *et al.* (1985) have shown that convertible bonds might resolve the agency problems associated with issuing stocks and bonds. They argue that creditors have incentives to force the firm into low-risk activities, while equity holders have incentives to adopt high-risk projects.[5] If these conflicts cannot be resolved, the firm might be forced to give up profitable investment projects. Convertible bonds represent a financing package of mixed risk incentives and go a long way toward resolving the conflicts between bondholders and stockholders. Thus, convertible bonds and bonds associated with warrants will have less restrictive debt covenants than will nonconvertible bonds.

[5]Using the option pricing concept, it can be shown that risky projects reduce the market value of risky bonds and increase the market value of stocks. Appendix 16A provides further discussion on these arguments.

Part V

Special Topics of Options and Futures

Chapter 17

Applications of Discriminant Analysis, Factor Analysis, Logistic Regression, and the KMV-Merton Model in Risk Analyses

Contents

17.1 Introduction

Financial risk can be divided into market risk, credit risk, and liquidity risk, among others. This chapter is about credit risk analysis. For example, credit rating models predict bankruptcy for firms, and credit scoring models predict default or insolvency for individuals.

Discriminant analysis, factor analysis, logistic regression, and the KMV-Merton model have been used to perform credit analysis for almost five decades. The main purposes of this chapter are to review and integrate the applications of discriminant analysis, factor analysis, logistic regression, and the KMV-Merton model in credit risk analysis. First, we will discuss how the discriminant analysis can be used for credit rating, such as calculating financial Z-score to determine the chance of bankruptcy of the firm. In addition, we also discuss how discriminant analysis can be used to classify banks into problem banks and non-problem banks. Second, we will discuss how factor analysis can be combined with discriminant analysis to perform bond rating forecasting. Third, we will show how both static and dynamic logistic regression techniques can be used to calculate the default risk probability. Fourth, we will discuss the KMV-Merton model and Merton Distance model for calculating default probability. Finally, we will compare all techniques discussed in this chapter and draw the conclusions and give suggestions for future research. Section 17.2 discusses how discriminant analysis can be used in loan credit analysis. Section 17.3 applies discriminant analysis to bankruptcy and financial distress analysis. Section 17.4 demonstrates how the factor analysis technique can be used to select useful financial ratios. Section 17.5 discusses how k-group discriminant analysis methods can be used to forecast bond ratings. In addition, a new method developed by Kao and Lee (2012) is also briefly discussed. Section 17.6 discusses how alternative logistic regressions can be used to calculate the default probability. Section 17.7 discusses the Merton Distance model and KMV-Merton model. In Section 17.8, we discuss how the Capital Structure Determination model can be used to improve Bharath and Shumway's model (2008) and naïve default probability. Section 17.9 discusses an empirical comparison. Finally,

Section 17.10 summarizes the results of this chapter. Appendix 17A discusses the logistic model and probit model. The SAS code for a hazard model in bankruptcy forecasting is shown in Appendix 17B. Appendix 17C demonstrates the application of Merton distance to a default model.

17.2 Literature Review

Bharath and Shumway (2008) have empirically compared the performance of three alternative models for estimating default probability. These three models are the Merton DD model, naïve DD model, and Moody's KMV model. They found that the naïve model performs at least as well as the two other models. The main reason for this finding has been discussed in Section (17.7.2).

Mai's dissertation (2010) has reexamined the four most commonly employed default prediction models: Z-score model (Altman, 1968), logit model (Ohlson, 1980), probit model (Zmijewski, 1984), and hazard analysis (Shumway, 2001). Her empirical results show that the discrete time hazard model adopted by Shumway (2001), combined with a new set of accounting ratio and market-driven variables, improves the bankruptcy forecasting power.

By using hand-collected business default events from the *Compustat* Annual Industrial database and publicly available press news, Mai (2010) has constructed a sample of publicly traded companies in one of the three U.S. stock markets between 1991 and 2006. With a cautiously chosen cutoff at 0.021 implying the bankruptcy probability level, the out-of-sample hazard model with stepwise methodology results in classifying 82.7% of default firms and 82.8% of non-default firms. This compares to the best results in Shumway (2001), which provides 76.5% classification of default firms, 55.2% in Altman (1993), 66.1% in Ohlson (1980), and 65.4% in Zmijewski (1984). It can be concluded that the resolution from her dissertation did better than the other 4 models.

The specification of logit and probit models can be found in Appendix 17B, and the SAS Code for the Hazard Model in Bankruptcy Forecasting can be found in Appendix 17C.

17.3 Credit Analysis

Two-group multivariate discriminant analysis (MDA) can be used to determine whether a customer's credit should be authorized or not, or to determine the financial soundness of an industrial firm, a bank, or an insurance company. Chapters 3 and 4 of Lee and Lee (2017) have discussed these applications in some detail.

In determining the trade credit policy of a firm, Mehta (1974) and Van Horne (2001) proposed a two-group discriminant analysis model to identify the "good account" from the "bad account." A linear discriminant function can be defined as

$$Y_I = AX_{1i} + BX_{2i}, \tag{17.1}$$

where Y_I is the index value for the ith account; X_{1i} is the ith firm's quick ratio; X_{2i} is the ith firm's total sales/inventory ratio; and A and B are the parameters or weights to be determined.

For purposes of formulating the original model, we extend open-book credit to all new credit applicants for a sample period, recording for each account the quick ratio and the total sales/inventory ratio and whether the account defaults in payment after a specified length of time. If the account defaults, it is classified as a bad account and the index is assigned the value of zero. If the account pays on time, it is classified as a good account and the index is assigned the value of one. With this information, we can apply a linear discriminant analysis with two independent variables. Based upon the sample data of X_1 and X_2, the coefficients A and B can be calculated by the following procedure:

The two equations used in solving for A and B of Equation (17.1) are defined as

$$S_{11}A + S_{12}B = D_1, \tag{17.2}$$

$$S_{12}A + S_{22}B = D_2, \tag{17.3}$$

where S_{11} = Variance of X_1, S_{22} = Variance of X_2, S_{12} = Covariance between X_1 and X_2, D_1 = Difference between the average of X_1's for good accounts and the average of X_1's for bad accounts, and D_2 = Difference between the average of X_2 for good accounts the average of X_2 for bad accounts.

Using Cramer's rule, we obtain

$$A = \frac{S_{22}D_1 - S_{12}D_2}{S_{22}S_{11} - S_{12}^2}, \tag{17.4a}$$

$$B = \frac{S_{11}D_2 - S_{12}D_1}{S_{22}S_{11} - S_{12}^2}. \tag{17.4b}$$

Based upon the estimated parameters, A and B, we need to determine the minimum cutoff value of the discriminant function. The aim here is to refuse credit to accounts with a value of Y below the cutoff value and to extend credit to accounts with a Y value above the cutoff. Theoretically, we wish to find the discriminant function value that is denoted by Y^* in Figure 17.1, where $Y(B)$ and $Y(G)$ are average discriminant function values for bad and good accounts, respectively.

Following Van Horne (2001), we start by calculating the Y_I for twelve accounts, as shown in Table 17.1, in ascending order of magnitude.

We see that there is an area of overlap for accounts 6, 2, 11, and 4, as shown graphically in Figure 17.1. We know that the cutoff value must lie between 1.64 and 1.96. For simplicity, we may want to use the midpoint, 1.80, as our cutoff value. In Figure 17.2, we can draw a discriminant boundary that most accurately classifies accounts into good and bad categories. Note, however, that two of the accounts, 11 and 12, are misclassified, given the cutoff value. Account 11 is

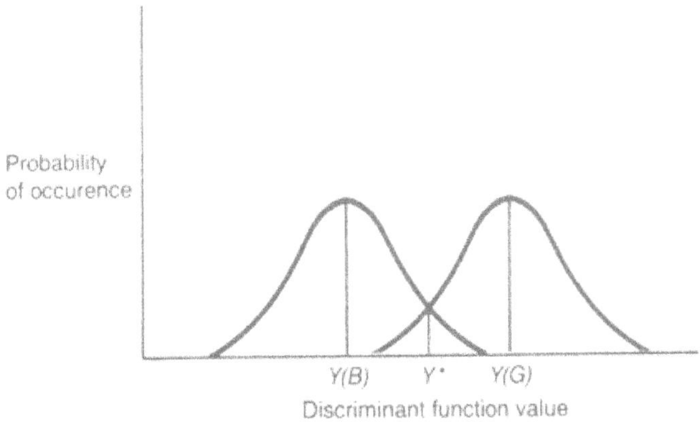

Figure 17.1 Universes of Good and Bad Accounts

Table 17.1 Status and Index Values of the Accounts

Account Number	Account Status	Y_i
7	Bad	0.81
10	Bad	0.89
2	Bad	1.30
3	Bad	1.45
6	Bad	1.64
12	Good	1.77
11	Bad	1.83
4	Good	1.96
1	Good	2.25
8	Good	2.50
5	Good	2.61
9	Good	2.80

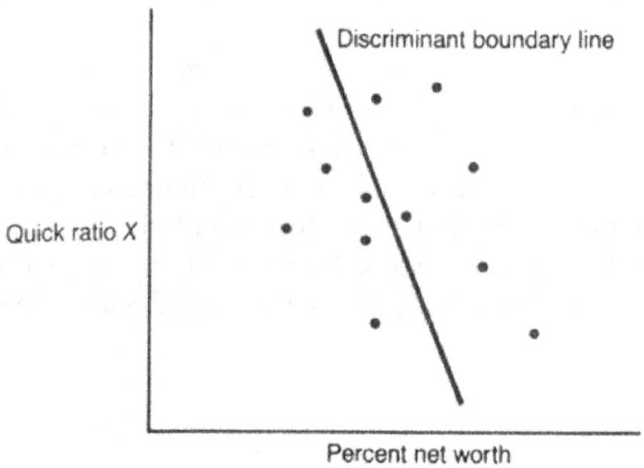

Figure 17.2 Discriminant Analysis of Accounts Receivable

classified by the graph as a good account when, in fact, we know it to be a bad account, while account 12 is classified as a bad account when, in fact, it was a good account.

These are Type I classification errors and Type II classification errors, respectively. Type I errors involve the rejection of the null hypothesis when it is true, while Type II classification errors involve the acceptance of the null hypothesis when it is false. For the sake of practicality, the analysis should assume an area of possible misclassification for indexes between 1.64 and 1.96. Accounts or firms falling within this range require further investigation and analysis.

If one has reason to believe that new credit applicants will not differ significantly from past ones whose performance has been analyzed, discriminant analysis can be used to select and reject credit sales customers. Using a minimum cutoff value, we reject all credit sales if the Y value for the credit applicant is less than 1.78. Using a 32-point range, we accept all credit sales where the prospective customer has a Y-value over 1.96 and reject applicants with Y-values below 1.64. For applicants with Y-values lying between those two values, we might want to obtain additional credit information, along with information as to the profitability of the sale, before making a decision.

In this credit analysis, Mehta (1974) used the quick ratio and the inventory turnover ratio to construct the index. He shows that there are four tasks to be faced by the manager in using the MDA for credit analysis:

(i) Determining significant factors,
(ii) Selecting the sample,
(iii) Assigning weights to factors to develop an index, and
(iv) Establishing cutoff values for the index.

Mehta regards the discriminant approach, the decision tree approach, and the conventional method as the three major approaches generally used by the credit department of a firm in making the credit-granting decision.

In assessing the risk of a request for credit, the conventional approach regards the three C's as relevant: character, capital, and capacity. This is a subjective credit analysis method, and it generally gives indeterminate and misleading results. Both the discriminant approach and the decision tree approach can supply financial managers with objective credit analysis results, and therefore are generally more useful than the conventional method in credit analysis. However, these two methods use a static analytic framework and assume that collection measures are given.

17.4 Bankruptcy and Financial Distress Analysis

For the past fifteen years, academicians and practitioners have used the linear discriminant function to analyze bankruptcy and financial distress for both industrial and financial firms. Here, we will discuss only the three most important studies: (1) Altman's (1968) bankruptcy analysis for industrial firms, (2) Sinkey's (1975) study of identifying problem banks from non-problem banks, and (3) Trieschmann and Pinches' (1973) analysis of the financial insolvency of insurance companies.

Altman's study included 33 manufacturers who filed bankruptcy petitions under Chapter X of the Bankruptcy Act during 1946–1965. These 33 firms were paired with 33 non-bankrupt firms based on similar industry and asset size. Asset size ranged between \$1 million and \$25 million. For each firm, 22 variables were initially chosen for analysis based on their popularity in the literature and their potential relevance to the study. These ratios were classified into five categories: liquidity, profitability, leverage, solvency, and activity. One ratio from each category was chosen for inclusion in the discriminant model. The variables used to obtain the results are as follows:

X_1 = Working capital/Total assets,
X_2 = Retained earnings/Total assets,
X_3 = EBIT/Total assets,
X_4 = Market value of equity/Book value of total debt, and
X_5 = Sales/Total assets.

The mean ratios of these five variables for the bankrupt group are –0.061, –0.626, –0.318, 0.401, and 1.500, respectively. The mean ratios for these five variables for the non-bankrupt group are 0.414, 0.355, 0.153, 2.477, and 1.900, respectively.

Altman's final estimated discriminant function is as follows:

$$Y_i = 0.012X_1 + 0.014X_2 + 0.033X_3 + 0.006X_4 + 0.999X_5. \quad (17.5a)$$

His results show that this discriminant function has done well in predicting non-bankrupt firms.

Using (i) the formula for the overall cost of misclassification (E) and (ii) the expected error rate as discussed in the previous chapters, Altman classified the initial sample. He concluded that all firms having a Z-score greater than 2.99 clearly fall into the non-bankrupt sector, while those firms having a Z-score below 1.81 are all bankrupt. The area between 1.81 and 2.99 will be defined as the zone of "ignorance" or the "*gray*" *area*. Although these are the original values proposed by Altman, in a more recent interview, he stated that a negative Z-score was now an indicator of potential bankruptcy.

Altman's original Z-score model requires a firm to have publicly traded equity and be a manufacturer. He uses a revised model to make it applicable for private firms and non-manufacturers. The resulting model is as follows:

$$Z = 6.56\frac{\text{Net working capital}}{\text{Total assets}} + 3.26\frac{\text{Accumulated retained earnings}}{\text{Total assets}} + 1.05\frac{\text{EBIT}}{\text{Total assets}} + 6.72\frac{\text{Book value of equity}}{\text{Total liabilities}}, \quad (17.5\text{b})$$

where $Z < 1.23$ indicates a bankruptcy prediction, $1.23 \leq Z \leq 2.90$ indicates a gray area, and $Z >$ indicates no bankruptcy.

By using Altman's final estimated discriminant function from Equation (17.5a), we now calculate JNJ's Z-score in the year 2020. First, we calculate X_1, X_2, X_3, X_4, and X_5 for JNJ as follows:

Working capital: Current assets – Current liabilities = 51,237 – 42,493 = 8,744

$$\begin{aligned} X_1 &= \text{Working capital/Total assets} = 8{,}744/174{,}894 = 0.05, \\ X_2 &= \text{Retained earnings/Total assets} = 113{,}890/174{,}894 = 0.65, \\ X_3 &= \text{EBIT/Total assets} = 16{,}698/174{,}894 = 0.095. \end{aligned}$$

Market value of equity is the total dollar value of a company's equity and is also known as market capitalization. This measure of a company's value is calculated by multiplying the current stock price by the total number of outstanding shares.

$$\text{Market value of equity} = 2,632.8 \times 157.38 = 414,350.1,$$

$$\begin{aligned} X_4 &= \text{Market value of equity/Book value of total debt} \\ &= 414{,}350.1/111{,}616 = 3.71, \\ X_5 &= \text{Sales/Total assets} = 82{,}584/174{,}894 = 0.47. \end{aligned}$$

Second, we substitute X_1, X_2, X_3, X_4, and X_5 into Equation (17.5a). We obtain the following Z-score for JNJ in the year 2020:

$$1.2 \times 0.05 + 1.4 \times 0.65 + 3.3 \times 0.095 + 0.6 \times 3.71 + 1 \times 0.47 = 3.99.$$

From the above calculation, the Z-score for JNJ in the year 2020 is 3.99. Since 3.99 is much larger than 2.90, the chance of JNJ becoming a bankrupt firm is almost equal to zero.

Sinkey's (1975) study of problem banks is another example of the use of a discriminant function in financial analysis. Sinkey draws a profile of characteristics associated with banks that may be in danger of failing, to develop an early warning system to help predict problem banks. The Federal Deposit Insurance Corporation wants to predict problem banks as early as possible in order to be able to advise banks of necessary financial management changes in time for them to maintain solvent operations. "Problem" banks are categorized according to the likelihood of their needing financial assistance. The three classes of problem banks and the composition of the firms studied are now discussed. These three classes are (i) serious problem–potential payoff (SPPP), (ii) serious problem (SP), and (iii) other problem (OP). SPPP represents an advanced problem bank that has at least 50% chance of requiring financial assistance in the near future. A bank whose financial condition threatens ultimately to obligate financial outlay by the FEIC unless drastic changes occur is classified as SP. And a bank with some significant weakness, with vulnerability less than class 2, but still calling for aggressive supervision and extraordinary concern by the FEIC is classified as OP.

Of the 110 banks analyzed, 90 were identified as SPPP in 1972 and 20 in 1973. Each problem bank was matched with a non-problem bank similar to it by (1) geographic market area, (2) total deposits, (3) number of banking offices, and (4) Federal Reserve membership status.

Over 100 variables were initially examined to see if there was a significant difference between the ratios of problem and non-problem banks on a univariate basis. Sinkey's study (1975) also presents a profile analysis (mean ratios for each group) of five ratios found to be highly significant over the 1969–72 period. These five variables represent the following dimensions of bank finances: (1) loan volume, represented by loans/assets; (2) capital adequacy, by loans/capital plus reserves; (3) efficiency, by operating expense/operating income; (4) sources of revenue, by loan revenue/total revenue; and (5) uses of revenue, by other expenses/total revenue. The details of Sinkey's profile analysis can be found in either Sinkey (1975) or Chapter 4 of Lee and Lee (2017).

Sinkey then applied the MDA technique to classify the banks based on their financial ratios. Separate discriminant functions were estimated for each year from 1969 through 1972. In general, six or seven variables were included in each function. Recall that a Type I error represents the prediction of a problem bank as a non-problem one, and that a Type II error represents the prediction of a non-problem bank as a problem one. Obviously, from the viewpoint of financial outlay, a Type I error is more costly to the FDIC. The prediction results of Type I, Type II, and Total errors are now discussed in some detail.

Type I errors for the years 1969 through 1972 are 46.36%, 42.73%, 38.18%, and 28.15%, respectively. Type II errors for the years 1969 through 1972 are 25.45%, 27.27%, 24.55%, and 21.36%, respectively. Total errors for the years 1969 through 1972 are 35.91%, 35.00%, 31.36%, and 24.76%, respectively.

In the years closer to a bank's classification as a problem bank, the discriminant model becomes better able to classify banks that were termed problems in 1971 and 1972. It is apparent that the potential exists for the banking agency to more efficiently allocate resources and analyze preexamination data through the implementation of an effective early warning system.

A third example of the application of a discriminant function in financial analysis is Orgler's (1970, 1975) dummy regression model for examining loan quality. His research sample contained 75 criticized loans and 225 non-criticized loans. The validation sample contained 40 criticized loans and 80 non-criticized loans. A final regression model is as follows:

$$\begin{aligned} Z_i = 1.1018 &+ 0.1017X_{1i} - 0.3966X_{2i} - 0.0916X_{3i} \\ &- 0.1573X_{4i} - 0.0199X_{5i} - 0.4533X_{6i}, \end{aligned} \tag{17.6}$$

where $X_1 = 0$: Unsecured loan, 1: Secured loan; $X_2 = 0$: Past interest payment due, 1: Current loan; $X_3 = 0$: Not audited firm, 1: Audited firm; $X_4 = 0$: Net loss firm, 1: Net profit firm; $X_5 =$ Working capital/Current assets; and $X_6 = 0$: Loan criticized by bank examiner, 1: Loan not criticized by bank examiner.

Orgler used two cutoff points to classify loans: $C_1 = 0.08$ and $C_2 = 0.25$. These two cutoff points gave three predicted categories for commercial loans:

$$\begin{aligned} \hat{Z}_i > C_2 &= \text{“Bad” loans}, \\ C_1 \leq \hat{Z}_i \leq C_2 &= \text{“Marginal” loan}, \\ \hat{Z}_i \leq C_1 &= \text{“Good” loan}. \end{aligned}$$

A fourth example of the application of a discriminant function in financial analysis is Trieschmann and Pinches' (1973) multivariate model for predicting financially distressed Property-Liability (P-L) insurers. Their paper is concerned with insurance company insolvency and the identification of firms with a high probability of financial distress. They use multiple discriminant analysis to classify firms into two groups (solvent or distressed). The model was able to correctly classify 49 out of 52 firms in the study. One solvent firm was classified as being distressed, while two of the distressed firms were classified as being solvent. Of the 70 variables the researchers felt might be important, the final model included only six. The discriminant model for identifying P-L firms with a high potential for financial distress is as follows:

$$\begin{aligned} Z = &-11.08576X_1 - 1.50752X_2 + 3.53606X_3 \\ &- 2.49824X_4 - 2.45352X_5 - 0.24492X_6, \end{aligned} \tag{17.7}$$

where $X_1 =$ Agents' balances/Total assets; a measure of the firms' accounts receivable management, $X_2 =$ Stocks at cost (preferred and common)/Stocks at market (preferred and common); measures investment management, $X_3 =$ Bonds at cost/Bonds at market; measures the firm's age, $X_4 =$ (Loss adjustment expenses paid + Underwriting expenses paid)/Net premiums written; a measure of a firm's funds flow from insurance operations, X_5 = Combined ratio; traditional measure of underwriting profitability, and X_6 = Premiums written direct/Surplus; a measure of the firm's sales aggressiveness.

The final discriminant model has an F-ratio of 12.559, which, with the appropriate degrees of freedom (6 and 45), is significant beyond the 0.005 level. Once it is established that the model does discriminate between distressed and solvent P-L insurance firms, the individual contribution of each of the variables can be examined using the t-test. The individual contribution is dominated by X_6, which is significant at the 0.0005 level; X_1, which is significant at the 0.005 level; and X_2 and X_4, which are significant at the 0.025 level. The discriminant model has been proved to be quite applicable to this sort of analysis. With further development of databases for analysis, future regulators should be in a better position to step in and to help potentially distressed firms well before bankruptcy threatens.

17.5 Applications of Factor Analysis to Select Useful Financial Ratios

Farrar (1962) and King (1966) have used the factor analysis technique to determine the important factors for security rates-of-return determination. King (1965) found that there are market factors, industry factors, and other factors that determine stock price behavior over time. Lloyd and Lee (1975) have used factor analysis to identify the subgroups for the thirty Dow-Jones industrial firms and to test the existence of Block Recursive Systems in asset pricing models. To test the existence of their arbitrage pricing theory (APT), Roll and Ross (1980) have used factor loadings of individual securities to show that many factors are involved in the return-generating process.

In financial ratio analysis, Johnson (1979) has used information factor loadings to test the cross-sectional stability of financial ratio patterns; Pinches and Mingo (1973) have used factor loading information to determine which variables should be used to estimate their n-group MDA for industry bond ratings. Then, Chen and Shimerda (1981) used factor analysis in the empirical determination of useful financial ratios.

The properties and characteristics of financial ratios have received considerable attention in recent years, with interest focused primarily on determining the predictive ability of financial ratios and related financial data. Principal areas of investigation have included (i) prediction of corporate bond ratings as explored by Horrigan (1965), Pinches and Mingo (1973), and Pogue and Soldofsky (1969); (ii) prediction of financial ratios by Lev (1969) and Frecka and Lee (1983); (iii) prediction of the suitability of the firm to merge, through an examination of the characteristics of merged firms by Simkowitz and Monroe (1971) and Stevens (1973); and (iv) anticipation of financial impairment by Altman (1968), Beaver (1968a, 1968b), Blume (1974), Tinsley (1970), and Wilcox (1971).

Using the information from factor loadings, Johnson (1979) classified 61 financial ratios for 306 primary manufacturers and 159 retailers into eight financial groups. The results of Johnson's study, and results obtained by Pinches *et al.* (1973) (PMC), and Pinches, Eubank, and Mingo (1975), suggest that meaningful, empirically based classifications of financial ratios can be isolated, and that the composition of these financial ratio groups is reasonably stable over the time periods investigated and across the two industry classifications examined. Similarly, Chen and Shimerda (1981) used factor loadings to study useful financial ratios, obtaining conclusions like those obtained by Johnson (1979). The detailed analysis done by Chen and Shimerda and Johnson can be found in Chapter 4 of Lee and Lee.

17.6 Bond Rating Forecasting

Pinches and Mingo (1973) (P&M) have developed and tested a factor analysis/multiple discriminant model for predicting bond ratings. They used factor analysis to screen the data in the manner discussed earlier. The details of these techniques have been discussed in Chapters 3 and 4 of Lee and Lee (2017). Here, we will use P&M's multiple discriminant results to show how a k-group discriminant function can be used to analyze the performance of bond ratings and predict future bond ratings.

The following six variables estimate the final discriminant functions:

X_1 = Subordination; the legal status of bonds,
X_2 = Years of consecutive dividends; indicates the stability of the firms' earnings,
X_3 = Issue size; reflects the size of the firm,
X_4 = (Net income + Interest)/Interest: five-year mean, indicates the ability of the firm to meet debt obligations,
X_5 = Long-term debt/Total assets: five-year mean; a measure of the capital structure of the firm, and
X_6 = Net income/Total assets; a measure of management's ability to earn a satisfactory return on investment.

These variables were chosen from a group of 35 through factor analysis. In all, 180 bonds were analyzed and randomly assigned to one of two sample groups — 132 forming the original sample for model development and 48 forming a holdout sample for testing purposes. P&M's model includes three discriminant functions that were significant at the 0.001 level (based upon Barlett's v-statistic). The structural form of these three functions is presented in the following:

$$\begin{aligned} Y_1 &= -0.329X_1 + 0.107X_2 + 0.100X_3 + 0.005X_4 - 0.270X_5 + 0.893X_6, \\ Y_2 &= 0.046X_1 + 0.218X_2 - 0.212X_3 - 0.264X_4 - 0.505X_5 - 0.762X_6, \\ Y_3 &= -0.128X_1 - 0.044X_2 - 0.138X_3 + 0.001X_4 + 0.320X_5 - 0.928X_6. \end{aligned} \tag{17.8}$$

The overall discriminating power of the model was determined by testing the equality of the group means. The calculated F-value for the MDA model is 17.225. As the tabled value (0.001) is 2.13, the calculated F-value permits rejection of the null hypothesis that the bonds came from the same population. With the overall conclusion that, *a priori*, the groups of bonds are significantly different, the six variables entering the final MDA model can be examined. The individual discriminating ability of each of the variables and their rank of importance in the various discriminant functions are presented in Chapter 4 of Lee and Lee.

The MDA model correctly rated 92 of the 132 bonds in the original sample, which corresponds to a correct prediction rate of 69.7%; this is analogous to the coefficient of determination (R^2) in regression analysis. If an analyst were interested only in the ability of the model to predict ratings within one classification (either higher or lower) of the actual rating, the model performed very accurately, classifying all but two of the bonds within one rating of the actual rating.

In another test of validity, the model was applied to the holdout sample. With this group, the model correctly rated 31 of 48 bonds (64.58%) and rated all 48 bonds within one rating higher or lower than the actual rating. To further validate the MDA model, a stratified random sample of 48 companies issuing bonds during the first six months of 1969 was gathered. The MDA model (developed from a sample of newly rated bonds issued in 1967 and 1968) was employed to predict the ratings on the new bonds issued in 1969. Twenty-seven of the 48 bonds were rated correctly, indicating that the model possesses future predictive ability.

The subordination status of a corporate bond [represented by a binary (0–1) variable] appears to be the most important variable among those that were examined in this study. If one were interested only in rating bonds as investment quality (AA, A, and BAA) or non-investment quality (BA and B), the best single predictor is the subordinated status of the bond. Based on this variable alone, correct ratings (investment vs. noninvestment quality) would have occurred 88.6% of the time for the original sample (117/132) and 83.3% of the time for the holdout sample (40/48).

The model performed very poorly for BAA-rated bonds. An analysis of the multiple range tests indicated that the inability of the MDA model to accurately predict BAA-rated bonds appears to be due to a lack of statistically significant differences in the quantifiable variables included in the model. Overall, though, the model's ability to discriminate between different bond ratings is fairly good, and it shows potential for application to the prediction of future bond ratings.

There are two major technical differences between the methods and procedures used in this section and those used in Sections 17.4 and 17.5. First, the MDA used in this section is a k-group instead of two-group analysis. Second, Pinches and Mingo's MDA analysis is predictive instead of descriptive in nature. Joy and Tollefson (1974) argue that MDA can be used for either predictive or descriptive purposes. They regard Altman's (1968) MDA application as a descriptive analysis instead of a predictive analysis. This comment can also apply to both Sinkey's and Trieschmann and Pinches' (1973) MDA analysis. Other related arguments can be found in Joy and Tollefson (1978) and Altman and Eisenbeis (1978).

The financial-ratio-based credit scoring model for a bond rating system requires the maximization of two conflicting objectives (i.e., the explanatory and discriminatory power, simultaneously), which had not been directly addressed in the paper by Pinches (1973). Therefore, Kao and Lee's (2012) paper has developed a hybrid multivariate credit scoring model that combines principle component analysis and Fisher's discriminant analysis using the MINIMAX goal programming technique so that the maximization of the two conflicting objectives can be compromised. The performance of alternative credit scoring models is analyzed and compared using a dataset from previous studies. They found that the proposed hybrid credit scoring model outperforms other alternative models in both explanatory and discriminatory powers.

For multiple-class prediction, a frequently used approach is based on ordered probit model. Hwang *et al.* (2008) show that this approach is not optimal in the sense that it is not designed to minimize the error rate of the prediction. Based upon the works by Altman (1968), Ohlson (1980), and Begley *et al.* (1996) on two-class prediction, Hwang *et al.* (2008) propose a modified ordered probit model. The modified approach depends on an optimal cutoff value and can be easily applied in applications. An empirical study is used to demonstrate that the prediction accuracy rate of the modified classifier is better than that obtained from the usual ordered probit model. In addition, we also show that not only are the usual accounting variables useful for predicting issuer credit ratings but that the market-driven variables and industry effects are also important determinants.

17.7 Ohlson's and Shumway's Methods for Estimating Default Probability[1]

Beginning in the 1980s, more complex estimation methods such as logit and probit were used to determine the likelihood of company bankruptcy. The logit model is a methodology that uses maximum likelihood estimation, or the so-called conditional logit model. Two well-known models using logit models to estimate the probability of bankruptcy are Ohlson (1980) and Shumway (2001), which we will discuss next. Ohlson discusses the following econometric advantages of the logit model over MDA used for the development of the Altman Z-score. MDA imposes certain statistical requirements on the distributional properties of the predictors, violation of which will result in invalid or poor approximations. For example, MDA assumes the same variance–covariance matrices of the predictors for both failed and non-failed group; it also requires normal distributions of failure predictors which bias against the use of indicator-independent variables. Moreover, the output of the MDA model is a score which has little intuitive interpretation. The matching procedure which is typically used in the MDA technique can result in losing useful information such as losing meaningful predictors. The use of logistic regression, on the other hand, essentially overcomes the weaknesses of MDA discussed above.

Ohlson (1980) used data available prior to the date of bankruptcy to ensure the strict forecasting relationships. His sample included 105 bankruptcies and 2,058 non-bankruptcies from the 1970s (1970–76). Among the 105 bankrupt firms, eight firms are traded in the New York Stock Exchange, 43 are traded in the American Stock Exchange, and 54 are traded in the over-the-counter market or regional exchanges. Nine variables defined in the following are used to develop the logit model:

[1]This section was written by Professor Lili Sun from the University of North Texas and Professor Bi-Huei Tsai from Yang Ming Chiao Tung University.

X_1 = Natural log of Total assets/GNP Implicit Price Deflator Index. The index assumes a base value of 100 for 1968,
X_2 = Total liabilities/Total assets,
X_3 = (Current assets − Current liabilities)/Total assets,
X_4 = Current assets/Current liabilities,
X_5 = One if total liabilities exceed total assets, zero otherwise,
X_6 = Net income/Total assets,
X_7 = Funds provided by operations/Total liabilities,
X_8 = One if net income was negative for the last two years, zero otherwise, and
X_9 = (Net income in year t − Net income in $t-1$)/(Absolute net income in year t+ Absolute net income in year $t-1$).

Three sets of coefficients are estimated using data one year prior to bankruptcy or two years prior to bankruptcy. Intuitively, the model with estimates computed using data one year prior to bankruptcy performs the best, which is expressed as follows:

$$\begin{aligned} Y = &-1.32 - 0.407X_1 + 6.03X_2 - 1.43X_3 + 0.0757X_4 \\ &- 2.37X_5 - 1.83X_6 + 0.285X_7 - 1.72X_8 - 0.521X_9, \end{aligned} \tag{17.9}$$

where $Y = \log[P/(1-P)]$, $P =$ the probability of bankruptcy.

Thus, the probability of bankruptcy (P) is calculated as $\exp(Y)/[1+\exp(Y)]$ exp, and the model becomes relatively easy to interpret.

Ohlson found that using a probability cutoff of 3.8% for classifying firms as bankrupt minimized Type I and Type II errors of the model presented in Equation (17.9). At this probability cutoff point, the model correctly classified 87.6% of his bankrupt firm sample and 82.6% of the non-bankrupt firms. Begley *et al.* (1996) applied Ohlson's logit model (1980) to predict bankruptcy for a holdout sample of 65 bankrupt and 1,300 non-bankrupt firms in the 1980s. They found substantially higher Type I and Type II error rates than those in the original studies. They reestimated the coefficients for each model using data for a portion of their 1980s sample. However, they found no performance improvement for the reestimated Ohlson model.

The logit model used by Ohlson (1980) is single-period static logit model. Shumway (2001) employed a discrete hazard model or multiple-period dynamic logit model.[2] The concept of the discrete time hazard model originates from the survival model and is widely used in the biological medication field. It was not until recent years that social science researchers started using it for analyzing variables' effect upon survival (e.g., Lancaster, 1992). Cox and Oakes (1984) calculate the hazard rate to estimate the likelihood of survival and survival time. Shumway (2001) elaborates the econometric advantages of a hazard model over a static binary logit model. First, hazard models control for each firm's period at risk, while static models do not. Second, hazard models exploit each firm's time series data by including annual observations as time-varying covariates. Third, hazard models produce more efficient out-of-sample forecasts by utilizing much more data. Shumway (2001) proves that a multi-period logit model is equivalent to a discrete time hazard model. Therefore, his model used multiple years of data for each sample firm and treated each firm as a single observation.

Moreover, Shumway (2001) also corrected the problem in the traditional approaches of bankruptcy forecasting, that is, previous studies that used only most of the accounting ratios used in the previous bankruptcy studies are found not significant. Shumway (2001) incorporated not only financial ratios but also market variables such as market size, past stock returns, and idiosyncratic returns variability as bankruptcy predictors.

The dependent variable in the prediction models is each firm year's bankruptcy status (0, 1) in a given sample year. In a hazard analysis, for a bankrupt firm, the dependent variable equals 1 for the year in which it files bankruptcy, and the dependent variable equals 0 for all sample years prior to the bankruptcy-filing year. The non-bankrupt firms are coded 0 every year they are in the sample.

The Shumway (2001) study employed all available firms in a broad range of industries, resulting in a sample of 300 bankrupt firms for the period of 1962–1992. The study found that a multi-period logit

[2]A statistical technique for determining "hazard functions," or the probability that an individual will experience an event within a particular time period, given that the individual was subject to the risk that the event might occur.

model outperformed MDA and single-period logit models, and that a combination of market-based and accounting-based independent variables outperformed models that were only accounting-based. The Shumway model with the incorporation of market-based and accounting-based predictors is expressed as follows:

$$Y = -13.303 - 1.982X_1 + 3.593X_2 - 0.467X_3 - 1.809X_4 + 5.79X_5, \tag{17.10}$$

where $Y = \log[P/(1-P)]$, $P =$ the probability of bankruptcy; $X_1 =$ Net income/Total assets; $X_2 =$ Total liabilities/Total assets; $X_3 =$ The logarithm of Each firm's market capitalization at the end of year prior to the observation year/Total market capitalization of NYSE and AMEX market; $X_4 =$ Past excess return as the return of the firm in year $t-1-$ The value-weighted CRSP NYSE/AMEX index return in year $t - 1$; and $X_5 =$ Idiosyncratic standard deviation of each firm's stock returns. It is defined as the standard deviation of the residual of a regression which regresses each stock's monthly returns in year $t-1$ on the value-weighted NYSE/AMEX index return for the same year.

To evaluate the forecast accuracy of the Hazard model presented in Equation (17.10), Shumway (2001) divided the test sample into ten groups based upon their predicted probability of bankruptcies using the model. The hazard model classifies almost 70% of all bankruptcies in the highest bankruptcy probability decile and classifies 96.6 of bankrupt firms above the median probability. Following Shumway (2001), researchers of bankruptcy prediction have been using multiple-period logit regression. For instance, Sun (2007) developed a multi-period logistic regression model and found this model outperforms auditors' going concern opinions in predicting bankruptcy. Saunders and Allen (2002) and Saunders and Cornett (2006) have discussed alternative methods for determining credit risk.

Hwang *et al.* (2008) use the discrete time survival model by Cox and Oakes (1984) to predict the probability of financial distress for each firm under study. The maximum likelihood method is employed to estimate the values of our model parameters. The resulting estimates are analyzed by their asymptotic normal distributions, and are used to estimate the in-sample probability of financial distress for each firm under study. Using such estimated probability, a strategy is developed to identify failing firms, and is applied to study the probability of bankruptcy in the future for firms listed in Taiwan Stock Exchange. Empirical studies demonstrate that our strategy developed from the discrete time survival model can yield more accurate forecasts than the alternative methods based on the logit model in Ohlson (1980) and the probit model in Zmijewski (1984).

17.8 Merton Distance Model and KMV-Merton Model

In this section, we will discuss Merton Distance Model, Naïve Merton Distance Model, and KMV-Merton Model.

17.8.1 *Merton distance model*

The Merton DD model produces a probability of default for each firm in the sample at any given point in time. To calculate the probability, the model subtracts the face value of the firm's debt from an estimate of the market value of the firm and then divides this difference by an estimate of the volatility of the firm (scaled to reflect the horizon of the forecast). The resulting Z-score, which is sometimes referred to as the distance to default, is then substituted into a cumulative density function to calculate the probability that the value of the firm will be less than the face value of debt at the forecasting horizon. The market value of the firm is simply the sum of the market values of the firm's debt and the value of its equity. If both these quantities were readily observable, calculating default probabilities would be simple. While equity values are readily available, reliable data on the market value of firm debt is generally unavailable. Appendix 17C explains how to resolve this issue.

Following Appendix 17C, the Merton distance to default can be calculated as

$$\mathrm{DD} = \frac{\ln\left(\frac{V}{F}\right) + (\mu - 0.5\sigma_V^2)T}{\sigma_V\sqrt{T}}, \tag{17.11}$$

where μ is an estimate of the expected annual return of the firm's assets, V is the total value of the firm, σ_V is the volatility of firm value, T is the time to maturity, F is the face value of the firm's debt, and r is the instantaneous risk-free rate. The corresponding implied probability of default, sometimes called the expected default frequency (or EDF), is

$$\pi_{\text{Merton}} = N\left(-\left(\frac{\ln\left(\frac{V}{F}\right) + \left(\mu - 0.5\sigma_V^2\right)T}{\sigma_V\sqrt{T}}\right)\right) = N(-\text{DD}), \tag{17.12}$$

where $N(\cdot)$ is the cumulative standard normal distribution function.

There are five variables in Equation (17.11), that is, μ, V, σ_V, T, and F. In these five variables, only V and σ_V are not observable. Following Bharath and Shumway (2008), in Appendix 17C, we will discuss how V and σ_V can be numerically estimated. In addition, we also discuss how DD can be estimated.

17.8.2 *A naïve Merton distance model*

To estimate Merton's distance model, it is required to implement it using the iterative procedure. To avoid solving Equations (17C.2) and (17C.5) by implementing the iterative procedure described in Appendix 17C, Bharath and Shumway (2008) construct a naïve predictor with two objectives. First, they want their naïve predictor to have a reasonable chance of performing as well as the Merton DD predictor, so they want it to capture the same information the Merton DD predictor uses. They also want their naïve probability to approximate the functional form of the Merton DD probability. Second, they want their naïve probability to be simple, so they avoid solving any equations or estimating any difficult quantities in its construction. They proposed the form for the naïve probability similar to the Merton DD model. None of the numerical choices of the naïve model is the result of any type of estimation or optimization as required by the original Merton DD model, which is defined in Equation (17.11).

For constructing a naïve probability, they first approximate the market value of each firm's debt with the face value of its debt (F),

$$\text{Naïve}D = F, \tag{17.13}$$

where naïve D represents the approximate market value of the firm's debt.

Since they assume that firms that are close to default have very risky debt, and the risk of their debt is correlated with their equity risk, they approximate the volatility of each firm's debt as

$$\text{Naïve } \sigma_D = 0.05 + 0.25 * \sigma_E, \tag{17.14}$$

where σ_D and σ_E represent the standard deviation debt and equity, respectively.

They include the five percentage points in this term to represent term structure volatility, and they include the 25% times equity volatility to allow for volatility associated with default risk. This gives them an approximation to the total volatility of the firm of

$$\begin{aligned}\text{Naïve } \sigma_V &= \frac{E}{E + \text{Naïve } D}\sigma_E + \frac{\text{Naïve } D}{E + \text{Naïve} D}\text{Naïve } \sigma_D \\ &= \frac{E}{E+F}\sigma_E + \frac{E}{E+F}(0.05 + 0.25 * \sigma_E). \end{aligned} \tag{17.15}$$

Next, they set the expected return on the firm's assets equal to the firm's stock return over the previous year,

$$\text{Naïve } \mu = r_{it-1}. \tag{17.16}$$

This allows them to capture some of the same information that is captured by the Merton DD iterative procedure described above. The iterative procedure is able to condition on an entire year of equity return data. By allowing their naïve estimate of μ to depend on past rate of returns, they incorporate the same information used by the Merton DD model.

The naïve distance to default is then

$$\text{Naïve DD} = \frac{\ln\left(\frac{E+F}{F}\right) + (r_{it-1} - 0.5\, \text{naïve } \sigma_V^2)T}{\text{Naïve } \sigma_V \sqrt{T}}. \tag{17.17}$$

This naïve alternative model is easy to compute; however, it retains the structure of the Merton DD distance to default and expected default frequency. It also captures approximately the same quantity of information as the Merton DD probability. Thus, examining the forecasting ability of this quantity helps them separate the value of solving the Merton model from the value of the functional form of π_{Merton}. Bharath and Shumway (2008) define a naïve probability estimate as

$$\pi_{\text{naïve}} = N(-\text{naïve DD}). \tag{17.18}$$

Bharath and Shumway (2008) argue that it is fairly easy to criticize their naïve probability. This is because their choices for modeling firm volatility are not particularly well motivated and their decision to use past returns for μ is arbitrary at best. However, to quibble with their naïve probability is to miss the point of their exercise. In their paper, they have empirically demonstrated that the predictive power of naïve model is as good as the Merton DD model. However, they suggest that a theoretical improved naïve model should be considered for future research.

Bharath and Shumway (2008) have found that their naïve model performs as well as the original Merton DD model. The following are a few comments on their findings:

(i) It is well known the functional form of the Black–Scholes original model is subject to specification biases. These include that the original Black–Scholes model assumes the firm value is log-normally distributed. In addition, Bharath and Shumway's (2008) empirical work assumes that volatility of firms is constant. Therefore, it is worthwhile to reconsider the use of the stochastic volatility type of the CEV model to reexamine the performance of the Merton DD model.

(ii) It is well known that the estimator can contaminate estimation risk. Therefore, the estimation risk might be larger than the measurement error which uses face value of bond to replace market value of bond.

In Section 17.8, we will propose a theoretically improved naïve model in terms of the capital structure determination models suggested by Titman and Wessels (1988), Chang and Lee (2009), Yang *et al.* (2010), Lee and Tai (2016), and others.

17.8.3 *KMV-Merton model*

The KMV Corporation developed the KMV-Merton model, which is frequently used in both practice and academic research. This model is an application of the Merton DD model which has been discussed in Section 17.8.1. Bharath and Shumway (2008) have pointed out that there are a number of things which differentiate the Merton DD model, which they test, from Moody's KMV. One important difference is that Merton's distance model uses Merton's (1974) model, while Moody's KMV uses a proprietary model that they call the KV model. Apparently, the KV model is a generalization of the Merton model that allows for various classes and maturities of debt. Bharath and Shumway (2008) use the cumulative normal distribution to convert distances to default into default probabilities. However, Moody's KMV uses its large historical database to estimate the empirical distribution of changes in distances to default and it calculates default probabilities based on that distribution. The distribution of distances to default is an important input to default probabilities, but it is not required for ranking firms by their relative probability. Therefore, several of our results will emphasize the model's ability to rank firms by default risk rather than its ability to calculate accurate probabilities. Moody's KMV may also make proprietary adjustments to the accounting information that they use to calculate the face value of debt. We cannot perfectly replicate the methods of Moody's KMV because several of the modeling choices made by Moody's KMV are proprietary information. As I discussed in Section 17.8.2, cumulative normal density function might not be appropriate for estimating the Merton DD model. I strongly believe the KMV model uses the distribution in terms of historical data and is more appropriate than the cumulative normal density function used by Bharath and Shumway (2008).

17.9 Capital Structure Determination and Naïve Default Probability

In this section, we will discuss how capital structure determination models can be used to theoretically improve the naïve default probability model as defined in Equation (17.17). Following Titman and Wessels (1988), Chang *et al.* (2009), Yang *et al.* (2010), and Lee and Tai (2016), we will define the capital structure determination model as follows.

Titman and Wessels (1988) and Chang *et al.* (2009) have used a single equation to estimate the determination of capital structure. Yang *et al.* (2010) and Lee and Tai (2016) have incorporated stock return information to simultaneously estimate the capital structure.

We can use Lee and Tai's (2016) model to estimate the capital structure. Then, we can use the information of estimation of capital structure and market value of the firm to estimate the value of debt as follows:

$$\text{Estimated debt} = \text{Estimated}\frac{\text{Debt}}{\text{Equity}} * \text{Market value of equity.} \tag{17.19}$$

To obtain the theoretical improved naïve model, we can replace Equation (17.13) by Equation (17.19). Then, we follow Bharath and Shumway's (2008) approach to obtain the modified naïve default probability estimator. The performance of this modified model and the original naïve model will be empirically tested in future research.

17.10 Summary and Concluding Remarks

The main purposes of this paper are to review and integrate the applications of discriminant analysis, factor analysis, and logistic regression in credit risk management. First, we have discussed how the discriminant analysis can be used for credit rating such as calculating the financial Z-score to determine the chance of bankruptcy of a firm. In addition, we have also discussed how discriminant analysis can be used to classify banks into problem banks and non-problem banks. Second, we have discussed how factor analysis can be combined with discriminant analysis to perform bond rating forecasting. Third, we have shown how the logistic regression technique can be used to calculate the default risk probability. Fourth, we have discussed the KMV-Merton model and Merton distance model for calculating default probability. Finally, we have compared all techniques discussed in previous sections and drawn conclusions and given suggestions for future research. We propose using the CEV option model to improve the original Merton DD model. In addition, we also propose a modified naïve model to improve Bharath and Shumway's (2008) naïve model.

Questions and Problems

1. Briefly discuss the basic concepts of linear combination for both deterministic and stochastic variables. Why are these concepts needed for financial planning and forecasting?
2. What is the purpose of discriminant analysis?
3. What techniques are used to derive the coefficients in MDA? What is the objective in deriving them?
4. For what purpose is principle component analysis used?
5. Of what value is factor loading to the financial analyst? What are some examples of factor loading?
6. How did Pinches and Mingo combine factor analysis and discriminant analysis in bond rating forecasting? How was their discriminant analysis different from previous examples?
7. Describe how Mehta and Van Horne used two-group discriminant analysis for credit analysis. How is the proper cutoff point determined? What tasks is the manager responsible for in doing credit analysis?
8. Briefly discuss the classification errors in Question 8 and their implications to this type of analysis.
9. Describe the application of factor analysis and factor loadings to classify financial ratios, as in the Johnson study of industrial firms. How are the factor scores determined?
10. Please describe Ohlson's (1980) and Shumway's (2001) models for estimating default probability in detail.
11. Please discuss the similarities and differences among Altman's (1968), Ohlson's (1980), and Shumway's (2001) approaches for credit analyses.
12. Please discuss the Merton distance model and the naïve alternative model in detail.
13. Please discuss the KMV Merton model in detail.
14. Please discuss how capital structure determination can affect naïve default probability.

Bibliography

Altman, E. I. (1968). Financial ratios, discriminant analysis, and the prediction of corporate bankruptcy. *Journal of Finance*, 23, 589–609.

Altman, E. I. (1982). Accounting implications of failure prediction models. *Journal of Accounting, Auditing, Finance*, 6(1), (Fall), 4–19.

Altman, E. I. (1984). The success of business failure prediction models. An international survey. *Journal of Banking and Finance*, 8(2), 171–198.

Altman, E. I. (1989). Measuring corporate bond mortality and performance. *Journal of Finance*, 44(4), 909–922.

Altman, E. I. (1993). *Corporate Financial Distress and Bankruptcy: A Complete Guide to Predicting and Avoiding Distress and Profiting from Bankruptcy.* New York, NY: Wiley.

Altman, E. I. (2000). Predicting financial distress of companies revisiting the Z-score and ZETA models. Working paper.

Altman, E. I., R. Haldeman and P. Narayanan (1977). ZETA analysis, a new model for bankruptcy classification. *Journal of Banking and Finance*, 1(1), 29–54.

Altman, E. I. and T. P. McGough (1974). Evaluation of a company as a going-concern. *Journal of Accounting*, 138(6), (December), 50–57.

Altman, E. I., G. Marco and F. Varetto (1994). Corporate distress diagnosis: Comparisons using linear discriminant analysis and neural networks. *Journal of Banking & Finance*, 18, 505–529.

Amemiya, T. (1981). The qualitative response models: A survey. *The Journal of Economic Literature*, 19(4), (December), 1483–1536.

Anandarajan, M., P. Lee and A. Anandarajan (2001). Bankruptcy prediction of financially stressed firms: An examination of the predictive accuracy of artificial neural networks. *International Journal of Intelligent Systems in Accounting, Finance and Management*, 10, 69–81.

Anderson, J. A. (1972). Separate sample logistic discrimination. *Biometrika*, 59, 19–35.

Barth, M. E., W. H. Beaver and W. R. Landsman (1998). Relative valuation roles of equity book value and net income as a function of financial health. *Journal of Accounting & Economics*, 25, 1–34.

Beaver, W. (1968a). Market prices, financial ratios and prediction of failure. *Journal of Accounting Research*, 6(2), 179–192.

Beaver, W. H. (1966). Financial ratios as predictors of failure. *Journal of Accounting Research*, 4, 71–111.

Beaver, W. H. (1968b). Alternative accounting measures as predictors of failure. *The Accounting Review*, 43, 113–122.

Beaver, W. H., M. F. McNichols and J. Rhie (2005). Have financial statements become less informative? Evidence from the ability of financial ratios to predict bankruptcy. *Review of Accounting Studies*, 10(1), 93–122.

Begley, J., J. Ming and S. Watts (1996). Bankruptcy classification errors in the 1980s: An empirical analysis of Altman's and Ohlson's models. *Review of Accounting Studies*, 1, 267–284.

Bharath, S. T. and T. Shumway (2004). Forecasting default with the KMV-Merton model. Working paper, the University of Michigan.

Bharath, S. T. and T. Shumway (2008). Forecasting default with the Merton distance to default model. *Review of Financial Studies*, 21(3), 1339–1369.

Bhandari, S. B., R. M. Soldofsky and W. J. Boe (1979). Bond quality rating changes for electric utilities: A multivariate analysis. *Financial Management*, 8, 74–81.

Billings, B. (1999). Revisiting the relation between the default risk of debt and the earnings response coefficient. *Accounting Review*, 74(4), 509–522.

Blume, M. P. (1974). The failing company doctrine. *Journal of Accounting Research*, 43, 1–25.

Chen, K. H. and T. A. Shimerda (1981). An empirical analysis of useful financial ratios. *Financial Management*, (Spring), 51–60.

Cielen, A., L. Peeters and K. Vanhoof (2004). Bankruptcy prediction using a data envelopment analysis. *European Journal of Operational Research*, 154(2), 526–532.

Clark, K. and E. Ofek (1994). Mergers as a means of restructuring distressed firms: An empirical investigation. *Journal of Financial & Quantitative Analysis*, 29(4), 541–565.

Cox, D. R. and D. Oakes (1984). *Analysis of Survival Data*. New York: Chapman & Hall.

Crosbie, P. and J. Bohn (2003). *Modeling Default Risk*. New York: Moody's KMV Company.

Denis, D., D. Denis and A. Sarin (1997). Ownership structure and top executive turnover. *Journal of Financial Economics*, 45, 193–221.

Diamond Jr., H. (1976). Pattern recognition and the detection of corporate failure. Ph.D. dissertation, New York University.

Dichev, I. (1998). Is the risk of bankruptcy a systematic risk? *Journal of Finance*, 53, 1131–1148.

Dimitras, A. I., S. H. Zanakis and C. Zopounidis (1996). Theory and methodology: A survey of business failure with an emphasis on prediction methods and industrial applications. *European Journal of Operational Research*, 90, 487–513.

Duffie, D. and K. Singleton (1999). Modeling term structures of defaultable bonds. *Review of Financial Studies*, 12, 687–720.

Drehmann, M., A. J. Patton and S. Sorensen (2005). Corporate defaults and large macroeconomic shocks. Working paper.

Farrar, F. S. (1962). *The Investment Decision Under Uncertainty*. Englewood Cliffs, NJ: Prentice Hall, Inc.

Falkenstein, E. G., A. Boral and L. Carty (2000). Riskcalc for private companies: Moody's Default model. As published in Global Credit Research.

Fitzpatrick, P. (1932). A comparison of the ratios of successful industrial enterprises with those of failed companies. *Certified Public Accountant*, 6, 727–731.

Foster, G. (1998). *Financial Statement Analysis*, 2nd ed. Englewood Cliffs, NJ: Prentice Hall, Inc.

Foster, B., T. Ward and J. Woodroof (1998). An analysis of the usefulness of debt defaults and going concern opinions in bankruptcy risk assessment. *Journal of Accounting, Auditing & Finance*, 13(3), 351–371.

Frecka, T. and C. F. Lee (1983) Generalized ratio generation process and its implications. *Journal of Accounting Research*, (Spring), 308–316.

Glennon, D. and P. Nigro (2005). Measuring the default risk of small business loans: A survival analysis approach. *Journal of Money, Credit, and Banking*, 37(5), 923–947.

Hillegeist, S. A., E. K. Keating and D. P. Cram (2004). Assessing the probability of bankruptcy. *Review of Accounting Studies*, 9, 5–34.

Hol, S., S. Westgaard and N. Wijst (2002). Capital structure and the prediction of bankruptcy. Working paper.

Honjo, Y. (2000). Business failure of new firms: An empirical analysis using a multiplicative hazards model. *International Journal of Industrial Organization*, 18(4), 557–574.

Hopwood, W., J. C. Mckeown and J. F. Mutchler (1984). A reexamination of auditor versus model accuracy within the context of the going-concern opinion decision. *Contemporary Accounting Research*, 10, 409–431.

Hopwood, W. S., J. C. Mckeown and J. P. Mutchler (1989). A test of the incremental explanatory power of opinions qualified for consistency and uncertainty. *The Accounting Review*, 64, 28–48.

Horrigan, J. O. (1965). Some empirical bases of financial ratio analysis. *The Accounting Review*, 40, 558–586.

Hwang, R. C., K. F. Cheng and C.-F. Lee (2009). On multiple-class prediction of issuer credit ratings. *Journal of Applied Stochastic Models in Business and Industry*, 25(5), 535–550.

Hwang, R. C., H. C. Wei, J. C. Lee and C. F. Lee (2008). On prediction of financial distress using the discrete-time survival model. *Journal of Financial Studies*, 16, 99–129.

Johnson, W. B. (1979). The cross-sectional stability of financial ratio patterns. *Journal of Financial and Quantitative Analysis*, 14, 1035–1048.

Jones, F. (1987). Current techniques in bankruptcy prediction. *Journal of Accounting Literature*, 6, 131–164.

Jones, S. and D. A. Hensher (2004). Predicting firm financial distress: A mixed logit model. *Accounting Review*, 79(4), 1011–1038.

Joy, O. M. and J. O. Tollefson (1975). On the financial applications of discriminant analysis. *Journal of Financial and Quantitative Analysis*, 10, 723–739.

Kao, L.-J. and C.-F. Lee (2012). Alternative method for determining industrial bond ratings: Theory and empirical evidence. *International Journal of Information Technology & Decision Making*, 11(6), 1215–1235.

Kiefer, N. M. (1988). Economic duration data and hazard functions. *Journal of Economic Literature*, 26, 646–679.

King, B. F. (1966). Market and industry factors in stock price behavior. *Journal of Business*, (Suppl.), 39(1), 139–190.

Lachenbruch, P. A. (1967). An almost unbiased method of obtaining confidence intervals for the probability of misclassification in discriminant analysis. *Biometrics*, 23(4), 639–645.

Lancaster, T. (1992). *The Econometric Analysis of Transition Data.* New York, NY: Cambridge University Press.

Lane, W. R., S. W. Looney and J. W. Wansley (1986). An application of the Cox proportional hazards model to bank failure. *Journal of Banking and Finance*, 10, 511–531.

Lau, A. H. L. (1987). A five-state financial distress prediction model. *Journal of Accounting Research*, 18, 109–131.

Lee, J. C. and C. F. Lee (2017). *Financial Analysis, Planning and Forecasting*, 3rd ed. Singapore: World Scientific.

Lee, C. F. and W. C. Yeh (2023). Financial statement analyses and firm valuation: Johnson and Johnson (JNJ) as a case study, in C. F. Lee, A. C. Lee and J. Lee (eds.), *Handbook of Investment Analysis, Portfolio Management, and Financial Derivatives.* Singapore: World Scientific Publishers.

Lee, C. F., A. C. Lee and J. Lee (2010). *Handbook of Quantitative Finance and Risk Management*. New York: Springer Academic Publishers.

Lee, C. F., A. C. Lee and J. Lee (2023). *Handbook of Investment Analysis, Portfolio Management, and Financial Derivatives*. Singapore: World Scientific.

Lee C. F. and J. Lee (2015). *Handbook of Financial Econometrics and Statistics*. New York: Springer Academic Publishers.

Lee, C. F. and J. Lee (2020). *Handbook of Financial Econometrics, Mathematics, Statistics, and Machine Learning*. Singapore: World Scientific.

Lee, J., C. F. Lee, J. R. Chang and L.-J. Kao (2023). *Essentials of Excel VBA, Python, and R: Financial Derivatives, Risk Management and Machine Learning*. New York: Springer Academic Publishers.

Lloyd, W. P. and C. F. Lee (1975). Block recursive systems in asset pricing models. *Journal of Finance*, 31, 1101–1113.

Mai, J. S. (2010). Alternative approaches to business failure prediction models. Essay I of Dissertation, Rutgers University.

Mehta, D. R. (1974). *Working Capital Management*. Englewood Cliffs, NJ: Prentice-Hall, Inc.

Merton, R. C. (1974). On the pricing of corporate debt: The risk structure of interest rates. *Journal of Finance*, 29, 449–470.

Molina, C. A. (2005). Are firms underleveraged? An examination of the effect of leverage on default probabilities. *Journal of Finance*, 3, 1427–1459.

Moyer, R. C. (1977). Forecasting financial failure: A re-examination. *Financial Management*, (Spring), 6(1), 11–117.

Ohlson, J. S. (1980). Financial ratios and the probabilistic prediction of bankruptcy. *Journal of Accounting Research*, 19, 109–131.

Orgler, Y. E. (1970). A credit-scoring model for commercial loans. *Journal of Money, Credit and Banking*, 2, 435–445.

Orgler, Y. E. (1975). *Analytical Methods in Loan Evaluation*. Lexington, MA: Lexington Books.

Penman, S. H. (2006). *Financial Statement Analysis and Security Valuation*, 3rd ed. New York, NY: McGraw-Hill/Irwin.

Pinches, G. E. and K. A. Mingo (1973). A multivariate analysis of industrial bond ratings. *Journal of Finance*, 28, 1–18.

Pinches, G. E., A. A. Eubank and K. A. Mingo (1975). The hierarchical classification of financial ratios. *Journal of Business Research*, 3, 295–310.

Pinches, G. E., K. A. Mingo and J. K. Caruthers (1973). The stability of financial patterns in industrial organizations. *Journal of Finance*, 28, 389–396.

Pinches, G. E., J. C. Singleton and A. Jahankhani (1978). Fixed coverage as a determinant of electric utility bond ratings. *Financial Management*, 8, 45–55.

Pogue, T. F. and R. M. Soldofsky (1969). What's in a bond rating? *Journal of Financial and Quantitative Analysis*, 4(2), 201–228.

Rao, C. R. (1952). *Advanced Statistical Methods in Biometric Research.* New York, NY: Wiley.

Roll, R. and S. A. Ross (1980). An empirical investigation of the arbitrage pricing theory. *Journal of Finance*, 35, 1073–1103.

Saretto, A. A. (2005). Predicting and pricing the probability of default. Working paper.

Sarkar, S. and R. S. Sriram (2001). Bayesian models for early warning of bank failures. *Management Science*, 47(11), 1457–1475.

Saunders, A. and L. Allen (2002). *Credit Risk Measurement: New Approaches to Value at Risk and Other Paradigms*, 2nd ed. New York, NY: Wiley.

Saunders, A. and M. M. Cornett (2013). *Financial Institutions Management: A Risk Management Approach*, 8th ed. New York, NY: McGraw-Hill/Irwin.

Scott, J. (1981). The probability of bankruptcy: A comparison of empirical predictions and theoretical models. *Journal of Banking and Finance*, 5, 317–344.

Shumway, T. (2001). Forecasting bankruptcy more accurately: A simple hazard model. *The Journal of Business*, 74, 101–124.

Simkowitz, M. A. and R. J. Monroe (1971). A discriminant analysis function for conglomerate targets. *Southern Journal of Business*, 6(1), (November), 1–16.

Singer, J. D. and J. B. Willett (1993). It's about time: Using discrete-time survival analysis to study duration and the timing of events. *Journal of Educational Statistics*, 18, 155–195.

Sinkey, J. F. (1975). A multivariate statistical analysis of the characteristics of problem bank. *Journal of Finance*, 30, 21–36.

Stevens, D. L. (1970). Financial characteristics of merged firms: A multivariate analysis. *Journal of Financial and Quantitative Analysis*, 5, 36–62.

Sun, L. (2007). A re-evaluation of auditors' opinions versus statistical models in bankruptcy prediction. *Review of Quantitative Finance and Accounting*, 28(1), 55–78.

Tam, K. Y. and M. Y. Kiang (1992). Managerial applications of neural networks: The case of bank failure predictions. *Management Science*, 38(7), 926–947.

Trieschmann, J. S. and G. E. Pinches (1973). A multivariate model for predicting financially distressed P-L insurers. *Journal of Risk and Insurance*, (September), 327–338.
Van Horne, J. C. (2001). *Financial Management and Policy*, 12th ed. Englewood Cliffs, NJ: Prentice Hall Inc.
Venuti, E. K. (2004). The going-concern assumption revisited: Assessing a company's future viability. *CPA Journal*, 74(5), (May), 40–43.
Vuong, Q. (1989). Likelihood ratio tests for model selection and non-nested hypotheses. *Econometrica*, 57(2), 307–333.
Wilcox, J. W. (1971). A simple theory of financial ratios as predictors of failure. *Journal of Accounting Research*, 9(2), (Fall), 389–395.
Zavgren, C. V. (1983). The prediction of corporate failure: The state of the art. *Journal of Accounting Literature*, 2, 1–38.
Zmijewski, M. E. (1984). Methodological issues related to the estimation of financial distress prediction models. *Supplement to Journal of Accounting Research*, 22, 59–68.

Appendix 17A: Logistic Model and Probit Model

The likelihood function for binary sample space of bankruptcy and non-bankruptcy is

$$l = \prod_{i \in s_1} P(X_i, \beta) \prod_{i \in s_2} (1 - P(X_i, \beta)), \tag{17A.1}$$

where P is some probability function, $0 \leq P \leq 1$, and $P(X_i, \beta)$ denotes probability of bankruptcy for any given X_i and β.

Since it is not easy to solve the selecting probability function P, for simplicity, one can solve the likelihood function in Equation (17A.1) by taking the natural logarithm. The logarithm of the likelihood function then is

$$L(l) = \sum_{i \in s_1} \log P(X_i, \beta) + \sum_{i \in s_2} \log(1 - P(X_i, \beta)), \tag{17A.2}$$

where S_1 is the set of bankrupt firms and S_2 is the set of non-bankrupt firms.

The maximum likelihood estimators for β_s can be obtained by solving $\underset{\beta}{\text{Max}}\, L(l)$.

In the logistic model, the probability of company i going bankrupt given independent variables X_i is defined as

$$P(X_i, \beta) = \frac{1}{1 + \exp(-\beta' X_i)}. \tag{17A.3}$$

The two implications here are as follows: (1) $P(\cdot)$ is increasing in $\beta' X_i$ and (2) $\beta' X_i$ is equal to $\log\left[\frac{P}{(1-P)}\right]$.

We then classify bankrupt firms and non-bankrupt firms by setting a "cutoff" probability attempting to minimize Type I and Type II errors.

In probit models, the probability of company i going bankrupt given independent variables X_i is defined as

$$P(X_i, \beta) = \int_{-\infty}^{(X_i,\beta)} \frac{1}{\sqrt{2\pi}} e^{-\frac{z^2}{2}} dz, \tag{17A.4}$$

17A.4 is the cumulative standard normal distribution function.

Maximum likelihood estimators from the probit model can be obtained similarly as in the logistic models. Although probit models and logistic models are similar, logistic models are preferred to probit models due to the nonlinear estimation in probit models (Gloubos and Grammatikos, 1998).

Appendix 17B: SAS Code for Hazard Model in Bankruptcy Forecasting

```
libname jess 'D:\Documents and Settings\MAI\Desktop\sas
code';
*test modified model's performance in the test sample;
*** Logistic Regression Analysis ***;
options pageno=1;
* Add prediction data set to original data;
data jess._prddata;
  _FREQ_ = 1;
```

```
  set jess.train_winsor1 jess.test_winsor1(in=inprd);
  _inprd_ = inprd;
  * set freq variable to 0 for additional data;
  if inprd then _FREQ_ = 0;
run;

proc logistic data=jess._prddata DESCEND;
  freq _FREQ_;
  model BPTSTATUS = NITA CASALES CACL CATA CASHTA LTDTA
    LSALES CAR LNMCP/
  ctable pprob=0.001 to 0.99 by 0.01;
  ** Create output data set for predictions **;
  output out=jess.pred p=phat;
  run;

  proc means data=jess._prddata;
  var NITA CASALES CACL CATA CASHTA LTDTA LSALES
  stress3 CAR LNMCP;
  run;

  data jess.out_sample;
  set jess.pred;
  if _FREQ_ = 0;
  run;

  data jess.count1_1;
  set jess.out_sample;
  if phat >=0.021 and bptstatus = 1;
  run;

  data jess.count1_2;
  set jess.out_sample;
  if bptstatus =1;
  run;

  data jess.count2_1;
  set jess.out_sample;
  if phat <0.021 and bptstatus = 0;
```

```
run;

data jess.count2_2;
set jess.out_sample;
if bptstatus =0;
run;
```

Appendix 17C: Application of Merton Distance to Default Model

Following Bharath and Shumway (2008), we will discuss how V and σ_V can be numerically estimated. The Merton DD model estimates the market value of debt by applying the classic Merton (1974) bond pricing model. The Merton model makes two particularly important assumptions. The first is that the total value of a firm follows geometric Brownian motion,

$$dV = \mu V dt + \sigma_V V dW, \tag{17C.1}$$

where V is the total value of the firm, μ is the expected continuously compounded return on V, σ_V is the volatility of firm value, and dW is a standard Wiener process. The second critical assumption of the Merton model is that the firm has issued just one discount bond maturing in T periods. Under these assumptions, the equity of the firm is a call option on the underlying value of the firm with a strike price equal to the face value of the firm's debt and a time to maturity of T. Moreover, the value of equity as a function of the total value of the firm can be described by the Black–Scholes–Merton formula. By put–call parity, the value of the firm's debt is equal to the value of a risk-free discount bond minus the value of a put option written on the firm, again with a strike price equal to the face value of debt and a time to maturity of T.

Symbolically, the Merton model stipulates that the equity value of a firm satisfies

$$E = VN(d_1) - e^{-rT} FN(d_2), \tag{17C.2}$$

where E is the market value of the firm's equity, F is the face value of the firm's debt, r is the instantaneous risk-free rate, $N(\cdot)$ is the cumulative standard normal distribution function, and d_1 is given by

$$d_1 = \frac{\ln\left(\frac{V}{F}\right) + (r + 0.5\sigma_V^2)T}{\sigma_V\sqrt{T}}, \tag{17C.3}$$

and d_2 is just $d_1 - \sigma_V\sqrt{T}$.

The Merton DD model makes use of two important equations. The first is the Black–Scholes–Merton equation (17C.2), expressing the value of a firm's equity as a function of the value of the firm. The second relates the volatility of the firm's value to the volatility of its equity. Under Merton's assumptions, the value of equity is a function of the value of the firm and time, so it follows directly from Ito's lemma that

$$\sigma_E = \left(\frac{V}{E}\right)\frac{\partial E}{\partial V}\sigma_V. \tag{17C.4}$$

In the Black–Scholes–Merton model, it can be shown that $\frac{\partial E}{\partial V} = N(d_1)$, so that under Merton model's assumptions, the volatilities of the firm and its equity are related by

$$\sigma_E = \left(\frac{V}{E}\right)N(d_1)\sigma_V, \tag{17C.5}$$

where d_1 is defined in Equation (17C.3).

The Merton DD model basically uses these two nonlinear equations, Equations (17C.2) and (17C.5), to translate the value and volatility of a firm's equity into an implied probability of default. In most applications, the Black–Scholes–Merton model describes the unobserved value of an option as a function of four variables that are easily observed (strike price, time to maturity, underlying asset price, and the risk-free rate) and one variable that can be estimated (volatility). In the Merton DD model, however, the value of the option is observed as the total value of the firm's equity, while the value of the underlying asset (the total value of the firm) is not directly observable. Thus, while V must be inferred, E is easy to observe in the marketplace by multiplying the firm's shares outstanding by its current stock price. Similarly, in the Merton DD model, the volatility of equity, σ_E, can be estimated but the volatility of the underlying firm, σ_V, must be inferred.

The first step in implementing the Merton DD model is to estimate σ_E from either historical stock returns data or from option-implied volatility data. The second step is to choose a forecasting horizon and a measure of the face value of the firm's debt. For example, it is common to use historical returns data to estimate σ_E, assume a forecasting horizon of 1 year ($T = 1$), and take the book value of the firm's total liabilities to be the face value of the firm's debt.

The third step is to collect values of the risk-free rate and the market equity of the firm. After performing these three steps, we have values for each of the variables in Equations (17C.2) and (17C.5), except for V and σ_V, the total value of the firm and the volatility of firm value, respectively.

The fourth, and perhaps most significant, step in implementing the model is to solve Equation (17C.2) numerically for values of V and σ_V. Once this numerical solution is obtained, the distance to default can be calculated as

$$\text{DD} = \frac{\ln\left(\frac{V}{F}\right) + (\mu - 0.5\sigma_V^2)T}{\sigma_V\sqrt{T}}, \tag{17C.6}$$

where μ is an estimate of the expected annual return of the firm's assets. The corresponding implied probability of default, sometimes called the expected default frequency (or EDF), is

$$\pi_{\text{Merton}} = N\left(-\left(\frac{\ln\left(\frac{V}{F}\right) + (\mu - 0.5\sigma_V^2)T}{\sigma_V\sqrt{T}}\right)\right) = N(-\text{DD}). \tag{17C.7}$$

If the assumptions of the Merton model really hold, the Merton DD model should give very accurate default forecasts. In fact, if the Merton model holds completely, the implied probability of default defined above, π_{Merton}, should be a sufficient statistic for default forecasts.

Simultaneously solving Equations (17C.2) and (17C.5) is reasonably straightforward. However, Crosbie and Bohn (2003) explain that "In practice the market leverage moves around far too much for (Equation (17C.5)) to provide reasonable results." To resolve this problem, we follow Crosbie and Bohn (2003) and Vassalou and Xing (2004) by implementing a complicated iterative procedure. First, we propose an initial value of $\sigma_V = \sigma_E[s/(E + F)]$ and we use this value of σ_V and Equation (17C.2) to infer the market value of each firm's assets every day for the previous year. We then calculate the implied log return on assets each day and use that returns series to generate new estimates of σ_V and μ. We iterate on σ_V in this manner until it converges (so the absolute difference in adjacent σ_Vs is less than 10^{-3}). Unless specified otherwise, the values of π_{Merton} are calculated by following this iterative procedure and calculating the corresponding implied default probability using Equation (17C.7).

Chapter 18

Exotic Options*

Contents

18.1 Introduction

In the previous chapters, the derivatives we introduced were standard options, and the content of their contracts was relatively simple. Although they can meet many investment needs that cannot be achieved in the spot market, the changes in the financial environment and investors' needs have also led to the emergence of many specialized options. Compared with the plain vanilla options, in response to various purposes today, which may be factors such as hedging, tax avoidance, or regulations, there are many non-standardized novelty

*This chapter was written by Jow-Ran Chang. Jow-Ran Chang is a Professor of Quantitative Finance at National Tsing Hua University.

products in the OTC markets. This phenomenon not only reflects the future trend of the market but also attracts more investors. Several common exotic options are Hull (2017), Zhang (1998), and YouTube video Bionic Turtle (2014).

Section 18.2 discusses binary options, Section 18.3 discusses chooser options, and Section 18.4 looks at path-dependent options. In Section 18.5, we talk about Monte Carlo simulation and Excel application. Finally, in Section 18.6, we summarize the chapter.

18.2 Binary Options

The concept of binary options, also known as digital options, is when the underlying price is within a predetermined price range, and the investor holding the option can obtain a fixed amount or an asset. However, if it is not within the determined range, the investor cannot get any return and loses the premium.

18.2.1 *Cash-or-nothing options*

18.2.1.1 *Cash-or-nothing call*

A fixed amount of cash would be paid when the underlying market price is greater than the strike price, but not when it is lower. The formula of the payoff at maturity is as follows:

$$\text{CNCall}_T = \begin{cases} \text{cash}, & \text{if } S_T > X, \\ 0, & \text{others.} \end{cases}$$

According to the risk-neutral valuation method, we can obtain the expected value of option returns at maturity assuming under the conditions of risk probability space, then discount to the current period with the risk-free rate. The formula is as follows:

$$\begin{aligned} \text{CNCall}_0 &= \mathrm{e}^{-rT}\hat{E}_0[\text{cash} \times I_{\{S_T > X\}}] \\ &= \mathrm{e}^{-rT} \times \text{cash} \times P(S_T > X) \\ &= \mathrm{e}^{-rT} \times \text{cash} \times N(d_2), \end{aligned}$$

where

$$d_1 = \frac{\ln\frac{S_0}{X} + (r - q + \frac{\sigma^2}{2})T}{\sigma\sqrt{T}},$$

$$d_2 = d_1 - \sigma\sqrt{T}.$$

18.2.1.2 *Cash-or-nothing put*

A fixed amount of cash would be paid when the underlying market price is lower than the strike price, but not when it is greater. The formula of the payoff at maturity is as follows:

$$\text{CNPut}_T = \begin{cases} \text{cash}, & \text{if } S_T < X, \\ 0, & \text{others.} \end{cases}$$

The valuation formula is as follows:

$$\begin{aligned} \text{CNPut}_0 &= \mathrm{e}^{-rT}\hat{E}_0\left[\text{cash} \times I_{\{S_T<X\}}\right] \\ &= \mathrm{e}^{-rT} \times \text{cash} \times N(-d_2). \end{aligned}$$

From the above formula, we find that as long as cash-or-nothing options are in the money, options holder can receive a fixed amount of return — the amount of which is not related to the difference between underlying and exercise price. Based on this characteristic, when the investor expects that a certain underlying "price" will rise to the extent of the strike price in the future period, but is uncertain about the extent of the rise, he can buy cash-or-nothing call options to lock in a fixed return. Even if the expectation is off, the investor loses only the cash or the premium cash-or-nothing options.

18.2.2 *Asset-or-nothing options*

18.2.2.1 *Asset-or-nothing call*

A value identical to the return of the underlying would be paid when the underlying market price is greater than the strike price, but not when it is lower. The formula of the payoff at maturity is as follows:

$$\text{ANCall}_T = \begin{cases} S_T, & \text{if } S_T > X, \\ 0, & \text{others.} \end{cases}$$

The valuation formula is as follows:

$$\begin{aligned} \text{ANCall} &= e^{-rT}\hat{E}_0[S_T \times I_{\{S_T>X\}}] \\ &= S_0 \times e^{-qT} \times N(d_1), \end{aligned}$$

where

$$\begin{aligned} d_1 &= \frac{\ln\frac{S_0}{X} + (r - q + \frac{\sigma^2}{2})T}{\sigma\sqrt{T}}, \\ d_2 &= d_1 - \sigma\sqrt{T}. \end{aligned}$$

18.2.2.2 *Asset-or-nothing put*

A value identical to the return of the underlying would be paid when the underlying market price is lower than the strike price, but not when it is greater. The formula of the payoff at maturity is as follows:

$$\text{ANPut}_T = \begin{cases} S_T, & \text{if } S_T < X, \\ 0, & \text{others.} \end{cases}$$

The valuation formula is as follows:

$$\begin{aligned} \text{ANPut}_0 &= e^{-rT}\hat{E}_0[S_T \times I_{\{S_T<X\}}] \\ &= S_0 \times e^{-qT} \times N(-d_1). \end{aligned}$$

18.3 Chooser Options

A chooser option literally means the exotic option possesses a contingent claim. The option holder can choose to transform the option into either a call option or a put option at a specific time period (t) before the option expiry (T).

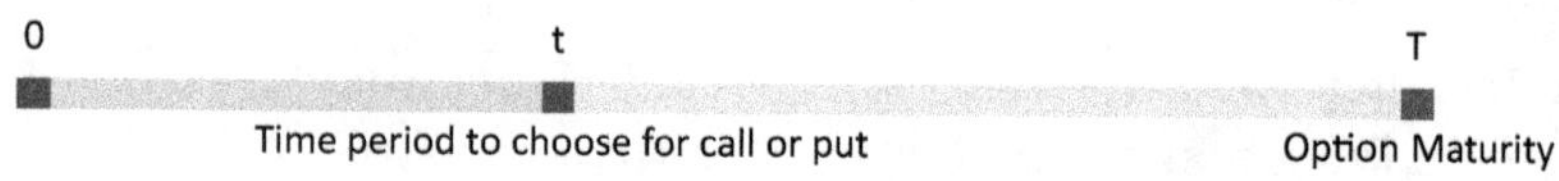

Therefore, option value w_t at time t is as follows:

$$\begin{aligned} w_t &= \max(c_t, p_t) \\ &= \max[c(X, T-t), c(X, T-t) - S_t e^{-q(T-t)} + X e^{-r(T-t)}] \\ &= c(X, T-t) + e^{-q}(T-t) \times \max[X e^{-(r-q)(T-t)} - S_t, 0] \\ &= c(X, T-t) + e^{-q(T-t)} \times p(X e^{-(r-q)(T-t)}, 0). \end{aligned}$$

From the concept above, the option value at time 0 is as follows:

$$\begin{aligned} w_0 &= c(X, T) + e^{-q(T-t)} \times p(X e^{-(r-q)(T-t)}, t) \\ &= S_0 e^{-qT} N(d_1) - X e^{-rT} N(d_2) + X e^{-rT} N(-d_2') - S_0 e^{-qT} N(-d_1'), \end{aligned}$$

$$d_1 = \frac{\ln \frac{S_0}{X} + (r - q + \frac{\sigma^2}{2})T}{\sigma\sqrt{T}},$$

$$d_2 = d_1 - \sigma\sqrt{T},$$

$$d_1' = \frac{\ln \frac{S_0}{X} + (r - q)T + \frac{\sigma^2}{2}t}{\sigma\sqrt{t}},$$

$$d_2' = d_1' - \sigma\sqrt{t}.$$

From this type of option contract design, it can be found that the chooser option is applicable to extremely uncertain market conditions, such as elections, wars, referendums, etc. Investors who hold this option will decide whether to turn into a call or a put based on whichever direction they deem favorable.

If the investor believes that the event will eventually be beneficial to the rising trend of the underlying asset, the chooser option can be turned into a call. Conversely, the chooser option can be turned into a put. Its payoff at maturity is similar to a long straddle strategy.

Example 18.1. Kevin buys a chooser option on a Taiwan-weighted stock index with a premium of 450 points. He can decide whether the chooser option is a call or a put 2 months before the option expires. The strike prices are both 5,200 points. What is the breakeven point of the chooser option?

There will be two breakeven points: when the Taiwan-Weighted Stock Price Index falls to 5,650 or 4,750 points as the option expires.

18.4 Path-Dependent Options

The payoff of path-dependent options will not only be affected by the price of the underlying asset at the expiry date but also depends on the path before the expiry date.

In the next section, we will discuss the valuation methods of three types of path-dependent options: Barrier Options, Asian Options, and Lookback Options.

18.4.1 *Barrier options*

Unlike standard-type options, the payoff of barrier options depends on whether the underlying asset price path has penetrated a certain level of barrier price. If the underlying asset price has reached the barrier, the option contract should initialize or terminate.

Barrier options can be divided into two categories: knock-in (KI) and knock-out (KO) options. KI means that if the price of the underlying asset penetrates the barrier price, then the option will initialize; KO means that when the price of the underlying asset reaches the barrier price, the option contract will terminate.

Based on the setting of the barrier price, the barrier options can also be split into two types: **Up** or **Down**. So, there will be eight combinations of barrier options in total. For example, a down-and-output (p_{do}) is a KO put, which means that if the price of the underlying asset is lower than the barrier price (S_b), the put will terminate. A down-and-in put (p_{di}) is a KI put, which means that the put will only initialize if the price of the underlying asset is higher than the barrier price (S_b).

For instance, for a **Down** barrier option, a standard-type put is equal to the sum of a down-and-out and a down-and-in put, $p = p_{\text{do}} + p_{\text{di}}$. It should be noted that for a barrier put option, S_b must be lower than the strike price X. If the barrier price is higher than the strike price, the put option will not be exercised, rendering setting the barrier price meaningless.

Determining whether the asset price has reached the barrier price can be continuously or periodically monitored. When evaluating the price of the barrier options, for the convenience of calculation and processing, it is usually assumed that the stock price is continuous. In practice, however, stock prices are not continuous, so periodic monitoring methods are used, for example, checking every minute whether a barrier price has been reached.

The evaluation of the barrier options is much more complicated than the standard-type European options. Some standard-type European barrier options have closed-form solutions, but American or non-standard barrier options do not, so application of some numerical methods must be used for evaluation. This section only covers the formulas of down-and-out call, down-and-in call and down-and-out put, down-and-in put. For the derivation of these formulas and the formulas of other barrier options, please refer to other books.

18.4.1.1 *Down-and-out/down-and-in call*

Down-and-out call's formula is as follows:

$$c_{\text{do}} = S_0\left[N(d_1) - \left(\frac{S_b}{S_0}\right)^{\delta+1} \times N(d_3)\right] - Xe^{-rT}\left[N(d_2) - \left(\frac{S_b}{S_0}\right)^{\delta-1} \times N(d_4)\right],$$

$$\delta = \frac{2r}{\sigma^2},$$

$$d_1 = \frac{\ln\frac{S_0}{X} + (r + \frac{\sigma^2}{2})T}{\sigma\sqrt{T}},$$

$$d_2 = \frac{\ln\frac{S_0}{X} + (r - \frac{\sigma^2}{2})T}{\sigma\sqrt{T}},$$

$$d_3 = \frac{\ln\frac{S_b^2}{XS_0} + (r + \frac{\sigma^2}{2})T}{\sigma\sqrt{T}},$$

$$d_4 = \frac{\ln\frac{S_b^2}{XS_0} + (r - \frac{\sigma^2}{2})T}{\sigma\sqrt{T}}.$$

The European Call price can be expressed as $c_{\text{BS}}(S_0, X, T) = S_0N(d_1) - Xe^{-rT}N(d_2)$ in the Black–Scholes form. Thus, we can simplify down-and-out call as follows:

$$c_{\text{do}} = c_{\text{BS}}(S_0, X, T) - \left(\frac{S_0}{S_b}\right)^{1-\delta} \times c_{\text{BS}}\left(\frac{S_b^2}{S_0}, X, T\right).$$

A standard-type option can be formed by passing a KO option and a KI option:

$$c_{\text{BS}}(S_0, X, T) = c_{\text{di}} + c_{\text{do}}.$$

Therefore, on the premise of knowing the value of the down-and-out call, the value of the down-and-in call can be easily deduced as follows:

$$\begin{aligned} c_{\text{di}} &= c_{\text{BS}}(S_0, X, T) - c_{\text{do}} \\ &= \left(\frac{S_0}{S_b}\right)^{1-\delta} \times c_{\text{BS}}\left(\frac{S_b^2}{S_0}, X, T\right). \end{aligned}$$

18.4.1.2 *Down-and-out/down-and-in put*

Down-and-output's formula is as follows:

$$\begin{aligned} p_{\text{do}} = X\mathrm{e}^{-rT}&\left\{N(d_4) - N(d_2) - \left(\frac{S_b}{S_0}\right)^{\delta-1}[N(d_7) - N(d_5)]\right\} \\ &- S_0\left\{N(d_3) - N(d_1) - \left(\frac{S_b}{S_0}\right)^{\delta+1}[N(d_8) - N(d_6)]\right\}, \end{aligned}$$

where $\delta = \frac{2r}{\sigma^2}$

$$d_1 = \frac{\ln\frac{S_0}{X} + (r + \frac{\sigma^2}{2})T}{\sigma\sqrt{T}}, d_2 = d_1 - \sigma\sqrt{T},$$

$$d_3 = \frac{\ln\frac{S_0}{S_b} + (r + \frac{\sigma^2}{2})T}{\sigma\sqrt{T}}, d_4 = d_3 - \sigma\sqrt{T},$$

$$d_5 = \frac{\ln\frac{S_0}{S_b} - (r - \frac{\sigma^2}{2})T}{\sigma\sqrt{T}}, d_6 = d_5 - \sigma\sqrt{T},$$

$$d_7 = \frac{\ln\frac{S_0X}{S_b^2} - (r - \frac{\sigma^2}{2})T}{\sigma\sqrt{T}}, d_8 = d_7 - \sigma\sqrt{T}.$$

Compared with the standard-type options, when the barrier price is reached, the contract will initialize and terminate. Therefore, this type of option may be voided, so its premium is usually cheaper.

18.4.2 *Asian options*

The Asian option differs from the European option in that the return (payoff) of the former is determined by the "average price" within a certain period.

Based on different exercise time periods, Asian options can be divided into European Asian Options and American Asian Options. The former can only be exercised at the expiry date, while the latter can be early exercised at any time before the expiry. The evaluation of the American Asian option is much more complicated in terms of path dependence, because it needs to consider the best time for exercising.

Asian options can be divided into two categories: One replaces the underlying asset price at maturity with the average of underlying asset prices (S_{ave}). For example, a European Asian Call Option with fixed strike is as follows:

$$c = \max(S_{\text{ave}} - X,\ 0).$$

A European Asian Put Option with fixed strike is as follows:

$$p = \max(X - S_{\text{ave}}, 0).$$

The other uses the average of underlying asset prices within a period to replace the original strike price. For example, a European Asian Call Option is as follows:

$$c = \max(S_T - S_{\text{ave}}, 0).$$

A European Asian Put Option is as follows:

$$p=\max(S_{\text{ave}}-S_T,\ 0).$$

The average price can be calculated in two ways: arithmetic mean and geometric mean. If the stock price is stated discretely, the arithmetic mean of the stock price is as follows:

$$A_{\mathrm{da}} = \frac{1}{n}\sum_{i=1}^{n} S(t_i).$$

If the stock price is continuous, the arithmetic mean of the stock price is as follows:

$$A_{\mathrm{ca}} = \mathrm{e}^{\frac{1}{T}\int_0^T \ln S(t)dt}.$$

As far as the geometric mean is concerned, if the stock price is discrete, the geometric mean of the stock price is as follows:

$$A_{\mathrm{dg}} = \left[\prod_{i=1}^{n} S(t_i)\right]^{\frac{1}{n}}.$$

If the stock price is continuous, the geometric mean of the stock price is as follows:

$$A_{\mathrm{cg}} = \frac{1}{T}\int_0^T S(t)dt.$$

Example 18.2. Kevin buys an Asian call option on the Taiwan-Weighted Stock Index. The expiration is one month, the strike price is 6,000 points, and the premium is 200 points. When it expires, the arithmetic average of the weekly closing prices is used as its settlement price. Assuming that the weekly closing price of the Taiwan-Weighted Stock Index is 5,980 points, 5,800 points, 5,970 points, and 6,000 points, should Kevin exercise the contract when it expires?

The arithmetic mean of the weekly closing price is (5,980 + 5,800 + 5,970 + 6,000)/4 = 5,937.5 (points), which is 6,000 points lower than the strike price, so Kevin will not exercise the contract and lose 200 points of premium.

If the stock price at the expiry is log-normally distributed, the stock price distribution of the geometric mean will also be a log-normal distribution, and the Black–Scholes model can still be used to calculate the price of the option.

If arithmetic mean is concerned, the stock price distribution will not be log-normally distributed; thus, the Black–Scholes model cannot be used to calculate the option price (no closed-form solution). The numerical method such as Monte Carlo simulation is preferred.

Since the Asian option takes the average price, it can prevent speculators from deliberately raising or lowering the price before the market closed. Since the fluctuation of the average price is usually lower than that of a certain time point, the premium is usually lower than standard-type options, so the Asian option is often used by FX dealers as a cost-saving hedging strategy.

18.4.3 *Lookback options*

The core of the lookback option is to allow the holder to look back on the history price performance of the underlying asset and choose the most favorable direction to exercise the contract. The return for a lookback option is related to the highest or lowest price of the underlying asset before the expiration of the option.

Lookback options can be divided into two categories: fixed strike price and strike price. A lookback option with a fixed strike price replaces the stock price on the expiry date based on the highest or lowest stock price in the past period. For example, the payoff for a European fixed strike price lookback call at maturity can be expressed as follows:

$$c = \max(S_{\max} - X, 0).$$

A European fixed strike price lookback put at maturity can be expressed as follows:

$$p = \max(X - S_{\min}, 0).$$

A lookback option with floating strike price determines the strike price based on the highest or lowest stock price during the effective period of the contract. For example, the payoff for a European floating strike price lookback call at maturity can be expressed as follows:

$$c = \max(S_T - S_{\min}, 0).$$

A European floating strike price lookback put at maturity can be expressed as follows:

$$p = \max(S_{\max} - S_T, 0).$$

Irrespective of a fixed or a floating strike price lookback call option, the holder can choose the most favorable direction depending on the underlying asset price, with more benefits than the standard-type option. As a result, the option premium is usually higher. Since the return of the lookback option is related to the highest or the lowest price in the underlying asset price path, it can be evaluated by using the Monte Carlo simulation method.

18.5 Monte Carlo Simulation and Excel Application

We have previously introduced the binomial tree and Black–Scholes formula for the pricing purposes of options. In this section, we will discuss another method for derivatives pricing: Monte Carlo simulation (Boyle, 1977; Boyle *et al.*, 1997; Brandimarte, 2013; YouTube video MomentsInTrading, 2013). This method can be applied to deal with derivatives and path-dependent options that do not have closed-form solutions.

18.5.1 *Application of Monte Carlo simulation on European options*

Under risk-neutral conditions, the value of the European option is to discount the return at maturity with the risk-free rate. Taking the call option as an example,

$$\begin{aligned} C &= \mathrm{e}^{-rT} \hat{E}_0 \max[S_T - X, 0] \\ &= \mathrm{e}^{-rT} \hat{E}_0 \max[S_0 \mathrm{e}^{\left(r-q-\frac{1}{2}\sigma^2\right)T+\sigma\sqrt{T}\varepsilon} - X, 0]. \end{aligned}$$

Therefore, with Monte Carlo simulation, we can evaluate the European call option by simulating the underlying asset price at maturity. The following describes the steps and concepts of the Monte Carlo simulation method in detail:

1. First, extract N standard normal random numbers from the random generator ε_i, $i = 1, 2, \ldots, N$, then with the formula $(S_T)_i = S_0 e^{(r-q-\frac{1}{2}\sigma^2)T+\sigma\sqrt{T}\varepsilon_i}$, we can calculate N stock prices at maturity.
2. With the stock price obtained in step 1, we can get N options payoff at expiry. For example, $\max[(S_T)_i - X]$ for call, $\max[X-(S_T)_i]$ for put.
3. Calculate the average of the N options payoff at maturity obtained in step 2. Take the call option as an example: $E(C_T) = \frac{1}{N}\sum_{i=1}^{N} C_i$.
4. Discounting the average value obtained in step 3 with the risk-free rate, we get the price of the option. Take the call option as an example: $C_0 = e^{-rT}E(C_T)$.

18.5.1.1 *VBA code*

In this section, we will explain how to apply Monte Carlo simulation by constructing a function to evaluate the European option: MCOptionValue. The parameters are as follows: iopt (1 for call, –1 for put), stock price (S), strike price (X), risk-free rate (r), dividend yield (q), time to maturity (tyr), volatility (sigma), and numbers of simulation (nsim).

```
Function MCOptionValue(iopt, S, X, r, q, tyr, sigma, nsim)
    Dim rnmut, sigt, sum, randns, S1, S2, payoff1, payoff2
    Dim i As Integer
    Randomize
    rnmut = (r - q - 0.5 * sigma ^ 2) * tyr
    sigt = sigma * Sqr(tyr)
    sum = 0
    For i = 1 To nsim
        randns = Application.NormSInv(Rnd)
        S1 = S * Exp(rnmut + randns * sigt)
        S2 = S * Exp(rnmut - randns * sigt)
        payoff1 = Application.Max(iopt * (S1 - X), 0)
        payoff2 = Application.Max(iopt * (S2 - X), 0)
        sum = sum + 0.5 * (payoff1 + payoff2)
    Next i
    MCOptionValue = Exp(-r * tyr) * sum/nsim
End Function
```

Application.NormSInv(Rnd) is the random normal numbers extracted from a random generator. S1 and S2 are the stock prices at maturity, and payoff1 and payoff2 are the returns of options at maturity. By accumulating the payoff N times as the variable sum, then taking the average and discounting to get MCOptionValue, we obtain the options price of the Monte Carlo simulation.

Likewise, we can get European call and put prices by creating a user interface, entering parameters, and pressing the run button.

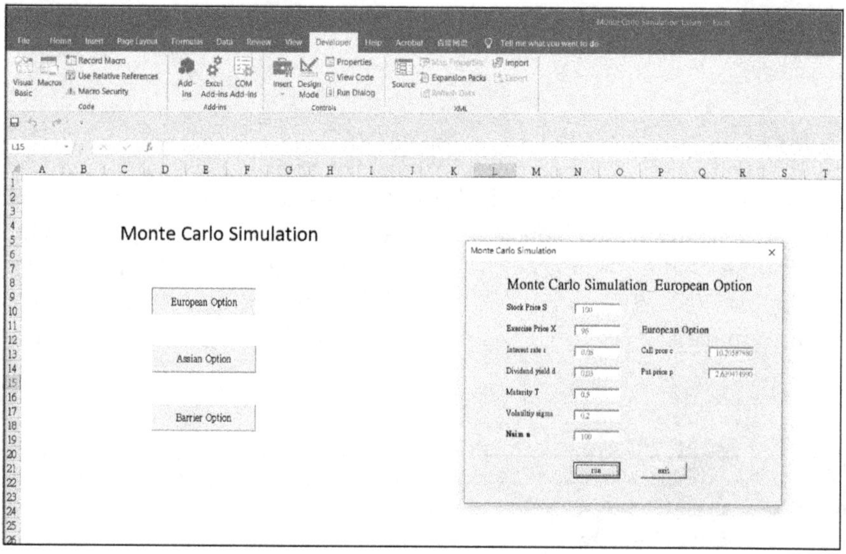

Since the Monte Carlo method is a simulation process, the generated random values will not be the same after each press of the run button. In addition, readers can also adjust the nsim value as number of simulations. When the number of simulations increases, the difference in the price of the option generated each time will be smaller, which means that when the number of simulations increases, the confidence interval will be smaller. The narrower it gets, the closer the option price to the Black–Scholes model.

18.5.2 *Applying Monte Carlo simulation for path-dependent options*

18.5.2.1 *Barrier options*

In this section, we will introduce how to simulate Geometric Brownian Motion describing the asset price variation. We first construct a function named AssetPaths with maturity T and N periods. The parameters are as follows: stock price (S), risk-free rate (r), dividend yield (q), time to maturity (tyr), volatility (sigma), numbers of period (nstep), and numbers of simulation (nsim). Output represents the stock price of each period.

```
Function AssetPaths(S, r, q, tyr, sigma, nstep, nsim)
     Dim dt, rnmut, sigt
     Dim i, j As Integer
     Dim spath()
     Randomize
     dt = tyr/nstep
     rnmut = (r - q - 0.5 * sigma ^ 2) * dt
     sigt = sigma * Sqr(dt)
     ReDim spath(nstep, 1 To nsim)
     For j = 1 To nsim
        spath(0, j) = S
        For i = 1 To nstep
            randns = Application.NormSInv(Rnd)
            spath(i, j) = spath(i - 1, j)
            * Exp(rnmut + randns * sigt)
        Next i
     Next j
     AssetPaths = spath
 End Function
```

Two loops are applied in this program. The outer loop represents each simulation, while the inner loop calculates the variation of stock price using the formula to obtain stock prices at each time node.

Having nsim traces of stock price, we are able to apply the Monte Carlo method to evaluate the down-and-out put. Then, we construct a function named DOPutMC, and the parameters are as follows: stock price (S), strike price (X), risk-free rate (r), dividend yield (q), time to maturity (tyr), volatility (sigma), barrier level (S_b), time periods (nstep), and numbers of simulation (nsim).

```
Function DOPutMC(S, X, r, q, tyr, sigma, sb, nstep, nsim)
    Dim payoff, sum
    Dim spath()
    ReDim spath(nstep, 1 To nsim)
    sum = 0
    spath = AssetPaths(S, r, q, tyr, sigma, nstep, nsim)
    For j = 1 To nsim
        payoff = Application.Max(X - spath(nstep, j), 0)
        For i = 1 To nstep
            If spath(i, j) <= sb Then
            payoff = 0
            i = nstep
            End If
        Next i
        sum = sum + payoff
    Next j
    DOPutMC = Exp(-r * tyr) * sum/nsim
End Function
```

The If...Then statement in the program is used to determine whether the stock price is lower than the barrier price (S_b). If the stock price is higher than the barrier price, the value of the put option is calculated; if the stock price is lower, the put option value is 0. Finally, we discount the put option price of each simulation to the present and calculate the average as the value of the down-and-output.

Similarly, through the design of the user interface, after inputting the parameter values in sequence, and pressing the run key, the value of the down-and-out put option of the barrier option can be obtained.

Provided in the following is the user interface of the function for calculating barrier options:

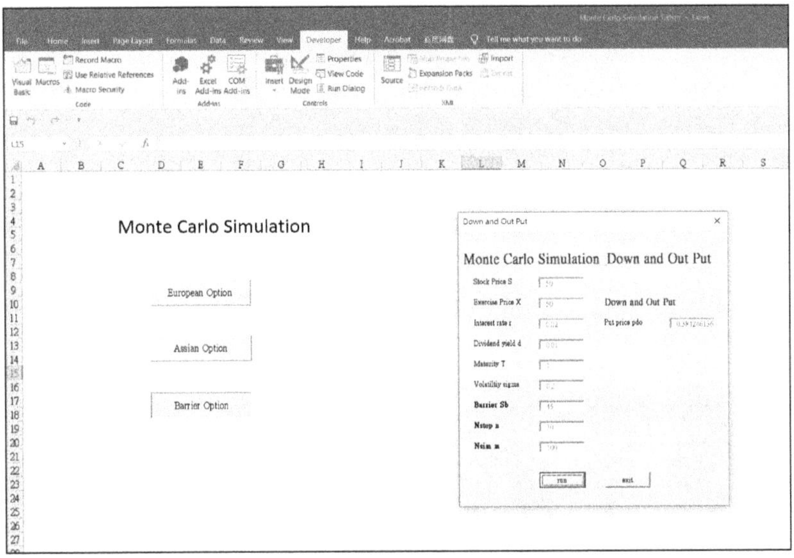

18.5.2.2 *Asian options*

We apply the Monte Carlo method to evaluate Asian options by using the previously defined function AssetPaths(S, r, q, tyr, sigma, nstep, nsim) and constructing another function AsianMC_S. The parameters are as follows: iopt (1 for call, –1 for put), stock price (S), strike price (X), risk-free rate (r), dividend yield (q), time to maturity (tyr), volatility (sigma), time periods (nstep), and numbers of simulation (nsim).

```
Function AsianMC_S(iopt, S, X, r, q, tyr, sigma, nstep, nsim)
    Dim payoff, sum, tot
    Dim spath()
    ReDim spath(nstep, 1 To nsim)
    Dim i, j As Integer
    sum = 0
    spath = AssetPaths(S, r, q, tyr, sigma, nstep, nsim)
    For j = 1 To nsim
        tot = 0
        For i = 1 To nstep
            tot = tot + spath(i, j)
        Next i
        payoff = Application.Max(iopt * (tot/nstep - X), 0)
        sum = sum + payoff
    Next j
    AsianMC_S = Exp(-r * tyr) * sum/nsim
End Function
```

Since the return of the Asian option depends on the average of the stock price over a period of time, the path of the stock price must be known before evaluating the Asian option, so the AssetPath function mentioned earlier is required.

Two loops are used in the whole program. The inner loop first accumulates the stock price of each cut period under the same path, and then averages the stock price during this period to calculate the option value (payoff) of the path. The outer loop then discounts the option value obtained by each path to the present and calculates the average as value of the Asian option.

Provided in the following is the user interface of the function for calculating Asian options:

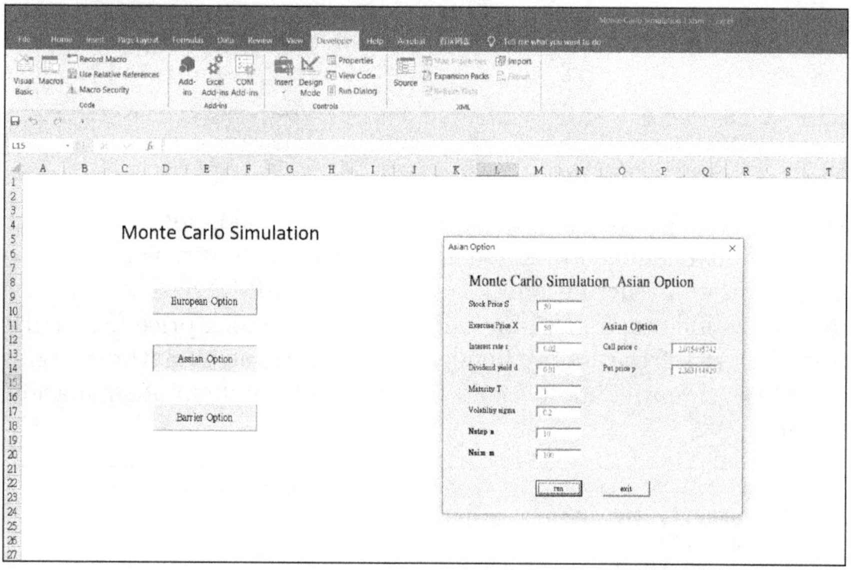

18.6 Summary

In this chapter, we have discussed some important exotic options, which include binary options, chooser options, and path-dependent options. Binary options include cash-or-nothing options and asset-or-nothing options. Path-dependent options include barrier options, Asian options, and lookback options. Finally, we also showed some Monte Carlo simulations and Excel applications.

Questions

1. Explain why an up-and-out call is worth zero when the strike is greater than the barrier.
2. Derive a decomposition of a vanilla call option into a cash-or-nothing option and an asset-or-nothing option.
3. How can a chooser option decompose into a call maturing at time t and a put maturing at time T?
4. Does a European fixed strike price lookback call become more valuable or less valuable as we increase the frequency with which we observe the asset price in calculating the maximum?
5. Explain why using Monte Carlo simulation to price an Asian option is better than using the binomial tree method.

Bibliography

Bionic Turtle (2014). Derivatives: Exotic Options, YouTube, https://www.youtube.com/playlist?list=PLB090C71F9516FDEE.

Boyle, P. P. (1977). Options: A Monte Carlo approach. *Journal of Financial Economics*, 4(3), 323–338.

Boyle, P., M. Broadie and P. Glasserman (1997). Monte Carlo methods for security pricing. *Journal of Economic Dynamics and Control*, 21(8–9), 1267–1321.

Brandimarte, P. (2013). *Numerical Methods in Finance and Economics: A MATLAB-Based Introduction*. New York: John Wiley & Sons.

Hull, J. C. (2017). *Options Futures and Other Derivatives*. New York: Pearson Global Edition.

MomentsInTrading (2013). Understanding and Creating Monte Carlo Simulation Step by Step, YouTube, https://www.youtube.com/watch?v=3gcLRU24-w0.

Zhang, P. G. (1998). *Exotic Options: A Guide to Second Generation Options*. Singapore: World Scientific.

Chapter 19

Real Option and Fuzzy Real Option*

Contents

19.1 Introduction

Large investments are capital projects of strategic importance which often have a long economic life cycle. They are characterized by many

*This chapter is a modification and expansion of the paper by Wang, S.-Y. and Lee, C.-F. (2010). A fuzzy real option valuation approach to capital budgeting under uncertainty environment. *International Journal of Information Technology & Decision Making*, 9(5), 695–713.

unknowns that are hard to foresee at their initial planning stage. Hence, the outcome of these investments may change during their long economic life, and the changes can be crucial since the larger the investments are, the more strategic importance they usually have. However, the information needed for capital budgeting is generally not known with certainty. Therefore, capital-budgeting procedures under uncertainty remain to be further developed. The sources of uncertainty may be the net cash inflow, the life of the project, the cash flow volatility, and/or the discount rate. Therefore, the traditional method to deal with capital budgeting under uncertainty is an important issue. Under the traditional view of capital budgeting under uncertainty, Lee *et al.* (2022) proposed the (i) risk-adjusted discount rate method, (ii) certainty-equivalent method, (iii) statistical distribution method, (iv) simulation method, and (v) decision tree method. In this chapter, we will show how the option pricing theory and model can be used to deal with capital budgeting under uncertainty. This approach is generally called real-option approach, which was first introduced in an article about corporate borrowing by Myers (1977), to analyze capital-budgeting decisions under uncertainty.

In practice, precise information concerning future investment projects is rarely available. Hence, a decision-maker does not have exact knowledge concerning future investment opportunities. Extensive studies have been undertaken to consider the capital-budgeting problems under risk. Traditional approaches to capital budgeting are based on the premise that probability theory is necessary and sufficient to deal with the uncertainty that underlies the estimates of required parameters. However, it is argued that in many circumstances this premise is invalid since the principal sources of uncertainty are often non-random in nature and are related to the fuzziness rather than the frequency of data. In order to correctly capture and quantify the underlying uncertainty present in non-statistical situations, the theory of possibility, an extension of the theory of fuzzy sets introduced by Zadeh (1965), can be used.

In this chapter, we will discuss real-option and fuzzy real-option approaches used to deal with investment decisions under uncertainty. In Section 19.2, we will discuss investment decisions under uncertainty. Real options will be discussed in Section 19.3. Section 19.4 will discuss fuzzy real-option valuation. The computational method and an example will be presented in Section 19.5. Section 19.6 will present the conclusions. Appendix 19A presents a fuzzy real-option valuation in terms of the binomial option pricing model, and Appendix 19B presents time state preference and the real-option approaches for capital budgeting under uncertainty.

19.2 Investment Decisions under Uncertainty

Capital-budgeting methods based on the Discounted Cash Flow (DCF) have been the primary instruments for investment decision-making. The most commonly used DCF-based method is the Net Present Value (NPV). Under static circumstances, DCF-based methods provide reliable results. However, the real-world situations are seldom static. Especially in cases of large investments with long economic lives, the static DCF-based methods fail to present a highly reliable picture of the profitability and possibilities offered by the investment project. As DCF-based methods have been the best thing available, "these methods have been used by managers for a long time."

Although there are many enhancements to the original formulae, the underlying unsatisfactory assumptions still exist. Hence, modified models are used which include the risk-adjusted discount rate method and the certainty-equivalent method. The risk-adjusted discount rate method simply extends the cash flow valuation model under certainty to the uncertainty case. The advantage of this method is that the valuation model gives us a formula that explicitly considers the uncertainty associated with future cash flows. Although the model does not specify exactly what constitutes the risk of the cash flows, it can be used to develop and explore the relationships among the variables of asset valuation models. On the other hand, the disadvantages of the risk-adjusted discount rate model are clear. The value of the risk-adjusted discount rate is only a subjective estimate, which could differ from person to person. Therefore, an objective determination of the value of a risky investment project will be almost impossible by simply applying this method.

While the risk-adjusted discount rate method provides a means for adjusting the basic riskless discount rate, an alternative method, the certainty-equivalent method, adjusts the estimated value of the uncertain cash flows. The underlying rationale is that, given a risky cash flow, the decision-maker will evaluate this risky cash flow by attaching an expected utility to that cash flow, that utility estimate being hypothesized to be equal to the utility derived from some certain amount. If a decision-maker performs this process for each cash flow, a series of certainty equivalents for the risky flows can be obtained. These two models should yield the same value for a given stream of cash flows. However, Robichek and Myers (1966) show that the risk-adjusted discount rate method tends to lump together the pure rate of interest, a risk premium, and time (through the compounding process), while the certainty-equivalent approach keeps risk and the pure rate of interest separate. This separation gives an advantage to the certainty-equivalent method.

Some economic factors, such as competition, inflation, consumer preferences, technological development, and labor market conditions, make it impossible to foretell the future. Consequently, the economic life, revenues, and costs of investment projects are less than certain. With risk, a firm is no longer indifferent between two investment proposals having the same internal rates of return or NPVs. Three related stochastic methods have been useful in capital-budgeting decisions, which are the probability distribution, decision tree, and simulation methods.

These methods have explicitly utilized the concepts of probability distributions and statistical distributions to carry out the analysis. If there is only a single accept–reject decision at the outset of the project, then a decision-maker can use either statistical distribution methods or simulation methods. If investment opportunities involve a sequence of decisions over time, a decision tree method can be used to perform the analysis. Decision tree is an analytical technique used in sequential decisions, where various decision points are studied in relation to subsequent chance events. This technique enables one to choose among alternatives in an objective and consistent manner. Simulation is another approach to confronting the problems of capital budgeting under uncertainty. Because uncertainty associated with capital budgeting is not restricted to one or two variables, every variable relevant to the capital budgeting decision can be viewed as a random variable. Facing so many random variables, it may be impossible to obtain tractable results from an economic model. Simulation is a useful tool designed to deal with this problem and is the closest we can get to modeling in cases of uncertainty. However, if risk reduction is a consideration, then the real option is a better alternative. The real-option approach also supports the determination of the timing for the investment and offers a comprehensive way of presenting the value of possibilities opened by the project, which can be further enhanced with frequently updated fuzzy cash flows.

The real-option approach is a methodology that calculates the value of an investment with techniques originally developed for valuation of financial options. This gives the possibility to take into consideration the managerial flexibility to act during the lifetime of an investment. The term real option was first introduced in an article about corporate borrowing by Myers (1997). Since then, more literature has been published to describe the different theoretical aspects of real options (Kulatilaka and Marcus, 1998; Dixit and Pindyck, 1994; Trigeorgis, 1995), as well as the managerial and strategic implications and applications of real options (Bowman and Hurry, 1993; Luehrman, 1998; Amram and Kulatilaka, 1999). Several case-based articles are also available to give further insight into real-world application (Kulatilaka, 1993; Nichols, 1994; Micalizzi, 1999).

19.3 Real Options

The concept of real options was first proposed by Myers (1977), who observed that the assets of many firms, in particular, investment projects with growth opportunity, may be expressed as a call option. Real options apply the analytical framework of financial options, which consider management flexibility and strategic flexibility overlooked in the traditional NPV approach and consider the irreversibility and deferability of investment decisions. Trigeorgis and Mason (1987) pointed out that corporate management frequently adopts the decision mechanism with considerable flexibility when dealing with highly uncertain, large investment projects. Thus, the valuation of such a project should include the traditional NPV plus the options value derived from management flexibility, which is termed "expanded NPV":

$$\text{Expanded NPV} = \text{Static NPV} + \text{Value of real option.} \quad (19.1)$$

Thus, the higher the uncertainty and the longer the investment period, the greater the discount rate and the smaller the NPV, but the drop in NPV will be offset by the value of the real option derived from management flexibility. That is why DCF-based evaluation methods[1] are often questioned by researchers. The NPV approach is suitable for the valuation of fixed cash flow investments, such as bonds, but does not express well when the investment project has uncertain factors, such as strategic moves and subsequent investment opportunities. The real-options approach can capture the value of latent profit opportunities brought about by such uncertainties.

In high-tech industries like biotechnology and semiconductor, the risks are high and cash flow is small, which may even be negative in the initial development of a new generation of technology. But when the product is accepted by the market and enters the mass production stage, cash flow is high, and the stock price of the company often rises sharply. It is as if these businesses are out of money in their initial stage and become in the money in the mass production stage, bringing substantial prospective profit opportunity for investors who put money into the firm at the initial stage. Therefore, the evaluation model for the high-tech investment project is different from the NPV method, which follows the theory of the higher the risk, the greater the discount rate and the smaller the NPV.

Luehrman (1998a, 1998b) indicated that information required for evaluation of investment projects using the real-options method is just expanded information for the traditional model and not difficult to obtain. Luehrman (1998a, 1998b) also suggested that the NPV method is "one-dimensional" thinking that evaluates whether the NPV of the underlying asset is greater than zero, while the real-options method is "two-dimensional" thinking, which takes into account the NPV of the underlying and the opportunity presented by uncertainties. Thus, in the evaluation of investment project with high uncertainty, the latter offers a better decision-making approach than other methods. Through the concept of flexibility in American options, the real-options approach allows the selection of optimal time points for exercise. The traditional evaluation techniques do not offer such flexible decision-making.

Given the high uncertainty in the high-tech industry, the investor or management needs to consider not only the R&D and

[1]Such as NPV and IRR.

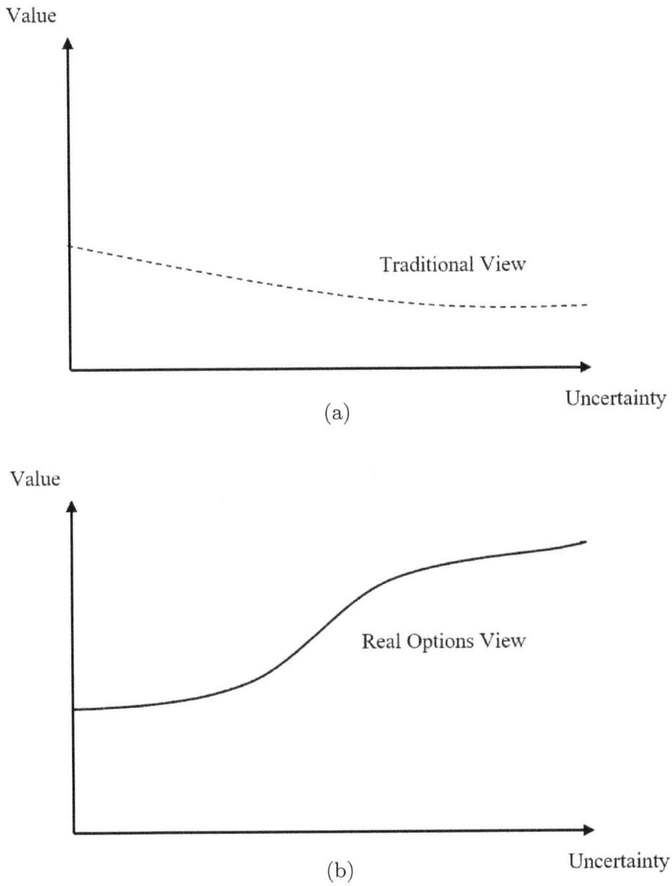

Figure 19.1 (a) Traditional View of the Value of Capital Budgeting under Uncertainty and (b) Real-Options View of the Value of Capital Budgeting under Uncertainty

manufacturing capabilities of the business but also the impact the product will be subjected to in the market. Amram and Kulatilaka (1999) suggested that the management should evaluate the extent of its ability to bear the uncertainty to explain the interaction between investment opportunity and uncertainty to make the optimal investment decision. Figure 19.1 is a perfect interpretation of the relationship between the value of investment opportunity and uncertainty as presented by Amram and Kulatilaka (1999); from the traditional viewpoint, an investment with high uncertainty will see its value fall as presented in Figure 19.1(a). But under the viewpoint of real options, the value of an investment opportunity increases with the decisions made by the management as the degree of uncertainty rises as presented in Figure 19.1(b). For the high-tech industry characterized by high growth, timely actions taken by the management in response to the uncertain conditions can create greater value for the entire investment project. Such a view is consistent with the suggestion of Trigeorgis (1996) that the real-options approach offers management flexibility and strategic flexibility.

Luehrman (1998a, 1998b) used option space[2] created by two-option value metrics of value to cost (NPVq) and volatility[3] to illustrate the technique of real options and locate the investment opportunity in the space for decision-making. Setting NPVq $= 1$ as the center of abscissa, Luehrman (1998a, 1998b) divided the option space into six regions as shown in Figure 19.2, each representing a different "level" of investment opportunity, which are

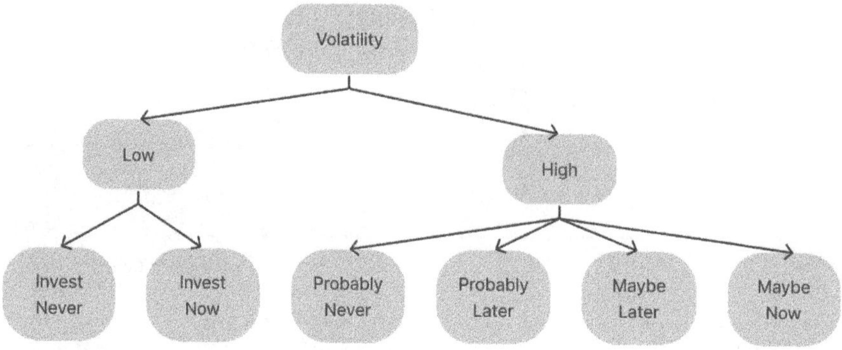

Figure 19.2 Two-Option Value Metrics of Value to Cost (NPVq) Equal to One under Different Degrees of Volatility

[2]Luehrman (1998a, 1998b) estimated value to cost (NPVq) by discounting the exercise price (X) at risk-free rate (r_f), which is defined as $\text{PV}(X)1/4\,X/(1pr_f)^t$ and then as "modified" NPV after deducting the present value of exercise price from the value of the underlying (S). The value to cost (NPVq) is the value of underlying asset divided by present value of exercise price, NPVq $1/4\ S/\text{PV}(X)$; when NPVq > 1, it represents the modified NPV being greater than zero; conversely, when NPVq < 1, the modified NPV is less than zero. The cumulative variance (σ^{2t}) is the variance of investment value multiplied by time.

[3]Defined as cumulative variance.

invest now, maybe now, probably later, invest never, probably never, and maybe later. Such a classification fully depicts the spirit of decision-making.

In the option space presented by Luehrman, the greater the NPVq, the higher the cumulative variance ($\sigma^2 t$) and the higher the value of the investment project; if NPVq > 1, the cumulative variance is small, indicating that other changes will be small in the future and the investment project may proceed right away. Alternately, projects with NPVq > 1 and small cumulative variance should not go ahead, while projects with large cumulative variance and relatively high uncertainty may be decided later after the inflow of new information. Projects with NPVq > 1 should not be executed immediately but should wait for the situation to clear up before making the decision. Using option value metrics for investment decision-making captures the NPV of the project and the value of opportunity under high risk. The two-dimensional model of real options is perfectly interpreted in the option space of Luehrman (1998a, 1998b).

19.3.1 *Treatment of non-traded assets*

The partial differential equation (PDE) for the pricing of derivative products derived under arbitrage-free argument may be applied regardless of whether the underlying asset is traded or not. Hull (1997) indicated that the Black–Scholes–Merton PDE does not contain the variable of risk preferences; that is, it assumes that the risk attitude of the investors is irrelevant to the underlying. Hence, the use of the risk-neutral evaluation method is meaningless in the evaluation of non-traded assets. In the real world, underlying assets to be valued are mostly non-traded assets that make the risk attitude of the investor an important factor. If the expected growth rate of the underlying asset is adjusted, it amounts to pricing the asset in a risk-neutral world.

Constantinides (1978) priced underlying asset with market risk in a world where the market price of risk is zero. He utilized the certainty equivalence approach to adjust the parameters in the model to effective value, that is, deducting risk premium and discounting the expected cash flows at the risk-free rate. The Constantinides model lets $\tilde{x}$ be cash flow, realized at the end of a period; hence, the risk-adjusted NPV given by the Capital Asset Pricing Model (CAPM) under the assumption of a single period is as follows:

$$\text{RANPV}(\tilde{x}) = \frac{\tilde{x}(\bar{r}_m - r_f)Cov(\tilde{r}_m, \tilde{x})/\sigma_m^2}{1 + r_f}, \tag{19.2}$$

where r_m, r_f, and σ_m are, respectively, market rate of return, risk-free return, and rate of market return shortfall. Under the assumption of zero market price of risk, $\bar{x}(\bar{r}_m - r_f)\,Cov(\tilde{r}_m, \tilde{x})/\sigma_m^2$ depicts the expected cash flow $\bar{x}$ which is adjusted to certainty-equivalent cash flows and discounted at the risk-free rate of return.[4] Merton (1973) showed that the equilibrium security returns satisfy the basic CAPM relationship. The derivation process of Constantinides (1978) was based on the equilibrium model, while the traditional PDE-based pricing models admit a no-arbitrage framework. These two models have different processes, but derive consistent results.

In handling the risk factors of uncertainty, Cox *et al.* (1985) suggested the use of certainty-equivalent cash flows, not the risk-adjusted discount rate. Trigeorgis (1993a, 1993b) also indicated that the contingent claim of asset can be priced in the real world of systemic risk by substituting the real growth rate with certainty-equivalent rate. The certainty-equivalent rate is obtained by deducting the risk premium from the original growth rate of the asset. Such an approach is the same as pricing in a risk-neutral environment. The expected return of all assets in a risk-neutral environment is risk-free return. But when the investor has certain risk preferences, the expected growth rate in equilibrium will differ from the original growth rate. Such a risk adjustment approach amounts to discounting certainty-equivalent cash flows at the risk-free rate of return, instead of adjusting the expected cash flows at the risk-adjusted rate.

19.3.2 *Dividend-like yield*

McDonald and Siegel (1984, 1985) discussed that since the rate of return derived from an option pricing equation should be consistent with capital market equilibrium, the results derived from the

---

[4] Cox *et al.* (1985) used the certainty-equivalent approach for risk adjustment, not risk-adjusted discount rate, that is, modifying the real expected growth rate to the certainty-equivalent growth rate by deducting discount premium from real expected growth rate.

Black–Scholes equation are independent of and irrelevant to the consideration of capital market equilibrium, and there exists a shortfall between the expected return and the required return. It is like a dividend yield, that is, only when the underlying asset does not pay any dividend and the expected return is equal to the market-required equilibrium return will the Black–Scholes equation be satisfied. The presence of this shortfall derived from CAPM consists of the conclusion of Constantinides (1978). Trigeorgis (1993a, 1993b) defined the shortfall as dividend-like yield (δ). Hence, if an investment project valued by the real-options model involves non-traded assets, the pricing model will contain a dividend-like yield, which differs from the pricing models for traded assets.

Real-options pricing models apply mostly in cases of non-traded assets. In a perfect market, we assume the existence of twin security, which is a traded asset having equivalent risk as the non-traded asset, paying fixed dividend, and satisfying CAPM. In such a case, the value of the non-traded asset using the PDE pricing model is determined under the risk-neutral environment. Thus, if there exists a twin security having the same financial risk as that for the non-traded asset, the real option can be priced.

Lin (2002) took into account the dividend-like yield in his real-options model in the valuation of venture capital projects. Although his model simulated value of the project based on assumed parameters, the paper had comprehensive discussion of dividend-like yield. Thus, under the assumption of perfect market, CAPM may be used for the estimation of dividend-like yield. Duan *et al.* (2003) proposed in a case study that dividend-like yield can be estimated using the cost of carry model that frees the estimation method from the restriction of perfect market assumption. In a case study using real data, they use the CAPM method to estimate dividend-like yields.

19.4 A Fuzzy Real-Option Valuation

19.4.1 *Fuzzy numbers*

From Zadeh (1965), $\tilde{A}$ is a convex fuzzy set if and only if its α-level set $\tilde{A}_\alpha = \{x : \mu_{\tilde{A}}(x) \geq \alpha\}$ is a convex set for all any α. Therefore, if $\tilde{\alpha}$ is a fuzzy number, then the α-level set $\tilde{\alpha}_\alpha$ is a compact (closed and bounded in R) and convex set; that is, $\tilde{\alpha}$ is a closed interval. The α-level set of $\tilde{\alpha}$ is then denoted by $\tilde{\alpha}_\alpha = [\tilde{\alpha}_\alpha^L, \tilde{\alpha}_\alpha^U]$. A fuzzy number $\tilde{\alpha}$ is said to be non-negative if $\mu_{\tilde{\alpha}}(x) = 0$ for $x < 0$. It is easy to see that if $\tilde{\alpha}$ is a non-negative fuzzy numbers, then $\tilde{\alpha}_\alpha^L$ and $\tilde{\alpha}_\alpha^U$ are all non-negative real numbers for all $\alpha \in [0, 1]$.

19.4.2 *Triangular fuzzy number*

The concept of triangular fuzzy number attempts to deal with real problems by possibility. The membership of a triangular fuzzy number is defined as follows (Figure 19.3):

$$\mu_{\tilde{A}}(x) = \begin{bmatrix} (x-L)/(M-L) \to L \le x \le M \\ (R-x)/(R-M) \to M \le x \le R. \\ 0, \quad \text{otherwise.} \end{bmatrix}$$

According to the characteristics of triangular fuzzy numbers and the extension principle put forward by Zadeh (1965), the operational laws of triangular fuzzy numbers, $\tilde{A} = (l_1, m_1, r_1)$ and $\tilde{B} = (l_2, m_2, r_2)$, are as follows:

(1) Addition of two fuzzy numbers $\oplus$

$$(l_1, m_1, r_1) \oplus (l_2, m_2, r_2) = (l_1 + l_2, m_1 + m_2, r_1 + r_2)$$

(2) Subtraction of two fuzzy numbers Θ

$$(l_1, m_1, r_1)\Theta(l_2, m_2, r_2) = (l_1 - r_2, m_1 - m_2, r_1 - l_2)$$

(3) Multiplication of two fuzzy numbers $\otimes$

$$(l_1, m_1, r_1) \otimes (l_2, m_2, r_2) \cong (l_1 l_2, m_1 m_2, r_1 r_2)$$

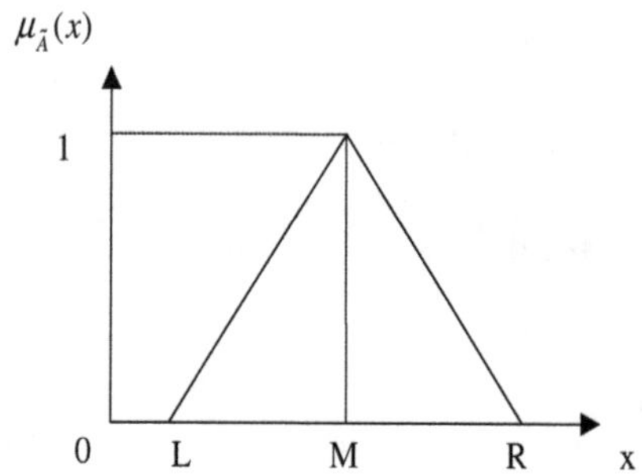

Figure 19.3 The Membership Function of the Triangular Fuzzy Number

(4) Multiplication of any real number k and a fuzzy number $\otimes$

$$k \otimes (l_1, m_1, r_1) = (kl_1, km_1, kr_1)$$

(5) Division of two fuzzy numbers $\emptyset$

$$(l_1, m_1, r_1)\emptyset(l_2, m_2, r_2) \cong (l_1/r_2, m_1/m_2, r_1/l_2)$$

19.4.3 *A real-option valuation*

A real option means the possibility for a certain period to either choose for or against making an investment decision, without binding oneself up front. The real-option rule is that one should invest today only if the NPV is high enough to compensate for giving up the value of the option to wait. Because the option to invest loses its value when the investment is irreversibly made, this loss is an opportunity cost of investing. While the ongoing evaluation effort is structured around key decision points, or triggered by changes in the business environment, it is a process in which the valuation, even the computing process, is not intended to provide a definite answer, but rather to provide decision-makers an ongoing dialogue about the project (Dahlberg and Porter, 2000). So, a process view of the real-option approach is a relevant task in analyzing the decision support needs.

Real options in option thinking are based on the Black–Scholes model as financial options. The option pricing theory is that you should invest today only if the NPV is high enough to compensate for giving up the value of the option to wait. Because the option to invest loses its value when the investment is irreversibly made, this loss is an opportunity cost of investing. Following Leslie and Michaels (1997), we will compute the value of a real option as

$$\text{ROV} = S_0 e^{-\delta T} N(d_1) - X e^{-rT} N(d_2), \tag{19.3}$$

where

$$d_1 = \frac{\ln(S_0/X) + (r - \delta + \sigma^2/2)T}{\sigma\sqrt{T}}, \quad d_2 = d_1 - \sigma\sqrt{T}$$

and where ROV denotes the current real-option value, S_0 is the present value of expected cash flows, X is the (nominal) value of fixed costs, σ quantifies the uncertainty of expected cash flows, and δ denotes the value lost over the duration of the option.

In real options, the options involve real assets. To have a real option means to have the possibility for a certain period to either choose for or against making an investment decision. Real options can be valued using the analog option theories that have been developed for financial options, but do not mean that they are the same. Real options are concerned about strategic decisions of a company, where degrees of freedom are limited to the capabilities of the company. In these strategic decisions, different stakeholders play a role, especially if the resources needed for an investment are significant and thereby the continuity of the company is at stake. In addition, it is quite different from traditional DCF investment approaches. The traditional methods make it very hard to make a decision when there is uncertainty about the exact outcome of the investment. And since these methods ignore the value of flexibility and discount heavily for external uncertainty involved, many interesting and innovative activities and projects are canceled because of the uncertainties.

If the result of NPV is negative, the company would obviously pass up the opportunity. But if we use the real-option valuation, the result may be different for the same case. Such a valuation would recognize the importance of uncertainty, which the NPV analysis effectively assumes away. The main question that a company must answer for a deferrable investment opportunity is how long we postpone the investment up to T time periods. To answer this question, Benaroch and Kauffman (2000) suggested the following decision rule for optimal investment strategy: Where the maximum deferral time is T, make sure that the investment (exercise the option) at time t is positive and attends its maximum value. Of course, this decision rule has to be reapplied every time new information arrives during the deferral period to see how the optimal investment strategy might change in light of the new information.

19.4.4 *A fuzzy real-option valuation under the Black–Scholes option pricing model*

We shall introduce a real-option rule in a fuzzy setting, where the present values of expected cash flows and expected costs are estimated by triangular fuzzy numbers, and determine the optimal exercise time by using the fuzzy real-option model. Usually, the present value of expected cash flows cannot be characterized by a single number. But managers are able to estimate the present value of expected cash flows by using triangular possibility distribution of the form $\tilde{F} = [f_l, f_m, f_r]$, that is, the most likely values of the present value of expected cash flows lie in the f_m (which is the core of the triangular fuzzy number $\tilde{F}$), f_r is the greatest value, and f_l is the smallest value for the present value of expected cash flows.

In a similar manner, one can estimate the expected costs by using a triangular possibility distribution of the form $\tilde{X} = [x_l, x_m, x_r]$, that is, the most likely values of expected costs lie in the interval x_m (which is the core of the triangular fuzzy number $\tilde{X}$), x_r is the greatest value, and x_l is the smallest value for expected costs.

In addition, the values are also influenced by the financial market, such as riskless interest rate (discount rate) and the volatility of cash inflow. We use historic data to estimate them by using a triangular possibility distribution of the form $\tilde{R} = [r_l, r_m, r_r], \tilde{\delta} = [\delta_l, \delta_m, \delta_r], \tilde{\sigma} = [\sigma_l, \sigma_m, \sigma_r]$, that is, the most likely values of discount rate, risk-adjusted discount rate, and the volatility of cash inflow lie in the interval r_m, δ_m, and σ_m (which is the core of the triangular fuzzy number $\tilde{R}$, $\tilde{\delta}$ and $\tilde{\sigma}$), respectively, r_r is the greatest value and r_l is the smallest value for discount rate, δ_r is the greatest value and δ_l is the smallest value for the risk-adjusted discount-rate, and σ_r is the greatest value and σ_l is the smallest value for volatility of cash inflow.

The information needed for capital budgeting is generally not known with certainty. The sources of uncertainty may be the net cash inflow, the discount rate, the life of the project, etc. Hence, in addition to considering the fuzzy volatility $\tilde{\sigma}$ and investing cost $\tilde{X}$, we also consider the fuzzy cash inflow $\tilde{F}$, fuzzy interest rate $\tilde{\delta}$, and $\tilde{R}$. In these circumstances, we suggest the use of the following formula for computing fuzzy ROVs:

$$\begin{aligned} &\tilde{\text{ROV}}(\tilde{F}, \tilde{X}, \tilde{\delta}, \tilde{R}, \tilde{\sigma}, T) \\ &\quad = \tilde{F} \otimes \mathrm{e}^{-\tilde{\delta}\otimes T} \otimes N(\tilde{d}_1) \Theta \tilde{X} \otimes \mathrm{e}^{-\tilde{R}\otimes T} \otimes N(\tilde{d}_2), \end{aligned} \tag{19.4}$$

where

$$\tilde{d}_1 = \frac{\ln(\tilde{F} \oslash \tilde{X}) \oplus (\tilde{R} \ominus \tilde{\delta} \oplus \tilde{\sigma}^2/2) \otimes T}{\tilde{\sigma} \otimes \sqrt{T}}, \tilde{d}_2 = \tilde{d}_1 \ominus \tilde{\sigma} \otimes \sqrt{T}$$

and, where $\tilde{F}$ denotes the probabilistic mean value of the present value of expected cash flows, $\tilde{X}$ stands for the probabilistic mean value of expected costs, $\tilde{\sigma}(\tilde{F})$ is the variance of the present value expected cash flows, $\tilde{\delta}$ stands for the risk-adjusted discount rate, $\tilde{R}$ stands for the discount rate, and T stands for the interval. Using the above formula for arithmetic operations on triangular fuzzy numbers, we find

$$\begin{aligned}\text{FROV} &= (f_l, f_m, f_r) \otimes \mathrm{e}^{-\tilde{\delta}\otimes T} \otimes N(\tilde{d_1})\Theta(x_l, x_m, x_r) \otimes \mathrm{e}^{-\tilde{R}\otimes T} \otimes N(\tilde{d_2}) \\ &= (f_l N(\tilde{d_1}) \otimes \mathrm{e}^{-\tilde{\delta}r\otimes T} - x_r N(\tilde{d_2}) \otimes \mathrm{e}^{-\tilde{R}r\otimes T}, f_m N(\tilde{d_1}) \otimes \mathrm{e}^{-\tilde{\delta}m\otimes T} \\ &\quad - x_m N(\tilde{d_2}) \otimes \mathrm{e}^{-\tilde{R}m\otimes T} \cdots + \cdots f_r N(\tilde{d_1}) \otimes e^{-\tilde{\delta}l\otimes T} \\ &\quad - x_l N(\tilde{d_2}) \otimes e^{-\tilde{R}l\otimes T}],\end{aligned} \tag{19.5}$$

where

$$\begin{aligned}\tilde{d_1} &= [(\ln f_l/x_r + r_l T - \delta_r T + \sigma_l\sigma_l T/2)/\sigma_r\sqrt{T} \\ &\quad \times (\ln f_m/x_m + r_m T - \delta_m T + \sigma_m\sigma_m T/2)/\sigma_m\sqrt{T} \\ &\quad \times (\ln f_r/x_l + r_r T - \delta_l T + \sigma_r\sigma_r T/2)/\sigma_l\sqrt{T}, \tilde{d_2} = \tilde{d_1}\Theta\tilde{\sigma} \otimes \sqrt{T}.\end{aligned}$$

In the following, we shall generalize the probabilistic decision rule for optimal investment strategy to a fuzzy setting: Where the maximum deferral time is T, make the investment (exercise the option) at time t^*; $0 \le t^* \le T$, for which the option, $\tilde{C}_{t^*}$, attends its maximum value,

$$\tilde{C}_{t^*} = \max_{t=0,1,\ldots,T} \tilde{C}_t = \tilde{F} \otimes e^{-\tilde{\delta}\otimes T} \otimes N(\tilde{d_1})\Theta\tilde{X} \otimes e^{-\tilde{R}\otimes T} \otimes N(\tilde{d_2}), \tag{19.6}$$

where

$$\tilde{F}_t = \text{PV}(\tilde{cf_0}, \tilde{cf_1}, \tilde{cf_T}, \tilde{\delta}) - \text{PV}(\tilde{cf_0}, \tilde{cf_1}, \tilde{cf_t}, \tilde{\delta}) = \text{PV}(\tilde{cf_{t+1}}, \tilde{cf_1}, \tilde{cf_T}, \tilde{\delta}),$$

that is,

$$\tilde{F}_t = \tilde{cf_0} + \sum_{j=1}^{T} \frac{\tilde{cf_j}}{(1+\tilde{\delta})^j} - \tilde{cf_0} + \sum_{j=1}^{t} \frac{\tilde{cf_j}}{(1+\tilde{\delta})^j} = \sum_{j=t+1}^{T} \frac{\tilde{cf_j}}{(1+\tilde{\delta})^j},$$

where $\tilde{cf_j}$ denotes the expected (fuzzy) cash flow at time j and $\tilde{\delta}$ is the risk-adjusted discount rate (or required rate of return on the project). However, finding a maximizing element from the set $\{\tilde{C}_0, \tilde{C}_1, \tilde{C}_T\}$

is not an easy task because it involves ranking of triangular fuzzy numbers.

In our computerized implementation, we have employed the following function to determine the expected fuzzy ROVs $\{\tilde{C}_l, \tilde{C}_m, \tilde{C}_r\}$ of triangular form:

$$E(C_t) = [(C_r - C_l) + (C_m - C_l)]/3 + C_l, \tag{19.7}$$

where C_r, C_m, and C_l are the largest, middle, and smallest values of the fuzzy ROVs, respectively.

19.5 Computational Method and Example

We give an example to compare and analyze the results of the capital-budgeting problem using a fuzzy real-option model, where the present values of expected cash flows, expected costs, the discount rate, the risk-adjusted discount rate, and volatility of cash inflows are estimated by triangular fuzzy numbers.

First, let us refer to Table 19.1 by Bonini (1975), where we consider a project requiring an initial outlay of \$10,000 (Column 1). In each of the following time periods (Columns 3, 5, and 7), the cash flow to be received is not known with perfect certainty, but the probabilities associated with each cash flow in each period are assumed to be known (Columns 2, 4, and 6), so that we are dealing with a case of risk, and not strict uncertainty. We note that Columns 4 and 6 are conditional probability figures, where the later periods' expected cash flows depend highly on what occurs in earlier time periods. Given our cash flow and simple probability estimates for Periods 1, 2, and 3, we find 27 possible joint probabilities (Column 8), each of which corresponds to a cash flow series. Thus, in the uppermost path, we find the joint probability 0.015 being associated with a cash flow of \$1,000 in Period 1, followed by cash flows of \$2,000 and \$3,000 in Periods 2 and 3, respectively. The returns and joint probabilities can be calculated similarly for the other 25 possible patterns.

While the primary hurdle in this process is in estimating the cash flows and the probabilities, we recognize that it is the NPV figures we are ultimately interested in. Table 19.2 gives the present value of the cash flows (PVA) and the NPV of the project for each cash flow series (NPV), where a constant 4% discount rate was employed.

Table 19.1 Illustration of Conditional Probability Distribution Approach

(1) Initial Outlay Period 0	(2) Initial Probability P (1)	(3) Net Cash Flow	(4) Conditional Probability $P(2\|1)$	(5) Net Cash Flow	(6) Conditional Probability $P(3\|2,1)$	(7) Cash Flow	(8) Joint Probability
					0.2	1,000	0.015
			0.25	2,000	0.5	2,000	0.0375
					0.3	3,000	0.0225
					0.2	2,000	0.03
10,000	0.3	2,000	0.5	3,000	0.5	3,000	0.075
					0.3	4,000	0.045
					0.2	3,000	0.015
			0.25	4,000	0.5	4,000	0.0375
					0.3	5,000	0.0225
					0.3	2,000	0.045
			0.3	3,000	0.4	4,000	0.06
					0.3	6,000	0.045
					0.3	4,000	0.06
	0.5	4,000	0.4	5,000	0.4	5,000	0.08
					0.3	6,000	0.06
					0.3	5,000	0.045
			0.3	7,000	0.4	7,000	0.06
					0.3	9,000	0.045
					0.25	4,000	0.0125
			0.25	5,000	0.5	6,000	0.025
					0.25	8,000	0.0125
					0.25	5,000	0.025
	0.2	6,000	0.5	7,000	0.5	7,000	0.05
					0.25	9,000	0.025
					0.25	7,000	0.0125
			0.25	8,000	0.5	9,000	0.025
					0.25	11,000	0.0125

Table 19.2 NPV and Joint Probability

t	PVA	NPV	Probability	Standard Deviation
1	4,661.2	−5,338.8	0.015	1,021.913
2	5,550.2	−4,449.8	0.0375	1,443.632
3	6,439.2	−3,560.8	0.0225	984.8824
4	6,474.76	−3,525.24	0.03	1,131.085
5	7,363.76	−2,636.24	0.075	1,544.94
6	8,252.76	−1,747.24	0.045	1,008.12
7	8,288.32	−1,711.68	0.015	577.6831
8	9,177.32	−822.68	0.0375	741.2431
9	10,066.32	66.32	0.0225	440.8144
10	8,297.84	−1,602.16	0.045	998.557
11	10,175.84	175.84	0.06	693.0202
12	11,953.84	1,953.84	0.045	223.0023
13	12,024.96	2,024.96	0.06	240.0801
14	12,913.96	2,913.96	0.08	25.77347
15	13,802.96	3,802.96	0.06	195.4392
16	14,763.08	4,763.08	0.045	372.9275
17	16,541.08	6,541.08	0.06	866.1388
18	18,319.08	8,319.08	0.045	1,127.269
19	13,948.04	3,948.04	0.0125	105.4258
20	15,726.04	5,726.04	0.025	430.2211
21	17,504.04	7,504.04	0.0125	502.9987
22	16,686.16	6,686.16	0.025	582.0294
23	18,464.16	8,464.16	0.05	1,220.687
24	20,242.16	10,242.16	0.025	1,144.282
25	19,388.72	9,388.72	0.0125	713.7123
26	21,166.72	11,166.72	0.025	1,290.468
27	22,944.72	12,944.72	0.0125	1,111.285

For example, when $t = 1$, the PVA $= [1{,}000/(1+4\%)^3+2{,}000/(1+4\%)^2 + 2{,}000/(1 + 4\%)] = 4{,}661.2$. The NPV $= 10{,}000 - \text{PVA} = 10{,}000 - 4{,}661.2 = -5{,}338.8$. From Columns (3) and (4), we found the worst NPV case is $-5{,}338.8$ with 0.015 fuzzy joint probability (Table 19.1), and the best NPV case is 12,944.72 with 0.0125 fuzzy joint probability. When we multiply each joint probability by the expected NPV associated with that probability, we obtain the expected NPV for the project as a whole, there shown to be \$2,517.18.

Table 19.3 Expected Fuzzy Real-Option Value

t	$\tilde{F}$	$\tilde{\sigma}(\tilde{F})$	FROV	$E(C_t)$
1	$\tilde{F}_1 = [2{,}617, 4{,}661, 6{,}705]$	$\tilde{\sigma}_1 = [960, 1{,}022, 1{,}084]$	$\tilde{C}_1 = [2{,}514, 4{,}523, 6{,}572]$	4,537
2	$\tilde{F}_2 = [2{,}663, 5{,}550, 8{,}437]$	$\tilde{\sigma}_2 = [1{,}182, 1{,}444, 1{,}705]$	$\tilde{C}_2 = [-7{,}495, 613, 8{,}106]$	408
3	$\tilde{F}_3 = [4{,}469, 6{,}439, 8{,}409]$	$\tilde{\sigma}_3 = [920, 985, 1{,}050]$	$\tilde{C}_3 = [-5{,}504, 2{,}984, -306]$	−2,932
4	$\tilde{F}_4 = [4{,}213, 6{,}475, 8{,}737]$	$\tilde{\sigma}_4 = [1{,}005, 1{,}131, 1{,}257]$	$\tilde{C}_4 = [-5{,}416, -2{,}779, 83]$	−2,704
5	$\tilde{F}_5 = [4{,}274, 7{,}364, 10{,}454]$	$\tilde{\sigma}_5 = [1{,}119, 1{,}545, 1{,}970]$	$\tilde{C}_5 = [-5{,}068, -1{,}849, 9{,}459]$	848
6	$\tilde{F}_6 = [6{,}237, 8{,}253, 10{,}269]$	$\tilde{\sigma}_6 = [906, 1{,}008, 1{,}110]$	$\tilde{C}_6 = [-3{,}243, -973, 1{,}590]$	−875
7	$\tilde{F}_7 = [7{,}133, 8{,}288, 9{,}444]$	$\tilde{\sigma}_7 = [531, 578, 624]$	$\tilde{C}_7 = [-2{,}361, -840, -915]$	−762
8	$\tilde{F}_8 = [7{,}695, 9{,}177, 10{,}660]$	$\tilde{\sigma}_8 = [731, 741, 752]$	$\tilde{C}_8 = [-1{,}786, -43, 2{,}004]$	59
9	$\tilde{F}_9 = [9{,}185, 10{,}066, 10{,}948]$	$\tilde{\sigma}_9 = [343, 441, 539]$	$\tilde{C}_9 = [-606, 707, 2{,}274]$	792
10	$\tilde{F}_{10} = [6{,}301, 8{,}298, 10{,}295]$	$\tilde{\sigma}_{10} = [901, 999, 1{,}096]$	$\tilde{C}_{10} = [-2{,}448, -556, 1{,}761]$	−414
11	$\tilde{F}_{11} = [8{,}790, 10{,}176, 11{,}562]$	$\tilde{\sigma}_{11} = [656, 693, 730]$	$\tilde{C}_{11} = [-685, 875, 2{,}808]$	999
12	$\tilde{F}_{12} = [11{,}508, 11{,}954, 12{,}400]$	$\tilde{\sigma}_{12} = [-8, 223, 454]$	$\tilde{C}_{12} = [7{,}109, 2{,}152, 0]$	3,087
13	$\tilde{F}_{13} = [11{,}545, 12{,}025, 12{,}505]$	$\tilde{\sigma}_{13} = [-19, 240, 499]$	$\tilde{C}_{13} = [6{,}864, 2{,}196, 0]$	3,020
14	$\tilde{F}_{14} = [12{,}862, 12{,}914, 12{,}966]$	$\tilde{\sigma}_{14} = [-394, 26, 446]$	$\tilde{C}_{14} = [7{,}347, 2{,}773, -5{,}913]$	1,402
15	$\tilde{F}_{15} = [13{,}412, 13{,}803, 14{,}194]$	$\tilde{\sigma}_{15} = [-85, 195, 476]$	$\tilde{C}_{15} = [7{,}361, 3{,}313, 0]$	3,558
16	$\tilde{F}_{16} = [14{,}017, 14{,}763, 15{,}509]$	$\tilde{\sigma}_{16} = [205, 373, 541]$	$\tilde{C}_{16} = [2{,}448, 3{,}862, 5{,}693]$	4,001
17	$\tilde{F}_{17} = [14{,}809, 16{,}541, 18{,}273]$	$\tilde{\sigma}_{17} = [818, 866, 914]$	$\tilde{C}_{17} = [2{,}801, 4{,}867, 7{,}576]$	5,081
18	$\tilde{F}_{18} = [16{,}065, 18{,}319, 20{,}574]$	$\tilde{\sigma}_{18} = [975, 1{,}127, 1{,}280]$	$\tilde{C}_{18} = [3{,}347, 5{,}808, 9{,}109]$	6,088
19	$\tilde{F}_{19} = [13{,}737, 13{,}948, 14{,}159]$	$\tilde{\sigma}_{19} = [-43, 105, 254]$	$\tilde{C}_{19} = [6{,}424, 3{,}211, 0]$	3,212
20	$\tilde{F}_{20} = [14{,}866, 15{,}726, 16{,}586]$	$\tilde{\sigma}_{20} = [323, 430, 537]$	$\tilde{C}_{20} = [2{,}633, 4{,}137, 6{,}179]$	4,316
21	$\tilde{F}_{21} = [16{,}498, 17{,}504, 18{,}510]$	$\tilde{\sigma}_{21} = [444, 503, 562]$	$\tilde{C}_{21} = [3{,}273, 5{,}005, 7{,}369]$	5,216
22	$\tilde{F}_{22} = [15{,}522, 16{,}686, 17{,}850]$	$\tilde{\sigma}_{22} = [523, 582, 641]$	$\tilde{C}_{22} = [2{,}777, 4{,}476, 6{,}844]$	4,699
23	$\tilde{F}_{23} = [16{,}023, 18{,}464, 20{,}906]$	$\tilde{\sigma}_{23} = [1{,}018, 1{,}221, 1{,}423]$	$\tilde{C}_{23} = [2{,}902, 5{,}276, 8{,}683]$	5,621
24	$\tilde{F}_{24} = [17{,}954, 20{,}242, 22{,}531]$	$\tilde{\sigma}_{24} = [1{,}025, 1{,}144, 1{,}263]$	$\tilde{C}_{24} = [3{,}561, 6{,}024, 9{,}561]$	6,382
25	$\tilde{F}_{25} = [17{,}961, 19{,}389, 20{,}816]$	$\tilde{\sigma}_{25} = [702, 714, 726]$	$\tilde{C}_{25} = [3{,}456, 5{,}480, 8{,}374]$	5,770
26	$\tilde{F}_{26} = [18{,}586, 21{,}167, 23{,}748]$	$\tilde{\sigma}_{26} = [1{,}125, 1{,}290, 1{,}456]$	$\tilde{C}_{26} = [3{,}571, 6{,}169, 9{,}993]$	6,578
27	$\tilde{F}_{27} = [20{,}722, 22{,}945, 25{,}167]$	$\tilde{\sigma}_{27} = [1{,}035, 1{,}111, 1{,}188]$	$\tilde{C}_{27} = [4{,}185, 6{,}811, 10{,}662]$	7,220

Note: Where t: time (in years), $\tilde{F}$: cash flow, $\tilde{\sigma}(\tilde{F})$: variance of the present value expected cash flows, FROV: fuzzy real-option value, $E(C_t)$: expected FROV.

If the probabilities of the cash flow do not know, then the cash flows become an uncertainty case. In $\tilde{X}_0 = [9{,}000, 10{,}000, 11{,}000]$, $\tilde{R} = [0.03,\ 0.04,\ 0.05], \tilde{\delta} = [0.02,\ 0.03,\ 0.04]$, we can use fuzzy real option to approach the capital budgeting under uncertainty. We use the above example and fuzzy real-option model to compute the expected fuzzy ROVs. From the above data, we transform them into the triangular fuzzy number and we substitute into Equation (19.5), then we get the FROV of Table 19.3.

For example, when $t = 1$, the PVA of Table 19.3 is $4{,}661.2 \pm 2\sigma$, for which the $\tilde{F} = (4{,}661.2 - 2 \times 1{,}021.913, 4{,}661.2, 4{,}661.2 + 2 \times 1{,}021.913) = [2{,}617, 4{,}661, 6{,}705]$. Then, we compute the $\tilde{d}_1$.

First,

$$\begin{aligned}\tilde{d}_1 &= [(\ln f_l/x_r + r_l T - \delta_r T + \sigma_l \sigma_l T/2)/\sigma_r\sqrt{T} \\ &\quad \times (\ln f_m/x_m + r_m T - \delta_m T + \sigma_m \sigma_m T/2)/\sigma_m\sqrt{T} \\ &\quad \times (\ln f_r/x_l + r_r T - \delta_l T + \sigma_r \sigma_r T/2)/\sigma_l\sqrt{T}].\end{aligned}$$

$$\begin{aligned}\tilde{d}_1 &= [(\ln(2{,}617/11{,}000) + 0.03 - 0.04 + 960 \times 960/2)/1{,}084 \\ &\quad \times (\ln(4{,}661/10{,}000) + 0.04 - 0.03 + 1{,}022 \times 1{,}022/2)/1{,}022] \\ &\quad \times \ln(6{,}705/9{,}000) + 0.05 - 0.02 + 1{,}084 \times 1{,}084/2)/960] \\ &= [425, 511, 612],\end{aligned}$$

$$\begin{aligned}\tilde{d}_2 &= \tilde{d}_1 \Theta \tilde{\sigma} \otimes \sqrt{T}\tilde{d}_2 = [(425 - 1{,}084),\ (511 - 1{,}022),\ (612 - 960)] \\ &= [-659, -511, -348].\end{aligned}$$

Then, we check the $N(\tilde{d}_1)$ and $N(\tilde{d}_2)$, substitute the value into Equation (19.5), and we can get

$$\begin{aligned}\text{FROV} &= (2{,}617, 4{,}661, 6{,}705) \otimes \mathrm{e}^{-(0.04,0.03,0.02)} \\ &\quad \otimes N(\tilde{d}_1)\Theta(11{,}000, 10{,}000, 9000) \otimes \mathrm{e}^{-(0.05,0.04,0.03)} \\ &\quad \otimes N(\tilde{d}_2) = [2{,}514, 4{,}523, 6{,}572].\end{aligned}$$

Lastly, using Equation (19.7), we can get the $E(C_1) = 4{,}537$. In addition, the values of $E(C_3)$, $E(C_4)$, $E(C_6)$, $E(C_7)$, and $E(C_{10})$ are negative, and these $E(C_t)$ will become zero.

When the environment is uncertain, with uncertain cash flows, the investor will face a distribution of future cash flows rather than a single-point estimate of future cash flow in each period. The method utilized to deal with these uncertain cash flows is that of the fuzzy real-option model. What would option valuation make of the same case? To begin with, such a valuation would recognize the importance of uncertainty, which the NPV analysis effectively assumes away. We use the fuzzy real-option model to evaluate the project in the same case, wherein holding the option also obliges one to incur the annual fixed costs of keeping the reserve active — let us say \$300. This represents a dividend-like payout of 3% (i.e., 300/1,000) of the value of the assets, the discount rate is around 4%, cost is around \$10,000, and dividend rate is around 3%; then, we obtain the expected fuzzy ROVs for the project as a whole, $\tilde{C}_{t^*} = \max_{t=0,1,\ldots,T} \tilde{C}_t$, where the maximum deferral time is $T = 27$, making the investment (exercise the option) at time t^*; $\leq t^* \leq T$, for which the option, $\tilde{C}_{t^*}$, there is shown to be \$7,220 at $t = 27$, which is positive and attends its maximum value.

19.6 Conclusions

The FROV will increase with the current value of increasing expected cash flow estimates. A proactive management can influence this by developing market strategies to enhance the sale and save the cost. If volatility of cash flow will increase, then the FROV will increase. Corporate management can be proactive and find ways to expand to new markets, product innovations, and innovation product combinations as end results of their strategic decisions. The longer the time to maturity, the greater will be the FROV. Proactive management can ensure this development by maintaining protective barriers, communicating implementation possibilities, and maintaining a technological lead. On the other hand, if the expected value of fixed costs goes up, the FROV will decrease as opportunities of operating with less cost are lost. This can be countered by using the postponement period to explore and implement production scalability benefits. An increase in risk-less returns will increase the FROV, and this can be further enhanced by closely monitoring changes in the interest rates. The FROV will decrease if value is lost during the postponement of the investment, but this can be countered by either creating business barriers for competitors or by better managing key resources.

Fuzzy capital-budgeting approaches allow cash flow estimates as fuzzy numbers and offer the means to integrate trend data into cash flows. Fuzzy cash flows can better reflect the uncertainty in the project. The integration of qualitative information into the process gives better support. The real-option approach also supports the determination of the timing for the investment, and offers a comprehensive way of presenting the value of possibilities opened by the project, which is further enhanced with frequently updated fuzzy cash flows. Finally, we would like to stress that advanced decision methods such as real options and fuzzy capital budgeting open the chance to explore the value of flexibility inside and outside a project, and give further insight into the real uncertainty of large investments. The uncertainty is genuine, that is, we simply do not know the exact levels of future cash flows. Without introducing the fuzzy real-option model, it would not be possible to formulate this genuine uncertainty. The proposed model that incorporates subjective judgments and statistical uncertainties may give investors a better understanding of the problem when making investment decisions.

Questions and Problems

1. Please discuss the traditional method to handle capital budgeting under uncertainty.
2. Please discuss the differences among expanded NPV and static NPV.
3. Please discuss the traditional view and real-option view on capital budgeting under uncertainty.
4. Please describe a fuzzy real-option valuation under the Black–Scholes option pricing model.
5. Please describe a fuzzy real-option valuation under the binomial option pricing model.
6. Please describe how Tables 19.1, 19.2, and 19.3 have been calculated.
7. In Equation (19B.9), if we know $P = \$2$ million, $R = 5\%$, $T = 10$ years, and initial cost of investment = \$1 million. Please calculate V_C.

Bibliography

Alonso, S., F. J. Cabrerizo, E. Herrera-Viedma and F. Herrera (2009). h-Index: A review focused in its variants, computation and standardization for different scientific fields. *Journal of Informetrics*, 3(4), 273–289.

Amram, M. and N. Kulatilaka (1999). *Real Options: Managing Strategic Investment in an Uncertain World.* New York: OUP.

Amram, M. and N. Kulatilaka (1999). *Real Options.* Boston: Harvard Business School Press.

Bellman, R. E. and L. A. Zadeh (1970). Decision-making in a fuzzy environment. *Management Science*, 17(4), B-141.

Benaroch, M. and R. J. Kauffman (2000). Justifying electronic banking network expansion using real options analysis. *MIS Quarterly*, 24(2), 197–225.

Bonini, C. P. (1975). Comment on formulating correlated cash flow streams. *The Engineering Economist*, 20(3), 209–221.

Bowman, E. H. and D. Hurry (1993). Strategy through the option lens: An integrated view of resource investments and the incremental-choice process. *Academy of Management Review*, 18(4), 760–782.

Cabrerizo, F. J., S. Alonso and E. Herrera-Viedma (2009). A consensus model for group decision making problems with unbalanced fuzzy linguistic information. *International Journal of Information Technology & Decision Making*, 8(01), 109–131.

Carlsson, C. and R. Fullér (2001). *Fuzzy Reasoning in Decision Making and Optimization*. Vol. 82. New York: Springer Science & Business Media.

Carlsson, C. and R. Fuller (2002). *Fuzzy Reasoning in Decision Making and Optimization*. Heidelberg: Physica Verlag.

Carlsson, C. and R. Fullér (2002). A position paper on the agenda for soft decision analysis. *Fuzzy Sets and Systems*, 131(1), 3–11.

Carlsson, C. and R. Fullér (2003). A fuzzy approach to real option valuation. *Fuzzy Sets and Systems*, 139(2), 297–312.

Constantinides, G. M. (1978). Market risk adjustment in project valuation. *The Journal of Finance*, 33(2), 603–616.

Cox, J. C., J. E. Ingersoll Jr and S. A. Ross (1985). An intertemporal general equilibrium model of asset prices. *Econometrica*, 53(2), 363–384.

Dahlberg, K. and R. S. Porter (2000). Get real. *Anderson Consulting Outlook Journal*, 2, 33–40.

Dixit, R. K., A. K. Dixit and R. S. Pindyck (1994). *Investment under Uncertainty*. Princeton: Princeton University Press.

Duan, C.-W., W. T. Lin and C. F. Lee (2003). Sequential capital budgeting as real options: The case of a new DRAM chipmaker in Taiwan. *Review of Pacific Basin Financial Markets and Policies*, 6(01), 87–112.

Dubois, D. and H. Prade (1987). Properties of measures of information in evidence and possibility theories. *Fuzzy Sets and Systems*, 24(2), 161–182.

Dubois, D. and H. Prade (1988). Representation and combination of uncertainty with belief functions and possibility measures. *Computational Intelligence*, 4(3), 244–264.

Hu, C. and S. Li (2009). Two-phase interactive satisfying method of fuzzy multiple objective optimization with linguistic preference. *International Journal of Information Technology & Decision Making*, 8(03), 427–443.

Hu, Y.-C. and F.-M. Tseng (2009). Mining simplified fuzzy if-then rules for pattern classification. *International Journal of Information Technology & Decision Making*, 8(03), 473–489.

Hull, J. C. (2003). *Options Futures and Other Derivatives*. London: Pearson Education India.

Kulatilaka, N. and A. J. Marcus (1988). General formulation of corporate real options. *Research in Finance*, 7, 183–199.

Kulatilaka, N. (1993). The value of flexibility: The case of a dual-fuel industrial steam boiler. *Financial Management*, 22(3), 271–280.

Lee, C. F. and S. Y. Wang (2010). A fuzzy real option valuation approach to capital budgeting under uncertainty environment. *International Journal of Information Technology & Decision Making*, 09(05), 695–713.

Lee, C. F., G. H. Tzeng and S. Y. Wang (2005). A fuzzy set approach to generalize CRR model: An empirical analysis of S&P 500 Index option, in *The First International Workshop on Multi-Attribute Portfolio Selection*, Helsinki/Stockholm, March 13–15, 2005.

Lee, C. F., J. Lee and M. Lee (2022). *Corporate Finance and Strategy, An Active Learning Approach*, Singapore: World Scientific.

Lee, C.-F., G.-H. Tzeng and S.-Y. Wang (2005). A new application of fuzzy set theory to the Black–Scholes option pricing model. *Expert Systems with Applications*, 29(2), 330–342.

Leslie, K. J. and M. P. Michaels (1997). The real power of real options. *The McKinsey Quarterly*, 3, 4.

Lin, W. T. (2002). Computing a multivariate normal integral for valuing compound real options. *Review of Quantitative Finance and Accounting*, 18(2), 185–209.

Luehrman, T. A. (1998a). Strategy as a portfolio of real options. *Harvard Business Review*, 76, 89–101.

Luehrman, T. A. (1998b). Investment opportunities as real options: Getting started on the numbers. *Harvard Business Review*, 76(4), (July–August 1998), 51–67.

McDonald, R. L. and D. R. Siegel (1985). Investment and the valuation of firms when there is an option to shut down. *International Economic Review*, 26(2), 331–349.

McDonald, R. and D. Siegel (1984). Option pricing when the underlying asset earns a below-equilibrium rate of return: A note. *The Journal of Finance*, 39(1), 261–265.

Merton, R. C. (1973). An intertemporal capital asset pricing model. *Econometrica*, 41(5), 867–887.

Micalizzi, A. (1999). Timing to invest and value of managerial flexibility schering plough case study, in *3rd Annual Real Options Conference*, Working paper. http://www.realoptions.org.

Myers, S. C. (1977). Determinants of corporate borrowing. *Journal of Financial Economics*, 5(2), 147–175.

Myers, S. C. and S. M. Turnbull (1977). Capital budgeting and the capital asset pricing model: Good news and bad news. *The Journal of Finance*, 32(2), 321–333.

Nichols, N. A. (1994). Scientific management at Merck: An interview with CFO Judy Lewent. *Harvard Business Review*, 72(1), 88–99.

Peng, Y., G. Kou, Y. Shi and Z. Chen (2008). A descriptive framework for the field of data mining and knowledge discovery. *International Journal of Information Technology & Decision Making*, 7(04), 639–682.

Rao, C. and J. Peng (2009). Fuzzy group decision making model based on credibility theory and gray relative degree. *International Journal of Information Technology & Decision Making*, 8(03), 515–527.

Robichek, A. A. N. and S. C. Myers (1966). Conceptual problems in the use of risk-adjusted discount rates. *Journal of Finance*, 12, 727–730.

Robichek, A. A. and S. C. Myers (1966). Conceptual problems in the use of risk-adjusted discount rates. *The Journal of Finance*, 21(4), 727–730.

Scholes, M. and F. Black (1973). The pricing of options and corporate liabilities. *Journal of Political Economy*, 81(3), 637–654.

Tanaka, H. and K. Asai (1984). Fuzzy linear programming problems with fuzzy numbers. *Fuzzy Sets and Systems*, 13(1), 1–10.

Trigeorgis, L. and S. P. Mason, Valuing managerial flexibility. *Midland Corporate Finance Journal*, 5(1), 1987, 14–21.

Trigeorgis, L. (ed.). (1995). *Real Options in Capital Investment: Models, Strategies, and Applications*. Praeger (Connecticut): Greenwood Publishing Group.

Trigeorgis, L. (1993). Real options and interactions with financial flexibility. *Financial Management*, 22(3), 202–224.

Trigeorgis, L. (1993a). The nature of option interactions and the valuation of investments with multiple real options. *Journal of Financial and Quantitative Analysis*, 28(1), 1–20.

Trigeorgis, L. (1996). *Real Options: Managerial Flexibility and Strategy in Resource Allocation*. Cambridge: MIT Press.

Zadeh, L. A. (1965). Fuzzy sets. *Information and Control*, 8(3), 338–353.

Zadeh, L. A. (1968). Probability measure of fuzzy events. *Journal of Mathematical Analysis and Applications*, 23(3), 421–427.

Appendix 19A: A Fuzzy Real-Option Valuation in Terms of Binomial Option Pricing Model

The main purpose of this appendix is to derive a Fuzzy Real-Option Valuation in terms of the binomial option pricing model. There are six sections in this appendix. Section 19A.1 discusses the basic model of a binomial type of real-option valuation model. Section 19A.2 reviews the probability of fuzzy events. The fuzzy real-option valuation model will be discussed in Section 19A.3. Section 19A.4 presents the N-step fuzzy option decision tree, and the computational method and examples will be presented in Section 19A.5. Finally, Section 19A.6 presents the conclusions of this appendix.

19A.1 *Real-option valuation*

Real option means the possibility to either choose for or against making an investment decision without binding oneself upfront. The real-option rule is that one should invest today only if the NPV is high enough to compensate for giving up the value of the option to wait. While the ongoing evaluation effort is structured around key decision points or triggered by changes in the business environment, it is a process in which the valuation is not intended to provide a definite answer, but rather to provide decision-makers an ongoing dialogue about the project (Dahlberg and Porter, 2000).

In real options, the options involve real assets. Real options can be valued using the analog option theories that have been developed for financial options, although they are not the same thing. Real options deal with strategic decisions of a company where degrees of freedom are limited to the capabilities of the company. In these strategic decisions, different stakeholders play a role, especially if the resources needed for an investment are significant and thereby the continuity of the company is at stake. Hence, it is quite different from traditional DCF investment approaches. Making decisions based upon the traditional methods is very hard when there is uncertainty about the exact outcome of the investment. In particular, since traditional methods ignore the value of flexibility and discount heavily for external uncertainty involved, many interesting innovative activities and projects are canceled because of the uncertainties.

Thinking in real options is based on the Black–Scholes model in financial options, which were discussed in previous chapters. The option pricing theory stipulates that one should invest today only if the NPV is high enough to compensate for giving up the value of the option to wait. Because the option to invest loses its value when the investment is irreversibly made, this loss is an opportunity cost of investing. In order to obtain the ROV from the cash flow, the details and inference process are explained below. Following the binomial option pricing model which was discussed in Chapters 7 and 8, we can compute the value of a real option as follows:

$$\mathrm{ROV} = F_0 B(n \geq a|T,p) - K(1+r)^{-T} B(n \geq a|T,p'), \qquad (19\mathrm{A}.1)$$

where p is the cash flow up probability such that

$$p = \frac{(1+r-d)}{u-d}, \quad p' = \frac{u}{1+r}p. \qquad (19\mathrm{A}.2)$$

The definitions of r, u, and d of Equation (19A.2) can be found in Appendix 7A.

ROV denotes the current real-option value; F_0 is the value of expected cash flows; $B(n \geq a|T,p)$ is the cumulative probability of having an in-the-money option (i.e., $n \geq a$), where the probabilities are the certainty-equivalent probabilities determined by the risk-free hedge portfolio; and $K(1+r)^{-T}$ is the discounted initial cash outflow. The option expires at time T and r is the risk-free rate (see Copeland and Antikarov, 2001, for details).

In the real world, the data sometimes cannot be recorded or collected precisely. For instance, if we ask a group of economists to predict the economic growth rate in the next year, their statements may be something like "approximately 3%," "should be 3–5%," "may be below 6%," etc. All of these statements can be characterized as fuzzy sets. Suppose that we introduce a selection procedure which will determine the probability that each economist will be selected; then, for each possible selection, their statements are fuzzy sets. Similarly, in a capital-budgeting model under uncertainty, the cash flow information can be specified as a special type of fuzzy number (triangular fuzzy numbers). Zadeh (1965), Dubois and Prade (1988), and

Carlsson and Fuller (2002) have investigated the usefulness of the fuzzy set theory in decision-making under uncertainty. Other studies involving decision-making use fuzzy modeling (Cabrerizo *et al.*, 2009; Rao and Peng, 2009) and fuzzy data mining (Peng *et al.*, 2008). The fuzzy capital-budgeting approaches allow cash flow estimates to be treated as fuzzy numbers, and in certain situations, fuzzy cash flows can better reflect the uncertainty in the project.

19A.2 *Probability of fuzzy events*

The concept of probability is employed in describing fuzzy events and in using sample information to make statistical inferences (Lee *et al.*, 2005). An event is an experimental outcome that may or may not occur. The probability of a fuzzy event is used to measure the chance, the degree of compatibility, or degree of truth.

19A.2.1 *Prior probability of fuzzy events*

In the ROV under uncertainty, the distributions of the primary variables are assessed subjectively. Therefore, a manager faces the problem of implicit fuzziness. It is difficult to measure the impreciseness with the concept of probability (Zadeh, 1965; Tanaka and Asai, 1984) because probability is used to measure randomness. Randomness is relevant to the occurrence or non-occurrence of an event, while fuzziness is relevant to the degree of an event (Bellman and Zadeh, 1970). According to the definition given by Zadeh (1965), a fuzzy set is used to describe the set of an event without clear boundaries. The membership function $\mu_{\tilde{A}} : X \to [0, 1]$ expresses the fuzzy set $\tilde{A}$ in set X where if element $x \in X$, then $\mu_{\tilde{A}}(x) \in [0, 1]$ expresses the grade of membership x (also, the degree of compatibility or degree of truth) of X in $\tilde{A}$, which maps X to the membership space. The greater the value of $\mu_{\tilde{A}}(x)$, the higher the grade of membership of x belonging to $\tilde{A}$. According to Zadeh (1968), when there is no extra sample information, the prior probability $P(\tilde{A})$ of fuzzy event $\tilde{A}$ can be defined as

$$P(\tilde{A}) = \sum_{i=1}^{I} \mu_{\tilde{A}}(x_i) \cdot P(x_i). \qquad (19A.3)$$

19A.2.2 *Posterior probability of fuzzy events*

Let $X = \{x_1, x_2, x_m\}$ be the sample information space. In S_k state, if the prior probability $P(x_j|S_k)$ of acquiring sample information x_j is known, then the posterior probability of acquiring sample information x_j is

$$P(S_k|x_j) = \frac{P(x_j|S_k) \cdot P(S_k)}{P(x_j)}. \tag{19A.4}$$

One could evaluate the sample information acquired through this method. However, it still involves the subjective opinion of managers. On the other hand, the posterior probability of the sample information with fuzziness can be calculated as shown in the following. Let the sample information space be $X = \{x_1, x_2, \ldots, x_m\}$, let $\{x_r\}$, $r = 1, 2, \ldots, m$ be an independent event, and let $\tilde{M} = \{\tilde{M}_1, \tilde{M}_2, \tilde{M}_J\}$ be the concept of fuzzy sample information. The posterior probability $P(S_k|\tilde{M}_j)$ is calculated in accordance with Bayes' rule after deriving $\tilde{M}_j$.

$$P(S_k|\tilde{M}_j) = \frac{P(\tilde{M}_j|S_k) \cdot P(S_k)}{P(\tilde{M}_j)},$$

where

$$P(\tilde{M}_j|S_k) = \sum_{r=1}^{m} P(x_r|S_k) \cdot \mu_{\tilde{M}_j}(x_r),$$

$$P(\tilde{M}_j) = \sum_{r=1}^{m} P(x_r) \cdot \mu_{\tilde{M}_j}(x_r),$$

therefore

$$P(S_k|\tilde{M}_j) = \frac{\sum_{r=1}^{m} P(x_r|S_k) \cdot \mu_{\tilde{M}_j}(x_r) \cdot P(S_k)}{\sum_{r=1}^{m} P(x_r) \cdot \mu_{\tilde{M}_j}(x_r)}. \tag{19A.5}$$

When fuzzy sample information exists, the occurrence probability of state S_k can be described using the above formula. Therefore, the concept of "fuzzy" to describe the ROV under fuzzy environment should be brought into the picture.

When the range of the membership function is improved to $\{0, 1\}$, then $\tilde{A}$ will be transformed to a crisp set A. The $\mu_{\tilde{A}}$ will be transformed into C_A (characteristic function). This kind of transformation in the ROV means that the estimates of the primary variable cash flows, risk rate, and the volatility of cash flow $(F,\ R,\ \sigma)$ are without fuzziness, that is, $\mu_{\tilde{A}}(x_i) = 1$ or 0. Under these circumstances, $\mu_{\tilde{A}}(x) = C_A(x) = 1$ if $x \in A$, or $\mu_{\tilde{A}}(x_i) = 0$, if $x \notin A$. Therefore, the probability for the occurrence of fuzzy event $\tilde{A}$ can be defined as

$$P(\tilde{A}) = \sum_{i=1}^{I} \mu_{\tilde{A}}(x_i) \cdot P(x_i) = \sum_{i=1}^{I} C_A(x_i) \cdot P(x_i) = P(A). \quad (19A.6)$$

According to the traditional probabilistic ROV, the decision space faced by a manager is $B = \{S, D, P(S_i), \text{ROV}(d_j, S_i)\}$. Therefore, under state S_i and sample information x_r, the expected FROV $\{\text{FROV}(d_j^*|x_r)\}$ of the optimal alternative is defined as

$$\begin{aligned} \text{FROV}(d_j^*|x_r) &= \underset{j}{\text{Min}} \left\{ \sum_{i=1}^{I} \text{ROV}(d_j, S_i) \cdot P(S_i|x_r) \right\} \\ &= \bigwedge_{j=1}^{J} \sum_{i=1}^{I} \text{ROV}(d_j, S_i) \cdot P(S_i|x_r). \end{aligned} \quad (19A.7)$$

When dealing with the actual ROV issues, a company not only faces a fuzzy sample information space but also stays in a fuzzy state space. For example, a manager forecasts future risk-free interest rate in accordance with the classification of "booming economy," "fair economy," or "recession." The definitions of "booming economy," "fair economy," and "recession" depend on the manager's subjective opinion. Therefore, the state space encountered by the manager also involves implicit fuzziness. Besides, the actions that the manager plans to take will cause the cash flow structure to fluctuate. Moreover, due to the company's environment, timing of the decision-making, and the inability to give it a trial, it is virtually impossible to sit and wait for a long time for the collection of perfect information. Under these circumstances, the alternative adopted by the manager for ROV under uncertainty contains fuzziness. In summary, the ROV, which a manager actually deals with, is in a fuzzy state with fuzzy sample information and fuzzy action. As a result, the company can be defined with fuzzy decision space $\tilde{B} = \{\tilde{F}, \tilde{A}, P(\tilde{S}), \mathrm{ROV}(\tilde{A}, \tilde{S})\}$, in which $\tilde{S} = \{\tilde{S}_1, \tilde{S}_2, \ldots, \tilde{S}_K\}$ stands for fuzzy state set; $\tilde{S}_k$, $k = 1, 2, \ldots, K$ stands for a fuzzy set in S; and $S = \{S_1, S_2, \ldots, S_I\}$ stands for the state set. S_i, $i = 1, 2, \ldots, I$ stands for a state of the state set. $\tilde{A} = \{\tilde{A}_1, \tilde{A}_2, \ldots, \tilde{A}_N\}$ stands for fuzzy action set; $\tilde{A}_n$, $n = 1, 2, \ldots, N$ stands for a fuzzy action set in D; $D = \{d_1, d_2, \ldots, d_J\}$ stands for action set; and d_j, $j = 1, 2, \ldots, J$ stands for an action or alternative available for the company. $P(\tilde{S}_k)$ is the prior probability of $\tilde{S}_k$; $\mathrm{ROV}(\tilde{A}, \tilde{S})$ is the evaluation function of $\tilde{A} \times \tilde{S}$.

The prior probability of fuzzy state $P(\tilde{S}_k)$ is defined as

$$P(\tilde{S}_k) = \sum_{i=1}^{I} \mu_{\tilde{F}_k}(S_i) \cdot P(S_i). \tag{19A.8}$$

Let $\tilde{M} = \{\tilde{M}_1, \tilde{M}_2, \ldots, \tilde{M}_J\}$ be the fuzzy sample information space in X. $\tilde{M}_j$, $j = 1, 2, \ldots, J$ is the fuzzy sample information; $X = \{x_1, x_2, \ldots, x_m\}$ is the sample information space; and $\{x_r\}$, $r = 1, 2, \ldots, m$ is an independent event.

The posterior probability of fuzzy state $\tilde{S}_k$ is defined in accordance with the posterior probability of fuzzy events after the fuzzy sample information $\tilde{M}_j$ is derived as

$$\begin{aligned} P(\tilde{S}_k|\tilde{M}_j) &= \sum_{i=1}^{I} \mu\tilde{S}_k(S_i) \cdot P(S_i|\tilde{M}_j) \\ &= \sum_{i=1}^{I} \mu_{\tilde{S}_k}(S_i) \cdot \frac{\sum_{r=1}^{m} P(x_r|S_i) \cdot \mu_{\tilde{M}_j}(x_r) \cdot P(S_i)}{P(\tilde{M}_j)} \\ &= \frac{\sum_{i=1}^{I} \sum_{r=1}^{m} \mu_{\tilde{S}_k}(S_i) \cdot \mu_{\tilde{M}_j}(x_r) \cdot P(x_r|S_i) \cdot P(S_i)}{\sum_{r=1}^{m} \mu_{\tilde{M}_j}(x_r) \cdot P(x_r)}. \end{aligned} \tag{19A.9}$$

19A.3 *A fuzzy real-option valuation*

In this section, we shall introduce a real-option rule in a fuzzy setting (Carlsson and Fuller, 2003), where the present value of expected cash flows is estimated by triangular fuzzy numbers. We will also

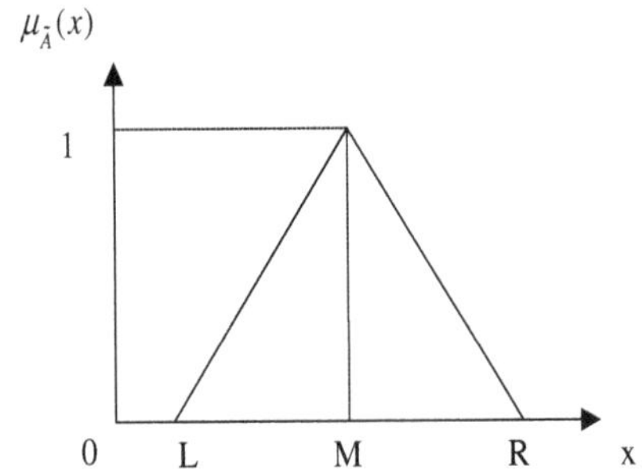

Figure 19A.1 The Membership Function of the Triangular Fuzzy Number

determine the optimal exercise time by using the fuzzy real-option valuation. To do so, we first briefly discuss the concept of triangular fuzzy number, followed by the combination of the binomial model and triangular fuzzy numbers to form a fuzzy decision tree.

As illustrated in Zadeh (1965), $\tilde{A}$ is a convex fuzzy set if and only if its α-level set $\tilde{A}_\alpha = \{x : \mu_{\tilde{A}}(x) \geq \alpha\}$ is a convex set for all α. Therefore, if $\tilde{\alpha}$ is a fuzzy number, then the α-level set $\tilde{\alpha}_\alpha$ is a compact (closed and bounded in R) and convex set; that is, $\tilde{\alpha}$ is a closed interval. The α-level set of $\tilde{\alpha}$ is then denoted by $\tilde{\alpha}_\alpha = [\tilde{\alpha}_\alpha^L, \tilde{\alpha}_\alpha^U]$. A fuzzy number $\tilde{\alpha}$ is said to be non-negative if $\mu_{\tilde{\alpha}}(x) = 0$ for $x < 0$. It is easy to see that if $\tilde{\alpha}$ is a non-negative fuzzy number, then $\tilde{\alpha}_\alpha^L$ and $\tilde{\alpha}_\alpha^U$ are all non-negative real numbers for all $\alpha \in [0, 1]$. The concept of triangular fuzzy number attempts to deal with real problems by possibility, as indicated in Figure 19A.1. The membership of a triangular fuzzy number is defined as follows:

$$\mu_{\tilde{A}}(x) = \begin{bmatrix} (x - L)/(M - L) \rightarrow L \leq x \leq M, \\ (R - x)/(R - M) \rightarrow M \leq x \leq R, \\ 0, \quad \text{otherwise.} \end{bmatrix}$$

According to the characteristics of triangular fuzzy numbers and the extension principle put forward by Zadeh (1965), the operational laws of triangular fuzzy numbers, $\tilde{A} = (l_1, m_1, r_1)$ and $\tilde{B} = (l_2, m_2, r_2)$, are as follows:

(1) Addition of two fuzzy numbers $\oplus$

$$(l_1, m_1, r_1) \oplus (l_2, m_2, r_2) = (l_1 + l_2, m_1 + m_2, r_1 + r_2)$$

(2) Subtraction of two fuzzy numbers Θ

$$(l_1, m_1, r_1)\Theta(l_2, m_2, r_2) = (l_1 - r_2, m_1 - m_2, r_1 - l_2)$$

(3) Multiplication of two fuzzy numbers $\otimes$

$$(l_1, m_1, r_1) \otimes (l_2, m_2, r_2) \cong (l_1 l_2, m_1 m_2, r_1 r_2)$$

(4) Division of two fuzzy numbers $\emptyset$

$$(L_1, m_1, r_1)\emptyset(l_2, m_2, r_2) \cong (l_1/r_2, m_1/m_2, r_1/l_2)$$

Usually, the present value of expected cash flows cannot be characterized by a single number. But managers are able to estimate the present value of expected cash flows by using triangular possibility distribution of the form $\tilde{F} = [f_l, f_m, f_r]$, that is, the most likely values of the present value of expected cash flows lie in the f_m (which is the core of the triangular fuzzy number $\tilde{F}$), f_r is the greatest value, and f_l is the smallest value for the present value of expected cash flows.

In addition, the values are also influenced by the financial markets such as risk-free interest rate (discount rate) and the volatility of cash inflows. We use historical data to estimate them by using a triangular possibility distribution of the form $\tilde{R} = [r_l, r_m, r_r]$, $\tilde{\sigma} = [\sigma_l, \sigma_m, \sigma_r]$, that is, the most likely values of risk rate and the volatility of cash inflow lie in the interval r_m and σ_m (which is the core of the triangular fuzzy number $\tilde{R}$ and $\tilde{\sigma}$), respectively, r_r is the greatest value and r_l is the smallest value for discount rate, and σ_r is the greatest value and σ_l is the smallest value for the volatility of cash inflows.

The information needed for capital budgeting is generally not known with certainty. The sources of uncertainty may be the net cash inflows, the discount rate, the cash flow volatility or the life of the project, etc. Hence, in addition to considering the fuzzy volatility, we also consider the fuzzy cash inflow $\tilde{F}$ and fuzzy interest rate $\tilde{R}$. Under these circumstances, we suggest the use of formulas described in the next section for computing FROVs.

19A.4 *N-step fuzzy decision tree*

We now combine the binomial model and triangular fuzzy number to form a fuzzy decision tree (Lee, Tzeng, and Wang, 2005). Assume that the decision tree will mature (project termination) in a given period and the cash flow is initially set to $F(t = 1)$. Cash flows can move up or down in the next period ($t = 2$). There are three possible scenarios in the up movement, $F_{ur}(= ur \cdot F)$, $F_{um}(= um \cdot F)$, or $F_{ul}(= ul \cdot F)$, and three scenarios in the down movement, $F_{dr}(= dr \cdot F)$, $F_{dm}(= dm \cdot F)$, or $F_{dl}(= dl \cdot F)$, depending on volatility. Hence, in each time interval, the cash flow moves from its initial value of F to one of the above six new values, F_{ur}, F_{um}, F_{ul}, F_{dr}, F_{dm}, or F_{dl}.

These six values are defined as follows:

F_{ur}: cash flow of up movement under the greatest volatility, $F_{ur} = F_0 \cdot [e^{(1+\rho)\sigma\sqrt{\Delta t}}]$,
F_{um}: cash flow of up movement under medium volatility, $F_{um} = F_0 \cdot [e^{\sigma\sqrt{\Delta t}}]$,
F_{ul}: cash flow of up movement under the smallest volatility, $F_{ul} = F_0 \cdot [e^{(1-\rho)\sigma\sqrt{\Delta t}}]$,
F_{dr}: cash flow of down movement under the greatest volatility, $F_{dr} = F_0 \cdot [e^{-(1-\rho)\sigma\sqrt{\Delta t}}]$,
F_{dm}: cash flow of down movement under medium volatility, $F_{dm} = F_0 \cdot [e^{-\sigma\sqrt{\Delta t}}]$,
F_{dl}: cash flow of down movement under the smallest volatility, $F_{dl} = F_0 \cdot [e^{-(1+\rho)\sigma\sqrt{\Delta t}}]$.

The FROV in maturity is $\tilde{\text{RO}}\text{V}_{ur} = \max(F_{ur} - X, 0)$, $\tilde{\text{RO}}\text{V}_{um} = \max(F_{um} - X, 0)$, $\tilde{\text{RO}}\text{V}_{ul} = \max(F_{ul} - X, 0)$, $\tilde{\text{RO}}\text{V}_{dr} = \max(F_{dr} - X, 0)$, $\tilde{\text{RO}}\text{V}_{dm} = \max(F_{dm} - X, 0)$, and $\tilde{\text{RO}}\text{V}_{dl} = \max(F_{dl} - X, 0)$.

To illustrate the process of obtaining the greatest volatility, we use the replicating portfolio approach found in the financial options. Let

$$mF + B = \text{ROV}, \tag{19A.10}$$

where m: the number of units of the underlying asset under the greatest volatility, B: amount invested in bonds under the greatest volatility.

Assume we buy m units of underlying asset under the greatest volatility and invest amount B in risky assets (bonds), (r_l, r_m, r_h); after one period, the value of the portfolio for up movement is $mF_{ur} + B(1 + \tilde{r}_h) = \tilde{\text{RO}}\text{V}_{ur}$ and the one for down movement is $mF_{dl} + B(1 + r_h) = \tilde{\text{RO}}\text{V}_{dl}$, where ur: the range of the greatest volatility of "up" movement. The movement from F to $F_{ur}(= ur \cdot F)$ is therefore an "up" movement under the greatest volatility, and dl: the range of the greatest volatility of "down" movement. The movement from F to $F_{dl}(= dl \cdot F)$ is therefore a "down" movement under the greatest volatility.

Suppose the value of the portfolio either under up or down movement is equal to the value of the corresponding FROV, we obtain

$$m = \frac{C_{ur} - C_{dl}}{F_{ur} - F_{dl}},$$

$$B = \frac{C_{ur} - mF_{ur}}{(1 + r_h)} = \frac{C_{ur} - \left(\frac{C_{ur}-C_{dl}}{F_{ur}-F_{dl}}\right) F_{ur}}{(1 + r_h)}$$

$$= \frac{\left(\frac{C_{ur}F_{ur}-C_{ur}F_{dl}-C_{ur}F_{ur}+C_{dl}F_{ur}}{F_{ur}-F_{dl}}\right)}{(1 + r_h)} = \frac{\left(\frac{C_{dl}F_{ur}-C_{ur}F_{dl}}{F_{ur}-F_{dl}}\right)}{(1 + r_h)},$$

where $P_u = \frac{(1+r_h)-dl}{ur-dl}$, $P_m = \frac{(1+r_m)-dm}{um-dm}$, $P_d = \frac{(1+r_l)-dr}{ul-dr}$.

The probabilities of three up movements are P_u, P_m, and P_d, while the probabilities of three down movements are $1 - P_u$, $1 - P_m$, and $1 - P_d$. In the above equations, $\tilde{\text{ROV}}_u$, $\tilde{\text{ROV}}_m$, and $\tilde{\text{ROV}}_d$ are the right, medium, and left values of the current fuzzy real-option price. So, we can get the FROV under the greatest volatility ($\tilde{\text{ROV}}_u$) as follows:

$$\tilde{\text{ROV}}_u = e^{-r_l \Delta t}[P_u \cdot \tilde{\text{ROV}}_{ur} + (1 - P_u) \cdot \tilde{\text{ROV}}_{dl}].$$

Similarly, we also can get the FROV under medium and the smallest volatility as follows:

$$\tilde{\text{ROV}}_m = e^{-r_m \Delta t}[P_m \cdot \tilde{\text{ROV}}_{um} + (1 - P_m) \cdot \tilde{\text{ROV}}_{dm}],$$

$$\tilde{\text{ROV}}_d = e^{-r_h \Delta t}[P_d \cdot \tilde{\text{ROV}}_{ul} + (1 - P_d) \cdot \tilde{\text{ROV}}_{dr}].$$

The process of the fuzzy decision tree can be stated as follows:

Step 1: Estimate ρ and σ values to compute the F_{ur}, F_{um}, F_{ul}, F_{dr}, F_{dm}, and F_{dl}. In other words, $\sigma(1 + \rho)$ is the volatility of the right value of up movement, $\sigma(1 - \rho)$ is the volatility of the left value of up movement, and $F_{ur}(= ur \cdot F)$, $F_{um}(= um \cdot F)$, and $F_{ul}(= ul \cdot F)$ are the degrees of up movement. In the down movement, $-(1 - \rho)$

is the volatility of the right value of down movement, $-\sigma(1+\rho)$ is the volatility of the left value of down movement, and $F_{dr}(= dr \cdot F)$, $F_{dm}(= dm \cdot F)$, and $F_{dl}(= dl \cdot F)$ are the degrees of down movement.

Step 2: Compute FROV from the fuzzy cash flow of $t = n$ to the FROV of $t = n$. We use the fuzzy cash flow at $t = n$ and the (nominal) value of fixed costs to compute the FROV. The process is the same with the binomial tree model. $\text{FROV}_n = \max(F_n - X, 0)$, where F_n is the fuzzy cash flow at time t and X is the (nominal) value of fixed costs.

Step 3: Compute the fuzzy real-option price from $t = n$ to $t = n-1$. Now, we integrate the fuzzy set with the binomial tree model and use a different probabilistic for different volatilities and interest rates. Here, $\tilde{\text{ROV}}_u$, $\tilde{\text{ROV}}_m$, and $\tilde{\text{ROV}}_d$ are the largest, middle, and smallest values of the fuzzy option price. Each node of the fuzzy option price has three option prices, not just a single one, as in the binomial tree model. So, we replace the fuzzy option prices $\tilde{\text{ROV}}_{ur}$ and $\tilde{\text{ROV}}_{dl}$ for the greatest volatility to get $\tilde{\text{ROV}}_u = \mathrm{e}^{-r_l \Delta t}[P_u \cdot \tilde{\text{ROV}}_{ur} + (1 - P_u) \cdot \tilde{\text{ROV}}_{dl}]$; $\tilde{\text{ROV}}_{um}$ and $\tilde{\text{ROV}}_{dm}$ for the medium volatility to get $\tilde{\text{ROV}}_m = \mathrm{e}^{-r_m \Delta t}[\tilde{\text{ROV}}_{um} \cdot P_m + \tilde{\text{ROV}}_{dm} \cdot (1 - P_m)]$; and $\tilde{\text{ROV}}_{ul}$ and $\tilde{\text{ROV}}_{dl}$ for the smallest volatility to get $\tilde{\text{ROV}}_d = \mathrm{e}^{-r_h \Delta t}[\tilde{\text{ROV}}_{ul} \cdot P_d + \tilde{\text{ROV}}_{dr} \cdot (1 - P_d)]$.

Step 4: Compute the FROV from $t = n-1$ to $t = n-2$. We use the same principle as the calculation of the fuzzy option price from $t = n$ to $t = n-1$ with three fuzzy option prices at $t = n-1$. We still use the same method for the FROV from $t = n$ to $t = n-1$, and the value we get at every node will have multiple FROVs.

Step 5: Compute the fuzzy option price from $t = n-2$ to $t = n-3, \ldots, t = 1$. The same principle applies to the FROV from $t = n-1$ to $t = n-2$. For computing one FROV, we shall generalize the probabilistic decision rule for the optimal investment strategy to a fuzzy setting: Here, T is the maximum deferral time and t^* is the time at which investment (exercise the option) is made; $0 \le t^* \le T$, for which the option, $\tilde{\text{ROV}}_{t^*}$, attends its maximum value.

$$\tilde{\text{ROV}}_{t^*} = \max_{t=0,1,\ldots,T} \tilde{\text{ROV}}_t$$

Table 19A.1 $\mu_{\tilde{F}_k}(S_i)$ and $P(S_i)$

	$S_i(R_t)$		
$\mu_{\tilde{F}_k}(S_i)/P(S_i)$	**3%**	**4%**	**5%**
$\mu_{\tilde{F}_1}(S_i)$	0.6	0.4	0
$\mu_{\tilde{F}_2}(S_i)$	0.2	0.7	0.1
$\mu_{\tilde{F}_3}(S_i)$	0.1	0.4	0.5
$P(S_i)$	0.3	0.5	0.2

However, to find a maximum element from the set $\{\text{R}\tilde{\text{O}}\text{V}_0, \text{R}\tilde{\text{O}}\text{V}_1, \ldots, \text{R}\tilde{\text{O}}\text{V}_T\}$ is not an easy task because it involves ranking of triangular fuzzy numbers.

In our computerized implementation, we have employed the following function to determine the expected FROVs $\{\text{R}\tilde{\text{O}}\text{V}_u, \text{R}\tilde{\text{O}}\text{V}_m, \text{R}\tilde{\text{O}}\text{V}_d\}$ of triangular form:

$$E(\text{R}\tilde{\text{O}}\text{V}_t) = \text{Max}\{[(\text{R}\tilde{\text{O}}\text{V}_u - \text{R}\tilde{\text{O}}\text{V}_d) + (\text{R}\tilde{\text{O}}\text{V}_m - \text{R}\tilde{\text{O}}\text{V}_d)]/3 + \text{R}\tilde{\text{O}}\text{V}_d, 0\},$$

where $\text{R}\tilde{\text{O}}\text{V}_u$, $\text{R}\tilde{\text{O}}\text{V}_m$, and $\text{R}\tilde{\text{O}}\text{V}_d$ are the largest, middle, and smallest values of the FROVs.

19A.5 *Computational method and example*

In the following sub-sections, we employ an example to describe the application of FROV under uncertainty.

19A.5.1 *Fuzzy state*

Assume that the manager is projecting possible risk rates in the next term for different future outlooks of the economy: "booming," "fair," and "recession." Suppose state set $S = \{S_1, S_2, S_3\}$, where S_i denotes the risk rate of ROV and the set represents a collection of fuzzy states. The probability of risk rate state can be illustrated in Table 19A.1. For example, when the economy is in the state of "booming," the probability of a 3% risk rate is 0.6.

Table 19A.2 $P(x_r|S_i)$

		x_r		
S_i	R_t (%)	\$3,000	\$5,000	\$7,000
S_1	3	0.25	0.3	0.25
S_2	4	0.5	0.4	0.5
S_3	5	0.25	0.3	0.25

Table 19A.3 $u_{\tilde{M}_j}(x_r)$ and $P(x_r)$

	x_r		
$\tilde{\mu}_{\tilde{M}_j}(x_r)/P(x_r)$	\$3,000	\$5,000	\$7,000
$\tilde{\mu}_{\tilde{M}_1}(x_r)$	0.3	0.2	0.25
$\tilde{\mu}_{\tilde{M}_2}(x_r)$	0.2	0.2	0.25
$P(x_r)$	0.5	0.4	0.5

19A.5.2 *Fuzzy sample information*

While F, K, T, and R can be derived directly from observation, calculation of σ requires the use of cash flow over some past periods of time. In response to recent cash flow fluctuations, the manager has readjusted the magnitude of fluctuation for the cash flow (σ). Based on historical statistics, σ is revised downward from its current level of 60% to 40%. Suppose the sample message space $X = \{x_1, x_2, x_3\}$, where x_r, $r = 1, 2, 3$ denotes the cash flow, and (x_r) is an independent event. The manager produces estimations based on two basic assumptions of "very high risk rate growth" and "relatively flat risk rate growth." Hence, the fuzzy sample message space can be expressed as $\tilde{M} = \{\tilde{M}_1, \tilde{M}_2\}$, where $\tilde{M}_1$ denotes very high risk rate growth and $\tilde{M}_2$ denotes a relatively flat risk rate growth. Giving historical information S_i, Table 19A.2 shows company's probability of the occurrence of x_r is $P(x_r|S_i)$. Table 19A.3 shows the prior of the membership function $u_{\tilde{M}_j}(x_r)$ and x_r for fuzzy sample message $\tilde{M}_j$, $j = 1, 2$ is $P(x_r)$.

From the above data, we can get the prior probability and posterior probability shown in Table 19A.4. Then, we can compute and analyze the results of FROV, assuming that the initial outlay, K, is \$10,000 and the net cash flows are \$3,000, \$5,000, and \$7,000 associated with each prior probability scenario. The probability and cash flow in fuzzy environment can be simplified as in Table 19A.4.

19A.6 *Conclusions*

The fuzzy capital-budgeting approaches allow the cash flow estimate to be fuzzy numbers. Fuzzy cash flows can better reflect the uncertainty in the project. The integration of qualitative information into the process gives better decision support. The fuzzy real-option approach also supports the determination of the optimal time to abandon the project, which the traditional method cannot do. The FROV thus offers a comprehensive way of presenting the value of possibilities opened by the project, which is further enhanced with frequently updated fuzzy cash flows. Finally, we would like to stress that advanced decision methods such as real options and fuzzy capital budgeting open the chance to explore the value of flexibility inside and outside a project, and give further insight into the uncertainty of large investments. The uncertainty is genuine, that is, we simply do not know the exact levels of future cash flows. Without introducing FROV, it would not be possible to formulate this genuine uncertainty. The proposed model that incorporates subjective judgments and statistical uncertainties may give managers a better understanding of the problem when making investment decisions.

The findings of this appendix and their implications for the managerial decision-making can be summarized as follows: (1) The FROV increases with increasing expected cash flow estimates; proactive management can influence this by developing market strategies to enhance the sales and trim the costs. (2) FROV increases with increasing fuzzy volatility; corporate management can be proactive and find ways to expand to new markets and product innovations as end results of their strategic decisions. (3) The longer the time to maturity, the greater the FROV; proactive management can make sure of this development by maintaining protective barriers and maintaining a technological lead. (4) An increase in risk-free rate of returns will increase the FROV, and this can be further enhanced by closely monitoring changes in interest rates. (5) The FROV will decrease if value is lost during the postponement of the investment,

Table 19A.4 Illustration of Conditional Probability Distribution Approach under Uncertainty

(1) Initial Outlay Period 0	(2) Prior Probability P (1)	(3) Net Cash Flow	(4) Posterior Probability $P(2\|1)$	(5) Fuzzy Net Cash Flow	(6) Fuzzy Conditional Probability $P(3\|2,1)$	(7) Fuzzy Cash Flow	(8) (8) Fuzzy Joint Probability
					0.2	1,000	0.015
			0.25	2,000	0.5	2,000	0.0375
					0.3	3,000	0.0225
					0.2	2,000	0.03
10,000	0.3	3,000	0.5	3,000	0.5	3,000	0.075
					0.3	4,000	0.045
					0.2	3,000	0.015
			0.25	4,000	0.5	4,000	0.0375
					0.3	5,000	0.0225
					0.3	2,000	0.045
			0.3	3,000	0.4	4,000	0.06
					0.3	6,000	0.045
					0.3	4,000	0.06
	0.5	5,000	0.4	5,000	0.4	5,000	0.08
					0.3	6,000	0.06
					0.3	5,000	0.045
			0.3	7,000	0.4	7,000	0.06
					0.3	9,000	0.045
					0.25	4,000	0.0125
			0.25	5,000	0.5	6,000	0.025
					0.25	8,000	0.0125
					0.25	5,000	0.025
	0.2	7,000	0.5	7,000	0.5	7,000	0.05
					0.25	9,000	0.025
					0.25	7,000	0.0125
			0.25	8,000	0.5	9,000	0.025
					0.25	11,000	0.0125

but this can be countered by either creating business barriers for competitors or by better managing key resources.

Appendix 19B: Time-State Preference and the Real-Option Approaches for Capital Budgeting under Uncertainty

The time-state preference model is one approach that can be used in capital budgeting under uncertainty. Breeden and Litzenberger (1978) have shown how option pricing theory can be applied to the time-state preference model in order to be used in capital budgeting under uncertainty. We will first look at a simple time-state preference model and then see how the option pricing model can be applied to time-state preferences for a single-period case. Then, we will look at the multiperiod cases.

Using estimates developed by Banz and Miller (1978) and Haley and Schall (1979), we shall use the following model[2]:

$$\mathrm{PV} = \sum_{s=1}^{n}\sum_{t=1}^{T}(V_{st})(Z_{st}), \tag{19B.1}$$

where V_{st} = current value (price) of a dollar for state s and time t, Z_{st} = present value of cash flow for state s and time t, and PV = present value of project.

We are considering introducing a new product that is a fad item and will be profitable to produce for only three years.

The expected cash flows for three different states of the economy, boom, normal, and recession, are shown in Table 19B.1.

Table 19B.1 Expected Cash Flows for Project, Z_{st}

State of Economy	Year 1	Year 2	Year 3
Boom	\$1,000	\$500	\$300
Normal	\$800	\$400	\$200
Recession	\$500	\$200	\$100

Using state prices developed from the option pricing model by Banz and Miller (1978) and substituting into Equation (19B.1), Haley and Schall obtained the following:

$$\begin{aligned} \text{PV} &= \$1,000(0.1672) + \$800(0.2912) + \$500(0.5398) \\ &\quad + \$500(0.1693) + \$400(0.2915) + \$200(0.5333) \\ &\quad + \$300(0.1686) + \$200(0.2903) + \$100(0.5313) \\ &= \$1,140. \end{aligned}$$

If the initial investment is less than \$1,140, the project has a positive NPV and should be undertaken.

To see how V_{st}, the time-state prices, are determined using the option pricing model, we will first look at the single-period case.

We assume we can define "states of the world" that are associated with payoffs from the market portfolio. In the three-state case used earlier, revision is defined as rates of return from −86.47% to 0.068%, normal is 0.068% to 20.428%, and boom is 20.428% to 171.83%.

By being able to define states in this manner, we can determine the historical frequency of occurrence of any state, we can have any number of states, and the state definitions are objective and easily understood. Let the current value of the market portfolio be M_0, and V_j an option that pays \$1 one period from now ($t = 1$) if $M_1 \geq M_j$ (M_j is a specified level). Breeden and Litzenberger (1978) show that V's value can be derived from the Black–Scholes model as the second partial derivative of the model with respect to the exercise price evaluated at an exercise price M_j. Therefore,

$$V_j = \mathrm{e}^{-i} N[d_2(M_j)], \tag{19B.2}$$

$$d_2 = \frac{+[(i - S_M^2/2]}{S_M}, \tag{19B.3}$$

where i = Interest rate, S_{M^2} = Instantaneous variance of the rate of return on the market portfolio, N = Probability of $d_2(M_j)$ obtained from a normal distribution.

The difference between this formula and that of a financial option lies in the differences in the options. This option has no exercise price, and the payoff when $M_0 \geq M_j$ is limited to \$1. Call options pay the differences between the stock price and the exercise price, which is unlimited.

Now. to put this model to use, we observe first that

$$\frac{M_0}{M_j} = \frac{1}{1 + r_{M_j}}, \tag{19B.4}$$

where r_{Mj} = Rate of return on the market portfolio for the period if $M_0 \geq M_j$.

Therefore, as r_{Mj} becomes negative, M_0/M_j becomes larger and so does $\ln(M_0/M_j)$. For a given i and S, the value of the option approaches certainty of paying off \$1 as r_{Mj} approaches -100%. As r_{Mj} gets larger (positive), the option becomes certain of not paying off and V_j value becomes zero.

When state S_j occurs, the option pays off \$1. This state S_j is defined as the range of rates of return on the market portfolio from r_{Mj} to $r_{M(j+1)}$. Given the assumption of perfect markets, the value of this option is

$$\Delta V_j = V_j - V_{j+1}. \tag{19B.5}$$

Substituting from Equation (19B.2), we have

$$V_j = \mathrm{e}^{-i}\{N[d_2(M_j)] - N[d_2(M_{j+1})]\} \tag{19B.6}$$

or, equivalently

$$v_j = \mathrm{e}^{-i}\{N[d_2(r_{M_j})] - N[d_2(r_{M_{j+1}})]\}. \tag{19B.7}$$

We can rewrite Equation (19B.5) as

$$V_j = v_j + V_{j+1}. \tag{19B.8}$$

Here, V_{j+1} is the value of the option that pays \$1 if $M_1 \geq M_{j+1}$ or, if the rate of return on the market portfolio $\geq r_{M,(j+1)}$, the only variables we need to estimate are i and S as shown by Haley and Schall.

As for the multiperiod state prices, we make some additional assumptions:

(a) State definitions are constant for all future periods under consideration.
(b) Transitions from one period to another follow a stationary market process.

(c) Everyone agrees on state definitions and that the transitions follow a stationary process.

These three assumptions mean that the probability that the rate of return of a market portfolio will be in a given state in period t depends only on the state into which it fell in period $(t-1)$. Also, the probability of going from state t to state $(t-1)$ does not vary with t.

The matrix of any future T periods is V^T, matrix V taken to the Tth power. A simple example of this is

		Next-Period State	
		High	**Low**
Current-Period State	**High**	H_H	H_L
	Low	L_H	L_L

For example, H_H and H_L are the current prices of \$1 received next period if the present state is high. The subscripts indicate whether the next period is high or low.

Looking at the matrix of status prices two periods from the present, V^2, we get

$$\begin{aligned} V^2 &= V\ V \\ &= \begin{bmatrix} H_H & H_L \\ L_H & L_L \end{bmatrix} \begin{bmatrix} H_H & H_L \\ L_H & L_L \end{bmatrix} \\ &= \begin{bmatrix} (H_H H_H + H_L L_H) & (H_H H_L + H_L L_L) \\ (L_H H_H + L_L L_H) & (L_H H_L + L_L L_L) \end{bmatrix}. \end{aligned}$$

Thus, if the state row is high and it is also high in time 2, the probability of \$1 to be in control two periods from now is given by $(H_H H_H + H_L L_H)$.

The economic explanation is as follows. We must first look at where we could be at time 1. At time 1, we can be high, H_H, or low, L_H. Looking at the present value (at time zero), we see that the right price of H is $H_H H_H + H_L L_H$, as described in the matrix above.

The basic theory of this approach is as follows:

(a) Given perfect capital markets with continuous trading, the state-contingent claims are implicit in option prices that conform to specific valuation equations.
(b) If states can be defined as ranges of the rate of return of the market portfolio, and transition from state is a stationary Markov process, state prices for any future period can be calculated from a matrix at single-period prices.
(c) Given the state prices for future periods, the state of payoffs from an investment can be solved using Equation (19B.1).

There exist three different approaches to deal with uncertainty: state preference, arbitrage, and mean variance. Generally, we regard state preference models as being impracticable for application in real-world decision-making. However, option pricing theory has made the application possible.

One of the major inputs for this type of application is an estimate of the market rate of return for each state of nature. Merton's (1980) time series approach "On Estimating the Expected Return on the Market" can be used to obtain estimates of market rates of return and its variances.

Copeland (2003), Amram and Kulatilaka (1999), and others have been using Equation (19B.9) to do real-option analysis:

$$V_c = P[N(d_1)] - \mathrm{e}^{-rt}E[N(d_2)], \tag{19B.9}$$

where V = value of option; P = present value annuity of future cash flow; r = continuously compounded annual risk-free interest rate; t = life of the project; E = initial cost of investment; $e = 2.71828\ldots$ is a constant; and $N(d_1)$ = probability that a standard normal random variable is less than or equal to d_i $(i = 1, 2)$, with

$$d_1 = \frac{\ln\left(\frac{P}{E}\right) + \left(r + \frac{\sigma^2}{2}\right)t}{\sigma\sqrt{t}} \tag{19B.10}$$

and

$$d_2 = \frac{\ln\left(\frac{P}{E}\right) + \left(r - \frac{\sigma^2}{2}\right)t}{\sigma\sqrt{t}} = d_1 - \sigma\sqrt{t}, \tag{19B.11}$$

where σ^2 = variance of future cash flow.

The real-option model defined in Equations (19B.9), (19B.10), and (19B.11) is similar to the financial option pricing model we defined earlier. The contract period for financial option is predetermined and cannot be changed. However, the lifetime of the project can be modified by the decision-maker. In other words, the managers can delay the project, that is, the managers have the flexibility to change the life of the project. Further discussion of the application of real options can be found in Ross *et al.* (2007).

Notes

1. This appendix heavily draws upon Haley and Schall (1979, 254–261), with permission from the publisher.
2. See Haley and Schall (1979, 218–229 and 253–261) for detailed discussion on the time-state preference model and its related issues.

Bibliography

Amram, M. and N. Kulatilika (1999). *Real Options: Managing Strategic Investment in an Uncertain World.* Boston: Harvard Business School Press.

Banz, R. W. and M. H. Miller (1978). Prices for state-contingent claims: Some estimates and applications. *Journal of Business*, 51(October), 653–672.

Breeden, D. T. and R. H. Litzenberger (1978). Prices of state-contingent claims implicit in option prices. *Journal of Business*, 51(October), 621–651.

Copeland, T. and V. Antikarov (2003). *Real Options: A Practitioner's Guide.* New York: Texere.

Duan, C. W., W. T. Lin and C. F. Lee (2003). Sequential capital budgeting as real options: The case of a new DRAM chipmaker in Taiwan. *Review of Pacific Basin Financial Markets and Policies*, 6(1), 87–112.

Haley, C. W. and L. D. Schall (1979). *The Theory of Financial Decisions*, 2nd ed. New York, NY: McGraw-Hill Book Company.

Lee, C. F., G. H. Tzeng and S. Y. Wang (2005a). A new application of fuzzy set theory to the Black–Scholes option pricing model. *Expert Systems with Applications*, 29(2), 330–342.

Lee, C. F., G. H. Tzeng and S. Y. Wang (2005b). A fuzzy set approach for generalized CRR model: An empirical analysis of S&P 500 index options. *Review of Quantitative Finance and Accounting*, 25(3), 255–275.

Merton, R. C. (1980). On estimating the expected return on the market: An exploratory investigation. *Journal of Financial Economics* 8(June), 323–361.

Ross, S. A., R. W. Westerfield and J. Jaffe (2008). *Corporate Finance*, 8th ed. New York, NY: McGraw-Hill/Irwin.

Wang, S. Y. and C. F. Lee (2022). A fuzzy real option valuation approach to capital budgeting under uncertainty environment, in Encyclopedia of Finance, 3rd edition, edited by Cheng-Few Lee and Alice Lee, *Encyclopedia of Finance*, pp. 1–24. Cham: New York: Springer International Publishing.

Chapter 20

Itô's Calculus: Derivation of the Black–Scholes Option Pricing Model*

Contents

*This chapter was written by Professor A. G. Malliaris, Loyola University of Chicago.

20.1 Introduction

The purpose of this chapter is to develop **stochastic calculus** (or more specifically as **Itô's calculus**) and to illustrate its application in the pricing of options. The topic is motivated by a desire to provide an *intuitive* understanding of certain probabilistic methods that have found significant use in financial economics. A rigorous presentation of the same ideas is provided briefly in Malliaris and Brock (1982) and more recently, Chalamandaris and Malliaris (2011).

Itô's calculus was prompted by purely mathematical questions originating in Wiener's work in 1923 on stochastic integrals and was developed by the Japanese probabilist Kiyosi Itô during 1944–1951. Two decades later, economists such as Merton (1973) and Black and Scholes (1973) started using Itô's stochastic differential equation to describe the behavior of asset prices. Because stochastic calculus is now used regularly by financial economists, some attention must be given to its mathematical meaning, its appropriateness in economic modeling, and its applications in economic modeling and finance.

These topics are discussed as follows. Section 20.2 discusses the Itô process and financial modeling, Section 20.3 discusses Itô's lemma, and Section 20.4 discusses the stochastic differential equation approach to stock price behavior. The pricing of an option is discussed in Section 20.5, and a reexamination of option pricing is talked about Section 20.6. Remarks on option pricing are given in Section 20.7, and finally in Section 20.8 we summarize the chapter. An alternative method to derive the Black–Scholes option pricing model is shown in Appendix 20A, and the present value of the partial expectation of the terminal stock price is shown in Appendix 20B.

20.2 The Itô Process and Financial Modeling

Stochastic calculus is the mathematical branch of random change in continuous time, unlike ordinary calculus, which deals with deterministic change. A key notion in stochastic calculus is the following equation:

$$dS(t,w) = \mu[t,S(t,w)]dt + \sigma[t,S(t,w)]dZ(t,w), \tag{20.1}$$

which is analogous to the ordinary differential equation $dS(t)/dt = \mu[t, S(t)]$. This section defines intuitively the Itô equation in Equation (20.1) and discusses its appropriateness to financial modeling.

A stochastic process is an Itô process if the random variable $dS(t, w)$ can be represented by Equation (20.1). The first term, $\mu[t, S(t, w)]dt$, is the expected change in $S(t, w)$ at time t. The second term, $\sigma[t, S(t, w)]dZ(t, w)$, reflects the uncertain term.

The Itô equation is a random equation. The domain of the equation is $[0, \infty) \times \Omega$, with the first argument t denoting time and taking values continuously in the interval $[0, \infty)$, and the second argument w denoting a random element taking values from a random set Ω. The range of the equation is the real numbers or real vectors. For simplicity, only the real numbers, denoted by R, are considered as the range of Equation (20.1). Because time takes values continuously in $[0, \infty)$, the Itô equation is a **continuous-time random equation**.

Although at first a real random variable $S\,(t, w) : [0, \infty) \times \Omega \to R$ is used — that is, a function having as domain $[0, \infty) \times \Omega$ and as range real numbers — Equation (20.1) expresses not the values of $S(t, w)$ but its infinitesimal differences $dS(t, w)$ as a function of two terms. For example, in finance, $S(t, w)$ denotes the price of a stock at time t affected by the state of the economy described by the random element w, and Equation (20.1) expresses the small changes in the stock price, $dS(t, w)$, at time t affected by the random element w. The mathematical meaning of this small difference can be explained as follows: $dS(t, w)$ may be viewed as the limit of large finite differences $\Delta S(t, w)$ as Δt approaches zero. Note that $\Delta S(t, w) = S(t + \Delta t, w) - S(t, w)$, where Δt denotes the difference in the change in time. Thus, the Itô equation expresses random changes in the values of a variable taking place continuously in time.

Moreover, these random changes are given as the sum of two terms. The first term, $\mu[t, S(t, w)]$, is called the **drift component** of the Itô equation, and in finance, it is used to compute the instantaneous expected value of the change in the random variable $S(t, w)$. Observe that $\mu[t, S(t, w)]$, as a function used in the computation of a statistical mean, is affected by both time and randomness. If at a given time t the expected change in $dS(t, w)$, expressed as $E[dS(t, w)]$, is desired, this can be answered by computing $E\{\mu[t, S(t, w)]dt\}$.

The second term $\sigma[t, S(t, w)]dZ(t, w)$ is itself the product of two factors. Each factor is important and needs special attention. The first factor, $\sigma[t, S(t, w)]$, is used in the calculation of the instantaneous standard derivation of the change in the random variable $S(t, w)$; it is a function of both time t and the range of values taken by $S(t, w)$. When $\sigma[t, S(t, w)]$ is squared to compute the instantaneous variance, it is usually called the **diffusion coefficient**; it measures the variability of $dS(t, w)$ at a given instance in time.

The second factor, $dZ(t, w)$, is called **white noise**; it models financial uncertainty in continuous time. Actually, $dZ(t, w)$ denotes an infinitesimal change in the **Wiener process**, $Z(t, w)\colon [0, \infty) \times \Omega \to R$, a process with increment that is statistically independent and normally distributed with mean zero and variance equal to the increment in time. In other words, for every pair of disjoint time intervals $[t_1, t_2], [t_3, t_4]$ with, say, $t_1 < t_2 \leq t_3 < t_4$, the increments $Z(t_4, w) - Z(t_3, w)$ and $Z(t_2, w) - Z(t_1, w)$ are independent and normally distributed random variables with means

$$E[Z(t_3, w) - Z(t_4, w)] = E[Z(t_2, w) - Z(t_1, w)] = 0,$$

and respective variances

$$\begin{aligned}\text{Var}[Z(t_4, w) - Z(t_3, w)] &= t_4 - t_3,\\ \text{Var}[Z(t_2, w) - Z(t_1, w)] &= t_2 - t_1.\end{aligned}$$

By convention, it is assumed that at time $t = 0$, the Wiener process is zero — that is, $Z(0, w) = 0$.

The two factors have been described separately; an intuitive explanation of the product of $\sigma[t, S(t, w)]$ and $dZ(t, w)$ is now presented. Because $\sigma[t, S(t, w)]$ measures the instantaneous standard derivation or volatility of $dS(t, w)$ and because $dZ(t, w)$ is an infinitesimal increment (which is, by definition, purely random with mean zero and variance dt), the expression of $\sigma[t, S(t, w)]dZ(t, w)$ is the product of two independent random variables, with

$$E\{\sigma[t, S(t, w)]dZ(t, w)\} = 0, \tag{20.2}$$

$$\begin{aligned}Var\{\sigma[t, S(t, w)]dZ(t, w)\} &= E\{\sigma[t, S(t, w)]dZ(t, w)\}^2\\ &= E\{\sigma^2[t, S(t, w)]dt\}.\end{aligned} \tag{20.3}$$

Therefore, the product $\sigma[t, S(t, w)]dZ(t, w)$ is a random variable with mean and variances given by Equations (20.2) and (20.3), which, for a given time t and state of nature w, yields a real number. This number may be either positive or negative depending on the value of $dZ(t, w)$ since $\sigma[t, S(t, w)]$ represents a measure of standard derivation and is always positive. Furthermore, the magnitude of the product $\sigma[t, S(t, w)]dZ(t, w)$ depends on the magnitude of each of the two terms. Indeed, the methodological foundation of the Itô model is that the uncertainty magnitude $dZ(t, w)$ is multiplied by $\sigma[t, S(t, w)]$ to produce the **total contribution of uncertainty**. Therefore, $\sigma[t, S(t, w)]dZ(t, w)$ describes the total fluctuation produced by volatility as this volatility is aggrandized or reduced by pure randomness.

This analysis explains why uncertainty given by $dZ(t, w)$ is being modeled as a multiplicative factor in the product $\sigma[t, S(t, w)]dZ(t, w)$: To repeat once again, the multiplicative modeling of uncertainty allows the generation of values for $dS(t, w)$ that are above or below the instantaneous expected value, depending on whether uncertainty is positive or negative, respectively. In other words, the product $\sigma[t, S(t, w)]dZ(t, w)$ can be viewed as the total contribution of uncertainty to $dS(t, w)$, with such uncertainty being the product of two factors: the instantaneous standard derivation of changes and the purely random white noise.

The conceptual components of the Itô process can now be collected to offer a more general interpretation of its meaning in finance. If at a given time t the possible future change in the price of an asset during the next trading interval is being evaluated, this change can be decomposed into two non-overlapping components: the *expected* change and the *unexpected* change. The expected change, $E[dS(t, w)]$, is described by $E\{\sigma[t, S(t, w)]dt\}$, and the unexpected change is given by $E\{\sigma[t, S(t, w)]dZ(t, w)\}$. As already noted, this unexpected change depends on the asset's volatility and pure randomness, and because uncertainty cannot be anticipated, the unexpected change is zero. This holds because $\sigma[t, S(t, w)]$ and $dZ(t, w)$ are independent random variables, and therefore, from Equation (20.2),

$$E\{\sigma[t, S(t, w)]dZ(t, w)\} = E\{\sigma[t, S(t, w)]\}E[dZ(t, w)] = 0,$$

because by definition $E[dZ(t, w)] = 0$. Thus, Equation (20.1), which was developed by mathematicians, captures the spirit of financial modeling admirably because it is an equation that involves three important concepts in finance: *mean*, *standard derivation*, and *randomness*.

However, Equation (20.1) captures the spirit of finance not only because it involves means, standard derivations, and randomness but, more importantly, because it also expresses key methodological elements of modern financial theory. In an elegant paper, Merton (1982) identified several foundational notions of the appropriateness of the Itô equation in modern finance:

(1) Itô's equation allows uncertainty not to disappear even as trading intervals become extremely short. In the real world of financial markets, uncertainty evolves continuously, and $dZ(t, w)$ captures this uncertainty because the value of $dZ(\Delta t, w)$ is not zero even as Δt becomes small. On the other hand, as trading intervals increase, uncertainty increases because by definition

$$\text{Var}[Z(t + \Delta t, w) - Z(t, w)] = \Delta t.$$

(2) Itô's equation incorporates uncertainty for all times. This means that uncertainty is present at all trading periods.
(3) The rate of change described by $\mu[t, S(t, w)]dt$ is finite, and uncertainty does not cause the term $\mu[t, S(t, w)]dZ(t, w)$ to become unbounded. These notions of the Itô equation are consistent with real-world observations of finite means, finite variances, and uncertainty (which evolve nicely by obtaining continuously finite values).
(4) Finally, all that counts in an Itô equation is the present time t. In other words, the past and future are independent. This notion expresses mathematically the concept of economic markets efficiency. That is, knowledge of past price behavior does not allow for above-average returns in the future.

Sample Problems 20.1 and 20.2 provide illustrations of the concepts discussed.

Sample Problem 20.1

Consider the following example of an Itô process describing the price of given stock:

$$dS(t, w) = 0.001\ S(t, w)dt + 0.025\ S(t, w)dZ(t, w).$$

If both sides are divided by $S(t,w)$ we get

$$\frac{dS(t,w)}{S(t,w)} = 0.001\ dt + 0.025\ dZ(t,w), \tag{20.4}$$

which gives the proportional change in the price of the stock. Assume that dt equals one trading period, such as one day. Using appropriate coefficients in Equation (20.4), dt could be denoted as one second. In Equation (20.4), the expected daily proportional change is given by

$$E\left[\frac{dS(t,w)}{S(t,w)}\right] = E[0.001\ dt + 0.025\ dZ(t,w)] = 0.001, \tag{20.5}$$

which means that at any given trading day, the price of the stock is expected to change by 0.1%. The standard derivation of the proportional change is $\sigma = 0.025$ or 2.5%.

What actually occurs at a given trading period depends on the evolution of the uncertainty as modeled by the normally distributed random variable $dZ(t,w)$, with mean 0 and variance 1. From the properties of the normal distribution, it can be deduced that although Equation (20.5) says that the expected daily proportional change is 0.001 and there is a 68.26% probability that the daily proportional change will be from $0.001 \pm (1)(0.025)$, or a 95.46% probability that it will be from $0.001 \pm (2)(0.025)$, or a 99.74% probability that it will be from $0.001 \pm (3)(0.025)$.

Sample Problem 20.2

This second example shows how the Itô equation combines the notion of a trading interval dt, the expected change in the price of the stock μ, the volatility of the stock μ, and pure uncertainty $dZ(t,w)$ to describe changes in the price of an asset. The same example will be used later to show the behavior of the price of the stock $S(t,w)$. Equation (20.5) illustrates only approximately the infinitesimal proportional change in the price of the stock and in order to obtain the solution of the stochastic differential equation (20.5), we need the following useful lemma.

20.3 Itô's Lemma

The preceding two sections dealt with the Itô process, both its intuitive mathematical meaning and its financial interpretation. This section presents briefly Itô's lemma of stochastic differentiation. By formally integrating Equation (20.1)

$$S(t,w) = S(0,w) + \int_0^t \mu(u,w)\,du + \int_0^t \mu(u,w)\,dZ(u,w), \quad (20.6)$$

this last equation describes Itô process in terms of the original random variable $S(t,w)$ rather than infinitesimal differences (differential form), as in Equation (20.1). Mathematically, Equations (20.1) and (20.6) are equivalent, and Equation (20.1) obtains clear meaning through integration, which is not developed here because of its complexity. Nevertheless, note that it is the second integral, $\int_0^t \mu(u,w)dZ(u,w)$, that presents the difficulties. The problem arises because uncertainty given by $dZ(u,w)$ in its limit does not have a precise meaning, and therefore the second integral cannot be treated like an ordinary Riemann integral. Itô's great accomplishment was to define the second integral as a random variable, that is, the limit in probability of a certain sequence of integrals of step functions multiplied by the uncertainty $dZ(u,w)$.

Suppose that a stochastic process is given by Equation (20.6) and that a new process $Y(t,w)$ is formed by letting $Y(t,w) = u[t, S(t,w)]$. Because stochastic calculus studies random changes in continuous time, the following question arises: What is $dY(t,w)$? This question is important for both mathematical analysis and finance. The answer is given in Itô's lemma.

Itô's Lemma. *Consider the non-random continuous function* $u(t,S)$: $[0,\infty) \times R \to R$ *and suppose that it has continuous partial derivatives* u_t, u_S, and u_{SS}.

Let

$$Y(t,w) = u[t, S(t,w)], \quad (20.7)$$

with

$$dS(t,w) = \mu[t, S(t,w)]dt + \sigma[t, S(t,w)]dZ(t,w). \quad (20.8)$$

Then, the process $Y(t, w)$ has a differential given by

$$\begin{aligned} dY(t, w) = \{&u_t[t, S(t, w)] + u_S[t, S(t, w)]\mu[t, S(t, w)] \\ &+\frac{1}{2}u_{SS}[t, S(t, w)]\sigma^2[t, S(t, w)]\}\, dt \\ &+u_S[t, S(t, w)]\sigma[t, S(t, w)]\, dZ(t, w). \end{aligned} \tag{20.9}$$

The proof is presented in Gikhman and Skorokhod (1969, pp. 387–389), and extensions of this lemma may be found in Arnold (1974, pp. 90–99). Here, the analysis is limited to three remarks:

(1) Itô's lemma is a useful result because it allows the computation of stochastic differentials of arbitrary functions. In this respect, Itô's formula is as useful as the chain rule of ordinary calculus.
(2) Given an Itô stochastic process $S(t, w)$ with respect to a given Wiener process $Z(t, w)$, and letting $Y(t, w) = u[t, S(t, w)]$ be a new process, Itô's formula gives the stochastic differential of $Y(t, w)$, where $dY(t, w)$ is given with respect to the same Wiener process — that is, both processes have the same source of uncertainty.
(3) An inspection of the proof of Itô's lemma reveals that it consists of an application of Taylor's theorem of advanced calculus and several probabilistic arguments to establish the convergence of certain quantities to appropriate integrals. Therefore, Itô's formula may be obtained by applying Taylor's theorem instead of remembering the specific result in Equation (20.6). More specifically, the differential of $Y(t, w) = u[t, S(t, w)]$, where $S(t, w)$ is a stochastic process with differential given by Equation (20.1), may be computed by using Taylor's theorem and the following multiplication rules:

$$dt \times dt = 0 \quad dZ \times dZ = dt \quad dt \times dZ = 0, \tag{20.10}$$

as

$$\begin{aligned} dY = u_t dt + u_S dS + \frac{1}{2}(dS)^2 = u_t dt, \\ + u_S(\mu dt + \sigma dZ) + \frac{1}{2}u_{SS}(\mu dt + \sigma dZ)^2. \end{aligned}$$

By carrying out these multiplications and using the rules in Equation (20.10), Equation (20.9) is obtained.

20.4 Stochastic Differential Equation approach to Stock Price Behavior

This section demonstrates how a stochastic equation can be used to describe the price behavior of an asset. We begin with Sample Problem 20.3.

Sample Problem 20.3

As a special case of Equation (20.1), consider

$$dS(t,w) = \mu S(t,w)dt + \sigma S(t,w)dZ(t,w), \tag{20.11}$$

in which μ and σ are constants as in Sample Problem 20.1. Assume that Equation (20.11) describes the price behavior of a certain stock with $S(0,w)$ given. The solution $S(t,w)$ of Equation (20.11) is given by

$$S(t,w) = S(0,w)\exp\left[\left(\mu - \frac{1}{2}\sigma^2\right)t + \sigma Z(t,w)\right]. \tag{20.12}$$

To show that the behavior of Equation (20.12) is the solution of Equation (20.11), use Itô's lemma as follows. First, start with Equation (20.12), which corresponds to the function $Y(t,w)$. In this case, Equation (20.12) is a function of t and $Z(t,w)$, and instead of Equation (20.8):

$$dZ(t,w) = 0 \cdot dt + 1 \cdot dZ(t,w).$$

Next, compute the first- and second-order partials denoted by S_t, S_Z, and S_{ZZ}:

$$\begin{aligned} S_t(t,w) &= \left(\mu - \frac{\sigma^2}{2}\right)S(t,w), \\ S_Z(t,w) &= \sigma S(t,w), \\ S_{ZZ}(t,w) &= \sigma^2 S(t,w). \end{aligned}$$

Collect these results and use Equation (20.9) to conclude that Equation (20.11) holds

$$\begin{aligned} dS(t,w) &= \left[\left(\mu - \frac{\sigma^2}{2}\right) S(t,w) + \sigma S(t,w)\cdot 0 + \frac{\sigma^2}{2} S(t,w)\cdot 1\right] dt \\ &\quad + \sigma S(t,w)\cdot 1 \cdot dZ(t,w) \\ &= \mu S(t,w)dt + \sigma S(t,w)dZ(t,w). \end{aligned}$$

This result is not only mathematically interesting but in finance it means that, assuming stock price is given by an Itô process as in Equation (20.11), Equation (20.12) holds as well. To see if Equation (20.12) accurately describes stock prices in the real world, rewrite it as

$$\ln \frac{S(t,w)}{S(0,w)} = \left(\mu - \frac{\sigma^2}{2}\right) t + \sigma Z(t,w), \tag{20.13}$$

which is a random variable normally distributed with mean $(\mu - \sigma^2/2)t$ and variance $\sigma^2 t$. This means that if the stock price follows an Itô process, it has a log-normal probability distribution. Such a distribution for stock price is reasonable because it is consistent with reality, where negative stock prices are not possible; the worst that can happen is that the stock price reaches zero. For a detailed analysis of the properties of a log-normal random distribution, see Cox and Rubinstein (1985, pp. 201–204); for a list of bibliographical references on the empirical distribution of stock price changes, see Cox and Rubinstein (1985, pp. 485–488). Sample Problem 20.4 provides further illustration.

Sample Problem 20.4

The analysis of this problem applies the results of the last two sections to the example in Sample Problem 20.1. Suppose that instead of Equation (20.11), Equation (20.14) is given. Then, Equation (20.12) describes the solution of Equation (20.14):

$$S(t,w) = S(0,w)\exp\left[\left(0.001 - \frac{0.025^2}{2}\right) t + 0.025 Z(t,w)\right]. \tag{20.14}$$

From Equation (20.14), the exact evolution of the price of the stock as influenced by a mean, a variance, time, and uncertainty is obtained.

Using Equation (20.14) for $t = 1$ to compute

$$E\left[\ln \frac{S(t,w)}{S(0,w)}\right] = \left(\mu - \frac{\sigma^2}{2}\right)t = \left[0.001 - \frac{(0.025)^2}{2}\right](0.1)$$

$$= 0.0006875, \tag{20.15}$$

$$\mathrm{Var}\left[\frac{S(t,w)}{S(0,w)}\right] = \sigma^2 t = (0.025)^2(0.1) = 0.000625, \tag{20.16}$$

which means that for a given trading day, the price of the stock is expected to experience a continuous change of 0.068% with a standard derivation of 0.025%. Computing Equations (20.15) and (20.16) for any t can be done easily; the same computations cannot be performed readily in Equation (20.4).

Sample Problem 20.5

Here, we give an intuitive description of Equation (20.1) with reference to Table 20.1 using Excel. In Table 20.1, we collect from Yahoo.com 40 recent daily closing Google Inc. prices. These prices are also illustrated graphically in Figure 20.1.

For modeling purposes, the Black–Scholes equation requires a mathematical expression for prices, such as shown in Table 20.1 and Figure 20.1. How can we check to see if the prices in these figures follow an Itô process? In Column 3 of Table 20.1, we compute the daily Google returns and calculate the average historical return of the 40 daily returns. This daily average is 0.000185, which annualized becomes $0.000185 \times 250 = 0.04625$. The volatility of these 40 returns is computed as the annualized standard deviation of daily returns and is computed as $0.011215 \times \sqrt{250} = 0.177324$. Both these calculations assume 250 trading days per year. To complete checking the prices in Table 20.1 to satisfy Equation (20.8), we solve for dZ. Since these prices are daily, we use the daily constant average return and constant daily volatility to obtain daily dZs in Column 4 of Table 20.1 using

$$dZ_i = \frac{r_i - \mu_{ri}}{\sigma_{ri}}.$$

We also compute the mean and variance of the dZ in the last column. Recall that earlier we postulated that $E(dZ) = 0$ and $\mathrm{Var}(dZ) = 1$ are assumed. Indeed, the mean and variance of the dZ values in Table 20.1 are as postulated.

Table 20.1 Daily Price Data for Google Inc.

Day	Price	r_i	dZ
1	610.21		
2	630.08	0.03256	2.91992
3	625.26	−0.00765	−0.66558
4	624.22	−0.00166	−0.13180
5	624.15	−0.00011	0.00651
6	628.15	0.00641	0.58794
7	624.5	−0.00581	−0.50160
8	616.44	−0.01291	−1.13427
9	616.5	0.00010	0.02519
10	618.38	0.00305	0.28841
11	614.29	−0.00661	−0.57323
12	610.98	−0.00539	−0.46394
13	610.15	−0.00136	−0.10462
14	612	0.00303	0.28686
15	611.04	−0.00157	−0.12336
16	600.36	−0.01748	−1.54193
17	600.99	0.00105	0.11008
18	616.79	0.02629	2.36063
19	616.5	−0.00047	−0.02541
20	619.91	0.00553	0.50970
21	611.08	−0.01424	−1.25354
22	611.83	0.00123	0.12594
23	626.77	0.02442	2.19377
24	631.75	0.00795	0.72496
25	639.63	0.01247	1.12868
26	624.18	−0.02415	−2.13721
27	616.69	−0.01200	−1.05344
28	616.87	0.00029	0.04253
29	616.01	−0.00139	−0.10780
30	614.21	−0.00292	−0.24403
31	616.44	0.00363	0.34024
32	613.5	−0.00477	−0.40874
33	609.07	−0.00722	−0.62733
34	602.12	−0.01141	−1.00093
35	604.35	0.00370	0.34674
36	593.97	−0.01718	−1.51493
37	598.86	0.00823	0.75057
38	601	0.00357	0.33513
39	598.92	−0.00346	−0.29208
40	602.38	0.00578	0.53162
41	604.23	0.00307	0.29035
μ_{ri}		−0.000185	
σ_{ri}		0.011215	
μ_{dz}			0
σ_{dz}			1

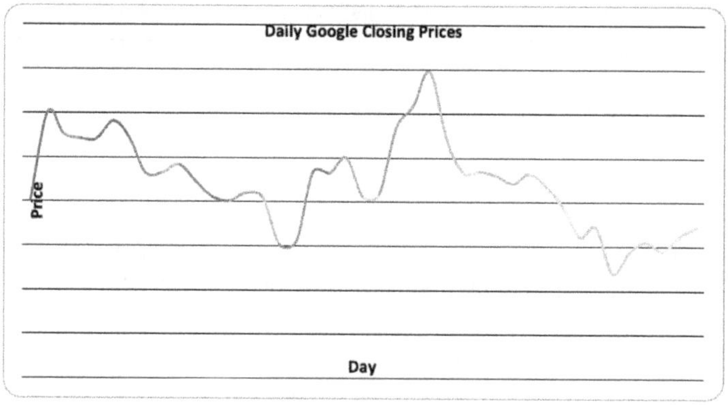

Figure 20.1 Daily Google Inc. Closing Prices

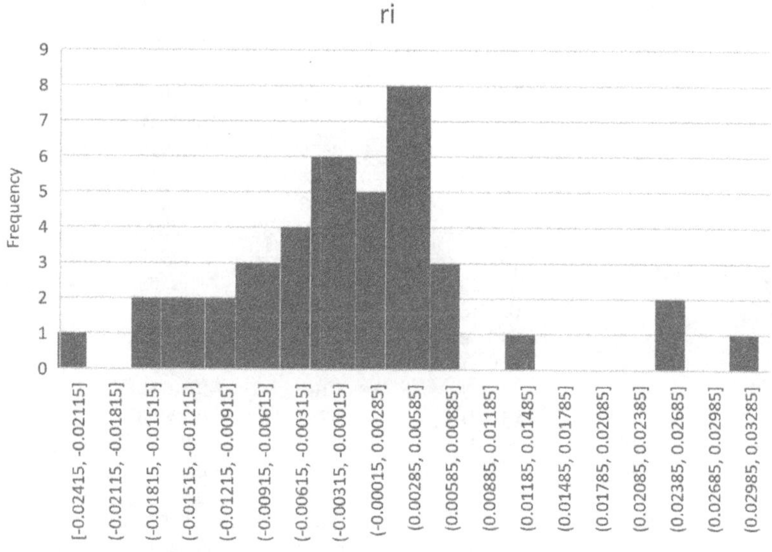

Figure 20.2 Frequency Distribution of Returns

Note that if we were to graph the distribution of Google stock prices, it would follow a log-normal distribution while its returns would follow a normal distribution. Furthermore, the daily dZs, as an approximation to the continuous random walk dZ of Equation (20.8), also are normally distributed with mean 0 and variance 1. Figures 20.2 and 20.3 are frequency approximations to a normal distribution and illustrate the distributions of returns and distributions of dZs of Table 20.1.

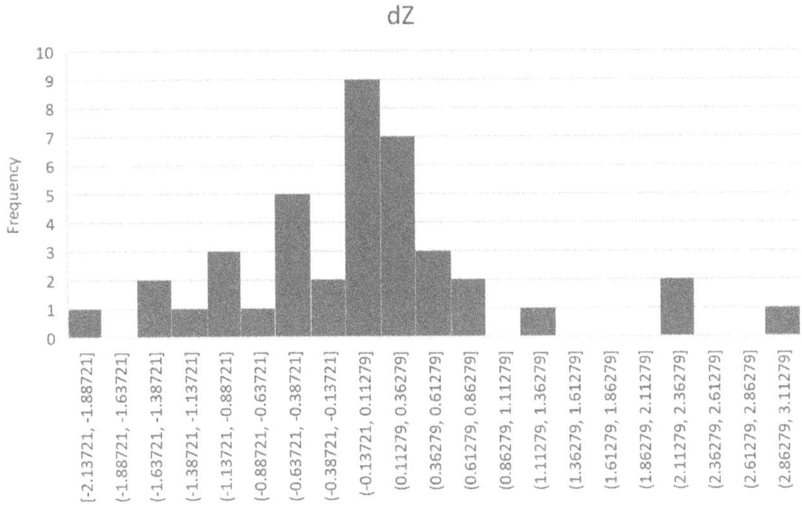

Figure 20.3 Frequency Distribution of Errors

20.5 The Pricing of an Option

An **option** is a contract giving the right to buy or sell an asset within a specified period of time subject to certain conditions. The simplest kind of option is the **European call option**, which is a contract to buy a share of a certain stock at a given date for a specified price. The date the option expires is called the **expiration date (maturity date)** and the price that is paid for the stock when the option is exercised is called the **exercise price (striking price)**.

In terms of economic analysis, several propositions about call option pricing seem clear. The value of an option increases as the price of the stock increases. If the stock price is much greater than the exercise price, it is almost certain that the option will be exercised; and, analogously, if the price of the stock is much less than the exercise price, the value of the option will be near zero and the option will expire without being exercised. If the expiration date is very far in the future, the value of the option will be approximately equal to the price of the stock. If the expiration date is very near, the value of the option will be approximately equal to the stock price minus the exercise price, or zero if the stock price is less than the exercise price. In general, the value of the option is more volatile than the price of the stock, and the relative volatility of the option depends on both the stock price and maturity.

The first rigorous formulation and solution of the problem of option pricing was achieved by Black and Scholes (1973) and Merton (1973). Consider a stock option denoted by C whose price at time t can be written:

$$C(t, w) = C[t, S(t, w)], \tag{20.17}$$

in which C is a twice continuously differentiable function. Here, $S(t, w)$ is the price of some stock upon which the option is written. The price of this stock is assumed to follow Itô's stochastic differential equation:

$$dS(t, w) = \mu[t, S(t, w)]dt + \sigma[t, S(t, w)]dZ(t, w). \tag{20.18}$$

Assume, as a simplifying case, that $\mu[t, S(t, w)] = \mu S(t, w)$ and $\sigma[t, S(t, w)] = \sigma S(t, w)$. For notational convenience, w is suppressed from the various expressions, and sometimes t as well. Therefore, Equation (20.18) becomes

$$dS(t) = \mu S(t)dt + \sigma S(t)dZ(t). \tag{20.19}$$

Consider an investor who builds up a portfolio of stocks, options on the stocks, and a riskless asset (e.g., government bonds) yielding a riskless rate r. The nominal of the portfolio, denoted by $P(t)$, is

$$P(t) = N_1(t)S(t) + N_2C(t) + Q(t), \tag{20.20}$$

where $N_1 =$ the number of shares of the stock, $N_2 =$ the number of call options, and $Q =$ the value of dollars invested in riskless bonds.

Assume that the stock pays no dividends or other distributions. By Itô's lemma, the differential of the call price using Equations (20.17) and (20.19) is

$$\begin{aligned} dC &= C_t dt + C_S dS + \tfrac{1}{2}C_{SS}dS^2 \\ &= (C_t + C_S\mu S + \tfrac{1}{2}C_{SS}\sigma^2 S^2)dt + C_S\sigma S dZ \\ &= \mu_C C dt + \sigma_C C dZ. \end{aligned} \tag{20.21}$$

Observe that in Equation (20.21)

$$\mu_C C = C_t + C_S\mu S + \tfrac{1}{2}C_{SS}\sigma^2 S^2, \tag{20.22}$$

$$\sigma_C C = C_S\sigma S. \tag{20.23}$$

In other words, $\mu_C C$ is the expected change in the call option price, and $\sigma_C^2 C^2$ is the variance of such a change per unit of time. Itô's lemma simply indicates that if the call option price is a function of a spot stock price that follows an Itô process, then the call option price also follows an Itô process with mean and standard derivation parameters that are more complex than those of the stock price. The Itô process for a call is given by Equations (20.22) and (20.23).

The change in the normal value of the portfolio dP results from the change in the prices of the assets because at a point in time the equations of option and stock are given — that is, $dN_1 = dN_2 = 0$. More precisely,

$$\begin{aligned} dP &= N_1(dS) + N_2(dS) + dQ \\ &= (\mu dt + \sigma dZ)N_1 S + (\mu_C dt + \sigma_C dZ)N_2 C + rQdt. \end{aligned} \tag{20.24}$$

Let w_1 be the fraction invested in stock, w_2 be the fraction invested in options, and w_3 be the fraction invested in the riskless asset. As before, $w_1 + w_2 + w_3 = 1$, that is, all of the funds available are invested in some type of asset. Set $w_1 = N_1 S/P$, $w_2 = N_2 C/P$, $w_3 = Q/P = 1 - w_1 - w_2$. Then, Equation (20.24) becomes

$$\frac{dP}{P} = (\mu dt + \sigma dZ)w_1 + (\mu_C dt + \sigma_C dZ)w_2 + (rdt)w_3. \tag{20.25}$$

At this point, the notion of **economic equilibrium** (also called **risk-neutral** or **preference-free pricing**) is introduced in the analysis. This notion plays an important role in modeling financing behavior, and its appropriate formulation is considered to be a major breakthrough in financial analysis.

More specifically, design the proportions w_1, w_2 so that the position is *riskless* for all $t \geq 0$ — that is, let w_1 and w_2 be such that

$$\text{Var} = \left(\frac{dP}{P}\right) = \text{Var}(w_1 \sigma dZ + w_2 \sigma_C dZ) = 0. \tag{20.26}$$

In the last equation, Var_t denotes variance conditioned on $S(t)$, $C(t)$, and $Q(t)$. In other words, choose $(w_1, w_2) = (\bar{w}_1, \bar{w}_2)$ so that

$$\bar{w}_1 \sigma + \bar{w}_2 \sigma_C = 0. \tag{20.27}$$

Then, from Equation (20.25), because the portfolio is riskless, it follows that the portfolio must be expected to earn the riskless rate of return, or

$$E_t\left(\frac{dP}{P}\right) = [\mu\bar{w}_1 + \mu_C\bar{w}_2 + r(1-\bar{w}_1-\bar{w}_2)]dt = r(t)dt. \quad (20.28)$$

Equations (20.27) and (20.28) yield the Black–Scholes–Merton equations:

$$\frac{\bar{w}_1}{\bar{w}_2} = -\frac{\sigma_C}{\sigma} \quad (20.29)$$

and

$$r = \mu\bar{w}_1 + \mu_C\bar{w}_2 - r\bar{w}_1 - r\bar{w}_2 + r, \quad (20.30)$$

which simplify to

$$\frac{\mu - r}{\sigma} = \frac{\mu_C - r}{\sigma_C}. \quad (20.31)$$

Because of the law of one price, Equation (20.31) says that the net rate of return per unit of risk must be the two assets and describes an appropriate concept of economic equilibrium in this problem. If this were not the case, there would exist an arbitrage opportunity until this equality held. Using Equation (20.31) and making the necessary substitutions from Equations (20.22) and (20.23), the partial differential equation of the pricing of an option is obtained:

$$\frac{1}{2}\sigma^2S^2C_{SS}(t,S) + rSC_S(t,S) - rC(t,S) + C_t(t,S) = 0. \quad (20.32)$$

The equation along with the boundary conditions for call options fully characterizes the call price: $C(S,T) = \text{Max}(0, S-X)$, $S \geq 0$, $0 \geq E \geq T$. The solution to the differential equation (20.32) given these boundary conditions is the Black–Scholes formula.

20.6 A Reexamination of Option Pricing

To illustrate the notion of economic equilibrium once again, consider the nominal value of a portfolio consisting of a stock and a call option on this stock and write

$$P(t) = N_1(t)S(t) + N_2(t)C(t), \tag{20.33}$$

using the same notation as in the previous section. Equation (20.33) differs from Equation (20.20) because the term $Q(t)$ has been deleted. Now, concentrating on the two assets of the portfolio — that is, the stock and the call option — and using Equations (20.33) and (20.21), the change in the value of the portfolio is given by

$$dP = N_1 dS + N_2 dC = N_1 dS + N_2[(C_t + \tfrac{1}{2}C_{SS}\sigma^2 S^2)dt + C_S dS]. \tag{20.34}$$

Note that $dN_1 = dN_2 = 0$, since at any given point in time the equations of stock and option are given. For arbitrary quantities of stock and option, Equation (20.34) shows that the change in the nominal value of the portfolio dP is stochastic because dS is a random variable. Suppose the quantities of stock and call option are chosen as

$$\frac{N_1}{N_2} = -C_S. \tag{20.35}$$

Note that C_S in Equation (20.35) denotes a hedge ration and is called **delta**. Then,

$N_1 dS + N_2 C_S dS = 0$, and inserting Equation (20.35) into Equation (20.34) yields

$$\begin{aligned} dP &= -N_2 C_S dS + N_2[(C_t + \tfrac{1}{2}C_{SS}\sigma^2 S^2)dt + C_S dS] \\ &= N_2(C_t + \tfrac{1}{2}C_{SS}\sigma^2 S^2)dt. \end{aligned} \tag{20.36}$$

Let $N_2 = 1$ in Equation (20.36) and observe that in equilibrium the rate of return of the riskless portfolio must be the same as the riskless rate $r(t)$. Therefore,

$$\frac{dP}{p} = rdt. \tag{20.37}$$

Equation (20.37) can be used to derive the partial differential equation for the value of the option. Making the necessary substitutions in Equation (20.36),

$$\frac{(C_t + \frac{1}{2}C_{SS}\sigma^2 S^2)dt}{-C_S S + C} = rdt,$$

which upon rearrangement gives Equation (20.32). Note that the option pricing equation is a second-order linear partial differential equation of the parabolic type. The boundary conditions of Equation (20.32) are determined by the specification of the asset. For the case of an option that can be exercised only at the expiration date t^* with an exercise price X, the boundary conditions are

$$C(t, S = 0) = 0, \tag{20.38}$$

$$C(t = t^*, S) = \text{Max}(0, S - X). \tag{20.39}$$

Observe that Equation (20.38) says that the call option price is zero if the stock price is zero at any date t. Equation (20.39) says that the call option price at the expiration date $t = t^*$ must equal the maximum of either zero or the difference between the stock price and the exercise price.

The solution of the option pricing equation for a call and a put option subject to the boundary conditions is given in Equations (20.40a) and (20.40b) for $T = t^* - t$, as

$$C(T, S, \sigma^2, X, r) = SN(d_1) - Xe^{-rT}N(d2), \tag{20.40a}$$

$$P(T, S, \sigma^2, X, r) = Xe^{-rT}(-N(d_2) - S(-N(d_1), \tag{20.40b}$$

where N denotes the cumulative normal distribution, namely,

$$N(y) = -\frac{1}{\sqrt{2\pi}}\int_{-\infty}^{y} \mathrm{e}^{-x^2/2}dx.$$

In Equation (20.40a), T is time to expiration (measured in years) and d_1 and d_2 are given by

$$d_1 = \frac{\ln(S/X) + (r + \frac{1}{2}\sigma^2)T}{\sigma\sqrt{T}}, \tag{20.41}$$

$$\begin{aligned} d_2 &= \frac{\ln(S/X) + \left(r - \frac{1}{2}\sigma^2\right)T}{\sigma\sqrt{T}} \\ &= d_1 - \sigma\sqrt{T}. \end{aligned} \tag{20.42}$$

It can be shown that

$$\frac{\partial C}{\partial T} > 0, \ \frac{\partial C}{\partial S} > 0, \ \frac{\partial C}{\partial \sigma^2} > 0, \ \frac{\partial C}{\partial X} < 0, \ \frac{\partial C}{\partial r} > 0. \tag{20.43}$$

These partial derivatives justify the intuitive behavior of the price of an option, as was indicated in the beginning of the previous section. More specifically, these partials show the following:

(1) As the stock price rises, so does the option price.
(2) As the variance rate of the underlying stock rises, so does the option price.
(3) With a higher exercise price, the expected payoff decreases.
(4) The value of the option increases as the interest rate rises.
(5) With a longer time to maturity, the price of the option is greater.

Before giving an example, it is appropriate to sketch the solution of Equation (20.32) subject to the boundary conditions of Equations (20.38) and (20.39). Let t denote the current trading period that is prior to the expiration date t^*. At time t, two outcomes can be expected to occur at t^*. (1) $S(t^*) > X$ — that is, the price of the stock at the time of the expiration of the call option is greater than exercise price, or (2) $S(t^*) \leq X$. Note that the first outcome occurs with probability $P_0 \equiv P[S(t^*) > X]$ and the second occurs with probability $1 - p$. Obviously, the only interesting possibility is the first case when $S(t^*) > X$, because this is when the price of the call has positive value. If $S(t^*) \leq X$, then $C(t^*) = 0$ from Equation (20.39). Again from Equation (20.39), if $S(t^*) > X$, then the price of the call option at expiration $C(t^*)$ can be computed from the expiration of Equation (20.39):

$$C(t^*) = E\{Max[0, S(t^*) - X]\} = E[S(t^*) - X]. \qquad (20.44)$$

What is the price of a call option if the first outcome materializes at t instead of t^*? This can be answered immediately by appropriate continuous discounting. Using Equation (20.44),

$$C(t) = \mathrm{e}^{-r(t^*-t)} E[S(t^*) - X]. \qquad (20.45)$$

Recall, however, that $C(t)$ in Equation (20.45) holds only with probability p. Combine both possibilities to write

$$\begin{aligned} C(t) &= p \cdot \mathrm{e}^{-r(t^*-t)} E[S(t^*) - X] + (1-p) \cdot 0 \\ &= p \cdot \mathrm{e}^{-r(t^*-t)} E[\,S(t^*)|\,S(t^*) > X] - p \cdot \mathrm{e}^{-r(t^*-t)} X. \end{aligned} \qquad (20.46)$$

Detailed calculations in Jarrow and Rudd (1983, pp. 92–94) show that because the price of the underlying stock is distributed lognormally, it follows that

$$p = P[S(t^*) > X] = N\left[\frac{\ln\frac{S(t)}{X} + (r + \frac{1}{2}\sigma^2)(t^* - t)}{\sigma\sqrt{t^* - t}}\right], \qquad (20.47)$$

$$p \cdot E[S(t^*)|\,S^* > X] = S(t)\mathrm{e}^{r(t^*-t)} N\left[\frac{\ln\frac{S(t)}{X} + (r + \frac{1}{2}\sigma^2)(t^* - t)}{\sigma\sqrt{t^* - t}}\right]. \qquad (20.48)$$

Combining Equations (20.47) and (20.48) with $T = t^* - t$ into Equation (20.46) yields Equation (20.40a).

It is worth observing that two terms of Equations (20.40a) and (20.40b) have economic meaning. The first term, $SN(d_1)$, denotes the present value of receiving the stock provided that $S(t^*) > X$. The second term gives the present value of paying the striking price provided that $S(t^*) > X$. In the special case when there is no uncertainty and $\sigma = 0$, observe that

$$N(d_1) = N(d_2) = N(\infty) = 1 \quad \text{and} \quad C = S(t) - \mathrm{e}^{-r(t^*-t)} X, \qquad (20.49)$$

that is, a call is worth the difference between the current value of the stock and the discounted value of the striking price provided $S(t^*) > X$; otherwise, the call price would be zero. When $\sigma \neq 0$ — that is, when uncertainty exists and the stock price is volatile — the two terms in Equation (20.49) are multiplied by $N(d_1)$ and $N(d_2)$, respectively, to adjust the call price for the prevailing uncertainties. These two probabilities can also be given an economic interpretation. As mentioned earlier, $N(d_1)$ is called delta; it is the partial derivative of the call price with respect to the stock price. $N(d_2)$ gives the probabilities that the call option will be in the money, as Equation (20.47) shows.

Assuming that investors in the economy have risk-neutral preferences, it will be possible to derive the Black–Scholes formula without using stochastic differential equations. Garven (1986) has shown that to derive Equation (20.40a) knowledge is required of normal and log-normal distributions and basic calculus, as presented in Appendix 20A.

Sample Problem 20.6

Equations (20.40a) and (20.40b) indicate that the Black–Scholes option pricing model is a function of only five variables: T, the time to expiration, S, the stock price, σ^2, the instantaneous variance rate on the stock price, X, the exercise price, and r, the riskless interest rate. Of these five variables, only the variance rate must be estimated; the other four variables are directly observable. A simple example is presented to illustrate the use of Equation (20.40). The values of the observable variables are taken from *Yahoo! Finance.*

On Wednesday, March 16, 2011, at 3:58 pm EDT, IBM Corp. had a stock price of \$152.93. The July 11 call option with a strike price of 150.00 was priced at \$10.50. We estimate the riskless rate at 0.25% from the U.S. Treasury bill rate. The only missing piece of information is the instantaneous variance of the stock price.

Several different techniques have been suggested for estimating the instantaneous variance. In this regard, the work of Latané and Rendleman (1976) must be mentioned; they derived standard derivations of continuous price-relative returns that are implied in actual call option prices on the assumption that investors behave as if they price options according to the Black–Scholes model. In the example, the implicit variance is calculated by using a numerical search to approximate the standard derivation implied by the Black–Scholes formula with these parameters: stock price $S = 152.93$, exercise price $X = 150$, time to expiration $T = 121/365 \times 0.3315$, riskless rate $r = 0.0025$, and call option price $C = 10.50$. The approximated implied volatility is found to be $\sigma = 0.264$.

Sample Problem 20.7

Using the information about the implied volatility presented above and a stock price of $S = 155$, we present the following example: Given $S = 155$, $X = 150$, $T = 0.3315$, $r = 0.0025$, and $\sigma = 0.264$, use Equation (20.40) to compute C. Using Equations (20.41) and (20.42), calculate

$$d_1 = \frac{\ln\left(\frac{155}{150}\right) + \left[0.0025 + \left(\frac{0.264^2}{2}\right)\right] 0.3315}{0.264\sqrt{0.3315}} = 0.29717,$$

$$d_2 = \frac{\ln\left(\frac{155}{150}\right) + \left[0.0025 - \left(\frac{0.264^2}{2}\right)\right] 0.3315}{0.264\sqrt{0.3315}} = 0.14517.$$

From a standard normal distribution table, giving the area of a standard normal distribution, $N(0.29717) = 0.616836$ and $N(0.14517) = 0.557923$. Finally,

$$C = 152.93 \times 0.616836 - 150e^{-0.0025*0.3315} \times 0.557923 = \$10.71.$$

These calculations show that as the price of the underlying stock increases from 152.93 to 155, the call price increases as indicated in Equation (20.43) from \$10.50 to \$10.71, while all other variables are the same.

Sample Problem 20.8

Using the information from the above example, we will calculate a call with a strike price of \$160 using Equation (20.40a):

$$d_1 = \frac{\ln\left(\frac{155}{160}\right) + \left[0.0025 + \left(\frac{0.264^2}{2}\right)\right] 0.3315}{0.264\sqrt{0.3315}} = -0.127419,$$

$$d_2 = \frac{\ln\left(\frac{155}{160}\right) + \left[0.0025 - \left(\frac{0.264^2}{2}\right)\right] 0.3315}{0.264\sqrt{0.3315}} = -0.268425.$$

From a standard normal distribution table, giving the area of a standard normal distribution, $N(-0.127419) = 0.449314$ and $N(-0.268425) = 0.394208$. Finally,

$$C = 152.93 \times 0.449314 - 160e^{-0.0025*0.3315} \times 0.394208 = \$9.63.$$

As expected, the price of this call option, $C = \$9.63$, with $X = 160$ has a lower calculated price than the call option with $X = 150$, as indicated in Equation (20.43).

This simple example shows how to use the Black–Scholes model to price a call option under the assumptions of the model. The example is presented for illustrative purposes only, and it relies heavily on the implicit estimate of the variance, its constancy over time, and all the remaining assumptions of the model. The appropriateness of estimating the implicit instantaneous variance is ultimately an empirical question, as is the entire Black–Scholes pricing formula. Boyle and Ananthanarayanan (1977) studied the implications of using an estimate of the variance in option valuation models and showed that this procedure produces biased option values. However, the magnitude of this bias is not large.

One additional remark must be made. The closeness of a calculated call option price to the actual call price is not necessarily evidence of the validity of the Black–Scholes model. Extensive empirical work has taken place to investigate how market prices of call options compare with prices predicted by Black–Scholes; see MacBeth and Merville (1979) and Bhattacharya (1980).

20.7 Remarks on Option Pricing

For a review on the literature on option pricing, see the two papers by Smith (1976, 1979). It is appropriate here to make a few remarks on the Black–Scholes option pricing model to clarify its significance and its limitation.

First, the Black–Scholes model for a European call as originally derived, and as reported here, is based on several simplifying assumptions:

(1) The stock price follows an Itô equation.
(2) The market operates continuously.

(3) There are no transaction costs in buying or selling the option or the underlying stock.
(4) There are no taxes.
(5) The riskless rate is known and constant.
(6) There are no restrictions on short sales.

Several researchers have extended the original Black–Scholes model by modifying these assumptions. Merton (1973) generalized the model to include dividend payments, exercise price changes, and the case of a stochastic interest rate. Roll (1977) had solved the problem of valuing a call option that can be exercised prior to its expiration date when the underlying stock is assumed to make known dividend payments before the option matures. Ingersoll (1976) studied the effect of differential taxes on capital gains and income, while Scholes (1976) determined the effects of the tax treatment of options on the pricing model. Furthermore, Merton (1976) and Cox and Ross (1976) showed that if the stock price movements are discontinuous, under certain assumptions, the valuation model still holds. These and other modifications of the original Black–Scholes analysis indicate that the model is quite robust about the relaxation of its fundamental assumptions.

Second, it is worth repeating that the use of Itô's calculus and the important insight concerning the appropriate concept of an equilibrium by creating a riskless hedge portfolio have let Black and Scholes obtain a closed-form solution for option pricing. In this closed-form solution, several variables do not appear, such as (1) the expected rate of return of the stock, (2) the expected rate of return of the option, (3) a measure of investor's risk preference, (4) investor expectations, and (5) equilibrium conditions for the entire capital market.

Third, the Black–Scholes pricing model has found numerous applications such as the following: (1) pricing the debt and equity of a firm; (2) the effects of corporate policy and, specially, the effects of mergers, acquisitions, and scale expansions on the relative values of the debt and equity of the firm; (3) the pricing of convertible bonds; (4) the pricing of underwriting contracts; (5) the pricing of leases; and (6) the pricing of insurance. Smith (1976, 1979) summarized most applications and indicated the original reference. See also Brealey and Myers (1988).

Fourth, Black (1976) showed that the original call option formula for stocks can be easily modified to be used in pricing call options on futures. The formula is

$$C(T, F, \sigma^2, X, r) = \mathrm{e}^{-rT}[FN(d_1) - XN(d_2)], \tag{20.50}$$

$$d_1 = \frac{\ln(F/X) + \frac{1}{2}\sigma^2 T}{\sigma\sqrt{T}}, \tag{20.51}$$

$$d_2 = \frac{\ln(F/X) - \frac{1}{2}\sigma^2 T}{\sigma\sqrt{T}}. \tag{20.52}$$

In Equation (20.50), F now denotes the current futures price. The other four variables are as before — time to maturity, volatility of the underlying futures price, exercise price, and risk-free rate. Note that Equation (20.50) differs from Equation (20.40) only in one respect: By substituting $\mathrm{e}^{-rT}F$ for S in the original Equation (20.40), Equation (20.50) is obtained. This holds because the investment in a futures contract is zero, which causes the interest rate in Equations (20.51) and (20.52) to drop out.

Fifth, three important papers by Harrison and Kreps (1979) and Kreps (1981, 1982) consider some foundational issues that arise in conjunction with the arbitrage theory of option pricing. The important point to consider is this: The ability to trade securities frequently can enable a few multiperiod securities to span many states of nature. In the Black–Scholes theory, there are two securities and uncountable many states of nature, but because there are infinitely many trading opportunities and because uncertainty resolves nicely, markets are effectively complete. Thus, even though there are far fewer securities than states of nature, markets are complete and risk is allocated efficiently. An interesting result of Harrison and Kreps (1979) is that certain self-trading strategies can create something out of nothing when there are infinitely many trading opportunities. The doubling strategies are the well-known illustrations of this phenomenon. Harrison and Kreps introduce the concept of a simple strategy to eliminate free lunches and conjecture that a non-negative wealth constraint could rule out the doubling strategies. Duffie and Huang (1985) gave an interpretation of admissible strategy as a limit of a sequence of simple strategies and used an integrability condition on the trading strategies. Dybvig and Huang (1986) showed that under certain conditions, the non-negative wealth constraints are functionally equivalent.

Finally, for an intensive survey of numerous empirical tests, see Galai (1983).

20.8 Summary

This chapter has discussed the basic concepts and equations of stochastic calculus (Itô's calculus), which has become a very useful tool in understanding finance theory and practice. By using these concepts and equations, the manner in which Black and Scholes derived their famous option pricing model was also illustrated.

Questions and Problems

1. Briefly describe Itô's lemma and Itô process.
2. Describe the meaning of the process of a stock price $S(t, w)$ that follows the stochastic process

$$dS(t, w) = \mu S(t, w)dt + \sigma S(t, w)dZ(t, w).$$

3. Derive the Black–Scholes call option model by using Itô's lemma and the stochastic process of a stock price $S(t, w)$ in Question 2.
4. Assume the stock price $S(t, w)$ in Question 2. What is the process of the variable $S^n(t, w)$? (Hint: Show that $S^n(t, w)$ also follows the same stochastic process.)
5. Assume the stock price $S(t, w)$ in Question 2. Let $\mu = 0.15$ and $\sigma = 0.2$ in the first two years and $\mu = 0.28$ and $\sigma = 0.35$ in the last year. Today, stock price is \$50.
   (a) What is the probability distribution of the stock price at the end of two years?
   (b) What is the probability distribution of the stock price at the end of three years?
6. Assume the stock price $S(t, w)$ follows the stochastic process

$$dS(t, w) = \mu dt + \sigma dZ(t, w).$$

Is this process more appropriate than the process in Question 2? Why or why not?

7. Assume the stock price $S(t, w)$ in Question 6. Let $\mu = 1.5$, $\sigma = 2$ and now the stock price is \$110.
   (a) What is the probability distribution of the stock price in the next year?
   (b) What are 95% confidence limits for the stock price in the next year?
8. Assume the stock price $S(t, w)$ in Question 2 again. Suppose the expected return of stock price equals 7% and volatility is 25% per year, and now the stock price is \$100.
   (a) What is the expected stock price at the end of six months?
   (b) What is the standard deviation of the stock price at the end of six months?
   (c) What is the expected stock price next year?
9. Assume the stock price $S(t, w)$ in Question 2 again. Derive the process of Y under the conditions as follows:
   (a) $Y = 3S(t, w)$
   (b) $Y = S^n(t, w)$
   (c) $Y = e^{r(T-t)}S(t, w)$.
10. Assume the stock price $S(t, w)$ in Question 5. What is the probability that the stock price will be greater than \$130 in two years?

Bibliography

Arnold, L. (1974). *Stochastic Differential Equation: Theory and Applications.* New York, NY: John Wiley & Sons.

Bhattacharya, M. (1980). Empirical properties of the Black-Scholes formula under ideal conditions. *Journal of Financial Quantitative Analysis*, 15(December), 1081–1105.

Black, F. (1976). The pricing of commodity contracts. *Journal of Financial Economics*, 3(January–March), 167–178.

Black, F. and M. Scholes (1973). The pricing of options and corporate liabilities. *Journal of Political Economy*, 81(May/June), 637–654.

Boyle, P. P. and A. L. Ananthanarayanan (1977). The impact of variance estimation in option valuation models. *Journal of Financial Economics*, 5(September), 375–387.

Brealey, R. and S. Myers (1988). *Principles of Corporate Finance*, 3rd ed. New York: McGraw-Hill.

Brennan, M. and E. Schwartz (1979). A continuous time approach to the pricing of bonds. *Journal of Banking and Finance*, 3(July), 133–155.

Brennan, M. and E. Schwartz (1978). Finite difference method and jump processes arising in the pricing of contingent claims: A synthesis. *Journal of Financial Quantitative Analysis*, 13(September), 461–474.

Courtadon, G. (1982). A more accurate finite difference approximation for the valuation of options. *Journal of Financial Quantitative Analysis*, 17(December), 697–705.

Cox, J. C. and S. A. Ross (1976). The valuation of options for alternative stochastic processes. *Journal of Financial Economics*, 3(March), 145–226.

Cox, J. C. and M. Rubinstein (1985). *Options Markets.* Englewood Cliffs, NJ: Prentice-Hall.

Duffie, D. and C. Huang (1985). Implementing Arrow-Debreu equilibria by continuous trading of few long-lived securities. *Econometrica*, 53(December), 1337–1356.

Dybvig, P. and C. Huang (1986). Optimal portfolios and positive wealth constraint. Yale University School of Management Working Paper.

Galai, D. (1983). A survey of empirical tests of option-pricing models, in M. Brenner (ed.), *Option Pricing*, pp. 45–80. Lexington, MA: Lexington Books.

Garven, J. R. (1986). A pedagogic note on the derivation of the Black–Scholes option pricing formula. *The Financial Review*, 21(November), 337–344.

Geske, R. and K. Shostri (1985). Valuation by approximation: A comparison of alternative option valuation techniques. *Journal of Financial Quantitative Analysis*, 20(March), 45–71.

Gikhman, I. and A. V. Skorokhod (1969). *Investment to the Theory of Random Processes.* Philadelphia, PA: W. B. Saunders.

Harrison, J. M. and D. M. Kreps (1979). Martingales and arbitrage in multiperiod securities markets. *Journal of Economic Theory*, 20, 381–408.

Harrison, J. and S. Pliska (1981). Martingales and stochastic integrals in the theory of continuous trading. *Stochastic Processes and Their Application*, 2, 261–271.

Ingersoll, J. E. (1976). A theoretical and empirical investigation of the dual purpose funds: An application of contingent claims and analysis. *Journal of Financial Economics*, 3(March), 83–123.

Itô, K. and H. McKean (1964). *Diffusion Processes and Their Sample Paths.* New York, NY: Academic Press.

Jarrow, R. and A. Rudd (1982). Approximate option valuation for arbitrary stochastic processes. *Journal of Financial Economics*, 10(November), 347–370.

Jarrow, R. and A. Rudd (1983). *Option Pricing.* Homewood, IL: R. D. Irwin.

Kreps, D. M. (1981). Arbitrage and equilibrium in economics with infinitely many commodities. *Journal of Mathematical Economics*, 8(March), 15–35.

Kreps, D. M. (1982). Multiperiod securities and the efficient allocation of risk: A comment on the Black–Scholes option pricing model, in J. J. McCall (ed.), *The Economics of Information and Uncertainty*, pp. 203–232. Chicago, IL: University of Chicago Press.

Latané, H. A. and R. J. Rendleman Jr (1976). Standard derivations of stock price ratios implied in option prices. *Journal of Finance*, 31(May), 369–381.

Lee, C. F., Y. Chen and J. Lee (2016). Alternative methods to derive option pricing models: Review and comparison. *Review of Quantitative Finance and Accounting*, 47(2), 417–451.

MacBeth, J. D. and L. J. Merville (1979). An empirical examination of the Black–Scholes call option pricing model. *Journal of Finance*, 34(December), 1173–1186.

Malliaris, A. G. and W. A. Brock (1982). *Stochastic Methods in Economics and Finance.* Amsterdam: North-Holland.

Merton, R. C. (1976). Option pricing when underlying stock returns are discontinuous. *Journal of Financial Economics*, 3(January–March), 125–144.

Merton, R. C. (1982). On the mathematics and economics assumption of continuous-time model, in W. F. Sharpe and C. M. Cootner (eds.), *Financial Economics: Essay in Honor of Paul Cootner*, pp. 19–51. Englewood Cliffs, NJ: Prentice-Hall.

Merton, R. C. (1975). Theory of finance from the perspective of continuous time. *Journal of Financial Quantitative Analysis*, 10(December), 659–674.

Merton, R. C. (1973). The theory of rational option pricing. *Bell Journal of Economics and Management Science*, 4(Spring), 141–183.

Roll, R. (1977). An analytic valuation formula for unprotected American call options on stocks with known dividends. *Journal of Financial Economics*, 5(May), 251–281.

Rubinstein, M. (1976). The valuation of uncertain income streams and the pricing of options. *Bell Journal of Economics*, 7(Fall), 407–425.

Scholes, M. (1976). Taxes and the pricing of options. *Journal of Finance*, 31(May), 319–332.

Smith, C. W. Jr. (1976). Option pricing: A review. *Journal of Financial Economics*, 3(January–March), 3–51.

Smith, C. W. Jr. (1979). Applications of option pricing analysis, in J. L. Bicksler (ed.), *Handbook of Financial Economics*. Amsterdam: North-Holland, pp. 79–121.

Appendix 20A: An Alternative Method to Derive the Black–Scholes Option Pricing Model

Perhaps it is unclear why it is assumed that investors have risk-neutral preferences when the usual assumption in finance courses is that investors are risk-averse. It is feasible to make this simplistic assumption because investors are able to create riskless portfolios by combining call options with their underlying securities. Since the creation of a riskless hedge places no restrictions on investor preferences other than non-satiation, the valuation of the option and its underlying asset will be independent of investor risk preferences. Therefore, a call option will trade at the same price in a risk-neutral economy as it will in a risk-averse or risk-preferent economy.

To derive the Black–Scholes formula, it is assumed that there are no transaction costs, no margin requirements, and no taxes; that all shares are infinitely divisible, and that continuous trading can be accomplished. It is also assumed that the economy is risk neutral.

In the risk-neutral assumptions of Cox and Ross (1976) and Rubinstein (1976), today's option price can be determined by discounting the expected value of the terminal option price by the riskless rate of interest. As was seen earlier, the terminal call option price can take on only two values: $S_t - X$, if the call option expires in the money, or 0 if the call expires out of the money. So, today's call option price is

$$C = \exp(-rt)\text{Max}(S_t - X, 0), \tag{20A.1}$$

where C = the market value of the call option, r = riskless rate of interest, t = time to expiration, S_t = the market value of the underlying stock at time t, and X = exercise or striking price.

Equation (20A.1) says that the value of the call option today will be either $S_t - X$ or 0, whichever is greater. If the price of stock at time t is greater than the exercise price, the call option will expire in the money. This simply means that an investor who owns the call option will exercise it. The option will be exercised regardless of whether the option holder would like to take physical possession of the stock. If the investor would like to own the stock, the cheapest way to obtain the stock is by exercising the option. If the investor would not like to own the stock, he or she will still exercise the option and immediately sell the stock in the market. Since the price the investor paid (X) is lower than the price he or she can sell the stock for (S_t), the investor realizes an immediate profit of $S_t - X$. If the price of the stock (S_t) is less than the exercise price (X), the option expires out of the money. This occurs because in purchasing shares of the stock the investor will find it cheaper to purchase the stock in the market than to exercise the option.

Assuming that the call option expires in the money, then the present value of the expected terminal option is equal to the present value of the difference between the expected terminal stock price and the exercise price, as indicated in Equation (20A.2):

$$\begin{aligned} C &= \exp(-rt)E[\text{Max}(S_t - X, 0)] \\ &= \exp(-rt)\int_x^\infty (S_t - X)h(S_t)dS_t, \end{aligned} \tag{20A.2}$$

where $h(S_t)$ is the log-normal density function of S_t. To evaluate the integral in Equation (20A.2), rewrite it as the difference between two integrals:

$$\begin{aligned} C &= \exp(-rt)\left[\int_x^\infty S_t h(S_t)dS_t - X\int_x^\infty h(S_t)dS_t\right] \\ &= E_x(S_t)\cdot\exp(-rt) - X\cdot\exp(-rt)\cdot[1 - H(X)], \end{aligned} \tag{20A.3}$$

where $E_x(S_t)$ = the partial expectation of S_t, truncated from below at x, and $H(X)$ = the probability that $S_t \leq X$.

Equation (20A.3) says that the value of the call option is the present value of the partial expected stock price (assuming the call expires in the money) minus the present value of the exercise price (adjusted by the probability that the stock's price will be less than the exercise price at the expiration of the option). The terminal stock price S_t can be rewritten as the product of the current price (S) and the t-period log-normally distributed price ratio S_t/S, so $S_t = S(S_t/S)$. Equation (20A.3) can also be rewritten as

$$C = \exp(-rt)\left[S\int_{x/s}^{\infty}\frac{S_t}{S}g\left(\frac{S_t}{S}\right)\left(\frac{dS_t}{S}\right) - X\int_{x/s}^{\infty}g\left(\frac{S_t}{S}\right)\left(\frac{dS_t}{S}\right)\right]$$

$$= S\exp(-rt)E_{x/S}\left(\frac{S_t}{S}\right) - X\exp(-rt)\left[1 - G\left(\frac{X}{S}\right)\right], \quad (20\text{A}.4)$$

where $g\left(\frac{S_t}{S}\right)$ = log normal density function of S_t/S, $E_{x/S}\left(\frac{S_t}{S}\right)$ = the partial expextation of S_t/S, truncated from below at x/S, and $G\left(\frac{X}{S}\right)$ = the probability that $S_t/S \leq X/S$.

Appendix 20B: Present Value of the Partial Expectation of the Terminal Stock Price

The right-hand side of Equation (20A.4) is evaluated by considering the two integrals separately. The first integral, $S\exp(-rt)E_{x/S}$ (S_t/S), can be solved by assuming the return on the underlying stock follows a stationary random walk. That is,

$$\frac{S_t}{S} = \exp(Kt), \quad (20\text{B}.1)$$

where K is the rate of return on the underlying stock per unit of time. Taking the natural logarithm of both sides of Equation (20A.5) yields

$$\ln\left(\frac{S_t}{S}\right) = (Kt).$$

Since the ratio S_t/S is log-normally distributed, it follows that Kt is log-normally distributed with density $f(Kt)$, mean $\mu_K t$, and variance $\sigma_K^2 t$. Because $S_t/S = \exp(Kt)$, the differential can be rewritten as $dS_t/S = \exp(Kt)tdK$. $g(S_t/S)$ is a density function of a log-normally distributed variable S_t/S; so, following Garven (1986), it can be transformed into a density function of a normally distributed variable Kt according to the relationship $S_t/S = \exp(Kt)$ as

$$g\left(\frac{S_t}{S}\right) = f(Kt)\left(\frac{S_t}{S}\right). \tag{20B.2}$$

These transformations allow the first integral in Equation (20A.4) to be rewritten as

$$S\exp(-rt)E_{x/S}\left(\frac{S_t}{S}\right) = S\exp(-rt)\int_{\ln(x/S)}^{\infty} f(Kt)\exp(Kt)tdK.$$

Because Kt is normally distributed, the density $f(Kt)$ with mean $\mu_K t$ and variance $\sigma_K^2 t$ is

$$f(Kt) = (2\pi\sigma_K^2 t)^{-1/2}\exp\left[-\tfrac{1}{2}(Kt-\mu_K t)^2/\sigma_K^2\right].$$

Substitution yields

$$\begin{aligned} &S\exp(-rt)E_{x/S}\left(\frac{S_t}{S}\right) \\ &\quad = S\exp(-rt)(2\pi\sigma_K^2 t)^{-1/2} \\ &\qquad \times \int_{\ln(x/S)}^{\infty} \exp[Kt]\exp[-\tfrac{1}{2}(Kt-\mu_K t)^2/\sigma_K^2 t]tdK. \end{aligned} \tag{20B.3}$$

The integrand of Equation (20B.3) can be simplified by adding the terms in the two exponents, multiplying and dividing the result by $\exp(-\frac{1}{2}\sigma_K^2 t)$. First, expand the term $(Kt-\mu_K t)^2$ and factor out t so that

$$\exp[Kt]\exp\left[-\frac{1}{2}(Kt-\mu_K t)^2/\sigma_K^2 t\right].$$

Next, factor out t so

$$\exp(Kt)\exp\left\{-\frac{1}{2}t\left[(K^2-2\mu_K K+\mu_K^2)/\sigma_K^2\right]\right\}.$$

Now, combine the two exponents

$$\exp\left\{-\frac{1}{2}t[(K^2 - 2\mu_K K + \mu_K^2 - 2\sigma_K^2 K)/\sigma_K^2]\right\}.$$

Now, multiply and divide this result by $\exp(-\frac{1}{2}\sigma_K^2 t)$ to get

$$\exp\left\{-\frac{1}{2}t\left[(K^2 - 2\mu_K K + \mu_K^2 - 2\sigma_K^2 K + \sigma_K^4 - \sigma_K^4)/\sigma_K^2\right]\right\}.$$

Next, rearrange and combine terms to get

$$\exp\left\{(-\frac{1}{2}t)\left[(K - \mu_K - \sigma_K^2)^2 - \sigma_K^4 - 2\mu_K\sigma_K^2\right]/\sigma_K^2\right\}$$
$$= \left[(\mu_K + \frac{1}{2}\sigma_K^2)t\right]\exp\left\{-\frac{1}{2}[Kt - (\mu_K + \sigma_K^2)t]^2/\sigma_K^2 t\right\}. \tag{20B.4}$$

In Equation (20B.4), $\exp[(\mu_K + \frac{1}{2}\sigma_K^2)t] = E(S_t/S)$, the mean of the t-period log-normally distributed price ratio S_t/S. So, Equation (20B.3) becomes

$$S\exp(-rt)E_{x/S}\left(\frac{S_t}{S}\right)$$
$$= SE\left(\frac{S_t}{S}\right)\exp(-rt)(2\pi\sigma_K^2 t)^{-1/2}$$
$$\times\int_{\ln(x/S)}^{\infty}\exp(Kt)\exp\left\{-\frac{1}{2}[Kt - (\mu_K + \sigma_K^2)t]^2/\sigma_K^2 t\right\}. \tag{20B.5}$$

Since the equilibrium rate of return in a risk-neutral economy is the riskless rate, $E(S_t/S)$ may be rewritten as $\exp(rt)$:

$$SE\left(\frac{S_t}{S}\right)\exp(-rt) = S\exp(rt)\exp(-rt) = S.$$

So, Equation (20B.5) becomes

$$S\exp(-rt)E_{x/S}\left(\frac{S_t}{S}\right) = S(2\pi\sigma_K^2 t)^{-1/2}\int_{\ln(x/S)}^{\infty}$$
$$\times\exp\left\{-\frac{1}{2}[Kt - (\mu_K + \sigma_K^2)t]^2/\sigma_K^2 t\right\}tdK. \tag{20B.6}$$

To complete the simplification of this part of the Black–Scholes formula, define a standard normal random variable y:

$$y = [Kt - (\mu_K + \sigma_K^2)t] \Big/ \sigma_K^2 t^{1/2}.$$

Solving for Kt yields

$$Kt = (\mu_K + \sigma_K^2)t + \sigma_K t^{1/2} y$$

and therefore

$$tdK = \sigma_K t^{1/2} dy.$$

By making the transformation from Kt to y, the lower limit of integration becomes

$$\left[\ln(x/S) - (\mu_K + \sigma_K^2)t\right] \Big/ \sigma_K t^{1/2}.$$

Further, simplify the integrand by noting that the assumption of a risk-neural economy implies

$$\exp\left[\left(\mu_K + \tfrac{1}{2}\sigma_K^2\right) t\right] = \exp(rt).$$

Taking the natural logarithm of both sides yields

$$\left(\mu_K + \tfrac{1}{2}\sigma_K^2\right) t = (rt).$$

Hence, $(\mu_K + \frac{1}{2}\sigma_K^2)t = (r + \frac{1}{2}\sigma_K^2)t$.

The lower limit of integration is now

$$-\left[\ln(S/x) + (r + \tfrac{1}{2}\sigma_K^2)t\right] \Big/ \sigma_K t^{1/2} = -d_1.$$

Substituting this into Equation (20B.6) and making the transformation to y yield

$$S\exp(-rt)E_{x/S}\left(\frac{S_t}{S}\right) = S\int_{-d_1}^{\infty} \exp\left(-\tfrac{1}{2}y\right)^2 \Big/ (2\pi)^{1/2} dy.$$

Since y is a standard normal random variable (distribution is symmetric around zero), the limits of integration can be exchanged:

$$\begin{aligned} S\exp(-rt)E_{x/S}\left(\frac{S_t}{S}\right) &= S\int_{\infty}^{-d_1} \exp\left(-\tfrac{1}{2}y^2\right) \Big/ (2\pi)^{1/2} dy \\ &= SN(d_1). \end{aligned} \tag{20B.7}$$

where $N(d_1)$ is the standard normal cumulative distribution function evaluated at $y = d_1$.

20B.1 *Present value of the exercise price under uncertainty*

To complete the derivation, the integrals that correspond to the term $X\exp(-rt)[1 - G(X/S)]$ must be evaluated. Start by making the logarithmic transformation:

$$\ln\left(\frac{S_t}{S}\right) = Kt.$$

This transformation allows the rewriting of $g(S_t/S)$ to $(S/S_t)f(Kt)$ as mentioned previously. The differential can be written as

$$d\frac{S_t}{S} = \exp(Kt)tdK.$$

Therefore,

$$X\exp(-rt)[1 - G(X/S)] = X\exp(-rt)\int_{\ln(X/S)}^{\infty} f(Kt)tdK$$

$$= X\exp(-rt)(2\pi\sigma_K^2 t)^{-1/2}\int_{\ln(X/S)}^{\infty} \exp[-\tfrac{1}{2}(Kt - \mu_K t)^2/\sigma_K^2 t]tdK. \tag{20B.8}$$

The integrand is now simplified by following the same procedure used in simplifying the previous integral. Define a standard normal random variable Z:

$$Z = \left[\frac{Kt - \mu_K t}{\sigma_K t^{1/2}}\right].$$

Solving for Kt yields

$$Kt = \mu_K t + \sigma_K t^{1/2} Z,$$

and $tdK = \sigma_K t^{1/2} dZ$. Making the transformation from Kt to Z means the lower limit of integration becomes

$$\frac{\ln(X/S) - \mu_K t}{\sigma_K t^{1/2}}.$$

Again, note that the assumption of a risk-neutral economy implies

$$\exp\left(\mu_K + \tfrac{1}{2}\sigma_K^2 t\right) = \exp(rt).$$

Taking the natural logarithm of both sides yields

$$\left(\mu_K + \tfrac{1}{2}\sigma_K^2\right) t = rt$$

or

$$\mu_K t = \left(r - \tfrac{1}{2}\sigma_K^2\right) t.$$

Therefore, the lower limit of integration becomes

$$\frac{-[\ln(S/x) + (r - \frac{1}{2}\sigma_K^2)t]}{\sigma_K t^{1/2}} = -(d_1 - \sigma_K t^{1/2})$$
$$= -d_2.$$

Substitution yields

$$\begin{aligned}
&x \exp(-rt)[1 - G(X/S)] \\
&\quad = x \exp(-rt) \int_{-d_2}^{\infty} \exp\left[-\tfrac{1}{2}Z^2 \Big/ (2\pi)^{1/2}\right] dZ \\
&\quad = x \exp(-rt) \int_{-\infty}^{d_2} \exp\left[-\tfrac{1}{2}Z^2 \Big/ (2\pi)^{1/2}\right] dZ \\
&\quad = x \exp(-rt) N(d_2), \qquad (20B.9)
\end{aligned}$$

where $N(d_2)$ is the standard normal cumulative distribution function evaluated at $Z = d_2$.

Substituting Equations (20B.7) and (20B.9) into Equation (20A.4) completes the derivation of the Black–Scholes formula:

$$C = SN(d_1) - X \exp(-rt) N(d_2). \qquad (20B.10)$$

This appendix provides a simple derivation of the Black–Scholes call option pricing formula. Under an assumption of risk neutrality, the Black–Scholes formula was derived using only differential and integral calculus and a basic knowledge of normal and log-normal distributions.

Chapter 21

Alternative Methods for Estimating Hedge Ratios: Theory and Empirical Results*

Contents

*This chapter is a modification of Chapter 74 of Lee, C.-F. and A. C. Lee (2022). *Encyclopedia of Finance*, 3rd ed. New York: Springer.

21.1 Introduction

A **future contract** is a standardized legal agreement between a buyer and a seller, who promise now to exchange a specified amount of money for goods or services at a future time. Of course, there is nothing really unusual about a contract made in advance of delivery. For instance, whenever something is ordered rather than purchased on the spot, a futures (or forward) contract is involved. Although the price is determined at the time of the order, the actual exchange of cash for the merchandise takes place later. For some items, the lag is a few days, while for others (such as a car) it may be months. Moreover, a futures contract imparts a legal obligation to both parties of the contract to fulfill the specifications. To guarantee fulfillment of this obligation, a "good-faith" deposit, also called **margin**, may be required from the buyer (and the seller, if he or she does not already own the product). This chapter both theoretically and empirically extends hedge ratios which have been discussed in Chapters 4 and 5.

There are five sections in this chapter. In Section 21.2, we present an overall view of hedge ratios. In Section 21.3, theories used for deriving the static optimal hedge ratios are carefully reviewed. Section 21.4 will use three alternative estimation methods to perform an empirical study to estimate minimal hedge ratios. Finally, in Section 21.5, we provide a summary. Appendix 21A presents the monthly data of S&P 500 index and its future from January 2005 to August 2020, and Appendix 21B explains the applications of R language in estimating three optimal hedge ratios.

21.2 Overall View of Hedge Ratios

Future contracts are frequently used to hedge spot contracts to reduce the risk. Therefore, hedge ratio estimation is important for risk management. One of the best uses of derivative securities such as futures contracts is to hedge the risk. For the last half century, both academicians and practitioners have shown great interest in the issue of hedging with futures; therefore, theoretical analysis and empirical investigation for future hedge ratio are important for both academicians and practitioners. This is quite evident from the large number of articles written in this area. In this section, we will review some important literature related to hedge ratio.

The main theoretical issue in hedging involves the determination of the optimal hedge ratio. However, the optimal hedge ratio depends on the particular objective function to be optimized. In this chapter, we will first carefully discuss different objective functions used to derive optimal hedge ratio. For example, one of the most widely used hedging strategies is based on the minimization of the variance of the hedged portfolio (e.g., see Johnson, 1960; Ederington, 1979; Myers and Thompson, 1989). This so-called minimum-variance (MV) hedge ratio is simple to understand and estimate. However, the MV hedge ratio completely ignores the expected return of the hedged portfolio. Therefore, this strategy is inconsistent with the mean-variance trade-off framework unless the individuals are infinitely risk averse or the futures price follows a pure martingale process (i.e., expected futures price change is zero).

Some more realistic strategies that incorporate both the expected return and risk (variance) of the hedged portfolio have been developed (e.g., see Howard and D'Antonio, 1984; Cecchetti *et al.*, 1988; Hsin *et al.*, 1994). These strategies are consistent with the mean-variance framework. In fact, it can be shown that if the futures price follows a pure martingale process, then the optimal mean-variance hedge ratio will be reduced to the MV hedge ratio.

Another aspect of the mean-variance-based strategies is that even though they are an improvement over the MV strategy, for them to be consistent with the expected utility maximization principle, either the utility function needs to be quadratic or the returns should be jointly normal. Unless these assumptions are valid, then the hedge ratio may not be optimal with respect to the expected utility maximization principle. Some research has solved this problem by deriving the optimal hedge ratio based on the maximization of the expected utility (e.g., see Cecchetti *et al.*, 1988; Lence, 1995, 1996). It should be noted that this approach requires the use of specific utility function and specific return distribution.

Attempts have been made to eliminate these specific assumptions regarding the utility function and return distributions. Some of them involve the minimization of the mean extended-Gini (MEG) coefficient, which is consistent with the concept of stochastic dominance (e.g., see Cheung *et al.*, 1990; Kolb and Okunev, 1992, 1993; Lien and Luo, 1993a; Shalit, 1995; Lien and Shaffer, 1999). Shalit (1995) shows that if the prices are normally distributed, then the MEG-based hedge ratio will be the same as the MV hedge ratio.

Recently, hedge ratios based on the generalized semivariance (GSV) or lower partial moments have been proposed (e.g., see De Jong *et al.*, 1997; Lien and Tse, 1998, 2000; Chen *et al.*, 2001). These hedge ratios are also consistent with the concept of stochastic dominance. Furthermore, these GSV-based hedge ratios have another attractive feature whereby they measure portfolio risk by the GSV, which is consistent with the risk perceived by managers, because of its emphasis on the returns below the target return (see Crum *et al.*, 1981; Lien and Tse, 2000). Lien and Tse (1998) show that if the futures and spot returns are jointly normally distributed and if the futures price follows a pure martingale process, then the minimum-GSV hedge ratio will be equal to the MV hedge ratio. Finally, Hung *et al.* (2006) have proposed a related hedge ratio that minimizes the Value at Risk associated with the hedged portfolio when choosing the hedge ratio. This hedge ratio will also be equal to the MV hedge ratio if the futures price follows a pure martingale process. However, the future price in general does not follow the pure martingale process; therefore, the generalized hedge ratio should be considered to improve the effectiveness of the hedging decision.

It should be noted that most of the studies mentioned above (except Lence, 1995, 1996) ignore transaction costs as well as investments in other securities. Lence (1995, 1996) derives the optimal hedge ratio where transaction costs and investments in other securities are incorporated in the model. Using a constant absolute risk aversion (CARA) utility function, Lence finds that under certain circumstances the optimal hedge ratio is zero; that is, the optimal hedging strategy is not to hedge at all.

In addition to the use of different objective functions in the derivation of the optimal hedge ratio, previous studies also differ in terms of the dynamic nature of the hedge ratio. For example, some studies assume that the hedge ratio is constant over time. Consequently, these static hedge ratios are estimated using unconditional probability distributions (e.g., see Ederington, 1979; Howard and D'Antonio, 1984; Benet, 1992; Kolb and Okunev, 1992, 1993; Ghosh, 1993). On the other hand, several studies allow the hedge ratio to change over time. In some cases, these dynamic hedge ratios are estimated using conditional distributions associated with models such as ARCH and GARCH (e.g., see Cecchetti *et al.*, 1988; Baillie and Myers, 1991; Kroner and Sultan, 1993; Sephton, 1993). The GARCH-based method has recently been extended by Lee and Yoder (2007) where a regime-switching model is used. Alternatively, the hedge ratios can be made dynamic by considering a multiperiod model where the hedge ratios are allowed to vary for different periods. This is the method used by Lien and Luo (1993b).

When it comes to estimating the hedge ratios, many different techniques are currently being employed, ranging from simple to complex ones. For example, some of them use a simple method such as the ordinary least squares (OLS) technique (e.g., see Ederington, 1979; Malliaris and Urrutia, 1991; Benet, 1992). However, others use more complex methods such as the conditional heteroscedastic (ARCH or GARCH) method (e.g., see Cecchetti *et al.*, 1988; Baillie and Myers, 1991; Sephton, 1993), the random coefficient method (e.g., see Grammatikos and Saunders, 1983), the cointegration method (e.g., see Ghosh, 1993; Lien and Luo, 1993b; Chou *et al.*, 1996), or the cointegration-heteroscedastic method (e.g., see Kroner and Sultan, 1993). Recently, Lien and Shrestha (2007), Maghyereh *et al.* (2019), and Sultan *et al.* (2019) have suggested the use of wavelet analysis to match the data frequency with the hedging horizon. Finally, Lien and Shrestha (2010) also suggest the use of multivariate skew-normal distribution in estimating the minimum-variance hedge ratio.

By now, it is clear that there are several different ways of deriving and estimating hedge ratios. In the next section, we will discuss alternative theories for deriving static hedge ratios. In addition, we will also use S&P 500 index future data to show how three different econometrics methods can be used to estimate hedge ratios.

21.3 Theories Used for Deriving the Static Optimal Hedge Ratios

By combining investments in the spot market and futures market to form a portfolio, we can eliminate (or reduce) fluctuations in its value by hedging. Consider a portfolio consisting of C_s units of a long spot position and C_f units of a short futures position.[1] Following Lee *et al.* (2013) and Chen *et al.* (2003), let S_t and F_t denote the spot and futures prices at time t, respectively. Since the futures contracts are used to reduce the fluctuations in spot positions, the resulting portfolio is known as the hedged portfolio. If the hedge ratio is discussed in terms of price changes (profits), then the profit on the hedged portfolio, ΔV_H, and the hedge ratio, H, is given by the following:

$$\Delta V_H = C_s \Delta S_t - H C_f \Delta F_t \quad \text{and} \quad H = \frac{C_f}{C_s}, \tag{21.1}$$

where $\Delta S_t = S_{t+1} - S_t$ and $\Delta F_t = F_{t+1} - F_t$.

The main objective of hedging is to determine and estimate the optimal hedge ratio (either h or H). It should be noted that optimal hedge ratio will depend on a particular objective function to be used. Hedge ratio can be classified into either static hedge ratio or dynamic hedge ratio.

It is important to note that in the above setup, the cash position is assumed to be fixed and we only look for the optimum futures position. Most of the hedging literature assumes that the cash position is fixed, a setup that is suitable for financial futures. However, when we are dealing with commodity futures, the initial cash position becomes an important decision variable that is tied to the production decision, which has been discussed by Lence (1995, 1996).

Static hedge ratio means the hedge ratio remains constant over time. Based upon Chen *et al.* (2003), there are nine static hedge ratios as follows: (a) Minimum-Variance Hedge Ratio, (b) Optimum Mean-Variance Hedge Ratio, (c) Sharpe Hedge Ratio, (d) Maximum Expected Utility Hedge Ratio, (e) Minimum Mean Extended-Gini Coefficient Hedge Ratio, (f) Optimum Mean-MEG Hedge Ratio, (g) Minimum Generalized Semivariance Hedge Ratio, (h) Optimum Mean-Generalized Semivariance Hedge Ratio, and (i) Minimum Value-at-Risk Hedge Ratio. In this section, we will discuss static hedge ratios (a), (b), (c), and (i) in detail. The information for the other five static hedge ratios can be found in Chen *et al.* (2003).

[1]Without loss of generality, we assume that the size of the future contract is 1.

21.3.1 *Minimum-Variance Hedge Ratio*

The most widely used static hedge ratio is the MV hedge ratio. Johnson (1960) derives this hedge ratio by minimizing the portfolio risk, where the risk is given by the variance of changes in the value of the hedged portfolio as follows:

$$\mathrm{Var}(\Delta V_H) = C_s^2\,\mathrm{Var}(\Delta S) + C_f^2\,\mathrm{Var}(\Delta F) - 2C_sC_fH\,\mathrm{Cov}(\Delta S, \Delta F).$$

The MV hedge ratio, in this case, is given by the following:

$$H_J^* = \frac{C_f}{C_s} = \frac{\mathrm{Cov}(\Delta S, \Delta F)}{\mathrm{Var}(\Delta F)}. \tag{21.2a}$$

Alternatively, if we use $\mathrm{Var}(R_h)$ to represent the risk of a hedged portfolio return (R_h), then the MV hedge ratio is obtained by minimizing $\mathrm{Var}(R_h)$ which is given by the following:

$$\mathrm{Var}(R_h) = \mathrm{Var}(R_s) + h^2\,\mathrm{Var}(R_f) - 2h\,\mathrm{Cov}(R_s, R_f).$$

where h is the so-called hedge ratio, and R_s and R_f are so-called one-period returns on the spot and futures positions, respectively. In this case, the MV hedge ratio is given by the following:

$$h_J^* = \frac{\mathrm{Cov}(R_s, R_f)}{\mathrm{Var}(R_f)} = \rho\frac{\sigma_s}{\sigma_f}, \tag{21.2b}$$

where ρ is the correlation coefficient between R_s and R_f, and σ_s and σ_f are standard deviations of R_s and R_f, respectively.

The attractive features of the MV hedge ratio are that it is easy to understand and simple to compute. However, in general, the MV hedge ratio is not consistent with the mean-variance framework since it ignores the expected return on the hedged portfolio. For the MV hedge ratio to be consistent with the mean-variance framework, either the investors need to be infinitely risk averse or the expected return on the futures contract needs to be zero.

21.3.2 *Optimum Mean-Variance Hedge Ratio*

Various studies have incorporated both risk and return in the derivation of the hedge ratio. For example, Hsin *et al.* (1994) derive the optimal hedge ratio that maximizes the following utility function:

$$\underset{C_f}{\text{Max}}\ V(E(R_h), \sigma; A) = E(R_h) - 0.5A\sigma_h^2, \tag{21.3}$$

where A represents the risk aversion parameter. It is clear that this utility function incorporates both risk and return. Therefore, the hedge ratio based on this utility function would be consistent with the mean-variance framework. The optimal number of futures contract and the optimal hedge ratio are given by the following:

$$h_2 = -\frac{C_f^* F}{C_s S} = -\left[\frac{E(R_f)}{A\sigma_f^2} - \rho\frac{\sigma_s}{\sigma_f}\right]. \tag{21.4}$$

One problem associated with this type of hedge ratio is that in order to derive the optimum hedge ratio, we need to know the individual's risk aversion parameter. Furthermore, different individuals will choose different optimal hedge ratios, depending on the values of their risk aversion parameter.

Since the MV hedge ratio is easy to understand and simple to compute, it will be interesting and useful to know under what condition the above hedge ratio would be the same as the MV hedge ratio. It can be seen from Equations (21.2b) and (21.4) that if $A \to \infty$ or $E(R_f) = 0$, then h_2 would be equal to the MV hedge ratio h_J^*. The first condition is simply a restatement of the infinitely risk-averse individuals. However, the second condition does not impose any condition on the risk averseness, and this is important. It implies that even if the individuals are not infinitely risk averse, then the MV hedge ratio would be the same as the optimal mean-variance hedge ratio if the expected return on the futures contract is zero (i.e., futures prices follow a simple martingale process). Therefore, if futures prices follow a simple martingale process, then we do not need to know the risk aversion parameter of the investor to find the optimal hedge ratio.

21.3.3 *Sharpe Hedge Ratio*

Another way of incorporating the portfolio return in the hedging strategy is to use the risk–return trade-off (Sharpe measure) criteria. Howard and D'Antonio (1984) consider the optimal level of futures contracts by maximizing the ratio of the portfolio's excess return to its volatility:

$$\underset{C_f}{\text{Max}}\ \theta = \frac{E(R_h) - R_F}{\sigma_h}, \tag{21.5}$$

where C_f is the level of futures contracts, $\sigma_h^2 = \text{Var}(R_h)$, and R_F represents the risk-free interest rate.

The classic one-to-one hedge is a naïve strategy based upon a broadly defined objective of risk minimization. The strategy is naïve in the sense that a hedging coefficient of one is used regardless of past or expected correlations of spot and futures price changes. Working's strategy brings out the speculative aspects of hedging by analyzing changes in the basis and, accordingly, exercising discrete judgment about when to hedge and when not to hedge. The underlying objective of Working's decision rule for hedgers is one of profit maximization. Finally, Johnson (1960), in applying the mean-variance criteria of modern portfolio theory, emphasizes the risk minimization objective but defines risk in terms of the variance of the hedged position. Although Johnson's method improves on the naïve strategy of a one-to-one hedge, it essentially disregards the return component associated with a particular level of risk. Rutledge (1972) uses both mean and variance information to derive hedge ratio.

Howard and D'Antonio (1984) use an objective function defined in Equation (21.5) to derive the hedge ratio as defined in Equation (21.6).

In deriving this hedge ratio, they use a mean-variance framework, and their strategy begins by assuming that the "agent" is out to maximize the expected return for a given level of portfolio risk. With a choice of putting money into three assets — a spot position, a futures contract, and a risk-free asset — the agent's optimal portfolio will depend on the relative risk–return characteristics of each asset. For a hedger, the optimal portfolio may contain a short futures position, a long futures position, or no futures position at all. In general, the precise futures position to be entered into will be determined by (1) the risk-free rate, (2) the expected returns and the standard deviations for the spot and futures positions, and (3) the correlation between the return on the spot position and the return on the futures.

$$\text{Hedge ratio } H = \frac{(\lambda - \rho)}{\gamma\pi(1 - \lambda\rho)}, \tag{21.6}$$

where $\pi = \sigma_f/\sigma_s$ = relative variability of futures and spot returns, $\alpha = \bar{r}_f/(\bar{r}_s - i)$ = relative excess return on futures to that of spot, $\gamma = P_f/P_s$ = current price ratio of futures to spot, $\lambda = \alpha/\pi = (\bar{r}_f/\sigma_f)/[(\bar{r}_s - i)/\sigma_s]$ = risk-to-excess-return relative of futures versus the spot position, P_s, P_f = the current price per unit for the spot and futures, respectively, ρ = simple correlation coefficient between the spot and futures returns, σ_s = standard deviation of spot returns, σ_f = standard deviation of futures returns, $\bar{r}_s$ = mean return on the spot over some recent past interval, $\bar{r}_f$ = mean return on the futures over some recent past interval, and i = risk-free rate.

Based upon Equations (21.6) and (21.1), Chen *et al.* (2003) have derived that the optimal number of futures positions, C_f^*, is given by the following:

$$C_f^* = -C_s \frac{\left(\frac{S}{F}\right)\left(\frac{\sigma_s}{\sigma_f}\right)\left[\frac{\sigma_s}{\sigma_f}\left(\frac{E(R_f)}{E(R_s)-R_F}\right) - \rho\right]}{\left[1 - \frac{\sigma_s}{\sigma_f}\left(\frac{E(R_f)\rho}{E(R_s)-R_F}\right)\right]}. \tag{21.7}$$

From the optimal futures position, we can obtain the following optimal hedge ratio:

$$h_3 = -\frac{\left(\frac{\sigma_s}{\sigma_f}\right)\left[\frac{\sigma_s}{\sigma_f}\left(\frac{E(R_f)}{E(R_s)-R_F}\right) - \rho\right]}{\left[1 - \frac{\sigma_s}{\sigma_f}\left(\frac{E(R_f)\rho}{E(R_s)-R_F}\right)\right]}. \tag{21.8a}$$

Again, if $E(R_f) = 0$, then h_3 reduces to the following:

$$h_3 = \left(\frac{\sigma_s}{\sigma_f}\right)\rho, \tag{21.8b}$$

which is the same as the MV hedge ratio h_J^*.

By analyzing the properties of λ, Howard and D'Antonio (1984) discern some important insights for the coordinated use of futures in a hedge portfolio. Numerically, λ expresses the relative attractiveness of investing in futures versus the spot position. When $\lambda < 1$, $\lambda = 1$, and $\lambda > 1$, the futures contract offers less, the same, and more excess return per unit of risk than the spot position, respectively. Since this analysis is being undertaken from a hedger's point of view, it is assumed that $\lambda < 1$. An assumption that $\lambda > 1$ would inappropriately imply that theoretically it is possible to hedge the futures position with the spot asset. In addition, they also consider the effect of the relationship of λ to ρ on the optimal hedge ratio, H. Other detailed analysis can be found in Table 4 of Howard and D'Antonio's (1984) paper.

21.3.4 *Minimum Value-at-Risk Hedge Ratio*

Hung *et al.* (2006) suggest a new hedge ratio that minimizes the Value at Risk of the hedged portfolio. Specifically, the hedge ratio h is derived by minimizing the following Value at Risk of the hedged portfolio over a given time period τ:

$$VaR(R_h) = Z_\alpha \sigma_h \sqrt{\tau} - E[R_h]\tau. \tag{21.9}$$

The resulting optimal hedge ratio, which Hung *et al.* (2006) refer to as zero-VaR hedge ratio, is given by

$$h^{VaR} = \rho \frac{\sigma_s}{\sigma_f} - E[R_f] \frac{\sigma_s}{\sigma_f} \sqrt{\frac{1 - \rho^2}{Z_\alpha^2 \sigma_f^2 - E[R_f]^2}}. \tag{21.10}$$

It is clear that if the futures price follows the martingale process, the zero-VaR hedge ratio would be the same as the MV hedge ratio.

21.4 Applications of OLS, GARCH, and CECM Models to Estimate Optimal Hedge Ratios

In this section, we will discuss three different approaches to estimating the optimum hedge ratios and apply these methods in practice to estimate the optimal stock index futures hedge ratio for S&P 500 index. We first introduce how to apply the ordinary least square (OLS) technique to estimating the optimum hedge ratios and discuss its limitations. Second, considering the heteroscedastic nature of the error term, the generalized autoregressive conditional heteroscedasticity (GARCH) technique is introduced to estimating the hedge ratios. In addition, we describe the cointegration and error correction method (CECM) to take into account the possibility of long-run equilibrium between spot and futures prices. Finally, we provide an empirical study on using OLS, GARCH, and CECM models to estimate the optimal stock index futures hedge ratios for the S&P 500 index through R language.

21.4.1 *OLS method*

The conventional approach to estimating the MV hedge ratio involves the regression of the changes in spot prices on the changes in futures price using the OLS technique (e.g., see Junkus and Lee, 1985). Specifically, the regression equation can be written as follows:

$$\Delta S_t = a_0 + a_1 \Delta F_t + e_t, \tag{21.12}$$

where the estimate of the MV hedge ratio, H_j, is given by a_1. The OLS technique is quite robust and simple to use. However, for the OLS technique to be valid and efficient, assumptions associated with the OLS regression must be satisfied. One case where the assumptions are not completely satisfied is that the error term in the regression is heteroscedastic. This situation will be discussed later.

Another problem with the OLS method, as pointed out by Myers and Thompson (1989), is the fact that it uses unconditional sample moments instead of conditional sample moments, which use currently available information. They suggest the use of the conditional covariance and conditional variance in Equation (21.2a). In this case, the conditional version of the optimal hedge ratio (Equation (21.2a)) will take the following form:

$$H_J^* = \frac{C_f}{C_s} = \frac{\mathrm{Cov}(\Delta S, \Delta F)|\Omega_{t-1}}{\mathrm{Var}(\Delta F)|\Omega_{t-1}}. \tag{21.2a}$$

Suppose that the current information (Ω_{t-1}) includes a vector of variables (X_{t-1}) and the spot and futures price changes are generated by the following equilibrium model:

$$\Delta S_t = X_{t-1}\alpha + u_t,$$
$$\Delta F_t = X_{t-1}\beta + v_t.$$

In this case, the maximum likelihood estimator of the MV hedge ratio is given by (see Myers and Thompson, 1989) the following:

$$\hat{h}|X_{t-1} = \frac{\hat{\sigma}_{uv}}{\hat{\sigma}_v^2}, \tag{21.13}$$

where $\hat{\sigma}_{uv}$ is the sample covariance between the residuals u_t and v_t, and $\hat{\sigma}_v^2$ is the sample variance of the residual v_t. In general, the OLS estimator obtained from Equation (21.12) would be different from the one given by Equation (21.13). For the two estimators to be the same, the spot and futures prices must be generated by the following model:

$$\Delta S_t = \alpha_0 + u_t, \quad \Delta F_t = \beta_0 + v_t.$$

In other words, if the spot and futures prices follow a random walk, then with or without drift, the two estimators will be the same. Otherwise, the hedge ratio estimated from the OLS regression (21.12) will not be optimal.

21.4.2 *GARCH method*

Ever since the development of the GARCH models, the OLS method of estimating the hedge ratio has been generalized to consider the heteroscedastic nature of the error term in Equation (21.12). In this case, rather than using the unconditional sample variance and covariance, the conditional variance and covariance from the GARCH model are used in the estimation of the hedge ratio. As mentioned above, such a technique allows an update of the hedge ratio over the hedging period.

Consider the following bivariate GARCH model (see Cecchetti *et al.*, 1988; Baillie and Myers, 1991):

$$\begin{bmatrix} \Delta S_t \\ \Delta F_t \end{bmatrix} = \begin{bmatrix} \mu_1 \\ \mu_2 \end{bmatrix} + \begin{bmatrix} e_{1t} \\ e_{2t} \end{bmatrix} \quad \text{and} \quad e_t|\Omega_{t-1} \sim N(0, H_t),$$

where Ω_{t-1} is all the available information up to time $t-1$. N denotes a bivariate normal distribution and H_t is a time-varying 2×2 positive-definite conditional variance–covariance matrix as follows:

$$H_t = \begin{bmatrix} H_{11,t} & H_{12,t} \\ H_{12,t} & H_{22,t} \end{bmatrix}.$$

The conditional MV hedge ratio at time t is given by $h_{t-1} = H_{12,t}/H_{22,t}$. This model allows the hedge ratio to change over time, resulting in a series of hedge ratios instead of a single hedge ratio for the entire hedging horizon.

In practice, it is necessary to model the conditional variance–covariance matrix and ensure the positive definiteness of H_t. Different models for H_t have been proposed in the literature, for example, Bollerslev (1988), Bollerslev *et al.* (1988), and Engle and Kroner (1995). Bollerslev (1988) built up a VECH-GARCH (1,1) model assuming that H_t is a linear combination of its own squared residual e'_{t-1} and past conditional variance–covariance variance H_{t-1} as follows:

$$\text{vec}(H_t) = C + A\,\text{vec}(e_{t-1}e'_{t-1}) + B\,\text{vec}(H_{t-1}),$$

where vec is the operator that stacks a matrix as a column vector. A and B are both 3×3 parameter matrices.

$$\text{vec}(H_t) = \begin{bmatrix} H_{11,t} \\ H_{12,t} \\ H_{22,t} \end{bmatrix} = \begin{bmatrix} c_{01,t} \\ c_{02,t} \\ c_{03,t} \end{bmatrix} + \begin{bmatrix} a_{11} & a_{12} & a_{13} \\ a_{21} & a_{22} & a_{23} \\ a_{31} & a_{32} & a_{33} \end{bmatrix} \begin{bmatrix} \varepsilon^2_{1,t-1} \\ \varepsilon_{1,t-1}\varepsilon_{2,t-1} \\ \varepsilon^2_{3,t-1} \end{bmatrix}$$

$$+ \begin{bmatrix} g_{11} & g_{12} & g_{13} \\ g_{21} & g_{22} & g_{23} \\ g_{31} & g_{32} & g_{33} \end{bmatrix} \begin{bmatrix} H_{11,t-1} \\ H_{12,t-1} \\ H_{13,t-1} \end{bmatrix}.$$

To simplify calculation, Bollerslev *et al.* (1988) suggest a diagonal VECH-GARCH (1,1) model where parameter matrices A and B are restricted to be diagonal.

$$\text{vec}(H_t) = \begin{bmatrix} H_{11,t} \\ H_{12,t} \\ H_{22,t} \end{bmatrix} = \begin{bmatrix} c_{11}^* \\ c_{12}^* \\ c_{22}^* \end{bmatrix} + \begin{bmatrix} a_{11}^* & 0 & 0 \\ 0 & a_{12}^* & 0 \\ 0 & 0 & a_{22}^* \end{bmatrix} \begin{bmatrix} \varepsilon_{1,t-1}^2 \\ \varepsilon_{1,t-1}\varepsilon_{2,t-1} \\ \varepsilon_{2,t-1}^2 \end{bmatrix} + \begin{bmatrix} g_{11}^* & 0 & 0 \\ 0 & g_{12}^* & 0 \\ 0 & 0 & g_{22}^* \end{bmatrix} \begin{bmatrix} H_{11,t-1} \\ H_{12,t-1} \\ H_{22,t-1} \end{bmatrix}.$$

21.4.3 *Cointegration and error correction method (CECM)*

The techniques described so far do not take into consideration the possibility that spot price and futures price series could be nonstationary. If these series have unit roots, then this will raise a different issue. If the two series are cointegrated as defined by Engle and Granger (1987), then the regression Equation (21.12) will be misspecified, and an error correction term must be included in the equation. Since the arbitrage condition ties the spot and futures prices, they cannot drift far apart in the long run. Therefore, if both series follow a random walk, then we expect the two series to be cointegrated in which case we need to estimate the error correction model (ECM). This calls for the use of the cointegration analysis. Therefore, the CECM should be used to estimate the hedge ratio.

The cointegration analysis involves two steps. First, each series must be tested for a unit root (e.g., see Dickey and Fuller, 1981; Phillips and Perron, 1988). Second, if both series are found to have a single unit root, then the cointegration test must be performed (e.g., see Engle and Granger, 1987; Johansen and Juselius, 1990; Osterwald-Lenum, 1992).

If the spot price and futures price series are found to be cointegrated, then the hedge ratio can be estimated in two steps (see Ghosh, 1993; Chou *et al.*, 1996). The first step involves the estimation of the following cointegrating regression:

$$S_t = a + bF_t + u_t. \tag{21.16}$$

The second step involves the estimation of the following ECM:

$$\Delta S_t = \rho u_{t-1} + \beta \Delta F_t + \sum_{i=1}^{m} \delta_i \Delta F_{t-i} + \sum_{j=1}^{n} \theta_i \Delta S_{t-j} + e_j, \quad (21.17)$$

where u_t is the residual series from the cointegrating regression. The estimate of the hedge ratio is given by the estimate of β. Some researchers (e.g., see Lien and Luo, 1993b) assume that the long-run cointegrating relationship is $(S_t - F_t)$, and estimate the following ECM:

$$\Delta S_t = \rho(S_{t-1} - F_{t-1}) + \beta \Delta F_t + \sum_{i=1}^{m} \delta_i \Delta F_{t-i} + \sum_{j=1}^{n} \theta_i \Delta S_{t-j} + e_j. \quad (21.18)$$

Alternatively, Chou *et al.* (1996) suggest the estimation of the ECM as follows:

$$\Delta S_t = \alpha \hat{u}_{t-1} + \beta \Delta F_t + \sum_{i=1}^{m} \delta_i \Delta F_{t-i} + \sum_{j=1}^{n} \theta_i \Delta S_{t-j} + e_j, \quad (21.19)$$

where $\hat{u}_{t-1} = S_{t-1} - (a + bF_{t-1})$; that is, the series $\hat{u}_t$ is the estimated residual series from Equation (21.16). The hedge ratio is given by β in Equation (21.18).

Kroner and Sultan (1993) combine the error correction model with the GARCH model considered by Cecchetti *et al.* (1988) and Baillie and Myers (1991) in order to estimate the optimum hedge ratio. Specifically, they use the following model:

$$\begin{bmatrix} \Delta \log_e(S_t) \\ \Delta \log_e(F_t) \end{bmatrix} = \begin{bmatrix} \mu_1 \\ \mu_2 \end{bmatrix} + \begin{bmatrix} \alpha_s(\log_e(S_{t-1}) - \log_e(F_{t-1})) \\ \alpha_f(\log_e(S_{t-1}) - \log_e(F_{t-1})) \end{bmatrix} + \begin{bmatrix} e_{1t} \\ e_{2t} \end{bmatrix}, \quad (21.20)$$

where the error processes follow a GARCH process. As before, the hedge ratio at time $(t-1)$ is given by $h_{t-1} = H_{12,t}/H_{22,t}$.

21.4.4 *Empirical studies*

Here, we apply OLS, GARCH, and CECM models in practice to estimate optimal hedge ratios through R language. Monthly data for the

Table 21.1 Summary Statistics

	Min	Max	Mean	Std Dev	Skewness	Kurtosis
SPOT	735.09	3,500.31	1,781.57	656.57	0.66	2.30
FUTURES	734.20	3,498.90	1,780.09	656.05	0.66	2.31
ΔS_t	−369.63	327.84	12.17	79.23	−0.76	7.92
ΔF_t	−381.40	332.70	12.16	80.34	−0.77	8.08
Observations	188					

Table 21.2 Hedge Ratio Coefficient Using the Conventional Regression Model

Variable	Estimate	Std Error	t-Ratio	p-Value
Intercept	0.1984	0.2729	0.73	0.4680
ΔF_t	0.9851	0.0034	292.53	<0.0001

S&P 500 index and its futures were collected from the Datastream database, with the sample consisting of 188 observations from January 31, 2005 to August 31, 2020. Summary statistics of the data is presented in Table 21.1.

First, in Equation (21.12), we use the OLS method by regressing the changes in spot prices on the changes in futures prices to estimate the optimal hedge ratio. The estimate of the hedge ratio obtained from the OLS technique is reported in Table 21.2. As shown in Table 21.2, we can see that the hedge ratio of the S&P 500 index is significantly different from zero, at a 1% significance level. Moreover, the estimated hedge ratio, denoted by the coefficient of ΔF_t, is generally less than unity.

Second, we apply a conventional regression model with heteroscedastic error terms to estimate the hedge ratio. Here, an AR(2)-GARCH(1,1) model for the changes in spot prices regressed on the changes in futures prices is specified as follows:

$$\Delta S_t = a_0 + a_1 \Delta F_t + e_t, e_t = \varepsilon_t - \varphi_1 e_{t-1} - \varphi_2 e_{t-2},$$
$$\varepsilon_t = \sqrt{h_t} \epsilon_t, h_t = \omega + \alpha_1 \varepsilon_{t-1}^2 + \beta_1 h_{t-1},$$

Table 21.3 Hedge Ratio Coefficient Using the Conventional Regression Model with Heteroscedastic Errors

Variable	Estimate	Std Error	t-Ratio	p-Value
Intercept	0.0490	0.0144	3.41	0.0007
ΔF_t	0.9994	0.0008	1,179.59	<0.0001
e_{t-1}	−0.9873	0.0109	−90.29	<0.0001
e_{t-2}	−0.9959	0.0145	−68.83	<0.0001
ω	0.0167	0.0098	1.71	0.0866
ε_{t-1}^2	0.3135	0.0543	5.78	<0.0001
h_{t-1}	0.6855	0.0530	12.94	<0.0001

where $\epsilon_t \sim N(0, 1)$ The estimated result of the AR(2)-GARCH(1,1) model is shown in Table 21.3. The coefficient estimates of the AR(2)-GARCH(1,1) model, as shown in Table 21.3, are all significantly different from zero, at a 1% significance level. This finding suggests the importance of capturing the heteroscedastic error structures in the conventional regression model. In addition, the hedge ratio of conventional regression with the AR(2)-GARCH(1,1) model is higher than the OLS hedge ratio for S&P 500 futures contract.

Next, we will apply the CECM model to estimate the optimal hedge ratio. Here, standard augmented Dickey–Fuller (ADF) unit roots and Phillips and Ouliaris (1990) residual cointegration tests are performed and the optimal hedge ratios estimated by ECM will be presented. Here, we apply the ADF regression to test for the presence of unit roots. The ADF test statistics, as shown in Panel A of Table 21.4, indicates that the null hypothesis of a unit root cannot be rejected for the levels of the variables. Using differenced data, the computed ADF test statistics shown in Panel B of Table 21.4 suggested that the null hypothesis is rejected, at the 1% significance level. As differencing one produces stationarity, we may conclude that each series is integrated of order one, I(1), process which is necessary for testing the existence of cointegration. We then apply a Phillips and Ouliaris (1990) residual cointegration test to examine the presence of cointegration. The result of the Phillips–Ouliaris cointegration test is reported in Panel C of Table 21.4. The null hypothesis of the Phillips–Ouliaris cointegration test is that there is no cointegration present. The result of the Phillips–Ouliaris cointegration test shows that the null hypothesis is rejected under the 1% significant

Table 21.4 Unit Roots and Residual Cointegration Tests Results

Variable	ADF Statistics	Lag Parameter	p-Value
Panel A. Level data			
Spot	−1.3353	1	0.8542
Futures	−1.3458	1	0.8498
Panel B. First-order differenced data			
Spot	−10.104	1	<0.01
Futures	−10.150	1	<0.01
Panel C. Phillips-Ouliaris cointegration test			
Phillips–Ouliaris demeaned	−60.783	1	<0.01

Table 21.5 Error Correction Estimates of Hedge Ratio Coefficient

Variable	Estimate	Std Error	t-Ratio	p-Value
ΔF_t	0.9892	0.0031	316.60	<0.001
$\hat{u}_{t-1}$	−0.3423	0.0571	−5.99	<0.001

level. This suggests that the spot S&P 500 index is cointegrated with the S&P 500 index futures.

Finally, we apply the ECM model in term of Equation (21.17) to estimate the optimal hedge ratio. Table 21.5 shows that the coefficient on the error correction term, $\hat{u}_{t-1}$, is significantly different from zero, at a 1% significance level. This suggests that the importance of estimating ECM, and in particular the long-run equilibrium error term, cannot be ignored in the conventional regression model. In addition, the ECM hedge ratio is higher than the conventional OLS hedge ratio for the S&P 500 futures contract. This finding is consistent with the results in Lien (1996, 2004) who argued that the MV hedge ratio will be smaller if the cointegration relationship is not considered.

Tables 21.2, 21.3, and 21.5 indicate that hedge ratios obtained from the OLS, GARCH, and CECM methods are 0.9851, 0.9994, and 0.9892, respectively. It is clear that hedge ratios from the three estimation methods are relatively similar. Therefore, the OLS result is sufficient for estimating the hedge ratio for index futures.

21.5 Summary

This chapter first discusses four different theoretical models, that is, the minimum-variance, mean-variance, expected utility, and Value-at-Risk methods. Then, we use S&P 500 data to show how three alternative estimation methods can be used to estimate hedge ratios. These three methods are the OLS method, GARCH method, and CECM. We found that the OLS method is sufficient for estimating hedge ratios.

The four theories discussed in this chapter are the (i) minimum-variance approach, (ii) mean-variance-based approach, (iii) Sharpe hedge ratio, and (iv) minimum value-at-risk hedge ratio. All these approaches will lead to the same hedge ratio as the conventional MV hedge ratio if the futures price follows a pure martingale process and if the futures and spot prices are jointly normal. However, if these conditions do not hold, then the hedge ratios based on the various approaches will be different; therefore, the user should carefully examine what kind of assumptions they will use.

Since the statistical properties of the MV hedge ratio are well known, it is easy to estimate and perform the statistical hypothesis test. For example, we can test whether the optimal MV hedge ratio is the same as the naïve hedge ratio. Since the MV hedge ratio ignores the expected return, it will not be consistent with the mean-variance analysis unless the futures price follows a pure martingale process. In general, if the martingale and normality condition do not hold, then the MV hedge ratio will not be consistent with the expected utility maximization principle in terms of mean and variance.

In order to make the hedge ratio consistent with the expected utility maximization principle, we can derive the optimal hedge ratio by maximizing the expected utility in terms of mean and variance. However, to implement such an approach, we need to assume a specific utility function such as the quadratic utility function, and we need to make an assumption regarding the return distribution. Therefore, different utility functions will lead to different optimal hedge ratios.

It should be noted that the derivation of the optimal hedge ratio discussed in this chapter does not incorporate transaction costs.

Furthermore, these derivations do not allow investments in securities other than the spot and corresponding futures contracts. As shown by Lence (1995), once we relax these conventional assumptions, the resulting optimal hedge ratio can be quite different from the ones obtained under the conventional assumptions. Lence's (1995) results are based on a specific utility function and some other assumptions regarding the return distributions.

In this chapter, we have also reviewed various ways of estimating the optimal hedge ratio. As far as the estimation of the conventional MV hedge ratio is concerned, there are many methods that have been proposed in the literature. These methods range from a simple regression method to complex cointegrated heteroscedastic methods.

In this chapter, we used S&P 500 index futures from January 2005 to August 2020 in terms of three estimation methods to estimate the hedge ratio. These three methods are the OLS regression method, GARCH method, and CECM. We also compared hedge ratio estimates from these three methods in some detail. The R programs used to estimate this empirical result can be found in Appendix 21B.

For those who are interested in research in this area, we would like to finally point out that one requires a good understanding of financial economic theories and econometric methodologies. In addition, a good background in data analysis and computer programming would also be helpful.

Questions and Problems

1. Please briefly discuss the following terms:
   a. Minimum-Variance Hedge Ratio
   b. Optimal Mean-Variance Hedge Ratio
   c. Sharpe Hedge Ratio
   d. Minimum Value-at-Risk Hedge Ratio
   e. Quadratic Utility Function
   f. Constant Absolute Risk Aversion Utility Function
2. Please discuss the relationships among the Sharpe hedge ratio, minimum-variance hedge ratio, and optimal mean-variance hedge ratio.

3. Please use the data presented in Appendix 21A to estimate the minimum-variance hedge ratio, optimal mean-variance hedge ratio, Sharpe hedge ratio, and minimum value-at-risk hedge ratio.
4. Please discuss the differences of methodologies used to estimate the OLS, GARCH, and CECM models to estimate hedge ratios.
5. Please reproduce the hedge ratios from Tables 21.2, 21.3, and 21.5 by using the data presented in Appendix 21A.

Bibliography

Baillie, R. T. and R. J. Myers (1991). Bivariate Garch estimation of the optimal commodity futures hedge. *Journal of Applied Econometrics*, 6, 109–124.

Benet, B. A. (1992). Hedge period length and ex-ante futures hedging effectiveness: The case of foreign-exchange risk cross hedges. *Journal of Futures Markets*, 12, 163–175.

Cecchetti, S. G., R. E. Cumby and S. Figlewski (1988). Estimation of the optimal futures hedge. *Review of Economics and Statistics*, 70, 623–630.

Chen, S. S., C. F. Lee and K. Shrestha (2003). Futures hedge ratios: A review. *The Quarterly Review of Economics and Finance*, 43(3), 433–465.

Chen, S. S., C. F. Lee and K. Shrestha (2004). An empirical analysis of the relationship between the hedge ratio and hedging horizon: A simultaneous estimation of the short-and long-run hedge ratios. *Journal of Futures Markets*, 24(4), 359–386.

Chen, S. S., C. F. Lee and K. Shrestha (2001). On a mean-generalized semivariance approach to determining the hedge ratio. *Journal of Futures Markets*, 21, 581–598.

Chen, S. S., C. F. Lee, F. L. Lin and K. Shrestha (2022). Three alternative methods for estimating hedge ratios. *Encyclopedia of Finance edited by Cheng-Few Lee and Alice Lee*, 3rd ed. New York: Springer.

Cheung, C. S., C. C. Y. Kwan and P. C. Y. Yip (1990). The hedging effectiveness of options and futures: A mean-Gini approach. *Journal of Futures Markets*, 10, 61–21.

Chou, W. L., K. K. Fan Denis and C. F. Lee (1996). Hedging with the Nikkei index futures: The conventional model versus the error correction model. *The Quarterly Review of Economics and Finance*, 36(4), 495–505.

Crum, R. L., D. L. Laughhunn and J. W. Payne (1981). Risk-seeking behavior and its implications for financial models. *Financial Management*, 10, 20–27.

De Jong, A., F. De Roon and C. Veld (1997). Out-of-sample hedging effectiveness of currency futures for alternative models and hedging strategies. *Journal of Futures Markets*, 17, 817–837.

Dickey, D. A. and W. A. Fuller (1981). Likelihood ratio statistics for autoregressive time series with a unit root. *Econometrica*, 49, 1057–1072.

Ederington, L. H. (1979). The hedging performance of the new futures markets. *Journal of Finance*, 34, 157–170.

Engle, R. F. and C. W. Granger (1987). Co-integration and error correction: Representation, estimation and testing. *Econometrica*, 55, 251–276.

Geppert, J. M. (1995). A statistical model for the relationship between futures contract hedging effectiveness and investment horizon length. *Journal of Futures Markets*, 15, 507–536.

Ghosh, A. (1993). Hedging with stock index futures: Estimation and forecasting with error correction model. *Journal of Futures Markets*, 13, 213–752.

Grammatikos, T. and A. Saunders (1983). Stability and the hedging performance of foreign currency futures. *Journal of Futures Markets*, 3, 295–305.

Howard, C. T. and L. J. D'Antonio (1984). A risk-return measure of hedging effectiveness. *Journal of Financial and Quantitative Analysis*, 19, 101–112.

Hsin, C. W., J. Kuo, and C. F. Lee (1994). A new measure to compare the hedging effectiveness of foreign currency futures versus options. *Journal of Futures Markets*, 14(6), 685–707.

Hsin, C. W., J. Kuo and C. F. Lee (1995). An empirical test of minimum-risk foreign currency hedges with futures and options. *Advances in Investment Analysis and Portfolio Management*, III.

Hung, J. C., C. L. Chiu and M. C. Lee (2006). Hedging with zero-value at risk hedge ratio. *Applied Financial Economics*, 16, 259–269.

Hylleberg, S. and G. E. Mizon (1989). Cointegration and error correction mechanisms. *Economic Journal*, 99, 113–125.

Johansen, S. and K. Juselius (1990). Maximum likelihood estimation and inference on cointegration — With applications to the demand for money. *Oxford Bulletin of Economics and Statistics*, 52, 169–210.

Johnson, L. L. (1960). The theory of hedging and speculation in commodity futures. *Review of Economic Studies*, 27, 139–151.

Junkus, J. C. and C. F. Lee (1985). Use of three stock index futures in hedging decisions. *Journal of Futures Markets*, 5(2), 201–222.

Kolb, R. W. and J. Okunev (1992). An empirical evaluation of the extended mean-Gini coefficient for futures hedging. *Journal of Futures Markets*, 12, 177–186.

Kolb, R. W. and J. Okunev (1993). Utility maximizing hedge ratios in the extended mean Gini framework. *Journal of Futures Markets*, 13, 597–609.

Koppenhaver, G. D. and C. F. Lee (1987). Alternative instruments for hedging inflation risk in the banking industry. *Journal of Futures Markets*, 7(6), 619–636.

Kroner, K. F. and J. Sultan (1993). Time-varying distributions and dynamic hedging with foreign currency futures. *Journal of Financial and Quantitative Analysis*, 28, 535–551.

Lee, C. F., E. L. Bubnys and Y. Lin (1987). Stock index futures hedge ratios: Test on horizon effects and functional form. *Advances in Futures and Options Research*, 2(1), 291–311.

Lee, C. F., J. E. Finnerty, J. Lee, A. C. Lee and D. H. Wort (2013). *Security Analysis, Portfolio Management, and Financial Derivatives*. Singapore: World Scientific Publishers, Inc.

Lee, C. F., K. Wang and Y. L. Chen (2009). Hedging and optimal hedge ratios for international index futures markets. *Review of Pacific Basin Financial Markets and Policies*, 12(4), 593–610.

Lee, C.-F. and A. C. Lee (2022). *Encyclopedia of Finance*, 3rd ed. New York: Springer.

Lee, H. T. and J. Yoder (2007). Optimal hedging with a regime-switching time-varying correlation GARCH model. *Journal of Futures Markets*, 27, 495–516.

Lence, S. H. (1995). The economic value of minimum-variance hedges. *American Journal of Agricultural Economics*, 77, 353–364.

Lence, S. H. (1996). Relaxing the assumptions of minimum variance hedging. *Journal of Agricultural and Resource Economics*, 21, 39–55.

Lien, D. and K. Shrestha (2007). An empirical analysis of the relationship between hedge ratio and hedging horizon using wavelet analysis. *Journal of Futures Markets*, 27, 127–150.

Lien, D. and K. Shrestha (2010). Estimating optimal hedge ratio: A multivariate skew-normal distribution. *Applied Financial Economics*, 20, 627–636.

Lien, D. (1996). The effect of the cointegration relationship on futures hedging: A note. *Journal of Futures Markets*, 16, 773–780.

Lien, D. (2004). Cointegration and the optimal hedge ratio: The general case. *The Quarterly Review of Economics and Finance*, 44, 654–658.

Lien, D. and X. Luo (1993a). Estimating the extended mean-Gini coefficient for futures hedging. *Journal of Futures Markets*, 13, 665–676.

Lien, D. and X. Luo (1993b). Estimating multiperiod hedge ratios in cointegrated markets. *Journal of Futures Markets*, 13, 909–920.

Lien, D. and D. R. Shaffer (1999). Note on estimating the minimum extended Gini hedge ratio. *Journal of Futures Markets*, 19, 101–113.

Lien, D. and Y. K. Tse (1998). Hedging time-varying downside risk. *Journal of Futures Markets*, 18, 705–722.

Lien, D. and Y. K. Tse (2000). Hedging downside risk with futures contracts. *Applied Financial Economics*, 10, 163–170.

Lin, F. L. (2023). A comparative analysis of hedging determination for three alternative international equity index futures. *Review of Pacific Basin Financial Markets and Policies*, 26(1), 1–22.

Maghyereh, A. I., B. Awartani and H. Abdoh (2019). The co-movement between oil and clean energy stocks: A wavelet-based analysis of horizon associations. *Energy*, 169, 895–913.

Malliaris, A. G. and J. L. Urrutia (1991). The impact of the lengths of estimation periods and hedging horizons on the effectiveness of a hedge: Evidence from foreign currency futures. *Journal of Futures Markets*, 3, 271–289.

Myers, R. J. and S. R. Thompson (1989). Generalized optimal hedge ratio estimation. *American Journal of Agricultural Economics*, 71, 858–868.

Osterwald-Lenum, M. (1992). A note with quantiles of the asymptotic distribution of the maximum likelihood cointegration rank test statistics. *Oxford Bulletin of Economics and Statistics*, 54, 461–471.

Phillips, P. C. B. and S. Ouliaris (1990). Asymptotic properties of residual based tests for cointegration. *Econometrica*, 58, 165–193.

Phillips, P. C. B. and P. Perron (1988). Testing unit roots in time series regression. *Biometrika*, 75, 335–346.

Rutledge, D. J. S. (1972). Hedgers' demand for futures contracts: A theoretical framework with applications to the United States soybean complex. *Food Research Institute Studies*, 11, 237–256.

Sephton, P. S. (1993). Hedging wheat and canola at the Winnipeg commodity exchange. *Applied Financial Economics*, 3, 67–72.

Shalit, H. (1995). Mean-Gini hedging in futures markets. *Journal of Futures Markets*, 15, 617–635.

Stock, J. H. and M. W. Watson (1988). Testing for common trends. *Journal of the American Statistical Association*, 83, 1097–1107.

Sultan, J., A. K. Alexandridis, M. Hasan and X. Guo (2019). Hedging performance of multiscale hedge ratios. *Journal of Futures Markets*, 39, 1613–1632.

Working, H. (1953). Hedging reconsidered. *Journal of Farm Economics*, 35, 544–561.

Appendix 21A: Monthly Data of S&P 500 Index and Its Futures (January 2005–August 2020)

Date	SPOT	FUTURES	C_spot	C_futures
1/31/2005	1,181.27	1,181.7	−30.65	−32
2/28/2005	1,203.6	1,204.1	22.33	22.4
3/31/2005	1,180.59	1,183.9	−23.01	−20.2
4/29/2005	1,156.85	1,158.5	−23.74	−25.4
5/31/2005	1,191.5	1,192.3	34.65	33.8
6/30/2005	1,191.33	1,195.5	−0.17	3.2
7/29/2005	1,234.18	1,236.8	42.85	41.3
8/31/2005	1,220.33	1,221.4	−13.85	−15.4
9/30/2005	1,228.81	1,234.3	8.48	12.9
10/31/2005	1,207.01	1,209.8	−21.8	−24.5
11/30/2005	1,249.48	1,251.1	42.47	41.3
12/30/2005	1,248.29	1,254.8	−1.19	3.7
1/31/2006	1,280.08	1,283.6	31.79	28.8
2/28/2006	1,280.66	1,282.4	0.58	−1.2
3/31/2006	1,294.83	1,303.3	14.17	20.9
4/28/2006	1,310.61	1,315.9	15.78	12.6
5/31/2006	1,270.09	1,272.1	−40.52	−43.8
6/30/2006	1,270.2	1,279.4	0.11	7.3
7/31/2006	1,276.66	1,281.8	6.46	2.4
8/31/2006	1,303.82	1,305.6	27.16	23.8
9/29/2006	1,335.85	1,345.4	32.03	39.8
10/31/2006	1,377.94	1,383.2	42.09	37.8
11/30/2006	1,400.63	1,402.9	22.69	19.7
12/29/2006	1,418.3	1,428.4	17.67	25.5
1/31/2007	1,438.24	1,443	19.94	14.6
2/28/2007	1,406.82	1,408.9	−31.42	−34.1
3/30/2007	1,420.86	1,431.2	14.04	22.3
4/30/2007	1,482.37	1,488.4	61.51	57.2
5/31/2007	1,530.62	1,532.9	48.25	44.5
6/29/2007	1,503.35	1,515.4	−27.27	−17.5
7/31/2007	1,455.27	1,461.9	−48.08	−53.5
8/31/2007	1,473.99	1,476.7	18.72	14.8

Appendix 21A. (*Continued*)

Date	SPOT	FUTURES	C_spot	C_futures
9/28/2007	1,526.75	1,538.1	52.76	61.4
10/31/2007	1,549.38	1,554.9	22.63	16.8
11/30/2007	1,481.14	1,483.7	−68.24	−71.2
12/31/2007	1,468.35	1,477.2	−12.79	−6.5
1/31/2008	1,378.55	1,379.6	−89.8	−97.6
2/29/2008	1,330.63	1,331.3	−47.92	−48.3
3/31/2008	1,322.7	1,324	−7.93	−7.3
4/30/2008	1,385.59	1,386	62.89	62
5/30/2008	1,400.38	1,400.6	14.79	14.6
6/30/2008	1,280	1,281.1	−120.38	−119.5
7/31/2008	1,267.38	1,267.1	−12.62	−14
8/29/2008	1,282.83	1,282.6	15.45	15.5
9/30/2008	1,166.36	1,169	−116.47	−113.6
10/31/2008	968.75	967.3	−197.61	−201.7
11/28/2008	896.24	895.3	−72.51	−72
12/31/2008	903.25	900.1	7.01	4.8
1/30/2009	825.88	822.5	−77.37	−77.6
2/27/2009	735.09	734.2	−90.79	−88.3
3/31/2009	797.87	794.8	62.78	60.6
4/30/2009	872.81	870	74.94	75.2
5/29/2009	919.14	918.1	46.33	48.1
6/30/2009	919.32	915.5	0.18	−2.6
7/31/2009	987.48	984.4	68.16	68.9
8/31/2009	1,020.62	1,019.7	33.14	35.3
9/30/2009	1,057.08	1,052.9	36.46	33.2
10/30/2009	1,036.19	1,033	−20.89	−19.9
11/30/2009	1,095.63	1,094.8	59.44	61.8
12/31/2009	1,115.1	1,110.7	19.47	15.9
1/29/2010	1,073.87	1,070.4	−41.23	−40.3
2/26/2010	1,104.49	1,103.4	30.62	33
3/31/2010	1,169.43	1,165.2	64.94	61.8
4/30/2010	1,186.69	1,183.4	17.26	18.2
5/31/2010	1,089.41	1,088.5	−97.28	−94.9
6/30/2010	1,030.71	1,026.6	−58.7	−61.9

(*Continued*)

Appendix 21A. (*Continued*)

Date	SPOT	FUTURES	C_spot	C_futures
7/30/2010	1,101.6	1,098.3	70.89	71.7
8/31/2010	1,049.33	1,048.3	−52.27	−50
9/30/2010	1,141.2	1,136.7	91.87	88.4
10/29/2010	1,183.26	1,179.7	42.06	43
11/30/2010	1,180.55	1,179.6	−2.71	−0.1
12/31/2010	1,257.64	1,253	77.09	73.4
1/31/2011	1,286.12	1,282.4	28.48	29.4
2/28/2011	1,327.22	1,326.1	41.1	43.7
3/31/2011	1,325.83	1,321	−1.39	−5.1
4/29/2011	1,363.61	1,359.7	37.78	38.7
5/31/2011	1,345.2	1,343.9	−18.41	−15.8
6/30/2011	1,320.64	1,315.5	−24.56	−28.4
7/29/2011	1,292.28	1,288.4	−28.36	−27.1
8/31/2011	1,218.89	1,217.7	−73.39	−70.7
9/30/2011	1,131.42	1,126	−87.47	−91.7
10/31/2011	1,253.3	1,249.3	121.88	123.3
11/30/2011	1,246.96	1,246	−6.34	−3.3
12/30/2011	1,257.6	1,252.6	10.64	6.6
1/31/2012	1,312.41	1,308.2	54.81	55.6
2/29/2012	1,365.68	1,364.4	53.27	56.2
3/30/2012	1,408.47	1,403.2	42.79	38.8
4/30/2012	1,397.91	1,393.6	−10.56	−9.6
5/31/2012	1,310.33	1,309.2	−87.58	−84.4
6/29/2012	1,362.16	1,356.4	51.83	47.2
7/31/2012	1,379.32	1,374.6	17.16	18.2
8/31/2012	1,406.58	1,405.1	27.26	30.5
9/28/2012	1,440.67	1,434.2	34.09	29.1
10/31/2012	1,412.16	1,406.8	−28.51	−27.4
11/30/2012	1,416.18	1,414.4	4.02	7.6
12/31/2012	1,426.19	1,420.1	10.01	5.7
1/31/2013	1,498.11	1,493.3	71.92	73.2
2/28/2013	1,514.68	1,513.3	16.57	20
3/29/2013	1,569.19	1,562.7	54.51	49.4
4/30/2013	1,597.57	1,592.2	28.38	29.5

Appendix 21A. (*Continued*)

Date	SPOT	FUTURES	C_spot	C_futures
5/31/2013	1,630.74	1,629	33.17	36.8
6/28/2013	1,606.28	1,599.3	−24.46	−29.7
7/31/2013	1,685.73	1,680.5	79.45	81.2
8/30/2013	1,632.97	1,631.3	−52.76	−49.2
9/30/2013	1,681.55	1,674.3	48.58	43
10/31/2013	1,756.54	1,751	74.99	76.7
11/29/2013	1,805.81	1,804.1	49.27	53.1
12/31/2013	1,848.36	1,841.1	42.55	37
1/31/2014	1,782.59	1,776.6	−65.77	−64.5
2/28/2014	1,859.45	1,857.6	76.86	81
3/31/2014	1,872.34	1,864.6	12.89	7
4/30/2014	1,883.95	1,877.9	11.61	13.3
5/30/2014	1,923.57	1,921.5	39.62	43.6
6/30/2014	1,960.23	1,952.4	36.66	30.9
7/31/2014	1,930.67	1,924.8	−29.56	−27.6
8/29/2014	2,003.37	2,001.4	72.7	76.6
9/30/2014	1,972.29	1,965.5	−31.08	−35.9
10/31/2014	2,018.05	2,011.4	45.76	45.9
11/28/2014	2,067.56	2,066.3	49.51	54.9
12/31/2014	2,058.9	2,052.4	−8.66	−13.9
1/30/2015	1,994.99	1,988.4	−63.91	−64
2/27/2015	2,104.5	2,102.8	109.51	114.4
3/31/2015	2,067.89	2,060.8	−36.61	−42
4/30/2015	2,085.51	2,078.9	17.62	18.1
5/29/2015	2,107.39	2,106	21.88	27.1
6/30/2015	2,063.11	2,054.4	−44.28	−51.6
7/31/2015	2,103.84	2,098.4	40.73	44
8/31/2015	1,972.18	1,969.2	−131.66	−129.2
9/30/2015	1,920.03	1,908.7	−52.15	−60.5
10/30/2015	2,079.36	2,073.7	159.33	165
11/30/2015	2,080.41	2,079.8	1.05	6.1
12/31/2015	2,043.94	2,035.4	−36.47	−44.4
1/29/2016	1,940.24	1,930.1	−103.7	−105.3
2/29/2016	1,932.23	1,929.5	−8.01	−0.6

(*Continued*)

Appendix 21A. (*Continued*)

Date	SPOT	FUTURES	C_spot	C_futures
3/31/2016	2,059.74	2,051.5	127.51	122
4/29/2016	2,065.3	2,059.1	5.56	7.6
5/31/2016	2,096.96	2,094.9	31.66	35.8
6/30/2016	2,098.86	2,090.2	1.9	−4.7
7/29/2016	2,173.6	2,168.2	74.74	78
8/31/2016	2,170.95	2,169.5	−2.65	1.3
9/30/2016	2,168.27	2,160.4	−2.68	−9.1
10/31/2016	2,126.15	2,120.1	−42.12	−40.3
11/30/2016	2,198.81	2,198.8	72.66	78.7
12/30/2016	2,238.83	2,236.2	40.02	37.4
1/31/2017	2,278.87	2,221.5	40.04	38.3
2/28/2017	2,363.64	2,362.8	84.77	88.3
3/31/2017	2,362.72	2,359.2	−0.92	−3.6
4/28/2017	2,384.2	2,380.5	21.48	21.3
5/31/2017	2,411.8	2,411.1	27.6	30.6
6/30/2017	2,423.41	2,420.9	11.61	9.8
7/31/2017	2,470.3	2,468	46.89	47.1
8/31/2017	2,471.65	2,470.1	1.35	2.1
9/29/2017	2,519.36	2,516.1	47.71	46
10/31/2017	2,575.26	2,572.7	55.9	56.6
11/30/2017	2,647.58	2,647.9	72.32	75.2
12/29/2017	2,673.61	2,676	26.03	28.1
1/31/2018	2,823.81	2,825.8	150.2	149.8
2/28/2018	2,713.83	2,714.4	−109.98	−111.4
3/30/2018	2,640.87	2,643	−72.96	−71.4
4/30/2018	2,648.05	2,647	7.18	4
5/31/2018	2,705.27	2,705.5	57.22	58.5
6/29/2018	2,718.37	2,721.6	13.1	16.1
7/31/2018	2,816.29	2,817.1	97.92	95.5
8/31/2018	2,901.52	2,902.1	85.23	85
9/28/2018	2,913.98	2,919	12.46	16.9
10/31/2018	2,711.74	2,711.1	−202.24	−207.9
11/30/2018	2,760.17	2,758.3	48.43	47.2
12/31/2018	2,506.85	2,505.2	−253.32	−253.1

Appendix 21A. (*Continued*)

Date	SPOT	FUTURES	C_spot	C_futures
1/31/2019	2,704.1	2,704.5	197.25	199.3
2/28/2019	2,784.49	2,784.7	80.39	80.2
3/29/2019	2,834.4	2,837.8	49.91	53.1
4/30/2019	2,945.83	2,948.5	111.43	110.7
5/31/2019	2,752.06	2,752.6	−193.77	−195.9
6/28/2019	2,941.76	2,944.2	189.7	191.6
7/31/2019	2,980.38	2,982.3	38.62	38.1
8/30/2019	2,926.46	2,924.8	−53.92	−57.5
9/30/2019	2,976.74	2,978.5	50.28	53.7
10/31/2019	3,037.56	3,035.8	60.82	57.3
11/29/2019	3,140.98	3,143.7	103.42	107.9
12/31/2019	3,230.78	3,231.1	89.8	87.4
1/31/2020	3,225.52	3,224	−5.26	−7.1
2/28/2020	2,954.22	2,951.1	−271.3	−272.9
3/31/2020	2,584.59	2,569.7	−369.63	−381.4
4/30/2020	2,912.43	2,902.4	327.84	332.7
5/29/2020	3,044.31	3,042	131.88	139.6
6/30/2020	3,100.29	3,090.2	55.98	48.2
7/31/2020	3,271.12	3,263.5	170.83	173.3
8/31/2020	3,500.31	3,498.9	229.19	235.4

Appendix 21B: Applications of R Language in Estimating Three Different Optimal Hedge Ratios

In this appendix, we show the estimation procedure on how to apply the OLS, GARCH, and CECM models to estimate optimal hedge ratios through R language. R language is a high-level computer language that is designed for statistics and graphics. Compared to alternatives, such as SAS, Matlab, or Stata, R is completely free. Another benefit is that it is open source. Users could head to http://cran.r-project.org/ to download and install R language. Based upon the monthly S&P 500 index and its futures as presented in Appendix 21A, the estimation procedures of applying R language to estimate the hedge ratio are provided as follows:

First, we use the OLS method in term of Equation (21.11) to estimate the minimum-variance hedge ratio. By using the linear model (lm) function in R language, we obtain the following program code:

```
SP500=read.csv(file="SP500.csv")
OLS.fit < - lm(C_spot~C_futures, data=SP500)
summary(OLS.fit)
```

Next, we apply a conventional regression model with AR(2)-GARCH(1,1) error terms to estimate the minimum-variance hedge ratio. By using the rugarch package in R language, we obtain the following program:

```
library(rugarch)
fit.spec <- ugarchspec(
variance.model = list(model = "sGARCH",
                      garchOrder = c(1, 1)),
mean.model = list(armaOrder = c(2, 0),include.mean = TRUE,
                  external.regressors= cbind(SP500$C_futures)),
                  distribution.model = "norm")

GARCH.fit <- ugarchfit(data = cbind(SP500$C_spot),
                       spec = fit.spec)
GARCH.fit
```

Third, we apply the ECM model to estimate the minimum-variance hedge ratio. We begin by applying an augmented Dickey–Fuller (ADF) test for the presence of unit roots. The Phillips and Ouliaris (1990) residual cointegration test is applied to examine the presence of cointegration. Finally, the minimum-variance hedge ratio is estimated by the error correction model. By using tseries package in R language, we obtain the following program:

```
library(tseries)
# Augmented Dickey—Fuller Test
# Level data
adf.test(SP500$SPOT, k = 1)
adf.test(SP500$FUTURES, k = 1)
# First-order differenced data
adf.test(diff(SP500$SPOT), k = 1)
adf.test(diff(SP500$FUTURES), k = 1)

# Phillips and Ouliaris (1990) residual cointegration test
```

```
po.test(cbind(SP500$FUTURES,SP500$SPOT))

# Engle--Granger two-step procedure
## 1. Estimate cointegrating relationship
reg <- lm(SPOT~FUTURES, data=SP500)
## 2. Compute error term
Resid <- reg$resid
# Estimate optimal hedge ratio using the error correction model
n=length(resid)
ECM.fit <-lm(diff(SPOT)~ -1 + diff(FUTURES) + Resid[1:n-1],
             data=SP500)
summary(ECM.fit)
```

Finally, we apply a multivariate GARCH(1,1)-BEKK model to estimate the dynamic minimum-variance hedge ratio.

```
library(mgarchBEKK)

estimated=BEKK(as.matrix(cbind(SP500$C_futures,SP500$C_spot)),

               order = c(1, 1))

estimated$est.params

estimated$asy.se.coef
```

Chapter 22

Alternative Methods for Determining Option Bounds: A Review and Comparison*

Contents

*This chapter is a modification of the paper by Lee *et al.* (2021). Alternative methods for determining option bounds: A review and comparison, in C.-F. Lee and J. Lee (eds.), *Handbook of Financial Econometrics, Mathematics, Statistics, and Machine Learning*, Singapore: World Scientific, pp. 917–945.

22.1 Introduction

Option pricing is a central issue in the derivatives literature. After the seminal papers by Black and Scholes (1973) and Merton (1973), there has been an explosion in option pricing models developed over the last five decades. Rather than proposing new option pricing models, some researchers establish option bounds with only modest assumptions on the price distribution, investors' preferences, and/or market frictions in accordance with the existence of incomplete markets. The main purposes of this chapter are (i) to expand the option bound, which has been briefly discussed in Chapter 9, and (ii) to review and discuss an alternative method for determining option bound.

Section 22.1 is an introduction, Section 22.2 presents the literature review, and Section 22.3 summarizes and compares the different mathematical techniques to derive option bounds. Section 22.4 discusses different approaches to tighten European options bounds. Section 22.5 reviews the option bounds for American options and Asian options. The empirical applications of option bounds can be found in Section 22.6. We conclude the chapter in Section 22.7. In Appendix 22A, we demonstrate a mathematical derivation of the option bounds. Appendix 22B shows tightening techniques of the option bounds, and in Appendix 22C, we discuss other option bounds.

22.2 Literature Review

We first review these major theoretical techniques and categorize them into four broad categories. Many different methods have been proposed to construct option bounds; however, they belong to one of these approaches:

(1) Search for arbitrage conditions (e.g., Merton, 1973; Handley, 2005).
(2) Stochastic dominance (e.g., Perrakis and Ryan, 1984; Perrakis, 1986; Levy, 1985; Henin and Pistre, 1998; Constantinides and Perrakis, 2002; Constantinides *et al.*, 2009).

(3) Linear programming approach (e.g., Ritchken, 1985; Ritchken and Kuo, 1988, 1989; Basso and Pianca, 1997; Ryan, 2003; Peña *et al.*, 2009).
(4) Semi-parametric or non-parametric approaches (e.g., Lo, 1987; Grundy, 1991; Zhang, 1994; Boyle and Lin, 1997; Lee *et al.*, 2002; Bertsimas and Popescu, 2002; Gotoh and Konno, 2002; Chazal and Jouini, 2008; Rodriguez, 2003; Lin *et al.*, 2012).

After identifying these major general models, their extensions and relations to each other are also briefly discussed. Many studies have attempted to further tighten the option bounds using a variety of approaches. In the second part of the chapter, we distinguish these models by their different tactics to tighten European option bounds:

(1) Imposing investor preferences and pricing kernel restrictions (e.g., Perrakis and Ryan, 1984; Ritchken, 1985; Levy, 1985; Ritchken and Kuo, 1989; Basso and Pianca, 1997, 2001; Mathur and Ritchken, 1999; Bernardo and Ledoit, 2000; Cochrane and Saa-Requjo, 2000; Bondarenko and Longarela, 2004; Huang, 2004; Mello and Pyo, 2006; Pyo, 2008; Christoffersen *et al.*, 2010).
(2) The selection of risk-neutral measures and the absence of arbitrage opportunities (e.g., Frey and Sin, 1999; Ryan, 2000; King *et al.*, 2005; Cont, 2006; Oancea and Perrakis, 2007; Chazal and Jouini, 2008; Pinar, 2009; Christoffersen *et al.*, 2010).
(3) Trading in markets with frictions (e.g., Henin and Pistre, 1998; Constantinides and Zariphopoulou, 1999, 2001; Masson and Perrakis, 2000; Constantinides and Perrakis, 2002; Constantinides *et al.*, 2009).

Following the discussion of the various approaches mentioned above, we next review how these methods were applied to tighten bounds for American options and other options. After the summary of option bounds for various kinds of options, we survey the empirical studies that apply the theoretical option bounds to different derivatives markets. The important results and data used in each paper are also briefly described. In contrast with many studies on European option bounds, recent papers working on either the extensions to

American options and other options or the empirical applications are just arising.

22.3 Mathematical Techniques to Derive Option Bounds

In this section, major mathematical methods used to derive option bounds are discussed in detail. The major techniques are classified into four broad categories: searching for arbitrage conditions, stochastic dominance, linear programming, and semi- and non-parametric approaches. For each category, we review its influential papers and describe the basic concepts of the derivation process to obtain option bounds.

22.3.1 *Arbitrage theory*

Merton (1973) derives option bounds by searching for arbitrage conditions. Given no arbitrage assumption and the constant risk-free interest rate, r, the upper and lower bounds for European options can be obtained without any particular assumptions as follows:

$$C_{\min}^{E} = \begin{cases} \max(S_0 - Ke^{-rT}, 0) & \text{without dividend case} \\ \max(S_0 - D - Ke^{-rT}, 0) & \text{with dividend case} \end{cases},$$

$$\text{and} \quad C_{\max}^{E} = S_0 \tag{22.1}$$

$$P_{\min}^{E} = \begin{cases} \max(Ke^{-rT} - S_0, 0) & \text{without dividend case} \\ \max(D + Ke^{-rT} - S_0, 0) & \text{with dividend case} \end{cases},$$

$$\text{and} \quad P_{\max}^{E} = Ke^{-rT}, \tag{22.2}$$

where $C_{\min}^{E}$ and $C_{\max}^{E}$ represent the lower and upper bounds for a European call option, respectively; $P_{\min}^{E}$ and $P_{\max}^{E}$ are the lower and upper bounds for a European put option, respectively. S_0 is the current price of the underlying asset, K denotes the strike price, and D represents the dividend payment.

Without any assumptions of the distribution of the underlying asset's price, the bounds for American options written on stock with non-dividend can be derived as follows:

$$C^A_{\min} = \max(S_0 - Ke^{-rT}, 0), \quad \text{and} \quad C^A_{\max} = S_0, \tag{22.3}$$

$$P^A_{\min} = \max(K - S_0, 0), \quad \text{and} \quad P^A_{\max} = K, \tag{22.4}$$

where $C^A_{\min}$ and $C^A_{\max}$ represent the lower and upper bounds for an American call option, respectively; $P^A_{\min}$ and $P^A_{\max}$ are the lower and upper bounds for an American put option, respectively.

The derivations of upper bounds for European and American call options are trivial. If the current underlying asset is not the value of these upper bounds, then the arbitrageur can easily earn riskless profit by purchasing the current underlying asset of call options and selling call options. The upper bounds for European and American put options can also be proven by the same arbitrage trading strategy.

To derive the lower bounds of European options, we consider the following investments:

Portfolio A: Purchase a European call option at price C_0 with strike price K and purchase Ke^{-rT} value of bond
Portfolio B: Purchase the underlying stock at price S_0
Portfolio C: Purchase a European put option at price P_0 with strike price$K$ and purchase the underlying stock at price S_0
Portfolio D: Purchase Ke^{-rT} value of bond

At maturity, Portfolio B and Portfolio D are worth S_T and K, respectively. The value of Portfolio A and Portfolio C will be $\max(S_T, K)$ where Portfolio A and Portfolio C are worth S_T if $S_T > K$ and worth K if $S_T \leq K$. Therefore, unless the current value of Portfolio A is at least as large as Portfolio B, there will be arbitrage opportunity. In the same way, Portfolio C should be always worth as much as Portfolio D. Hence, we can obtain the following relations:

$$C_0 + Ke^{-rT} \geq S_0 \quad \text{and} \quad P_0 + S_0 \geq Ke^{-rT}$$

or

$$C_0 \geq S_0 - Ke^{-rT} \quad \text{and} \quad P_0 \geq Ke^{-rT} - S_0. \tag{22.5}$$

Then, the lower bounds of European options are derived. Since American call options are never exercised early if the underlying asset is without dividend payment, the upper and lower bounds for American call options are the same as the bounds of European call options. However, an American put option should be larger than $K - S_0$ since it can be exercised at any time. Handley (2005) investigates the extension of Merton's (1973) approach to the options with dividends. The tighten upper bound for European and American call options with dividends under an arbitrage opportunity framework is determined by the comparison between dividend payment and strike price.

22.3.2 *Stochastic dominance*

There are two ways to derive option bounds in stochastic dominance: one is to utilize second-degree stochastic dominance (SSD), and the other one is to use SSD with the consideration of a riskless asset (called second-degree stochastic dominance with riskless asset — SSDR). Two methods are introduced in detail in this section.

22.3.2.1 *Second-degree stochastic dominance*

The concept by Perrakis and Ryan (1984) to obtain the option bounds involves looking for the SSD relationship between different portfolios. SSD allows the universal ranking of distributions among risk-averse individuals. The criterion is stated as follows:

Let X and Y be two random variables whose cumulative distributions are F_X and F_Y, respectively. Then, F_X dominates F_Y by SSD if and only if

$$\int_{-\infty}^{z} [F_Y(t) - F_X(t)]dt \geq 0,$$

for all z.

Any risk-averse expected utility investor prefers a second-degree stochastic dominant investment to a dominated alternative.

Based on Rubinstein's (1976) equation of the valuation of uncertain income streams, Perrakis and Ryan (1984) assume that the normalized conditional expected marginal utility of the consumptions is a non-increasing function of price change (Y). The option bounds can be obtained by comparing the values of three portfolios. Assume an investor has wealth endowment S_0 that can only be invested in one of these portfolios:

Portfolio A: *One share of stock at price* S_0
Portfolio B: *One call option on the stock at price* C_0 *with strike price* K*, and* $S_0 - C_0$ *invested in the riskless asset with risk-free rate,* r
Portfolio C: S_0/C_0 *call options on the stock at price* C_0 *with strike price* K

The values of these three different portfolios are represented as a function of Y as follows:

$$\textbf{Value of Portfolio A} = S_0 + Y,$$

$$\textbf{Value of Portfolio B} = (S_0 - C_0)(1 + r) + \text{Max}(S_0 + Y - K, 0),$$

$$\textbf{Value of Portfolio C} = \frac{S_0}{C_0}(\text{Max}(S_0 + Y - K, 0)).$$

By comparing Portfolio A and Portfolio B to derive the lower bound and comparing Portfolio A and Portfolio C to derive the upper bound, the bounds of a European call option for a single period can be shown as

$$C_{\min}^{E} = \text{Max}\left(0, S_0 + \frac{1}{1+r}\left[-K + \int_0^K F_Y(w - S_0)dw\right]\right), \quad (22.6)$$

$$C_{\max}^{E} = S_0 + \frac{S_0}{S_0 + E[Y]}\left[-K + \int_0^K F_Y(w - S_0)dw\right], \quad (22.7)$$

where $F_Y(w - S_0)$ is the cumulative probability distribution of price change Y for $Y \in [-S_0, \infty)$. The option bounds are functions of the initial stock price S_0, the exercise price K, the riskless rate of interest, r, and the distribution of stock price change, $F_Y(Y)$.

In the following, Perrakis (1986) extends the results of Perrakis and Ryan (1984) by tightening the bounds with the restrictions that the one-period return (of per dollar investing in the underlying stock) is finite and has a strictly positive lower limit. In addition, the bounds for American put option are also developed within the framework of Perrakis and Ryan (1984).

22.3.2.2 *Second-degree stochastic dominance with riskless asset*

Distinct with Perrakis and Ryan's (1984) option bounds, which are obtainable by applying the second-degree stochastic dominance method, Levy (1985) applies the concept of SSDR to derive the upper and lower bounds for European options. Levy (1985) assumes that the investors' preferences belong to the set of all non-decreasing concave utility function and the underlying assets are those with non-negative consumption beta. Let F_c and F_s be the cumulative distributions of the terminal wealth investing in a European call option and its underlying asset. If borrowing and lending at the risk-free rate are allowed, which is a crucial assumption to derive relative narrower bounds, then an investor may find that ***any*** combination of the underlying asset with the riskless asset is dominated by ***some*** combination of European call option with the riskless asset even though neither F_c nor F_s dominates each other without the riskless asset. That is, in the presence of a riskless asset, if every risk-averse investor prefers to hold the investment F_c rather than the investment F_s, then F_c is said to dominate F_s by SSDR.

Therefore, the European call option bounds can be obtained by using the intuition that the lower (upper) bound of a European call option is derived in such a way that F_c (F_s) exactly does *not* dominate F_s (F_c). The criterion of SSDR is stated as follows:

Let F_c and F_s be the two cumulative distributions with the pth quantile, $Q_{F_C}(p)$ and $Q_{F_S}(p)$, respectively. Then, F_c dominates F_s in the SSDR if and only if

$$\operatorname*{Inf}_{0\le p<p_C}\frac{\int_0^p[Q_{F_S}(w)-r]dw}{\int_0^p[Q_{F_C}(w)-r]dw}\ge\operatorname*{Sup}_{p_C<p\le 1}\frac{\int_0^p[Q_{F_S}(w)-r]dw}{\int_0^p[Q_{F_C}(w)-r]dw},$$

where p_C is the value which solves $\int_0^{p_C}[Q_{F_C}(w)-r]dw=0$.

Levy (1985) proves that the cumulative distribution of the return of a European call option, F_c, dominates the cumulative distribution of the return of its underlying asset, F_s, in the SSDR if and only if

$p_c \le p_S$, where p_c and p_s are the values that solve

$$\int_0^{p_c} [Q_{F_C}(w) - r]dw = 0 \quad \text{and} \quad \int_0^{p_S} [Q_{F_S}(w) - r]dw = 0. \quad (22.8)$$

The lower bounds of a European call option, $C^E_{\min}$, then can be solved by using Levy's (1985) dominance theory. In order to avoid such dominance, we must set $p_c > p_S$. Therefore, one can solve for a European call option price, C_0, that equates this condition, and then concludes that the market price of a European call option must be greater than such a value. Using this line of reasoning, it can be shown that

$$C_0 \ge C^E_{\min} = S_0 - \frac{K}{r} + \frac{1}{rp_C} \int_0^K (K - S_T)f(S_T)dS_T, \qquad (22.9)$$

where C_0 denotes current price of a European call option; S_0 denotes current price of the underlying asset; S_T is the future price of the underlying asset at expiration day, T; K and r represent the strike price and risk-free rate, respectively; p_c is the value that solves $\int_0^{p_c}[Q_{F_C}(w) - r]dw = 0$; and F_c is the cumulative distribution of the return of a European call option.

Similarly, the upper bound of a European call option, $C^E_{\max}$, can be obtained by considering the dominance of the price of the underlying asset over the price of a European call option in SSDR. By using Levy's (1985) dominance theory and setting $p_S > p_c$, the upper bound of a European call option, $C^E_{\max}$ can be shown as[1]

$$C_0 \le C^E_{\max} = \frac{S_0}{E(S_T)} \int_K^{\infty} (S_T - K)f(S_T)dS_T, \qquad (22.10)$$

where S_T is the future price of the underlying asset at expiration day, T; $E(S_T)$ is the expected value of the underlying asset at expiration day; C_0 denotes current price of a European call option; S_0 denotes current price of the underlying asset; and K and r represent the strike price and risk-free rate, respectively.

Some classic puts on debt instruments can be viewed as calls with a concave payoff of the underlying interest rate since the bond price

[1]The detailed derivation process can be found in Levy's (1985) paper.

is a decreasing convex function of the interest rate. It is essential to understand the option bond of a call on bond. Hence, Henin and Pistre (1998) use second-order stochastic dominance arguments to study calls where the payoff is a concave function of the underlying asset. They derive bounds on option prices, whose exercise payoff is a concave function of the difference between the underlying asset and strike price. Later, Constantinides and Perrakis (2002) derive the tighter option bounds of European options by using stochastic dominance arguments. They utilize the zero-net-cost portfolio which consists of a riskless bond, a stock, and European call (or put) options and assume the concave utility function for investor preference to derive the bounds of the European option price. Their option bounds can be viewed as a generalization of a single-period model to a multiperiod economy since they are independent of the trading frequency.

Constantinides, Jackwerth, and Perrakis (2009) utilized the theoretical stochastic dominance method to test whether the S&P 500 index options market is rational or not. In the stochastic dominance framework, the investors are risk averse and their preference is to maximize their expected utility. This utility function is a concave and increasing function of the wealth and the wealth is monotone increasing in the stock return.

22.3.3 *Linear programming*

The development of linear programming is driven by its applications in economics and management. The standard form of a linear programming problem can be written as

$$\text{Maximize } \mathbf{c}^{\mathbf{T}}\mathbf{x} \text{ subject to } \mathbf{A}\mathbf{x} \leq \mathbf{b} \quad \text{and} \quad \mathbf{x} \geq 0. \tag{22.11}$$

In other words, linear programming is a technique for optimization of a linear objective function, subject to linear equality and linear inequality constraints. Any vector $\mathbf{x}$ satisfying the constraints of the linear programming problem is called a feasible solution of the problem. Linear programming is an important branch of applied mathematics that solves a wide variety of optimization problems. The biggest advantage of linear programming is that it always achieves the optimal solution if one exists.

Ritchken (1985) proposes using linear programming that places constraints on the time preference, risk aversion, and state probabilities. Under some specific set of assumptions, the price of a European call option can be viewed as the objective function to be optimized and formulated by a linear program. Then, the lower and upper bounds of a European call option can be obtained by minimization and maximization of the objective function in linear programming problem.

In an incomplete market, the prices of the state securities are not unique. To replicate Merton (1973)'s result, Ritchken (1985) assumes investors always prefer more to less, which implies the positive value of the current price of the specific pure state security that pays out \$1 at maturity day if this specific state occurs. The option bounds are, therefore, obtained by solving the following linear programming problem:

$$\text{Minimize (or Maximize)}\, C_0 = \sum_{i=1}^{n} c_i e_i,$$

$$\text{subject to} \sum_{i=1}^{n} s_i e_i = S_0 \quad \text{and} \quad \sum_{i=1}^{n} e_i = B_0 \quad \text{with} \quad e_i \geq 0, \tag{22.12}$$

where e_i is the current price of a pure state i security that pays out \$1 at maturity date if state i occurs; s_i is the value of the underlying security in state i; c_i is the value of a European call option in state i; and S_0 and B_0 are current values of the underlying security and a portfolio containing all state securities, respectively. The European call option with strike price K at maturity date T is defined as

$$c_i = \text{Max}(0,\, s_i - K),\, i = 1, 2, \ldots, n. \tag{22.13}$$

By minimizing and maximizing Ritchken's (1985) linear programming problem, the bounds of a European call option can be shown as follows:

$$C_{\max}^{E} = S_0 - \frac{KS_0}{s_{j^*}},$$

$$C_{\min}^{E} = \frac{[(c_{i^*} s_{i^*+1} - c_{i^*+1} s_{i^*}) B_0 + (c_{i^*+1} - c_{i^*}) S_0]}{s_{i^*+1} - s_{i^*}}, \tag{22.14}$$

where s_{j^*} is the largest possible price of the underlying asset; S_0 and B_0 are current values of the underlying security and a portfolio containing all state securities, respectively; K is strike price; and s_{i^*} and c_{i^*} represent the values of the underlying asset and call option, respectively, at state i^* in which i^* is chosen such that $s_{i^*+1} > \frac{S_0}{B_0}$ and $s_{i^*} < \frac{S_0}{B_0}$.

To achieve narrower bounds, one can require additional assumptions. For example, in addition to investors preferring more wealth to less, Ritchken (1985) assumes that investors are risk averse and there exists a set of ex-ante consensus probabilities for the states:

$$e_i = \pi_i d_i, \ i = 1, 2, 3, \ldots, n, \tag{22.15}$$

where d_i is the state discount factor that is non-increase with respect to wealth and π_i is ex-ante consensus probabilities that state i occurs. The bounds of a European call option are then obtained by solving the following linear programming problem:

$$\text{Minimize (or Maximize) } C_0 = \sum_{i=1}^{n} c_i \pi_i d_i, \tag{22.16}$$

$$\text{subject to} \sum_{i=1}^{n} s_i \pi_i d_i = S_0 \quad \text{and} \quad \sum_{i=1}^{n} \pi_i d_i = B_0,$$

$$\text{with} \quad d_1 \geq d_2 \geq d_3 \geq \cdots \geq d_n \geq 0.$$

where e_i is the current price of a pure state i security that pays out \$1 at maturity date if state i occurs; s_i is the value of the underlying security in state i; c_i is the value of a European call option in state i; d_i is the state discount factor that is non-increase with respect to wealth; π_i is *ex ante* consensus probabilities that state i occurs; and S_0 and B_0 are current values of the underlying security and a portfolio containing all state securities, respectively.

Following Ritchken (1985), Ritchken and Kuo (1988) propose the application of the single-period linear programming option model to handle multiple periods. Ritchken and Kuo (1988) obtain identical upper bounds and tighter lower bounds than Ritchken (1985). Ritchken and Kuo (1989) further consider the additional preference restrictions on the investors with third-order or above stochastic dominance criteria. They also apply a decreasing absolute risk aversion (DARA) dominance rule in a state preference context. With the two restrictions, the closed-form analytical solutions for the option bounds are not obtained, but a simple numerical example is presented.

The behavior of the DARA lower bound for the option price is not wholly explored by Ritchken and Kuo (1989). Basso and Pianca (1997) analyze the general rule of DARA dominance. They solve the optimization DARA problem in the case of three states of nature, proving that the optimal solution satisfies the nonlinear constraint as equality. This solution is obtained through an exponential-like utility function having constant absolute risk aversion (CARA).

Basso and Pianca (1997) reconsider the following maximization and minimization problem:

$$\text{Minimize (or Maximize) } C_0 = \sum_{i=1}^{n} c_i e_i,$$

$$\text{subject to} \sum_{i=1}^{n} s_i e_i = S_0 \quad \text{and} \quad \sum_{i=1}^{n} e_i = B_0,$$

$$\text{with} \quad (e_1 e_2 e_3, \ldots, e_n) \in D, \tag{22.17}$$

where the set D depends on the stochastic dominance rule adopted and is determined by the assumptions made on the utility function. For example, given a utility function with DARA character, the set D is constrained by the following:

$$e_i \geq 0, i = 1, 2, \ldots, n,$$

$$e_i \geq e_{i+1}, i = 1, 2, \ldots, n-1,$$

$$e_i e_{i+2} \geq e_{i+1}^2, i = 1, 2, \ldots, n-2. \tag{22.18}$$

Recently, Peña *et al.* (2009) showed that the problem of computing sharp upper and lower static arbitrage bounds on the price of a European basket option, given the prices of other similar options, can also be cast as a linear program. The linear program formulations readily yield super-replicating (sub-replicating) strategies for the upper-bound (lower-bound) problem. The dual counterparts of the linear program formulations in turn yield underlying asset price distributions that replicate the given option prices and the bound on the new basket option's price. In the special case when the given option prices are those of vanilla options on the underlying assets, they show that the linear program formulations admit further simplifications. In particular, for the upper-bound problem, they derive closed-form formulas for the basket's price bound and for the corresponding super-replicating strategy. In addition, their linear program approach admits efficient modeling of additional features such as basket options with negative weights, bid–ask spreads, transaction costs, and diversification constraints.

22.3.4 *Semi-parametric and non-parametric methods*

The option bounds discussed so far are derived by "parametric" methods. Although Perrakis and Ryan (1984) obtain bounds for all stock price distributions with a non-negative beta property, the actual values of the bounds depend on the specific stock price distribution. Similar to Perrakis and Ryan (1984), the bounds of Levy (1985) obtained by using SSDR are also parametric methods. In addition, Ritchken's (1985) linear programming approach also requires parametric assumption of the state probabilities to calculate values for the bounds. In contrast to the previous discussed method, semi-parametric and non-parametric methods discussed in this section do not require strong assumptions in models and just need the historical data to derive option bounds.

22.3.4.1 *Semi-parametric method*

Different from parametric methods, Lo (1987) initiated literature on "semi-parametric" bounds on option prices. The option bounds derived by Lo (1987) depend only on the mean and variance of the terminal stock price and not on the entire distribution, that is, they are "semi-parametric."

Relying on the mathematical inequality provided by Scarf (1958), Lo (1987) derives the boundary of option prices. For the underlying asset price, S_t, with constant mean μ and constant standard deviation σ, the upper bound of a European call option, $C^E_{\max}$, can be written as

$$C^E_{\max} = \begin{cases} \dfrac{\mu^2(\mu - K) + \mu\sigma^2}{\mu^2 + \sigma^2} & \text{if } K \leq \dfrac{\mu^2 + \sigma^2}{2\mu}, \\ \dfrac{1}{2}\left[\mu - K + \sqrt{(\mu - K)^2 + \sigma^2}\right] & \text{if } K > \dfrac{\mu^2 + \sigma^2}{2\mu}. \end{cases} \tag{22.19}$$

The important feature of this equation is that the upper bound of the call option depends only on the first two moments of the price distribution.

Zhang (1994) sharpens Lo's (1987) bounds by using the assumption that the underlying stock price is continuously distributed. Assume the terminal stock price S_T with cumulative distribution $F(S_T)$ satisfying the moment conditions:

$$\int_0^\infty dF(S_T) = 1, \int_0^\infty S_T dF(S_T) = \mu, \int_0^\infty S_T^2 dF(S_T) = \mu^2 + \sigma^2. \tag{22.20}$$

Based on these constraints, the upper bound, $C^E_{\max}$, and lower bound, $C^E_{\min}$, of a European call option can be obtained as follows:

$$C^E_{\max} = \frac{1}{2}\left[\mu - K + \sqrt{(\mu - K)^2 + \sigma^2}\right],$$

$$C^E_{\min} = \begin{cases} \mu - \frac{K\mu^2}{\mu^2+\sigma^2} & \text{if} \quad K \leq \mu + \frac{\sigma^2}{\mu} \\ 0 & \text{if} \quad K > \mu + \frac{\sigma^2}{\mu} \end{cases}. \tag{22.21}$$

Lee *et al.* (2002) further extend Zhang's (1994) moment conditions by incorporating third and fourth moments to capture skewness and kurtosis characteristics of the underlying stock price since most empirical findings indicate that the distribution of stock return is often fat-tailed and excess kurtosis. The results for the upper bounds of a European call option of Lee *et al.* (2002) can be categorized into three parts:

$$C^E_{\max} = \begin{cases} \sigma\left(\frac{\eta(F_{S_T}(K))^3}{a}\right)^{1/4} & \text{when} \quad \mu = K, \\ \kappa_4(\mu - K) & \text{when} \quad \mu > K, \\ \varpi_4(K - \mu) & \text{when} \quad \mu < K, \end{cases} \tag{22.22}$$

where $a = 1 + \left(\frac{F_{S_T}(K)}{1-F_{S_T}(K)}\right)^3$ and η is the kurtosis of the underlying asset price distribution. $F_{S_T}(K)$ denotes the cumulative function of any distribution for the underlying asset when S_T equals the strike price K at maturity and κ_4 is the largest real root of the quadratic equation: the largest real root of the quadratic equation $ax^4 - 4x^3 + 6x^2 - 4x + b = 0$ and ϖ_4 is the largest real root of the quadratic equation $ax^4 + 4x^3 + 6x^2 + 4x + b = 0$, $b = 1 - \phi F^3(K)$, $\phi = \frac{\eta\sigma^4}{(\mu-K)^4} + \frac{4K\sigma^3}{(\mu-K)^3} + \frac{6\sigma^4}{(\mu-K)^2} + 1$.

Besides Zhang (1994) and Lee *et al.* (2002), several papers tried to extend or generalize Lo's (1987) approach. Grundy (1991) derived option bounds by considering higher moments of the underlying asset's distribution. Grundy's (1991) upper bound of a European call option can be derived by the given knowledge that the value of the nth moment multiplied by the nth power of current price of underlying asset should be equal to the nth power of the value of the underlying asset at maturity date. Boyle and Lin (1997) apply Lo's (1987) semi-parametric method to a European call option on the maximum of several assets and a lookback option. Bertsimas and Popescu (2002) also extend Lo's (1987) upper bound of a European call option by considering the correlation between European call options with different strike prices. Lo's (1987) approach is also improved by Gotoh and Konno (2002). They propose an efficient cutting-plane algorithm which can efficiently solve the semi-definite programming problem associated with the bound depending on the first n moments. Chazal and Jouini (2008) put constraints on the two first risk-neutral moments and use some qualitative information on the risk-neutral measure in order to improve the bound of Lo (1987).

22.3.4.2 *Non-parametric method*

The advantages of the non-parametric method used in the derivation of option bounds are not assumptions of the underlying stock's distribution, interest rates, or volatility in the option pricing framework. Rodriguez (2003) uses a non-parametric method and a single analytical framework to derive the option bounds. Rodriguez (2003) states that the disparate methods applied to option bounds can be viewed as a single analytical framework with the synthesis lying in the derivation of call option bounds, which depends on the discount factor of its corresponding put option. The general expression for the value of a European call option in a single analytical framework can be written as

$$C_0 = S_0 - Ke^{-rT} + R_p \int_0^K F(S_T)d(S_T), \tag{22.23}$$

where r is risk-free rate, $F(S_T)$ is the cumulative distribution function of underlying stock price, and R_p is the discount factor of its corresponding put option. Given the suitable lower bounds of the put's discount factor, Rodriguez (2003) provides a tighter lower bound than previous work.

Lin, Chen, and Palmon (2012) derived a tighter lower bound and reinterpret Ritchken's (1985) upper bound of European options under a non-parametric framework. The only variable used in these bounds is the dollar beta of an option which is defined as the covariance between an option price and its underlying asset's price over the variance of its underlying asset's price. Lin *et al.* (2012) utilize the general classical asset pricing model with a stochastic kernel to derive the lower bound at time t for a European call option as follows:

$$C^E_{t,\min} = D_{t,T}E[C_T] + \beta_C\{S_t - D_{t,T}E[S_T]\}, \tag{22.24}$$

where $\beta_C = \frac{\text{Cov}(C_T,S_T)}{\text{Var}(S_T)}$ denotes the dollar beta of the call option and $D_{t,T}$ is the risk-free discount factor and can be written as $D_{t,T} = e^{-r(T-t)}$ if the risk-free rate is non-stochastic. The lower bound of a European put option can be derived by the put–call parity as follows:

$$P_t = C_t + D_{t,T}K - S_t \geq C^E_{t,\min} + D_{t,T}K - S_t = P^E_{t,\min}. \tag{22.25}$$

By substituting the lower-bound formula of a European call option, we can get

$$P^E_{t,\min} = D_{t,T}E[P_T] + \beta_P\{S_t - D_{t,T}E[S_T]\}, \tag{22.26}$$

where $\beta_P = \frac{\text{Cov}(P_T,S_T)}{\text{Var}(S_T)} = 1 - \beta_C$ denotes the dollar beta of the put option and can be calculated by the dollar beta of the call option. By using the histogram method to calculate the expected payoffs of the stock and the option, lower bounds of European options can be obtained under the non-parametric framework.

22.4 Methods to Tighten Bounds for European Options

In this section, we review the previous studies that attempt to tighten bounds for European options by adding assumptions on investors' preference, adding restrictions on pricing kernel, selecting some risk-neutral measures, and adding frictions in financial markets. The tightened bounds for European options in markets with frictions are also discussed in detail.

22.4.1 *Restrictions on investor preferences and pricing kernel*

The assumptions of investor behaviors and the related pricing kernel (called a state-contingent discount factor or stochastic discount factor) have paved the way for tightening option bounds (Perrakis and Ryan, 1984; Levy, 1985; Ritchken, 1985; Ritchken and Kuo, 1989; Mathur and Ritchken, 1999; Basso and Pianca, 1997, 2001; Mello and Pyo, 2006; Pyo, 2008). Kimball (1990) deeply and stringently discussed the standard risk aversion (SRA) concept to explain that investors will reduce current expense and save more for the uncertainty of future income. Therefore, previous papers usually assume risk-averse investors in markets to obtain narrower option bounds. The following are some examples: non-decreasing concave utility functions used in Levy (1985), assumption of DARA used in Ritchken and Kuo (1989) and Basso and Pianca (1997), application of SRA rules in Basso and Pianca (2001), and non-increasing absolute risk aversion utility functions utilized in Mathur and Ritchken (1999).

If the investor preference (utility function) is given, the pricing kernel in each state can be constructed by the discounted marginal utility of wealth in that state divided by the expected marginal utility. Thus, we can use this pricing kernel to evaluate all securities including options as well. By incorporating the no-arbitrage assumption, the option bounds can be obtained by searching minimum and maximum option prices which are determined by the pricing kernel (Ritchken, 1985; Ritchken and Kuo, 1989; Basso and Pianca, 1997, 2001; Mello and Pyo, 2006). Mello and Pyo (2006) and Pyo (2008) employ the minimax deviation approach to derive the bounds for real options in accordance with the risk preference of the decision-maker.

An alternative way to apply the pricing kernel technique to the derivations of option bounds is to investigate the characteristics of pricing kernel. Bernardo and Ledoit (2000) propose "gain–loss ratio bounds" for options by linking pricing kernel to the gain–loss ratio of the investment's excess payoff, that is, the ratio of positive expected value of excess payoff to its expected negative value. Narrow option bounds can be obtained by maximizing the gain–loss ratio. Cochrane and Saa-Requejo (2000) link the volatility of the pricing kernel to Sharpe ratio. They propose "good-deal bounds" for options that lower (upper) option bounds are the minimization (maximization) of option prices under the constraints of the volatility of pricing kernel less than Sharpe ratio of the option. Bondarenko and Longarela (2004) further modify "good-deal bounds" for an option in which its underlying asset follows the stochastic volatility model. Huang (2004) generalizes option bounds by using the elasticity of the pricing kernel and shows that Cochrane and Saa-Requejo's (2000) approach is a special case of Huang's (2004) approach when the underlying asset follows log-normal distribution. Christoffersen *et al.* (2010) show that using a quadratic equivalent martingale measure (EMM) and GARCH framework can also derive good-deal bounds on option prices.

22.4.2 *The existence of a risk-neutral measure and the absence of arbitrage*

Besides giving investors' preferences to pursue the tightening of option bounds, there is an alternative way to pursue narrower bounds under a risk-neutral measure (or called an EMM). In an arbitrage-free and complete financial market, the price of an option can be evaluated by the expected value of its discounted cash flows under a risk-neutral measure if the price processes of the underlying asset are specified. For example, by assumption of the log-normal distribution of the underlying asset, European-style options can be obtained in closed-form formulas by Black and Scholes (1973) and Merton (1973).

However, there is no unique specified risk-neutral measure to accurately evaluate option prices because of the lack of precise information on the underlying asset dynamics. Chazal and Jouini (2008) adopt a duality approach to derive the upper bound of European call option when the underlying asset dynamics are not specified. Rather than applying the restrictions to distributions and investor's preferences, Ryan (2000) analyzes arbitrage opportunities based on the existing set of options with the same maturity. By using Ritchken's (1985) linear programming method, the bounds of an options in Ryan (2000) are subject to the constraining prices of the underlying asset, the riskless asset, and other observed options with the same underlying asset and same maturity date.

Another stream considers the underlying asset's fluctuations to search for the tightening option bounds (Christoffersen *et al.*, 2010). Many studies utilize a stochastic volatility model or other advanced approach to precisely capture the movements of the underlying asset and then obtain option prices in accordance with this specification assumption (Hull and White, 1987). Frey and Sin (1999) determine the maximum and minimum of the set of possible European option prices for a large class of stochastic volatility models under the no-arbitrage assumption. Lupu (2006) used Monte Carlo simulation to estimate tightening option bounds when the underlying asset follows a jump-diffusion process. Oancea and Perrakis (2007) also extend the stochastic dominance approach by Perrakis and Ryan (1984) to derive narrow option pricing bounds under the different assumptions of the underlying asset following a jump-diffusion process, a stochastic volatility model, or a GARCH process. However, uncertainty of the model of the underlying asset dynamics might be subject to the model risk problem (Cont, 2006). Thus, the calibration of option bounds under the specified price process of the underlying asset should be taken into account (King *et al.*, 2005; Pinar, 2009).

22.4.3 *Trading in financial markets with frictions*

In an incomplete market, using the no-arbitrage argument to price options will lead to the problem of frictions such as the transaction costs of dynamic replicating strategies (Leland, 1985; Bensaid *et al.*, 1992; Edirisinghe *et al.*, 1993) and the derivation of option bounds (Henin and Pistre, 1998; Constantinides and Zariphopoulou, 1999, 2001; Masson and Perrakis, 2000; Constantinides and Perrakis, 2002; Constantinides *et al.*, 2009). In this section, we review some studies that have investigated the tightening bounds derived by adding the consideration of market imperfections such as transaction costs or bid–ask spreads.

Henin and Pistre (1998) use this stochastic dominance method to derive bounds of European concave option prices incorporated with transaction costs and dividend payments on underlying assets. A concave option is one whose exercise payoff is a concave function of the difference between the underlying asset and the strike price. The bounding conditions for European concave options only depend on the final distribution of the stock price which has adjusted to dividends. The transaction costs only affect the initial costs of the replication strategy because of its European style. Instead of dealing with transaction costs directly, Masson and Perrakis (2000) pursue the tight option bounds by the consideration of the bid–ask spread of option prices. Their upper and lower bounds follow two different risk-neutral distributions related to the implied volatilities of observed ask and bid option prices, respectively.

Many studies concentrate the analysis on option bounds in an incomplete market with proportional transaction costs. Constantinides and Zariphopoulou (1999, 2001) derive the bounds for option prices with proportional transaction costs and investors' preferences. Constantinides and Perrakis (2002) extend Constantinides and Zariphopoulou's (1999, 2001) approach under the stochastic dominance framework. Their tight upper bound of the reservation write price of a call option is related to the transaction costs of selling and purchasing a stock. On the other hand, their tight lower bound of the reservation purchasing price of a put option is also based on the factors of transaction costs and the return rate on the bond. The advantages of the bound formulas are as follows: (1) These bounds of European options can be viewed as a generalization of single-period model to a multiperiod economy since they are independent of the trading frequency. (2) The upper (lower) bound on the write price of a put (call) option can be derived from the upper (lower) bound on the write price of a call (put) option and the put–call parity. Furthermore, the bounds of European option price also can compute the implied volatility bounds. Constantinides and Perrakis (2002) show the implied volatility skew of the bounds on European options; that is, the implied volatility of both upper and lower bounds is decreasing in the strike-to-price ratio. Constantinides, Jackwerth, and Perrakis (2009) also consider market frictions involved in the trading frequency, bid–ask spread, and the transaction costs into the derivations of European option bounds under the assumption that traders' assets consist of a riskless bond, a stock with cash dividends over time, and European options. They conclude that the S&P 500 index option market is not rational because the empirical results violate stochastic dominance. The detailed results are discussed in the section of empirical applications.

22.5 The Option Bounds for American Options and Asian Options

In this section, the previous studies that investigate the option bounds for American options, Asian options, currency cross-rate options, and real options are reviewed in detail.

22.5.1 *American option bounds*

American option valuation requires one to consider not only the option pricing problem itself but also simultaneously the determination of the early exercise boundary. Most previous papers use the lattice model to estimate American options because a closed-form function for American-style options does not exist. A lattice model is a tree model with nodes to represent the time and state spaces of underlying assets in order to approximate the American option price. Practical implementation involves numerical methods that may become computationally burdensome, in particular when there are multiple state variables. Carr, Jarrow, and Myneni (1992) derive the upper bound for American put options as a European put option plus a fixed premium. Chaudhury and Wei (1994) studied the bounds on American future options. Broadie and Detemple (1996) derive the lower bound of the American call option by using the lattice model where the optimal exercise boundary of the American call option is set as one of the nodes on a binomial tree. Perrakis (1986) applies the bounds by Perrakis and Ryan (1984) to obtain the bounds for an American put option that can be represented in the binomial model.

In contrast with the heavy computational burden in the lattice method, Chen and Yeh (2002) derived closed-form upper bounds under a stochastic interest rate, stochastic volatility, and jump model. Chung and Chang (2007) further generalized Chen and Yeh's (2002) upper bounds to solve the case of inadequate upper bounds for American options when the interest rate is smaller than the dividend yield. They also extended their upper bounds to American options with several underlying assets. Handley (2005) utilized the arbitrage strategy to derive the upper-bound American call options with multiple known dividends. The arbitrage strategy for American call options is like a trade-off decision between the underlying asset's dividend received and the value of an American call option exercised on ex-dividend date before maturity. Based on this insight, Handley (2005) derived the upper bounds for American call options which depend on the value of dividends received compared to the strike price of the contract.

In addition, some studies obtained the tightening bounds for the American option in an incomplete market. Perrakis and Lefoll (1997, 2000, 2004) investigated the American option bounds with proportional transaction costs in lattice method framework. Constantinides and Perrakis (2007) extended the bounds by Constantinides and Zariphopoulou (1999, 2001) to American option markets with transaction costs in the stochastic dominance framework.

22.5.2 *Asian option bounds*

An Asian option is a kind of exotic option which has been presented in Chapter 18 and its prices are determined by the average underlying prices over the whole period, not only dependent on the price of the asset at the maturity date. Even though there is no closed-form solution for an Asian option, the bounds of an Asian option can be derived by replication of a portfolio incorporated with other related financial derivatives. Nielsen and Sandmann (2003) express bounds of an Asian call option as the portfolio of delayed payment European call options which depend on the exercise price of the Asian option. By using put–call parity, the bounds of an Asian put option can be derived as well. Vanmaele *et al.* (2006) investigate bounds for Asian options under the assumption that the underlying asset follows log-normal distribution. They employ the bounds approach proposed by Kaas *et al.* (2000) for sums of random variables and then obtain computable bounds for Asian options. Asian option bounds can not only appropriately evaluate the prices of Asian options but can also be applied to hedging strategies. Nielsen and Sandmann (2003) and Vanmaele *et al.* (2006) also discuss hedging positions based on their Asian option bounds.

22.6 Empirical Applications

In this section, we survey the papers that apply option bounds in empirical work. The data and major results in each study are briefly described and categorized by markets of underlying assets.

22.6.1 *Equities and equity indices*

The options with underlying assets in equity market are the most investigated and priced in both academia and industry. The option bounds can be used to price the options which the underlying assets are traded in equity market. Chung *et al.* (1997) used option data with either stock price or index as the underlying asset from 1987 to 1989 to test the law of one price proposed by Chen and Welch (1991) that options are redundant if they can be replicated by its underlying stock. According to Chung *et al.*'s (1997) major results, they found that the distributions of trading volumes for options on both stock and index are bound in a narrow range when underlying assets remain constant. The narrow width of option trade price bands not only confirms Chen and Welch's (1991) single-price law, but also supports the sense of using option bounds to price option price without complex option models.

The option pricing bounds also can be transferred to the bounds of Black–Scholes-implied volatilities to compare the implied volatilities of stock options and test market efficiency. Cochrane and Saa-Requejo (2000) use the S&P 500 index options which expired at the end of June, September, and December, 1996, to compare the implied volatilities with the implied volatilities of their option bounds. The results show that Cochrane and Saa-Requejo's bounds are only valid for at-the-money options. Masson and Perrakis (2000) use the implied volatilities of observed ask and bid call options on S&P 500 during 1993–1995 and obtain tight option bounds. These option bounds are only less than 0.2% observations. Constantinides, Jackwerth, and Perrakis (2009) utilize implied volatility criteria based on the Constantinides and Perrakis (2002) option bound model to test whether the S&P 500 index options market is rational or not. It is the first large-scale empirical investigation of whether the observed cross sections of 1-month S&P 500 index option prices over 1986–2006 are consistent with various economic models that explicitly allow for a dynamically incomplete market and an imperfect market that recognizes trading costs and bid–ask spreads. They used both the unconditional distribution and the conditional distribution of the stock returns to avoid the fact that the problem of mispricing the S&P 500 index options in the Black–Scholes–Merton model (BSM) contributes to the assumption of log-normal distribution of the index returns. The unconditional distribution of the stock returns is based on the historical date; on the other hand, the conditional distribution of the stock returns can be calculated by three different ways: the GARCH(1,1) process, Black–Scholes implied volatility method, or Chicago Board Options Exchange Volatility Index (VIX) data. Their results show the significant number of stochastic dominance violations, and the violations decrease before the crash but increase after the crash. It implies that the options market is not becoming more rational over time, particularly after the crash. In particular, the empirical findings are that the implied volatility of options bounds is smooth in the pre-crash period but becomes steep in the post-crash period. Moreover, in contrast with the usage of information on the implied volatilities of options, Lin *et al.* (2012) apply the relationship between option prices and their underlying prices to derive option bounds under the non-parametric framework. Lin *et al.* (2012) use the call option prices on the S&P 500 and the prices of the S&P 500 index during the period of June 1988 to December 1991 to estimate the bounds for the S&P 500 index options that 10% observations violate their lower bound.

22.6.2 *Index futures*

Constantinides *et al.* (2011) utilize the stochastic dominance bounds derived by Constantinides and Perrakis (2009), which consider incomplete and imperfect markets involved in the bid–ask spread and the transaction costs into the derivation of the bounds for American options as the benchmarks for trading strategy in the market of American options on the S&P 500 index futures. Constantinides *et al.* (2011) test whether the options on the S&P 500 index futures from 1983 to 2006 are profitable by only using the violations of option bounds as signals for trading. Their major findings are as follows: (1) There are significant violations of upper bounds in the bid price of American call options rather than American put options. (2) The trading strategy of selling (buying) options when they violate the upper (lower) bounds is profitable in the market of American options on the S&P 500 index future. Without the given probability distribution of the S&P 500 index futures, the empirical results in Constantinides *et al.* (2011) are not affected by the estimation error and model misspecification problem of the underlying asset's return.

22.6.3 *Foreign exchange rates*

Chung and Wang (2008) derive the bounds of a currency cross-rate option under risk-neutral conditions. By using the no-arbitrage pricing approach, the bounds of a currency cross-rate option can be presented as the combination of other two currency options on related dollar rates. Chung and Wang (2008) use daily OTC currency option prices from 11 March 1999 to 11 January 2001 and test the bounds of a currency cross-rate option on euros/British pounds (€/£) by using two other currency options on US dollars/British pounds ($/€) and US dollars/euros ($/£), respectively. The results show that the bounds of a currency cross-rate option have powerful explanations on its market prices. Therefore, the persistent relationships between the market prices of a cross-rate option and its bounds can be applied to hedging strategies.

22.6.4 *Real options*

In Chapter 19, we have shown how the option pricing theory can be used to do capital budgeting decisions under uncertainty. Since real options are involved in capital budgeting decisions which are distinct characteristics from other options, the risk preference of the decision-maker is an important factor in pricing real-option bounds.

Mello and Pyo (2006) and Pyo (2008) employ the minimax deviation approach incorporated with risk-averse utility functions to obtain real-option bounds in the incomplete market. Their numerical results show that their minimax bounds are more efficient and narrower than the other two approaches, gain–loss ratio bounds by Bernardo and Ledoit (2000) and good-deal bounds by Cochrane and Saa-Requejo (2000).

22.7 Conclusion

In this chapter, we provided a comprehensive literature review of option bounds. Option bounds can be generally obtained with fewer assumptions on the investor's preferences and/or the underlying asset's price processes. The studies on option bounds are categorized either by their mathematical techniques to derive the bounds or by their different approaches to tighten the bounds. The most important mathematical methods for deriving option bounds include searching for arbitrage conditions, stochastic dominance, linear programming, and semi-parametric and non-parametric methods. The bounds on option prices can be further tightened using a variety of approaches including imposing restrictions on investor preferences or pricing kernels, the selection of risk-neutral measures, and consideration of market frictions. We also surveyed the papers that have applied option bounds to different empirical applications. These option bounds have also been shown to be useful in many areas, such as providing qualitative properties of option prices and screening market data for mispricing.

Questions

1. Please discuss the stochastic dominance approach to derive option bound.
2. Please discuss the linear programming approach to derive option bound.
3. Please discuss the semi-parametric and non-parametric approaches to derive option bound.
4. Please discuss different methods that can be used to tighten bounds for European options.

5. Please describe option bound for American options and Asian options.
6. Please briefly discuss how option bound has been used to conduct empirical studies for equity, equity index, index future, and foreign exchange rate.

Bibliography

Basso, A. and P. Pianca (1997). Decreasing absolute risk aversion and option pricing bounds. *Management Science*, 43, 206–216.

Basso, A. and P. Pianca (2001). Option pricing bounds with standard risk aversion preferences. *European Journal of Operational Research*, 134, 229–260.

Bensaid, B., J.-P. Lesne, H. Pagès and J., Scheinkman (1992). Derivative asset pricing with transaction costs. *Mathematical Finance*, 2, 63–86.

Bernardo, A. E. and O. Ledoit (2000). Gains, loss and asset pricing. *Journal of Political Economy*, 108, 144–172.

Bertsimas, D. and I. Popescu (2002). On the relation between option and stock prices: A convex optimization approach. *Operation Research*, 50, 358–374.

Black, F. and M. S. Scholes (1973). The pricing of options and corporate liabilities. *Journal of Political Economy*, 81, 637–654.

Blume, M. (1971). On the assessment of risk. *Journal of Finance*, 26, 1–10.

Bondarenko, O. and I. Longarela (2004). Benchmark good deal bounds: An application to stochastic volatility models of option pricing. Working Paper, Stockholm School of Economics.

Boyle, P. P. and X. S. Lin (1997). Bounds on contingent claims based on several assets. *Journal of Financial Economics*, 46, 383–400.

Brennan, M. (1979). The pricing of contingent claims in discrete time models. *Journal of Finance*, 34, 53–68.

Broadie, M. and J. Detemple (1996). American option valuation: New bounds, approximations and a comparison of existing methods. *Review of Financial Studies*, 9, 1211–1250.

Carr, P., R. Jarrow and R. Myneni (1992). Alternative characterizations of American put options. *Mathematical Finance*, 2, 87–106.

Chaudhury, M. and J. Wei (1994). Upper bounds for American futures options: A note. *Journal of Futures Markets*, 14, 111–116.

Chaudhury, M. (2006). Upper bounds for American options. *Research in Finance*, 23, 161–191.

Chazal, M. and E. Jouini (2008). Equilibrium pricing bounds on option prices. *Mathematics and Financial Econometrics*, 1, 251–281.

Chen, D. M. and R. L. Welch (1991). Empirical option price bands on the Chicago Board Options Exchange and the redundancy of options. *Advances in Quantitative Analysis of Finance and Accounting*, 1(b), 161–182.

Chen, R. R. and S. K. Yeh (2002). Analytical upper bounds for American option prices. *Journal of Financial and Quantitative Analysis*, 37, 117–135.

Christoffersen, P., R. Elkamhi, B. Feunou and K. Jacobs (2010). Option valuation with conditional heteroskedasticity and nonnormality. *Review of Financial Studies*, 23, 2139–2183.

Chung, S. L. and H. C. Chang (2007). Generalized analytical upper bounds for American option prices. *Journal of Financial and Quantitative Analysis*, 42, 209–227.

Chung, S. L. and Y. H. Wang (2008). Bounds and prices of currency cross-rate options. *Journal of Banking and Finance*, 32, 631–642.

Chung, T. Y., R. L. Welch and D. M. Chen (1997). On the distribution of CBOE option trade prices occurring between consecutive stock trades. *Review of Quantitative Finance and Accounting*, 9, 269–288.

Cochrane, J. and J. Saa-Requejo (2000). Beyond arbitrage: Good-deal asset price bounds in incomplete markets. *Journal of Political Economy*, 108, 79–119.

Constantinides, G. M. and S. Perrakis (2007). Stochastic dominance bounds on American option prices in markets with frictions. *Review of Finance*, 11, 71–115.

Constantinides, G. M. and S. Perrakis (2002). Stochastic dominance bounds on derivatives prices in a multiperiod economy with proportional transaction costs. *Journal of Economic Dynamics and Control*, 26, 1323–1352.

Constantinides, G. M., J. C. Jackwerth and S. Perrakis (2009). Mispricing of S&P 500 index options. *Review of Financial Studies*, 22, 1227–1277.

Constantinides, G. M., M. Czerwonko, J. C. Jackwerth and S. Perrakis (2011). Are options on index futures profitable for risk-averse investors? Empirical evidence. *Journal of Finance*, 66, 1407–1437.

Constantinides, G. M. and T. Zariphopoulou (1999). Bounds on prices of contingent claims in an intertemporal economy with proportional transaction costs and general preferences. *Finance and Stochastics*, 3, 345–369.

Constantinides, G. M. and T. Zariphopoulou (2001). Bounds on derivative prices in an intertemporal setting with proportional transactions costs and multiple securities. *Mathematical Finance*, 11, 331–346.

Cont, R. (2006). Model uncertainty and its impact on the pricing of derivative instruments. *Mathematical Finance*, 16, 519–547.

Cox, J. C., S. A. Ross and M. Rubinstein (1979). Option pricing: A simplified approach. *Journal of Financial Economics*, 7, 229–263.

De la Peña, V. H., R. Ibragimov and S. Jordan (2004). Option bounds. *Journal of Applied Probability*, 41A, 145–156.

Edirisinghe, C., V. Naik and R. Uppal (1993). Optimal replacement of options with transactions costs and trading restrictions. *Journal of Financial and Quantitative Analysis*, 28, 117–138.

Frey, R. and C. A. Sin (1999). Bounds on European option prices under stochastic volatility. *Mathematical Finance*, 9, 97–116.

Gotoh, J. and H. Konno (2002). Bounding option prices by semi-definite programming: A cutting plane algorithm. *Management Science*, 48, 666–678.

Grundy, B. D. (1991). Option prices and the underlying asset's return distribution. *Journal of Finance*, 48, 1045–1069.

Handley, J. C. (2005). On the upper bound of a call option. *Review of Derivatives Research*, 8, 85–95.

Henin, C. and N. Pistre (1998). Stochastic dominance arguments and the bounding of the generalized concave option price. *Journal of Futures Markets*, 18, 629–670.

Huang, J. and Z. Zhang (2009). Option bounds and second order arbitrage opportunities. Working paper.

Huang, J. (2004). Option pricing bounds and the elasticity of the pricing kernel. *Review of Derivatives Research*, 7, 25–51.

Hull, J. and A. White (1987). The pricing of options on assets with stochastic volatilities. *Journal of Finance*, 42, 281–300.

Jackwerth, J. C. and M. Rubinstein (1996). Recovering probability distributions from option prices. *Journal of Finance*, 51(5), 1611–1631.

Kaas, R., J. Dhaene and M. J. Goovaerts (2000). Upper and lower bounds for sums of random variables. *Insurance: Mathematics and Economics*, 27, 151–168.

Kimball, M. S. (1990). Precautionary saving in the small and in the large. *Econometrica*, 58, 53–73.

King, A. J., M. Koivu and T. Pennanen (2005). Calibrated option bounds. *International Journal of Theoretical and Applied Finance*, 8, 141–159.

Lee, C. F., P. Zhang and A. C. Lee (2002). Bounds for options prices and the expected payoffs with skewness and kurtosis. *Advances in Quantitative Analysis of Finance and Accounting*, 10, 117–138.

Lee, C. F., Z. Zhong, T. Tai and H. Chuang (2021). Alternative methods for determining option bounds: A review and comparison, in C.-F. Lee and J. Lee (eds.), *Handbook of Financial Econometrics, Mathematics, Statistics, and Machine Learning*, Singapore: World Scientific, pp. 946–966.

Leland, H. E. (1985). Option pricing and replication with transactions costs. *Journal of Finance*, 40, 1283–1301.

Levy, H. (1985). Upper and lower bounds of put and call values: Stochastic dominance approach. *Journal of Finance*, 40, 1197–1218.

Lin, H. C., R. R. Chen and O. Palmon (2012). Non-parametric method for European option bounds. *Review of Quantitative Finance and Accounting*, 38, 109–129.

Lo, A. W. (1987). Semi-parametric upper bounds for option prices and expected payoffs. *Journal of Financial Economics*, 19, 373–387.

Lupu, R. (2006). Option bounds for multinomial stock returns in jump-diffusion process - a Monte Carlo simulation for a multi-jump process. *Romanian Journal of Economic Forecasting*, 2, 58–71.

Masson, J. and S. Perrakis (2000). Option bounds and the pricing of the volatility smile. *Review of Derivatives Research*, 4, 29–53.

Mathur, K. and P. Ritchken (1999). Minimum option prices under decreasing absolute risk aversion. *Review of Derivatives Research*, 3, 135–156.

Mello, A. and U. Pyo (2006). Minimax asset price bounds in incomplete markets. Working paper.

Merton, R. C. (1973). Theory of rational option pricing. *Bell Journal of Economics and Management Science*, 4, 141–183.

Nielsen, J. A. and K. Sandmann (2003). Pricing bounds on Asian options. *Journal of Financial and Quantitative Analysis*, 38, 449–473.

Oanceal, I. M. and S. Perrakis (2007). Stochastic dominance and option pricing in discrete and continuous time: An alternative paradigm. Working paper.

Peña, J., J. C. Vera and L. F. Zuluaga (2009). Static-arbitrage lower bounds on the prices of basket options via linear programming. *Quantitative Finance*, 10, 1–9.

Perrakis, S. and P. J. Ryan (1984). Option pricing bounds in discrete time. *Journal of Finance*, 39, 519–525.

Perrakis, S. (1986). Option bounds in discrete time: Extensions and the pricing of American put. *Journal of Business*, 59, 119–125.

Perrakis, S. (1993). Option pricing for multinomial stock returns in diffusion and mixed processes. *Canadian Journal of Administrative Sciences*, 10, 68–82.

Perrakis, S. and J. Lefoll (1997). Derivative asset pricing with transaction costs: An extension. *Computational Economics*, 10, 359–376.

Perrakis, S. and J. Lefoll (2000). Option pricing and replication with transaction costs and dividends. *Journal of Economic Dynamics and Control*, 22, 1527–1561.

Perrakis, S. and J. Lefoll (2004). The American put under transactions costs. *Journal of Economic Dynamics and Control*, 28, 915–935.

Pınar, M. C. (2009). Measures of model uncertainty and calibrated option bounds. *Optimization*, 58, 335–350.

Pyo, U. (2008). Real option pricing and bounds in incomplete markets. *The Engineering Economist*, 53, 4–41.

Ritchken, P. and S. Kuo (1989). On stochastic dominance and decreasing absolute risk averse option pricing bounds. *Management Science*, 35, 51–59.

Ritchken, P. H. (1985). On option pricing bounds. *Journal of Finance*, 40, 1219–1233.

Ritchken, P. H. and S. Kuo (1988). Option bounds with finite revision opportunities. *Journal of Finance*, 43, 301–308.

Rodriguez, R. (2003). Option pricing bounds: Synthesis and extension. *Journal of Financial Research*, 26, 149–164.

Rubinstein, M. (1976). The valuation of uncertain income streams and the pricing options. *Bell Journal of Economics and Management Science*, 7, 407–425.

Ryan, P. J. (2000). Tighter option bounds from multiple exercise prices. *Review of Derivatives Research*, 4, 155–188.

Ryan, P. J. (2003). Progressive option bounds from the sequence of concurrently expiring options. *European Journal of Operational Research*, 151, 193–223.

Scarf, H. (1958). A min-max solution of an inventory problem. *Studies in the Mathematic Theory of Inventory and Production*, 5(5), 201–209.

Vanmaele, M., G. Deelstra, J. Liinev, J. Dhaene and M. J. Goovaerts (2006). Bounds for the price of discrete arithmetic Asian options. *Journal of Computational and Applied Mathematics*, 185, 51–90.

Zhang, P. G. (1994). Bounds for option prices and expected payoffs. *Review of Quantitative Finance and Accounting*, 4, 179–197.

Zuluaga, L. F., J. Peña and D. Du (2009). Third-order extensions of Lo's semi-parametric bound for European call options. *European Journal of Operational Research*, 198, 557–570.

Appendix 22A: Mathematical Derivation of the Option Bounds

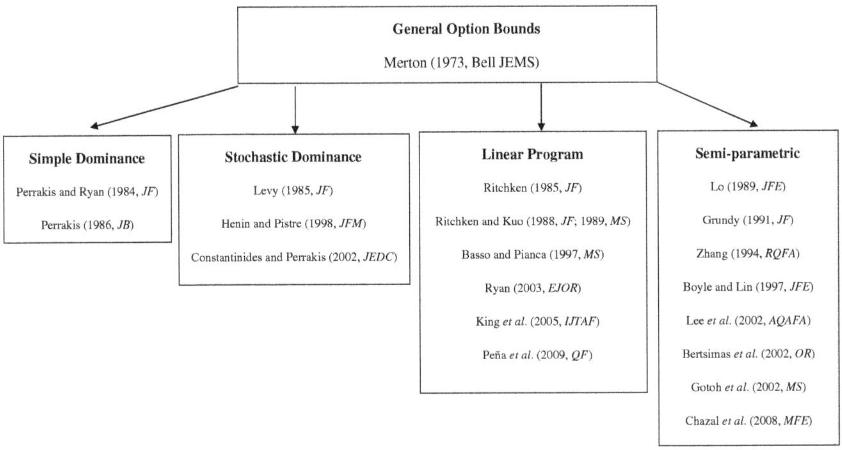

Appendix 22B: Tightening Techniques of the Option Bounds

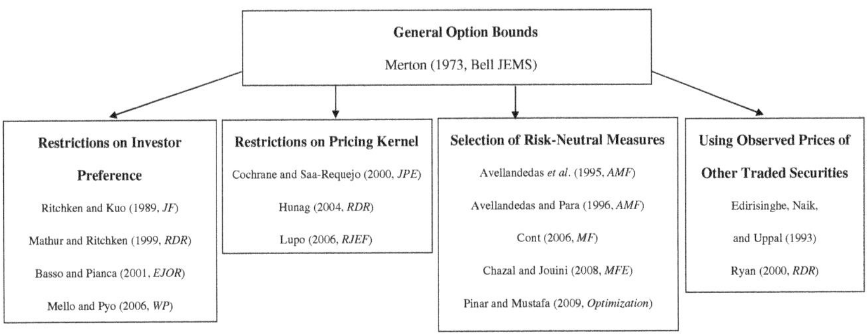

Appendix 22C: Other Option Bounds

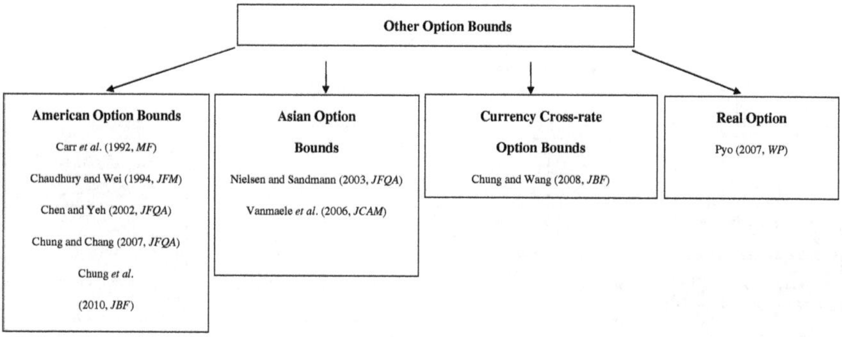

Author Index

D

E

F

M

T

U

V

Subject Index

D

G

H

I

N

O

T

U

V

W

Y

Z

Printed in the USA
CPSIA information can be obtained
at www.ICGtesting.com
LVHW020741011123
762154LV00002B/3